SOCIAL PSYCHOLOGY

SOCIAL PSYCHOLOGY

2nd Edition

Eliot R. Smith

Purdue University

Diane M. Mackie

University of California, Santa Barbara

PSYCHOLOGY PRESS
· Taylor & Francis Group ·
ALERE FLAMMAM

USA	Publishing Office:	PSYCHOLOGY PRESS
		A member of the Taylor & Francis Group
		325 Chestnut Street
		Philadelphia, PA 19106
		Tel: (215) 625-8900
		Fax: (215) 625-2940
	Distribution Center:	PSYCHOLOGY PRESS
		A member of the Taylor & Francis Group
		7625 Empire Drive
		Florence, KY 41042
		Tel: (800) 634-7064
		Fax: (800) 248-4724
UK		PSYCHOLOGY PRESS
		A member of the Taylor & Francis Group
		27 Church Road
		Hove
		E. Sussex, BN3 2FA
		Tel: +44 (0)1273 207411
		Fax: +44 (0)1273 205612

Social Psychology, 2/E

2 3 4 5 6 7 8 9 0

Printed by Courier, Kendallville, IN. Cover design by Joan Wendt. Figure illustration by Lineworks.

A CIP catalog record for this book is available from the British Library.
    The paper in this publication meets the requirements of the ANSI Standard Z39.48-1984 (Permanence of Paper).

Library of Congress Cataloging-in-Publication Data
Smith, Eliot R.
    Social psychology/by Eliot Smith and Diane Mackie. —2nd ed.
        p. c.m
    Includes bibliographical references and index.
    ISBN 0-86377-587-X (case : alk. paper)
    1. Social psychology.   I. Mackie, Diane M.   II. Title
HM1033.S55   1999
302—dc21   99-42560
                                                                            CIP

About the Authors

Eliot Smith earned his B.A. and Ph.D. at Harvard University. He taught at the University of California, Riverside, before moving in 1982 to Purdue University, where he is now Professor of Psychological Sciences. A distinguished researcher, he has held numerous research grants and is author of more than 75 book chapters, journal articles and reviews. Besides this textbook, he has written two books, *Research Methods in Social Relations, 6th edition* (with Charles Judd and Louise Kidder) and *Beliefs about Inequality* (with James Kluegel). He has chaired the Social and Group Processes research review committee of the United States National Institute of Mental Health, and served as associate editor of the Journal of Personality and Social Psychology and as a member of the editorial boards of several major social psychology journals. This experience has given him a broad view of the best research in every area of social psychology. Professor Smith's scholarly interests center on person perception, stereotyping, and intergroup relations. Professor Smith is married to Pamela Grenfell Smith, a Web designer and freelance writer. They share a love of music, travel, and dogs with their daughter Miranda, a graduate student in cultural anthropology, and son Thomas, a high school student.

Diane M. Mackie is Professor of Psychology and Communication at the University of California, Santa Barbara, where she was honored with a 1994 Distinguished Teaching Award and was listed as one of "Ten Terrific Teachers" by UCSB students in 1995. Dr. Mackie grew up in New Zealand, received her BA and MA at the University of Auckland, and then worked as a researcher for a year in Geneva. She received her PhD in social psychology from Princeton University in 1984. These opportunities to become steeped in both European and North American traditions of social psychology are reflected in her interest in integrating different perspectives and areas in her research and in this textbook. She is editor of *Affect, Cognition, and Stereotyping* (with David L. Hamilton) and author of more than 60 articles and chapters on persuasion, social influence, group interaction, and intergroup processes. Dr. Mackie is an Associate Editor of *Group Processes and Intergroup Relations* and serves on the Editorial Boards of several leading journals in psychology and marketing. She has reviewed grants for the U.S. National Science Foundation, Social Sciences and Humanities Council of Canada and the Australia Research Council. Among her many honors are an American Psychological Association Young Psychologist Award in 1989, the Western Psychological Association's Outstanding Young Researcher Award in 1992, and the Rocky Mountain Psychological Association's Psi Chi Keynote Speaker Award in 1999. However her greatest (and busiest) honor by far is being Mom to a terrific three year old, Alexander Mackie.

To our parents
Curtis and Elaine Smith
and
David and Joan Mackie

Contents in Brief

Social Psychology in Applied Settings

This brief index provides a ready reference to major application sections integrated within the chapters. Other shorter discussions of applied topics also appear throughout the book.

Contents

Preface

"No wise fish would go anywhere without a porpoise" claims *Alice in Wonderland*'s Mock Turtle. "Why, if a fish came to ME, and told me he was going on a journey, I should say 'With what porpoise?'" Had the Mock Turtle asked us our purpose in undertaking this textbook writing journey, the answer would have been simple. We wanted to convey to an undergraduate audience some of our excitement about and appreciation for the richness and variety of human social behavior, by presenting social psychology in a conceptually integrated way. Both of us have felt frustration at textbooks that portray social behavior as a list of interesting but unrelated phenomena explained by numerous never-to-be-heard-from-again theories. We have felt disappointment when laboratory studies are presented in isolation from "real world" settings—the courtroom, school, supermarket, or hospital—where real applications take place. And we have been concerned that the very special nature of social psychology as the interface between the individual and the social world becomes lost in treatments that emphasize one of these aspects over the other.

Our purpose, then, has been integration. Our goal is to present both social behavior and the science that studies it in a conceptually and thematically integrated way. We want to show students not just the wonderfully diverse *what* of social behavior, but the impressively orderly and organized *how* and *why* of it. Our pursuit of these goals is reflected in three ways of weaving together the content of this book.

Three Types of Integration

INTEGRATION OF DIVERSE TOPICS THROUGH UNIFYING PRINCIPLES. Eight basic principles that apply to social behavior emerge and re-emerge in the text. The two most fundamental ones are that people construct their social reality and that social influence pervades social life. Simply put, people help define their social environments at the same time their social environments influence them. In addition, we structure our discussion of people's interaction with their social world by introducing three overarching motivational principles and three processing principles that direct and determine thoughts, feelings, and actions. The powerful effects of these principles give coherence to our descriptions of research findings and theoretical approaches in every area of social psychology. By focusing on these core ideas, students can enhance their conceptual understanding of social psychology and can take away from the course knowledge that is applicable to their everyday lives.

INTEGRATION OF THE SOCIAL AND THE COGNITIVE. Our discipline was founded—indeed broke away from its parent field of psychology—on the idea that people's behavior depends on their perceptions and interpretations of social situations. Recent research in social cognition has started to spell out in detail how these cognitive processes operate. But social psychologists are also aware that social motives, interpersonal relationships, and emotional attachments to group membership guide and direct everything people do. The intertwining of social processes with cognitive processes is the essential tension of human social behavior, and we have made it a central theme of our textbook. The theme is reflected in the social and cognitive nature of the unifying principles. It is reflected again in the research data we describe: we have made a special effort to bring together the contributions of both North American and European social psychologists, who have emphasized somewhat different aspects of the cognitive/social interface. Finally, it is mirrored in our special focus on cultural, ethnic, and national similarities and differences in social behavior.

INTEGRATION OF BASIC SCIENCE AND APPLICATIONS. Historically, social psychology has focused simultaneously on advancing theory and addressing important social problems. In our book we stress that the same underlying processes of social perception, social influence, and social relations operate in the experimental laboratory, field research, and people's everyday lives. In each chapter we describe the practical implications of the theory and research being discussed. We do so with examples such as:

- A discussion of polygraph usage next to a section on nonverbal cues to deception.

- An overview of jury decision-making in the chapter on group influence.

- A discussion of Pygmalion in the classroom as part of the presentation of self-fulfilling processes.

- An account of subliminal advertising following the description of persuasion and counterargument.

These applications should stimulate students to think about the breadth and generality of the underlying processes, reinforcing the idea that ours is an integrated field.

In formulating and pursuing these integrative goals we have been inspired by the example set by Krech and Crutchfield's famous 1948 social psychology text. Despite the huge differences between the social psychology of their day and ours, their approach and ours are similar in several key ways. Most fundamentally, Krech and Crutchfield also aimed at a systematic, integrated treatment. They stressed the linkages between basic and applied research: "The basic guiding principle has been that a theoretically sound social psychology is also a practically valid and immediately useful social psychology" (p. vii). Finally, they emphasized the role of both social and cognitive processes in social behavior, drawing particularly on what was the most active area of cognitive psychology in their time: the study of perception. The ideas presented in the Krech and Crutchfield text had a profound influence on those who taught us social psychology and who instilled in us in turn a passion for combining, intertwining, and integrating the social and the cognitive.

The impetus for an integrated treatment of social psychology is the same today as it was a half century ago. There is an esthetic pleasure in showing students how the diverse findings of our field fit together in an intellectually coherent way. As people who care deeply about our field, we take pride in demonstrating social psychology's growth as a science and the accumulation of knowledge about social behavior. The integrative enterprise also reveals the existence of a number of fascinating yet underresearched areas. For example, huge amounts of research have examined the impact of attitudes on behavior. Though the effect of *norms* on behavior is equally great—and arguably greater—only a scattering of existing studies address this relationship.

However, the most important benefits of integration are pedagogical: showing students social psychology as an integrated whole, rather than as a list of topics that happen to share a label, makes our field both *easier to understand* and *more applicable*. As the same few principles emerge again and again in diverse topic areas, these ideas serve as a coherent organizing framework for particular findings and theories. Many studies of science education support the integrated approach. Science is most effectively taught to students of all ages not by cramming them full of "facts" but by stressing integrative themes, presenting findings in their context, and showing theories together with their applications (Tobias, 1990; Celis, 1993). Thus, all students should find our text enjoyable and understandable. We believe that our approach will enable them to do well in the course and also to take away ideas that will help them to understand themselves and others better throughout their lives.

Organization of the Text

After two chapters that introduce the field of social psychology and the conceptual basis of its research methods, the remaining chapters are organized into three broad topic areas that build one on another: social perception, social influence, and social relations. Within each of these areas are four chapters.

In terms of the book's integrative principles, the material on social perception (chapters 3–6) naturally emphasizes the role of cognitive processes, but it continually reinforces the idea that all cognition is socially influenced—even such basic and personal ideas as what we think about the self. The section on social influence (chapters 7–10) naturally focuses on the role of social processes, but it stresses that the effects of social processes are also mediated through cognitive processes—as, for example, the amount of effort people devote to processing persuasive arguments. Finally, the section on social relations (chapters 11–14) illustrates the ways that social and cognitive processes are inextricably intertwined as they influence the ways we get to know and like other people, cooperate in groups, and harm or help others. The book ends with a brief Epilogue that summarizes the major themes and reflects on some of their interrelationships and applications.

Although this organization seems to us to enhance the thematic presentation of concepts and topics, the integrated nature of the material allows instructors considerable flexibility in organizing the course. The instructors' manual suggests several different teaching sequences that emphasize different approaches to the material—without surrendering the advantages of integration. For example, those who wish to focus on the "social" before the "psychology" will find that the social influence section can easily precede the social perception chapters.

In keeping with our integrated approach, there are no separate chapters on "law," "business," or "education." Instead of relegating these interesting topics to a "back of the bus" position, we have integrated applications of social psychological theories and research results throughout the book. In this way, we hope to reinforce and strengthen the idea that exactly the same processes studied by researchers in their labs operate in applied settings to produce socially significant effects. Further, we operate with a broad definition of what is "applied," considering not only major societal institutions like law and business, but also such topics as personal relationships and divorce, media violence and aggression, social support and health, cooperation in solving environmental problems, "choking under pressure" in sports, conflicts in international relations, and the effectiveness of advertising. Text sections focusing on such applied topics are flagged by blue boxes before their headings. For the convenience of instructors who wish to devote lecture time specifically to summing up the implications of social psychology for one or more applied areas, and for students with a special interest in a particular area, a topical index to applications is on page ix.

Features to Enhance Learning

Our text has a number of special features to aid the student's learning.

FOCUS ON PRINCIPLES. The emergence and re-emergence of the basic principles are noted by the repetition of key words or phrases designed to activate and re-activate these concepts in students' minds. To further the idea that the same principles recur again and again, we provide margin references to related points in other chapters. These references direct students who are interested in conceptual parallels between different topics to look either forward or back in the text to find them, citing specific pages.

INTEGRATIVE REFLECTIONS. The end of the narrative of each chapter is devoted to *Concluding Comments*, our reflections on some larger issues raised by the chapter, on interrelations among chapters, or on special aspects of the way the principles play themselves out in the chapter. In these sections we step back a bit from the details of a particular topic, and place it in its larger context, both in theoretical terms and in its relation to our everyday lives.

ORGANIZATIONAL FEATURES. Each chapter opens with an outline of the chapter's main headings, followed by an introduction to the key problems and topics to be discussed. In addition, each major section within the chapter begins with a short preview to give the reader an idea of what is coming. Such advance organizers provide a simple structure that helps students understand material as they read it for the first time. For example, by identifying the main ideas of the section, the preview allows students to focus their initial reading on grasping those ideas rather than becoming sidetracked by details.

GRAPHICAL FEATURES. In line with our emphasis on the principles that underlie the diversity of behavior, explanations are often supplemented by graphical flow-charts, representations of key processes that demonstrate how and why such behavior arises. Results from key studies are also shown in the form of easy-to-understand bar charts.

OTHER FEATURES. A running glossary defines the most significant terms and concepts on the pages on which they occur. All entries are repeated in a cumulative glossary at the end of the book for convenient reference. Finally, the end of each chapter also features a verbal summary that includes the key terms, for review and reference.

Supplements that Accompany the Text

The *Instructor's Resources*, by Angela Lipsitz of Northern Kentucky University, provides extended outlines, lecture suggestions, discussion topics, classroom demonstrations, handouts, and lists of audiovisual materials for each chapter of the text. To help develop student appreciation of the integrated approach to social behavior, this manual includes extended coverage of how the basic principles are manifest in each chapter, and how each chapter builds on and develops themes from earlier chapters. There are also suggestions for teaching the material in different sequences, and for using the text to provide an extended focus on specific areas of application. In addition, the manual suggests several ways in which the issues of differences within and between cultures discussed throughout the text might be highlighted.

A *Test Bank* that includes both multiple-choice and essay questions covering the material in each chapter is also available from Psychology Press. Questions emphasize concept acquisition, understanding of underlying processes and principles, integration of material within the chapter, and application of chapter material to everyday situations, as well as assessing factual knowledge. [Psychology Press provides both a printed Test Bank and computerized test-generation systems that use these questions as a data base.]

Acknowledgments

As the Mock Turtle no doubt knew, it takes more than just a porpoise to allow wise fish to complete a journey. We owe thanks to many, many people who have helped us not just to make the journey but to become wise fish. First, our friends, students, and colleagues at the University of California, Santa Barbara and Purdue University have provided advice and social support—Chris Agnew, Jim Blascovich, Don Carlston, Nancy Collins, Denise Driscoll, Alice Eagly, Kurt Frey, Dave Hamilton, Sarah Hunter, Janice Kelly, Stan Klein, Brenda Major, Sarah Queller, Duane Wegener, and Crystal Wright were particularly important to us. The many undergraduate students who participated in classroom tests of various drafts of the manuscript were also extremely helpful to us—even their occasional puzzled looks provided useful feedback. The all-engrossing process of writing a book always becomes an imposition on family, friends, and companions. We are grateful to Pamela Smith, Miranda Smith, Tom Smith, and Alex Mackie for putting up with us and giving us perspective on our work. We promise to be in a better mood from now on, to talk about something else every once in a while, and to stop trying to use them as examples in the book.

We have been lucky indeed to have worked with the many dedicated and talented people at Psychology Press. We began with the conviction that a textbook taking an integrated approach to social psychology could be written. We thank J. George Owen, good friend and incomparable next-door neighbor, for encouraging us in this process and Gün Semin for steering us toward Psychology Press. Director of Publishing Alison Mudditt shared our vision for the book and helped make it a reality. Beth Gallagher served as our developmental editor, clarifying and improving our writing at every turn. Phyllis Fisher played a similar role for the first edition, and many traces of her able assistance remain in this second edition. Ed Cilurso applied his formidable powers of organization as production manager for the project.

Many of our colleagues and friends generously gave their time to review portions of this text. We are particularly grateful to those who have used the first edition in their classrooms over the years, and for the comments, suggestions, and encouragement that they have passed along to us. To all those who reviewed various portions of the manuscript, and whose insightful comments have often gently shaped and smoothed the ideas we present here, our heartfelt thanks:

Christopher Agnew, *Purdue University*
Judith Allen, *Drake University*
Scott Allison, *University of Richmond*
Roy Baumeister, *Case Western Reserve University*
Ellen Berscheid, *University of Minnesota*
Herbert Bless, *University of Mannheim*
Galen Bodenhausen, *Northwestern University*
Rupert Brown, *University of Kent at Canterbury*
Peter Carnevale, *University of Illinois, Urbana-Champaign*
Chris Crandall, *University of Kansas*
John Dovidio, *Colgate University*
Peter Gray, *Boston College*
John Harvey, *University of Iowa*
Alex Haslam, *Australian National University*

Tory Higgins, *Columbia University*
Michael Hogg, *University of Queensland, Australia*
L. Rowell Huesmann, *University of Michigan, Ann Arbor*
Lucy Johnston, *University of Canterbury, New Zealand*
Martin Kaplan, *Leiden University, Holland*
Janice Kelly, *Purdue University*
Bill Klein, *Colby College*
Neil Macrae, *University of Bristol*
Norman Miller, *University of Southern California*
Richard Petty, *Ohio State University*
Dean Pruitt, *State University of New York at Buffalo*
David Schroeder, *University of Arkansas*
Norbert Schwarz, *University of Michigan, Ann Arbor*
Constantine Sedikides, *University of Southampton*
Gün Semin, *Free University of Amsterdam*
Jeffrey Sherman, *Northwestern University*
Tom Tyler, *New York University*
Michaela Waenke, *Psychology Institute, Heidelberg, Germany*
Daniel Wann, *Murray State University*
Kipling Williams, *University of New South Wales, Australia*

Finally, we would like to thank each other for the many benefits of co-authorship. Through our collaboration on each section and sometimes each sentence of the text, we believe we have accomplished a sort of integration through teamwork. We learned to respect and admire each other's different strengths and talents, to appreciate each other's different views of the field, and to blame each other when deadlines were missed! We also became much better friends in the process.

To The Student

As you begin your study of social psychology, you may be wondering what this field is all about, and how it relates to your own personal experiences. You are in for a treat, because it is a fascinating field that has much to do with you. Our goal in writing this book is to convey some of the excitement and satisfaction that comes with understanding more about your own and others' social behavior.

One of the reasons that social psychology is so fascinating is that the limitless variety of social behavior we see around us every day can be understood as effects of a few basic principles. Rather than asking you to memorize a large number of unrelated ideas, we have tried to write a book that makes those basic principles easy for you to *see, understand, remember,* and *apply* in your own life. We have sought to accomplish this by

- Clearly *identifying* the most basic principles so that you can distinguish them from the many interesting (but less important) facts, studies, and comments.

- *Illustrating* the way the basic principles apply to a wide range of situations, including research studies and people's everyday lives.

In our years of studying and teaching, we have found that certain ways of approaching written material can greatly facilitate learning. Based on that experience, we have included a number of features in each chapter to assist you. The basic premise underlying these features is that *effective studying and learning is an active process*. You won't get much out of this or any other textbook if you try to rush through a whole chapter rapidly and passively, the way you might approach a mystery novel. You should divide up the chapter into chunks, read each chunk more than once, and reflect on what you have read. Here are some suggestions on how to do that.

- Start by reading the chapter title and looking at the outline of headings. Read the chapter introduction. Browse through the photos, cartoons, figures, and tables. This process will give you a general overview of the chapter's content.

- Every chapter contains several major sections. Work on one section at a time, paying particular attention to the *previews* (brief shaded sections that follow major headings), a unique feature that offers a capsule survey of the information that follows. By giving you an idea of what is coming, the previews make it easier to understand the material the first time you read it. The previews will tell you the main ideas of the section, to help you avoid getting bogged down in details or mistaking a subsidiary point for the key idea.

- Keep alert for appearances of the basic principles. By focusing on these core ideas, you will be able to build an integrated and coherent picture of social psychology's research findings and theories. To remind you of the basic principles, we use the same key words or phrases whenever an example of their operation arises.

- Follow up on the *margin references* whenever they interest you or when you are not sure you remember an idea or argument. This feature is designed to remind you of related points elsewhere in the book and to point out similarities or parallels between chapters, helping you to link new material to what you already know.

- The important terms and concepts of the field are presented in **boldface** and are defined in the margin of the page on which they appear. Psychologists use technical terms for precision in writing. Don't try to memorize their definitions on first reading; it is more important first to understand the gist of what you are reading. You will find it helpful, however, to learn these terms on second reading and to review them when studying for an exam. An alphabetical glossary of terms and definitions can be found at the back of the book.

- After you have finished studying each of the chapter's main sections, read the concluding comments and the summary. If anything in the summary seems unfamiliar or unclear, reread the relevant section of the text.

Finally, we urge you to enjoy yourself. Think about what you are reading and what it means for your own life, and for society at large. Ask questions about what you read, and pose your own questions about what issues need to be thought about next by social psychologists—perhaps by you! We think social psychology is fascinating. We hope that what you learn here will convince you of that too.

How to use this book

This new edition of *Social Psychology* has been thoughtfully designed to present textbook material in a user-friendly manner. Eliot Smith and Diane Mackie have provided a fascinating mix of broad concepts and specific examples. Our challenge as the publisher is to present them to you in a clean, easy-to-read format that draws attention to important information but does not distract from the important framework the authors have created. These pages illustrate some of the most important features that should be utilized when teaching or reading this book.

> Theme tables at the end of each chapter summarize the most important applications of the basic principles

Because scientific theories are invented rather than discovered, the scientific enterprise draws on its practitioners' creativity and imagination. The greatest contributions of Galileo, Newton, Darwin, and Einstein were not new data, but deep insights into new conceptions of reality that organized and explained existing evidence. On a more mundane level, creativity is also a crucial ingredient as scientists devise ways to test existing theories. A clever study, like a novel theory, is a product of creative imagination as well as disciplined hard work. As any social psychologist will tell you, this is one of the main reasons why doing research is fun.

Science is a human activity. Needless to say, then, it cannot be completely logical and unbiased. Just as scientists, like all humans, construct a version of reality based on bits and pieces of evidence, so are scientists, like all humans, subject to biases. Cultural values, political and religious views, and personal preferences may influence the problems that scientists choose to study or the theories they find congenial or abhorrent. Further, once a scientist creates or endorses a theory, it is likely to influence the way he or she evaluates research. A researcher may uncritically applaud some studies because their results support a "pet" theory, while dismissing less supportive studies as methodologically flawed or inadequately generalizable. Still, the standards and procedures of science, especially its public nature and its emphasis on the possibility of bias, limit the effects of such biases. And the danger of bias recedes even further when a number of studies conducted by scientists with diverse theoretical orientations in various places converge to support a theory.

This text now turns from "how we find out" to "what we know" about social behavior. However, the transition is not as drastic as you might think. As chapter 1 pointed out, all of us, scientists and nonscientists alike, are constantly constructing theories to help explain what we experience. As you will see throughout this text, these processes are at work when people watch a football game, read a political advertisement, or deal with conflict in a relationship. One of the most important applications of these processes occurs when we get to know someone, when we form impressions of what others are "really like." Just as scientists try to explain "the facts" theoretically, we all gather information about others and try to make sense of it by forming a coherent impression. The information we gather and the way we put it together can have a dramatic impact on how we act and react to the others around us.

CHAPTER 2 THEMES

- **Construction of Reality**
  Scientific theories are developed to summarize and explain observed patterns of behavior.

- **Pervasiveness of Social Influence**
  Scientists are influenced not only by the rules and customs of science but also by personal and cultural values and goals.

- **Striving for Mastery**
  Scientists attempt to understand and predict natur

SUMMARY

> Chapter summaries recall the major points stressed in the text, and synthesize specific concepts into larger themes

Research Questions and the Role of Theory. Research questions are provoked by curiosity about why people act the way they do. In turn, this curiosity often reflects concern about important social problems. Social psychologists seek to develop

Putting It All Together: Multiple Guides for Behavior   413

FIGURE 10.9   Attitudes and norms affect deliberately planned behavior

Belief that behavior produces good outcomes

Wearing a helmet protects a bicyclist against head injuries.

Belief about others' view of behavior

Everyone else wears a helmet and they think I should too.

■ According to the theory of planned behavior, people's attitudes, perceived norms, and their perception of their own control combine to produce a considered intention to act. This intention, in turn, guides behavior. (Based on Ajzen & Fishbein, 1977, 1980.)

Attitude toward behavior

I want to wear a helmet.

Perceived control over behavior

I can wear a helmet if I choose to. (I can afford one, can find a store that sells them, etc.)

Norm regarding behavior

I ought to wear a helmet.

Intention to perform behavior

I'm going to wear a bike helmet.

Actual behavior

I wear a bike helmet.

You may have noticed that in discussing both the direct and more deliberate impact of norms and attitudes on behavior, we have used examples in which attitudes and norms suggest the same action. Although attitudes and norms often converge, this is not always the case, of course. Milgram's participants obviously *hated* what they did, even as they bowed to the norm of obedience. You may earnestly desire a quiet Saturday afternoon by yourself but nevertheless fulfill your social commitment to help your friend move. How do we behave when attitudes and norms are at odds?

When Attitudes and Norms Conflict: Accessibility Determines Influence

Whether attitudes or norms have more influence on behavior depends on their relative accessibility for a particular behavior, in a particular situation, and for a particular person.

Norms, like attitudes, can guide behavior only if they are activated. When a relevant attitude is very accessible, it comes to mind easily, and behavior falls in line with it, as we saw in chapter 8. And, as the research described in this chapter has demonstrated, this fundamental principle applies to norms

---

Flow charts within chapters clarify processes and emphasize relationships

Highlighted previews offer short summaries of major sections and help to focus reading

Margin cross-references remind you of the connections among topics and the similarity of processes underlying different social behaviors

Major coverage of applied topics is highlighted in the text and indexed at the beginning of the book

Key terms are defined in a running glossary

Forming First Impressions: Cues, Interpretations, and Inferences   71

no effect on people's interpretations of Donald. People apparently do not use just any accessible cognitive representation to interpret information; rather, the accessible representation must be *applicable* to the information.

Activating a cognitive representation to increase its accessibility and make it more likely to be used is called *priming*. The effects of priming can be long-lasting and rather subtle. Concepts that have been primed can remain accessible and influence later interpretations for as long as 24 hours (Srull & Wyer, 1980). Their impact does not even depend on people's awareness of the activation! To demonstrate this, John Bargh and Paula Pietromonaco (1982) showed some participants neutral words, while others saw words related to the trait of hostility. Then both groups read a description of a character's ambiguous behaviors. When the groups' responses were compared, those primed with the hostility-related words interpreted the behaviors as more hostile and aggressive. The interesting twist is that the presentation of the priming words was so brief—a mere flash on a computer screen—that the participants could not say what the words were. Even when people are unable to identify a word consciously, encountering the word can still make cognitive representations accessible and influence the interpretation of later information. Other similar studies have confirmed this remarkable finding (Niedenthal, 1990). So even if you just glimpse the Clint Eastwood poster out of the corner of your eye without consciously registering it, it might make you interpret behaviors as aggressive.

ACCESSIBILITY FROM FREQUENT ACTIVATION: CHRONIC ACCESSIBILITY. What toys are usually found lying at the top of the toy box? The ones that get dragged out and played with every day. The same is true of thoughts. The frequent use of a cognitive representation over days, months, or years can make it *chronically accessible* (Bargh, Bond, Lombardi, & Tota, 1986; Higgins, 1996). When this happens, people repeatedly use the same concepts in interpreting others' behavior. For example, intelligence might always be important in one person's judgments, whereas friendliness or helpfulness might matter more to someone else. In fact, people can more easily recognize information relevant to their "favorite" traits and can remember it better than unrelated information (Bargh & Thein, 1985; Higgins, King, & Mavin, 1982). Imagine, for instance, that you observed someone performing many behaviors: greeting friends, going to a party, studying in the library, and working at a part-time job. If friendliness is chronically accessible for you, you would be more likely to notice and later remember the first two of these behaviors. Another observer for whom intelligence is a chronically accessible concept would more easily notice and remember the time the person spent in the library.

□ **ACCESSIBILITY AND SEXISM IN A JOB INTERVIEW.** Television and print advertisements often use sex to sell products like beer and automobiles, implicitly promising the intended male consumers that attractive women will flock around them if they purchase the correct product. Do such ads make thoughts about women as sex objects more accessible? Might this priming even affect men's behaviors if they interviewed female candidates for a job? Laurie Rudman and Eugene Borgida (1995) showed one group of male students a series of TV commercials that the researchers felt portrayed women

FIGURE 3.3   What is this man experiencing?

■ Emotional expressions are some of the easiest signals for humans to understand. But before you come to a firm conclusion, turn the page.

Chapter 7, especially pages xxx to xxx, will discuss the thought-provoking possibility that our attitudes might similarly be influenced without our awareness.

Priming. The activation of a cognitive representation to increase its accessibility and thus the likelihood that it will be used

1

What Is Social Psychology?

In the fall of 1951, Princeton University's undefeated football team played Dartmouth College in a particularly hard-fought game. The teams were long-term rivals, and the game started rough and went downhill from there. Penalties punctuated the game, and fights left players on both sides with serious injuries before Princeton finally won. One month later, two social psychologists asked Princeton and Dartmouth undergraduates to view a film of the game (Hastorf & Cantril, 1954). The responses were astonishing. Princeton fans and Dartmouth supporters reported seeing events so differently that they might have been watching different games. Princeton students saw a constant barrage of Dartmouth violence and poor sportsmanship, with Princeton players occasionally retaliating in self-defense. Dartmouth students rated the teams as equally aggressive but saw their battered team's infractions as understandable responses to brutal Princeton attacks. One Dartmouth alumnus who watched the film saw so few Dartmouth violations that he concluded he must have been sent an edited copy of the film.

Perhaps these findings are not really so astonishing if you consider that fans of opposing teams hardly ever agree on the impartiality of the umpiring. Similarly, partisan observers of political debates almost always proclaim their own candidate "the winner," and proud parents at the school music contest often disagree with the judges' decision. Yet consider the profound questions that these findings raise. If the world is objectively "out there" for all to see, how can observers reach such different conclusions about what seems to be the same event? Why do we so often end up seeing exactly what we expected to see, and how then can we decide what "really" happened? Can the same innocent feelings of belonging that make us see our team, our candidate, or our child in such positive terms also produce biased judgments, unfair decisions, and unequal treatment of others?

Thirty years after Hastorf and Cantril's study, researchers at Vanderbilt University asked two groups of students to consider the difficult issue of whether convicted criminals should be given probation as an alternative to imprisonment (Axsom, Yates, & Chaiken, 1987). One group of students had a special reason to be concerned with the issue: They had been led to believe that the probation policy might soon be introduced in their area. For the other group, the issue was merely academic—the policy was not being considered for their community. The researchers told the students that, to help them make up their minds, they would hear a tape of a local candidate speaking in favor of the issue at a political rally. What the students were not told was that the researchers had actually prepared four quite different tapes. On one tape, the candidate put forward compelling evidence in support of probation while an enthusiastic audience warmly applauded his words. On a second, the same effective presentation elicited scattered hisses, boos, and heckling from the audience. A third tape had the candidate giving rambling, specious, and disjointed arguments, which were met with enthusiastic applause from the audience. And on the fourth tape, the weak arguments were greeted by boos and hissing.

When the researchers polled the students whose interest in the probation issue was merely academic, the impact of the audience's taped response was clear. Students in this group who heard either of the tapes on which the audience greeted the candidate's position with enthusiasm adopted the position themselves, and those who heard the tapes on which the audience voiced disdain rejected the candidate's position. A completely different pattern of responses emerged among students who expected the issue to affect their community. These students focused on the content of the speech. They were swayed if they heard the candidate give cogent arguments but remained unpersuaded if the arguments were weak—regardless of the applause or hisses of the taped audience. Why were the reactions of other people so compelling to some students and so unimportant to others? Why did some participants "go with the flow" while others considered the issues carefully? Did some students care less than others about being right, or were all of the students trying to take different paths to the "truth?"

Like the Vanderbilt students, we are all bombarded daily by attempts to persuade us: advertising campaigns, paid political messages, even the cajoling of friends and family. Consider the last time you were persuaded by one of these attempts. What approach was used by the person who persuaded you? Did that person present you with the hard facts, or did he or she play on your emotions? If you were told that "everyone else" had already joined the parade, would you be more likely to go along or more likely to rebel? Or would it depend on the issue?

Questions like those raised by these studies lure social psychologists into their labs every day in search of reliable answers. Social psychology offers a special perspective on human behavior, because the social aspects of human behavior—the ways that people's thoughts and actions are affected by other people—can be both powerful and puzzling. Our goal in this book is to give you some insight into how people act, and why they act the way they do, by introducing you to some of the many questions social psychologists ask about social behavior, the ways they go about answering those questions, and the answers they have found. We know that you will find these questions intriguing and hope that the often surprising conclusions will make you want to delve more deeply into these compelling issues.

Our first step will be to provide a definition of *social psychology*: to chart out the territory we will be covering and to give you a glimpse of what makes the terrain so fascinating. We next describe how social psychology developed its special perspective on human behavior. Like other fields of human inquiry, contemporary social psychology is a product of its own history and of the history of the societies in which it developed. With a quick survey of the past behind us, we then map out the territory ahead. The final part of the chapter provides a sneak preview of the material we cover in the rest of this book. To help you find your way with confidence, we point out some signposts and landmarks to look for along the route.

A Definition of Social Psychology

Social psychology is the scientific study of the effects of social and cognitive processes on the way individuals perceive, influence, and relate to others. Notice that social psychology is defined as a science, that social psychologists are as keenly interested in underlying social and cognitive processes as they are in overt behavior, and that the central concern of social psychology is how people understand and interact with others. Let us consider each of these components in turn.

The Scientific Study . . .

Social psychologists, like other scientists, gather knowledge systematically, by means of scientific methods. These methods help to produce knowledge that is less subject to the biases and distortions that often characterize common-sense knowledge.

This shaded text is a brief preview of the section that follows. For advice on how you can use it to improve your efficiency in studying the text, turn back to the "To the Student" section in the Preface.

Of course, you have been studying social behavior all your life. Everyone uses common sense and "street smarts" to make sense of the social world they inhabit because we all want to make good friends, reach mutually satisfying decisions, raise children properly, hire the best personnel, and live in peace and security rather than in conflict and fear. How does the social psychologist's approach differ from our everyday approaches? The answer is found in methods, not goals (Fletcher & Haig, 1990). Although scientific researchers and common-sense observers share many goals—both wish to understand, predict, and influence people's thoughts and behavior—their methods for achieving those goals differ greatly.

As common-sense observers, people often reach conclusions about social behavior haphazardly, based on their own or others' experiences. Therefore common-sense knowledge is sometimes inconsistent, even contradictory. You may have heard, for example, that "opposites attract," and also the reverse, that "birds of a feather flock together." As scientists, on the other hand, social psychologists study social behavior systematically, seeking to avoid the misconceptions and distortions that so often afflict our common-sense knowledge. Of course, even scientific knowledge is not infallible. The history of science shows that many conclusions proposed as scientific truths are eventually overturned by new observations or new insights. But as you will see in chapter 2, scientific conclusions are sounder and more resistant to challenge than common-sense knowledge because they are based on systematic methods of gathering information and are constructed with an awareness of the possibility of error.

Social psychology. The scientific study of the effects of social and cognitive processes on the way individuals perceive, influence, and relate to others.

. . . of the Effects of Social and Cognitive Processes. . .

The presence of other people, the knowledge and opinions they pass on to us, and our feelings about the groups to which we belong all deeply influence us through social processes, whether we are with other people or alone. Our perceptions, memories, emotions, and motives also exert a pervasive influence on us through cognitive processes. Effects of social and cognitive processes are not separate; they are inextricably intertwined.

A first date, a classroom presentation, a job interview, a problem-solving session with co-workers: What do these situations have in common? Each is a situation in which others observe us or interact with us, influencing our thoughts, feelings, and behavior. We try to make a good impression, to live up to the standards of the people we care about, to cooperate or compete with others as appropriate. These examples show the operation of social processes. **Social processes** are the ways in which the people around us, the groups to which we belong, our personal relationships, the teachings of our parents and culture, and the pressures we experience from others all affect our thoughts, feelings, and actions.

Cognitive processes, on the other hand, are the ways in which our memories, perceptions, thoughts, emotions, and motives guide our understanding of the world and our actions. Note that emotion and motivation are intrinsic parts of every cognitive process, just as are memory and thought. Modern social psychology rejects the misleading opposition—dating back to ancient Greek philosophers—between pure, rational thought and irrational emotions. Cognitive processes affect every aspect of our lives, because the content of our thoughts, the goals toward which we strive, and the feelings we have about people and activities—all the ways we act and react in the social world—are based on what we *believe* the world is like.

Though we have defined them separately, in reality social and cognitive processes are inextricably intertwined. To illustrate their intimate connections, consider these two points.

First, social processes affect us even when others are not physically present: We are social creatures even when alone. Faced with an important decision, we often stop to think about the possible reactions of absent friends, relatives, or fellow group members, and these thoughts can also influence us. Even during many of our most private activities—studying, practicing a musical instrument, exercising, or showering—we are motivated by our concern for what others think of us. Think about the last time you rode an elevator in which you were the only passenger. We bet you stood facing the doors, just as you would have if other people had been physically present. Because our group memberships become part of who we are, they influence us even when other group members are absent. Whether other supporters are present or not, we rise to the defense of our party's political platform and feel elated about our college team's victory. We react in this way because *our* party or *our* college has become a basic part of *our* identity. In cases like these, by considering the *group in the individual*, social psychologists examine how people are affected by their knowledge of what is expected of them, that is, by their knowledge about the be-

---

Social processes. The ways in which input from the people and groups around us affect our thoughts, feelings, and actions.

Cognitive processes. The ways in which our memories, perceptions, thoughts, emotions, and motives influence our understanding of the world and guide our actions.

■ **Group influence far from the group.** These Egyptian soccer players are celebrating a goal scored in a 1999 World Cup match in America. Although engaged in a sporting competition, and far away from their homeland, they so thoroughly accept their Muslim faith that they stop and pray after the goal. For all of us, beliefs, attitudes, and practices endorsed by the groups to which we belong strongly affect our thoughts, feelings, and actions. This is true even when we are far away from other group members.

liefs, attitudes, and actions that are considered appropriate for members of their group.

Second, the social processes that affect us even when others are physically present depend on how we *interpret* those others and their actions, and therefore on the operation of cognitive processes. The impact of other people's arguments or comments in a group discussion depends on how we think and feel about their statements: Is the argument strong and compelling, or shaky and questionable? Does a particular comment indicate that the other person has thought seriously about the issue or is the comment ill considered or even offensive? By studying the *individual in the group*, researchers gain insights into how people are affected by others who are physically present, whether they offer friendly hugs or scornful glares, provide trustworthy information or try to deceive, lead by example or wait for someone to follow. But in all these cases, the way others affect us depends on our own thoughts and feelings.

Whether we are alone or together with others, then, both social and cognitive processes operate together to affect everything we think, feel, and do.

. . . on the Way Individuals Perceive, Influence, and Relate to Others

Social psychology focuses on the effects of social and cognitive processes on the way individuals perceive, influence, and relate to others. Understanding these processes can help us comprehend why people act the way they do, and it may also help solve important social problems.

Social psychology seeks to understand the social behavior of *individuals*, a focus that distinguishes it from sociology, political science, and other social sciences. The cognitive and social processes we have just described affect individuals as they perceive, influence, and relate to others. Consequently, these processes shape all forms of social behavior, including some that are significant concerns in today's world. Here are some examples of social behaviors that are important concerns and some questions social psychologists might ask about them.

- *Why do many marriages end in divorce?* A social psychologist might study divorce as an outcome of the social and cognitive processes of conflict in marriages. The research might focus on questions like the following: How do couples interpret events that put the relationship under stress? What alternatives to the relationship do they believe they have? What types of actions in the course of an argument determine whether one partner storms angrily out of the house or allow the couple to kiss and make up after a fight? Whereas sociologists might study the effects of unemployment on divorce rates in a society, social psychologists might instead examine the ways that being unemployed causes conflict and divorce, by affecting how the partners think about their relationship or how they try to influence one another.

- *How do door-to-door salespeople sell products?* Have you ever found yourself, as a salesperson departed from your door, holding an item that you never wanted and wondering how you were manipulated into purchasing it? A social psychologist would be interested in knowing the social and cognitive processes that induced you to buy. For example, how can a sales pitch expertly play on the consumer's needs, desires, or feelings of guilt or obligation? In contrast, an economist might study whether newspaper advertisements or door-to-door sales techniques produce more total sales.

- *What causes outbreaks of ethnic violence?* An historian or journalist might document the unique events that sparked a particular conflict. To the social psychologist, however, intergroup hostility stems from fundamental aspects of the ways people think about and interact with members of different groups. These include both people's competition for concrete resources (like jobs and political clout) and people's attitudes, emotions, and actions toward their own and other social groups. Social psychologists would ask whether the ways people categorize individuals into groups, the stereotypes they form about others, their preferences for people "just like them," or their feelings of power or powerlessness contribute to intergroup hostility.

Thus, social psychology seeks an understanding of the reasons people act the way they do in social situations. Such an understanding helps us explain events in our own lives: that disastrous first date, the successful job interview, the loneliness of being the new kid on the block, the hesitation we feel before making a major decision. It also helps us comprehend the factors that contribute to the complex events of our times: crime and violence, ethnic unrest and civil war, the spread of the AIDS epidemic, the destruction of the global environment. And if we understand how people are influenced by social and cognitive processes, we can begin developing solutions for such pressing social problems. For example, knowing that stereotypes and prejudice about members of other religious groups may have contributed to violent conflict in Lebanon or Northern Ireland suggests that changing those beliefs might help to prevent recurrences. In fact, social-psychological research has been instrumental in exposing workplace discrimination (Fiske, Bersoff, Borgida, Deaux, & Heilman, 1991) and recommending procedural changes to lessen biases in courtrooms (Kassin & Wrightsman, 1985). It has suggested policies to deal with violence and explicit sex in the media (Donnerstein & Linz, 1986) and to improve classroom environments for minorities and women (Steele, 1992). It has also been influential in finding ways to change perceptions of the risks of AIDS (Fisher & Fisher, 1992) and in developing programs to reduce international tensions (Lindskold, 1986). Thus the social-psychological perspective invites us not only to understand but also to act on that understanding.

Historical Trends and Current Themes in Social Psychology

How did social psychology come to develop its particular point of view? Like any field of knowledge, social psychology is a product of its past. The current focus of its research reflects historical events of the 20th century, changing societal concerns, and developments in other scientific fields, as well as changes in the techniques social psychologists have used in their research. This brief survey of the field's history will place the field in context and serve as a partial explanation for where social psychology stands today.

Social Psychology Becomes an Empirical Science

Soon after the emergence of scientific psychology in the late 19th century, researchers began considering questions about social influences on human thought and action.

From the time of the ancient Greeks, the study of the human condition was considered to be the domain of philosophy. Like social psychologists today, early philosophers recognized the impact that other people can have on individual behavior. Plato, for example, speculated about the "crowd mind," arguing that even the wisest individuals, if assembled into a crowd, might be transformed into an irrational mob. Through the ages, philosophers continued to theorize about the workings of the human mind—and they still do—but the development of social psychology had to await the emergence of its parent discipline, the science of psychology. This new field was born in the late 19th century, when a few researchers in Germany, impressed by laboratory methods being used by physiologists, began to employ experimental techniques to understand mental processes like sensation, memory, and judgment.

The experimental investigation of social-psychological issues began soon afterward, as researchers in North America, Britain, and France began the task of systematically measuring how behavior is influenced by the presence of others. A study published in 1898 by an American researcher, Norman Triplett, is sometimes cited as the first research study in social psychology (G. W. Allport, 1954a). Triplett, having noticed that swimmers and cyclists performed better when competing against their rivals than when practicing by themselves, wondered whether the presence of other people has a generally beneficial effect on performance. To find out, he asked schoolchildren to wind fishing line onto reels as quickly as possible, with and without others present. Sure enough, the children's performance improved in the presence of others. This interesting finding, however, appeared to contradict a conclusion that Max Ringelmann, a French agricultural engineer, had reached in an even earlier study conducted in the 1880s. Ringelmann found that when people worked together to pull on a rope or push on a cart, they put less effort into the task than when they worked alone (Ringelmann, 1913). The study of group effects on performance still continues today, and we now know that Ringelmann's and Triplett's results are not necessarily inconsistent. As you will see in chapter 12, the presence of others often facilitates performance when individual contributions are easily identified, but it reduces performance when people are "lost in a crowd."

For the first social psychologists, this puzzle was just one among many questions about how people influence one another. Early researchers also tackled questions about how facial expressions and body movements reveal people's feelings, how people conform to the suggestions of others, and the role that experimenters might play in influencing the outcomes of research (Haines & Vaughan, 1979). The first two textbooks bearing the name *Social Psychology* appeared in 1908. One of these, by psychologist William McDougall, argued that all social behavior stems from innate tendencies or instincts, an idea that was popular throughout psychology at the time. The other, by sociologist E. A. Ross, took up the theme that was soon to become social psychology's central concern: that people are heavily influenced by others, whether those others are physically present or not.

Social Psychology Splits From General Psychology Over What Causes Behavior

Throughout much of the 20th century, North American psychology was dominated by behaviorism, but social psychologists maintained an emphasis on the important effects of thoughts and feelings on behavior.

Although it arrived on the coattails of general psychology, social psychology soon developed an identity distinct from that of its parent discipline. Early in the 20th century, North American psychology as a whole became dominated by the behaviorist viewpoint. This perspective, exemplified by the work of John B. Watson and B. F. Skinner, denied the scientific validity of explanations for behavior that invoke mental events like thoughts, feelings, and emotions. For radical behaviorists, a legitimate science of human activity could be based only on the study of observable behavior as influenced by observable environmental stimuli.

Most social psychologists, however, resisted the behaviorist view that thoughts and feelings had no place in scientific explanations. They accepted the behaviorists' argument that the ultimate goal of science is to explain behavior, but their studies showed that behavior could not be explained without taking into account people's thoughts and feelings. Social psychologists learned that individuals often hold divergent views of, and react in different ways to, the same object or idea, be it a football game, a political candidate, or capitalism. Such findings could be explained only by differences in individuals' attitudes, personality traits, impressions of others, group identifications, and emotions (F. H. Allport, 1924). Behaviorists were certainly right in their belief that external stimuli can influence behavior. However, social psychologists maintained that the effect of any stimulus depends on how individuals and groups *interpret* it. Right from the start, then, social psychology was distinctive in its conviction that understanding and measuring people's perceptions, beliefs, and feelings is essential to understanding their overt behavior (E. E. Jones, 1985).

The Rise of Nazism Shapes the Development of Social Psychology

In the 1930s and 1940s, many European social psychologists fled to North America, where they had a major influence on the field's direction. Significant questions generated by the rise of Nazism and the Second World War shaped research interests during this period.

It has been said that the one person who has had the most impact on the development of social psychology in North America is Adolf Hitler (Cartwright, 1979). Ironic though this observation is, it contains important elements of truth. In fact, both the events that precipitated the Second World War and the war itself had a dramatic and lasting impact on social psychology.

As Nazi domination spread across Europe in the 1930s, a number of psychologists fled their homelands to continue distinguished scientific careers in North America. This influx of European researchers consolidated social psychology's special emphasis on how people interpret the world and how they are influenced by others. Most European researchers were trained not in the behaviorist tradition that was prominent in North America but in Gestalt theory, which took for granted the role cognitive processes play in our interpretations of the social world. Around the same time, researchers became increasingly impressed by anthropologists' accounts of the pervasiveness of cultural influences on people's thoughts and behavior. It fell to social psychologists to identify the mechanisms by which such influences occurred, and they soon developed techniques to perform realistic studies of complex social influences in the laboratory. Muzafer Sherif's (1936) elegant experiments, for example, showed that a social group can influence even a person's perception and interpretation of physical reality, as you will see in chapter 9 of this text.

But the war's effect on social psychology went beyond bringing a new group of skilled researchers to North America. Revelations of Nazi genocide led a horrified world to ask questions about the roots of prejudice (Adorno, Frenkel-Brunswik, Levinson, & Sanford, 1950). How could people feel and act on such murderous hatred for Jews, Gypsies, homosexuals, and members of other groups? These questions still resonate today as the world contemplates "ethnic cleansing" in the former Yugoslavia; ethnic conflicts in the Congo, Azerbaijan, and South Africa; and "gay bashing" on the streets of North American cities.

Conditions created by the Second World War also drew social psychologists into the search for solutions to immediate practical problems. With food in short supply and rationing in full swing, the U.S. government asked social psychologists how to convince civilians to change their eating habits: to eat less steak and more kidneys and liver, to drink more milk, and to feed their babies cod-liver oil and orange juice (K. Lewin, 1947). Social psychologists were also called on to help the military maintain troop morale, improve the performance of aircraft and tank crews (Stouffer, 1949), and teach

■ **Social influences on scientific concerns.** This German photograph from 1938 shows an advertisement for a special edition of *Der Stürmer* with the headline "Jews Are Criminals." Many of the social psychologists who fled Nazi-dominated Europe were horrified at the Nazis' success in swaying the public mind against the Jews. These concerns triggered lifelong efforts to understand the roots of prejudice, the causes of obedience, the power of propaganda, and other social issues.

troops to resist enemy propaganda—and even to brush their teeth regularly (Hovland, Janis, & Kelley, 1953).

Social psychologists fell to applied research with a will, realizing that they would be able to develop and test general theories of behavior even as they solved practical problems. As we will see in Chapter 10, Kurt Lewin (1947) found that active participation in discussion groups, by establishing behavior in a social context, was more effective in changing what women fed their families than passive listening to lectures on the topic. Lewin's findings are still successfully applied in support groups like Weight Watchers, Overeaters Anonymous, and many other organizations. Samuel Stouffer's (1949) research on American soldiers' morale showed that it depended more on the soldiers' interpretations of how they were doing compared to other enlisted men than on how well they were actually doing. Satisfaction with the rate of promotion, for example, was sometimes lower in units with higher-than-average promotion rates. Stouffer suggested that in these units the soldiers' expectations of promotion were high, setting them up for disappointment if others were promoted but they were not. The importance of comparisons with others and ways comparisons can lead to feelings of relative deprivation are still important topics in current social-psychological research. And, though we may be amused by Carl Hovland's assignment of devising ways to persuade GIs to brush their teeth regularly, current theories of persuasion build on his original demonstrations that persuasion depends on who delivers the message, who receives the message, and how the message is processed (Hovland and others, 1953).

During this crucial period of research and theory building, the work of one social psychologist in particular embodied the themes that characterized the young discipline. Kurt Lewin, one of the scientists who had fled Hitler, held that all behavior depends on the individual's *life space,* which he defined as a subjective map of the individual's current goals and his or her social environment (K. Lewin, 1936). Perhaps you can see how Lewin's ideas sum up two of social psychology's enduring themes: that people's subjective interpretation of reality is the key determinant of their beliefs and behaviors and that social influences structure those interpretations and behaviors. Lewin's work also reflected the close link between research aimed at understanding the underlying social and cognitive causes of behavior and research aimed at solving important social problems, a link that will receive considerable attention throughout this book. Lewin had a gift for conducting research that combined the testing of theories with the solving of problems. As he put it, "There is nothing so practical as a good theory" (K. Lewin, 1951, p. 169).

Growth and Integration

During the 1950s and 1960s, social psychology grew and flourished, moving toward an integrated theoretical understanding of social and cognitive processes and toward further applications of social-psychological theory to important applied problems.

Both basic and applied social psychology flourished during the prosperous 1950s and 1960s. Backed by expanding university enrollments and generous government grants, researchers addressed a great variety of topics central to understanding social behavior. Research contributions during this period laid the foundations of what we now know about self-esteem, prejudice and stereotyping, conformity, persuasion and attitude change, impression formation, interpersonal attraction and intimate relationships, and intergroup relations, all still key topics within social psychology today.

By the 1970s, social psychology had developed a set of reliable and repeatable findings, which is a mark of scientific maturity. The time was ripe for both internal integration, the melding of various specific topic areas into broader explanations of behavior, and external integration, increasing attention to neighboring scientific fields and to significant social concerns. And so the movement toward integration began.

INTEGRATION OF COGNITIVE AND SOCIAL PROCESSES. The study of cognitive processes became a natural framework for integration both within and outside social psychology. As the tight grip of behaviorism on North American psychology was finally broken, a cognitive revolution got under way (Neisser, 1967). Cognitive themes and theories swiftly gained attention in experimental, developmental, personality, and even clinical psychology. Of course, the cognitive revolution was no revolution for social psychology. Cognitive themes such as the importance of people's interpretations in shaping their reactions to events were familiar to social psychologists because their foundations had been laid decades earlier in Allport's, Sherif's, and Lewin's work in the 1930s and in Stouffer's and Hovland's studies in the 1940s. Concepts such as attitudes, norms, and beliefs, already common currency in social psychology, began to be applied to new areas of study: personal relationships, aggression and altruism, stereotyping and discrimination. These applications were greatly facilitated during the 1970s and 1980s by the adoption of research techniques that had been found to be valuable by cognitive psychologists studying perception and memory. Thus, theoretical concerns and proven experimental methods converged as researchers in many areas of social psychology focused on the study of cognitive processes (E. E. Jones, 1985).

Concern with cognitive processes is only one side of the coin, however. Social psychologists have always been aware that social processes, including personal and group relationships and social influence, also impinge on everything people do. True, our behavior is a function of our perceptions and interpretations and our attitudes and beliefs, but those factors in turn are fundamentally shaped by our relationships to others, our thoughts about their reactions, and the group memberships that help us define who we are (Markus, Kitayama, & Heiman, 1996). Scientific understanding of the way social and cognitive processes work together to mold all social behavior has benefited from the increasing integration of North American social psychology with European social psychology, where the impact of social group memberships has long been a dominant theme (Doise, 1978; Moscovici, 1980; Tajfel, 1978). Today, researchers in all domains of social psychology are weaving together the effects of cognitive and social processes to provide explanations of people's experience and behavior.

INTEGRATION OF BASIC SCIENCE AND SOCIAL PROBLEMS. Can technological advancement by itself offer solutions to such global threats as resource depletion, environmental pollution, war and ethnic conflict, and overpopulation? Many people believe the answer to that question is no. Instead, solving such massive problems requires profound changes in human behavior.

Social psychologists are attacking these and other crucial social problems, and this attack will require their best theoretical efforts. In this regard, social psychologists are lucky. Scientists in many other fields have to choose whether they will work on purely theoretical issues or apply their theoretical knowledge to practical problems. A materials scientist, for example, may seek to understand the nature of the molecular bonds that produce stronger materials, but it is the engineer who will use the new materials to design an improved wind-turbine blade. Social psychologists do not have to make this kind of choice. It is difficult to think of a single area of social-psychological research that does not have some application to significant social issues. Whether social psychologists are looking at close relationships or divorce, altruism or aggression, attitude change or the effectiveness of advertising, intergroup conflict or its resolution, they simultaneously address the basic theoretical questions that spur pure scientific curiosity and the important phenomena that affect our daily lives.

Traditionally, many psychologists have thought of basic and applied research as distinct, even opposite, areas, with applied research taking a back seat to basic research. This stance is foreign to contemporary social psychology. Because virtually all social-psychological research is relevant to significant social issues, it is simultaneously basic and applied. The same underlying social and cognitive processes operate wherever people perceive, influence, and interact with each other, both inside the research laboratory and outside it, in schools, factories, courtrooms, playgrounds, boardrooms, and neighborhoods. For this reason, as we describe theories and research areas throughout this text, we will also discuss their applied implications. As you will see, talented researchers are studying social-psychological processes in many applied settings, with a particular focus on major issues relevant to health, education, law, the environment, and business. We have created special section headings to help you locate discussions of particularly important applications to areas such as the following.

- *Health.* Good health is just a matter of good diet, regular exercise, and lucky genes, right? Wrong. The emotions we experience, the amount of stress we encounter from daily hassles, our ability to find love and acceptance in close relationships, and even the way we feel about ourselves can influence our bodies as well as our minds. When public health officials promote exercise and fight drug abuse, when hospitals allow patients more control over their treatments, and when support groups speed recovery from illness, addiction, and grief, social-psychological processes are playing a part in producing sound minds in sound bodies.

- *Education.* As teachers teach and students learn, more is being communicated than just Spanish and geography. Teachers' expectations can shape their pupils' self-esteem, self-confidence, and even their actual performance. Classroom activities can encourage competition or cooperation and can eliminate or exacerbate ethnic and gender stereotypes. No wonder that for some the classroom is an open field of opportunity, whereas for others it is a minefield of adversity and disappointment.

- *Law.* How do the police extract confessions? Do lie detectors really work? Is a defendant in suit and tie more credible than one in prison fatigues? How might leading questions and inadmissible evidence influence a juror's thinking? Does the minority opinion of a dissenting juror ever sway jury verdicts? From crime to conviction, social-psychological processes are at work as police enforce laws, juries weigh evidence, and societies try to distribute justice.

- *Environment.* Japanese commuters buy whiffs of oxygen from coin-operated machines in subways, yields of Atlantic fisheries decline, and American motorists waste hours in traffic jams. These human dimensions of environmental change are among those motivating social psychologists to discover how individuals can be encouraged to conserve energy or to recycle used materials. Others are working hard to determine the ways groups can be convinced to cooperate in harvesting renewable resources instead of overexploiting and destroying them.

- *Business.* From advertising to sales techniques to the pitfalls of managerial decision making, social-psychological processes are the gears that drive the wheels of business. Consider, for example, the way effective leadership can mold diverse individuals into a smoothly functioning work team, while ineffective leadership generates only conflict, dissatisfaction, and low productivity.

In social psychology, the everyday world is not just a place to test discoveries made during laboratory research. Instead, social psychologists regard issues that are important outside the laboratory—ethnic conflict, the AIDS epidemic, crime and aggression, declining productivity, global interdependence—as both a source of theoretical ideas and a target for solutions (J. Rodin, 1985).

How the Approach of This Book Reflects an Integrative Perspective

Not surprisingly, given the way social psychology has developed, our conception of social psychology is an integrated one. In this text we share with you our view of social psychology as a field that integrates not only the cognitive and the social but also basic theory and applied research. We believe that all the diversity and richness of human social behavior can be understood in terms of a few fundamental social-psychological processes. These processes flow from eight principles: two fundamental axioms, three motivational principles, and three processing principles.

As we describe specific topics like attraction, aggression, altruism, and attitude change, we will show you how all these forms of social behavior flow from the interaction of these same fundamental principles. At the same time, seeing these principles at work in different settings, producing apparently different forms of social behavior, will enhance your understanding of their meanings and implications. Here we give you just a quick introduction to these basic principles and the processes that flow from them.

Two Fundamental Axioms of Social Psychology

Two fundamental axioms of social psychology are that people construct their own reality and that social influences are pervasive.

Two fundamental axioms, or most important principles, integrate all the topics in this text. The first is that *people construct their own reality*. The second is that *social influence pervades all social life*.

CONSTRUCTION OF REALITY. At first glance, studying social behavior may seem to be an exercise in the obvious. As we go through our daily routines, we trust that we are seeing the world around us as it is—that an objective reality exists "out there" for all to see. When we join friends to watch a ball game or to eat dinner in a restaurant, we assume that we all see the same game and hear the same enjoyable dinnertime conversation. When we meet someone new, we quickly form an impression of what he or she "is like." And when we see someone raise a fist, furrow a brow, or slump in a chair, we know what the behavior means because "actions speak louder than words." Because we assume that our impressions are accurate and true, we usually expect anyone else who meets the same person, goes on the same date, or sees the same action to share those impressions.

Every now and then, however, we are forced to think twice. Discovering how different the reactions of others can be to the "same" social event overturns our usual lack of awareness of the extent to which we construct our own reality. Try reminiscing with one of your parents about what happened on your first day of school, and you may discover that your memories of the details of that milestone in your lives are quite different. Or, if you are a sports fan, compare your recollection of an important game with

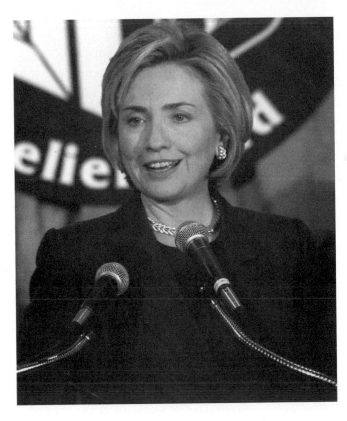

■ **Who is this woman?** Is Hillary Rodham Clinton a calculating manipulator or a victim of nasty gossip? A cutthroat political climber or a cookie-baking mom? Or is she none of these? The answer depends on who is doing the perceiving—conservative detractors, the liberal media, her family, or Clinton herself. What seems real to us is socially constructed and, like beauty, is in the eye of the beholder.

the view of the opposing team's fans and see if you agree about what happened. At such times we discover that we do not, in fact, share the same experience. A fist can be raised in intimidation or triumph, and a furrowed brow can indicate depression or concentration. What is real for each of us is a **construction of reality,** shaped in part by cognitive processes (the way our minds work) and in part by social processes (input from others who are actually present or whose presence we imagine).

Cognitive processes operate as we piece together fragments of information, draw inferences from them, and try to weave them into a coherent whole. We may hear a speaker deliver a series of arguments, note the audience's response, draw inferences about how others feel, and decide whether the message is worth our close consideration. In this sense, a person's view of the world is certainly in the eye—or the ear—of the beholder.

Social processes enable us to influence and be influenced by the views of others as we pursue agreement about the nature of reality. Within the groups that are important to us, agreement is our standard for interpreting and responding to events. For example, most members of Western societies enjoy kissing, although the meaning of the kiss varies, depending on whom we kiss and how. But when the Thonga of southeast Africa first saw Europeans kissing, they were disgusted by what they regarded as "eating each other's saliva and dirt" (Hyde, 1979, p. 18). Whether we are Thonga cattle herders or North American college students, we tune in to others' interpretations—our parent's views about kisses or the cheers or boos of an audience listening to a speech—and we use those interpretations as the basis for our own responses. In this sense, a person's view of the world is at least in part a reflection of what is seen in the eyes of others.

Construction of reality. The axiom that each person's view of reality is a construction, shaped both by cognitive processes (the ways our minds work) and by social processes (input from others either actually present or imagined).

PERVASIVENESS OF SOCIAL INFLUENCE. We could probably all agree that other people influence our public behavior and that our actions in turn can influence what others say and do. Having supporters at our back gives us a bit more courage to speak out; face-to-face confrontations with detractors may frighten us into silence.

Recall, however, that we said earlier that others can influence us even when we are alone. The **pervasiveness of social influence** means that other people influence virtually all of our thoughts, feelings, and behavior, whether those others are physically present or not. Our thoughts about others' reactions and our identification with social groups mold our innermost perceptions, thoughts, feelings, motives, and even our sense of self. Do you proudly think of yourself as a Celtics fan, a member of your temple, a citizen of Canada? Our allegiances may be small scale, such as membership in families, teams, and committees, or large scale, including affiliations based on race, ethnicity, religion, gender, or the society and culture in which we live. But whether the group is large or small, our membership in it provides a frame and a filter through which we view social events. The Dartmouth–Princeton game had a particular meaning for students from each school and a quite different meaning for people who felt no allegiance to either team. Even among those on the same side, the game meant different things to the team members and their fans.

We sometimes experience social influence as social pressure, as when we encounter an aggressive salesperson or are berated for holding out on an otherwise unanimous jury. But social influence is most profound when it is least evident: when it shapes our most fundamental assumptions and beliefs about the world without our realizing it. The reactions of the Princeton and Dartmouth fans were certainly shaped and biased by their school allegiances, but were the fans aware of that influence? Probably not. We would not expect anyone to think, "I'd better interpret that tackle as vicious because my friends will reject me if I don't." Social influences have surrounded us since infancy, and it is therefore no surprise that we usually are unaware of their impact. Does the fish know it swims in water? Sometimes it takes a shift in perspective to make us aware of the impact of social influence. Such shifts are familiar to all of us: A rebellious teenager becomes a parent and imposes a curfew on his own teenagers; a die-hard Braves fan moves from Atlanta to Toronto and eventually joins with her new co-workers to support the Blue Jays. Even then, such changes often seem so natural that we attribute them not to social influence but to the demands of the situation, for example, reasoning that the Blue Jays are just the best team. Throughout this text, you will see evidence of the powerful effect social influence has in molding the reality we construct for ourselves—and therefore our thoughts, feelings, and actions—whether we are together with others or alone with our thoughts.

Three Motivational Principles

As they construct reality and influence and are influenced by others, people have three basic motives: to strive for mastery, to seek connectedness with others, and to value themselves and others connected to them.

> **Pervasiveness of social influence.** The axiom that other people influence virtually all of our thoughts, feelings, and behavior, whether those others are physically present or not.

As individuals and groups construct reality while influencing and being influenced by others, they direct their thoughts, feelings, and behaviors toward three important goals.

PEOPLE STRIVE FOR MASTERY. Mastery refers to understanding ourselves and the world around us and applying that understanding to help us control outcomes in our lives. Each of us **strives for mastery**: We seek to understand and predict events in the social world in order to obtain many types of rewards. Achieving mastery is an important incentive in our attempt to form and hold accurate opinions and beliefs about the world, because accurate beliefs can guide us to effective and satisfying actions. For example, if you want the last available part-time job at the campus bookstore, forming an accurate impression of the manager's needs and knowing yourself well enough to give a convincing account of your qualifications may help you get the job. Similarly, insightfully diagnosing business problems and successfully understanding students' and faculty members' needs may help you keep such a job. In many everyday decisions, individuals and groups choose to act in ways that appear likely to lead to the most rewarding results, guided by the most reliable and accurate information we can muster.

PEOPLE SEEK CONNECTEDNESS. In **seeking connectedness,** each person attempts to create and maintain feelings of mutual support, liking, and acceptance from those they care about and value. For members of groups in conflict, such as Israelis and Palestinians, actions that benefit their group often seem even more important than civil peace and an end to conflict. Apparently, conforming to group standards, even standards that have destructive consequences for people outside the group, fulfills a need for belonging and connectedness. But the consequences are not always destructive. This same fundamental motive cements the relationships that bring joy and meaning to our lives, linking us to our teammates, families, friends, and lovers.

PEOPLE VALUE "ME AND MINE." The motivational principle of **valuing "me and mine"** means that we are motivated to see ourselves and anything or anyone connected to us, such as our families, teams, nations, or even possessions, in a positive light. Even people with life-threatening illnesses can maintain a positive view of themselves by comparing themselves with others who are even worse off. Our biased views of those who are connected to us often explain why members of different groups see the same events in very different ways. A Princeton fan may view the Dartmouth quarterback's broken leg as an accident—unfortunate, but part of the game of football and certainly not something that reflects badly on the Princeton team. A Dartmouth supporter might blame the injury on a viciously dirty tackle, clear evidence that the Princeton team is incapable of good sportsmanship. Little wonder that these fans came away from the game with very different views of it, views that emphasized the positive characteristics of their own teams and let them feel good about themselves.

Three Processing Principles

The operation of social and cognitive processes is described by three processing principles: Established views are slow to change, accessible information has the most impact, and processing is sometimes superficial but at other times goes into great depth.

In seeking rewards and connectedness and in valuing me and mine, people and groups gather and interpret information about the world in which they live. Three principles describe the cognitive and social processes that oper-

Striving for mastery. The motivational principle that people seek to understand and predict events in the social world in order to obtain rewards.

Seeking connectedness. The motivational principle that people seek support, liking, and acceptance from the people and groups they care about and value.

Valuing "me and mine." The motivational principle that people desire to see themselves, and other people and groups connected to themselves, in a positive light.

■ **Conservatism: What people think is slow to change.** In 1999, Nancy Ruth Mace became the first female graduate of The Citadel, which for 153 years had been an all-male military college. The road to this accomplishment, however, was paved with adversity. The college's first female student, Shannon Faulkner, dropped out after only six days in 1995. Two other women who entered with Mace in 1996 dropped out after one semester, citing cruel hazing and unfair treatment by male students who did not believe women could measure up to their college's valued traditions.

Conservatism. The processing principle that individuals' and groups' views of the world are slow to change and prone to perpetuate themselves.

Accessibility. The processing principle that the information that is most readily available generally has the most impact on thoughts, feelings, and behavior.

Superficiality versus depth. The processing principle that people ordinarily put little effort into dealing with information, but at times are motivated to consider information in more depth.

ate as we construct a picture of reality, influence other people, and are influenced by them.

CONSERVATISM: ESTABLISHED VIEWS ARE SLOW TO CHANGE. Conservatism is the principle that individuals' and groups' views of the world are slow to change and prone to perpetuate themselves. The Princeton supporters, convinced that their Tigers were the better team, interpreted what they saw through the filter of their beliefs. Their selective perceptions thus supported their views of reality, as did the influence of their group, the equally biased fans around them. Examples of conservatism are almost endless: the first impressions we form of job applicants, the stereotypes we harbor about other groups, or preferences we nurture for the brand of peanut butter Mom always bought. But in all these cases and more, the principle is the same: established knowledge tends to perpetuate itself. In the chapters to come you will see why prior beliefs, expectations, and preferences are so hard to change, and you will become more aware of the consequences of their resiliency. You will also appreciate the enormous amount of effort needed to budge them at all.

ACCESSIBILITY: ACCESSIBLE INFORMATION HAS THE MOST IMPACT. From football games to political debates, every social situation provides an incredibly rich array of information—so rich that we could not consider all its details. Consequently, we are likely to consider, remember, and use only a tiny fraction of the potentially relevant information when we make judgments or decisions. **Accessibility** is the principle that whatever information is most readily available to us usually has the most impact on our thoughts, feelings, and behavior. In many situations, what comes most easily to mind is what we were already thinking. So, to return to the football example, Dartmouth stalwarts used their conviction that their team is good as a basis for their judgments of what happened. In other situations, we base our judgments on the information that is most easily noticed and interpreted. For many of the students who listened to the probation speech without expecting to be personally affected, enthusiastic applause or disapproving whistles were the most noticeable and had the most impact on their judgments.

SUPERFICIALITY VERSUS DEPTH: PEOPLE CAN PROCESS SUPERFICIALLY OR IN DEPTH. Much of the time, people seem to operate on automatic, putting little effort into forming a superficial picture of reality and relying heavily on whatever information is most accessible. But sometimes, particularly when we notice that events fail to match our expectations or when our important goals are threatened, we take the time and trouble to process information more extensively. These are examples of the principle of **superficiality versus depth.** Confronted with an opposing point of view—one that clearly contradicted their own—students who cared about probation reconsidered their positions. They reviewed the arguments and based their opinions on the content of the speeches rather than on the circumstances of their presentation. Disagreement or rejection challenges not only our sense of mastery and understanding but also our feelings of connectedness, triggering anxiety and uncertainty. Threats to any of our important goals may motivate us to consider information in more depth and to think hard about our own beliefs and actions.

The interrelationships among the eight basic principles of social psychology are summarized in Figure 1.1.

FIGURE 1.1   Interrelations among the eight basic principles of social psychology

The person

Motivational principles
Striving for mastery
Seeking connectedness
Valuing "me and mine"

Processing principles
Conservatism
Accessibility
Superficiality versus depth

Construction of reality

Pervasiveness of social influence

The social world

■ Two fundamental axioms link the individual person to the social world. Each person constructs his or her own picture of social reality, which then guides all thoughts, feelings, and actions. At the same time, the pervasiveness of social influence affects virtually all aspects of the person. Three motivational principles and three processing principles determine both the nature of the constructed reality and the nature of the social influence.

Common Processes, Diverse Behaviors

In combination, these eight principles account for all types of social behavior, including thoughts and actions that are useful and valuable as well as those that are misleading and destructive.

It would be wonderful if these cognitive and social processes guaranteed accurate social thinking, positive social emotions, and successful social interaction. Unfortunately, this is not the case. As our examples demonstrate, exactly the same processes that produce useful and valuable outcomes in some situations produce misleading and destructive outcomes in others. Our ability to construct reality allows us to see our world as a coherent and meaningful place, but it also opens the door to bias and misinterpretation. Social influences sometimes provide us with safety in numbers, but they also may lead us like lambs to the slaughter. The drive for connectedness and the value we place on me and mine can give us the warm glow of belonging, but it can also prompt us to reject, devalue, and exclude others not in our chosen circle. Basing decisions on accessible information often produces extremely efficient decision making but sometimes leads to bad decisions. Even when we contemplate information as thoughtfully as possible, we are not always guaranteed an accurate decision. Sometimes the very act of thinking about things can slant our interpretations and introduce mistakes without our being aware of the problem.

Human behavior is not always as simple as it seems, but neither is it impenetrable to scientific inquiry or impossible to understand systematically. In fact, although social behavior is incredibly diverse, this diversity results from the operation of these same few processes. Thus, as you move from chapter to chapter in this text, watch for these principles at work. We offer some help by calling attention to the principles and general themes of the book. In addition, we make special efforts to present theories and research findings as interrelated sets of ideas by placing cross-references to related ideas in the margins. We know that disconnected items of information are hard to remember and do not contribute much to a real *understanding* of social behavior. We would like you to see this text as an integrated story of (a) the fundamental social and cognitive processes that operate as human beings perceive, influence, and interact with others, and (b) the way social psychologists learn about these processes, both in the laboratory and in the world of everyday life. It is a fascinating story, and we hope you will learn much about yourself and others as you follow it through the text.

Plan of the Book

The first two chapters of this text are an introduction to social psychology, covering the "Why?" and the "How?" of our science. The remainder of the book explores the "What?" of social psychology—the topic areas that make up the discipline. In this chapter we have tried to convey *why* social psychologists ask the questions they do. Chapter 2 tells more about *how* they seek answers.

- *Asking and Answering Research Questions.* Have we convinced you already that peoples' interpretive processes and social surroundings may bias what they know? Scientists are no exception. Chapter 2 describes the logical checks and balances built into the structure of science that help researchers guard against subjectivity and bias.

Chapters 3 through 14 explore *what* social psychologists study. Following our definition of social psychology, we deal in turn with how individuals perceive others (chapters 3–6), influence others (chapters 7–10), and relate to others (chapters 11–14).

Chapters 3 through 6 focus on *social perception,* the way we come to know and understand the basic elements of our social world: individuals and social groups.

- *Perceiving Individuals.* From fleeting impressions of passing strangers to the intimate familiarity of our best friend, chapter 3 deals with knowing and understanding other people.

- *The Self.* What person is probably most important, most near and dear to each of us? Chapter 4 describes how we understand the self.

- *Perceiving Groups.* In chapter 5, we investigate the beliefs and feelings people develop about social groups like working women, Russians, schoolteachers, or Muslims.

- *Social Identity.* Chapter 6 brings these topics together in a discussion of how we come to see ourselves *as* members of a social group, and how a group can become part of the self.

Social influence is the impact each of us has on others, and it is the topic of chapters 7 through 10. The elements of social psychology do not occur in isolation: Each of us is constantly influencing and being influenced by others. Others affect us whether they are in our face, like an aggressive salesperson, or on our minds even when we are alone.

- *Attitudes and Attitude Change.* Advertisements aim at our pocketbooks, political campaigns play on our fears, debates appeal to our reason. Do they change our minds? If so, how? Chapter 7 gives some answers to questions like these.

- *Attitudes and Behavior.* Under the right circumstances, attitudes both reflect and guide behaviors. Chapter 8 tells a tale of the mutual influence of attitudes and behaviors.

- *Groups, Norms, and Conformity.* A different kind of mutual influence is the focus of chapter 9. Here we examine how groups reach agreement and why that agreement has such compelling effects on group members.

- *Norms and Behavior.* Chapter 10 describes the effects of groups on what people do, not just on what they think. Bringing all the chapters of this section together, we describe how attitudes and group influences combine to affect behavior.

In the final four chapters we concentrate on *social relations*, the bonds that link us one to another, as individuals and as groups. Whether we are bound by attraction or cooperation, or shackled by aggression and conflict, our relations with others can pull us together or drive us apart.

- *Liking and Loving.* Chapter 11 takes a close look at feelings of attraction to other people and the formation and development of close and loving relationships. We also review what social psychology can tell us about why relationships flourish or wither.

- *Interaction in Groups.* Small groups—management committees, paramedic teams, juries, and others—do most of society's work. Chapter 12's topic is how we interact with others in small groups, and how groups work to accomplish shared tasks.

- *Aggression and Conflict.* Who can watch the evening news without being struck by the many conflicts that pit person against person or group against group? In chapter 13 we analyze the path of such conflicts: how they can arise, escalate, and, sometimes, be resolved.

- *Helping and Cooperation.* Dramatic incidents of selfless heroism or more commonplace acts of cooperation that benefit others: Why do they occur? Chapter 14 examines the conditions under which we help other people and our reasons for doing so.

The text ends with an epilogue, a brief concluding comment that summarizes the major themes and reflects on some of their interrelationships and applications.

As you read this book, we invite you to join us in seeing social-psychological principles at work in people's actions and interactions. Seeing events around you in this framework is the first and most essential step toward *becoming* a social psychologist and having the fun of doing research that advances our knowledge of how social-psychological principles work and of applying the principles to real and important problems. But you do not have to do research to use your new knowledge to understand why your friends act as they do, how other people influence you, or what accounts for group conflicts around the world. We hope you will come to appreciate both the usefulness and the excitement of social psychology.

S U M M A R Y

 A Definition of Social Psychology. Social psychology is the scientific study of the effects of social and cognitive processes on the way individuals perceive, influence, and relate to others. Like other scientists, social psychologists gather knowledge systematically by means of scientific methods. These methods help produce knowledge that is less subject to the biases and distortions that often characterize common-sense knowledge.

The physical presence of other people, the knowledge and opinions that they pass on to us, and our feelings about the groups to which we belong all deeply influence us through **social processes**, whether we are with other people or alone. Our perceptions, memories, emotions, and motives also influence us through **cognitive processes**. Effects of social and cognitive processes are not separate; they are inextricably intertwined.

All types of social behavior, including individuals' perceptions of, influences on, and relationships with others, reflect the operation of social and cognitive processes. Understanding these processes can help us comprehend why people act the way they do, and it may also help solve important social problems.

Historical Trends and Current Themes in Social Psychology. Social psychology emerged soon after the beginning of scientific psychology in the late 19th century, when researchers began considering questions about social influences on human thought and action. Through much of the 20th century, North American psychology was dominated by behaviorism, but social psychologists maintained an emphasis on the important effects of thoughts and feelings on behavior.

In the 1930s and 1940s, many European social psychologists fled to North America, where they had a major influence on the field's direction. Throughout this period, significant questions inspired by the rise of Nazism and the Second World War shaped research interests.

During the 1950s and 1960s, social psychology grew and flourished, moving toward an integrated theoretical understanding of social and cognitive processes and toward further applications of social-psychological theory to important applied problems.

How the Approach of This Book Reflects an Integrative Perspective. Social psychology is a field that integrates not only the cognitive and the social but also basic theory and applied research. All the diversity and richness of human social behavior can be understood in terms of eight basic principles. Two fundamental axioms of social psychology are that people **construct their own reality** and that **social influences are pervasive**. Three motivational principles are that, as they construct reality and influence and are influenced by others, people **strive for mastery**, or understanding and control of their environment; **seek connectedness** with others; and **value "me and mine."** People's thoughts and actions are also influenced by three processing principles. One is **conservatism**: Established views are slow to change. Another is **accessibility**: Easily accessed information has the most impact. The final principle is **superficiality versus depth**: People can process superficially or in depth. In combination, these eight principles account for all types of social behavior, including thoughts and actions that are useful and valuable as well as those that are misleading and destructive.

Plan of the Book. This text has four main sections. Chapters 1 and 2 introduce social psychology and its typical research methods. Chapters 3 through 6 focus on social perception, the ways that people interpret and understand other people, themselves, and social groups. Chapters 7 through 10 deal with social influence, the ways that people and groups affect each other as they interact and communicate. Chapters 11 through 14 describe the social relations that lead people to form relationships, work together in groups, and help and hurt each other.

2

Asking and Answering Research Questions

Imagine winning the state lottery. Or receiving a promotion after only 5 months in your new position. Or getting a would-be buyer to meet your price on the sale of your used car. How do you think you would react to these events? Most people would anticipate being very happy. Now imagine finding out that you have a life-threatening illness, that you have stayed in the same job for years and still have little hope of advancement, or that you got much less for your used car than you had hoped for. You probably would predict that you would be quite unhappy about these alternatives. It might surprise you to learn that social-psychological research has shown that these intuitively obvious conclusions are not always true. Lottery winners are soon no happier than the rest of us (Brickman, Coates, & Janoff-Bulman, 1978). Those receiving rapid promotions are often more dissatisfied than people with less chance of advancement (Stouffer, Suchman, DeVinney, Star, & Williams, 1949). Patients with serious illnesses often show remarkably good spirits (J. V. Wood, Taylor, & Lichtman, 1985). And the money actually gained or lost in negotiation with others has little to do with people's satisfaction about the outcome (Loewenstein, Thompson, & Bazerman, 1989).

Most people find these research findings pretty surprising. Common sense tells us that good outcomes make people feel happy, contented, and satisfied, and that negative events or failures make us unhappy. But conclusions based on scientific research are not always the same as those we reach using everyday common sense or intuition. And when those conclusions differ, which should you trust: research findings or common sense? Are research findings really more dependable, trustworthy, or accurate than our everyday understanding of social behavior?

These kinds of questions are at the heart of this chapter. Social psychology is an *empirical science,* meaning that its theories and conclusions about social behavior rest on the results of research. Like other scientists, most social psychologists believe that scientific research methods produce answers that are more likely to be trustworthy and unbiased than those we arrive at through everyday common sense, hunches, and intuitions. Why? It is not that scientists are perfectly objective logicians like *Star Trek*'s Mr. Spock or Commander Data. On the contrary, scientists are human, too, and they are just as vulnerable as anyone else to preconceptions, prejudices, and wishful thinking. But this is exactly why scientific methods are so important. Most people are unaware of the biases in their everyday thinking and knowledge, and they therefore fail to guard against them. Because scientists know that biases can distort their reasoning and their findings, they use research methods specifically designed to counter such slips in thinking.

Most of this chapter is dedicated to describing the lengths to which social psychologists go to try to keep their research free from bias and error. Their goal is to reach general conclusions about human social behavior that are as trustworthy as possible. Understanding the practical and logical steps researchers take to reach this goal will help you grasp *why* social psychologists do the sorts of research you will read about in this book. It will also help you to judge which research findings should be taken seriously and when research you read about in newspapers falls short of its goal.

But good science is about more than just producing trustworthy and general results. Social-psychological research is a human enterprise, in which people are both the investigators and the investigated. This situation inevitably raises issues of values and ethics. How should research participants be treated? Are there research questions that should not be pursued? Should the results of research be made known to everyone, no matter how they will use those results? No researcher can ignore these questions, and neither should any consumer of social-psychological research. As you read this chapter and the rest of this text, you may wish to reflect on the values implicit in social psychologists' work and on how your own values guide your reactions to the topics and results that we will discuss. Clarifying ethical and value stands about research issues is just as important to good science as carefully following the rules of the scientific method.

A Note to the Student on How to Use This Chapter

Research methods can seem dry and abstract, compared to the richness and excitement of the substance of social psychology. Although some familiarity with research methods is essential for understanding how social psychologists reach their conclusions about people's social behavior, instructors may use this chapter in different ways. Some may assign this chapter early in the course, corresponding to its place in the book. Others may ask you to read this chapter after two or three substantive chapters, so that your knowledge of some meaningful and important studies can serve as background for deeper understanding of research methods. Other instructors may not assign this chapter at all, preferring to describe research methods in lectures or handouts.

Whatever your instructor's approach, we add one piece of advice. Through the book, as you read about particular studies, you may wonder what justifies the research conclusions, or feel concerned about the well-being of participants in the study. When issues like these arise in your mind, it is a good idea to turn back to this chapter as a resource to help you think about the issues. So if you question a study's conclusion that violence in the media can *cause* people to become more aggressive, you might want to look at the section on experimental designs and the strength of causal inferences on pages 35–36. Or if you wonder how a study using North American college students as participants can shed light on the reactions of other kinds of people or people in other cultures, see the section on the generalizability of research on pages 39–40. These examples illustrate some ways this chapter can serve as a resource for understanding how and why research is conducted, throughout the entire course.

Research Questions and the Role of Theory

Origins of Research Questions

Research questions are provoked by curiosity about why people act the way they do. In turn, this curiosity often reflects concern about important social problems.

Research is almost always provoked by curiosity: the researcher's desire to know the answer to some question about events, ideas, and people. Some questions are provoked by unexpectedly negative or positive events. Well-publicized events such as the brutality of ethnic warfare in the former Yugoslavia and the global outpouring of aid for African famine victims provoke questions about hatred and altruism. The mass suicide of Marshall Applewhite and his Heaven's Gate followers cause social psychologists, like other observers, to ask how patterns of obedience are established. And the way rescuers work together to help victims of earthquakes, floods, hurricanes, and fires stimulates researchers' curiosity about processes leading to cooperation. But research ideas also stem from questioning the mundane and the accepted—the everyday events that affect the lives of all of us. Why do women still earn less than men performing the same jobs? How good are people at judging others' characters? How can city managers convince more motorists to carpool? Is breaking up really hard to do, even if you are the breaker-upper rather than the broken-up-with?

Part of what makes a person choose to become a social psychologist is a healthy store of curiosity about why people act the way they do. Notice, however, that many of these questions go beyond mere curiosity. Many social psychologists try to explain and solve social problems that have a major impact on many people's lives: racial prejudice, gender discrimination, depletion of environmental resources, violence, unhealthy lifestyles, and depression. And although individual events and people may provoke their research questions, social psychologists do not strive merely to understand *specific* events or *specific* individuals. They seek instead to discover general principles that explain the behavior of many people in many situations. From those principles will flow an understanding of why behavior occurs and under what conditions.

What Is a Scientific Theory?

Social psychologists seek to develop scientific theories to explain social behavior. A scientific theory is a statement about the causal relationships among abstract constructs. It is a statement that holds for specified types of people, times, and settings.

To conduct their research, social psychologists have to translate specific questions about individuals and events into general statements about social behavior. Consider, for example, some of the research referred to at the beginning of this chapter. One study interviewed women diagnosed with breast cancer and noted whether they compared themselves to others who were adjusting better or worse to the disease (J. V. Wood and others, 1985). In another study, business school students engaged in a mock negotiation with an opponent, then learned that the opponent was happy or sad about the outcome (Loewenstein and others, 1989). What was the point of these exercises? Were the researchers concerned only about the behavior of particular cancer patients, or about specific students involved in one set of negotiations? Not at all. The real goal of these studies was not to gauge the reactions of particular individuals in particular situations but rather to test a general social-psychological theory about human behavior. In fact, all the research referred to in the introduction to the chapter was testing some aspect of *social comparison theory*, the idea that people evaluate their abilities, opinions, and outcomes by comparing themselves to others (Festinger, 1954). All of our judgments about ourselves, as slow or smart, right or wrong, winners or losers, are affected by our comparisons of our own abilities, attitudes, and outcomes to those of others.

Information gleaned from comparison to others has a major impact on what people think and how they feel about themselves, as described in chapter 4, pages 120 to 122.

Theories provide general explanations for social behavior. More formally, a **scientific theory** satisfies three requirements:

- It is a statement about *constructs*.
- It describes *causal relations*.
- It is *general in scope*.

Let us look more closely at each part of this definition.

Scientific Theory. A statement that satisfies three requirements: It is about constructs; it describes causal relations; and it is general in scope, although the range of generality differs for different theories.

Constructs. Abstract and general concepts that are used in theories and that are not directly observable.

1. *Theories are about constructs.* **Constructs** are abstract concepts like "anxiety," "aggression," or "self-esteem." "The knowledge of others' attitudes" and "the evaluation of one's own attitudes" are two constructs that feature in social comparison theory. Each of these constructs is abstract, in that it cannot be directly observed. You cannot see knowledge or touch an evaluation.

2. *Theories describe causal relations.* Theories describe causal relations among constructs. A theory states that a change in one construct (the cause) produces a corresponding change in another construct (the effect). Social comparison theory is a theory about cause and effect: Our knowledge of other people's outcomes, performances, or opinions *causes* changes in how we evaluate our own outcomes, performances, or opinions.

   Because theories offer reasons to explain why events occur, they are very powerful. If we know that one state or event causes another, we can take practical steps, known as interventions, to change behavior or solve problems. The knowledge that people evaluate their own abilities and attitudes by reference to those of other people, for example, could have a variety of practical applications. A city might decide to saturate the community with posters featuring the names and photos of city residents who form car pools. Social comparison theory would predict that knowing that their neighbors are committed to car pooling might cause other residents to decide to share rides. Similarly, medical personnel who work with patients with treatable forms of cancer might encourage those patients to compare themselves with other people who have more serious forms of the disease. Such a comparison might help them to cope better with their illness. Both of these strategies are made possible by research showing that comparisons between our own experiences and those of other people actually cause us to feel and act in certain ways.

3. *Theories are general in scope.* Theories are intended to be general in scope, applying to many people in different settings and times. However, the range of applicability may vary from one theory to another. Social comparison theory, for example, is intended to be a broadly applicable statement about how all people evaluate many aspects of their life. And, indeed, judging one's own experience in the context of what happens to others does appear to be a general human characteristic, although reactions to the comparison may differ in different cultures (Moghaddam, Taylor, & Wright, 1993).

Other theories, however, have a more limited scope. Perhaps they pertain only to males, or only to people raised in some Asian cultures. The more generally applicable a theory is, the more useful it is because it will hold for many different kinds of people in many different situations and at many different times. Currently, however, little is known about just how broadly many social-psychological theories can be applied (M. H. Bond, 1988; Markus, Kitayama, & Heiman, 1996). This important issue of the generality of theories is explored in more detail later in this chapter.

Testing Theories: From Theory to Research

Theories are not worth much unless they are tested, and so the ultimate goal of research is to test theories. This testing allows social psychologists to assess whether a theory offers a good explanation of human behavior. Theories can be evaluated only on the basis of *valid* research: research that is trustworthy because the researcher has taken pains to exclude bias and error. How can researchers be sure their research is valid and can provide evidence for or against theories? It turns out that valid research is guided by the three properties of theories just described (T. D. Cook & Campbell, 1979; Judd, Smith, & Kidder, 1991).

1. Because theories deal with *constructs*—abstract concepts—researchers have to be sure the specific observations they make in their studies are in fact relevant to those constructs. For example, researchers studying how social comparisons affect cancer patients' adjustment to their illness must have some way to accurately measure the patients' adjustment.

2. Because theories describe *causal relations,* researchers have to be sure they know the causes of any changes in behavior they find in their studies Research must allow the conclusion that the cancer patients' successful adjustment is due to the social comparisons they make, rather than to some other, extraneous cause.

3. Because theories are *general* in scope, researchers have to be sure they have learned something about how people in general, not just a few individuals, think, feel, and act. Conclusions about effects of social comparisons on patients' adjustment would be most valuable if they held for those with many types of disease (not just cancer), and to patients who are treated at home as well as in hospitals, for example.

Research that meets these three criteria is said to have *construct validity, internal validity,* and *external validity.* As we shall see, all three of these criteria are essential links in the logical chain by which research supports theory. Although decisions about every aspect of research may have implications for all three forms of validity, construct validity has the most to do with the way constructs are measured, internal validity with the design of a study, and external validity with the populations and settings used in the research.

Construct Validity and Approaches to Measurement

To provide a valid test of a theory, research must have construct validity, which means that the independent and dependent variables used in the research must correspond to the intended theoretical constructs. Construct validity is endangered if participants behave in ways they think are socially desirable. Researchers ensure construct validity by measuring independent and dependent variables in many different ways.

The researcher's first task is to make sure that the research has good **construct validity,** meaning that the events that occur in the research setting actually correspond to the theoretical constructs under investigation. This is not always an easy task.

Remember that cause and effect constructs are abstract concepts (like anxiety or social comparison) that are not directly observable. Their presence or absence has to be inferred through observable variables (factors on which people can vary). Variables that are considered to be causal factors are called **independent variables.** Variables representing effects are called **dependent variables.** The term *dependent* indicates that the study has been designed to see how this variable depends on the independent variable.

An example can help clarify these terms. Let's consider a theory called *realistic conflict theory.* This theory states that hostility between social groups is caused by direct competition for limited resources. Researchers have tried to study the abstract construct of "competition for limited resources," for example, by measuring people's belief that their department and another department are pitted against each other for a share of an organizational budget. The theory suggests that this belief (the study's independent variable) will cause another construct, "hostility between social groups," to increase. To measure this construct, researchers have looked at dependent variables such as negative stereotypes, insults, refusal to help, and acts of aggression that rival groups direct toward each other. If the concrete inde-

Construct validity. The extent to which the independent and dependent variables used in research correspond to the theoretical constructs under investigation.

Independent variable. A concrete manipulation or measurement of a construct that is thought to influence other constructs.

Dependent variable. A concrete measurement of a construct that is thought to be influenced by other constructs.

■ **The Rattlers and the Eagles.** These archival photographs show two groups of boys who participated in Muzafer Sherif's famous study testing realistic conflict theory, to be described in chapter 13. On the left, the boys compete in a tug of war, an activity that corresponds to the construct of competition for limited resources because only the winning group received prizes. On the right, the boys cooperate to solve a problem with the water tank. This activity reflects the theoretical construct of cooperation for common goals, which the study found can reduce intergroup conflict.

pendent and dependent variables used in the research correspond to the intended theoretical constructs, the researchers will be able to draw valid conclusions about those constructs.

Construct validity has two parts. First, independent and dependent variables must correspond to the *intended* construct, and second, they must not correspond to *other* constructs. As you will see in the pages that follow, much of the ingenuity in social-psychological research goes into selecting and refining ways to measure important theoretical constructs without measuring other, unintended constructs.

THREATS TO CONSTRUCT VALIDITY. Unfortunately, ensuring construct validity is a pretty tall order. A common problem is that a variable may be affected by other influences besides the construct that it is intended to measure. Suppose researchers tried to measure intergroup hostility by asking workers in the organization how much they liked members of the competing department. Workers might be unwilling to admit that they hate their co-workers, so their ratings might not honestly reflect their feelings of hostility. This threat to construct validity is called **social desirability response bias:** people's tendency to act in ways that make them look good (M. J. Rosenberg, 1969). Consider another example. A researcher wishing to measure the construct of conscientiousness might ask the following questions: Are you a punctual person? Do you keep your promises? Do you carry your share of responsibilities in group projects? The problem is that most people's responses to such questions would reflect both their appraisal of their conscientiousness and their tendency to say good things about themselves. The researcher might think she is measuring conscientiousness, but in fact she also would be measuring people's desire to look good. Social psychologists must be constantly on guard against the threat of social desirability as well as other biases in their measurements. This is particularly true when researchers are interested in attitudes or behaviors that might meet with some social disapproval, such as stereotyping, prejudice, aggression, or unusual opinions or lifestyles.

Social desirability response bias. People's tendency to act in ways that they believe others find acceptable and approve of.

Sally Forth

© Reprinted with special permission of King Features Syndicate.

ENSURING CONSTRUCT VALIDITY. Researchers take great pains to avoid compromising the construct validity of their studies. They do so by choosing their measurements very carefully and by using multiple measures.

1. *Using the best measure for the purpose.* Researchers try hard to choose measurement techniques that tap the construct under investigation but minimize other influences. Measures used in research fall into a few distinct categories, each with its own strengths and weaknesses. *Self-report measures,* which rely on asking the individual about his or her thoughts, feelings, or behaviors, are probably the best available source of information about beliefs, attitudes, and intentions. But they are also particularly susceptible to social desirability biases, especially if the topic is a sensitive one. Thus, asking people overt questions about their racial prejudice might not produce answers with high construct validity (Dunton & Fazio, 1997).

A researcher studying racial prejudice might decide, therefore, that a better technique for his particular study would be to use *observational measures:* to directly watch and record people's behavior. The researcher could watch, for example, how close a participant stood or sat next to a person of another race and whether people participating in intergroup interactions displayed relaxed smiles or nervous fidgeting. Observational measures often have good construct validity, particularly when participants are unaware of being observed. Of course, if the research setting is public or if participants know they are being observed, social desirability biases could still undermine construct validity.

Performance measures are most appropriate for some research goals. *Performance measures* ask participants to perform some task as well as they can, for example, by answering questions as rapidly and accurately as possible or by recalling as much as they can about information presented earlier. A performance measure of prejudice might require participants to read a complicated description of a character's successes and failures and then to recall everything they could from the story. If participants recalled mostly successes when they believed the character was White but mostly failures if the same character was described as Hispanic, the researcher might conclude that the participants were prejudiced against Hispanics.

Because people usually just try to perform as well as they can on such tasks, social desirability tends to be less of a problem than it is with self-report or observational measures.

Like any good carpenter or chef, a social psychology researcher must choose the right measurement tool for the job at hand. Measures that prove to be particularly precise and effective ways of assessing constructs often become quite popular in research, as ones with less construct validity fall by the wayside. But even the best available measure might not by itself guarantee construct validity.

2. *Using multiple measures.* Because different kinds of measures have different strengths, the best way a researcher can ensure construct validity is to use *multiple measures.*

The use of multiple measures increases researchers' confidence in their findings. To understand why, imagine you wanted to be sure your boss was in a good mood before you asked for time off. You check her expression for a smile and conclude she probably is feeling fine. Because you really are not sure, however, you ask a co-worker, who reports that the supervisor has been quite amicable. Still, you decide to see if she chooses to work out during her lunch hour—usually a good sign of an upbeat mood. Each of these very different means of gathering information has its own unique problems, but the accumulated evidence all points to the fact that your boss is feeling pretty chipper. You can see how your conviction that you were actually reading the supervisor's mood accurately would grow with each converging piece of evidence, even though no single piece of evidence could be conclusive in itself. When different measures produce the same results it works the same way: Researchers can be reasonably confident that they are measuring the intended construct and nothing else.

Now imagine for a moment that you are part of a research team trying to test the impact of positive or negative mood on helping. How could you assess the dependent variable construct, helping? You can probably think of a number of different possibilities. You might ask people about their intentions to help. Alternatively, you could count the number of spilled papers they retrieve or tally the dollars they donate to a worthy cause. A third possibility is to time how long it takes the research participants to come to another person's aid. These are diverse measures of willingness to help. Which should you use? Your best choice might be "all of the above." By using so many diverse measures of willingness to help, researchers increase the likelihood that the construct of helping will be adequately measured.

Internal Validity and Types of Research Design

To provide a valid test of a theory, research must allow observers to conclude that changes in the independent variable actually caused changes in the dependent variable. If both the independent and dependent variables are measured, the research may lack internal validity because many other unknown factors could affect the research results. Random assignment of participants to groups followed by manipulation of independent variables allow the researcher to draw stronger conclusions about cause and effect.

The conditions under which intergroup contact can undermine prejudice and help resolve intergroup conflict are described in chapter 5, pages 190 to 197, and chapter 13, pages 542 to 545.

A good test of a theory provides solid evidence about cause and effect. Research has high **internal validity** if the researcher can confidently conclude that a change in the independent variable *caused* a change in the dependent variable. Whether or not such a conclusion can be drawn depends primarily on a study's *research design,* which specifies how research participants will be selected and treated. Some types of research designs offer a higher level of internal validity than do others.

THREATS TO INTERNAL VALIDITY. The major threat to internal validity is that factors other than changes in the independent variable may be present and may be causing the observed changes in the dependent variable. Eliminating all such alternative factors is often very difficult, as you will see in the following example.

The *contact hypothesis* is a theory that states that casual, friendly contact with members of a different ethnic group increases liking for that group (G. W. Allport, 1954b). One obvious way of testing this idea involves investigating the impact of important, naturally occurring, causal variables, such as a person's contact with different groups in the neighborhood, on liking for various groups. Rudolf Kalin and J. W. Berry (1982) did just that, using data from a public opinion survey. The survey asked what Canadians thought of English-speaking and French-speaking Canadians, Canadian Native Americans, and Canadians of German, Jewish, Italian, and Ukrainian descent. Kalin and Berry compared the survey data with information from the Canadian Census to establish which ethnic groups lived in the same neighborhoods as the various survey respondents. Their results showed that people who lived in areas with a relatively high percentage of a particular group liked that group more than did people who lived far away from members of the group. This study is an example of a **nonexperimental research** design, a design in which researchers simply measure both the independent variable (in this case, neighborhood ethnic composition) and the dependent variable (people's opinions of groups).

Unfortunately, nonexperimental designs are vulnerable to many threats to internal validity. For example, measurement of the independent variable in this survey does allow researchers to identify participants who live near many French-speaking Canadians and participants who do not. However, the nonexperimental design cannot rule out the possibility that these two groups of participants may differ in many other unknown ways. As a result, even if the groups differ in their general favorability toward French-speaking Canadians, researchers cannot confidently state the cause of that difference. Although highly favorable responses may be due to the causal impact of frequent contact with the group in the participants' neighborhood, other factors besides increased contact could also be the cause. In fact, you can probably think of several alternative explanations. For example, rather than contact causing the liking, liking may cause the contact. That is, people who hold more positive views of a group might choose to move into or remain in areas in which many members of that group live. Another explanation may be that people who live in a particular neighborhood share other personal characteristics, such as a particular type of social background, that influence both where the people live and how they feel about ethnic diversity.

In a nonexperimental design it is always possible that people who differ on the intended independent variable may also differ in other unin-

Internal validity. The extent to which it can be concluded that changes in the independent variable actually caused changes in the dependent variable in a research study.

Nonexperimental research. A research design in which both the independent and dependent variables are measured.

■ **Yes, but is it internally valid?** Many nonexperimental studies find that children exposed to violent television or video games are more aggressive than those who are not. Unfortunately, these designs lack internal validity. Their results cannot tell us whether what the children are watching causes aggression, or whether aggressive children prefer such video games and television programs. To establish the causal role of TV and video game violence, social psychologists have turned to experimental research designs with high internal validity, as discussed in chapter 13.

tended ways. Each additional difference offers an alternative explanation for any results researchers find. And each alternative explanation for differences in the dependent variable threatens the internal validity of the research.

ENSURING INTERNAL VALIDITY. Given the vast number of differences that characterize humankind, is it possible to set up a research design that ensures that groups of people can be expected to differ only in the way the researcher intends? Amazingly, the answer is yes. This feat can be accomplished by using an **experimental research** design. Two aspects of experimental design are crucial for internal validity: First, participants are *randomly assigned* to experimental groups (sometimes called *conditions*). Random assignment of the participants in a study is distinct from random selection of participants from some larger set of people, a topic that we will discuss later in this chapter. Second, after the random assignment takes place, the independent variable is *manipulated* (or intentionally varied) rather than simply measured. Here is how these two processes work.

First, researchers divide participants into groups that are equivalent. To do so, they use a technique similar to a lottery or a flip of a coin to assign participants to different groups. **Random assignment** gives every person who is a participant in an experiment exactly the same chance of ending up in any given experimental group. Random assignment of participants ensures that the groups are approximately equivalent in every way. Suppose you started out with 20 people, 10 men and 10 women, and randomly divided them into two groups by flipping a coin for each person. Would it be likely that all of the women would end up in one group and all the men in the other? It could happen, but it is extremely unlikely; in fact, this outcome would occur less often than once in 500,000 times. Because the coin has the same chance of landing head-up each time it is flipped, every person has an equal chance of being assigned to the "heads" group. In the end, each group will probably have a roughly even number of males and females. The same logic applies not just to gender but to all attributes of the individuals who are being assigned: their age, eye color, friendliness, shoe size, and even other characteristics the researcher would not think of or could not measure. So, on the average, random assignment creates groups that are approximately equivalent to one another before the manipulation is applied.

Experimental research. A research design in which researchers randomly assign participants to different groups and manipulate one or more independent variables.

Random assignment. The procedure of assigning participants to different experimental groups so that every participant has exactly the same chance as every other participant of being in any given group.

This sets the stage for the second important step in an experimental design: The researcher now manipulates, or intentionally varies, the independent variable so that participants in the different conditions are exposed to different treatments. Because the groups were expected to be equivalent to begin with, this procedure creates groups that differ *only* in terms of the independent variable. Finally, the researcher measures the dependent variable. Now it is reasonable to conclude that any observed differences in the dependent variable were caused by the independent variable, simply because no other differences between the groups are expected to exist. Of course, manipulations as well as measures must have good construct validity for an experiment to be meaningful. That is, a good manipulation (like a good measure) must successfully cause changes in the desired theoretical construct, but not in other, unintended constructs.

Donna Desforges and her associates (1991) used an experimental design when they set out to test the contact hypothesis. These researchers randomly assigned some participants, U.S. college students, to work cooperatively with a person described as a former mental patient. (The "patient" was actually a *confederate,* a research assistant playing a specific role in the study.) Other participants simply sat in the same room with the person. The students who interacted with the individual came to hold more positive beliefs about former mental patients than the beliefs expressed by students who simply worked in the same room. We can be confident that the interaction caused this difference because the groups of students who received these two treatments were created by random assignment and therefore can be expected to be equivalent in every other way.

EXPERIMENTAL VERSUS NONEXPERIMENTAL RESEARCH DESIGNS. A researcher who wishes to test a theory may choose either an experimental or a nonexperimental design. In general, experimental designs offer higher internal validity and therefore permit stronger tests of the causal relations between constructs. If a nonexperimental study shows that the dependent variable and independent variable go together, that result is consistent with a causal theory. For example, Kalin and Berry's (1982) finding that people who lived in ethnically diverse neighborhoods are lower in ethnic prejudice is certainly consistent with the contact hypothesis. The result does not provide strong support for the theory, however, because factors other than the independent variable could also be causing the observed pattern of results. Experimental designs provide stronger tests of theory because the combination of random assignment and manipulation of the independent variable rule out virtually all alternative explanations.

Why, then, would a researcher ever use a nonexperimental design? The reasons are quite straightforward. First, some theoretically important inde-

TABLE 2.1. Advantages and Disadvantages of Nonexperimental and Experimental Designs

Type of validity	Nonexperimental design	Experimental design
Internal validity	*Low,* because the lack of random assignment and manipulation means that alternative explanations for results may be possible.	*High,* because random assignment and manipulation allow alternative causal explanations to be ruled out.
Construct validity	*High,* if powerful effects of real-life variables— including those that cannot practically or ethically be manipulated—can be studied in their natural contexts.	*Low,* when practical or ethical constraints render manipulations weak or artificial. *High,* when manipulations can adequately vary theoretically important constructs.

pendent variables, like gender, ethnicity, or area of residence, obviously cannot be intentionally varied. Thus, Kalin and Berry could not practically have assigned people to live in neighborhoods near or far from members of other ethnic groups. Second, for ethical reasons, researchers must not manipulate variables like participants' relationships with their marriage partner, or their feelings of depression, or the degree of their ethnic prejudice. And, finally, other research manipulations just cannot be as powerful as the variation in constructs found in everyday life. For example, no experimental study of the effects of television watching on aggression could faithfully reproduce the accumulated effect of watching 4 or more hours of television every day for a period of 10 or 20 years. For all these reasons, nonexperimental designs are sometimes the most appropriate. Table 2.1 summarizes the advantages and disadvantages of experimental and nonexperimental designs.

External Validity and Research Populations and Settings

> To provide a valid test of a theory, research must have external validity, meaning that its results can be generalized to other people, settings, and times. Some theories apply to many different kinds of people and places, whereas others apply more narrowly. When a theory is intended to apply to a particular population and setting, external validity is ensured by conducting studies using that population and setting. When a theory is intended to apply generally *across* different people, places, and times, external validity is ensured by conducting repeated tests of the theory in diverse populations, settings, and cultures.

Research is usually conducted with a single type of participant at a single time and in a single location. Research has **external validity** if its results can be assumed to generalize, that is, to hold for other types of participants, other times, or other places relevant to the theory.

The results of the study by Desforges and her associates (1991), for example, offer support for the contact hypothesis. But you might wonder whether these results would be found *only* if the participants were North American college students, or *only* if the contact group was former mental patients. One of the important functions of research is to determine just how broadly theories generalize. Recall from the earlier discussion in this chapter that the more generalizable a theory is, the more powerful it is because it explains the behavior of many different people in many different situations. But not all theories claim to hold true for all people in all places (T. D. Cook & Campbell, 1979; Kruglanski, 1975): Some research aims at generalizing *to* specific people in specific places. Most of the research you will read about in this text, however, seeks to generalize more broadly *across* various kinds of people, places, and times.

GENERALIZING *TO* VERSUS GENERALIZING *ACROSS* PEOPLE AND PLACES. In some research, a specific target population and setting is the researcher's primary interest. Applied research, where the goal is to use scientific findings to solve immediate practical problems, often falls into this category. For example, researchers have long known that when people have a sense of control over their situation they cope better with stress. A physician might wonder whether an increased sense of control could help seriously ill patients cope better when they are hospitalized. A study that attempts to an-

> **External validity.** The extent to which research results can be generalized to other appropriate people, times, and settings.

swer this question has a specific and relevant population and setting. Only people hospitalized with serious illnesses can be used as participants if the goal is to answer this particular research question. In fact, as a result of such studies, giving hospitalized patients some control over their situation is now a widely used technique for helping them deal with stressful medical procedures (Pranulis, Dabbs, & Johnson, 1975).

Most research you will read about in this text does not attempt to generalize *to* a single, specific target population or setting. Instead, as you will see, the research goal is usually a broader sort of generalization *across* various factors. One way to think about this goal is to ask the questions: Does the research have implications for many types of people in various places at more than one time period? Does the research apply, for example, to women as well as men? To Israelis and Koreans, as well as North Americans? To people living in the year 2020 as well as those living today? A typical study is conducted with a limited number of participants of a particular type— usually college students—in one location at one point in time. Few people would be interested in research results that applied only to those participants at that time and place. The key question therefore becomes: Exactly what aspects of the research conclusions will successfully generalize?

Let us return to the example of the North American college students who engaged in a cooperative learning task in the laboratory with a person they believed was a former mental patient. Those students came to hold more favorable beliefs about one group, former mental patients (Desforges and others, 1991). What generalization can be drawn from this finding, assuming it passes the tests of construct validity and internal validity? One could ask whether exactly the same finding would be obtained among Ethiopian college students, among Israeli sixth graders, and among adults in Papua-New Guinea. But social-psychological researchers rarely study participant populations as diverse as these; indeed, the very concept of a "former mental patient" would be meaningless to some of these groups. The reason is that this is not precisely the right question to ask about generalizability. Whether the study's *specific findings* can be directly generalized is not the crucial issue.

What is the appropriate generalization? To answer that question, we need to recall the fundamental reason why a study like that of Desforges and her associates is conducted. That study was not aimed at generalizing *to* some target population or setting. Nor was it intended to reveal some modestly interesting fact about people's opinions of former mental patients, that is, about the specific dependent variable used in the study. Instead, the goal was to test a *theory* regarding causal relations among abstract constructs. In this case, the theory states that under specific conditions, friendly interaction with individual group members often causes positive changes in people's attitudes and beliefs about the group. This theoretical level defines the generalization that is expected. So we would not expect all kinds of people all around the world to hold the same views about former mental patients. We would, however, expect to find that similar processes of belief and attitude change are caused by friendly interaction with group members, at least until further research demonstrates limitations on the generalizability of the results.

Recall that we emphasized in chapter 1 that you should seek to learn general principles about social psychology rather than a long list of findings of specific studies. In exactly the same way, researchers hope that the underlying principles, rather than the details of the findings, will generalize from one population and setting to other appropriate ones. Figure 2.1 illustrates this idea: The results of a study are not applied directly to another population or setting but are used to support a general theory, which in turn has implications for other people and places (Mook, 1980).

EXTERNAL VALIDITY AND RESEARCH PARTICIPANTS. Recall that if research has external validity, its results can be assumed to hold for other types of participants, other times, or other places relevant to the theory. The first major threat to such generalizations thus involves the types of *people* studied. One problem is the use of participants who are unrepresentative of all the people to whom a theory is intended to apply. College students differ in many ways from the average person. For example, compared with the general population, they tend to be younger and more intelligent; they probably have less stable close relationships; they are still involved in forming new roles and images of themselves; and they are less likely to have experienced serious illness, divorce, or parenthood. Can researchers assume that *all* research findings obtained with college student participants will generalize to all other types of people? Of course not.

As we have said, however, researchers ordinarily do not wish to generalize specific findings. Their usual goal is to generalize a broader conclusion about underlying causal processes. So one would not expect, for example, to find that the issues responsible for arguments and conflict were the same for both college dating couples and older married couples. Nevertheless, the effect of arguments on the partners' satisfaction with their relationships

FIGURE 2.1   Research results generalize through theories

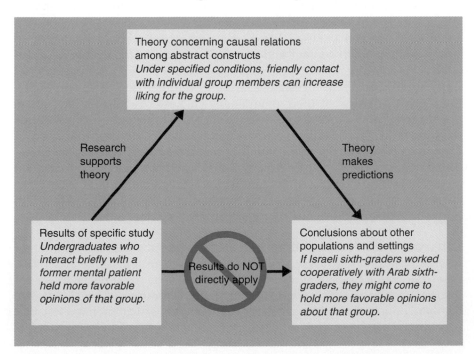

Theory concerning causal relations among abstract constructs
Under specified conditions, friendly contact with individual group members can increase liking for the group.

Research supports theory

Theory makes predictions

Results of specific study
Undergraduates who interact briefly with a former mental patient held more favorable opinions of that group.

Results do NOT directly apply

Conclusions about other populations and settings
If Israeli sixth-graders worked cooperatively with Arab sixth-graders, they might come to hold more favorable opinions about that group.

■ Most studies are conducted to test theories. The theory may then make predictions that apply to different people and places. The results of a particular study are not generalized *directly*, but they have implications for other people, times, and places to the extent that the results support a valid and general theory.

might be similar for both kinds of couples. Or, to use another example, students may not have as many well-developed social roles as older people, but the process by which students form their views of themselves and the effects of those views on behavior may be the same for many groups of diverse people. Thus generalizing about causal explanations is more justifiable than generalizing about the content of thoughts and behavior.

The social-psychological processes that are most likely to operate in similar ways among diverse groups of people are the most basic processes. Research has shown that these include the ways people respond to social influence from others, use the most accessible information, and seek mastery over their environment and connectedness with other people. As you will see in later chapters, these are the sorts of processes many social psychologists have investigated, often using college students as participants because they are easily accessible. Still, the only way to be really sure that research conclusions generalize is to repeat the research with different types of participants because, as you will see, sometimes even conclusions about processes cannot be generalized.

CULTURES AND EXTERNAL VALIDITY. People who have traveled in a country other than their own can testify that patterns of social behavior differ, and anthropologists' scientific observations confirm this conclusion. Since social psychology remains largely a Western phenomenon, do the research conclusions of social psychologists generalize across the world's societies and cultures? Once again, the answer is, "It depends." We can answer this question only by examining the specific set of research conclusions that we expect to generalize. Consider the observation that people tend to have certain expectations, or stereotypes, about what other social groups are like. Though the stereotypes that French and Australian citizens (for example) have of the English will probably be very different, the way the two groups of people develop those stereotypes and how they use them are likely to be very similar. Culture strongly dictates the *content* of people's thoughts and actions. The processes by which that content is developed and used, however, are more likely to be generalizable.

Sometimes both content and processes can differ for members of different cultures. For example, members of Western cultures are particularly likely to think of themselves as separate from other people and to define themselves in terms of their uniqueness. In Eastern cultures like Japan, people tend to think of themselves as linked to others, and they define themselves in terms of their relationships to others (Markus, Kitayama, & Heiman, 1996). The different content of their self-concepts leads to several differences in the ways Westerners and Easterners process information about the self, respond to social conflict and disagreement, and experience emotions. Any theory on these topics that has been formulated and tested in only one type of culture may not generalize to members of other cultures.

EXTERNAL VALIDITY AND LABORATORY RESEARCH. As noted earlier, the representativeness of participants is one factor that can limit generalizability. A second major factor is the setting or place in which the research is conducted. Each research setting, whether in the laboratory or outside it, has advantages and disadvantages that arise from its particular characteristics.

Most social-psychological research is conducted in the laboratory because the researcher can control this setting. In the laboratory, the researcher

If you are interested in how and why people form stereotypes, why they are so resistant to change, and what can be done to overcome that resistance, look at chapter 5, where these topics are covered.

can randomly assign participants to different conditions, manipulate independent variables while keeping other factors constant, and measure dependent variables with high construct validity. The chief virtue of the laboratory setting is that experimental designs with high internal validity are most easily implemented there.

But the lab also has a down side. One disadvantage is the short time span of most studies, which usually last no more than a few hours. Another is the somewhat artificial quality of many laboratory manipulations and measures. A researcher may, for example, ask participants to donate to another student the points they earn in the experiment and then count those points and use them as a measure of the concept of helping. You might wonder how well such measures correspond to nonlaboratory examples of helping, like volunteering 3 hours a week at the church food pantry.

Another potential weakness of the laboratory for external validity is that participants probably pay much more attention to the information provided in the laboratory than they would in some other context. In laboratory research on persuasion, for example, participants read persuasive messages and their attitudes are measured. Different kinds of messages can then be shown to be more or less effective. But outside the laboratory people do not go around reading every persuasive communication they see! Do you read every political poster on every lawn in your neighborhood? Or every ad for cold medicine in your bus or subway car? In everyday life outside the lab, the effectiveness of any persuasive message depends crucially on its ability to attract your attention. Thus, when different processes operate in laboratory and nonlaboratory settings, theories supported by findings from the laboratory may not apply to nonlaboratory settings.

A final disadvantage of laboratory settings is that participating in research may itself elicit special motives. When people are aware that they are being studied, they may start to wonder, "What are they trying to get at here?" and their perceptions of the purpose of the research (whether the perceptions are accurate or wildly off base) may then affect their behaviors.

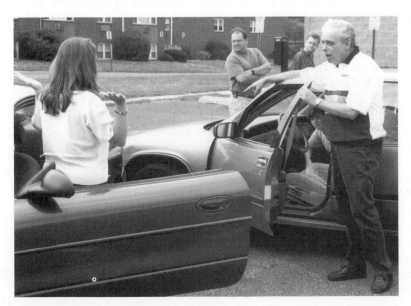

■ **Ensuring construct validity by getting real.**
To ensure that participants' reactions to manipulations are not contaminated by their beliefs about how they should act in a laboratory setting, social psychologists sometimes stage incidents in public to gauge people's natural reactions. Here a man pretends to verbally abuse a young woman. How might you react if you came upon this scene?

Behaviors that are based on the participant's perceptions of the research purpose are said to be influenced by **demand characteristics.** Demand characteristics threaten construct validity because elements of the experiment other than the intended construct—the participants' impressions of what the researcher wants or expects—may affect the participants' behavior (Orne, 1962; Rosenthal, 1969). When research takes place in a strange and novel environment like the laboratory, people are remarkably sensitive to subtle cues that tell them how they are expected to act. This effect was clearly demonstrated in a study in which participants were asked to judge the degree of success or failure shown in a series of photographed faces (Rosenthal & Fode, 1963). One group of participants was guided through the study by a researcher who had been led to believe that the photos represented "successful" faces. The second group worked with a researcher led to believe that the same photos showed faces of "failure." Both researchers followed identical procedures and gave their participants identically worded instructions. Though participants were told nothing about the photos, they could pick up clues about the expected responses from the researchers' subtle nonverbal behaviors. In each group, the participants' evaluations of the photos corresponded exactly to the researcher's expectations. Because their responses reflected not only the intended construct (perceptions of the photos) but also demand characteristics (the responses the researcher seemed to expect), this study demonstrates how construct validity can be compromised.

To counteract demand characteristics, researchers often exercise extra precautions with members of the research team who will have contact with participants. These team members are prevented from knowing the responses that are expected from any particular participant. This precaution is taken so that the team members cannot subtly and unintentionally communicate those expectations to the participant. In addition, as you will see later in this chapter, researchers often attempt to conceal the true purpose of their research from participants and, in some cases, may even mislead participants about the purpose. Despite all these precautions, any research that takes place in the laboratory always has to be carefully scrutinized for the potential impact of demand characteristics.

EXTERNAL VALIDITY AND NONLABORATORY RESEARCH. The strengths and weaknesses of *field research*—research that takes place outside the laboratory—complement those of laboratory research. Field researchers can study the long-term effects of such variables as relationship development or public health campaigns. They can measure concrete, powerful variables. For example, instead of counting the points students donate in experiments, they can count donations of blood as a measure of helping. Field researchers can also study the effects of an earthquake prediction, an alarming event that could not ethically or practically be reproduced in a laboratory. Thus, field research often has good construct validity: The variables used in the research correspond to the intended theoretical constructs. And if random assignment and manipulation of independent variables can be implemented in the field, the use of an experimental design can also provide good internal validity. That means that the researcher can confidently conclude that the manipulations of the independent variables caused the change in the dependent variables. However, for practical reasons, carrying out experiments outside the laboratory is often very difficult. As a result, most field studies are nonexperimental in design.

Demand characteristics. Cues in a research setting that lead participants to make inferences about what researchers expect or desire and that therefore bias how the participants act.

Field research, whether experimental or nonexperimental, can have high external validity if it avoids triggering the special processes, such as demand characteristics or concern for social desirability, that often occur in the laboratory setting. However, you should not make the mistake of assuming that research conducted in field settings always has more external validity than laboratory research. Diverse field settings, such as hospitals, airport departure lounges, and office cafeterias, also have particular characteristics that influence people's thoughts, motives, and actions in specific ways. Research conducted in one of these settings may or may not generalize to another, just as laboratory research may or may not generalize to a field setting.

ENSURING EXTERNAL VALIDITY. The keys to achieving external validity, then, depend on the underlying research purpose.

1. *If the goal is to generalize to some specific target population and setting, the participants and setting must be representative of the target.* For example, if the goal is to see how assembly-line workers respond to changes in a supervisor's behavior, a study of assembly-line workers in their factory would be the most useful and appropriate.

2. *If the goal is to generalize across people, places, and times, the best way to do so is to repeat the research in multiple settings and with multiple populations, including people from different cultures.* Most of the research you will read about in this text is concerned with generalizing across people and places. Ultimately, as social psychology adopts a more integrative perspective and becomes less bound by Western culture, two important consequences will follow. Cultural variables, such as East–West differences in self-conceptions, will be incorporated into theories so that cultural differences in social behavior can be explained rather than merely described. In addition, more research will be performed in diverse cultural settings, so that such broadly integrative theories can be developed and tested. Indeed, social psychology is currently moving in these directions (M. H. Bond, 1988; Markus, Kitayama, & Heiman, 1996; Moghaddam and others, 1993). Throughout this book, we will report the results of cross-cultural research whenever it throws new light on our understanding of the social and cognitive processes that influence human behavior.

Construct, internal, and external validity pertain to different aspects of the research process, are threatened by different factors, and are ensured by different types of strategies. Table 2.2 summarizes the most important characteristics of the three types of validity.

■ **Cultural differences: When can research findings be generalized?** These Chinese workers are participating in a corporate-sponsored exercise program. Their notion of "working out" differs greatly from what someone from a Western culture would envision. Social psychologists—aware that not all research findings generalize across cultures—have started to explore cultural effects on many scientific theories. These new findings are discussed throughout this book.

Evaluating Theories: The Bottom Line

Theories become generally accepted if the results of multiple valid studies show them to be superior to rival theories. Sometimes theories that seem to compete are in fact complementary explanations of events. Social-psychological research cannot help but be influenced by researchers' personal beliefs and cultural values. However, the rigorous use of research methods is our best hope for excluding the biases and errors that characterize everyday thinking.

TABLE 2.2. Properties of Theories and Corresponding Characteristics of the Three Forms of Research Validity

Property of theory	Corresponding type of validity	Threats to validity	Relevant aspects of research	Ideal research characteristics
A theory deals with abstract constructs.	Construct validity: Observable variables used in research match the theoretical constructs.	Participants may respond in socially desirable ways or act in accordance with perceived demands.	Measures and manipulations	Multiple measures; multiple manipulations
A theory proposes causal relations among constructs.	Internal validity: Relationship among observable variables is due to postulated causal process.	Alternative causal explanations may be possible.	Designs	Experimental designs
A theory is general in scope, although the range varies across theories.	External validity: Research results can be obtained with many types of people, times, and settings.	Findings may apply to only limited types of people, times, or settings.	Populations and settings	Multiple replications

Theories about social behavior ultimately stand or fall on the basis of how well they are supported by the results of valid research. As shown in Figure 2.2, the process involves a logical chain in which all three types of validity play a part. And just as a chain can be no stronger than its weakest link, each type of validity is crucial if research is to provide support for a theory.

Of course, no theory ultimately stands or falls on the basis of a single study. The results of any one study might have been influenced by simple mistakes by the researcher, the use of particular manipulations or measures, poor internal validity, special characteristics of the participants, or even chance variation. Indeed, researchers' attempts to increase one form of validity (for example, internal) often decrease other forms (external or construct validity). Kalin and Berry's (1982) survey testing the contact hypothesis in the field had high construct and external validity, as it measured long-term and powerful intergroup contact in the general population. But, as we pointed out earlier, that study had low internal validity because many differences other than degree of contact might explain the results. In contrast, the test of the same theory in a laboratory setting by Desforges and others (1991) had high internal validity because participants were randomly assigned to different levels of contact. But that study, in turn, had questionable construct and external validity, given the artificial nature of the laboratory cooperative learning task.

THE IMPORTANCE OF REPLICATION. Because no single study can be fully convincing by itself, researchers seek to **replicate,** or reproduce, the results of prior research. Indeed, scientists are required to report the procedures and methods used in their studies so that other researchers can repeat the research. The most important replications produce the same results by using different manipulations of the theoretical constructs in studies carried out in different settings with different participant populations.

Replication. Conducting new studies in an effort to provide evidence for the same theoretically predicted relations found in prior research.

FIGURE 2.2 The role of research validity in supporting theory

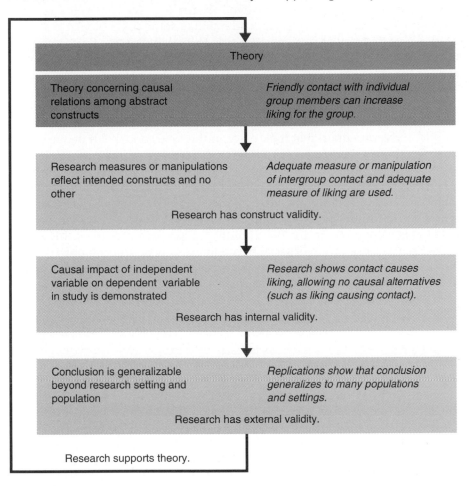

Theory

| Theory concerning causal relations among abstract constructs | Friendly contact with individual group members can increase liking for the group. |

| Research measures or manipulations reflect intended constructs and no other | Adequate measure or manipulation of intergroup contact and adequate measure of liking are used. |

Research has construct validity.

| Causal impact of independent variable on dependent variable in study is demonstrated | Research shows contact causes liking, allowing no causal alternatives (such as liking causing contact). |

Research has internal validity.

| Conclusion is generalizable beyond research setting and population | Replications show that conclusion generalizes to many populations and settings. |

Research has external validity.

Research supports theory.

■ To test a theory, researchers must follow a logical chain. Only if the research has high construct validity, strong internal validity, and good external validity can the theory be supported with confidence. Any weak link breaks the inferential chain.

Because replications provide such convincing support for theories, social psychologists often compare the results of different tests of the same theory. They perform these comparisons using *meta-analysis,* a systematic technique for locating relevant studies and summarizing their results (H. Cooper, 1990; Rosenthal, 1991). Meta-analysis allows researchers to examine the generality of results across replications conducted by different researchers using diverse methods, settings, and participant populations. When many such studies all produce similar results, they provide stronger evidence for or against theories. Thus, for example, because studies as different as Kalin and Berry's (1982) survey and Desforges and her associates' (1991) laboratory tests show the same result, we can have greater confidence that intergroup contact does indeed increase liking. Because replication is so important, you will often see more than one study or the results of a meta-analysis cited to support conclusions reported in this text.

COMPETITION WITH OTHER THEORIES. The theories that social psychologists propose to explain social events or processes sometimes compete with and contradict each other. Eventually, one theory may stand out among all the others as being more consistent with replicated research findings. This victory may be only temporary, however. Research in social psychology, like that in other sciences, is ongoing, and any day some psychologist may propose a new theory that is even better able to explain the set of research findings. For this reason scientists avoid applying the term *proven* to a theory. At best, a theory is *generally accepted*, a phrase that points to the importance of social consensus—the judgment made by the community of scientists.

In some cases, theories that first compete to explain research findings turn out to provide complementary explanations of events. Consider, for example, the competition that took place in the 1960s and 1970s between two theories that seemed to explain why attitudes often change to reflect people's behavior. In a series of studies, participants were assigned the task of writing an essay supporting a position they initially opposed. Researchers demonstrated that after the participants wrote the essay, their attitudes often became more similar to the view they had advocated in their writing (Goethals, Cooper, & Nacify, 1979; Linder, Cooper, & Jones, 1967). To explain these changes, one group of social psychologists, those who supported *cognitive dissonance theory,* argued that when people choose to act inconsistently (such as writing an essay they disagree with), the inconsistency creates psychological tension. The tension can be resolved, they proposed, if attitudes change to become consistent with behavior (moving toward the stand taken in the essay). In contrast, proponents of *self-perception theory* suggested that such changes occurred merely because people observed their own behavior and inferred their attitudes from their behavior. "I agreed to write the supportive essay, therefore I suppose I must have a supportive attitude."

Although researchers conducted many studies and compared the predictions of the two theories, they were not able to settle the controversy. Cognitive dissonance theory and self-perception theory were each supported by some results, and neither theory gained general acceptance at the expense of the other. Finally, researchers Russell Fazio, Mark Zanna, and Joel Cooper (1977) noticed an interesting difference between the two sets of findings. Most successful tests of self-perception theory occurred when people behaved in ways not too inconsistent with their original attitudes. But the successful tests of cognitive dissonance theory seemed to be those

Peanuts

Peanuts © United Features Syndicate, reprinted with permission.

in which people were induced to act in a way that directly opposed their initial convictions. This observation led Fazio, Zanna, and Cooper to suggest that the two theories offer a complementary understanding of the effect of behavior on attitudes. Perhaps self-perception processes operate to change attitudes when behavior is mildly different from initial attitudes. Cognitive dissonance processes, on the other hand, might kick in when behavior is so divergent from original attitudes that the discrepancy is upsetting. Further research confirmed their suggestions. Thus two theories that started out as seeming competitors now work together to provide a better understanding of the interplay between action and attitudes, as you will see in chapter 8.

GETTING THE BIAS OUT. Perhaps you can see now why scientists prefer to believe well-supported theories, even if they sometimes conflict with common sense. Research methods are designed to exclude many biases and errors by maintaining concern with all three forms of validity.

1. *Concern for construct validity*—making sure that observable events are good measures of general constructs—helps researchers avoid incorrect interpretations of specific events. Consider, for example, a conversation in which a New Yorker has trouble communicating with a person from the deep South. New Yorkers tend to speak faster than people from other areas of the United States, particularly those from the South, and they leave shorter pauses between "turns" in the conversation (Tannen, 1990). If the New Yorker interprets the difficulty of conversing with a Southerner as a sign that the Southerner is a bit slow-witted, rather than as an effect of different group standards for speech, an error of construct validity has affected this common-sense interpretation.

2. *Concern for internal validity*—being certain that one event causes another—makes it less likely that researchers will fall into the everyday trap of failing to consider alternative explanations. For example, if you see a man fidgeting nervously while waiting to be called in for a job interview, you might assume that he is basically an anxious person. That assumption, however, does not consider the fact that anyone waiting for an important interview is likely to feel nervous. Research needs to exclude such alternative explanations for behavior before citing the behavior as good evidence for or against a theory.

In fact, people often jump quickly to the conclusion that behavior reflects personality, without looking for alternate explanations. You'll find out why in chapter 3, pages 74 to 76.

3. *Concern for external validity*—being sure an observation can be generalized—makes it clear why we should not base conclusions about human nature on our own limited and usually unrepresentative experience. A Southerner visiting Manhattan may be brushed aside by a rude New Yorker who grabs the only available taxi during a downpour. If the Southerner concludes that all New Yorkers are rude, an error in external validity has been made. Such a broad generalization is hardly justified on the basis of one obnoxious individual.

But you should not assume that scientists always successfully achieve their objective of excluding bias and error from their research methods. On the contrary, the scientific enterprise is full of judgment calls that open the door to such influences as researchers' personal attitudes and beliefs, cultural beliefs, educational background, scientific training, or religious, moral, and political views. Scientists, after all, are human beings and are no more able than anyone else to stand outside their culture and society and evaluate theories with a pure, detached rationality (Gould, 1978). Thus, they tend to prefer theories that are consistent with their culture's generally accepted beliefs and values. For example, the 1935 *Handbook of Social Psychology* contained chapters on the "negro," the "red man," the "white man," and the "yellow man." The contents reflected the unquestioned assumptions of that time—assumptions that most people today would regard as offensively racist and sexist.

Feminist psychologists have pointed out some cultural assumptions about women and men that have crept unnoticed into scientific practice (Hare-Mustin & Marecek, 1988; McGrath, Kelly, & Rhodes, 1993; Peplau & Conrad, 1989; C. W. Sherif, 1979). For example, in some areas of research, such as the study of achievement motivation, the conclusions have been based almost entirely on responses of male participants. Although deciding to limit the participant pool to males may have allowed the researchers to avoid some complexities, other unwanted consequences may have resulted. For example, unique aspects of women's behavior may never be discovered if results from men are assumed to generalize to all humans. And even if such differences are discovered, they may be interpreted as mere deviations from the male "standard" rather than legitimate parts of the human standard (Denmark, Russo, Frieze, & Sechzer, 1988).

Nevertheless, their fundamental reliance on research findings has often enabled social psychologists to expose and overturn generally accepted myths and falsehoods. For example, many social psychologists participated in preparing a statement presented to the U.S. Supreme Court in the 1954 *Brown v. Board of Education* case. Challenging the prevailing acceptance of "separate but equal" education for Whites and Blacks, the statement summarized research evidence showing that racially segregated schools could never be equal. That statement contributed to the Court's landmark decision to overturn legally enforced school segregation (Klineberg, 1986). Science is a human enterprise with no guarantees of objectivity. Nevertheless, its research techniques are the best ways yet devised to limit the effects of bias.

The Role of Ethics and Values in Research

Social psychology is both similar to and different from other scientific disciplines. Like all scientists, psychologists have responsibilities to the scientific community. Scientists must not falsify or misrepresent their procedures or data. They must avoid personal attacks in scientific controversies, while engaging in full, no-holds-barred debates on theoretical and empirical issues. And they must allocate credit fairly for scientific work. They must not plagiarize other scholars' work, and in publications, they must give credit to all who earned it by working on the research project. Good science depends on the integrity of each researcher, and serious violations of these rules of conduct are not tolerated.

But social psychology shares with the other social and behavioral sciences a special element. Recall that the statement was made earlier in the chapter that in social psychology, humans are both the investigators and the investigated. In social-psychological research, there are people filling out questionnaires as well as devising them, people exposed to independent variables as well as manipulating them, and people in front of the camera as well as at the controls. The inherently people-packed nature of social-psychological research means that researchers often must grapple not only with research problems and scientific responsibility but also with issues of values and ethics. When designing and conducting studies that might provide answers to questions about human behavior, researchers must always ask whether the end justifies the means. Do the research results justify the experiences of the research participants? And when the results are in hand, another question must be answered. If those findings can easily be applied to society as a whole, will the results of research be used in a socially responsible way? The issues of fairness to research participants and of social responsibility are a special part of social psychologists' scientific training (Ethical Principles, 1992).

Being Fair to Participants

Researchers seek to treat their participants fairly, often ensuring that participants know what they will experience in the study and agree to it in advance. However, to avoid biases when sensitive topics are investigated, researchers sometimes deceive participants about various aspects of the study. If deception is used, participants must be given information about research procedures and purposes at the conclusion of the study.

One of social psychology's best-known experiments began about 30 years ago when Philip Zimbardo of Stanford University signed up male volunteers between 17 and 30 years of age to participate for pay in a study of "prison life" (Haney, Banks, & Zimbardo, 1973; Zimbardo, Banks, Haney, & Jaffe, 1973). Some of the men were randomly assigned to be prison guards and others to be prisoners. Unexpectedly, the "prisoners" were taken into custody by real police officers, fingerprinted, and taken to the "prison," which had been set up, complete with barred cells, in the basement of the psychology building. Dressed in shapeless prison smocks and wearing ankle chains, the prisoners were at the mercy of any rules the "guards" cared to invent and enforce. As time passed, the cruelty and abusiveness of the guards and the passivity and dehumanization of the prisoners increased. The experiment soon went out of control: First one prisoner, then another, was released with depressive or psychotic symptoms. In the end, the entire experiment had to be terminated less than halfway through its planned duration.

Unexpected as they were, the results of the experiment led Zimbardo to conclude that the institutional roles of prisoner and guard caused the sometimes shocking behaviors in his prison. It was not the personalities of these initially normal, well-adjusted men that produced the results.

The finding was no doubt important; perhaps, by extension, the same conclusion applies to what happens daily inside actual prison walls. But did the results justify the research participants' experiences, which were far more difficult and stressful than they had expected? When it became clear that the participants were given almost no details about the research project at the time they signed up, it appeared that the study violated a number of the special obligations psychologists have to their research participants.

Primary among those obligations, of course, is to avoid harming participants. Potential harm can come from several different sources. Self-reports or observations may reveal things about participants that they would not wish to have publicly known. In most studies, this threat is routinely averted by keeping participants' responses completely anonymous and unidentifiable. Another source of harm is that people can be upset or distressed by their participation in research, as they were in the Zimbardo study. Participants may experience intense distress when they are involved in potentially doing harm, are required to make difficult decisions, or are placed in situations over which they have no control. They also may be upset by their own reactions to events, as the fake prison guards may have been when they realized how easily they had become brutal.

Research on topics as divergent as helping and stereotyping often causes distress when participants later realize that their actions were so-

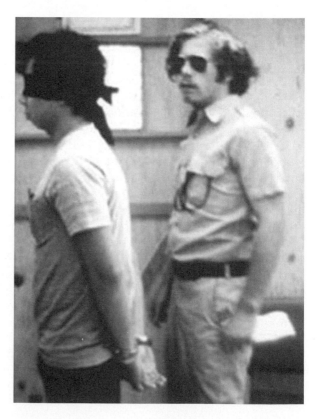

■ **Do research ends justify means?** In this photo of the Stanford prison experiment, a student assigned to the role of prisoner is handcuffed, blindfolded, and searched. Although these experiences caused considerable psychological distress, the results of the experiment provided important information about the sometimes frightening power of social roles and institutions. Such an experiment could not be conducted today. Yet the same questions about research remain: Can the social significance of results justify studies in which participants have unpleasant experiences? Can the same questions be asked in less potentially damaging ways? What do you think?

cially undesirable. This is a dilemma social psychologists face: They want their research to address many important issues, but in such research some participants may discover potentially damaging information about themselves or others. How, then, can researchers ethically proceed with their studies? The answer is by obtaining participants' **informed consent,** and social psychologists arrived at that answer partly in response to concern over studies like the Stanford prison project. Researchers must now help protect participants against the possibility of harm by telling participants they can withdraw from a study without penalty at any time. And they must give any volunteer enough information about the research to allow the person to make an informed decision about participating. "Without penalty" means that participants (often college students) cannot be coerced into participating, and any rewards resulting from participation, such as earning course credit, must be made available in alternative ways, such as through conducting library research. "Informed consent" does not mean participants are told everything about the research. They do not need to know the specific theory being tested, the rationale for the procedures, or other technical details. Participants must, however, be informed about and consent to the experiences they personally will undergo, such as filling out personality questionnaires, watching a videotape of erotic scenes, or participating in a group discussion. People who know they are free to participate and know what will happen to them if they do participate can freely choose to avoid any procedure they consider potentially harmful. How many of Zimbardo's participants do you think would have agreed to the experiment had they been informed in advance?

THE USE OF DECEPTION IN RESEARCH. Because of the importance of informed consent, ethical questions arise when researchers use *deception* to keep participants in the dark about various aspects of the research. Most instances of deception are relatively trivial. Participants are often told in advance what they will experience during the study (for example, watching a brief video clip and filling out a questionnaire) without being told the exact purpose of the study or the details of the procedure until their participation is complete.

In other cases participants are actually misled about what will happen to them. Charles Hardy and Bibb Latané constructed an elaborate ruse to compare people's efforts on a task when they thought they were working alone versus their efforts in the presence of others. The researchers told participants the study concerned the effects of sensory deprivation on noise production. This explanation provided a rationale for having the participants wear earphones and blindfolds so that they had to rely on a researcher's word as to whether they were alone or with others. When told to yell and clap as loudly as they could, participants made less noise when they thought a second person was performing with them, compared to when they thought they were working alone (Hardy & Latané, 1986). Although deception was involved, its consequences were rather minor. But not all deception is this benign. In Stanley Milgram's famous study of obedience to authority, which we will discuss in detail in chapter 10, participants were led to believe that they were giving increasingly strong electric shocks to another person. That

This drop-off in individual effort often found in groups, called *social loafing*, is discussed in detail in chapter 12.

Informed consent. Consent voluntarily given by an individual who decides to participate in a study after being told what will be involved in participation.

individual cried out in pain, demanded that the procedure be stopped because he had a heart condition, and ultimately fell silent, suggesting that he might be unconscious or even dead. Of course, none of this was true, but because participants believed it, the entire experience was extremely stressful for them.

Why would social psychologists engage in such practices? The point of deception, whether trivial or consequential, is to combat demand characteristics and social desirability biases while gathering information about socially important topics. Think honestly about how you would act if a researcher told you, "This study concerns the effects of racial prejudice on reactions to requests for help," or "We are testing the ways failure at an important task can affect people's self-esteem." Perhaps you and everyone else would refuse to participate, and thus these topics could never be studied. Even if you did agree to participate, how could you prevent your knowledge of the topic from affecting your responses? Perhaps you might try, with the best of intentions, to help confirm the researcher's expectations. Or you might act in the most socially acceptable way you could think of. Either of these reactions, which are responses to factors other than the researcher's intended causal construct, would invalidate the research findings.

Most researchers argue that many social-psychological topics, such as helping, aggression, racial and gender prejudice, and conformity, are so sensitive that deception is often necessary to produce valid results. Yet the use of deception frequently makes it impossible to obtain truly informed consent, and it runs counter to most peoples' ideas about honest and fair treatment of others. Once again the question arises: Does the end justify the means? Most researchers are willing to use deception as a last resort when they judge the research topic to be highly important and when no other alternatives are feasible. Even then, they try to keep deception to a minimum, and they inform participants of the deception as soon as possible through **debriefing.** Debriefing has several goals.

- The participant can raise questions and concerns about the research, and the researcher can address them.

- The researcher can fully explain any necessary deception.

- The researcher and participant can discuss the overall purpose and methods of the study, thereby enhancing the educational value of research participation.

- The researcher can detect and deal with any possible negative effects of the research.

Debriefing. Informing research participants—as soon as possible after the completion of their participation in research—about the purposes, procedures, and scientific value of the study, and discussing any questions participants may have.

Because most of its goals are important even for nondeceptive research, debriefing is now customary in most research. When deception is involved, however, debriefing is particularly important. If a participant is led to believe that he or she has failed at an important task, for example, the deception is carefully explained and every effort is made to ensure that participants leave the study feeling no worse than when they entered (L. Ross, Lepper, & Hubbard, 1975). In response to a heightened concern with ethical issues, the studies that social psychologists perform today usually have little potential for long-lasting harm. That was not always true of earlier studies. Consider the prison experiment again, for example. These researchers offered their participants extensive debriefing, but you may wonder whether any after-the-fact explanations could fully eliminate lasting ill effects of such powerful experiences (Baumrind, 1964; Milgram, 1964). Fortunately, most research shows that debriefing can provide deceived participants with more positive attitudes both about themselves and about research activities (Y. M. Epstein, Suedfeld, & Silverstein, 1973; S. S. Smith & Richardson, 1983; W. C. Thompson, Cohen, & Rosenhan, 1980). To do so, the debriefing must be thorough and professional, emphasize the importance of the research, and treat participants with respect.

When it comes to making difficult decisions about research ethics, a researcher is not forced to rely solely on his or her individual judgment. Since the mid-1970s, universities and other research institutions have established Institutional Review Boards. These committees, whose members include both scientists and members of the community, review and approve research plans before the research is conducted. They have the power to ask for changes in the plan or even to deny approval if they believe a study may harm participants. Despite some researchers' initial fear that the approval process would interfere with worthwhile research, it has worked smoothly in most instances. The greater ethical sensitivity that exists today, which was sparked largely by controversy over a few well-publicized studies like Zimbardo's, means that some types of study can probably no longer be performed. Take a moment to think about how you, as a member of a review board, would weigh the social and scientific importance of a study like Zimbardo's against the undoubted stress it would cause to participants.

Being Helpful to Society

Researchers have obligations as citizens and members of society to make choices about what topics to study and how their findings should be applied. Although social-psychological research cannot decide moral or ethical questions, valid research can provide relevant evidence to inform individual and societal decision making about such issues.

Like every individual, each scientist has his or her own conception of responsibility to society and to humanity. Social psychologists have long focused on major social issues like poverty, prejudice, pollution, and peace because we believe that our discipline can contribute to solving these problems. As you read this book you will see some of the results of this research.

Of course, psychologists often disagree about social and political issues. In the area of research, these differences often show up as disagreements over how science can best serve society. For instance, one researcher who studies persuasion may firmly believe that advertising offers major economic benefits by informing consumers about available products and services. Another researcher may believe just as firmly that advertising manipulates and exploits consumers, that it creates limitless desires for this year's model and encourages people to spend money on products they do not truly need. Given their differences, these two researchers would presumably also disagree on the appropriate application of social-psychological research on persuasion. The first might act as a consultant, assisting companies that want to use the research to make their advertising more effective. The second might instead use the same research findings to develop ways to teach children to resist the lure of ads for faddish toys. And a third researcher might take a middle ground, endorsing the use of knowledge of persuasion processes as legitimate in public health campaigns to encourage healthier lifestyles but opposing their use in selling consumer products. These three views represent disagreements about how science can best serve society.

In practice, every researcher must come to her or his own decisions about how research findings should be applied. Psychologists can refuse to participate in research they find morally objectionable and can encourage others to do the same. Many researchers, for example, question the benefit of conducting research designed to show gender or ethnic differences, especially in politically and legally sensitive areas like leadership potential or propensity to aggression.

Social psychology is an empirical science, and as such it is designed to answer empirical questions. The results of research will not answer questions of morality and ethics: whether abortion is right or wrong, whether or when aggression is justified, or how much our individual freedoms should be curtailed by a government's concern for the population as a whole. Such issues must be decided by every individual—scientist and nonscientist alike—through the democratic political process. But we can hope that this political process is informed by the results of valid scientific research where it is relevant. This is one role that social psychology can play in the larger society. Although research cannot tell us whether abortion is right or wrong, it can tell us who has abortions and why, how women make such difficult decisions, how they adjust to the experience, and whether it has effects on their later emotions, attitudes, and behaviors. These are all issues that may enter into individuals' moral judgments.

CONCLUDING COMMENTS

Chapter 1 described how each of us, individually and as a member of social groups, constructs his or her own picture of reality. Scientists are no different from anybody else in this respect, even as they ply their trade. Relying on inference, deduction, and generalization, they draw on fragmentary, incomplete, and sometimes contradictory bits of research evidence to construct a coherent picture of reality. A scientific theory—a statement about unobservable causal relationships among abstract constructs—is intended to be such a picture.

Because scientific theories are invented rather than discovered, the scientific enterprise draws on its practitioners' creativity and imagination. The greatest contributions of Galileo, Newton, Darwin, and Einstein were not new data, but deep insights into new conceptions of reality that organized and explained existing evidence. On a more mundane level, creativity is also a crucial ingredient as scientists devise ways to test existing theories. A clever study, like a novel theory, is a product of creative imagination as well as disciplined hard work. As any social psychologist will tell you, this is one of the main reasons why doing research is fun.

Science is a human activity. Needless to say, then, it cannot be completely logical and unbiased. Just as scientists, like all humans, construct a version of reality based on bits and pieces of evidence, so are scientists, like all humans, subject to biases. Cultural values, political and religious views, and personal preferences may influence the problems that scientists choose to study or the theories they find congenial or abhorrent. Further, once a scientist creates or endorses a theory, it is likely to influence the way he or she evaluates research. A researcher may uncritically applaud some studies because their results support a "pet" theory, while dismissing less supportive studies as methodologically flawed or inadequately generalizable. Still, the standards and procedures of science, especially its public nature and its emphasis on the possibility of bias, limit the effects of such biases. And the danger of bias recedes even further when a number of studies conducted by scientists with diverse theoretical orientations in various places converge to support a theory.

This text now turns from "how we find out" to "what we know" about social behavior. However, the transition is not as drastic as you might think. As chapter 1 pointed out, all of us, scientists and nonscientists alike, are constantly constructing theories to help explain what we experience. As you will see throughout this text, these processes are at work when people watch a football game, read a political advertisement, or deal with conflict in a relationship. One of the most important applications of these processes occurs when we get to know someone, when we form impressions of what others are "really like." Just as scientists try to explain "the facts" theoretically, we all gather information about others and try to make sense of it by forming a coherent impression. The information we gather and the way we put it together can have a dramatic impact on how we act and react to the others around us.

CHAPTER 2 THEMES

- **Construction of Reality**
  Scientific theories are developed to summarize and explain observed patterns of behavior.

- **Pervasiveness of Social Influence**
  Scientists are influenced not only by the rules and customs of science but also by personal and cultural values and goals.

- **Striving for Mastery**
  Scientists attempt to understand and predict nature.

S U M M A R Y

 Research Questions and the Role of Theory. Research questions are provoked by curiosity about why people act the way they do. In turn, this curiosity often reflects concern about important social problems. Social psychologists seek to develop scientific theories to provide explanations for social behavior. A **scientific theory** is a statement about causal relationships among abstract, general **constructs.** It is a statement that holds for specified types of people, times, and settings.

Testing Theories: From Theory to Research. To provide a valid test of a theory, research must have three types of validity. **Construct validity** means that the **independent variables** and **dependent variables**—the concrete manipulations or measures used in the research—must correspond to the intended theoretical constructs. Construct validity is threatened by **social desirability response bias** if participants act in ways they think are socially desirable. Researchers ensure construct validity by manipulating and measuring independent and dependent variables in many different ways.

To provide a valid test of a theory, research must also have **internal validity** so that observers can conclude that changes in the independent variable actually caused changes in the dependent variable. In **nonexperimental research** in which both independent and dependent variables are measured, the research may lack internal validity because many other unknown causal factors could affect the research results. **Random assignment** of participants to groups, followed by manipulation of independent variables, defines **experimental research.** Experiments allow researchers to draw stronger conclusions about cause and effect.

Finally, research must have **external validity,** meaning that its results can be generalized to other people, settings, and times. Some theories apply to many different kinds of people and places, whereas others apply more narrowly. When a theory is intended to apply *to* a particular population and setting, external validity is ensured by conducting studies using that population and setting. When a theory is intended to apply more generally *across* different people, places, and times, external validity is ensured by conducting **replications,** repeated tests of the theory in diverse populations, settings, and cultures.

Theories become generally accepted if the results of multiple valid studies show them to be superior to rival theories. Sometimes theories that seem to compete are in fact complementary explanations of events. Social-psychological research cannot help but be influenced by researchers' personal beliefs and cultural values. However, striving to maximize all three forms of validity is our best hope for excluding the biases and errors that characterize everyday thinking.

The Role of Ethics and Values in Research. Researchers seek to treat their participants fairly, often ensuring that participants know what they will experience in the study and agree to it in advance, a procedure called **informed consent.** However, to avoid biases when sensitive topics are investigated, researchers sometimes deceive participants about various aspects of the study. If deception is used, participants must be given information about research procedures and purposes in a **debriefing** at the conclusion of the study.

Researchers have obligations as citizens and members of society to make choices about what topics to study and how their findings should be applied. Although social-psychological research cannot decide moral or ethical questions, valid research can provide relevant evidence to inform individual and societal decision making about such questions.

3

Perceiving Individuals

If you woke one morning to discover you were a patient in a mental hospital, would anyone be able to tell that you were perfectly sane? The question sounds like material for a bad movie or a nightmare, and a classic study by David Rosenhan (1973) suggests an unsettling answer. Rosenhan arranged for individuals with no clinical dysfunction to be admitted to 12 different psychiatric hospitals. After gaining admission by saying they heard nonexistent voices, the individuals acted as normally as possible in the hospitals. In clinical interviews they honestly reported their personal backgrounds and experiences, although without mentioning their connection with Rosenhan. During hospital stays averaging over 2 weeks, *not one* pseudopatient was detected as an impostor by the hospital staffs! Could it be that the psychologists and other staff members, expecting patients to be mentally ill, saw only what they expected to see? Such effects of expectations are one important reason our judgments are sometimes terribly inaccurate.

Surely, though, the evidence of our everyday lives contradicts the findings of Rosenhan's study. As a student of social psychology, you are probably an interested observer of other people's behavior, and you probably believe that you do reasonably well at understanding other people and forming judgments about them. Indeed, research shows that in many situations, our impressions of other people can be quite accurate. For example, people can make fairly accurate judgments even about strangers, assessing their poise, warmth, and sociability after just a few minutes of observation (Funder & Colvin, 1988). Even in the Rosenhan experiment, some people were making pretty good judgment calls: Although hospital staff members seemed blind to the psychological normality of the pseudopatients, other *patients* often suspected them of being sane.

What accounts for the puzzling mixture of accuracy and inaccuracy in our perceptions of other people? Why do we immediately like some people and dislike others on first meeting them, sometimes without even knowing the reasons? This chapter explores the ways that people construct, maintain,

■ **Different cues, different person?**
We are used to thinking of others as having fixed personalities and attributes. This businesswoman's physical appearance, body language, and behavior all contribute to impression we form of her, as does the context in which we interact with her. It is likely that people meeting her in her favorite pub will have a different view of her as pictured below than her coworkers do when they see her as pictured above.

Cognitive representation. A body of knowledge that an individual has stored in memory.

and change their impressions of others. First, we describe how people rely on general knowledge plus some convenient principles to form impressions of strangers. Surprisingly, these judgments are often quite accurate, at least accurate enough to let people move smoothly through most everyday social encounters.

Sometimes, however, we need to go beyond snap judgments to form detailed impressions of others. Mental health workers must decide which patients are really ill; employers must decide which job applicants are right for their business needs; and teachers must decide which students know the material. And of course, all of us like some people more than others, and these feelings affect us as we decide whom to befriend or work with.

Does giving more thought to impressions increase their accuracy? Not necessarily, because, as this chapter explains, our motives and expectations can slant our judgments. Although Juliet may spend a lot of time thinking about Romeo, you probably would ask someone else if you wanted an impartial picture of his personality. As you will see, once our minds are made up, we find it hard to see, let alone accept, evidence that contradicts our views.

Of course, sometimes we have to face facts that are clearly inconsistent with our impressions. What happens then? Our discussion concludes with a description of the ways we can change impressions to accommodate contradictory evidence. How we handle inconsistency has important consequences for the accuracy of our impressions—and therefore for the success of our dealings with others.

Forming First Impressions: Cues, Interpretations, and Inferences

Try to answer a few questions about the people pictured in Figure 3.1. Who is more likely to listen to alternative rock than modern jazz? Which person has a stock portfolio to keep track of? Which person would *you* choose to get together with for lunch? You can probably answer such questions fairly readily and with some confidence. These are among the different aspects of an impression of another person. Impressions include many elements, including the person's behaviors and physical appearance (Carlston, 1994). However, the core elements are how much we like the person and our perceptions of what the person is "really like," including their underlying personality characteristics, personal goals, and values.

Our knowledge about people's characteristics and the ways they are related to one another is one type of **cognitive representation**, a term for a body of knowledge an individual has stored in his or her memory (E. R. Smith, 1998). We have cognitive representations of situations, people, and social groups. For example, our knowledge of what typically happens at a child's birthday party is a cognitive representation. Our impressions of specific individuals are cognitive representations, and so are our beliefs about members of particular occupations, nationalities, and ethnic groups. Because our stored knowledge influences virtually all of our social beliefs and behaviors, the effects of various types of cognitive representations are described throughout this text.

What is the purpose of forming impressions of situations, social groups, or individual people? The answer is that impressions guide our actions in ways that meet our needs for both concrete rewards and connected-

FIGURE 3.1   What are your impressions of these people?

■ Physical appearance offers many cues to people's personality and preferences, but these cues are interpreted through our *own* prior beliefs. Which of these people would you predict listens to alternative rock music? Who do you think reads up on stock market trends? What might you think of the woman on the right?

ness to other people. An impression that someone is generous might lead you to approach her (rather than someone else) for a loan until payday. An impression that someone else is smart might encourage you to choose that person as a study partner. And general positive or negative impressions—our liking for some people and distaste for others—influence our choices of companions to spend time with or share our personal thoughts and feelings with, and ultimately, what close relationships we form. Thus, the impressions that we construct guide us along the paths of our social lives.

The Raw Materials of First Impressions

Perceptions of other people begin with visible cues, including physical appearance, nonverbal communication, and overt behavior. Familiarity also affects impressions, generally leading to increased liking. Cues that stand out and attract attention in the particular context in which they occur are particularly influential.

The raw materials of first impressions are the way people look and how they act. However, these cues are informative only because we believe that appearance and behavior reflect personality characteristics, preferences, and lifestyles. This section focuses on the knowledge that guides our first impressions of others: the aspects of a person's appearance and behavior that call particular representations to mind, and the kinds of personal characteristics that are associated with those aspects of appearance and behavior.

IMPRESSIONS FROM PHYSICAL APPEARANCE. According to tennis star Andre Agassi, "Image is everything." It may not be everything to everyone, but physical appearance certainly influences our impressions of other people, as it probably influenced your reactions to the photos in Figure 3.1. After all, the way people look is usually our first and often our only cue to what they are like. Our ideas about the meaning of physical appearance are endless. Direct eye contact elicits trust, whereas shifty eyes evoke suspicion. Blondes are sociable and fun-loving, but redheads are fiery and quick-tempered. People who wear glasses are scholarly and those with silvery hair are distinguished. People rely on many beliefs like these when they meet a stranger, even though most are unsupported by research. Still, some aspects of impressions based on appearance may be surprisingly accurate (Zebrowitz & Collins, 1997).

Physical beauty, particularly a beautiful face, calls up a variety of positive expectations. Apparently people assume that "what is beautiful is good" (Dion, Berscheid, & Walster, 1972) or, as the German poet and philosopher Johann Schiller wrote over a century ago: "Physical beauty is the sign of an interior beauty, a spiritual and moral beauty" (1882). We expect highly attractive people to be more interesting, warm, outgoing, and socially skilled than less attractive people (Eagly & Makhijani, 1991; Feingold, 1992).

For these reasons, physical appearance is an important element in people's attraction to strangers. In a classic study, Elaine Walster and her colleagues (Walster, Aronson, Abrahams, & Rottman, 1966) randomly paired college men and women for an evening of talking and dancing. The researchers unobtrusively rated each student's attractiveness and social skills, and they also obtained their grades and their scores on intelligence and personality tests. After the evening ended, the researchers asked the students how satisfied they were with their dates. The partner's physical attractiveness was by far the most important influence on both men's and women's satisfaction. It also strongly influenced the likelihood that the men would contact their partners to seek another date. None of the other variables measured in this study—intelligence, social skills, or personality differences—had a similar influence on liking for the partner.

Well, you may say, physical attractiveness may be important to college students in a dating context, but does it have more general effects? The answer is yes. When elementary-school teachers in one study were shown information about some children, including their photos, the teachers rated the more attractive youngsters as possessing more intelligence and academic potential (Clifford, 1975). Strangers are more likely to give help to a physically attractive person than to one who is less attractive (Benson, Karabenick, & Lerner, 1976). More attractive defendants have lower bail set in misdemeanor cases (Downs & Lyons, 1991), and if they are convicted, they receive lighter prison sentences (Stewart, 1985). Apparently justice is not blind, after all! Even young children prefer their physically attractive peers, while regarding unattractive youngsters as unfriendly and aggressive (Dion & Berscheid, 1974). Clearly, physical beauty has a pervasive influence on our perceptions and evaluations of other people, even when dating and romance are not at issue.

Beauty is not the only physical characteristic that influences perceptions of other people. Certain patterns of facial features can also function this way. Some people have *baby-faced* features: large, round eyes, high eyebrows, and a small chin. In studies conducted in both the United States and Korea, Diane Berry and Leslie McArthur found that baby-faced adult males were viewed as more naive, honest, kind, and warm than males of more mature facial appearance (Berry & McArthur, 1985; McArthur & Berry, 1987). Because of these perceptions, baby-faced adults are less likely to be recommended for jobs that require mature characteristics like shrewdness or leadership ability, but are more likely to be chosen as dates by people who like to dominate others (Hadden & Brownlow, 1991; Zebrowitz, Tenenbaum, & Goldstein, 1991). People with baby faces even seem to view *themselves* as possessing relatively childlike psychological characteristics (Berry & Brownlow, 1989).

☐ **PHYSICAL APPEARANCE IN THE WORKPLACE.** Liking based on physical appearance can have an impact on our everyday work lives. One study compared physically attractive and unattractive job candidates and found that the attractive candidates were more likely to be hired by college students role-playing employment interviewers (Cash & Kilcullen, 1979). Another researcher found that newly hired professional men taller than 6 feet 2 inches received starting salaries 10 percent higher than those given to men under 6 feet (Knapp, 1978).

Attractiveness may be a mixed blessing for women in the workplace, however. One study asked people to evaluate a fictitious assistant vice president of a corporation on the basis of a photo. Some of them saw a photo of an attractive male; others saw a less attractive male. Still other research participants saw an attractive or an unattractive female. The participants rated the attractive male as higher in ability than the unattractive one, but the reverse was true for female photos (Heilman & Stopeck, 1985). According to the researchers, participants suspected that an attractive woman might have been promoted because of her appearance rather than her ability.

IMPRESSIONS FROM NONVERBAL COMMUNICATION. Did your mother tell you that the proper way to greet people was to "stand up straight, look them in the eye, smile, and shake hands firmly"? If so, she knew how much information is communicated by facial expressions, eye contact, and body language. In general, people who more readily express their feelings non-verbally are liked more than less expressive individuals (Friedman, Riggio, & Casella, 1988). Specific aspects of nonverbal behavior are important for impression formation as well. Members of Western cultures, at least, tend to like people who orient their bodies toward us—facing us directly, leaning toward us, nodding while we speak—and we believe that they like us (Mehrabian, 1972). We also tend to like people who look at us with dilated pupils, which are generally a sign of interest and attention (Niedenthal & Cantor, 1986). People who make frequent eye contact are perceived as honest, straightforward, friendly, and likable (Kleinke, Meeker, & LaFong, 1974), whereas those who avoid eye contact are seen as unfriendly, shifty, or perhaps shy (Zimbardo, 1977). Of course, too much eye contact—staring—can be unpleasant and often conveys anger or hostility (Ellsworth & Carlsmith, 1973).

Body language offers a special insight into people's moods and emotions (Ekman, Friesen, & Ellsworth, 1972). In such diverse cultures as those of Germany, Hong Kong, Japan, Turkey, and the United States, people express sadness and happiness, fear and anger, surprise and disgust with similar bodily postures and facial expressions, and they interpret them in similar ways (Ekman and others, 1987). Based on such findings, researchers concluded that emotional expression is a kind of universal language. However, recent findings show that despite some general agreement, interpretations of emotional expressions often differ between Western and non-Western cultures, particularly for the emotions of surprise, sadness, and disgust (Markus, Kitayama, & Heiman, 1996; Russell, 1994).

As we will see in chapter 4, the very basis of emotions—whether they arise from a person's private feelings or from a network of social relationships—also differs from one culture to another.

DETECTION OF DECEPTION. Have you ever wondered how people can be gullible enough to lose their savings to a con artist who has told them some outrageous lie? Or how an instructor could believe some far-fetched excuse spun by one of your classmates? Perhaps you told yourself that you could never be so easily deceived. Maybe not, but detecting lies is not always easy.

Paul Ekman and Wallace Friesen (1974) suggest that liars often give themselves away with nonverbal cues, but those cues are not the ones we usually watch for. Most people look for evidence of deception in a liar's face or words, when in fact these are what the liar can easily control (DePaulo, Lassiter, & Stone, 1982; Ekman & Friesen, 1974). The best cues are a quivering or high-pitched tone of voice or restless movements of the hands and feet. People who pay attention to those cues are relatively successful at detecting deception.

Can people be trained to pay attention to the correct cues? To find out, Ekman and Maureen O'Sullivan (1991) compared four groups of professional deception detectors: police detectives and agents from the U.S. Customs Service, the Central Intelligence Agency, and the Secret Service. When asked to judge whether an individual shown on film was making true or false statements, the Secret Service agents outperformed all others. The other professional law-enforcement personnel were no better at detecting deception than untrained students who also saw the films. The researchers suggested that Secret Service agents' training, which includes scanning

■ **Telling the truth.** When President Clinton went on television in front of the nation to deny ever having an inappropriate relationship with White House intern Monica Lewinsky, millions of people believed him; his deception had proven almost impossible to detect. What clues might you look for to gauge the authenticity of a statement?

crowds to detect threats to the president and other high officials, may sensitize them to valid cues to deception.

The fact that people tend to use the wrong cues in assessing truthfulness may also account for a seemingly paradoxical finding: Under some circumstances, the less information people receive, the better they are at detecting deception. For example, people can detect deception better when they see only the speaker's body on videotape than when they see both the body and face. Focusing on the easily controlled face apparently leads them astray (Zuckerman, DePaulo, & Rosenthal, 1981). Similarly, people who observe someone speaking usually pay most attention to the speaker's words and consequently are relatively poor at detecting the body's hints at deception. One study found that research participants who are distracted by a difficult cognitive task, which prevents them from giving full attention to the speaker's words, are better at detecting deception than participants without any distraction (Gilbert & Krull, 1988).

Given the difficulty of detecting deception, perhaps it is not surprising that some people have looked for more mechanical means of exposing dishonesty.

☐ **LIE DETECTION IN THE LEGAL SYSTEM.** "Accused Embezzler Passes Lie Detector Test—Denies Any Wrongdoing." The "lie detector" in the headline is a polygraph, a device that measures signs of physiological arousal, such as rapid breathing, increased heart rate, and sweating, as the test taker answers questions. Because people cannot completely control these responses, they are assumed to reveal the extra stress and effort of lying. However, current research evidence suggests that polygraph examinations are not precise enough to warrant their widespread use. In one study, for example, polygraph examiners correctly detected 75% of guilty suspects, but they also declared guilty 37% of those who were actually innocent (Lykken, 1985; Saxe, Dougherty, & Cross, 1985).

Nevertheless, polygraph tests continue to be widely used. Much of their apparent effectiveness may derive from superstitions about the device rather than from its inherent accuracy. Some criminal suspects who anticipate that their lies will be detected may decide to confess when confronted with a polygraph examination (Lykken, 1985). Similarly, some dishonest job seekers may avoid employers who screen applicants with the polygraph.

IMPRESSIONS FROM FAMILIARITY. Most of us tend to develop positive feelings about the people we encounter frequently in our everyday lives (Festinger, Schachter, & Back, 1950; Zajonc, 1968). Of course, such encounters may lead to an acquaintanceship or even friendship, as we will discuss in chapter 11. But even when little or no interaction takes place, mere exposure to another person increases liking. Richard Moreland and Scott Beach (1992) demonstrated this effect when they arranged for four women to attend varying numbers of sessions of a large college lecture course. The women sat quietly and took notes without interacting with any of the students. At the end of the semester, students in the course viewed slides of the women and answered questions about their impressions of them. The students thought the women they had seen more often were more interesting, attractive, warm, and intelligent than the women who had attended fewer class sessions. The students also thought they would like the more familiar women better and would enjoy spending time with them. As you can see, familiarity alone can be one basis for developing a positive impression and feelings of liking for another person.

IMPRESSIONS FROM BEHAVIOR. Physical appearance and familiarity are important factors, but the most genuinely useful resource for developing an impression of another person is the individual's behavior. If you know that someone donates hours of free time working in a local food bank, you may reasonably conclude that the person is caring, altruistic, and philanthropic. If you find out that someone stole money from a cash register at work, you can probably assume that he or she is dishonest. Like these examples, many behaviors are strongly linked to particular personality traits. Indeed, people are often advised to judge others by their deeds, not by their appearance or their words. (The processes by which people draw inferences from others' behaviors will be described in detail shortly.)

WHICH CUES CAPTURE ATTENTION? Imagine sitting in the cafeteria idly watching those around you. What cues might attract your attention? You might notice that one person makes loud and nasty comments to the clerk at the cash register, that another drinks three cups of coffee in quick succession, and that a third towers over all the other people in the room. Characteristics that are different stand out, and this is true for all kinds of characteristics, including behaviors such as making rude comments or physical cues like tallness. Or suppose you learn that someone has two hobbies: playing tennis and keeping snakes as pets. You will probably find the person's unusual taste in pets more revealing than the more commonplace athletic interests. If you were going to buy this person a book as a gift, would you be more likely to choose one on snakes or on tennis? Research suggests you'd go for herpetology (Nelson & Miller, 1995).

In cases like this, what makes a characteristic stand out is its rarity or uniqueness. **Salience** refers to a cue's ability to attract attention in its context. Of course, a cue that is unusual or unexpected in one context may be

---

Salience. The ability of a cue to attract attention in its context.

FIGURE 3.2   Salient cues dominate impressions

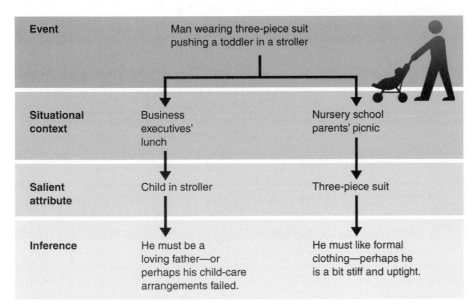

Event	Man wearing three-piece suit pushing a toddler in a stroller	
Situational context	Business executives' lunch	Nursery school parents' picnic
Salient attribute	Child in stroller	Three-piece suit
Inference	He must be a loving father—or perhaps his child-care arrangements failed.	He must like formal clothing—perhaps he is a bit stiff and uptight.

■ Our impression of the same individual may differ greatly from one situation to another because attributes that stand out in one context may go unnoticed in another. An attribute that is salient in its context may give rise to inferences that become part of our first impression of a person.

quite normal in another, as Figure 3.2 shows. The person who towered over everyone might be salient in the cafeteria but not on the basketball court, surrounded by equally tall team members. Thus, attributes that stand out in one context may be unnoticed in another. When we have information about a person's physical appearance, their nonverbal communication, and some of their behavior, those aspects that are salient are likely to grab our attention and provide the basis for first impressions.

Unusual and salient characteristics not only make a difference in our impressions of others, but also help us define ourselves, as you will see in chapter 4, pages 107 to 108.

Interpreting Cues

Cues have no meaning in themselves. Instead, they are interpreted in the light of our stored knowledge about people, behaviors, traits, and social situations. Stored knowledge that is linked to the cue itself or is easy to bring to mind is most likely to be used in interpreting cues.

We seem to leap effortlessly from the cues of appearance, body language, and behavior to liking or disliking a person, and to conclusions about his or her inner characteristics. Yet none of the cues we use in perceiving people have much meaning in themselves. No behavior, appearance, gesture, or expression indicates a person's inner qualities *directly*. Instead, even our first impressions rely on rapid but seemingly effortless cognitive processes (Gilbert, 1998). These processes operate spontaneously even when we are not specifically trying to make sense of another individual, that is, even when we are processing superficially rather than devoting a lot of thought to the issue.

The first step in processing is interpreting the cues themselves: deciding whether a wrinkled brow reflects menace or puzzlement, or whether a lie is an act of deceit or of loyalty. Two crucial kinds of stored knowledge help us make these decisions: the associations we have already learned, and the thoughts that are currently in our mind.

THE ROLE OF ASSOCIATIONS IN INTERPRETATION. On learning that someone was caught stealing money from the cash register at the local convenience store, most people would immediately conclude that the person is dishonest. Why do we jump to that conclusion? The answer has to do with the strong link that exists between two cognitive representations. Our concept of stealing money is **associated**, or linked, to our knowledge about the trait of dishonesty. When we think about stealing, the associated trait of dishonesty is *activated*, or brought to mind. To understand why association is important, imagine a child's toy box containing a jumble of all kinds of toys, among them a paddle connected by a string to a rubber ball. If you pull the paddle out of the box (think of this as hearing about the behavior of stealing) you can be sure the ball (the associated trait of dishonesty) will soon follow.

Associations can arise from *similarity in meanings* between two cognitive representations, like the similarity between the act of stealing and the concept of dishonesty. However, even unrelated ideas can become associated if they are repeatedly *thought about together*. Thus, Lennon and McCartney, cops and robbers, and Windows and Microsoft have become associated concepts for most of us. Of course, these learned connections depend on the culture that surrounds us. Suppose a co-worker expresses agreement when you voice objections to his new plans, but then goes ahead with the plans anyway. A North American might decide that the co-worker is insincere, but in Japan the same behavior, agreeing with criticism, is regarded as simple politeness. As this example suggests, members of different cultures have different associations and therefore arrive at different interpretations for the same behavior (Markus and others, 1996).

Once we form an association, it links the two cognitive representations just as the string links the paddle to the ball. If either of the linked representations comes to mind, the other will usually come to mind also. Because of these patterns of stored associations, some cues are easier to interpret than others. For example, the act of turning in money that was found in a lonely spot with no witnesses is so closely connected with our idea of honesty that we would be hard pressed to interpret the behavior in any other way. Similarly, superior performance in the decathlon immediately conjures up the idea of athleticism. In cases like these, people spontaneously think of the associated trait when they comprehend a behavior, even if they are not specifically trying to form an impression of the person (Uleman, Hon, Roman, & Moskowitz, 1996). For example, in one study participants examined photos of people together with written descriptions of behaviors that strongly implied a trait. Even if instructed simply to familiarize themselves with these materials rather than to form impressions of the pictured individuals, the participants' responses later in the study showed that they had made trait inferences based on the behaviors (Carlston & Skowronski, 1994).

THE ROLE OF ACCESSIBILITY IN INTERPRETATION. The meaning of a behavior is not always so clear. Imagine discovering that someone you know had shared test answers with a classmate. How would you interpret that behavior? This act of sharing could reflect either helpfulness or dishonesty,

Association. A link between two or more cognitive representations.

and you might have difficulty choosing one interpretation over the other. In such cases, we tend to rely on relevant information we currently have in mind. And the principle of **accessibility**, which we introduced in chapter 1, means that the knowledge that comes to mind most easily and rapidly—that is, the most accessible knowledge—has the most powerful influence on the interpretaton of behavior or other cues. Going back to our toybox metaphor, accessible toys are those near the top of the pile, whereas the less accessible ones are buried near the bottom.

The more accessible the knowledge, the more likely it is to come to mind automatically, without our consciously trying to retrieve it, and the more likely it is to guide our interpretation of cues (Higgins, 1996). Thus, someone whose ideas about helpfulness are highly accessible may interpret the act of sharing answers as a helpful act. Another person, perhaps an instructor for whom the concept of academic dishonesty is more accessible, might see the same behavior as dishonest—a quite different interpretation. Among the factors that influence the accessibility of knowledge are concurrent activation by other sources and recent and frequent past activation.

ACCESSIBILITY FROM CONCURRENT ACTIVATION OF KNOWLEDGE. Whatever thoughts are in our mind when we are forming an impression may activate cognitive representations, making them highly accessible and likely to affect our interpretations. For instance, generally positive or negative information may be made accessible by our current moods. Thus, moods have a well-documented impact on how we react to others. People in a happy and cheerful mood see both their own and others' behavior through rose-colored glasses, evaluating all behavior more positively than do people in neutral moods (Isen, 1987; Williamson & Clark, 1989). The converse is also often true: Being in a blue mood sometimes gives everything a negative tinge.

Our expectations also act as accessible knowledge that can powerfully influence our interpretations of behaviors or other information. In a classic demonstration of the effects of expectations, Harold Kelley (1950) arranged for a guest instructor to conduct 20-minute discussions in psychology courses. Before the guest's appearance, the students were given background information about the guest instructor. Though they were unaware of it, different students were given different background information. One group of students learned that the guest instructor was "a very warm person, industrious, critical, practical, and determined." The other group was informed that he was "a rather cold person, industrious, critical, practical, and determined." All students then had an extensive opportunity to observe the instructor's actual behavior during the discussion. When the students later rated his personality, the results clearly demonstrated the effects of expectation. Students who expected the instructor to be warm rated him as more considerate, informal, sociable, popular, good-natured, humorous, and humane than did those who expected a colder individual.

The effects of expectations on social perception are pervasive (Harris, 1991; Rosenthal, 1985). Supporters of opposing candidates in presidential debates expect that their own candidate will show statesmanlike behavior and leadership potential and will win the debate. And when the debate is over, each group of supporters is usually sure that they saw just that (Kinder & Sears, 1985). Doctors and nurses in psychiatric facilities expect disturbed behavior from their patients, and that is usually what they think

■ **A kiss is just a kiss.** Or is it? In fact, accessible knowledge influences the way in which any action is interpreted, and thus cultural ideas about appropriate behavior change the interpretation of the action. In North America a scene like this—where Boris Yeltsen greets a visiting dignitary—might have an entirely different meaning.

An important source of expectations about other people is their social group memberships (age, gender, ethnicity, occupation, and the like). The powerful effects of such expectations will be discussed in detail in chapter 5.

they find. Presumably this effect of expectations explains the failure of hospital staff members to identify David Rosenhan's (1973) pseudopatients as sane. The situation calls to mind the exchange between Alice and the Cheshire Cat in *Alice in Wonderland*:

> *Said the Cat: "We're all mad here. I'm mad. You're mad."*
> *"How do you know I'm mad?" said Alice.*
> *"You must be," said the Cat, "or you wouldn't have come here."*

Our expectations based on the situation in which a behavior occurs can often help us interpret the behavior. Look at the photo in Figure 3.3, for example. Is the man's face twisted in pain or expressing violent anger? Yaacov Trope (1986) found that people answer such questions in different ways, depending on what they know about the situation. Trope showed students photos of people wearing ambiguous facial expressions together with information about the context. The same expression looked grief-stricken to students who were told the photographed person was attending a funeral but was interpreted as tearful laughter by those who thought the person was at a comedy performance. Indeed, situational information can override even relatively unambiguous facial expressions when people interpret others' emotions (Carroll & Russell, 1996).

ACCESSIBILITY FROM RECENT ACTIVATION. A toy that a child has recently used can be found near the top of the toy chest. Similarly, a cognitive representation that has recently been brought to mind also remains accessible for a time (Wyer & Srull, 1989). Therefore, anything that brings an idea to mind, even coincidental or chance events, can make it accessible and influence our interpretations of behavior. Imagine walking down the street with a friend and noticing in passing a movie poster featuring Clint Eastwood in an aggressive pose. Could the poster increase the accessibility of your cognitive representations related to hostility and aggression? If so, might it influence your interpretations, leading you to see hostility in an ambiguous remark made by your friend when none was intended?

The answer to both of these questions is yes. To demonstrate this effect, Tory Higgins and his colleagues (Higgins, Rholes, & Jones, 1977) asked students to memorize several words. One group memorized words related to the positive trait *adventurous*, while another group learned words related to the negative trait *reckless*. This procedure was intended to activate students' stored knowledge about one or the other of these two traits, thereby making that knowledge accessible in the next step of the experiment. Then, in what students thought was an unrelated experiment, they read a description of Donald, who had climbed Mount McKinley, gone white-water kayaking, and driven in a demolition derby. Later, the two groups were asked to describe Donald's activities. Their descriptions showed that the first group of students, for whom *adventurous* was accessible, saw Donald's behavior as daring, whereas those who had focused on words relating to *reckless* saw his behavior as foolhardy and rash. Correspondingly, the "adventurous" students evaluated Donald more positively than the "reckless" group.

Higgins and his colleagues (1977) wondered whether this effect would occur if any positive or negative word was made accessible. They used the same procedure with traits like *obedient* or *disrespectful*, but activating these traits had no effect on people's interpretations of Donald. People apparently do not use just any accessible cognitive representation to interpret information; rather, the accessible representation must be *applicable* to the information.

Activating a cognitive representation to increase its accessibility and make it more likely to be used is called **priming**. The effects of priming can be long-lasting and rather subtle. Concepts that have been primed can remain accessible and influence later interpretations for as long as 24 hours (Srull & Wyer, 1980). Their impact does not even depend on people's awareness of the activation! To demonstrate this, John Bargh and Paula Pietromonaco (1982) showed some participants neutral words, while others saw words related to the trait of hostility. Then both groups read a description of a character's ambiguous behaviors. When the groups' responses were compared, those primed with the hostility-related words interpreted the behaviors as more hostile and aggressive. The interesting twist is that the presentation of the priming words was so brief—a mere flash on a computer screen—that the participants could not say what the words were. Even when people are unable to identify a word consciously, encountering the word can still make cognitive representations accessible and influence the interpretation of later information. Other similar studies have confirmed this remarkable finding (Niedenthal, 1990). So even if you just glimpse the Clint Eastwood poster out of the corner of your eye without consciously registering it, it might make you interpret behaviors as aggressive.

ACCESSIBILITY FROM FREQUENT ACTIVATION: CHRONIC ACCESSIBILITY. What toys are usually found lying at the top of the toy box? The ones that get dragged out and played with every day. The same is true of thoughts. The frequent use of a cognitive representation over days, months, or years can make it *chronically accessible* (Bargh, Bond, Lombardi, & Tota, 1986; Higgins, 1996). When this happens, people repeatedly use the same concepts in interpreting others' behavior. For example, intelligence might always be important in one person's judgments, whereas friendliness or helpfulness might matter more to someone else. In fact, people can more easily recognize information relevant to their "favorite" traits and can remember it better than unrelated information (Bargh & Thein, 1985; Higgins, King, & Mavin, 1982). Imagine, for instance, that you observed someone performing many behaviors: greeting friends, going to a party, studying in the library, and working at a part-time job. If friendliness is chronically accessible for you, you would be more likely to notice and later remember the first two of these behaviors. Another observer for whom intelligence is a chronically accessible concept would more easily notice and remember the time the person spent in the library.

☐ **ACCESSIBILITY AND SEXISM IN A JOB INTERVIEW.** Television and print advertisements often use sex to sell products like beer and automobiles, implicitly promising the intended male consumers that attractive women will flock around them if they purchase the correct product. Do such ads make thoughts about women as sex objects more accessible? Might this priming even affect men's behaviors if they interviewed female candidates for a job? Laurie Rudman and Eugene Borgida (1995) showed one group of male students a series of TV commercials that the researchers felt portrayed women

FIGURE 3.3 What is this man experiencing?

■ Emotional expressions are some of the easiest signals for humans to understand. But before you come to a firm conclusion, turn the page.

Chapter 7, especially pages 283 to 286, will discuss the thought-provoking possibility that our attitudes might similarly be influenced without our awareness.

Priming. The activation of a cognitive representation to increase its accessibility and thus the likelihood that it will be used.

■ **The social context of interpretation.** Even our understanding of emotional expression is influenced by the social context. Now that you know that Italian boxer Giovanni Parisi is celebrating his newly awarded super-lightweight title, his look is not one of anguish or sorrow, but of victory.

as sex objects, while another group saw commercials for similar products (such as beer or cars) that lacked sexist imagery. The students then were asked, as a favor to the experimenter, to interview a female student (actually a confederate) for a job assisting the research project. The students who had viewed the sexist ads (compared to the nonsexist ones) sat closer to the interviewee and asked her more personal and inappropriate questions. After the interview, they recalled more about her physical appearance, but less about the information she had revealed in the interview. They also rated her as more friendly, but as less competent in terms of her potential job duties! Finally, the interviewee (who did not know which priming video each man had viewed) rated how much she felt the interviewer had been looking at her body and how sexually motivated he was. These ratings were also higher for the men who had watched the sexist commercials. It seems that the concept of viewing women as sex objects can be primed, affecting men's judgments and behavior toward real women over whom they may hold power. It is worth pondering the fact that in this study, the priming stimuli that produced these effects were typical, everyday TV commercials, not extreme or pornographic materials.

As you have seen in the last several pages, accessibility has many sources, and it works in many ways to alter the interpretation of a given behavior, as summarized in Figure 3.4. In fact, as you will see throughout this book, the principle of accessibility has implications for many of our thoughts and actions, not only for our impressions of others.

Characterizing the Behaving Person: Correspondent Inferences

People often assume that others have inner qualities that correspond to their observable behaviors. This assumption is frequently made even when external factors could have influenced the behaviors.

Sometimes off-the-cuff interpretations shaped by associations and accessible cognitive representations are enough for us. If we never expect to interact with a person again, we may not go beyond interpreting their looks or their behaviors. Sometimes circumstances require us to take a second step: applying our characterization of behavior to the behaving person. Does a

FIGURE 3.4   Accessibility shapes inferences about behavior

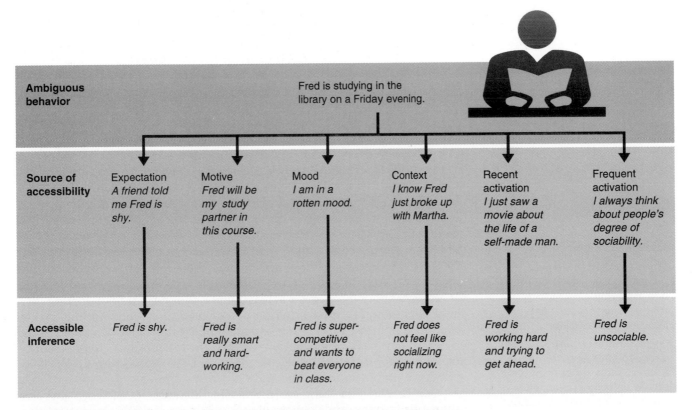

■ The same behavior can give rise to a variety of inferences, depending on what cognitive representations are accessible for the observer. Expectations, motives, and moods are just some of the many factors that can influence accessibility.

menacing expression reveal a dangerous person? Does deceitful behavior imply that the person is untrustworthy? Characterizing someone as having a personality trait that corresponds to his or her behavior is called making a **correspondent inference**. When a correspondent inference follows the initial interpretation of a behavior, it completes a *first impression*, an initial cognitive representation of what the other person is like (Gilbert, Pelham, & Krull, 1988; Trope, 1986).

WHEN IS A CORRESPONDENT INFERENCE JUSTIFIED? According to Edward Jones and Keith Davis (1965), correspondent inferences are justified when three conditions hold true:

- *The individual chooses to perform the behavior.* No one should conclude that a child forced to write a pleasant thank-you note for an unloved birthday gift actually feels grateful.

- *The behavior has few effects that distinguish it from other courses of action.* The fewer effects that a behavior shares with other possible choices, the easier it is to decide which effect motivated the behavior. For example, if a person chooses a college in sunny Florida over an identical campus in the chilly Midwest, we would be justified in seeing the choice as reflecting a love of warm weather. However, if the Florida school also has a better reputation, that muddies the inferential waters—it is no longer clear whether the person loves sunshine or status.

- *The behavior is unexpected rather than expected or typical.* When it is not fashionable to be patriotic, one can reasonably assume that neighbors who fly their country's flag outside their home feel strongly about the issue. The unexpectedness of the behavior increases our confidence in the leap from behavior to a trait inference.

THE CORRESPONDENCE BIAS: PEOPLE ARE WHAT THEY DO. In a study designed to test these ideas about correspondent inferences, Edward Jones and Victor Harris (1967) found some unexpected results. Each participant in the study read an essay favoring or opposing Fidel Castro's communist regime in Cuba. Some were told that the writer of the essay had freely chosen what position to take. When asked to guess the writer's real opinion, these participants naturally assumed that it mirrored the position taken in the essay.

Other participants learned that the writer was given no choice: The position had been assigned. You might expect these individuals to realize that a required essay, like a dictated thank-you note, carries no information whatsoever about the writer's actual opinion. But they did not. Instead, like those who thought the essay writer had a choice, the second group of participants concluded that the writer actually held the views expressed in the essay, as Figure 3.5 shows. In other words, they made an unjustified correspondent inference when they inferred that the writer's opinion corresponded with the writer's behavior.

Our tendency to draw correspondent inferences even when they are not justified, for example, when other possible causes of the behavior exist, is known as the **correspondence bias**. Another term for the correspondence bias is *fundamental attribution error* (Ross, 1977). The correspondence bias

Correspondent inference. The process of characterizing someone as having a personality trait that corresponds to his or her observed behavior.

Correspondence bias. The tendency to infer an actor's personal characteristics from observed behaviors, even when the inference is unjustified because other possible causes of the behavior exist.

FIGURE 3.5   The correspondence bias: People are what they do

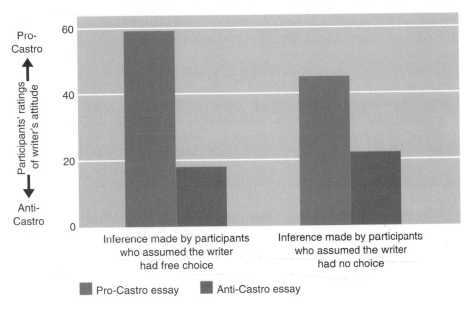

Inference made by participants
who assumed the writer
had free choice

Inference made by participants
who assumed the writer
had no choice

■ Pro-Castro essay   ■ Anti-Castro essay

■ Participants who read an essay and thought the writer had freely chosen the position were likely to infer that the writer's true position corresponded to that advocated in the essay (left bars). However, they were nearly as likely to make the same inference when they knew that the writer had no choice about the position (right). People often leap to the conclusion that behaviors reflect inner characteristics, when situational forces are truly responsible. (Based on Jones & Harris, 1967.)

has been demonstrated repeatedly, both inside and outside the social psychology laboratory (Gilbert, 1998; Jones, 1990). People tend to assume that the behaviors they observe must reflect the actors' inner characteristics even though other aspects of the situation could explain those behaviors.

☐ **CORRESPONDENCE BIAS IN THE WORKPLACE.** The correspondence bias has serious implications for fairness in the workplace. If others see us as having personal characteristics that fit with our behaviors, impressions of us can be shaped by behaviors we are instructed to perform (Ross, Amabile, & Steinmetz, 1977). Consider the results of a study in which groups of five participants were assigned in an obviously random way to two "manager" and three "clerk" positions (Humphrey, 1985). For a couple of hours, the managers made decisions, read documents, dictated letters to customers, and performed other varied and challenging tasks. Meanwhile the clerks filed papers, alphabetized cards, and filled out forms in triplicate, being given little opportunity to make decisions or display initiative. When the participants rated each other at the end of the study, they did not recognize that the randomly assigned roles conveyed no information about their personal characteristics or abilities. Managers and clerks alike believed that managers were assertive and decisive, with real leadership potential. Even the clerks predicted that managers would be more successful than clerks in their real-life future careers.

When the correspondence bias occurs, roles make the person. Given this bias, how likely is it that even a highly competent secretary will ever be seen as having what it takes to be an effective manager?

LIMITS ON THE CORRESPONDENCE BIAS. Despite its power and pervasiveness, the correspondence bias does not inevitably affect our impressions of other people. Consider the following situation: You are waiting in line at a

It is the correspondence bias—our belief that people's acts reflect their inner qualities rather than situational pressures—that makes some of the most central and important research results in social psychology so unexpected and therefore compelling. For example, it is this bias that makes it seem paradoxical that perfectly ordinary people often follow orders to carry out actions that injure innocent victims (chapter 10, pages 395 to 402).

movie theater to see the latest comedy hit. As the audience from the previous showing streams out of the theater, you notice someone grinning broadly and chuckling. The correspondence bias would suggest that you should see him as a jolly person, but do you think that is what you would do? Rather, you would probably take his reactions as evidence that the movie is funny, drawing an inference about the situation rather than the person! This is what Douglas Krull (1993) found. As in this example, when people are specifically motivated to find out about the situation, the correspondence bias is reduced or reversed. Perhaps in the Jones and Harris (1967) study, the correspondence bias emerged because the research participants generally assumed that they were supposed to draw conclusions about the person (the writer's true attitude toward Castro) rather than the situation (being instructed to write an essay).

Culture also sets limits on the correspondence bias. In Western cultures, individuals are seen as independent and autonomous, responsible for their own thoughts, feelings, and actions (Markus, Kitayama, & Heiman, 1996; Nisbett, 1987). Thus, Western observers naturally tend to assume that people's inner dispositions cause their behaviors, leading to the correspondence bias. In non-Western cultures, particularly in Asia, people are assumed to be interdependent with, rather than independent from, their groups (P. B. Smith & Bond, 1993). Causes of thoughts, emotions, and actions are more often assumed to be located in the group or social context rather than within an autonomous individual. In such cultures, the correspondence bias is somewhat less prevalent, although research participants in China, Korea, and Japan do display the bias to some extent (Fiske, Kitayama, Markus, & Nisbett, 1998). As in Krull's studies (1993), when observers pay attention to potential situational causes of a behavior, they are less likely to immediately leap to an inference that the actor possesses the corresponding trait.

FIGURE 3.6   The processes involved in constructing a first impression

■ Although forming a first impression seems immediate and effortless, it involves processes of noticing salient cues, interpreting them, and making correspondent inferences about the person's characteristics.

Though our snap judgments about other people seem to just "come to us," in reality we actively construct them, though without effort, intention, or even much ability to control their emergence. The construction follows the steps summarized in Figure 3.6, proceeding from initial cues to correspondent inferences.

Beyond First Impressions: Systematic Processing

Think back to the last time someone paid you a particularly outrageous compliment. Did you buy it? Perhaps you took the compliment at face value and, drawing a correspondent inference, decided that the person had a particularly high opinion of you. Probably, however, you were not quite so naive. Astute observers know that people say and do things for many reasons: the desire to flatter others, the demands of social situations, or the wish to receive something in return. Because we know that actions do not always reflect the inner person, we sometimes try to avoid the correspondence bias, correcting our first impressions by considering other possible causes of behaviors (Gilbert and others, 1988).

Initial impressions formed with minimal effort and thought on the basis of just one or two obvious attributes, such as impressions based on the assumption that inner characteristics correspond directly to observed behavior, are one example of **superficial processing**. But sometimes a quick glance at another person does not tell us all we want to know. Then we may think more deeply and take more information into account in the hope of forming a more adequate impression, a process termed **systematic processing**.

Processing systematically requires two ingredients. One is *motivation*: Only when people have some reason to form a deeper or more complex impression will they generally expend the effort to go beyond superficial processing. The second ingredient is the *ability* to process thoroughly: adequate time to think, freedom from distractions, and so on. When both motivation and ability to process are in the mix, systematic processing is likely to result. And as we will see throughout this book, this is true not only when people are forming impressions of others. In many different areas of life—when we are reading advertisements and thinking about buying a new product, or when we are interacting with a member of a stereotyped group—the extent to which people think systematically can be crucial in determining the outcomes.

Causal Attributions

To go beyond a first impression, people must engage in more extensive thought, particularly to explain others' behaviors. People are likely to consider potential causes that are linked to the behavior or are generally accessible, salient in context, or suggested by the pattern of available information.

In the process of person perception, the systematic processing that people perform when they are willing and able includes making **causal attributions**: judgments about the cause of a behavior or an event. In fact, making

Superficial processing. Relying on accessible information to make inferences or judgments, while expending little effort in processing.

Systematic processing. Giving thorough, effortful consideration to a wide range of information relevant to a judgment.

Causal attribution. A judgment about the cause of a behavior or other event.

inferences about the causes of people's behaviors is central to our perception of other people, for example, when we try to interpret an unexpected compliment by thinking about whether it reflects the speaker's true opinion or an effort at flattery. We draw on many types of information as we think about others' actions and attempt to understand why they have occurred.

ATTRIBUTIONS TO ASSOCIATED CAUSES. Recall that associations play an important role in the way we form first impressions. Associations also affect the ways we think more deeply about other people, but in a slightly different way. In reaching a deeper understanding of people, we do not superficially link behaviors with corresponding traits. Instead, we use associations between behaviors and their possible causes. For example, people distinguish between behaviors that are actions and behaviors that are experiences, and associate them with different types of causes (Brown & Fish, 1983; McArthur, 1972). Actions are seen as caused mostly by actors, as you may see if you try to complete the following sentence: "Romeo serenaded Juliet because . . ." Did you begin the next phrase with the word *he*? Perhaps you said something like, ". . . he wanted to win her heart." Experiences, however, are usually attributed to the stimulus rather than to the actor. So you would probably finish the sentence "Romeo loved Juliet because . . . " with a phrase beginning with the word *she*: ". . . she had such admirable qualities."

Some behaviors are so closely associated with a particular situation that the causal role of the situation becomes obvious. We are most likely to see this causal role when we possess general knowledge about what is expected in a given situation, cognitively represented in a *script*. For example, undergraduates generally agree on the script for that familiar situation known as "dating." It includes such elements as "female greets male at the door," "they go to a movie," "male takes female home," "they kiss" (the element on which most students agree), and "they say good night and thank date" (Pryor & Merluzzi, 1985). People often learn scripts for unfamiliar situations by observing others. If your first Weight Watchers' meeting opens with everyone congratulating each other on how good they look, you can conclude that the situation demands these behaviors.

Scripts tell us what behaviors are normal and expected in given situations, and when an expected behavior occurs, such as wearing jeans and a funny T-shirt to a picnic, it can be attributed to the demands of the situation. In contrast, behaviors that are unexpected, such as wearing the jeans and T-shirt to a formal dinner party, demand more attributional thought, and we may end up explaining them in terms of the personal characteristics of the actor.

CULTURAL DIFFERENCES IN ATTRIBUTIONS. People from different cultures, of course, learn to associate behaviors with different types of causes. When Joan Miller (1984) looked at the way children and adults from the United States and India explained behaviors, she found striking cultural differences. Only adults from the United States were likely to attribute behavior to the actor's general personality traits. For example, adult Americans explained examples of cheating and dishonesty on the basis of the actor's general traits, like competitiveness or selfishness. Adults from India and children from both countries placed more emphasis on other characteristics of the actor, such as his or her roles and social relationships. Cheating might be explained by the fact that the actor was unemployed and needed money, or that he had a history of conflict with his victim. The American children used more trait-based explanations with increasing age, however, suggesting that they learned this pattern from their culture over time. In another study, Morris and Peng (1994) described a murder case to Americans and Chinese and asked them to explain the event. The Americans tended to say things like, "He was a psycho." In contrast, Chinese perceivers did not attribute the event to causes within the actor, but located the cause in the social relationships between the murderer, his victim, and the larger social context.

These attributional differences reflect the fact that, as we noted earlier, different cultures incorporate quite different assumptions about the basic nature of human beings. In Western cultures, people are seen as independent and autonomous, responsible for their own actions. Many non-Western cultures, in contrast, portray individuals as interdependent with their groups and social contexts, rather than as separate from them (Markus and others, 1996). These differences in basic conceptions of people are mirrored in the explanations that people from different cultures provide for behaviors.

People in cultures like the United States tend to think of others in terms of their traits, and those in more interdependent cultures, such as India, emphasize roles and social relationships. This difference is also evident when people think about themselves, as you will see in chapter 4, especially pp. 114 to 116.

ATTRIBUTIONS TO ACCESSIBLE CAUSES. The more accessible a potential cause, the more likely it is to be cited as an explanation of behavior. Thus, William Rholes and John Pryor (1982) reasoned, priming should influence people's causal attributions, just as it can affect their initial interpretations of behaviors. To test their hypothesis, the researchers first exposed students to words like *aviator* or *rug*, to make those concepts more accessible in memory. They then asked the students to explain hypothetical events, such as "The pilot liked the carpet." Those who had been primed with *aviator* attributed the behavior to the actor, while those who had seen *rug* attributed the behavior to the stimulus object. More accessible causes are more likely to be seen as responsible for an event.

ATTRIBUTIONS TO SALIENT CAUSES. The more noticeable or attention-getting a potential cause is, the more likely it is to be used to explain behavior. And what is noticeable can depend literally on the perceiver's point of view. To demonstrate the impact of salience on attribution, Shelley Taylor and Susan Fiske (1975) arranged an experiment in which six students watched a two-person conversation from different viewing positions, as Figure 3.7 shows. When questioned about what they had seen, the students attributed a greater causal role to the person they were directly watching. They gave that person higher ratings for dominating the conversation and dictating its tone and outcome.

Salient features, whether they are people we are focusing on, bright colors, moving images, loud voices, or any other outstanding feature, can draw our attention, thereby turning a potential cause into the probable cause (McArthur & Post, 1977; Robinson & McArthur, 1982). Salience has these effects not only when people make quick, relatively unthinking judgments, but even when they make an effort to think carefully and be accurate (E. R. Smith & Miller, 1979).

Consider the implications of these findings for courtroom proceedings. Imagine jurors watching a videotape of a suspect confessing while being interrogated by police. Was the confession voluntary (attributable to the

FIGURE 3.7   Salient causes dominate impressions

■ In this study, two people held a conversation as six others watched. The observers were seated so two could most easily see participant *A*, two faced participant *B*, and two could see both participants equally well. The results? The observers attributed a greater causal role to the participant they were directly watching than to the other participant. (Adapted from Taylor & Fiske, 1975, copyright © 1975 by the American Psychological Association. Adapted by permission.)

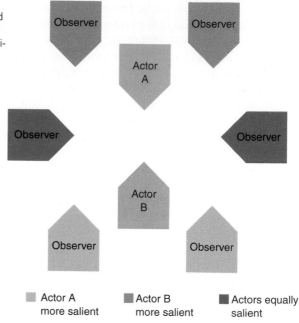

■ Actor A more salient   ■ Actor B more salient   ■ Actors equally salient

suspect) or was it coerced by pressure from the detectives? Salience can affect observers' answers to this question, as one study showed. Some observers saw a confession with the video camera focused on the suspect, and others saw the same interaction from a viewpoint that focused mainly on the interrogating detective. The first group judged the confession to be more voluntary and less coerced (Lassiter & Irvine, 1986). Is it any wonder that police agencies that are videotaping interrogations almost always focus the camera on the suspect?

ATTRIBUTIONS BASED ON COVARIATION INFORMATION. Knowledge stored in the mind—cognitive representations that are activated by associations, accessibility, or salience—does not always provide ready answers to causal questions. Observing a behavior, such as a graduate student flattering a professor (as graduate students do from time to time) may not immediately bring any particular causal attribution to mind. In such situations, people can try to ascertain the cause of the event by collecting *covariation information*, information about potential causal factors that are present when the event occurs and absent when it does not.

Harold Kelley (1967) considered three major categories of possible causes of a social event like flattery. First, he suggested, the behavior might be explained by something about the actor. Thus, the graduate student might be insecure about his standing in the department and might respond by flattering all professors frequently. Second, the behavior might be due to something about the stimulus or target of the behavior. Perhaps this professor is known to be susceptible to flattery. Third, the behavior might be caused by something about the particular situation or circumstances. Perhaps the graduate student plans to ask this professor for a letter of recommendation later in the day.

How do people decide which kind of attribution to make? Kelley (1967) argued that people look for the possible cause that covaries uniquely with the event. The one that is present when the behavior occurs and is absent when the behavior is absent wins the causal sweepstakes. Therefore, an observer would seek out *distinctiveness* information (whether the student flatters other people), *consensus* information (whether other people flatter the professor), and *consistency* information (whether the student flatters the professor under other circumstances).

You can probably guess some of the predictions that derive from Kelley's reasoning. Assume the professor, like a social magnet, seems to draw flattery from everyone, including this rather reserved student who rarely flatters anyone. In that case, most people would conclude that something about the professor is causing the flattery, as can be seen in Table 3.1. But perhaps that is not the case. Perhaps the student flatters lots of people, most other people do not flatter the professor, and the student flatters her every time they meet. In that case, there is probably something special about the graduate student that explains the flattery. Given these pieces of information, people would attribute the behavior to the actor. As a third possibility, maybe the flattery occurred only today but did not occur last week, and few people in the history of the department have ever flattered this professor, who in fact is quite an unpleasant person. In this final case, most people

TABLE 3.1. Information About the Presence or Absence of Potential Causes Influences Attributions

Event *The graduate student flatters a professor*

	Situation A	Situation B	Situation C
Consensus	High *Almost everyone flatters this professor.*	Low *Almost nobody flatters this professor.*	Low *Almost nobody flatters this professor.*
Distinctiveness	High *The graduate student does not flatter anyone else.*	Low *The graduate student flatters almost everyone.*	High *The graduate student does not flatter anyone else.*
Consistency	High *The graduate student flatters this professor almost all the time.*	High *The graduate student flatters this professor almost all the time.*	Low *The graduate student does not flatter this professor on most occasions.*
	↓	↓	↓
Attribution	*Something about the professor (stimulus)*	*Something about the graduate student (person)*	*Something about the particular time or situation (circumstances)*

would see the graduate student's behavior as due to some particular situation or circumstance (McArthur, 1972). Perhaps the student is, after all, about to request a letter of recommendation.

Using Attributions to Correct First Impressions

> When external factors appear to have caused behavior, people may attempt to correct an initial inference about the actor's characteristics. This correction takes time and cognitive effort, however, so it often does not occur.

Attributional thinking may lead us to revise our initial correspondent inferences; that is, we may become less confident that the actor's inner characteristics correspond to his or her behavior. This process is termed *discounting*, which refers to reducing a belief in one potential cause of behavior, such as the flatterer's true opinion, because there is another viable cause, his need for a favor (Kelley, 1972). When you see your classmates sweating and biting their fingernails as they await the calculus exam, the associated trait of anxiety immediately springs to mind. Processing superficially, you may go on to draw a correspondent inference: to form a first impression that the students are nervous people. However, if you think more systematically about the circumstances in which the behavior is occurring—the looming examination—you might take a third step and correct your initial impression by discounting, concluding that the nail biters may not be such nervous Nellies after all.

This third step seems so logical and sensible that one might wonder why people so often fall prey to the correspondence bias, even when situational causes are quite obvious. The answer lies in the fact that the first two steps, labeling the behavior and characterizing the person, are relatively easy, but the third step, using causal reasoning to correct the impression, is difficult (Gilbert, 1991). In fact, the first two steps may occur automatically, without any conscious effort. In contrast, causal reasoning usually takes time and effort and, as we all can testify, things that take more time and effort often do not get done at all.

Daniel Gilbert and his colleagues (1988) have demonstrated that extra effort is required to discount an initial impression. In their experiment, students watched a videotaped interview of an obviously nervous woman, with the sound turned off. The topics she was supposed to be discussing were displayed as subtitles on the TV screen. One group of students believed the interview centered on such highly personal, anxiety-provoking topics as "My sexual fantasies" or "My most embarrassing moment." Another group thought she was discussing innocuous matters like "My favorite vacation." After seeing the interview, all students were asked to rate how anxious a person the woman was in general. A correspondent inference would suggest that because the woman showed signs of nervousness, she must be a nervous type. However, the researchers reasoned, those who knew of a situational cause for her anxiety—the personal topics—should engage in discounting. And, indeed, their ratings of her general level of anxiety were lower than those of the students who thought the topics were mundane.

Two additional groups of students in the experiment went through exactly the same procedure with one exception: The researchers required these students to memorize the topics the woman was supposed to be discussing. Gilbert and his colleagues predicted that this distracting activity would leave them with insufficient cognitive resources to engage in effortful discounting. As expected, the distracted students failed to discount their initial impressions. That is, they rated the woman as an anxious type even though they successfully memorized the anxiety-provoking topics (see Figure 3.8). Apparently, because the memory task absorbed some of their cognitive resources, they never went back to change their initial correspondent inferences, even though the role of situational factors, the anxiety-producing topics, was quite obvious. As this study shows, unless we are willing and able to process information systematically, the principle of conservatism applies: We stick with our first impressions.

All the typical demands of everyday interaction—trying to remember other people's names and faces, planning what we want to say, or working to create a good impression—also require considerable cognitive capacity. Thus, interaction itself may limit our ability to form accurate impressions of the people with whom we interact, leaving our impressions very much at the mercy of the behaviors we happen to see people perform first.

Putting It All Together: Forming Complex Impressions

One person's impression of another individual usually includes several characteristics. People may infer additional traits based on their knowledge or observations of the individual. The multiple components of an impression may become linked as people attempt to infer causal connections among them. Overall evaluations, too, are usually constructed by integrating multiple aspects of an impression.

Our everyday encounters with other people are likely to reveal more about them than just a single characteristic. How, then, do we develop coherent overall impressions? Imagine being introduced to Paul at a city council meeting. As you chat, you find that in addition to his involvement in city

FIGURE 3.8   Correcting impressions is hard work

Participants' ratings of woman's level of anxiety

Ratings by participants who performed no extra task

Ratings by participants distracted by extra task

■ Woman discussed "sensitive" topics   ■ Woman discussed "innocuous" topics

■ Participants who could focus their attention on their judgments rated a woman as a less anxious person when they knew she was discussing sensitive topics (left). In contrast, participants who were distracted by an additional task failed to discount (right). Those who believed the topics were sensitive assigned approximately the same ratings as those assigned by participants who believed the topics were innocuous. (Based on Gilbert and others, 1988.)

politics, Paul sells salad dressing and popcorn, acts in movies, contributes to newspaper advertisements for political causes, writes to his congressional representative regularly, and drives race cars. How would you put together all this information into an overall impression of Paul? We form our overall impressions by integrating multiple characteristics, whether they are traits or evaluations of the person.

INTEGRATING TRAIT INFORMATION. We usually expect certain traits to go together. Knowing that an acquaintance is generous, for example, often leads us to expect that he will be warm as well. These patterns of associations among traits, called *implicit personality theories* (Schneider, 1973), can guide the development and elaboration of complex impressions of others. For example, if you conclude that Paul is daring because he drives race cars, you might immediately conclude that he also is reckless or dominating because most people associate these traits with the trait daring (Rosenberg, Nelson, & Vivekananthan, 1968). In general, people seem to think that most positive traits are related to each other and that negative traits form another distinct group. When people rely on their implicit personality theories, they may infer that a person has many positive qualities on the basis of a single good one, and they may expect a lot of negative characteristics if they learn about one bad quality. Learning that someone is pessimistic, most people would expect him or her to also be irritable, cold, vain, and finicky. The fact that trait associations are structured in this way illustrates the central role of evaluation in our thinking about other people.

The general patterns of implicit personality theories are widely shared within a culture, but an individual may also make certain idiosyncratic trait inferences, depending on his or her own experiences (E. R. Smith & Zárate, 1992). For example, suppose you have a friend who is both exceptionally clumsy and quite reliable. If you meet someone else who is clumsy you might infer that this person is also reliable (Andersen & Cole, 1990; Lewicki, 1985). These two traits would be associated for you because they are both included in your cognitive representation of your friend, even though they are not connected in most people's implicit personality theories. In addition, you would probably like the person because of his or her resemblance to your friend (Andersen & Baum, 1994).

As we observe or infer more and more characteristics of an individual, we try to organize what we know and create an overall impression that is a complex and interlinked whole. For example, if you notice that several behaviors have similar trait implications, you may think about them together. This reflection, in turn, may cause the behaviors to become associated in your mind. For example, you may realize that Paul's behaviors of attending the council meeting, supporting the political ad campaigns, and writing letters to his congressional representative all reflect political activism. David Hamilton and his colleagues (Hamilton, Katz, & Leirer, 1980) suggest that behaviors that represent the same trait are linked into associated clusters in memory as people mentally organize their impressions of others. Supporting this idea, these researchers found that when people were asked to recall behaviors of a person they had earlier read about, they often recalled a number of behaviors reflecting the same trait in sequence, followed by behaviors linked to a different trait, and so on.

We may also make sense of a person's diverse behaviors and traits by creating causal links among them (Park, 1986; Prentice, 1990). You may know, for example, that a star athlete is quick-tempered. You might assume that she has a burning competitive drive that causes both her athletic successes and her outbursts of temper. These processes of inferring additional traits and linking multiple traits and behaviors into an integrated whole thus allow us to build impressions that are unified and coherent, not just lists of seemingly unrelated characteristics.

INTEGRATING EVALUATIONS. Most of the people we meet in everyday life are neither saints nor axe murderers, but have some positive and some negative characteristics. How do we put together our admiration for someone's artistic talents, positive feelings about their attractive appearance, and dismay at their occasional rude behavior into an overall evaluation? We could simply average the evaluations and conclude that overall, two positives and one negative lead to a mildly positive impression. However, we tend to give negative information more weight than positive information when we integrate impressions in this way, a pattern termed a *negativity effect* (Fiske, 1980; Skowronski & Carlston, 1989). We do this because negative information is generally surprising and unexpected—after all, more people are generally polite than rude. Therefore, the negative information seems more extreme and informative than comparable positive information.

However, particularly when we are thinking carefully and systematically about another person, we usually go beyond simply averaging our evaluations of their characteristics. We try to construct a more meaningful type of integration, just as we integrate traits into a complex and causally linked overall impression. In this case the first information we learn may be used as a basis for interpreting and evaluating other information. If we first learn that the person is an artist, for instance, when we notice the occasional rudeness, it may become just an aspect of "the artistic temperament," perhaps even acquiring a neutral or positive evaluation. As this example suggests, evaluations of traits or other personal characteristics are not fixed and constant, but depend on the total impression of the person (Hamilton & Zanna, 1974).

The Accuracy of Considered Impressions

Even considered impressions may not be completely accurate. When people devote extra thought to forming an impression, biases may still limit their accuracy, and the extra efforts may only confirm an existing positive or negative view. Unless people are aware of such biases in social perception, they are unlikely to try to correct them.

When we go beyond a first impression, both making attributions and integrating multiple behaviors and traits require considerable thought. What might motivate the expenditure of all this cognitive effort? And will the extra effort guarantee that considered impressions are unbiased, valid conceptions of what the person is really like?

MOTIVATION TO BE ACCURATE. Accuracy is one of the strongest motivations for working hard on forming an impression. Suppose you have a new acquaintance, Tom, and you are sure your friend will like Tom. You realize that your friend might hold you responsible if he invites Tom to come along to a party and Tom turns out to be a bore. If it is important to be accurate because you will be held accountable, you will probably make an extra effort to gather information (Kruglanski & Freund, 1983). This effort sometimes allows us to overcome the effects of an initial expectation (Neuberg, 1989).

We can also be particularly motivated to form accurate perceptions of people when we will have to work with them (Flink & Park, 1991; Srull & Brand, 1983). In one study, students learned that they would shortly have to meet a man who had previously been hospitalized for schizophrenia. Some of the students were told they would simply meet him, but others believed that they would work cooperatively with him on a joint task (Neuberg & Fiske, 1987). The students then received an information sheet describing the man's personal background, hobbies, and so on. Those who expected to cooperate with him spent more time reading about his personal characteristics, and used that additional information in forming their impressions. In contrast, the others spent less time reading about the man's attributes and formed an impression that was based almost entirely on the schizophrenia diagnosis.

Suspicion about someone's motives may also cause us to think before leaping to a correspondent inference, as Steven Fein (1996) demonstrated. Students read a speech on a controversial issue that was supposedly the work of an applicant for a summer internship. One group was told that the writer had freely chosen the side of the issue supported by the speech, and that the views given in the speech matched the position of the professor who would be evaluating the writer's application. Apparently inferring that the applicant might have been trying to curry favor, the students drew no inferences about the writer's personal position. In contrast, another group of students were told that the writer had been assigned the position without having any choice. Like the participants who read essays about Castro in the original Jones and Harris (1967) study, this group fell prey to the correspondence bias: They inferred that the writer privately held the position espoused in the speech. Suspicion of ulterior motives evidently motivates people to think hard about the causes of behavior, which reduces their susceptibility to the correspondence bias.

MOTIVES BESIDES ACCURACY. Extra efforts that people devote to processing information about others are not always in the service of accuracy. One study showed that when perceiving another person accurately might create interpersonal problems, people may be motivated to avoid accuracy. Jeffry Simpson and his colleagues (Simpson, Ickes, & Blackstone, 1995) had members of dating couples evaluate photographs of highly attractive opposite-sex individuals and then attempt to guess each other's thoughts and feelings about the task. When the situation posed a threat to the couple's relationship (for example, when the relationship was insecure), these guesses were relatively inaccurate. Accuracy is not always the primary goal of person perception!

At times our judgments are inaccurate because our hopes and desires guide our search for and our interpretation of facts (Kruglanski & Freund, 1983; Kunda, 1990). In one study, for example, students evaluated the trivia knowledge of a man whom they expected to be either their competitor or their partner in a trivia contest. All students had watched him answer a few practice questions correctly. Those who expected to be the man's future partners rated his trivia ability higher than did those who expected to compete with him (Klein & Kunda, 1992).

As these studies show, our approach is sometimes a lot like that of an attorney constructing the best possible case for a client (Baumeister & Newman, 1994). Rather than conducting an unbiased search with accuracy as the only goal, we hunt for evidence that supports our preferred conclusion. And because behavior is often ambiguous, we often find just what we are seeking. If the trivia player is to be our partner, we focus on how much knowledge his answers displayed; if we will have to compete with him, we instead emphasize how easy the practice questions were. When our search succeeds, we remain unaware of the biases in the search process and we blissfully forget that, had we searched with different goals, we might have unearthed a very different body of evidence.

AWARENESS OF BIAS. Most of the time we remain blind to our biases, accepting the world we perceive at face value. We think that what we see is what actually is, because we are so good at constructing a coherent representation of reality (Gilbert, 1998). And we ordinarily get along well enough relying on our construction of reality (Fiske, 1993). But sometimes, perhaps when we compare notes with another person who sees things differently, we realize that our views may be biased. Awareness of bias may motivate us to devote extra effort to thinking about other people (Lombardi, Higgins, & Bargh, 1987; Strack, Schwarz, Bless, Kubler, & Wanke, 1989). Have you ever had a friend give a glowing description of someone you regarded as narrow-minded, hostile, and uncouth? Disagreement often motivates us to think hard to determine the truth, or at least to convince ourselves that other people's interpretations and judgments, not our own, are biased. If disagreement never surfaces, however, we may feel quite satisfied with the impressions we form. We operate on the motto "If it ain't broke, don't fix it," and we generally do not even try to correct our impressions.

Even when awareness of a potential bias makes us try to correct our impressions, a lack of time or cognitive resources may undermine our best intentions and leave us unable to make the correction (Martin, Seta, & Crelia, 1990). Only when both motivation and cognitive ability are available will we attempt to counteract potential biases. At that point, our attempted correction will depend on our beliefs about the nature and direction of the bias. For example, suppose you meet someone on a brightly sunny spring day when your boss has just given you a big raise. If you are aware that you are in a terrific mood and believe that it might bias your impression in a positive direction, you will probably attempt to correct your impression of the person by making it more negative: trying to cancel out the assumed bias (Wegener & Petty, 1995). The net result of this process may be a more accurate judgment, but only if your theory about the direction and size of the bias is relatively correct.

Figure 3.9 summarizes all the processes involved in impression formation, from noticing cues to interpreting them, inferring traits, and integrating multiple traits to form an overall impression. What is surprising is how little aware we usually are of all this processing. Our impressions of others

FIGURE 3.9   From snap judgments to complex impressions

Event:	Student in hallway shakes fist at professor	
Information used	**Process**	**Resulting representation**
Appearance or behavior cues	Noticing salient cues	*He shook his fist.*
Associated or accessible cognitive representation	Interpreting cues	*He did something hostile.*
	Making a correspondent inference	*He is a hostile person.*
Knowledge about causes	Attributional processing	*He is upset because his low grade might keep him out of law school, so perhaps he is not a hostile person.*
Implicit personality theories Additional observed behaviors or other information	Inference of additional personal characteristics	*He is hostile and ambitious.*
Knowledge about causes	Construction of causal links that relate and integrate known and inferred characteristics	*He is hostile because he is ambitious.*

seem to be formed immediately, rarely requiring much thought. But in fact, this sense of immediacy actually reflects the unobtrusive efficiency with which our interpretive processes construct our picture of reality.

The Impact of Impressions: Using, Defending, and Changing Impressions

Once we have formed an impression of another person, whether it is a snap judgment or a thoughtful construction, and whether it is biased or accurate, we use it to guide our judgments and social interactions. Thus, once we have concluded that the next-door neighbor is a generous fellow, we trust that our interpretation represents objective reality. And even if these impressions are biased, they take on reality as we act on them.

Impressions and Judgments

Once an impression is formed, it becomes a basis for judgments and behaviors. Sometimes judgments about others rest on simple, superficial processing; at other times people engage in extensive processing, attempting to put together the implications of all relevant information.

Imagine that you need to find several housemates. As you interview a few candidates, you may develop complex, well-articulated impressions of each of them. Whom should you pick? What aspects of your impressions will influence your decision? Sometimes only a single aspect of an impression really matters. If the only thing you care about is a compatible lifestyle (similar tastes in music, similar preferences for late hours), the happy-go-lucky night person may seem to be your best bet. If a shared interest in animal rights is your most important criterion, you certainly will not choose the woman in the fur coat. Often, however, more than one aspect of your impression seems important. You want someone you like, who has a compatible lifestyle, but you also want that person to be financially responsible—someone who will not stick you with bills for unpaid rent and telephone calls each month. How do we make judgments about others on the basis of our impressions of them?

SUPERFICIAL PROCESSING: USING A SINGLE ATTRIBUTE. Decisions based on a single accessible or salient characteristic require minimal effort and thought. You might pick the best-looking person who turns up to see your apartment or base your decision on some other equally obvious characteristic, ignoring all other considerations. Having to make a decision quickly or without full attention might force such superficial processing even if you would prefer a more systematic approach.

When people process quickly and superficially, they generally rely on their past judgments and evaluations of an individual, rather than on the underlying evidence that led to those judgments in the first place (Carlston & Skowronski, 1986). For example, on learning that your congressional representative takes conservative positions on several issues, you may form the judgment that she is a conservative. If a new issue, such as capital punishment, becomes a topic for political discussion, you probably will assume that she will take an equally conservative stand. If you make this assumption, you will be relying on your past judgment rather than on specific statements the representative may have made about capital punishment. In fact, when we use our past judgments we may not even bother to retrieve from memory or reconsider the specific facts on which those judgments were based (Hastie & Park, 1986; Sherman & Klein, 1994).

Our tendency to rely on our past judgments and evaluations makes us slow to change our thinking and can lead us into trouble. For example, people tend to rely on their past judgments even if those judgments were made under circumstances that create bias. If a doting mother asked for an

■ **Tell us her story.** Is this young woman a vegetarian? Is she a college English major? Is she an environmentalist? The facts tell us that relatively few young women are any of those things, but research has found that even if you know this, it won't change your assumptions about her. Most of us make assumptions influenced by a base-rate fallacy: Our theories about individuals have more impact on our judgments than information about what most people are like.

opinion of her rather ordinary son, most of us would find it difficult to describe him in anything except positive terms. Interestingly, giving such a slanted description may affect our private impressions of the son (Higgins & McCann, 1984; Sedikides, 1990). Rather than thinking again about the evidence, people tend to draw on their previous descriptions of others, forgetting or ignoring the fact that these descriptions were shaped by the demands of an audience.

SYSTEMATIC PROCESSING: INTEGRATING MULTIPLE FACTORS. When we apply for jobs or loans, we all hope that those evaluating the application will process it with conscientiousness and depth, taking account of more than one of our characteristics. As noted earlier, when people know their decisions matter and when accuracy is extremely important to them, they often do carry out such systematic processing (Neuberg, 1989; Neuberg & Fiske, 1987). One way of combining multiple factors is termed the *algebraic* approach. It is similar to the way an "ideal" consumer decides which appliance or automobile to buy: examining the *Consumer Reports* table of each brand's advantages and disadvantages and weighting each feature according to its importance for the particular decision (Anderson, 1981). For example, if you are considering someone as a potential date, you might assess the person in terms of a variety of individual qualities, some similar to and some different from those you would consider for a potential study partner.

Alternatively, people may integrate multiple items of information in a less mechanical way. Instead of evaluating each attribute independently, people may attempt to fit the information together into a meaningful whole. In this integration process, one item may subtly change the meaning of others (Asch, 1946; Asch & Zukier, 1984). For example, suppose one person

Is described as intelligent and cold, and another as intelligent and warm. The very meaning of intelligent seems to differ in these two descriptions, connoting something like "calculating" or "sly" when combined with cold, but taking on the meaning of "wise" in the context of warm. When people use this *configural* approach to evaluate a person's multiple attributes, their overall judgment may depend on the particular way they combine the attributes. As mentioned earlier in this chapter, integrating multiple characteristics often involves causal reasoning, as when we infer that coldness leads people to use their intelligence in self-centered ways, making them seem calculating.

Defending Impressions

Impressions tend to resist change, partly because an initial impression can alter the interpretation of later information. As a result, impressions may even survive the discrediting of the information on which they were based. Impressions shape overt interaction as well as judgments. They often lead people to seek consistent information or even to elicit confirming actions from others.

Once formed, our impressions of others can influence both our private judgments about those individuals and our interactions with them. As we obtain further information, we may slant our interpretations to maintain our impressions unchanged. And as we treat people in ways that reflect our existing impressions and expectations, we may produce in them the very behavior we expect to see. The principle of conservatism can be seen clearly here: Once formed, our beliefs about other people are slow to change, in part because they tend to maintain themselves.

IMPRESSIONS SHAPE INTERPRETATIONS. Suppose you are watching the quiz show *Jeopardy*. One contestant gives quick correct answers early in the show but cools off as the questions continue. Another contestant starts out with a series of wrong answers and then improves. By the first commercial break, they have an equal number of right and wrong answers. Which contestant seems more intelligent to you? If you are like most people, you will give the edge to the one who started strongly (Jones, Rock, Shaver, Goethals, & Ward, 1968). Our initial impressions can set up an expectation that shapes our interpretations of later information: The early information has a greater impact, in what is called a *primacy effect* (Asch, 1946).

In an illustration of the lasting effects of initial impressions, Bernadette Park (1986) arranged for small groups of strangers to meet together repeatedly over a 7-week period. After the first meeting, and periodically after that, participants wrote descriptions of one another. Week after week, first impressions dominated these profiles. The characteristics noted after the very first meeting turned up repeatedly, even though the first impressions were based on little information. Apparently, initial impressions biased the participants' interpretations of later behavior. Putting your best foot forward right from the start is much easier than trying to change others' opinions once you have put your foot in it.

■ **First impressions are lasting impressions.** Massachusetts Senator Edward Kennedy's political connections and insider experience would seem to make him a likely candidate for U.S president. But his chances of success may have been limited by lingering doubts about his behavior more than 30 years ago, when he left the scene of an accident in which a passenger was killed.

IMPRESSIONS RESIST REBUTTAL. Because our impressions can shape the interpretation of later information, their effects can persist even if the initial impression is discovered to be false. This distortion is called the *perseverance bias* (Lord, Lepper, & Preston, 1984). To investigate this bias, Lee Ross and his colleagues (Ross, Lepper, & Hubbard, 1975) arranged for female students to observe others performing a decision-making task. Some observers received false feedback that made it appear that the decision maker performed quite well, getting 24 of 25 items correct. Others learned that the decision maker performed poorly, with only 10 correct items. The experimenter then revealed that the feedback had been randomly determined and had no relation to the decision maker's actual performance. However, even after the observers learned of this deception, their ratings of the decision makers' ability and their predictions of future performance still showed the effects of the now-discredited feedback. For example, observers who initially thought a decision maker had succeeded predicted that she would get an average of 19 items correct on a future trial; conversely, observers who initially saw failure predicted only 14.5 for the same decision maker. As this experiment shows, once beliefs have influenced our interpretation of other information, it is difficult to undo their effects completely if we later learn the beliefs are false (Gilbert, Krull, & Malone, 1990; Gilbert & Osborne, 1989). No wonder that it is notoriously difficult to counteract rumors after they get started (Rosnow & Fine, 1976).

The most effective way to reduce or eliminate the perseverance bias is to explicitly consider the opposite possibility (Lord and others, 1984). Learning that the supposed 24 of 25 score was false had little effect on the observers in Ross's study. However, considering the possibility that the individual might have actually performed quite poorly could have reduced the bias.

☐ **PERSEVERANCE IN THE COURTROOM.** When legally inadmissible evidence is introduced in courtroom proceedings, it can be stricken from the official trial record. The judge may even instruct jurors to disregard it. Unfortunately, jurors cannot wipe the information from their minds as easily as the court reporter can expunge the record. In fact, research has found that inadmissible evidence does influence jurors' deliberations and verdicts (Thompson, Fong, & Rosenhan, 1981). The same is true of discredited evidence. In one mock-trial study, for example, one group of participants saw minimal evidence against the defendant, and only 18% voted for conviction. A second group saw the same evidence plus an eyewitness identification of the defendant; in that group, 72% voted for conviction. A third group, after receiving all this information, learned that the eyewitness was legally blind and was not wearing his glasses at the time he claimed to have seen the defendant. This discrediting information had virtually no impact, however. In the third group the conviction rate decreased only to 68% (Loftus, 1974). The perseverance bias means that, as in this example, information may have effects that persist even after the information is found to be false.

SELECTIVELY SEEKING IMPRESSION-CONSISTENT BEHAVIOR. Most of us are somewhat inconsistent in our behaviors; for instance, we may act shy at some times and outgoing at others. What would happen if someone expected you to be outgoing and attempted to test that belief? He or she might ask you leading questions about occasions when you were outgoing, for example, when you were the center of attention at a large party or particularly enjoyed a social gathering (Snyder & Swann, 1978). As you recounted such instances, the questioner's initial hypothesis would seem to be confirmed. But was it? If the questions had focused on the times you felt shy and avoided other people, you would have been able to report on those equally well. Any hypothesis about another person could probably be confirmed if tested in this way.

Actually, people do not always ask biased or leading questions to test their beliefs about others. Given a choice, they often prefer questions that are diagnostic, that is, questions whose answers will provide information about the truth or falsity of the hypothesis (Trope, Bassok, & Alon, 1984). For example, a diagnostic question to assess whether someone is outgoing could take the following form: "Would you rather attend a large party or have a quiet get-together with one or two close friends?" Unlike the earlier example, this question would not necessarily produce a false confirmation of an initial hypothesis. However, coming up with properly diagnostic questions is often difficult unless the questioner is aware of alternatives to the given hypothesis (Higgins & Bargh, 1987; Hodgins & Zuckerman, 1993). As we have already seen, a strategy of "considering the opposite"— thinking about the possibility that the person might be quiet and retiring rather than outgoing—can reduce biases (Trope & Mackie, 1987).

CREATING IMPRESSION-CONSISTENT BEHAVIOR: THE SELF-FULFILLING PROPHECY. Suppose you believe, for whatever reason, that people from the southern United States tend to be gracious and friendly. When you meet a Southerner,

FIGURE 3.10   Expectations create confirmation: The self-fulfilling prophecy

■ Once we have formed an impression of another person, our expectations often lead us to behave in ways that elicit expectation-confirming behaviors.

you will probably act warmly, and the person will naturally reciprocate (Snyder, Tanke, & Bersheid, 1977). You will probably end up liking the person, just as you thought you would. Of course, the outcome might be quite different if your initial expectation was that Southerners would be hostile and unfriendly. As this example demonstrates, we do more than just ask other people about their behaviors. Our initial impressions may actually *create* corresponding behaviors. When a person's expectation about another causes that person to act in ways that confirm the expectation, the process is called a **self-fulfilling prophecy** (Darley & Fazio, 1980; Merton, 1948). Figure 3.10 portrays an example of this process.

Of course, if people were aware of their influence on others, they might try to discount that influence to improve the accuracy of their impressions. However, people sometimes fail to recognize even their clear and overt influences on others. To demonstrate this point, researchers set up an interview situation in which interviewers and interviewees read questions and answers from fixed scripts (Gilbert & Jones, 1986). The questions concerned politics; the prepared answers reflected a conservative or liberal viewpoint. The interviewer read each question and then pushed a "Liberal" or "Conservative" button, as specified by the script, to signal which answer the interviewee should read. Of course, by pushing the buttons, the interviewers themselves controlled the answers they heard. But did they recognize their own influence? No. They rated the interviewees as conservative when most of their answers were conservative, and liberal when most answers were liberal. It is surprisingly difficult for people to recognize the effects of their own actions on others, and without such awareness we cannot correct our impressions to improve their validity.

☐ **SELF-FULFILLING PROPHECY IN THE CLASSROOM.** Self-fulfilling prophecies can operate anywhere: at home, on the job, and in the classroom. In studies pioneered by Robert Rosenthal and his colleagues, researchers gave schoolteachers the names of some pupils in their classes who were expected to "bloom" intellectually over the next few months (Rosenthal, 1985; Rosenthal & Jacobson, 1968). Actually, the students had been selected at random. Later in the school year all the students were tested. Multiple studies using

Self-fulfilling prophecy. The process by which one person's expectations about another become reality by eliciting behaviors that confirm the expectations.

this technique have shown that children identified as "bloomers" tend to perform better than their classmates—on objective tests, not just in the teachers' own estimation. The teachers' high expectations for these children are somehow translated into actual achievement over the course of a few months. The reason may be that teachers give students more attention and more challenging assignments when they expect them to perform at a high level (Cooper & Good, 1983). These types of teacher behaviors improve students' performance.

LIMITS ON THE SELF-FULFILLING PROPHECY. How vulnerable are we to the effects of other people's expectations, particularly those of people such as teachers or employers, who have some power over us? To some extent, the answer to that question is determined by our self-views, our awareness of the views others have of us, and our social motives in the situation.

When the person being perceived has strong views about him- or herself, the self-fulfilling effects of a perceiver's expectations become weaker. William Swann and Robin Ely (1984) demonstrated this fact in an ingenious experiment in which they created a conflict between a perceiver's expectations and the other person's own self-views. The researchers paired previously unacquainted female students, selecting one as a target and the other as a perceiver. Some of the targets were self-described introverts and others were extroverts. Some of each group had great confidence in their self-knowledge, whereas others were less confident. The perceiver in each pair was led to have the opposite expectation about the target; for some, the expectation was held with great confidence and for others, with some tentativeness. Perceivers interviewed the targets three times, and then both women's impressions were assessed. Whose views exerted the most force? Most of the time, those of the target: Perceivers usually changed their original impression to match the target's self-views. The effects of the self-fulfilling prophecy emerged only when the target initially had been uncertain about her self-views and the perceiver confidently believed the reverse. In such cases, the self-fulfilling prophecy influenced both the target's overt behavior and her self-views.

Self-fulfilling prophecies can also be foiled when targets are aware of the perceivers' expectations. If you met someone who expected you to be uncertain and naive, would you make a special effort to show your independence and sophistication? Many people would react just this way. Indeed, research shows that people who are aware of others' unfavorable expectations about them often succeed in disconfirming those expectations (Hilton & Darley, 1985).

Third, self-fulfilling prophecies are weaker when the targets are motivated to convey accurate impressions, rather than trying to make the interaction go smoothly and pleasantly (Snyder & Haugen, 1995). This finding suggests that when targets confirm perceivers' expectations, it is often out of their general desire for social acceptance and connectedness.

Thus, the self-fulfilling prophecy does not affect everyone equally. Like the schoolchildren in Rosenthal's studies, some people—those who are uncertain about their self-views, are unaware of others' beliefs, or want to make interactions run smoothly—are especially vulnerable to shaping by others' expectations.

Dealing With Inconsistent Information

People sometimes encounter information that is clearly inconsistent with an impression. They may attempt to explain it away in various ways, or they may take it into account and assume that the other person has changed. Most of the time, however, impressions of others' personal characteristics are stable and difficult to change.

Consider the many mental tricks you may use to sustain your impression of another person. Believing that Albert is intelligent, you notice only his ground-breaking discoveries in science. When his behavior is ambiguous, you interpret it as being smart rather than stupid. Sometimes you seek out evidence of his intelligence, questioning him about his latest ideas on relativity rather than about the times he forgot where he parked his car. You may even create the opportunity for Albert to be smart by giving him his own lab, a supply of freshly sharpened pencils, a supercomputer, and all the coffee he can drink. Then, one day, Albert does something so remarkably stupid—so unambiguously inconsistent with your belief—that there can be no denying it. How would you handle this conflict? You could explain away this inconsistency, defending your original impression to the death. Or you could take account of the information in ways that make your impression of Albert more accurate.

RECONCILING INCONSISTENCIES. When we encounter inconsistent and contradictory information about someone, it challenges our two central social motives. Our sense of mastery and understanding is threatened by the unexpected information, and our ability to maintain a relationship or social interaction with the person may also be thrown into doubt. Inconsistent information is therefore generally unwelcome (Olson, Roese, & Zanna, 1996). This is why we often prefer to gloss over and ignore it, continuing to process superficially rather than paying attention to the inconsistency. However, important inconsistencies are likely to trigger systematic processing, when people have adequate time to devote to the task (Hamilton, Driscoll, & Worth, 1989; Srull, Lichtenstein, & Rothbart, 1985).

How would you react, for example, if one friend told you that a classmate is kind and another friend said that the same person is hostile? When people in one study were presented with such contradictory trait descriptions and asked to describe their impressions in their own words, they creatively integrated the seemingly inconsistent traits (Asch & Zukier, 1984). They decided, for example, that the person was hostile to most people but kind to family members, or that the person masked a hostile disposition with an appearance of kindness.

When people make the effort to reconcile inconsistent and contradictory information, it has several effects on cognitive processing and memory.

1. *People spend more time thinking about unexpected behaviors than about expected ones.* For example, if you read that your liberal state senator is fighting for a conservative position such as a reduction in the minimum wage for young workers, you might pay extra attention, although you might quickly pass over more expected news of his support of several liberal causes (Belmore & Hubbard, 1987).

2. *People try to explain unexpected behaviors.* Thus, you might begin to wonder why the senator supports reducing the minimum wage. Perhaps you will decide that he supports this measure because it will provide more jobs for the poor and disadvantaged, whose cause he generally favors. As we noted earlier, people are more likely to make causal attributions about unexpected events than about events that are normal and expected (Hastie, 1984).

3. *Extra processing improves people's ability to recall inconsistent behaviors.* The special attributional processing that we give to inconsistent behaviors may help us remember them better than the behaviors consistent with our expectations (Hastie & Kumar, 1979; Srull, 1981). In fact, any behaviors that people explain can be better recalled at a later time, compared with behaviors that people read but do not explain (Hastie, 1984). This is true whether the behaviors are consistent or inconsistent with the person's expectations.

Even when people make an effort at reconciliation, their impressions of others do not always change. For example, in a study conducted in the Netherlands, inconsistent behaviors (such as negative behaviors performed by a generally well-liked person) had no effect on people's impressions (Vonk, 1995). One reason is that the extensive processing may be directed at explaining away the inconsistency. If unexpected behaviors can be attributed to situational factors, the initial impression can be maintained intact (Crocker, Hannah, & Weber, 1983). Thus, a battered woman might defend her impression that her abusive partner is basically a good person by attributing his occasional violence to external factors, such as the effects of alcohol or, sadly, even some behavior of her own.

ALTERING IMPRESSIONS: IS FUNDAMENTAL CHANGE POSSIBLE? By now, you may be pretty pessimistic about the possibility of ever changing an established impression. Because so many processes tend to maintain our views, it is not surprising that even long weeks of interaction can leave people's initial impressions largely intact (Kenny, 1991; Park, 1986). Is fundamental change in impressions ever possible? Linda Silka's (1989) research offers some reason for optimism. Silka's participants read the life history of a young woman who appeared, at least on the surface, to change greatly. Lany Tyler was a high school cheerleader who, although she initially failed to win admission to college, eventually obtained a Ph.D. and became a Princeton University professor of history. Those asked to write about how Lany had changed had no trouble identifying examples, noting that she changed "from the stereotypical 'social butterfly' to an intellectually geared individual" (p. 126). This finding suggests that when people are actively looking for change in an individual, they are able to perceive it. Indeed, faced with inconsistent information for which no situational explanations are obvious, people often make sense of the behaviors by assuming that the person's beliefs, attitudes, motivation, or ability has changed (Allison, Mackie, Muller, & Worth, 1993; Silka, 1989).

Other research results point to a more qualified conclusion, however. Susan Babey and her colleagues (Babey, Queller, & Klein, 1998) gave students information about a person who changed over time, starting out with mostly intelligent behaviors but ending with mostly unintelligent ones. As expected, students who saw only the first part of the information (the intelligent behaviors) formed a corresponding impression of the person. Students who also saw the later, less intelligent behaviors revised this initial impression and concluded that the person was actually fairly stupid. However, the researchers found evidence that this new impression did not completely *replace* the original impression in the students' memory. Instead, both impressions seemed to be maintained simultaneously, though the more recently formed one was more accessible. To understand the implications of the continued presence of the original impression, imagine how these students might react if they once again learned of some intelligent behaviors performed by the person. If they had truly and completely changed their impressions they would be surprised a second time by this new information. It seems more likely, though, that they would say "There, I knew it all along," demonstrating that the original impression was still present and able to reemerge under the right conditions. This research suggests that impression change is not only rare but, even when it occurs, may often be incomplete.

CONCLUDING COMMENTS

As you reflect on the evidence presented in this chapter, you may conclude that biases in impressions are pretty hard to overcome. Most of the time that is true. We get a lot of mileage out of the simple general principle that behavior reflects personality. Yet we also know that human nature is more complicated than this rule would indicate. When accuracy is of the utmost importance, we attend fully, process carefully, and are rewarded with more accurate impressions of other people. But why is accurate person perception so likely to be the exception rather than the rule in our daily life? Why are simple principles, with all their possibilities of bias, usually more than adequate for our needs?

First, in many cases, our needs for accuracy in day-to-day person perception are modest. Correspondent inferences work perfectly well if our encounters with people are limited to particular situations or roles. For example, your assumption that the office bookkeeper is a quiet and restrained person on the basis of his office demeanor will not create problems if the office is the only place the two of you interact, though you might be surprised to see how he acts at a wild party. We can ignore people's individual personalities and still interact successfully with them if their behaviors are governed largely by the power of social situations and roles.

Second, people's behavior in particular situations often accurately reflects their personalities because they choose to be in most situations in which they find themselves. Suppose you watch someone telling jokes at a comedy try-out. Technically, it might be correct that her provocative, lively, and funny behaviors are called for by this situation. But since the would-be comedian *chose* the situation, it is probably reasonable to assume that she is a lively, funny person. Thus, a correspondent inference works just fine.

Third, correspondent inferences are often accurate because other people offer us accurate cues to their true nature, at least as they themselves perceive it. As you will see in the next chapter, being perceived accurately by others is rewarding, and being misperceived is frustrating and uncomfortable. So the lover of baroque music might wear a J. S. Bach T-shirt to let us know. Even if the cues a new acquaintance offers do not ring quite true, it is often wise to go along for the ride, accepting rather than challenging the person. Certainly the interaction will go more smoothly if we save the other's face.

Thus, people's tendency to take others' behaviors or observable cues at face value can grease the wheels of social interaction, and this tendency usually lets us get along quite well. Still, going beyond first impressions to seek greater accuracy in person perception is sometimes important. When choosing a housemate, we want to predict a variety of compatible behaviors accurately on the basis of a few items of background information and a brief conversation. Serving on a jury, we want to decide whether the defendant or the accuser is telling the truth.

In the final analysis, both accurate and inaccurate impressions flow from the same underlying *processes* that people use as they attempt to understand others. Therefore, it is these processes that social psychologists seek to understand. They include tapping our stored knowledge to make quick inferences about observed behaviors, thinking about the causes of behaviors or other events, integrating multiple items of information into a single judgment, and reconciling inconsistencies. People use these basic processes not only to understand other people, but also to understand other social objects. In the chapters that follow we will discuss how similar processes operate as we perceive and interpret ourselves (chapter 4), our own and other social groups (chapter 5), consumer products and social issues (chapter 7), our loved ones (chapter 11), even our enemies (chapter 13). Nothing in the nature of these processes necessarily leads to either accurate or inaccurate judgments. Accuracy depends more on the circumstances in which the processes are applied: the amount of useful information available, the applicability of the person's knowledge, the amount of effort the person is willing and able to put in, and whether the goal is to be accurate or to form a particular impression. Our perceptions of *all* social objects, including other people, are not determined solely by their observable characteristics. Instead, they also reflect our own individuality and uniqueness as perceivers: our motives and biases, our cognitive limitations, and the content and accessibility of our preexisting knowledge.

CHAPTER 3 THEMES

- **Construction of Reality**
  Our impressions of others are constructions based on our own selection and interpretation of cues.

- **Pervasive Social Influence**
  General knowledge shaped by our culture and past experiences enters into our impressions of others.

- **Striving for Mastery**
  Accurate understanding of others helps us deal successfully with them.

- **Conservatism**
  Once formed, an impression of another person tends to perpetuate itself by affecting our interpretations and our interactions.

- **Accessibility**
  The most salient cues and our most accessible knowledge contribute the most to our impressions.

- **Superficiality Versus Depth**
  Sometimes we are content with first impressions and snap judgments, but sometimes we strive to understand others more deeply.

SUMMARY

Forming First Impressions: Cues, Interpretations, and Inferences. Perceptions of other people begin with visible cues, including physical appearance, nonverbal communication, and overt behavior. Familiarity also affects impressions, generally leading to increased liking. Cues that are **salient**—that stand out and attract attention in the context in which they occur—are particularly influential.

These cues have no meaning in themselves, but are interpreted in the light of our existing knowledge or **cognitive representations** of people, behaviors, traits, and social situations. A representation that is **associated** with the cue itself or is **accessible** and easy to bring to mind is most likely to be used in interpreting cues. Accessibility can stem from the person's expectations, moods, or the situational context, or from recent activation (termed **priming**) or frequent activation of the representation.

When processing **superficially**, people often make **correspondent inferences**, assuming that others have inner qualities that correspond to their observable behaviors. In fact, people often make correspondent inferences even when situational causes actually account for behaviors, a pattern termed the **correspondence bias**.

Beyond First Impressions: Attribution and Integration. To go beyond a first impression, people must engage in more **systematic** thought, particularly to make **causal attributions** for behavior. People usually consider potential causes that are associated with the behavior, generally accessible, salient in context, or suggested by the pattern of available information.

When external factors appear to have caused behavior, people may attempt to correct their initial correspondent inference about the actor's characteristics. This correction takes time and cognitive effort, however, so it often does not occur.

An impression of another person usually includes several characteristics. People may infer additional traits based on their knowledge or observations of the individual. The multiple components of an impression may become linked as people attempt to infer causal connections among them. Overall evaluations, too, are usually constructed by integrating multiple aspects of an impression.

Even considered impressions may not be completely accurate. When people devote extra thought to forming an impression, biases may still limit their accuracy, and the extra efforts may only confirm an existing positive or negative view. Unless people are aware of such biases in social perception, they are unlikely to try to correct them.

The Impact of Impressions: Using, Defending, and Changing Impressions. Once an impression is formed, it becomes a basis for judgments and behaviors. Sometimes judgments about others rest on simple, superficial processing; at other times, people engage in systematic processing, attempting to put together the implications of all relevant information.

Impressions tend to resist change, partly because an initial impression can alter the interpretation of later information. As a result, impressions may survive even the discrediting of the information on which they were based. Impressions shape overt interaction as well as judgments. They often lead people to seek consistent information or even to elicit confirming actions from others, creating a **self-fulfilling prophecy**.

Still, sometimes people encounter information that is clearly inconsistent with an impression. They may attempt to explain it away in various ways, or they may take it into account and assume that the other person has changed. Most of the time, however, people's impressions of others' personal characteristics are stable and difficult to change.

4

The Self

Stroll past the popular psychology shelves in any bookstore, and you will be encouraged to *Celebrate Your Self, Be Your Best, Know Yourself,* and *Develop Your Potential.* You will be offered advice on *Making Peace With Yourself, Taking Control,* and *How to Raise Your Self-Esteem.* And you will find that you should be *Honoring the Self, Asserting Yourself, Healing Yourself,* and even *Talking to Yourself.* As these titles indicate, one of the most important life tasks you face is understanding who you are, discovering that special mix of qualities that, like your fingerprints, distinguishes you from others and makes you unique. What you think of yourself, how you feel about yourself, and the ways you choose to express yourself influence virtually all aspects of your life. In this chapter we examine the processes that help us not only to acquire accurate self-knowledge but also to protect and enhance that image we label "self."

What is this "self" anyway? Since ancient times philosophers have admonished: "Know thyself," for *the self is an object of knowledge.* You may be confident that you are shy or honest or intelligent or attractive. You may feel that, all things considered, you are a pretty decent human being. But how did you come to know these things about yourself? The first part of this chapter looks at the way we form our impressions of the self, how we come to know what we are like, and how we feel about ourselves. As you will see, the way we form impressions of the self is very similar to the way we perceive other people. However, we bring more biases to the process of self-perception. For most of us, although the self-portraits we paint are accurate in a general way, they are also colored by powerful motivational pressures to think well of ourselves.

Why do we need to know who we are? The reason is that self-knowledge is crucial in *directing and regulating our thoughts, feelings, and behaviors.* Self-knowledge lets us seek out situations that match our capabilities: Knowing ourselves to be good at tennis, we welcome the opportunity to compete on the court. Similarly, goals that are important in defining who we are direct our emotional responses to events. For example, valued accomplishments arouse pride and joy, while events that threaten or thwart us evoke the prick of fear or the sting of anger. And when we choose to coach Little League on the weekends or volunteer to lead tours through the art museum, our sense of self guides our behavior as we try to show others the kind of person we are. In the second section of the chapter we see the self in action, directing our interpretations and interactions with the social world.

In the final section of this chapter we consider what happens when our sense of self is challenged—when what happens is not what we planned, hoped for, or expected. Will juggling a career and parenthood, fighting rush-hour traffic, or struggling to make ends meet be too much for you? How do people cope with sudden illness, the loss of a job, a house once full of children becoming an "empty nest"? The last part of the chapter examines our attempts to cope with stresses, failures, and inconsistencies. As you will see, the way we defend ourselves against threats and disappointments influences not only our emotional well-being but also our physical health. In orchestrating our thoughts, feelings, and behaviors, in coordinating the person we see from the inside with the person others see from the outside, our sense of self becomes a special glue that holds body and soul together.

Constructing the Self-Concept: What We Know About Ourselves

Self-knowledge has two components: the self-concept, what we know about ourselves, and self-esteem, how we feel about ourselves. Although these parts of our self seem as familiar and comfortable as a favorite pair of jeans, both in fact are constantly developing and changing as our experiences, life circumstances, and social surroundings change. In fact, just as our impressions of other people are constructions based on a few available cues and our own general knowledge, self-knowledge is also actively constructed rather than simply or directly "known." Indeed, if complete self-understanding were easily attained, philosophers would not have to advise us to seek the self, therapists would not spend hours helping people get in touch with themselves, and bookstore self-help shelves would not be nearly so well stocked.

Sources of Self-Knowledge

People construct self-knowledge in much the same way that they form impressions of others, using similar types of information and similar interpretive processes. People often infer their own characteristics from their observed behaviors. They also use thoughts and feelings and other people's reactions to form opinions about themselves. Finally, people compare themselves to others to learn what characteristics make them unique.

The **self-concept** is the set of all an individual's beliefs about his or her personal qualities. We piece together self-knowledge over time from our interpretations of many different kinds of information.

DRAWING INFERENCES FROM OUR BEHAVIOR. "How do I know what I think until I see what I say?" asked British author E. M. Forster. His tongue-in-

Self-concept. All of an individual's knowledge about his or her personal qualities.

cheek comment captures the key idea of Daryl Bem's (1967) **self-perception theory**: We can learn things about ourselves by observing our own behavior. When we contemplate our church attendance and conclude we are religious, or star in a community theater production and decide we are extroverted, self-perception processes are at work (Rhodewalt & Agustsdottir, 1986; Salancik & Conway, 1975).

People are most likely to draw inferences about themselves from behaviors that they see themselves as having freely chosen. These behaviors are driven by *intrinsic motivation:* We are doing what we want to do rather than what we have to do. In contrast, when a behavior is performed as a means to some external end, it is governed by *extrinsic motivation*. Not only does such a behavior reveal less about our inner qualities, but we often lose pleasure in performing it (Deci, 1971; Harackiewicz, 1979).

Ironically, providing external rewards often undermines intrinsic motivation, as Mark Lepper and his colleagues (Lepper, Greene, & Nisbett, 1973) have demonstrated. They introduced preschool children to an attractive new activity: drawing with colorful felt-tip markers. After drawing for a while, some children received a previously promised "Good Player" certificate, others unexpectedly received the same certificate, and still others received nothing. One to two weeks later, the markers were placed in the children's regular classroom. The amount of free time each child spent playing with the markers was recorded as a measure of their intrinsic motivation. The children who had not been rewarded and those who had received the unexpected reward retained their motivation, drawing for 16% of the time or more. In contrast, children who expected and received an award used the markers for an average of only 8.6% of their free time.

The researchers explained their drop in motivation in terms of self-perception. Children who saw themselves drawing pictures when a reward had been promised must have concluded that they drew for the reward, not just for the pleasure of creating the picture. In contrast, drawing with no anticipation of reward allowed other youngsters to infer that the activity must be interesting and enjoyable. External rewards can undermine intrinsic motivation, particularly when they are perceived as bribes that externally control behavior, rather than as bonuses that demonstrate competence and mastery (Deci, 1975).

We do not actually have to carry out behaviors to engage in self-perception processes: Even imagined behaviors can do the trick. Imagine for a moment doing various things to help preserve the environment, perhaps recycling aluminum cans or car pooling twice weekly. Try to picture yourself actually doing something like this. Do you now see yourself as a more environmentally aware person? Research suggests that imagining these behaviors might lead you to such a conclusion (C. A. Anderson & Godfrey, 1987). Of course, if you had been asked to imagine yourself taking 30-minute showers or keeping the thermostat at 80 degrees in winter, you might have come to the opposite conclusion about yourself.

What explains these findings? Thinking about actual or imagined behavior increases the accessibility of related personal characteristics. Thus, you might imagine solving a puzzle and then reflect on your good spatial memory, recalling that you loved to play with puzzles as a child. As thoughts like these come to mind, they become the basis for a self-inference: "I am very good at solving puzzles." Interestingly, seeing the self as possessing relevant traits may improve not only your confidence, persistence,

■ **Practice for the mind as well as the body.** World-famous tenor Luciano Pavarotti during a break from one of his equally famous rehearsals. During rehearsal he prepares body and mind for demanding performances, not only singing those golden high notes but also visualizing an actual stage performance. Research has shown that visualizing in this way is an effective practice technique.

Self-perception theory. The theory that we make inferences about our personal characteristics on the basis of our overt behaviors when internal cues are weak or ambiguous.

and effort, but also your actual performance on the task (Campbell & Fairey, 1985). Athletes and sports psychologists have put such findings to work in training routines that incorporate imagery. For example, in one study, runners were divided into two groups. One group was given strength training on an exercise bicycle; the other was not. Some members of each group were also instructed to imagine themselves sprint-racing (Van Gyn, Wenger, & Gaul, 1990). Of course, sweating on the exercise cycles improved all the runners' performances, but those who also imagined themselves sprinting later obtained better race times than those who did not.

DRAWING INFERENCES FROM THOUGHTS AND FEELINGS. No one knows you as well as you know yourself, right? Perhaps this is because our most significant clues to self-knowledge are our private reactions to the world: our thoughts and feelings. Even self-perception theory states that people draw inferences from their own behaviors only when internal cues, such as thoughts and feelings, are weak. These cues can tell us more about ourselves than our overt behavior does, precisely because thoughts and feelings are less influenced by external pressures (Andersen & Ross, 1984). Attending your best friend's wedding may prompt you to act like the life and soul of the party, but your inner feelings of envy and loss tell you more about yourself. One study underlines the importance of thoughts and feelings for self-knowledge (Andersen, 1984). Some observers in the study heard participants talk about their thoughts and feelings in various everyday situations, while others heard participants describe only their behaviors in those situations. The observers then wrote down their impressions. Observers who listened to descriptions of thoughts and feelings formed impressions that matched the participants' own self-concept more accurately than the impressions recorded by observers who heard only about behaviors. This finding suggests that our thoughts and feelings can play a bigger role than behaviors in our inferences about what we are like.

EFFECTS OF OTHER PEOPLE'S REACTIONS. Other people's views of us also contribute to the development of the self-concept. In 1902, the sociologist Charles H. Cooley coined the phrase the "looking-glass self" to indicate that one source of our self-knowledge is other people's reactions to us. These reactions serve as a kind of mirror, reflecting our image so that we, too, can see it (Felson, 1989). Parents coo over us. Peers belittle us. Relatives note with pleasure that we remind them of devout Aunt Agatha. Reactions like these tell us we are cute, clumsy, or religious.

One study supported the concept of the looking-glass self when it compared the behaviors of three groups of schoolchildren. Teachers and others repeatedly told some of the children that they *were* tidy. Children in another group were repeatedly instructed that they *should be* tidy, and the third group was not told anything special. The researchers then observed how much litter each group spread around. The tidiest youngsters were those in the first group. Labeled as tidy, they behaved accordingly, reflecting their new self-concept (R. L. Miller, Brickman, & Bolen, 1975).

Like the self-fulfilling prophecy (discussed in chapter 3), the looking-glass self involves an observer's reactions that influence someone else's behavior and self-concept (D. T. Miller & Turnbull, 1986). Chapter 3 noted that self-fulfilling prophecies mainly affect people who are uncertain of their

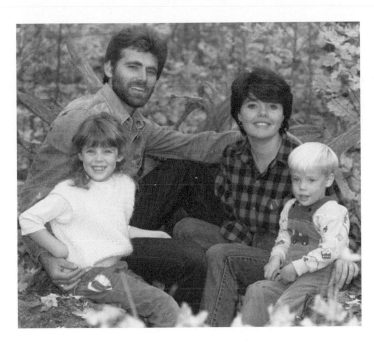

■ **A real standout.** People tend to describe themselves in terms of the characteristics that make them different from those around them. Thus, the little boy is probably quite conscious of his blond hair, which distinguishes him from all the members of his dark-haired family.

actual self-concept, and the same is true with the looking-glass self. Thus, others' reactions have the largest effects on young children (as in the study just described) or others who lack firm self-concepts. For most adults, in contrast, self-views rely more on other types of evidence, such as comparisons with other people, and are only weakly related to the opinions of other people (Malloy & Albright, 1990; Shrauger & Schoeneman, 1979). Perhaps part of the reason for the weakness of these effects is that we are often unaware of what other people actually think about us (Kenny & DePaulo, 1993).

SOCIAL COMPARISON. If you, as a moderately skilled chess player, want to know how good you really are, your best approach is not to listen to what other people tell you about your playing skills, but to play a lot of games and see how many you win. This approach makes sense, because according to **social comparison theory**, the self-concept is often shaped by comparisons between ourselves and others. This theory was initially proposed by Leon Festinger (1954), who assumed that people want to evaluate themselves accurately and that they therefore seek out *similar* others for comparison. Thus, you will learn more by comparing your game with that of opponents with similar skills than by judging yourself against either Garry Kasparov or a rank beginner. In fact, however, multiple motives lead people to compare themselves to others, including not only the desire for accurate self-evaluations but also desires for empathy and connectedness, for inspiration from others' outstanding performances (Lockwood & Kunda, 1997), or for positive feelings about themselves (Helgeson & Mickelson, 1995).

By revealing what physical or social attributes distinguish us from familiar or similar others, social comparisons are important in allowing us to construct a sense of our own uniqueness. The attributes that distinguish us from most others often become defining features of the self. A left-hander is more likely to think of handedness, a personally distinguishing attribute, than is a right-handed person. Children writing self-descriptions are likely to

> **Social comparison theory.** The theory that people learn about and evaluate their personal qualities by comparing themselves to others.

FIGURE 4.1   Sources of self-knowledge

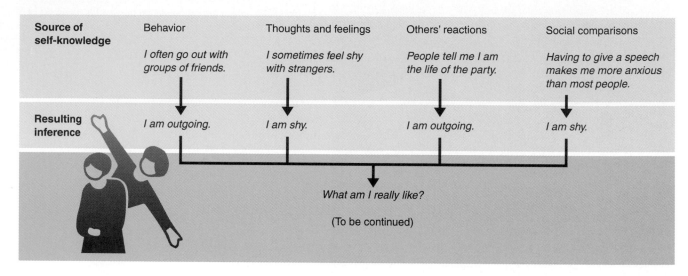

■ Because no one is totally consistent all the time, multiple sources of information about ourselves may lead to potentially conflicting inferences, which will eventually have to be integrated.

Chapter 6 will deal with the aspects of self-knowledge, such as our membership in social groups, that we share in common with other people.

mention characteristics, such as wearing glasses or being short, that mark them as unusual in their family or classroom (W. J. McGuire & McGuire, 1981; W. J. McGuire & Padawer-Singer, 1978). By summarizing the ways in which we differ from others, social comparison permits us to construct a self-concept that gives each of us a strong sense of being unique and distinctive.

Figure 4.1 shows the many sources of self-knowledge. Note that social influences are pervasive even as we are constructing the self and learning what makes us unique.

Knowledge About Self and Other People: The Same or Different?

Despite the general similarity between the ways people learn about themselves and about others, self-knowledge is richer and more detailed than knowledge about others. People can observe themselves in more situations and have better access to private thoughts and feelings. People also tend to explain their own and other people's behaviors differently, attributing their own actions to properties of the situation or the stimulus, while generally explaining others' actions by their personal characteristics. However, even people's explanations for their own behaviors may be inaccurate.

Most of the time, the cues we use to learn about ourselves are the same sorts of cues we use to learn about others. For instance, we draw inferences from our own behaviors, and we monitor other people's reactions to us. Our reliance on similar sorts of cues creates important similarities between our knowledge about the self and about others, but there are differences as well, particularly in the amount of knowledge we have and in the inferences we draw from it.

DIFFERENCES IN AMOUNT OF KNOWLEDGE. We usually have a greater quantity and variety of information about ourselves than we have about others. For example, we see ourselves in a wider range of situations and for more time than we observe anyone else. This fact probably explains why we view ourselves as quite variable and flexible, whereas we view other people as more set in their ways (T. L. Baxter & Goldberg, 1987). Asked to state whether they are serious or carefree, for example, most people will describe themselves and those they know well by saying, "In-between," or "It depends." But they freely characterize those they know less well as closer to the extremes (Prentice, 1990; Sande, Goethals, & Radloff, 1988). Interestingly, people seem to realize that observers are likely to see them as less variable and more consistent than the way they see themselves (Krueger, Ham, & Linford, 1996).

DIFFERENCES IN ATTRIBUTION. Because we have greater access to our own reactions, we are more aware of the impact people, places, and events have on us than of the impact they have on others. As a result, we may draw different inferences about the causes of behaviors. Recall for a moment the last time you became really angry and yelled at someone. Why did you act the way you did? Try to answer the same question about the last person who became irate at you. Why did he or she do that?

If you are like most people, you answered these similar questions in very different ways. In explaining your own aggressive actions, you probably pointed to external factors, perhaps saying that the person you became angry with had been really annoying and provocative. Answering the same question about someone else, you probably cited that person's personal characteristics: He or she is just an aggressive type who boils over easily. Why the difference? People tend to attribute their own choices to situational

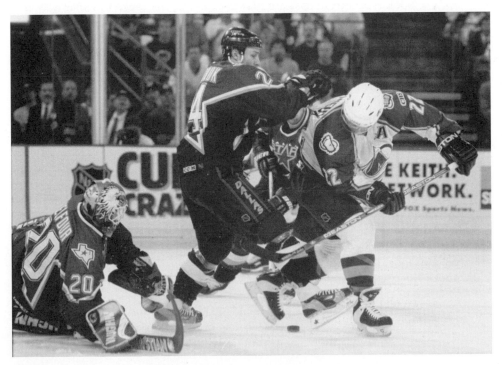

■ **Actor–observer differences in attribution.** While trying to stop this shot, Dallas Stars defender Richard Matvichuk would probably see his hit on Colorado Avalanche right winger Claude Lemieux (22) as caused by the rough-and-tumble competition of intense playoff action. Observers, however, might attribute such incidents to the aggressive nature of the player.

factors but to make *correspondent inferences*—assumptions that behavior reflects personality characteristics—for others. Such **actor–observer differences in attributions** for behavior have been found repeatedly (Gioia & Sims, 1985; E. E. Jones & Nisbett, 1972). You can find a small sample of these differences by reading a few letters to Ann Landers in your local newspaper. Watch how people seeking advice tend to explain their own actions by citing external reasons, and to explain others' behaviors by describing those people's personal characteristics (Schoeneman & Rubanowitz, 1985).

Why are people so prone to these actor–observer differences in attribution? Differences in salience and assumed comparisons are two important factors.

1. *Whatever grabs our attention stands out.* When we witness another person's behavior, that person is salient: He or she is the focus of attention and stands out against the background (Heider, 1958; Storms, 1973). In contrast, when we act, we literally look out at the world, so the stimulus or trigger for our action is the salient factor. You see the snake in the grass as causing your sudden jump, whereas a passerby focuses mainly on your startle response and may conclude that you are an easily frightened person.

2. *Different sets of causal alternatives are considered for the self and for others.* When asked why something occurred, people consider alternative causes, but they consider different alternatives for the self and for others (Kahneman & Miller, 1986; McGill, 1989). For example, if someone asks you why you liked the latest John Grisham thriller, you will probably assume that the questioner means why you liked it *as compared to other books*. Obviously, then, it would be reasonable to cite the aspects of the novel that distinguish it from others. But if someone asks why a friend of yours liked the same book, you might assume that the questioner seeks to learn why this friend *among all other people* liked the book, and so you might cite some of your friend's unique personal characteristics (McGill, 1989). The difference in assumed comparisons for self and others produces very different answers (Wells & Gavanski, 1989).

SIMILARITIES IN ACCURACY. Although we know more about ourselves than about others, that knowledge is not always sufficient to let us make more accurate judgments about ourselves than about others. In fact, being the leading authority on the topic does not guarantee that we are always aware of why we think, feel, and act the way we do (Nisbett & Wilson, 1977). Consider the efforts of 50 students who for 5 weeks kept diaries of their positive and negative moods and tried to identify the sources of those moods. They recorded many potential causes, such as whether the weather was sunny or wet and whether it was a Monday or a weekend day. Another group of students was simply asked to describe how these factors *generally* affect people's moods. Despite their efforts at self-analysis, the diary keepers' reports about the causes of their own moods were no more accurate than the blind guesses of people who did not know them (Wilson, Laser, & Stone, 1982). Apparently, all the participants relied on general causal theories, like the idea that rainy days and Mondays cause blue moods, even if they were explaining their own moods. Self-knowledge does not guarantee insight into

Actor–observer differences in attribution. The tendency to attribute our own behaviors to situational causes while seeing others' acts as due to their inner characteristics.

our own unique actions and reactions: We use our general knowledge about human behavior to interpret ourselves as well as others.

Multiple Selves

Because people see themselves in a wide range of situations and roles, self-knowledge is organized around multiple roles, activities, and relationships. People vary in the number and diversity of "selves" that they believe they possess.

As information about the self accumulates from all these different sources, we become aware that we have many different "selves." We begin to see that some of our behaviors, thoughts, and feelings depend on what we are doing and who our companions are (Markus & Wurf, 1987). For instance, most of us probably act and feel differently when we are working with our office mates—perhaps more responsibly and less playfully—than we do when we are with family and close friends. Social comparisons also vary from situation to situation. Someone who is one of the least polite people at work may be the most polite family member at home. Others' reactions also differ. Older relatives may view a 40-year-old physician as a youngster, but his co-workers may see him as a mature leader in the field of transplant surgery.

How do we deal with all this varying and potentially confusing information? We organize it according to our various roles, activities, and relationships (Carver & Scheier, 1981; James, 1890; T. B. Rogers, 1981; Stryker, 1980). Thus, a woman might consider herself *studious* in academic situations, *hardworking* at the office, and *fun-loving* when relaxing with a group of friends. Each of these different *self-aspects* summarizes what she believes she is like in a particular domain, role, or activity. Other self-aspects may reflect additional roles and activities such as sister, lover, chess player, or jogger (Hoelter, 1985).

People differ in **self-complexity**, or the number and diversity of the self-aspects that they develop for different situations, roles, or relationships. People with only a few, relatively similar, self-aspects are said to have low self-complexity, while people with many independent self-aspects are described as high in self-complexity (Linville, 1985). When college admissions committees look for "well-rounded" applicants, they are probably looking for individuals with high self-complexity. Such applicants might describe themselves not only in terms of their academic achievements but also as participants in other roles or activities: sports, volunteer work, school governance, art, or music. Examples of high and low self-complexity are shown in Figure 4.2. As you will see later, self-complexity has major implications for both mental and physical well-being.

Putting It All Together: Constructing a Coherent Self-Concept

People try to fit the diverse elements of self-knowledge together in a way that seems coherent and stable. Coherence can be attained by making accessible only limited aspects of the self at any given time, by selectively remembering past acts, by explaining away inconsistencies, and by focusing on a few central traits.

Self-complexity. The number and diversity of the self-aspects that people develop for different roles, activities, and relationships.

FIGURE 4.2   Examples of self-concepts that are high and low in self-complexity

High self-complexity self-concept

In relationships
*outgoing, playful,
reflective, mature,
assertive,
emotional,
competitive*

With friends
*humorous, relaxed,
assertive,
individualistic,
outgoing,
soft-hearted,
not studious*

At school
*quiet, studious,
organized, mature,
industrious*

With my family
*individualistic,
emotional, playful,
mature, assertive,
unconventional*

By myself
*quiet,
individualistic,
industrious,
organized*

Low self-complexity self-concept

At the dorm
*relaxed, playful,
humorous, imaginative,
disorganized*

At home
*relaxed, humorous,
not studious, affectionate,
irresponsible, playful*

In activities
*relaxed, assertive,
affectionate, imaginative,
outgoing, helpful*

■ The hypothetical individual at the top sees herself as having five self-aspects, characterized by relatively distinct sets of traits. The person at the bottom possesses only three self-aspects, with a greater degree of overlap: Note that some traits (like "relaxed" or "playful") are seen as applying to most or all self-aspects. (Adapted from Linville, 1987, p. 667, copyright © 1987 by the American Psychological Association. Adapted by permission.)

Self-knowledge does not come to us in final form, neatly wrapped with ribbon and bow. Instead, the label warns: "Some assembly required." When we construct a self-concept from disparate pieces of self-knowledge derived from our multiple roles and social interactions, the pieces may not fit together very well. You may be an eager participant in one class but unmotivated in another. You may think of yourself as a good father but a failure as a husband. You may be a vociferous team leader but reserved off the field. Like the pieces of a Lego set, a person's self-aspects must be assembled into a coherent whole if the individual is to have a sense of unity and constancy. People use a number of strategies to construct this coherent sense of self (Baumeister, 1998).

COHERENCE THROUGH LIMITED ACCESSIBILITY. Imagine for a moment a house in which every room is furnished in a different style: a country kitchen, a southwestern bedroom, a stately traditional living room. If you stood in a central hallway viewing all the rooms at once, the house would truly be a hodgepodge. But if you stepped into one room and closed the door, the decor would be coherent and the ambience comfortable. We often deal with inconsistencies among the various parts of our self-concept in the same way: We relax comfortably in one role because other inconsistent roles are out of sight and out of mind.

What opens and closes the doorways between our several selves? The accessibility of different parts of our self-knowledge is the key. In one study, researchers asked biased questions to induce students to reflect on either their past introverted or extroverted behaviors (Fazio, Effrein, & Falender, 1981). Increasing the accessibility of a biased subset of the self-concept in this way not only caused the students to rate themselves as more introverted or extroverted (depending on their experimental condition), but even made them behave accordingly. As this experiment demonstrates, most people have different and even inconsistent bits of self-knowledge potentially available, but it is the self-knowledge that is currently accessible that will govern thoughts and behavior. Thus, for example, at work you may see yourself as logical, persistent, and authoritative, ignoring other traits (such as *fun-loving* or *carefree*) that characterize your leisure-time self. Different self-aspects will be accessible in work versus play situations, so you will rarely be uncomfortably aware of potential inconsistencies.

COHERENCE THROUGH SELECTIVE MEMORY. As people think about their past, they reconstruct an autobiography that integrates their various self-aspects and characteristics (Bruner, 1986; Gergen & Gergen, 1988). For example, people whose behavior has changed from shy to outgoing may retrieve a biased set of autobiographical memories in which they were always outgoing (M. Ross & Conway, 1986). Reconstruction, like a totalitarian government's rewriting of history, deals with inconsistencies by erasing them (Greenwald, 1980). This strategy gives the person a sense of self that *feels* coherent over time, even if it fails to accurately record the facts of personal history. Michael Ross (1989) speculates that adults' frequent reminiscences (particularly to their misbehaving children) about their own praiseworthy, responsible childhood may be a product of reconstruction. As a responsible adult, it is easy to misremember one's child self as having been equally responsible and to forget incidents of childish carelessness.

COHERENCE THROUGH ATTRIBUTION. Would it surprise you to learn that your co-workers find you rather changeable—quiet and deferential one moment but bossy and domineering the next? If you are like most people, it probably would. You might reply that of course you are deferential when the boss is around, but when she is not, somebody has to get things organized. We explain our behaviors as reasonable responses to situations, so we are unlikely to see variations in our behavior as significant signs of instability. As pointed out earlier, most people attribute their own behavior to circumstances, not to stable, general personality traits (E. E. Jones & Nisbett, 1972). This tactic enables us to interpret our inconsistent behavior as a result of inconsistent circumstances, not of our inconsistent selves.

COHERENCE THROUGH SELECTING A FEW KEY TRAITS. People also construct a unified and enduring sense of self by noting a few core attributes that they believe characterize them uniquely among people and consistently across situations. These important and distinctive personal characteristics form the *self-schema* (Markus, 1977). Once a particular characteristic is incorporated into the self-schema, people notice and process information about it very efficiently. For example, people whose self-schema includes a trait like *helpful* can answer questions like "Are you helpful?" more quickly than other individuals (Markus, 1977). People tend to see evidence for these core traits even in their most mundane behaviors, thereby reinforcing their sense of a stable and unitary self (Cantor & Kihlstrom, 1987). Thus, you might see confirmation for your view of yourself as helpful even in a trivial interaction like giving directions to a stranger on campus. And, as we will see, people are quick to reject feedback that is inconsistent with their self-schema, thereby increasing their sense of consistency even further (Markus, 1977; Swann & Hill, 1982).

FIGURE 4.3   Reconciling inconsistencies: Forming a coherent self-concept

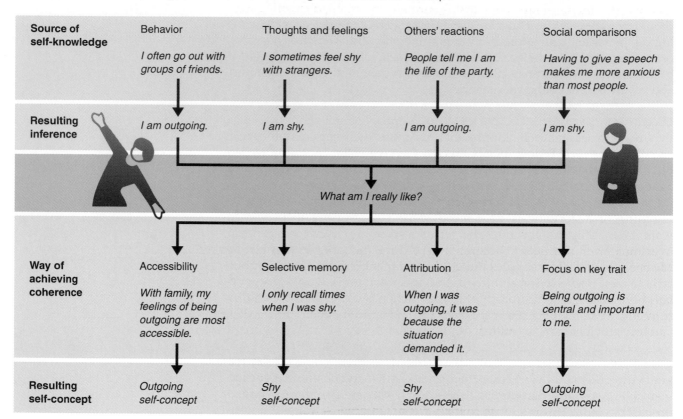

Source of self-knowledge	Behavior	Thoughts and feelings	Others' reactions	Social comparisons
	I often go out with groups of friends.	*I sometimes feel shy with strangers.*	*People tell me I am the life of the party.*	*Having to give a speech makes me more anxious than most people.*
Resulting inference	*I am outgoing.*	*I am shy.*	*I am outgoing.*	*I am shy.*

What am I really like?

Way of achieving coherence	Accessibility	Selective memory	Attribution	Focus on key trait
	With family, my feelings of being outgoing are most accessible.	*I only recall times when I was shy.*	*When I was outgoing, it was because the situation demanded it.*	*Being outgoing is central and important to me.*
Resulting self-concept	*Outgoing self-concept*	*Shy self-concept*	*Shy self-concept*	*Outgoing self-concept*

■ We have several ways to reconcile inconsistencies in the process of forming a stable and coherent self-concept. Different people select different strategies from among these alternatives.

As we saw earlier, different sources often provide mixed information about the self. But Figure 4.3 illustrates the several ways that people can construct a self-concept that is coherent and meaningful.

Cultural Differences in the Self-Concept

Cultures influence the type of self-concept that people construct. Members of Western, independent cultures stress the self-schema, traits that generally describe them across situations, while those in interdependent cultures emphasize their roles and relationships with others.

Imagine two recalcitrant 4-year-olds, each steadfastly refusing to taste the carrots. "Just try them," coaxes one mother, "vegetables help you grow up big and strong. You want to be big and strong, don't you?" The other caregiver tries a different tactic: "Think of the farmer who grew the carrots so you could have them to eat. He will be so disappointed if you don't like them. Just a taste, to make the farmer happy!" Perhaps you recognize one or the other of these strategies. In fact, the first "you-oriented" approach is more often used by parents in cultures that emphasize individuality, whereas the second strategy reflects the "other-directed" concerns of community-oriented cultures. Do cultures with such different emphases also foster different conceptions of the self?

Although members of all cultures seek a coherent sense of the self, Hazel Markus and Shinobu Kitayama (1991; Markus, Kitayama, & VandenBos, 1996) have suggested that different cultures offer diverse visions of what a self is like. In many of the countries of North America and Western Europe, people tend to see the self as independent, separate from other people, and revealed primarily in inner thoughts and feelings. North American students writing self-descriptions tend to list general attributes that mark them as unique or distinctive individuals, such as "I am intelligent" or "I am musical"—the sort of characteristics that make up the self-schema.

In contrast, people in the *interdependent* cultures found in many parts of Asia, Africa, and South America tend to see the self as connected with others and revealed primarily in social roles and relationships. Chinese students are more likely than Westerners to define themselves in terms of relationships, roles, or attributes they share with others, such as "I am a daughter" or "I am Buddhist" (Trafimow, Triandis, & Goto, 1991). Because relationships with others are so important, members of interdependent cultures rely on self-aspects—their social roles and relationships with others—to define the self, not on self-schemata (Cousins, 1989; Markus & Kitayama, 1991). In one study demonstrating this difference, Cross and others (Cross, Kanagawa, Markus, & Kitayama, 1995) gave Japanese and American college students questionnaires asking them to describe themselves in different social contexts, such as in a professor's office, with a friend, or alone. American students were more likely than Japanese to describe themselves using general traits such as *optimistic* or *warm*. Moreover, their descriptions varied less than those of the Japanese students across the different contexts. For example, a Japanese student might mention academic characteristics such as *smart* in the professor's office context, but not in other settings. Table 4.1 shows some of the contrasts between independent and interdependent cultural views of the self.

TABLE 4.1. Some Differences Between Construction of the Self in Independent and Interdependent Cultures

Feature	Independent culture	Interdependent culture
Definition of the self	Unique individual, separate from social context	Connected with others in mesh of social roles and relationships
Structure of the self	Unitary and stable, constant across situations and relationships	Fluid and variable, changing from one situation or relationship to another
Important features	Internal, private self (abilities, thoughts, feelings, traits)	External, public self (statuses, roles, relationships)
Significant tasks	Being unique Expressing yourself Promoting your own goals Being direct (saying what's on your mind)	Belonging, fitting in Acting appropriately Promoting group goals Being indirect (reading others' minds)

Source: Adapted by permission from "Culture and the self: Implications for cognition, emotion, and motivation," by H. Markus and S. Kitayama, *Psychological Review, 98,* p. 230. Copyright © 1991 by the American Psychological Association.

■ **A match made by culture.** Many Western women may wonder at Masake Owado's choice of mate. The princess, shown here in an official wedding photo, gave up a brilliant diplomatic career and her legal existence as a person to marry Japan's Crown Prince Naruhito. From the point of view of Japanese culture with its valuing of connectedness to others and the greater good of the group, the choice may not have been so hard to understand.

Thus, cultures tell us much about the kinds of selves we should have (Markus & Kitayama, 1991). Cultures like those of Europe and North America emphasize independence, and people in those societies see themselves as unique, characterizing their individuality in traits represented by words such as *honest, responsible*, or *outgoing*. In contrast, in interdependent cultures like Japan, the emphasis is on connectedness to others; instead of general traits and characteristics, relationships with specific persons and groups are most important. Indeed, a Japanese person will experience social connections and ties to others as the core of the self, even if those linkages conflict with his or her inner feelings. Japanese people who thought about themselves as most North Americans do and who acted accordingly would be considered at least antisocial, and perhaps even mentally ill. It is paradoxical that our seemingly most private possession—our sense of who we are— is so thoroughly molded by our cultural groups and by the people around us.

In all cultures, though, the primary function of self-knowledge is the same. For people to survive and flourish, they must adapt successfully to their environment, particularly the social environment consisting of other people. Self-knowledge is a crucial aid in that adaptation. Knowing our unique configuration of talents and social ties allows us to choose goals that we can reasonably attain, avoid situations that make us miserable, and act in ways that play up our strong points while compensating for our shortcomings (Higgins, 1996b). Self-knowledge is most helpful in guiding our adaptation if it is accurate. If we held inflated ideas of our own capabilities, we might be tempted into situations that demanded more than we could produce, setting ourselves up for disappointment and failure. Accuracy is one important goal as we construct our self-knowledge, then, but as we will see, it is not the only goal.

Constructing Self-Esteem: How We Feel About Ourselves

Self-esteem. An individual's positive or negative evaluation of himself or herself.

The self-concept is *what we think* about the self; **self-esteem**, the positive or negative evaluation of the self, is *how we feel* about it (E. E. Jones, 1990a).

Self esteem is reflected in people's agreement or disagreement with statements like: "I feel I'm a person of worth," or "On the whole, I am satisfied with myself" (M. Rosenberg, 1965). Why is self-esteem important? Our level of self-esteem plays a role in the crucial adaptive function of the self: It tells us from moment to moment and from year to year how we are doing in constructing a positively valued self that lets us function well, attaining concrete rewards and fostering connectedness with others.

Balancing Accurate Self-Knowledge and Self-Enhancement

Accurate self-knowledge regarding our capabilities and preferences is important for guiding us through our lives in ways that suit our needs and abilities. But accuracy is not the only consideration in evaluating the self: We are also greatly influenced by motivational pressures to think well of the self. These motivations color and bias many of our thoughts and feelings.

Self-esteem summarizes how we are doing at using our self-knowledge to navigate the world and achieve our goals. To see how this works, consider that to successfully regulate anything, such as your financial life, it is important to keep track of your current standing, for example with a bank statement showing your balance at the end of each month. Like a bank statement that shows how well you are managing your income and expenses, self-esteem is a signal of how well you are doing in successfully adapting to your own social world (Leary, Tambor, Terdal, & Downs, 1995). It tracks the net result of your successes and failures, achievements and difficulties, as well as your acclaim or rejection by important other people (Baldwin & Sinclair, 1996). But to serve its proper role in monitoring the self-regulation process, self-esteem should be a relatively accurate reflection of how you are doing. What use would be an inaccurate bank statement that showed you with thousands of dollars more than you really have? It would only encourage you to overspend and leave you with an empty account and a pile of bounced checks.

Yet here is a puzzle. Despite the clear value of accurate knowledge about how we are doing, people generally tend to inflate their own abilities and accomplishments, seeking to elevate their self-esteem. For example, pick a few traits—honesty, social sensitivity, and leadership, for example—and ask some people to rate themselves on each. You will probably find few people who rate themselves below average on any one (let alone on all) of these qualities. Researchers have found that most people rate themselves above average on a variety of characteristics, including things like managerial ability, driving skills, and health habits (Larwood & Whittaker, 1977; Svenson, 1981; Weinstein, 1987). This self-enhancing tendency has been termed the "Lake Wobegon effect," after the humorist Garrison Keillor's mythical town where "all the children are above average." Of course, the vaguer the criteria for a characteristic, the easier it is for people to see themselves as above average. Thus, we are more likely to believe we are better than average in sensitivity, discipline, or sophistication than in punctuality, a trait easily measured against the clock (Dunning, Meyerowitz, & Holzberg, 1989). For the same reason, people are more likely to estimate that they are above average on dimensions of morality than on dimensions

Calvin and Hobbes by Bill Watterson

CALVIN AND HOBBES © 1992 Watterson. Dist. By Universal Press Syndicate

of intellectual performance (Allison, Messick, & Goethals, 1989). People's high views of themselves even extend to things they own or are attached to in some way (Beggan, 1992). If you're like most people, you probably even prefer letters that occur in your name to other letters (Nuttin, 1987)!

These and other findings reflect our desire to view ourselves in a positive light. Thus, as we will see in the next few sections, our level of self-esteem often reflects compromises between accurate self-evaluation and unrealistic self-enhancement. Many types of events and experiences affect self-esteem, as we tally our successes and failures, compare ourselves to others, and evaluate ourselves against internal standards. Though these types of information could allow us to form reasonably accurate assessments of how we stand, at the same time **self-enhancing biases** sneak into the processes of gathering and interpreting information (Kunda, 1990).

Evaluating Personal Experiences: Some Pain but Mainly Gain

Events that affect us positively or negatively influence our self-esteem, but we try in several ways to accumulate more positive than negative experiences.

Remember how happy you felt the first time you beat your regular opponent at tennis? And how your image of yourself plunged on the day you broke up with your first love? Experiences like these can raise or lower self-esteem at a moment's notice. However, self-enhancing biases can color the impact of our experiences on self-esteem. Almost without thinking about it, most of us stack the deck so that life produces more gain and less pain.

First, we choose situations in which we can shine. One of the authors of this text is a member of a choir and regularly chooses to sing in public; the other takes care to avoid embarrassment by putting a great distance between herself, choirs, and even occasional invitations to Karaoke nights. Most of us tend to abandon relationships that make us miserable, hobbies that we are unskilled at, and careers that do not allow us to flourish. Instead, our life choices often move us into domains that let us be all that we can be.

We also inflate our contributions to joint efforts or projects. In part, this bias may stem from the natural workings of memory. It is easy to remember one's own contributions to a joint project; the hours others worked are

Self-enhancing bias. Any tendency to gather or interpret information concerning the self in a way that leads to overly positive evaluations.

naturally less vivid. However, people inflate their own contributions to a lesser extent when a project ends in failure (M. Ross & Sicoly, 1979). If overestimating were due only to superior memory for one's own actions, then the overestimate should occur to an equal extent when a project fails. Since it does not, we can infer that the tendency stems at least in part from a self-enhancing motive to overestimate one's positive contributions.

For reasons like these, though our assessment of each individual experience may be largely accurate, most of us amass more positive experiences than negative ones, both in reality and in memory.

PERSONALITY DIFFERENCES IN THE IMPACT OF EXPERIENCES. Individuals differ both in the way they react to positive and negative events and in the impact such events have on their self-esteem. Patricia Linville's (1985) research demonstrated that the effect of positive and negative events is exaggerated for people who are low in self-complexity, that is, those who see themselves as having relatively few distinct self-aspects. Linville set up an opportunity for her participants to experience success or failure. Compared with participants with higher self-complexity, those with low self-complexity experienced both more positive moods after success and more negative moods after failure, as Figure 4.4 shows. Those low in self-complexity also had larger changes in self-esteem after a success or failure experience. Other research, however, suggests that the effects may be more limited, holding only for those who are high in self-complexity for their *positive* attributes, not negative attributes (H. J. Morgan & Janoff-Bulman, 1994; Woolfolk, Novalany, Gara, Allen, & Polino, 1995).

Why may high self-complexity protect people from swings in mood and self-esteem? Linville argues that a good or bad event, such as an argument or a reconciliation with a loved one, is likely to have a *direct* effect on only one or two self-aspects (one's view of oneself as a supportive confidant, for

FIGURE 4.4 Self-complexity influences mood

■ In one study of the influence of self-complexity, success or failure had a marked impact on the mood of individuals who were low in self-complexity (left bars). Note, in contrast, the narrower range of good and bad feelings these events produced in individuals with high self-complexity (right bars). (Data from Linville, 1985.)

example, or as a family-oriented spouse). If people have many independent self-aspects, only a small portion of their self-concept will be affected by an event. Such people may reflect, "Well, I may be hopeless when it comes to romance, but at least I am still a good writer and a great basketball player." In contrast, a single positive or negative event will color a major portion of the self-concept of a person with relatively few self-aspects, and that person will therefore experience events relatively intensely. So when our lives go really well, we may benefit from having a relatively simple self-concept because our highs will be higher. But for most of us, life experience is a mix of good and bad events, and we probably should try not to "put all of [our] eggs in one cognitive basket" (Linville, 1985, p. 94).

Carolin Showers (1992) has found that reactions to good or bad events are also affected by the ways that positive and negative information is organized into self-aspects. Some people keep positive and negative information about the self well separated, so that each self-aspect includes mostly positive or mostly negative beliefs. In people with this *compartmentalized* pattern, events (like winning a hard-fought tennis match) that increase the accessibility of a thoroughly positive self-aspect (such as an "athletic self") will flood the person with positive self-knowledge. A great mood will likely result. However, this type of self-organization has a vulnerability: An event that activates a largely negative self-aspect may lead to an extreme negative mood. In contrast, suppose the person's self-knowledge was organized in more *integrated* fashion, with both positive and negative beliefs associated with the athletic self as well as other selves. For example, the person might realize that she is a great tennis player but no good as a distance runner. Then the same event would activate a more evaluatively mixed set of self-views, and the person's reaction would be more subdued. Like high self-complexity, an integrated self-organization will generally lead to less extreme moods in response to positive or negative events.

Social Comparisons: Better or Worse Than Others?

We also evaluate ourselves by making comparisons with others. These comparisons also are sometimes self-enhancing.

Self-esteem, like the self-concept, depends on social comparisons. Consider, for example, the plight of a young man who recently enrolled in one of our universities with a basketball scholarship. He is an athlete of above-average talent who is expected, in time, to make real contributions to the team. The problem is that his older brother, who played at the same school 2 years earlier, was a major star and is now beginning a career as a professional. It seems inevitable that the young man will be compared to his older brother.

How might these comparisons influence the player's self-esteem if his performance is not equal to his brother's? Abraham Tesser's (1988) model of *self-evaluation maintenance* suggests two possible reactions. They both depend on the *closeness* of the other person, for example, the fact that the star player was a brother rather than a cousin, and the *importance* or centrality of the attribute in question for the person's self-concept. Suppose the young man was planning to compete in track and field instead of basketball. Then he would be likely to feel good because of the reflected glory of his brother's impressive accomplishments. But if playing basketball is an important and central part of the younger brother's self-concept, disappointment stemming from the comparison could overwhelm his pleasure in his brother's success. In fact, being outperformed by a sibling or close friend may be even more painful than being beaten by a stranger, because the likelihood of social comparison is greater. Sometimes we want to bask in a loved one's reflected glory; at other times the glare of his or her achievement is just too painfully illuminating.

As the example illustrates, we are not always free to choose whom to compare ourselves with (J. V. Wood, 1989). Most of us have probably had the unfortunate experience of performing in public, for example, at a track meet, speech contest, or piano recital, immediately after the local superstar turned in a superb performance. This kind of inescapable comparison can induce feelings of envy and resentment and can lower self-esteem (Salovey & Rodin, 1984; Tesser & Collins, 1988). However, forced comparisons can have positive as well as negative consequences. Consider the top three competitors in an Olympic event, all of whom are awarded medals. The silver medalist naturally compares him- or herself to the winner, and probably doesn't feel good about coming in second. However, for the bronze medalist, the most natural comparison is to the fourth-place competitor, who gets no medal at all! Based on these ideas about social comparison, Victoria Medvec and her colleagues (Medvec, Madey, & Gilovich, 1995) coded videotapes of the 1992 Summer Olympic Games. Indeed, they found that the facial expressions of the bronze medal winners—who had performed less well in absolute terms—were happier than those of the silver medal winners.

Chapter 6, pages 212 to 213, will discuss in more detail the ways in which connections with other people can help us feel good or bad about ourselves.

BIASED COMPARISONS: DEFINITELY BETTER THAN OTHERS.
Social comparisons sometimes help us gain an accurate picture of our skills and abilities, but we often attempt to avoid comparisons that make us look bad. One common tactic we employ is establishing distance between ourselves and those who are successful. We do this by either downplaying our similarities to them or backing off from our relationships with them (Tesser, 1988). Another form of protection involves *downward comparisons*, which involve comparing ourselves with others who are in some way less fortunate or less successful. An average grade on the calculus final looks better in the light of the failing grades some students received. A not-so-exciting home life sure beats the misery experienced by recently divorced friends. In fact, people who learn that they have some positive attribute tend to underestimate the number of others who share the same characteristic—a bias that fosters a sense of superiority (Goethals, Messick, & Allison, 1991). Even when the situation is objectively pretty grim, it helps to know that life could be worse. Interviews with breast-cancer patients, for example, found that they compared themselves with others who were worse off: people whose disease was not responding to treatments, or those who lacked social support or contracted the disease at a comparatively young

"Of course you're going to be depressed if you keep comparing yourself with successful people."

age (S. E. Taylor & Lobel, 1989). Buoyed by such comparisons, most cancer patients think they are better off than their peers (S. E. Taylor, Falke, Shoptaw, & Lichtman, 1986).

Internal Standards for the Self: Self-Guides

Self-evaluation also involves comparing the self with internal standards. The outcomes of these comparisons can lead to positive or negative feelings about the self. Although our thoughts are turned outward most of the time, some events create heightened awareness of the self, including our internal standards and whether we measure up to them. Focusing attention on the self makes self-discrepancies obvious.

Do you know someone who, despite her many accomplishments, nevertheless feels she is a fake who will soon be caught, or a high achiever who is constantly worried that he does not measure up? If so, you realize that self-esteem is affected not only by what happens to us but also by what happens inside us. This is because our self-knowledge includes not only conceptions of what we are like, but also personal standards toward which we strive. Tory Higgins (1987) calls these personal standards *self-guides*. Self-guides come in two flavors: the *ideal self* (the person we would like to be) and the *ought self* (the person we feel we should be; Higgins, 1987; Markus & Nurius, 1986). Ideal self-guides include the traits that help you match your aspirations; ought self-guides include those that help you meet your obligations. Self-guides are the part of the self-concept most closely and directly tied to the self-regulatory function (Higgins, 1996b).

According to Higgins's **self-discrepancy theory**, the difference between who we think we actually are and our self-guides influences our emotional well-being and ultimately our self-esteem (Strauman & Higgins, 1988). For example, a self-discrepancy could arise if you would ideally like to be slender and athletic, but think you actually are a corpulent couch potato. Ideal selves represent positive outcomes toward which people strive, or *promotion goals* (Higgins, 1998). Discrepancies from ideal selves produce feelings of disappointment, sadness, and dejection, but when people actually attain promotion goals, they feel joy or elation. The emotional consequences are different, however, if the discrepancy concerns an ought self, as Figure 4.5 shows. Ought selves generally involve negative outcomes that people try to avoid, or *prevention goals*: For example, you may feel that you ought to avoid divorce or being fired from a job. Discrepancies from an ought self, or failures to accomplish prevention goals, lead to emotions of anxiety and agitation. Accomplishing these goals produce feelings of relief and relaxation.

Notice that the very same goal, such as staying married, might represent an ideal for one person and an ought for another person. This is because it can be thought of as either a promotion goal ("maintaining a happy marriage") or a prevention goal ("avoiding marital conflict and divorce"). In terms of the emotional impact of failing to attain the goal, what matters is the way the individual thinks about it. In fact, some people generally tend to cast most of their life goals as ideals to be approached, while other people generally think of goals as avoiding negative outcomes. These types of indi-

Self-discrepancy theory. The theory that people evaluate themselves against internal "ideal" and "ought" standards, producing specific emotional consequences.

FIGURE 4.5   Summary of self-discrepancy theory

Discrepancy	Actual self/ideal self (failure to match aspirations)	Actual self/ought self (failure to match obligations)
Emotional reactions	Disappointment Sadness Lowered physiological arousal	Guilt Embarrassment Heightened physiological arousal
Long-term effects	Lowered self-esteem Depression Poor immune function Illness	Lowered self-esteem Anxiety Poor immune function Illness

■ Discrepancies between the actual self and ideal or ought self-guides give rise to specific emotions. They also have long-term negative consequences that affect the body as well as the mind.

viduals differ in the types of negative emotions to which they are vulnerable: either sadness and dejection, or anxiety and tension (Higgins, Shah, & Friedman, 1997).

Not only emotional reactions but also behavioral strategies depend on how people think about their goals. In one study, students were asked which of several strategies for friendship they would use. The choices included some strategies that involved seeking positive outcomes, such as being generous and supportive with friends, and some that involved avoiding negative outcomes, such as not losing contact with friends or not gossiping about them. Consistent with their general tendency to focus on promotion or prevention goals, those students who emphasized ideals chose more of the positive strategies, while those who emphasized oughts chose more of the negative ones (Higgins, Roney, Crowe, & Hymes, 1994).

Even when goals are externally provided, whether they are framed in terms of seeking success or avoiding failure makes a difference in our emotional reactions. When people are told that they will be rewarded if they succeed at a task, they are likely to experience disappointment upon failure or joy upon success. If told instead that they will *not* be rewarded if they *fail* at the task—instructions that objectively describe exactly the same situation—they feel anxiety if they fail and relaxation if they succeed (Higgins, 1998). Thus, people's focus on ideal or ought selves represents one important aspect of a more general orientation toward approaching positive outcomes versus avoiding negative outcomes. This motivational orientation has implications for emotions as well as for the actual behavioral strategies that people use.

FOCUSING ON SELF-DISCREPANCIES. In extreme cases, self-discrepancies trigger negative emotions that can lead to a cycle of sadness and anxiety, lowered self-esteem, and even depression (Csikszentmihalyi & Figurski, 1982; Pyszczynski & Greenberg, 1987). Certain thoughts and situations can exaggerate our awareness of discrepancies from our self-guides, and some people are generally highly aware of them.

1. *Self-focusing thoughts.* Thinking about our inner standards can make us aware of our self-discrepancies, activating the typical emotions in

response. Those standards can be brought to mind by specific people who represent them, as Mark Baldwin and his colleagues (Baldwin, Carrell, & Lopez, 1990) demonstrated. The researchers primed some research participants, who were Roman Catholic college students, by exposing them very briefly to a scowling photo of Pope John Paul II. As an experimental control, other participants saw a similarly grim-faced photo of social psychologist Robert Zajonc, whose unfamiliar face would not be associated with any particular standards for these students. When later asked to evaluate themselves, the practicing Catholics who had seen the photo of the Pope felt worse about themselves, whereas participants who saw Zajonc displayed no such effect.

2. *Self-focusing situations.* Do you know someone who hates being photographed or having his or her voice recorded? The reason may be that these situations focus our attention inward on ourselves. Most of the time our thoughts are turned outward. However, talking about ourselves, being scrutinized by an audience or a camera, even catching sight of ourselves in a mirror, can create **self-awareness**, directing our attention to our internal standards and heightening our awareness of whether we measure up to them. According to the *theory of self-awareness*, focusing attention on the self makes self-discrepancies obvious, which is why it is often unpleasant (Carver & Scheier, 1981; Duval & Wicklund, 1972). Research supports this proposition: People often report feeling relatively unhappy when thinking about themselves (Csikszentmihalyi & Figurski, 1982).

TABLE 4.2. Examples of Items Used to Measure Private Self-Consciousness

1. I'm always trying to figure myself out.
2. I reflect about myself a lot.
3. I never scrutinize myself.
4. I'm alert to changes in my mood.
5. I'm constantly examining my motives.

Note: A person who agrees with items like 1, 2, 4, and 5, and disagrees with item 3 and similar items is probably high in private self-consciousness. The actual scale contains many more than five items, so it can more accurately classify people as high or low in private self-consciousness.

Source: From "Public and private self-consciousness: Assessment and theory," by A. Fenigstein, M. F. Scheier, & A. H. Buss, *Journal of Consulting and Clinical Psychology, 43,* p. 524. Copyright © 1975 by American Psychological Association. Reprinted by permission.

---

3. *Self-focusing individuals.* People differ in the tendency to devote attention to the self. Table 4.2 shows some examples of statements used to measure *private self-consciousness*, the tendency to focus on one's own internal states and feelings. Compared with people low in self-consciousness, those who are high are more likely to be aware of, and to try to cope with, any discrepancy between their actual self and their internalized standards (Carver & Scheier, 1981). This increased awareness means that negative self-related information leads to stronger feelings of distress and sadness (Scheier & Carver, 1977).

BIASED ESTIMATES OF HOW WE MEASURE UP. But wait, you might be thinking, no one is perfect. Since we all live with self-discrepancies, why do we not feel

Self-awareness. A state of heightened awareness of the self, including our internal standards and whether we measure up to them.

terrible all the time? One reason is that we do not notice self-discrepancies when our personal standards are inaccessible. Certain thoughts, certain situations, and certain people can bring self-discrepancies to mind, but as day-to-day events unfold we usually do not dwell on how we are measuring up. And even when we do engage in self-analysis, we hardly ever gather all the relevant evidence. Unlike a good detective, we stop short of a thorough search. How do we end up gathering a sample of evidence that is usually biased in our favor?

For one thing, the outcome often determines the evidence. Memories that come to mind most easily are those associated with the outcome being considered (Kunda, 1990). If you are gauging your career success, your past achievements will come to mind more readily than your failed opportunities. As a result, you would conclude you have been pretty successful. Of course, if you had searched instead for career failures, you might have found some of those, too.

In addition, we generally access successes and suppress failures. Because it is pleasant to linger over our successes and not so comfortable to think about our failures, our positive memories will be retrieved more frequently than our negative memories, and therefore will become more accessible (Kunda, 1990).

Thus, as we try to pull together relevant evidence, most information we bring to the surface will probably suggest how good we are. In one demonstration of this self-enhancing bias in memory, students were led to believe that either extroversion or introversion was a desirable characteristic (Sanitioso, Kunda, & Fong, 1990). When the students then recalled relevant past behaviors, they described more memories of the sort they believed to be desirable. Success and failure do not have to be very important to bias our recall. People who were led to believe that tooth-brushing has negative effects on health remembered brushing their teeth less frequently in the past than others who thought brushing was a healthy practice (M. Ross, McFarland, & Fletcher, 1981).

Why Self-Enhance?

Despite the value of accurate self-knowledge, self-enhancement occurs for two primary reasons. Some actions that appear self-enhancing are aimed at actual self-improvement, reflecting successful self-regulation. And high self-esteem can be an important resource that protects us against stress and threats to the self.

We noted earlier that successful dealings with the social world demand self-knowledge that is accurate and self-esteem that is an unbiased indicator of how we are doing. But if that is true, why do we try to create and maintain positively biased views of ourselves? The answer has two parts.

First, some of the ways people strive for high self-esteem really amount to efforts at self-improvement. For example, you might work hard to learn to play a musical instrument to ensure that your public performances will be successful, earning you applause and boosted self-esteem. To return to our earlier analogy of self-esteem as a statement giving your bank balance, people may try to increase their income or reduce their spending as a way to increase their balance. In fact, this is simply an example of successful self-regulation, with self-esteem (or the bank balance) telling us how well we are doing in attaining our valued goals.

Second, self-esteem has value above and beyond its usefulness as an indicator of our level of success in our commerce with the world. People prefer to feel good about themselves—to value "me and mine." For example, high self-esteem is associated with generally positive emotions and a lower likelihood of depression (J. D. Campbell, Chew, & Scratchley, 1991; Tennen & Affleck, 1993). And, as we will see later in this chapter, high self-esteem not only feels good but has real positive effects on our lives, acting as a kind of resource that can buffer us from some of the blows of fortune. For both of these reasons, people often process information about the self in ways that favor a positive view. In other words, despite the clear usefulness of knowing one's bank balance accurately, we suspect that if people guessed how much they had in the bank on any given day, more estimates would be high than low.

Thus, as Figure 4.6 summarizes, self-esteem reflects a compromise between the stern mirror of accurate self-assessment and some self-enhancing biases that give our image a positive tilt and a rosy glow. We often avoid situations in which we do not perform well, refuse to compare ourselves with more successful others, and fail to notice that we are not all that we could or should be. Even if our inadequacies become obvious, however, we are not without resources. Later in the chapter you will see that failures, inconsistencies, and shortcomings set off some of the self's best defense mechanisms.

FIGURE 4.6   Events, self-evaluation, and self-enhancement

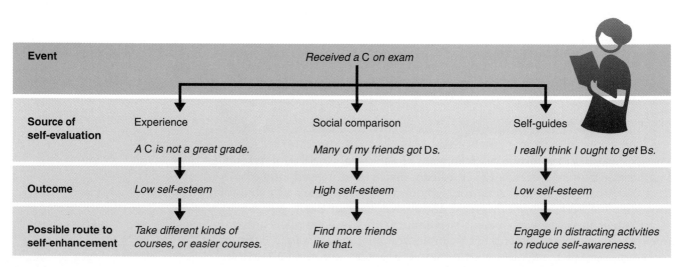

Event		Received a C on exam	
Source of self-evaluation	Experience *A C is not a great grade.*	Social comparison *Many of my friends got Ds.*	Self-guides *I really think I ought to get Bs.*
Outcome	*Low self-esteem*	*High self-esteem*	*Low self-esteem*
Possible route to self-enhancement	*Take different kinds of courses, or easier courses.*	*Find more friends like that.*	*Engage in distracting activities to reduce self-awareness.*

■ Many self-relevant events are neither intrinsically positive nor intrinsically negative. Instead, they must be interpreted and evaluated. The evaluation process may lead to increases or decreases in self-esteem, and it almost always leaves room for the operation of self-enhancing biases.

Self Esteem in Cultural Context

As with most other aspects of the self, self-enhancing biases operate somewhat differently in different cultures. Independent cultures emphasize positive individual characteristics as the source of self-esteem, while interdependent cultures stress connectedness to others. Despite these differences, self-esteem functions in all cultures to indicate how well we are meeting our most important motives for mastery and connectedness.

Since so many aspects of the self differ between independent and interdependent cultures, you may be wondering whether biases related to self-esteem operate in the same way in all cultures. In fact, recent evidence from interdependent Asian cultures shows intriguing differences from the patterns typically found in North America and Western Europe. Shinobu Kitayama and his colleagues (Kitayama, Markus, Matsumoto, & Norasakkunkit, 1997) observe that although self-enhancement is common among Americans, Japanese people and other Asians are less prone to this bias. For example, Japanese students (whether in Japan or studying in America) score lower on self-esteem questionnaires than American students do. Japanese people may even reverse the self-enhancing bias, showing a greater tendency to accept negative rather than positive information about the self (Kitayama, Takagi, & Matsumoto, 1995).

Does this mean that members of interdependent cultures are psychologically unhealthy? Kitayama and his colleagues (1997) argue otherwise. They propose that the sensitivity to negative information about the self that is found in interdependent cultures actually serves as a form of self-criticism, which is ultimately meant to improve one's actions and ability to fit in harmoniously with others. In North America and other independent cultures, the view of the self as autonomous and separate from others means that positive personal attributes are the fundamental source of personal worth. In this cultural setting, self-enhancement is natural. In contrast, in interdependent cultures, connectedness among individuals and groups is emphasized over personal autonomy. The value of the self is not measured by outstanding individual characteristics, but by adjustment to others' expectations and shared ideals. Thus in Japanese schools, it is common for classes to take time at the end of a day to reflect on the ways they have failed to meet class goals, either as individuals or as a group (Lewis, 1995). Such self-criticism is both a way of affirming one's acceptance of shared social standards and a way of seeking to remedy deviations from those standards. From this perspective, self-criticism is just as natural a way of enhancing the value of the self in interdependent cultures as overt self-enhancement is in independent cultures. And, interestingly, Japanese students show a preference for letters that are included in their own names—a relatively subtle and indirect measure of self-esteem—just as Americans do (Kitayama & Karasawa, 1997)

Despite such cultural variations, the function of self-esteem is the same for everyone. The ups and downs of self-esteem are not just meaningless fluctuations. Rather, self-esteem serves a crucial function as the self regulates our thoughts, feelings, and behavior: It signals how well we are doing in fulfilling our fundamental social motives for mastery of our environment and connectedness with others (Leary and others, 1995). People differ in their relative sensitivity to these two motives, with men's self-esteem more influenced by successes or failures involving mastery and women's self-esteem more affected by connectedness (Josephs, Markus, & Tafarodi, 1992). Cultural differences are important as well, as just described (Markus & Kitayama, 1991). For everyone, though, success and acceptance (that is, events that help us feel in charge and connected to others) make us feel particularly good about ourselves, while failure, rejection, and loss can knock us to our knees. And, as you will see later, people with high and low self-esteem differ significantly in the ways they respond to and cope with all kinds of life experiences.

Effects of the Self: Directing Thoughts, Feelings, and Behavior

What a difference a self makes! Once we know what we think about ourselves, self-knowledge becomes resistant to change by new information. At the same time, self-knowledge starts to regulate many important aspects of our lives, particularly our emotions and our behavior.

The Self and Thoughts About Ourselves and Others

The self-concept, once formed, is relatively difficult to change. People avoid or actively reject information that is inconsistent with their established self-views. Self-knowledge also serves as a framework for perceiving other people, and influences what types of social information we will remember.

Once the self-concept has been constructed, the familiar principle of conservatism comes into operation, and we become much less open to new information about the self. A young child might begin to think of himself as tidy after noticing that he picks up his room a few times, but once the self-concept is firmly established, people no longer have to make inferences from their behaviors to decide who they are (S. B. Klein & Loftus, 1993; Schell, Klein, & Babey, 1996). In fact, most of the time inconsistent behaviors have little impact on firmly established self-knowledge (Chaiken & Baldwin, 1981; Fazio and others, 1981). Other people's reactions also play less of a role after self-knowledge in a particular domain becomes entrenched (B. P. Allen, 1988). Feedback inconsistent with an established self-concept is avoided, distrusted, or resisted—even if it is flattering (Markus, 1977; Swann & Read, 1981). This function of the self is important in creating our sense of a stable personal identity, making us subjectively the same person when we awaken each morning. In fact, people with an unstable or fluctuating self-concept tend to have low self-esteem and high emotional reactivity to daily events (Campbell, 1990; Campbell & Lavallee, 1993), illustrating the value of having a secure and certain sense of self.

An established self-concept influences not only the way we think about ourselves but also the way we perceive and remember social information in general. For example, when we perceive other people we tend to notice and use information that is important in our own self concept (Markus, Smith, & Moreland, 1985; Sedikides & Skowronski, 1993). So if you think of yourself as honest, you may be particularly likely to note other people's honest or dishonest behaviors, and to use that information in making judgments about them. The self-concept also affects memory. When we process information in relation to the self-concept, for example by making judgments about whether a series of traits describe the self or not, we remember those traits better than we do if we make other judgments, such as whether the traits are positive or negative (Symons & Johnson, 1997). The self-concept tells us what types of social information are particularly important to us, so it serves as an organizing framework for perceiving and remembering information about people in general.

The Self and Emotions: For Me or Against Me?

Emotions are sparked by interpretations of self-relevant events and their causes. Emotions signal the occurrence of significant events and motivate us to act in response, for example, to flee from danger. As they perform this self-regulation function, emotions involve the whole self, body and mind: They activate facial expressions, physiological responses, subjective feelings, and overt behaviors.

Emotions mark the most meaningful moments of our lives. Feelings like pride, anxiety, joy, fear, or anger signal that something important is happening (Zajonc, 1998). Fear signals that a danger must be escaped; joy lets us know that a positive outcome should be celebrated. The intrusive quality of emotions forces us to pay attention to significant events, even as the positive or negative quality of the emotion indicates the nature of the event. Emotions also direct behavior toward a goal. For example, fear turns our efforts toward escaping from threat, and anger toward harming the target. Because of their intrusiveness, emotions often seem to "just happen" to us, but as we shall see, they actually depend on the perceiver's interpretation of both the self and the external world.

WHERE DO EMOTIONS COME FROM? Emotions are complex and multifaceted and involve the entire self, body and mind. When you feel angry, your heart pounds and blood rushes to your face. You want to strike out at the target of your anger. You believe deeply that he or she injured you without cause. Thoughts, feelings, bodily reactions, and desires for action are tied together in patterns that characterize different emotions. Which of these many components is primary in *causing* the emotion? Psychologists have offered different answers to this question over the years. A century ago, William James (1884) argued that sensations from the skin and muscles were the chief causes of the experience of emotion. A generation ago, Stanley Schachter and Jerome Singer (1962) identified emotion as the product of physiological arousal plus a belief concerning its cause.

The prevailing view today is that emotions are caused by cognitive appraisals of a self-relevant object or event (Arnold, 1960; Frijda, 1986; Roseman, Spindel, & Jose, 1990; Tomaka, Blascovich, Kibler, & Ernst, 1997; Weiner, 1985). A **cognitive appraisal** is an interpretation of an event, including both the

Cognitive appraisal. An individual's interpretation of a self-relevant event or situation that directs emotional responses and behavior.

causes of the event and how the event affects the self. Different appraisals of the same situation can produce different emotions, as is illustrated in Figure 4.7 for the everyday event of feeling hungry and finding the refrigerator empty. Two types of appraisals are particularly important in influencing emotions.

1. *Our appraisal of the event's positive or negative implications for the self.* Actions and events that we interpret as supportive of ourselves and our goals produce positive emotions such as joy, hope, and gratitude. If you were trying to lose 10 pounds to fit into a new swimsuit but had just succumbed to the temptation of finishing off yesterday's chocolate cake, you might be relieved to find an empty refrigerator. But how would you feel if the shelves were empty because the food money had run out and your paycheck was not due for another 2 days? You probably would be both angry and frightened by this event. Actions and events that threaten, frustrate, or repel us evoke negative emotions like fear, anger, and disgust.

2. *Our appraisal of who or what caused or controlled the event.* Was someone to blame, or was the event beyond everyone's control? And did you bring about the event, or was someone else responsible? The emotions you feel and the actions you subsequently take will be quite different depending on your answer to those two questions. If the refrigerator is empty because you worked so many overtime hours that the stores closed before you could get to them, you will have one set of responses. But if your housemate failed to contribute his share of the grocery money and shopping chores, your feelings and actions will be quite different. Figure 4.7 shows how our appraisal of credit or blame affects emotions (Weiner, 1985).

Like all interpretations, appraisals are flexible, not cut and dried. As we saw in chapter 3, many factors can influence how we appraise events, including the context, accessible thoughts, and transient moods. And, as always, other people's reactions play a large role in our appraisals. A toddler who trips over her feet may burst into either tears or giggles, depending on whether others gasp with concern or laugh. When other people seem to judge that a situation warrants calmness or dejection or goofy lightheartedness, we often follow suit (Schachter & Singer, 1962).

Culture also strongly affects the ways we interpret events and therefore the kinds of emotions we feel. Japanese people, for example, are more likely than Westerners to report feeling emotions like connectedness, indebtedness, and familiarity, which tie the self to important others (Markus & Kitayama, 1991). Despite such cultural differences, researchers assume that at least a few "basic" emotions are common to all human cultures, although there is not full consensus on what these emotions are (Wierzbicka, 1994; Zajonc, 1998).

Because so many factors influence our appraisals, we can be misled about the emotions we are feeling and about their causes. You might believe you are angry with your child because of her annoying behavior, when the true cause of your anger is your run-in with your boss earlier in the day. An experiment by James Olson (1990) demonstrated this point by misleading participants about the cause of their anxiety. Everyone in the experiment expected to be exposed to "subliminal noise" as they were videotaped while

FIGURE 4.7   Appraisals dictate emotional reactions to events

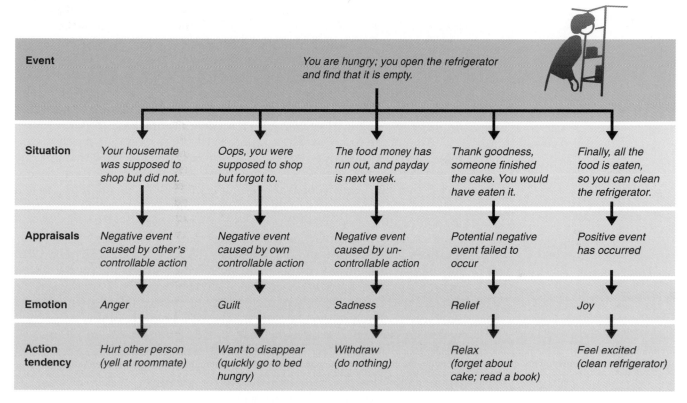

Event		You are hungry; you open the refrigerator and find that it is empty.		
Situation	Your housemate was supposed to shop but did not.	Oops, you were supposed to shop but forgot to.	The food money has run out, and payday is next week.	Thank goodness, someone finished the cake. You would have eaten it.	Finally, all the food is eaten, so you can clean the refrigerator.
Appraisals	Negative event caused by other's controllable action	Negative event caused by own controllable action	Negative event caused by un-controllable action	Potential negative event failed to occur	Positive event has occurred
Emotion	Anger	Guilt	Sadness	Relief	Joy
Action tendency	Hurt other person (yell at roommate)	Want to disappear (quickly go to bed hungry)	Withdraw (do nothing)	Relax (forget about cake; read a book)	Feel excited (clean refrigerator)

■ Here are examples of different emotions and action tendencies arising from different appraisals of the same event—in this case, opening the refrigerator and finding that it is empty.

delivering a speech. Some people were told the noise would arouse them physiologically, and others were told it would relax them. Although no noise was played, the participants' beliefs about it still influenced their emotions. Those who thought the noise would arouse them rated themselves as less anxious and made fewer speech errors than those who expected to be relaxed by the noise. Apparently those who expected arousal attributed their stage fright to the "noise," whereas those who expected relaxation had no such excuse. Thus, like other aspects of self-knowledge, the emotions we experience and our beliefs about their causes actually reflect our appraisals. And appraisals are often based on salient cues: conspicuous features, people, or events that may or may not correspond to the true causes of our emotions (Reisenzein, 1983).

APPRAISALS, EMOTIONS, BODILY RESPONSES: ALL TOGETHER NOW. Our appraisals of events not only cause our emotions but also affect many aspects of our body and mind. People in many different cultures smile when they feel happy, frown when they feel sad, and wrinkle their brow when they feel angry (Ekman and others, 1987). Physiological systems come on line, revving us up or calming us down. We are motivated to act: to strike back in anger, escape in fear, or move closer in happiness. Some of these action tendencies, like attack and flight, appear to be universal and biologically determined. Other emotional behaviors are, of course, learned and differ from one culture to another (Frijda, Kuipers, & ter Schure, 1989; Markus & Kitayama, 1991).

Emotions also affect thinking, focusing us on the content of our appraisals. Thus, in the grip of extreme rage you may be totally focused on the thought of how your antagonist mistreated you and how he deserves to have his lights punched out (Keltner, Ellsworth, & Edwards, 1993). Strong emotions of any sort, positive or negative, can create intense arousal that limits people's ability to pay attention to other events (Easterbrook, 1959).

All of these components—appraisals, bodily responses, subjective feelings, and emotionally driven behavior—become so associated that any one aspect can engage all the rest. If your heart is pounding, your face is contorted in a snarl, and your fists are tightly clenched, you are likely to feel anger, just as anger provokes those same responses. Because our inner feelings and outward expressions of emotion are so intertwined, bodily signs of emotion often intensify emotional feelings (Adelmann & Zajonc, 1989; Ekman, 1992). Fritz Strack and his colleagues (Strack, Martin, & Stepper, 1988) ingeniously demonstrated this point by having participants write with a pen either clenched tightly between their teeth or held loosely between pursed lips. These maneuvers force expressions resembling a smile and a scowl, respectively, although participants were unaware of this fact. (Try it yourself.) The experimenters then asked both groups to assign ratings to a series of cartoons, telling how funny they were. The participants holding the pen between their teeth in a "smile" assigned higher ratings than did those holding the pen "scowlingly" between their lips.

If an emotional facial expression promotes emotional experience, it stands to reason that an inconsistent expression will reduce the intensity of the emotion. Have you ever been in a clutch situation and been terrified you might fail? Perhaps you were about to speak to a large audience. Did you take a couple of long deep breaths to calm yourself down or lock your face in a determined grin? If so, you were trying to take advantage of the way emotions often follow bodily expressions.

As Figure 4.8 shows, emotions tie together all aspects of body and soul, action and thought (De Rivera, 1977; Shaver, Schwartz, Kirson, & O'Connor, 1987).

The Self in Action: Regulating Behavior

Sometimes people act in ways that express their true inner selves. At other times, people are concerned with shaping others' opinions in order to gain power, influence, or approval. But even behaviors intended for others' consumption may end up influencing people's private views of themselves.

Since her arrival on the music scene over a decade ago, Madonna has changed her appearance frequently and dramatically. Yet, from the days of her Marlene Dietrich look to the publication of her aptly titled book, *Sex*, Madonna's every marketing, musical, and fashion move has conveyed the same image of devil-may-care sexual independence. What

FIGURE 4.8 Components of emotions

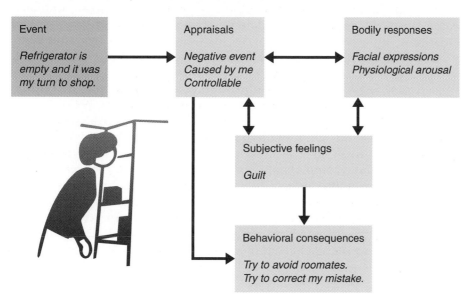

Event	Appraisals	Bodily responses
Refrigerator is empty and it was my turn to shop.	Negative event Caused by me Controllable	Facial expressions Physiological arousal

Subjective feelings

Guilt

Behavioral consequences

Try to avoid roomates.
Try to correct my mistake.

■ When events are appraised as self-relevant, the resulting emotion has many components: cognitive appraisals, physiological responses, and subjective feelings. Each component can affect the others, and all may contribute to emotionally driven behaviors.

motivates her behavior? Is she really an inherently sexual person whose fame allows her to express her true nature to her thousands of fans across the globe? Or is Madonna the consummate actress, carefully crafting her behavior to convey an impression she believes will buy her the greatest success in the marketplace?

If there is one domain where the impact of who we are and how we feel is dramatic, it is in our interactions with others. Our sense of self guides us as we act in ways that convey and reaffirm who we actually are, or select our behaviors to convey particular impressions and achieve particular goals.

SELF-EXPRESSION: I AM WHAT I AM. When people engage in **self-expression**, they attempt to demonstrate their self-concept through their actions. Self-expression confirms and reinforces the individual's sense of self and also conveys it to other people. If you think of yourself as a committed animal rights activist, you may see many of your behaviors—volunteering at the Humane Society or campaigning to stop unnecessary cosmetics testing—as expressions and affirmations of that self-concept. Research shows that, if given a choice, most people prefer to enter social situations that allow them to act in a way consistent with their self-concept (M. Snyder & Gangestad, 1982), and prefer relationship partners who agree with their own self-images (Swann, Hixon, & de la Ronde, 1992). Thus, an outgoing man may accept invitations to parties, and an organized woman may take a job that offers clearly structured tasks. As we will see later in this chapter, self-expression is so beneficial to us that it can even serve as a powerful coping strategy when we are under stress.

SELF-PRESENTATION: I AM WHAT YOU WANT ME TO BE. Sometimes we try to create a desirable impression, whether we believe the impression is accurate or not. Thus, another motive for choosing particular behaviors is

> **Self-expression.** A motive for choosing behaviors that are intended to reflect and express the self-concept.

self-presentation, trying to shape other people's impressions of us in order to gain power, influence, or approval (Jones & Pittman, 1982; Tedeschi, 1981). Most people care about conveying a positive impression to others. After all, attracting a desirable date or impressing a job interviewer can have a real impact on the course of our lives. Even in less crucial situations, we usually want to show the world a face it can like, admire, and respect. In fact, *ingratiation*, trying to convey the impression we are likable, and *self-promotion*, trying to convey an impression of competence, are two of the most common goals of social interaction (Arkin, 1981; Leary, 1995).

We all have had so much practice trying to win approval and respect that ingratiation and self-promotion should be easy. To be seen as likable, we go out of our way to help, to fit in with the other person's wishes, and to deliver charming compliments. To be seen as competent, we play up our strong points, mention our accomplishments, and display our knowledge. But self-presentation is fraught with potential pitfalls; taken too far, these qualities become blatant flattery or unseemly boasting. For advice on how to ingratiate yourself smoothly and subtly, look at Table 4.3. Illustrating the dangers of self-presentational efforts, in one study that took place in India, a hypothetical character who discussed a possible promotion with his boss in an ingratiating fashion was rated as both less likable and less competent than a character who did not try to ingratiate (Pandey & Singh, 1986). But notice that in this study the research participants were observing from the sidelines; they were not themselves the targets of ingratiation. In general, ingratiation has little effect on observers' liking for the ingratiator, but strong effects on the target (Gordon, 1996). It can be difficult to resist flattery aimed directly at you!

FROM SELF TO BEHAVIOR, AND BACK AGAIN. Self-presentation can amount to a sort of "trying a self on for size," perhaps acting in a way that is consis-

---

TABLE 4.3. The Self-Presenter's Handbook, Lesson 1: How to Make Others Like You Without Being Obvious

Don't let others notice that you are conforming to their opinions. (Or, if you are going to try to get in someone's good books, keep it credible.)
- Disagree on trivial issues, agree on important ones.
- Be wish-washy when you disagree, forceful when you agree.

Be modest (selectively).
- Make gentle fun of your standing on unimportant traits.
- Put yourself down in areas that don't make much difference.

Keep your need for others' approval under wraps.
- Don't conform or flatter someone in a situation where it is expected—for example, when talking to your boss just before annual raises are handed out.
- Use these tactics only when you really need to.
- Get others to do the self-presentation for you—for example, in letters of reference.

Bask in others' reflected glory if you can.
- Make casual references to connections with winners.
- Link yourself to losers only when it cannot be used against you.

Source: Adapted from *Interpersonal perception*, by E. E. Jones, 1990, San Francisco: Freeman, p. 184.

Self-presentation. A motive for choosing behaviors intended to create in observers a desired impression of the self.

tent with an ideal "wanna be" self (Baumeister, 1982). Adolescents, for example, may experiment with such selves as "rebel," "intellectual," or "environmental activist." These experiments can have lasting effects because self-presenters often end up influencing themselves just as much as their audience. For example, when people are instructed to present themselves as extraverted, they then give themselves higher ratings on that dimension (Gergen, 1965; Jones, Rhodewalt, Berglas, & Skelton, 1981; Schlenker, 1985). Interestingly, the presence of an audience is crucial in shaping effects of self-presentation. Schlenker and his colleagues (Schlenker, Dlugolecki, & Doherty, 1994) had participants prepare for an interaction in which they would present themselves in a certain way to other people, but then the interaction never took place. In contrast to participants who actually engaged in the self-presentation, these participants showed minimal change in their self-concepts. Just recalling past extraverted actions may be enough to alter the self-concept (C. A. Anderson & Godfrey, 1987), but making a self-presentation before an audience has stronger effects, illustrating the fundamentally interpersonal nature of the self. These studies show effects of even a single self-presentation, but sorting out the portrayal from the self may be even more difficult as the performance becomes routine. We would do well to heed sociologist Erving Goffman's warning: Choose your self-presentations carefully, for what starts out as a mask may become your face (Goffman, 1959).

PERSONALITY DIFFERENCES IN BEHAVIOR: SELF-MONITORING. Although everyone engages in both self-expression and self-presentation, people show stable preferences for one or the other. This individual difference is called **self-monitoring** (M. Snyder, 1974). High self-monitors typically shape their behaviors to project the impression they think their current audience or situation demands. Low self-monitors behave in ways that express their internal attitudes and dispositions, and they therefore behave more consistently from audience to audience and situation to situation. You might like to answer the questions in Table 4.4 to see whether you tend to be high or low in self-monitoring.

The importance of personality differences in self-monitoring was demonstrated by a study of people's reactions to success or failure at a rather

---

TABLE 4.4. Examples of Items Used to Measure Self-Monitoring

1. I have considered being an entertainer.
2. In a group of people I am rarely the center of attention.
3. I have trouble changing my behavior to suit different people and different situations.
4. I guess I put on a show to impress or entertain people.
5. I may deceive people by being friendly when I really dislike them.

Note: People who agree with items 1, 4, and 5 and disagree with items 2 and 3 are probably high in self-monitoring. The actual scale contains many more than five items, so it can more accurately classify people as high or low in self-monitoring.

Source: Reprinted by permission from "The self-monitoring of expressive behavior," by M. Snyder, 1974, *Journal of Personality and Social Psychology, 30,* p. 531. Copyright © 1974 by the American Psychological Association.

Self-monitoring. A personality characteristic defined as the degree to which people are sensitive to the demands of social situations and shape their behaviors accordingly.

FIGURE 4.9   What a difference a self makes

■ Once formed, a person's self-concept influences his or her thoughts, feelings, and actions.

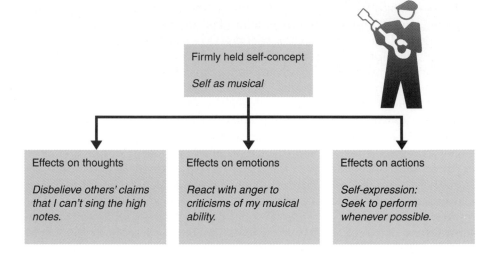

Firmly held self-concept

Self as musical

Effects on thoughts

Disbelieve others' claims that I can't sing the high notes.

Effects on emotions

React with anger to criticisms of my musical ability.

Effects on actions

Self-expression: Seek to perform whenever possible.

peculiar task: portraying themselves as corrupt and immoral individuals (E. E. Jones, Brenner, & Knight, 1990). In a simulated job interview, each participant pretended to be an ambitious, selfish person who would be suitable for a "cutthroat position in a dog-eat-dog environment." Some participants learned that their act was convincing by overhearing comments like "He wouldn't mind selling his mother down the river." Others learned they had failed in their portrayals. High self-monitors felt better about themselves when they succeeded at the task, even though success meant convincing others that they were corrupt. Apparently creating an "appropriate" impression was more important than being true to who they really were. In contrast, low self-monitors felt better about themselves after *failing* at this task. They appear to prefer being seen as they truly are instead of successfully, even profitably, putting on a false face.

Once we have constructed a sense of self, we begin to use it to regulate many aspects of our lives. Our self-concept tends to resist change and to influence our thoughts, emotions, and behavior. Figure 4.9 summarizes some of the effects of the self.

Defending the Self: Coping With Stresses, Inconsistencies, and Failures

Our sense of self is our most valued possession, and we certainly treat it that way. We use it continually, as both a guide for action and an aid in interpreting others' reactions to us. We keep it polished and in good repair as we enhance our self-esteem and present our best face to others. And, as we shall see, we strive to defend our sense of self against all comers. When events set off our security alarms, we may respond in two different ways. We may attempt to deal with what set off the alarm, or we may try to change the way it makes us feel.

Threats to the Well-Being of the Self

When threatened by external events or negative feedback, people must defend their sense of who and what they are. Major failures and disasters obviously threaten the self, but so do inconsistent information and daily hassles and stresses. Threats to the self affect not only emotional well-being but also physical health. The most damaging threats are those we appraise as uncontrollable.

Anything that contradicts our sense of who we are and how we feel can cause us to question our impression of the self. Three types of events pose especially significant threats. *Failures*—flubbing the driver's test, ending a marriage in divorce—expose us to negative feedback about who we are and what we do. *Inconsistencies*—illness in a usually healthy person, an empty nest for an at-home mom—provide us with information that contradicts who and what we thought we were. Events do not have to be negative to be inconsistent. Because they change our lives, even joyous occasions like getting married or becoming a parent also require changes in the self-concept. Finally, *stressors* threaten the well-being of the self because they seem to exceed our resources for dealing with them. Stressors obviously include major crises like the death of a spouse or a house fire. But stress also arises from the small but relentless grind-you-down frustrations and hassles of daily life, the boredom of routine, the pressures of the rat-race. All these events call our sense of self into question.

EMOTIONAL AND PHYSICAL EFFECTS OF THREAT. Failures, inconsistencies, and stressors arouse the gamut of negative emotions. Experiences like losing a loved one to illness or being fired from a job for poor performance activate the most intense emotions: terror, crushing depression. Such threats to the self may have additional negative effects. People with unrealistically

■ **On their own but out of control.** Crowded dormitory rooms are a reality in many colleges today, and crowding is a potent source of stress that can produce anxiety and physical illness, as well as low grades. But just as control can reduce the effects of many other sources of stress, control—in the form of choosing one's own roommates—reduces the effects of crowding.

inflated self-views, which may be especially unstable and highly vulnerable to negative information, are the most likely to turn to violence and aggression (Baumeister, Smart, & Boden, 1996; Bushman & Baumeister, 1998). Similarly, people whose self-concept is much higher than their friends' ratings of them—who are most likely to have their lofty views challenged from time to time—tend to have poor social skills, and the negative effects on mental health may last for years (Colvin, Block, & Funder, 1995).

Threats to the self do not affect only our emotions. Research over the past 20 years has convinced even the sometimes-skeptical medical community that such events also contribute to physical illness (Salovey, Rothman, & Rodin, 1998). Major setbacks adversely affect our health, but so do everyday minor hassles: arguing with a best friend, receiving a parking ticket, having to wait in line at the bank. Threats to the self bring us down, tick us off, and also alter our immune responses, nervous-system activity, and blood pressure—the kinds of physiological changes that contribute to illness (S. Cohen, Doyle, Skoner, & Fireman, 1995; O'Leary, 1990; J. Rodin & Salovey, 1989). For example, one study found that when people were reminded of significant self-discrepancies, levels of "natural killer" cell activity in their bloodstream decreased (Strauman, Lemieux, & Coe, 1993). These immune-system cells are important in defending the body against viral infections and cancers.

It is the negative emotions we experience in response to threats that put physical health at risk. People who habitually respond to failures, setbacks, and stresses with negative emotions are the most likely to suffer physically (Watson & Pennebaker, 1989). One of the best-known examples of this finding is the Type A behavior pattern, which is associated with risks of heart disease in both men and women (Booth-Kewley & Friedman, 1987; Thoresen & Low, 1990). The Type A pattern includes ambitiousness, competitiveness, rapid speech style, hostility, and anger, but not all of these characteristics are harmful to health. Anger and hostility appear to be the most important risk factors (Booth-Kewley & Friedman, 1987). People who react with rage to everyday annoyances, such as noticing that the person before them in the 10-items-or-less line at the supermarket has 11 items in the shopping cart, may be at greatest risk from heart disease (Angier, 1990a).

THREAT AND APPRAISALS OF CONTROL. We must respond to frustrations, shortcomings, hassles, disasters, or any event we appraise as a threat. By far the most threatening events, however, are those we judge to be out of our control (Rodin & Salovey, 1989). Think about how the perception of control might affect some of your own responses. Do you feel more comfortable driving a car or riding in an airplane? Most people choose driving even though flying is as much as 10 times safer than driving, as measured in deaths per mile. Our deep-seated preference for control is one reason for this perverse response. When our basic motive to master our environment is called into question, a vital part of our sense of self is threatened. Feeling that events are beyond one's control increases the likelihood of many kinds of negative outcomes, including worker "burnout" and the perception of overcrowding in dormitories and prisons (Paulus, 1988; Pines, Aronson, & Kafry, 1981). For example, if you were assigned roommates in a dormitory suite, you would probably feel more crowded than if you roomed with the same number of individuals whom you had picked yourself. Not surprisingly, the anxiety and frustration that accompany lack of control take their toll on physical well-being. Uncontrollable stressful events are much more hazardous to health than controllable ones (Fleming, Baum, & Weiss, 1987; Kiecolt-Glaser & Glaser, 1988; Salovey and others, 1998).

☐ **CONTROL AND DEPRESSION.** Perhaps the most negative result of repeated experiences of lack of control is *learned helplessness* (Abramson, Seligman, & Teasdale, 1978; M. E. P. Seligman, 1975). Animals and humans that have endured uncontrollable outcomes often give up attempting to control their fate (M. E. P. Seligman & Maier, 1967). In one study in which people were exposed to inescapable bursts of noise, they later failed to protect themselves from noises they could easily have stopped (Hiroto, 1974). Learned helplessness can undermine people's efforts to master their situations. For example, people who work on insoluble problems or experience uncontrollable failures may give up trying, even in situations where their efforts might be of use. Part of the reason may be that repeated thoughts, such as "I can't do anything" or "My efforts are useless," and the associated sad and hopeless emotions interfere with the thought processes that would help people actually gain control (Sedek & Kofta, 1990).

Findings such as these have led researchers to argue that appraisals of events as uncontrollable contribute to *clinical depression*, a psychological disorder characterized by negative moods, low self-esteem, pessimism, and a disruption of thinking, sleeping, eating, and activity patterns (Abramson and others, 1978). Figure 4.10 shows how the process works. A negative event or situation that occurs is appraised as both uncontrollable and laden with widespread implications for many areas of the person's life. The expectation of lack of control produces learned helplessness.

FIGURE 4.10 Attributions, learned helplessness, and depression

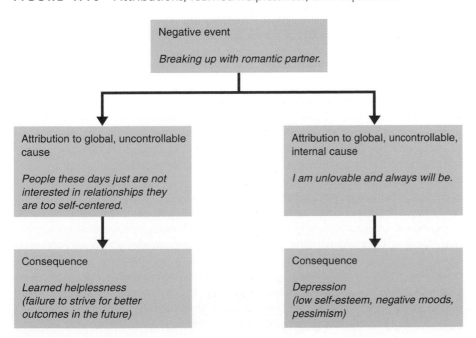

■ When a negative event is seen as due to a general and uncontrollable cause, people may give up and stop trying—a symptom of learned helplessness. Depression results when the cause of a negative event is seen not only as global and uncontrollable but also as internal.

But learned helplessness is only part of depression. If global, enduring, uncontrollable events are also attributed to internal causes, that is, perceived to be "my fault," depression is the likely result (Abramson and others, 1978). For instance, in explaining the break-up of a romantic relationship, a person might conclude that he is now and always will be completely and totally unlovable. This explanation robs him of control in his present situation and of any hope of finding a future loving relationship. Research shows that people who use this *depressive attributional style* are more likely than others to become depressed when things go wrong in their lives (C. A. Anderson, Jennings, & Arnoult, 1988). The effects can last for years and can damage physical as well as mental health. Peterson and his colleagues (C. Peterson, Seligman, & Vaillant, 1988) examined interviews of men recorded when they were college students in the early 1940s, coding their attributions about negative events as depressive or not. The men were medically examined from time to time over the ensuing decades, with highly consistent results: The men who had explained negative events more pessimistically in their early 20s experienced poorer physical and mental health even into their 60s.

Defending Against Threat: Emotion-Focused Coping

To defend against threats, people sometimes try to manage their emotional responses to threat through escape, distraction, redefinition of an event's importance, or self-expression.

Though learned helplessness may keep people from doing anything about events that are appraised as threats to the self, people ordinarily respond with **coping strategies**, efforts to reduce the negative consequences produced by threatening events. In one common type of coping response, *emotion-focused coping*, people attempt to deal with the negative emotions associated with the event, perhaps by escaping or avoiding the threatening situation. Faced with family discord, for example, a person could ignore the problem or become immersed in some distracting hobby or activity. How do these strategies of emotion-focused coping work?

ESCAPING FROM THREAT: SHIPPING OUT. When events conspire to bring home our failures and shortcomings, a common first impulse is to ship out rather than shape up. After all, escape mercifully terminates the painful awareness of inadequacies (Gibbons & Wicklund, 1982). Experimental evidence bears out the idea that people who have fallen short of a personal standard will make a quick exit from the stressful situation—if they can. In one study, an experimenter told participants that they had scored very well or very poorly on a test of intelligence and creativity and then asked them to wait 5 minutes for a second experimenter. For half of the participants, the waiting room was equipped with a mirror and videocamera, both designed to induce self-awareness. Did the combination of embarrassing self-discrepancies (scoring poorly on the test) and self-awareness (finding oneself in front of mirror and camera) make escape look like the best option? Apparently so. The people who scored poorly and were told to wait in the specially equipped room left significantly sooner than did other participants (Duval & Wicklund, 1972).

Coping strategies. Efforts undertaken to reduce negative consequences of self-threatening events.

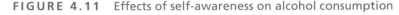

FIGURE 4.11   Effects of self-awareness on alcohol consumption

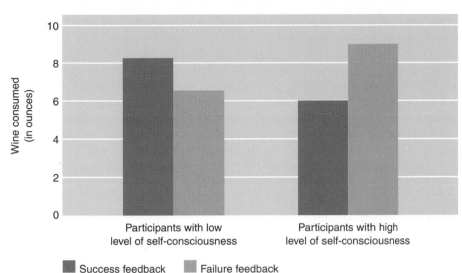

- Participants who were high in self-consciousness and learned that they failed on a task drank more wine than students in the other three conditions—presumably to blot out painful awareness of their shortcoming. In contrast, successful students who were high in self-consciousness drank the least of any group. They probably wanted to avoid dulling their good feelings about themselves. (Data from Hull & Young, 1983.)

IGNORING THREAT: ANYTHING TO TAKE MY MIND OFF IT. Sometimes attempts to avoid painful self-knowledge and the pressures of uncontrollable events produce a new set of negative effects. People drink, take drugs, and engage in "just for kicks" risky behavior for many reasons, but sometimes these activities are attempts at blotting out the self, eliminating the uncomfortable consequences of self-discrepancies (Baumeister, 1991). For example, Jay Hull (1981) found that people really can "drown their sorrows" with alcohol: Alcohol consumption reduces self-awareness.

Based on this finding, Hull and Robert Young (1983) reasoned that people who have experienced failure might use alcohol to escape from self-awareness, while people who had succeeded would not. To test this idea, they selected students who were high or low in self-consciousness and gave them bogus success or failure feedback on intellectual tasks. They then offered them a chance to escape from their feelings, disguised as a wine-tasting task. The researchers subsequently measured the amount of wine consumed. As Figure 4.11 shows, the highly self-aware participants who had experienced failure drank significantly more than those in the other three groups. Similarly, studies of alcohol use among high school students show that consumption is highest among those who are both high in self-consciousness and low in academic performance (Hull, Young, & Jouriles, 1986). Of course, using alcohol to reduce self-awareness can create problems of its own. Alcohol consumption contributes to serious health risks. The short-term solace it may offer to people under stress is overshadowed by the role it plays in overall stress-related health damage.

DOWNPLAYING THREAT: ACCENTUATE THE POSITIVE, ELIMINATE THE NEGATIVE. Fortunately, people have available more constructive strategies than drinking alcohol to help them cope with failures and shortcomings. One way to manage the negative consequences of poor performances is to downplay their importance. Faced with irrefutable evidence of our couch-potato behavior and our selfish motives, we may decide that slimness and generosity are not all they are cracked up to be. We may also downgrade their importance compared with areas in which we do excel, reasoning that those other areas of life are the ones that are really important (Lewicki, 1984). Research shows, for example, that the more highly skilled people are on dimensions like academic ability, social skills, or artistic ability, the more important they think those dimensions are (Pelham, 1991).

Reaffirming who we are, by expressing the personal characteristics we see as most important and value most highly, can also help us cope with failure, uncertainty, and stress (Steele, 1988). Shelley Taylor (1983) found that breast-cancer patients who were facing the possibility of death often expressed and reaffirmed what they regarded as their most basic self-aspects. Some individuals quit dead-end jobs, while others turned to writing poetry or reaffirmed significant relationships.

☐ **PROTECTING SELF-ESTEEM IN THE CLASSROOM.** Downplaying the importance of domains in which we experience failure may bring benefits for self-esteem, but sometimes the costs are tremendous. Claude Steele (1992, 1997) has argued that high failure and dropout rates among African-American students are due at least in part to their need to protect themselves against the unremittingly negative feedback that many receive in school. Faced with teachers who expect them to fail, labeled as "at risk," and seeing their culture marginalized, some Black students may resist measuring themselves against the goals and values of an educational system that does not welcome them. One form of resistance can involve a change in self-concept, so that academic success is no longer important to self-esteem. Unfortunately, withdrawal of academic interest and effort sets off a self-fulfilling spiral of failure. As Steele (1992) puts it, this method of defending self-esteem, "like a pain-killing drug, . . . undoes [the] future as it relieves [the] vulnerability" (p. 74).

Supporting Steele's views, research has shown that African-American college students' beliefs about the importance of academic achievement in their lives are an important factor in predicting their college grades—even more important than their level of academic preparation for college (Nisbett and others, 1992, cited in Steele, 1992). Self-esteem protection of this type is undoubtedly a common cause of academic failure among students of all ethnic and socioeconomic backgrounds. Schools might consider these findings as they search for new educational strategies that build opportunities for academic success into the curriculum. By giving students positive feedback, these strategies may not only boost self-esteem but also increase the value they place on academic achievement.

WORKING THROUGH THREAT: SELF-EXPRESSION. "Sometimes I wonder how all those who do not write, compose, or paint can manage to escape the madness, the melancholia, the panic fear which is inherent in the human situation." As novelist Graham Greene realized (1980, p. 285), self-expression helps people cope emotionally. Even such simple forms of self-expression as talking about the feelings produced by threatening events can help overcome some of their emotional and physical costs (Bulman & Wortman, 1977; Tait & Silver, 1989).

James Pennebaker (1997) has championed the idea that bringing to the surface deeply buried stressful events can help alleviate some of their negative effects. In one dramatic illustration of this idea, he and his colleagues asked some students to write about personally traumatic life events that they had never before discussed, and they asked others to write about trivial topics (Pennebaker, Kiecolt-Glaser, & Glaser, 1988). The students were assured that their names would not be connected to what they wrote. On the 4 successive days of the experiment, the first group dealt with extremely significant events in their lives, including such traumas as the sudden death of a sibling or childhood sexual abuse. Not surprisingly, they reported more negative emotions and more physical discomforts (headaches, muscle tension, pounding heart) at the time, compared with participants who wrote about unimportant topics. However, physiological measures showed that immune-system functioning was superior among students who wrote about traumas. This health benefit persisted for 6 weeks, during which these students visited the university health center less often than did the other participants. Many other studies have replicated these powerful effects. The health effects seem to stem not simply from writing about the distressing events but from the understanding and self-insight that result. In these studies the most benefits flowed to those who increased across the writing sessions in their use of "causal" words like *because* and *reason* and "insight" words like *understand* and *realize* (Pennebaker, 1997). That is, it was not the writers who used a lot of these words all along, but those who initially used few of them but then increased their use who seemed to derive the maximum benefit from writing about their experiences.

Of course, although these participants benefited in the long run, the immediate impact of writing about traumatic events was negative. Before agreeing to participate in this study, the students were warned that they might be asked to write about extremely upsetting events. In addition, researchers conducting studies of this type are always prepared to refer for counseling any participants who become overly distressed. Traumatic events do, of course, harm the victim in many ways, and merely thinking and writing about the event cannot remove all its negative effects. But disclosure can at least help reduce the costs of suppressing and inhibiting painful thoughts, and it is often the first step toward appraising negative events differently (Horowitz, 1987). As you will see, reappraising events is one way to cope directly with problems.

Attacking Threat Head-On: Problem-Focused Coping

Sometimes people respond to threats directly, attempting to reinterpret or remove the negative event or situation itself. Strategies include re-assessing evidence, making excuses, seeking to take control, or directly attacking the problem.

Focusing on the emotional responses produced by threats to the self can help us to feel good about ourselves, but sometimes we prefer tackling events head on. *Problem-focused coping* directs people's cognitive, emotional, and behavioral resources toward reinterpreting the event as nonthreatening (rather than just trying to manage emotional reactions to the threat), or toward physically removing the event.

BIASED EVALUATION: WHAT PROBLEM? As teachers, we have to tell you that we don't get many visits from students who got an A but think the test was unfair. Usually, it's those who do less well who think the test did not reveal their true abilities. When people receive any negative information—not just a bad test score—they may reject it out of hand or at least question its validity in order to dismiss any threat to the self. Tom Pyszczynski and his colleagues (Pyszczynski, Greenberg, & Holt, 1985) studied this strategy in a laboratory experiment in which women took a test of "social sensitivity." Regardless of their actual performance, some women were told that they had done well and others that they had performed poorly. They were then invited to read and evaluate two research reports, one supporting the validity of the social sensitivity test, the other questioning it. As you might have guessed, evaluations of the two research reports were determined by the supposed scores on the test. Those who had "succeeded" thought the supporting study was the better of the two; those who had "failed" came to the opposite conclusion. This kind of biased evaluation of self-relevant information can help us cope with our failures and shortcomings: A threat redefined can be a threat defeated.

MAKING EXCUSES: IT'S NOT MY FAULT. What happens when our worst fears are realized and we do fail a test, get caught out in a lie, or get pulled over for speeding on the expressway? Although we have all wished the earth would open up and swallow us under such circumstances, our usual recourse is to apologize, offer excuses, and try to pick up where we left off. Whenever an action ends in disaster and threatens our self-concept, a good excuse is worth its weight in gold.

Why are excuses so important? The answer has to do with *self-enhancing attributions* that distort people's explanations for successes and failures (Mullen & Riordan, 1988). Most people like to take credit for their successes and notable accomplishments and to attribute failure to external causes. A good grade on an exam reflects well on our intelligence and motivation, while a failing grade is surely due to poorly written test items, an emergency at home, a sudden bout of the flu, or even loud music playing down the hall (D. T. Miller & Ross, 1975). "I missed the appointment because my car broke down." "The dog ate my homework." "That old football injury got in my way."

SELF-HANDICAPPING. A good excuse can be even more valuable if it is lined up before the performance: If we do fail, our defense is already in place. Charles Snyder and his colleagues found that people often use disclaimers like shyness, anxiety, ill health, or disruptive events when they anticipate failing at an important task (C. R. Snyder & Higgins, 1988; C. R. Snyder, Smith, Augelli, & Ingram, 1985). Letting others think we are shy, sick, or under stress seems preferable to conveying the impression that we are unlikable or incompetent.

If verbal excuses help us save face, could the creation of actual barriers to successful performance do the same? Strange as it may seem, some people actually sabotage their own performances to provide excuses for subsequent failures. The strategy is called *self-handicapping* (Berglas & Jones, 1978). To see how and why self-handicapping might work, imagine that you have been bragging for months about your chicken curry, and now your friends are finally coming over for dinner. It suddenly occurs to you that your culinary skills may not quite match those you have advertised. Is there any way out? One possibility is self-handicapping: You could intentionally arrange to run out of a crucial ingredient for the curry. In attributional terms, self-handicapping is a no-lose proposition: Observers' impressions of your skill will be even more positive than they otherwise would be, regardless of the dinner's failure or success. If the curry is not so great, your reputation as a great cook will be saved as your friends blame the disaster on the missing ingredient rather than on your poor skills. If the dinner is wonderful anyway, your culinary expertise will appear even more impressive. But remember, you purchased this attributional benefit of self-handicapping at the cost of lowering your real probability of good performance: You chose probable failure rather than the attributional consequences of *possible* failure (Baumgardner & Brownlee, 1987).

TAKING CONTROL OF THE PROBLEM. If external attributions usually help us to save face, what do you make of the following finding? In one survey of U.S. residents, people who regarded themselves as poor or economically struggling were questioned about their attributions for their situation and about their general emotional well-being. Poor people who believed they had had a fair chance to achieve felt more pride and joy and less guilt and disappointment about their lives than those who believed that external forces had held them back (E. R. Smith & Kluegel, 1982). That is, even when their outcomes are negative, people often feel better if they think they have control. Blaming external factors for failures might let you off the hook momentarily, but interpreting as *controllable* the forces that influence your life will put you back in charge for the long term.

Consider what happened, for example, when Ellen Langer and Judith Rodin decided to see what difference a small degree of control would make to the well-being of a sample of nursing-home residents (1976; Rodin & Langer, 1977). The daily routine in most nursing homes is highly regulated, and residents' ability to control their own lives is limited. Langer and Rodin encouraged a randomly selected group of residents in one home to control such matters as the movies they chose to attend and the location of plants placed in their rooms. Compared with other residents who did not have these opportunities for control, the participants in the study felt better and remained healthier longer, as can be seen in Figure 4.12. Feelings of control are so important that we attempt to exert control whenever we can (R. W. White, 1959). In fact, we often exaggerate the amount of control we possess, even in situations actually ruled by chance (Langer, 1975). For example, most people who play the state lottery prefer to pick their "lucky number," even though any number would have an equal chance of winning.

What gives people the feeling that they can control events in their lives? One crucial ingredient is their confidence in their ability to deal with a particular area, such as passing exams in psychology or successfully managing their social life. This confidence in our ability to produce the outcomes we desire is termed *self-efficacy* (Bandura, 1986). Self-efficacy is particularly strongly linked with the way people explain their *failures*: whether they explain them in terms of controllable or uncontrollable causes. If the bank bounces one of your checks for the third time this month and you explain it by saying, "Oh, I just can't keep a checkbook balanced; I'm no good

FIGURE 4.12   How increased control can affect well-being

■ Eighteen months after a group of nursing-home residents were given increased control over small aspects of their daily lives, the staff rated them as more vigorous and more sociable than a comparison group of patients, as shown on the left scale. Correspondingly, control led to an improvement in physical health over the 18-month period, while the health of the comparison group had deteriorated, as shown on the right scale. (Data from Rodin & Langer, 1977.)

at finance," you are pointing to your supposed lack of ability—an uncontrollable cause. If you blame the situation on your lack of effort or attention, you are pointing to a potentially controllable cause. Such an explanation for a failure should lead you to try harder to keep track of your deposits and withdrawals, which may result in fewer overdraft fees in the future.

The same principle apparently works for elementary-school students, too. Children who are taught to view their failures as a consequence of either their lack of effort or their use of ineffective strategies—not the uncontrollable factor of low ability—improve in persistence and classroom performance (Dweck, 1986). And children who are given a sense of control over their own behavior are less aggressive than children whose every action is externally constrained (R. M. Ryan & Grolnick, 1986). This finding is particularly dramatic because it contradicts the usual assumption that externally imposed rewards and punishments are the best means of reducing aggression.

☐ **CONTROL AND LIFE GOALS**. The issue of who is in control is central even when people set overall directions for their lives. Take a moment to contemplate your most important long-term objectives and goals. Do these aspirations reflect your own internally guided choices, or are they goals that other people have selected for you? Consistent with the general benefits of control, actions and goals that we choose for ourselves benefit us psychologically more than those that are externally imposed, according to an intriguing recent study. Tim Kasser and Richard Ryan (1996) asked people to rate the importance they personally attached to several different life goals. These goals included some that the researchers classified as intrinsic or self-chosen, such as positive relationships with friends and family, community service, or health, as well as some goals the researchers viewed as involving external approval or rewards, such as financial success, fame, and physical attractiveness. The researchers also measured several forms of physical and psychological well-being, including physical symptoms and depression. Consistent results emerged in separate studies of undergraduate students and of adults from 18 to 79 years old. Those who attached more importance to the intrinsic goals tended to have better well-being and lower levels of depression and psychological distress, compared to those whose aspirations were classified as more extrinsic. It seems that striving for wealth, fame, and beauty is *not* a sure route to happiness. Instead, people whose most important goals reflect intrinsic values, goals involving such things as relatedness to others and community service, have the best life outcomes overall.

SOLVING THE PROBLEM: RISING TO THE CHALLENGE. The negative feelings aroused by failures, self-discrepancies, and stress can have positive motivational consequences. We do not always ship out; sometimes we decide to shape up. For example, the painful nature of self-discrepancies can motivate

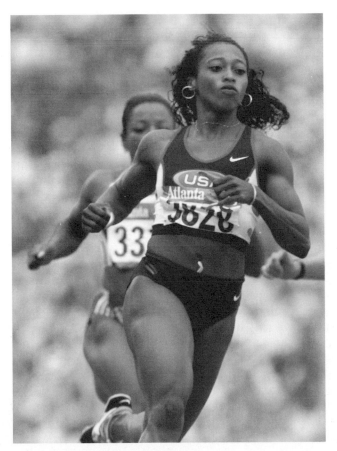

■ **Rising to the challenge.** Only a year before she won Olympic gold, Gail Devers couldn't walk. After a diagnosis of a thyroid condition provided an explanation for a variety of debilitating symptoms, Devers struggled to overcome their effects and get back into the kind of shape that allowed her to win this competitive race. Her friends and family credit her high self-esteem and the support of her trainer for the turnaround.

people to change themselves, to live up to their own ideals and self-guides. Self-awareness often makes people behave in ways consistent with their own personal values (Gibbons, 1978). Startled by being labeled as a couch potato, the former star quarterback might decide to substitute an hour of lifting weights for an hour of watching TV reruns. When we can attribute bad outcomes to controllable factors, we can activate strategies designed to change our performance. If you decide that your low grade was due to a lack of preparation rather than an inability to understand the material, setting up a regular study time may help you prepare for the next exam well in advance. When people try to change, the support and encouragement of others—a spouse or a group of friends, for instance—is generally crucial (Heatherton & Nichols, 1994). This fact underlines the social and interpersonal nature of the self: Whether we are trying to change our overt behavior, our self-esteem, or the way we think about ourselves, these changes depend on our social surroundings.

How to Cope?

The individual's resources as well as characteristics of the threatening situation dictate the best response to threats. No single type of response is always best, but many types of coping can help overcome the threat, preserve psychological well-being, and protect physical health.

As we have seen, there are many ways to cope with threats to the self. Both problem-focused and emotion-focused coping can improve psychological well-being and lessen the health damage caused by threatening events (F. Cohen, 1984; Kiecolt-Glaser, Fisher, & Ogrocki, 1987). But which type works better? The answer depends on who is being threatened—the individual and the resources she or he brings to the situation—and also on the nature of the threat, particularly its controllability.

SELF-ESTEEM AS A RESOURCE FOR COPING. Different people have different cognitive and emotional resources at their disposal to aid in coping. Self-esteem is not only an indicator of how well we are meeting our fundamental social motives for mastery and connectedness, but also an important resource for coping with threats to the self. Those with high self-esteem roll out a formidable arsenal of weapons to defend against threats. For example, they fight negative feedback, setbacks, or stress with an aggressive use of self-enhancing biases and problem-focused coping (J. D. Brown, 1986; S. Epstein, 1992; Josephs, Larrick, Steele, & Nisbett, 1992). They compare themselves with others who are worse off and make self-enhancing attributions for their failures and shortcomings. A challenge to one aspect of the self-concept, such as interpersonal sensitivity, may be met with affirmation of another aspect: generosity, athletic prowess, or intellectual acumen (Steele, 1988). Finally, a strong sense of control lets people with high self-esteem tackle problems head-on. The successful use of this impressive array of self-enhancing biases and coping strategies restores and maintains high self-esteem so the whole cycle can begin again (S. E. Taylor & Brown, 1988). Like a reflection in a series of fun-house mirrors, high self-esteem leads to self-enhancement and successful coping, which restore high self-esteem, which triggers self-enhancement, and so on. No wonder, then, that people with high self esteem have more stable levels of self esteem and clearer self concepts (J. D. Campbell, 1990), and also respond to threat with far fewer emotional and physical symptoms than do those with low self-esteem (J. D. Brown & Smart, 1991).

If you have ever interacted with someone who has low self-esteem, however, you may have noticed a completely different set of reactions. Rather than predicting that the rain clouds will be followed by spring flowers, people with low self-esteem seem resigned to permanent flood conditions. Indeed, depressed people and those with low self-esteem are much less likely to self-enhance than others (Alloy & Abramson, 1979; S. E. Taylor & Brown, 1988). They make downward comparisons less often, remember more negative things about themselves, and assume they have less control over events.

So it is clear that everyday decisions—whether to apply for graduate school, try out for the band, or ask a popular classmate for a date—are very different proposals for different individuals, depending on their level of self-esteem. Great rewards might follow from taking these actions, but individuals with low self-esteem may be unable to take the risk because they are highly sensitive to the possibility of failure and embarrassment (Leary, Barners, & Griebel, 1986). "To the person high in self-esteem . . . the world is an oyster bed of opportunities to enhance themselves, but to the person low in self-esteem, it is a minefield that can humiliate and depress" (Josephs, Larrick, et al., 1992, p. 35). The differences between the ways people with high or low self-esteem approach events can compound across a lifetime. One study illustrates striking effects of the everyday boosts or blows to self-esteem that come from having initials that spell positive words (like WIN or JOY) or negative words (ILL or PIG). Researchers looked at death certificates of California men (because men's initials ordinarily do not change at marriage) and found that those whose initials spelled or resembled positive words lived longer and were less likely to commit suicide, compared to men whose initials made either meaningless or negative words (McConnaughey, 1998). This fascinating finding underlines the importance of self-esteem in the ways we deal with daily threats and ultimately in our physical health.

CONTROLLABILITY AND COPING. The best way to cope depends on the characteristics of the threat as well as on those of the threatened person. Depend-

Calvin and Hobbes by Bill Watterson

CALVIN AND HOBBES © 1992. Watterson. Dist. By Universal Press Syndicate.

FIGURE 4.13   Ways of coping and their effects

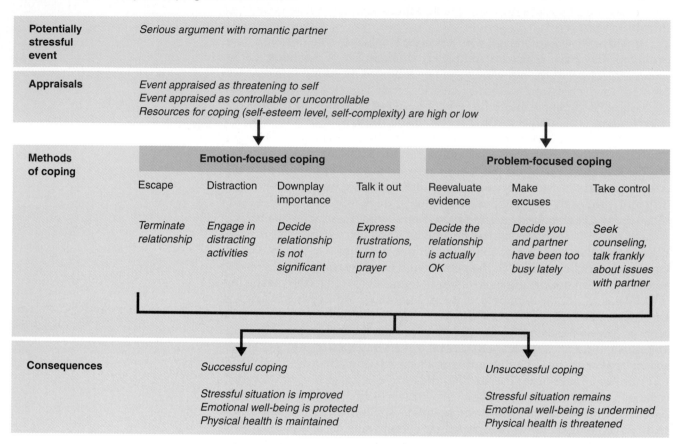

Potentially stressful event	*Serious argument with romantic partner*

Appraisals	*Event appraised as threatening to self* *Event appraised as controllable or uncontrollable* *Resources for coping (self-esteem level, self-complexity) are high or low*

Methods of coping

Emotion-focused coping				Problem-focused coping		
Escape	Distraction	Downplay importance	Talk it out	Reevaluate evidence	Make excuses	Take control
Terminate relationship	*Engage in distracting activities*	*Decide relationship is not significant*	*Express frustrations, turn to prayer*	*Decide the relationship is actually OK*	*Decide you and partner have been too busy lately*	*Seek counseling, talk frankly about issues with partner*

Consequences

Successful coping

Stressful situation is improved
Emotional well-being is protected
Physical health is maintained

Unsuccessful coping

Stressful situation remains
Emotional well-being is undermined
Physical health is threatened

■ Appraisals of a self-threatening event—particularly of its controllability—and of one's coping resources influence the selection of coping strategies. Successful or unsuccessful coping may influence emotional well-being and physical health—as well as affecting the concrete stressful situation itself.

ing on their appraisals of the threat and of their own resources, people can choose among many possible coping strategies, as Figure 4.13 shows. Every style of coping, however, has costs as well as benefits. The most important appraisal is of a threat's controllability. Controllable threats, those that one is confident in being able to handle, really represent *challenges* rather than threats (Blascovich & Tomaka, 1996). People's emotional responses to challenges are generally positive or only mildly negative, and physiological responses (including heart-rate changes, for instance) are geared toward successful mobilization and effective action. With challenges, problem-focused coping might work best, even if it increases immediate distress (S. M. Miller & Mangan, 1983). In contrast, when threats are appraised as uncontrollable, escape, distraction, and other forms of emotion-focused coping may be the only effective ways to deal with them (Folkman, 1984). Unlike challenges, threats elicit negative feelings and physiological responses that are ineffective and perhaps even health-damaging.

But the difference between a threat and a challenge is not so much in the event itself as in the way one looks at it. In one study Joe Tomaka and his colleagues (1997) gave students a mental arithmetic task, introducing the task for some students by stressing the need for both speed and accuracy (making the task somewhat threatening) and for others by asking them to think of the task as "a challenge" and to think of themselves as "someone capable of meeting that challenge." This simple difference in instructions for the very same task elicited the physiological response patterns characteristic of threats versus challenges. Once again, as we have seen so many times in this chapter, the way people regard the stressful event is crucial.

Aid in fighting stress also comes from external sources. The presence of others who give support, advice, and assistance can help ward off the negative consequences of threat. We see how this happens in chapter 11, pages 443 to 445.

CONCLUDING COMMENTS

 We started the chapter by saying that one of the most important life tasks each of us faces is understanding both who we are and how we feel about ourselves. Philosophers have long admonished us to "know thyself," the first aspect of this important task. An accurate understanding of our individual abilities, preferences, and talents enables us to choose the partners, pastimes, and professions that suit us best. It lets us know where we fit in the social world and provides a starting point in any attempt at change or improvement. But psychologists know that it is not enough to "know thyself." Self-esteem is equally central in our lives. Viewing the self as both good and in control—even in exaggerated ways—protects our emotional and physical well-being as we cope with inconsistencies, failures, and stress. Whenever we think about the self, we are faced with two, sometimes conflicting, motives: enhancing the self and accurately evaluating the self.

The dual needs for accurate self-knowledge and positive self-esteem play themselves out in a variety of ways that were discussed throughout this chapter. Sometimes we seek accurate assessments of the self; at other times we engage in biased searches or interpretations to come up with self-enhancing information. Sometimes we compare ourselves with similar others and sometimes with others who are worse off than we are. Sometimes we choose our behaviors to accurately reflect the person we believe we are, but at other times we try to create a positive impression of ourselves. Even the ways we defend ourselves against such threats as negative feedback, obvious shortcomings, and large and small stressors provoke the same dilemma. The warm glow of positive thinking infuses us with strength to clear life's many hurdles, but escaping into a fantasy world of self-enhancement can just as easily set us up for a fall. Taking negative feedback at face value can help us to deal constructively with, and possibly to overcome, our failures and shortcomings. But it can also be painful.

Does this mean we are caught in a no-win situation, forced to make trade-offs between reality and illusion, happiness and depression? Are our choices limited to being eternal optimists, happy but out of touch, or hard realists, on top of the facts but miserable because of it? Fortunately, we have other options. The recipe for a healthy sense of self calls for both accurate self-knowledge and protective self-enhancement, in just the right amounts at just the right times. Weighing these ingredients may be the most important aspect of constructing and maintaining the self. The correct measure of self-enhancement keeps our spirits high and our body healthy, while a judicious amount of self-assessment keeps our goals realistic and our efforts focused in the best direction. A good dollop of self-evaluation tells us what we need to do, a splash of self-enhancement gives us the courage to do it.

CHAPTER 4 THEMES

- **Construction of Reality**
  We construct an impression of the self, based on a multitude of cues.

- **Pervasiveness of Social Influence**
  Our perceptions of other people and their reactions to us pervasively influence our self-concept and self-esteem.

- **Striving for Mastery**
  Perceiving that we control our environment helps mental well-being and physical health.

- **Valuing Me and Mine**
  Self-enhancing biases shape our self-concept and elevate self-esteem.

- **Conservatism**
  Once formed, the self-concept is resistant to change and well defended against threats.

- **Accessibility**
  The self-concept and self-esteem depend on information and experiences that come readily to mind.

SUMMARY

 Constructing the Self-Concept: What We Know About Ourselves. People construct the **self-concept** in much the same way that they form impressions of others, using similar types of information and similar interpretive processes. People often infer their own characteristics from their observed behaviors, as **self-perception theory** notes. They also use thoughts and feelings and other people's reactions to form opinions about themselves. Finally, **social comparison theory** describes how people compare themselves to others to learn what characteristics make them unique.

Despite the general similarity of the ways people learn about themselves and others, self-knowledge is richer and more detailed than knowledge about others. People can observe themselves in more situations and have better access to private thoughts and feelings. People also tend to explain their own and other people's behaviors differently, producing **actor–observer differences in attribution**. They attribute their own actions to properties of the situation or the stimulus, while generally explaining others' actions by their personal characteristics. However, even people's explanations for their own behaviors may be inaccurate.

Because people see themselves in a wide range of situations and roles, self-knowledge is organized around multiple self-aspects representing roles, activities, and relationships. People vary in **self-complexity**, the number and diversity of "selves" that they believe they possess.

People try to fit the diverse elements of self-knowledge together in a way that seems coherent and stable. Coherence can be attained by making accessible only limited aspects of the self at any given time, by selectively remembering past acts, by explaining away inconsistencies, and by focusing on a few central traits. Cultures influence the ways in which people seek coherence. Members of Western, independent cultures stress the self-schema, traits that generally describe them across situations, while those in interdependent cultures emphasize their roles and relationships with others.

Constructing Self-Esteem: How We Feel About Ourselves. Accurate self-knowledge regarding our capabilities and preferences is important for guiding us through our lives in ways that suit our needs and abilities. But accuracy is not the only consideration in evaluating the self: **Self-esteem** is also greatly influenced by motivational pressures to think well of the self. These motivations color many of our thoughts and feelings about the self through **self-enhancing biases**.

Events that affect us positively or negatively influence our self-esteem, but we try in several ways to accumulate more positive than negative experiences. We also evaluate ourselves by making comparisons with others. These comparisons also are sometimes self-enhancing. In addition, **self-discrepancy theory** describes how people compare themselves with their own internal standards. The outcomes of these comparisons can lead to positive or negative feelings about the self. Although our thoughts are turned outward most of the time, some events create **self-awareness**, a state of heightened awareness of the self, including our internal standards and whether we measure up to them. Focusing attention on the self makes self-discrepancies obvious.

Despite the value of accurate self-knowledge, self-enhancement occurs for two primary reasons. Some actions that appear self-enhancing are aimed at actual self-improvement, reflecting successful self-regulation. And high self-esteem can be an important resource that protects us against stress and threats to the self.

Like most other aspects of the self, self-enhancing biases operate somewhat differently in different cultures. Independent cultures emphasize positive individual characteristics as the source of self-esteem, while interdependent cultures stress connectedness to others. Despite these differences, self-esteem functions in all cultures to indicate how well we are meeting our most important motives for mastery and connectedness.

Effects of the Self: Directing Thoughts, Feelings, and Behavior. The self-concept, once formed, is relatively difficult to change. People avoid or actively reject information that is inconsistent with their established self-views. Self-knowledge also serves as a framework for perceiving other people and influences what types of social information we will remember.

The self regulates many aspects of our lives. Emotions are sparked by **cognitive appraisals** of self-relevant events and their causes or controllability. Emotions signal the occurrence of significant events and motivate us to act in response, for example, to flee from danger. As they perform this self-regulation function, emotions involve the whole self, body and mind: They activate facial expressions, physiological responses, subjective feelings, and overt behaviors.

The self also directs behavior. Sometimes people engage in **self-expression**, acting in ways that express their true inner selves. At other times, people are concerned with **self-presentation**, attempting to shape others' opinions in order to gain power, influence, or approval. The personality variable of **self-monitoring** reflects the degree to which people seek one or the other of these two general goals. But even behaviors intended for others' consumption may end up influencing people's private views of themselves.

Defending the Self: Coping with Stresses, Inconsistencies, and Failures. When threatened by external events or negative feedback, people must defend their sense of who and what they are. Major failures and disasters obviously threaten the self, but so do inconsistent information, daily hassles, and stresses. Threats to the self affect not only emotional well-being but also physical health. The most damaging threats are those we appraise as uncontrollable.

Faced with threats, people respond with **coping strategies**. Sometimes they try to manage their emotional responses to threat through escape, distraction, redefinition of an event's importance, or self-expression. At other times, people respond to threats directly, trying to reduce the negative consequences of self-threatening events. Possible strategies are reinterpreting evidence, making excuses, seeking to take control, or directly attacking the problem.

The individual's resources, including self-esteem and self-complexity, as well as characteristics of the threatening situation, dictate the best response to threats. No single type of response is always best, but many types of coping can help overcome the threat, preserve psychological well-being, and protect physical health.

5

Perceiving Groups

Cedric Holloway sat in his car outside the Great Western Bank in Tamarac, Florida, poring over the current interest rates for certificates of deposit and money market funds. Earlier in the day, the 20-year-old chef's helper had visited the Great Western twice trying to decide how to invest the $1,000 he had saved. Suddenly his car was surrounded by sheriff's deputies, guns drawn. Holloway was ordered out of the car, handcuffed, and read his rights. Why? Because bank employees, suspicious that the young man was planning to rob their branch, had called the police. After 45 minutes of questioning, the police accepted Holloway's explanation and released him (L. Williams, 1991).

Were the officers justified in suspecting that the man parked outside the Florida bank was a potential bank robber? Or was Holloway, who is Black, approached, accused, and arrested because of discrimination? The term **discrimination** refers to positive or negative behavior directed toward a social group and its members. Of course, people are usually concerned with negative behaviors—with discrimination *against* a specific group—but discrimination against one group inevitably amounts to discrimination in favor of others. For example, the former South African system of apartheid—legally enforced segregation—victimized Blacks while preserving the power and wealth of the small White minority. Apartheid and many other forms of discrimination are illegal in the United States, but many people still find themselves ill-treated because of their group memberships. Physical attacks, vandalism, harassment, and threats against Jews, Blacks, Asian Americans, and gay men and lesbians have been widely reported in recent years, leading some communities to pass laws providing extra punishment for "hate crimes" (Garofalo, 1997; Green, Glaser, & Rich, 1998). Economic discrimination victimizes women and people of color when they try to purchase a used car, rent or purchase a home, or negotiate a salary (Abrams, 1991; Goldin, 1990; W. E. Schmidt, 1990). And, as Cedric Holloway and most young Black men are well aware, non-Whites' experiences with the criminal justice system differ substantially from those of most Whites (D. A. Bell, 1973; Silverstein, 1965).

> **Discrimination.** Any positive or negative behavior that is directed toward a social group and its members.

155

Unfortunately, discrimination seems to be found everywhere around the globe. Turks and other foreigners living in Germany have been victims of verbal abuse, beatings, arson, and murder by neo-Nazis and teenage "skinheads" (Moseley, 1998). People of Korean descent living in Japan—even those whose families have resided there for generations—are barred from voting and are required to carry alien registration cards at all times and to report their addresses to the government (Sterngold, 1992). French Canadians feel oppressed by the English-speaking majority; Canadian Mohawk Indians feel oppressed by French Canadians. Tamils in Sri Lanka, women in Afghanistan, and Blacks in South Africa have little access to adequate schooling, health care, or political power.

What leads one group of people to victimize another? Religious thinkers, political leaders, social scientists, and others have searched for an answer to this important question. Social psychologists believe that the underlying processes leading to discrimination usually include **prejudice**, the positive or negative evaluation of a social group and its members. Once again, people's concern is most often with negative evaluations, which range all the way from mild dislike to blind hatred. As you will see in the first part of this chapter, prejudice is complex and multifaceted, and its roots can be traced to cognitive and social processes that guide our every interaction with groups. So many processes contribute to prejudice, in fact, that we will need two chapters (chapters 5 and 6) to tell the whole story.

In this chapter we start with the very basis of prejudice: the way in which people divide the world into social groups. We then consider the **stereotypes**, or impressions that people form of groups by associating particular characteristics and emotions with particular groups (Eagly & Mladinic, 1989; D. L. Hamilton, 1981). The sometimes biased and often sketchy impressions we form of groups can permeate our thinking and become a basis for both prejudice and discrimination. For example, many White Americans associate Black men with characteristics like violence and criminal behavior. In Cedric Holloway's case, this stereotype was translated into prejudice (the negative interpretation of Holloway's motives) and discrimination (his mistreatment by bank employees and the police).

Is it possible to eliminate the stereotypical thinking that contributes to prejudice? Will a young Black man parked outside a bank ever just fade into the crowd, attracting no more and no less suspicion than other bank customers do? The answer is a cautious but optimistic yes. Stereotypes can be changed, though it does not happen easily. Initial impressions of groups, like first impressions of individuals, tend to have lasting power. Established stereotypes often influence thoughts and actions in ways that make stereotypes resistant to modification. But as you will see in the final section of this chapter, the defenses protecting stereotypes from change can be breached under some conditions. Negative stereotypes can then be replaced by more favorable impressions, and prejudice can be replaced by more positive evaluations.

The Social and Cognitive Roots of Prejudice

It is discouragingly easy to find examples of racism, sexism, and other "-isms" throughout the world—examples like those just described of prejudice based on race, ethnicity, age, gender, religion, and sexual preference. To explain these

Prejudice. A positive or negative evaluation of a social group and its members.

Stereotype. A cognitive representation or impression of a social group that people form by associating particular characteristics and emotions with the group.

findings, we need to understand how prejudice arises and how groups become the target of everything from mild dislike to contemptuous hatred.

What Causes Prejudice?

Prejudice, the positive or negative evaluation of a social group and its members, has at times been viewed as the product of distorted thinking in a few troubled individuals. But both social and cognitive factors contribute to prejudice. One important source of prejudice is people's beliefs about a group's positive or negative characteristics.

Prejudice can be "hot" or "cold." Virulent hatred for other groups, such as that espoused by the Nazis or the Ku Klux Klan, is easy to recognize. It shows itself in burning crosses, campaigns of "ethnic cleansing," pogroms, and massacres. Unfortunately, the very obviousness of this type of bigotry and hatred may blind us to a more insidious type of prejudice based on the calm assumption that certain groups just "do not have what it takes" and should therefore be excluded from desirable positions, wealth, or power. This quieter, cooler form of prejudice is at work when sports-team owners profit from the performance of Black athletes on the field but can never find a "qualified" Black for a front-office job. And it is present when a construction union maintains an all-male membership by keeping women out of apprenticeship programs, or when a real estate agent steers prospective home buyers who are Hispanic to particular neighborhoods. Such discriminatory actions are carried out calmly, routinely, and without any of the familiar overt signs of bigotry. But even though no hooded robes or swastika armbands are anywhere in sight, very real harm is suffered by those on the receiving end. Prejudice wears so many different faces that it is no wonder that no single cause of prejudice has been found.

THE AUTHORITARIAN PERSONALITY EXPLANATION. Some of social psychologists' first systematic attempts to explain prejudice were triggered by the genocidal policies of the Nazis during the Second World War (Ashmore & Del Boca, 1981). The extreme nature of that prejudice and discrimination seemed to call for equally extreme explanations. Drawing on the work of Sigmund Freud, researchers theorized that hatred of other groups is abnormal. In one influential study, Theodor Adorno and his colleagues (Adorno, Frenkel-Brunswik, Levinson, & Sanford, 1950) argued that prejudice has its roots in the inner conflicts of those with *authoritarian personalities*—people who cannot accept their own hostility, believe uncritically in the legitimacy of authority, and see their own inadequacies in others. Thus, the theorists argued, prejudice protects these individuals from an awareness of their painful inner conflicts and self-doubts. To understand Adorno's position, imagine, for example, an authoritarian athletic coach who doubts his own abilities but is not consciously aware of those feelings. His response to a lost game might be to see his players as clumsy and incompetent and to heap blame on them for their loss.

There is something psychologically satisfying about the authoritarian personality explanation of prejudice. If prejudice is rooted in the mental and emotional deviance of certain individuals, it becomes the exception rather than the rule, a problem *other* people have. Unfortunately, despite its appeal, this explanation does not stand up against the accumulated evidence

Freud would agree!!

(Billig, 1976). Some individuals' extreme prejudice may in fact flow from deep inner conflicts, as Adorno described (Esses, Haddock, & Zanna, 1993). Unfortunately, however, as the examples cited at the beginning of the chapter suggest, prejudice seems to be the rule and not the exception. In fact, it is so pervasive that social psychologists have come to a more mundane, but also more consequential, conclusion: Prejudice most often grows out of the same social and cognitive processes that affect all aspects of our lives.

SOCIAL AND COGNITIVE PROCESSES AS EXPLANATIONS. Our social interactions and interrelations with others influence not only the way we divide people into groups but also our thoughts and feelings about those groups. When the only women that male executives deal with are those in subordinate positions, the resulting patterns of interaction contribute to prejudice by reinforcing views of women as dependent and unsuited for leadership. When children learn bigotry from their parents or peers, they are following the example of these loved or respected others because they want to feel connected to those others. But the result is prejudice.

Prejudice reflects cognitive as well as social processes, because it is also a by-product of our perception of the world and our efforts to make sense of it. We deal with the social world by clumping together people who seem similar and by treating all members of a group in the same way. These tendencies promote perceptions of groups as very different from each other. And, of course, cognitive processes are not always unbiased. The way we think usually promotes our self-interest by protecting "me and mine." Nor is it always just chance that we gather and interpret information in a way that seems destined to confirm and perpetuate, rather than overthrow, our established beliefs and prejudices.

Both the social and cognitive processes that generate stereotypes and prejudice are pervasively affected by our own group memberships. This happens in many ways, as we learn whom to interact with and befriend, how to look at the world, and why our groups are superior to others. Thus, some Japanese people who dislike Koreans might do so not because of any specific negative stereotype but because they act out the wish to see their own group as superior by putting other groups down. This aspect of our desire to see "me and mine" in a positive light is responsible for the most malignant forms of group hatred and appalling discrimination. The connections between our sense of self and our group memberships, and their implications for the way we treat other groups, are so important that they receive full treatment in the next chapter, chapter 6.

Conflicts between groups often intensify prejudice and discrimination. Chapter 13, pages 519 to 535, describes the often explosive consequences of intergroup conflict and competition.

Targets of Prejudice: Social Groups

Any group that shares a socially meaningful common characteristic can be a target for prejudice. Different cultures emphasize different types of groups, but race, religion, gender, age, social status, and cultural background are important dividing lines in many societies.

Social group. Two or more people who share some common characteristic that is socially meaningful for themselves or for others.

Stereotypes, prejudice, discrimination: We have been talking about processes that depend on identifying people as members of social groups. But what is it that turns "people" into "members of social groups"? A **social group** is two or more people who share some common characteristic that is socially meaningful for themselves or for others (Shaw, 1976; Tajfel & Turner, 1979; J. C. Turner, 1981). The key phrase here is *socially meaningful*. People who share just any attribute, such as pedestrians who happen to be waiting in the same place to cross the same street, do not qualify as a social group (D. L. Hamilton & Sherman, 1996). Categories of people who share socially meaningful attributes—college students, Quakers, the "working poor," white-collar criminals, environmentalists—are groups, however. In fact, individuals who believe they share socially significant attributes are a group even if others do not think of them that way. Likewise, people who are seen by others as sharing meaningful similarities are a group even if they themselves do not hold that view. Recent immigrants who see themselves as blending into their new culture are often disappointed when their new compatriots think of them as "foreigners." Social groups exist very much in the eyes of their beholders.

Socially meaningful characteristics, of course, can change from time to time and from culture to culture. If several British and French men and women are discussing dating, they will probably think of themselves and each other primarily as members of the groups "men" or "women." If the topic shifts to the new Euro currency, however, the implicit lines of group membership will probably shift as well. These people may now see themselves and each other as members of national groups that are affected differently by European economic union.

Even though rapid changes in perception of group membership are possible, each society and culture generally emphasizes particular group distinctions. In most North American and European countries today, those considering the issues of stereotypes and prejudice are likely to think of "racial" groups. And because most research on these issues has been conducted in North America and Europe, most focuses on racial stereotypes and prejudice, particularly on Whites' perceptions and reactions to Blacks. Interestingly, though, the concept of "race" originated fairly recently (around the middle of the 19th century) to provide a pseudoscientific justification for socially determined differences in the treatment of different groups (Gould, 1981). Thus, race is largely a social concept with little, if any, biological mean-

Members of some groups have much more in common than shared features. Interaction and shared goals also affect group members' beliefs, feelings, and behavior in important ways, as you will see in chapters 9 and 12.

■ **Multiple group memberships.** Listening to the tour guide and snapping shots of landmarks, these people share the socially meaningful characteristics of "tourists." But several of them share memberships in other social groups. Thus, under different circumstances they could be categorized in terms of their family membership, age, ethnicity, or gender.

ing (Dobzhansky, 1973). For most of human history, religion has been the characteristic that elicited the most prejudice and discrimination, and this is still true today in many parts of the world (G. W. Allport, 1954b, p. xi). In Lebanon, for example, the characteristic that matters is whether a person is Muslim or Christian; in Northern Ireland, Catholic or Protestant identity is what counts. In still other places, cultural background is the trigger for prejudice. The Chinese, for example, have historically been prejudiced against the Japanese, the Japanese against the Koreans, and so on.

Social Categorization: Dividing the World Into Social Groups

People identify individuals as members of social groups because they share socially meaningful features. Social categorization is helpful because it allows people to deal with others efficiently and appropriately. However, social categorization also exaggerates similarities within groups and differences between groups, and hence it forms the basis for stereotyping.

"Doggie," says the 2-year-old, pointing to a horse. "Doggie," she says again as she spies a cat. This common mistake reflects an attempt at categorization, the process of recognizing individual objects as members of a category because they share certain features. Categorization is the process by which we group things or people, and it is an intrinsic part of the way we think about and try to understand the world. We know the elm in our backyard and the oak across the street are both trees because they share features that characterize deciduous trees. "Satisfaction" and "Hey Jude" go together because they are both classic rock-and-roll hits. In the same way, we divide the enormous number of individuals we meet into groups, lumping them together on the basis of their shared socially relevant features. Instead of individuals, they become men, women, Whites, Flemish, Jews, elderly persons, single mothers, or blue-collar workers. **Social categorization** occurs when people are perceived as members of social groups rather than unique individuals. Gender, ethnicity, and age are obvious bases for social categorization, but they are not the only attributes we use. Name tags, uniforms, or tools of the trade, for example, help us categorize people by occupation, whereas accent and speech dialect may identify an individual's nationality, regional background, or social class.

Why does social categorization occur? It is a useful, even essential tool—one that enables us to master our environment and function effectively in society (S. E. Taylor, 1981; Wilder, 1986). Think, for example, what you gain when you categorize the man standing by the library stacks as a librarian (Andersen & Klatsky, 1987; C. F. Bond & Brockett, 1987). First, you can infer that he will help you locate a book, check it out, and even keep the place quiet so you can study. That is, knowing that this individual is a member of the group "librarians" tells you he has many characteristics shared by members of that group, even if they are not immediately obvious. Second, categorization allows you to ignore unimportant information. You can focus on what is relevant—his knowledge of books and where they are kept—without having to notice the color of his suit or wonder about his political leanings, food preferences, or lifestyle. Social categorization saves you the effort of having to deal with all the unique aspects of every individual you meet, when they are

Social categorization. The process of identifying individual people as members of a social group because they share certain features that are typical of the group.

irrelevant to your interaction. Thus, categorization has a dual purpose: It provides useful information that cannot immediately be perceived, and it allows us to ignore unnecessary information (Bruner, 1957).

However, as victims of prejudice and discrimination know well, categorization also has negative side effects. Social categorization makes all members of a group seem more similar to each other than they would be if they were not categorized (McGarty & Penny, 1988; Tajfel & Wilkes, 1963). This is true whether people sort others into groups on the basis of real differences or of arbitrary and trivial characteristics. The librarian who breeds cocker spaniels and the librarian who writes movie scripts seem more similar if we focus only on their shared group membership as librarians. Because of this increased similarity, people often overestimate group members' uniformity and overlook their diversity (G. W. Allport, 1954b; Brigham, 1971; Wilder, 1981). Thus, we go from a world in which some professors are forgetful to one in which all professors are absentminded, and we move beyond the news that a majority of the voters have cast their ballots for a right-wing Republican to the idea that the electorate is uniformly conservative (Allison & Messick, 1985).

Social categorization also exaggerates differences between groups. Thinking about Martina Hingis and Pete Sampras as members of different gender or ethnic groups makes them seem more different than if we think of them both as world-champion tennis players. In fact, once we categorize people into groups, we become more aware of the characteristics that make one group different from another rather than of those that make them similar (Krueger & Rothbart, 1990). For example, in the United States men are slightly more aggressive than women, yet impressions of gender groups vastly overestimate that small difference (C. L. Martin, 1987). These negative aspects of social categorization are presumably responsible for the fact that people who are most concerned with accurately categorizing others into groups also tend to be the most prejudiced against those groups (Blascovich, Wyer, Swart, & Kibler, 1997). Social categorization brings the world into sharper focus, but the exaggeration of similarities within groups and differences between groups is the price we pay for better resolution.

Measuring Stereotypes and Prejudice

Stereotypes can be measured by asking plain questions or in more subtle ways that make it difficult for people to hide prejudiced feelings. However, people who reveal stereotypes or prejudice in subtle ways while overtly denying them may not be dishonest; they may actually hold conflicting views.

How can researchers assess the stereotypes that people hold of social groups, or the level of prejudice that they feel? A generation or two ago this was a relatively easy task: Researchers could just ask people, and generally received honest answers (D. Katz & Braly, 1933). However, more recently, people have become less likely to endorse group stereotypes or to openly reveal prejudice against racial or other groups (Devine, 1989; Dovidio & Fazio, 1992). Does this mean that stereotyping and prejudice have actually declined over time, or just that people are now less likely to be honest about such socially sensitive matters?

Researchers have used several techniques to try to answer this important question. One approach is the use of questionnaires that attempt to assess prejudice in a disguised manner, by asking about political and social attitudes relevant to the group in question. For example, people might be asked how they feel about affirmative action programs for Blacks as an indirect way of measuring their prejudice toward that group. However, recent research shows that the disguise is relatively ineffective; people who desire to hide their prejudiced feelings alter their responses on such measures (Dunton & Fazio, 1997). As we will see later in the chapter, researchers have also found subtle and indirect ways to measure the automatic activation of stereotypes and positive or negative feelings when people think about or encounter members of specific groups. Such methods allow the investigation of stereotypes and prejudice even when the individuals involved do not wish to reveal or acknowledge them.

Research using such subtle measurement techniques has consistently found that many people who deny harboring stereotypes or prejudice, apparently with great sincerity, nevertheless show tell-tale signs of these phenomena. Are these individuals just being dishonest (with their questioners, and perhaps even with themselves)? The answer may be no. As we will see, this pattern of overt denial combined with subtle indications of the presence of stereotypes and prejudice may actually reflect the fact that many people have learned stereotypes from an early age—from parents, the media, the culture in general—yet are honestly attempting to escape their influence (Devine, 1989). Unfortunately, their good intentions cannot always be carried out.

Forming Impressions of Groups: Establishing Stereotypes

There are many similarities between the ways we form impressions of individuals (as described in chapter 3) and the ways we form impressions of groups. Yet there are also subtle differences that contribute to the special properties of group stereotypes (D. L. Hamilton & Sherman, 1996). To understand these special properties we must first answer two questions: What kinds of characteristics are included in stereotypes? Where do these stereotypes come from?

The Content of Stereotypes

Many different kinds of characteristics are included in stereotypes, which can be positive or negative. Some stereotypes accurately reflect actual differences between groups, though in exaggerated form. Other stereotypes are completely inaccurate.

STEREOTYPES INCLUDE MANY TYPES OF CHARACTERISTICS. Walter Lippmann, a journalist who introduced the current meaning of the term *stereotype* in 1922, saw stereotypes as "pictures in the head," simplified mental images of what groups look like and what they do. Stereotypes often do incorporate physical appearance, typical interests and goals, preferred activities and occupations, and similar characteristics (Andersen & Klatzky, 1987; Brewer,

1988; Deaux & Lewis, 1983, 1984). Yet they usually go well beyond what groups *look* like or *act* like. Stereotypes more often make statements about what groups *are* like: the personality traits group members are believed to share, and the emotions and feelings group members arouse in others.

Early research on stereotypes found that college students held well-developed beliefs about the traits characterizing various ethnic groups (D. Katz & Braly, 1933). Considerable social pressure now exists against the public expression of such beliefs, but stereotypes have not disappeared. Do you have a mental image of the "typical" college professor, accountant, or truck driver? Or, if you are an English Canadian, what is your view of French Canadians? Research suggests you may think of them as talkative, excitable, and proud (Gardner, Lalone, Nero, & Young, 1988), whereas French Canadians may describe you as educated, dominant, and ambitious (Aboud & Taylor, 1971). Russians view men of Caucasian nationalities—Georgians, Armenians, and others from the mountainous Caucasus region—as brazen, flashy, criminally inclined, and likely to accost respectable women in the street (Bohlen, 1992). According to a recent study of 300 U.S. communities, a majority of respondents believes that Blacks are less industrious, intelligent, and even patriotic than Whites, despite the dramatic overrepresentation of Blacks in the armed forces ("Poll Finds," 1991).

Gender stereotypes are held even more strongly and confidently than ethnic stereotypes (Jackman & Senter, 1981). Most people describe women as sensitive, warm, dependent, and people-oriented, whereas men are considered dominant, independent, task-oriented, and aggressive (Ashmore, 1981; Spence, Deaux, & Helmreich, 1985). In fact, these gender stereotypes are found in similar forms among adults and children in North and South America, Asia, Africa, Europe, and Australia (J. E. Williams & Best, 1982).

Group stereotypes also incorporate the emotions that group members arouse in others. For example, observers may regard members of one group with feelings of disgust and repulsion, a second group with fear and apprehension, and yet a third with respect and admiration (Mackie & Hamilton, 1993). As a result, the first group may be labeled "disgusting," the second "hostile," and the third "admirable." As we will see shortly, our emotions can have important effects on our actual face-to-face interactions with members of stereotyped groups.

STEREOTYPES CAN BE EITHER POSITIVE OR NEGATIVE. As these examples make clear, stereotypes can include positive as well as negative characteristics. You may wonder, though, why we should be concerned with positive beliefs about groups. After all, positive stereotypes may represent attributes, such as women's sensitivity, that group members themselves value and take pride in claiming. Still, even positive stereotypes can have negative consequences. Consider the belief, widespread among White American college students, that Asian Americans are straight-*A* students. One problem with that stereotype is its implication that everyone in the group is the same, and, as chapter 4 showed, people generally prefer to be thought of in terms of their unique personal characteristics.

A second problem created by positive stereotypes is that they may set unrealizably high standards, so that an Asian-American student who gets average grades may be regarded as particularly dull (E. R. Smith & Ho, 1999). Finally, positive stereotypes can create a backlash, as Harry Duh, a Stanford University biology major, discovered the day he dressed as a "typical Asian nerd." Duh, who walked around campus with a bulging backpack, hitched-up pants, and pocket calculator, was harassed by Whites and shunned by his embarrassed ethnic peers ("1-day nerd," 1992). American Jews face a similar backlash because many people believe that they are richer and more powerful than non-Jews and that their influence in society should be curtailed (T. Lewin, 1992).

The psychological consequences of stereotyping are overestimated uniformity and rigid expectations, and the social translation of those consequences is prejudice and discrimination. This connection warrants our continued concern with stereotypes, regardless of whether they are positive or negative.

STEREOTYPES CAN BE ACCURATE OR INACCURATE. Perhaps even more important than whether stereotypes are positive or negative is the issue of whether they are accurate or inaccurate. No good yardstick is available for measuring the accuracy or inaccuracy of most stereotypes. There is no solid evidence, for example, on the relative frequency with which Georgian versus Russian men accost female passers-by. In addition, many concepts included in common stereotypes, for example, "clannish," "lazy," or "dirty," are so subjective as to be virtually meaningless.

Nevertheless, other aspects of stereotypes can be measured against "reality," and when they are, researchers find some to be accurate in direction if not in degree. This is not surprising since people often join together in clubs, political parties, professional associations, and other groups precisely because they share attitudes, feelings, and beliefs. This self-sorting process creates real group differences that may be reflected in stereotypes. Social customs also help create accurate stereotypes by prescribing what men and women, teenagers and retirees, and different racial groups can or should think, feel, and do. For example, as Table 5.1 shows, many gender stereotypes accurately describe the direction of differences that research has identified between men's behavior and women's behavior, although in exaggerated form (Eagly, 1995; C. L. Martin, 1987). Similarly, Black and White college students' stereotypes of these two groups on attributes such as "dance well," "have high SAT math scores," and "self-centered" generally differ in the same direction as the group members' self-descriptions (C. S. Ryan, 1996).

Yet stereotypes can also be *in*accurate. Consider an early study of Californians' stereotypes of Armenian Americans (LaPiere, 1936). The researcher compared official statistics on this small, segregated minority with popular stereotypes about their behavior. Whereas Californians claimed that Armenians were constantly in trouble with the law, records showed that only about 1.5% had arrest records, compared with about 6% of the rest of the population. Similarly, Californians believed Armenians were more likely to be on welfare than working. In fact, only 1 of every 500 Armenians had applied for welfare, while the proportion for all Californians was five times higher. As another example, many people hold the stereotype that men are more effective leaders than women. A re-

TABLE 5.1. Do Gender Stereotypes Reflect Actual Gender Differences? Results from Meta-Analyses

Gender stereotypes	Differences identified by research
Aggressiveness: (male) aggressive (female) soft-hearted	Men are more aggressive than women overall. The difference is larger for physical than for psychological aggression, and in situations in which aggression may be dangerous.
Influenceability: (male) independent (female) submissive, dependent	Women are more influenceable than men. The difference is larger for influence exerted by a group than for persuasive messages, and larger when the topic is regarded as "masculine."
Emotionality: (male) strong, tough (female) affectionate, anxious, emotional, sensitive, sentimental	Women are more nonverbally expressive and more nonverbally sensitive than men.
Leadership style: (male) autocratic, dominant (female) sensitive, emotional	As leaders, women are more democratic and men are more autocratic. The difference is larger in laboratory studies than in studies of leadership in real, ongoing organizations.

Sources: Stereotypes—J. E. Williams and Best (1982); Meta-analyses of research on gender differences—Eagly (1987), Eagly and Johnson (1990).

cent meta-analysis of the research, in contrast, found no sex differences (or even small differences favoring women) in leadership effectiveness in business, educational, or government organizations (Eagly, Karau, & Makhijani, 1995).

Finally, there is one sense in which every stereotype is inaccurate: when it is viewed as applying to *every* member of a group. Not every French Canadian is talkative; not every woman is emotional; not every Asian American is a straight-*A* student. So it is an error for anyone to confidently assume that an individual member of a group possesses all of the group's stereotypic qualities. Clearly, acting on inaccurate or exaggerated stereotypes has a tremendous potential for harm.

But whatever their content—positive characteristics or negative ones, accurate descriptions or inaccurate distortions—stereotypes are a very real part of our daily lives. Each of us could reel off dozens of well-known stereotypes. Used-car dealers cannot be trusted; the French are great lovers. Nobel-winning physicist Leon Lederman, in advocating a TV series to humanize the image of physicists, said: "Scientists fall in love. But when was the last time you saw a physicist on TV galloping off into the sunset with a beautiful woman?" ("The Romance," 1995). Think about this for a moment. Did you notice Lederman's assumption that a physicist is a heterosexual man?

Where do these stereotypes come from? In most cases, we learn these things from interaction, either with members of the stereotyped group or with other people who tell us about the group.

Forming Stereotypes Through Personal Experience

Stereotypes learned through personal experience with group members may be biased because people pay attention to extremes or inaccurately perceive groups' characteristics. Social roles often shape group members' behaviors, but people attribute the behaviors to group members' inner characteristics. The emotions generated by interaction with certain groups can also become part of stereotypes about those groups.

The world is getting smaller. In central Europe, boundaries between nations and peoples are suddenly permeable. Residents of Germany, France, and Italy are more often coming face to face with immigrants about whom they know little: Albanians, Mozambicans, Arabs, Namibians, and Turks. Changes in U.S. immigration patterns have created a similar situation. The new family moving into the apartment across the hall might be Vietnamese Hmong, the new student assigned to your section might be Lithuanian, and the new sales representative joining your company might be from El Salvador.

As people encounter groups for the first time, their interactions with the newcomers can become the basis of stereotypes. In the absence of other information, idiosyncratic experiences with only one or two Hmong, Lithuanians, or Salvadorans are used to construct a personal stereotype of the group. And even if people interact with more than one member of an unfamiliar group with the genuine intention of forming an accurate, unbiased impression, the interactions themselves often generate exaggerated stereotypes (Rothbart, Dawes, & Park, 1984).

Surprisingly, encounters with individual group members can affect stereotypes even when the group is well known and stereotypes are well established. Henderson-King and Nisbett (1996) demonstrated such an effect by arranging for White students to observe a confederate, pretending to be another experimental participant, behave in a rude and hostile manner toward the experimenter. In some cases the confederate was Black and in other cases White, while in a third condition no hostile interaction took place. The participants were then asked to conduct a mock interview of another student for a position of residence hall counselor. They were given a list of suggested questions and told that the interview could last up to 20 minutes. The student to be interviewed turned out to be Black. The participants who had previously seen another Black's negative behavior ended the interview much sooner (after an average of just 8 minutes) compared to those who had seen a White behaving in the same obnoxious fashion or who had seen no negative behavior at all (about 10½ minutes). Evidently, a single group member's negative acts can activate negative thoughts and feelings about the entire group, even when the group is familiar.

Fortunately, this effect can work to make feelings about a group more positive as well. Galen Bodenhausen and his colleagues (Bodenhausen, Schwarz, Bless, & Waenke, 1995) demonstrated that when people have recently thought about well-liked Blacks (such as Bill Cosby or Oprah Winfrey), their opinions on issues related to Blacks' position in American society become more positive. Findings like these suggest that positive or negative impressions of individual group members form an important part of people's overall impressions of a group (E. R. Smith & Zárate, 1992).

But this fact raises a puzzle. Why do firsthand observations of group members—seemingly the most trustworthy form of information—often lead to impressions of their groups that are biased and exaggerated? There are several reasons.

PEOPLE NOTICE SOME MEMBERS MORE THAN OTHERS. Next time you are at a party, stand back a little and glance around the room. Whom are you most likely to notice, even in passing? The guest in the tuxedo, when everyone else is wearing blue jeans? Or the very tall woman standing over by the window? If these people stand out, it is because our attention is typically drawn to what is unusual, unexpected, or salient (L. Z. McArthur, 1981). For this reason, distinctive individuals can have a disproportionate impact on the formation of group stereotypes, as Myron Rothbart and his colleagues (Rothbart, Fulero, Jensen, Howard, & Birrel, 1978) demonstrated. One group of participants in their experiment read a list of the actions of 50 men, 10 of whom had committed nonviolent crimes. A second group of participants read the same list, but the criminal actions of the 10 men were violent and salient. The participants were later asked how many men from each group had committed crimes. Compared with those exposed to the nonviolent crimes, participants exposed to the violent crimes thought that more group members had committed crimes. Similarly, recall the appalling death toll in the bombing of a U.S. Government office building in Oklahoma City, for which Timothy McVeigh was convicted. This event probably had a huge impact on people's opinions of the "militia movement" of antigovernment activists, even though McVeigh represents only one member of that group.

SOME INFORMATION ATTRACTS MORE ATTENTION THAN OTHER INFORMATION. Even if a few extremes stand out, why do our impressions of groups remain unchanged when we encounter other group members whose appearance or actions are quite ordinary? The answer is that biases in processing lead us to form an association between unusual or distinctive characteristics and rare or infrequently encountered groups. These processes can operate even if we have no prior stereotype of a group, so they can generate a stereotype more or less out of thin air.

Suppose you move to a new city and discover that the residents there classify themselves as Eastsiders or Westsiders, but you have no idea what characteristics are associated with these categories. As you read the "Police Blotter" column in the local newspaper, you notice that more Eastsiders than Westsiders are mentioned. Most members of each group are named for innocent reasons, such as reporting a mysteriously broken car window or having a cat stranded in a tree, but about a third of each group are named as crime suspects. What impressions would you form of the two groups?

According to David Hamilton and Robert Gifford (1976), you might overestimate the incidence of crime among the Westsiders, the smaller group. Your overestimate would illustrate the creation of an *illusory correlation*, a perceived association between two characteristics that are not actually related. In a demonstration of the illusory correlation, Hamilton and Gifford asked participants to read a series of sentences, each describing a desirable or undesirable behavior performed by a member of Group A or Group B. For both groups, more desirable behaviors were reported than undesirable ones: The ratio was about two positive behaviors for every negative one. Overall, participants saw more sentences about Group A than about Group B. When participants were asked their impressions of the groups, they liked Group B less.

They had formed an illusory correlation by perceiving a link between the two relatively infrequent and distinctive characteristics: undesirable behavior, and membership in the group about which they had read less often.

What explains this surprising bias in our perceptions of groups? Researchers have found that when something occurs infrequently, it becomes distinctive and people pay attention to it. When one of the behavior descriptions involves two distinctive characteristics occurring *together*—a Group B member doing something antisocial—it really stands out. These behaviors may attract special attention when people encounter them (D. L. Hamilton & Sherman, 1989). Or they may have a disproportionate impact when people combine what they know into judgments about the groups (E. R. Smith, 1991). Either way, these doubly distinctive behaviors have the greatest impact on the impressions we form of groups.

Could these processes contribute to the formation of stereotypes outside the laboratory? They could, particularly when people have only limited encounters with members of a group that is numerically small or segregated. Even if criminal acts are equally rare among members of a large group and those of a small group, observers may form an illusory correlation, judging the small group to be more criminal than the larger group. Remember the Californians' stereotypes of the unfortunate Armenians? Though only a small proportion of that minority group was involved in crime, observers tended to see Armenians as constantly running afoul of the law.

SOCIAL ROLES TRIGGER CORRESPONDENCE BIASES. Regardless of how often we encounter a group, what we see the group doing has a big impact on our impressions. Yet even this kind of firsthand observation can lead to biased stereotypes when a group's social role shapes the behavior that can be observed. Consider a new stereotype that the citizens of Moscow seem to have developed recently. In increasing numbers, farmers from the sunny lands of Azerbaijan, Georgia, Dagestan, and other regions of the Caucasus are setting up stalls in major Russian cities to sell fresh fruits, vegetables, chickens, and other goods that are scarce or unavailable in ordinary food stores. But far from welcoming this new source of food, Russians are turning against the Caucasians, resentful of their apparent prosperity and the high prices they charge. Russians have overturned Caucasians' stalls in the markets and scrawled slogans like "Russia for the Russians" on walls. One Russian woman commented, "In my view, frankly, they deserve to get beaten up. These southerners are so brazen that it gets to the point where an average Russian man can't take it anymore" (Bohlen, 1992).

This upsurge in prejudice based on stereotypes of the Caucasians as brazen and dishonest may involve social roles. Most Russians interact with Caucasians only in their role of produce vendor, and the Caucasians' behavior is constrained by that occupational role. Because the Russians remain largely oblivious to the effects that the role has on the farmers' behavior, they form a stereotype that reflects the characteristics of the role. Of course, Russian vegetable buyers are not unique in this regard. Most of us form our impressions of doctors by watching a doctor care for us or for a loved one, or of ministers or rabbis by watching one perform a religious ceremony. Our stereotypes of particular groups typically reflect the social roles occupied by those groups (D. T. Campbell, 1967; Eagly, 1987). Consider the following facts.

- In the Middle Ages, money handling was one of very few occupations open to Jews, who soon came to be seen as excelling in this occupation for reasons of personality, that is, because they were inherently "sharp" and "frugal." These same traits have been attributed to many other groups: the Chinese in Indonesia and Malaysia, Muslim merchants in eastern and southern Africa, Korean merchants in Black neighborhoods in the United States, and now produce sellers from the Caucasus in Russia. What do these wildly diverse groups have in common? They all fill the same "middleman" economic niche in their societies (Pettigrew, 1968). Apparently the role produces the assumed personality characteristics, rather than the other way around.

- In virtually every society, socioeconomically disadvantaged groups, regardless of their ethnicity, are seen as ignorant, lazy, loud, dirty, and carefree. In the United States this stereotype has been applied to a number of groups in the last century: first to poor Irish immigrants, then to the first wave of Italian immigrants, and more recently to Puerto Rican and Mexican Americans (Pettigrew, 1968; L. Ross & Nisbett, 1990). As the economic position of a group rises, stereotypes about them change and, like hand-me-down clothing, the lower-class stereotype is passed on to some new and less fortunate group.

- Stereotypes adapt rapidly as a group's roles change. Such changes are especially obvious in times of war or hardship, as we shall see in chapter 14. As peace is replaced by war, the Germans become "Huns" and the Japanese "Japs." And as war is replaced by peace, German ruthlessness becomes German efficiency, and Japanese cunning becomes Japanese ingenuity.

FIGURE 5.1   Social roles shape stereotypes

Social, cultural, economic, political, and historical factors create social roles.

↓

Social roles are assigned to groups.
Caucasian farmers sell produce in Russian cities.

↓

Group members perform role-appropriate behaviors.
Farmers charge as much as they can, and some become prosperous.

↓

Through correspondence bias, role-associated behaviors are attributed to personality characteristics.
These farmers are greedy and flashy people.

↓

Stereotype of group forms.
Caucasians are by nature greedy and flashy.

■ The roles allocated to a particular group influence group members' behavior. Based on that behavior, observers are likely to be influenced by the correspondence bias—ignoring the effects of the roles and attributing the behavior to the group members' personality characteristics. These characteristics then become part of the stereotype of the group.

How and why people fall prey to the correspondence bias when making inferences was discussed in chapter 3, pages 74 to 76.

As all these facts suggest, stereotypes do not reflect what groups are actually like. Instead, they reflect the roles groups play in society relative to the perceiver. The correspondence bias leads people to see behavior as reflecting others' inner dispositions, even if roles or situational contingencies truly cause the behavior. As can be seen in Figure 5.1, the outcome is the formation of a stereotype.

SOCIAL ROLES AND GENDER STEREOTYPES. Males' and females' differing social roles also contribute to gender stereotypes (Eagly, 1987). (Look back at Table 5.1 for some examples.) The process works like this: Virtually all societies assign men and women to somewhat different roles and occupations. In Western cultures, men are more often employed outside the home, while women are more likely to be responsible for home and family. Employee roles demand the kinds of traits—task-orientation, assertiveness, rationality—that characterize the traditional male stereotype. In contrast, the role of homemaker requires those qualities—sensitivity, warmth, gentleness—that characterize the female stereotype (Eagly & Steffen, 1984). Thus, if men and women tend to act in ways that are appropriate for their roles, observers who note those differences and fail to make allowances for the effects of roles may conclude that men are *by nature* task oriented, and women interpersonally oriented.

A clever laboratory study by Curt Hoffman and Nancy Hurst (1990) demonstrated this process. Students read descriptions of fictitious groups of "Orinthians" and "Ackmians" who supposedly inhabit a distant planet. Most Orinthians were described as involved in child care, whereas Ackmians were mainly employed outside the home. All child-care workers (regardless of group membership) were described as typically nurturant, affectionate, and gentle, and all employees as typically competitive and ambitious. However, participants asked to guess these creatures' typical psychological characteristics attached traits to the groups rather than to the roles, and assumed that Orinthians (not child-care workers) were nurturant and Ackmians (not employees) were competitive (see Figure 5.2). That is, each group was seen as having psychological characteristics appropriate for the group's typical role. Once the stereotype was formed, participants applied it even to individual group members whose occupations clashed with the stereotype: they saw an employed Ackmian as more competitive and ambitious than an employed Orinthian. This finding suggests that the different typical social roles of men and women contribute to shaping earthly gender stereotypes. The effect is not inevitable, however. Mark Schaller and his colleagues (Schaller, Asp, Rosell, & Heim, 1996) found that people can be trained to avoid these inferential errors.

INTERACTIONS AND EMOTION. Roles are not the only things that shape and constrain people's interactions. Whenever people move outside their own group, they enter unknown social territory. This happens, for example, when people travel to a foreign country, rise from the blue-collar ranks to middle management, or encounter ethnic newcomers in their neighborhoods. Feelings of uncertainty and concern often arise when people interact with novel groups, and these feelings can influence the stereotypes people form.

Dutch adults described just these feelings when asked about their everyday dealings with Surinamers, Turks, and Moroccans, groups that recently have immigrated in large numbers to the Netherlands (Dijker, 1987).

FIGURE 5.2   Roles and stereotypes on a distant planet

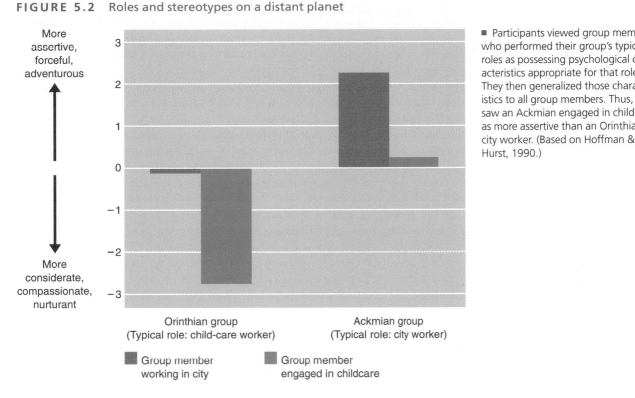

More assertive, forceful, adventurous

More considerate, compassionate, nurturant

Orinthian group
(Typical role: child-care worker)

Ackmian group
(Typical role: city worker)

Group member working in city

Group member engaged in childcare

■ Participants viewed group members who performed their group's typical roles as possessing psychological characteristics appropriate for that role. They then generalized those characteristics to all group members. Thus, they saw an Ackmian engaged in child care as more assertive than an Orinthian city worker. (Based on Hoffman & Hurst, 1990.)

According to the respondents, interactions with these groups produced anxiety, and the interactions with Moroccans and Turks—the groups culturally most different from the native-born Dutch—also provoked feelings of irritation. North American college students responded the same way when asked to imagine what emotions they might experience in a casual conversation with someone of a different race (Vanman & Miller, 1993). The most frequently reported emotion was irritation, followed closely by dislike, apprehension, and anxiety. Other research shows that the presence of another man they know to be homosexual can make heterosexual men nervous and uncomfortable (L. A. Jackson & Sullivan, 1989).

Why are interactions across group lines so often tinged with arousal and anxiety? In intergroup interactions, ignorance is not bliss. For example, Walter Stephan and Cookie Stephan (1985) found that the less Asian Americans and Whites in Hawaii knew about each other's groups, the more anxious and irritated they felt when they met. The same researchers obtained similar results when they investigated interactions between Latinos and Whites in New Mexico. Not knowing what to do or say and not knowing how another person will react usually creates awkwardness, frustration, and impatience. Yet, with only 51% of Whites working with members of other races and only 47% socializing with members of other races outside of work, ignorance and unfamiliarity continue to be the rule ("Opinion Watch," 1991).

When even relatively benign cross-group interactions cause anxiety and irritation, imagine the strength of emotion that is generated when groups

More of the factors that increase the emotional intensity of prejudice become obvious in chapter 6, pages 224 to 227, and chapter 13, pages 532 to 535.

threaten one another, compete for scarce resources, and violate one another's values (Tyler & Smith, 1998). Under these circumstances, powerful emotions become associated with group encounters, and anxiety, irritation, and awkwardness are soon overwhelmed by fear, anger, frustration, and revulsion. The emotions provoked by uncomfortable intergroup encounters then become an integral part of a stereotype (E. R. Smith, 1993; E. R. Smith & Ho, 1999). When group interaction is repeatedly accompanied by negative emotion, bad feelings are soon transferred to the group itself through the process of classical conditioning. *Classical conditioning* occurs when a person or object that has been repeatedly paired with a particular emotion begins itself to elicit the emotion. After several uncomfortable interactions, the emotions arising from the encounter become associated with the group, so that seeing group members, hearing the group mentioned, or even thinking about the group will itself reactivate the emotion. An individual who repeatedly experiences disgust, fear, or hatred in interactions with group members eventually will view the group as *intrinsically* disgusting, threatening, or loathsome.

Of course, being ill at ease is hardly the majority's prerogative. On the contrary, finding oneself on alien social territory is both a more common and a more negative experience for minority group members than for majority group members (Lord & Saenz, 1985). Anyone stands out in such circumstances, and the smaller the minority, the more its members stand out (Mullen, 1987), and therefore the greater their discomfort.

One potential benefit of school desegregation is that it provides an increased range of informal contexts in which members of different groups can meet with ease. Unfortunately, however, desegregated classrooms often empty out into resegregated cafeterias and playgrounds, where members of the same group congregate to the exclusion of others (Schofield, 1978). Perhaps one reason for this voluntary self-segregation is people's desire to minimize the discomfort of being in different social surroundings: Being constantly on one's guard can take its toll. In recent years, historically Black colleges have experienced a surge in applications from Black students, including many of the nation's very best students who could attend any college they chose (Radin, 1992). The main reason seems to be the students' desire *not* to stand out as different, to be able to relax and focus on studies in an emotionally supportive environment.

Forming Stereotypes Through Social Learning

Social learning contributes to stereotypes. Stereotypes and discriminatory behavior are often accepted and endorsed as right and proper by members of a particular group. Group members learn such stereotypes from family, friends, and the media.

Personal encounters are not the only way we form impressions of groups. In the United States, for example, many people believe from the bottom of their hearts that welfare recipients often drive Cadillacs. Most have never actually seen this phenomenon, but they just know that it is true. Examples like this suggest that stereotypes do not always depend on direct experience. They often come ready-made and prepackaged, and we learn them in particular social, economic, cultural, religious, and political contexts (Stangor & Schaller, 1996).

LEARNING STEREOTYPES FROM OTHERS. Parents, teachers, and peers offer us our first lessons about group differences. By age five, for example, most children have begun to develop clear-cut racial attitudes (Goodman, 1952; Rosenfield & Stephan, 1981). Parents and teachers do not have to teach hate explicitly, although they sometimes do. Children can pick up stereotypes and prejudice simply by observing and imitating their elders: listening to disparaging group labels or derogatory jokes that elicit approving laughter, following family rules against playing with those "other" children. With experiences like this, no wonder that young children's ideas about racial groups are highly similar to those of their parents and friends (Epstein & Komorita, 1966; Patchen, Davidson, Hofmann, & Brown, 1977; W. G. Stephan & Rosenfield, 1978).

Parents' and teachers' words and deeds reflect **social norms**, generally accepted ways of thinking, feeling, or behaving that people in a group agree on and endorse as right and proper (Thibaut & Kelley, 1959a). When stereotypes and prejudices are deeply embedded in the social norms of a culture, people learn them naturally as a part of growing up. In fact, those who adhere most closely to their culture's social norms also show the most prejudice (Pettigrew, 1958). A study of White U.S. soldiers during the Second World War, a time when military units were racially segregated, underscores the extent to which social norms can underlie prejudice. Asked whether their units should remain segregated, about 80% said yes, reflecting the current popular view. In contrast, fewer than half said they had personal objections to working in the same unit with Black soldiers (Stouffer et al., 1949). Thus, nearly 40% who had no personal objections to working side-by-side with Blacks unquestioningly accepted the prejudiced norms. The power of norms is probably one reason that when President Harry S Truman's postwar desegregation of the U.S. armed forces reversed the norm, the change was accomplished relatively easily.

LEARNING STEREOTYPES FROM THE MEDIA. The expression of group norms in art, literature, drama, and film reflects and thus reinforces the stereotypes deeply ingrained in a culture. This pattern is found in today's rap music and other forms of confrontational art (Nields, 1991), but it also occurred in William Shakespeare's plays, written over 350 years ago. Othello is called "thick lips" because he is Black. Shylock is spat on because he is a Jew. Lady Macbeth wishes to be unsexed because women are weak. Richard III attributes his evil to his physical deformity, and King Lear is reviled because he is old.

Today's cultural medium of choice is television, of course. On an average day, North American children watch 3 hours of television, and during those hours children receive a mixed message. Prime-time entertainment television has, for example, reversed the traditional invisibility of people of color. *The Cosby Show*, which portrayed the family life of a Black doctor and lawyer and their children, ranked as the most popular show in the United States for more than 5 years. However, news and documentary programs send different messages. One study of Philadelphia local TV news found that in comparison to actual crime statistics, Blacks are overrepresented as crime suspects while Whites are more often portrayed as crime victims (Romer, Jamieson, & de Coteau, 1998). Media portrayals generally follow common stereotypes in depicting Blacks as poor (Gilens, 1996). And Blacks

■ **Learning stereotypes from those you love.** Children can learn stereotypes and prejudice by imitating those they trust and by conforming to the norms of the groups they belong to. This can happen long before they understand the consequences of such beliefs.

How norms form, and why we generally go along with our group's norms, are considered in detail in chapters 9 and 10.

Social norms. Generally accepted ways of thinking, feeling, or behaving that people in a group agree on and endorse as right and proper.

remain nearly invisible in major national magazine ads, although they make up 11% of all magazine readers. One study of advertisements appearing in 27 national magazines between 1988 and 1991 found that only about 3% of the models were Black, and most of those were depicted as athletes, musicians, or objects of charity (Rothenberg, 1991).

Media portrayals of other groups are no better. The elderly are generally depicted in highly stereotypic terms as frail, unattractive, and useless (A. Williams & Giles, 1998). Asian Americans appear frequently in television ads (in over 8% of commercials, compared to their 3.6% of the U.S. population), but are usually cast in stereotypic ways. Consistent with the "work ethic" stereotype, Asian Americans are generally portrayed in business settings and only rarely in home or family settings (C. R. Taylor & Stern, 1997). Differences between Chinese, Japanese, and Koreans are minimized or ignored. Latinos fare equally poorly. Though they constitute 9% of the U.S. population, they were only 1% of characters portrayed in the 1992 TV season, and of these characters, 16% committed crimes, twice the percentage of other groups ("Study Shows," 1994). All in all, media stereotyping and underrepresentation send a strongly biased message (Rothenberg, 1991).

☐ **GENDER STEREOTYPES AND THE MEDIA**. Media messages about women can be summed up in a single word: *contradictory*. On the one hand, television programming increasingly has portrayed women in realistic or counter-stereotypic roles. Popular dramatic and comedy series often feature strong female characters who are competent, assertive, independent, and successful in their careers. However, during the commercial breaks a different type of message comes through. Analyses of French-language television ads in Quebec and radio ads in Australia replicate findings from the U.S.: Commercials typically reinforce gender stereotypes (Dalcourt, 1996; Hurtz & Durkin, 1997). For example, male voice-overs predominate when the voice of an "expert" is required. Men and women generally sell gender-stereotypic products: Men sell lawnmowers and computers, women sell shoes and toilet bowl cleaners. And even more than ads, children's cartoons represent the pinnacle of gender stereotypes. In the United States (T. L. Thompson & Zerbinos, 1995) and Hong Kong (Chu & McIntyre, 1995), cartoons consistently show boys as active, rough, and often violent, while girls are shown as home-oriented, concerned with their appearance, and interested in boys.

Not all media images are as blatant as the eager woman receiving instructions on how to clean the toilet bowl or the male superhero rescuing the helpless woman. Some images reinforce gender stereotypes in more subtle ways. After inspecting thousands of photographs appearing in news magazines in 12 different countries, Dane Archer and his colleagues (D. Archer, Iratani, Kimes, & Barrios, 1983) reported that men's faces were much more likely to be portrayed prominently than were women's faces. A similar bias was found in women's magazines such as *Ms.* and *Good Housekeeping* (Nigra, Hill, Gelbein, & Clark, 1988). One possible explanation for this curious difference is that it flows from a cultural concern with women's whole bodies. Women's bodies are more likely to be shown than are men's, reducing the relative prominence of their faces in photographs. Another possible factor is the traditional stereotype of the male as thoughtful and rational, traits often symbolized by shots of the head. Regardless of the reason, the bias in portrayals has a subtle effect on perceptions. When Archer asked people to evaluate photos, they judged both male and female models with visually prominent heads and faces to be more intelligent and ambitious (D. Archer and others, 1983).

Do such portrayals matter? Experimental studies suggest that the answer is yes. Florence Geis and her colleagues (Geis, Brown, Jennings, & Porter, 1984; Jennings, Geis, & Brown, 1980) showed college women one of two sets of television commercials. One set depicted men and women in traditional roles, with the woman playing an alluring and subordinate role. In the other set the roles were reversed, with the man shown as subordinate and seductive. The young women who watched the traditional commercials later expressed lower self-confidence, less independence, and fewer career aspirations than did those who watched the nontraditional commercials. Meta-analyses summarizing many studies support the conclusion that media content increases viewers' acceptance of gender stereotypes (Herrett-Skjellum & Allen, 1996). If media portrayals can subtly influence viewers' thinking about themselves as men and women, it is undoubtedly true that they can similarly affect our thinking about members of other groups as well.

Forming Stereotypes That Justify Inequalities

The stereotypes prevalent in a society often serve to justify existing social inequalities. They do so by portraying groups as deserving their social roles and positions on the basis of their own characteristics.

We have seen that people develop stereotypes as they interact with members of other groups and as they learn the beliefs and norms prevalent in their own group. These two sources of information usually work together to reinforce each other and, ultimately, to reinforce the perception that members of different groups are naturally suited for the roles they play. Most cultures, for example, assign nurturing roles to women, so perceivers see women as "naturally" nurturing. As we have seen, this perception reflects the correspondence bias: People fail to realize that women's roles demand nurturing behaviors, and so they attribute the behaviors to women's personalities (Eagly, 1987). The stereotype that women are "naturally" suited to nurturing is further strengthened as people learn what society teaches about women. This stereotype soon becomes the basis for an inference with even more serious consequences. The belief that women have the right stuff to care for others then becomes a justification for retaining them in that role: They have the perfect qualifications. Most stereotypes, like this example, justify groups' existing places and roles in society as right, natural, and inevitable (Jost & Banaji, 1993; Yzerbyt, Rocher, & Schadron, 1997).

Every society maintains inequalities that benefit some groups and hurt others. Sunni Muslims rule Iraq and deny power to their more numerous Shi'ite counterparts. In Taiwan, people from mainland China who fled the Communists in 1949 still dominate native Taiwanese. Gaps in income and opportunity between men and women and between most Whites and people of color persist in the United States. As stereotypes reflecting these differences have developed, they have justified and rationalized the underlying inequalities (Pettigrew, 1980). Historically, women and people of color have often been viewed in ways that justified their treatment as childlike, unintelligent, and weak, and thus in need of direction and guidance (Hacker, 1951).

Why do we slide so quickly down the slope from behavior to stereotype to justification of inequality? One reason may be the widespread belief that the world is just and that people therefore deserve what they get and get what they deserve. This *just-world belief* (Lerner, 1980) leads people to blame victims for their misfortunes. This effect was demonstrated by one study in which students watched a woman apparently receive painful electric shocks (Lerner & Simmons, 1966). Did they react with sympathy toward this unfortunate victim? On the contrary, most derogated the victim, concluding that she must have done something to deserve her suffering. Rape victims, victims of spouse abuse, and people with AIDS often suffer the same fate (Carli & Leonard, 1989; Hunter & Ross, 1991), as do those whose social roles confine them to subordinate positions. It is no surprise, then, that people who believe more strongly that the world is just also tend to be prejudiced against gays and other groups (Crandall & Cohen, 1994). Believing that groups' positions in society are somehow deserved, fitting, or justified lets us off the hook morally, as Martin Luther King (1967) observed so astutely:

> It seems to be a fact of life that human beings cannot continue to do wrong without eventually reaching out for some rationalization to clothe their acts in the garments of righteousness. And so, with the growth of slavery, men had to convince themselves that a system which was so economically profitable was morally justifiable. The attempt to give moral sanction to a profitable system gave birth to the doctrine of white supremacy. (p. 72)

Blaming victims is a way to maintain our view of the world as understandable and controllable and of ourselves as good and deserving. It is comforting to believe that bad things happen only to bad people: that AIDS is a punishment for taking drugs or for a gay lifestyle, or that poor people are lazy and shiftless (Furnham & Gunter, 1984; R. Robinson & Bell, 1978). Indeed, two thirds of White Americans believe that the reason Blacks generally have worse jobs, lower incomes, and poorer quality housing than Whites is that they lack the motivation to do better (Kluegel & Smith, 1986). Without beliefs that justify and rationalize inequalities, we would have to face the unsettling thought that bad things could easily happen to us.

Trait by trait, emotion by emotion, our personal experiences and the teachings of others help us construct a coherent impression of the social groups around us. As you can see in Figure 5.3, the information we weave together is a product both of our own personal interactions and of the influence of others. If group impressions were nothing more than neutral descriptions, it would be hard to imagine them provoking prejudice and discrimination. But the content of stereotypes is far from neutral. When we think of men as aggressive, of immigrants as cliquish, or of Scots as thrifty, those terms have evaluative implications, whether positive or negative, mild or extreme. Moreover, stereotypes often incorporate emotions we associate with groups. We see some groups not only as hostile, stubborn, aggressive, and deviant but also as frightening, frustrating, threatening, and repulsive. Once stereotypes are firmly established, they take on a life of their own, provoking prejudiced judgments and directing discriminatory behavior.

FIGURE 5.3   Multiple sources of stereotypes

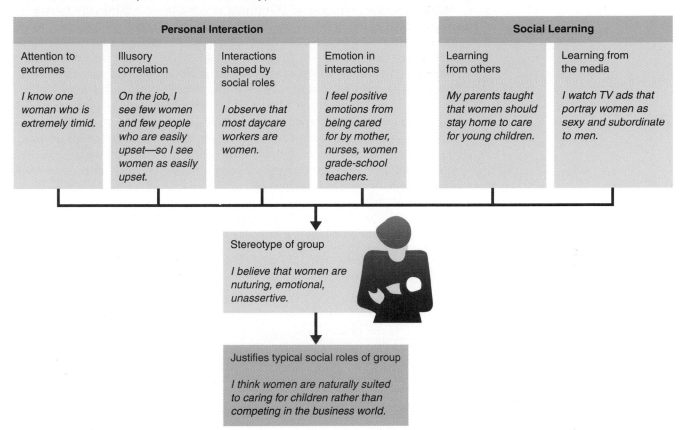

Personal Interaction				Social Learning	
Attention to extremes *I know one woman who is extremely timid.*	**Illusory correlation** *On the job, I see few women and few people who are easily upset—so I see women as easily upset.*	**Interactions shaped by social roles** *I observe that most daycare workers are women.*	**Emotion in interactions** *I feel positive emotions from being cared for by mother, nurses, women grade-school teachers.*	**Learning from others** *My parents taught that women should stay home to care for young children.*	**Learning from the media** *I watch TV ads that portray women as sexy and subordinate to men.*

Stereotype of group

I believe that women are nuturing, emotional, unassertive.

Justifies typical social roles of group

I think women are naturally suited to caring for children rather than competing in the business world.

■ People's impressions of groups are formed by their personal interactions with group members and by what they learn from others. Multiple sources of information often converge to support a stereotype that justifies the social roles typically held by group members.

Using Stereotypes:
From Preconceptions to Prejudice

Stephen Carter, a professor at Yale Law School who is Black, described the following encounter at a conference.

> *A dapper, buttoned-down young white man glanced at my name tag, evidently ignored the name but noted the school, and said, "If you're at Yale, you must know this Carter fellow who wrote that article about thus-and-so." Well, yes, I admitted. I did know that Carter fellow slightly. An awkward pause ensued. And then the young man, realizing his error, apologized. . . . "Oh," he said, "you're Carter."* (Carter, 1991, p. 56)

The young man's assumptions about race and academic excellence had been embarrassingly revealed. As Carter notes, "Since this young man liked the article, its author could not, in his initial evaluation, have been a person of color. He had not even conceived of that possibility, or he would have glanced twice at my name tag" (p. 57).

Once a stereotype exists, it influences what people think and how they behave toward members of stereotyped groups. In fact, stereotype effects are so pervasive that they can even affect our judgments of inanimate objects! When computers are programmed to "talk" with synthesized male voices, people take their evaluations more seriously than if they use female voices; on matters related to relationships, people prefer advice given by a computer in a female voice. This is true even when people are specifically told that a male programmer created the software in the first place (Reeves & Nass, 1995). Stereotypes can have this impact whether we are making snap judgments of others quickly and with minimal thought—like the young man at the conference—or making considered judgments involving extensive processing of information.

Activation of Stereotypes and Effects on Judgment

Once established, a stereotype can be activated by obvious cues, use of group labels, or the presence of a group member, especially a minority in a social situation. Some stereotypes are learned so well and used so often that their content comes to mind automatically. When a stereotype is activated, it often causes us to treat people as interchangeable members of their group rather than as individuals.

A stereotype can influence judgments or actions only if it comes to mind. Does this happen frequently? You bet it does! The very first thing we notice about other people is often their group memberships, and once a category is activated, the associated stereotype comes to mind as well. In fact, some categories seem so important that we use them to classify people even when they appear irrelevant to the social context. Consider the first thing most people ask the parents of a newborn: Is it a girl or a boy? Regardless of the social context, perceivers almost always note general categories like gender, race, and age (Brewer, 1988; Stangor, Lynch, Duan, & Glass, 1992).

WHAT ACTIVATES STEREOTYPES? The more obvious and salient the cues to category membership, the more likely it is that the category and its related stereotypes will come to mind. Indeed, women with a highly feminine physical appearance and dress are perceived as also having highly feminine natures (Deaux & Lewis, 1984; Forsyth, Schlenker, Leary, & McCown, 1985). The deliberate use of pejorative group labels, national nicknames, or ethnic slurs can bring stereotypes to a listener's mind at once (Greenberg & Pyszczynski, 1985).

A category often becomes particularly salient when only a single member of the group is present. Consider an increasingly common occurrence: A woman is hired as a member of a previously all-male work crew, or a single Latino student joins a class or seminar. Because of their salience, such solo appearances draw much more attention, and the extra attention usually leads to particularly stereotypic perceptions. A solo male seems more masculine and a solo female more feminine than they would in a more evenly split group (S. E. Taylor, 1981; S. E. Taylor, Fiske, Etcoff, & Ruderman, 1978). Field studies in work organizations have recorded the same effects (Kanter, 1977). "Token" integration of a workplace or other social setting—admitting a single member of a previously excluded group—can thus increase the likelihood of stereotyped thinking rather than decrease it.

STEREOTYPES CAN BE ACTIVATED AUTOMATICALLY. If reminders of group membership surround us, the ease with which race, gender, age, and role categories come to mind can set off a vicious cycle. The more often a category is used, the more accessible it becomes; the more accessible it is, the more it is used (Higgins, 1996a; Stangor and others, 1992). In fact, a stereotype sometimes becomes so well learned and so often used that its activation becomes automatic. Cues that relate to group membership can bring stereotypic information to mind, even if the perceiver does not consciously notice the group membership at all!

One recent study by Lorella Lepore and Rupert Brown (1997) supports the view that stereotypes can be automatically activated. Using British university students as participants, the researchers presented the words *Blacks, reggae, dreadlocks,* and other words associated with Black people in Britain. These words appeared on a computer screen in extremely brief flashes, so brief that participants could not consciously read them or even tell that words were being flashed at all. For other participants, only nonsense letter strings appeared on the screen. Next, each participant read a description of a

■ **Stereotypes at work.** This model's "hardened criminal" appearance is calculated to activate stereotype-consistent information. If "fear" makes our need for "maximum protection" salient and inspires us to head for the hardware store, the advertisement will have achieved its goal.

In chapter 3, page 71, we described evidence that words that could not be consciously read nevertheless could bring related beliefs to mind, without the perceiver's awareness.

person that was ambiguously related to traits included in the British Black stereotype, such as athletic and aggressive. Finally, the participants rated this person on these stereotypic traits, as well as other traits. Results showed that participants who had been primed with words related to Blacks rated the person in more stereotypic fashion. This effect was stronger for those who had been identified (by a separate questionnaire) as relatively high in anti-Black prejudice.

These results show that the group labels presented as primes activate group stereotypes among highly prejudiced participants, making them more likely to see ambiguous behaviors as related to the stereotypic traits. The automatic nature of this stereotype activation is demonstrated by the occurrence of the effect when the participants could not consciously read the prime words. Wittenbrink, Judd, and Park (1997) reported similar findings using American participants and words related to the stereotype of Blacks in the United States. However, everyone may not experience automatic stereotype activation to an equal extent. Like Lepore and Brown (1997), Wittenbrink and his colleagues found automatic stereotype activation to be stronger among participants who were revealed by standard pencil-and-paper measures to be more highly prejudiced against Blacks.

FEELINGS ABOUT GROUPS CAN BE ACTIVATED AUTOMATICALLY. Can general positive or negative feelings about a group, as well as the specific trait information contained in stereotypes, also be activated automatically? One approach to this question involves physiological measurement (Cacioppo, Petty, Losch, & Kim, 1986). Facial electromyography (EMG) measures electrical activity in the facial muscles that create expressions such as smiles or frowns, as shown in Figure 5.4. Electrical activity can be measured even when changes in facial expressions are not visible, and evidence suggests that these measurements can accurately assess people's automatically activated positive or negative feelings about social groups (Vanman, Paul, Ito, & Miller, 1997). However, this approach requires specialized equipment, a carefully controlled environment, and extremely cooperative research participants.

In another recently developed approach, Russell Fazio and his colleagues (Fazio, Jackson, Dunton, & Williams, 1995) use a priming technique in which participants see images of Black or White faces on a computer screen, followed by positive or negative words (like *sunshine* or *disease*). Their task is simply to press one of two keys as rapidly as possible to indicate whether the word is positive or negative. For most participants, responses to positive words are

FIGURE 5.4   Facial electromyography (EMG): An indirect measure of attitudes

■ When people react positively to an attitude object, activity in the zygomatic muscles increases, whereas negative responses are accompanied by increased activity in the corrugator muscles. Although this activity cannot be observed with the naked eye, it can be measured by electrodes placed at the indicated positions. (Adapted from Petty & Cacioppo, 1986, p. 42.)

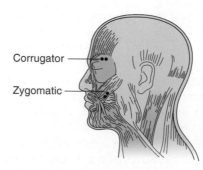

Corrugator

Zygomatic

FIGURE 5.5 The Implicit Association Test

Sequence	Task Name Instructions: For specific type of stimulus, press left or right response button	Examples of stimuli and correct responses
1	**Black-White Names** Black name - Left White name - Right	Meredith - Right Tashika - Left Betsy - Right
2	**Pleasant-Unpleasant Words** Pleasant word - Left Unpleasant word - Right	poison - Right gift - Left disaster - Right
3	**Initial Combined Task** Black name or pleasant word - Left White name or unpleasant word - Right	Peggy - Right evil - Right Ebony - Left miracle - Left
4	**Reversed Black-White Names** Black name - Right White name - Left	Courtney - Left Shereen - Right Tia - Right
5	**Reversed Combined Task** Black name or unpleasant word - Left White name or pleasant word - Right	peace - Left Latisha - Right filth - Right Nancy - Left

■ The Implicit Association Test (IAT; Greenwald, McGhee, & Schwartz, 1998) involves a series of tasks, performed in the indicated order. Each task involves making a response by pressing one of two buttons (labeled Left and Right in this figure) for each of a number of names or words presented on a computer screen. The computer records how long it takes to complete a fixed number of trials of each task. This figure shows the use of the IAT to measure people's evaluations of Blacks versus Whites as an example, but the same approach can be adapted to measure evaluations of any two groups.

The first two tasks (sequence numbers 1 and 2) are quite easy, and participants are able to respond rapidly. When responses to both names and words are required (as in the combined tasks 3 and 5), however, performance may be easy or difficult, depending on the way the responses go together. For most White participants, the combination shown as sequence number 3 (where Black names and pleasant words require the same response) is much more difficult than the combination in sequence number 5 (where White names and pleasant words are given the same response). By measuring how much longer it takes participants to complete the more difficult combination task compared to the other one, researchers are able to assess how strongly the participants associate the Black category with negative evaluations and the White category with positive ones. It is very difficult, if not impossible, for participants to intentionally alter their patterns of responses in order to conceal their evaluations of the categories.

To read more about the Implicit Association Test or to try it for yourself, visit the IAT website, http://depts.washington.edu/iat/

faster following a White person's face, and responses to negative words are faster following a Black face (Fazio and others, 1995). The magnitude of this difference serves as a measure of the individual's relative evaluation of Blacks and Whites, which is very difficult if not impossible for the person to control or conceal. Another technique, the Implicit Association Test (IAT), also measures people's automatic associations of social groups with positive or negative evaluations (Greenwald, McGhee, & Schwartz, 1998). The IAT is described in Figure 5.5.

Interestingly, these measures of people's automatic evaluations of groups, in contrast to the priming measures of the automatic activation of stereotype

■ **Impact of stereotypes on judgments.** It's situations like this that illustrate just how wrong we might be if stereotypes bias our judgments. If you judged Manon Rheaume, shown in this picture suiting up to play for the Tampa Bay Lightning professional hockey team, according to the stereotype usually associated with women (see p. 165), you might be in for a shock!

traits, are generally unrelated to questionnaire measures of prejudice. So it is not necessarily the most overtly biased people who have the strongest automatic negative reactions to a group. As we will see shortly, this pattern does not always mean that people's overt responses are dishonest, meant to hide their "true" but socially unacceptable negative feelings. Instead, many people genuinely reject stereotypes and prejudice and sincerely want to treat other groups equally—while still showing automatic activation of negative thoughts and feelings about those groups, perhaps as a long-lasting residue of lessons learned in childhood.

IMPACT OF STEREOTYPES ON JUDGMENTS. Once activated, stereotypes or feelings can serve as a basis for making judgments or guiding action toward a group. Thus, Fazio and others (1995) showed that participants with more readily activated negative feelings about Blacks behaved in a less friendly manner toward an experimental assistant who happened to be Black. A stereotype may even be the *only* consideration if the perceiver is processing superficially. Thus, individuals identified as group members may be seen as possessing all the features associated with the group, while their unique personal characteristics are overlooked (M. J. Rodin, 1987; Rothbart & John, 1985). Have you ever had an experience like this? As you sit down to dinner with friends at a restaurant, the waiter introduces himself, describes the specials, and passes out menus. He returns later to take the dinner orders and soon after delivers the meals. But if you later realize that you need extra silverware, you may be dismayed to find that you cannot identify your waiter. Having interacted with him only in terms of his "serving" qualities, you may have no idea what he actually looks like.

This embarrassing experience can occur because a focus on one group membership (whether an occupational, racial, or gender group) causes us to ignore other, competing group memberships (Macrae, Bodenhausen, Milne, & Jetten, 1994). As a result, all members of the group become just the same. Being treated as an anonymous, interchangeable group member is a common experience for victims of stereotyping and prejudice. Debbie Allen, the actress, once entered a Beverly Hills jewelry store but found that the clerk would not show her any merchandise, assuming that no Black could afford what the store had to sell. Virtually every woman professor or business manager can tell stories about being mistaken for the secretary; many a male Hispanic homeowner can recall times when he was out working in his yard, and passersby assumed he was the hired gardener.

Trying to Overcome Stereotype Effects

People may try to overcome the effects of stereotypes by suppressing stereotypic thoughts or correcting for their impact on judgments. However, both of these tactics require motivation and cognitive capacity, so they are unlikely to succeed if we are short of time or burdened by strong emotions.

Evidently, we are often in danger of making stereotypic snap judgments because common and well-learned stereotypes can be activated automatically. If the content of stereotypes comes to mind unbidden, and can influence our thoughts, feelings, and behaviors every time we encounter a group member, can people do anything to overcome stereotype effects?

The answer seems to be yes. Even though negative stereotypic infor mation may be activated whenever a particular category comes to mind— at the mere sight or sound of a group member—negative judgments about the group or its members are not inevitable. The activation of a category brings certain information to mind, but we do not have to rely on this information alone. Instead, people can make conscious efforts to avoid thinking of stereotypes, or to revise and correct any judgments that they suspect may have been influenced by stereotypes (Devine, 1989).

SUPPRESSING STEREOTYPIC THOUGHTS. Think back to the last time you had a conversation with a member of a group about which you had well-learned negative stereotypes. Naturally, during the conversation you probably worked hard to avoid expressing any stereotypic thoughts or feelings. However, your well-intentioned efforts at suppressing the stereotype might have had negative results later! This conclusion rests on fascinating research by Neil Macrae and his colleagues (1994). The British students who participated in this study were shown a photograph of a skinhead, a member of a social group linked to extremely negative stereotypes, and were asked to write a paragraph about a day in this person's life. Half were told to avoid using any stereotypes or preconceptions, while the other half were not given any special instructions. Those who were told to suppress the stereotype clearly were able to do so: Their paragraphs were less stereotypic than those written by the other participants. Next, the participants were told that they would meet the skinhead in person, and were taken into another room where a coat and other items (evidently belonging to the skinhead) were draped over a chair, making it appear that he had left the room momentarily. Participants selected a seat for themselves, and the distance from the skinhead's supposed seat was measured. Those who had earlier suppressed the negative skinhead stereotype now chose to sit farther away from the skinhead!

Other studies found similar results when people suppressed stereotypes on their own because they believed that using stereotypes was inappropriate, rather than because of an experimenter's instruction (Macrae, Bodenhausen, & Milne, 1998). Consistent with other research suggesting that once-suppressed thoughts often rebound and become even more accessible (Wegner, 1994), suppressing a stereotype may make its content more likely to influence our thoughts and feelings later. Thus suppression may not be the best approach to avoiding stereotype effects on our thoughts and judgments (Monteith, Sherman, & Devine, 1998).

CORRECTING STEREOTYPIC JUDGMENTS. A different approach involves correction rather than suppression. If we think that an unwanted stereotype may have influenced our thinking, we can try to correct for its effects, for example, by trying hard to be pleasant (Wegener & Petty, 1997). A generation ago Gordon Allport (1958) quoted two college students writing anonymously about their feelings about groups:

> *Intellectually, I am firmly convinced that this prejudice against Italians is unjustified. And in my present behavior to Italian friends I try to lean over backwards to counteract the attitude. But it is remarkable how strong a hold it has on me. (p. 310)*

These prejudices make me feel narrow-minded and intolerant and there-fore I try to be as pleasant as possible. I get so angry with myself for having such feelings, but somehow I do not seem to be able to quench them. (p. 311)

Patricia Devine (1989) argues that these quotations capture exactly what most nonprejudiced people do. She believes that virtually everyone is affected by the negative content of early learned and deeply ingrained racial stereotypes, but that some people try to overcome their insidious consequences by correcting their judgments. Thus, being unprejudiced may not mean never having stereotypic thoughts or feelings come to mind, but rather acknowledging them and making a conscious effort to avoid being influenced by them. Like trying to break any bad habit, this work is not easy, for it requires people to wrestle with inner conflicts between the negative stereotypes they have learned and the nonprejudiced views they also hold (I. Katz & Hass, 1988).

When well-intentioned people try to correct judgments that they suspect may have been affected by stereotypes, they may even make judgments of stereotyped group members that are overly positive. This outcome was observed in studies by Kent Harber (1998). In these studies, White college students read essays that were intentionally filled with major stylistic flaws and content errors, and gave feedback to the supposed essay writers. When the participants believed the writer was a Black student, the feedback was more positive and supportive than when the writer was believed to be White. In cases like this, people may alter their judgments to avoid appearing prejudiced—not only to others, but even more important, to themselves.

LESS CAPACITY, MORE STEREOTYPING. Unfortunately, we cannot always succeed even when we try to suppress or correct stereotypic judgments. Like any thorough, detailed processing of available information, overcoming the effects of stereotypes requires opportunity as well as motivation (S. T. Fiske & Neuberg, 1990). As we have seen before, stereotyping is often easy, but processing people's unique individual characteristics or correcting our judgments takes more effort. Therefore conditions that drain people's cognitive capacity make it more likely that unwanted stereotypes will affect their judgments.

For example, people who must make quick decisions about others are more likely to rely on stereotypes than are those who can take their time (Freund, Kruglanski, & Shpitzajzen, 1985; Kruglanski & Freund, 1983). In one study, the less time people had, the more likely they were to rely on gender stereotypes in deciding among male and female job candidates (Bechtold, Naccarato, & Zanna, 1986). It's worth pondering the fact that police officers who must make snap judgments in life-threatening situations may base their decisions on the stereotypes that are most salient at that moment.

Lack of time is not the only factor that can limit our ability to correct for stereotypes. Sometimes information is just too complex to process adequately. Under such circumstances, people may rely on stereotypes as their best bet for making the judgments, even if they have plenty of time and the consequences of their decisions are important. In one mock jury trial, for example, participants role-playing jurors based their decisions on their unfavorable stereotypes of the Latino defendant when the information relevant to making the judgment was complex. They did not show stereotypic biases when the information was presented in a simpler way (Bodenhausen & Lichtenstein, 1987).

Almost anything that diminishes an individual's cognitive capacity can also increase the impact of stereotypes on judgment. Are you a morning person or a night person? In either case, you probably realize that at certain times of day your thinking is not at its best. Galen Bodenhausen (1990) wondered whether time of day could have an impact on stereotyping. He used a questionnaire to measure whether participants were "morning types" or "evening types" and then assigned them randomly to experimental sessions that met at 9 a.m., 3 p.m., or 8 p.m. Their task was to read several items of evidence about a fictitious character named either *Roberto Garcia* or *Robert Garner,* who was accused of assault. After reading the evidence, participants were asked about Garcia/Garner's guilt. When people were scheduled for their worst times, they were more prone to rely on their stereotypic expectations that Latinos are aggressive and to assert that the Latino individual had committed the crime (see Figure 5.6). So morning people: Beware of stereotyping others after lunch. And night people: Watch what you think in the morning!

MORE EMOTION, MORE STEREOTYPING. If the impact of stereotypes is magnified when decision making is difficult, what happens when emotions like anxiety, irritation, or anger cloud our judgment? If you suspect that stereotyping will get worse, you are right, as recent research shows (Mackie & Hamilton, 1993). By disrupting careful processing and short-circuiting attention, strong emotions increase our reliance on stereotypes (Dijker, 1987;

FIGURE 5.6 Stereotyping by the clock?

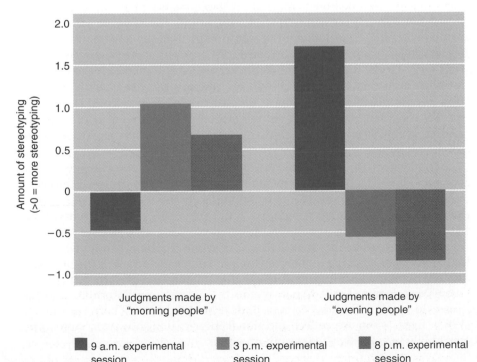

■ At people's nonpreferred times of day, they were more likely to fall back on ethnic stereotyping. For morning people, the stereotype of Latinos as aggressive had its greatest effect on their judgments of guilt in the afternoon and evening. For night owls, the effect of the stereotype was greatest in the morning. (Based on Bodenhausen, 1990.)

C. W. Stephan & Stephan, 1984). For example, fear, anxiety, and sadness increase the impact of stereotypic expectations on perceptions of individual group members (D. L. Hamilton, Stroessner, & Mackie, 1993; H.-S. Kim & Baron, 1988; Wilder & Shapiro, 1988), and they decrease recognition of differences among group members (Stroessner & Mackie, 1992). In one study of the effect of anger on stereotyping, students playing mock jurors were asked to decide the guilt or innocence of a defendant whom some believed to be a Latino and others thought was ethnically nondescript (Bodenhausen & Kramer, 1990, cited in Bodenhausen, 1993). Students who were made to feel angry by an experimental manipulation before reading the evidence were more likely to deliver a guilty verdict against the Latino defendant than against the other defendant. In contrast, those who were not angered treated the two defendants the same.

Beyond Simple Activation: Effects of Stereotypes on Considered Judgments

Even when people make considered judgments, established stereotypes exert an effect. People tend to look for stereotype-confirming, not disconfirming, evidence and to interpret ambiguous information as stereotype-consistent. People may even elicit stereotype-consistent information from others by the way they interact with them.

We have seen that people often use stereotypes when they are in a hurry, when they make judgments without much thought, or when they are emotionally upset. Unfortunately, stereotypes also leave their mark even when people try to gather more information. Stereotypes often guide our decisions because we believe they allow us to make valid judgments. If you need help in a store, identifying a store clerk—any store clerk—is the first step in getting that help. Similarly, if you are sick or injured, your physician stereotype helps you by indicating the type of person who can provide aid. People have two reasons for feeling confident that their stereotyped judgments are correct. First, any information that is consistent with expectations will tend to increase confidence that those expectations are correct. And, as you will see, stereotypes can bias the information people process, producing apparent consistency. Second, consensus creates confidence. A socially shared stereotype boosts our confidence by letting us know that other people agree with our beliefs and react in the same way we do.

In many situations, of course, confidence in a stereotype is not enough. We need to see beyond group membership and consider personal characteristics, reactions, or emotions. For example, in choosing an employee, competency is more important than gender, and in choosing a friend, shared tastes and preferences are more important than race. So in some situations—when the judgment is important and when we choose to devote attention to the task—we may try to go beyond group stereotypes and collect further information about people as individuals (Fiske & Neuberg, 1990; M. L. Hoffman, 1986; M. J. Rodin, 1987). When we do this, stereotypic information is less likely to come to mind (Macrae, Bodenhausen, Milne, Thorn, & Castelli, 1997). Even when we collect additional information, however, stereotypes can subtly bias the way we see other people.

We discussed the conditions that lead people to go beyond their initial expectations to consider others as individuals in chapter 3, pages 77 to 88.

SEEKING EVIDENCE TO CONFIRM THE STEREOTYPE: JUST TELL ME WHERE TO LOOK. How do stereotypes distort our considered judgment of others' behaviors, reactions, and feelings? One source of bias is our stereotypic expectations: We tend to notice and remember what we expect to see. For one thing, when people are given both stereotypic and stereotype-inconsistent information about a person, they tend to spend more time reading and thinking about the stereotypic information (Neuberg & Fiske, 1987). If they are allowed to select what information they will receive, they tend to ask for stereotype-consistent information (L. Johnston & Macrae, 1994).

Stereotypic biases affect not only the information we seek out and attend to, but also what we remember. Recall from chapter 3's discussion of person perception that when we are especially motivated to pay attention to an *individual*, we carefully process unexpected information and remember it particularly well (Hastie & Kumar, 1979). For example, suppose you have an impression of an individual as generally self-centered, but then observe the person volunteering four consecutive weekends to work on building a Habitat for Humanity house. As we described in chapter 3, you are likely to think hard about this unexpected behavior, and you will probably remember it particularly well when you think about the person again. This special processing of unexpected behaviors is less likely to occur with groups (D. L. Hamilton & Sherman, 1996). That is, if you think of a group as self-centered but learn that a group member volunteered for Habitat, you are unlikely to devote the same kind of special processing to the inconsistent behavior or to remember it well. In fact, you may remember mostly stereotype-consistent information (D. L. Hamilton & Rose, 1980; Rothbart, Evans, & Fulero, 1979). This memory bias means that once a stereotype is in place, people may falsely recall that the stereotype was confirmed in their actual encounters with group members. As D. L. Hamilton and Rose (1980) concluded, believing is seeing. When bias molds people's observations and memories so that they fit their stereotypes, the stereotypes grow even stronger (Rothbart & John, 1985; Wilder & Shapiro, 1984).

INTERPRETING EVIDENCE TO FIT THE STEREOTYPE: WELL, IF YOU LOOK AT IT THAT WAY. The implications of a good deal of the information we gather are not immediately obvious. As Cedric Holloway sat in his car outside a bank, who could say whether he was pondering his financial future, planning a robbery, or merely taking a nap? When information is ambiguous, activation of a stereotype influences our interpretation of the behavior (or of the individual performing the behavior), making it seem consistent with the stereotype (Darley & Gross, 1983).

In a study demonstrating this point, Andrew Sagar and Janet Schofield (1980) showed schoolchildren stick-figure drawings of children who were identified as Black or White, and described each stick-child's behavior. For example, a picture of two students sitting one behind the other in a classroom was accompanied by the following description: "Mark was sitting at his desk, working on his social studies assignment, when David started poking him in the back with the eraser end of his pencil. Mark just kept on working. David kept poking him for a while and then he finally stopped." When David was Black, the children saw his behavior as more mean and threatening than when he was White. Thus the same behavior was interpreted differently depending on who the actor was and what stereotype his group membership evoked.

Stereotypes can similarly influence our interpretations of others' behavior in everyday situations, as an episode recounted to author Studs Terkel (1992) demonstrates. A White man described how his wife, driving down the street in a Black neighborhood, noticed that the people on the street corners were all gesturing at her forcefully. Frightened, she closed the car windows and drove very determinedly through the area. Only after several blocks did she discover that she was going the wrong way on a one-way street and that the pedestrians had merely been trying to help her.

If stereotypes can bend our interpretation of behaviors in one direction or another, some group impressions may be almost impossible to counteract. If a group is reputed to be cunning, anything it does could be considered further evidence of a duplicitous nature. During the Second World War, California governor Earl Warren regarded the *absence* of evidence of subversion among Japanese Americans as the most ominous sign that they were planning surprise attacks of sabotage.

COMPARING INFORMATION TO STEREOTYPIC STANDARDS: THAT LOOKS GOOD FOR A GROUP MEMBER. At 5 feet 10 inches, Sarah is more likely to be called "tall" than Samuel, who is also 5 feet 10. This is just common sense; Sarah is indeed tall *for a woman.* But this example illustrates one additional way stereotypes can affect our judgments: by shifting our standards for judgments, at least on characteristics like "tall" or "smart" or "athletic" that involve a strong subjective element. Monica Biernat and Melvin Manis (1994) illustrated this effect when they had students judge essays on stereotypically "masculine" or "feminine" topics supposedly written by a woman or a man. Letter grades given to the essays revealed, as expected, that gender-congruent essays were evaluated more highly; for example, Joan's essay on eye makeup received a higher grade than the identical essay supposedly written by John. Yet the students' ratings of the essays on a subjective scale (for example, from "poor" to "excellent") showed no differences by the author's supposed gender. Evidently the students believed that John's essay on the feminine topic, while not as good as Joan's, was still "good" *for a man.* Group stereotypes (for example, that men would not be expected to know much about makeup) affect the standards used to assign such subjective ratings. Looking at this finding another way, it is interesting to realize that even when members of different groups are rated the same—as when the subjective scale was used in this study—stereotypes may still be operating, subtly affecting not only people's perceptions of group members but also the standards they use to make and express their judgments (Kobrynowicz & Biernat, 1997).

CONSTRAINING EVIDENCE TO FIT THE STEREOTYPE: THE SELF-FULFILLING PROPHECY. Not only do people seek out stereotype-consistent behavior, they may even elicit it. One of us observed just such a situation when he was in graduate school. Two of his fellow students who had co-authored a paper ran into the professor who had given them their assignment. The professor immediately engaged the male student co-author in conversation, spending several minutes complimenting him on the paper and discussing a few of its fine points. The woman student stood by, silently fuming. So did the observer, because he knew that the woman was by far the more talented student and suspected that three quarters of the work on the paper was hers. Yet the professor, stereotypically assuming that the male student was the primary author, was holding a conversation that reinforced his opinion that the male student could talk intelligently on the topic while the female student had nothing to say.

When stereotypes lead us to act in ways that produce the very behaviors that confirm our expectations, the stereotype becomes a *self-fulfilling prophecy*. Recall from chapter 3 that when people interact with someone about whom they hold a particular expectation, they often induce that person to confirm the expectation (M. Snyder, Tanke, & Berscheid, 1977). Similarly, people's actions often elicit information that confirms and maintains their group stereotypes. When we ask women about their family and men about their job, our behavior produces responses that are likely to tell us what we already know. Alternatively, we may simply not bother to gather much specific information from people who are members of a stereotyped group. In one study, perceivers who held a stereotypic expectation about someone sought less information from them in an interview, asking fewer questions than when the target person was not described as a member of a stereotyped group (Trope & Thompson, 1997).

☐ **SELF-FULFILLING PROPHECIES IN SCHOOL AND AT WORK.** The self-fulfilling nature of stereotypes can set up a chain reaction in which not only the perceiver's beliefs but also the actual behavior of members of the stereotyped groups are affected (Word, Zanna, & Cooper, 1974). In the classroom, the consequences can be devastating. For this reason, researchers have intensively studied the effects of teachers' expectations on student performance. Expectations may be based on social categorizations like gender, race, or social class, or on personal characteristics like physical attractiveness (M. J. Harris, 1991). When teachers' expectations for students are high, they tend to treat them with more warmth, teach them more material, and give them more chances to contribute to discussions and answer questions in class. These differences translate directly into differences in student achievement (M. J. Harris & Rosenthal, 1985). Such findings make it clear why we should be concerned about studies like one undertaken in a New York City suburb. That research indicated that teachers' expectations for Black children are consistently lower than for White children, regardless of the children's actual abilities (S. I. Ross & Jackson, 1991). Similarly, a 1992 review shows that classroom teachers generally give more attention and encouragement to boys than to girls (Wellesley College Center for Research on Women, 1992).

Self-fulfilling prophecies operate in the workplace, too. An employer's preconceptions can predetermine the outcome of applications for job openings. For example, interviewers who believe that a particular candidate is not suitable for a position are likely to probe for negative information (Binning, Goldstein, Garcia, & Scatteregia, 1988), whereas those with positive preconceptions tend to spend time gaining and giving positive information (Phillips & Dipboye, 1989). In one study, White participants interviewed Black or White applicants. When dealing with Blacks, they conducted briefer interviews and sat farther away, causing the applicants to react in a less confident and effective manner (Word and others, 1974). Self-fulfilling prophecies also restrict the opportunities of employees already on the job. Employers can generate confirmations of their stereotypes in a number of subtle ways. A supervisor who regularly interrupts his female subordinates is clearly communicating to them that their contributions are unimportant, damaging their

FIGURE 5.7   Stereotypes are self-perpetuating

```
                         ┌──────────────────────────┐
                         │   Stereotype of group     │
                         │                           │
                         │ Professors are absent-minded. │
                         └──────────────────────────┘
```

Stereotype of group

Professors are absent-minded.

Condition: Attention is low or emotion is high.

Condition: Attention is focused and additional information is considered.

Seek stereotypic information

Think of times when Snerdly forgot appointments.

Interpret ambiguous information as stereotypic

Snerdly forgot an obscure citation.

Elicit stereotypic behavior

Don't bother telling Snerdly about the meeting because you assume he'd forget anyway.

Stereotypic snap judgment

Professor Snerdly is absent-minded.

Stereotypic considered judgments

Professor Snerdly is absent-minded.

■ Whether people make snap judgments or attempt to process information more carefully, stereotypes shape their thoughts and action. In most cases, the result seems to confirm and perpetuate the stereotype.

self-confidence. A boss who delegates responsibilities to his female staff but then checks up on every detail is not only advertising his distrust but also denying the women the opportunity to prove their competence.

No wonder then, that group stereotypes, like other cognitive representations, tend to perpetuate themselves and to be slow to change. When people process superficially, stereotypes alone can dictate their judgments. When people process more extensively, stereotypes influence what they see and how they interpret it. Either way, the outcome is likely to be a judgment consistent with the stereotype, as Figure 5.7 demonstrates.

Changing Stereotypes: Overcoming Bias to Reduce Prejudice

Even though people sometimes selectively gather, interpret, and elicit information so that their stereotypes are confirmed, they may eventually have an experience that unambiguously contradicts their impression of a group. For example, a member of a group regarded as hostile and clannish may move into the neighborhood and turn out to be unobjectionable, even pleasant. Could getting to know likable individual group members change negative stereotypes of another group? Somehow, we like to think that stereotypes are born out of ignorance, so that simply learning more about a group will put them to rest.

That simple idea—that contact with individual members who violate the group stereotype should bring about its downfall—is the basis of one of the

■ **Pursuing a dream to overcome a stereotype.** These athletes are lining up in the 100-meter final of a major track and field competition. The competition is the Gay Games, and in addition to competing for the gold medal, these athletes are hoping to break the stereotype that gay men are not interested in athletics or competition, and are somehow less fit to be athletes.

oldest and most researched theories of stereotype change. The **contact hypothesis** suggests that under certain conditions, direct contact between members of different groups can reduce intergroup stereotyping, prejudice, and discrimination (G. W. Allport, 1954a). When members of different groups socialize, perhaps they can exchange the kind of information that undermines stereotypic thinking. Getting to know group members on a one-to-one-basis should make it obvious that they do not fit the group stereotype. In the face of this inconsistent information, common sense says that the stereotype should change.

Barriers to Stereotype Change: Is Contact Enough?

Even when contact with members of a group allows people to obtain information that is blatantly inconsistent with a stereotype, stereotypes may remain unchanged. This is because people can explain away the inconsistency, create a new category for exceptions to the rule, and see the behavior of unusual group members as being irrelevant to the group stereotype.

Unfortunately, reality is not as straightforward as common sense. Consider, for example, the high level of contact between men and women, police officers and gang members, Palestinians and Israelis. None of these contact situations has been a prejudice-reduction success story. The problem lies in the fact that contact in and of itself—even contact that contradicts a stereotype—may not undermine a stereotype (G. W. Allport, 1954a; Amir, 1969; W. G. Stephan, 1987). In fact, exposure to inconsistent information can trigger powerful mechanisms that protect established stereotypes from change.

Contact hypothesis. The theory that certain types of direct contact between members of hostile groups will reduce stereotyping and prejudice.

EXPLAINING AWAY INCONSISTENT INFORMATION. Well-intentioned authors of uplifting stories for young people sometimes devise plots in which the

■ **If it doesn't fit, explain it away.** In the male-dominated sport of bullfighting, women like Christina Sanchez are beginning to achieve some success. Despite assertions by some of her male colleagues that "Women can only handle so much animal," Sanchez in 1996 passed Spain's toughest test and earned the elite "matador" designation.

hero holds a negative stereotype about Group X, meets an X, after some initial misunderstandings gets to know the X as a person, and finally decides the stereotype was wrong and X's are as likable as anybody else. The idea that a stereotype can be changed by a single inconsistent experience, a process called *conversion* (Rothbart, 1981), is appealing. But the plot somehow seems contrived. Does true conversion occur so easily?

One barrier to stereotype change is the fact that when people even notice information that fails to fit their expectations, they often just explain it away. Information that is in some way discrepant often makes us look hard for its causes, and thus makes it likely that we will find some "special circumstances" to explain it. If we interpret friendly and positive behaviors performed by a member of a disliked group as just the result of special circumstances, we will not accept the behaviors as a reflection of the actor's true nature (Crocker, Hannah, & Weber, 1983; Gordon & Anderson, 1995). Consider the responses of students asked to explain why a college student succeeded on an object recognition task (Deaux & Emswiller, 1974). When the task involved recognizing "feminine" objects like a double boiler, participants made the same attributions about a man or a woman who did well. However, when the task involved recognizing "masculine" objects such as an auto jack, the man's success was attributed to his ability. Why did people say a women succeeded? They attributed this outcome to good luck! The participants—both males and females—implicitly denied a woman credit for her success on the masculine task. This study is an example of a more general finding that women who succeed in a "man's world" are often viewed as highly motivated or very lucky, rather than as very able (Heilman & Stopek, 1985). Encountering a few successful women, or individuals who violate other stereotypes, generally does not change the minds of prejudiced observers.

COMPARTMENTALIZING INCONSISTENT INFORMATION. Even when inconsistent information is too plentiful to be explained away, people can still defend their stereotypes by resorting to specific **subtypes**: social categories that are narrower than broad groups like *men* or *Latinos*. For example, German students have different stereotypes for subtypes of women, such as "chick," housewife, career woman, and "woman's libber" (Eckes, 1994). Older people are also categorized into common subtypes such as respected elder statesman, sweet grandmother, and inactive senior citizen (Brewer, Dull, & Lui, 1981).

Although these differentiated categories permit the perceiver to formulate fine-grained expectations about different group members, they also protect stereotyped beliefs from change. If we place a group of people who are exceptions to the rule in a new category, the old rule can remain inviolate. Male executives who work alongside highly competent female colleagues can form a "career woman" subtype that allows them to maintain a more general belief that *most* women cannot succeed in business (Rothbart & John, 1985; Weber & Crocker, 1983). Similarly, we can maintain our view that outstanding physical feats are the province of the young if we compartmentalize stereotype-inconsistent older people in special subtypes. We merely create an exceptions-to-the-rule category for people like John Glenn, who at age 76 took another space trip 38 years after he became the first American to orbit the earth, or Johnny Kelly, who completed his 57th Boston marathon at age 83.

DIFFERENTIATING ATYPICAL GROUP MEMBERS: CONTRAST EFFECTS. Stereotype-inconsistent information can be defused in yet a third way. If we cannot explain away inconsistencies or create new subtypes, we may defend our stereotypes by seeing stereotype-disconfirming individuals as remarkable or exceptional people. When stereotypic expectations serve as a background against which individual group members are judged, people who do not behave as expected seem even more different, creating what is called a *contrast effect*. In one study, for example, researchers created stereotypes of patients in a mental hospital. They had college students read statements, supposedly written by the hospital's patients, that revealed the patients as either severely disturbed or only mildly disturbed (Manis, Nelson, & Shedler, 1988). The students then read statements by other patients who showed a moderate level of pathology. Because of the contrast with their expectations, those who had been led to expect severe disturbance judged these new patients to be only mildly ill, whereas those who expected only mild disturbance thought the new patients were extremely ill. Similar processes probably explain why people's stereotypes of an employed woman are quite different from those for a "typical woman" and are very similar to their impression of an employed man. People apparently assume that employed women have actively chosen that role and that only the most ambitious and independent women—the ones most unlike the rest of their group—would so choose (Eagly & Steffen, 1984).

Through contrast effects, members who deviate from expectations for their group seem even more different from the rest of the group than they really are. As a result, perceivers can easily decide that these unusual people are not true group members at all: Their difference makes them exceptions to the rule. As such, they have little bearing on people's impressions of the group as a whole (Rasinski, Crocker, & Hastie, 1985; Rothbart & John, 1985).

Subtype. A narrower and more specific social group, such as housewife or feminist, that is included within a broad social group, like women.

Overcoming Stereotype Defenses: The Kind of Contact That Works

> Effective contact has to provide stereotype-inconsistent information that is repeated (so that it cannot be explained away), that involves many group members (so that subtyping is prevented), and that comes from typical group members (so that contrast will not occur). When these conditions exist, contact does reduce stereotypes and improve intergroup relations.

Positive and cooperative intergroup contact can not only change stereotypes, but also help resolve ongoing conflict between groups. Thus, we will return to the question of what kinds of contact are most effective when we consider intergroup conflict in chapter 13, pages 542 to 545.

Given all the barriers to stereotype change, can contact ever alter our stereotypes and reduce prejudice? We have seen that contact by itself is not enough to bridge the gap of ignorance separating stereotypes from reality. The answer seems to lie in the kind of contact that occurs (S. W. Cook, 1985; W. G. Stephan, 1987). To allow the kind of information exchange that undermines stereotypic thinking, contact situations must expose people to information that cannot be explained away, subtyped, or contrasted.

REPEATED INCONSISTENCY: AN ANTIDOTE FOR "EXPLAINING AWAY." One counterstereotypic act can easily be explained away. The sales manager who expects inferior performances from women might attribute a woman sales rep's single week of outstanding sales just to extra effort or sheer luck. However, if the strong performance continues week after week, these attributions become harder to support. When behavior remains stable over time and circumstances, attributions to the person are warranted. Thus, stereotype change requires counterstereotypic behaviors to be performed more than once or twice. Of course, this places a special burden on members of stereotyped groups. They cannot afford to perform poorly, even once, for fear that a failure will reinforce rather than change others' stereotypes (Steele, 1992).

Chapter 3, pages 80 to 82, described how highly consistent behaviors are interpreted as due to stable characteristics of the person, such as ability, rather than to circumstances or other temporary factors.

WIDESPREAD INCONSISTENCY: AN ANTIDOTE FOR SUBTYPING. Even if the sales manager in the previous example changes his impression of that particular woman sales rep, he may still maintain his stereotype by simply compartmentalizing her as a member of a small subgroup of highly competent women. When behaviors are performed by just a few individual group members, perceivers may create a subtype to insulate their general stereotype from change. To illustrate how this defense can be overcome, Reneé Weber and Jennifer Crocker (1983) gave people information about many behaviors performed by members of a group. Some learned that just a few group members performed stereotype-inconsistent behaviors; the other members' actions were all in line with the stereotype. These participants did not change their overall stereotype of the group, presumably because they categorized the few inconsistent individuals into a new subtype (Johnston & Hewstone, 1992). In contrast, other participants who learned that the same number of inconsistent behaviors were spread out over a large number of group members were more likely to change their stereotype. In the latter case, the inconsistent individuals could not be considered a subtype: Too many group members had unusual, counterstereotypic features.

BEING TYPICAL AS WELL AS INCONSISTENT: AN ANTIDOTE FOR CONTRAST EFFECTS. People have other weapons besides subtypes to use in defense of their stereotypes. Recall that group members who violate the stereotype may simply be considered highly unusual individuals—so atypical that their characteristics have no impact on impressions of "typical" group members (Johnston & Hewstone, 1992). This defense can be overcome if individual stereotype violators provide strong and consistent reminders of their group membership. In one study, college students interacted with a confederate posing as a student from a rival college. The students initially disliked people from the other school, but this particular interaction was positive and friendly. The students' general beliefs about those attending the rival school, however, became more positive only if the confederate acted and dressed in ways perceived to be "typical" of the rival college (Wilder, 1984). If the confederate did not display such highly typical characteristics, the friendly interaction had no impact on students' general views about the other college.

This finding poses a dilemma for group members who wish to change others' negative stereotypes by being a positive example of their group. The very accomplishments and valued attributes that make you a *positive* example may make you less of an *example*, by making you less typical of the group in the eyes of an observer who holds negative stereotypes (Desforges and others, 1991; Rothbart & John, 1985). Indeed, any sort of extensive personal information about you, whether positive or negative, can make you seem less of a group member (Fein & Hilton, 1992). As others get to know you as an individual, they may fail to generalize their positive feelings about you to other members of your group. If your goal is stereotype change, therefore, you should repeatedly remind others of your group membership, so that they cannot treat you as an exception to the rule.

PERSONAL RELATIONSHIPS MAKE CONTACT EFFECTIVE. When interaction involves the right kind of contact—contact that blocks attribution, subtyping, and contrast effects—stereotypes can change. The key ingredient may be contact that encourages the development of a real personal relationship involving positive feelings and sharing of thoughts and feelings—in other words, a friendship—rather than a mere nodding acquaintanceship (Pettigrew, 1998). Stephen Wright and his colleagues (S. C. Wright, Aron, McLaughlin-Volpe, & Ropp, 1997) set out to test this idea in a laboratory study, by first creating conflict between experimentally created groups and then trying friendly contact as a way of reducing it. College students were randomly assigned to two teams that then participated in a series of problem solving and creativity competitions. Though this procedure alone often suffices to build conflict, as you will see in chapter 13, the experimenters helped it along in various ways. For example, each team was asked to provide an evaluation of the other team's problem solutions, and the experimenters covertly edited these to leave only negative comments before delivering them to the team that had been evaluated. After steps like these had built up negative feelings between the groups, one member from each group was selected, ostensibly as part of an unrelated study, to participate in a dyadic getting-to-know-you task that established feelings of personal closeness. Finally, all members of both groups, after learning about the experimentally created friendship between these individual members, again rated both groups.

The results of this experimentally created contact were clear. The individual members who built up a close relationship with the opposite-group partner rated that group more positively. Perhaps of greater importance, the other group members did so as well! It seems that not only having a member of another group as a friend, but even *knowing that someone else* from your group has a member of the other group as a friend, is sufficient to reduce negative feelings about that group. This optimistic conclusion has been confirmed in additional studies (S. C. Wright and others, 1997).

Other laboratory research has demonstrated similar positive effects of intergroup contact. Donna Desforges and her associates (1991) set up a 1-hour laboratory session in which participants interacted with a confederate posing as a former mental patient, a member of a group about which the participants had negative stereotypes. The contact was structured to be cooperative in nature, and as a result friendship budded, and the students came to like their partners. They also developed improved attitudes toward former mental patients in general.

□ **INTERGROUP CONTACT IN THE NEIGHBORHOOD.** Finding that friendly contact breaks down stereotypes in the controlled conditions of the laboratory is one thing, but can the right kind of contact break down prejudice in other settings, too? Several studies suggest that reductions in prejudice are associated with increased everyday contact.

The 1950s were a period of large-scale desegregation of public housing units in the United States, creating the conditions for research on the effects of living near members of other groups. Morton Deutsch and Mary Collins (1951) studied the responses of White families assigned to live alongside Black families as well as Whites living in all-White buildings. When the groups were compared, those living in desegregated housing, and particularly those who lived closest to Black families, had more positive feelings about Blacks. Such contact also dissolved stereotypes about the previously unknown group. Two Canadian researchers obtained similar results when they matched national survey data on prejudice with census information on the racial composition of residential neighborhoods (Kalin & Berry, 1982). People felt relatively positive about the groups that lived nearby, suggesting again that informal, everyday contact reduces prejudice.

Finally, Thomas Pettigrew (1997) analyzed survey data from Britain, France, the Netherlands, and Germany. People were asked whether they had any friends who were members of racial groups with common negative stereotypes (such as Turkish immigrants in Germany or North Africans in France). Those with such friendships were also less prejudiced against the outgroup, to a greater extent than could be explained by the simple fact that less prejudiced individuals would be more likely to form such friendships in the first place. The effects of a cross-group friendship were not even limited to the specific group: A French person who had an Algerian friend became less predjudiced not only against Algerians, but against other groups as well (Pettigrew, 1997). In fact, heroic Gentiles who risked their lives rescuing Jews from the Nazis seem to have had more cross-group friendships in their own childhoods (Oliner & Oliner, 1988). Thus the results of nonexperimental studies of contact and friendship in the neighborhood converge with experimental findings from the laboratory. Contact can reduce group prejudice and stereotyping, but it has to be the right kind of contact: contact that permits the development of friendships across group lines.

Chapter 2, pages 44 to 45, describes why replication of findings inside and outside the laboratory increases researchers' confidence that contact of the right kind does in fact reduce prejudice.

FIGURE 5.8   Possible fates of stereotype-inconsistent information

■ Inconsistent information will not always lead people to change or reject their stereotypes, because people have many ways to defend stereotypes against such information (shown on the left side of figure). However, these defenses can be overcome if the inconsistent information appears in the right patterns, or if the individual intentionally chooses not to rely on the stereotype (right side). In some circumstances, stereotypes can be changed.

Before we review the bottom line for changing stereotypes, we should pause to consider for a moment that not all stereotypes ought to be changed. If you have a stereotype that neo-Nazis are evil, but meet a member of that group who smiles politely and acts pleasant, should this experience alter your stereotype? Most of us would say no. And a Frenchman may not want to change the stereotype that the French are good cooks, any more than a Marine would disavow his group's stereotype of toughness and bravery.

Many individuals, though, in keeping with today's social norms, have decided that they do not endorse or wish to use stereotypes of racial, gender, religious, or ethnic groups of the sort that were commonly accepted in past decades. In such cases, when we wish to change stereotypes, it is possible but not easy. Although many factors conspire to keep stereotypes in place, exposure to the right kinds of information can eventually beat down the defense mechanisms that protect stereotypes from change. Even when old stereotypes are activated, people can choose to counter them with nonprejudiced thoughts, feelings, and behaviors. Figure 5.8 shows both the factors that make stereotypes resistant to change and the factors that can finally overcome that resistance. Although it is sometimes difficult to find situations that have all the necessary ingredients working together, contact of the right type can break down negative stereotypes and engender warm feelings of friendship with particular individuals. When this kind of contact is extensive and sustained, those positive feelings can become generalized to the group as a whole, changing stereotypes and reducing prejudice.

CONCLUDING COMMENTS

 One theme that has surfaced repeatedly in this book is that our social knowledge is slow to change and tends to perpetuate itself. Stereotypes offer perhaps the most dramatic illustration of this principle, for they perpetuate themselves in two different ways.

First, within each individual, the effects of stereotypes mean that believing is seeing. Stereotypes color our perceptions so that unclear or ambiguous events are quickly interpreted in line with the stereotype. If we think politicians are self-serving, we might decide that any action they take is made only for its publicity value. When we read in the newspaper that our member of Congress donated $100 to the local orphanage, for example, we then conclude that the donation was meant to attract media attention. Even when we try to think hard and process carefully, stereotypes shape the information we seek out, remember, and use to make judgments. We might question the politician about foreign junkets rather than efforts on behalf of the district, or we might remember negative campaign tactics rather than sponsorship of important legislation. Even when inconsistent information comes our way, we are likely to defend our stereotypes by explaining away inconsistencies, forming subtypes, or contrasting a particular individual as a praiseworthy exception to the rule.

Of course, none of these self-fulfilling and defensive tendencies are intentional. No one consciously decides, "I want to maintain my biased and stereotypic view of politicians, so don't confuse me with the facts!" Instead, our stereotypes, like our other cognitive representations, constitute the picture of reality we have constructed for ourselves. And for this reason, their effects are below the level of our awareness. We don't *try* to defend and maintain our stereotypic beliefs, it just happens that way most of the time.

The pervasiveness and power of the self-fulfilling quality of stereotypes within each person's head is only half of the complete story: Stereotypes perpetuate themselves and resist change in society as well. As we have seen, stereotypes generally reflect the roles society allocates to members of the stereotyped group. If more women than men care for children, if members of one ethnic group tend to be small shopkeepers while most members of another group hold unrewarding jobs as menial laborers, those roles will become the raw material of stereotypes. People are likely to end up believing that women are nurturant, that the first ethnic group is greedy and grasping, and that the second group is lazy and dirty. Stereotypes track social roles both because the roles limit the behaviors that we observe individual group members performing, and because the culture and media generally foster the idea that personal characteristics fit roles. Thus

CHAPTER 5 THEMES

- **Construction of Reality**
  We construct impressions of social groups based on our interactions with group members and what we learn from others.

- **Pervasiveness of Social Influence**
  These interactions and the things we learn are shaped by society and culture.

- **Striving for Mastery**
  Stereotypes often reflect individuals' actual social experiences.

- **Conservatism**
  Stereotypes perpetuate themselves by shaping both the way we think and the way we act.

- **Superficiality Versus Depth**
  Stereotypes influence judgments made quickly with little thought and also judgments made by collecting further information.

the circle is closed. Because people believe groups are naturally suited for the roles they play, those beliefs become the justification for keeping the groups in those roles. Social change that would alter groups' roles is seen as a violation of the natural order of things, becoming morally wrong as well as impractical.

Thus stereotypes have self-fulfilling force not only in an individual's head but also in society. Because stereotypes operate on two levels, changing them will demand alterations not only in the way we think, but also in the way we live. We need to consciously reflect on the extent to which social roles and other external constraints determine not only other people's actions but also our own. Equally, we need to interact with members of all groups in more varied contexts, to see them in more diverse roles, and to work toward change in social inequalities that are reflected in and rationalized by stereotypes.

Could changes like these allow us to retain the benefits of social categorization while eliminating the costs of stereotypes? We would still perceive groups, but we would know each group for its positive and valued characteristics. Perhaps all groups would respect and value all other groups, a goal that is implicit in the concept of multiculturalism. Unfortunately, another factor stands in the way of developing a society in which all groups are equally valued and respected: We all show strong preferences for the groups to which we belong. In chapter 6 we consider the consequences of this preference for the way we think about and act toward others and ourselves.

S U M M A R Y

 The Social and Cognitive Roots of Prejudice. Discrimination, or treatment of individuals based on their group memberships, and **prejudice**, evaluations of individuals as group members, or evaluations of social groups, are significant problems in the world today. Prejudice has at times been viewed as the product of distorted thinking in a few troubled individuals. But both social and cognitive factors contribute to prejudice. One important source is people's **stereotypes**: positive or negative beliefs about a group's characteristics.

Any **social group** that shares a socially meaningful common characteristic can be a target for prejudice. Different cultures emphasize different types of groups, but race, religion, gender, age, social status, and cultural background are important dividing lines in many societies. People identify individuals as members of social groups because they share socially meaningful features. This process of **social categorization** is helpful because it allows people to deal with others efficiently and appropriately. However, it also exaggerates similarities within groups and differences between groups, and hence it forms the basis for stereotyping.

Stereotypes can be measured by asking plain questions or in more subtle ways that make it difficult for people to hide prejudiced feelings. However, people who reveal stereotypes or prejudice in subtle ways while overtly denying them may actually hold conflicting views rather than being dishonest.

Forming Impressions of Groups: Establishing Stereotypes. Many different kinds of characteristics are included in stereotypes, which can be positive or negative. Some stereotypes accurately reflect actual differences between groups, though in exaggerated form. Other stereotypes are completely inaccurate.

Stereotypes can be learned through personal experiences with groups members. However, these stereotypes may be biased because people pay attention to extremes or inaccurately perceive groups' characteristics. Social roles often shape group members' behaviors, but people attribute the behaviors to group members' inner characteristics. The emotions generated by interaction with groups can also become part of stereotypes about those groups.

Social learning also contributes to stereotypes. Stereotypes and discrimination are often accepted and endorsed as right and proper by members of a particular group, becoming **social norms**. Group members then learn these beliefs and behaviors from family, friends, and the media.

The stereotypes prevalent in a society often serve to justify existing social inequalities. They do so by portraying groups as deserving their social roles and positions on the basis of their own characteristics.

Using Stereotypes: From Preconceptions to Prejudice. Once established, a stereotype can be activated by obvious cues, use of group labels, or the presence of a group member, especially as a minority in a social situation. Some stereotypes are learned so well and used so often that their content comes to mind automatically.

Once activated, a stereotype can lead to snap judgments about the group member. People may try to overcome the effects of stereotypes by suppressing stereotypic thoughts or correcting for their impact on judgments. However, both of these tactics require motivation and cognitive capacity, so they are unlikely to succeed if we are short of time or burdened by strong emotions.

Even when people make considered judgments, established stereotypes exert an effect. People tend to look for stereotype-confirming, not disconfirming, evidence and to interpret ambiguous information as stereotype-consistent. People may even elicit stereotype-consistent information from others by the way they interact with them.

Changing Stereotypes: Overcoming Bias to Reduce Prejudice. Research on how stereotypes may be changed in society has focused on the **contact hypothesis,** the idea that under certain conditions, contact with members of a stereotyped group may reduce stereotyping and prejudice. Mere contact is not sufficient. Even when people obtain information that is blatantly inconsistent with a stereotype, stereotypes may remain unchanged because people explain away the inconsistency, create a new **subtype** for exceptions to the rule, and see the behavior of unusual group members as irrelevant to the group stereotype.

To be effective, contact has to provide stereotype-inconsistent information that is repeated (so it cannot be explained away), that involves many group members (so subtyping is prevented), and that comes from typical group members (so contrast will not occur). When these conditions exist, contact does reduce stereotypes and improve intergroup relations.

People who consciously reject prejudice are able to overcome the effects of automatically activated stereotypes. They do so by devoting conscious thought to seeking disconfirming information and correcting their judgments.

6

Social Identity

As part of your participation in a psychological experiment, you learn that you will be videotaped being interviewed about various social and academic aspects of your life as a student. To show you what the interview will be like, the researcher plays another participant's videotape. The interview unfolds to show a student who appears almost incredibly successful: earning straight A's in premed courses, well dressed and attractive, full of self-confidence—yet still coming across as likable and not arrogant. Now you are given a questionnaire asking you to rate yourself in comparison to other college students in academic ability, social competence, and so on. With the superstar interview still echoing in your mind, wouldn't your ratings perhaps be a little below the top of the scale? In contrast, suppose you saw a real loser instead of the superstar. The same actor (for the interviews were staged, of course) portrayed a sloppily dressed, unmotivated individual who came across as socially awkward, slow talking, and even slower thinking. Wouldn't your self-ratings go up a bit in this case?

What we have just described is a typical social comparison experiment. Many such studies confirm that exposure to another person's outstanding performance lowers people's self-ratings, while witnessing a poor performance raises them. Marilynn Brewer and Joseph Weber (1994), though, added a new twist to this type of study when they also manipulated group membership. Before seeing the videotape, each participant took a bogus test classifying him or her into one of two personality types, one that was said to include 80% of college students and the other only 20%. The videotaped actor was also said to belong to one or the other group. Did group membership affect the outcomes of the social comparison? It certainly did. When the videotaped interviewee was a member of the larger group, social comparison had its typical effect: Participants felt bad if the performance was great and good if it was terrible, regardless of their own group membership. But consider what happened when the videotaped student belonged to the minority group:

We described the effects of social comparison on the self in chapter 4, pages 107 to 108.

- For a majority group participant, a videotape of a minority interviewee had no effect whatever on the participant's self-concept. It seems that majority group members simply do not compare themselves to minorities.

- Even more striking, minority group participants who saw a minority interviewee reacted in the *opposite* way from the usual social comparison process. They felt *good* if their fellow group member gave a great performance, and bad if he or she looked terrible! Could it be that people in this situation do not compare themselves as individuals against other individuals, but raise or lower their self-esteem in accordance with the positive or negative image the other person's performance gives to their group?

As these findings show, being a member of a group influences many of our thoughts, feelings, and actions. You may feel good or bad about yourself depending on the specific groups that come to your mind. Being part of the Filipino community or the swim team, being a woman or a member of any other group can boost or lower self-esteem if we identify with the group. Group memberships are an essential part of the self.

Group membership can confer tremendous benefits. Groups give us a sense of belonging and worth, of being valued for who we are (Tajfel, 1972). As group members, we can bask in the glow of achievements other than our own and feel at home in a haven of similarity and understanding. A sense of group membership that connects us to others is the basis for our participation in social life. It even protects our mental well-being and physical health, as you will see in chapter 11. Group membership supports our needs for mastery as well as connectedness. Our groups can offer us support and confidence in our ways of understanding the world (Festinger, 1954; Hogg & Abrams, 1993), a topic that will receive much more attention in chapter 9.

The many benefits of group belonging come at a cost, however. Because our groups are so important for defining the self, we need to see them as attractive, valued, and successful. Unfortunately, valuing our own groups often entails preferring them over other groups. Regard, esteem, and liking for *in-groups*—groups to which we belong—are often coupled with disregard, derogation, and dislike for *out-groups*. As sociologist William Graham Sumner (1906) said long ago, "loyalty to the in-group, . . . [and] hatred and contempt for outsiders . . . all grow together" (p. 13). From school rivalries to ethnic prejudice to national patriotism, both the exaltation of in-groups and the belittling of out-groups reflect the importance of group membership for each of us.

These all-but-inseparable positive and negative sides of our group memberships will be explored throughout this chapter. The chapter first describes the way people come to view social groups as aspects of the self: how we learn what group memberships mean, and what factors conspire to make a particular membership significant at any given time. The chapter then turns to the consequences of placing ourselves and others in social categories. Once a group membership is activated, it affects the way we see and respond to ourselves and others. Shared group membership tends to make us view other in-group members as similar to ourselves and as likable, so we try to treat them justly and fairly. In contrast, we often respond to out-group members with indifference, active dislike, or even overt discrimination.

The chapter concludes with a discussion of the effects of belonging to a group that others look down upon. Being chubby or speaking with an accent are enough to evoke scorn in elementary-school classrooms and playgrounds. Being mentally ill, old, homeless, or on welfare can provoke dislike and avoidance among adults. Such negative group identities can take their toll, on individuals and groups. But this outcome is not inevitable, and the chapter concludes by describing how people resist the implications of a negative identity and even work to change society's evaluation of their groups.

Categorizing Oneself as a Group Member

Some group memberships are so important that they become a basic part of our view of ourselves. Try asking a friend to take a piece of paper and write 10 different sentences beginning "I am . . ." When people perform this task they typically list some individual characteristics such as "I am outgoing" or "I am tall," but they also list group memberships: "I am a woman," "I am Taiwanese." In fact, most people list more group than individual characteristics (M. H. Kuhn & McPartland, 1954). The term **social identity** refers to those aspects of our self-concept that are derived from our knowledge and feelings about the group memberships that we share with others (M. Rosenberg, 1979; Tajfel, 1972). Social identity turns "I" into "we"; it extends the self out beyond the skin to include other members of our groups. The process of seeing oneself as a member of a group is known as **self-categorization** (J. C. Turner, Hogg, Oakes, Reicher, & Wetherell, 1987). Self-categorization is flexible and can readily shift. Depending on the social context, for example, sometimes you may see yourself as a woman, other times as a student, and still other times as a unique individual, with group memberships temporarily receding into the background.

Although some group memberships are only fleetingly important—being part of the "white shirts" team in a lunch-hour basketball game, for example—most group memberships are stable and enduring. Membership in gender and ethnic groups lasts a lifetime. Being a member of the Duran or the Jackson family, or being Muslim, Roman Catholic, or Buddhist, or being a Connecticut Yankee or a Southern Belle can be nearly as long-lasting. How do we learn what characteristics are associated with those groups?

Learning About Our Groups

People learn about the groups to which they belong in the same ways that they learn the characteristics of other groups: by observing other group members or from the culture.

We learn about our own groups in the same ways that we learn stereotypes of other groups: Lessons come from parents, teachers, peers, and the media. However, our most important lessons generally come from fellow group members and what they do. Consider your first job. What did it mean to become part of the team in the typing pool, on the factory floor, or in corporate headquarters? Whom did people ask for help when something went wrong? Did they joke around, or was the atmosphere pretty serious? Probably you figured out what it meant to be an employee in your company

Social identity. Those aspects of the self-concept that derive from an individual's knowledge and feelings about the group memberships he or she shares with others.

Self-categorization. The process of seeing oneself as a member of a social group.

To review the kinds of information on which we base impressions of groups, see chapter 5, especially pages 166 to 177.

By turning to chapter 4, pages 109 to 110, you can remind yourself of the reasons for this actor–observer difference in attributions.

■ **Welcome to who you are.** As this young Lenape girl performs the movements of a traditional Native American dance, she also learns what it means to be Lenape. So it is with every group. As socialization processes teach them history, traditions, and customs, young members absorb even deeper lessons: who they are and what their group stands for.

primarily—maybe only—by watching others. To illustrate the importance of interaction with group members, one study tracked sorority pledges' perceptions of their groups over an academic year and found that these women saw their groups in increasingly stereotypic terms as they got to know them better (C. S. Ryan & Bogart, 1997). Learning by watching others is particularly important when group membership is transitory and situation-bound. Today the "white shirts" may be ball hogs, always looking for a chance to shoot; tomorrow they may be team-spirited and ready to pass the ball.

What we and other group members do often depends on our cultural roles. In any society, members of a group may occupy particular roles that influence who they are. In the United States, for example, women are only 1% of automobile mechanics and carpenters and 8% of engineers, compared to 79% of cashiers, 84% of elementary school teachers, and 93% of nurses (Wootton, 1997).

Does a group's assignment to certain roles and occupations have an impact on group members' views of themselves? The answer is a qualified yes. People may not make direct inferences about their own characteristics on the basis of role-constrained behaviors as readily as observers do. Still, roles affect the individuals who hold them because as people enact their roles, they acquire role-related skills and develop tendencies to behave in certain ways. These skills and tendencies in turn make those behaviors, and correspondent self-inferences, more likely. A woman's experiences raising young children may leave her better able to interpret nonverbal behaviors or to comfort people when they are distressed. A man's experiences with aggression, perhaps in military service or organized sports, may leave him with the belief that aggressive behaviors are often effective. Thus, performing a role based on gender or on membership in some other group can shape our future behaviors and, ultimately, our self-knowledge (Eagly, 1987).

Accessibility of Group Memberships

Knowledge about group memberships may be activated by direct reminders, such as group labels; by the presence of out-group members; by being a minority; or by intergroup conflict. Group membership is particularly significant in some cultures and for some individuals, who tend to see the world in terms of that group membership.

No matter how extensive our knowledge about the characteristics of our groups, that knowledge will have little impact unless the group membership comes to mind. Imagine that you are a male Midwestern feminist, or a female Canadian conservative. Perhaps you are also musically talented, nearsighted, and love Cajun food. Under what circumstances will your gender, politics, or other group memberships be more important than your individual attributes? And which group membership will matter? Researchers have found that a variety of social and cognitive factors conspire to make a particular group membership accessible. Let's look at some of these factors.

DIRECT REMINDERS OF MEMBERSHIP. If someone calls you "Reverend," or "nerd," or "dumb jock," you are reminded directly and quite vividly about your social identity. Honorary titles or pejorative labels bring group membership home in a hurry (Billig & Tajfel, 1973; Charters & Newcomb, 1958).

Being offered a "senior citizen" discount at a restaurant or movie theater may be an unwelcome reminder of one's age (Stock, 1995). For this reason, some people in their 60s still pay the full admission price for a movie, refusing to take advantage of the discount! Often, however, the process is more subtle. Circumstances remind us of our similarities with others, and this activates knowledge of group membership. The mere presence of other in-group members can be a potent reminder (Doise & Sinclair, 1973; Wilder & Shapiro, 1991). Just hearing another New Zealand accent is enough to make one of the authors of this text "feel" like a New Zealander, and seeing someone in a Harvard T-shirt reminds the other author of his New England background. When group similarities are highlighted, as when a team wears uniforms or when members coordinate their actions for a common goal, membership and all it entails become even more accessible. This process is powerful enough to overcome important cross-cutting categorizations (Gaertner, Mann, Dovidio, Murrell, & Pomare, 1990). So White and Surinamese soccer players join together on the Dutch national team, and Republicans and Democrats coordinate their talents on a town planning committee.

PRESENCE OF OUT-GROUP MEMBERS. The presence of out-group members can also be a forcible reminder of shared group membership, as one of the authors discovered at a recent conference. He was standing with a dozen or so social psychologists in a hallway between conference sessions, chatting over coffee. Suddenly three strangers walked by; their nametags identified them as members of an association of bank loan officers, attending their own conference in the same hotel. Their presence made us even more aware of what we social psychologists had in common. The fact that out-group members' presence emphasizes the importance of an in-group's social identity was demonstrated in a study conducted in Belgium. Two groups of Belgian university students were asked to write descriptions of typical students of Belgian and North African origin. For one group, the experimenter who made this request was a North African; for the other, the experimenter was Belgian. The responses of the students who wrote in the presence of an out-group member, the North African experimenter, revealed greater identification with their in-group, Belgians (Marques, Yzerbyt, & Rijsman, 1988). Apparently the presence of even a single out-group member is enough to increase our focus on in-group membership.

When outsiders are present, resourceful group members sometimes put their mouth where their membership is, using language to emphasize their identification with their group. For example, when French-speaking Canadians were confronted with English-speaking Canadians in one experiment, the French speakers either broadened their accents to indicate their usual use of their native language or switched to that language altogether (Bourhis, Giles, Leyens, & Tajfel, 1978). Ethnic languages are important sources of social identity, as attempts by French speakers in Canada, Catalans in Spain, and Welsh nationalists in Britain to preserve their languages all attest.

BEING A MINORITY. If a few out-group members arriving on the scene can make in-group membership accessible, imagine the impact when they actually outnumber the in-group. In chapter 4 we noted that people are more likely to think of themselves in terms of individual characteristics that are unusual or distinctive in their social group (W. J. McGuire & Padawer-Singer, 1978). The same principle operates at the group level: People are more likely to think of themselves in terms of their memberships in smaller groups than in larger ones (Mullen, 1991; S. E. Taylor et al., 1978; Turnbull, Miller, & McFarland, 1990). The study by Brewer and Weber (1994) described at the beginning of this chapter illustrated this point, showing that members of a minority group were more likely than members of a majority to base their self-esteem on the performance of a fellow group member.

Similarly, consider the results obtained when William McGuire and his colleagues (W. J. McGuire, McGuire, & Winton, 1979) asked grade-school children to talk for 5 minutes about themselves and carefully coded these self-descriptions. As can be seen in Figure 6.1, the researchers found that boys and girls from households where their gender was in the minority were more likely to mention gender than were children from households where their gender made up the majority. Similarly, children whose ethnic group constituted a minority at school were more likely to mention their ethnicity in informal self-descriptions than were children who were part of the ethnic majority (W. J. McGuire, McGuire, Child, & Fujioka, 1978). Think about your

You may recall a similar point from chapter 5, pages 178 to 179: A solo member of a group tends to be perceived by observers in terms of that group membership.

■ **A unique car with unique owners?**
Sharing unusual characteristics can make those characteristics socially significant. Owners of the distinctive Volkswagen New Beetle have achieved group status: They find themselves honking at each other on the freeway and gathering in parking lots to discuss their cars.

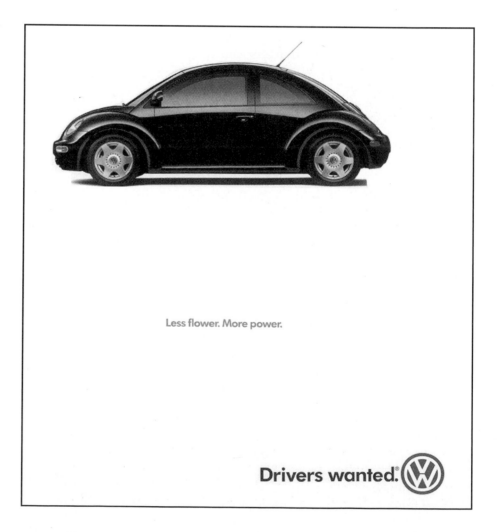

Less flower. More power.

Drivers wanted.

FIGURE 6.1   Being in the minority matters

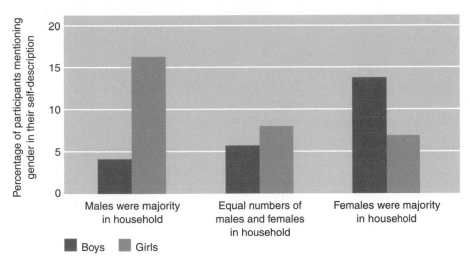

- In this study, grade-school children spoke for five minutes in response to the instruction "Tell us about yourself." Notice that both boys and girls were more likely to mention their gender if their gender was a minority at home. (Based on W. J. McGuire and others, 1979.)

friend's completions of the "I am . . ." sentences. Did your friend list group memberships that make him or her different from most other people?

CONFLICT OR RIVALRY. Although all of these reminders can make a social identity accessible, probably the most potent factor that brings group membership to mind is conflict or rivalry between groups (Doise & Weinberger, 1973; Ryen & Kahn, 1975). One experiment set up a discussion on a social issue, either between a male and a female participant who disagreed on the issue or between two men and two women, who disagreed along gender lines (Hogg & Turner, 1987). In the second condition, because the conflict was along group lines, participants identified more strongly with their groups, for example, by rating themselves as more typical of their sex. Even a news report of rivalry can remind us of group loyalties. In one study, exposure to a campus newspaper headline like "Humanities, Science Majors at Odds Over Core Program" was enough to increase the accessibility of students' identity as scientists or humanists (V. Price, 1989). Thus, conflict is perhaps the most powerful factor in making a group membership accessible.

Chapter 13 will describe the several vivid demonstrations of the effects of intergroup conflict on group identification, including the famed "Robbers Cave" study.

CULTURAL DIFFERENCES IN THE IMPORTANCE OF GROUP MEMBERSHIP. Group membership does not exist in a vacuum, of course, but has an importance that depends on the cultural context. Interdependent cultures, like most in Asia, South America, and Africa, foster and reinforce views of the self in group terms (Markus, Kitayama, & Heiman, 1996). People from these cultures tend to see themselves as members of larger groups or categories—perhaps as workers at a particular plant, graduates of a certain school, or inhabitants of a specific village. In such societies, family units are often multigenerational and employment relationships may last a lifetime.

In contrast, people who live in the United States, Canada, Northern Europe, and other individualistic cultures are encouraged to think of themselves in comparatively idiosyncratic terms, for example, as tall, dark, and handsome. They tend to value freedom, personal enjoyment, and the achievement of individual goals, while viewing group memberships as temporary and changeable (Bellah, Madsen, Sullivan, & Tipton, 1985). Members of these societies have high divorce rates and often seem comfortable switching churches or employers. Thus, cultural differences can affect whether people think of themselves more often as individuals or as members of groups, and by so doing, they can create corresponding differences in social behavior (Markus & Kitayama, 1991). But as we will see throughout this chapter, even in individualistic cultures in which group memberships are seen as more fluid and less omnipresent, group memberships make a big difference to people's ways of thinking about themselves and those around them.

PERSONALITY DIFFERENCES IN GROUP MEMBERSHIP IMPORTANCE. Every time you think of yourself as a group member—as, perhaps, a Texan, a psychologist, or a single mother—the mere thought increases the likelihood that you will think of yourself that way again. A group membership that is personally very significant—religious identification for a member of the clergy, party affiliation for a politician, or racial or ethnic group membership for a civil rights leader—will be frequently activated and highly accessible. This accessibility produces reliable and predictable differences in the way each of us habitually sees ourselves and others. For example, people for whom

FIGURE 6.2   Factors that make a social identity accessible

■ Many factors can increase the accessibility of a particular group membership. Not only obvious reminders, like group labels or intergroup conflict, but even relatively subtle factors like the presence of out-group members can activate our knowledge of group membership. A particular membership that is significant in the general culture or is personally important to an individual may be highly accessible virtually all the time.

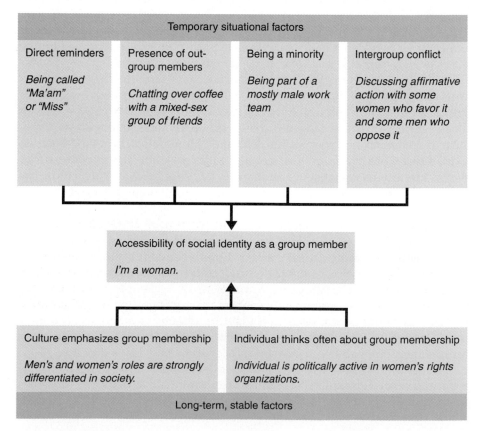

gender is chronically important and accessible have "male" or "female" as part of their self-schema (S. Bem, 1981). Accordingly, these individuals tend to perceive, and to react to, themselves and others in terms of gender rather than other social attributes (Frable, 1989). Similarly, people who are more racially prejudiced or more prone to use racial stereotypes seem more concerned with categorizing others by race (Blascovich et al., 1997; Zárate & Smith, 1990). Figure 6.2 summarizes all the factors that can make a social identity accessible.

To remind yourself of the consequences of having a particular trait as part of the self-schema, see chapter 4, especially page 113.

Me, You, and Them: Effects of Social Categorization

Does it really make a difference if we see ourselves as Mexican Americans, Californians, lefties, or libertarians? It certainly does! When group memberships surface, they influence the way we see ourselves and others, making a huge difference in what we think, how we feel, and what we do.

"I" Becomes "We": Social Categorization and the Self

Activated knowledge about a group membership has multiple effects on people's self-concept and self-esteem. People tend to see themselves as typical group members. Group memberships also influence people's moods and self-esteem as they feel bad about their groups' failures or good about their successes. Relatively small groups typically have the greatest effects.

SEEING ONESELF AS A GROUP MEMBER. Seeing oneself as a group member means seeing oneself as typical of the group; in effect, it means stereotyping *oneself* (J. C. Turner and others, 1987). One experiment demonstrated this effect by having some students listen to a discussion in which one group presented pro-environmental attitudes. Some of the students were about to join the group voicing the positive attitudes, while others knew they would not be joining. The students who were going to join the group rated themselves as higher in environmental awareness than did the other students who heard the same discussion (Mackie, 1986). In another study, Dutch university students were presented with a comparison that was potentially threatening to their group; for example, psychology students were asked to compare their own group to physics students on intelligence (Spears, Doosje, & Ellemers, 1997). The way students responded to this threat depended on their initial level of identification with their group. Students who identified only weakly avoided the threat by dissociating themselves from the in-group. But students who strongly identified with their group tended to self-stereotype, showing group solidarity by rating themselves as highly typical of their group. Evidently, factors that activate people's group identity—even threatening social comparisons—can cause people to see themselves in group-stereotypic terms.

When people see themselves as typical members of a group, this perception, just like any other aspect of the self-concept, directs their thoughts and actions. This process may be responsible for the finding that when laboratory groups include men, women speak more tentatively than they do in all-female groups (Carli, 1990). The presence of men apparently makes the women's identity as females accessible, causing many of them to act in ways that they regard as typical of women, such as by avoiding assertive speech. In fact, acting in gender-stereotypic ways tends to make people feel good about themselves (W. Wood, Christensen, Hebl, & Rothgerber, 1997).

☐ **ACCESSIBILITY OF GENDER IDENTITY IN THE CLASSROOM.** If group memberships can affect people's behavior in a situation as transient as a research discussion group, what is the likely long-term impact of highly accessible gender roles? College enrollment statistics suggest that they may influence women's and men's career and educational choices. In coeducational schools, men tend to major in the hard sciences and mathematics, and women in the humanities and fine arts. These majors are consistent with traditional stereotypes of men and women, which a mixed-sex environment renders more accessible. In contrast, compared with their counterparts in coeducational schools, women in women's colleges are more likely to major in science or math, and men in men's colleges, in the arts or humanities (E. R. Smith, 1977). Though many factors no doubt contribute to explaining outcomes like these, could the reduced salience of gender in single-sex schools reduce the impact of gender stereotypes on men's and women's choices of major?

LIKING OURSELVES: SOCIAL IDENTITY AND SELF-ESTEEM. We have all experienced it: We feel great when our team wins. When France beat the fa-

■ **Basking in reflected glory.** When we identify with a group, their emotional ups and downs become our own. Like these Danish soccer fans, we are not only happy to join in a victory celebration, we are happy *because* our team has won.

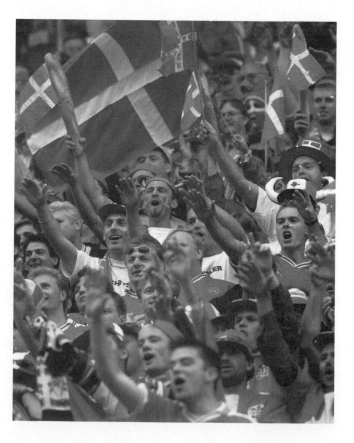

vored Brazilian team to win the 1998 World Cup soccer championship, hundreds of thousands poured into the streets of Paris for a frenzied celebration, many with their faces painted with the tricolor flag. Why? We experience emotions on behalf of our groups because group memberships are a part of our social identity (E. R. Smith, 1993). When good things happen to our team, our school, or our city, we feel good—about life and about ourselves. Recall that in the experiment described at the outset of this chapter, the same process made members of a minority group feel good or bad depending on the performance of a fellow group member (Brewer & Weber, 1994).

Strivers for positive self-esteem that we are, we play up group memberships that make us feel good about ourselves (Tesser, 1988). Robert Cialdini and his co-workers (1976) investigated this tendency to **BIRG**, or *bask in the reflected glory* of a positive group identification, by counting "in-group" clothing worn on school days following football games. At seven universities they found that students wore more school sweatshirts, baseball caps, scarves, and pins if the football team won than if it lost.

You may recall from chapter 4, pages 118 to 125, that, in the same way, people tend to play up the idiosyncratic characteristics they feel good about.

To test their hypothesis that links to a positive group membership serve to raise self-esteem, Cialdini and his colleagues (1976) gave students a brief general-knowledge test and temporarily raised or lowered their self-esteem by manipulating the results. Some randomly selected students were told falsely that they had performed poorly on the test, and others were told that they had done well. The students were then asked, seemingly incidentally, to describe the outcome of a recent game. In their descriptions, the students who thought they had failed the test were more likely to associate themselves with winning teams (referring to them as "we") and to dissociate themselves from losing teams (referring to them as "they"), than were students who believed they had done well and whose self-esteem was intact. Thus, people BIRG as a way of restoring positive self-regard, and they do so particularly when self-esteem is threatened.

BALANCING INDIVIDUALITY AND CONNECTEDNESS. As we saw in chapter 4, people generally like to see themselves as unique individuals, distinct from others. Yet they are also motivated to seek connectedness and similarity with others. Can people balance these two seemingly incompatible needs? In fact, group membership can simultaneously satisfy both. Perceiving the differences between our group and other groups provides feelings of being unique and special, while seeing the similarity among members within our group can help us feel connected and similar (Brewer, 1991). Though individual and cultural differences influence the relative strengths of these opposing motives, the best balance for most people most of the time involves membership in relatively small groups. Another study confirmed this idea by showing that people's self-esteem is highest when they can both have pride in their in-groups and feel respected by the other members of those groups (H. J. Smith & Tyler, 1997). A group that is too small might not be an adequate basis for group pride, but in a group that is too large, the person might be too anonymous to attain much respect. Relatively small groups seem to provide the best balance between similarity and group identification on the one hand and uniqueness and recognition for one's individual qualities on the other (Brewer, 1991).

BIRG (bask in reflected glory). A way of boosting self-esteem by identifying oneself with the accomplishments or good qualities of fellow in-group members.

Others Become "We": Social Categorization and the In-Group

When group membership is highly accessible, people see other in-group members as similar in their central group-linked characteristics. However, extensive personal interaction (when group membership is not activated) also provides knowledge about their unique and diverse personal characteristics. People like fellow in-group members and tend to treat them in fair, humane, and altruistic ways, seeing the other members as similar to themselves in their goals and interests.

An accessible group membership is not just an aspect of the individual self, like height or chess-playing ability. Instead, this aspect of *social* identity links the individual to others, influencing the way the person thinks, feels, and acts toward other in-group members.

PERCEIVING FELLOW IN-GROUP MEMBERS. When we think about fellow in-group members, what is uppermost in our minds? When group membership is accessible, we think mostly about the features we believe we share with the group, thereby causing us to see other in-group members as similar to ourselves. In one demonstration of this effect, students were assigned to groups ostensibly on the basis of their artistic preferences. They were then asked to guess the extent to which other in-group members shared their own personal characteristics and preferences (V. L. Allen & Wilder, 1979). As expected, the students assumed that all members of the group would be very similar in art preferences. Surprisingly, they also thought that in-group members' interests, activities, and even personality traits would match their own. Anything that increases the accessibility of group membership—being a minority, engaging in competition, even just making judgments about another group, for example—further enhances this assumed similarity (Haslam, Oakes, Turner, & McGarty, 1995; N. Miller & Brewer, 1986; B. Simon, 1992).

Although a highly accessible shared group membership leads us to focus on our similarities with other in-group members, we also manage to learn quite a lot about other in-group members' personal qualities—the things that make them unique as individuals. This awareness of specific, personal attributes develops as we interact with other members in a variety of contexts and situations (J. C. Turner and others, 1987). It is particularly acute when personal rather than group identities are most salient, as when a group of close friends chats together over dinner.

Knowing about others' unique characteristics helps us to find our own place in the group. As chapter 4 noted, we define our personal selves in terms of what makes us distinct from others (W. J. McGuire and others, 1978; Park & Rothbart, 1982). Among your fellow students you may be the serious one, the conservationist, the lover of country music. Of course, to make these differentiations you have to pay attention to the personality, passions, and preferences of your fellow in-group members. In doing so, you learn a lot about them—so much that when group membership is not highly accessible, you are likely to see your group as quite diverse in characteristics *not* related to group membership (Park & Judd, 1990).

LIKING IN-GROUP MEMBERS: TO BE US IS TO BE LOVABLE. Because they share our attributes, fellow in-group members become part of "me and mine" and so we like them, usually much more than we like out-group members. Asked to evaluate essays or creative solutions to problems, people treat their own group's work more generously than out-group products. They choose to interact with and to befriend members of their own rather than of another group (Brewer, 1979; Brewer & Silver, 1978). Even people assigned to groups on a trivial or random basis evaluate their own group as more positive and desirable than other groups, and the in-group bias is stronger yet when the groups are real and meaningful (Mullen, Brown, & Smith, 1992).

Indeed, the very concept "we" seems to have positive connotations, as compared with the concept "they" (Perdue, Dovidio, Gurtman, & Tyler, 1990). People think that nonsense syllables (like *xeh*) that have been paired with the word *we* have more positive meanings than syllables paired with the word *they*. Participants also respond more quickly to positive words that follow the prime *we* than to those that follow *they*, when the prime words are flashed too quickly to be consciously read. Both of these findings suggest that the label *we* automatically activates positive associations that facilitate the recognition of other positive words. In a clever study of the consequences of these effects for intergroup behavior, students were asked to read a description of the task that they were to perform with other individuals. For one group of participants, this task was described as "something *we* all have to do *our* best on"; for other participants it was "something *they* have to do *their* best on." When asked to imagine the quality of the interaction and the likability of the other participants, those who had been exposed to the in-group pronouns had more positive expectations than those who had read out-group pronouns (Dovidio & Gaertner, 1993).

It may have occurred to you that attraction to other in-group members is somehow different from "ordinary" feelings of liking for another individual. After all, attraction usually depends on getting to know someone—on recognizing their desirable personal characteristics and your common interests. In contrast, attraction in group situations seems to depend merely on the knowledge of shared group membership (J. C. Turner, Sachdev, & Hogg, 1983). Indeed, people often prefer others who belong to their own group even if those people would not be especially likable on the merits of their individual characteristics alone. This pattern has been observed in many types of groups, including work groups and the members of an Australian football team (Hogg, Cooper-Shaw, & Holzworth, 1993; Hogg & Hardie, 1991). In a sense, in-group members are liked not as individuals but as representatives of the liked group (Clement & Krueger, 1998).

GIVING IN-GROUP MEMBERS AN ATTRIBUTIONAL ADVANTAGE. This special kind of liking leads us to give fellow in-group members the benefit of the doubt when we make attributions about their behaviors. Unfortunately, we are not nearly so generous with out-group members (Islam & Hewstone, 1993). Consider the responses of Hindu office workers who were presented with descriptions of either a Hindu person or a Muslim person behaving in a socially desirable or undesirable way, for example, a shopkeeper being particularly generous or cheating a customer (D. M. Taylor & Jaggi, 1974). When Hindus explained the actor's behavior, they demonstrated *group-serving attributional biases*. That is, they attributed positive behavior by Hindus and negative actions by Muslims to enduring personality traits, in statements like "Hindus are generous" or "Muslims are basically cheats." Conversely, they attributed negative behavior by Hindus and positive behavior by Muslims to fleeting situational causes, such as "The Hindu

You might have noticed that the attributions we make about our groups are just like the self-enhancing attributions we make as individuals. To check the parallels for yourself, see chapter 4, pages 144 to 145.

cheated him because the man has been stealing from his store," or "The Muslim was generous because he thought the man worked for the authorities." Another study found that English schoolboys at private schools believe they and their comrades fail only because they do not try, but they think students in other schools fail because they are stupid (Hewstone, Jaspars, & Lalljee, 1982). People everywhere make positively biased attributions for the behaviors of the in-group, but they do not do so for the out-group (Pettigrew, 1979).

Bias favoring the in-group can be found in the very language people use to describe others' actions. Anne Maass and her colleagues (Maass, Salvi, Arcuri, & Semin, 1989) prepared cartoon drawings depicting positive actions by in-group and out-group members. Asked to describe the actions, participants gave relatively concrete and specific descriptions of out-group behavior, whereas the in-group descriptions were more abstract and general. If an out-group member comforted a lost child on a crowded street, participants said "he *talked to* the child," or some similarly specific statement. The same action by an in-group member elicited "he *helped* or *cared for* the child." The researchers argue that the concreteness of the out-group descriptions implicitly casts the behaviors as ungeneralizable, one-of-a-kind instances, while the more abstract terms used for in-group actions emphasize their links to the actor's positive general characteristics, such as helpfulness or caring. Another study found that people answer questions about positive attributes of the in-group or negative attributes of the out-group on the basis of their general impressions of those groups. But when asked about negative in-group or positive out-group characteristics, the participants tried to recall specific behaviors from memory (J. W. Sherman, Klein, Laskey, & Wyer, 1998). Like the linguistic bias just described, this judgment strategy implicitly frames unexpected types of behaviors (such as negative acts by in-group members) as isolated, specific occurrences, that is, as exceptions to the rule rather than the general rule.

TREATING THE IN-GROUP RIGHT: JUSTICE AND ALTRUISM. If in-group members are lovable and similar to us, we will want to treat them as we ourselves would like to be treated. Indeed, people sometimes act in ways that seem to make no sense from the perspective of individual costs and benefits. Parents scrimp and save to leave an inheritance for their children. Soldiers sacrifice their lives for their comrades or their country. From the perspective of a social group, however, actions like these make a great deal of sense. Groups prosper when their members are willing to subordinate personal interests to the group and to help other members in times of need. This has been true since members of many early hunting societies shared the meat from large animals among the whole group (A. P. Fiske, 1992). When group memberships are uppermost in people's minds, they often act in these altruistic ways, showing more concern for treating others fairly than for getting the largest share of rewards (Tyler, Lind, Ohbuchi, Sugawara, & Huo, 1998).

When people see the world through the lens of their group memberships, what is best for the group blurs together with what is best for the individual. As "I" becomes "we," the distinction between self-interest and group interest vanishes (J. C. Turner and others, 1987). This merging of perceived individual and group interests constitutes the psychological basis for fair and altruistic behavior. Over a century ago Charles Darwin (1871/1909) argued that morality derives originally "from the social instincts": Actions are judged good or

It is this unification of self-interest and group-interest that makes altruistic and self-sacrificing behavior possible, as we will see in chapter 14. It is also the basis of effective functioning of small interacting groups, a topic discussed in detail in chapter 12.

FIGURE 6.3 Social identity turns others into "we"

■ When a shared group membership is accessible, it has positive effects on the way we see, evaluate, and treat other group members.

bad "solely as they obviously affect the welfare of the tribe." When people think of themselves as members of a family, community, ethnic group, or nation, they feel *like* and feel *for* fellow in-group members. As a result, treating those others with fairness and compassion—indeed, treating others as they themselves would like to be treated—becomes easy, natural, and the right thing to do (Deutsch, 1973, 1990; Staub, 1978; Struch & Schwartz, 1989).

An accessible group membership makes other in-group members part of "me and mine." Shared group membership has dramatic effects on the way we think about, evaluate, and behave toward other members, as shown in Figure 6.3.

Others Become "They": Social Categorization and the Out-Group

People see out-groups as quite uniform and homogeneous. People also dislike, devalue, and discriminate against out-group members, depending on the extent to which they are seen as threatening to the in-group. When the out-group is simply different, it elicits mild dislike. When the out-group is seen as outdoing the in-group, this more serious threat results in resentment, dislike, and overt discrimination. Out-groups that are seen as severe threats to the in-group elicit murderous hatred, discrimination, aggression, or moral exclusion.

The comedian Emo Phillips (cited in D. L. Hamilton & Mackie, 1990) describes a conversation with a suicidal man threatening to jump off a bridge:

I said, "Are you a Christian or a Jew?" He said, "A Christian." I said, "Me too. Protestant or Catholic?" He said, "Protestant." I said, "Me too. What franchise?" He says "Baptist." I said, "Me too. Northern Baptist or Southern Baptist?" He says, "Northern Baptist." I said, "Me too. Northern Conservative Baptist or Northern Liberal Baptist?" He says, "Northern Conservative Baptist." I said, "Me too. Northern Conservative Fundamentalist Baptist or Northern Conservative Reformed Baptist?" He says, "Northern

Conservative Fundamentalist Baptist." I said, "Me too. Northern Conservative Fundamentalist Baptist, Great Lakes Region, or Northern Conservative Fundamentalist Baptist, Eastern Region?" He says, "Northern Conservative Fundamentalist Baptist, Great Lakes Region." I said, "Me too. Northern Conservative Fundamentalist Baptist, Great Lakes Region, Council of 1879 or Northern Conservative Fundamentalist Baptist, Great Lakes Region, Council of 1912?" He says, "Northern Conservative Fundamentalist Baptist, Great Lakes Region, Council of 1912." I said, "Die, heretic!" and I pushed him over. (D. L. Hamilton & Mackie, 1990, p. 10)

Emo Phillips makes comic what more often is tragic: the tendency to hate and mistreat those who are not members of our in-group, regardless of how similar to us they may seem to outsiders. Just as feeling good about our groups often involves giving them the edge over others, bringing our group up in the world sometimes means putting others down. Unfortunately, anthropological evidence suggests that this tendency to put other groups down is the rule rather than the exception in intergroup relations. Throughout human history and in every human culture, esteem, consideration, and favoritism await in-group members, whereas disdain, discrimination, and domination are often the fate of those categorized as out-group members (LeVine & Campbell, 1972). The process that culminates in these outcomes begins with a perception of out-group members as all alike: faceless people who lack individuality.

PERCEIVING THE OUT-GROUP AS HOMOGENEOUS: "THEY'RE ALL ALIKE!" A member of an Isla Vista, California, band explained, "Los Angeles bands are all homogeneous. Seattle bands all sound like Seattle bands. But Isla Vista music is more original. Bands here play all kinds of music!" (Lagerquist, 1992). You should have no difficulty finding other examples of this **out-group homogeneity effect:** the tendency to perceive out-group members as "all the same" compared to the relatively more diverse in-group. People of European origin typically see the widely diverse groups of Native Americans as "all the same" while finding great diversity and variety among those of European descent. Brothers in one fraternity find members of other houses just as they expected them but do not think they themselves fit their own group's stereotype (Linville, Fisher, & Salorey, 1989; Mullen & Hu, 1989). Thus the tendency to see out-groups as relatively homogeneous is quite widespread. What accounts for this effect?

One obvious potential explanation involves numbers: We usually know more in-group members than out-group members, and we are therefore more aware of their diversity. The more students you know on your campus, for example, the better your chances are of coming across a wide variety of individuals, such as the vegetarian gourmet cook, the athlete majoring in engineering, and the antinuclear activist. No wonder the in-group seems more diverse than the students at another, less familiar college (Linville and others, 1989). But lack of familiarity with the out-group cannot be the whole story. In fact, even members of laboratory groups, meeting under carefully controlled conditions so that participants have equal information about their own and other groups, see their fellow group members as more varied than members of other groups (Judd & Park, 1988; Mackie, Sherman, & Worth, 1993). And in studies that follow the development of group impressions as people get to know each other by interacting over many weeks, increasing familiarity often

Out-group homogeneity effect. The tendency to see the out-group as relatively more homogeneous and less diverse than the in-group.

FIGURE 6.4   It is easier to remember us than them

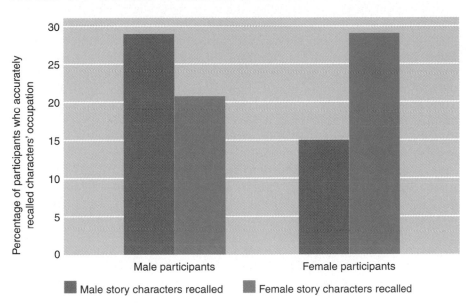

Male participants   Female participants

■ Male story characters recalled   ■ Female story characters recalled

■ In this study, men and women were asked to read a "newspaper story" and, at a later time, to recall information about the main characters. As you can see, men more easily recalled the occupations of male characters, whereas women more easily recalled female characters' occupations. (Based on Park & Rothbart, 1982.)

makes people view groups as increasingly homogeneous (Oakes, Haslam, Morrison, & Grace, 1995). On the basis of studies like these, it is clear that familiarity alone cannot fully explain the out-group homogeneity effect.

Another important factor is the relatively constrained nature of typical interactions with out-group members. The very presence of an outsider may be enough to make the group close ranks and present a unified front. In fact, people's exposure to out-groups often takes place in settings where no individual interaction is even possible, for example, when students from a rival school attend a sports event en masse. In such settings one can easily gain the impression that out-group members are pretty much all alike. In contrast, in-group interactions are likely to be relatively more varied, relaxed, and informal (Rothbart, Dawes, & Park, 1984). Moreover, you probably have a greater likelihood of meeting in-group members again in the future compared to out-group members. This means that even if the same information is available, you may be more motivated to remember in-group members' names and one or two other facts about them (Srull & Brand, 1983). As a result, in-group members' unique roles, traits, and opinions can emerge, so members are seen in more differentiated terms.

Finally, as we stated earlier, people habitually focus on the personal characteristics that make them unique and different from others. Within the in-group, this means that we learn a lot about others' characteristics in the process of finding out what differentiates us from them. But we can feel unique and different from out-group members just by noting their group-defining characteristics, such as ethnicity, gender, nationality, or university affiliation (J. C. Turner and others, 1987). In a study demonstrating this effect, Bernadette Park and Myron Rothbart (1982) asked students to read brief newspaper stories about men and women. When they later were asked to recall as much as they could about the protagonists, they remembered more personal details, such as occupation, about same-sex than about opposite-sex individuals (see Figure 6.4).

Although these cognitive and social processes mean that out-groups are usually perceived as more homogeneous than in-groups, there are interesting exceptions to the rule. When the in-group is a minority, it tends to be perceived as more homogeneous than the majority out-group, by outsiders and by its own members (R. Brown & Smith, 1989; B. Simon & Brown, 1987). But even this exception can be explained by the same processes outlined earlier. People who belong to a small minority may know even more members of the majority out-group than members of their own small in-group. They often see majority individuals in a wide variety of roles and situations, and they can expect to interact with them as frequently as with members of their own small group. And, if the majority commands more power and resources than the minority, minority group members may have to depend upon the majority and will have to be careful to treat individual majority group members in appropriate ways. For all these reasons, members of minority groups typically have strong reasons for recognizing fine distinctions among members of the majority group, as well as among members of their own in-group (S. T. Fiske, 1993).

And as we have already seen, group membership is more often on the minds of minorities than of majorities (Mullen, 1991). Its accessibility in turn causes people to see themselves as typical group members and to act accordingly (B. Simon & Hamilton, 1994). In this way minority status sometimes increases actual, as well as perceived, uniformity of thought and action.

□ OUT-GROUP HOMOGENEITY IN THE LEGAL SYSTEM. The out-group homogeneity effect extends even to the perception of physical characteristics, and this can have destructive effects. People can recognize the faces of members of their own ethnic group more easily than the faces of members of other groups, an effect called the *cross-race identification bias* (Anthony, Copper, & Mullen, 1992; Bothwell, Brigham, & Malpass, 1989). Apparently, members of other groups "all look alike." In one study, Texas convenience store clerks were asked to identify three male customers—actually experimental confederates—who had stopped by to make a purchase earlier in the day. One confederate was Black, another was Mexican American, and the third was Anglo American. The shop clerks were also members of these three ethnic groups. As Figure 6.5 shows, the clerks made more accurate identifications of the customer belonging to their own group than they did of the customers from the other two groups (Platz & Hosch, 1988). As familiarity with a group grows, so too does identification accuracy (A. G. Goldstein & Chance, 1985). No wonder, then, that criminal defendants and their attorneys often question the accuracy of eyewitness identifications across ethnic group lines.

The tendency to see members of the out-group as all alike may in itself be relatively harmless, but it sets the stage for worse feelings and behavior. You need only look at any newspaper, turn on the television newscast, or flip back to the examples in chapter 5 to see ample evidence that groups treat other groups badly, in ways ranging from mild dislike and overt discrimination all the way to domination, exploitation, and massacre. As we will see, one important factor in the way out-groups are treated is how much threat they seem to pose to the in-group.

EFFECTS OF MERE CATEGORIZATION: DISCRIMINATION FAVORING THE IN-GROUP.
For ethnic conflict in Kosovo or Rwanda, or any of the other manifold exam-

FIGURE 6.5   Inaccuracy in cross-ethnic identification

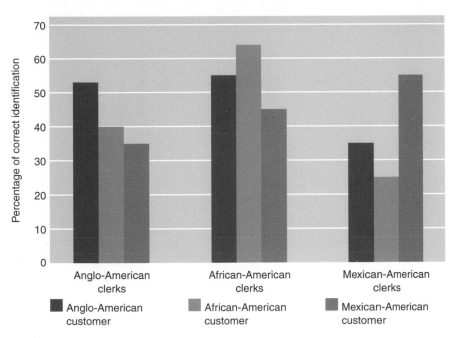

■ Convenience store clerks who were either Anglo American, African American, or Mexican American tried to identify customers that researchers had sent to visit their store earlier. The three customers also belonged to one of the three ethnic groups. As shown here, clerks were best able to identify customers from their own group. (Based on Platz & Hosch, 1988.)

ples of one group's maltreatment of another, multiple explanations can be offered. These include negative stereotypes, mutual ignorance and fear, unjust distribution of resources, and a history of conflict. However, perhaps the most sobering body of social-psychological research on the issue reaches a startling conclusion: Explanations like these are not necessary. Discrimination can occur when a dividing line simply creates two groups, even in the absence of these common sources of antagonism.

In one of the experiments that initially demonstrated this point, a number of English boys aged 14 to 16 were assigned to Group *X* or Group *W* on the basis of a coin toss (Billig & Tajfel, 1973). The groups had no defining characteristics, and members did not know which other individuals were in each group. There was no basis for in-group or out-group stereotypes, and the groups had no history of conflict or antagonism—indeed, no history at all. For all these reasons, this situation was appropriately labeled a **minimal intergroup situation**. After being assigned to a group, each boy was given the opportunity to distribute rewards worth a small amount of money to two other individuals. For example, he might be asked to divide, in any way he wanted, 15 points between two other boys, who were identified only as "Member number 49 of the *W* group" and "Member number 72 of the *X* group."

The late European social psychologist Henri Tajfel devised this procedure as a baseline for further comparisons. He planned to go beyond merely categorizing participants into groups, and to add other ingredients, such as negative stereotypes or conflict over resources, one at a time until prejudice and discrimination developed. However, the results in the baseline situation confounded the researchers' expectations. Even in this minimal situation, the boys favored their own group: They awarded more points to members of their in-group than to boys in the out-group. They

Minimal intergroup situation. A research situation in which people are categorized, on an arbitrary or trivial basis, into groups that have no history, no conflicts of interest, and no stereotypes.

Cartoon © Jules Feiffer

were not always blatantly unfair; for example, of the 15 points, boys awarded an average of 8.08 to the in-group and 6.92 to the out-group. However, the bias in favor of the in-group was consistent, and this finding was replicated in many other similar studies (Brewer, 1979; Mullen and others, 1992). Simple categorization into groups seems to be sufficient reason for people to dispense valued rewards in ways that favor in-group members over those who are "different."

DISCRIMINATION AND SOCIAL IDENTITY. What explains the favoritism found in minimal intergroup situations? Were people simply seeking material gain for the in-group? Tajfel was not so sure. His further explorations of behavior in minimal intergroup situations revealed a startling tendency: Participants often favor the in-group over the out-group *even when doing so costs the in-group in absolute terms.* For example, Tajfel gave some of his participants a choice between option *A*, which allocates 11 points to an in-group member and 7 to an out-group member, and option *B*, which gives 17 points to each. Many preferred option *A*, which gave the in-group an edge over the out-group, even though choosing *A* instead of *B* cost the in-group 6 points (Tajfel, Billig, Bundy, & Flament, 1971). These results and others show that the expectation of rewards is not the driving force behind intergroup discrimination (Gagnon & Bourhis, 1996). Other studies of minimal groups showed that members give their own group higher ratings on positive traits, evaluations of performance, and inferences of morality (Brewer, 1979). Apparently group members want to make their groups better, stronger, and more lovable in any way available to them.

These findings led Tajfel to propose that just as we strive to view our individual selves positively, we also want to view our social identities in positive terms. This idea was the basis for **social identity theory**, which argues that people's motivation to derive positive self-esteem from their group memberships is one driving force behind in-group bias (Tajfel and others,

Social identity theory. The theory that people's motivation to derive positive self-esteem from their group memberships is one driving force behind in-group bias.

1971) Preferring the in-group over the out-group becomes a way of expressing regard for the in-group, and it is therefore a way of feeling good about oneself (M. Rubin & Hewstone, 1998). Interestingly, studies show that people in minimal intergroup situations do not discriminate when allocating negative outcomes (like unpleasant blasts of noise) as they do when handing out praise or money (Otten, Mummendy, & Blanz, 1996). Evidently benefiting the in-group with more than its share of good things gives a greater boost to self-esteem than forcing the out-group to absorb most of the bad.

Group memberships have many benefits: They give us a sense of belonging and connectedness, as well as helping us to master and understand the world correctly. (We will discuss these other benefits in more detail in chapter 9.) However, enhancing self-esteem is indeed one of the most important effects of group membership, as social identity theory holds. The finding that people can increase their self-esteem by discriminating against out-groups has been repeatedly confirmed (Lemyre & Smith, 1985; Oakes & Turner, 1980; M. Rubin & Hewstone, 1998). And people are particularly likely to choose this tactic when their self-esteem has recently suffered a blow. In a study by Steven Fein and Steven Spencer (1997), for example, some participants were given false negative feedback on a supposed intelligence test. They then read a detailed description about a young actor's struggles to begin a career in New York City. If the description of the actor implied that he was probably gay, participants who had been made to feel bad about themselves rated the actor in highly negative and stereotypic terms. The ratings were more positive if the actor was described as heterosexual, or if the participant had received no negative feedback. Other kinds of threat, like being reminded of their own mortality, can also increase people's tendency to express biased views of out-groups (Nelson, Moore, Olivetti, & Scott, 1997).

But in the minimal intergroup situation, where is the threat that might spur people to discriminate against the out-group? In fact, being categorized in one of two unknown groups constitutes a threat to most people. Consider the experimental situation from the participant's point of view. You are assigned to a totally meaningless group and referred to by a code number rather than by name. Your only possible source of identity is the in-group/out-group distinction, and even the in-group cannot provide much of a positive identity because it is indistinguishable from the out-group. The results of one study demonstrated that this type of categorization can indeed be threatening. In the study, some participants were categorized as member 16 of an unknown "Red group," while others were assigned the personal code number 16 but were not categorized. Those assigned to an unknown group were found to have lower self-esteem than the other participants (Lemyre & Smith, 1985). The lost self-esteem was restored only by the opportunity to discriminate in favor of the in-group—to say, in effect, that the difference between the in-group and the out-group is that the in-group is *better*.

EFFECTS OF PERCEIVED DISADVANTAGE: LET'S COMPETE WITH THEM. Threats to a group occur not only within the laboratory but also in the outside world of everyday life, where they have the same effect of triggering intergroup discrimination. The effects differ, however, depending on the relative status positions of the groups (Ellemers & van Knippenberg, 1997; Mullen and others, 1992). When higher-status groups are threatened, they tend to discriminate on dimensions that are centrally relevant to the group distinction. Thus, common stereotypes applied by the economically successful to groups with lower economic standing involve traits like laziness, lack of ambition, and unintelligence—traits seen as quite relevant to economic position and success. In contrast, lower-status groups show more discrimination on other dimensions that are less directly relevant to status. So lower-class groups frequently evaluate themselves more favorably than higher-class out-groups on dimensions like friendliness, cooperativeness, or likability (Sachdev & Bourhis, 1991).

In general, unequal status amplifies intergroup discrimination. If groups perceive themselves as losing out to an out-group that is higher in status, more powerful, more prosperous, or more favored by government programs, they often turn from mild dislike to stronger emotions. Anger, resentment, and support for overt discrimination against the out-group are frequent outcomes. For example, Whites in the United States who regard their racial group as threatened by out-groups tend to oppose interracial marriage, affirmative action, the use of busing to desegregate schools, and welfare spending (J. M. Jones, 1992; Sears & Allen, 1984).

EFFECTS OF EXTREME THREAT: THEY THREATEN US, SO LET'S ATTACK FIRST. One evening in October 1998, two men lured Matthew Shepard, a 21-year-old college student in Laramie, Wyoming, from a bar out to their pickup truck. Driving out of town, they beat Shepard severely, fracturing his skull with a blow from a pistol butt. Finally they burned him, then left him tied to a fence in near-freezing temperatures. When a passerby found him 18 hours later he was rushed to a hospital, but he never regained consciousness and died several days later. The two attackers did not know Shepard personally, and they had no history of disagreement or conflict with him. Their only motive for this brutal crime was that Shepard was gay. What can explain this kind of hatred? Stereotypes can produce group prejudice, as we discussed in chapter 5, and Shepard's attackers probably believed that gay men have a variety of negative characteristics. But can stereotypes fully account for such murderous hatred?

When prejudice turns from dislike to extreme hatred, it usually reflects the perception that what "they" stand for threatens everything that "we" stand for. When people see such extreme threat, they usually respond in two interrelated ways. First, they exalt in-group symbols and values. Past or present group leaders, flags, slogans, and the group's historical accomplishments are glorified and cast in a totally positive light. Second, they derogate, hate, and attack the out-group they perceive as threatening. Hatred for outsiders that arises in connection with the exaltation of in-group symbols, whether the hatred is directed against homosexuals, women, immigrants, or racial, ethnic, or religious groups, is termed **symbolic prejudice** (Kinder, 1986; Sears, 1988). Recall that in the minimal intergroup situation, preferences for the in-group are relatively mild, taking the form of favoring the in-group with good things but usually not giving the out-group an unfair share of punishments (Mummendey and others, 1992). However, extreme group threat ties together glorification of the in-group and hatred for the out-group into an ominous package (Branscombe & Wann, 1994). This pattern was found, for example, in a study of South African Blacks' attitudes toward Afrikaner Whites, the group that had been the strongest supporters of the former apartheid system (Duckitt & Mphuthing, 1998).

A prime example of symbolic prejudice took place when the Communist regime in the former Yugoslavia began to fail around 1990. People

Symbolic prejudice. Hatred for out-groups that arises, together with the exaltation of in-group symbols, in response to perceived threat.

■ **Symbolic prejudice.** Some of the most virulent intergroup hatred arises from reverence for an in-group's cherished values when out-groups threaten those values. Here a group of Iraqis express their rage they hold towards the United States' policies by burning something of great symbolic significance—the U.S. flag.

of Serbian descent felt themselves threatened by Croatians and Muslims, though the groups had been living peacefully side by side. Following a strongly nationalist leader, Slobodan Milosevic, Serbians began proclaiming the historic rights of their people and remembering past martyrs and Serbian blood shed in many wars over the centuries. In actions that were chillingly reminiscent of Nazi atrocities, the Serbians then launched military campaigns aimed at "ethnic cleansing," creating a new, larger homeland by killing members of other groups or driving them from their homes and lands. In just one attack in 1992, heavy shelling drove out or killed three quarters of the 120,000 inhabitants of the city of Mostar. In the overall conflict, including wars in Bosnia and Kosovo, hundreds of thousands were killed and literally millions of people were made homeless refugees.

The exaltation of in-group values and symbols not only goes hand in hand with mistreatment of out-groups but also is used to justify it (Esses, Zanna, & Haddock, 1993; Sears, 1988). In the 18th and 19th centuries, for example, some Christian leaders cited biblical passages as evidence that slavery was divinely sanctioned (Swartley, 1983). Of course, many of their contemporaries posed the opposite argument, that slavery contradicted the basic message of the Bible. Apologists for slavery took such arguments as assaults on in-group values, as Albert Taylor Bledsoe did in his defense of slavery in 1860: "The history of interpretation furnishes no examples of more willful and violent perversions of the sacred text than are to be found in the writings of the abolitionists. They seem to consider themselves above the scriptures. . . . They put themselves above the law of God" (Swartley, 1983, p. 49). Today, some people are using similar arguments to oppose antidiscrimination protection for homosexuals. When people perceive threats to their groups, esteem and reverence for in-group symbols are often accompanied by prejudice against out-groups—which is justified by reference to those very symbols.

As these examples indicate, wherever you see virulent hatred of out-groups and support for outright discrimination, you can *always* expect to find the perception that the out-groups pose extreme threats to the cherished in-group. James Ridgeway (1991), author of a book on hate groups in the United States, described the manifestation of these feelings at a meeting with Ku Klux Klan (KKK) leaders:

FIGURE 6.6   Social identity turns others into "them"

Out-group seen as homogeneous	An identifiable out-group		
Germans tend to see Turks as "all alike."	Turkish workers in Germany.		

Out-group seen as different from in-group	Out-group seen as outdoing in-group	Out-group seen as seriously threatening in-group
Some Germans see cultural and religious differences.	Some Germans believe Turks take Germans' jobs.	Some Germans believe their country should be ethnically pure.

Mild dislike for out-group	Dislike and resentment for out-group; support for action against group	Extreme hatred for out-group; potential for violent action
Some Germans avoid Turks or discriminate against them in minor ways.	Some Germans support immigration limits, write anti-Turkish slogans on walls.	Some German neo-Nazi "skinheads" assault and murder Turks.

■ Out-group members tend to be seen as "all alike." In addition, they are often disliked and victimized by discrimination, depending on the magnitude of threat they are seen as posing to the in-group. Negative reactions may range from mild dislike, due to the simple perception of difference, to extreme hatred or even genocide when the in-group's very existence is believed to be threatened.

You could feel the hatred. In this delusional world, I realized, fear and hatred grew together: fear of a world that had left them behind, in which they could participate only marginally; hatred of the people they believed had caused them to lose out. . . . Everybody was after you. You were the only one left. Death was everywhere: figuratively, in terms of the White race perishing; and literally, as you fought, threatened, intimidated, and killed to "save" your people. (p. 5)

MORAL EXCLUSION. Groups like the KKK, which carry discrimination to its extreme, view out-groups as fundamentally inferior to the in-group—as subhuman and outside the domain in which the rules of morality apply (Opotow, 1990). History records numerous instances in which slaves, women, racial and religious minorities, and enemies of the nation or ruling power have been treated as fundamentally inferior to those who held power. This attitude allows us to suspend behaviors we usually consider both human and humane, such as helping others and treating them fairly and justly. These rules of justice and civility depend on seeing oneself and others as members of a larger community, and they therefore may not apply to out-group members (T. R. Tyler & Lind, 1990). When this perception is held by a powerful in-group, while members of relatively powerless groups are excluded from the scope of moral principles, the stage may be act for extreme intergroup oppression, massacre, or genocide (Opotow, 1990; Sachdev & Bourhis, 1991).

Moral exclusion can begin with symptoms that appear relatively benign, such as a belief in the in-group's moral superiority. The disease quickly spreads, however. In-group members may portray the out-group in subhuman terms, often by labeling them as vermin, barbarians, or even germs "infecting" the pure in-group, or by dismissing their ability to experience human sentiments like pain or grief. Destructive actions against the out-group may be rationalized by the idea that "they brought it on themselves" or by self-justifying comparisons with horrible atrocities committed by others. The actions may be given euphemistic and misleading labels, like Hitler's genocidal "final solution" or the Serbian "ethnic cleansing." Finally, group members reject personal responsibility for hateful or destructive acts by appealing to the in-group's welfare as a source of higher moral authority. These aspects of moral exclusion often play a role in the dynamics of intergroup conflict, which we will discuss in chapter 13.

People's reactions to out-groups usually stop short of virulent hatred and moral exclusion. Still, as shown in Figure 6.6, the reactions, though they range from mild to intense, are always negative. Moreover, prejudice and discrimination against out-groups are found in all cultures (LeVine & Campbell, 1972), and they may be even stronger in the interdependent cultures of Asia and Africa than in Western, independent cultures (Hsu, 1983; Moghaddam et al., 1993). Dislike, distrust, and discrimination seem to be intrinsic parts of the way people respond to out-groups: They are inextricably linked to the esteem and favor that in-groups enjoy.

When Group Memberships Are Negative

What are the costs of belonging to a group that is disliked, discriminated against, or excluded from the scope of moral principles? Members of these groups are likely to suffer from unequal economic opportunity, lack of access to quality education and medical care, and poor living conditions. In the United States, for example, the infant mortality rate for Blacks is more than twice the average for Whites; in fact, it is worse than the rate in Malaysia. Forty-three of every 100 Black children live in poverty, and nearly half of the murder victims in the United States are Black.

Group membership can impose other important costs as well, and the price is paid in decreased self-esteem and emotional well-being. If a group becomes part of the member's view of the self, what are the effects of belonging to a *stigmatized*, or negatively evaluated, group (Crocker, Major, & Steele, 1998)? Does membership inevitably drag down the individual? Or can the group become a source of pride for its members even when others look down on them?

Stigmatization is not just a problem for members of small minority groups like homosexuals or Blacks. Most of us belong to one or more groups that society devalues and stigmatizes, at least in certain contexts—women, people of color, the elderly, recent immigrants, people with AIDS, the overweight, the disabled, the unemployed, the addicted; the list seems endless. If you cannot think of any negatively regarded groups that you belong to yourself, perhaps reading the questions in Table 6.1 will give you a sense of what others experience.

TABLE 6.1. Turning the Tables: Questions Implying that Group Membership is Abnormal and Devalued

1. What do you think caused your heterosexuality?
2. When and how did you decide you were a heterosexual?
3. Is it possible that heterosexuality is just a phase you may grow out of?
4. Is it possible your heterosexuality stems from a neurotic fear of others of the same sex?
5. If you've never slept with a person of the same sex, is it possible that all you need is a good same-sex lover?
6. To whom have you disclosed your heterosexual tendencies?
7. Why do heterosexuals feel compelled to seduce others into their lifestyle?
8. Why do you insist on flaunting your heterosexuality? Why can't you just be who you are and keep quiet about it?
9. Why do heterosexuals place so much emphasis on sex?
10. There seem to be very few happy heterosexuals. Techniques have been developed that might enable you to change. Have you considered aversion therapy?
11. Considering the menace of hunger and overpopulation, can the human race survive if everyone were heterosexual like yourself?
12. Despite social support of marriage, the divorce rate is still 50 percent. Why are there so few stable relationships among heterosexuals?

Note: This questionnaire has been used in sensitivity-training workshops to provoke discussion. Does it give you a sense of what it might feel like to belong to a group that most people dislike and regard as abnormal?

Source: From *Working It Out: The Newsletter for Gay and Lesbian Employment Issues.*

Effects of Stigmatized Group Memberships

Negative stereotypes about the abilities of a group's members can become self-fulfilling, actually harming the members' performances. In addition, belonging to a devalued group poses a threat to self-esteem.

EFFECTS ON PERFORMANCE. Realizing that others think that your group does not have what it takes to perform well in some area is a psychological burden in itself. But recent research shows that this type of **stereotype threat** can actually act as a self-fulfilling prophecy, bringing about confirmation of the stereotype. To examine this process, Claude Steele and Joshua Aronson (1995) used the common stereotype that Black Americans are unintelligent and academically untalented. They gave Black and White students a difficult test, telling some that it was highly related to intellectual ability and telling others that the test was "just a laboratory exercise." When the test was described as an unimportant exercise, or when the research participants were not asked to record their race on the experimental materials, Black students performed as well as White students (when appropriate statistical adjustments were made for the students' individual levels of academic preparation, as measured by their SAT scores). But in the condition that posed a stereotype threat—when the test was said to tap intellectual ability and the student's race was explicitly identified—Black students scored more poorly than Whites. Similar effects have been found with a different group with a different stereotype about performance: women, and the idea that women are less able than men at math (Spencer, 1994). Women

Stereotype threat. The fear of confirming others' negative stereotype of your group.

perform worse than men when presented with very difficult math tests under standard instructions, but this difference vanishes if the participants are simply told that on "this particular test" research has found that there is no gender difference in performance! Another study with Asian women as participants found that subtly activating either their gender identity (associated with a low-performance stereotype) or their ethnicity (associated with high performance) caused the threat-related performance deficit to increase or disappear (Shih, Pittinsky, & Ambady, 1999).

What accounts for these unsettling effects? Steele and his colleagues believe that the very knowledge that other people hold a negative stereotype about your group's performance can bring the stereotype to mind, creating anxiety and crippling actual performance (Steele & Aronson, 1995). You may worry, for example, that any mistake you make will not only harm you personally, but will reflect negatively on your whole group, confirming the invidious stereotype in the minds of observers. Simone Young, one of the first women to conduct major symphony orchestras around the world, said: "Somehow, if a man gets in front of an orchestra and does a bad job, people say 'Well, we won't have him back again.' But if a woman fails, they say, 'See what happens when you have a woman conductor.'" (Tommasini, 1996). Thus, for example, imagine a 75-year-old person who momentarily forgets an acquaintance's name (as we all do from time to time). Realizing that this confirms a stereotype of the elderly as forgetful, the person may be flooded with high levels of anxiety that will make memory even worse.

Providing people with an external excuse for a potential poor performance can reduce stereotype threat and its effects on performance. When R. P. Brown and Josephs (1999) gave male and female students a difficult math test, the standard gender difference in performance emerged. However, if a faked computer problem eliminated the students' chance to do practice problems before taking the test, the women's performance improved. With an external excuse available for a possible poor performance, the women had no reason to fear that failure would confirm the gender stereotype. Because stereotype threat is not an issue for men in the area of math performance, the excuse had no effect on the men's test scores.

EFFECTS ON SELF-ESTEEM. However negative the effects on task performance, belonging to a socially devalued group can have effects on self-esteem that are more subtle, but perhaps ultimately even more severe. Because social group membership contributes so directly to individual self-identity, belonging to a negatively regarded group can take its toll on the individual. Kenneth Clark, a distinguished social psychologist whose research contributed to the 1954 U.S. Supreme Court decision mandating school desegregation, commented, "Human beings . . . whose daily experience tells them that almost nowhere in society are they respected and granted the ordinary dignity and courtesy accorded to others, will, as a matter of course, begin to doubt their self worth" (K. B. Clark, 1965, p. 64).

Clark was right to be worried, for feelings about group membership do have a major impact on the emotional and physical well-being of members of stigmatized groups. One group of researchers measured Black and White students' personal self-esteem, their feelings about their group memberships, and symptoms of depression (Luhtanen & Crocker, 1992). For Whites, low personal self-esteem was the key factor that increased the risk of depression.

This is not the first time we have seen that feeling bad about oneself can produce symptoms of depression. Look back at chapter 4, pages 139 to 140.

For Blacks, in contrast, *collective self-esteem*—positive or negative feelings about group membership—was more strongly related to depression than was personal self-esteem (Luhtanen, Blaine, & Crocker, 1991). That is, among Black students with similar levels of individual self-esteem, those who were less proud and happy about their group membership were more likely to be depressed. Writers like Malcolm X (1966) have eloquently described their struggles in coming to terms with their ethnic identity, integrating socially stigmatized group membership into a positive overall sense of self. And negative feelings arising from group membership are not limited to socially disadvantaged groups. Even members of dominant groups like men, when reminded of their group's privileges and advantages over women, can have their self-esteem lowered by feelings of guilt (Branscombe, 1998; Doosje, Branscombe, Spears, & Manstead, 1998).

Wouldn't you expect that belonging to a group that many people look down on, despise, and discriminate against would bring *you* down? Then consider this puzzle: Individual members of many stigmatized groups, including Blacks, people with developmental disabilities, and people who are facially disfigured, have self-esteem that is just as high as that of individuals who are not members of these groups (Crocker & Major, 1989). Clearly, at least some members of negatively regarded groups can defend and enhance their self-esteem. How are they able to value themselves in a society that devalues their groups?

Defending Individual Self-Esteem

Belonging to a group that is disliked and discriminated against by others can have a major impact on the individual. But this experience does not inevitably lead to lowered self-esteem, because people can attribute negative reactions to others' prejudice or make most of their social comparisons against fellow in-group members.

USING ATTRIBUTIONS TO ADVANTAGE. A Black person described a common dilemma to a White reporter.

> *If you go into a restaurant and get totally lousy service, you know it's for one reason. They do totally lousy service. I go into a restaurant and I get totally lousy service, I don't know why. . . . Is it because we're black or is it because . . . it's a bad service person?* (Duke & Morin, 1992)

When a member of a devalued group is treated badly, attributional ambiguity is created: The treatment might have been due to group membership. The same uncertainty arises in more significant form when group members are rejected for jobs, promotions, or bank loans. People in these situations are free to attribute others' behavior to prejudice against their group.

One clever experiment demonstrated that people often see another person's behavior as a response to a stigma, even when the stigma could not possibly have had any effect (Kleck & Strenta, 1980). Participants were made up to look as if they had a large and disfiguring facial scar, which they examined in a mirror before the experimenter applied "moisturizer." Without the participants' knowledge, the moisturizer they thought would "set their make-up" in fact removed the scar. Participants then spent several minutes with a second person to assess the effects of the disfigurement on social interaction. Those who falsely believed they were disfigured thought their scar had a tremendous effect on how they were treated, even though their partners were of course unaware of the stigma. People who permanently belong to stigmatized groups, like the Black restaurant patron, always have group membership accessible as a potential explanation for the way others treat them.

Of course, attributing negative outcomes to others' prejudice against one's group can protect self-esteem against the negative psychological effects of failure (Crocker & Major, 1989; Crocker and others, 1998). However, the strategy, like many of the self-enhancing biases described in chapter 4, also carries a cost. First, negative feedback is sometimes realistic, and discounting it can prevent accurate self-assessment and self-improvement. Second, the strategy may breed a sense of hopelessness and a loss of control: If one always expects to be treated primarily as a group member, no personal action will make any difference (Ruggiero & Taylor, 1995).

Third, attributing other people's reactions to group membership can destroy trust in positive feedback. Are praise and promotions signs of respect and admiration for one's accomplishments, or are they due to sympathy, pity, and resigned affirmative action? Research suggests that members of stigmatized groups are likely to suspect the latter—to discount positive feedback and attribute honors and accomplishments to others' efforts to appear unprejudiced. Unfortunately, these cynical views are sometimes right. Leaning over backwards to avoid seeming prejudiced, people sometimes inflate their evaluations of members of disliked out-groups compared to their ratings of in-group members who turn in the same performance (Crocker, Voelkl, Testa, & Major, 1991).

One study demonstrates both the costs and benefits of this attributional strategy. Black students participated in a "study of friendship development" with a White same-sex evaluator. Some students believed the evaluator seated in the next room could see them (the blinds on a window between the two rooms were up), while others knew the evaluator could not see them (the blinds were down). After exchanging self-description forms with the partner, participants received either a very favorable or very unfavorable response that was supposedly from the partner but was actually prepared by the researchers. Black students who received negative feedback were more likely to attribute the evaluation to prejudice—thereby protecting their self-esteem—when the blinds were up than when the blinds were down. However, they also distrusted the evaluator's positive response when the blinds were up, assuming that it might reflect leaning over backward. A positive response increased the Black students' self-esteem when they could not be seen, but actually *decreased* it when they could be seen (Crocker and others, 1991).

Thus, belonging to a stigmatized group can be a buffer against the chill of negative feedback, but it also barricades you from the warm pleasure usually derived from positive feedback. Perhaps it is awareness of these costs that keeps some members of stigmatized groups from making attributions to others' prejudice unless the evidence is virtually unavoidable. In one study, women who received negative feedback from a male generally blamed the low quality of their performance rather than the man's potential sexism, unless other information established with virtual certainty that the man was prejudiced (Ruggiero & Taylor, 1995).

☐ **ATTRIBUTIONAL AMBIGUITY IN THE WORKPLACE.** Not knowing how to interpret feedback can create serious workplace problems for people with disabilities, women, and other groups. For example, if a few wheelchair users are hired at a typical business, they draw more than their fair share of attention. Like members of other groups, they may feel that their every move is scrutinized and that their behavior reflects not only on themselves but on all people with disabilities (Pettigrew & Martin, 1987).

In some cases, an employee may suspect that he or she is a *token*, a single group member hired in order to avoid more thoroughgoing change. Consider the dilemma this suspicion creates: In these circumstances, people find it hard to trust feedback because outcomes seem to be determined by group membership. For example, women managers who believe they were hired because of their gender show lower organizational commitment and job satisfaction and higher role stress than women who believe they were hired for their abilities (Chacko, 1982).

In an experimental demonstration of this effect, one group of men and women were told that they were selected for a leadership role because they had scored well on leadership potential tests. Another group learned that they had been selected because the experimenter "needed more" of their gender in leadership positions (Heilman, Simon, & Repper, 1987). Later, the participants learned that they had either succeeded or failed on the leadership task. As can be seen in Figure 6.7, women selected on the basis of gender rather than merit devalued their own leadership ability, regardless of whether they performed well or poorly as leaders. The women in this condition also reported less interest in persisting as leaders. In contrast, men did not show such self-doubts, whether they believed their selection reflected merit or gender-based preference. Members of groups that are typically devalued and discriminated against are the most at risk from attributional ambiguities involving performance feedback.

FIGURE 6.7   Preferential treatment can lead to self-doubt among women

■ Men or women were led to believe that they were chosen as leaders either on the basis of merit or through gender-based preferential treatment. They were then told that they either succeeded or failed on a leadership task. When male participants rated their own leadership ability, as the left bars show, their ratings were about equal in all conditions. However, women who thought that they had been chosen on the basis of gender doubted their own leadership ability—whether they had succeeded or failed. (Based on Heilman and others, 1987.)

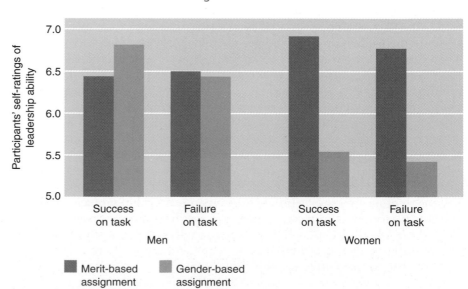

MAKING THE MOST OF INTRAGROUP COMPARISONS. Chapter 4 showed that social comparisons are an important source of self-evaluation. Thus, is it any wonder that a female middle manager in a large firm might choose to think of herself as "one of the highest-ranking women here at Acme Corporation" rather than to compare herself to the male members of top corporate management (Major, 1994)? This kind of in-group comparison is also typical of ethnic groups. One study found that Black schoolchildren who compared themselves mainly with other Blacks had higher self-esteem than those who compared themselves with White children (M. Rosenberg & Simmons, 1971). Intragroup comparisons not only boost self-esteem by showing us that we are better off than some others, they also remind us of in-group members who are doing particularly well—even if we are not. When given the opportunity to choose others for comparisons, schoolchildren from low-status groups in both New Zealand and the United States often name other in-group members who are high performers in the social, academic, or athletic domains (Aboud, 1976; Mackie, 1984). And recall that in the social comparison study cited at the beginning of this chapter, members of a minority group got a boost from a fellow group member's good performance (Brewer & Weber, 1994).

WOMEN'S SELF-ESTEEM: WHAT'S SO SPECIAL ABOUT GENDER? We now have a partial solution to the puzzle posed earlier: Members of stigmatized groups, such as Blacks, can use several strategies to maintain levels of self-esteem equal to that of the dominant group, in this case, Whites. However, another puzzle remains. Even though they also can use all of the strategies we have discussed, women seem to have lower self-esteem than men (Freiberg, 1991a; Skaalvik, 1986). The gender gap in self-esteem initially arises in adolescence, when teachers and other adults often discourage girls from academic pursuits while giving boys more attention and more challenging assignments in class.

The self-esteem difference has real consequences: Girls are much more likely than boys to lower their career aspirations, feeling that they are "not smart enough" to fulfill their dreams (Freiberg, 1991a). These findings remind us that psychological strategies of self-esteem defense are not always sufficient when teachers and other powerful people behave differently toward students from different groups. The findings also suggest that the same strategies may not work equally well for all groups (Frable, 1997). Why is gender different from other important group memberships? One reason may be that gender roles are learned extremely early in life and are reinforced by parents and peers. As a result, both men and women usually place a high value on behaving in accordance with these roles and may see gender as a more central aspect of the self than other group memberships (S. T. Fiske & Stevens, 1993).

Social Mobility: Escaping Negative Group Membership

If self-protective strategies are insufficient, people can attempt to escape from membership in a negatively regarded group. They can psychologically disidentify with the group, for example, by playing down group memberships that reflect badly on them or by regarding themselves as atypical group members. Another option is to dissociate, to escape physically, by "passing" or keeping group membership hidden "in the closet."

■ **Formulating self-esteem.** Young girls like these participating in a girl's "Future Frontiers" program are as interested in science and math as their male peers. But by adolescence, differential treatment by adults may have begun to take its toll on self-esteem. Often reacting to a teacher's belief that they are not smart enough to do things they may have excelled at in elementary school, young women begin to doubt their own abilities. They may then see career choices in math or science as out of reach. A program like this is attempting to reverse such trends.

When strategies intended to buffer self-esteem against the implications of negative group membership prove ineffective, people may turn to more long-term solutions involving either social mobility or social change (Tajfel & Turner, 1979). **Social mobility** is a strategy involving individual escape from membership in a negative group, either through disidentification (creating a psychological distance between oneself and the group) or through dissociation (physically escaping the group). Social mobility frees the individual from many of the costs of group membership and leaves the group's situation as a whole unchanged in the short run. Social change, in contrast, involves direct efforts to improve society's evaluation of the entire group. Note, however, that large amounts of individual social mobility may also create social change over time. For example, as increasing numbers of women overcome stereotypes and discrimination to enter previously male-dominated occupations, their actions may, over time, alter societal stereotypes of women. Recall that the roles typically held by group members are often reflected in stereotypes of the group (Eagly, 1987).

DISIDENTIFICATION: PUTTING THE GROUP AT A PSYCHOLOGICAL DISTANCE. Social mobility can be purely psychological, as when people *disidentify*, or minimize their personal connections to the group. One strategy is to avoid reminders of membership in a stigmatized group, as a laboratory study demonstrated (C. R. Snyder, Lassegard, & Ford, 1986). Students participated in a group problem-solving session and each group received success feedback, failure feedback, or no feedback at all. The experimenter then announced that they could take home team badges that advertised their group membership. Would team performance influence pride of membership? Apparently so. Over half of the members of groups that succeeded or received no feedback took badges home. But only 9% of those on a losing team welcomed the opportunity to announce their membership in it.

People can also disidentify from a group by publicly criticizing and devaluing an in-group member's poor performance. This reaction, termed *cutting off reflected failure*, or **CORFing**, makes it clear that the critic regards

Social mobility. The strategy of individual escape, either physical or psychological, from a stigmatized group.

CORF (cut off reflected failure). The act of criticizing or distancing oneself from an in-group or a group member who is viewed negatively.

the poor performance as unrepresentative of the group. For example, imagine that you (a law student) have to evaluate speeches given by a fellow law student and by a philosophy student. If the law student's speech was third-rate, your self-categorization with him would put you in an uncomfortable situation. Under these circumstances, you might be inclined to CORF—to downgrade the in-group speaker, rating her even more negatively than an out-group member who performed equally poorly. By doing so, you will make it clear that this in-group member's performance is not representative of your group. Marques and Yzerbyt (1988) obtained exactly this pattern of results. People rated successful in-group members higher, and poorly performing in-group members lower, compared with out-group members. When the previously cheering fans turn to booing and hissing the home team's losses with even more enthusiasm, perhaps part of their motivation is to psychologically distance themselves from poor performance (Branscombe, Wann, Noel, & Coleman, 1993).

Yet a third way of disidentifying is to consider *oneself* to be an exception rather than a typical group member. For example, many women acknowledge that women in general are discriminated against but insist that discrimination does not affect them personally (Crosby, Pufall, Snyder, O'Connell, & Whalen, 1989). The same pattern of beliefs is found among many other groups, including French-speakers in Quebec and immigrants to Canada from Haiti and India (D. M. Taylor, Wright, Moghaddam, & Lalonde, 1990). However, groups differ in the extent to which their individual members see themselves as escaping discrimination. Black students in one study were more likely than Asian students to attribute a poor grade assigned by a potentially prejudiced evaluator to actual prejudice (Ruggiero & Taylor, 1997). Of course, there could be many reasons for this belief, and it is certainly possible that some individual group members are fortunate enough to escape discrimination personally. But the belief is held most often by those who identify least strongly with their groups, suggesting that the belief serves, at least in part, as a psychological distancing mechanism (Crosby and others, 1989; H. J. Smith & Spears, 1996).

One fascinating study suggests that disidentification has a potential cost. Ferdman (1989) presented managers in an organization with videotapes of an interview with a Hispanic manager. Some saw an interview in which the individual discussed only personal, individuating information, with no explicit mention of his ethnicity. In another version of the interview the Hispanic man also described how important his group identity was to him and mentioned his participation in several Hispanic organizations. Those who watched the second version of the interview evaluated the man more positively, implying that people who play down their group memberships risk negative responses from others.

DISSOCIATION: PUTTING THE GROUP AT A PHYSICAL DISTANCE. Whereas disidentifying takes place in the mind, dissociating involves actual escape from a disadvantaged group or concealment of group membership. This form of social mobility occurs, for example, when immigrants cast off their cultural and linguistic heritage and become indistinguishable members of a new nationality. Gays or lesbians who are "in the closet" are concealing their group membership. A related strategy of some historical importance is "passing," a pattern in which light-skinned individuals of African ancestry

■ **"The critical and fundamental point is that ethnic background and/or composition should NOT make a difference. It does NOT make a difference to me. The bottom line is that I am an American . . . and proud of it!"** When Tiger Woods pounced on the professional golf circuit, winning the Masters at the young age of 21 and even getting his own Wheaties box, every aspect of him was suddenly in the spotlight, including his African-American/Asian heritage. As his quote illustrates, Woods wants to be admired for his individual talents and not merely in terms of his group memberships.

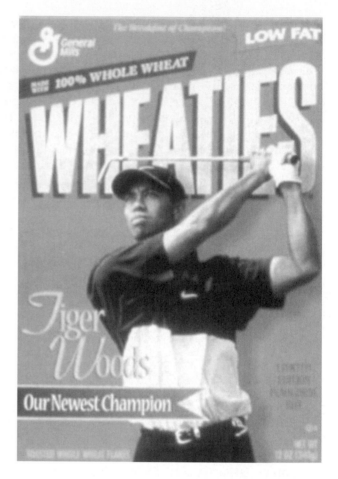

adopted a White identity, or American Jews adopted anglicized names and the customs of Gentile society (K. Lewin, 1948).

How successful is escape as a solution to membership in a negatively evaluated group? The answer seems to be that it is a mixed blessing. The individual does reap some personal benefits, such as freedom from discrimination, but for some, these benefits may be outweighed by the strategy's potential costs. New members of a group often suffer the isolation of not being thought quite the same as those "born to it." In addition, concealing group membership can be lonely and dangerous. The heartache of having to join in the laughter at anti-gay or racist jokes might be surpassed only by anxiety at being "outed." To deal with the problems of living with a concealed stigmatized identity, a recent study suggests that the potential anonymity provided by the Internet can help. Results found that interactive discussions on newsgroups devoted to group support can be an important source of identity for those with concealable stigmatized group memberships (such as drug addiction or homosexuality). Comparing people who participate in such newsgroups with participants in similar support newsgroups for nonconcealable stigmas (such as stuttering or being overweight), Katelyn McKenna and John Bargh (1998) found that the newsgroups involving concealable characteristics were more important to the lives of their members and had greater impact on their member's emotions and behavior. In effect, participation in the new-group increased members' acceptance of their identity, replacing feelings of isolation and just being different.

Finally, those who conceal their group membership give up opportunities to influence others' thinking about their group. U.S. Representative Barney Frank kept his homosexuality secret when he was first elected to Congress. He recalls that when he lobbied his colleagues on gay issues, "They would say 'Ah, you're right. But you know, it's not that important.' The pain gay people felt was unknown. We were hiding it from them. How the hell are they supposed to know when we were making damn sure they didn't?" (Schmalz, 1992).

Disidentification and dissociation are not viable options for many group members, leaving them only the option to turn and fight. Instead of separating from the group, either psychologically or physically, group members can directly attack society's negative evaluation of their group. Their aim is a change in social identity through concrete social change.

Social Change: Changing the Intergroup Context

Sometimes group members attempt to change society's evaluation of their in-group. They may redefine group characteristics in positive terms, engage in direct intergroup conflict or struggle, or seek to overturn the in-group/out-group distinction altogether.

Strikes, protest marches, and struggles in the courts and legislatures to outlaw discrimination are familiar tactics of the civil rights movement in the United States. These tactics reflect a social change strategy of confronting and challenging the hierarchy of group domination. **Social change** refers to the strategy of improving the overall societal situation of a group held in low esteem. Social change is preferred by people who identify strongly with their group and see themselves as typical members. Rather than changing only their personal situation, they wish to, and believe they can, change the way society regards their group as a whole (Tajfel & Turner, 1979). The main tactics employed by these determined group members are social creativity, social competition, and recategorization.

SOCIAL CREATIVITY. When faced with a negative identity on one dimension, groups can introduce and emphasize alternative dimensions on which the in-group is superior. A group of French boys at a summer camp showed this kind of *social creativity* when they found themselves in a hut-building contest with another team that had better construction materials (Lemaine, 1974). Realizing their inability to construct a large and sturdy structure, they created an elaborate garden around their mediocre cabin and asked the judges to consider them the garden-building winners. By introducing a new dimension of competition, the group maintained its superiority and distinctiveness. Similarly, players on the last-place team in a competitive ice hockey league cannot make a claim on skill and competitiveness, but they may be able to think of themselves as "cleaner" and more sportsmanlike than other teams. For one team, adopting this belief served to maintain the players' self-esteem, even though it seemed to correspond very little with reality—observers and coaches viewed the last-place team as one of the "dirtiest" in the league (Lalonde, 1992). In studies involving both laboratory-created and real-life

Social change. The strategy of improving the overall societal situation of a stigmatized group.

groups, Jackson and others (L. A. Jackson, Sullivan, Harnish, & Hodge, 1996) found that social creativity strategies were used more when the group boundaries were relatively fixed. When boundaries were permeable, social mobility became a preferred strategy.

Some women show social creativity by accepting society's definition of femininity and seeking a positive group identity through its distinctive positive characteristics. For example, they may emphasize dimensions of achievement that they view as specifically feminine, such as nurturing or peacemaking (Branscombe, 1998). This "cultural feminism" does not directly challenge social definitions of gender roles, but it does proclaim the value of feminine qualities and strengthen collective self-esteem. Along the same lines, a gay pride movement has emerged, with an emphasis on celebrating the accomplishments of gays and lesbians, particularly in artistic and cultural fields. "Black is beautiful!" was one group's statement that distinctive characteristics that have been derogated by the majority, such as skin color, language, or cultural heritage, can be redefined as a source of pride (Bourhis and others, 1978).

SOCIAL COMPETITION. Sometimes groups attempt to build in-group solidarity and oppose domination by the out-group, by taking direct action to improve the relative position, status, power, and resources of the in-group. When they do so, they are engaging in *social competition* by directly seeking to change the conditions that disadvantage them. This is the strategy that leads to in-group bias, when a group member gives the in-group an edge over the out-group by allocating his or her group more resources, evaluating in-group products more positively, and judging the in-group to be morally and socially superior. Of course, what looks like opportunity for advancement to disadvantaged groups often appears as a threat to a dominant group. Earlier, we saw that favored groups respond with increased levels of prejudice and discrimination against out-groups when they see those groups as threats. Thus, social competition strategies are likely to provoke a backlash from powerful groups.

Groups engage in these strategies when they believe they can make a difference and improve their situation in concrete ways (Tajfel & Turner, 1979) or when their members strongly identify with the group (B. Simon and others, 1998).

Social competition strategies take many forms. They include the strategy of radical feminism (e.g., Kate Millett, 1970) and the pressure for racial self-sufficiency and separatism advocated by the Nation of Islam. Everywhere in society, lobbies and advocacy organizations seek social changes that will benefit particular groups. The American Association of Retired Persons and Gray Panthers mobilize efforts on behalf of seniors. Groups such as the Coalition of Citizens with Disabilities and Mainstream, Inc. lead "wheelchair rebellions." Radical gay and lesbian organizations such as Queer Nation actively combat gay bashing, antigay prejudice, and negative portrayals of homosexuals in the media while lobbying for open and equal opportunities for their group. Individuals as well as organizations can engage in social competition strategies, for example, by creating informal associations of group members aimed at community building and mutual support. Individuals can also speak out against stereotypes, prejudice, and discrimination whenever they encounter them: in ethnic slurs, sexist jokes, or "old boy" hiring practices in organizations.

RECATEGORIZATION: CHANGING THE DEFINITION OF IN-GROUP. Social change can also come through transcending group categorizations. In most business organizations, for example, there will be both male and female members among both the senior staff and the junior staff. Thus, some individuals who are out-group members on one dimension will be in-group members on another; the categorizations by professional status and gender cut across each other (Doise, 1978). What impact does *cross-categorization* have on in-group bias? To find out, one experimenter set up groups in which out-group members on one dimension were in-group members on another dimension. When such a cross-categorization was introduced, intergroup discrimination against members of partially overlapping in-groups was greatly reduced (Vanbeselaere, 1991). This technique cannot completely wipe out discrimination, however. The male senior staffers may expand their in-group to include senior females or junior males, bestowing on them the many benefits of in-group membership. In this sense, cross-categorization also produces recategorization, but the female junior staff remain outside even the redrawn group boundaries.

Thus, one promising way to transcend group antipathies is to form new inclusive in-groups from which esteem and identity can be derived (S. Feshbach & Singer, 1957; Gaertner, Dovidio, Anastasio, Bachman, & Rust, 1993). Laboratory demonstrations using experimentally created minimal groups have confirmed that blurring boundaries can coalesce groups into one larger overarching structure, thereby reducing bias and discrimination. Samuel Gaertner and his colleagues (Gaertner, Mann, Murrell, & Dovidio, 1989) found, for example, that intergroup relations were improved when members of two subgroups were placed at alternating seats around a table and when they gave the joint group a new and separate name. However, creating new, inclusive in-groups does not necessarily mean denying the importance of the former group memberships.

These recategorization strategies are important weapons in the fight against intergroup conflict. We discuss their implications for reducing conflict in chapter 13, pages 543 to 545.

"COLOR-BLINDNESS" OR VALUING GROUP DIFFERENCES? How many times have you heard someone say "I don't care if he's black, white, green, or purple—I'll judge him by his job performance!" Statements like these express a "color-blind" ideology, the idea that race should not affect the way people are treated, and should therefore be disregarded and even actively ignored (Schofield, 1986). This ideology fits well with the emphasis on individual achievement that prevails in independent cultures, so it has a strong appeal to many people. It may be an appropriate and desirable approach in some organizations where job performance can be objectively measured and used to rank and reward people independent of their race or other group memberships. And some have advocated the color-blind approach because of a concern that an emphasis on group differences may foster intergroup hostility and prejudice. The limited evidence that is available, however, does not support that fear. One study of Dutch schools that included significant numbers of Turkish as well as Dutch children found that in classrooms where teachers incorporated lessons about ethnic discrimination and cultural differences, the children evaluated the out-group more favorably (Kinket &

Verkuyten, 1999). Although this study is nonexperimental and cannot establish causality, the effect held regardless of other important factors such as the relative numbers of Dutch and Turkish students in the classroom. Thus, the results cast doubt on the idea that acknowledging group differences will inevitably increase intergroup bias.

In addition, color-blind ideology has important disadvantages. First, in schools and many other settings, including even the workplace, the values of getting to know about other cultures and learning to live and work alongside culturally different individuals are important, perhaps even as important as individual task performance. Janet Schofield (1986) found that color-blind ideology impeded such learning, for example, by keeping schoolchildren and teachers from capitalizing on their cultural diversity to enrich their perspectives.

Second, color-blind ideology desensitizes members of a dominant group to the value placed on group membership by members of minority or disadvantaged groups. Charles Judd and his colleagues (Judd, Park, Ryan, Brauer, & Kraus, 1995) found that many White Americans professed color-blindness, refusing with apparent sincerity even to acknowledge that Whites and Blacks differ in important ways. Yet the Blacks in the same study regarded their group membership as quite meaningful and important to them. Based on their life experiences, most of them were convinced that race *does* matter in America, and used their group membership as a source of pride. From this perspective, color-blindness denies an important social identity and may even translate into a demand for assimilation, that is, for members of minority groups to adopt the values and customs of the dominant White group so that all may live harmoniously side by side. Of course, this position is unlikely to appeal to Blacks who value their own group membership. In fact, when Whites who see themselves as unprejudiced assert with all good intentions that group memberships are irrelevant and should be ignored, Blacks may regard this refusal to recognize and honor valued group differences as just the newest form of prejudice.

Clearly, a balance is required. Members of different groups can share common goals and work together, while simultaneously maintaining their own group memberships as sources of identity and esteem. Despite its appeal, a color-blind ideology that denies both the reality and the value of group differences is not the answer to intergroup conflict and misunderstanding.

One Goal, Many Strategies

Those who most strongly identify with a group tend to choose social change rather than social mobility strategies. However, no single approach is always best for dealing with a negatively evaluated group membership, just as no single coping strategy is uniformly the best way to handle threats to the individual self.

As you can see in Figure 6.8, there is more than one way to cope with the threat to social identity posed by negative group memberships. No one way is always better or worse than others; like the strategies for coping with

FIGURE 6.8   How can I value myself when others devalue my group?

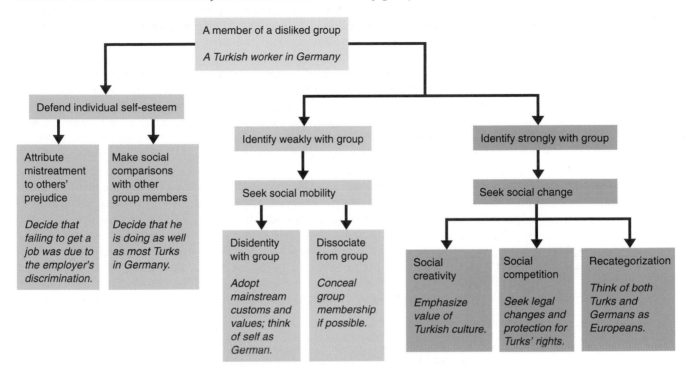

■ Members of groups that suffer dislike and discrimination try to defend their individual self-esteem. In addition, they may seek escape from their group through social mobility or seek to improve the whole group's situation through social change, depending on the strength of their identification with the group.

threats to the individual self that were described in chapter 4, the effectiveness of each method depends on many factors. The size of a group, the resources its members control, the ease or difficulty of concealing group membership, and the personal significance of group membership for each individual will all influence how people respond (Eberhard & Fiske, 1996). It is no surprise, then, that different groups tend to prefer distinct strategies for coping with the disdain that others feel for them (Frable, 1997).

Strength of group identification is the single most important factor that tilts people toward using social mobility versus social change strategies (Tajfel & Turner, 1979). In studies with Dutch university students conducted by Naomi Ellemers and her colleagues (Ellemers, Spears, & Doosje, 1997), for example, those who were led to identify strongly with a low-status group were less likely to seek individual mobility out of the group. They also perceived their group as homogeneous, a display of group solidarity that is associated with collective action such as social competition. Interestingly, the relative permeability of the group boundary had little or no effect on people's commitment to the group or use of mobility. Thus, the strength of people's psychological attachment to their group seems to be crucial in their choices among strategies (B. Simon and others, 1998).

At times, multiple forces push and pull people in different directions. For example, many Blacks feel a fundamental tension between the desire to maintain in-group solidarity and the desire for individual advancement in White-dominated society. Deep, often emotional disagreements have sprung up between advocates of various strategies. It seems to some that "in order to be accepted by Whites they must give up everything that is Black; that if they played basketball before they now have to play golf" (L. Williams, 1991b). Yet those who seek professional advancement sometimes "fear that if you are successful you will be too alienated from Black people," according to Cornel West, a Princeton University professor (Cary, 1992). The different strategies of social mobility and social change often contradict each other. Nevertheless, all aim at improving the group's situation and any one of them may be appropriate for a particular individual or group, given the unique social situation.

In thinking about the ways in which people cope with *being* a likable member of a devalued group, you may have noticed some similarities with the ways in which people deal with *meeting* a likable member of a disliked group (discussed in chapter 5). These parallels, detailed in Table 6.2, are no accident. They reflect the fundamental principle that group member-

TABLE 6.2. Three Types of Responses to a Likable Member of a Disliked Group

Response	*Knowing* a likable member of a disliked group	*Being* a likable member of a disliked group
See the individual as unrepresentative of the group; separate beliefs about the group from beliefs about the individual.	Exclude the individual from the group by seeing him or her as a special type of the general category (*subtyping*) or by seeing him or her as extremely different from typical category members (*contrasting*).	Remove the self from the group, either psychologically by down-playing group membership as an aspect of the self (*disidentification*) or physically by escaping from or concealing group membership (*dissociation*).
See the individual as representative of the group; use beliefs about the individual to modify beliefs about the group.	See the likable individual as a typical group member, improving the evaluation of the group (*stereotype change*).	Attempt to make society's evaluation of the group more positive (*social change*). Interpret the group and its history, culture, and other distinctive aspects in positive terms (*social creativity*) or struggle to change the group's generally low status and power in society (*social competition*).
Change the lines of social categorization.	Merge the out-group into a larger in-group.	Expand the in-group to include former out-groups.

ships influence our thoughts and feelings about individual group members, whether the individual is someone else or the self.

CONCLUDING COMMENTS

 Social identity is central to every aspect of social behavior, just as this chapter occupies a central place in this text. The concept of social identity, as discussed in this chapter, makes clear how intertwined are people's knowledge about groups, their conceptions of themselves, and their impressions of others. Group memberships not only shape the ways we perceive our own and other groups, but also fundamentally affect the ways we perceive other individuals and ourself. Not only do we see ourselves in group terms and act in accordance with in-group standards and norms, but as in-groups become part of the self, we think about our groups in many of the same ways that we think about ourselves as individuals. For example, various biases lead us to view not only ourselves but also our groups through rose-colored glasses.

Social identities anchor us in the social world by connecting us to other people—people whom we otherwise might have little reason to trust, to like, or even to know at all. Because relationships are encouraged and even made possible by our assumptions about what we have in common, group belonging and identification provide a truly social basis for thinking, feeling, and acting. Thus, understanding group membership is vital for understanding many aspects of social behavior. As you will see in later chapters, the effects of our groups on our beliefs, opinions, and behavior; on our close and loving relationships with other individuals; and on the ways we act in face-to-face groups all depend crucially on the ways we accept and identify with in-groups. No wonder, then, that we often feel lost and adrift when we lose important social identities, as when we are expelled or fired, or when our social identities are threatened, for example, when we experience discrimination and realize that others devalue our group. We may still be the individuals we always were, but important parts of our whole selves have been damaged or have disappeared because our place in the social world is lost or threatened.

Negative views of out-groups sprout from the same roots as people's positive views of themselves and their own kind. The biased stereotypes of groups that were discussed in chapter 5 are only part of the underpinning of prejudice and discrimination. Disregard and maltreatment of others are supported by our social and psychological investment in our own groups as well. When group membership is most important, out-group members are only faceless outsiders; their individuality is of little concern to us. We see "them" as all the same and as totally different from us in their goals, values, and beliefs. As we will see, this way of thinking is an important basis for both aggression and intergroup conflict.

Perhaps understanding how group membership can contribute to hurtful and destructive human behavior will help provide solutions to some of

CHAPTER 6 THEMES

- **Construction of Reality**
  We construct the self using our knowledge about our social groups.

- **Pervasiveness of Social Influence**
  This construction process imports social influences into the very core of the self.

- **Seeking Connectedness**
  Group memberships that we share with others are rewarding.

- **Valuing Me and Mine**
  We positively value the groups to which we belong as well as our individual self.

these problems by redefining in-groups and out-groups. Whether the effects of social identity are good or bad, the fundamental fact remains that our sense of self extends beyond our skin to encompass some people and exclude others, with powerful implications for how we see and treat others and ourselves.

SUMMARY

 Categorizing Oneself as a Group Member. Group membership can turn into a **social identity** when it becomes a significant part of a person's self-concept through the process of **self-categorization**. People learn about the groups to which they belong in the same ways that they learn the characteristics of other groups: through observation of other group members or from the culture.

Knowledge about group memberships may be activated by direct reminders, such as group labels; by the presence of out-group members; by being a minority; or by intergroup conflict. Group membership is particularly significant in some cultures and for some individuals, who tend to see the world in terms of that group membership.

Me, You, and Them: Effects of Social Categorization. Activated knowledge about a group membership has multiple effects on people's self-concept and self-esteem. People tend to see themselves as typical group members. Group membership also influences people's moods and self-esteem, as they feel bad about their group's failures or **BIRG** (bask in reflected glory) when their group succeeds. Relatively small groups typically have the greatest effects on their members' feelings.

When group membership is highly accessible, people see other in-group members as similar in their central group-linked characteristics. However, extensive personal interaction (when group membership is not salient) also provides knowledge about their unique and diverse personal characteristics. People like in-group members and tend to treat them in fair, humane, and altruistic ways because people see them as similar to themselves in their goals and interests.

In contrast, the **out-group homogeneity effect** causes people to see out-groups as quite uniform and homogeneous. People also dislike, devalue, and discriminate against out-group members, depending on the extent to which they are seen as threatening the in-group. When the out-group is simply different, it elicits mild dislike. This effect can be demonstrated even in the **minimal intergroup situation**, in which mere categorization results in mild discrimination against the out-group. According to **social identity theory**, people respond in this way to derive self-esteem from their in-group membership.

When the out-group is seen as outdoing the in-group, this more serious threat results in resentment, dislike, and overt discrimination. Out-groups that are seen as severe threats to the in-group elicit **symbolic prejudice**, which often goes hand in hand with murderous hatred, discrimination, aggression, or moral exclusion.

When Group Memberships Are Negative. Negative stereotypes about a group's ability can become self-fulfilling, actually harming the group members' performances when **stereotype threat** is present. In addition, belonging to a group that others dislike or discriminate against poses a threat to self-esteem. However, people can defend self-esteem by attributing negative reactions to others' prejudice or by making most of their social comparisons against fellow in-group members.

If these strategies are insufficient to protect individual self-esteem, people can use **social mobility** strategies: attempting to escape their membership in a stigmatized group. They can psychologically disidentify with the group, for example, by playing down group membership or by regarding themselves as atypical group members. **CORFing** (cutting off reflected failure) is one way to distance oneself from a negatively regarded group membership. Another option is to dissociate: to escape physically, by "passing" or keeping group membership hidden "in the closet."

Sometimes group members adopt **social change** strategies, attempting to alter society's evaluation of their in-group. They may redefine group characteristics in positive terms, engage in direct intergroup conflict or struggle, or seek to overturn the in-group/out-group distinction altogether. No one approach is always best for dealing with a negatively regarded group membership, just as no single coping strategy is uniformly the best way to handle threats to the individual self.

7

Attitudes and Attitude Change

What do the following events have in common? New Zealand rugby legend Sean Fitzpatrick recommends that "Kiwis" invest more in their own country; subsequently, requests to buy shares in the initial public offering of Auckland International Airport stock exceed all expectations. U.S. president Bill Clinton goes on national television to urge the American public to consider his inappropriate relationship with an intern as part of his private life rather than a legitimate public concern. A cigarette manufacturer launches an international advertising campaign featuring cartoon character Joe Camel, who quickly becomes more familiar to children than the Disney character Mickey Mouse. Religious groups seek converts on street corners, scientists dispute evidence for a well-established theory, and friends argue over the best place to buy snow tires.

In all of these cases, a person or a group is trying to develop, maintain, or change the attitudes of others. An **attitude** is any cognitive representation that summarizes our evaluation of an *attitude object*, which may be the self, other people, things, actions, events, or ideas (W. J. McGuire, 1985; Ostrom, 1969; Zanna & Rempel, 1988). People can—and do—hold attitudes about just about anything. You may realize from this definition that we have already dealt with some attitudes in earlier chapters. Liking for others, discussed in chapter 3, is an attitude about other individuals; self-esteem (chapter 4) is an attitude about ourselves; and prejudice (chapters 5 and 6) reflects attitudes toward our own and other groups. Although chapters 7 and 8 focus on attitudes about objects, issues, events, ideas, and actions, what we say in these two chapters can also be applied to evaluations of ourselves, other people, and social groups. Because attitudes are so pervasive, the study of *attitude change*—how attitudes form and how they can be modified—has been a central concern in social psychology since the discipline began. Both this chapter and the next focus on the development, mainte-

Attitude. A cognitive representation that summarizes an individual's evaluation of a particular person, group, thing, action, or idea.

nance, and change of attitudes and on the important impact attitudes have on what we think, feel, and do.

This chapter begins by asking what attitudes are and why we form them. Knowing the kinds of information upon which attitudes are based opens the way to thinking about **persuasion,** the process by which attitudes are developed, reinforced, or changed by communications. As you will see, persuasive communications can be subtle or direct, funny or frightening, intriguingly innovative or boringly repetitious. They may appeal to cold logic or play on emotions. Some we find easy to resist, whereas others immediately push our persuasion buttons.

What makes some persuasive messages effective while others fail to change our minds? It won't surprise you to know that the answer lies in the way people process persuasive communications. As you will see in the second and third sections of the chapter, how carefully we consider persuasive information determines what kinds of messages are effective, for what kinds of people, under what kinds of conditions. Responding thoughtfully to persuasive communications can also make the difference between being at their mercy and resisting their appeals. As you will see in the final section of the chapter, despite the sophistication of many of the techniques used to influence us, whether we are persuaded or not is largely up to us.

Attitudes and Their Origins

Do you agree with laws that ban smoking on airplanes? Should more Eastern European countries be allowed to join NATO? Do you think that brand-name products are superior to generic ones? Do the benefits of socialized medicine outweigh its drawbacks? Should women in the military be allowed to serve in combat? The answers people give to these kinds of questions reflect their attitudes, or evaluations of attitude objects. Because our evaluations of attitude objects can be favorable, neutral, or unfavorable, attitudes are said to have a positive, neutral, or negative *direction*. And, just as they differ in direction, attitudes also differ in *intensity*, reflecting whether the evaluation is moderate or extreme.

Like other mental representations discussed in earlier chapters, attitudes can't be weighed, watched, or observed under microscopes. Social psychologists have to infer an attitude's direction and intensity on the basis of people's expressions of their thoughts, feelings, or behaviors. The most straightforward approach to attitude measurement is to ask people to give *self-reports:* to say what they think. Consumer surveys, political polls, and even our daily exchange of opinions with friends and family are forms of self-reports. Social psychologists use attitude scales to assess people's views. An *attitude scale* is a series of questions that provides precise and reliable information about how strongly people agree or disagree with, favor or oppose, or like or dislike any attitude object (Dawes & Smith, 1985). Respondents choose among options that range from an extreme negative evaluation through a neutral point to an extreme positive evaluation, thus assessing intensity and direction. Researchers have to be quite careful constructing such scales. Especially before they are well established, the attitudes that people report can be easily influenced by how attitude questions are worded ("Is Pepsi better than Coke?" compared with "Do you pre-

Persuasion. The process of forming, reinforcing, or changing attitudes by communication.

for Pepsi to Coke?") and the response alternatives people are given. For example, people may well express a different opinion of an attitude object when they rate it on an evaluative scale that runs from "positive" at one end to "negative" at the other, compared to when they rate it on a scale that has "extremely positive" and "extremely negative" as its endpoints (Schwarz, 1999). Social psychologists also use *observations* of behavior to gauge attitudes. For example, they might infer direction of attitude from whether people will volunteer to stuff envelopes for a campaign to save the spotted owl, and intensity from how many envelopes they are willing to stuff (Deci, 1975; Wilson & Dunn, 1986).

Self-report techniques and observational measures become less useful when people hold unpopular attitudes that they may want to hide or deny (D. T. Campbell, 1963). When people suspect that their attitudes differ from what most other people think, or from what other people think is good, people are reluctant to express their true attitudes. As noted in chapter 2, social psychologists have developed a number of techniques to get around people's desire to look good.

Some self-report techniques guarantee anonymity, so participants need not fear being publicly identified with a particular attitude. Others use measures that subtly reveal attitudes without the participants' knowledge (Hammond, 1948; Pratkanis, 1989). One such technique is designed to use response time to uncover people's implicit attitudes: by looking at the time people take to make a particular response to an attitude object, researchers can tell if people typically see the object as positive or negative, regardless of what they say about it (Greenwald and others, 1998).

Still other techniques increase the honesty of participants' answers by convincing them that their "true" physiological reactions about issues such as drug and alcohol use and safe-sex practices, for example, are being measured (Jamieson & Zanna, 1983; Quigley-Fernandez & Tedeschi, 1978; Wech, Lundstrom, & Moore, 1989). Facial electromyography (EMG) has also permitted precise measurements of both the intensity and the direction of attitudes on such sensitive campus issues as alcohol possession or dorm visitations (Cacioppo & Petty, 1979; Cacioppo et al., 1986).

■ **Tell us what you think.** Like this interviewer, most social psychologists measure attitudes using self-report techniques—a method that relies on people expressing their intensity and direction of their opinions openly and honestly.

The use of measures to assess implicit attitudes towards social groups was discussed in Chapter 5, pages 179 to 182.

Attitude Formation: Why and How?

People form attitudes because they are useful in mastering the social environment and in expressing important connections with others. Attitudes are assembled from three types of information: beliefs about the object's positive or negative characteristics, feelings and emotions about the object, and information about past and current actions toward the object. Once an attitude has been formed, it becomes closely linked to the representation of the object.

What's your opinion of ice cream? How do you feel about the country in which you were born? We expect that you can answer these questions without much thought. Many attitudes are so well established and so frequently used that people can express them and act on them without a second thought. But even familiar things that now elicit almost a knee-jerk evaluative response were once confronted for the first time. Where do attitudes come from? Why do we construct attitudes toward almost every object in our social world? And how do we come to favor one idea and resist another, to like one object and dislike something else?

WHY ATTITUDES FORM. Not surprisingly, we develop attitudes because they are useful to us (D. Katz, 1960; M. B. Smith, Bruner, & White, 1956). First, attitudes help people master the environment. Attitudes toward chocolate ice cream and calculus classes, for example, help us successfully negotiate our interactions with these attitude objects in two ways. The *object appraisal function* (also known as the *knowledge function*) of attitudes helps organize and simplify our experience, orienting us to the important characteristics of an attitude object so we can deal with it efficiently. Attitudes can also have an *instrumental,* or *utilitarian,* function, steering us toward objects that will help maximize our rewards and reach desired goals while avoiding undesirable situations or events. Both these functions help us master the environment.

Attitudes are useful to us in a second way as well. They help people express their real selves, voice their convictions, show what they stand for, and affirm their significant relationships. This *social identity function* (or *value-expressive function*) of attitudes helps people gain and maintain connectedness with others. Attitudes on environmental, social, or religious issues help us define who we are.

These two important functions of attitudes are not mutually exclusive. Many attitudes serve both object appraisal and social identity functions, although not necessarily to the same degree. Attitudes toward practical objects like a new hot water heater or a down vest, for example, may serve the purpose of object appraisal much more than that of social identity. Attitudes about religious practices, a cherished memento from childhood, or the animal rights movement, on the other hand, are probably more expressive of a person's identity (Shavitt, 1990). Because attitudes may serve different functions, we might form multiple attitudes about one and the same object (A. Liberman & Chaiken, 1996; Tourangeau, Rasinski, Bradburn, & D'Andrade, 1989). We may have a different attitude about our local club sweatshirt, for example, when our team loses the soccer finals (when the shirt serves identity functions) than when the shirt keeps out the cold on a chilly night (serving a utilitarian function).

CULTURAL DIFFERENCES IN ATTITUDE FUNCTIONS. Cultural differences also influence what functions attitudes serve, and thus why particular attitudes form. As we first pointed out in chapter 3, independent cultures, like those found in North America, tend to emphasize individualism, whereas interdependent cultures, such as those found in Asia, are more concerned with group harmony and belongingness. It's not surprising, then, that persuaders in different cultures rely on different kinds of appeals to make these functions salient. After examining the advertisements in popular American and Korean magazines, Sang-pil Han and Sharon Shavitt (1993) concluded that American ads appealed more to individual benefits, personal success, and independence. These ads used slogans like: "The art of being unique," or "You, only better," or "A leader among leaders." In contrast, Korean advertisements emphasized group benefits, interpersonal harmony, and family integrity. Slogans like: "We have a way of bringing people together,"

We encountered attitudes that serve the value-expressive or social identity function in chapter 6, pages 224 to 226. Value-expressive attitudes are so centrally tied to our definitions of ourselves and our groups that any threat to them becomes a threat to the self and to the group.

"Sharing is beautiful," and "We devote ourselves to our contractors" were more typical in Korean ads. The cultural differences were also reflected in judgments of the persuasiveness of the advertisements, as the results of a second study demonstrated. American participants tended to find individually oriented ads more persuasive than family- or group-oriented ads. Judgments made by Korean participants reversed this pattern. Political advertising in the United States and Korea show the same cultural differences (Tak, Kaid, & Lee, 1997).

THE BUILDING BLOCKS OF ATTITUDES. As people encounter information about an attitude object (either by interacting with it or by hearing about it from friends, family, teachers, or the media), they build a cognitive representation of it. This representation can include cognitive, affective, and behavioral information associated with the object (Trafimow & Sheeran, 1998; Zanna & Rempel, 1988).

1. *Cognitive information is what people know about an attitude object—the facts and beliefs they have about it.* Perhaps the high incidence of lung cancer among smokers has convinced you that cigarette smoking causes disease. This belief constitutes cognitive information about this attitude object, cigarette smoking.

2. *Affective information consists of how people feel about the object—the feelings and emotions the attitude object arouses.* Experiencing nausea or anger when you are in a smoky closed area qualifies as affective information associated with cigarette smoking.

3. *Behavioral information comprises knowledge about people's past, present, or future interactions with the attitude object.* The fact that you do not smoke constitutes behavioral information consistent relevant to cigarette smoking.

Any of these types of information can contribute to an attitude. An opinion about a common European currency that is based on its advantages and disadvantages for economic expansion, for example, is based on cognitive information. Other attitudes might similarly reflect the consideration of mainly cognitive information (Fishbein & Ajzen, 1975), especially if they are formed on the basis of hearsay rather than direct experience (Millar & Millar, 1996). On the other hand, affective information has the edge in many attitudes (Abelson, Kinder, Peters, & Fiske, 1982; Edwards & von Hippel, 1995; Zajonc, 1980). Many affective reactions reflect an inborn preference for pleasure over pain, and this can provide the basis for some attitudes (Tesser, 1993). Under emotion-arousing circumstances, affective information may also be the key factor in determining attitudes. In attitudes toward donating blood, for example, feelings play a bigger role than do cognitions (Breckler & Wiggins, 1989). Information about past behavior can also dominate attitudes, particularly if that behavior becomes habitual. Donating to the Multiple Sclerosis Fund year after year, for example, is likely to have a powerful influence on attitudes toward the charity (Fazio & Zanna, 1981). Although attitudes can be based on just one type of information, most attitudes probably reflect a mixture of the building blocks (Breckler & Wiggins, 1989; Zanna & Rempel, 1988).

Because impressions of ourselves, others, and other groups discussed in earlier chapters are also attitudes, they too are based on cognitive, affective, and behavioral information. In chapter 5, for example, we saw that what we think group members are like, how we feel about them, and our actions toward them could all contribute to prejudice.

PUTTING IT ALL TOGETHER. How do evaluative summaries—attitudes—emerge from all the information that accumulates about attitude objects? When it comes to building attitudes, consistency is the name of the game. People typically form attitudes that are consistent with most of what we know, feel, and experience, as Figure 7.1 suggests (Feather, 1969; M. Rosenberg, 1956). The presence of positive information about an attitude object typically results in a positive attitude (Festinger, 1957; Heider, 1944). Similarly, the presence of negative beliefs, feelings, or behaviors produces a negative attitude.

Of course, the different pieces of information that accumulate do not always imply a consistent evaluation of an attitude object. Most people know arguments on both sides of major social issues, such as immigration control, the death penalty, and environmental management (Judd & Kulik, 1980; Pratkanis, 1984). Having evaluatively mixed beliefs and feelings toward particular attitude objects is also a common experience. For example, you might think blood drives are an excellent idea at the same time that you feel nauseated at the sight of a hypodermic needle (Breckler & Wiggins, 1989; Chaiken & Baldwin, 1981). Such *ambivalent* attitudes contain both positive and negative reactions to the attitude object (I. Katz, 1981; Priester & Petty, 1996; M. M. Thompson & Zanna, 1995; Tourangeau and others, 1989). Since 1990, more and more U.S. citizens report conflicted attitudes toward abortion, so that now almost 60% can be characterized as favoring the right to an abortion, but being unhappy about it (Reibstein, 1998).

How do people put all this varying information together? People seem to employ two strategies to combine their attitude-relevant pieces of information into a single evaluation. In the first, we weight each piece of infor-

FIGURE 7.1 Attitude formation and measurement

■ If you learn that George Strait donates money to several charities, feel relaxed when you listen to his music, and know that you would drive over one hundred miles to see him in concert, you are likely to form a positive attitude toward the popular country singer. The attitude in turn will influence thoughts, feelings, and observable behaviors. Researchers draw on these effects to measure the underlying attitude.

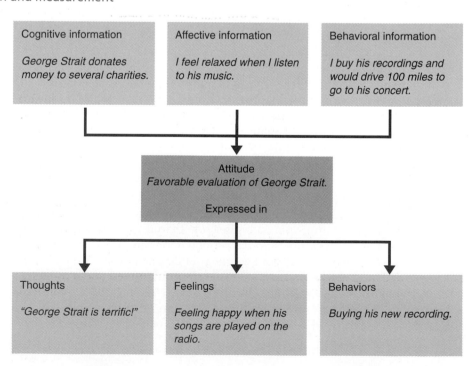

mation according to its value and importance and then combine all the pieces algebraically, either by adding them all up or by taking their average (N. H. Anderson, 1981; Fishbein & Azjen, 1975). In the other approach, we try to configure the information into a meaningful whole, letting each piece influence the others rather than evaluating each item independently. Regardless of which strategy is used, the direction and intensity of our attitudes reflects the number and importance of cognitive, affective, and behavioral building blocks we accumulate.

But if inconsistent information pulls them in both directions, why don't most people form middle-of-the-road, wishy-washy attitudes on most issues? In fact, this situation is probably the exception rather than the rule. Consistency is a powerful force in human thinking, and some basic social-psychological processes help us avoid or resolve inconsistencies so that consistency rules the day.

These algebraic and configural approaches to integrating information were first discussed as ways we make judgments about individuals. See chapter 3, page 85.

1. *Our information base is usually lopsided.* Sometimes we avoid inconsistencies by collecting one-sided information. Because people usually share the same opinions held by their family and friends, day-to-day interactions provide a one-sided view of the issues. If everyone in your home, club, and church group is politically conservative, for example, you will hear a great deal of support for that point of view. Because we typically think the views of those associated with us are right and true, we are likely to weight them heavily. Another source of one-sided information is set in motion by our initial reactions to people, places, and things. If, for example, your first early encounter with lima beans, bean sprouts, or guavas is largely negative, you might adopt an avoidance strategy. In doing so, you prevent yourself from gathering further information that might contradict your lopsidedly negative information base. Often, we are exposed to affective information before encountering cognitive information (as when we have a gut reaction to a new colleague before even getting to know what she is like). Because of this, affective information may dictate not only the direction of many attitudes, but also the kind of information they are based on.

2. *Accessible information determines attitudes.* Accessible information—information that comes most easily to mind or that grabs our attention—can dominate an attitude judgment. In one demonstration of this point, researchers deliberately planted conservative or liberal ideas in participants' minds by getting them to answer certain questions, and then looked at the impact of these ideas on their judgments (Tourangeau & Rasinski, 1988). The participants, Chicago-area women, were divided into two groups. The women in one group were first asked their opinions about conservative issues, like the value of hard work. The other group was asked to respond to liberal issues, like government's responsibility for the plight of the poor. Both groups were then encouraged to present their own views on social spending. Sixty-two percent of the respondents primed with conservative values stated that the government spent too much money on social programs. In contrast, only 46% of the respondents primed with liberal values expressed similar beliefs. Why the difference? The information made accessible by the earlier questions— thoughts supporting liberal or conservative values—tipped participants' attitudes in the liberal or the conservative direction.

Information that is accessible because it is perceptually salient also exerts a strong effect on attitude judgments. Our preferences for and evaluations of our favorite foods probably relate much more to their obvious sensory appeal than to their hidden nutritional benefits. Similarly, the accessibility of motives and goals can determine our attitudes. If you are buying a car for utilitarian reasons, one model's excellent fuel economy and sound maintenance record will be salient, and your attitude toward the car will be positive. On the other hand, if you think that what you drive reflects who you are, the same model's vinyl seats and plastic accessories will make your attitude toward it negative. Thus whatever is uppermost in our minds can determine our attitudes.

LINKING ATTITUDES TO THEIR OBJECTS. As soon as an evaluative summary about an attitude object forms, it becomes part of our cognitive representation of the object, just like other pieces of information, as can be seen in Figure 7.2. Not surprisingly, then, thinking about almost any object about

FIGURE 7.2   Linking an attitude to the object

■ People form attitudes based on cognitive, affective, and behavioral information about an attitude object. Once the attitude is formed, it too becomes associated with the mental representation of the attitude object, as shown in the center panel. If the attitude is repeatedly activated, perhaps because the person encounters the object frequently, the attitude's link to the object will be strengthened (bottom panel). As a result, the attitude is more likely to be retrieved and used whenever the attitude object is encountered.

After consideration of information

After repeated activation of attitude

which an attitude has been formed also brings to mind the positive or negative evaluation associated with it (Bargh, Chaiken, Raymond, & Hymes, 1996). The more frequently we think about our attitude toward the object, the closer and stronger the link between object and attitude becomes. This tight coupling has three important consequences. First, the stronger the link, the more automatically the attitude pops to mind whenever we think about the object (Fazio, 1986). For example, we don't just think about a spider, but about a squishy creature that repulses us. In fact, we may not be able to think about the object without our prejudged evaluation coming to mind, even if we wanted to. Second, the stronger the link, the more likely it is that our attitude will become a shorthand substitute for what we know and how we feel about the attitude object. When people ask you what you think of country singer George Strait, your attitude tells you: "I like him," without your having to think about the cognitions, feelings, and behaviors that initially generated your reaction (Lingle & Ostrom, 1979). Third, the stronger the link, the less vulnerable the attitude is to the influence of accessible information. When an attitude is well established and immediately accessible, it need not be constructed from information that is ready in our minds or in the context (Petty, Preister, & Wegner, 1994).

Superficial and Systematic Routes to Persuasion: From Snap Judgments to Considered Opinions

Although we form attitudes because they are useful to us, other people also find our attitudes useful. In the marketplace, political arena, or classroom— wherever you go—you will find people trying to influence you to develop new attitudes or change old ones. And if positive beliefs, feelings, or behaviors produce positive attitudes, and negative beliefs, feelings, and behaviors produce negative attitudes, the persuader's task should be quite straightforward. *Rational messages,* which focus on the attitude object's attributes, can provide cognitive building blocks for a new attitude. *Emotional appeals* can be designed to associate feelings with the attitude object, in turn influencing attitudes. To ensure that you will love their product, scorn drug use, or support socialized medicine, all persuaders need to do is provide you with important cognitive or affective information consistent with the attitude they want you to develop. Right?

Actually, it's not that simple. Like the proverbial horse that can be led to water but cannot be convinced to drink, people can be provided with information but cannot always be convinced to think or at least to think deeply. Shelly Chaiken (1980, 1987) and Richard Petty and John Cacioppo (1981, 1986) have argued that people deal with information about attitude objects in two different ways: They scan it somewhat superficially, or they consider it systematically. When people engage in *superficial processing,* they rely on accessible or salient information to make rather simple inferences about the attitude object. When people engage in *systematic processing,* they go beyond simple cues and also consider the strength of the arguments and their implications for the evaluation of the attitude object. As we shall see, both kinds of processing—superficial and systematic—can change attitudes, but they do so in very different ways and under different conditions.

These two types of processing should sound familiar, because superficial and systematic processing also come into play when we make judgments about other individuals (chapter 3, pages 77 to 85) and about members of groups (chapter 5, pages 182 to 190).

Superficial Processing: Persuasion Shortcuts

When people do not give persuasive communications much thought, various superficial aspects of the persuasive appeal can lead to attitude change. For example, people may agree with messages from attractive or expert sources or with familiar or long messages. They might also be influenced by positive or negative objects or events associated with the attitude object, or by other feelings they are experiencing.

When you thumb absentmindedly through a magazine, you pay very little attention to the actual words on the printed page. Nevertheless, despite the superficiality of your processing, some information is getting through. You may notice the beautiful people using a product, the amount of evidence that supports an advertising claim, or the irritating or appealing photos in an advertisement. An advertisement may evoke feelings of nostalgia, sentimentality, disgust, or fear. A persuasive setting may feature inviting smells and cheerful music or glaring lights and uncomfortable temperatures. Because such simple pieces of information are themselves associated with and activate positive or negative evaluations, they can act as **persuasion heuristics.** People engaged in *heuristic processing* can come to like or dislike the attitude object based on such simple cues, without having to consider information about it in any depth (Chaiken, 1980, 1987). Some of these persuasion heuristics have the effect of changing the cognitive base of attitudes, leading us to think the attitude object has positive qualities. Other heuristics change the affective building blocks of attitudes, giving us positive feelings about the attitude object. When people are processing superficially, both affective and cognitive cues can influence their attitudes. When people form attitudes based on persuasion heuristics rather than careful thinking about the attitude object, Petty and Cacioppo (1981, 1986) describe them as taking a *peripheral route to persuasion.*

LINKING AFFECTIVE INFORMATION DIRECTLY TO THE ATTITUDE OBJECT. Some attitude objects, such as perfumes, baby products, and vacations, inevitably appeal to the emotions. Think of the pleasure associated with powdering a baby or lying on a sun-drenched beach. No wonder ads for these products play on our emotions. But emotional appeals can also influence our attitudes about emotionally neutral products. The happily splashing baby can sell faucets as well as baby powder. Political candidates can reminisce about their childhoods to promote policy changes. And classical compositions can become theme songs for wines, automobiles, and long-lasting batteries. Why do advertisers want babies, nostalgia, and well-loved music in their ads? If positive events are repeatedly associated with an attitude object, the attitude object soon comes to elicit the feelings associated with those events (Zanna, Kiesler, & Pilkonis, 1970). This general process is called *classical conditioning,* and it is demonstrated in Figure 7.3.

Classical conditioning is the backbone of the emotional appeal, or "soft sell." As one advertising expert put it: "It sets off the product as something pretty wonderful by draping around it as many . . . pleasant associations as possible" (Martineau, 1957, pp. 13–14). Of course, persuasion professionals need to be careful that a positive association in one culture translates when their campaign goes international. Baby food manufacturer Gerber, for ex-

Classical conditioning can occur between any pairs of stimuli. We discussed the impact of classical conditioning on reactions to social groups in chapter 5, page 172.

Persuasion heuristic. An association of superficial cues with positive or negative evaluations, which allows people to evaluate an object quickly and without much thought.

FIGURE 7.3   Classical conditioning and attitude formation

■ Suppose that people encounter a neutral object in conjunction with a stimulus that they evaluate positively or negatively. After this happens a few times, the feelings produced by the stimulus become associated with the object, resulting in the formation of an attitude.

ample, has done well in the U.S. market by labeling their product with an adorable smiling baby. Using the same packaging in the African market was not a success: Because of the low literacy rate, products there are often labeled with a picture of their contents!

Perhaps classical conditioning explains the popularity of the business lunch and the fund-raising dinner; associating a sales pitch or an appeal for a donation with good food may well increase its persuasiveness. One early experiment supports this idea. Students who were given snacks of peanuts and soft drinks while listening to persuasive messages about controversial issues expressed more agreement with the issues than did those who were not given the snacks (Janis, Kaye, & Kirschner, 1965).

Music may have the same effect. Popular songs evoke a special set of emotions and memories, and associating an attitude object with them capitalizes on classical conditioning to boost evaluations (Galizio & Hendrick, 1972). In one study that gauged the effect of popular music on attitudes toward products, students in a management class watched what they believed to be an ad agency's pilot version of an advertisement for a ball-point pen (Gorn, 1982). The ad offered minimal information about the pen, but it was accompanied in one condition by popular rock-and-roll music and in the other by classical Indian music, which initial testing showed that the students disliked. When students were later allowed to choose a pen as a reward for their participation in the study, they were much more likely to choose the pen that had been accompanied by the popular rock-and-roll music. Encouraging customers to rely on their emotional reactions rather than thinking carefully about the product can boost evaluations—and sales.

Of course, classical conditioning works the same way when negative events are associated with an attitude object. When several people died in the United States after someone tampered with bottles of Tylenol, the painkiller became associated in people's minds with danger and death. To restore Tylenol's reputation as "the pain reliever doctors and hospitals trust most," its manufacturers had to rebuild the association of Tylenol with safety and reliability. This required a persistent and widespread campaign.

☐ **AFFECTIVE ASSOCIATIONS AND POLITICS.** If association with a positive stimulus can sell products, can it also sell politicians? Brian Mullen and his associates (1986) asked this question after discovering an intriguing connection between newscasters' smiles and political attitudes. Using videotapes of the three major network news anchors, the researchers counted how often the newscasters smiled as they reported on Ronald Reagan and Walter Mondale, candidates in the 1984 U.S. presidential election. Although the content of the commentary was not biased in favor of either candidate, Peter Jennings of the television network ABC did smile more when he mentioned Ronald Reagan. After the election, Mullen and his colleagues polled voters around the country to find out what news program they watched and how they voted. The results showed that the percentage of ABC viewers who had voted for Reagan was higher than that of viewers who watched CBS or NBC (two other television networks). Could Jennings's smile actually have helped Reagan win? Because the study had a nonexperimental design, it was impossible to pinpoint the direction of the influence. Watching Jennings might have increased support for Reagan, but it is also possible that Reagan supporters watched Jennings because they noticed he liked their candidate.

To try to determine the direction of the influence, Carolyn Copper and her associates (1993) performed an experimental study in which students were randomly assigned to watch one of three versions of a simulated news broadcast. Each program included the same special report on the views of hypothetical Democratic and Republican congressional candidates, but the timing of the newscaster's smiles was varied. Smiles occurred when the announcer mentioned either the Republican candidate or the Democratic candidate or neither candidate. Participants—self-identified as Republicans or Democrats—watched one version of the newscast and then rated the newscaster and both candidates. Of course, regardless of the newscaster's facial expression, students preferred candidates from their own party. But the newscaster's smile did make a difference. First, it affected participants' evaluations of the newscaster himself. They liked him more if he smiled while mentioning their candidate, suggesting that partisan Reagan supporters might well have watched Jennings because he seemed to like their candidate. Second, smiling had a small but reliable effect on degree of preference for a candidate. Participants liked the opposition candidate more and their own candidate less if the newscaster smiled while reporting on the opposition candidate.

THE ATTRACTIVENESS HEURISTIC: AGREEING WITH THOSE WE LIKE. If a pleasant smile can be persuasive, imagine the power of an attractive face or a winning personality. Advertisements often pair an attitude object with a popular or attractive figure, betting that someone who turns our heads can also change our minds. These communicators make no claim to expertise, so why are they persuasive? Attractive people are well-liked people, and we often agree with people we like (Benson, Karabenic, & Lerner, 1976; Chaiken, 1987; Insko, 1981) and believe that people we like are right (Byrne, 1971).

Associating someone we like with the attitude object makes us think that it too is likable. No wonder that Roger Ailes (1988), adviser to both the Reagan and Bush U.S. presidential campaigns, calls likability a persuasive "magic bullet": "If you could master one element of personal communication that is more powerful than anything . . . it is the quality of being likable. . . . If your audience likes you, they'll forgive just about everything else" (p. 81).

He seems to be right. Not surprisingly, voters like candidates they find physically attractive (M. L. Patterson, Churchill, Burger, & Powell, 1992; S. W. Rosenberg, Kahn, & Tran, 1991). Research also demonstrates that attractive people get their way more easily. One study, for example, showed that attractive people are more persuasive than those who are less attractive (Chaiken, 1979). The researcher arranged for male and female college students to solicit signatures for a petition asking the university to stop serving meat at breakfast and lunch. Attractive communicators obtained signatures from 41% of the students they approached, compared with a 32% success rate for those who were less attractive. So attractiveness serves as a persuasion cue: If Joe Montana likes Isotoner gloves, or Paula Abdul drinks Diet Coke, consumers will want to buy those products—at least that is the hope of the advertiser.

When advertisers use attractive communicators, they usually make them the most prominent feature of the appeal. Does putting the focus on a

These aren't the only advantages that attractive people have over the rest of the population. See chapter 3, pages 62 to 63, and chapter 11, pages 420 to 423.

■ **The attractiveness heuristic.**   Milk producers know that ads like this one featuring supermodel Tyra Banks use the persuasive power of an attractive source to make magazine readers buy milk without having to think carefully about its benefits.

communicator's attractiveness increase our reliance on the attractiveness heuristic? Apparently so. Suzanne Pallak (1983) showed two groups of women the same article, which urged donations in support of the arts. One of the groups also saw a vivid color photo of an attractive man who had supposedly written the article. Other students saw only a blurred photocopy of the man's photograph. Although the arguments were exactly the same, women for whom the communicator's attractiveness was made salient were much more persuaded than were women for whom the man's appearance was not so obvious.

THE FAMILIARITY HEURISTIC: FAMILIARITY DOES MAKE THE HEART GROW FONDER. There's nothing more comforting than the presence of old friends, repeated rituals, familiar surroundings. In fact, repeated exposure to a stimulus increases people's liking for it. Consider what happened, for example, when Robert Zajonc (1968) showed college students unfamiliar "Turkish words" like *saracik* and *dilikli* different numbers of times and asked them to pronounce the word. When they were later asked to guess how positive or negative each word was, people rated more positively the words they had seen more often. This **mere exposure effect,** the finding that people prefer things to which they have been more frequently exposed, is one of the most replicated findings in social psychology. This association between familiarity and goodness is so powerful that it operates even when people are unaware of whether or how often they have seen the stimulus before. In fact, the mere exposure effect is even stronger when people are unaware of how frequently they have been exposed to the stimuli (Bornstein, Leone, & Galley, 1987; Kunst-Wilson & Zajonc, 1980).

Perhaps because of the positive and reassuring feelings associated with familiarity, familiar stimuli can also be more persuasive. People judge sentences that they have heard before (even in the context of a prior experimental task) to be more credible and valid (Arkes, Hackett, & Boehme, 1989; Hasher, Goldstein, & Toppino, 1977). They are more persuaded by a weak message that has been recently repeated than by one they are hearing for the first time (Garcia-Marques, 1999). And even framing arguments in terms of familiar idioms and metaphors makes the arguments more convincing than phrases conveying the same information in more literal form. In one study, for example, Daniel Howard (1997) presented college students with a message urging them to begin financial planning for retirement soon. The content of the persuasive message was summarized using either familiar phrases or more literal arguments. For example, some students received the advice: "Don't bury your head in the sand" and "Don't put all your eggs in one basket." Others were told: "Don't pretend a problem doesn't exist" and "Don't risk everything on a single venture." Use of the familiar phrases was more effective: Those hearing the more commonplace advice developed more positive attitudes toward financial planning.

FEELINGS AS HEURISTIC CUES: IF I FEEL GOOD, I MUST LIKE IT. Affective information about an attitude object—how the object makes us feel—is an important component of our attitude toward it. When people evaluate a persuasive appeal superficially, their attitudes can reflect just their current feelings, rather than any other information. Norbert Schwarz and Jerry Clore (1983, 1988) refer to reliance on current feelings to evaluate an attitude object as the "How do I feel about it?" heuristic. When the attitude ob-

Mere exposure effect. People's tendency to prefer objects to which they have been more frequently exposed.

ject actually elicits the feelings, for example, when being with a date makes you feel good or sky-diving makes you feel sick, this shortcut makes sense. But when people process superficially, feelings that exist quite independently of a persuasive appeal or an attitude object can get mixed up with the attitude object itself. Sometimes people just feel good, perhaps because the sun is shining, the memories are sweet, the music is upbeat, or they just received a compliment. Or they feel bad—maybe a friend is ill or they failed a test. Under these circumstances, the "How do I feel about it?" heuristic means that people like whatever they evaluate when they are feeling good and dislike whatever they evaluate when they are feeling bad. Evidence for this process is plentiful. Students evaluate their lives more positively when interviewed on sunny, upbeat days than they do on rainy, downbeat days. Uninterested listeners are more accepting of persuasive messages when they are happy than when they are not happy. And pleasant music influences consumers' product preferences when choice has no real consequence (Gorn, 1982; Petty, Schumann, Richman, & Strathman, 1993; Schwarz & Clore, 1983).

Obviously, this process can sometimes lead us astray. Consider, for example, this cautionary tale. Researchers in Illinois conducted a telephone poll on the need for comprehensive exams for graduating college students, calling some students on sunny days and some on gloomy days (Sinclair, Mark, & Clore, 1991). Regardless of whether the caller offered sound or weak arguments for the proposal, the good weather group, who were assumed to be in a good mood, were more likely than the others to support the institution of exams. In this case, it seemed that feelings that might have been caused by the weather got mixed up with evaluations of the arguments, making them seem more persuasive. In fact, when experimenters subtly pointed out the possible source of these unrelated feelings (by asking: "How's the weather down there?"), the weather had no impact on participants' attitudes. Like other heuristics, the "How do I feel about it?" cue is most powerful when people process only superficially.

THE EXPERTISE HEURISTIC: AGREEING WITH THOSE WHO KNOW. "Life on other solar systems is entirely possible!" Imagine that this sentence had caught your attention as you flipped through the television channels on a Sunday afternoon. You soon discover that the source of the intriguing statement is a talk-show guest, a farmer who claims he has been taken for multiple rides on a spaceship. Would you nod in agreement or snort with derision? Imagine now that you had heard this same sentence as part of the television series *Cosmos*, created by the late Carl Sagan, professor of astronomy and space science at Cornell University. Would your reaction be different?

Research suggests that it would. Because communicators with excellent credentials usually offer cogent arguments, people often associate them with opinions that should be respected: Experts know what they are talking about. On the basis of this association, the *expertise heuristic* leads people to accept the validity of a claim on the basis of *who* says it, instead of carefully analyzing *what* is said (Hovland & Weiss, 1951; Maddux & Rogers, 1980; Sternthal, Dholakia, & Leavitt, 1978).

Why is Carl Sagan an expert source while the space-traveling farmer is not? To be credible, communicators must be competent. *Competence* refers to proof of the communicator's accomplishment or status in a particular field.

The Far Side by Gary Larson

Like a lot of dogs, I often have problems finding thrown objects in high grass... That's why I use the new ACME Stick-be-Found.

Dog Endorsements

When an ad features Renaldo in action on the soccer field, a robed judge banging a gavel in a wood-paneled courtroom, or a stethoscope-bedecked doctor writing prescriptions, its creators are hoping to capitalize on the expertise heuristic. One early demonstration of this simple association between occupation and competence compared the persuasive powers of a judge and a drug dealer (Kelman & Hovland, 1953). Participants were told that one or the other had recommended relatively lenient treatment of a juvenile delinquent. As you might expect, they found the judge more persuasive than the drug dealer.

Occupation is not the only cue that suggests competence. Research findings indicate that fast talkers also convey an image of expertise. As long as people can understand the gist of a message, the faster the message is delivered, the more objective, intelligent, and knowledgeable the communicator is seen to be (MacLachlan & Siegel, 1980; N. Miller, Maruyama, Beaber, & Valone, 1976). Rapid delivery makes it harder for listeners to tell a strong appeal from a weak one (S. M. Smith & Shaffer, 1995). In fact, running television ads at 120% of their normal speed can increase the persuasiveness of weak commercials (D. L. Moore, Hausknecht, & Thamodaran, 1986). There are limits to these effects, however. If delivery is so rapid that the meaning of the message is lost, persuasion is undermined. And when listeners really care about the topic, they are less likely to let a fast talker influence their attitudes (S. M. Smith & Shaffer, 1995).

People expect expert communicators not only to know the facts but also to tell the truth (Eagly, Wood, & Chaiken, 1978). Thus, after competence, *trustworthiness* is the most important characteristic a credible communicator can have. That is why communicators sometimes earn persuasion points by presenting both sides of an issue; the strategy makes them seem well informed and fair minded (R. A. Jones & Brehm, 1970). Trustworthiness is also the goal when advertisers arrange for their audience to "sit in on" or "overhear" product testimonials and "slice of life" endorsements. If the communication seems to happen by accident, rather than being tailored specifically for the listener's ears, the casual observer is likely to think it is true and to be influenced by it (Walster & Festinger, 1962).

Of course, we are likely to be taken in by these ploys only if we are processing very minimally. If we devote even a little more attention to the communication, we might be prompted to ask *why* a particular source is advocating a particular position (Eagly, Chaiken, & Wood, 1981). Such attributional processing can undermine a communicator's apparent trustworthiness. Imagine, for example, that an advertisement for Sergio Tacchini sportswear featuring tennis star Martina Hingis prompts you to wonder why Hingis endorses the product. Does Hingis promote that brand because of the quality of the product? Could it be that this particular line of sportswear is so terrific that Hingis cannot help but recommend it? If the ad leads to the belief that the communicator's position reflects the stimulus object's actual qualities—deciding that Hingis endorses Tacchini because the clothes are so good—such a *stimulus attribution* produces persuasion (Eagly and others, 1978). If the advocate seems to have ulterior motives, however, people become suspicious. If they recognize that Hingis—like Venus Williams with Reebok, Patty Schnyder with Adidas, and Mirjana Lucic with Fila—is well paid for an endorsement, they may find the ad less persuasive: Maybe it's the money talking, not the quality

Attributional processing (processing concerned with discovering the causes for behavior) and the conditions that lead to stimulus attributions were discussed in chapter 3, pages 77 to 82.

of the gear. Attributional processing may explain why people are particularly impressed when communicators seem to speak or act against their own best interests (Knight & Weiss, 1980). We would probably be persuaded if we learned that Martina Hingis owns stock in a competitive sportswear company but feels compelled to recommend Sergio Tacchini because of its quality.

THE MESSAGE-LENGTH HEURISTIC: LENGTH EQUALS STRENGTH. Even the form of a persuasive appeal can lead us to associate an attitude object with positive qualities if we are processing superficially. Perhaps you have noticed over the years that longer campaign speeches seem more convincing than briefer ones. Such observations might produce a simple *message-length heuristic:* The longer the message, the more valid it appears to be. Ads that pointedly number "the 25 best reasons" to prefer a product are trying to invoke this heuristic. Table 7–1 describes another persuasion technique that encourages people to rely on the sheer number of arguments supporting a particular position.

Of course, quantity does not always mean quality, and the focus on numbers can blind us to the inadequacy of the reasoning. Imagine the following scenario. You are waiting in line at the photocopy machine when you are approached by someone wanting to cut ahead of you. Her request is relatively small: She wants to make only five copies. Would you find her simple request persuasive? About 60% of students waiting in line to use the copy machine at the City University of New York (CUNY) did (Langer,

---

TABLE 7.1. Length Equals Strength: The Ben Franklin Close

A *close* is a persuasive technique that "closes a deal." A salesperson using the Ben Franklin close would begin with a story like this:

> As you know, Ben Franklin has always been considered one of the wisest men America has ever had. Whenever he felt himself in a situation where he couldn't quite make up his mind, he felt pretty much as you do now. If it was the right thing, he wanted to be sure he did it. If it was the wrong thing, he wanted to be just as sure that he avoided it. Isn't that about the way you feel?
>
> So here's what he would do to arrive at a decision. He would take a clean sheet of paper and draw a line down the middle, like this. On one side of the line he would list all the reasons why he should make a "yes" decision and on the other side of the line he would list all the reasons against making this decision. When he was through, he would count the reasons that he was able to tally on each side, and his decision was made for him. Why don't we try it here and see what happens?

As the customer attempts to come up with reasons for buying the product, the salesperson helps suggest and list reasons. When it comes to producing reasons for the other side, however, the salesperson leaves the customer to work alone. Often it will be difficult for one person to generate more reasons than two people can. With the sheet of paper showing more reasons "for" than "against," the customer can be influenced by the message-length heuristic.

Source: Adapted with permission of Lexington Books, an imprint of Macmillan Publishing Company, from J. Jacoby (1984). Some social psychological perspectives on closing. In J. Jacoby & C. S. Craig (Eds.), *Personal selling* (pp. 73–92). Copyright © 1984 by Lexington Books.

Blank, & Chanowitz, 1978). Now imagine that the would-be line cutter not only made the same request but also explained that she was in a rush. Would this legitimate argument in favor of letting her go ahead be even more persuasive? If you say yes, you agree with the CUNY students, 94% of whom agreed to the request when given a good reason.

These findings suggest that the quality of a message increases persuasiveness, but is that always the case? If people are processing heuristically—relying on whether the request is long or not, for example—maybe anything that *sounds like* an argument or reason will do. In fact, other people were approached by the woman with a request and an empty explanation that only sounded like a reason: "Excuse me, I have five pages. May I use the Xerox machine, because I have to make some copies?" Ninety-three percent of those approached this way agreed to let her go ahead! When people rely on the message-length heuristic, a longer message, no matter what it says, seems compelling (Petty & Cacioppo, 1984). As you will see later, however, when a request is substantial enough to provoke more extensive processing, for example, if the person had to make fifty copies instead of five, people will think more carefully about the reason.

Other superficial aspects of persuasive appeals can also act as heuristics. Many people are strong believers in the "you get what you pay for" heuristic: When items like perfume, wine, and jewelry are sold for higher prices, we think they are of better quality (McConnell, 1968; R. A. Peterson, 1977). And many people are particularly impressed by speeches or advertisements that contain numbers, graphs, or equations, perhaps because they convey an air of scientific objectivity (Chaiken, 1987). Perhaps this explains why political candidates often bring statistics when they take their platform to the people.

Most of the time, the associations that underlie persuasion heuristics allow us to effectively decide what we think about the attitude objects we encounter. Experts usually know what they are talking about, and a long message often yields more relevant information than a short one. If the attitude object makes us feel good, it probably is good. After all, the usefulness of these cognitive and affective cues led people to develop the heuristics in the first place. Sometimes, however, superficial processing of a persuasive communication may not provide enough convincing information. Or we may want to know more about the attitude object than superficial processing provides. Under these circumstances we move into high gear, and we process information in depth.

Systematic Processing of Persuasive Communications

Sometimes people do carefully consider the content of arguments presented in a persuasive communication. When people pay attention to a message, understand its content, and react favorably to it, persuasion occurs. Attitudes resulting from such careful consideration are much more resistant to later change than most attitudes produced by superficial processing.

When people process systematically, they begin to think about aspects of the attitude object that go beyond the immediate evaluations associated with communicators and messages. They turn their attention to evaluating the quality of the information provided about the attitude object and to thinking about what they are being told in relation to what they already know. It's not that systematic processors don't notice the presence of heuristic cues in the persuasion setting. But as they start to take notice of other information as well, the impact of superficial factors on attitudes becomes less important. How does this increase in thinking affect persuasion?

PROCESSING MESSAGE CONTENT. Thoroughgoing systematic processing involves paying increased attention to the strength and quality of the arguments that communicators use to advocate a particular position or object (Chaiken, 1980, 1987; Petty & Cacioppo, 1981, 1986). Because thinking carefully about the content of the message is so important in systematic processing, Petty and Cacioppo (1981, 1986) have called it the *central route to persuasion.* Over the years, researchers have gained considerable knowledge about the steps involved in systematic processing and how they influence persuasion (McGuire, 1969).

1. *Attending to the message.* In one popular French commercial for an all-purpose adhesive, the glue is applied to the soles of the announcer's shoes and he is hung upside down from the ceiling. In a recent North American ad, a mid-size truck is pushed off a suspension bridge to dangle on a bungee cord. The reason advertisers go to such lengths is that they realize that getting the audience's attention is the first crucial step in bringing about persuasion, a fact Carl Hovland and his colleagues at Yale University recognized long ago (Hovland, Lumsdaine, & Sheffield, 1949; Hovland, Janis, & Kelley, 1953). It's also a step that is easier said than done. Because people are bombarded by so many persuasive messages—more than three to four hundred a day from the mass media alone (Aaker & Myers, 1987)—most messages receive at best a superficial once-over. Television advertisers have the upper hand here: The use of both vision and sound makes their ads more attention grabbing than messages delivered on radio or in print (Andreoli & Worchel, 1978). But all professional persuaders know that, if they are to keep their candidate in the spotlight or make their product's packaging stand out from the rest, they must quickly snare the audience's attention, giving them a reason to watch and listen. As David Ogilvy (1983) concluded from his years of advertising experience, "People screen out a lot of commercials because they start with something dull. When you advertise fire extinguishers, open with the fire" (p. 111).

2. *Comprehending the message.* Although getting the audience's attention is a critical first step in communicating, attention does not always guarantee comprehension. Reading or hearing an argument does not mean we understand it. Research indicates, in fact, that much of the persuasive information aimed at us goes right over our heads. In one survey, for example, consumer psychologist Jacob Jacoby and his colleagues (Jacoby, Hoyer, & Sheluga, 1980) found that adults misunderstood 30% to 40% of the information presented in 30-second television segments. Comprehension of printed magazine ads and articles is somewhat better (Chaiken & Eagly, 1976), which may explain why they have more effect on attitudes (McGuire, 1985). But even here, misunderstandings are still quite frequent (Jacoby & Hoyer, 1989). So the golden rule for most media persuasion is: Keep it simple.

■ **Systematic processing might stop this child's suffering.**   The effectiveness of this ad is enhanced because it encourages systematic processing. The photo draws our attention to the easy-to-understand arguments, while the questions provoke active elaboration of message content. Systematically processed appeals usually result in attitudes that persist over time and resist further attempts to change them.

3. *Reacting to message content.* People do not just passively soak up information; they react to it, sometimes favorably and sometimes unfavorably. Whether the persuasive communication is your doctor's recommendation regarding a treatment regimen or your best friend's pitch to borrow your car, you will do more than just listen to it if it has engaged your attention and you understand it. You will think about whether you agree or disagree with the persuader's arguments. Favorable reactions might include merely registering agreement ("Walking for a half hour per day sounds good to me") or developing the supportive information even further ("Yes, well, Sara really is a very careful driver"). Negative reactions may range from simply disagreeing with some point ("Oh, pleeease!") to developing a detailed set of counterarguments. The process of generating such favorable and unfavorable evaluative reactions to the content of a message is called **elaboration**. These reactions can be affective as well as cognitive, reflecting feelings associated with the attitude object and additional characteristics that the object might have. One study presented messages favoring the use of animals in medical experiments to students who opposed their use. Faced with such a message, participants produced as many affective responses (like "Children dying unnecessarily makes me want to cry") as cognitive ones ("I realize now that some drug effects can't be modeled by computers"). In fact, when the content of the message was itself emotional (using arguments like "How would you feel if your child died

Elaboration. The generation of favorable or unfavorable reactions to the content of a message.

because the medical research hadn't been done?") rather than ratio
nal, more affective than rational responses were produced (Rosselli,
Skelly, & Mackie, 1995).

4. *Accepting the message*. If a systematically processed message stimulates favorable cognitive or affective elaborations, it will be persuasive. If the arguments evoke unfavorable reactions, the message will
   fail to persuade (Greenwald, 1968; Petty, Cacioppo, & Goldman,
   1981). Thus people's *reactions* to the content of the message can be
   even more important than the content itself. In effect, people persuade themselves.

If carefully processed arguments provoke positive elaborations, the
more arguments there are, the more attitude change there will be. By the
same token, greater numbers of carefully processed specious arguments
will produce more negative responses than would result from only a few
silly arguments. To assess the impact of systematic thinking about strong
and weak arguments on persuasion, one study presented students with different numbers of arguments in favor of instituting comprehensive examinations for graduating college students—a popular attitude issue in persuasion research (Petty & Cacioppo, 1984). Strong arguments—ones that
typically prompt favorable elaborations—in this experiment included statements like the following: "Graduate schools and law and medical schools
are beginning to show clear and significant preferences for students who received their undergraduate degrees from institutions with comprehensive
exams." Weak arguments, which typically elicit unfavorable elaborations,
included such statements as, "Graduate students have always had to take a
comprehensive exam in their major area before receiving their degrees, and
it is only fair that undergraduates should have to take them also." Some students heard three weak arguments and others heard nine weak arguments.
A third group heard three strong arguments, and a fourth group, nine
strong ones. All students then gave their own opinions on the comprehensive exams issue. The results indicated that when students were processing
systematically, they found three strong arguments persuasive and nine even
more so. In contrast, a few weak arguments were unimpressive, and many
weak arguments were a real turn-off. When communicators attempt to influence us with really bad arguments, we may even respond by moving in a
direction opposite the one intended. This change is called a *boomerang effect.*

Compelling arguments aren't always provided for us, but persuasion
can still occur when just thinking about an attitude issue brings more and
more relevant evidence and arguments to mind. When this happens, merely
thinking about the issue can lead to favorable or unfavorable evaluations of
the information we consider, which in turn produce either more persuasion
or a boomerang effect (Tesser, 1978).

THE CONSEQUENCES OF SYSTEMATIC PROCESSING. Systematic thinking has
implications for the kinds of information on which attitudes are based.
When people process systematically, they go beyond the immediate evaluations associated with persuasion cues and also evaluate the quality of information the message provides about the attitude object. When both heuristic
cues and information about message content are available, which deter-

mines our attitude? What happens if persuasion cues suggest a glowing endorsement, but message content suggests resounding rejection? If an expert endorses a dubious product, for example, the expertise heuristic and careful processing of message content tilts us in different attitudinal directions. The effect of additional attention to, comprehension of, and elaboration of message content will usually win the day. Especially if the arguments offered are unambiguously weak or strong, careful thinking about, for example, the famous commencement speaker's long-winded but hackneyed advice will leave us unconvinced, whereas we might find ourselves persuaded by the cogent campaign analysis of the unknown political commentator.

When message content is not so convincingly strong or weak, however, even systematic processors can still be affected by heuristic cues. The presence of an expert source might bias reactions to an ambiguous message, making elaborations more favorable. Having a nonexpert deliver the same message might bias reactions in the opposite direction. In these cases lots of thinking goes on, but the thinking is tilted in one direction more than the other, and a similarly slanted attitude results (Chaiken & Maheswaran, 1994).

Systematic thinking has other effects on attitudes as well. When attitudes change because information is carefully attended, comprehended, and elaborated, all this mental work helps write the resulting attitudes almost indelibly in memory (Chaiken, 1980; Petty, Cacioppo, Haugtvedt, & Heesacker, 1986). In fact, the new attitudes become so firmly fixed that they are little affected by the passage of time (Boninger, Brock, Cook, Gruder, & Romer, 1990; Chaiken, 1980; Pratkanis, Greenwald, Leippe, & Baumgardner, 1988). Compared with attitudes that change through heuristic processing, systematically altered attitudes are also resistant in the face of new material. In one demonstration of this advantage, individuals were presented first with a message suggesting that a new artificial sweetener was safe, and then with an equally strong message from a different source suggesting that it was not. The individuals who responded to the first message with considerable issue-relevant thinking were less influenced by the second message (Haugtvedt & Petty, 1992; Wu & Shaffer, 1987). Trial lawyers, political candidates engaged in debate, and disputing siblings arguing their case to a parent should all find these results very useful. If the audience is going to hear both sides of an issue, is it better to present your case first or last? If you have strong arguments and you expect people to do a lot of thinking about them, it's best to go first. If people put a lot of thought into changing their mind on the basis of your appeal, they are much more likely to resist the opposite point of view (Haugtvedt & Wegener, 1994).

Superficial and Systematic Processing: Which Strategy, When?

People process messages systematically only when they have both the motivation and the cognitive capacity to do so. The relevance of the message to important goals determines motivation. Cognitive capacity is available when people have adequate ability to process and can do so without distraction.

So what is the best strategy if you want to change someone's mind about something? Whether you are addressing your constituents, launching a new business, or trying to get your family to adopt a sensible diet, any strategy that evokes systematic processing seems to be the best bet for both persuader and persuadee. For the persuader, systematic processing guarantees long-term and resistant attitude change: Once you have won their minds, you will keep their allegiance. For the consumer of persuasive communications, careful processing gives us greater confidence in the validity of our attitudes.

Why, then, don't people process systematically all the time? Unfortunately, there is a catch. Systematic processing of persuasive appeals does not come easily. Like systematic processing of any other kind of information, it requires a substantial investment of effort and processing capacity. In fact, whether communications are processed superficially or systematically depends on two factors: people's motivation and their cognitive capacity to think carefully about the content of the message.

HOW MOTIVATION INFLUENCES SYSTEMATIC PROCESSING. Motives like mastery, connectedness, and protecting a positive view of ourselves play an important role in how we approach persuasive communications. Imagine the plight of a small company's purchasing manager given the responsibility of selecting and purchasing new computer equipment to be used for product design. The decision is a crucial one: The company needs to upgrade to stay competitive, but if it goes over budget there could be a real problem with cash flow. This is the manager's first real test as purchasing manager, and her reputation for mixing technical smarts with an eye for a bargain is on the line. How will she decide which product line uses her company's money most effectively? She probably will react as we all would. When it's important that we form accurate evaluations, and when the attitudes and opinions we form reflect directly on us, systematic processing is our greatest ally.

1. *The importance of being accurate.* When we are being held accountable for our preferences and are concerned about making the correct decision, the mastery motive will predominate and issues of accuracy will be central. The product manager will need solid evidence to justify her choice of computer system, because others will hold her accountable. She may also fear that if she chooses a faulty piece of equipment, the costs of being incorrect could be severe. Compared with people who have no one to answer to, accountable message processors and those anxious to avoid being wrong will process persuasive communications more thoroughly, think more about the information, and be more concerned with integrating new information as it comes to light (Kruglanski, 1988; Tetlock, 1983, 1985).

   Accuracy concerns can also be triggered when the evidence seems mixed. Imagine that you have been looking forward to seeing a newly released movie and you discover that your local paper has panned it. Siskel and Ebert also give it two "thumbs down," and you decide not to see it. But then one of your friends says it is the best movie he has seen in a long time. Now your confidence in your judgment wavers, and you start looking for new input. Perhaps you ask your friend about the plot and characters, or you seek out several additional reviews. When persuasive communications advocate inconsistent positions, as they do in this example, people move from casual to careful processing. People are motivated to undertake a detailed analysis of all aspects of the communication when they encounter arguments that do not fit or conclusions that do not follow (Chaiken, Liberman, & Eagly, 1989; Festinger, 1957; Maheswaran & Chaiken, 1991).

2. *The importance of self-relevance.* An old Chinese proverb says, "Tell me and I'll forget; involve me and I'll understand." People's tendency to carefully process personally relevant information is nothing new. When information is relevant to something that affects us, we want to know all about it. The product manager, for example, knows her decision will affect more than the company's bottom line. With her own reputation at stake, she will be motivated to pay careful attention to the information presented by the competing systems manufacturers.

In a demonstration of the influence of self-relevance on persuasion, researchers asked groups of students to listen to a speech dealing, again, with the issue of whether comprehensive exams should be required for graduation (Petty and others, 1981). Some groups heard a speech composed of strong and valid arguments advocating the exams, whereas other groups were given rather weak and silly arguments. Some groups were led to believe the speech had been delivered by an expert communicator—a Princeton University professor of education—whereas others were told the source was a nonexpert—a local high school junior "interested" in such issues. The most important manipulation was one of self-relevance. Some groups of students were told the exam would be implemented at their own school, which meant that they personally would be affected. Other groups were told the exams were planned for another institution, and thus they were personally less relevant. Perhaps you can guess how this manipulation of relevance influenced students' reactions. Those who thought the plan would not affect them processed the communication superficially. Relying on the expertise heuristic, they responded favorably to the expert communicator and unfavorably to the nonexpert, regardless of the message's content. As you can see in Figure 7.4, however, the message had quite a different impact on students who thought the exam proposal would affect them personally. These students were motivated to pay careful attention to the quality of the arguments. This systematic processing led them to accept strong and compelling arguments and to reject weak and specious ones, regardless of who espoused them.

The relevance of personal goals almost always increases systematic processing of relevant information. Consider a connectedness goal like having a pleasant interaction. When students in one study were given such a goal, they were particularly likely to express opinions similar to those of their interaction partners. But this outcome wasn't the result of a lack of thought. In fact, the students put quite a lot of effort into thinking about their partner's point of view. But the fact that they were motivated to agree with the partner biased this extra thinking toward positive elaboration of the partner's position (Chen, Shechter, & Chaiken, 1996).

CAPACITY FACTORS THAT INFLUENCE SYSTEMATIC PROCESSING. Even when we are highly motivated, we may encounter obstacles to systematic process-

FIGURE 7.4   Effects of motivation on message processing

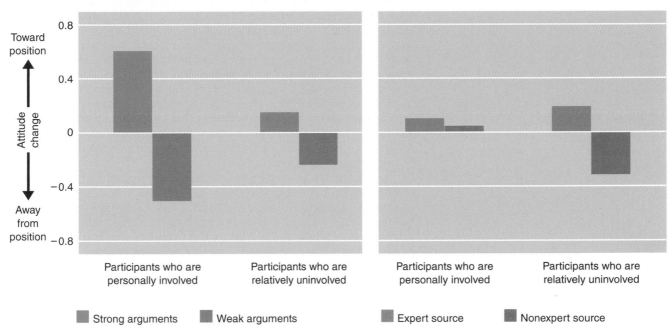

■ In this study, some participants were highly involved in the issue and others were uninvolved. They heard strong or weak arguments, presented by an expert or nonexpert source. Notice that the strength of the arguments made more difference to highly involved participants (graph on left). In contrast, the expertise of the source had more influence on the less involved participants (graph on right). (Data from Petty and others, 1981.)

ing. Imagine the product manager spreading the dozen or so computer brochures out on her desk. Each describes different product lines in different ways; each computer system offers different features for different prices. Will she be able to understand and evaluate every claim? Even when people want to process systematically, they are not always able to do so.

1. *The ability to process.* Sometimes, people just do not have the mental resources to take in and evaluate all the available information. Even the most motivated processors of persuasive communications occasionally have difficulty understanding all the complex and rapidly presented information offered in print, radio, and television commercials. This is particularly true when, as in the product manager's case, the information is technical, there is too much of it, or it has multiple dimensions on which alternatives differ (Janis & Rife, 1959). Consider, for example, a group of college students from a community rocked both by the murders of two local teenage girls and the reduced sentence given one of those convicted as the result of a plea bargain (in plea bargaining, an accused person agrees to plead guilty to a less serious charge, usually in exchange for information that will convict another, or in exchange for a particular sentence). When presented with strong or weak arguments supporting the wider use of plea bargaining to reduce court backlogs, the students were highly motivated to evaluate them thoroughly and probably to disagree with them (Hafer, Reynolds, & Obertynski, 1996). Why then, did some of them end up agreeing with the position advocated by a

judge with a Harvard Law School pedigree and 15 years of experience, regardless of whether his arguments were weak or strong? The answer lay in the complexity of the legal arguments used to support plea bargaining. In one set of conditions, the students listened to either weak or strong arguments that used layperson's terms, common terms, and simple grammatical structures. Indicating their high motivation and thorough evaluation of the messages, students who read strong arguments were somewhat persuaded, whereas those presented with weak arguments completely dismissed them. But in another set of conditions, the students were presented with the same strong and weak arguments framed in legal jargon and complex grammar. Despite their motivation, these processors just couldn't comprehend and evaluate the information, and their attitudes ended up reflecting source expertise.

Children are at even more of a disadvantage in this area. Young children often have enough ability to understand a message but lack the critical capacity to evaluate it. Many of them trust television to tell the truth, and they do not always know when programs stop and advertisements begin. They know the brand names and their jingles but they cannot remember the specific details of the ad. As a result, they are particularly prone to fall for the inducements served up with children's programs (Liebert & Spratkin, 1988; Palmer & Dorr, 1980). These problems are even more serious in countries where children have limited media exposure, such as India (Unnikrishnan & Bajpai, 1996). As children grow older and more experienced, they learn to evaluate information more critically and become less easily persuaded (Boush, Friestad, & Rose, 1994).

2. *The opportunity to concentrate.* No matter how motivated or expert we are, our ability to process systematically is diminished if we cannot concentrate. Ready and willing to understand and evaluate all the relevant material, our hapless manager is suddenly interrupted by the phone. As she hangs up, a co-worker stops by wanting to discuss a purchase order. Then her boss reminds her that the departmental meeting begins in an hour. These continual distractions, as you undoubtedly know from your own experience, will reduce her ability to process information carefully.

By reducing our critical ability, distractions can decrease the effectiveness of strongly persuasive communications because we are not able to elaborate them favorably. To make matters worse, distraction exerts the opposite effect on weak communications. It makes weak communications more persuasive because it reduces people's cognitive capacity, thereby making it difficult for them to counter flawed arguments or demolish shaky logic (Petty, Wells, & Brock, 1976). And because of this reduced ability to process message content carefully, people are more influenced by superficial cues. When distracted, for example, people are more influenced by the expertise heuristic: Their attitudes reflect the presence of a credible source more than their nondistracted counterparts (R. A. Baron, Baron, & Miller, 1973; S. B. Kiesler & Mathog, 1968). No wonder the old advertising motto recommends: "If you have nothing to say, distract them!"

As some of these studies were described, you might have realized that some of the same factors that produce influence via superficial processing can also be persuasive when systematic processing occurs. For example, a long message might be particularly compelling because of the "length equals strength" heuristic. But those same lengthy arguments might provide ammunition for attitude change if they are processed systematically. Because many pieces of information in the persuasion setting can be processed either superficially or systematically, persuasion-relevant information can play multiple roles when it comes to changing attitudes (Petty & Wegener, 1998).

PERSONALITY DIFFERENCES IN RESPONSES TO PERSUASIVE COMMUNICATIONS. Although motivation and ability to process persuasive communications often depend on the situation, individuals also differ in how willing and able they are to process systematically. One such difference seems to be how much people enjoy thinking itself. People differ, for example, in the degree to which they enjoy puzzling over difficult problems, resolving inconsistencies, and searching for the right answers. Those who enjoy such activities are said to have high *need for cognition* (Cacioppo & Petty, 1982; A. Cohen, 1957). This need is indicated by people's responses to statements like the ones in Table 7.2.

Research has found that individuals with a high need for cognition are more likely than others to put time and effort into processing persuasive communications. In one study demonstrating this point, participants read a strongly or weakly argued editorial. The higher their need for cognition, the more likely they were to respond favorably to strong arguments and to be unmoved by weak ones (Cacioppo, Petty, & Morris, 1983). As you might expect, people with a low need for cognition are relatively more responsive to heuristic cues, like the expertise of a communicator (Cacioppo & Petty, 1984).

Another kind of personality difference influences the sorts of messages that people find personally relevant. For example, because high self-monitors are so conscious of how others evaluate them, they zero in on image-focused appeals that show how a product can help them impress others. Low self-monitors, on the other hand, hold attitudes that allow them to express who they are, and thus are more attuned to value-expressive appeals. Howard Lavine and Mark Snyder (1996) demonstrated the difference self-

To remind yourself of other characteristics of typical high and low self-monitors, reread chapter 4, pages 135 to 136.

TABLE 7.2. The Need for Cognition Scale: Sample Items

1. I find satisfaction in deliberating hard for long hours.
2. Learning new ways to think doesn't excite me very much.
3. I like tasks that require little thought once I've learned them.
4. I would prefer complex to simple problems.
5. The notion of thinking abstractly is appealing to me.
6. More often than not, more thinking just leads to more errors.

Note: These are sample items from the Need for Cognition Scale, which assesses how much people enjoy engaging in effortful cognitive activities. People who agree with items 1, 4, and 5 and disagree with items 2, 3, and 6 would be regarded as high in need for cognition. The actual scale used in research contains many more than six items, so it can more accurately classify people as high or low in need for cognition.

Source: From "The need for cognition" by J. T. Cacioppo & R. E. Petty, 1982, *Journal of Personality and Social Psychology, 42,* pp. 116–131. Copyright © 1982 by the American Psychological Association. Reprinted by permission.

FIGURE 7.5   "This is who I am" versus "Image is everything": Self-monitoring and persuasion

■ High and low self-monitors reacted in different ways to appeals that advocated voting in an upcoming election. High self-monitors had more positive attitudes when they received an image-focused appeal, whereas low self-monitors were more positive when the message stressed value expressive reasons to vote. (Data from Lavine & Snyder, 1996).

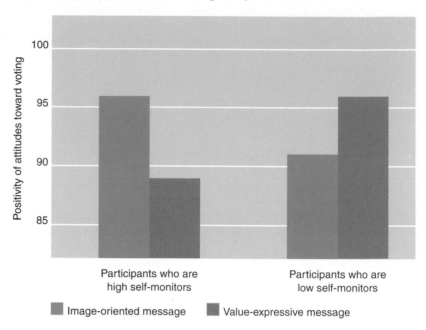

monitoring could make in a study that compared reactions to messages that advocated voting in local and presidential elections. The image-focused appeal contended that voting enhances a person's status, popularity, and attractiveness, and noted that a majority of the recipient's peers were planning to vote in an upcoming election. In contrast, the value-expressive message pointed out that voting provides a way of supporting liberty and democracy, and affords the opportunity to put attitudes and beliefs into action. The results of the study appear in Figure 7.5. As the researchers expected, high self-monitors had more positive attitudes toward voting when the message appealed to image. In contrast, low self-monitors were more positive when the message focused on value expression. Importantly, those exposed to messages tuned to their individual motivational preferences were also more likely to ask for information about the candidates and more likely to actually vote. How do such motivationally matched appeals produce these persuasive benefits? First, both high and low self-monitors pay more attention to and spend more time processing arguments that further their goals (DeBono, 1987; DeBono & Harnish, 1988). Second, both groups see those functionally relevant arguments as stronger and more compelling than arguments that don't speak to their goals (Lavine & Snyder, 1996).

In many situations, of course, differences among individuals in motivation and capacity go hand in hand to determine how extensively a particular message will be processed and how great its impact will be. For example, when prelaw students are more persuaded by legalistic arguments than by other evidence, both the motivating force of self-relevance and the ability factor of extra background knowledge are probably at work (Cacioppo, Petty, & Sidera, 1982). Similarly, expertise in an area often reflects both inter-

FIGURE 7.6   Conditions for systematic processing

■ When people have both motivation and capacity, they are likely to process persuasive messages systematically by elaborating the arguments, and the result is enduring attitude change.

est in thinking about and ability to deal with particular material (W. Wood, 1982; Wood, Kallgren, & Preisler, 1985). These individual differences are why messages that match people's motives and abilities are so effective.

In summary, both motivation, which is highest when a message taps into goals that are important for an individual, and capacity, which depends on ability and freedom from distraction, are prerequisites for systematic processing. Perhaps you can see now why most persuasive communications are processed superficially. As Figure 7.6 shows, the kind of careful message processing that produces long-term attitude change depends on both motivation and capacity.

The Persuasive Power of Emotion

"Reach out and touch someone." "Mazda: It just feels right." "Welcome to our world. Step into our heart." These advertising slogans are designed not just to provide facts or feelings about attitude objects, but to make us feel good. The strategy is an obvious one: Aren't people in good moods particularly easy to persuade? Both popular belief and professional practices based on them suggest that the answer is yes. But if making people feel good makes persuasion more likely, why would an antismoking appeal ever feature a tiny premature baby, crisscrossed by tubes and bandages, screaming in an incubator? Or a toothpaste ad show diseased gums and decaying teeth? Do scenes and ideas that make us feel bad also have persuasive power? In fact, the answer is that both feeling good and feeling bad (or anxious or angry or guilty) can either increase or decrease persuasion depending on the circumstances. And these persuasive consequences can occur regardless of whether such feelings are aroused in association with the attitude object, or whether we are feeling good or bad for completely unrelated reasons. As you will see, because moods and emotions have impacts on motivation and capacity, they can increase or decrease our vulnerability to persuasion.

Feeling Good but Not Always Thinking Straight

Positive and negative feelings can influence people's motivation and their ability to process persuasive messages systematically. When positive mood decreases motivation and capacity, it lowers the impact of message content on attitudes and increases the impact of heuristic cues.

The evidence linking good mood and persuasiveness is quite mixed. We have already seen that when people base their evaluations on emotions, positive feelings will produce positive attitudes. People in good moods are more likely to comply with requests than unhappy people, particularly if the requests are impolite (Forgas, 1998). And if being in a good mood while thinking about arguments makes you evaluate them favorably, a good mood can increase persuasion (Petty and others, 1993; Wegener, Petty, & Smith, 1995). Other studies indicate, however, that a positive mood can make persuasion *less* likely to occur (Isen & Levin, 1972; Wegener and others, 1995). What explains these differences?

Part of the answer is that people in a good mood are less likely than people who feel neutral or sad to process the contents of persuasive appeals systematically (Mackie, Asuncion, & Rosselli, 1992; Schwarz, Bless, & Bohner, 1991). This in turn means that the attitudes of people in positive moods are more likely to reflect associations based on heuristic cues. Consider what happened, for example, when some students unexpectedly won a dollar in a lottery—a pleasant event that raised their spirits—while others simply answered questions about lotteries (Worth & Mackie, 1987). All students then read and evaluated a speech about acid rain supposedly delivered by a delegate to an environmental conference. Whereas those in a neutral mood accepted strong arguments and rejected weak ones, happy processors were equally impressed by weak and strong arguments. They also fell prey to the expertise heuristic, agreeing with a message delivered by a prestigious source and ignoring an appeal from a disreputable communicator.

This finding demonstrates part of the relationship between positive mood and persuasion. Since being in a good mood often decreases careful, systematic processing, a happy person is more likely to succumb to an expert or attractive source, a long or "scientific-looking" message, or other heuristic cues. Someone in a good mood is also less likely to see through weak arguments and to counter flawed assumptions. And because of the "How do I feel about it?" heuristic, the mood itself can act as a cue, so happiness can deliver a doubly persuasive whammy. At the same time, rational arguments may have little impact on the happy person. If you want to persuade your parents that you need a costly school ring, tailor your arguments to their mood. If your arguments are weak, pick a day when their spirits are high. But if you have compelling arguments to offer, wait until they are in a neutral mood, when you can count on their careful attention.

What is it about feeling good that leads to superficial processing? The answer has to do with the impact of mood states on motivation and cognitive capacity.

1. *Positive mood and motivation.* When people feel good, they may see no need to process carefully. They have no motivation to engage in systematic processing: Their good mood tells them that everything is just fine. Their heuristically based conclusions may seem perfectly adequate because positive mood makes them feel confident (E. J. Johnson & Tversky, 1983), informs them that their situation holds no danger for them (Bless and others, 1996; Schwarz and others, 1991), or indicates that how they have acted in the past will suffice again now (Garcia-Marques, 1999). They may not want anything to interfere with their good spirits—not even the effort of careful thought (Isen & Levin, 1972; Mischel, Ebbessen, & Zeiss, 1973). The powerful impact that good feelings have on motivations to process is demonstrated by studies that increase persuasive processing by changing the goals associated with positive mood. For example, if processors are led to believe that good mood indicates that they are enjoying a task, rather than that they are performing it adequately, they process more deeply (L. L. Martin, Ward, Achee, & Wyer, 1993). And if people believe that reading particular information will help them maintain or improve a positive mood, they think about that material more extensively (Wegener and others, 1995). Such systematic processing can, of course, lead to more persuasion if message content is compelling.

2. *Positive mood and capacity.* When people feel good they may also find it hard to concentrate. Think about the last time something wonderful happened to you. Did you turn it over and over in your mind? Some research suggests that a good mood might reduce systematic processing because people's minds are full of other thoughts. In demonstrating this point, researchers have given happy people extra time to process arguments (Mackie & Worth, 1989) and have helped them focus on key aspects of the message (Bless, Bohner, Schwarz, & Strach, 1990). Both of these strategies made it easier for happy people to evaluate persuasive communications.

Fear Appeals and Persuasion: Make Me Worry, Make Me Agree

In the right dosage, anxiety can motivate people to process, but an excess of fear can decrease motivation and drain cognitive capacity, undermining systematic processing.

Fear is by far the most common negative emotion that influence agents exploit. When advertisements remind us that body odor, bad breath, or dandruff could make us social pariahs, they are playing on our fears. When politicians tell us that their opponent is soft on crime or in the pocket of special-interest groups, they are using "fear and smear" scaremongering to garner votes. Many public health campaigns also use scare tactics in the hope of reducing dangerous behaviors like smoking during pregnancy, sunbathing, and drinking before driving. Can people really be frightened into accepting a persuasive message?

To answer this question, researchers have compared reactions to messages that invoke different degrees of anxiety. In one of the earliest studies of the effects of fear, the idea that people could be scared into agreement did not fare well (Janis & Feshbach, 1953). In that study, one group of students received graphic personalized warnings of the dangers posed by lack of dental hygiene. For example, tooth decay was said to lead to "secondary infections and diseases such as arthritic paralysis, kidney damage, or total blindness." This message provoked intense fear but little change in attitudes. In fact, it was less effective than the mildly fear-inducing appeal seen by other students. Does this mean that fear was an ineffective persuasion weapon? Once again, the answer to this question lies in thinking about motivation and capacity. In explaining the results of this study, Carl Hovland and his colleagues (1953) focused on the amount of fear that a persuasive message elicits. Foreshadowing what social psychologists now know to be true, they argued that the level of fear influences motivation and ability to process a message, and this in turn influences attitude change.

1. *Fear and motivation.* First, fear appeals must engage the right motives. If a message does not arouse any anxiety, no need for mastery, connectedness, or protecting me and mine is aroused, and the message is ignored as irrelevant. Just the right amount of anxiety can activate all these goals, motivating people to pay attention in the hope that the anxiety-provoking event can be eliminated. For a fear appeal to be effective, the audience must also be convinced that the threatened negative consequences will happen, and will happen to them, thus engaging personal relevance (Leventhal, 1970; R. W. Rogers & Mewborn, 1976). Efforts to promote seat-belt usage illustrate this point. Appeals that show the mangled bodies of unprotected accident victims and send the message that "this could happen to *you*" are much more effective than those without the personal connection (R. W. Rogers, Deckner, & Mewborn, 1978; R. W. Rogers & Mewborn, 1976).

   Provoking too much fear, however, will turn audiences off. If people feel overwhelmed or unable to escape, self-protective motives may mean they ignore the message or belittle, deny, and contradict the threatening information (Janis & Terwilliger, 1962). This kind of reaction is called *defensive avoidance.* To overcome defensive avoidance a message must contain clear information on how to avoid the danger, which encourages mastery. Thus, the most effective fear-inducing messages are those that incorporate reassuring instructions on how to eliminate the anxiety (Hovland, Janis, & Kelley, 1953; Robberson & Rogers, 1988; R. W. Rogers, 1983). One study, for example, looked at responses to fear-inducing messages about preventing tetanus. The messages varied, with some arousing high fear, some moderate fear, and others no fear at all. In addition, some contained specific instructions about where to get an inoculation and others did not (Leventhal, Singer, & Jones, 1965). The high-fear messages inspired more positive attitudes toward getting shots than did the low-fear or no-fear messages. But only those people who received messages that both aroused fear and included specific information about how to obtain a shot were more likely than other students to respond by getting a tetanus inoculation.

2. *Fear and capacity.* Anxiety also influences the ability to process persuasive information. As their fear increases in intensity, people find it harder and harder to concentrate on message content and to evaluate it. In fact, high levels of stress impair performance on complex cognitive tasks like systematic processing (Darke, 1988). Christopher Jepson and Shelly Chaiken (1990), for example, found that how carefully a message is processed depends on how much the target fears its contents. Their participants were college students who varied in their level of fear of cancer. The message, which advocated regular cancer check-ups, contained a number of reasoning errors. Very fearful participants showed several signs of superficial processing. They detected fewer errors, recalled less of the message, and responded with fewer elaborations of message content than did readers with little fear. These responses occurred even though there was no sign that fearful participants were *avoiding* the message; they just didn't seem to be able to do a very good job. In contrast, relatively unfearful readers processed the message carefully.

The bottom line? Fear works, but only in the right dosage and in the right combination. Fear has to be motivating without being debilitating. It works only if the threatened outcome is believable, and if the recommended change is both attainable and certain to bring relief. It takes just the right mixture to get people to increase seat-belt use, decrease smoking, and get cancer check-ups.

Other emotional states can also influence our susceptibility to persuasion. When was the last time you heard: "You'd do it if you loved me/were a good father/knew how much I'd sacrificed for you!"? Unfortunately, moderate levels of guilt can activate connectedness and self-protection motives that make us more likely to accept and like products or ideas that provide solutions to that guilt. In one study, for example, working mothers—prime targets of guilt appeals—responded more favorably to advertisements for a microwaveable dinner if the ad evoked moderate guilt about time away from their children than if it did not play the guilt card at all. Such guilt also increased their intention to buy the product (Coulter & Pinto, 1995; Pinto & Priest, 1991). Like anxiety, however, too much guilt can backfire. Ads that play too heavily on guilt tend to induce anger, and anger has its own implications for persuasion. If anger is directed at the source ("How dare they try to make me feel that way?"), the persuasiveness of the appeal is undermined (Coulter & Pinto, 1995). Anger can also reduce the ability to think carefully, undermining the effectiveness of an appeal that demands careful processing. But such reduced ability to process can make angry people more likely to be influenced by heuristic cues like the expertise or credibility of a source (Bodenhausen, Sheppard, & Kramer, 1994). And if anger is aroused by the perception of unfairness, messages that promise redress of such injustice can be particularly seductive (Butler, Koopman, & Zimbardo, 1995).

Thus, both positive and negative emotions can increase or interfere with persuasion, depending on the circumstances. And just as the number of arguments presented can produce persuasion via either superficial or

FIGURE 7.7   Emotions can increase persuasion or interfere with it

■ Both positive and negative emotions can set many different processes in motion. Depending on the particular circumstances and whether the person is processing superficially or systematically, the result may be increased or decreased persuasion.

systematic processing, so too do feelings play multiple roles when it comes to changing attitudes. The ways in which feelings influence attitudes are summarized in Figure 7.7.

Defending Attitudes: Resisting Persuasion

Strong arguments compel us; positive feelings placate us; expert and attractive sources inspire us; fear and guilt move us. When it comes to filling our heads or emptying our pockets, communicators have a number of powerful persuasion tools at their disposal. Yet one of the reasons that social psychologists study attitude change so closely, and one of the reasons that persuasion professionals spend so much money and effort on advertising, is that attitudes don't change willy-nilly. We don't have a complete change of heart and mind with every ad, every appeal, every communication. How do we resist these ever-present inducements to change our attitudes?

Forewarning Means Forearming

Being forewarned of a persuasion attempt can help people resist persuasion. Having previous experience with related arguments is also a successful defense against persuasion.

One factor that builds our resistance to persuasive attempts is knowing that we are the target of one. When people expect others to try to change their attitudes, they marshal arguments to mount a good defense (C. A. Kiesler & Kiesler, 1964; Petty & Cacioppo, 1977, 1979). For example, Hiromi Fukada (1986) exposed two groups of participants to a persuasive message. One group had been warned that a persuasive attempt would take place; the other group did not receive the warning. A comparison of the two groups' reactions to the message showed that those who were warned were able to counter the persuasive claims with arguments of their own and, not surprisingly, were less persuaded than the other group. Other studies also indicate that the more time people have to prepare a defense of their views, the more successfully they resist persuasion (Freedman & Sears, 1965).

INOCULATION: PRACTICE CAN BE THE BEST MEDICINE. Do we have to wait for a warning, or can we protect ourselves in advance against persuasive arguments? William McGuire (1964) has suggested that the most effective way to resist persuasion is to rehearse counterarguments. He drew an analogy to medical inoculations, which stimulate the body's defenses by exposing the person to weak doses of an infection. According to McGuire, immunity to arguments can be obtained in the same way. The strategy seems to work, as was demonstrated when a team of researchers tackled the difficult issue of preventing smoking among young teenagers. Knowing that peer pressure often initiates first-time smoking, these researchers had older students "inoculate" younger ones against typical peer-pressure tactics (McAlister, Perry, Killen, Slinkard, & Maccoby, 1980). In a series of sessions in the seventh grade and again in the eighth grade, the younger students learned to resist pressures to smoke with such counterarguments as: "I'd be a real chicken if I smoked just to impress you." When the research team followed the students' progress over the next few years, they found that the inoculated students were much less likely to begin smoking than were a similar group of seventh graders who had received no training in resistance, as can be seen in Figure 7.8. Other research has confirmed that inoculation techniques are quite effective in reducing teenage smoking (Flay and others, 1985; Hirschman & Leventhal, 1989) and in the Drug Abuse Resistance Education (DARE) program administered in schools across the United States (DeJong, 1987). Inoculation aimed at children and early adolescents is particularly effective if it works to refute peer criticisms of actions the children are already taking, so that their current antismoking and anti-drug-use behaviors are positively reinforced (Pfau, 1995).

FIGURE 7.8 Inoculating teenagers against smoking

■ In this study, seventh- and eighth-graders were "inoculated" by older students who gave them practice in resisting prosmoking arguments that peers might use. Compared with students in another school who did not receive this treatment, the inoculated students were much less likely to smoke by the ninth grade. (Data from McAlister and others, 1980; Telch and others, 1982.)

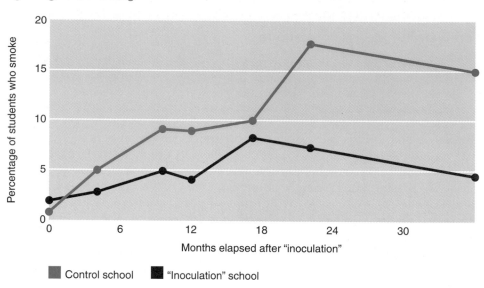

■ Control school   ■ "Inoculation" school

□ **INOCULATION AND ADVERTISING EFFECTIVENESS.** Messages that give us practice in warding off opposing opinions have an added advantage: They strengthen our existing views (Batson, 1975; C. A. Kiesler, 1971). Advertisers are well aware of the effectiveness of this strategy. Refuting the claims of the competition and demonstrating one's own superiority is common advertising practice (Belch, 1981; W. L. Wilke & Farris, 1975). In an ad for laundry bleach, Vivid is compared to Clorox, and the advertiser performs a demonstration meant to show that Vivid gets whites even whiter. "Inoculation" ads are also more effective in overcoming people's objections to various safety-promoting behaviors. For example, although driver's-side airbags that inflate on impact reduce automobile injuries, campaigns to promote them are often stymied by people's fears of potential malfunctions or of unintended injuries caused by the bags' sudden inflation. Ads that allay people's fears about such dangers will be much more successful than ads that merely tout the devices' advantages (Szybillo & Heslin, 1973).

Can inoculation help 4- to 8-year-old couch potatoes resist the advertisements on Saturday morning television? Norma Feshbach (1980) thought so. Feshbach gave small groups of elementary-school children in Los Angeles lessons on how to deal with the claims made in the barrage of Saturday morning commercials. They listened to the claims and then discussed them. They played with the toys and found that they often could not make them do what the ads said they could. When they realized that some of the claims were more fantasy than fact, the children learned to view the advertisements (and perhaps the programs) with a slightly more cynical eye. Similar techniques have been used to inoculate adults against the smear campaigns sometimes used in political contests, since well-crafted inoculation ads have the added benefit of protecting a message source against credibility slippage in the face of later attacks (Burgoon, Pfau, & Birk, 1995; Pfau & Burgoon, 1988; Pfau, Kenski, Nitz, & Sorenson, 1990).

Resisting attitude change in this way depends on being motivated and capable of the considered thought that can fight off a persuasion attempt. When people don't care about a particular attitude issue, they are less likely to resist claims about it—if they even bother to listen to the persuasive appeal in the first place. Attitudes related to important personal goals are much harder to change (Borgida & Howard-Pitney, 1983; Krosnick, 1988a). When attitudes are important, people are motivated to resist the threat to self-image and self-interest that changing them entails (Chaiken, Pomerantz, & Giner-Sorolla, 1995; Pomerantz, Chaiken, & Tordesillas, 1995). They are also motivated to build up an informational base that supports their views and gives them ammunition to fight off challenges to those views (Pfau and others, 1997; M. Ross, McFarland, Conway, & Zanna, 1983; W. Wood and others, 1985). Similarly, people need capacity to counteract a persuasive attempt. Without the ability, time, or opportunity to marshal arguments for the defense, people are more vulnerable to appeals that try to change their minds. Unfortunately, people tend to overestimate both their invulnerability to persuasive appeals and their ability to generate effective arguments to counter them (Wilson, Gilbert, & Wheatley, 1998; Wilson, Houston, & Meyers, 1998). Such cavalier attitudes make the task of the professional persuader much easier!

Subliminal Persuasion

Subliminal persuasion gains some of its power because people do not realize they are the target of a persuasive attempt. But careful consideration of attitude objects can weaken the effects of subliminal information.

Resisting attitude change by thinking a lot about it also depends on awareness. We cannot fight persuasion attempts if we don't know we are being persuaded: As an old Nepalese proverb says, "You cannot fight a tiger you cannot see." What would happen, then, if professional persuaders were able to bombard you with persuasive messages of which you were not even aware? Can we be persuaded without even knowing it?

In the fall of 1957, moviegoers in Fort Lee, New Jersey, became unwitting targets of just such a hidden persuasion campaign. As they sat watching a feature film, the words "Eat popcorn" and "Drink Coca Cola" appeared several times on the screen for just a fraction of a second. Although the words appeared too quickly to be seen by the audience, an 18% increase in drink sales and a 50% increase in popcorn sales was reported (Brean, 1958). Could *subliminal messages,* ones too faint or fast for people to be consciously aware of them, really have such impact?

Plenty of people think so. In a recent poll, 61% of North Americans surveyed thought that subliminal additions to advertisements could persuade them to buy products they do not want (Muller, 1991). In one sample of college students, nearly 80% believed that a subliminal message would be able to influence them in an undesirable way (Wilson and others, 1998). Entrepreneurs have recently sold $50 million worth of subliminal self-help tapes, mostly to middle-class buyers under 45. These tapes typically contain soothing New Age music interspersed with inaudible and fleeting instruc-

By permission of Johnny Hart and Creators Syndicate, Inc.

tions to "Relax, be happy" or reminders like, "You are good, you are capable, you are calm." Inmates at Utah's South Point Prison reportedly listen to subliminal tapes designed to quell criminal impulses. Members of the Texas Rangers' pitching staff use custom-made cassettes to increase their on-the-mound confidence. Security personnel are also apparently convinced of the technique's effectiveness: The canned music piped into department stores in your area may well contain such subaudible messages as "I am honest. I will not steal" (Natale, 1988).

Research evidence for the persuasive power of subliminal messages is more mixed. Considerable doubt has been cast on the apparent increase in popcorn and soda sales at the New Jersey movie theater. Not only could the results not be replicated (T. E. Moore, 1982; Weir, 1984), but later evidence suggested the results were fabricated (Wahl, 1989). But laboratory studies provide clear evidence that people can be influenced by exposure to information of which they are not aware. People exposed to a stimulus multiple times like it more than a novel stimulus, even when exposure is subliminal. People who see objects accompanied by a subliminal "smiley face" like them more than objects accompanied by a subliminal frowning face (Niedenthal, 1990). And people agree more often with others whose photos they have seen subliminally. In one study, for example, researchers arranged for students to participate with two experimental confederates in making what was supposed to be a series of group decisions. The confederates had been instructed to disagree on most of the judgments, leaving the real participant in the uncomfortable position of casting the tie-breaking vote by siding with one of the two confederates. Students in a control condition agreed with each confederate about half the time. But a different pattern emerged among people in the experimental condition. They formed coalitions with one confederate much more often than with the other. The difference was attributable to the subliminal influence of photographs of one confederate that participants in the experimental condition had been exposed to during a slide show prior to the discussion session. Although they were not aware of their exposure to the photos, these participants were more likely to side with this "familiar" face during the discussions, presumably because of the mere exposure effect (Bornstein and others, 1987).

HOW SUBLIMINAL INFLUENCE CAN BE RESISTED. Although research evidence suggests that our attitudes may be vulnerable to subliminal information, those same research findings make clear the limits on such influence. First, in laboratory studies of subliminal effects, researchers have to work hard to ensure that participants focus closely on the region in which subliminal stimuli are presented. In the normal confusion of everyday environments, such narrow focusing is unlikely, and so the messages probably would not receive even minimal processing.

Second, subliminal effects are obtained with a limited range of stimuli. Humans are more likely to encode pictures (especially faces), even when paying little attention to them, than to similarly encode words, for example. So, although pictures of buckets of popcorn and cups of soda might be effective subliminal stimuli, it is no wonder that the words "Eat popcorn" had a much weaker impact. Research on the way we process sounds also suggests limits on subliminal influence. Because people process sounds sequentially, it is highly unlikely that humans are capable of decoding "subliminal" verbal messages recorded backwards or at high speed (Merikle, 1988). Since such stimuli would be impossible to interpret even if they were presented above the threshold of conscious awareness, how could they possibly be effective when presented subliminally?

The research evidence provides little support for people's belief in the power of subliminal self-help tapes. For example, one comparison of different subliminal tapes showed that their effect depended not on their content but on what people expected to hear (Greenwald, Spangenberg, Pratkanis, & Eskenazi, 1991). In this study, participants listened every day for 5 weeks to a tape with a subliminal message ostensibly designed either to improve memory or to boost self-esteem. The researchers introduced an interesting twist, however, when they reversed the labels on half of the tapes. This meant that half the participants listening to a self-esteem tape thought they were listening to a memory tape and half the participants listening to a memory tape thought they were listening to a self-esteem tape. Objective measures were taken at the end of the 5-week period. Although everyone's memory scores had improved slightly, the content of the subliminal tapes made no difference in memory or in self-esteem, as shown in Figure 7.9. But participants' self-ratings did not reflect these findings. Participants thought their memory or self-esteem had improved if they had listened to an appropriately labeled tape, even though, in half the cases, the label was wrong.

Expectations obviously have powerful influences on social behavior, as we have already seen in earlier chapters. But these subliminal tapes had no persuasive power to brainwash listeners without their knowing it.

The third line of evidence that limits the power of subliminal stimuli to determine our attitudes and behavior is perhaps the most important of all. Even if subliminal stimuli have a potential impact on our attitudes, this potential is quickly nipped in the bud when conscious processing takes place (Bargh, 1989; S. Murphy & Zajonc, 1993). What we *know* to be true erases any "vague feeling" we might have. Although we might be influenced by information outside of awareness, the influence is eliminated if we know why and how we might be being influenced (Lombardi, Higgins, & Bargh, 1987). Consider the mere exposure effect, for example. When we are unaware of our exposure, the more we see something, the more we like it. But when we are conscious of the fact that we are seeing the same stimulus over and over again, little or no increase in liking is found (Bornstein, Kale, & Cornell, 1990).

The fact that conscious processing dominates subliminal influences means that what we *want* to do is much more powerful than any "hidden urges" we might experience. Consider what happened when students who were generally high or low in competitiveness were exposed to words related to competitiveness (*mean, hostile,* and *cutthroat,* for example) or to neutral words, without their awareness of it (Neuberg, 1989a). Playing a game later, the competitive students exposed to the competitive words acted more aggressively than did competitive students exposed to the neutral words. But the more important finding was that noncompetitive participants were uninfluenced by mere exposure to the aggressive words. These students' values were not overridden by subliminal influence. On the contrary, their behavior was determined by how they wanted to act, not how they were subtly urged to act.

Such results show that conscious processing typically overrides the impact of subliminal events. That in turn means that it is unlikely that subliminal influence can make us do anything we do not want to do, as long as some thinking is involved. But that thinking is the key: To resist

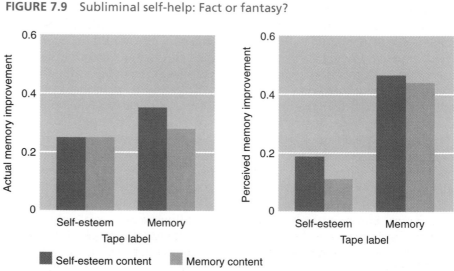

FIGURE 7.9   Subliminal self-help: Fact or fantasy?

■ In this study, participants listened for 5 weeks to self-help tapes that were sold to improve either self-esteem or memory. Labels on half the tapes were switched so that half the people who were actually listening to a memory tape thought they were listening to a self-esteem tape, and vice versa. The results showed that actual memory scores (left-hand graph) and participants' ratings of their memory abilities (right-hand graph) both improved when participants *thought* they were listening to memory improvement tapes, regardless of the content of the tapes. (Data from Greenwald and others, 1991.)

persuasion on important issues, we must put time and effort into our judgments.

CONCLUDING COMMENTS

 Persuasion has a pretty bad reputation. We often associate advertising with attempts to make us buy products we do not want or cannot afford. Political campaigns often seem little more than attempts to package and sell candidates who might not prevail if considered on their merits. Classic literature like George Orwell's *1984* warns us that by controlling information and playing on feelings, totalitarian governments may even persuade their citizens that the history they remember never really happened. Nowhere is concern about persuasion more obvious than in the public's fear that subliminal stimuli might influence us against our will.

Realizing that persuaders do not always have our best interests at heart is healthy: It pays to remember that we can be misled. And it helps if we know what we are up against. The citizens of ancient Greece and Rome were schooled in the art—and artifice—of argumentation. But most of today's citizens, unless they take classes in social psychology or communication, are taught little about the different ways in which attitude change can come about. Perhaps the most important lesson to be learned from the research discussed in this chapter is that influence does not have to be something that others do to us: Whether we are persuaded or not lies largely in our own hands, or at least in our own heads.

When we do not care about or cannot cope with persuasive messages, we may well be influenced by emotional appeals, celebrity endorsements, and the use of complicated statistics. Of course, such simple cues work pretty well for us most of the time. But sometimes circumstances demand careful evaluation of a communication. When we are motivated by concerns about mastery and connectedness, we pay attention, try to make sense of the information presented to us, and think it through carefully. This kind of careful thinking, responding, and reacting can help a persuasion attempt to flourish or can let it wither away. Just as careful thought can flesh out a first impression into a coherent and balanced view of another individual, or take us beyond stereotypes and prejudices to more individualized conceptions of groups and their members, so careful thinking can prove a persuasion cue wrong and show a tear-jerker to be nothing more than a manipulative tug on the heartstrings. Because *our* knowledge, attention, and careful processing determine whether our attitudes will change, it is important to remember that we quite literally persuade ourselves.

Realizing our role in attitude change enables us to view persuasion as an empowering process rather than an overpowering one. In ancient Greece, the Sophists believed that persuasion was needed to lay bare the advantages and disadvantages of any object, and Aristotle argued that persuasion was needed to ensure that everyone came to see what was true and good. Persuasion does not have to involve deception, confusion, and trick-

CHAPTER 7 THEMES

- **Construction of Reality**
  We construct attitudes based on our beliefs, feelings, and behaviors about objects.

- **Pervasiveness of Social Influence**
  In this construction process, we draw heavily on persuasive communications from others.

- **Striving for Mastery**
  Attitudes help us master our environment and obtain rewards.

- **Seeking Connectedness**
  Attitudes also help us express our connectedness with groups or ideas we value.

- **Conservatism**
  An existing attitude shapes our interpretations in ways that confirm the attitude.

- **Superficiality Versus Depth**
  Attitude change may result when we process persuasive messages superficially or when we think about them in more depth.

ery. The same processes that sometimes sell us inferior products and disreputable politicians are also at work when charitable organizations raise money for good causes, when public service messages improve the population's health, and when parents pass their values along to a new generation. And if we react to important appeals in an open but critical way, persuasion can be used to inform rather than confuse and to broaden rather than restrict our appreciation of attitude objects.

SUMMARY

 Attitudes and Their Origins. People form **attitudes** because they are useful in mastering the social environment and in expressing important connections with others. Attitudes are assembled from three types of information: beliefs about the object's positive or negative characteristics, feelings and emotions about the objects, and information about past and current actions toward the object. Once an attitude has been formed, it becomes closely linked to the representation of the object.

Superficial and Systematic Routes to Persuasion: From Snap Judgments to Considered Opinions. When people are targets of **persuasion,** they sometimes do not give persuasive communications much thought. In this case, various superficial aspects of the persuasive appeal can lead to attitude change. For example, people may be influenced by **persuasion heuristics,** leading them to agree with messages from attractive or expert sources or with long messages, or to be influenced by positive or negative objects or events associated with the attitude object or by other feelings they are experiencing. The **mere exposure effect** means that people also tend to form positive attitudes toward familiar objects.

Sometimes people do carefully consider the content of arguments presented in a persuasive communication, in a process termed **elaboration.** When people pay attention to a message, understand its content, and respond to it in a favorable way, persuasion may occur. Attitude change resulting from such careful consideration lasts longer than change produced by superficial processing.

People process messages systematically only when they have both the motivation and the cognitive capacity to do so. The relevance of the message to important goals determines motivation. Cognitive capacity is available when people have adequate ability to process and can do so without distraction.

The Persuasive Power of Emotion: Using Emotion to Persuade. Positive and negative feelings can influence people's motivation and their ability to process persuasive messages systematically. When positive mood decreases motivation and capacity, it lowers the impact of message content on attitudes and increases the impact of heuristic cues.

Using negative emotions like fear to bring about persuasion can be complex. In the right dosage, anxiety can motivate people to process, but an excess of fear can decrease motivation and drain cognitive capacity, undermining systematic processing.

Defending Attitudes: Resisting Persuasion. People often seek to resist persuasion, and one of their best weapons is awareness. Being forewarned of a persuasion attempt can help people resist persuasion. Having previous experience with related arguments is also a successful defense against persuasion. Subliminal persuasion gains some of its power because people do not realize they are the target of a persuasive attempt. But careful consideration of attitude objects can weaken the effects of subliminal information.

8

Attitudes and Behavior

Most of us assume that what we think or feel on the inside influences what we do on the outside—that attitudes influence behavior. We take for granted that our political views affect our vote for a candidate, our food preferences influence our selections at the supermarket, and our personal likes and dislikes dictate our choice of friends. Social psychology provides considerable evidence for this view. As pointed out in previous chapters, our impressions of others have an impact on a variety of behaviors: on whom we hire or fire, acquit or convict, treat as healthy or mentally ill. Similarly, our attitudes toward our own and other groups can determine whether we treat an individual with fairness or subject that person to discrimination.

Attitudes and behaviors are quite often predictably related like this for two very good reasons. The first is that *actions influence attitudes:* Given the right conditions, our actions can change our attitudes. Collecting cans for recycling can help develop caring attitudes toward environmental conservation; donating some loose change to a panhandler can generate positive attitudes toward the homeless. In the first part of this chapter, we will consider two different ways in which behaviors can become building blocks for attitudes. Sometimes people notice what they are doing, make simple inferences about it, and bring their attitudes into line with their actions. At other times, for example, when their behavior has more serious consequences, people work hard to justify or rationalize their actions, and this too can result in attitude change. Thus, because our attitudes are changed by our actions, it's not surprising that actions and attitudes go hand in hand.

The second reason attitudes and behaviors are predictably related is that *attitudes influence actions.* Attitudes dictate how we look at attitude objects, and this in turn determines how we act toward them. You may recall examples of this process from earlier chapters: Seeing their team as the most talented, the fans turn out for every game. Noticing only the immigrant's differences, the bigot refuses to hire him. Focusing on their child's positive qualities, the doting parents indulge his foibles and pamper him. The process by which our attitudes trigger action sometimes happens in an almost knee-jerk fashion, with very little forethought. On other occasions, the process is more deliberate. When this happens, our attitudes produce intentions to act in particular ways, and much time, effort, and thought is exerted to make good on those intentions. The means by which attitudes shape and direct behavior is the topic of the second part of the chapter.

To say that attitudes and behaviors are predictably related does not mean, however, that they will always be in lockstep. We do sometimes act against our personal convictions. We raid the children's Halloween candy when we mean to diet. We watch action movies even though we hate media violence. We buy trucks for our nephews and dolls for our nieces despite our long-standing opposition to gender stereotypes. We act in these contradictory ways for two reasons. First, several important processes have to occur before attitudes can affect behavior. What has to happen, and when will attitudes play a more or less important role in guiding behavior? These questions, which have important implications for attitudes and behaviors in clinical, business, and educational settings, are addressed in the final section of this chapter.

Second, attitudes are only one of several factors that can affect behavior. Sometimes the impact of attitudes is weakened or even overwhelmed by particular circumstances and particular situations. One of the most powerful reasons attitudes are sometimes unrelated to behaviors is that actions are also influenced by social norms. These shared standards of appropriate behavior may differ from personal attitudes, and in such cases, behaviors don't always reflect attitudes. In fact, the impact that norms exert on behavior is so important that we will cover that topic in chapters 9 and 10.

Changing Attitudes With Actions

Have you ever found yourself in a brand new role? Perhaps you were appointed office coordinator for the United Fund pledge drive or elected president of a student organization dedicated to reducing class size. A new position demands new actions and new ways of interacting with people, and these new actions soon spawn new attitudes. When Seymour Lieberman (1956) followed the careers of male factory workers, he found just such a change. Workers promoted to foremen soon showed increased sympathy for management's viewpoint; in contrast, those newly elected to union offices adopted more hard-line union positions. Lieberman's findings show the tremendous impact of career choices: Careers can dictate conduct, which in turn can determine character. Even playing a part can change attitudes. For example, students playing the role of U.S. advisers in international negotiation games often develop hard-line pro-American positions (Trost, Cialdini, & Maas, 1989). If such transitory roles can exert this influence, it's no wonder that "taking on" the personalities of the roles they play is an occupational hazard for some actors and actresses (Magnusson, 1981). Actor Leonard Nimoy, portrayer of the coolly logical Vulcan on the series *Star Trek*, was even prompted to write a book proclaiming, *I Am Not Spock*. Apparently novelist George Eliot was correct: "Our deeds determine us as much as we determine our deeds."

The effects of behavior on attitudes are not limited to the job arena. Almost any kind of action can influence attitudes (R. K. White, 1971). People end up liking those they help (Blanchard & Cook, 1976) and disliking those they hurt (Davis & Jones, 1960; Glass, 1964). Even saying something that another person wants to hear can be enough to change an attitude. In one study demonstrating this point, participants were asked to describe a man to someone who supposedly either liked or disliked him (Higgins & Rholes, 1978). When participants believed the listener liked the man, they said more good things about him than when they thought the listener did not like him. These statements also colored the participants' own attitudes. Those who had given glowing descriptions ended up liking the man better than those who had described him less favorably. (Now that you know this, you might be tempted to improve your professor's opinion of you by asking her to write you a strong letter of recommendation!)

As these studies illustrate, behavior can be an important part of the information on which we base our attitudes. Just as novel beliefs and feelings can change our opinions about an attitude object (chapter 7), so too can new actions contribute to new attitudes. How does information about our actions exert an influence on our attitudes? By now you probably will not be surprised to learn that it is a matter of processing. People deal with information either superficially or systematically, depending on their ability to process and the relevance of the information to important goals and motives. We process information about our own behavior the same ways. Sometimes people take what they do at face value and make simple action-to-attitude inferences. Under other circumstances, especially if the behavior has serious consequences, people move to a deeper consideration of the implications of their actions.

■ **Action across attitude gaps.** This boy is trying to teach this woman about the Internet as part of a junior-senior computer class. The goal of the class isn't simply to help senior citizens grasp computers, but also to change attitudes of both participants, reducing one dimension of the "generation gap."

From Action to Attitude via Superficial Processing

Behavior is an important part of the information on which people base attitudes. If behaviors change, attitudes can also change. When people process superficially, attitudes can be based on associations with actions or on inferences from actions. Like other forms of superficial processing, actions only affect attitudes in this way when people lack the motivation or ability to process more thoroughly.

At the most superficial level of processing, even simple muscle movements can influence attitudes because the actions are associated with agreement or pleasure or approach (or their opposites). When they like something, people tend to smile, nod their heads, and move the object toward them. In contrast, disliked objects elicit frowns, head shaking, and distancing movements (Eibl-Eibesfeldt, 1972; Ekman, 1971; Solarz, 1960). Such movements become associated with liking or disliking, and when they occur in the presence of an attitude object, the liking and disliking can rub off. Consider, for example, a study in which participants were asked to pull up or push down on a bar while thinking about whether they liked or disliked "foreign" (actually nonsense) words like *begrid, plicen,* and *triwen* (Priester, Cacioppo, & Petty, 1996). Pulling up on the bar approximated the muscle movements that typically bring objects closer, whereas pushing down on the bar approximated the muscle extension used in pushing objects away. Those who pulled up on the bar liked the words more than those who pushed down on it. Perhaps the cultural ritual of gripping a hand in greeting works to give newcomers a subtly positive boost.

The impact of such activity in more complex social situations can be seen in an ingenious study by Gary Wells and Richard Petty (1980) that demonstrated how nodding and shaking the head affects attitudes. To see if participants would infer their attitudes from such head movements, the researchers led them to believe they were testing the sound quality of stereo headphones during jogging or bike riding. To simulate jogging, some participants were asked to move their heads up and down; to simulate bicycling, others moved their heads from side to side. These actions were carried out as they listened through headphones to an editorial, ostensibly broadcast from the campus radio station, that advocated increases or decreases in college tuition. As you can see in Figure 8.1, the gestures had an impact. Head nodders were relatively supportive of the position advocated in the broadcast, whereas head shakers opposed the position. In addition, head nodders recognized and encoded positive words more quickly and easily, whereas head shakers recognized and encoded negative stimuli more quickly and easily (Foerster & Strack, 1996).

SELF-PERCEPTION THEORY. When people are aware of their actions—when they believe that smiling indicates being amused or that eating indicates liking food, for example—they can make straightforward inferences from action to attitude. Darryl Bem's *theory of self-perception* (1972) explains the impact of actions on attitudes by suggesting that people infer their attitudes by observing their own behaviors and the situations in which those actions occur. You may have experienced self-perception processes yourself. Have

Chapter 4 (pages 104 to 106) described this process at work as people infer their own personal characteristics, like traits and dispositions, from their actions.

FIGURE 8.1 Head movements and opinions: Inferring attitudes from actions

■ In this study, participants nodded their heads up and down or shook them from side to side while listening to a speech calling for raised or lowered tuition. As you can see, their gestures influenced their attitudes. The nodders (darker bars) were more supportive of the position taken in the message than the shakers (lighter bars). (Data from Wells & Petty, 1980.)

you ever contemplated your growing collection of Bob Marley cassettes and suddenly realized you had developed a taste for reggae? Or, noting that you are spending more and more time at the gym, have you decided that you are committed to the benefits of regular exercise?

Researchers have mimicked such situations experimentally by asking participants to focus on particular aspects of their previous behavior and then measuring their attitudes. In one study, for example, Gerald Salancik and Mary Conway (1975) used questions about the frequency of religious observance to draw participants' attention to their own performance or lack of performance of religious behaviors. One group of students was asked questions that prompted them to reflect on the many religiously oriented behaviors they had performed, such as attending a house of worship or occasionally reading a religious publication. Another group of students were asked questions that led them to think about the many times they had failed to act in a religious way: failure to attend services regularly, to pray every day, and so forth. The researchers then asked the students about their attitudes toward religion. Those who had reflected on their performance of religious behaviors reported favorable attitudes toward religion, whereas those who had been made aware of their failure to act did not. As predicted by self-perception theory, participants inferred their attitudes from the kinds of behaviors they reviewed.

Advertisers and sales personnel have been quick to take advantage of the connection between behavior and attitude change. They sponsor slogan-writing contests that induce thousands of people to spend hours describing the benefits of particular products. They offer free samples, often counting on people to conclude that they must like the product—why else would they have agreed to use it? They offer their products to game shows, assuming that having contestants compete avidly for their goods will make

The Far Side by Gary Larson

Darren's heart quickened: Once inside the home, and once the demonstration was in full swing, a sale was inevitable.

those products seem valuable. Sales personnel are content with a small purchase from their customer, knowing that one small commitment to a product will often result in larger and larger sales. Thus, the simple process of self-perception has become a popular—and effective—social influence technique.

THE FOOT-IN-THE-DOOR TECHNIQUE: WOULD YOU MIND DOING ME A SMALL FAVOR? A particularly clever ploy that takes advantage of people's tendency to judge their own behavior at face value is called the **foot-in-the-door technique.** As the name implies, this social influence technique reflects the tactics of door-to-door salespeople who literally need to get a foot in the customer's door. It involves getting people to perform a small act consistent with an intended goal—an act that opens the way for further influence. Jonathan Freedman and Scott Fraser (1966) demonstrated the technique's effectiveness when they approached female householders in California and asked them to sign a petition supporting safe driving. Nearly all complied. Then, about 2 weeks later, they contacted the same group of women, and some who had never been approached before, with a big request: Would they agree to let the experimenters place a large, ugly "Drive Safely" sign in their front yards? The rate of agreement among those who had gone along with the first small request was three times that of those who had not received the first request.

How does the foot-in-the-door technique work? Why would the relatively inconsequential act of signing a petition translate into a costly commitment to obscure one's house behind an unattractive billboard? The answer is that performance of the initial behavior triggers self-perception processes, and the presence of an action-consistent attitude is inferred. This new attitude then makes agreement with the second request more likely, but only if all the conditions are right. Research suggests that two conditions are crucial if the foot-in-the-door technique is to influence attitudes.

- *Performing the initial request must be meaningful.* Initial requests cannot be trivial. They have to be large enough to allow people to draw an inference about their support for a particular cause. Sometimes the person using the foot-in-the-door technique may find it necessary to draw the inference for the target. In one study, people who donated to a charity after a first request were explicitly told: "You are the kind of person who supports charitable causes." This group of donors was much more likely to give a second generous donation than were donors whose first gift was received without comment (Kraut, 1973).

If the initial request is significant enough, however, the target person will probably draw the inference unassisted. The more

Foot-in-the-door technique. A technique for increasing compliance with a large request by first asking people to go along with a smaller request.

people agree to do, the greater the chance that they will see their actions as evidence of their support of the cause. So actually signing a petition is more effective than merely expressing interest; completing a form as if one were placing an order works better than agreeing to consider a product. Of course, initial requests cannot be so large that people will refuse them. In this case, self-perception processes can boomerang and work against further change. If people view their refusal as evidence that they oppose the cause, the stage will be set for further refusals of future requests (DeJong, 1979).

- *Performing the initial request must seem purely voluntary.* As we saw in chapter 4, people are quick to see their own behavior as determined by environmental forces. Not surprisingly, this tendency undermines the operation of self-perception processes. If attending religious services or donating to a cause is forced on you by parental insistence or your need for a tax shelter, you are unlikely to make the inference that you indeed have attitudes consistent with your actions (DeJong, 1979). You may recognize some irony here. Although we are used to thinking that we like what we are rewarded for, it is often the case that behaviors undertaken for external rewards fail to translate into internal preferences. Only when the initial choice seems ours alone, rather than being attributable to the reward, are we likely to infer that we must hold an action-consistent attitude.

You may recall another example of inferences being more important than actual rewards from our discussion of intrinsic motivation in chapter 4, page 105.

☐ **SELF-PERCEPTION PROCESSES AND CHARITABLE GIVING.** With its ability to turn small commitments into large convictions, the foot-in-the-door technique is particularly helpful to those trying to solicit charitable donations of time, money, and effort. One study demonstrated how well this strategy can work for a good cause. The researcher called some residents of Bloomington, Indiana, and asked them if, hypothetically, they would volunteer to spend 3 hours collecting for the American Cancer Society (ACS). Three days later, a second experimenter called the same people and actually requested help for ACS. More than 31% of those responding to the earlier request agreed to help. Compared with the 4% of a similar group of townspeople who were willing to help when approached directly, this represented an increase of more than 700% in the volunteer rate (S. J. Sherman, 1980). In a similar study of donors in Israel, 92% of those who signed a petition supporting recreational facilities for the handicapped donated money to the cause when contacted 2 weeks later, compared with a rate of 53% among people who had not made the earlier commitment (Schwarzwald, Bizman, & Raz, 1983). The impact of the foot-in-the-door technique was again demonstrated when people who had made an appointment to give blood were induced to give a verbal restatement of their commitment simply by being asked: "We'll count on seeing you then, OK?" The show-up rate for the group increased from the usual 62% to 81% (Lipsitz, Kallmeyer, Ferguson, & Abas, 1989). When commitments affect self-perception, small public-spirited behaviors produce staunch public-minded volunteers.

FROM ACTIONS TO ATTITUDES SUPERFICIALLY. Although our actions often lead us to quickly and easily infer that we hold attitudes associated with them, in fact we are not constantly at the mercy of the wily persuaders who coax us to change our attitudes by changing our behavior. These simple associations between actions and attitudes have an effect only when people process superficially. Although arm movements influence ratings of unknown objects like nonsense words, they have no effect on evaluative judgments of "real" words about which students have already thought (Priester and others, 1996). When actions have implications for attitudes that are important for mastery or connectedness—motives that make people process systematically—self-perception processes do not operate (Bem, 1963). This difference was demonstrated in a study in which researchers led students to think about some small anti-environmental actions they had performed. Students who were initially neutral on the issue did indeed infer that they opposed conservation. But students with well-established pro-environmental attitudes did not infer a new attitude merely because they were asked to focus on some attitude-inconsistent past behaviors (Chaiken & Baldwin, 1981).

Indeed, simple action-to-attitude inferences are made only if the consequences are not particularly serious. To demonstrate this point, one researcher compared women's "gut reactions" to pictures of men under two circumstances: One group of women expected to meet one of the men, whereas the other group did not (S. E. Taylor, 1975). As she viewed each photo, each woman received fake feedback allegedly revealing her physiological reaction to each man. The feedback falsely indicated that the woman's heart beat faster when she viewed some photos but not others. When asked to evaluate the men, the women who did not anticipate meeting them used their supposed reactions to infer their attitudes: They reported liking the men who seemingly "made their hearts beat faster." But the women for whom the ratings had real consequences—those who thought they would meet the man they rated most favorably—were unwilling to base their evaluations on their physiological responses alone.

As these studies show, actions lead us to adopt associated attitudes only when people are thinking rather superficially about their attitudes. When behavior has serious implications, of course, people tend to think much more systematically. Just as high motivation increases systematic processing of persuasive communications, high stakes also cause us to think much more carefully about the implications of our behavior. This does not mean that behavior that is inconsistent with important attitudes never influences those attitudes, however. As you are about to see, even when people are processing quite extensively, the knowledge that they acted inconsistently can nevertheless result in changed attitudes.

Cognitive Dissonance: Changing Attitudes to Justify Behavior

When freely chosen actions violate important or self-relevant attitudes, the inconsistency produces an uncomfortable state of tension and arousal, which can motivate people to change their attitudes to make them consistent with their behavior. Because this kind of attitude change involves extensive processing, it is often long-lasting.

People's actions sometimes contradict attitudes that are important to them and that have long-term consequences for them. Consider the following example. During the Korean War, many U.S. soldiers were interned in Chinese communist prisoner-of-war camps. These men went to their captivity fiercely opposed to the communist way of life. Nevertheless, some of them were induced to author lists of "problems with America," espouse some of the benefits of communism, and perform other small but significant acts of support for communism.

When contradictions between important attitudes and behaviors arise, people do not unthinkingly accept their actions as indications of their underlying attitudes. Instead, they reflect deeply on their behavior. Does this careful thinking prevent their actions from having any impact on their attitudes? On the contrary. There is often dramatic evidence of attitude change. For example, many soldiers returning from Chinese prisoner-of-war camps had changed their opinion of communism enough to believe that, while it might not work in North America, communism "is a good thing for Asia" (Schein, 1956; H. A. Segal, 1954). Let's see why.

THE THEORY OF COGNITIVE DISSONANCE. In 1957, Leon Festinger, a brilliant young social psychologist, argued that when people become aware that their attitudes, thoughts, and beliefs ("cognitions") are inconsistent with one another, this realization brings with it an uncomfortable state of tension called **cognitive dissonance.** Cognitive dissonance often follows when behavior conflicts with a prior attitude: when, for example, people love their country but cooperate with its enemies. Festinger did more than just suggest that inconsistencies cause discomfort. He also offered a bold new proposal: that people's motivation to reduce the unpleasant side effects of inconsistency often produces attitude change. According to cognitive dissonance theory, tensions caused by differences between important actions and attitudes are often reduced by adjustments we make to our thinking, not to our behavior.

In the decades following Festinger's proposal, literally hundreds of experiments have verified the existence and effects of dissonance. Those experiments have also helped clarify the processing steps involved when dissonance turns actions into attitude change (Cooper & Fazio, 1984; Petty & Wegener, 1998). According to the accumulated research, four steps are necessary for actions to produce dissonance and for that dissonance to produce attitude change.

1. *The individual must perceive the action as inconsistent.* In Festinger's view, the very inconsistency of attitude and action was enough to produce dissonance. Some recent evidence suggests that this is true (Harmon-Jones, Brehm, Greenberg, Simon, & Nelson, 1996; R. W. Johnson, Kelly & LeBlanc, 1995). But is inconsistency in and of itself sufficient to cause such discomfort? Perhaps only actions that produce negative consequences, or even the possibility of negative outcomes, create the potential for dissonance arousal (J. Cooper & Brehm, 1971; Goethals et al., 1979; Scher & Cooper, 1989). If the action has no effects, like simply reflecting on reasons why communism may be better than capitalism, dissonance should not be aroused because no harm has been done. But dissonance would be provoked if the list of reasons produced could be used to

> **Cognitive dissonance.** An unpleasant state caused by people's awareness of inconsistency among various beliefs, attitudes, or actions.

persuade other prisoners, for example. Other research suggests that only actions inconsistent with our positive image of ourselves have the power to arouse dissonance (E. Aronson, 1969; Baumeister, 1982; Greenwald & Ronis, 1978; Steele, 1988). Actions that violate our sense of self-integrity (like lying or cheating) should produce discomfort, for example (Steele, 1988). In fact, from this perspective, even behaviors that are consistent with attitudes may provoke dissonance if they are inconsistent with positive self-regard (Stone, Wiegand, Cooper, & Aronson, 1997). For example, if arguing that people should conserve water makes conservationists aware that they themselves sometimes misuse resources, they might experience dissonance.

Of course, all of these situations involve inconsistency with attitudes, self concepts, or standards that are important to the individual. It is this inconsistency, regardless of its exact source, that is the first step on the road to dissonance arousal.

2. *The individual must take personal responsibility for the action.* Dissonance is aroused only when an internal attribution is made, that is, when we perceive ourselves as having freely engaged in the attitude-discrepant behavior. When we are coerced by severe threat or driven by large rewards, we can attribute the action to an external cause, which will forestall dissonance arousal. If, for example, the Chinese had used torture to force cooperation, the prisoners' collaborative behavior would not have aroused dissonance. But instead of using coercion, the captors offered very small prizes for participation in "essay-writing contests," which the prisoners were free to refuse to enter. Laboratory research has confirmed the effectiveness of these tactics. Students *asked* to write an essay inconsistent with their personal beliefs about free speech experienced considerable dissonance, whereas those required to write the essay or promised large rewards for doing so showed no signs of dissonance arousal (Linder, Cooper, & Jones, 1967). Taking personal responsibility is so central to producing dissonance that those individuals who routinely attribute their behavior to external causes don't experience dissonance like those who see actions as internally driven (Stalder & Baron, 1998).

3. *The individual must experience physiological arousal.* Just as Festinger suggested, dissonance seems to be experienced as an uncomfortable state of physiological arousal. Robert Croyle and Joel Cooper (1983) measured this arousal by attaching electrodes to participants' fingers while they participated in an essay-writing study. One group of participants was asked to write essays that were consistent with their personal opinions (proattitudinal) and another group wrote essays that were not consistent with their attitudes (counterattitudinal). The experimenter told these participants that it was their choice, but that it would greatly facilitate the research if they would agree to write the requested essays. Virtually all of them complied with the request. Two other groups of participants were simply told to write proattitudinal or counterattitudinal essays. The researchers expected dissonance to be aroused only when people freely chose to engage in attitude-discrepant behavior, that is, when they were asked to write a counterattitudinal essay but given the choice not to. The results confirmed their hypotheses. Only partici-

pants who saw themselves as freely choosing to write counterattitudinal essays showed increases in physiological arousal. Other research using psychophysiological techniques has confirmed that dissonance is experienced as a feeling of unpleasant arousal (Elkin & Leippe, 1986; Losch & Cacioppo, 1990). If any of the wartime prisoners realized they had written anti-American essays of their own free will, they undoubtedly felt quite upset.

4. *The individual must attribute the arousal to the action.* Cognitive dissonance does not occur simply because people feel aroused. They must attribute that arousal to the inconsistency between their attitudes and their actions (J. Cooper & Fazio, 1984). This point has been demonstrated by studies in which people were tricked into believing that the discomfort they felt was due to something else: fluorescent lights that malfunctioned, a pill they ingested, electric shocks they were anticipating, or prism goggles they were required to wear (J. Cooper, Zanna, & Taves, 1978; Fazio et al., 1977; Losch & Cacioppo, 1990; Pittman, 1975). In such cases, the discomfort has no implications for the inconsistencies between attitudes and actions. But when people correctly attribute their discomfort to the inconsistency between attitude and action, their attention is focused on that inconsistency.

Just as people are motivated to eliminate uncomfortable physiological states like hunger and thirst, they want to reduce the discomfort of dissonance. When attitudes and behaviors are uncomfortably inconsistent, something has to change. Because freely chosen behavior and its negative consequences are hard to take back or deny, we can restore consistency most easily by changing our attitude. Unable to take back or deny the evidence of their small acts of collaboration, some American prisoners of war came to see things more and more from their Chinese captors' point of view. In fact, when the war was over, 21 prisoners who were given permission to return to the United States chose to remain in China. It is only when attitudes are brought into line with actions that dissonance is finally eliminated. This whole process of dissonance arousal and its eventual reduction through attitude change is summarized in Figure 8.2.

In certain circumstances, then, people who behave in an attitude-discrepant way change their attitudes to conform to their actions. This does not occur only in dramatically life-altering situations such as internment in prisoner-of-war camps. Dissonance theory provides a simple explanation for a wide variety of situations in which such changes occur in day-to-day interactions in classrooms and clinics and on sales floors. When people perform behaviors that are inconsistent with important attitudes, the dissonance triggers justification processes that produce attitude change. In the next sections, we explore the attitude change that occurs when people try to justify acting in an attitude-inconsistent way, expending considerable effort, making tough decisions, or failing to practice what they preach.

JUSTIFYING ATTITUDE-DISCREPANT BEHAVIOR: I HAVE MY REASONS! Imagine that you are a participant in a very boring experiment. For what seems like hours you perform meaningless and repetitive tasks. First, the experimenter

FIGURE 8.2   Four steps to dissonance

■ For dissonance to result in physiological arousal and ultimately in attitude change, four steps must occur.

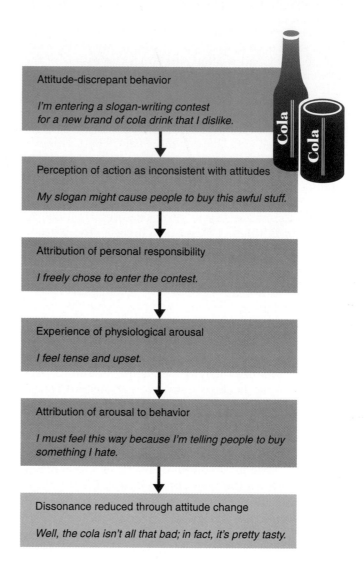

gives you a pegboard containing 48 square pegs and asks you to give them a quarter turn to the left, a quarter turn back to the right, a quarter turn to the left again, back to the right, and so on, again and again. Just as you are sure you will die of boredom, you are instructed to change tasks. But the next task is no better: Now you are instructed to remove pegs from the board, put them back, take them off, put them back on. Finally (mercifully) the experiment is over. But just as you are about to leave, the experimenter requests your help. A graduate student assistant who was supposed to motivate participants in a different condition of the experiment has not arrived on time. Will you fill in, and tell the next participant how much you enjoyed the experiment? The experimenter even offers to pay you $1 for doing so.

FIGURE 8.3 It must have been as interesting as I said: Justifying attitude-discrepant behavior

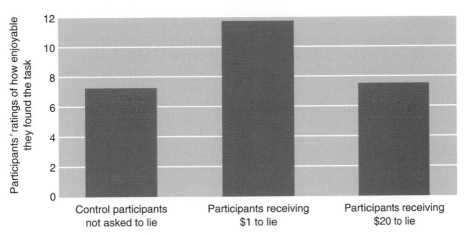

■ All participants in this classic study performed an exceedingly boring task. However, only those who freely chose to lie by saying the task was enjoyable for an insufficient reward (middle bar) reduced dissonance by bringing their attitudes into line with the lie. (Data from Festinger & Carlsmith, 1959.)

If you agree, the classic conditions for dissonance have been set up. An attitude-discrepant behavior (lying about the experiment) with potentially negative consequences (the next person's unrealistic expectations about the study) has been performed with insufficient external justification (the payment of $1). Thus dissonance will be aroused, and you will probably change your attitude about the experiment.

According to dissonance theory, attitude change is the most likely outcome when there is *insufficient justification*, that is, when people perform an attitude-discrepant behavior for a small reward. Behavior is justified and dissonance is eliminated because the attitude about the task ("After all, the experiment did have scientific merit, it was a challenge rather than a bore") changes to match the behavior ("And that's what I told the next participant"). In their classic study of just such a situation, Festinger and J. Merrill Carlsmith (1959) confirmed this prediction. As you can see in Figure 8.3, control participants who were not asked to mislead the next participant rated the experimental task as pretty boring. So did participants paid $20 to lie about the experimental task: They had plenty of external justification for what they said to the next participant. In contrast, those who agreed to mislead others for the insufficient justification of a single dollar reduced dissonance by changing their attitudes.

Just as a small reward is insufficient justification for attitude-discrepant behavior, so a small punishment is *insufficient deterrence* for attitude-discrepant *nonbehavior*. Dissonance theory predicts that when a threatened punishment is mild, people will change their attitudes to convince themselves that they do not want to act in whatever way they are not supposed to, and research bears out this prediction. In one study, 4-year-old children were threatened with severe or mild punishment if they played with an attractive robot toy (E. Aronson & Carlsmith, 1963). When given freedom to play with any toy in the experimenter's absence, all children avoided the forbidden toy. However, when asked to evaluate the toys, only the children faced with mild punishment justified their avoidance by derogating the toy.

Children given the severe warning still liked it. If you can get someone to resist temptation with just a little threat, dissonance processes might fool them into thinking they really were not tempted at all.

JUSTIFYING EFFORT: I SUFFERED FOR IT, SO I LIKE IT. Perhaps you have a friend who seems to get caught up in bad relationships. If so, you may have noticed that as the relationship worsens, your friend makes even more sacrifices, and as the partner grows more hurtful, your friend becomes more committed. Why do people sometimes come to like what they suffer for? Cognitive dissonance provides an explanation: People change their attitudes to justify their suffering. Members of groups who undergo severe initiation rituals value their groups more highly than those accepted without initiation (E. Aronson & Mills, 1959). People prefer difficult experimental tasks they perform for rude instructors over those they perform for personable ones (Rosenfeld, Giacalone, & Tedeschi, 1984).

Suffering is not the only kind of "work" that requires justification. Almost any kind of effort can result in dissonance-reducing attitude change. Danny Axsom and Joel Cooper (1985) demonstrated the practical benefits of this *effort-justification effect* in a clever study involving overweight females. Some of these individuals, all of whom had volunteered in response to a newspaper advertisement, worked on difficult and effortful perceptual and auditory tasks during a 3-week training period on weight reduction; others performed relatively easy and pleasant versions of the same tasks during the weekly sessions. Nothing was done in either of these conditions to explicitly encourage the women to diet, although all were encouraged to keep track of what they ate and were weighed regularly. Six months later, participants were contacted again and reweighed. Results showed that the high-

Dilbert by Scott Adams

Dilbert © United Features Syndicate, reprinted with permission.

effort group had lost an average of 8.55 pounds, compared with only .07 pounds for the low-effort group. This difference was found again when participants reported their weight 1 year later. Perhaps the women justified the difficulty of the tasks they agreed to do by deciding that weight loss was important to them. Other research confirms the idea that the more you put into something, whether in time, money, pain, or effort, the more you value it (Wicklund & Brehm, 1976).

JUSTIFYING DECISIONS: OF COURSE I WAS RIGHT! Every difficult decision we make—to return to work or to stay at home with our children, to major in science or in the humanities, to expand our business into a new district or to consolidate local gains—has advantages and drawbacks. Whenever we make decisions, we give up some things in order to gain others. By definition, then, decisions involve dissonance. When people give up options freely, they experience *decisional dissonance:* tension between the alternative they have chosen and all the attractive features of the alternatives they have given up. According to dissonance theory, people try to reduce such tension by strengthening their positive evaluations of the chosen option and disparaging the unchosen alternative.

To show this process at work, Jack Brehm (1956) asked female students to evaluate several small appliances as part of a supposed study of consumer preferences. After they rated a toaster, a coffee pot, a radio, and other products, the students were allowed to choose one product in payment for their participation. Some participants had a chance to choose between two products they had found almost equally desirable—a dissonance-invoking dilemma. After receiving their chosen product and completing some other tasks, the women were asked to evaluate all the products again. Their ratings offered strong support for dissonance theory: The women now evaluated the product they had chosen much more positively than the item they rejected.

Dissonance processes help people in a variety of decision-making situations convince themselves that what they did was right. Racetrack patrons are much more confident about their chances of winning *after* laying their money down than they are *before* doing so (Knox & Inkster, 1968; Younger, Walker, & Arrowood, 1977). Voters leaving the polling booth are more positive about the candidate they support than are voters entering it (Frenkel & Doob, 1976; D. C. Regan & Kilduff, 1988). And people who start to smoke again after quitting for a while perceive smoking to be less dangerous to their health, compared to their views when they decided to stop and to the views of those who continue to abstain (Gibbons, Eggleston, & Benthin, 1997).

JUSTIFYING ATTITUDE-CONSISTENT BEHAVIOR: I'M NO HYPOCRITE! Imagine being asked to tell a group of high school students the dangers of having unprotected sexual intercourse and to persuade them to use condoms to prevent the spread of AIDS. Now imagine that just having taken such action, you are asked to make a list of the occasions in which you yourself might not have used a condom. Having just advocated their use, being reminded of your own failure to use condoms might produce a high state of dissonance. Preaching what you might not be practicing is one recipe for hypocrisy, and a considerable threat to self-esteem. What's the best way to restore your faith in yourself? Perhaps it is starting to practice what you preached. That's certainly what Aronson and his colleagues (E. Aronson, Fried, & Stone, 1991; Stone and others, 1997) found when they put college students in just such a position. Compared to other students who merely wrote speeches or thought about their own condom use, those in the hypocrisy conditions were much more likely to report increasing their use of condoms and to actually buy condoms when given the opportunity. The dissonance created by provoking such hypocritical behavior has also been used to improve water conservation and increase donations to homeless shelters.

THE PROCESSING PAYOFF: DISSONANCE CREATES PERSISTENT ATTITUDES. The effort to justify inconsistent behavior prompts people to consider many arguments they might otherwise have ignored. In fact, the information marshaled in the justification process is one source of the new behavior-consistent attitude (Greenwald, 1968). In one study, for example, young women who smoked were encouraged to act out the part of a fellow smoker who had been diagnosed with cancer—a role that was highly inconsistent and uncomfortable (Janis & Mann, 1965). Playing the role required them to concentrate on and build a strong set of arguments against smoking. The arguments soon overwhelmed their prior attitudes; when contacted more than 18 months later, they were smoking much less (Mann & Janis, 1968). Chinese prison officials used a similar approach to stabilize the new anti-American attitudes of U.S. prisoners of war. Those who agreed with their Chinese captors' suggestion that the United States was not perfect were asked to indicate some of the reasons this was true and then to discuss those reasons in more depth, expanding on or defending them. At each stage, the men had to work harder to generate information inconsistent with their original attitudes—information that then helped bolster their new views about communism (Schein, 1956).

Given the extensive processing of information required to reduce dissonance, it is no surprise that attitude change brought about by dissonance reduction can be long-lasting. As we saw in chapter 7, the more carefully information is processed, the longer the resulting attitude change will last. Carefully considering the justifications for one's initially inconsistent behavior has the same impact. Arguments are marshaled, new evidence is generated, action is rationalized, and challenges are successfully countered. All of these processes help solidify the new behavior-consistent attitude and inoculate it against further change. Recall that participants in the weight-loss experiment described earlier, who must have spent considerable time and effort justifying their participation in the difficult training tasks, were still showing signs of changed attitudes more than a year later (Axsom & Cooper, 1985). In the same way, the young children who had resisted playing with the attractive toy robot on the basis of minimal deterrance still shunned the toy several weeks later (Freedman, 1965).

Attitude change brought about by dissonance processes can be just as powerful outside the laboratory as in it. In the late 1960s, young men in the United States were randomly assigned lottery numbers in the military draft, and those who received low numbers were the first to be called up. Men

■ **At last   the dissonance diet!**   Does this award-winning plate of "Twice Fried Salami" look appealing? If you answer no, you may have been influenced by campaigns designed to cut cholesterol consumption. Information about the health effects of eating tasty high-fat foods can trigger the unpleasant arousal associated with dissonance. And one way to reduce such dissonance is to alter one's attitude, turning former favorites into something quite different.

who volunteered for military service through the Reserve Officer Training Corps (ROTC) program could ordinarily avoid being sent to Vietnam, where most draftees ended up. Barry Staw (1974) took advantage of this naturally occurring "experiment" by tracking the attitudes of men who joined ROTC before being assigned their lottery numbers. Staw predicted that ROTC enrollees who subsequently received low numbers, which, if they had not enrolled, would have resulted in their being among the first to be drafted and sent to Vietnam, would feel justified in their decision to enroll in ROTC. Men who received high numbers probably would have escaped the draft even if they had not joined ROTC, and so would have had less justification for joining—classic dissonance-producing conditions. Sure enough, the high-number ROTC men apparently engaged in considerable processing aimed at reducing dissonance and restoring cognitive consistency. Over a year later, these men liked ROTC better and performed better in it than those with low draft numbers.

☐ **DISSONANCE PROCESSES AND RESISTING MEDIA INFLUENCE.** The same dissonance-reduction processes have helped children resist the effects of violence-ridden Saturday morning television, as Rowell Huesmann and his colleagues (Huesmann, Eron, Klein, Brice, & Fischer, 1983) demonstrated. The first time they tried to teach children to be critical of television violence, the researchers used lectures and demonstrations. These strategies had no effect on the children: Neither their attitudes nor their behavior changed. But when the researchers put the power of dissonance to work, the outcome was quite different. They persuaded the children to "volunteer" to make a videotape to help "other kids" who had been "fooled by television" or who had "got into trouble for imitating what they saw on TV." In acting out antitelevision messages for no reward, the children had to justify attitudes inconsistent with their own behavior, a process that apparently helped them persuade themselves. Although they continued to watch as much television as the control participants did, they reported a change in attitude: They were less interested in violent television and less impressed by it. Their behavior changed as well. While the control participants became increasingly aggressive, the experimental children did not. For these children, watching no longer meant doing.

ALTERNATIVES TO ATTITUDE CHANGE. You may have noticed that many experimental tests of dissonance theory set up situations in which attitude change is the only avenue by which cognitive consistency can be reestablished. Festinger (1957) was the first to point out, however, that people can reduce dissonance in other ways if they have the opportunity. Imagine that you have just broken a month-long diet by eating an entire bag of chocolate chip cookies. Rather than changing your prodieting attitude, you could dissipate dissonance at any point in the four steps of the arousal and reduction process. One strategy would be to minimize the inconsistency by trivializing the attitude-discrepant behavior ("A few cookies won't make any difference"; L. Simon, Greenberg, & Brehm, 1995) or adding cognitions to make it consonant ("Actually, you have to treat yourself once in a while or you just can't stay on a diet"). As an alternative, you might try minimizing personal responsibility: "The cookies were a gift; not eating them would be rude." Or you could attribute your dissonance-induced arousal to something other than your inconsistent behavior: "This diet is making me feel grouchy," thereby feeling no need to reestablish consistency between word and deed.

Measures taken to reduce the uncomfortable tension of arousal can sometimes be harmful. Claude Steele and his colleagues (Steele, Southwick, & Critchlow, 1981) have demonstrated that people may reduce dissonance by using alcohol. These researchers persuaded students to write an essay favoring a big tuition increase—an action clearly inconsistent with their attitudes. Displaying the usual dissonance-induced attitude change, participants became more supportive of the fee hike, except in one condition. Right after writing the essay, some students participated in a "taste-test" in which they drank beer or vodka. These participants showed none of the usual signs of dissonance and failed to change their attitudes. The researchers believe that drinking alcohol eliminated the unpleasant tension of dissonance, so attitude change never occurred. Their conclusion was that alcohol and drug use may be habitual and health-damaging ways in which some people avoid or reduce the tension cognitive dissonance creates in their lives (Steele, 1988; Steele & Southwick, 1985).

Fortunately, a more constructive avenue of reduction is often available. Because the actions and attitudes that trigger dissonance are usually important or self-relevant, people can reduce the uncomfortable tension associated with such inconsistencies by reaffirming their positive sense of self-worth and integrity (Dietrich & Berkowitz, 1989, as cited in Eagly & Chaiken, 1993; Schlenker, 1982; Steele & Liu, 1983). Perhaps offering people who have just committed an attitude-discrepant act the opportunity to say: "Hey, I really am a good person, you know" could eliminate attitude change.

Researchers have tested this idea by giving people the chance to donate money, offer help, or reaffirm important values and self-identities just after they acted in ways inconsistent with their attitudes (Dietrich & Berkowitz, 1997; Steele & Liu, 1983; Tesser & Cornell, 1991). In one study, for example, researchers recruited as participants college students, some of whom were science majors and some of whom were not (Steele, 1988). All participants were asked to rate 10 popular record albums, and they then were given the choice of keeping either their fifth- or sixth-ranked album—a classic decisional-dissonance situation. Participants were then asked to prepare for a second experiment, in which about half of the them would be required to don white lab coats. Then came a surprise task: Everyone was asked to rate all the albums again. Consistent with dissonance theory, most participants reduced the dissonance created by making their earlier difficult choice by evaluating their chosen record more highly than the one they had not chosen. But different results were found for one particular group of students, the science majors who had been asked to wear lab coats, a symbol of their values and training. Science students given this opportunity to reaffirm their positive self-identity showed no signs of the usual dissonance-induced attitude change. The potential distress aroused by performing actions inconsistent with a positive view of ourselves can often be dissolved by an act that underscores our sense of identity.

With many alternatives available, how do people decide how to reduce dissonance? People tend to use whatever means of reducing dissonance is most accessible. For example, people tend to use the reduction opportunity that presents itself first (J. Aronson, Blanton, & Cooper, 1995; L. Simon and others, 1995). Direct ways of reducing dissonance (such as changing inconsistent cognitions) are preferred over indirect ways (Stone and others, 1997). Self-affirmation is easier for individuals who have many "affirmational resources," such as a large number of alternative positive self-concepts that can be at the ready when one self-image is threatened (Steele, Spencer, & Lynch, 1993). This variety is important because affirming works best in domains unrelated to the dissonance-causing event. In fact, affirmation of the very standards that were violated in the first place can make dissonance worse, not better. For example, lying and then affirming your sense of self

You may recall a similar point from chapter 4, pages 140 to 141: Some people seem to drink alcohol to reduce the awareness of unpleasant discrepancies between their current selves and their ideal or ought selves.

FIGURE 8.4 Alternatives to dissonance and attitude change

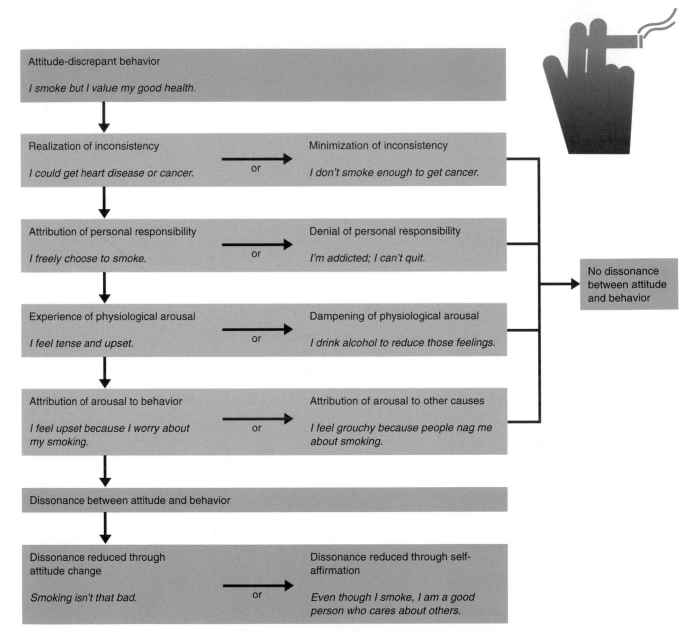

Attitude-discrepant behavior

I smoke but I value my good health.

Realization of inconsistency

I could get heart disease or cancer.   or

Minimization of inconsistency

I don't smoke enough to get cancer.

Attribution of personal responsibility

I freely choose to smoke.   or

Denial of personal responsibility

I'm addicted; I can't quit.

Experience of physiological arousal

I feel tense and upset.   or

Dampening of physiological arousal

I drink alcohol to reduce those feelings.

Attribution of arousal to behavior

I feel upset because I worry about my smoking.   or

Attribution of arousal to other causes

I feel grouchy because people nag me about smoking.

No dissonance between attitude and behavior

Dissonance between attitude and behavior

Dissonance reduced through attitude change

Smoking isn't that bad.   or

Dissonance reduced through self-affirmation

Even though I smoke, I am a good person who cares about others.

■ An attitude-discrepant behavior may lead to dissonance arousal through the four steps described earlier in the chapter. However, at each step alternatives exist that will block the arousal of dissonance. Even if dissonance is aroused, it can be reduced by self-affirmation instead of by attitude change.

as an honest person might make the need for self-justification even more pressing (Blanton, Cooper, Skurnick, & Aronson, 1997). So self-affirmation in an entirely unrelated domain is an easier and more effective route for reducing dissonance.

Figure 8.4 shows the entire sequence of steps by which dissonance arousal leads to attitude change, and the alternative processes that can either block the arousal of dissonance or reduce dissonance through self-affirmation rather than attitude change. As you can see, behavior that is inconsistent with attitudes can lead to many outcomes, not only to attitude change.

DISSONANCE AND CULTURE. Dissonance seems to arise when an important aspect of the self—a valued attitude, a central self-definition, a well-established standard of behavior—is violated. Because the self is viewed differently in different cultures, however, as we saw in chapter 4, you might expect that dissonance would be aroused differently in different cultures. That's just what research recently conducted by Steven Heine and Darrin Lehman (1997) suggests. They asked Canadian and Japanese participants to rank a number of compact discs (CDs) and then offered them either their 5th or 6th ranked disc to take home. Remember that making such a decision provokes dissonance: Choosing one option means freely giving up all the positive qualities of the other option. Such dissonance is typically resolved by reevaluating the chosen alternative more positively. When Canadian participants were asked to rerank the CDs after making their choice, that's just what they did. Japanese participants did not show this effect. Their rerating of the CDs showed no tendency to justify their choice.

Four culturally relevant explanations are possible for this result. First, because the Japanese sense of self tends to be interdependent, the possibility of having made a bad choice (as long as it has implications only for the self) may not be as psychologically threatening to a Japanese as a self-esteem violation is to an American. On the other hand, a violation of the interdependent sense of self might be just as arousing. Second, if behavior is seen as constrained more by circumstance than by personality in Japanese culture, some of the prerequisites for dissonance may be harder to achieve. There is some evidence, for example, that Japanese participants make more external attributions for inconsistent behavior, thus short-circuiting the dissonance process (Sakai & Andow, 1980). Third, the ownership of particular CDs or other consumer goods might be seen as more important to self-image in North America, compared to other, less consumer-oriented cultures (P. L. Murphy & Miller, 1997). Finally, it is possible that such inconsistencies are less likely to produce dissonance because Japanese culture, unlike Western culture, places less emphasis on maintaining positive self-esteem (Kitayama, Markus, & Matsumoto, 1995).

As we have seen, behaviors can have an impact on attitudes whether we engage in superficial processing or extensive processing. Whenever behaviors are inconsistent with previously established attitudes, self-perception processes or dissonance-reduction processes can come into play to change attitudes in the direction of actions. As you read the studies conducted to test the operation of self-perception and dissonance processes, and thought about the kinds of behaviors they were trying to explain, you may have realized that, in many cases, both processes provided viable explanations. In fact, whether self-perception or dissonance was *the* correct explanation for the changes that followed attitude-inconsistent behavior was a source of great controversy among social psychologists. The experiments

You may recall that this study was first discussed in chapter 2, pages 46 to 47, as an example of how theories might complement rather than compete with each other.

that this controversy triggered gradually made it clear that very different processes were involved in their operation. These differences were explicitly tested when Russell Fazio and his colleagues (1977) compared the conditions under which attitudes changed in response to behaviors that were only mildly or severely discrepant with previous attitudes. When freely chosen but inconsistent actions were relatively trivial, i.e., when they did not violate cherished self-images or important attitudes, changed attitudes were inferred with little or no effort: Self-perception processes explained the change that occurred under these conditions. In contrast, freely chosen attitude-discrepant actions that had important implications triggered emotional arousal and extensive thinking as participants worked to justify their attitudes. In these cases, attitudes changed in the service of dissonance reduction. Under different conditions and via different processes, both superficial and systematic thinking provide means by which behaviors (as well as the thoughts and feelings discussed in chapter 7) determine our attitudes. Once attitudes are well established, however, they in turn start to influence what people do.

Guiding Actions With Attitudes

"Attitudes determine for each individual what he [or she] will do" wrote Gordon Allport more than half a century ago (Allport, 1935, p. 806). This basic tenet of social psychology—that attitudes direct behavior—is the driving force behind decades of research on how attitudes can be formed and changed. After all, if attitudes guide actions, then knowing something about people's attitudes permits the prediction of behavior. And if attitudes guide actions, changing attitudes—about ourselves, others, objects, events, and issues—permits behavioral change. The patient with a more positive self-view will treat herself with greater dignity, the convert to a religion will act on the teachings of the faith, and the duly impressed customer will follow through and buy the latest TV, computer, or pick-up truck.

Research has provided a lot of evidence to justify these optimistic statements. Attitudes often do go hand in hand with behaviors. Attitudes toward politicians closely predict voting (Schuman & Johnson, 1976). Attitudes about social drinking dictate how much wine, beer, and spirits people are likely to consume (Kahle & Berman, 1979). Pregnant women's attitudes about breastfeeding versus bottlefeeding accurately foretell how their babies will be fed at 6 weeks of age (Manstead, Plevin, & Smart, 1984; Manstead, Proffitt, & Smart, 1983). Attitudes influence behaviors that range from blood and organ donations to use of contraception or illegal drugs to participation in psychology experiments and cleaning up the environment. In a recent meta-analysis of 88 studies, Stephan Kraus (1995) confirmed that attitudes have a significant and substantial impact on future actions.

Perhaps because we so often assume that attitudes and behavior go hand in hand, we are jolted when they seem glaringly inconsistent. Consider a recent example. Deepak Chopra is an educator, author, and spiritual leader with an international following for his message that personal spiritual energy can be channeled toward harmony and belonging. Yet whenever his teachings are challenged, Chopra's hardball response includes threatening to sue, suing, and countersuing. "I'm not practicing what I preach, and I'm ready to admit it," he says (Reibstein & Gideonse, 1997).

Laboratory studies have also documented similar inconsistencies between attitude and action. One early study, for example, found large discrepancies between college students' attitudes about cheating and their actual behavior (Corey, 1937). Having ascertained their attitudes toward cheating, researchers gave students an opportunity to cheat by asking them to grade their own tests. Actually, the true/false tests had already been graded, so the difference between the real grade and the one students reported could be used as an index of cheating. Under these tempting circumstances, many students did in fact cheat. More important from a theoretical point of view, however, was the absence of a relationship between students' attitudes about cheating and their actual cheating. Those who were strongly opposed to cheating were just as likely to cheat as those who were not so opposed. Other studies have shown similar gaps between attitudes and behavior. And these experimental inconsistencies were just as jolting to social psychologists as personal examples of attitude–action inconsistency are in everyday life. Faced with research results that sometimes told two different stories, some social psychologists suggested that the concept of attitudes should be abandoned altogether (Wicker, 1969).

This was clearly an overreaction. But the challenge did cause social psychologists to think carefully about the role of attitudes in eliciting, modifying, and inhibiting behavior. Rather than asking: "Do attitudes guide behavior?" (to which the answer seemed to be, "Sometimes"), researchers began asking: "How do attitudes guide behavior?" By understanding *how* behavior was influenced by attitudes, they hoped to learn *when* attitudes would influence behavior. This change in tactics led to new findings about the processes by which attitudes are translated into action.

How Attitudes Guide Behavior

Established attitudes can sometimes guide behaviors in a very direct way. Attitudes bias perceptions, thereby making attitude-consistent information about objects, people, and events more obvious and attitude-consistent behavior more likely. Attitudes also influence behavior in a more considered way by prompting intentions to act in certain ways. Intentions in turn can trigger planning that makes attitude-consistent behavior more likely.

Have you ever argued with someone whose mind is made up, perhaps a friend who is sure that her candidate is best, or a parent who is convinced that he knows what's right for you? If you have had this common experience, you know that people with established opinions seem to see the world in only one way. Even more obviously, they are committed to acting on their opinions, as candidate preferences are transformed into dedicated campaigning and firm child-rearing attitudes turn into a refusal to let you borrow the family car. Social psychologists have asked just what it is about attitudes that produces this increase in attitude–behavior consistency. Their answers suggest that attitudes are linked to behaviors in two different ways. Sometimes attitudes seem to trigger consistent behaviors quite directly, with little or no intervening thought. On other occasions, however, attitudes influence behaviors only after extensive and deliberate consideration of intentions.

ATTITUDES GUIDE BEHAVIORS WITHOUT MUCH THOUGHT. Sometimes attitude–behavior connections seem to occur without any effortful thought. Consider, for example, the way participants responded to the opportunity to choose five small snacks (such as a Mounds candy bar, Dentyne gum, a packet of raisins) as payment for participation in an experiment (Fazio, Blascovich, & Driscoll, 1992). Earlier in the session, participants had indicated whether they liked or disliked a large number of products, including the offered snacks. Participants who held well-formed attitudes about the snacks (as indicated by the speed of their responses) were much more likely to make choices consistent with their attitudes than were the participants who were uncertain of their likes and dislikes (as indicated by their slow responses). Well-formed attitudes guided action quite directly: Preferred snacks were chosen and less-favored snacks were left on the table. What is it about the presence of an attitude that can guide behavior in this automatic fashion?

1. *Attitudes focus attention: Tell me where to look.* In the summer of 1973, the U.S. Senate Judiciary Committee held a series of hearings to investigate illegal activities during then-President Richard Nixon's reelection campaign. Media reports of the so-called Watergate investigation were generally unfavorable to Nixon, who subsequently resigned. Researchers who interviewed members of the public before, during, and after the hearings discovered an intriguing pattern of behavior. Although those who had voted for Nixon's opponent eagerly followed the media coverage, Nixon supporters avoided news about the hearings whenever they could (Sweeney & Gruber, 1984). Not surprisingly, both groups maintained their original opinions about the two men. This is a common outcome. Attitudes tend to narrow people's focus of attention, orienting them to information that is most in line with what they already believe and away from evidence that contradicts it (Fazio, 1986; Frey, 1986). In fact, like blinders on a horse, our attitudes seem to guide our attention toward consistent evidence and away from inconsistent information. No wonder that behavior then follows from "the evidence."

2. *Attitudes bias interpretation: Tell me what to see.* Attitudes not only selectively focus attention, they also affect the interpretation of information. They do so by creating a bias in favor of supporting information. First, information that is close to an established attitude is often seen as resembling the attitude exactly, a process called *assimilation*. So if a newspaper article ranked your school or college as the second most prestigious in the state, you might in fact see this as further confirmation of your view that yours is the best college around. On the other hand, information that is quite discrepant with your view—perhaps the article ranked your institution way down on the list—is often seen as even more inconsistent with the attitude than it actually is, a process called *contrast*. As you will see, such discrepant information is usually rejected out of hand as totally invalid.

Attitudes also bias interpretation in a second way. People's well-entrenched views seem to lead them to distort ambiguous evidence so that their original attitudes are supported. For example, Charles Lord and his colleagues (C. G. Lord, Ross, & Lepper, 1979) showed two supposed research studies to Stanford undergraduates who supported or opposed capital punishment. One study provided evidence that capital punishment deters crime, a position consistent with an attitude supporting the death penalty. The second study contradicted the first and confirmed the views of the death penalty opponents. Both studies had several strong points but also some obvious weaknesses. As can be seen in Figure 8.5, both the supporters and the opponents of capital punishment judged whichever study was consistent with their own views to be much more convincing than the other one. And while reading the same body of conflicting information, the two groups not only reached different conclusions but also increased their disagreement with each other. Supporters of the death penalty now believed even more strongly in capital punishment, whereas its opponents were even more firmly opposed, making it much more likely that they would act in line with their original opinion. Rather than moderating a well-established opinion, exposure to mixed or ambiguous information can sometimes intensify the opinion, making it even more extreme (D. Kuhn & Lao, 1996; Munro & Ditto, 1997). Whenever established attitudes come to mind, they affect what we see and how we see it.

Sometimes, then, our attitudes bias our perceptions (Fazio, 1986, 1990). This process increases the likelihood that behavior consistent with the attitude will be elicited in a rather straightforward way. If attitudes bias percep-

We have seen before that well-established views influence our thoughts and behaviors in ways that confirm those views. In chapter 3, pages 91 to 95, for example, we described why first impressions can be so lasting, and in chapter 5, pages 186 to 190, why stereotypes are so persistent.

Calvin and Hobbes by Bill Watterson

Calvin and Hobbes © 1990. Watterson. Dist. by Universal Press Syndicate.

FIGURE 8.5   Established attitudes guide interpretation of attitude-relevant information

■ Undergraduates who supported or opposed the death penalty evaluated two studies whose results supported or undermined the idea that the death penalty has a deterrent effect. Both the supporters and opponents of capital punishment judged the study consistent with their views to be more convincing than the other study. (Data from Lord, Ross, & Lepper, 1979.)

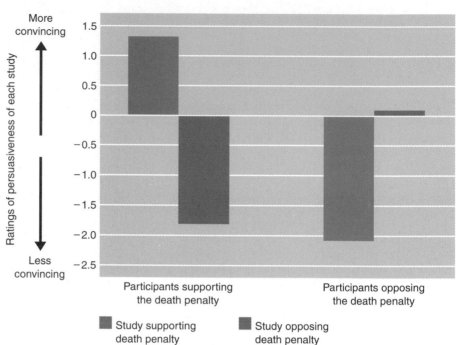

tions of attitude objects, a favorable attitude makes the positive qualities of the object more obvious. If a negative attitude comes to mind, however, the object's unfavorable attributes are most salient. For those who love ice cream, the sight of a large bowl of it brings to mind its delicious flavor and smooth, creamy taste. Those who dislike it are likely to think of its many calories and high fat content. If people then respond to the qualities of the objects that are most salient to them, attitude-consistent behaviors are likely to follow (Eagly & Chaiken, 1993). Focusing on flavor and taste will probably lead to spoon wielding; focusing on calories and fat makes backing firmly away from the table more likely.

In sum, attitudes about objects can directly influence actions. Attitudes direct our attention to particular aspects of an object and influence our interpretations of the object. As a result, attitude-consistent behavior is more likely, and people can act on their attitudes in a relatively straightforward manner. At other times, however, attitudes play a role in a more complex sequence of action-producing events.

ATTITUDES GUIDE BEHAVIOR THROUGH CONSIDERED INTENTIONS. Attitudes can also guide behavior in a much more considered and thoughtful way. When people deliberately attempt to make their behavior consistent with their attitudes, they usually put considerable effort into forming intentions to act in a particular way (Ajzen & Fishbein, 1980). For example, if your old clunker keeps breaking down and you have formed a positive attitude toward buying a new car, you may thoughtfully consider a great deal of information as you form an intention to act.

Once intentions are in place, they are the single most important predictor of actual behavior (Fishbein & Ajzen, 1975). This is the central idea of the *theory of reasoned action,* which argues that attitudes, together with social norms, as we discuss in chapter 10, are an important source of intentions, which in turn produce behavior. Thus, knowing a person's intentions, whether they are to buy a new car within the next year or to finish a term paper by Friday, gives us the best chance of accurately predicting the person's future behavior: purchasing the car or completing the assignment. Indeed, intentions to act have been found to be good predictors of a wide variety of important social behaviors, including donating blood, voting, using family planning techniques, attending church, eating out, practicing dental hygiene, having an abortion, smoking cigarettes, and participating in on-the-job training (Sheppard, Hartwick, & Warshaw, 1988; Van den Putte, Hoogstraten, & Meertens, 1996).

Intentions help translate attitudes into behavior by bringing to mind all we know about performing the intended behavior (L. Sternberg, 1990). Intentions can range from the very general to the very specific, and the level at which we think about our intentions determines the kind of information about potential behaviors that will be activated (Wegner & Vallacher, 1986). For example, a very general intention—"Time to lose some weight!"—brings to mind various options by which this intention can be carried out, such as cutting back on fats and sugars, signing up for a weight-loss program, or taking an aerobics class. But a very specific intention—"I intend to reduce my fat intake to no more than 30% of my daily calories"—is likely to activate corresponding specific behavioral information focused on fat reduction: "Eat more fruits and grains." Forming more specific intentions often helps us carry out desired behaviors because more specific behavioral options come to mind, but broad intentions allow us more flexibility (Vallacher & Wegner, 1987). It is perhaps not surprising, then, that thinking about behaviors that have to be performed in the near future tends to be more specific, whereas thinking about distant actions tends to be more abstract and general (N. Liberman & Trope, 1998).

Once intentions have been formed and relevant behavioral information has been activated, the next step is planning (Gollwitzer & Moskowitz, 1996). Each behavioral option that comes to mind might be weighed and considered until the optimal way of carrying through on the intention is selected. Even quite specific and mundane intentions, like picking up milk at the convenience store on the way home, require the selection and planning of a number of intermediate steps. Imagine how much more complicated it might be to carry through on an intention like reducing fat intake to 30% of daily calories. Successful execution of the intention might entail finding out which foods contain fat, learning to prepare meals without fat, dealing with cravings for fatty foods, and so forth.

With intentions in place, behavioral knowledge activated, and plans selected, we are ready to carry out intended behavior if an opportunity presents itself. Of course, once we start acting, our actions may or may not accomplish our intention. For this reason, people monitor their behavior against their intentions: If the behavior seems to reduce the gap between the present state and the desired state, the behavior continues until the goal is attained. If, on the other hand, the action seems ineffective, it may be increased in intensity, replaced by a new plan, or eventually abandoned altogether (Carver & Scheier, 1990; Gollwitzer, 1996). As part of this monitoring process, people mentally keep track of intentions that they haven't yet made good on. Studies show that people respond more quickly to material related to incomplete intentions than those that have been successfully carried out, indicating that unfulfilled goals and plans are more accessible (Marsh, Hicks, & Bink, 1998).

Emotions are also part of the system that regulates action and monitors goal attainment. Positive emotions can motivate intentions and plans and signal successful completion of subgoals, whereas negative emotions indicate frustration or failure and prompt revision of current attempts to reach the goal (Oatley & Johnson-Laird, 1987; N. L. Stein, Liwag, & Wade, 1996). In one study of 406 Dutch men and women trying to avoid weight gain, Richard Bagozzi, Hans Baumgartner, and Rik Pieters (1998) showed how all these factors worked together to help people turn positive attitudes into attitude-consistent behavior. The positive emotions participants anticipated experiencing on reaching their goals helped promote intentions and plans to exercise and diet, which in turn contributed to successful performance of such behavior. Men who exercised more lost more weight, and women who dieted more lost more weight, indicating the impact of behavior on goal attainment. Reaching their goals made people feel good, and so emotions fed back to keep attitudes, intentions, plans, and behavior on track.

By influencing intentions, then, attitudes can guide attitude-consistent behavior in a more considered and thoughtful way. This does not mean that attitudes, intentions, and plans are deliberately formed anew each time you enter a new situation (Ajzen & Fishbein, 1980). An intention, and a plan to carry it out, may have been formed quite deliberately and systematically at some time in the past and might pop into mind almost automatically whenever a relevant attitude object or particular situation is confronted (Gollwitzer & Schaal, 1998). A patriotic attitude, for example, may at one point have led to the conscious intention of saluting the national flag whenever it passes by in a parade, but that behavior may now, after many repetitions, be performed virtually without thought.

When do attitudes trigger consistent behaviors directly versus deliberately? Circumstances undoubtedly have a big impact on whether attitudes influence behavior in a relatively direct manner or through the more thoughtful process of intention formation and planning, the two routes shown in Figure 8.6. It is probably obvious that thinking about attitudes in relation to intentions, and about intentions in relation to behavior, requires a lot more effort and concentration than responding in a knee-jerk fashion to salient features of an attitude object. In fact, the motivation and opportunity to engage in such thinking dictates the route by which attitudes affect behavior (Fazio, 1990). When careful consideration is not possible because immediate action is necessary, or when your choice will have no serious consequences, behavior may follow quite straightforwardly from how the attitude object is viewed. When the stakes are high and extensive thinking is possible, however, attitudes may influence behavior through their impact on intentions.

FIGURE 8.6   Direct and indirect routes from attitude to behavior

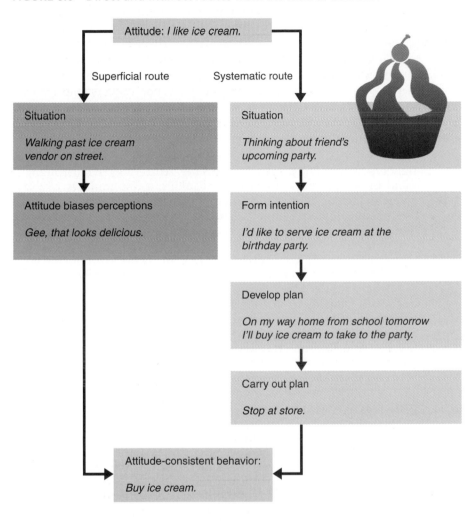

■ Attitudes can influence behavior relatively automatically by influencing people's immediate perceptions. At other times, the effect of attitudes on behavior occurs with more thought when people plan and carry out intentions that result in attitude-consistent behavior.

When Do Attitudes Influence Action?

If attitudes are to guide actions, attitudes must be readily accessible, appropriate to the intended behavior, and useful. Attitudes can be made accessible by deliberate thought, self-awareness, or frequent use. Only attitudes specific to a particular behavior will be able to guide that behavior. Attitudes are more likely to guide behavior when they offer an adequate solution to a problem. Finally, behavior is more likely to reflect attitudes if people both believe they have control and actually do have control over behavior.

Answering the question of *how* attitudes guide actions has helped social psychologists understand *when* attitudes will do so. During the course of research, some conditions crucial for attitudes' impact on actions have become clear. Knowing these conditions may help design interventions that assist people in acting on their constructive and socially useful attitudes. How do attitudes get to be part of the equation?

ATTITUDE ACCESSIBILITY: ATTITUDES MUST COME TO MIND. To have any effect on behavior, attitudes about objects, events, people, or ideas must come to mind at the right time (Fazio, 1990; S. J. Kraus, 1995). Some people's inner convictions seem to be more accessible to them most of the time. Low self-monitors, for example, for whom expressing the true self is important, have more accessible attitudes than high self-monitors (DeBono and Snyder, 1995; Kardes, Sanbonmatsu, Voss, & Fazio, 1986). Not surprisingly, then, low self-monitors are more likely to practice what they preach (Kraus, 1995). But you don't have to be a low self-monitor to show such consistency. There are a number of other ways in which attitudes can be brought to mind at the right time to influence behavior.

1. *Deliberately making attitudes accessible.* Attitudes can be brought to mind by a deliberate effort, so that taking a few minutes to think about an appropriate attitude increases its impact on behavior. Mark Snyder and William Swann (1976) demonstrated this idea in a study of attitudes toward affirmative action employment policies. Undergraduate men served as jurors in mock sex-discrimination trials. Some of the men were given "a few minutes to organize your thoughts and views on the affirmative action issue" before hearing the case, whereas others were not. Only those who were first induced to bring their attitude to mind reached verdicts consistent with their attitudes (which had been measured in a separate session 2 weeks earlier). And, as other researchers have found, even overhearing someone else discussing an issue is enough to make attitudes come to mind, and thus to increase the impact they have on behavior (Borgida & Campbell, 1982).

   Of course, people do not always recognize the relevance of a particular attitude (M. Snyder, 1982). In these cases, being reminded of the relationship of an attitude to the task at hand can increase the attitude's impact on behavior. To demonstrate this point, Mark Snyder and Deborah Kendzierski (1982) set up another mock trial, also of a sex-discrimination case, in which jurors were or were not reminded of their own attitudes before coming to a verdict. One group of mock jurors was encouraged to think about their views on affirmative action before being presented with the case. Another group of participants was not only encouraged to review their attitudes but was specifically informed that the issue of affirmative action, and thus their attitudes toward it, were relevant to the case they were about to hear. A third group received no reminder at all. Compared with the third group, the participants in the two groups that received reminders reached verdicts that were more consistent with their prior attitudes. In addition, the participants explicitly reminded that their attitudes were relevant to the judgment at hand showed even greater consistency between attitude and verdict than did those who were merely encouraged to think about their attitudes.

   The opposite result—decreased consistency between attitude and behavior—may occur when people are led to deliberate about something *other* than the relevant attitude right before making a behavioral choice. Imagine, for example, that you have always loved posters of August Macke's prints because the vivid colors make you feel so cheerful. If allowed to choose a poster to take home as a reward for participation in an experiment, your positive attitude would probably guide you to pick a Macke. But what if right before you made the choice, you were required to analyze your thoughts or beliefs about the poster—to focus on its artistic merit or its fit with the color scheme in your living room, rather than just the affective reactions on which your attitude was based? Thinking about something other than the relevant attitude might disrupt the attitude–behavior link. In one experiment that tested this idea, one group of students was asked to analyze their thoughts about various art posters. Compared with students who were not required to analyze their thoughts, they were more likely to take home a poster they originally had not liked, and they also were more likely to regret their choice later (Millar & Tesser, 1986; Wilson and others, 1993). When the relevant attitude is not uppermost in the actor's mind at the time action is called for, its impact on behavior is reduced.

2. *Making attitudes accessible through self-awareness.* Making people *self-aware* also makes it more likely that important attitudes will come to mind. When people hear their own voices, see themselves unexpectedly in a shop window or store mirror, stand in front of an audience, or become the center of attention in a group, they are reminded of the extent to which they measure up to their inner convictions (Duval & Wicklund, 1972; Gibbons, 1978).

    Does such a reminder promote attitude–behavior consistency? In a further exploration of the conditions under which college students give in to the urge to improve a test score, Ed Diener and Mark Wallbom (1976) looked at the impact of self-awareness on the temptation to cheat. Their participants were given anagrams to solve and told that the timed task was a test of intelligence. Left alone in the exam room (but surreptitiously observed), 71% of the students worked after hearing a bell that indicated the time was up. When other students carried out the same task either in front of a large mirror or while listening to their own tape-recorded voices, only 7% cheated. Next time you notice the mirrored walls and alcoves of a large department store, consider the possibility that their presence provides shoppers with opportunities to become momentarily self-aware, particularly about their attitudes about honesty.

3. *Making attitudes accessible automatically.* The more often attitudes are deliberately brought to mind and reflected upon, the more likely they are to produce consistent behavior (Fazio, Chen, McDonel, & Sherman, 1982). It's not surprising, then, that attitudes built up by interaction, practice, and direct experience with attitude objects are also likely to direct consistent behavior (Fazio & Zanna, 1981). The same is true of attitudes formed on the basis of considerable issue-relevant thinking (Leippe & Elkin, 1987; Petty, Haugtvedt, & Smith, 1995; W. Wood, Rhodes, & Beik, 1995). This is why well-established and frequently used political attitudes are much more likely to predict voting (Kallgren & Wood, 1986) than are less well established and less frequently used attitudes. Similarly, environmental and racial attitudes that are well established are good predictors of ecological behavior and discrimination (Davidson, Yantis, Norwood, & Monano, 1985; Krosnick, 1988b).

Using an attitude a lot makes it more potent because the attitude becomes more accessible (Fazio and others, 1982). It becomes more accessible because use strengthens the link between the attitude and its appropriate attitude object. The more closely and strongly representations of attitudes and attitude objects are linked, the more likely it is that the attitude will come to mind whenever the attitude object is encountered (Fazio, 1989). Many fac-

If you have forgotten what we mean by the link between an attitude object and the attitude associated with it, refer to Figure 7.2 on page 254 for a quick refresher. Recall that because of that link, thinking about almost any object also brings to mind the positive or negative evaluation associated with it.

tors can strengthen attitude-object links. Some such connections might be partially innate to help us take immediate action whenever we perceive a dangerous stimulus (Frijda et al., 1989; Tesser, 1993). Others are built up through constant activation, deliberation, discussion, and action (Fazio, 1989). Regardless of how the links between attitudes and their attitude objects are formed, attitudes that are automatically activated are much more likely to exert a spontaneous influence on behavior than are attitudes that must be deliberately called to mind (Fazio & Zanna, 1981).

☐ **ATTITUDE ACCESSIBILITY IN CLINICAL SETTINGS.** Research on the attitude–behavior link has practical implications for dealing with bad habits like nail biting or overeating. Familiar situations often evoke particular behaviors without our pausing to consider them. Habits are behaviors that are triggered in particular situations so automatically that people "find themselves" in the middle of acting before they realize they have acted (Triandis, 1977, 1980). Smokers, for example, often notice they are smoking but do not recall having decided to smoke or lighting the cigarette (Ikard, Green, & Horn, 1969).

People can gain attitudinal control over these impulses, but only with tremendous effort. To do so, attitudes must be deliberately activated over and over again in high-risk situations (McFall, 1977). Every time you bite your finger nails when you feel put on the spot, or grab a candy bar as you pass a vending machine, you have to take a few moments to organize your thoughts and views and bring those important attitudes to mind. Former smokers, drinkers, and drug users face an even tougher battle. The first smoke, hit, or drink taken by smokers, heroin addicts, and alcoholics who "fall off the wagon" usually happens in a high-risk situation, like a bar, in which the habitual behavior previously occurred (Hunt, Matarazzo, Weiss, & Gentry, 1979). Because developing and activating appropriate attitudes can be hard at first, programs attempting to break such old habits often recommend that addicts initially avoid the triggering situation.

Of course, good habits can be learned and strengthened by activating attitudes over and over again. If you want to bring your behavior into line with your new pro-environmental views or eliminate your tendency to form stereotyped judgments, focusing for a few moments on the relevant attitudes before you act will increase the chances that those worthy attitudes will guide your behavior (Devine & Monteith, 1993). With lots of practice, positive attitudes can become so firmly attached to their attitude objects that they come spontaneously to mind, bringing the appropriate behavior with them. Seatbelt use becomes much more likely when people, because of repeatedly performing the behavior in a given situation, automatically reach for the belt as they sit down in the vehicle.

ATTITUDE COMPATIBILITY: THE RIGHT ATTITUDE MUST COME TO MIND. For an attitude to guide behavior, the right attitude must come to mind at the right time. Acting according to attitudes would be a lot easier if life were simple and a single attitude were relevant to each attitude object. Alas, that is rarely the case. Think about the issue of environmental conservation. You may favor conservation as a general principle, but that is not your only environmental attitude. You probably have several related and increasingly specific attitudes toward implementation, e.g., toward downsizing landfills, using recycled aluminum cans versus glass or plastic bottles, or cutting down on automobile emissions. It isn't enough if just any vaguely related attitude comes to mind when we contemplate action—how we feel about glass bottles is irrelevant at the gas pump. Only an attitude appropriate and relevant for a particular behavior can be expected to influence that behavior.

To influence a specific behavior, specific attitudes must come to mind (Eckes & Six, 1994; M. Kim & Hunter, 1993; Kraus, 1995). When researchers tried to predict whether women would use birth-control pills during a 2-year period, they found that the women's specific attitudes about birth-control pills were better predictors than their attitudes toward birth control in general (Davidson & Jaccard, 1979). On the other hand, attitudes about birth control in general are better predictors of whether *any* form of birth control will be used than are attitudes about a specific method (Ajzen & Fishbein, 1977). Specific attitudes guide specific behaviors, whereas behaviors in general are better predicted by general attitudes. Whether you want to improve health habits, change environmental practices, or increase support for worthy causes, it is important to bring an attitude compatible with the desired behavior to mind.

Research by Charles Lord and his colleagues (C. G. Lord, Lepper, & Mackie, 1984; Lord & Lepper, in press; Sia, Lord, Blessum, Ratcliff, & Lepper, 1997) makes a similar point. These researchers asked male undergraduates whether they would be willing to show a hypothetical transferring student, John B., around the Princeton campus. John was identified (ostensibly by a counseling psychologist at his current school) as being gay. Would participants' attitudes about gays influence their willingness to spend time with John? The researchers hypothesized that this would be true only if John matched the students' expectations of typical gay men. To test this idea, participants were asked to read a description of John that either closely matched or largely disconfirmed their stereotype. When John's description matched students' preconceptions, their attitudes (whether positive or negative) toward gays were highly correlated with their willingness to interact with him. Participants acted in line with their attitudes. When John did not appear to match the preconception, their attitudes had no impact. Attitude–behavior consistency can only be expected when the attitude object (what or whom you think about when asked your opinion) and the target of behavior (what or whom you act toward when given the opportunity) are the same (Ajzen, 1996).

ATTITUDE FUNCTIONALITY: ATTITUDES PROVIDE THE EASIEST ROUTE TO A DECISION. Why are we so ready to act on relevant and accessible attitudes? One reason is that much of the time, deciding what to do is not easy. The amount of information about where to go to graduate school, which vacation to take, or whom to befriend is overwhelming. When understanding and evaluating all the behavioral options is difficult, or a decision is needed quickly, we may welcome a decisional shortcut. Under these conditions, attitudes that easily come to mind have an advantage in guiding how we react because they offer a handy evaluative summary of the attitude object. Perhaps this is why attitudes are more likely to influence decisions when evidence is ambiguous and people are under time pressure than when a leisurely choice between clear-cut options is possible (A. Liberman, de la Hoz, & Chaiken, 1988). Internal pressures such as excitement, anxiety, and distress also make it more likely that people will rely on their attitudes when making decisions (Suedfeld & Tetlock, 1977; P. E. Tetlock, 1985).

Finally, reliance on well-established attitudes can make decisions easier. Researchers recently demonstrated this effect by giving participants a series of trials in which they had just 4 seconds to look at a pair of abstract paintings and

Recall a similar finding from chapter 5, pages 184 to 186. People are more likely to rely on stereotypes and make discriminatory judgments when they are overwhelmed with information or under the pressure of a deadline.

■ **A clear choice?**   This wide selection of bottled waters illustrates how attitudes affect decision making. How does a consumer choose among products when there is no clear evidence of one product's superiority? It is likely most bottled water consumers base their decisions on factors that have nothing to do with product quality, such as recognition of a brand name or seeing a more attractive label.

select the picture they preferred (Fazio and others, 1992). Individuals who had previously had a chance to inspect each painting and decide how much they liked it, in other words, those with established attitudes, found the task easy. Another group of participants had also seen the paintings previously but had been asked to identify each painting's primary color rather than to form an attitude. These participants found the 4-second choice difficult and stressful.

WHEN ATTITUDES ARE NOT ENOUGH.   For a useful and relevant attitude to guide behavior, of course, more is required than having it come to mind. People do not act on attitudes if they believe performance of the behavior is beyond their control (Liska, 1984). Perceptions of *personal control*—whether people feel capable of action—thus have a big influence on attitude-consistent intentions and behavior. When people perceive that they can control their behavior, attitudes can become highly effective in mobilizing and sustaining effective action. A sense of control has been shown to facilitate effective weight loss (Sheppard and others, 1988), performance of breast self-examinations (Alagna & Reddy, 1984), and the expectation and achievement of success at stopping smoking (Eiser & Sutton, 1977; Eiser, van der Pligt, Raw, & Sutton, 1985). In contrast, overeaters who believe obesity is due to hormonal factors, smokers who attribute their behavior to addiction, and drivers who believe being in a car wreck is a matter of fate have no reason to follow through on even a relevant attitude and therefore do not do so (Ajzen & Madden, 1986; Bandura, 1982; Eiser & van der Pligt, 1986; Ronis & Kaiser, 1989). Such findings led Icek Ajzen (1991) to propose that perceptions of choice work along with attitudes to produce the intentions that then drive or derail attitude-consistent behavior.

The impact of perceiving control over one's actions will be discussed further in chapter 10, pages 411 to 413.

Of course, even when our attitudes are positive, our intentions are firm, and we perceive ourselves to be in control, unforeseen circumstances or lack of ability can prevent us from following through on behavior. A would-be voter who cannot get transportation to the polls cannot translate his political attitudes into action. Many useful and much-wanted consumer products are so expensive that desire cannot be translated into ownership. And even if we *believe* we have control, we sometimes just do not have enough *actual*

FIGURE 8.7 When do attitudes guide behavior?

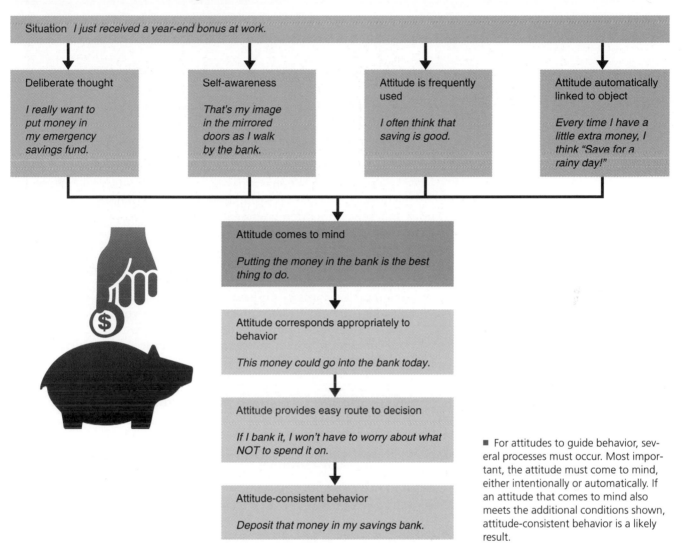

Situation *I just received a year-end bonus at work.*

Deliberate thought

I really want to put money in my emergency savings fund.

Self-awareness

That's my image in the mirrored doors as I walk by the bank.

Attitude is frequently used

I often think that saving is good.

Attitude automatically linked to object

Every time I have a little extra money, I think "Save for a rainy day!"

Attitude comes to mind

Putting the money in the bank is the best thing to do.

Attitude corresponds appropriately to behavior

This money could go into the bank today.

Attitude provides easy route to decision

If I bank it, I won't have to worry about what NOT to spend it on.

Attitude-consistent behavior

Deposit that money in my savings bank.

■ For attitudes to guide behavior, several processes must occur. Most important, the attitude must come to mind, either intentionally or automatically. If an attitude that comes to mind also meets the additional conditions shown, attitude-consistent behavior is a likely result.

control to carry through on our attitudes and intentions. This is particularly true when attitude-consistent behavior requires social interaction, that is, when we need other people to help us act on our attitudes. An uncooperative spouse may sabotage the best-laid plans to discipline the children. An old-fashioned boss may squash attempts to introduce a parental-leave policy in a company. Intentions to conserve energy and lower utility bills may be undermined by family members who leave on lights and open windows in air-conditioned rooms. Although attitudes are personal, we often need interpersonal cooperation to carry through on them.

No wonder, then, that it's a long step from saying to doing. Whether we are deciding what to eat for breakfast or whether to join the armed forces, a behavioral decision, like all judgments large and small, depends on the information that goes into it. Attitudes are an important element in the behavioral equation, but they are seldom the only source of information relevant to action. As Figure 8.7 shows, attitudes are most likely to influence actions when the attitude comes to mind, when the attitude is appropriate, when it provides the easiest route to a decision, and when attitude-consistent behavior is not constrained in any other way. When we understand how attitudes influence behaviors, we come to see some of the complexities involved in getting attitudes to influence behavior in everyday situations.

CONCLUDING COMMENTS

A greater understanding of how our inner selves fit with our outer selves—of how behaviors can shape attitudes and attitudes can shape behaviors—is one of the most significant contributions that social-psychological research offers us. Research on attitudes and behaviors often goes against the accepted wisdom. Consider these counterintuitive findings.

- Most people would *never* guess that behavior has an impact on our attitudes. Yet when we casually give money to the homeless person on the corner, or murmur support for the boss's unworkable plan, we may be helping to change our own opinions. As the research discussed in this chapter has demonstrated, subtle situational and interpersonal pressures can produce marked changes in our attitudes.

- Most of us would *probably* guess that what we are rewarded for, we will come to like. Yet self-perception and dissonance theory teach us that sometimes less is more. It is when external rewards are missing, when we suffer pains to reach our goals, and when we give up alternatives with many positive benefits that we are likely to form the most positive attitudes.

- Most of us would *certainly* guess that, by and large, we act on our attitudes. Much of human activity is marked by a motive for consistency—why else would we experience dissonance when our attitudes and behaviors are inconsistent? We certainly expect other people to follow through on their convictions. After all, we work hard to change customers' minds in order to change their purchases. We try to raise employees' morale in order to boost their productivity; we take pains to eliminate prejudice in order to eliminate discrimination. All of these efforts assume that there is an attitude–action connection, and there is good reason to assume it. Yet this relationship is not one on which we can casually rely. Attitudes are just one of the factors that have to come to mind to influence perceptions, intentions, plans, and, ultimately, behavior.

As researchers continue to specify the conditions under which attitudes do influence behavior, however, their findings also reaffirm their optimism. Knowing *how* attitudes influence behavior means that we can have some control over *when* they do. Such knowledge has important personal and societal consequences. Recall from chapter 5 that in their battle against prejudice and discrimination, some individuals try to inhibit the impact of their initial responses and consciously bring to bear more egalitarian attitudes. Similar processes could be involved when managers evaluate workers' performance and when jury members form impressions on which they acquit or convict

CHAPTER 8 THEMES

- **Construction of Reality**
  Our actions are guided by the attitudes we have constructed toward the world.

- **Pervasiveness of Social Influence**
  Both our attitudes and our behavior are shaped by other people and by our social surroundings.

- **Accessibility**
  Attitudes can guide behavior only when they come to mind.

- **Superficiality Versus Depth**
  The effect of behavior on attitudes, and also the effect of attitudes on behavior, can reflect either superficial processing or more thoughtful systematic processing.

defendants. The research described in this chapter suggests ways both to suppress the influence of some attitudes and to increase the influence of others. When we want attitudes to be potent, they must come to mind readily, be related to the behavioral options at hand, and provide an adequate solution to the behavioral dilemma. Weak connections between attitude and object, competition from other attitudes, and a lack of control over the desired behavior will all reduce the impact of attitudes on behaviors.

Of course, the influence of social norms can also reduce this impact. Social norms often conflict with people's personal inclinations. Yet, information about others' standards of appropriateness is vital for effective social functioning—so vital that these standards often override personal attitudes to determine social behavior. The development of social norms and the impact they have on behavior are the focus of the next two chapters.

S U M M A R Y

Changing Attitudes With Actions. Behavior is an important part of the information on which people base attitudes. If behaviors change, attitudes can also change. When people process superficially, they infer their attitudes by observing their own behaviors and the situations in which the behaviors occur. At such times, people often infer the presence of an attitude that is consistent with their behavior. For example, in the **foot-in-the-door technique,** people who are induced to comply with a small request come to view themselves as having corresponding attitudes. If they are later faced with a larger request from the same source, they are more likely to grant it than are people who never received the initial request.

When freely chosen actions violate important or self-relevant attitudes, the inconsistency produces an uncomfortable state of tension and arousal, termed **cognitive dissonance.** This can motivate people to change their attitudes to make them consistent with their behavior, to value highly what they have worked hard for, and to emphasize the positive aspects of options they have chosen. Because this kind of attitude change involves extensive processing, it is often long-lasting.

Guiding Actions With Attitudes. Established attitudes can sometimes guide behaviors in a very direct way. Attitudes bias perceptions, thereby making attitude-consistent information about objects, people, and events more obvious and attitude-consistent behavior more likely. Attitudes also influence behavior in a more considered way by prompting intentions to act in certain ways. Intentions, in turn, can trigger planning, which makes attitude-consistent behavior more likely.

If attitudes are to guide actions, they must be readily accessible, appropriate to the intended behavior, and useful. Attitudes can be made accessible by deliberate thought, self-awareness, or frequent use. Only attitudes that are specific to a particular behavior and that offer an adequate solution to a problem are likely to guide behavior. Finally, behavior is more likely to reflect attitudes if people both believe they have control and actually do have control over their behavior.

9

Groups, Norms, and Conformity

In August of 1990, scandal rocked the French political scene. The annual conference of the French Socialist party had seemed a success at first, with well-attended talks and an enthusiastic reception for the party platform. Then, on the third day of the conference, some members of the audience mistakenly approached reporters to ask for their payments. In doing so, they revealed a gap between appearances and reality. A cabinet minister had hired students, unemployed actors, and day laborers to pose as an enthusiastic audience at the otherwise sparsely attended affair.

As you can imagine, the minister's deception sparked outrage and he was forced to resign in disgrace (Tempest, 1990). But while he may not have been able to make his plan succeed, the minister's strategy in fact revealed him as a keen observer of social behavior. He had realized that people are profoundly influenced by others' reactions, and that salting an audience with a few noisy supporters can effectively sway the opinions of many other people.

Politics is not the only sphere in which other people's reactions to something affect the way we think and act about it. Such social influence affects every aspect of our lives. Consider, for example, the bursts of "audience" laughter blended into the soundtracks of TV comedies. When jokes and slapstick routines are accompanied by canned laughter, people find them funnier and laugh longer and harder (Fuller & Sheehy-Skeffington, 1974; Smyth & Fuller, 1972). Bartenders, street musicians, church ushers, and collectors for charitable agencies use a similar ploy. They know that putting dollar bills in their tip jars and collection boxes will substantially increase the flow of contributions. Social influence is at work when we revise our way of speaking or change our wardrobes to keep "up to date." Companies can rise or fall because their products become the latest craze or a market failure. Whether or not an individual chooses to donate blood, live with someone rather than marry, or abuse alcohol on a college campus can all depend on the number of others who have also chosen to do so.

■ **Defining reality and defining identity.** Group members—no matter what their age—soon come to share similar thoughts, experience similar emotions, and act in similar ways. The power of group norms rests on two important human motivations: to master our environment by seeing the world accurately and to achieve a sense of belonging and connectedness with others.

When groups interact closely to perform tasks, their feelings and behaviors can change quite markedly, as you will see again in chapter 12.

Face-to-face group. Two or more individuals who interact and influence each other.

The impact of others' thoughts, feelings, and behavior is usually positive and appropriate. In fact, a basic premise of social life is that many heads are better than one. We rely on juries to decide the fate of people accused of crimes. We trust boards of directors to run schools, businesses, and charitable organizations. We use community standards—what's accepted by a majority of people in the community—to define what is obscene. These arrangements reflect our trust that collective wisdom will emerge from the mutual interaction and influence of multiple individuals in a group.

Sometimes, however, our willingness to go along with other people's beliefs, opinions, or actions has a negative consequence. If the artificial enthusiasm of the French minister's "hired hands" had been more influential than the content of the party leaders' speeches, the real Socialists would have been led astray. Failing to ask questions in a lecture because nobody else does, littering highways and forests because others leave their trash behind, and taking part in a riot are all examples of situations in which taking cues from others can be personally or socially destructive.

Questions about how others shape our perceptions, feelings, attitudes, and actions have interested social psychologists for decades. And, not surprisingly, they have found that the groups to which people belong have a pervasive and far-reaching impact. Remember that *social groups* are made up of people who share socially relevant characteristics or features like gender, age, or an interest in the environment. Members of such groups may or may not actually interact with one another. Members of **face-to-face groups,** on the other hand, interact with one another directly. This gives them the power to dramatically affect one another's thoughts, feelings, and behaviors. In this chapter we explore the processes that occur when groups of individuals interact with one another to influence each other and reach agreement. We begin by considering two related questions: Why do groups seek to reach consensus, or agreement, and why do people accept influence from others? You will see that part of the answer to these questions is that people want to *understand and master* their social worlds—to see things the right way, hold correct opinions, and do the right thing. People also want to be *connected* to others, to be liked and valued by those whose opinions they respect. When a group comes to an agreement, it leaves people with feelings of both mastery and connectedness.

We then turn to the question of *how* agreement is reached. For example, how are the differing opinions of 12 individual jury members forged into a verdict that all can accept? How are the jurors' individual views represented in the final group decision? As you will see, the processes of social influence are reciprocal. Individuals contribute their views to the group consensus, and the consensus influences each individual's views. When the group decision-making process is at its most effective, the consensus reached by the group incorporates multiple views and reflects the best available evidence.

Mere agreement does not guarantee a positive outcome, however. Sometimes groups reach agreements that reflect neither careful consideration of information nor openness to divergent opinions. When groups make such decisions and act on them, the consequences can be disastrous. Knee-jerk business decisions can lead to bankruptcy. The wrong choice by a flight crew can cause an airplane crash. An ill-considered jury verdict can free the guilty or convict the innocent. In the final two sections we consider how such negative outcomes occur and how they can be avoided. Groups that foster dissent rather than squelch it often reach agreements that are worthy guides for their members' thoughts, feelings, and behavior.

Conformity to Social Norms

The Formation of Social Norms

> Because people are profoundly influenced by others' ideas and actions, interaction causes group members' thoughts, feelings, and behaviors to become more alike. Whether a judgment task is clear-cut or ambiguous, individual members' views converge to form a social norm. Norms reflect the group's generally accepted way of thinking, feeling, or acting.

When people interact in a group, their thoughts, emotions, and actions tend to converge, becoming more and more alike until they are identical, or nearly so. Consider, for example, Muzafer Sherif's (1936) classic demonstration of a group's power to affect its members' beliefs. Each participant in Sherif's experiment first sat alone in a totally dark room and focused on a single point of light. As the participant watched, the light seemed to jump erratically and then disappear. Seconds later the participant again saw the light appear, move, and disappear. Each time the light appeared, the observer had to estimate how far it moved. In fact, the light did not move at all. Because a dark room provides no points of reference, a stationary point of light appears to career in a jagged circle, an optical illusion called the *autokinetic effect*.

Given the ambiguity of the situation, it is not surprising that the participants' original distance estimates differed, ranging from an inch or so to nearly a foot. These numbers changed dramatically, however, when participants returned to the lab during the following few days to judge the light's movement, this time as members of three-person groups. As they heard one

FIGURE 9.1 How consensus develops

■ These three typical individuals in Muzafer Sherif's experiment entered the group with varied views about the apparent movement of the light, as indicated by their initial judgments. Note how their estimates in the group sessions gradually converged until they were identical. (Data from Sherif, 1936.)

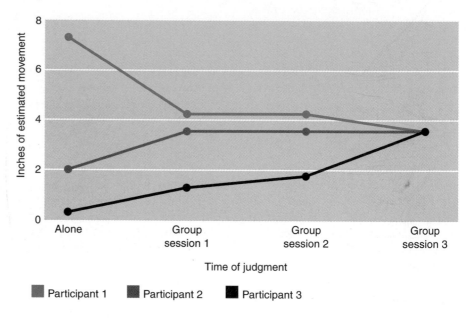

Participant 1   Participant 2   Participant 3

another's estimates of the light's movement, group members' responses began to converge until they were nearly identical (see Figure 9.1). And these shared estimates had lasting power: As much as a year later, these participants continued to use the common response when judging the light, even when alone (Rohrer, Baron, Hoffman, & Schwander, 1954; Stasson & Hawkes, 1995).

In coming to this collective opinion, or consensus, group members established a social norm about the movement of the light. As you may recall from chapter 5, a *social norm* is a generally accepted way of thinking, feeling, or behaving that people in a group agree on and endorse as right and proper (Thibaut & Kelley, 1959a). You may refer to a social norm as "tradition," "public opinion," "the way we do things," "fashion," or "a well-known fact." Social norms are similar to attitudes in that both are cognitive representations of appropriate ways of thinking, feeling, and acting in response to social objects and events. But whereas attitudes represent an *individual's* positive or negative evaluations, norms reflect *group* evaluations of what is true or false, appropriate or inappropriate. Thus, for example, a parent's love for his or her children is an attitude, whereas the idea that parents should love their offspring is a social norm. Social norms formed from group consensus can range from the trivial (such as what a group finds funny) to the profound (a group's standards of morality). And, as Sherif's experiment shows, social norms even influence the way we perceive the world around us.

You may be thinking that Sherif stacked the deck in favor of social influence and against individual independence. After all, the experimental situation was highly ambiguous. Participants could not measure the light's movement, and they received no feedback about right and wrong answers. Under these conditions, what else could the participants do but rely on the responses of others? But these very features—high ambiguity, no physical

FIGURE 9.2 Asch's line judgment task

Standard line

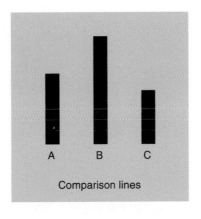

A   B   C

Comparison lines

■ Participants had to decide which comparison line—*A*, *B*, or *C*—was identical to the standard line for 18 different sets of lines. On certain trials, confederates agreed on obviously wrong answers—in this case, *A* or *C*. Participants conformed to this incorrect consensus about a third of the time. (Adapted from Asch, 1955.)

means of testing reality, and no one clearly right answer—characterize many important questions people must answer in their lives outside the laboratory. For example, what is an acceptable risk in building a nuclear power plant or designing an infant's car seat? How accident-proof must a nuclear power plant be, considering the high costs of building and running it? What is an acceptable trade-off between car-seat affordability and performance in an accident? Is short-term corporate profit the proper yardstick for measuring an automobile manufacturer's success, or should long-term effects on the environment and on customer loyalty be considered? In all these cases, the agreement among *social* sources of information defines the appropriate answer.

Do groups still influence people when a decision is not ambiguous, that is, when physical and other nonsocial sources of information are available? Surprisingly, the answer is yes. Solomon Asch (1951, 1955) provided one of the earliest and most convincing demonstrations of this point, although at the time he did not intend to do so. The suggestibility of Sherif's participants disturbed Asch, and he hypothesized that if a judgment task were unambiguous, social influence would be eliminated.

Imagine being in Asch's experiment. Along with eight other people, you are shown two cards marked with lines like those in Figure 9.2. A single straight line, called the standard line, appears on one card, and three comparison lines of different lengths appear on the other. Your task is to state out loud which of the three lines is the same length as the standard line. For each of 18 different sets of comparison lines, group members will answer in order of seating, and you are next to last. The task seems simple: The test lines clearly differ from one another, and for the first few trials everyone agrees on the correct line. But on the next trial, all of the other participants, each responding in turn, agree unanimously on an obviously wrong answer. Now it's your turn to respond. Faced with a conflict between the evidence of your senses and the opinions of your peers, how do you respond?

As you have probably guessed, the other "participants" in Asch's experiments were confederates coached to make incorrect responses on certain trials. On 12 of the 18 experimental trials, the confederates unanimously agreed on a wrong answer, responding together that either a shorter

■ **Huh? Why don't we agree?** It's not hard to identify the real participant in this photograph from one of Solomon Asch's original experiments on conformity. Faced unexpectedly with unanimous disagreement from the rest of the group, participant Number 6 peers anxiously at the line matching task. What powerful social influences might make him accept the group norm over the evidence of his senses?

or a longer line matched the standard line. Despite the ease of the task, the confederates' wrong answers had a considerable impact on the real participants' responses, and they also produced a good deal of anxiety. Three quarters of the participants echoed the confederates' choice on at least 1 trial, and half agreed with an obviously wrong answer on 6 or more trials. Only a hardy 25% stood up for what their eyes were telling them on all 12 of the critical trials. Why did so many yield? When questioned later, some participants who went along with the group told Asch they felt bewildered and were concerned about looking ridiculous. Others said they quite literally "couldn't believe their eyes" and assumed that the group was correct. Even those who remained independent reported discomfort and were still looking for ways to reconcile their judgments with those of the majority when the experiment ended.

The essential results of Sherif's and Asch's studies—that people are influenced by and often adopt the opinions of other group members—have been replicated many times. But Sherif's and Asch's findings on the powerful impact of others' reactions are also demonstrated daily as groups all around us make decisions. Members of the school council debate and decide on school policy. Union representatives hammer out an agreement on a management offer. A group of friends negotiates about where to have dinner. Whether the judgment task is clear-cut or ambiguous, whether the group is large or small, whether prior opinions are held with more or less conviction, group members typically offer, exchange, and accept various points of view until consensus evolves.

Public Versus Private Conformity

Conformity is the convergence of individual responses toward group norms. Conformity occurs for two important reasons: because people believe that the group is right and because they want the group to accept and approve of them. Most of the time people adopt group norms as their own, believing them to be correct and appropriate. Sometimes, however, people publicly conform to norms they do not privately accept.

The convergence of individuals' thoughts, feelings, and behavior toward a group norm is called **conformity** (V. L. Allen, 1965; C. A. Kiesler & Kiesler, 1969). Most of the time, this tendency to let other people's reactions and responses guide our own occurs because we privately accept the group's view, believing it to be both a correct and an appropriate model for our own position. When people are truly persuaded that the group is right, and when they willingly accept group norms as their own beliefs, **private conformity** occurs. When participants in Sherif's study adopted their group's standard opinion regarding the movement of the light, even though there was no pressure to do so, they showed private conformity. So too did these students in Asch's experiment—who truly believed that the group was correct.

Sometimes, however, conformity occurs because we feel we have no choice but to go along with social norms. **Public conformity** occurs when people respond to real or imagined pressure and behave consistently with norms that they do not privately accept as correct. Public conformity is also sometimes called *compliance.* Public conformity produces only a surface change: People pretend to go along with the group norm in what they say or do, but privately they do not think the group is right. People publicly conform because they fear ridicule, rejection, incarceration, or worse. Those of Asch's participants who reluctantly accepted the incorrect majority view to avoid seeming ridiculous were publicly conforming, as are political dissidents who survive by paying lip service to the party line even though they do not agree with it. Although public conformity in the face of heavy-handed group pressure does occur, private acceptance of group norms is far more prevalent and powerful. Because we usually see others as valid and valued sources of knowledge about the world, we often privately conform to social norms without even intending to do so.

☐ **CONFORMITY AND CONFESSIONS IN THE INTERROGATION ROOM.** As the classic studies of conformity show, uncertainty makes us particularly vulnerable to social influence. This fact has not been lost on police interrogators who may be interested in eliciting confessions from recalcitrant criminal suspects. Common interrogation practices include conducting lengthy interviews in bare rooms lacking any other source of social support, while confronting the suspect with a version of reality that he or she may eventually come to accept. On the one hand, a detective might lull a suspect into confessing by pretending to be on his or her side, blaming the victim, citing extenuating circumstances, and downplaying the consequences of the alleged crime. On the other hand, the detective may make distorted or false claims about incriminating evidence and exaggerate the seriousness of the crime and possible punishments. It is also common to bring other people into the interrogation to help convince the suspect to confess or to "confirm" the presence of damning evidence. In other words, the suspect is subjected to the pressure of considerable social influence.

Such tactics are apparently so successful that even the innocent have been led to confess. In one highly publicized case, for example, New York police had to release a suspect who had confessed during an interrogation when the physical evidence later exonerated him (J. Hoffman, 1998).

Confessions from the innocent can be elicited even outside the police interrogation room. In a clever demonstration of the power of social influence,

Conformity. The convergence of individuals' thoughts, feelings, or behavior toward a social norm.

Private conformity. Private acceptance of social norms.

Public conformity. Overt behavior consistent with social norms that are not privately accepted.

Saul Kassin and Katherine Kiechel (1996) had college students type letters on a computer keyboard, ostensibly as part of a study of reflex speed. Some students had to complete the task at a very high rate of speed, whereas others could type the letters at a more leisurely pace. All participants were warned not to hit the ALT key, as doing so could crash the computer.

About a minute into the task, the computer malfunctioned, and the distressed experimenter accused the student of hitting the forbidden key. When the student initially denied the charge, the experimenter continued to press: "Did you hit the ALT key?" He then turned to a confederate and asked, "Did you see anything?" In one condition, the confederate reported seeing nothing, but in another condition, the confederate "admitted" that she had seen the student press the forbidden key. At this stage, the experimenter demanded that the students sign a handwritten confession ("I hit the ALT key and caused the computer to crash. Data were lost"). Sixty-nine percent agreed to do so. Of course, such behavior might have reflected mere public conformity. To see if any students actually began to believe their own confession, the researchers secretly recorded the way in which the students later described the incident to a confederate who was unaware of the purpose of the study. Analysis of the content of these conversations indicated that 28% of the participants came to see themselves as guilty, showing private conformity to the social reality with which they had been presented. Importantly, private conformity was much more likely to occur when the (false) witness agreed with the experimenter that the student was guilty, and especially when the fast pace of the task left students uncertain about what had actually happened. Just as in the classic conformity studies, uncertain participants were particularly likely to accept the responses of others, even if it meant confessing to a "crime" that initially they were all sure they hadn't committed!

CONFORMITY AND CULTURE. Because the results of Sherif's and Asch's studies tell us so much about the relationship between individual and group, attempts have been made to replicate their results in many different cultures and countries. The relatively high levels of conformity found in the original studies were surprising partly because individualistic cultures (like the predominant cultures in the United States and Europe) put such a high value on individual autonomy. In such cultures, both public and private conformity have somewhat negative overtones. Nonetheless, more than 97 replications of Asch's procedure in the United States indicate that even individualistic North Americans are less autonomous and more subject to group influence than they would like to believe.

Conformity is seen quite differently in interdependent or collectivist cultures such as those found in India or Japan. In interdependent cultures, individuals see themselves as an integral part of the group and view conformity as a kind of social glue (Markus & Kitayama, 1991). It is not surprising, then, that when studies like Sherif's and Asch's are replicated in interdependent cultures—with Fijians, Lebanese, Japanese, and Zimbabwean Bantus, for example—the degree of conformity to group norms is usually higher than that found in individualistic cultures (P. B. Smith & Bond, 1993a). In fact, a meta-analysis of 133 studies conducted in 17 different countries provided evidence that the degree to which a culture endorses individualistic or collective values is the biggest influence on the extent of conformity (R. Bond & Smith, 1996). The more collectivist the culture, the more conformity to the responses of others occurs.

The Dual Functions of Conformity to Norms: Mastery and Connectedness

Advertisers, market specialists, and campaign managers have been quick to use the idea that people rely on others' views and often adopt others' behaviors. Slice-of-life scenes—the hidden camera recording family breakfasts with Eggo waffles, the testimonial from the schoolteacher with the Excedrin headache—provide us with models of people "just like us" who are solving problems and improving their lives. Headlines that shout: "Only two left at this price!" or "Get yours now while supplies last!" convey just how desirable such sought-after products must be. In one demonstration of such effects, college students preferred cookies they thought were in short supply because they were popular with others over the same cookies described as being in plentiful supply (Worchel, Lee, & Adewole, 1975). And putting their money where their mouths were, students were willing to pay more for the scarce cookies. Why are we so influenced by what others are thinking, feeling, and, presumably, eating? Why do we conform to others' views at all? And why are the views of others "just like us" particularly important? Why do we seem to care more what some people think and not worry too much about others?

Expecting Consensus

> Private conformity comes about because we expect to see the world the same way most others see it. In fact, we often assume that most other people share our own opinions and preferences. Agreement with others increases our confidence that our views are correct, whereas disagreement undermines that certainty.

The key factor in our conformity to norms is our *expectation of agreement*. We usually expect other people to see the world the same way we do. In fact, people tend to overestimate the extent to which others agree with their views of the world, a phenomenon called the **false consensus effect** (Gilovich, 1990; Mullen and others, 1985). To see the effect in action, ask a number of people to tell you whether they prefer 1960s music to 1990s music and to estimate the percentage of other people who share their preference. Your respondents, no matter which opinion they express, will probably guess that most people agree with them. People generally see their own preferences as reasonable responses to the world, and so they assume that any "reasonable" person will share them. (After all, who wouldn't choose the Beatles over Celine Dion?)

At the same time, we usually expect to see the world the same way others do. When other people share our views, their agreement increases our confidence that we see things the right way. Our expectation of consensus is fulfilled and no action needs to be taken. In contrast, disagreement with others, and especially disagreement with a consensus, can be a startling disconfirmation of our view of the world and our place in it. Disagreement leaves us uncertain, uncomfortable, and, as Sherif and Asch demonstrated, vulnerable to social influence until a new consensus is formed. How does the consensus represented in a norm help us to avoid that uncertainty and discomfort?

False consensus effect. The tendency to overestimate others' agreement with one's own opinions, characteristics, and behaviors.

The Dual Functions of Conformity to Norms

Agreeing with others not only assures people that they are in contact with a common reality but also gives them the feeling of belonging with others. Although particular circumstances can make one goal more important than the other, usually agreement with a group of similar others simultaneously fulfills the motives for both mastery and connectedness.

NORMS PROVIDE REALITY INSURANCE. Norms are important because we need other people to help us construct an appropriate view of reality. Other people's reactions tell us what the world is like. Imagine, for example, that you made both an apple pie and a peach pie for a family get-together. If everyone came back for seconds on the peach pie but there were no repeats on the apple, it would be natural to infer that your peach pie was a success but your apple was not as good as usual. When everyone prefers the peach pie, we make the attribution that the characteristics of the pie itself, rather than any idiosyncrasy of the eaters, determine its positive reception. That is, consensus tells us something about reality. If we believe that group norms are correct, then conforming to them satisfies our need for mastery (Crano, Gorenflo, & Shackleford, 1988; E. E. Jones & Gerard, 1967). In such cases, the group has *informational influence,* meaning that its members conform to it because they believe its norms reflect reality (Deutsch & Gerard, 1955).

Some of the most convincing demonstrations of the importance of a consensus in shaping beliefs about reality come from variations on Asch's experimental procedure. When Asch increased or decreased the number of confederates who agreed on the incorrect line judgment, he found that the amount of influence the group exerted increased as the size of the group increased, but only up to a point. As you can see in Figure 9.3, an incorrect answer given by one person had very little effect. Two confederates giving the same incorrect answer elicited some conformity from the study participants, but a consensus among three confederates led participants to agree with their obviously incorrect answer about 33% of the time. Adding more than three confederates, however, did not lead to further increases in con-

FIGURE 9.3   The importance of consensus

■ Amassing a consensus of three people around an obviously incorrect answer caused considerable conformity among real participants in this variation on Asch's procedure. Once the consensus was established, however, adding to it did not make much difference. A unanimous group of fifteen confederates caused no more conformity than a unanimous group of three. (Data from Asch, 1955.)

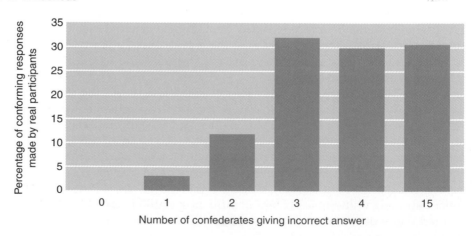

formity. Once an adequate consensus has formed, adding to the size of that consensus apparently has no further effect (Insko, Dreenan, Soloman, Smith, & Wade, 1983).

If consensus exerts such an important influence on an individual's views, breaking the consensus should undermine the group's influence. To test this idea, Asch arranged for one of the confederates to agree with the real participant. He found that the presence of an ally dramatically decreased conformity. This was true even when the dissenter gave a different incorrect answer or dropped out after a few responses (Allen & Bragg, 1965 [as cited in V. L. Allen, 1975]; Allen & Wilder 1972 [as cited in V. L. Allen, 1975]). When there is no longer a consensus about reality, the group loses its power to persuade.

Why were Asch's participants so responsive to the majority's views? For that matter, why are most people so dependent on group norms for reality insurance? First, consensus diminishes the possibility of individual error. One person can easily see things incorrectly, make the wrong decision, or come to a false conclusion, but multiple others are unlikely to do so (Allen, 1965, 1975; Asch, 1951). In fact, when the task in Asch's study was made more difficult (by making the standard and comparison lines more similar), people relied even more heavily on the views of inaccurate confederates, even when given incentives to be as accurate as possible (R. S. Baron, Vandello, & Brunsman, 1996). Thus the consensus of others is seen as the "best bet" when reality is ambiguous. Second, consensus ideally involves replication—different people come to the same conclusion after reviewing the evidence—and that replication is reassuring. As an old Spanish proverb says, "If three people call you an ass, put on a bridle!" If different people take different paths to the same conclusion, it is likely to be valid (Festinger, 1950; H. H. Kelley, 1967). Even in science, our ideal of an objective domain of knowledge, a finding is only considered valid if has been replicated and agreed upon by individuals with scientific training and knowledge.

Because we depend so much on agreement with others, disagreement causes surprise, confusion, and, eventually, uncertainty and self-doubt (Asch, 1956). Disagreement undermines our confidence in our view of reality. Finding themselves in the situation of Asch's participants, most people would be anxious and unsure and would begin to doubt their own perceptions and to consider the group consensus as possibly correct. Thus, there is a potential for informational influence whenever people find themselves at odds with others with whom they expect to agree. Under these conditions, agreeing with the group consensus helps reestablish our confidence that we are indeed in touch with reality.

The role of consensus in the process by which scientists seek validity is discussed in chapter 2, especially pages 44 to 47.

NORMS GIVE US FEELINGS OF CONNECTEDNESS. In many religious communities, children who have reached an appropriate age go through some kind of ceremony, such as the Christian First Communion, the Jewish Bar or Bat Mitzvah, or the Hindu Sacred Thread ceremony. After these rituals, they are considered ready to participate fully in the rites of their community. The new members learn, though formal instruction or by observing others, how to speak, what thoughts and feelings are appropriate, and how to act. Knowing and following these standards allows them to take their place and fulfill their roles in the group. They experience a proud sense of belonging, as full members of their religious community.

■ **All for one and one for all.** The more closely knit the group and the more strongly individuals value their membership, the more powerful the effect of group norms. Here Army recruits learn "the Army way." Developing total devotion to group norms is part of their training so that individual members won't forget their role or desert their group in times of danger.

What people gradually learn in such situations are group norms. By adopting such norms, we demonstrate our commitment and connections to our new associates and our pride in "who we are." A group has *normative influence* when members conform to it to attain a positive and valued social identity (Deutsch & Gerard, 1955). Normative influence thus satisfies our needs for connectedness.

The desire to be a valued member of a group is so strong that people typically adopt group norms whenever they identify with a group. For example, when discussing cases together, mock jurors are much more likely to uphold the norm "innocent until proven guilty" than they are when they judge the same cases alone (MacCoun & Kerr, 1988; Tindale & Davis, 1983). Groups, whether long-standing (like religious groups) or transitory (like juries), reward conformity to their norms. For example, people who endorse group norms most strongly are often admired as more intelligent, competent, confident, and sincere (Eisenger & Mills, 1968; Levinger & Schneider, 1969). So, just as disagreement undermines our confidence that we view reality correctly, being out of step with group norms undermines the secure social identity we derive from belonging to a group. And just as moving toward the group consensus helps reestablish the perceived accuracy of our views, conforming to group norms helps reconfirm our sense of identity.

MASTERY, CONNECTEDNESS, OR BOTH? Groups usually have both an informational and a normative function. That is, they help their members figure out what the world is like and they encourage members to think and act alike. We adopt group norms not only because we think they reflect reality but also because we want to express our identity with groups we value (Kelman, 1961). These dual functions make conformity to norms very useful. In fact, Nobel prize winner Herbert Simon (1990) argues that the tendency to adopt group norms is the product of evolution. Because norms convey knowledge about how to cope effectively with the social and physical world, and because norms connect people together, individuals who adopt group norms are probably at a survival advantage. Although the mastery and connectedness benefits of norms usually go hand-in-hand, the balance may be tipped toward one function or the other under particular circumstances (Kaplan & Wilke, in press).

1. *When the need for mastery prevails.* The need for mastery (that is, to be right and to make accurate judgments) takes precedence over the need for connectedness when a group is faced with an *intellective task*. Intellective tasks, such as visual judgments, mathematical problems, or general knowledge questions, are those that have one verifiably correct solution that requires physical judgments or statements of fact. For example, a town planning committee may be asked to recommend the most cost-efficient brand of bus to buy. After purchase price, reliability, maintenance requirements, and fuel efficiency have all been researched and weighed, one manufacturer's product will probably emerge as the "best buy." When groups are engaged in intellective tasks, with their focus on facts and information, reaching a valid consensus is the top priority. In these circumstances, the reality-testing function of conformity is particularly important (Kaplan & Miller, 1987; Stasser & Stewart, 1992).

2. *When the need for connectedness prevails.* In value-laden judgmental tasks, the identity functions of conformity become more salient (Kaplan & Miller, 1987). Judgmental tasks require decisions about social and personal issues ranging from big questions, like whether government spending for social welfare programs should be cut back, to small ones, like which movie a couple should see. Consider what is involved when the town planning committee must decide whether to buy foreign-made or domestically produced buses. The group task now involves economic patriotism as well as cost effectiveness. Expressing connectedness may be more important than establishing mastery when coming to a decision.

   The connectedness function of consensus may also be more likely to prevail among female group members. Because of their typical roles in our culture, women tend to be more attentive than men to social relationships and interpersonal feelings (Eagly, 1987). Therefore, the connectedness function of norms may be more salient for women than for men. Women may see consensus as a way to facilitate interaction among group members and to create positive feelings of identity. Research does suggest that women are more easily influenced than men are, particularly in face-to-face interactions (R. Bond & Smith, 1996). This finding may reflect women's greater concern with the connectedness functions of group agreement (Becker, 1986; Eagly & Carli, 1981).

As you will see in chapter 12, page 492, female leaders are more likely to involve all group members in group decisions, again reflecting their greater concern with connectedness in groups.

Although the motive for either mastery or connectedness prevails in some situations, agreement with a group of similar others usually fulfills both motives simultaneously. When other people share our views, their agreement fulfills our need for mastery of the world: It increases our confidence that we hold correct opinions, experience appropriate feelings, and do the right thing. And because we depend on others to define and endorse the ideas, values, and expectations that are the basis for the smooth operation of the social system, their agreement also strengthens our feelings of connectedness with those whose opinions we respect. Thus, the reality-seeking and identity-seeking motivations for conformity work together most of the time.

Whose Consensus? The Impact of Reference Groups

People expect to agree with those who share attributes relevant to the judgment at hand. Agreeing with such a group ensures that people are in contact with a common reality and gives them the feeling of being valued. These goals are particularly important in close-knit groups, thus increasing conformity.

Do you expect to agree with everyone about everything? Of course not. Rather, if you need support for a decision or evaluation, you turn to the people you believe are an appropriate source of information for the particular judgment (Moscovici, 1976; J. C. Turner, 1982; J. C. Turner and others, 1987). These people are called a **reference group.** The reference group you turn to depends on the kind of judgment or evaluation you are making. Recall that intellective tasks require physical judgments or statements of fact. Because many people have the knowledge and skills to verify the solutions to intellective tasks, most other people can serve as a reference group for such tasks. If the task involves, for example, visual judgments, as Sherif's and Asch's experimental tasks did, people expect to agree with any other people who have reasonably good eyesight. Because such tasks have a single answer, and because so many people can serve as a reference group for them, the expectation that most other people will agree on intellective tasks is very strong (S. A. Insko and others, 1983; Kaplan & Miller, 1987).

The appropriate qualifications of reference group members for value-laden judgment tasks are somewhat different. The people we accept as an appropriate source of information for these social and personal issues are those who share similar values, attitudes, and relationships. In such cases, people usually expect to agree with peers, family, and others who share their tastes and pastimes (Goethals & Nelson, 1973; Gorenflo & Crano, 1989). Because we are so likely to turn to others like us when making such decisions, sales professionals can use it to their advantage. Many sales programs teach trainees to try to match the customer's speech patterns, nonverbal behavior, and even dress, if possible. Similarity on even these superficial dimensions can give a salesperson the credibility of a valued reference group member (Woodside & Davenport, 1974).

If the judgmental task involves politics, morality, or social justice, our lifelong membership in national, ethnic, religious, age, or political groups can provide a ready-made reference group, whether we are French Canadians, Southern Baptists, Generation Xers, or Democrats. In fact, many of our most cherished and fiercely held convictions are norms rooted in and shared by membership in highly valued groups (Boninger, Krosnick, & Berent, 1995). In contrast, we do not expect to agree with people we dislike or with out-group members (S. J. Sherman, Chassin, Presson, & Agostinelli, 1984). It is not surprising, then, that people are far more af-

To remind yourself of how membership in even a minimal group can affect our thoughts and actions, see chapter 6, especially pages 220 to 223.

Reference group. Those people accepted as an appropriate source of information for a judgment because they share the attributes relevant for making that judgment.

fected by social influence from in-group than from out-group members (Mackie, Worth, & Asuncion, 1990; J. C. Turner, 1982). For example, the finding that members of collectivist cultures show more conformity holds only if the sources of influence are other in-group members (P. B. Smith & Bond, 1993a).

Persuasive appeals from in-group members are also treated differently than those from out-group members. First, if we associate an in-group source with perceptions of validity, we are more likely to accept its views: "If my group thinks this, it must be right!" Such superficial acceptance of in-group messages is particularly likely when the persuasive appeals deal with issues that are not centrally relevant to group membership (Mackie, Gastardo-Conaco, & Skelly, 1992). When information is more relevant and important to group memberships, persuasive appeals from in-group members are processed more systematically than appeals from out-group members. Students in one study read a persuasive appeal on an environmental issue made by either a fellow schoolmate or a student from another university. Some participants received persuasive appeals comprised of strong and compelling arguments, while others heard in-group or out-group messages that were weak and specious (Mackie and others, 1990). The position advocated in the strong in-group messages was accepted, whereas weak in-group messages were rejected, showing that careful thinking about the content of the appeals had occurred. In contrast, messages from out-group members had little impact, regardless of argument quality. The finding that in-group communications receive more systematic processing than out-group messages has been confirmed many times (Budesheim, Houston, & DePaola, 1996; van Knippenberg & Wilke, 1991, 1992; W. Wood, Pool, Leck, & Purvis, 1996).

Any group with the qualifications appropriate to making the relevant judgment can act as a reference group. But the more characteristics group members share, the more closely they interact, and the more each member identifies with the group, the greater the reference group's impact. Groups whose members are tightly knit and identify strongly with the group are said to be highly *cohesive:* Many shared factors act like glue to keep them together (Cartwright & Zander, 1960). The more cohesive the group, the greater the expectation of agreement, and the greater the influence of group norms.

INCREASING THE IMPACT OF REFERENCE GROUPS. Maybe you have noticed how enthusiastically delegates to party conventions support the platform, or how wildly new converts at a revival meeting embrace the group's creed. The reason for their special conviction is that both kinds of motivations—mastering reality and expressing connectedness with others—are activated when circumstances make people especially conscious of their group

"*How would you like me to answer that question? As a member of my ethnic group, educational class, income group, or religious category?*"

memberships. In these examples, of course, the physical presence of other group members is key. Being around others like us highlights all the features we share in common, thus making very salient the group's role as a reference group for testing reality. At the same time, all those shared features bring concerns about identity and connectedness to mind. No wonder, then, that the double motivational whammy of having other group members present increases conformity to group norms (Crutchfield, 1955; Reid, 1983; Skinner & Stephenson, 1987).

This finding, that people agree even more strongly with the group when in its midst than in private, is often interpreted as meaning that groups produce only public conformity, not private conformity. However, the evidence does not support this claim. Conformity to group norms occurs even in private (V. L. Allen, 1965; Deutsch & Gerard, 1955; S. A. Insko and others, 1983). After all, the Republican delegate's fierce belief in free enterprise does not disappear when she comes home from the convention; the new convert's faith does not falter just because the revival meeting ends. And remember that participants in Sherif's study used the group norm as their personal standard as much as a year later, when they were asked to judge the light movements in the absence of other group members. You do not need to have other group members present to be highly aware of your group membership or to conform to group norms. Conformity occurs because the group is part of the individual—as a social identity that is part of the self—as well as because the individual is part of the group.

The formation and transmission of group norms is one of the most powerful examples of how we work together with others to socially construct a shared view of reality. As can be seen in Figure 9.4, the needs for mastery and connectedness guide our reactions to informational and normative influence from the group as we try to reach consensus on a multitude of judgments and decisions.

These findings might remind you of similar results discussed in chapter 6, pages 211 to 213. Although the physical presence of group members can strongly affect our perceptions of ourselves and others, such effects also occur whenever we think about ourselves as group members, whether or not others are present.

FIGURE 9.4   Motives behind private conformity

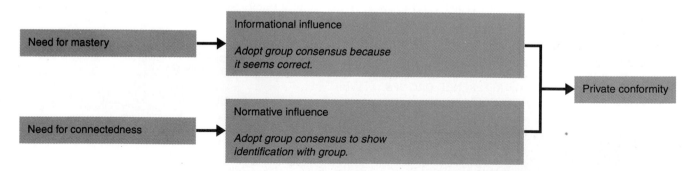

■ People adopt a group consensus as their own private belief because they wish both to hold correct opinions and to show their identification with a group they value and respect. These two processes are termed *informational influence* and *normative influence*.

How Groups Form Norms: Processes of Social Influence

Every year in early spring, admissions committees in hundreds of colleges and universities across the United States gather to discuss the current crop of applicants. In institutions like ours, roundtable discussions determine who will be invited to join the freshman class in the fall and who will be sent an "I'm sorry to inform you" letter. As members of the admissions committee meet and talk together, each contributes some of his or her views and ideas to the group, and each hears what others think and how they react. Gradually the group forms a consensus, agreeing on who should be accepted and who will be rejected. In these groups and others, the group norms forged from this kind of give and take sometimes reflect a middle-of-the-road consensus. But the merging of individual arguments can also move the consensus away from the center and toward the extreme.

Group Compromise: Taking the Middle Ground

When group members are initially split on an issue, group discussion usually results in convergence on a moderate position.

You might expect that a middle-of-the-road compromise would be the most likely outcome when people share their views. For example, just as Sherif's participants converged on a middling estimate of how far the light moved in the darkened room, people with extremely positive or negative evaluations of a particular candidate might move toward more moderate views when faced with arguments that oppose their original evaluations. Surprisingly, though, this outcome is rare in group discussions. Such compromise usually happens only when a group's views are evenly split, with roughly half the members supporting an issue and half opposing it (Burnstein & Vinokur, 1977; Wetherell, 1987).

When group discussion does produce a compromise, the position reflected in the final group norm is more moderate than the initial views of its individual members, an effect called *depolarization*. The convergence of estimates by those in Sherif's study demonstrates depolarization. Look back at Figure 9.1 and you will see that each group member ultimately moves toward a moderate group norm that is near the average of the members' initial opinions. The same pattern can be seen when an admissions application initially elicits an equal number of supporters and opponents. Opinions will converge toward a moderate position, which may or may not be good enough to gain admission for the would-be student.

Group Polarization: Going to Normative Extremes

When a majority of group members initially favors one side of the issue, discussion usually moves the group to an even more extreme position.

An even division of opinion is a rare phenomenon in group decision making. More commonly, a majority of group members initially favor a particular point of view. One large-scale study of jury proceedings, for example, found that a majority initially favored acquittal or conviction in all but 10 of 225 trials studied (Kalven & Zeisel, 1966). Why do groups initially lean in one direction or another? Often their views are influenced by the weight of the evidence. A student with good academic preparation and well-rounded extracurricular activities will appeal to the majority of admissions committee members, for example. And frequently the initial point of view actually defines the group. Individual members of the local Sierra Club probably joined because they favor conservation and thus share similar opinions on the endangered spotted owl. Similarly, members of a neighborhood watch committee can be expected to share views about local law enforcement.

What kind of final consensus can we expect when most members of a group initially share an opinion? If you participate in admissions discussions long enough, you begin to notice a reliable pattern. Imagine that a candidate with some potential is being discussed. Someone points out her solid but not startling academic credentials. Another notes that her GPA improved over her high school years, even as she took on extracurricular activities. A third mentions that the candidate is on his "accept" list, at which point a fourth chips in with "Uh huh, I gave her a high rating, too." A particularly strong letter of recommendation is reread, and the group agrees enthusiastically on acceptance: The candidate is excellent. Seen at first as merely having potential, the candidate is now a superior applicant. And, of course, movement in the opposite direction can also happen. When the majority of committee members lean toward rejection, talking about credentials seems only to doom the candidate further. In the context of group discussion, the good gets better and the bad gets worse.

The first to notice this unexpected effect of group discussion was a young graduate student named James Stoner (1961). Stoner asked business school students to respond to a series of fictitious "choice dilemmas," in which they had to decide between a cautious course of action with a small potential benefit and a risky option with a large payoff. For example, imagine having to decide between staying in a job that offers security and moderate yearly raises, versus taking a better paying job with a new firm that could go out of business in a year or two. Stoner found that when people work together in groups on this kind of problem, they opt for more risky actions than when they make decisions alone. This finding was originally called the *risky shift*.

Surprisingly, Stoner's results had little to do with the perception of risk. Other researchers soon demonstrated that if most people initially prefer a cautious line of action, group discussion produces a more cautious outcome. Similar patterns of group shifts emerged under a variety of circumstances. For example, if most members of a group initially are racially prejudiced, group interaction and discussion tends to increase their prejudice. If most members initially are not prejudiced, then group discussion shifts them further in the direction of egalitarian views (Myers & Bishop, 1971). Findings such as these have led to the conclusion that the various shifts are part of a general phenomenon, group polarization. **Group polarization** occurs when the group's initial average position becomes more extreme following group interaction (Moscovici & Zavalloni, 1969).

Group polarization. The process by which a group's initial average position becomes more extreme following group interaction.

☐ **POLARIZATION IN THE JURY ROOM.** Group polarization can operate whenever like-minded individuals interact. In one demonstration of its impact on jury deliberation, David Myers and Martin Kaplan (1976) asked mock juries made up of U.S. college students to assess the guilt of defendants in traffic felony cases. The researchers manipulated the strength of the evidence, so that in some groups a majority initially favored conviction, whereas in others a majority initially favored acquittal. In the pro-conviction groups, discussion increased the likelihood that the defendant would be found guilty. In the pro-acquittal groups, the reverse occurred. Similar results were found in a study of Japanese students serving as mock jurors (Isozaki, 1984).

Research confirms that group polarization takes place among real jurors deciding real cases. In their survey of jury decisions, Kalven and Zeisel (1966) found that in 209 of 215 cases, the final outcome favored the position of the initial majority. The authors of the study offer an interesting metaphor for the impact of group discussion: "The deliberation process might be likened to what the developer does for an exposed film: it brings out the picture" (p. 489). This is a far cry from the compromise, middle-of-the-road, or depolarized position we might intuitively expect groups to adopt.

Explaining Polarized Norm Formation

When people process superficially, merely relying on others' positions can produce polarization of group norms. Under these conditions, the majority consensus in the group is seen as reflecting reality and as defining what good group members are like. This viewpoint gives the majority position a persuasive advantage. When people process systematically, both others' positions and arguments work together to make polarized group norms more likely. Majority arguments are more numerous, receive more discussion, seem more compelling, and are presented more persuasively. All these factors give majority views a persuasive advantage.

How do social psychologists explain the formation of polarized group norms? The key lies in the fact that most groups have majorities that favor one side of the issue over the other. We have seen that when people make judgments or decisions, they are sometimes influenced by simple associations, whereas at other times they think deeply about the alternatives. Both superficial and systematic processing also characterize our reactions to information about others' opinions during group interaction. Sometimes we notice where others stand and go along with the majority without worrying about their reasons. If, for example, you and some friends are choosing a restaurant and you do not particularly care what you eat, you may pay no attention to claims about the quality of the food and service and simply throw your support behind the majority. But if you are in a situation in which your decision will matter a great deal (for example, as a member of an admissions committee or a jury), you probably will consider more than just the other members' positions. You will also want to understand their reasons, evidence, and arguments. In this case, the persuasive effects of the majority of others' opinions can be even stronger. Regardless of whether superficial or systematic processing occurs, however, extreme group norms are the likely result. Let's see why.

SUPERFICIAL PROCESSING: RELYING ON OTHERS' POSITIONS. Sometimes people know only *what* others think but not *why* they came to their conclusions (R. S. Baron & Roper, 1976). The way norms are formed in these situations usually reflects the fact that people rely on the ready-made consensus alone. That is, consensus is used as a heuristic: It provides a shortcut to the position that people believe to be both correct and appropriate, without their having to do a lot of hard work figuring out the right answer. People rely on consensus in this way both to help them master the social environment and to meet needs for connectedness. Both motives for relying on other's views alone can produce an extreme group norm.

1. *Consensus and mastery.* Agreeing with a consensus fulfills people's desire for mastery of their social world—their desire to hold the correct views. Because people believe that a consensus reflects reality, group consensus is associated with reality: If most people think something is correct, then it probably is. Like other simple mental shortcuts, consensus can be assumed correct almost automatically when people are not thinking too hard. This means people often accept a consensus even when other available information might warn them not to.

   In one laboratory demonstration of the power of the consensus heuristic, students listened to strong or weak arguments that were presented in a speech supporting probation as an alternative to imprisonment (Axsom, Yates, & Chaiken, 1987). During the presentation, one group of students heard several bouts of loud clapping and cheers from the audience listening to the speech; another group of students heard only scattered applause and occasional jeering. Some students in each of the two groups were told that the new probation policies would not affect them personally. As a result, these listeners were less involved and less attentive, and they were also very much influenced by the apparent consensus. When others cheered, these students agreed with the probation policy, even if the arguments were weak. When others jeered, they disagreed with the policy, even if the arguments were strong. Other research shows a similar reliance on the mere existence of consensus (Reingen, 1982). When undecided or dissenting members of a group adopt the majority consensus, whether apparent or real, the group's average position moves toward the extreme, and the result is group polarization.

   If you now recall the anecdote about the French cabinet minister from the beginning of this chapter, you will appreciate just how well he understood social psychology, if not politics. He knew that audience members who devoted no real effort to evaluating the Socialist party platform would be persuaded by, and would then adopt, the apparent consensus of the paid supporters who applauded so noisily.

2. *Consensus and connectedness.* Because people care about their membership in groups, they often want to be the best possible members of their group. Any group member who values his or her group membership naturally wants to represent the group ideal (Codol, 1975). In fact, most members of cohesive groups think of themselves not as average but as superior representatives of their groups (Myers

You may recall that this experiment was cited in chapter 1, pages 1 to 2, as an interesting example of social-psychological research.

& Lamm, 1976). Thus, for example, most business executives think of themselves as more ethical than the average executive, and most editors think their grasp of grammar is better than that of their average colleague (Allison et al., 1989). However, others' views may not support the opinions we hold of ourselves. Sometimes hearing what others think reveals that we are not as far above average as we thought we were. This realization may in turn prompt a speedy adoption of a more extreme position so that we can again become above average on important dimensions within the group (Singleton, 1979). As more and more group members adopt this strategy, the group norm grows more extreme.

Even when others' positions are all we know, our desire for mastery and our wish to be valued by important others make us want to agree with, and even go beyond, the majority's view. Group members who hold the minority position shift to adopt the majority consensus. Members of the majority may move even farther toward the extreme. Together, these two processes make group polarization a likely outcome of norm formation as the average position in the group grows more extreme.

SYSTEMATIC PROCESSING: ATTENDING TO BOTH POSITIONS AND ARGUMENTS. When the evaluations that a group makes are important or affect the group directly, group members move their processing into high gear. They consider not just the preferences of others but also their supporting arguments and evidence. You might think that such careful processing would never produce the exaggerated or extreme norms that occur in group polarization. In fact, however, systematic processing makes group polarization even more likely.

In the lively interchange that characterizes most group discussions, preferences and the arguments for those preferences are aired simultaneously. Imagine, for example, that you are a jury member listening to another juror argue, "Well, if the defendant was at work, as his foreman testified, he could not possibly have arrived home before 6:30, and the doctors said that the victim was already dead by then." Although this statement reviews relevant evidence, it also reveals the juror's opinion. If, instead of laying out her position, the juror had merely voiced her opinion that the defendant was innocent, you might still have been able to figure out the unstated arguments supporting that view. When a jury or another group is deeply engaged in resolving a dilemma, both *what* other group members believe and *why* they believe it become important considerations. The resulting attention given to *both* arguments and positions gives even more of a persuasive edge to the position initially favored by the majority of other group members, which moves the norm towards polarization. Several forces join together to make this happen.

1. *Majority arguments are more numerous.* The greater the number of people who hold a particular viewpoint, the more numerous the arguments favoring that position are likely to be. Imagine a situation in which your philanthropy committee is planning a fundraiser. Since most members favor a silent auction, more people speak in favor of that activity and more evidence is given supporting it than any other activity. Not surprisingly, the effect of hearing this lop-

sided set of appeals, particularly the novel and compelling ones, is to further strengthen group members' views. This in turn produces polarization. The idea that initial preferences bias the kinds of arguments discussed and thus make the group's view more extreme is called the *persuasive arguments explanation* of group polarization (Burnstein & Vinokur, 1977; Kaplan & Miller, 1987). The degree of polarization depends on the novelty and quality of the evidence. When group members hear persuasive arguments that they had not previously considered, they move toward the majority position and the group norm becomes more extreme (Hinsz & Davis, 1984).

2. *Majority arguments get more discussion.* When people think that others share their views, they are more likely to express them (Glynn, Hayes, & Shanahan, 1997; Schittekatte, 1996). Arguments endorsed by more than one group member are much more likely to be discussed than ideas endorsed by only a single person. In one demonstration of this effect, Garold Stasser and his colleagues (Stasser, Taylor, & Hanna, 1989) asked students to read different sets of information about candidates for president of a student body. Some information was given to all members of the group, but other information was given to just one person. When the group met to evaluate the candidates, they discussed 46% of the shared information but only 18% of the unshared information. Not only was the unshared information less likely to be raised with the group, but even when it was, it was less likely to be discussed and evaluated. This bias occurs even when discussion members are experts highly involved in the decision-making process, as when physicians diagnose medical cases (Larson, Christensen, Abbott, & Franz, 1996), and even when researchers structure the discussion, instituting rules to make the group discuss all the facts available to them. In fact, such instructions resulted in an even more intense focus on the shared information (see Figure 9.5). Group members apparently believe that the in-

FIGURE 9.5 Let's talk about something we all know

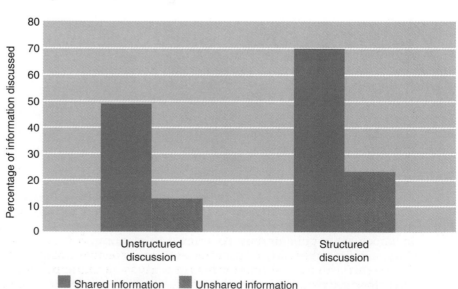

■ Students asked to evaluate candidates were much more likely to discuss information that everyone in the group shared than they were to discuss information known to only one member of the group. When rules were instituted to structure the discussion, the shared information was even *more* likely to be discussed. (Data from Stasser and others, 1989.)

formation on which they all agree is the information most relevant to the issue under discussion. This tendency is particularly strong with judgmental rather than intellective tasks (Stasser & Stewart, 1992). The bias toward discussing shared rather than individually held information is bound to strengthen the majority's case—after all, by definition, majority arguments are shared viewpoints, whereas minority arguments are likely to be unique, dissenting views. As such biased discussions confirm the majority position and convince some minority members, the group norm is likely to become more extreme.

3. *Majority arguments seem more compelling.* When several people make the same argument, it has extra impact. Thus, for example, three different people voicing an identical argument are more persuasive than a single person who repeats the same argument three times (Harkins & Petty, 1983). This bias reflects the tendency of people to pay particular attention to replication (different people coming to the same conclusion) compared to repetition (the same person repeating the conclusion). The fact that different people with different perspectives reach the same conclusion makes that conclusion seem particularly compelling. Such replication also provides social validation: The information that one group member raises can be "confirmed" by another group member who also has that information. At the same time, the validity of unshared information is called into question because it cannot be independently verified by others (D. D. Stewart & Stasser, 1995). In fact, any group member whose information is widely shared (and can thus be confirmed again and again by other group members) exerts considerable influence in the group (Kameda, Ohtsubo, & Takezawa, 1997). Consistent with this bias is the finding that people rate as more persuasive, and respond more favorably to, those arguments with which "most people" or "a majority" agree: If most people buy the argument, it must be a good one (Erb, Bohner, Schmalzle, & Rank, 1998; McLachlan, 1986; Singleton, 1979). Thus, the arguments put forward by a majority in a group discussion seem particularly persuasive, and their influence moves the group further toward the extreme.

4. *Majority arguments are presented more compellingly.* Majority arguments also seem to be presented in ways that make them particularly persuasive. Information that many group members share is raised much earlier in discussions than unshared information (Larson and others, 1996). This gives it two persuasive advantages. First, if a discussion is cut short, unshared or minority information may not be heard at all. Second, information considered toward the beginning of discussions has more impact than information introduced later on (Hogarth & Einhorn, 1992). In addition, group members, especially males, use a less cautious and more argumentative style of advocacy when they are members of the majority than when they are in the minority (N. L. Kerr, MacCoun, Hansen, & Hymes, 1987). Perhaps this explains why other group members see those expressing the majority opinion as more confident and intelligent than those who disagree with it (McLachlan, 1986). Thus, not only do group members hear more arguments in favor of the majority view, but those arguments are also more confidently and effectively presented. The result once again is that the majority seems more compelling, it wins more converts to its cause, and group polarization takes place.

FIGURE 9.6   Why a consensus is influential: Processes underlying group polarization

Majority in group takes a particular position

Most members of the dorm social committee favor purchasing big-screen TV.

Process superficially

Process systematically

Consensus and mastery	Consensus and connectedness
The majority is probably right.	*I'll go along to be a good group member.*

Most arguments favor the majority	Majority arguments are discussed more	Majority arguments seem more persuasive	Majority arguments are presented persuasively
I see more and more advantages of the TV.	*The advantages are mentioned again and again.*	*The arguments seem very convincing.*	*People seem quite confident about their reasons.*

Advocates of minority viewpoints are won over, and majority views are strengthened and reinforced

Group polarization takes place: Average position in group moves toward the extreme

Buying the big-screen TV seems the obviously correct thing to do.

■ When a majority in a group initially leans in a particular direction, their consensus tends to influence others in a variety of ways—whether the group members process superficially or think about the issues in more depth. As the majority position attracts converts from the other side and majority members find their beliefs further strengthened and reinforced, the group's average position moves in the direction favored by the majority initially. Group polarization has occurred.

In summary, when group members engage in systematic processing, the existence of consensus makes majority arguments more persuasive, and this persuasive advantage in turn strengthens the consensus. As members of the minority jump onto the majority bandwagon, majority members move toward even more extreme views, and polarization is the inevitable consequence. The process is summarized in Figure 9.6. As you may recall from our discussions of attitudes in chapter 7, systematic processing is even more likely to produce private acceptance and lasting change of attitudes than is superficial processing. Group norms formed through systematic processing have the same capacity to produce private acceptance and enduring change, as you will see in chapter 10.

☐ **GROUP NORMS IN CLINICAL SETTINGS.** People seeking support and personal change often use the power of group norms to help them achieve their goals. People frequently choose this path when coping with a serious illness, the death of a loved one, or a substance-abuse or weight-control problem. Support and self help groups are voluntary groups whose members meet to discuss their thoughts and feelings, share their problems, and develop ways of coping on a day-to-day basis (Forsyth, 1990). Alcoholics Anonymous (with more than 1 million members worldwide), Weight-Watchers, and Parents Without Partners all use the power of group norms to change group members' perceptions and, frequently, their behaviors. One study randomly assigned overweight women to one of two treatment programs. One group received step-by-step instructions on exercise and diet, and the other group attended self-help meetings. Later, the women's diet progress was compared. Researchers found that those in the self-help groups were not only more optimistic about losing weight and more motivated to do so but also more likely to act on their positive attitudes: They consumed less fat and exercised more. These changed attitudes and behaviors translated into an average weight loss of 9 pounds for those in the self-help groups, compared with less than 1 pound for the others (Jason, Greiher, Naylor, Johnson, & Van Egeren, 1991). Another study evaluated the effectiveness of a support group and AIDS education program designed for people under treatment for drug addiction. Compared with a matched control group that received no specific AIDS education, people who attended support groups had more positive attitudes toward condom use and actually used condoms more often (Magura and others, 1991).

Self-help groups work so effectively for reasons that should now be familiar. As members conform to the group norms, they obtain both a sense of mastery and a feeling of connectedness to valued others. As they share information, recount their personal histories, and explain their particular experiences, participants can learn many concrete, useful lessons. Among these are how others cope with their problems, what programs and resources are available to group members, and why people with their particular problem feel the way they do. At the same time, groups give members a feeling of being valued. The group offers comradeship in the recognition that all members are fighting a common battle. And it offers support in the opportunity to express emotions freely with no fear of rejection. Individual successes are cheered, and failures are accepted with sympathetic understanding (Yalom, 1985). Can you think of ways to use the power of group norms to support other types of constructive personal and social change?

Conformity Pressure: Undermining True Consensus

Because people place such a high value on group consensus, they sometimes succumb to group pressure, with disastrous results. As we have seen, relying on one another when we make judgments and decisions—when we do so in a way that avoids personal bias, provides reassuring replication, and considers all information thoroughly—can give us a handle on reality and connect us firmly to our groups. But groups sometimes short-circuit such processes, coercing their members and ignoring dissenting voices no matter how worthy these opinions might be. When that happens, group consensus can lead to invalid and unreliable decisions, even when individual members have the knowledge and skills to come up with the right ones.

When Consensus Seeking Goes Awry

Consensus implies that opinions are valid only when consensus is achieved in the right way. A consensus cannot be trusted if it arises from unthinking reliance on others' positions, contamination by shared biases, or public conformity. Such a consensus offers only the illusion of unanimity.

A decision is not necessarily valid merely because it is based on a consensus. Consider the decision to market the drug Thalidomide, which caused tragic birth defects; or the production of the flawed Hubble space telescope; or the operating procedures that led to the Chernobyl nuclear power plant disaster. All these decisions depended in large part on group input, but all had serious flaws. Were they perhaps marred by faulty consensus seeking? As you will see, if a consensus is to provide trustworthy information about reality, the consensus has to be achieved in the right way.

CONSENSUS WITHOUT CONSIDERATION: UNTHINKING RELIANCE ON CONSENSUS. If we merely rely on the presence of consensus, we can be influenced by an unreliable or even a manipulated consensus. In 1990, key members of the U.S. Senate may have fallen prey to a manipulated consensus when they squashed legislation designed to reduce fuel inefficiency, air pollution, and dependency on foreign oil. This surprising action apparently represented legislators' views that "the people" did not want such changes. Senators had received thousands of letters opposing the bill, and they relied on this consensus when deciding how to vote. If they had processed information

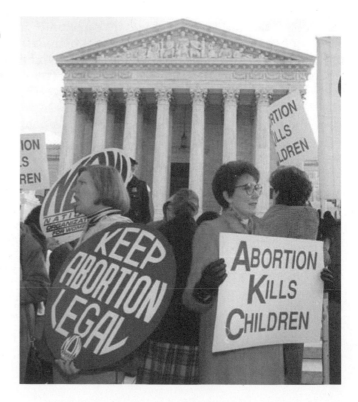

■ **Unthinking reliance on apparent consensus.** Why are these women on opposite sides of the abortion debate holding signs? Each of their respective groups normally shows up at the same times and places—and normally in large numbers—such as at this Washington, D.C. rally. The potential power of the consensus heuristic is clearly undermined by this fact. Their presence actually illustrates that there is no clear consensus on this issue.

more carefully, they might have realized that corporate consultants had orchestrated the apparent consensus (Waldman, 1991).

Many studies have demonstrated how easily people adopt an apparent consensus, even when relevant information is weak. The apparent endorsement of a staged audience can increase acceptance of a persuasive appeal, even when the accompanying arguments are weak (Axsom and others, 1987). Similarly, the effects of canned laughter can make jokes, particularly bad jokes, seem funnier than they seem without the laughter (Nosanchuk & Lightstone, 1974). Group members who unthinkingly go along with an apparent consensus are often led astray.

CONSENSUS WITHOUT INDEPENDENCE: CONTAMINATION. The idea that a consensus provides reality insurance rests on an assumption: We believe we can trust the consensus because multiple individuals, who considered the evidence independently and from diverse perspectives, have reached the same conclusion. Although we acknowledge that one person might be influenced by a particular bias, it seems unlikely that so many people with so many different perspectives will all make the same mistake.

Because of the importance of this assumption, people are often on the lookout for shared biases that might contaminate group decisions. In one study, for example, students trying to decide a mock court case watched the videotaped views of six people before giving their own opinions about the defendant's guilt or innocence. Some listeners heard the people on the tape described as two "groups" of three; others believed they were hearing six independent individuals. The opinions of the taped speakers had less effect on the decisions of students who believed them to be two groups than they did on the other participants (Wilder, 1977). Why? Perhaps the participants suspected contamination, thinking that the groups of speakers might have shared a bias or influenced each other. Consistent with this interpretation, another study showed that the mere perception that a group of confederates was a committee reduced their influence on participants' opinions. The confederates' views were persuasive only when it was made clear that the committee members represented diverse perspectives—that their individual views had not been contaminated by undue influence or a shared bias (Harkins & Petty, 1987).

You may sense a contradiction here. On the one hand, we trust a consensus when independent and separate individuals endorse it; the convergence of their differing perspectives on the same position confirms the validity of that position. On the other hand, as you may recall from the discussion earlier in this chapter, we really expect to agree only with those who share our characteristics. If we disagree with people who are different from us, it is easy to write them off as confused, ignorant, or just plain wrong.

How can these contradictory statements be reconciled? We seem simultaneously to demand that group members be different and independent (so their consensus indicates validity) and similar and in accord (so they remain members of the in-group). In fact, simultaneous similarity and difference is just what we need. We need others to be *similar* to us in terms of the features relevant to making the judgment so that agreement with them will tell us about reality. But we need them to be *different* from us in every other possible way so that no other shared feature can be responsible for biasing everyone's judgment (Gorenflo & Crano, 1989).

To refresh your memory about the reasons people see in-groups as more diverse than out-groups, review chapter 6, pages 218 to 220.

This simultaneous similarity and difference is part of what makes in-groups so much more persuasive than out-groups (Mackie and others, 1990). People usually see members of their own group as similar on characteristics that define the group but as variable and different in other ways. Thus an English major might see other English majors as sharing an appreciation for language and a love of literature, but interacting with them would reveal that they differ greatly in terms of hobbies, political views, food preferences, and so forth. In contrast, people see out-group members as all alike: To English majors, those dance majors all seem the same.

David Wilder (1990) devised a clever experiment to demonstrate that this perception of simultaneous similarity and difference helped in-groups to be more persuasive than out-groups. Participants listened to an audiotape of some in-group and some out-group members presenting their views on an issue. As the tape played each speaker's comments, participants viewed a slide of that speaker's face. Then the researcher played a tape of each person's arguments again and asked participants to match each speaker's picture with his or her arguments. Participants also indicated how much they agreed with the views expressed by the group they had listened to.

The results showed that participants could accurately match in-group members' faces to their arguments: They seemed able to keep track of each in-group member as a distinct and separate individual making distinct and separate arguments. In contrast, students could not match the out-group members with their arguments. Although they might have remembered that an out-group member made a particular point, they had no idea which

FIGURE 9.7   How in-groups become more persuasive than out-groups

■ In-groups offer simultaneous similarity and difference. They are viewed as similar on attributes that are crucial for the judgment but as diverse in other ways. As a result, in-groups are more persuasive than out-groups.

In-group	Out-group
Other members seem similar on attributes relevant to judgment but different in all other ways.	Group members seem all alike.
Listener can keep track of individuals and their arguments.	Listener can't remember who said what.
Their arguments seem distinct and independent.	Their arguments all seem the same; listener suspects contamination.
Their arguments are persuasive.	Their arguments are unpersuasive.
In-group has influence.	Out-group has little influence.

speaker had made the point. These different perceptions of in-group and out-group members translated into very different amounts of influence. Participants saw in-group members as distinct individuals putting forward independent arguments and coming to the same conclusion. Thus the in-group seemed to provide replication for and social validation of the view they advocated. Not surprisingly, then, participants were persuaded by the in-group consensus. In contrast, participants seemed to lump out-group members together, seeing them as faceless figures droning the party line over and over again. No wonder they found the out-group's views unpersuasive. As Figure 9.7 illustrates, thinking of the in-group as simultaneously similar and diverse makes their individual views seem independent and in turn renders their shared consensus persuasive. In contrast, the sameness of the out-group heightens the perception that their views might be contaminated, and it decreases their ability to exert influence.

CONSENSUS WITHOUT ACCEPTANCE: PUBLIC CONFORMITY. The most dangerous threat to the ideal of consensus formation is public conformity, which we earlier defined as people behaving consistently with norms that they do not privately accept as correct. When some of Asch's participants went along with norms that they did not believe were correct, they were demonstrating public conformity. Motivated by the desire to avoid wrath or ridicule, these students followed the motto, "go along to get along" (Deutsch & Gerard, 1955; H. H. Kelley, 1952), and their public conformity destroyed the reliability of the consensus.

Public conformity reflects people's recognition that groups dispense rewards to members who go along with the consensus and punish members who do not. People who disagree with other group members often anticipate negative reactions (Gerard & Rabbie, 1961), and their fears are well founded. When Stanley Schachter (1951) set up an experiment in which a confederate persistently disagreed with other group members, he found that the group first tried hard to win over the deviant. When this failed, the group ignored his views, assigned him to undesirable tasks, and suggested that he be excluded from the group.

Even jurors experience the pressure to conform. In the first trial of four White Los Angeles police officers accused of beating the Black motorist Rodney King, one juror went public to describe the extreme pressures she felt from other members of the jury. Bullied and ridiculed for her dissenting opinion by the majority who favored acquittal, and worn down by 7 days of deliberation, she commented that other jurors' "eyes weren't open, and I said to God, 'If you could give me one more person on my side, I would know'" ("A juror describes," 1992). Could any statement more clearly demonstrate Asch's finding that a single supporter helps people resist pressure from a majority? When another person changed positions and offered her support, the dissenting juror was able to deadlock the jury on a single charge against one officer despite acquittals on all other charges. Jurors have admitted capitulating under group pressure in other recent cases, including the convictions of boxer Mike Tyson and ex-Panamanian strongman Manuel Noriega ("California Case," 1992).

Unfortunately, because public conformity brought about by fear, exhaustion, or the desire to please cannot easily be distinguished from real acceptance, it can influence others. When everyone publicly adheres to a norm

FOR BETTER OR WORSE © United Feature Syndicate

that no one privately endorses, _pluralistic ignorance_ exists. Such ignorance abounds in many areas of daily life, even in the classroom. Have you ever been afraid to ask a question because the silence of your classmates led you to believe that everyone but you understood the teacher? Many of the other students undoubtedly were feeling exactly the same way but made the same false assumption you did (D. T. Miller & McFarland, 1987).

Pluralistic ignorance may also contribute to such significant social problems as widespread alcohol abuse on college campuses. One study supporting this idea reported that most students engaged in behaviors, such as excessive drinking or bringing liquor to parties, that suggested more acceptance of alcohol use than they actually felt. As a result, most students believed that their peers were more comfortable with heavy drinking than the peers actually were (Prentice & Miller, 1993). The evidence indicated that everyone was drinking more than they actually wanted to because they thought that everyone else approved of that behavior! If students had discussed their real opinions on this issue, the impression that "everyone" accepts alcohol abuse might have been dispelled. Positive changes in actual behavior might also have followed.

Consensus Seeking at Its Worst: Groupthink

When groups become more concerned with reaching consensus than with making the right decision, actions based on their norms can be disastrous. Groupthink can be avoided when minority as well as majority viewpoints are considered.

The Florida weather was unusually chilly on January 28, 1986, as the U.S. space shuttle _Challenger_ was launched with a crew of seven, including schoolteacher Christa McAuliffe. Seventy-three seconds after liftoff, a fiery explosion caused by the failure of a rubber O-ring in a booster rocket killed everyone on board and set back the U.S. space program for years. Investigations proved that the accident had not been an unforeseeable freak event. Indeed, only hours before launch, engineers from the company that built the booster rocket had urgently warned the National Aeronautics and Space Administration decision team that extremely cold temperatures might cause the O-ring to fail. Yet NASA proceeded with the launch—a tragic error that graphically displayed many of the ways that group consensus can go wrong (Esser, 1998; Esser & Lindoerfer, 1989; Moorhead, Ference & Neck, 1991).

How could trying to achieve group consensus hinder rather than help a good decision, as it apparently did in this case? Irving Janis (1972, 1982) asked this question over 20 years ago and set about analyzing the decision making that led various U.S. presidents and their groups of advisers to make some ill-advised policy decisions. In studying decision making by Franklin D. Roosevelt and his advisers prior to Pearl Harbor, by John F. Kennedy and his advisers prior to the invasion of the Bay of Pigs in Cuba, and by Richard M. Nixon and his advisers prior to their decision to cover up their responsibility for the Watergate break-in, Janis noticed that each situation was marked by an overpowering pressure for unanimity. As a result, the group becomes more interested in reaching agreement than in how that agreement is achieved. Janis (1972) applied the term **groupthink** for situations in which the desire to reach consensus interferes with effective decision making. A presidential commission investigating the *Challenger* disaster found that NASA's decision making was flawed by an emphasis on agreement rather than dissent—the essence of groupthink (Presidential Commission, 1986). Analyses of other recent events suggest that this tendency might have contributed to poor decisions in as wide a range of cases as escalation of the Viet Nam war, a resolution by the Kent State Board of Trustees to build a gymnasium at the site at which several students had been shot, and decisions made by management teams of top Fortune 500 companies, in addition to the launch of the *Challenger* space shuttle (Esser, 1998; Hensley & Griffin, 1986; McCauley, 1989; R. A. Peterson, Owens, Tetlock, Fan, & Martorano, 1998).

CAUSES AND CONSEQUENCES OF GROUPTHINK. According to Janis, group consensus seeking was most likely to go awry when a highly cohesive group of individuals worked under pressure to make decisions. Under these conditions, group members were likely to force conformity, selectively withhold dissenting information, suppress independent thinking, and prematurely rationalize or justify their position. These groups were also likely to perceive themselves as invulnerable, moral, and superior to other groups. Later researchers tried to provide more quantitative analyses of groupthink situations (Tetlock, Peterson, McGuire, Chang, & Feld, 1992) and to devise laboratory tests of Janis's ideas. Results of these studies support the idea that groupthink is affected by many of the same factors that affect all situations in which groups form consensus (Raven, 1998). For example, the more strongly people identify with the group itself, the more likely groupthink is to occur (Hogg & Hains, 1998; Mullen, Anthony, Salas, & Driskell, 1994; M. E. Turner, Pratkanis, Probasco, & Leve, 1992). Other research supports the idea that groupthink is associated with decision-making procedures that bias or suppress information processing (Kameda & Sugimori, 1993; Moorhead & Montanari, 1986; Schafer & Crichlow, 1996) and that it often occurs when groups overestimate their abilities and effectiveness (Whyte, Saks, & Hook, 1997).

Many of the more recent findings do not completely support Janis's analysis of the causes and consequences of groupthink. What they do suggest, however, is just what it is about groupthink situations that can pro-

Groupthink. Group decision making that is impaired by the drive to reach consensus regardless of how the consensus is formed.

duce potentially bad decisions. Consensus formation typically increases the validity of decisions while contributing to positive social identity. But consensus confers these benefits only if it achieved in the right way. A consensus cannot be trusted if it arises from unthinking reliance on others' positions, contamination by shared biases, or public conformity. Yet these conditions are common when groups care more about reaching consensus than about how consensus is reached. Consider, for example, how groupthink can undermine the guarantees that consensus usually offers.

1. *Consensus is achieved without considering all the available information.* Because reaching consensus is all that counts and pressures for agreement are so strong, group members devise multiple ways to avoid exposure to dissenting information. Doubting members engage in *self-censorship*, voluntarily suppressing their doubts and criticisms. Occasionally a *mindguard* emerges: someone who shields group members from unwelcome information that might destroy their confidence in the consensus. With only supporting evidence and ideas available, *collective rationalization* takes over. The group engages in justifying and bolstering its decision, strengthening consensus rather than testing it.

   In the *Challenger* case, the engineers concerned about the potential failure of *O*-rings in cold weather were not allowed to present their doubts to those higher up the chain of command (Esser & Lindoerfer, 1989). They were asked to prove absolutely that the booster would not work, which of course was impossible. In the end, self-appointed mindguards shielded the top NASA decision makers from any knowledge of the engineers' reservations.

2. *Consensus is contaminated because members' views are not independent.* Groups whose members share similar backgrounds and similar points of view are most likely to fall prey to groupthink. Despite this danger, such groups often isolate themselves from outside influences and different perspectives, thereby making it more likely that shared biases will corrupt their decision making. Some group members may approach others in private and squash their expression of dissatisfaction, sometimes by appeals to "think like an ingroup member." At one point in the *Challenger* decision-making process, a top executive did just that: Declaring that "a management decision" had to be made, he appealed to his engineering vice president to "take off his engineering hat and put on his management hat." In other words, the vice president was being told to think as management thought and to come to the management decision, rather than considering the issue from the engineering—or any other—point of view.

3. *Consensus is achieved by public conformity without acceptance.* When groupthink operates, conformity pressure is often intense. Tolerance for any kind of disagreement is low, and dissenters are harshly brought into line or "cut out of the loop." Faulty consensus processes often start with voice votes among members, which permits powerful and respected members of the group to state their opinions before discussion takes place (Moorhead & Montanari, 1986). If a majority of the group falls into line, any dissenter is then faced with a situation very much like that of Asch's participants in the line-matching task, and many apparently go along in public

FIGURE 9.8 Groupthink undermines the validity of consensus

- For consensus to be valid, it has to be attained in the right way. Groupthink produces a biased consensus that may be out of touch with reality.

without being privately convinced (McCauley, 1998). As the presidential commission noted, the NASA decision team was publicly polled in the final launch decision meeting, while the corporate executives, who knew of the engineers' concerns, listened. In turn, each team member recommended launch. In the face of such apparent consensus, the executives said only that they could not give an unqualified "go" (Presidential Commission, 1986). Unfortunately, this was not interpreted as a strong vote against the mission, and the launch proceeded.

As can be seen in Figure 9.8, these groupthink processes produce an illusion of unanimity, rather than a true consensus. Everyone thinks that everyone else accepts the group position, so pluralistic ignorance also reigns. The apparent consensus in turn validates the group's judgment: "All reasonable people" would have reached the same conclusion. In fact, the process producing consensus has gone horribly awry. Relevant information has not been processed, shared biases have produced contamination, and a group decision that should be based in fact actually reflects fantasy. In the case of the *Challenger* launch, the consequences of fantasy were fatal.

REMEDIES FOR GROUPTHINK. How can the dangers of groupthink be combated? The answer to this question depends, of course, on what causes groupthink. If faulty decision making involves consensus without consideration, consensus via contamination, and consensus that reflects conformity, groups can take the following precautions.

1. To ensure adequate consideration of alternatives, open inquiry and dissent must be actively encouraged. Yea-sayers eager to rubber-stamp their superiors' preferences must be excluded, and devil's advocates should be appointed to ensure that weaknesses in the group's favored position are pointed out and that opposing views are heard.

2. To avoid contamination by shared biases, outsiders can be brought in to validate the group's decisions. Different groups with different perspectives could work simultaneously on the same problem, or the group could break into subgroups that take different points of view.

3. To reduce conformity pressures that contribute to apparent consensus, public votes should be the exception rather than the rule. The role of the leader should be minimized, and self-criticism and the voicing of doubts and objections should be encouraged.

Many of these solutions were recommended by Janis (1982) on the basis of his analysis of situations in which groups make effective decisions. Do such precautions prevent groupthink? Janis concluded that they do. After faulty group decision making culminated in the ill-fated Bay of Pigs invasion of Cuba in 1961, President Kennedy changed the way his team of advisers made policy recommendations. First, he insisted on full discussion of the pros and cons of each possible course of action, encouraging the expression of niggling doubts and skeptical dissent. In fact, he unofficially appointed his brother, Attorney General Robert Kennedy, as devil's advocate for the group. Robert Kennedy's job was to challenge the group's decisions, point out possible flaws in their reasoning, and find fault with their conclusions. Second, to avoid contamination from shared biases, the president arranged for his advisers to meet in two separate subgroups. Disagreement between the groups was taken as a signal that one group's thinking might be faulty or that more than one solution to a problem might be viable. At the very least, having two solutions to consider often provoked a lively debate and ensured that as many views as possible were put on the table. Finally, President Kennedy dropped his former practice of stating his personal preferences at the beginning of a meeting; instead, he withheld them until others had aired their own views. At times he even insisted that the group meet without him to ensure that public conformity to his views could not contribute to an illusion of unanimity.

When a new foreign policy crisis developed in October 1962, the new practices were in place. In response to the discovery of Soviet missile-launching sites in Cuba, Kennedy's Executive Committee met for 5 days, debating possible responses. Finally, after considering and rejecting many alternatives, after consulting with experts, after second-guessing themselves every step of the way, the committee recommended a blockade of Cuban ports, which opened the way for a resolution of the conflict. Eventually, the Soviets agreed to dismantle the missile bases in return for a U.S. promise not to invade Cuba.

The fact that such solutions and practices might improve group decision making should not surprise you. They are calculated, after all, to increase the odds that any consensus is reached with full consideration, without contamination, and without compliance. Many of these solutions are designed to achieve these goals by ensuring that minority views are given their due. In fact, inclusion and consideration of minority points of view are crucial to achieving valid judgments and good decisions in groups.

Minority Influence: The Value of Dissent

Consider the obvious idea that the earth travels around the sun. What we now consider "obvious" was once the scandalous heresy of a single scientist, Galileo. Similarly, the norm that women should have the right to vote and own property was once championed by only a few hardy women and even fewer men. Despite the strength of majorities, minority opinions sometimes win the day. Even when the majority is not swayed by the minority, exposure to minority dissent plays a crucial role in ensuring the validity and connectedness functions of social norms.

Successful Minority Influence

Minority views can sway the majority. To be influential, the minority must offer an alternative consensus, remain consistent, strike the right balance between similarity to and difference from the majority, and promote systematic processing.

Minority viewpoints can alter the consensus reached in a group. But to achieve their victories and convince the majority to reconsider, minorities must turn the processes of social influence to their own advantage.

OFFERING AN ALTERNATIVE CONSENSUS. Just as a majority's power lies in its command of consensus, the main source of a minority's power is its potential to undermine the majority's consensus and to promote an alternative consensus. Because group members expect to agree, a minority can exert influence by undermining confidence in the correctness of the consensus (Asch, 1956; Moscovici, 1980). Sometimes the exceptional credentials or charisma of a single person like Galileo or Martin Luther King may be able to sway others to the cause. But most of the time a lone dissenter has little impact on the group. To make the majority sit up and take notice, the alternative view must be a consensus in its own right. That is, it must be adhered to by more than one person. It must also be presented in such a way that the majority takes it seriously.

1. *Minorities are most influential when they agree among themselves.* Do you remember the California juror quoted earlier, who prayed for just "one more person on my side" ("A juror describes," 1992)? Just as Asch found that influence began when majorities of two or three formed, so researchers have shown that minority factions of two or three are more influential than a lone dissenter in mock juries (Tindale, Davis, Vollrath, Nagao, & Hinsz, 1990). Increasing numbers espousing the minority position engender more minority influence (W. Wood, Lundgren, Ouellette, Busceme, & Blackstone, 1994). The agreement of multiple group members on a single position apparently signals that the position is a viable alternative (Moscovici & Lage, 1976; Nemeth, Wachtler, & Endicott, 1977).

2. *Minorities are most influential when they are consistent.* Because majorities are hardly ever swayed immediately, a minority must remain loyal to its consensus over time (Moscovici, 1980; Nemeth & Wachtler, 1983). Many researchers have demonstrated that behavioral consistency is essential in giving a minority clout (Wood and others, 1994). The first to do so were Serge Moscovici and his colleagues (Moscovici, Lage, & Naffrechoux, 1969), who devised a mirror image of Asch's line-matching task. They asked groups of six (four participants and two confederates) to judge the color of a series of unambiguously blue slides. When the confederates insisted on all 36 trials that the slides were green, a small but significant number of participants joined them in this error. However, when the minority wavered, calling the slides green on only 24 of the 36 trials, they had no influence on the majority. Other researchers have found that consistent minorities can influence others in mock jury deliberations (Nemeth & Wachtler, 1974) and in discussions of such social issues as feminism, the death penalty, and homosexuality (Maass & Clark, 1983; Maass, Clark, & Haberkorn, 1982; Paichelier, 1976). Consistency is important because it conveys commitment to the viability of an alternative position. Taken too far, however, the minority's consistency may be interpreted as rigidity or intractability, which leads to a rapid decline of their influence (Mugny, 1975; Mugny & Papastamous, 1980).

When a minority successfully challenges the majority view, the effect can extend beyond the single immediate issue, pushing majority group members to be more open-minded in the future. In fact, seeing a minority express opposition in one situation might even give majority members the courage of their convictions in other situations. One study looked at the effects of hearing a minority point of view on people's later ability to resist conformity pressure (Nemeth & Chiles, 1988). Students made color perception judgments in the presence of a confederate who made dissenting judgments—calling a blue slide green—all the time, some of the time, or not at all. They later participated in a study like the Asch line-matching task, in which the majority agreed on an obviously incorrect response. Up against this unanimous majority, students who had not been exposed to any prior dissent conformed to the majority 70% of the time. But those who had viewed minority dissent in an earlier experiment were much more likely to insist on the correct response. In fact, as can be seen in Figure 9.9, the more consistent the earlier observed dissent had been, the less students later conformed to the group norm.

NEGOTIATING SIMILARITY AND DIFFERENCE. Advocates of minority views face a dilemma. To influence the majority viewpoint, they must offer a consensus that clearly differs from the majority position. At the same time, however, dissenters will not be heard if they are perceived as too different from the majority and therefore not part of the in-group, or if they are judged to be lacking in the qualifications for making the judgment (Gorenflo & Crano, 1989; J. C. Turner, 1991). Indeed, dissenters are often ignored, disliked, and rejected (Levine, 1980; Mugny, 1982). How can minorities successfully navigate this fine line? According to John Turner (1982; David & Turner, 1996) and William Crano (Alvaro & Crano, 1996; Crano & Alvaro, 1998), the minority first has to establish itself as a part of the in-group before

FIGURE 9.9 Learning independence from dissent

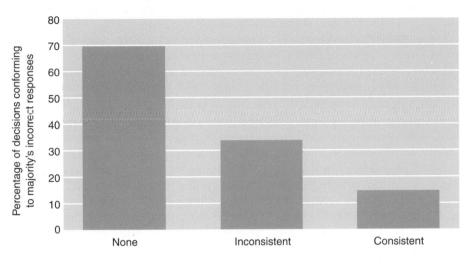

In the presence of confederates who made unanimous but obviously incorrect judgments on a line-matching task, participants who had not been exposed to a dissenting minority in a previous study conformed 70% of the time. But those who had previously witnessed minority dissent conformed much less often. The more consistent the earlier dissent had been, the more independence participants showed. (Data from Nemeth & Chiles, 1988.)

it receives any scrutiny. Edwin Hollander (1958, 1985) suggested that minorities could establish this in-group credibility by first agreeing with the group on important issues. This enables other group members to then show respect for their views on other issues—even deviations from the party line. Research confirms that members who first agree and then dissent are more persuasive than those who challenge the group immediately (Bray, Johnson, & Chilstrom, 1982; Lortie-Lusier, 1987). As Hollander describes it, the dissenters must first build up "points," or *idiosyncrasy credits*, before they can spend them.

Recall that a majority consensus loses some of its power if group members are thought to share a common bias. Minority influence is similarly reduced if the minority viewpoint seems contaminated or if out-group memberships are made salient. *Double minorities*—those who hold a viewpoint different from that of the majority and who differ from the majority in an obvious way—are at a particular disadvantage. This is especially true if the dissenting viewpoint is apparently related to the dissenter's group membership. When gay advocates lobby for affirmative action laws or mothers petition their employers for child-care facilities, opponents can too easily dismiss their claims. Why? Because the claimants' shared attribute—sexual orientation, motherhood, or other minority group characteristics—can be portrayed as a factor that may bias the claimants' views and raise questions about their self-interest (Mugny & Papastamous, 1980). In such cases, the majority may assume that the minority viewpoint is invalid. The viewpoint will seem much stronger if its advocates represent a comparatively diverse group of people, as when both gays and nongays campaign for unbiased hiring or when parents and nonparents join in supporting daycare centers.

Chapter 7, pages 262 to 263, described the attributional processes that weaken the impact of arguments when they seem to be governed by the source's self-interest.

PROMOTING SYSTEMATIC PROCESSING. Serge Moscovici (1980) has suggested that when minorities manage their dissent effectively, other group members are more likely to systematically process their arguments. He believes that their plausible alternative creates uncertainty about reality and that this stimulates thinking among majority members. The majority seeks additional information and processes it in greater depth (Nemeth, 1995). In this sense, minority dissent promotes systematic processing.

Evidence that minorities can make majorities process carefully comes from a clever study in which students were confronted with confederates who were either a majority or a minority in a given experimental session (Nemeth, Mayseless, Sherman, & Brown, 1990). The real participants and the confederates listened to three lists of words. After hearing each list, they took turns naming a category represented by some words on the list. For example, if the list contained many names of birds and a few names of fruit, "birds" was the obvious response and was usually named by the real participants. The confederates, however, did not name the obvious categories. In some conditions, the rigged majority of confederates named the less obvious category (fruit), whereas in other conditions the rigged minority named it. The consistency with which the confederates responded with the unusual category name was also varied. In some conditions, the nonobvious category was mentioned only once, and in others it was mentioned consistently on all three trials. At a later time, the real participants were asked to recall words from all the lists. The results showed that they could recall more words from lists in which a minority rather than a majority mentioned the nonobvious category, suggesting that exposure to a minority point of view had made them process those words more carefully (see Figure 9.10). Recall was particularly good when the minority consistently mentioned the nonobvious category on all three trials, suggesting that a consistent minority was the most likely to make participants process systematically.

Other evidence also shows that hearing minority views makes majority members look more deeply at an issue. Deborah Gruenfeld (1995; Gruenfeld, Thomas-Hunt, & Kim, 1998) studied the extent to which U.S. Supreme Court decisions considered multiple perspectives on a problem, recognized

FIGURE 9.10   Minority consistency encourages systematic processing

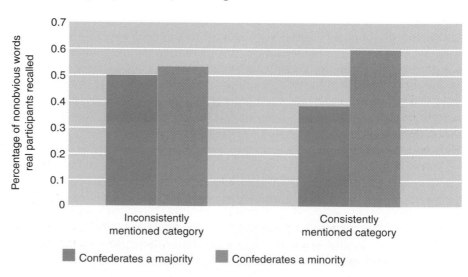

■ In this study, researchers used confederates who gave nonobvious answers in a series of three trials. When a minority rather than a majority mentioned a nonobvious category of words on a list, participants could more easily recall the words at a later time—suggesting that they thought about them more thoroughly. Recall was particularly good when the minority consistently mentioned the nonobvious category on all three lists, rather than on only one. (Data from Nemeth and others, 1990.)

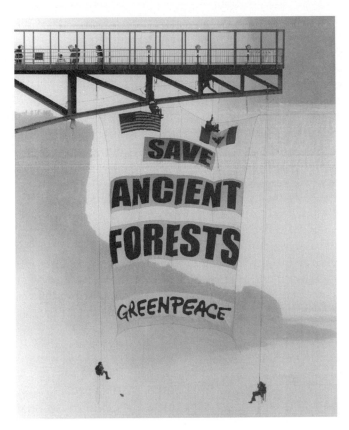

■ **Hanging tough to make others think.** When those holding minority views take a clear, consistent stand—even when opposed by others—they can make the majority think deeply about the issues involved. When members of the environmental group Greenpeace engage in repeated dangerous acts like bungee-jumping off this Niagara Falls tower to unveil a sign, they demonstrate solid commitment to their cause in a way that can promote systematic thinking, and attitude change, in the majority.

that reasonable arguments exist on both sides of an issue, and integrated these various perspectives and arguments in a coherent position. Decisions marked by these characteristics were seen as reflecting higher levels of complex thought than decisions marked by more rigid application of simple rules. Compared to decisions that were unanimously supported, and compared to dissenting decisions issued by minorities, nonunanimous majority decisions showed higher levels of complexity, regardless of whether the decisions were made privately or announced publicly. Confronting minority views prompted the majority to develop deeper and more considered judgments, compared to when such opposition was lacking.

Under most circumstances, such systematic processing leads to private acceptance of any attitude change that results. When a majority presents compelling reasons for lowered school tuition, for example, those who systematically process their arguments usually come to support lowered fees as well. But minorities don't always produce change in such a direct way. In fact, research suggests that, compared to majority advocacy, minority appeals result in less change on directly related issues but more change on indirectly related issues (Perez & Mugny, 1990; W. Wood and others, 1994). Indirectly related issues can be thought of as ones similar, but not identical, to the focal attitude issues. For example, a minority argument for lowered school tuition may not produce support for lower fees, but might increase support for more financial aid for students. A minority appeal to liberalize abortion laws may not be endorsed, but might enhance tolerance for contraception use. Why might such indirect changes occur?

First, given the powerful mastery and connectedness functions of the majority norm, group members resist openly agreeing with the deviant viewpoint on the main issue of contention (W. Wood and others, 1996). But the fact that they systematically process the minority message may well have consequences for other related issues. Perhaps considering the minority message in depth triggers change on those other issues, even if change on the main issue is blocked (Alvaro & Crano, 1997; Crano & Chen, 1998). This explanation for minorities' ability to bring about indirect change thus focuses on the systematic processing that minority viewpoints generate. All that processing brings about attitude change, but not on the issue tackled head-on by the minority.

Second, minority dissent may also produce indirect change because it encourages people to be more creative. Because they are not so concerned with agreeing with minority sources, people hearing their messages may think more broadly, considering alternatives, going beyond the information given, and diverging from the topic at hand (Nemeth, 1985; Nemeth & Kwan, 1987). This may allow them to see novel connections and to look at things with a fresh perspective. While these divergent ideas may not lead to change on the main issue at hand, they may bring about changes in loosely related topics (Crano & Chen, 1998; Kaplan & Miller, in press).

☐ **MINORITY INFLUENCE IN THE JURY ROOM.** As we have seen, the expression and consideration of minority views can be vital to preventing groupthink and forming a valid consensus. And this principle has important implications for jury deliberations. In 1972, the U.S. Supreme Court ruled that states could allow juries to give verdicts that command only majority support, holding that there is neither legal nor historical basis for requiring unanimity. Unfortunately, this ruling makes it possible for a majority to ig-

■ **Turning minorities into majorities.** In the film "Twelve Angry Men" (shown here with the cast from the 1998 version), a juror finds himself alone in voting for acquittal in a murder trial. He presents his minority view with such consistency and confidence that he convinces the other members to consider the evidence systematically—and eventually change their minds. In real jury rooms, establishing an alternative consensus and maintaining it with consistency and confidence are so difficult that minorities rarely win over majorities.

nore minority views. An initial majority would have no need to convince the minority to go along with its position, nor any strong reason to listen to the minority's arguments. Could loosening the requirement of unanimity have weakened minority influence and perhaps even have lessened the quality of jury decisions?

To investigate these issues, Charlan Nemeth (1977) divided University of Virginia students into mock juries and asked them to reach a verdict about the guilt or innocence of a defendant charged with murder. Nemeth made sure that each group included some students who initially favored acquittal and others who favored conviction. Some of the juries were forced to deliberate until they reached a unanimous verdict, while others were allowed to bring in a verdict with only a two-thirds majority. The groups forced to consider and respond to minority points of view not only deliberated longer but also were more confident about their eventual decisions. These mock jurors recalled more of the evidence, suggesting that they had considered it more thoroughly than those in the nonunanimous juries. Even more importantly, they were more likely to change their initial views on the case than were members of groups allowed to bring in a two-thirds majority opinion. Similar results were found when more than 800 Massachusetts citizens recruited from the jury rolls participated in mock jury discussions after watching a videotaped trial (Hastie, Penrod, & Pennington, 1983). When unanimity was not required, jurors usually terminated their deliberations as soon as they reached the required majority.

These findings suggest that loosening the unanimity requirement does weaken minority influence and thus may have reduced the quality of a jury's deliberations. Of course, it is possible that the participants in these studies, aware that they were involved in research, acted differently than jurors in a real trial. Perhaps real jurors, knowing that their judgments would affect the lives of real people, would give careful consideration to each juror's point of view even if a unanimity rule did not force them to do so. The authors of the Supreme Court decision assumed that they would. Still, it appears that a unanimity rule both increases the likelihood that minority views will contribute to the final group consensus and improves the quality of group consensus formation.

Processes of Minority and Majority Influence

By and large, majorities and minorities influence others by the same processes. They elicit public compliance, encourage systematic processing of the evidence, and offer positive social identities.

Do majorities and minorities influence others using fundamentally different processes? Serge Moscovici (1980) thought so. He argued that minorities induce a process of validation, in which group members carefully process information to try to understand *why* dissenters hold their particular views. In fact, he argued, calling attention to their logical arguments is the dissenters' only recourse because they cannot offer either the validity-ensuring or the identity-confirming benefits of majority positions. In contrast, majority arguments induce a relatively superficial comparison process because people generally want to go along with the crowd, at least in public (Moscovici &

FIGURE 9.11   Minorities use consensus to attain influence

■ Minorities as well as majorities can influence others when they offer a consensus that represents the convergence of diverse views and is built on the systematic processing of relevant evidence.

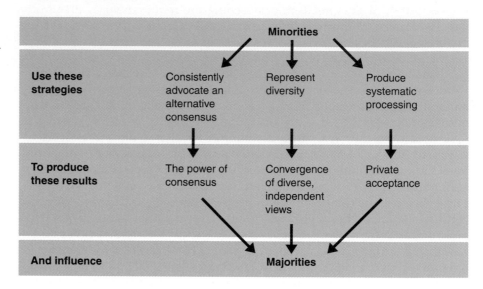

Personnaz, 1980; Mugny, 1982). According to Moscovici, listeners focus on *what* majority members say, so that they can quickly comply and earn the rewards of being valued members of the team. Thus minorities, when successful, bring about private conformity, whereas majorities generate public conformity.

How are we to evaluate Moscovici's arguments? First, majority positions and arguments, as well as minority views, can both be privately accepted (Baker & Petty, 1994; Mackie, 1987; W. Wood and others, 1994)—we have already described research demonstrating this point. At the same time, it is easy to find examples of situations in which minorities, like majorities, elicit mere public conformity. Majorities may control rewards, but minorities can dispense punishments. One need only listen to the screaming 4-year-old who helps the family decide not to eat out that night. So both majorities and minorities can produce public and private conformity.

Second, although majorities offer group members positive identities as good team players, not everybody wants to be a member of the establishment team. A minority identity of deviance and rebellion can also be appealing. Can you imagine circumstances in which you might prefer a deviant image to a staid, conservative, respectable one? When being avant garde, innovative, or socially progressive is important, minority opinions offer a positive identity and minorities have a relatively strong influence (Nemeth, 1986; Paichelier, 1976). At the same time, although majority agreement is usually associated with reality, consistent disagreement from a minority can trigger concerns about the validity of the majority position. Thus it seems that both majority and minority influence can occur to satisfy concerns about both mastery and connectedness.

Finally, as we have seen, both majority and minority messages are reacted to in knee-jerk fashion under some circumstances. At other times, both types of appeal apparently provoke extensive thinking. So it seems that both majority and minority influence can come about through superficial or systematic processing.

Thus, although Moscovici's ideas have generated new ways of thinking about majority and minority influence, he may have overstated the differences between the processes underlying the two forms of influence (Kruglanski & Mackie, 1990; Latané & Wolf, 1981). Although majority influence might be more likely to produce direct change while minority influence produces indirect change, the processes by which they do so are the same ones. Both can elicit mere public compliance, both can induce people to process information about their positions and their arguments, and both can offer the rewards of a positive self-image, whether that image is of a solid team member or a free-thinking innovator. In fact, as can be seen in Figure 9.11, minorities are influential when their dissent offers a consensus, avoids contamination, and triggers private acceptance—the same processes by which all groups achieve influence. By and large, majorities and minorities achieve influence by pulling the same levers.

CONCLUDING COMMENTS

 Among the most important characteristics of group interaction are the formation, transmission, and change of group norms. When group members interact, they offer opinions and arguments and listen to others voicing their views, until finally a consensus emerges. Individuals are highly motivated to have their beliefs, feelings, and actions reflect reality. When participating in a discussion with similar others who share the same information, they fully expect to agree with one another. When such agreement fails to materialize, people are puzzled, distressed, and uncertain. Thus social dissent opens the way for social influence.

This view of group influence makes clear that both social and cognitive processes confer validity on group norms. The social process is the give-and-take interaction that occurs as the group works out a consensus. The cognitive process is the independent evaluation of information carried out by each group member. Maximal validity—maximal certainty about our view of reality—depends on both processes.

In many important ways, scientists are engaged in a reality-construction enterprise that is just like everyone's day-to-day attempts to understand social and physical reality. Recall our discussion of scientific method in chapter 2. Just as people try to construct social reality by forging agreement with fellow group members, social psychologists use many of the same strategies to ascertain the truth about social behavior. Every individual researcher has his or her own personal biases that, despite all efforts to be objective, might influence research strategies, results, and interpretations.

Scientists often come to an experimental test as partisan adherents of a favorite theory. How to discover the truth? The scientific community's solution, like that of other social groups, is to seek consensus. Regardless of researchers' different theoretical perspectives, tests of theories and evaluations of information should ultimately converge on the same outcome. And reaching the same conclusion from different theoretical starting points, using different techniques, and with different participants, offers strong evidence for the validity of the shared conclusion. Such convergence increases

---

CHAPTER 9 THEMES

- **Construction of Reality**
  Individuals and groups construct consensus about what is true and good.

- **Pervasiveness of Social Influence**
  This construction process involves conformity and mutual influence among group members.

- **Striving for Mastery**
  Conformity helps us to hold valid opinions because the convergence of many opinions often means correctness.

- **Seeking Connectedness**
  Conformity helps us feel connected to and valued by other group members.

- **Conservatism**
  Positions supported by a majority in a group usually attract more supporters and do not readily change.

- **Superficiality Versus Depth**
  People process the opinions of other group members either in superficial ways or with careful consideration.

our certainty that we are learning about a phenomenon that is real to all of us and independent of our preconceived views. All the norms and procedures of science are intended to promote systematic processing and the acceptance of positions based on the underlying evidence rather than on public conformity. This in turn means that minority influence should be maximized, allowing for the acceptance of new insights and innovations.

True consensus is achieved only when a variety of opinions are processed from multiple points of view and are accepted only after being proved valid by such processing. When we think about how consensus is forged, we can see that true consensus should be constantly undergoing revision. The current norm should be constantly open to new ideas that might challenge the status quo. We should listen to minority opinions instead of closing our minds and finding comfort in majority support for our existing view. When new ideas become too threatening to the status quo, groups often try to expel the deviants from the group. But as we have seen, the expression and consideration of minority views is crucial to the development of reliable group norms. Thus it is important to nurture diverse and different voices in any group: The validity of a group's norms depends on their being forged from the consideration of many points of view.

SUMMARY

 Conformity to Group Norms. Because people are profoundly influenced by others' ideas and actions, interaction causes the thoughts, feelings, and behaviors of members of **face-to-face groups** to become more alike. Whether a judgment task is clear-cut or ambiguous, individual members shift their views toward the group consensus to form a social norm. Norms reflect the group's generally accepted ways of thinking, feeling, and acting.

Conformity is the convergence of individual responses toward group norms. Conformity occurs for two reasons: because people believe that the group is right and because they want the group to accept and approve of them. Most of the time people engage in **private conformity,** adopting group norms as their own because they believe them to be correct and appropriate. Sometimes, however, people display **public conformity,** acting consistently with norms they do not privately accept.

The Dual Functions of Conformity to Norms: Mastery and Connectedness. Private conformity comes about because we expect to see the world in the same way similar others see it. In fact, we often assume that most other people share our opinions and preferences, a tendency known as the **false consensus effect.** Agreement with others increases our confidence that our views are correct, whereas disagreement undermines that certainty.

Agreeing with others both ensures that people are in contact with a common reality and gives them the feeling of being valued. Although particular circumstances can make one goal more important than the other, usually agreement with a group of similar others fulfills the motives for both mastery and connectedness simultaneously.

People expect to agree with those who share attributes relevant to the judgment at hand. Agreeing with such a **reference group** ensures that people are in contact with a common reality and gives them the feeling of being valued. These goals are particularly important in close-knit groups, which further increases conformity.

How Groups Form Norms: Processes of Social Influence. When group members are initially split on an issue, group discussion results in convergence on a moderate position. But when a majority of group members initially favor one side of the issue, discussion usually results in **group polarization,** in which the group moves to an even more extreme position.

When people process superficially, merely relying on others' positions can produce polarization. Under these conditions, the majority consensus in the group is seen as reflecting reality and as defining what good group members are like. This viewpoint gives the majority position a persuasive advantage.

When people process systematically, both members' positions and their arguments and evidence work together to produce polarization. Majority arguments are more numerous, receive more discussion, seem more compelling, and are presented more persuasively. All these factors give majority views a persuasive advantage, thus pushing the group toward the extreme.

Conformity Pressure: Undermining True Consensus. Consensus suggests that opinions are valid only when consensus is achieved in the right way. A consensus cannot be trusted if it arises from unthinking reliance on others' positions, on contamination by shared biases, or on public conformity. Such a consensus offers only the illusion of unanimity. When groups become more concerned with reaching consensus than with reaching a valid conclusion, actions based on their norms can be disastrous. **Groupthink** can be avoided when both minority and majority viewpoints are considered.

Minority Influence: The Value of Dissent. Minority views sometimes can sway the majority. To be influential, the minority must offer an alternative consensus, remain consistent, strike the right balance between similarity with and difference from the majority, and promote systematic processing.

By and large, majorities and minorities influence others by the same processes. They can elicit public compliance, encourage systematic processing of their arguments, and offer positive social identities.

10

Norms and Behavior

I meant what I said and I said what I meant. An elephant's faithful, one hundred percent." With these words Horton the Elephant, the hero of the Dr. Seuss children's classic *Horton Hatches the Egg*, reminds himself of his promise to help Mayzie Bird hatch her egg. Mayzie takes off for Florida, abandoning both the egg and Horton, but Horton, one hundred percent faithful, sits on the egg for a whole year.

Like most children's books, *Horton Hatches the Egg* has a moral as well as a good story line. Horton keeps his end of the bargain, even though Mayzie shamelessly takes advantage of him. In life, as in story land, we usually fulfill our obligations, return favors to those who help us, and obey authority—even when such actions are personally costly or harmful. How are we to understand these important aspects of human interaction? Not surprisingly, the answer involves social norms. Through the processes we described in chapter 9, all human groups establish and teach *social norms:* generally accepted ways of thinking, feeling, and behaving that people agree on and endorse as right and proper. Social norms reflect a group's view of the world, itself, and others, and they have a powerful effect on almost all aspects of our behavior. Of course, groups create laws and sanctions—systems of reward and punishment—to enforce appropriate standards of behavior among their members. But as you will see in the first part of this chapter, norms are powerful precisely because they usually control group members' behavior without any kind of outside enforcement. For most of us, norms are so well learned and privately accepted that when a norm is activated its standards automatically govern our behavior. Thus, most of the time people do what the social customs and conventions of their group prescribe because they *want* to, not because they *have* to.

Some of the most powerful norms reflect deeply held beliefs about how members of a group should treat one another. Norms about reciprocity dictate that people should repay others' kindnesses or favors. Norms about interpersonal commitment direct us to keep our word, stand by our promises, and be trustworthy and reliable. Norms about obedience command us to obey those

■ **Norms are powerful.** These Puerto Rican workers are marching as part of a general strike demanding better working conditions. Their obedience to the police there to control them is an example of acceptance of a powerful social norm, respect for authority figures. However, their protest is itself an example of people banding together to reject a norm in their society, the government-sanctioned work standards.

to whom society has given legitimate authority. Because norms like reciprocity, commitment, and obedience are so important in regulating human interaction, we discuss them in detail in three major sections of the chapter.

What happens when others exploit our tendency to follow our groups' rules? Like Horton, we may find ourselves in trouble. If an opponent makes a meaningless concession, our impulse to reciprocate can trap us into giving up something of real value. Salespeople sometimes use this trick to entice us into unintended commitments. And throughout history malevolent authorities have used norms to make people act obediently in the service of great evil. Hitler's death camps, Stalin's secret police, and Argentinean dictators' death squads were all institutions that could not have functioned without the norm of obedience.

If norms have such power, can people successfully rebel against them? We saw in chapter 9 that considering diverse points of view can sometimes change group norms, even those that are fully accepted and widely endorsed. The same strategy of careful thinking can help us resist inappropriate attempts to use norms against us. Because we are subject to a variety of norms that offer sometimes contradictory suggestions about how we should act, every influence situation is open to interpretation. By understanding how norms influence our actions, by questioning the norms that others assume *should* guide our behavior, and by deliberately considering which norms apply to each situation, people can successfully resist normative pressure.

Of course, norms are not the only cognitive structure that helps guide behavior. As you may recall from chapter 8, attitudes also have a potent influence on what we do. The final section of this chapter shows that norms and attitudes usually operate together to guide behavior. Because so many of our attitudes are also a product of our memberships in groups, these attitudes rarely conflict with norms. Sometimes, however, norms and attitudes suggest different courses of action, and then the outcome depends on which of them comes to mind more easily. Whether or not an employee's personal beliefs leads her to "blow the whistle" on a company's way of doing business or whether a young man's personal convictions cause him to challenge the state's authority to draft him into the military will depend on the mix of social norms and individual attitudes that are brought to bear in the situation. To understand how all these forces affect our actions, however, we have to begin at the beginning. How do norms influence our behavior, and why do they have such a powerful effect on what we do?

Norms: Effective Guides for Social Behavior

Kurt Lewin (1943) was one of the first social psychologists to demonstrate the powerful effect of group norms on behavior. During the Second World War, traditional cuts of meat like steaks and chops were scarce and, when available, very expensive. To keep the civilian population healthy, the U.S. government wanted people to consume more liver, kidneys, and other unfamiliar organ meats. Commendable as this goal was, U.S. citizens found it hard to swallow at the dinner table. Pamphlets extolling the nutritional value of these meats, newspaper stories appealing to patriotism, even public lectures by expert nutritionists had little impact on well-entrenched food-buying and eating habits. Lewin believed that changes in such habits could be accomplished only by changing the prevailing norms. That is, he suspected that only the development of a new shared consensus about what was appropriate to eat would change people's behavior. To test this idea, he brought homemakers together in small groups to discuss in depth such questions as how to cook the new cuts and how to overcome family members' resistance. In the course of these discussions, group members' willingness to try the new foods increased, and this produced a shift in norms, just as we described in chapter 9. A follow-up survey showed that over 30% of the discussion group members actually tried the unusual foods, compared with only 3% of homemakers who listened to a lecture advocating the same course of action (but who had no idea how other people just like them reacted to the new foods). Norms thus had an impact that information alone could not achieve. How do norms come to influence behavior, and why are they so effective?

How Norms Guide Behavior

Norms must be brought to mind before they can guide behavior. They can be activated by deliberate reminders or by subtle cues, such as observations of other people's behavior.

No norm, attitude, or other cognitive representation can influence behavior unless it comes to mind. Norms, like attitudes, can be activated either by deliberate reminders or by subtle cues. Deliberate reminders of appropriate norms are all around us. The sign in the library requests, "Quiet, please." The reluctant child is instructed, "Do as you're told!" And the announcer at the Olympic medal award ceremony states, "Please rise for the playing of the national anthem." Not surprisingly, this direct approach pays off in norm-based behavior. In one demonstration of this effect, Robert Cialdini and his colleagues (Cialdini, Reno, & Kallgren, 1990) placed handbills on the windshields of cars parked at their campus library. Some handbills activated antilittering norms in a straightforward way, announcing, "April Is Keep Arizona Beautiful Month. Please Do Not Litter." Others delivered a message irrelevant to littering: "April Is Arizona's Fine Arts Month. Please Visit Your Local Art Museum." Unobtrusive observers counted (and we hope picked up) the handbills thrown to the ground. Twenty-five percent of those receiving the irrelevant message discarded it before getting into the car, compared with only 10% of those receiving the direct reminder about antilittering norms.

FIGURE 10.1   Effect of activated norms on littering

■ In this study, people littered least when they observed someone sullying a clean environment, and they littered most when they saw trash being thrown into an already dirty environment. Researchers explain this paradox in terms of norm accessibility: The litterer's behavior called attention to the prevailing norm, whether cleanliness or messiness, and the norm, in turn, influenced behavior. (Data from Cialdini and others, 1990.)

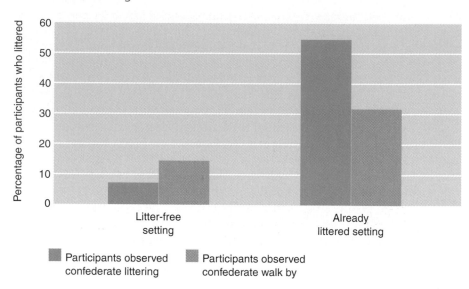

Although deliberate reminders effectively bring norms to mind, our behavior is usually influenced by less direct means. More often, people, places, or proceedings provide subtle cues that activate norms, which in turn guide behavior. The silence of others in libraries and in churches keeps our own voices hushed; the raucous cheering of basketball and football fans lets us know it's fine to yell. We slow down at the sight of flashing lights and pull over at the sound of a siren. The first few notes of the national anthem bring us to our feet, and the dimming of lights at a concert settles us down.

☐ **NORMS AND THE ENVIRONMENT.** Most of us have had the experience of having someone drop trash on the floor or the ground near us. When this happens, probably the first things that spring to mind are norms about such actions: Is littering acceptable behavior or not? Direct reminders, like a sign posting the fines for littering, offer an easy guide, but your surroundings may also offer clues about the prevailing norm. Heaps of discarded trash suggest that other people have found it acceptable to litter, whereas a pristine environment implies norms against such behavior. Researchers have found that people are more likely to litter in messy environments than in surroundings that are clean and free of trash (Krauss, Freedman, & Whitcup, 1978). And the more salient the reminder of the norm is, the greater its impact will be.

One study demonstrating this point placed participants in one of two settings: One was littered, the other was clean (Cialdini and others, 1990). The researchers found that more participants littered in the dirty environment than in the clean one. These actions are evidence that prevailing norms have a big impact on behavior. For other participants in the same environments, researchers drew attention to the norms regarding littering by having a confederate walk by and drop a piece of trash. Those who saw the confederate litter the clean environment littered even less than those in the same environment with no confederate. In contrast, the confederate's littering made participants throw even more trash into the dirty environment (see Figure 10.1). Evidently, the confederate's behavior made the norm implied by the state of the environment—whether neatness or messiness—even more accessible, and in doing so, it increased behavior consistent with the norm.

In a second study by the same researchers, making the norms accessible in a different way had the same impact. In this study, observers compared behavior in three environments: One was completely clean, one was marred by a single piece of trash, and one was covered with litter. The single piece of trash seemed to make people really think about the prevailing antilittering norm, which in turn led them to litter even less than when the environment was completely clean. The greatest amount of littering occurred in the already spoiled environment.

Could it be that a single act of littering is the best prevention for littering? Although seeing a person litter a clean environment does make us more aware of antilittering norms, Cialdini and his associates (1990) are not advocating preventive littering. Clean environments stay clean for long periods, and when one person finally drops something, littering becomes even less likely. So starting with a perfectly clean environment is the best way to ensure maximum impact of antilittering norms on behavior. As the researchers note, it's about time the concept of norms was recycled to help clean up the environment.

Why Norms Guide Behavior So Effectively

Norms are sometimes enforced by rewards and punishments. More often, however, people follow norms because they seem right, they are endorsed by the behavior of other group members, they are frequently activated, and they offer solutions to problems.

Why do we resist the impulse to litter a clean environment, especially when littering is probably easier than using a wastebasket or recycling? And why should anyone return a favor? After all, accepting benefits from others and never giving anything back can be highly profitable, at least in the short run. Why do people adhere to social norms at all?

ENFORCEMENT: DO IT, OR ELSE. The most obvious reason we conform to social norms is that groups sometimes use a carrot-and-stick approach—rewards and punishments—to motivate people to adhere to group standards. Norms are important, often vital, to the smooth functioning of groups, and groups take quite seriously their need to identify and stop norm violators. In fact, people are better at detecting violations of social norms (which often have more serious social consequences) than they are at detecting violations of logic (Cosmides, 1989). You soon notice the colleague who never puts money into the office coffee fund while you dutifully pay for your daily mug of java.

Groups handle norm violations by embodying their norms in legal statutes or moral canons: by specifying behaviors that are legitimate and those that are not. Societies take such action not only out of concern for any particular wronged individual but to reinforce the importance of the norm to the group as a whole. And, as we saw in chapter 9, groups often attempt to maintain conformity to social norms by withdrawing social acceptance and support from norm violators. Bucking social convention can be both a lonely and a painful activity.

Using rewards and punishments may be the most obvious way groups can establish and maintain norm-consistent behavior, but it is also the least effective. First, the carrot-and-stick approach may produce public compliance, but it is less likely to bring about private acceptance of norms. When those who are merely complying publicly with group norms escape group surveillance, watch out! Second, no society can afford enough monitors to enforce all appropriate norms on all its citizens all of the time, to say nothing of the problem of who will monitor the monitors.

INTERNALIZATION: IT'S RIGHT AND PROPER, SO I DO IT. Although using rewards and punishments can be effective, behavior often matches norms for a much more powerful reason: Most norms are internalized, and they thus seem to be both the right thing and the proper thing to do. People accept group consensus as truly reflecting reality and expressing the kind of people they are, and thus norm-based actions are a way of maintaining a shared reality and expressing group identity. As any parent can testify, it takes considerable time and effort to teach new group members which behaviors are appropriate, and why. Children are taught to ask before they borrow someone else's property, to show respect toward people in authority, and a seemingly endless list of other dos and don'ts. Luckily for parents, rules that benefit the group usually benefit the individual, which makes persuasion a lot easier. The North American immigrant in England, for example, accepts with little resistance the norm that he must drive on the left side of the road to avoid injuring himself and others. Of course, the individual benefits of social rules are not always so immediately clear. Nevertheless, these norms—the norm of obedience, for example, or the norm of social responsibility—become deeply ingrained through the process of socialization. Part of the process of learning what it means to be a group member is accepting and following group norms. Adhering to such norms not only feels like the right and proper thing to do but also makes people feel respected by others whose opinions they value.

CONSENSUS AND SUPPORT: WE'RE ALL DOING IT, SO I'LL DO IT TOO. Because other members of our groups endorse the same norms, their presence promotes rather than interferes with normative behavior. Remember from chapter 8 that our intentions to act in line with our attitudes are sometimes undermined by others who do not share our convictions. We may intend to be cooperative, but a persistently aggressive opponent may make it difficult to carry out that intention. Some activities inherently require the participation of others, and almost any behavior can be undermined if others actively oppose it. With normative behaviors, this is not a problem: Those around you are likely to be openly supportive, either because they share the same set of norms or because they are likely to be engaged in the same behaviors themselves. All of your fellow Sierra Club members will clean up the campsite before leaving, and they expect similar behavior from you.

FREQUENT ACTIVATION: SOMETHING MADE ME THINK ABOUT IT, SO I DO IT. As we interact with other members of our group, we are often reminded of its norms. The more often a cognitive representation comes to mind, the more impact it can have on behavior. No wonder, then, that norms influence a lot of behavior: Because norms are associated with groups, any reminders of belonging to the group can bring its norms to mind. The presence of fellow group members, hearing the group's language or seeing its symbols, and even the presence of out-group members can activate group norms and increase norm-consistent behavior. Put the average soccer fan in national team colors, surrounded by other supporters in the bleachers, for example, and watch for behavioral signs of increased patriotism. And note what happens when the opposition team takes the field! Because people are so often reminded of their group memberships by choice or circumstance, norms have lots of opportunities to influence behavior.

ACTION HEURISTICS: I DO IT BECAUSE IT MAKES MY LIFE EASIER. Like other cognitive representations, norms help us make decisions or decide on actions when the relevant information is very complicated or our emotions are running very high. If deciding how to distribute resources is particularly difficult, for example, people might rely on the norm of equality— "everyone gets an equal share"—to come to a decision without further thought. Even in the hubbub of the Fourth of July or Boxing Day barbecue, six adults will understand that if each takes one of the six ears of corn, the food will be shared equally (Allison & Messick, 1990).

☐ **THE INFLUENCE OF NORMS IN THE WORKPLACE.** Aware of the effectiveness of norms in guiding behavior, social psychologists were quick to realize that permitting groups to establish their own norms might help solve a familiar workplace dilemma: how to introduce changes in production procedures without loss of productivity, lowered morale, or outright hostility from workers. In one early experiment demonstrating this point, researchers compared workers' responses to three different ways of introducing changes into production routines at a small rural pajama factory (Coch & French, 1948). Workers in the control group were merely informed about the new procedures. Quite predictably, they reacted with dismay: Productivity dropped dramatically and turnover increased. Workers in a second group were allowed to choose group representatives to teach them the new techniques. This group representation helped: Morale stayed high and productivity, after an initial decline, returned to original levels. In a third group every worker became a "special operator" who was responsible for figuring out the best ways to make the changes in production. In this condition, then, all the workers were able to participate in and contribute to decisions about the changes. In short, they developed a group norm about how the changes should be made. The results in this total participation condition were dramatic. Morale stayed high, and the initial drop in productivity lasted only a day. After that, productivity climbed steadily until it was 15% higher than before the changes were introduced.

Helping establish norms for one's own group has the same dramatic effect today that it had in the 1940s. One more recent study of machine operators in a U.S. factory showed that employees who contributed to decisions about their work environment were more productive and less often absent than workers in a comparison group (Marks, Mirvis, Hackett, & Grady, 1986). In fact, as you can see in Figure 10.2, participants' productivity got better and better during the 2-year study. This study used a nonexperimental design: Workers could not be randomly assigned to decision-making or comparison conditions, so some threats to internal validity cannot be ruled out. However, as Figure 10.2 shows, the two groups had very similar productiv-

The reasons why internal validity may be low in nonexperimental designs were discussed in chapter 2, pages 35 to 37.

FIGURE 10.2   Group norms can affect workplace productivity

■ In this study of machine operators in a U.S. factory, some workers helped establish norms for their own group by participating in quality circles. Compared with those who did not participate, members of the quality circles showed superior productivity over the two years of the study. (Data from Marks and others, 1986.)

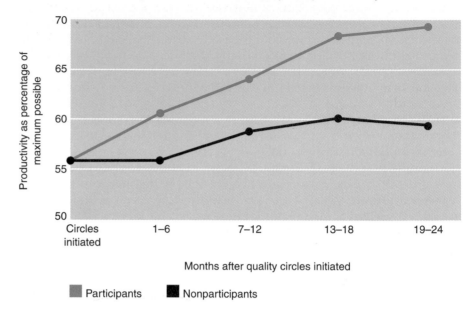

ity levels before the study began, raising our confidence that the differences observed later were due to participation in the new work organization.

Many countries have used this participative decision-making approach with great success. Automobile manufacturing workers in Japan and Sweden, for example, have long participated in *quality circles,* small groups of employees who meet regularly to discuss improvements in the production process and the work environment. This approach has been partially credited with these nations' ability to produce large numbers of high-quality products very efficiently.

Deindividuation: When Norms Overwhelm

When individuals see themselves purely in terms of group identity, their behavior is likely to be guided by group norms alone. The result can be either antisocial or prosocial behavior, depending on what norms are currently accessible.

Group norms do not always produce socially responsible behavior. Consider groups of British "soccer hooligans," for example, who have developed norms of extreme partisan support, violence against opposing fans, and vandalism following team victories. Such behavior is often triggered when groups of fans congregate, and it reaches fever pitch when one group of fans, decked out in the team colors and waving team flags, confronts equally fanatical supporters of other teams. The fact that violent behavior such as this often occurs in such group settings made early observers speculate that being in a crowd changes the rules of human behavior, making it less rational, more volatile, and often more violent (LeBon, 1908).

Some researchers have argued that crowds have this effect because they promote anonymity and the feeling that normative standards of conduct do not apply (Festinger, Pepitone, & Newcomb, 1952). Some evidence supports the idea that crowds make antisocial behavior easier. In one study, for example, Philip Zimbardo (1970) had college students dress in identical overalls and hoods that concealed their faces. He assumed this anonymity would produce a state of *deindividuation,* or the feeling that one's personal and individual identity has become lost in the crowd. Compared to other students who wore normal clothing, whose faces were visible, and who wore name tags, the deindividuated students delivered stronger electric shocks to another student. Of course, such behavior may have resulted from practical considerations. Being anonymous and unidentifiable—wearing a hood or mask, being concealed by darkness, or melting into the crowd—makes it less likely that someone will be arrested and punished for vandalism, looting, assault, or arson.

Note that this view assumes that group norms elicit merely public conformity or compliance, and that as soon as surveillance is impossible, normative behavior ceases. But being an unidentifiable face in the crowd could also undermine the power of internalized norms. If deindividuation reduced self-awareness, it could also reduce the accessibility of internal standards for behavior (Diener, 1980). By this reasoning, deindividuation will always lead to socially unacceptable behavior.

But does deindividuation always lead to antisocial responses? If the crowd turns into a rock-throwing mob, deindividuation should cause people to join in. But what if the crowd is rushing to pull victims out of the rubble after an earthquake? Will deindividuation stop people from engaging in this altruistic activity, as early research suggested? Not according to Steven Reicher (1987). Reicher argues that rather than *reducing* self-awareness, being part of a crowd *increases* people's tendencies to see themselves as group members. Furthermore, he believes that being anonymous and indistinguishable increases feelings of shared group membership still further. Under these conditions, group norms become maximally accessible; the only thing group members think about are what the other group members around them are thinking, saying, and doing.

Far from arguing that deindividuation frees people from normative constraints, this view suggests that deindividuation increases the power of group norms over behavior: People, acting purely as group members, end up thinking and doing what the group does. In this view, then, deindividuation would increase rather than decrease the tendency of individual members to join in any kind of group behavior, whether that behavior is tearing down goal posts or rescuing earthquake victims.

Research evidence supports this group-centered view of deindividuation. In a recent meta-analysis of 60 studies, Tom Postmes and Russell Spears (1998) found that deindividuation increased normative behavior rather than antisocial behavior. That is, deindividuation increases whatever behavior is typical of the group. Consider, for example, the results of a study that varied the accessible norms in a situation in which people's anonymity was also manipulated (R. D. Johnson & Downing, 1979). Some groups of participants in this study dressed in robes and hoods designed to activate negative associations, such as thoughts about the disguises worn by the racist Ku Klux Klan organization or the hoods worn by executioners. Other groups of participants dressed in nurse's uniforms, outfits that activated positive associations with helping and caring. In addition, some groups of "executioners" and "helpers" were anonymous—their outfits covered their faces—whereas others were identifiable. All participants had

Chapter 4, pages 123 to 124, described how self-awareness increases the accessibility of behavioral standards, or "self-guides," and thereby increases people's tendency to act in accordance with those standards.

■ **Deindividuation: The power of group norms.** When group membership dominates thinking, a likely outcome is blind conformity to in-group norms. In Britain, soccer fans, often wearing team colors and fueled by beer, have established norms of violence, including destruction of property and attacks on opposing fans that have sometimes led to deaths. These British soccer fans are destroying their own field after an announcement that a popular local team was relocating.

to decide the level of shock to deliver to another person for failing a task. As can be seen in Figure 10.3, anonymous participants in the Klanlike costume delivered higher levels of shock than those who were identifiable, replicating Zimbardo's findings with hooded participants. But the anonymous participants in nurses' uniforms delivered *lower* levels of shock when they were unidentifiable than when their faces and name tags were visible.

These findings suggest that deindividuation does not universally "free" people to follow their "basic" antisocial impulses. Instead, deindividuation makes people act in accordance with whatever group identification is accessible at the time: being a member of a looting mob, a Manchester United soccer supporter, a KKK member, or even a nurse.

The Norm of Reciprocity: Treating Others as They Treat You

Winnie the Pooh, hero of the much loved British children's stories, gently instructs one of his fellow inhabitants of the Hundred Acre Wood: "When someone does something nice for you, you're supposed to do something nice for them in return. That's called friendship." Actually, it's called the norm of reciprocity. The **norm of social reciprocity** directs us to return to others the goods, services, and concessions they offer to us. According to the sociologist Alvin Gouldner (1960), almost all societies endorse some form of reciprocity norm, and only a few members of society—the very young, the sick, or the old—are exempt from it. The universality of this norm is not surprising; it benefits both individual group members and the group as a whole. Individuals gain because the norm helps ensure fairness: Any resources they share will be returned by others. The group benefits because reciprocity strengthens the bonds that hold it together, building trust and commitment among its members.

Norm of social reciprocity. The shared view that we are obligated to return to others the goods, services, and concessions they offer to us.

FIGURE 10.3 Deindividuation makes people act in accordance with accessible group norms

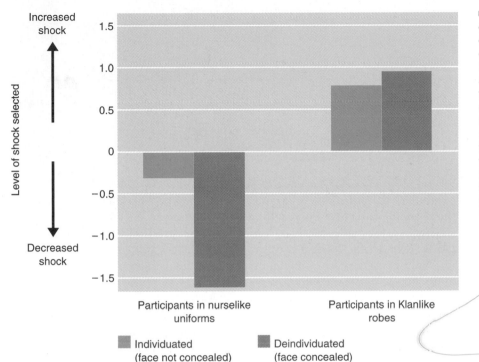

Level of shock selected

Increased shock

Decreased shock

Participants in nurselike uniforms

Participants in Klanlike robes

Individuated (face not concealed)

Deindividuated (face concealed)

■ Participants in this experiment could increase or decrease the levels of shock by 1, 2, or 3 units. When dressed in nurselike uniforms, participants selected lower levels of shock, and deindividuation magnified this tendency. In contrast, participants dressed in Klanlike robes tended to increase shock levels, and deindividuation increased this tendency still further. Deindividuation does not always lead to antisocial behavior, but it does make people more likely to follow currently salient norms. (Data from R. D. Johnson & Downing, 1979.)

Returning Favors

One of the most prevalent social norms directs us to return to others favors, goods, and services that they offer to us. This norm can sometimes be activated to our disadvantage.

The offer of some valued resource triggers the norm of reciprocity, which directs us to give something in return. This means we are obliged to return gifts, favors, and compliments, even if they are unsolicited (H. Wilke & Lanzetta, 1970, 1982). Consider the power of a small, unsolicited favor to increase giving, as demonstrated by one laboratory study (D. T. Regan, 1971). As each male participant settled to his supposed task of making aesthetic judgments, he was joined by a confederate who was trained to be either particularly friendly or rather rude. In one condition, the confederate returned from a break with two bottles of cola and offered one to the participant; in another condition he returned empty-handed. The confederate later asked the participants to purchase some 25-cent raffle tickets. As you can see from Figure 10.4, participants bought the most raffle tickets when the confederate had done them an unsolicited favor, even though at the time a bottle of cola cost much less than the 25-cent ticket. Notice also that the norm of reciprocity was so strong that it prevailed even when the confederate was unlikable. In fact, the power of the norm of reciprocity is so great that people even feel

■ **Teaching the norm of reciprocity.** Because it benefits the group and its members, the norm of reciprocity is often an explicit part of group socialization. These youngsters are learning the value that their group places on cooperative exchanges of ideas, feelings, and communication.

compelled to return the favors of a stranger who has been forced to help them out (Goranson & Berkowitz, 1966). The power of the norm is strongest right after we have received the favor and gradually tails off (Burger, Horita, Kinoshita, Roberts, & Vera, 1997).

Salespeople, market managers, and survey researchers are well aware of the power of unsolicited gifts. When was the last time you received a free sample of a product through the mail, were offered a free aerobics session at a newly opened health club, or were sent a dollar as an incentive to fill out a long questionnaire? These techniques activate the feeling that you should do something in return: buy the product, enroll at the health club, or complete and return the questionnaire. And the technique seems to work. Door-to-door sales increase when households receive products to try for a day or two without charge. When a salesperson eventually follows up with a call, customers typically buy as many as half the products they have sampled (Cialdini, 1984). Sending a dollar bill along with a survey questionnaire in-

FIGURE 10.4   Banking on the norm of reciprocity

■ In this experiment, some participants were treated to a bottle of cola by a likable or an unlikable confederate. Later, the confederate tried to sell participants raffle tickets. Participants who had received the unsolicited favor from the confederate bought more raffle tickets, even though they cost more than the drinks. They honored the norm of reciprocity—returning favors, goods, and services that others offered them—even when they did not like the confederate much. As these results show, honoring the norm of reciprocity can sometimes lead to returning a favor more valuable than the one received. (Data from D. T. Regan, 1971.)

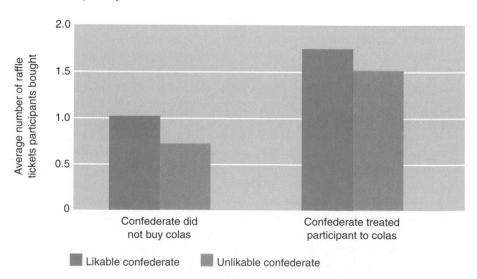

creases the number of people who complete it from about 25% to over 50% (May, 1976). The norm of reciprocity works in the supermarket, too. The feeling that you are obliged to buy several packets of frozen waffles after accepting a delicious sample morsel—complete with whipped cream—keeps products moving briskly (Packard, 1971).

Despite these sometimes less-than-beneficial consequences, social groups must maintain reciprocity norms. Without such norms, people might never help one another or develop close relationships. And, as you will see later, we can protect ourselves against misuse of the norm of reciprocity by trying not to follow it—or any other rule of conduct—without reflecting on the meaning of our action.

The Norm of Reciprocity for Concessions

Concessions are also supposed to be reciprocated. This can leave us vulnerable when influencers make concessions following our refusal to comply with a large demand—we feel obligated to make a concession in return. Because people believe in the norm of reciprocity, behaviors based on these concessions are often stable over time.

THE DOOR-IN-THE-FACE TECHNIQUE. One day a young man of about 14, casually dressed but freshly scrubbed, appeared at the front door of one of the authors. He informed her that he represented a national service organization dedicated to helping local high school youths resist the temptations of easily available drugs and alcohol. The plan was to get local householders to "adopt" a youth: him. For 1 month he would spend 10 hours a week cleaning, gardening, or performing other household chores in return for an hourly wage of $4, which would be paid to the organization. She would adopt him to help America's youth, wouldn't she?

Not that she didn't want to support America's youth, but working full time and on a tight budget, she was used to doing her own cleaning and gardening. "Well," she started weakly, "I'm not home all day, and I'm not sure . . . I'm really not sure . . . No, I don't think I can do that."

"Well, Ma'am," the young man replied, "we are offering householders like yourself an alternative way to help. If you can't help us out on the adoption program, a donation would be acceptable."

"Just a minute, I'll get my purse," she responded, feeling relieved that she had avoided having someone come to her house every day for a month. Then, as the young man walked away with her check for $20, the light dawned: She had been the target of the door-in-the-face technique. The young man had expertly manipulated social norms to increase the likelihood of her making a donation.

The **door-in-the-face technique** consists of making a large request and following its refusal with a concession that invokes the norm of reciprocity (Cialdini and others, 1975). The ploy gets its name from the fact that the requester wants the door to be slammed so that he or she can retreat from the initial request. In fact, the first request is always for something much greater than requesters actually want, leaving room for them to back down, thereby putting pressure on the other person to reciprocate with a concession.

The door-in-the-face technique is extremely effective. In one investigation of the technique, researchers asked two groups of students to volunteer

Door-in-the-face technique. A technique in which the influencer makes an initial request so large that it will be rejected, and follows it with a smaller request that looks like a concession, making it more likely that the other person will concede in turn.

Calvin and Hobbes by Bill Watterson

Calvin and Hobbes © 1985 Watterson. Distributed by UNIVERSAL PRESS SYNDICATE. Reprinted with permission. All rights reserved.

for a worthy cause (Cialdini and others, 1975). The researchers approached some students—the control group—as they walked across campus and asked if they would be willing to accompany a group of teenage delinquents on a 2-hour trip to the local zoo. Not surprisingly, the idea of spending several hours with an unspecified number of potentially uncooperative teenagers had little appeal, and only 17% agreed. Other students were first asked to spend *2 years* serving as personal counselors to juvenile delinquents. When all refused this long-term commitment, the request was downgraded to the 2-hour zoo trip. This technique induced 51% of the participants to agree—more than three times the number in the control group.

The door-in-the-face technique will activate the norm of reciprocity only if three conditions exist (Cialdini and others, 1975). First, the initial request must be large enough that it is sure to be refused but not so large that it will breed resentment or suspicion. Second, the target must be given the chance to compromise by *refusing* the initial request and complying with the second request. Finally, the second request must be related to the first request and come from the same person, who must be seen as making a personal concession (Mowen & Cialdini, 1980; Schwarzwald, Raz, & Zvibel, 1979).

Once it is clear that the requester has made a concession, the target is on the spot. The sense that the other person is really giving something up makes the target of the request feel guilty—am I acting appropriately? Am I creating a negative impression? How can I make up for it? (O'Keefe & Figge, 1997). Agreeing to the second request gives the target an opportunity to repair a damaged sense of self (Pendleton & Bateson, 1979; Steele, 1975). When targets believe that a compromise has been made and that agreeing to it is the best way to restore self-respect, the door-in-the-face technique can be a powerful tool in closing a deal.

□ **RECIPROCITY OF CONCESSIONS ON THE SALESFLOOR.** Merchandise managers count on the norm of reciprocity when they offer discounts or special deals. They expect customers who have been given 10% or 15% off the price of a sweater or who have accepted a free child's toy with every hamburger to respond by buying more sweaters and more hamburgers. Their expectations are usually rewarded. Two favorite methods retailers use to activate the norm of reciprocity for concessions are the "that's-not-all" technique and the strategy of selling the top of the line.

1. *The that's-not-all technique.* In this ploy, the requester starts with an inflated price and then shifts to a better deal without even waiting for a refusal. The concession technique of immediately offering a discount or bonus has been called the *that's-not-all technique.* And it is effective, as Jerry Burger (1986) showed. He set up a table at a bake sale and offered cupcakes at $1.25 each—a price he immediately reduced to $1.00. Buyers bought more cupcakes when they thought they were getting a bargain than they did when the cupcakes were simply sold for $1.00 with no previous "markdown." Burger achieved similar success when he "sweetened the pot" by offering a free cookie with every cupcake. In both cases, the seller offered the buyer a little more, and the norm of reciprocity for concessions helped clinch the sale.

2. *Selling the top of the line.* Retailers also use a concession technique called *"selling the top of the line."* A salesperson using this strategy tries to interest the customer in the most expensive model of a product and then, if the sale is not made, directs the customer to the next-cheaper item. As the salesperson gives up trying to sell the preferred product, the consumer reciprocates by spending more than he or she intended. Does the technique work? Cialdini (1984) cites an excerpt from *Consumer Reports* that suggests that the answer is yes:

> *If you were a billiard-table dealer, which would you advertise— the $329 model or the $3,000 model? The chances are you would promote the low-priced item and hope to trade the customer up when he comes to buy. But G. Warren Kelley, new business promotion manager at Brunswick, says you would be wrong [and] has actual sales figures from a representative store. . . . During the first week, customers . . . were shown the low end of the line . . . and then encouraged to consider more expensive models. . . . The average table sale that week was $550. . . . However during the second week customers . . . were led instantly to a $3,000 table, regardless of what they wanted to see . . . and then allowed to shop the rest of the line. . . . The result . . . was an average sale of over $1,000. (Cialdini, 1984, p. 58)*

From the door-in-the-face technique, through the that's-not-all technique, to selling the top of the line, all these influence strategies rely on the same principles. Regardless of whether it is a smaller request, a special deal, or lowered expectations, people presented with a concession are nudged by the norm of reciprocity to respond with concessions of their own.

LONG-TERM CONSEQUENCES OF RECIPROCATING CONCESSIONS. Do the targets of these shifts from large to small requests resent being the victims of such an approach? Far from it. In fact, people who comply with the door-in-the-face technique are more likely to carry out the agreed-on behaviors than are those who make the same commitment without refusing a prior request. In one study in which the commitment involved 2 hours of work without pay in a community mental health agency, 85% of those in the door-in-the-face group actually reported for duty, compared with only 50% of the volunteers from the control group (R. L. Miller, Seligman, Clark, & Bush, 1976). Similar results were found in a study of participation in a blood drive (Cialdini & Ascani, 1976). A heightened sense of having acted consistently with the norm of reciprocity apparently moves people to complete the agreed-on behavior. Once again, privately accepted norms have a powerful effect on actual behavior.

The Norm of Commitment: Keeping Your Promises

"You're only as good as your word." "Don't make promises you cannot keep." "Put your money where your mouth is." These nuggets of folk wisdom reflect a key component of social life: the **norm of social commitment.** This norm requires us to stand by our agreements and fulfill our obligations. If your friend agrees to save your seat while you buy popcorn, she is obligated to protect it from encroachment. If you agree to subscribe to the Sunday paper, you must pay the delivery person when he or she comes to collect. Social contracts help ensure that members of a group or society behave in socially acceptable ways.

One study demonstrated the lengths to which people will go to maintain a commitment (Moriarty, 1975). The scene was a crowded New York beach. In one condition, the researcher made an explicit social contract with neighboring sunbathers: He asked them to keep an eye on his radio while he was away for a short time. In the control condition, the researcher only interacted socially with his neighbors; he asked them for the time before leaving. A few minutes later, a confederate pretended to steal the radio. Did the norm of social commitment affect behavior? Indeed it did. Ninety-five percent of the people who agreed to watch the radio tried to stop the thief, with some even running after the thief to retrieve it. In contrast, only 20% of the uncommitted bystanders bothered to intervene. In a replication of the study, a pocketbook was left for a few minutes in a booth at a fast-food restaurant, with similar results. The bystanders who helped were those who had made a prior commitment to do so.

Like the norm of reciprocity, norms governing commitment allow groups and societies to function effectively. Group members can trust one another, agreements can be long-lasting rather than fleeting, and future planning can be based on other people's stated intentions. Not surprisingly, norms of social responsibility may be even stronger in interdependent cultures and groups. One study, for example, found that Indian participants regarded social responsibility as a moral imperative rather than a personal choice. American participants were more likely to think that the norm could be avoided, unless it involved life-threatening need or immediate family (J. G. Miller, Bersoff, & Harwood, 1997).

Even in individualistic cultures, however, the norm of social commitment is strong enough that it, like the norm of reciprocity, can also be used to entrap us if we follow it unthinkingly. Like poor old Horton, who was ex-

Norm of social commitment. The shared view that people are required to honor their agreements and obligations.

ploited by Mayzie Bird, we can end up tending someone else's nest instead of our own.

The Low-Ball Technique

The obligation to honor agreements can make people vulnerable to influence when they make a deal and then find out there are hidden costs. People usually stick to the deal even though it has changed for the worse.

Our tendency to honor interpersonal commitments, and the corresponding expectation that others will honor their commitments to us, are so ingrained that we stand by agreements even when the deal has changed to our disadvantage. Imagine the following scenario. An acquaintance asks if you will help her move her few belongings to a small apartment in your neighborhood on Saturday morning. You agree, but when you turn up, you find that she has a new plan. She is now moving into a house with one of her friends in a new location across town, so each trip will take about 2 hours. And the deal seems to include collecting her friend's belongings and helping her move in as well. Suddenly, a couple of hours work on a Saturday morning has turned into a mammoth moving experience that will probably take all day. Like Horton the Elephant, you have been "low-balled." The **low-ball technique** is used when an influencer secures an agreement with a request but then increases the size of that request by revealing hidden costs. How would you respond in such a situation?

If the findings of social-psychological research are any indication, you would probably spend the day helping your acquaintance move. In one study demonstrating the low-ball technique, experimenters phoned students and asked them to participate in an experiment for extra credit. Some students were told the bad news up front: The experiment was to start at 7 a.m. Knowing that, only 31% were willing to participate. Other students were low-balled: They were first asked to make a commitment to participate, and those who agreed were then told about the early starting time. Yet, 56% of these students agreed to participate, a significantly higher percentage than in the other group. Having made a deal, the students were reluctant to break the commitment, even though the deal had changed (Cialdini, Cacioppo, Bassett, & Miller, 1978).

Long-Term Consequences of Commitment

People stick by their commitments for several reasons. They feel obligated, and being inconsistent makes them feel uncomfortable. They also add new thoughts, feelings, and behaviors to help support and bolster their action.

The power of the low-ball technique can influence behavior over the long term as well as in the short run. Consider the way in which Michael Pallak and his colleagues (M. S. Pallak, Cook, & Sullivan, 1980) used low-balling to encourage energy conservation. After finding that merely asking families to conserve natural gas had no impact on their fuel use, these researchers offered an incentive to produce the desired commitment to saving fuel. The

Low-ball technique. A technique in which the influencer secures agreement with a request but then increases the cost of honoring the commitment.

deal was that families who saved fuel would get their names in the paper as energy-conscious, public-minded citizens. It worked. In the very first month, each family saved an average of 422 cubic feet of natural gas. Then came the low ball. The researchers withdrew the incentive, sending a letter to each family saying it would be impossible to publish their names. Was the commitment strong enough to keep the families saving without the incentive? Apparently so. The researchers found that during the following 3 months, the families continued to conserve at the original rate or an even better one.

Why do people stay the course? Several processes conspire to make people stick by their commitments even when a deal has changed.

1. *Fulfilling social commitments.* We initially fall for the low-ball technique because we feel an obligation to fulfill our social contracts. The importance of this obligation can be seen in the effectiveness of a particular variant on the low-ball strategy, which is common practice among dealers of new and used cars. It is often the case that the customer and salesperson make an excellent deal, only to have "the boss" raise the price significantly. Despite the additional charges, most customers stick by their commitment to the salesperson. In fact, low-balled victims are often very apologetic to salespeople for even considering backing out of a deal whose terms have changed (Cialdini, 1984).

   One reason this particular ploy is successful is that it cleverly sustains the customer–salesperson relationship and the obligations that go with it. Having an outsider—"the boss," "management," "my supervisor"—be responsible for overturning the agreement maintains the customer's feelings of social obligation to the salesperson; after all, it's not the salesperson's fault the deal is changing. Committed to the original arrangement, the hapless buyers feel honor-bound to fulfill their social contracts.

2. *Maintaining a positive self-image.* It's not only our commitment to others that leads us to make good on a contract that now favors the other party. Our commitment to maintaining a positive view of ourselves helps too. We may know that the deal is weakened. We may even want to back out of an obligation. But we carry through because we have difficulty reconciling such behavior with our sense of being trustworthy and reliable members of society. Even though it might be wise to walk away from a deal that is now less desirable, the discrepancy between our past commitment to the deal ("I gave my word!") and our possible withdrawal from it ("I'm thinking of backing out!") creates an uncomfortable arousal. This arousal is *cognitive dissonance*, which you will recognize from chapter 8. The only way to reduce the discrepancy is to grit our teeth and fulfil the commitment.

3. *Bolstering the original commitment.* When *cognitive bolstering* occurs, the original commitment is strengthened by the addition of supportive new thoughts, feelings, and behaviors. First, people think of all the possible benefits the new behavior or product could provide. Even though its price has gone up, the new car will still make vacations much easier, and now we can save money on groceries by shopping at the supermarket instead of the convenience store. Second, people start to think of the object as their own (it's my

first car and it's new, shiny, and attractive), which gives it special value and makes it harder to give up even if the deal changes (Beggan, 1992). Third, actually performing the behavior or interacting with the object offers additional rewards. Perhaps there are unexpected savings on gas, or the latest model's reduced pollution makes people feel they are helping clean up the environment. As these bolstering processes go to work, many other new thoughts, feelings, and behaviors come to support the original course of action.

The way these processes work together to bind people to a deal even though it changes are illustrated in Figure 10.5. At first, buying the car depends purely on the great price the salesperson offers. But soon, many other reasons to stay the course come into being. With all these new cognitions, feelings, and actions supporting the new behavior, changing the original deal and removing the original incentive makes little difference. Just as the fuel-saving householders deprived of the opportunity for publicity found many other reasons to justify their continued energy conservation, so the customer now sees many reasons other than the original sales price that justify buying the new car.

Sales personnel are quick to provide opportunities for these bolstering processes to kick in. After the original commitment to buy, for example, the client may be allowed to try the new car out for the weekend. Taking rela-

FIGURE 10.5   Cognitive bolstering and maintaining commitment

■ The original decision to purchase a new car may have been based mainly on the great deal the salesperson offered (left panel). Given time, the customer generates several additional reasons that also support the decision, as shown in the middle panel. When the customer is low-balled, these other reasons may sustain the decision, even after the initial reason vanishes.

tives and friends out for a drive makes potential ownership a matter of public record, draws attention to the car's many benefits, and increases feelings of ownership, all of which make the customer's commitment to the car even stronger. Sales personnel refer to this kind of tactic as "the puppy dog close:" Most people who spend time with a puppy find it hard to return it to the pet store.

Thus, the norm of social commitment, like the norm of reciprocity, is intended to foster group cohesion and support, but it can sometimes serve antisocial ends. We can reap the benefits of conservation as our heating bills decline, or we can suffer the consequences when we pay more than we need to for a new car. This double-edged quality is an inherent attribute of social norms, as it is of other cognitive representations, such as stereotypes and biased self-perceptions. But perhaps nowhere is the tension between possible societal good and the potential for harm more salient than in the case of the norm we discuss next, that of obedience to authority.

The Norm of Obedience: Submitting to Authority

For millions of people around the world, the war-crimes trial of Adolf Eichmann raised deep questions about human nature (Arendt, 1965). As one of Hitler's top officials during the Second World War, Eichmann sent millions of European Jews, Gypsies, homosexuals, Communists, mental patients, and Christian Scientists to their deaths in Nazi concentration camps. To his Israeli captors and to the worldwide audience, Eichmann's behavior seemed incomprehensibly evil. Surely such monstrous behavior reflects total depravity, extreme cruelty, or pathological hatred.

Yet, like countless people who have slaughtered others in the line of "duty," Eichmann appeared quite normal, even boring. He described himself as a good family man who had lived quite blamelessly before the rise of the Nazi regime. He said he had nothing in particular against the Jews. Over and over again, he claimed he was "just following orders." Eichmann's defense did not save his life: He was found guilty and hanged for crimes against the Jewish people and humanity. But genocidal policies are still with us today, and so the questions about human nature raised by Eichmann's actions and his trial still linger. Is torture or murder something that any of us might do on command?

Among those fascinated by the trial was the North American social psychologist Stanley Milgram. A firm believer in cultural differences, Milgram doubted that behavior like Eichmann's could occur in cultures where rugged individualism and independence were valued. He believed that members of such cultures would resist group pressure to obey orders, especially if those orders meant that someone else would get hurt. Once he had finalized the procedures for a control condition—a situation in which participants were merely instructed to harm another without any group pressure to do so—Milgram planned to test his hypotheses about conformity and obedience in many different countries. But the startling responses of participants in this control condition put Milgram's plans on hold. Understanding when and why people obeyed authority, even if doing so harmed others, became Milgram's main concern, and his findings became perhaps the best known and most controversial in social psychology.

Milgram's Studies of Obedience

In one of the best-known experiments in psychology, people obeyed orders to deliver shocks to an unwilling and clearly suffering victim. They obeyed these orders even though they were not forced to do so.

■ **The victim in Milgram's experiment.** In a simple experiment with powerful implications, Stanley Milgram studied obedience by asking participants acting as "teachers" to deliver electric shocks to a "learner," shown here being fitted with electrodes and strapped into a chair. The results of the experiment demonstrated the often startling power of widely accepted social norms on behavior.

Using advertisements in a New Haven, Connecticut, newspaper, Milgram recruited men from all walks of life to participate in his experiment in return for a small payment. When each volunteer arrived in the laboratory on the Yale University campus, he was introduced to a middle-aged man, a confederate pretending to be another participant. The experimenter explained that the purpose of the study was to demonstrate the effects of punishment on learning, and he said that one of the participants would serve as teacher and the other as the learner for the session. A rigged drawing assigned the real participant to the role of teacher. His job was to teach the pupil word pairs and to punish any incorrect response by delivering an electric shock to the pupil's wrist. As the teacher watched, the pupil was strapped without protest into a chair in an adjoining room and electrodes were taped to his wrist. To "test the equipment," the experimenter gave the teacher a low-voltage shock, enabling him to experience the small, mildly unpleasant feeling that the learner would be subjected to in the early stages of the experiment.

Back in the experimental room, the experimenter explained the operation of the equipment. To deliver a shock, the teacher merely had to flick one of the switches on the shock generator. There were 30 switches, in 15-volt increments ranging from 15 volts (labeled "slight shock") to 450 volts (ominously marked only with *XXX*). The teacher was to start with the lowest level of shock and move to the next higher level with each mistake. The shocks may be "painful," the experimenter said, "but do not cause permanent tissue damage." The experimenter stood beside the teacher as the experiment began.

The pupil's initial mistakes were met with only low levels of shock. But as incorrect responses mounted, so did the voltage. Soon, grunts of pain came from the pupil's room, but he continued trying to learn the word pairs. At this stage, the teachers typically showed visible signs of distress and tried to stop the experiment. But the experimenter was unrelenting, repeating only that the teacher must continue. Finally, at the 300-volt level, the learner pounded on the wall in protest and refused to answer further questions. Most teachers sighed with relief at this point, believing the experiment was over. Instead, the experimenter announced that silence was to be considered an incorrect answer and punished. Teachers' protests were met with the response: "The experiment requires that you continue." As the shocks increased and the learner pounded ever more feebly on the wall, the experimenter urged the teacher onward, saying, "You have no choice, you must go on." Finally, even the pounding stopped. Anguished teachers typically raised the possibility of injury, but the experimenter never wavered, insisting, "The responsibility is mine. Please continue."

■ **Obedience rules.** Even when the learner's pain and distress were obvious, teachers often went along with the experimenter's implacable demands that they continue giving shocks. Why did so many people obey?

As is now widely known, most of the participants did continue. In one study, 68% of them delivered shocks all the way to the 450-volt level (Milgram, 1963). Far from demonstrating that ordinary people would resist the dictates of authority, the experiment showed the opposite. The results astounded scientists and nonscientists alike. When Milgram described his experimental procedure to middle-class adults, college students, and psychiatrists, most guessed that only a few people in a thousand would obey the experimenter to the end. Yet more than two thirds of the participants agreed to perform actions they found repulsive.

Attempting to Explain Obedience: Was It the Time, the Place, the People?

The destructive obedience of Milgram's participants was not due to personality defects, hard-hearted unconcern about the victim, or suspicion that the experiment was rigged. In fact, obedience in nonexperimental settings can be just as high, and authorities command as much obedience in recent studies as they did 40 years ago in Milgram's experiments.

Why did so many people obey? Were Milgram's participants particularly heartless individuals, hardened urbanites too calloused to care for others? Could they have seen through the deception and realized that no shocks were actually delivered? These explanations seem implausible in the face of the reactions of the participants themselves. Milgram's teachers experienced extraordinary distress as the experiment progressed. They trembled, pleaded to be allowed to stop, muttered to themselves, stuttered when they spoke, laughed nervously, dug their nails into their flesh, and offered to take the learner's place. Clearly, they fully believed that the shocks were real, and they cared deeply about the learner's suffering.

In fact, the potential harm to the hapless participants in Milgram's experiments attracted severe ethical criticism when the results were published (Baumrind, 1964). The critics first pointed to the participants' severe distress, asking whether the trauma of the experience could have lasting aftereffects—effects that could not be dissipated by a postexperimental debriefing. They also raised questions about the debriefing itself. What would be the effect on people of realizing that they had been thoroughly hoaxed and that they were capable of committing great harm when told to? Critics questioned whether these insights might decrease the participants' trust in others or their self-esteem (Baumrind, 1964; Schlenker & Forsyth, 1977).

Milgram (1964, 1977) responded by arguing that the debriefing was carefully and sensitively conducted. Participants appeared greatly relieved (rather than upset) upon realizing the true nature of the experiment, and they came to believe the research purpose was worthwhile. In a follow-up questionnaire sent to participants some months after their participation, 84% reported positive feelings about their participation, 15% reported neutral feelings, and only 1.3% described negative feelings. Despite these seemingly reassuring findings, the distress experienced by Milgram's participants was one impetus for the introduction of "informed consent" procedures in psychological experimentation. Participants must now be given enough information about an experiment so that they can make an informed decision about participation.

The nature and purpose of informed consent were discussed in chapter 2, page 51.

The fact that Milgram's participants felt so badly about the punishments they believed they were inflicting makes it unlikely that they obeyed because they were cruel or heartless. Nor can their behavior be explained by their status as adult males in one particular society. Milgram's procedure has since been replicated in several different countries with women as well as men, and children as well as adults, in the role of teacher (Askenasy, 1978; V. L. Hamilton & Sanders, 1992, 1995; Meeus & Raaijmakers, 1986; Shanab & Yahra, 1977). Most participants expressed considerable distress at what they were asked to do, yet most also continued to obey.

If high levels of obedience cannot be attributed to the participants' character, could it be a consequence of the nature of the experimental setting itself? Perhaps people who feel that obedience is appropriate in a protected laboratory environment would never dream of carrying out harmful orders in settings outside the laboratory. Unfortunately, obedience to authority occurs in many other settings.

☐ **OBEDIENCE IN MEDICAL SETTINGS.** In most medical settings, unquestioning obedience to the physician is the normal state of affairs. No one overrules the doctor—not the patient, not nurses, and not interns. Doctors have been accused of attempting to maintain this power differential by insisting on giving the orders even when nurses know more about the case than they do (Ashley, 1976; L. Stein, 1967). What happens, then, when doctors make mistakes? Does anyone question them?

To find out, researchers looked at nurses' responses when a "doctor" gave an unreasonable order (Hofling, Brotzman, Dalrymple, Graves, & Pierce, 1966). The "physician" phoned 22 different nurses' stations at different hospitals, identifying himself as a physician at the hospital. He instructed the nurse, who was alone at the station, to deliver 20 milligrams of the drug Astrogen to a specific patient. Such an instruction violated hospital policy in several ways. Prescriptions were supposed to be given in person, not over the phone. The drug had not been cleared for use on the particular ward. The requested dosage was twice the maximum listed on the container. Finally, the "doctor" giving the order was unknown to the nurse. Despite all these red flags, all but one of the nurses immediately prepared to obey. The norm of obedience overpowered their considerable medical training. No wonder, then, that the number of American patients dying from medication errors continues to grow. Many researchers attribute such problems largely to the unquestioning deference to authority that doctors demand and nurses accept (David & Cohen, 1981; Lesar & others, 1997).

Hospitals are not the only other settings in which obedience is the norm. In fact, many recent studies indicate that "organizational obedience"—obedience that occurs in bureaucratic hierarchical organizations—may occur at even higher levels than suggested by Milgram's studies. In one study, for example, 77% of the students who were playing the role of board members advocated the continued marketing of a potentially dangerous drug if they believed that the chairman of the board, to whom they were accountable, favored this decision (Brief, Dukerich, & Doran, 1991). In another, North American business students derogated the credentials of qualified African-American job applicants and recommended against interviewing them, if given "instructions from the company's president" that favored giving the job to a White American (Brief, Buttram, Elliott, Reizenstein, & McCline, 1995). And in a series of more than 19 experiments in which Dutch participants were ordered to interfere with the performance of another person who was interviewing for an important job, Wim Meeus and Quinten Raaijmakers (1986, 1987) found greater obedience than comparable conditions produced in the Milgram experiment. These findings show that obedience to authority is just as likely today as it was 40 years ago; people were not just more obedient "back then." All in all, the research record indicates that obedience to authority can occur regardless of participant, culture, setting, or time: Milgram's results cannot be explained away by the time, the place, or the people involved.

The Norm of Obedience to Authority

The obligation to obey a legitimate authority figure invoked by the norm of obedience had a powerful effect on behavior in Milgram's experiment. Conditions that decreased the accessibility of the obedience norm or increased attention to other norms (such as social responsibility) also decreased obedience.

If none of these factors (personality, setting, culture, or time) can explain the obedience Milgram found, what does? When he observed participants' responses to the systematic manipulation of various features of the experimental procedure, Milgram became increasingly convinced that the explanation lay in the power of the social situation to activate a norm of obedience (Milgram, 1963, 1974). The **norm of obedience to authority** is the shared view that people should obey commands given by a person with legitimate authority. "Legitimate" and "authority" are important parts of this definition. *Legitimacy* derives from the group: The group endows the authority figure with the might and right to give orders, and the group assigns to its members the responsibility of obeying. *Authority* derives from status, not from any particular person. When a private salutes a major in the army, for example, he or she is saluting the senior officer's rank, a gesture symbolizing the authority the major holds over the private.

Obedience to authority is sometimes enforced, as when military courts stand ready to enforce obedience to authoritative orders. Most often, however, obedience is motivated by private feelings of obligation, as was the case in Milgram's experiment. The experimenter represented legitimate authority, and his presence activated the norm of obedience; that is, participants believed the experimenter had the legitimate right to tell them what to do and that they had an equal duty to obey him. Several of Milgram's experimental variations support this explanation.

AUTHORITY MUST BE LEGITIMATE. In one experiment, Milgram put a confederate posing as a participant in the experimenter's role. The experimenter then left the room. With the authority figure gone, the results were dramatically different from those in the original experiment. Teachers now ignored the confederate and refused to deliver the shocks. When the confederate feigned disgust and tried to deliver the shocks himself, the teachers protested vigorously. Some went so far as to unplug the shock generator so it could not be used. Similar results were found in the study of obedience in

Norm of obedience to authority. The shared view that people should obey those with legitimate authority.

FIGURE 10.6 Conditions for obedience

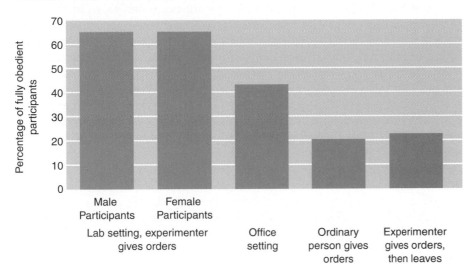

■ By changing experimental conditions to make the norm of obedience more or less accessible, Milgram showed the power of the norm on behavior. In the laboratory, in the presence of the authoritative experimenter, fully 65% of men and women followed his orders. But in conditions that reduced the salience of the norm—such as a less "official" location, or a nonlegitimate authority giving orders, or the absence of any authority figure—obedience was reduced. (Data from Milgram, 1974.)

which Dutch participants were ordered to harass an applicant being interviewed for an important job. In a control condition in which the experimenter was absent, not a single participant obeyed. But when the experimenter was present and ordered participants to follow instructions, 92% succeeded in ruining the candidate's chances of getting the job (Meeus & Raaijmakers, 1986).

In these experiments, the authority figure was easy to recognize, as is the case in many real-life situations. Medical doctors wear white lab coats and sling stethoscopes around their necks; police officers, firefighters, and paramedics wear uniforms and identification badges. These symbols are usually enough to activate the norm of obedience to authority. In one experiment demonstrating the power of a uniform, a "stranger"—actually an experimental confederate—asked passersby on a busy city street to comply with an unusual request, for example, to pick up garbage or move to the other side of a bus-stop sign (Bickman, 1974). Half the time, the stranger wore ordinary clothes; the rest of the time he wore a security guard's uniform. Clothes made the authority figure: Many more people did his bidding when he was dressed in a uniform than when he wore street clothes. To test the limits of the power of an authority figure, the confederate approached passersby, pointed to a man about 50 feet away, demanded that they give him a dime for a parking meter, and then turned and *walked away*. Despite the fact that he was out of sight, 92% of the pedestrians followed his orders when he was wearing a uniform, compared with 49% when he was wearing street clothes.

It should not come as a surprise that Milgram's experimenter wore a white lab coat, embodying the authority of the expert research scientist pursuing knowledge. Whether by presence or by uniform, the more salient the authority figure, the more likely people are to obey, as can be seen in Figure 10.6.

AUTHORITY MUST ACCEPT RESPONSIBILITY. Recall that when some of the "teachers" in Milgram's experiments had qualms about continuing, the experimenter reminded them that he took full responsibility, and this was often enough to maintain obedience. When all responsibility is ceded to the authority, people enter what Milgram called *the agentic state:* They see themselves as merely the agent of the authority figure. When this displacement of responsibility occurs, people don't think of themselves as agents of their own action, and thus, the self-monitoring mechanisms of trying to match internal or external standards or guides for behavior are short-circuited (Bandura, Barbaranelli, Caprara, & Pastorelli, 1996). Responsibility can sometimes be diffused as well, as when authorities divide reprehensible behavior into small subtasks, each of which may be performed by a different person and each of which may in and of itself seem harmless (Kelman, 1973). When responsibility is displaced or diffused, people ignore the possibility that they could or should control their own behavior. In fact, the assumption of responsibility is crucial to the power of the authority figure. Both people who obey and observers who view obedient subordinates attribute responsibility for obedience to the authority figure (V. L. Hamilton & Sanders, 1995; Meeus & Raaijmakers, 1995). Only when participants believe that they, not the authority, are responsible for their actions does obedience drop off (Tilker, 1970).

Individuals differ in the extent to which they abdicate responsibility when faced with orders from an authority figure. Some individuals believe that citizens owe legitimate authorities unquestioning obedience if society is to function effectively: These individuals deny that subordinates have responsibility for the effects of orders they carry out. In contrast, other people believe that individuals never give up the responsibility to control their own behavior (Kelman & Lawrence, 1972). Table 10.1 shows some of the kinds of statements these two types of people endorse. The idea that individuals always maintain the right and duty to refuse an illegal order is part of the military code of conduct: Although soldiers are ordinarily expected to obey superior's orders, they are required to resist orders that are "manifestly illegal" or that a reasonable person would know to be illegal (Department of the Army, 1956).

THE NORM OF OBEDIENCE MUST BE ACCESSIBLE. As fully socialized members of society, Milgram's participants initially accepted without question their

---

TABLE 10.1. Individual Differences in Assertion of Responsibility

1. I feel obligated to protest both vigorously and publicly if the government does something that is morally wrong.
2. If you have doubts about an official order, the best thing is to do what is required of you, so you will stay out of trouble.
3. The most valuable contribution a citizen can make is to maintain an active and questioning approach toward government policies.
4. One reason for supporting the U.S. government is that anarchy will result if there are too many critics.

NOTE: People differ in the extent to which they believe that individuals maintain personal responsibility when an authority figure orders them to do something. Responsibility asserters tend to agree with items like 1 and 3 and to disagree with items like 2 and 4. In contrast, responsibility deniers agree with items such as 2 and 4 and disagree with 1 and 3. Many more than four items would be used in a real test of such differences.

Source: From *Crimes of obedience: Toward a social psychology of authority and responsibility* by H. C. Kelman & V. L. Hamilton, 1989, New Haven, CT: Yale University Press.

obligation to administer mild shocks. But when events took a turn for the worse, many of them began to express concern about the victim and about their role in his suffering. As we saw in chapter 9, such uncertainty usually causes people to question current interpretations of reality and the norms based on them. But the experimenter quashed the teachers' protests, focusing implacably on the norm of legitimate authority. His escalating prompts—"You must continue," "The experiment requires that you continue," "You have no choice"—made obedience seem an appropriate response to the situation. His calm confidence in the face of both the teachers' indecision and the learner's apparent suffering further reinforced the idea that obedience was typical, normal, and expected behavior. By insisting on only one interpretation of the situation, the experimenter focused the participants exclusively on the norm of obedience. With no social support for alternative interpretations of events, most participants fell into line, following the experimenter's directions. As you will soon see, social support can make a difference in resisting normative pressures to obey.

OTHER NORMS MUST BE LESS ACCESSIBLE. When you think about how distressed the teachers felt, even as they obeyed, it becomes clear that these people were experiencing a normative conflict. Milgram may have been playing on their commitment to the norm of obedience, but they could not have been unaware of the norm of social responsibility, which exhorts us to help, not harm, others—especially those in need. In fact, Milgram deliberately provoked the conflict when, for example, he had the pupil cry out and bang on the wall in distress. Knowing that they should have gone to the pupil's aid, teachers agonized over the appropriate behavior. In most of the experimental variations, Milgram tipped the balance in favor of the norm of obedience.

Wondering what would happen if alternative norms were made accessible, Milgram reduced the physical distance between the teacher and the pupil. He reasoned that this would increase the accessibility of the norm of social responsibility as the pupil's suffering was brought "up close and personal" (see Figure 10.7). And it did. When the learner and the teacher were

FIGURE 10.7 Undermining obedience by making incompatible norms salient

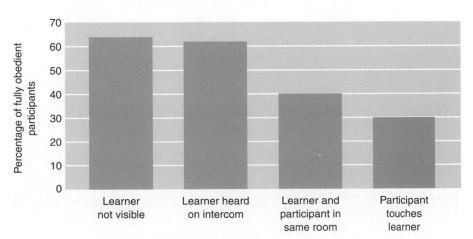

■ The norm governing obedience to legitimate authority held tremendous sway in Milgram's experimental situation. But it was not the only norm brought into play in the situation. When experimental variations focused participants' attention on the suffering of the learner, the norm of social responsibility—our obligation to give aid to those who need it—reduced the level of obedience. (Data from Milgram, 1974.)

in the same room, only 40% of participants obeyed. As Milgram gradually brought teacher and pupil closer together, the pupil's suffering became less avoidable and obedience decreased.

Milgram's experiment mimicked life: It is easier to drop a bomb from a plane than to kill a person with a bayonet, and it is easier to shuffle papers decreeing a death than to actually torture or kill someone (Silver & Geller, 1978). The same Eichmann who sat in his office dispassionately consigning people to their deaths reportedly was sickened when he was actually forced to tour the concentration camps.

From Experimental Obedience to Social Atrocities

Outside the laboratory, norms like the obligation to obey orders are often reinforced by other social-psychological processes such as a gradual entrapment into acts of escalating violence, self-justification and blaming the victim, and intergroup hatred and hostility. In these instances, obedience becomes destructive, and norms are used to justify inhumane treatment.

Milgram's research on obedience was provoked by the horrors of the Holocaust. But his findings do not offer a complete explanation for the kinds of brutality and cruelty that characterize social atrocities. His research, and many subsequent studies, confirm the powerful effects that adherence to norms like obedience to authority can have on our behavior and its potential for eliciting antisocial, as well as prosocial acts. Powerful as it is, the norm of obedience cannot alone account for the kind of destructive behavior that occurs in such dark moments in human history. In fact, many social-psychological processes combine with destructive obedience to produce atrocities like the Nazi extermination of Jews, the Tiananmen Square massacre, the ethnic cleansing policies in Bosnia and Kosovo, the Pinochet reign

■ **Obedience and atrocities.** Protestors stand over the bodies of students slaughtered in China's 1989 Tiananmen Square massacre. Fearful of social upheaval when students demanded rights of free speech, the Chinese government ordered soldiers to forcibly put down the demonstration. The power of obedience led young soldiers to carry out these orders and murder students exactly their own age.

of terror in Chile, sanctioned genocide in Cambodia, and the My Lai massacre ordered by U.S. commanders in the Vietnam War.

ESCALATION, ENTRAPMENT, AND ROUTINIZATION. As powerful as the norm of obedience to authority is, other aspects of the situation in which the norm was invoked also contributed to the destructive behavior of Milgram's participants. The gradually escalating sequential nature of the teacher's task also helped bind the participants to continuing obedience (S. J. Gilbert, 1981). The process worked like this. First, the norm of social commitment was used against the participants: They were low-balled. They unwittingly committed to a course of action that initially seemed quite benign; the shocks were quite weak and were intended to improve learning. Participants did not know that the learner would make so many mistakes that the shocks would become very strong. Second, the participants' initial compliance confirmed in their own minds the experimenter's right and authority to direct their actions. Having acknowledged the experimenter as a legitimate authority, participants found it increasingly difficult to refuse his gradually escalating demands. Third, participants' initial obedience to the early small requests left them with no legitimate basis to refuse the larger requests. When the command to give a 45-volt shock has been obeyed, why should a command to give a 60-volt shock be disobeyed?

In this way, participants in obedience experiments, and many others who commit crimes of politically and socially sanctioned evil, are led from the acceptable to the unthinkable, gradually (Kelman & Hamilton, 1989; Staub, 1989). At the extreme, repetition of evil acts, especially in the context of the agentic state, becomes routine, and, as the perpetrator becomes more deeply entrapped, almost mundane.

SELF-JUSTIFICATION AND BLAMING THE VICTIM. As behavior becomes more and more destructive, people may experience a state of cognitive dissonance. They undoubtedly see themselves as kind, caring, decent people, as we are all motivated to view ourselves. But as the inconsistency between their self-concept and their actual harmful behavior increases, they must also experience an unpleasant arousal and an increasing motivation to reduce that arousal. With little hope of reconciling these inconsistencies through self-deception—the harmful nature of their actions is quite clear—people are often motivated to provide other justifications for their behavior. They may focus on the positive implications of being a reliable and obedient agent or on the superior knowledge and wisdom of the authority, or they may reconstrue the activity as promoting a positive goal. Many acts of aggression are justified in terms of defending honor and reputation, for example (D. Cohen & Nisbett, 1994). Such moral justifications are often cloaked in euphemistic language, such as "the final solution" or "ethnic cleansing" (Bandura and others, 1996). Unfortunately, of course, any of these efforts at reconciliation maintain people's tendency to obey.

To remind yourself of the nature and consequences of cognitive dissonance, refer to chapter 8, pages 299 to 311.

Individuals who obey harmful orders sometimes react with anger, dislike, and hostility toward the authority figure that directed their behavior (M. P. Johnson & Ewens, 1971). However, people are less likely to react against the authority when they accept obedience as legitimate. More probable, and far more chilling in its consequences, is the response of *blaming the victim:* People come to believe that those being hurt somehow deserve to be punished. In fact, derogating the victim is a common means of reducing dissonance about one's role in another person's suffering (Perry, Williard, & Perry, 1990). As we saw in chapter 4, people tend to attribute their own behavior to situational factors, especially if they behave badly. The tendency to blame victims stems from a widely held belief in a "just world," the idea that the universe is a just and orderly place where people "get what they deserve" (Lerner, 1980). Such "just world" beliefs prompt thoughts that victims must in some way have "asked for trouble," provoked it, or brought it on themselves in some way (Lerner & Miller, 1978). Of course, such beliefs are designed to protect the believer: If the world is not a just place, anyone could fall victim to the cruel twists of fate.

The tendency to blame the victim seems strongest when we ourselves are the instrument of another person's pain. Indeed, Milgram (1974) reported that many of his participants, after delivering the maximum amount of shock, cruelly criticized the pupil with comments like "He was so stupid and stubborn, he deserved to get shocked." As Milgram noted, "Once having acted against the victim, these subjects found it necessary to view him as an unworthy individual whose punishment was made inevitable by his own deficiencies of intellect and character" (p. 10). Blaming the victim may be the most potentially dangerous consequence of carrying out destructive orders. As it occurs, the target—once an innocent victim harmed only reluctantly—becomes a person deserving of abuse.

HOSTILITY TO AND DEVALUATION OF OUT-GROUPS. Massacres, atrocities, torture, and extermination often take place in a context of virulent hatred and intergroup hostility. This hatred leads to moral exclusion, in which the victims are so dehumanized that norms like social reciprocity, responsibility, and commitment no longer seem to apply. The usual protections for those suffering and the aggressor's usual inhibitions seem to fall by the wayside (Bandura and others, 1996; Staub, 1989). In a world where "ethnic cleansing" and "genetic purity" become justifications for acts of savagery, repression, and brutality, we must be especially vigilant about the kinds of intergroup contexts that allow such ideas first to germinate, and then to flourish.

Thus many social-psychological processes combine to set the stage for social atrocities. Obedience to authorities, the entrapment that results from increasingly inhumane acts, and the tendency to justify one's own and one's group's actions can combine to cause individuals to commit acts of stunning evil (Kelman, 1973; Staub, 1989).

Normative Trade-Offs: The Pluses and Minuses of Obedience

Like all norms, the obligation to obey authority figures can be used for good or evil purposes.

Although the norm of obedience can be exploited for great evil, acceptance of legitimate authority is essential for the optimal functioning of society. Almost every group, whether an informal group of friends or a complex society, develops roles and functions that give some members authority over others. Imagine what would happen if people made individual and inde-

The nature and origins of just world beliefs were discussed in chapter 5, page 176.

Chapter 6, especially pages 224 to 227, described the often appalling consequences of morally excluding an outgroup.

pendent decisions about which side of the road they would drive on, what language they would speak, whether they would contribute to the defense of their group, or what principles of justice they would uphold. As Milgram points out, obeying legitimate authority has many advantages for every individual.

Perhaps the most important lesson we can take away from Milgram's studies is just how hard it is to resist the power of deeply ingrained and widely shared norms. Indeed, his findings make clear the often unexpected and unanticipated power of social situations. Obedience works well most of the time and, for that reason, resisting authority is very difficult. Neither Milgram himself nor any of those who read descriptions of his studies had any idea of the degree of obedience he would find. You may find it difficult to imagine that under similar circumstances you could act the same way Milgram's participants did. Yet the social-psychological processes invoked in this situation—activation of the norm of obedience, exclusion of other norms that might guide behavior, gradual commitment to a particular course of behavior, and justification of it—proved to be an overpowering combination.

Rebellion and Resistance: Fighting Back

An ad appearing in the newspapers of a small southeastern Michigan town sought paid participants for "market research involving group discussion of community standards" (Gamson, Fireman, & Rytina, 1982). Those who responded met in groups of nine with the representatives of Manufacturer's Human Relations Consultants, Inc. (MHRC) at a local Holiday Inn. The coordinator, a young man in a business suit, explained that MHRC was conducting research for a major oil company involved in legal action against the manager of a local gas station. To give the court a picture of "community standards"—what local people believed to be right and wrong—MHRC would videotape the group while it discussed various issues relevant to the case. After signing a consent form and being paid for their participation, participants learned that the oil company had terminated the manager because he was living with a woman to whom he was not married. The company claimed that this behavior offended community standards. For his part, the manager stated that his private life was none of the company's business, and that the company had sent investigators after him because he had criticized their pricing policies in a televised interview. After starting the video camera, the coordinator instructed the group to discuss the manager's behavior and then left the room for 5 minutes.

When the coordinator returned, he stopped the camera and gave the group a second discussion topic: Would they be reluctant to do business with the manager because of his lifestyle? This time, he asked three of the nine group members to take a stand against the manager's behavior. Two more filming sessions followed: In the first, three additional people were asked to criticize the manager's behavior, and in the last, all nine of the participants were asked to take a stand against the manager. Participants were then given an affidavit to sign, permitting MHRC to edit the videotape and use it in court. Only then were participants free to leave. As you may have guessed by now, this was a research study, conducted by William Gamson and his colleagues.

How do you think participants responded? On the basis of Milgram's findings, we might expect them to obey the researchers' instructions about what to discuss and what position to take. But they didn't. Only 1 of the 33 groups of participants in the study allowed the procedure to be completed. In all the other cases, group members challenged the coordinator's authority to make them act in a blatantly unfair and potentially harmful manner. Rather than attacking the manager as instructed, some participants remained silent during the videotaping sessions. When they were not openly defying the coordinator—refusing to participate or to sign the final affidavit—they were arguing with him, calling into question the rationale and justification for the procedure. In 25 of the 33 groups, a majority of members refused to sign the final affidavit. Nine groups threatened action against MHRC, such as publicizing the abuse in the local newspaper. Even in the 8 groups in which most people signed, participants refused to cooperate with some parts of the procedure.

Why were the participants in this study able to take a stand, while Milgram's participants seemed unable to resist the norm of obedience to authority? By examining how groups that rebelled differed from those that did not, Gamson and his colleagues found that three processes—reactance, systematic processing, and using norms against norms—led to resistance rather than capitulation.

Reactance: Enough Is Enough

> People can resist being manipulated by norms. People fight against threats to freedom of action when norms are not privately accepted or seen as appropriate.

Look at the *Calvin and Hobbes* cartoon on the next page! If you've just done so, you've seen Calvin illustrate reactance. But if you decided you would just keep reading for a while before looking at the cartoon, then you just demonstrated reactance yourself. People often respond to attempts to limit their choice with **reactance,** a desire to restore threatened freedom of action (Brehm, 1966). Reactance is common when people lose the opportunity to choose goods, services, or products. Banning a book or a recording in one part of the country ensures record-breaking sales elsewhere; reports that a movie is censored abroad is a sure-fire boost to domestic box office receipts. Therapists find that highly reactant clients respond poorly to advice such as "Try not to think about it!" (Dowd and others, 1988; A. E. Kelley & Nauta, 1997). Warning labels (WARNING: "The U.S. Surgeon General has determined that eating high fat products increases your risk of heart attack") on familiar products can sometimes make people want to try them more rather than less (Bushman, 1998). And every parent knows that the best strategy is sometimes "reverse psychology": telling children to stay in the house when you really want them to choose to go outside to play.

Heavy-handed social pressure often raises the red flag of reactance. It certainly did so in the MHRC study. Some individuals, feeling that their behavioral freedom was being threatened, simply walked out of the experiment. Reactance also explains people's anger when they feel unfairly beholden to someone else—unsolicited favors make it difficult to refuse to do something in return. In fact, some people avoid accepting favors from others, simply to ward off the possibility that someone will try to "cash in" on reci-

Reactance. The motive to protect or restore a threatened sense of behavioral freedom.

Calvin and Hobbes by Bill Watterson

procity (Eisenberger, Cotterell, & Marvel, 1987; M. S. Greenberg & Westcott, 1983). And, like Calvin and the MHRC participants, people often choose to do just the opposite of what they are requested if they feel their personal freedoms are being restricted by orders or influence.

Why do people respond with reactance to a simple request but not to an order to shock another person? In this case, the answer has to do with perceptions of legitimacy of authority. When normative pressure is perceived to be inappropriate or illegitimate, reactance is triggered. In Milgram's experiments, the experimenter was perceived to be a legitimate authority. In the MHRC study, however, some participants disputed the market consultant's right to tell them what they should say and do. In such cases, reactance eventually pushes us to resist and say "Enough is enough."

Unfortunately, however, reactance is unlikely to help with resistance to norms that we accept as legitimate and appropriate in the situation. We privately accept most norms that are used against us, even when they are used with a heavy hand. We acknowledge their appropriateness and relevance to be applied in the situation. The participants in Milgram's study struggled because norms they endorsed and accepted were applied in a way that seemed legitimate, at least at first. If a norm is seen as right and proper, its imposition is not seen as an infringement on our freedom. Such norms bypass the reactance aroused by inappropriate threats to our freedom.

Systematic Processing: Thinking Things Through

One of the best defenses against normative pressure is to think things through to make sure that a proffered norm is actually applicable.

By now you may not be surprised to learn that thinking is one of your best defenses against normative pressure. During the breaks in which the experimenter left the room, the participants in the MHRC study were given the opportunity to step back from the situation and consider what was going on, and many of them realized that unfair normative pressures were being applied. Thinking things through is not always easy, of course. Situations involving normative pressure often create anxiety and stress, and as anxiety mounts, we may be unable to think clearly. To avoid undue pressure, it's of-

Recall that systematic processing played the same role in reducing the impact of superficial cues automatically activated in persuasion settings (chapter 7, pages 267 to 268).

ten a good idea to try to give yourself a "cooling off" period before you make a commitment, reciprocate a favor, or obey an order. Even then, systematic thinking about the situation is important. The following strategies can help you fend off unfair normative pressure.

1. *Question how norms are being used.* Recognizing how norms operate and how they can be used against you is a good starting point. When you realize that a norm is being used against you, it loses its power (Cialdini, 1993). In fact, explicitly drawing attention to the other side's questionable tactics helps prevent their recurrence (R. Fisher & Ury, 1981). So if you believe you are being low-balled, let the culprit know you understand the tactic. By doing so, you may embarrass the other person and encourage forthright negotiation. Even more important, you will free yourself from forced feelings of obligation. Realizing that "the boss's" change in the terms of a sale is part of a low-ball plan frees you from the norm of social commitment: The agreement the salesperson made with you was just part of a strategy, not an honest deal. Questioning the way a norm is being used is also a good tactic when you are feeling obligated as much by the norm of obedience as by the person giving orders. At that point, try considering whether this norm is being used appropriately or not. In fact, the now-widespread knowledge about the results of Milgram's obedience studies might decrease the proportion of people who would obey if similar studies were carried out today (S. J. Sherman, 1980). Thus, the very knowledge of how people are effectively influenced by norms is also the most effective defense against that influence.

2. *Question claims about relationships.* You do not need to automatically accept another person's claim regarding his or her relationship with you. A good defense is questioning that claim. Does the person giving orders really have the authority to command you? Maybe not. Is the salesperson really your ally and advocate, fighting against an intractable "boss" who won't approve the deal? Probably not. And make sure that you are both abiding by the same rules of normative behavior. As part of the low-ball tactic, the salesperson often claims to be unable to make the deal without consulting the boss. This setup means that you have the power to make concessions, but the other person does not. As the old saying goes, "What's mine is mine; what's yours is negotiable!" In cases like this, insist on dealing directly with the person who can make a binding agreement (R. Fisher & Ury, 1981).

3. *Question others' views of the situation.* One of the most important lessons that social psychology can teach is that all situations are open to multiple interpretations. Your definition of what happened may be just as valid as the other person's. Did she really do you a favor? Do you really owe one in return? Don't automatically accept her version of "the facts"; instead, suggest that all assertions be objectively and independently verified before they become part of "the deal." And before buying into someone else's view of how you should behave, consider all the norms and attitudes that might be relevant. Balance such norms as obedience and social commitment against social responsibility.

The willingness of participants in the MHRC study to question others' views of the situation was central to their successful resistance. The coordinator brought two norms to bear on group members: the norm of legitimate obedience to authority and the norm of social commitment. If group members accepted the coordinator's legitimacy and their commitment to participate, they were likely to comply. But if they reinterpreted the coordinator's authority as illegitimate—after all, they were being asked to lie in taped testimony to be shown in court—they were likely to resist. As one participant put it, "I mean, we signed something that said, 'Yes, we're being taped,' but we didn't sign something that said, 'Yes, we're being taped to display something—an opinion—that we may not [agree] with.' " And when the coordinator invoked the norm of commitment, arguing that participants had contractual obligations to fulfill, the groups who rebelled asserted the norm of social responsibility: their obligation to protect the manager.

Remember from chapter 9 that the best group norms grow out of consideration of multiple points of view. If your interpretation of a situation differs from the one being presented, suggest some alternatives. Others may agree with you, or, at the very least, the person trying to influence the group will have to defend his or her interpretation. The sooner you offer an alternative the better, because the longer you buy into the other person's definition of the situation, the harder it will be to resist, and the sooner you suggest a different interpretation, the freer others will feel to resist the social pressure (Gamson and others, 1982; Modigliani & Rochat, 1995).

Using Norms Against Norms

Another effective defense is to use norms against norms: to forge or exploit an alternative consensus that a different course of behavior is the appropriate one.

As you may have noticed, the participants in the MHRC study had potential allies in their resistance, whereas Milgram's participants had to grapple with the experimenter's orders all alone. The presence of others and the opportunity this affords to form and affirm group norms of resistance is the most crucial factor in creating rebellion (Gamson, 1992; B. Simon, 1998). In every MHRC group in which discussion produced a consensus against compliance, group resistance to the coordinator followed. The coordinator's absence during taping sessions gave the group an opportunity to air their doubts and to find out that others felt the same way they did. To help build and strengthen the norm of resistance, participants stressed their shared views and bolstered their solidarity by referring to the group as "we." Consider, for example, the following interaction, when the coordinator applied pressure for agreement, and a group member responded, explicitly addressing him in the name of the group.

> Coordinator: *Apparently you didn't understand. It's necessary for you to talk as if you actually are a member of the community who's offended . . .*
> Member: *I think you didn't understand it. We do understand it and we don't want to go on record, even pretending that we agree with what we're saying. We don't. All three of us feel the same way. I think every one of us feels that way here.* (Gamson and others, 1982, p. 102)

Group support for alternative interpretations of a situation allows members to break free from the power of inappropriate norms in a wide range of situations. In fact, when Milgram provided his otherwise solitary participants with an ally, obedience was dramatically reduced. The shared disobedience apparently constituted a consensus that the norm of obedience did not apply.

Events outside the laboratory have also confirmed that group consensus and social support are crucial to successful rebellion. In a replication of the study in which nurses were given false prescription orders, for example, only 2 of 18 nurses were willing to follow an inappropriate instruction from a doctor—if they were allowed to talk to other nurses first (Rank & Jacobsen, 1977; Redfern, 1979). And group consensus was responsible for one of the few successful protests against the totalitarian policies of the Nazis. In 1943, 2,000 Jewish men and women married to Aryan Germans were incarcerated in an administrative center in the heart of Berlin. An angry group of spouses, mostly women, soon gathered outside the building on the Rosenstrasse, crying out for the prisoners' release. Despite periodic threats of gunfire from armed guards, the group staged the protest day and night for a week, as the crowd grew ever larger. Individual dissent was impossible, but participants reported feeling a deep sense of solidarity and group determination in their protest. Incredibly, the prisoners were finally released when Joseph Goebbels decided that the simplest way to deal with the rebellion was to give in to the obvious will of the masses. At a time when individuals were executed for offenses as minor as telling an anti-Nazi joke, only a collective undertaking had any chance of success (Stoltzfus, 1992). As the historian Michael Walzer observed: "Disobedience . . . is always a collective act" (Walzer, 1970, p. 4).

In terms of cause and cure, destructive obedience is like groupthink. In each case a natural and usually beneficial process—obedience to authority or conformity to a majority—goes awry. You may recall that the way to prevent or cure groupthink is to create conditions that enhance minority influence, especially the presentation of alternatives that promote careful, systematic processing of information. In the same way, the key to the prevention or cure of destructive obedience lies in creating alternatives. In particular, it consists of forming or reaffirming a more appropriate and applicable group norm. Perhaps this is what Thomas Jefferson had in mind when he reminded James Madison that "a little rebellion, now and then, is a good thing, and as necessary in the political world as storms in the physical."

To remind yourself of the nature and causes of groupthink, glance back at chapter 9, pages 358 to 361. And to see how minority influence can help prevent these problems, look back at pages 363 to 368 of that chapter.

Putting It All Together: Multiple Guides for Behavior

Most of the behaviors that social psychologists study are voluntary; that is, people can decide whether to perform them. Of course, we sometimes lack the resources, ability, knowledge, or opportunity to do what we want to do (Ajzen & Madden, 1986). Usually, however, behavior is shaped by the way people define situations and by social influence exerted by others. Thus, how situations are perceived—both by the individual and by his or her groups—is enormously influential in determining what behaviors occur. In chapter 8, we saw how and why individual attitudes—summary evaluations of how a person thinks, feels, and acts toward an attitude object—influence behavior. In this chapter, we have seen how social norms—shared ideas about appropriate ways to think, feel, and act—can exert a powerful effect on behavior. Each of these concepts tells only half the potential story, however. The full story is that attitudes and norms, although they sometimes operate individually to direct behavior, can work together to exert a combined influence on our actions.

Both Attitudes and Norms Influence Behavior

Attitudes and norms often work together to influence behavior, either by triggering behavior directly or by combining to influence intentions to act, which in turn direct behavior. People's perception of control over the behavior is also an important influence on intentions and thus on behavior.

To understand the complexity of influences on human social behavior, we need to keep in mind that attitudes and norms can combine to influence behavior by two different routes. They may trigger behavior directly and almost automatically, or they may operate indirectly, by influencing our intentions to act (Fazio, 1986; Ouellette & Wood, 1998).

THE DIRECT ROUTE. Attitudes and norms can guide behavior rather simply and directly, especially when we do not give matters much systematic thought. At such times, activated attitudes may affect our perceptions of attitude objects, and activated norms may serve as decision heuristics. Together, the attitudes and norms can color our perceptions and influence our behavior in an immediate and automatic way. For example, a person who holds a negative attitude toward an out-group member may be more aware of the out-group member's hostility-provoking characteristics. At the same time, a norm that says "protect the in-group" may be activated, and the attitude and norm together may lead directly to aggressive behavior. Attitudes and norms are especially likely to affect behavior directly when the resources and motivation to process deeply are not available. As Figure 10.8 illustrates, behavior may then follow quite simply and without much thought.

THE INDIRECT ROUTE. Sometimes attitudes and norms combine with other factors in a much more deliberate way as we form our intentions to act and then try to follow through on these intentions. The idea that multiple influences combine in this way to guide behavior is central to the **theory of planned behavior** (Ajzen & Fishbein, 1977, 1980). Like the theory of reasoned action described in chapter 8, the theory of planned behavior suggests that people tend to act in line with their intentions. According to the theory of planned behavior, intentions are a function of three factors: attitudes about the behavior, social norms relevant to the behavior, and perceptions of control over the behavior.

Let us look at each of these factors in turn, using an example. If an expectant mother believes that breastfeeding will protect her baby from disease, and if she feels happy about such closeness with her infant or has nursed previous children successfully, her *attitude* toward breastfeeding is likely to be positive. Social norms would have their influence in such a situation because people wonder what significant reference groups, such as close friends, co-workers, experts, and family, would like or expect to see happen in this situation. If, for example, the mother knows that both her sis-

Theory of planned behavior. The theory that attitudes, social norms, and perceived control combine to influence behavior.

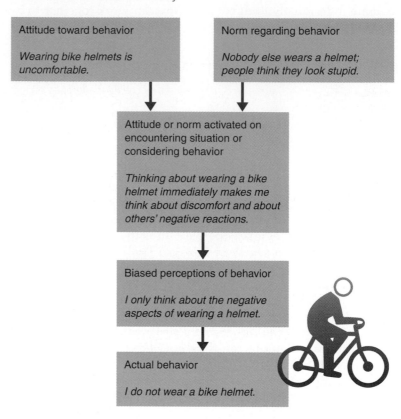

FIGURE 10.8 Attitudes and norms affect behavior automatically

■ When we do not give matters much systematic thought, both attitudes and norms can color our perceptions, influencing behavior in a relatively immediate and automatic way.

In chapter 4, pages 138 to 140, we saw that a sense of control and mastery was an important component of a healthy sense of self. Here we see it is an important prerequisite to effective functioning in the world.

ters chose to nurse their babies, and if most of her friends also have chosen to do so, she will perceive *social norms* as supporting breastfeeding. Finally, the theory of planned behavior suggests that people explicitly take into account their perceived control over behavior: A sense of control is necessary before positive attitudes and supportive norms translate into action. Only if a woman has confidence in her ability to nurse her baby successfully and perceives herself as being able to control the outcome of her actions by her efforts will she perceive herself as having *control* over breastfeeding (Manstead & Van Eekelen, 1998). With attitudes, norms, and perceived control in place, she will form the intention to breastfeed her baby.

Figure 10.9 illustrates the way behavior is influenced by attitudes, perceived norms, and perceptions of control associated with particular behaviors. By carefully measuring these three factors, researchers have used the theory of planned behavior to predict occupational choice, consumer purchasing decisions, blood donations, dietary changes, attendance at religious services, and participation in psychotherapy. In one study of attitudes and norms relating to the use of alcohol, marijuana, and hard drugs, researchers found that both attitudes and norms influenced students' intentions, which in turn influenced their self-reported behavior (Bentler & Speckart, 1979). Consistent with the theory, attitudes and norms influence only the behaviors that people consider to be under their control. If a smoker sees his behavior as due to an uncontrollable addiction, for example, norms and attitudes will have little effect on the behavior (Ajzen & Madden, 1986; Bandura, 1977a).

FIGURE 10.9   Attitudes and norms affect deliberately planned behavior

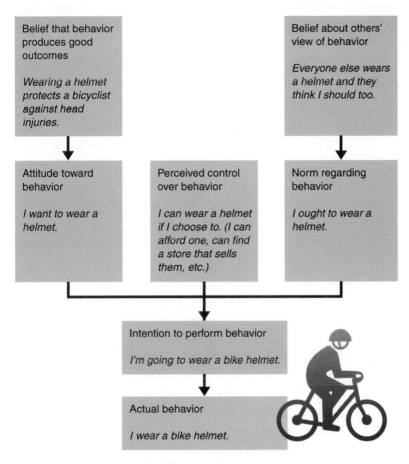

■ According to the theory of planned behavior, people's attitudes, perceived norms, and their perception of their own control combine to produce a considered intention to act. This intention, in turn, guides behavior. (Based on Ajzen & Fishbein, 1977, 1980.)

You may have noticed that in discussing both the direct and more deliberate impact of norms and attitudes on behavior, we have used examples in which attitudes and norms suggest the same action. Although attitudes and norms often converge, this is not always the case, of course. Milgram's participants obviously *hated* what they did, even as they bowed to the norm of obedience. You may earnestly desire a quiet Saturday afternoon by yourself but nevertheless fulfill your social commitment to help your friend move. How do we behave when attitudes and norms are at odds?

When Attitudes and Norms Conflict: Accessibility Determines Influence

Whether attitudes or norms have more influence on behavior depends on their relative accessibility for a particular behavior, in a particular situation, and for a particular person.

Norms, like attitudes, can guide behavior only if they are activated. When a relevant attitude is very accessible, it comes to mind easily, and behavior falls in line with it, as we saw in chapter 8. And, as the research described in this chapter has demonstrated, this fundamental principle applies to norms as well: Activated norms have a powerful influence on behavior. When attitudes and norms disagree, their impact on behavior, whether direct or indirect, depends on their relative accessibility: Whichever is more accessible will have the greater influence on behavior. And the relative accessibility of attitudes and norms depends on a number of different factors.

1. *The behavior in question.* Behaviors differ in the extent to which they are governed by norms and attitudes. In general, normative concerns are more likely to influence behaviors that are performed in public, involve others, and are crucial to the well-being of the group. Most groups, for example, have rules about safeguarding food and water, protecting others' property, controlling aggression and sex, exchanging social resources, keeping social commitments, and respecting authority (Maccoby, 1980). Individual attitudes tend to have more influence over private, individual behaviors: how we wear our hair, the way we shave in the privacy of our own bathrooms, and whether we have a strawberry or a chocolate ice-cream cone.

2. *The person in question.* Individuals differ in the extent to which they are responsive to social norms versus private attitudes. As you might expect, people who identify closely with membership in a particular group are more sensitive to and more influenced by the social norms of that group (Terry & Hogg, 1996; Trafimow & Finlay, 1996). This finding can also be generalized to cultures. Members of collective cultures tend to have group identities that are more accessible, and thus are more typically attuned to group norms (Triandis, 1994; Trafimow, Triandis, & Goto, 1991). People who are highly concerned with what others think of them, like high self-monitors, for example, are also more likely to show behavior that reflects norms rather than attitudes. In one study, Lynn Miller and Joseph Grush (1986) asked 226 students about their attitudes, their perception of social norms, and their actual behaviors at school. These researchers also had their participants complete self-consciousness and self-monitoring scales. They found that students high in self-consciousness (reflecting particular sensitivity to and awareness of their own attitudes) and low in self-monitoring (indicating a relative lack of interest in other people's expectations) showed high consistency between their attitudes and their behavior. In contrast, participants low in self-awareness and high in self-monitoring showed just the opposite pattern: Their behavior corresponded much more highly with social norms. Thus, for some people, attitudes are more likely to guide behavior because these people are constantly aware of their attitudes. For others, social norms are uppermost in their minds and tend to guide their behavior.

3. *The situation in question.* Situational factors can also determine whether norms or attitudes prevail. Attitudes and norms can be manipulated independently, and thus one can be made to predominate over the other (Trafimow & Fishbein, 1994a, 1994b). For example, one study showed that accessibility is a function of who is watching your behavior (Froming, Walker, & Lopyan, 1982). Students completed a questionnaire twice, first giving their own attitudes toward punishment and then indicating what they thought their peers thought, that is, what they perceived as the relevant social norms. Later in the term, they participated as "teachers" in a learning experiment similar to Milgram's, in which they believed they were delivering short electric shocks to a failing "pupil." There were three conditions in the experi-

ment. Some participants delivered the shocks in front of a mirror, some before an audience of their classmates, and others before an audience of advanced psychology students. In the presence of their own image in the mirror, which increases self-awareness and activates people's private attitudes, the participants' behavior was relatively consistent with their attitudes. But in the presence of the audiences, their behavior was more consistent with norms.

Neither attitudes nor norms predominate for all behaviors, for all people, in all situations. Whether their impact is direct or indirect, relevant attitudes can limit or modify the powerful influence of norms on behavior. Similarly, norms that are activated and considered can restrict or change individual attitudes being expressed in behavior. In our daily lives, multiple social norms and a variety of personal attitudes contribute to how we perceive a given set of circumstances and, thus, to the way we behave. Will an employee blow the whistle on his company's illegal dumping of chemical waste? Will a young mother nurse her baby or use formula? Will a soldier carry out orders she suspects are illegal? When the behavior is perceived as controllable, the answer will depend on the particular mix of norms and attitudes that are brought to mind as each individual interprets his or her situation.

CONCLUDING COMMENTS

 Social psychology has always aimed at understanding the intricate interplay between social thoughts, social feelings, and social behavior. One thing that makes achieving such a goal difficult is the incredible diversity of human behavior. On the one hand are behaviors like stepping on the brake when the traffic light turns red—behaviors so automatic that they take no conscious thought. On the other hand are decisions about choosing a particular college or voting for a particular candidate—behaviors that require an agonizingly careful scrutiny of available information. As we hope you have seen in this and the three previous chapters, the differences between these two types of behaviors are more apparent than real. It is easy to see how cognitive processes and social influences contribute to the kinds of carefully reasoned actions that follow the consideration of a variety of relevant attitudes and norms. But even automatic behaviors are influenced by the way we and others interpret and define social situations. You won't stop at the traffic signal unless you recognize the red light and interpret its meaning appropriately. And how you interpret the red light is governed to a large degree by social conventions and norms: Must you stay motionless until the light changes to green or can you turn right if the way is clear? Even your knowledge that the color red means "stop" is a cultural norm. Like carefully considered behaviors, apparently automatic actions are also influenced by both cognitive and social processes. Whether automatic or carefully thought through, then, all behavior is susceptible to the same principle of accessibility: The more readily the relevant attitude or norm comes to mind, the more impact it will have on behavior.

Although norms and attitudes affect behavior in the same ways, norms have a slight edge over attitudes. Indeed, if you think about it, you will probably be surprised to find how much more often when norms and attitudes

CHAPTER 10 THEMES

- **Construction of Reality**
  Every situation can be interpreted in multiple ways, making different norms applicable.

- **Pervasiveness of Social Influence**
  Social norms influence our actions, even when we are not physically in the group.

- **Striving for Mastery**
  Following norms helps us to obtain rewards from others.

- **Seeking Connectedness**
  Following norms helps us to feel like good group members.

- **Accessibility**
  Increasing the accessibility of norms increases their impact on behavior.

- **Superficiality Versus Depth**
  Resisting the effects of norms sometimes requires extensive thought.

conflict, you follow norms rather than your attitudes. You do what you *should* do rather than what you *want* to do. Part of the impact of norms comes from the fact that they are group-based, and thus the presence of group members is a cue that activates them. And because norms come from the group, norm-consistent behavior is likely to be supported and rewarded, rather than undermined. Although norm-consistent behavior can be maintained by threats or rejection, the pressure to conform usually comes from the inside: from our acceptance of group norms as the right and proper way to think, feel, and act. Thus we construct a world of right and wrong, good and bad, that is reflected in the norms and attitudes we develop and maintain. Effective social influence really stems from the ability to create and then make accessible cognitive structures that make desired behavior more likely to occur.

Factories, corporations, and businesses have begun to reap the benefits of encouraging groups to form and maintain their own standards of behavior, as have individuals joining self-help support groups. The power of social norms might be used with equal success in other social areas, not as rules imposed from above but as a grass-roots movement that builds from the small group level. In neighborhoods, for example, norms involving conservation and recycling might be established and made effective, just as block organizations and neighborhood watch groups have successfully developed standards of pride and caring for property and crime-free activity. Standards of curiosity and respect for learning might be reinforced in classrooms if students themselves participated in establishing norms for classroom behavior. As social and environmental problems escalate, such techniques could help produce much-needed change.

SUMMARY

 Norms: Effective Guides for Social Behavior. Norms must be brought to mind before they can guide behavior. They can be activated by deliberate reminders or by subtle cues, such as observations of other people's behavior. Norms are sometimes enforced by rewards and punishments. More often, however, people follow norms because they seem right, because they are endorsed by the behavior of other group members, because they are frequently activated, and because they offer solutions to problems.

When individuals see themselves purely in terms of group identity, their behavior is likely to be guided by group norms alone. The result can be either antisocial or prosocial behavior, depending on the norms that are currently accessible.

The Norm of Reciprocity: Treating Others as They Treat You. The **norm of social reciprocity** directs us to return to others favors, goods, and services similar to those they offer to us. This norm can sometimes be activated to our disadvantage when people give us small favors to induce us to return something of greater value.

Concessions made during negotiations are also supposed to be reciprocated. This can leave us vulnerable when influencers use the **door-in-the-face technique,** making a concession following our refusal to comply with a large demand. We feel obligated to make a concession in return. Because people believe in the norm of reciprocity, behaviors based on these concessions are often stable over time.

The Norm of Social Commitment: Keeping Your Promises. The **norm of social commitment** directs us to honor our agreements. It can make people vulnerable through the **low-ball technique,** when they make a deal and then discover there are hidden costs. People usually stick to the deal even though it has changed for the worse.

People stand by their commitments for several reasons. They feel obligated to do so, and being inconsistent makes them uncomfortable. They also add new thoughts, feelings, and behaviors to help support and bolster their action.

The Norm of Obedience: Submitting to Authority. In one of the best-known experiments in psychology, people obeyed orders to deliver shocks to an unwilling victim who was clearly suffering. They obeyed these orders even though they were not forced to do so. The destructive obedience of Milgram's participants was not due to personality defects, hard-hearted unconcern about the victim, or suspicion that the experiment was rigged. In fact, obedience in nonexperimental settings can be just as high, and authorities command as much obedience in recent studies as they did 40 years ago in Milgram's experiments.

The obligation to obey a legitimate authority figure invoked by the **norm of obedience to authority** had a powerful effect on behavior in Milgram's experiment. Conditions that decreased the accessibility of the norm of obedience or increased attention to other norms (such as social responsibility) also decreased obedience. Outside the laboratory, norms like the obligation to obey orders are often reinforced by other social-psychological processes such as a gradual entrapment into acts of escalating violence, self-justification and blaming the victim, and intergroup hatred and hostility. In these instances, obedience becomes destructive, and norms are used to justify inhumane treatment. But obedience has positive as well as negative effects.

Rebellion and Resistance: Fighting Back. People can resist being manipulated by norms. People display **reactance** by fighting against threats to their freedom of action when they do not privately accept norms or when they believe they are inappropriate.

One of the best defenses against normative pressure is to think things through to make sure that a proffered norm is actually applicable. Another effective defense is to use norms against norms: to forge or exploit an alternative consensus that a different course of behavior is the appropriate one.

Putting It All Together: Multiple Guides for Behavior. Attitudes and norms often work together to influence behavior, either by triggering behavior directly or by combining to influence intentions to act, which in turn direct behavior. According to the **theory of planned behavior,** people's perception of control over the behavior is also an important influence on intentions and, thus, on behavior.

When attitudes and norms disagree, their influence on behavior will depend on their relative accessibility for a particular behavior, in a particular situation, and for a particular person.

11

Liking and Loving

For most people, a happy marriage and a good family life are two of the most important elements of their lives. And for good reasons: Research findings suggest that close relationships with other people can make us healthy as well as happy. Consider the following findings:

- Compared to people in troubled marriages, those who are happily married have immune systems that ward off infections more effectively (Kiecolt-424 and others, 1987).

- The more college roommates like each other, the fewer colds and flu outbreaks they suffer (Goleman, 1992).

- The chances of surviving for more than 1 year after a heart attack are more than twice as high among elderly men and women who can count on two or more people for emotional support than among those who do not have this support (Berkman, Leo-Summers, & Horwitz, 1992).

No wonder, then, that people's feelings about their relationships have a bigger impact on their overall satisfaction with their lives than do their job, income, community, or even physical health (A. Campbell, Converse, & Rodgers, 1976). In fact, close relationships are so important to people's well-being that the end of a relationship can be psychologically and physically devastating (Hemstrom, 1996; Stroebe & Stroebe, 1986).

In this chapter we describe how our relationships with others develop and change over time. We begin by looking at the factors that spark initial attraction—in everyday language, liking—between people and motivate them to try to know each other better. You will see that once two people begin interacting on a regular basis—chatting on the phone and sharing meals and other activities—feelings of attraction based on personal characteristics become less important than feelings about the relationship and about what each partner gets out of it.

As two people's lives become interlinked and each comes to know the other more deeply, casual acquaintanceship is transformed into close friendship. Just as an important in-group can become part of the self, so does the partner in a close relationship. And just as group norms influence what we do, the partner's thoughts, feelings, and behavior influence our own. Each partner responds directly to the other's joys and sorrows, and each in turn feels deeply known, understood, and accepted by the other. These elements of caring and psychological intimacy characterize many kinds of loving relationships—between best friends, parents and children, romantic partners, and spouses. Sexual feelings, like hot peppers in an antipasto salad, are powerful additional ingredients that spice some relationships.

Of course, difficulties eventually arise in any relationship. When conflicts are handled constructively, relationships can endure and deepen over the years. If conflict leads to a break-up, however, the pain can be swift and sure. In the final section of the chapter we consider the causes of problems in relationships and the ways people deal with them.

Initial Attraction

Newly arrived in a strange city or a freshman dorm, you look at the strangers around you and wonder: "Who will be my friends?" How do we form new connections and turn nodding acquaintances into pals and partners? In cultures that emphasize voluntary relationships instead of lifelong, unchangeable group memberships, the first step in getting to know a stranger is often sparked by feelings of *attraction* or liking (Berscheid & Reis, 1998). As mysterious as attraction seems, it follows rules: People are usually attracted to those they find physically attractive and to those with whom they interact frequently.

Physical Attractiveness

The formation of a relationship is often spurred by feelings of attraction or liking for another person. Attraction to strangers is strongly influenced by perceptions of physical attractiveness.

Everyone likes to look at beautiful people. Julia Roberts, Kevin Costner, and Denzel Washington are movie stars because of their good looks as well as their acting talents. Thinking about people like these suggests that physical attractiveness is a characteristic that some lucky people just *have*. But this view is an overstatement. For one thing, members of different cultures differ greatly in the physical characteristics they consider attractive. When anthropologists surveyed more than 200 non-Western societies, they could not find a single characteristic that was considered attractive everywhere (Ford & Beach, 1951). For example, some societies value slimness in women, while others consider plumpness more attractive. Even within 20th century North America, shifts in standards of physical beauty have been documented (Banner, 1983). Thus, definitions of physical attractiveness are culturally shaped.

Even among members of the same culture, attractiveness seems to be partly in the eye of the beholder, as well as in the characteristics of the per-

■ **Beauty is in the eye of the beholder.** What is considered attractive differs not only across cultures and time, but can even vary widely within the same culture and time.

son being observed. Studies have demonstrated that the observer's liking for a person can influence perceptions of physical attractiveness. In one study, for example, men and women looked at a photo of a woman and read information about her personality traits. When they then judged her physical attractiveness, those who read that her personality was likable judged her to be more attractive than those who learned that she was dislikable (Owens & Ford, 1978). Similarly, women rate photos of men who are described as acting in agreeable and altruistic ways as more physically attractive, compared to the same photos linked with less positive behaviors (Jensen-Campbell, Graziano, & West, 1995). In other words, liking someone will help you see the person's beauty.

EFFECTS OF PHYSICAL ATTRACTIVENESS. Despite these points, there is some degree of consensus on people's physical attractiveness, and as we described in chapter 3, attractiveness can influence people's attitudes and behaviors in a wide range of social situations, even on the job. Why do we like to be around beautiful people? One obvious reason is the sheer esthetic pleasure we obtain from looking at them. However, that is not the only reason. In chapter 3 we described the common stereotype that attractive people are warm, friendly, and socially confident (Eagly, Ashmore, Makhijani, & Longo, 1991). And this stereotype may become self-fulfilling, as a study by Mark Snyder, Elizabeth Tanke, and Ellen Berscheid (1977) illustrated. These researchers showed male college students a photo of a woman with whom they would supposedly have a telephone conversation. The photos were rigged: Some students saw an image of a highly attractive woman; others saw a woman who was less attractive. Each participant then held an actual conversation with a female student who knew nothing of this ruse. When other students later listened to tape recordings of the two sides of the conversation, they found that the men's behavior varied, depending on which photo they had seen. Men who thought the partner was a very attractive woman acted more sociable, interesting, warm, and outgoing than those who thought she was less attractive. Naturally, the women responded to these different conversational patterns: Those whose partners thought they were attractive also acted more sociable, animated, and confident. The results of this study suggest that when we think people are attractive, we interact with them in a way that brings out the best in them.

The ways our interactions with people can cause them to become what we expect them to be—creating a self-fulfilling prophecy—were detailed in chapter 3, pages 93 to 95.

Attractiveness enhances social interaction in everyday life, not just in artificial experimental situations. For example, college students' attractiveness is related to the pleasantness they perceive in their everyday social interactions (Reis and others, 1982). Thus, we tend to like attractive people not only because we enjoy looking at them, but also because our interactions with them may generally be positive and pleasant.

WHO CARES ABOUT PHYSICAL ATTRACTIVENESS? Physical attractiveness is not equally important to everyone. Among both men and women, high self-monitors—those who care about acting in socially appropriate ways and fitting in with situational demands—place an especially high value on physical attractiveness in relationship partners. In contrast, low self-monitors are likely to seek partners with desirable personality traits and other inner qualities (M. Snyder, Berscheid, & Glick, 1985). This personality difference influences not only the way people select dating partners but also the way they choose among "job applicants": High self-monitors pay more attention to physical attractiveness and low self-monitors attend more to the applicant's personality (M. Snyder, Berscheid, & Matwuchuk, 1988).

Gender also plays a role. In romantic relationships, men attach more importance to physical attractiveness than women do, while women care more about qualities related to status, ambition, and financial success (Feingold, 1990, 1992). In "lonely hearts" personal columns, for example, more men than women specify that they are looking for attractive romantic partners. This concern for physical attractiveness is a characteristic *of men* as perceivers rather than a preference *about women* as partners. One source of evidence for this statement is a study of gay and lesbian advertising for partners. The gay men tended to specify attractiveness as a desired trait in a partner, whereas the lesbian women did not (Deaux & Hanna, 1984).

Evolutionary psychologists have advanced a potential explanation for this gender difference. In species (like humans) where the costs of pregnancy, nursing, and childrearing fall mainly on women, males and females have somewhat different ways of maximizing the transmission of their genes to the next generation (Trivers, 1972). Because their parental investment is relatively small, men maximize their reproductive success simply by having a large number of healthy children. For this reason, their best bet is to seek reproductive partners who are young (because young women are the most fertile) and free from diseases and genetic defects. Female beauty is argued to be an indicator of these qualities, explaining why psychological mechanisms have evolved that lead men in particular to seek attractive mates (D. M. Buss, 1994). In contrast, their greater parental investment makes it beneficial for women to be more selective than men in choosing partners, and they can maximize their reproductive success by preferring men who are able and willing to commit resources to them and their children. Thus, it is argued, women value indicators of men's resources, such as dominance, social status, and wealth, above physical attractiveness (D. M. Buss, 1994).

Though this evolutionary reasoning accounts neatly for the observed gender differences in mate preferences, it has not gone unchallenged. For one thing, women may prefer men with resources simply because in virtually every culture women themselves directly control few resources (J. A. Howard, Blumstein, & Schwartz, 1987). Consistent with this notion, in cultures where women have relatively more power, they also place less emphasis on resources relative to physical attractiveness in men (Gangestad, 1993).

(And supermarket tabloid stories often seem to pair fabulously rich female movie stars with young, physically attractive men who possess no particularly evident resource potential.)

Another question about the evolutionary explanation arises from the fact that little research on mate preferences has distinguished between the attributes that people desire for short-term versus long-term, committed relationships (Berscheid & Reis, 1998). For a short-term relationship, both men and women appear to care equally about attractiveness (Sprecher, 1989). In contrast, for a long-term relationship men are nearly as selective as women are, which is inconsistent with the parental investment theory (Kenrick, Sadalla, Groth, & Trust, 1990; P. C. Regan, 1998). Finally, the gender difference in preferences for physical attractiveness is larger in people's self-reports of what they want in a partner than in studies that assess people's actual behavioral choices (Feingold, 1992a). This finding also poses a challenge for parental investment theory, since (like any evolutionary theory) it makes direct predictions for what people *do* rather than for what they *say*. It is beyond question that evolved differences could affect men's and women's orientations toward mate selection, but the details of those differences, and the ways they interact with culture and learning, are not yet fully known.

■ **The closeness of connectedness.** Relationships need not involve romantic feelings to provide us with feelings of connectedness. More commonly we gain support, closeness, and a sense of identity from those with whom we share enjoyable activities or intimate revelations.

Positive Interaction

People are attracted to those with whom they have positive interactions. Interaction helps people master the world, and it also helps people find connectedness. In addition, interaction leads to familiarity, which increases liking. Similarity also increases attraction by making positive interaction more likely, by suggesting that the other person likes the individual in return, and by validating the individual's beliefs and attitudes.

Most of us like the people we work with every day, regardless of their physical attractiveness. We also like people who share our backgrounds, tastes, attitudes, and values. Why do we usually like people we frequently interact with and people who are similar to us?

INTERACTION SPELLS LIKING . . . MOST OF THE TIME. Suppose you have a new job, and you are assigned a desk near another worker. As the days pass, your neighbor shows you the ropes and you begin eating lunch together. You will probably end up liking this person better than your other co-workers, a pattern suggested by a clever study by Chester Insko and Midge Wilson (1977). In this study, small groups of three students, either three men or three women, sat facing each other in a triangular pattern. Two of the three held a get-acquainted conversation for 5 to 15 minutes while the third person silently observed. Then one of that pair had a similar conversation with the third person. Finally, each student reported how much he or she liked the other two members of the group. Although everyone obtained exactly the same information about everyone else (because the observer always heard the conversation between the other two), participants preferred group members with whom they had actively interacted. They liked them more, thought them more similar to themselves, and thought that their interaction partner liked them better in return.

Studies outside the laboratory confirm that people who interact frequently, even if they are thrown together by sheer chance, tend to like each other. A classic study of residents in a married-student housing complex found that friendships tended to form among those who lived near one another (Festinger, Schachter, & Back, 1950). The most popular residents were those whose apartments were located near the stairs or close to the mailbox area, where they had extra opportunities to interact with others. College roommates also tend to like each other, even if they do not initially share the kinds of characteristics that usually lead to attraction (Newcomb, 1961). Proximity leads to friendship even in the classroom. One study found that police trainees who were alphabetically assigned to classrooms and seats tended to form friendships with classmates whose names were in their part of the alphabet (M. W. Segal, 1974).

WHY INTERACTION INCREASES LIKING. We saw in chapters 6 and 9 that people enjoy belonging to valued in-groups for two basic reasons. Our groups can help us master the world—grasping reality and obtaining individual rewards—as others cooperate with us, validate our beliefs and attitudes, and aid us in seeing the world correctly. Groups also help us enjoy a sense of connectedness and belonging. The same reasons usually make interaction with other people enjoyable, and therefore lead us to like those people (Bakan, 1966; Cantor & Malley, 1991; McAdams, 1985).

1. *Interacting with others helps us master the world.* If you stop to think about why you enjoy being with other people, your first reason will probably be that it's often just plain interesting and fun. Debating politics far into the night, cheering together at sports events, and sharing what you know in joint study sessions are activities that meet our personal needs in many ways. Some ways are obvious: The study session may help improve test grades. Other benefits are not quite so obvious. Discussing a personal worry with a close friend can help us understand and cope with trying circumstances and with our own reactions to them. Thus, particularly when we are under stress, we seek to compare our own feelings and reactions with those of other people so that we can better understand ourselves (Rofé, 1984; Schachter, 1959). Similarly, when we feel uncertain of our opinions and beliefs, we may seek out others to test the validity of our views (Wheeler, 1974). When interacting with someone is rewarding in any of these ways, the result is the same: We tend to like the person (Rusbult & van Lange, 1996).

2. *Interacting with others helps us feel connected.* Interacting with another person who treats us with warmth, acceptance, and respect can confirm our sense of being connected to others (McAdams & Bryant, 1987; Reis & Patrick, 1996). This sense of relatedness and attachment to the other person is another important reward of interaction—one that, as we shall see, increases in importance as relationships deepen.

3. *Familiar others seem likable.* A third reason for liking those we frequently interact with is simple familiarity—the *mere exposure effect* (Bornstein and others, 1987). In fact, even when no actual interaction takes place, familiarity has positive effects, as Richard Moreland and Scott Beach (1992) demonstrated. As we described in Chapter 3, they had women sit in on varying numbers of lectures in a large class. The other students in the class thought the women who had attended

FIGURE 11.1   Interaction leads to attraction

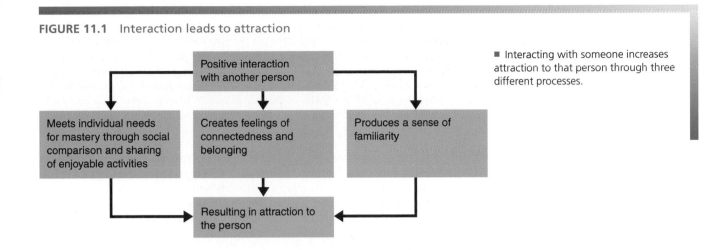

■ Interacting with someone increases attraction to that person through three different processes.

more often were more likeable and attractive. The research suggests that even in the absence of interaction, familiarity can lead to both liking and perceived similarity. For all three of the reasons just listed, we tend to like people we interact with a lot, as Figure 11.1 suggests.

WHAT ABOUT NEGATIVE INTERACTION? At this point you may be remembering a particularly obnoxious roommate or next-door neighbor and thinking that frequent interaction certainly does *not* always lead to liking. You're right: When interaction fails to meet our needs or even harms us, it will lead to disliking. More negative interaction just spells more annoyance if you have to spend time with someone who holds offensive political views, or to share a dorm room with someone who constantly plays rock music while you like only rap (or vice versa). Research supports this common-sense idea. When asked to name the people they most disliked, participants in one study named individuals who lived near them (Ebbesen, Kjos, & Konecni, 1976). And incompatible musical tastes are one of the most important reasons for dissension between college roommates, so much so that one college application form asks students to "cross out any music you cannot tolerate" so that rooms can be assigned accordingly (Abramovitch, 1997). Fortunately, most people seem to be more likable than annoying, so interaction more often leads to attraction than to repulsion (Rosenbaum, 1986).

BIRDS OF A FEATHER: LIKING SIMILAR OTHERS. Because you interact frequently with your nearby co-worker, and because her advice is so useful, you probably will end up liking her. However, as you get to know other people in the office over the next few months, you may identify someone who seems to be more similar to you, more "your type." This person may support the same candidate in the local election, share your love of opera, and come from the part of the country you call home. You probably will end up liking this person, too, for similarity breeds attraction (Newcomb, 1961). Though we all have heard that, like the north and south poles of magnets, "opposites attract," research shows that this is not true for people (Berscheid & Reis, 1998). Similarity leads to attraction for three main reasons.

1. *We tend to interact with people who are similar to us.* "Birds of a feather flock together" is one of those old sayings that often holds true: People tend to interact with similar others. For example, pairs of best friends in high school and members of dating couples in college tend to be similar on many variables, including age, religion, race, and social class (C. T. Hill, Rubin, & Peplau, 1976; Kandel, 1978). Shared interests obviously create opportunities for interaction: Academically motivated students meet others of their kind at the library, fanatical golfers find their like at the golf course, and environmentalists find one another at Sierra Club meetings. Similarity also makes it more likely that the interaction will be positive. You will have no problem finding topics of common interest to discuss with fellow Sierra Club members, and you won't argue about whether to save the endangered spotted owl. Similarity, like proximity, thus increases opportunities for positive interaction, which, as we just saw, spells liking.

2. *We assume that similar others will like us.* If we know that someone is similar to us, we usually assume that person will like us (E. Aronson & Worchel, 1966). And being liked by someone is one of the strongest reasons for liking that person (Condon & Crano, 1988).

3. *Similar others validate our beliefs and attitudes.* One of the earliest lines of research on attraction showed that people like similar others even before they have met them. Participants in studies conducted by Donn Byrne (1971) were given a questionnaire on social and political attitudes supposedly completed by another student. The closer the stranger's attitudes were to their own, the more the participants liked the unknown individual. You may think it strange to study attraction without having people meet other real people, but consider the ways in which the research situation mirrors real life. If you, a political liberal, were new in town and wanted to make friends, you might avoid the Conservative Club and show up at the Liberal League meeting. You would do so because you expect to find people with attitudes similar to your own—and thus likable people—among the Liberal League members.

The reason we like people with attitudes and beliefs similar to our own is that we tend to view our own characteristics as desirable. Thus those who share them have the *right* attitudes (LaPrelle, Hoyle, Insko, & Bernthal, 1990). If you favor affirmative action, you will probably like other people who share that attitude—not just because they agree with you but because their attitude suggests what you see as an appropriate concern for the disadvantaged in society. Other people's support for our views is rewarding because it validates our own opinions (Byrne, 1971).

In summary, if two people are similar, they are more likely to have positive interactions, to believe that they are liked in return, and to reinforce each other's attitudes and beliefs. For all these reasons, similarity tends to create attraction.

This tendency and other self-serving biases were introduced in chapter 4, pages 117 to 126.

Liking, Similarity, and Interaction: Mutually Reinforcing Processes

Similarity, liking, and interaction all tend to influence one another. As a result, relationships tend to deepen and intensify over time.

FIGURE 11.2 The mutually reinforcing effects of interaction, similarity, and liking

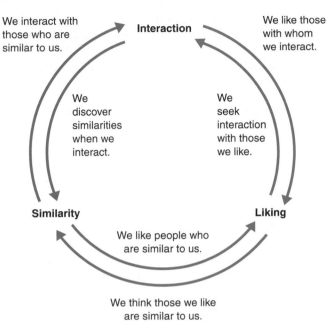

■ Interaction, similarity, and liking all tend to influence one another. Thus, if any one of these factors starts a relationship, the other two will tend to contribute to a self-sustaining spiral of friendship.

As Figure 11.2 shows, interaction, liking, and similarity are all tied together in our everyday lives (Berscheid & Reis, 1998).

- Similarity encourages interaction, and when people interact, they discover more similarities. For instance, getting-acquainted conversations tend to involve a search for common friends, activities, or interests (C. A. Insko & Wilson, 1977).

- Interaction creates liking, and liking leads to more interaction because we seek out the company of those we enjoy. Further, the fact that two people spend time together suggests that each finds the other likable and enjoyable. And knowing that someone likes you is a powerful reason for being attracted to them: It boosts self-esteem and demonstrates your value as a person (C. A. Insko and others, 1973). Even when people do not interact, familiarity can cause liking as well as perceived similarity (Insko & Wilson, 1977; Moreland & Beach, 1992).

- Similarity and liking also go together. We like those who are similar to us; we think those we like are similar to us; and we assume that people who *are* similar to us will like *us* (Condon & Crano, 1988).

Each of these three factors, similarity, liking, and interaction, can cause increases in all the others. Thus a relationship initially may be sparked by chance proximity, by perceptions of similarity, or by transitory feelings of attraction that lead to an initial encounter. But once it gets going, all three factors come into play, and the acquaintanceship will tend to progress toward friendship.

From Acquaintance to Friend: Relationship Development

If a group of strangers shares a few minutes of conversation, what kinds of feelings do you think they will have about each other? Not surprisingly, almost everyone will find a few individuals especially attractive or friendly. Some people will also have idiosyncratic preferences: Erica may be especially attracted to people with red hair, and Jeff may find Joe's sense of humor objectionable. On such short acquaintance, however, the factors that make Jeff dislike Joe will have little to do with Joe's feelings about Jeff.

If the same people interacted for weeks, months, or years, the patterns of liking would be very different (Kenny, 1994). Although particularly attractive and friendly people may still be quite popular, preferences will mostly reflect the unique history of the interactions between specific pairs of individuals. Erica may like Jeff even though he is not particularly popular with others, because he shares her passion for science-fiction novels. People's feelings will probably also be mutual. If Erica likes Jeff, Jeff will also like Erica. Patterns like this demonstrate the existence of *relationships.* As relationships develop, the purely individual characteristics that are central causes of attraction among strangers become much less important.

What turns acquaintances into friends? The answer involves both of the key motives we have already discussed: the need to master the social environment and the need for connectedness with others (Baumeister & Leary, 1995; Cantor & Malley, 1991). Friendship develops through interactions that fulfill these two needs. Partners exchange rewards, helping each other find individual satisfactions, and they exchange self-disclosures, getting to know each other in increasingly intimate ways.

Exchanges of Rewards: What's In It for Me?

As a relationship begins to develop, the partners exchange rewards. As the relationship deepens, they may shift to offering rewards to benefit the partner and to show caring.

For voluntary relationships such as friendships or romances to develop and deepen, *each* partner must receive benefits and rewards. Perhaps you have known someone who was always asking for a loan of a few dollars but never paid you back, or someone who always wanted to tell you his troubles without ever asking in return if you had had a good or a bad day yourself. If so, you probably tried to escape from those relationships unless they provided you with other types of rewards—maybe the chronic borrower was a witty raconteur, always fun to be around. As these examples illustrate, the rewards that each partner gets from interaction are key in determining the course of the relationship (Rusbult & van Lange, 1996). People who do not know each other intimately may share activities that directly reward both partners. For example, two acquaintances may frequently play tennis because they both enjoy the game. Or two people may directly exchange benefits. For example, one may cook a gourmet dinner for a classmate in return for an evening's tutoring help with a tough calculus assignment. Casual relationships that work this way are termed **exchange relationships,** because people offer benefits to their partners in order to receive benefits in return (M. S. Clark & Mills, 1979).

In contrast, close friends or others who have **communal relationships** are directly concerned for each other's welfare, and they provide benefits to demonstrate that they care rather than to receive benefits in exchange. The shift from an exchange to a communal orientation marks an important transition point in relationship development. Often a relationship is brought to this transition point when one person acts in ways that are typical of a communal relationship, signaling his or her desire to move in that direction. Thus, if you regard an acquaintance as a potential friend, you may signal your desire for a closer relationship by offering a favor or picking up the check for a shared restaurant dinner (Lydon, Jamieson, & Holmes, 1997). In fact, people may act in these ways even with a stranger, if they are attracted to the person and desire a relationship (M. S. Clark & Mills, 1979). But such gestures often leave the recipient uncertain about the individual's desires and intentions. Is the offered favor a genuine invitation to a closer relationship or something else, even an attempt at manipulation? Uncertainty and anxiety may cloud both partners' feelings about the transition (Lydon and others, 1997). If all goes well, the partner may read the intended meaning correctly and the relationship may progress further toward closeness. In contrast, if the partner refuses to accept the favor or insists on paying it back at the first available opportunity, that amounts to a statement that a closer relationship is not desired. In either case, actions take on special meanings in the context of the transition from acquaintanceship to a close friendship: They signal whether each partner takes an exchange or communal approach to the relationship.

Self-Disclosure

Relationship development also includes exchanges of self-disclosures as the partners come to know each other better. Self-disclosures increase liking and offer opportunities for sympathetic, supportive responses.

"I hate this cold weather." "I can't believe how much money I just spent on groceries." Relatively impersonal topics like these are the kinds of things you might discuss with acquaintances. On the other hand, "My alcoholic father used to beat me," or "I don't know if I'm smart enough to make it in grad school" are the kinds of intimate disclosures we usually share only with close and trusted friends. Self-disclosures include facts about one's life and situation, as well as inner thoughts, feelings, and emotions (Morton, 1978). Both the depth of self-disclosure (the level of intimacy of the information) and the breadth (the range of topics) increase as a relationship develops (Altman & Taylor, 1973; Z. Rubin, Hill, Peplau, & Dunkel-Schetter, 1980).

EFFECTS OF SELF-DISCLOSURE. Disclosing something about yourself makes both strangers and friends like you more (Collins & Miller, 1994). This fact probably explains why salespeople often self-disclose to their customers, offering cute stories about their children or pets. It may also explain why peo-

Exchange relationship. A relationship in which people exchange rewards in order to receive benefits in return.

Communal relationship. A relationship in which people reward their partner out of direct concern and to show caring.

ple who readily express their feelings nonverbally are liked more than less expressive individuals (Friedman, Riggio, & Casella, 1988). But self-disclosure can go too far: Those who disclose more than is appropriate for the closeness of the relationship make others uncomfortable (Wortman, Adesman, Herman, & Greenberg, 1976). Just as when an acquaintance offers a favor, the reason for the self-disclosure is uncertain: Does it express a desire to deepen the relationship?

You may recall our discussion of other implications of the norm of reciprocity from chapter 10, pages 384 to 390.

When people are entrusted with a self-disclosure, the norm of reciprocity prescribes that they should respond in kind. For example, when someone describes sad personal experiences to you, you might recount similar events from your own life. Thus self-disclosures, like rewards, are often exchanged in a relationship (R. L. Archer, 1980). This is particularly true in the early stages of acquaintance, as one experiment demonstrated. When participants were asked to respond to a stranger's note with one of their own, the topic they wrote about tended to match the level of intimacy in their correspondent's note (Derlega, Wilson, & Chaiken, 1976).

People do not always respond in kind to self-disclosures, however. Nor do we always want them to. Indeed, when we talk about our bad experiences, shortcomings, or anxieties, we usually expect to receive empathy, support, and acceptance in return (Reis & Patrick, 1996). Good friends often respond in just this way, saying things like, "That must have been terrible for you." A listener who responds with sympathetic concern to an intimate self-disclosure is liked better than one who simply reciprocates with a self-disclosure (Berg & Archer, 1980). As confidences elicit sympathy and support, self-disclosure leads to *self-validation*, the warm feeling of being truly known and accepted by the listener.

Self-disclosures bring other benefits besides self-validation to a relationship. Coordinating mutual activities is easier when each partner knows something of the other's abilities and preferences. And deeper mutual understanding lets each partner meet the other's needs more easily. Self-disclosure also signals trust, because in a particular relationship we may disclose things that we would not want the whole world to know.

There is a strong gender difference in the intimacy level of self-disclosure, as in so many other aspects of relationships. Women self-disclose more than men, particularly by revealing their feelings and emotions (Dindia & Allen, 1992; Morton, 1978). As Figure 11.3 shows, the difference is largest in same-sex friendships: Women disclose much more to other women than men do to other men (Reis, 1986). When men do engage in self-disclosure early in a heterosexual relationship, it can be part of an effort to make the relationship more intimate (Derlega, Winstead, Wong, & Hunter, 1985). In contrast, women's disclosures seem to reflect their existing feelings about the relationship, rather than their intention to move toward greater intimacy (Adams & Shea, 1981).

As two people interact over time, the course of the relationship comes to depend on the way they treat each other. As they exchange rewards, they feel good about themselves and each other. As they share intimate information, they grow in mutual understanding, demonstrate trust, and obtain support and self-validation. Each partner's liking for the other now depends on the way the exchanges of rewards and self-disclosures operate in the relationship. If the processes continue smoothly, casual friendship may

FIGURE 11.3 Gender and the intimacy of interaction

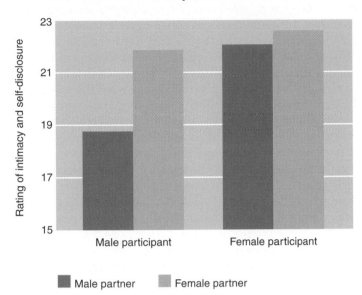

■ In this study, college students filled out brief questionnaires rating the intimacy of all their social interactions within a given time period. As the figure shows, interactions involving a female participant or a male participant and a female partner—that is, any interaction that involved a female—tended to be more intimate and self-disclosing than interactions between two males. (Data from Reis, 1986.)

be transformed into a close relationship. And, paradoxically, psychological closeness transforms the nature of the self-disclosure and exchange processes that produced closeness in the first place.

Close Relationships

Of your hundreds of relationships with other people, only a handful truly count as close. Are they the relationships that evoke the most positive feelings? Not necessarily. For example, you probably have felt high regard and strong attraction for someone who will always remain distant, such as a movie star or a teacher. Or you may have been in a close relationship with a sibling or a romantic partner that at times was so filled with conflict that your feelings were mostly negative. For reasons like these, researchers define a **close relationship** not in terms of positive feelings but as a connection involving strong and frequent interdependence in many different areas of life. **Interdependence** means that each partner's thoughts, emotions, and behaviors influence the other's (H. H. Kelley and others, 1983; Rusbult & van Lange, 1996).

There are three main types of interdependence. *Cognitive interdependence* means thinking about the self and partner as inextricably linked parts of a whole—a relationship—rather than as separate individuals (Agnew, van Lange, Rusbult, & Langston, 1998). Cognitive interdependence is strongly tied to feelings of intimacy and to the relationship's stability over time (Aron, Aron, & Smollan, 1992).

Behavioral interdependence means that each person has a great deal of influence on the partner's decisions, activities, and plans. Moreover, the partners usually spend a lot of time together, and they share a number of different activities. According to a study by Ellen Berscheid, Mark Snyder, and

Close relationship. A relationship involving strong and frequent interdependence in many domains of life.

Interdependence. A situation in which each person's thoughts, emotions, and behaviors influence those of other people.

Allan Omoto (1989), when people's lives are interlinked in these ways, the relationship tends to endure over time. Moreover, the extent of behavioral interdependence is a strong predictor of how long the relationship will last, even stronger than the couple's positive feelings for each other.

Affective interdependence refers to the affective bond that links close relationship partners. The feelings are usually warm and positive but not always; whether positive or negative, interdependence means that each partner's emotional well-being is deeply affected by what the other does.

Cognitive, behavioral, and affective interdependence thus reflect the special ways that relationships help people meet their fundamental needs for connectedness with others and for mastery and rewards. Though they are all important aspects of relationship closeness, they are somewhat separate; a particular relationship may be higher on one dimension and lower on others.

When people think about themselves mostly as members of a couple, share major parts of their lives, and are linked by strong emotional ties, are we talking about love? Trying to define *love* may be a fool's game, and indeed most relationship researchers have avoided doing so (Shaver & Hazan, 1988). Nevertheless, two intrepid researchers, Arthur Aron and Elaine Aron (1991), have defined *love* as the "thoughts, feelings, and actions that are associated with a desire to enter or maintain a close relationship with a specific person" (p. 26). This formal definition emphasizes the desire for closeness, that is, interdependence, and, like our everyday use of the word *love*, covers relationships with kin and nonromantic friendships as well as romantic relationships (Meyers & Berscheid, 1997). That is, a close relationship can involve the secure, trusting attachment of *companionate love* or the intense sexual attraction of *romantic love* (Hatfield, 1988). Because all close relationships share the basic properties of cognitive, behavioral, and affective interdependence, we consider what research tells us about those common processes before discussing what is special about romantic and sexual relationships.

Research on Close Relationships

By necessity, most research on close relationships uses nonexperimental designs that leave some ambiguity about causal relations among variables.

As you read this section of the chapter, you will notice that most research on close relationships uses nonexperimental designs. For obvious reasons, people cannot be randomly assigned to have high or low levels of variables like commitment to their partners, nor can relationships be randomly assigned to last for years or break up quickly. The impracticality of random assignment rules out experimental designs and weakens conclusions about the direction of cause and effect. For example, researchers have found that in romantic relationships, the frequency of sexual intercourse is higher among couples who are generally satisfied with their relationship. This observation may mean that sexual activity increases relationship satisfaction, but it could also mean that couples who are generally satisfied with their relationship tend to have intercourse more often. Researchers are sometimes able to overcome such ambiguities by studying relationships over time, which may allow them to determine the order in which processes occur.

When people are interdependent with the other members of a face-to-face group, it has many types of effects on their behavior, as we describe in chapter 12.

Cognitive Interdependence: The Partner Becomes Part of the Self

As a relationship develops, it may evolve into a close relationship, with extensive interaction and strong mutual influence. A desire for closeness with a particular other person seems to correspond to what people generally mean by "love." In a close relationship, the partner is incorporated into the self, each partner rewards the other to show caring, and a strong emotional attachment arises.

In the intense and frequent interaction that marks a close relationship, partners learn a lot about each other: She can repair her car; he once cheated on an important exam. As each partner becomes increasingly familiar with intimate and varied information about the other, something important happens: The differences that typically exist between self-knowledge and knowledge about the partner are erased. Consider some of the self–other differences that melt away in a close relationship.

The differences that usually exist between knowledge of the self and knowledge of another person were described in chapter 4, pages 108 to 111.

1. *People know what they think and feel but are usually unaware of others' thoughts and feelings.* Self-disclosure and extensive interaction, however, gives a person access to his or her partner's inner life. In a close relationship, people often have the sense that they know just what their partners are thinking (Ickes & Simpson, 1997).

2. *People perceive themselves in a wide range of situations, whereas their opportunities to observe others are relatively restricted.* The shared intimacy of a close relationship changes that, as each partner learns about almost every aspect of the other person's life.

3. *People have a different perspective on themselves (as actors) than on others (as observers).* In a close relationship, however, self-disclosure allows each partner to share the other person's perspective and to know the reasons behind the other person's behaviors and preferences.

4. *People can control their own actions but not those of other people.* Interdependence in a close relationship narrows this gap, as each partner tries to shape his or her own behavior to take the other person's wishes into consideration.

As the typical differences between the cognitive representations of the self and the partner are reduced or eliminated, knowledge of the partner becomes more like self-knowledge. This process represents a sort of expansion of the self beyond the individual to incorporate the partner (Aron, Paris, & Aron, 1995). If Romeo wrote a description of Juliet, for example, he would probably include descriptions of her private thoughts, feelings, and reactions, and he would discuss how she responds differently to different situations (Prentice, 1990). Contrast this with the way people usually describe unfamiliar others, by including little information about thoughts and feelings and assuming that the person behaves consistently across situations.

As the boundaries between self and other break down, mental representations of the self and partner are linked into a single unit, the defining feature of cognitive interdependence (Agnew and others, 1998). For example, people use *we* to refer to themselves and the partner, just as they do

To remind yourself of how a group can similarly become part of the self, refer to chapter 6, pages 211 to 213.

with an in-group with which they identify. In one study demonstrating the linkage of partner and self, people were asked to fill out two questionnaires listing 90 trait words, like *dominant* or *anxious.* The participants completed one questionnaire reporting whether these words described themselves, and a second describing their spouses. Later, the participants again rated whether each of the 90 terms described themselves, while a computer recorded the amount of time they took to respond to each item. The researchers then compared the speed of responding and the number of "errors" (changes from the participant's earlier response) for those traits on which participants had rated themselves as similar to their spouses and for those traits on which participants had rated themselves as different from their spouses. Participants were slower in responding and made almost twice as many errors on the traits where they thought they differed from their spouses (Aron, Aron, Tudor, & Nelson, 1991). The researchers concluded that people's representations of themselves and their spouses are intertwined, so much so that the connection can lead to confusion and slow down someone's ability to report, for instance, that he is not assertive when his wife is. A recent study replicated this finding and showed that the amount of slowing on traits on which people differ from their relationship partner was larger for those people who rated their relationships as closer (E. R. Smith, Coats, & Walling, 1999).

In a close relationship, therefore, the partner—whether a best friend, parent, or romantic partner—becomes linked to the person's self-concept. Self-definition as a member of the twosome, and the support and validation provided by the partner, become important to the person's identity, just as a significant group membership becomes important. The merging of self and partner means that the two processes that drive the development of casual relationships—the exchange of rewards and the increase of mutual knowledge stemming from reciprocal self-disclosure—begin to operate in different ways. The linkage of partner to self fundamentally changes the ways in which we meet our basic needs within a close relationship.

Behavioral Interdependence: Transformations in Exchange

Relationship closeness alters the way partners exchange rewards. In a close relationship, partners reward each other to show affection and because they want to make the partner happy.

Why would you do a favor for a close friend? Probably not because you expect the favor to be immediately repaid, but in order to show that you care and because you *want* to make your partner happy. In close relationships, the exchange of rewards proceeds differently and has a different meaning than it does in more casual relationships.

CHANGES IN THE DISTRIBUTION OF REWARDS. Caring about the partner's feelings—wanting to make him or her feel good—can complicate decisions about what to do. Suppose, for example, you have a yen to take in a classic Federico Fellini film on a Friday night. If your partner prefers the latest Terminator epic, you have to consider that preference as well as your own in deciding on the evening's entertainment. We solve minor coordination problems like this many times each day, usually without even seeing them as problems. We do so because the nature of exchange is transformed in a close relationship (H. H. Kelley, 1979; Rusbult & van Lange, 1996). People do not just do whatever they would prefer as individuals and ignore the partner's wishes, or give in to the partner and expect direct reciprocation in the future. Instead, people directly respond to their partners' wishes. After all, if your partner is part of yourself, his or her needs and desires become indistinguishable from your own.

In a study demonstrating this point, participants divided up a set amount of money between themselves and another person (Aron and others, 1991). As Figure 11.4 shows, people gave themselves considerably more than they gave to a stranger. When the other person was their best friend, however, they gave the friend just about the same amount as they gave themselves. The experimenters told some participants that the money would be sent to the friend with a note explaining the participant's role, while other participants were told that their friends would receive the money and an explanation that did not mention the participant's name. People were equally generous to the friend in both cases, indicating that they were not motivated only by a desire to avoid upsetting their friends. Rather, people really want to benefit a close friend just as much as they want to benefit themselves. Indeed, one's best friend is part of "me and mine."

Closeness alters not only the reasons for exchanging rewards but also the types of benefits the partners bestow on each other. Material rewards are typically exchanged in relationships that are not close, whereas love and emotional support are more often the coin of close relationships (Hays, 1984; Lloyd, Cate, & Henton, 1982). And the more deeply the partners know one another, the more finely the rewards can be tuned to the loved one's specific needs and preferences. For example, new roommates who have just

FIGURE 11.4   Treating a best friend like the self

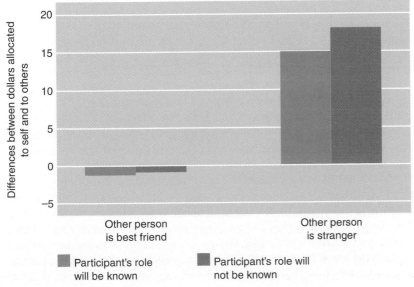

■ In this study, participants were given a sum of money to divide between themselves and another person. As the left bars show, when the other person was their best friend, the participants gave that person slightly more than they gave themselves—regardless of whether the friend would know of their role in the allocation. In contrast, when the other person was a stranger, the right bars show that participants gave considerably more to themselves than to that person. (Data from Aron and others, 1991.)

met seek a rough balance in the total amount of rewards they exchange, regardless of type. But as time passes and their relationship deepens, they are more likely to give each other the specific types of benefits that each values most: help with math homework, companionship for an evening at the movies (Berg, 1984).

ATTRIBUTIONS IN CLOSE RELATIONSHIPS: IT'S THE THOUGHT THAT COUNTS. Your 6-year-old son or your young brother gives you a wonderful Christmas present: a lumpy pottery bowl he fashioned and painted himself. The bowl is downright ugly and you don't have any idea what you will do with it. We bet, though, that you will still enjoy it because you appreciate the feelings behind the gift. In close relationships, it's the thought that counts. The ways the partners treat each other become less important than the *feelings and intentions* that those acts convey, just as the youngster's gift indicates his high regard for you (H. H. Kelley, 1979). The principle holds true on the negative side as well. A relatively minor sin like arriving late for a date, which might be shrugged off by a mere acquaintance, may be seen as indicating a lack of caring in a close relationship and may precipitate a major crisis.

Fortunately, attributions in close relationships are generally biased in a positive direction. As we saw in chapter 4, our attributions for our own behaviors are often self-serving, and because a close relationship partner is part of "me and mine," the same self-serving biases apply to the partner. We inflate the significance of our partner's positive behaviors, linking them to his or her sterling qualities or loving feelings: "How much he must care about me!" We usually minimize the partner's negative behaviors, explaining them away as due to situational causes like a bad day at work or minor failings like a poor memory (Fletcher & Fincham, 1991). In fact, idealized, highly positive views of the partner—perceptions that are even more positive than the partner's own self-views—are typically found in romantic relationships that deeply satisfy the partners and last a long time (S. L. Murray, Holmes, & Griffin, 1996).

Affective Interdependence: Intimacy and Commitment

> Ongoing processes of self-disclosure and sympathetic support lead to feelings of trust, closeness, and acceptance. As closeness increases, the partners feel a growing sense of commitment to each other.

Just as closeness transforms the exchange of rewards and the way partners think about themselves and each other, it also fundamentally changes the partners' feelings. A sense of intimacy grows, and the partners' commitment to the relationship deepens.

PSYCHOLOGICAL INTIMACY. Perhaps the most important component of close relationships is **intimacy.** This is defined as a positive emotional bond that includes understanding and support (Hatfield, 1988; Reis & Patrick, 1996). If asked about your feelings toward your closest friends or family members, you probably would use words like *caring, warmth,* and *acceptance.* You feel happy when you are with the partner and may feel low or even distressed when you are apart (Bowlby, 1969). These feelings are displayed in mutual

Intimacy. A positive emotional bond that includes understanding and support.

understanding and support, and a desire to share with and help the partner (Sternberg & Grajek, 1984). Intimacy develops slowly over time and is nourished by interactions involving self-disclosure, support, and validation (M. S. Clark & Taraban, 1991; Reis & Patrick, 1996). This is why it is difficult to imagine a truly intimate relationship springing up between two people "at first sight," no matter how strong their mutual attraction might be.

Let's consider the process that builds and reflects intimacy in a close relationship. The first step is self-disclosure, particularly regarding feelings or deeply personal reactions. Arriving home in the evening, you might tell your partner, "My computer crashed today and then the boss chewed me out because some important files got lost. I don't know how much longer I can handle this job." Instead of simply reciprocating with another self-disclosure, your partner is likely to try to convey acceptance, acknowledgment, and understanding (Derlega and others, 1976), and this type of responsiveness is the second step in the process. It is important that the partner respond to the emotional content of the self-disclosure rather than to the surface issues. For example, you probably wouldn't find it very satisfying if the partner started talking about ways to keep your computer from crashing. The most responsive messages not only incorporate the content of the self-disclosure (to show understanding) but go beyond it to express positive feelings (Burleson, 1994).

Such truly responsive replies have several effects on the original discloser, which constitute the third step in the intimacy process. You feel *understood* when your partner correctly perceives and acknowledges your feelings. You also feel *valued and esteemed* by your partner's acceptance and responsiveness. Interactions that let you feel known and validated (Berg & Archer, 1980) may give you the strength to go back to work the next day and face your temperamental hard disk and curmudgeonly boss.

As the partner becomes part of the self, the partner's esteem for you becomes just like your own self-esteem. You feel good when your partner both knows and likes you. Intimate interactions of this sort are therefore deeply linked with positive emotions of warmth and caring. The self-disclosure/ responsiveness process strengthens positive emotional bonds and also demonstrates positive feelings because people are unlikely to self-disclose deeply or to respond appropriately *unless* they care for the partner. The linkage between psychological intimacy and positive emotions is so profound that developmental psychologist John Bowlby (1969) has suggested that it has an evolutionary basis. An innate system binds infants emotionally to their mothers or other caregivers by leading them to feel good when in contact with the caregiver and anxious or distressed when apart. This type of emotional bond keeps helpless infants close to their caregivers. The same psychological system may have an important influence on feelings toward friends and romantic partners in adult life (Hazan & Shaver, 1987).

Feelings of warmth, connectedness, and caring are so important to people that psychological intimacy is perhaps the most central reward of a close relationship (Reis & Patrick, 1996). As John Harvey and Julia Omarzu (1997, p. 225) wrote, "Perhaps there is no act more endearing to a partner than that of trying diligently over time to know the partner and use that knowledge toward enhancement of the relationship. This is an act that makes people feel special, treasured, and nurtured. Many of us will live our lives having few if any experiences with others who made us feel this way."

COMMITMENT. Intimacy may draw people closer, but it is commitment that holds a relationship together over time. **Commitment** includes a long-term orientation toward the relationship, reflecting the intention and desire to maintain the relationship for the long term, as well as a strong emotional bond to the partner (Agnew and others, 1998). Caryl Rusbult (1983) argues that commitment is the central force that keeps people working to promote and maintain their partnership.

Committed partners feel comfortable relying on each other for intimacy, advice, and support (Kobak & Hazan, 1991). Each believes that the other is trustworthy, responsive, and available when needed, and that his or her support can bring comfort in times of distress. Commitment involves actions as well as feelings, for it affects people's intentions, desires, and plans for the future. Being committed means, for instance, wanting the relationship to last for a long time. The different aspects of commitment, such as thinking of the implications of current actions for the relationship's future and intending to stay in the relationship for the long term, usually go together (Rusbult, Martz, & Agnew, 1998).

What creates and maintains commitment to a relationship? Rusbult (1983) argues that it emerges from three factors that all tend to increase as relationships deepen over time. As Figure 11.5 shows, one factor is personal *satisfaction* with the relationship: recognition of the rewards it brings, such as the opportunity to make intimate self-disclosures, express sexuality, experience emotional involvement, find companionship for enjoyable activities, and feel secure, worthy, and validated (Drigotas & Rusbult, 1992). But people evaluate these outcomes not in absolute terms but by comparing them with the rewards they believe would be available in alternative relationships, a standard termed the *comparison level for alternatives* (Thibaut & Kelley, 1959b), which is the second factor affecting commitment. If you see your relationship as offering unique rewards that you think would be unavailable from other relationships, you are likely to be strongly committed to it.

Negative forces can be as important as positive ones in maintaining commitment. Psychological or financial factors often pose barriers to leaving a relationship (Levinger, 1991; Rusbult, 1983). For example, people contemplating divorce face the embarrassment of having to admit to friends that the relationship failed, and they must cope with the financial, emotional, and legal difficulties of breaking up a home and family. They also confront the loss of their investments of time, energy, and self-disclosures that they have made in the relationship. They may even lose mutual friends or treasured possessions. Barriers like these are the third factor that influences commitment, and they can help maintain a relationship even if satisfaction is low.

Commitment usually grows as a relationship continues. As the partners' intimacy increases, they are likely to derive increasing satisfaction from the relationship, and they begin to perceive alternative relationships as less desirable and less available. In fact, compared with those who are dating casually, heterosexual college students who are committed to a dating relationship tend to see opposite-sex others as physically less attractive (Simpson, Gangestad, & Lerma, 1990). Needless to say, this means that they also see their partner as relatively more attractive (J. G. Miller and others, 1997). For all these reasons, relationships that involve stronger feelings of

Commitment. The combined forces that hold the partners together in an enduring relationship.

FIGURE 11.5 Factors influencing commitment to a relationship

| Rewards from relationship

I enjoy being with her—she helps me feel good when I'm low. | Potential rewards from alternative relationships

I don't like dating around; no one else is so appealing. | Investments that would be lost if relationship ended

We have lots of mutual friends; it would be hard to break up our CD collection. | Costs of leaving relationship

Parting would involve lots of tears; I'd hate to have to tell our friends we broke up. |

Satisfaction with relationship

Barriers to leaving relationship

Commitment to relationship

I am comfortable relying on her; I want the relationship to last a long time.

■ Commitment depends on satisfaction with the relationship relative to its potential alternatives. Commitment is also strengthened by perceived barriers to leaving the relationship. (Based on Rusbult, 1983.)

commitment last longer, even when they are studied over a period of 15 years (Bui, Peplau, & Hill, 1996).

Types of People, Types of Relationships

People differ in the ways they approach close relationships. Securely attached individuals are comfortable relying on the partner for support and acceptance. Avoidant individuals fear reliance on others, and anxious individuals worry that the partner will not be available and responsive. Gender and culture also play a role. Most relationship research has been conducted in Western, independent cultures.

In a committed close relationship, psychological intimacy allows caring partners to share self-disclosures and to comfort and support each other. However, some people are more comfortable than others with intimacy, trust, and reliance on a partner.

ATTACHMENT STYLES. Take a look at the three self-descriptions in Table 11.1, and decide which one most closely fits you. A questionnaire like this was used in a pioneering study by Cindy Hazan and Philip Shaver (1987) to classify adults as having one of several distinct **attachment styles.** Their study was based on the assumption that, as we have already mentioned, people have built-in tendencies to form emotional attachments to others, beginning in infancy (Bowlby, 1969). Although this psychological mecha-

Attachment styles. People's basic securely attached, avoidant, or anxious orientation toward others in close relationships.

nism is common across all people, our differing lifetime experiences teach us different lessons about what to expect from close partners. If other people (including caregivers in childhood and romantic partners in adulthood) generally are attentive and responsive to our needs, we will come to hold different beliefs and emotional tendencies than if we find other people unresponsive or inconsistent. In fact, even infants display different types of attachment to their mothers (Ainsworth, Blehar, Waters, & Wall, 1978).

The many ways in which our prior knowledge influences our perceptions and interpretations are described in chapter 3, pages 67 to 72.

Attachment styles summarize people's general beliefs about the self, other people, and the nature of relationships (Fletcher & Fincham, 1991; Surra & Bohman, 1991). Like all knowledge structures, these beliefs in turn affect people's perceptions and evaluations of their current relationships (Baldwin, 1992). Thus, attachment styles have been found to relate to many aspects of people's loving relationships (Shaver, Hazan, & Bradshaw, 1988).

Findings regarding attachment orientations are often presented in terms of the three distinct types shown in Table 11.1, though in reality people can be described by a continuous range of values (Fraley & Waller, 1998). *Securely attached* people, about 59% of the adult population (Mickelson, Kessler, & Shaver, 1997), are the most likely to feel happiness and trust in their relationships, are highest in self-esteem, and are the least likely to fear closeness. Those categorized as *avoidant* (about 25%) fear closeness and are less accepting of their partners than are those in the other groups. As adults, avoidants are more prone than the other groups to alcohol or drug abuse (Mickelson and others, 1997). Finally, the 11% classed as *anxious* are most prone to emotional extremes: Compared with others, they feel more jealousy and passion and a greater desire for merging with the partner. Shaver and his colleagues (1988) also found that the three groups held different basic beliefs about self and others. For example, securely attached people are most likely to agree that "I am easier to get to know than most people" and that "people are generally well intentioned and good-hearted."

Do attachment styles actually have effects on the way close partners give and receive support? A fascinating study of dating couples by Jeffry Simpson and his colleagues (Simpson, Rholes, & Nelligan, 1992) examined this question. The researchers separated the couple and led the woman to a waiting room, where she was told that she would soon undergo "experimental procedures that arouse considerable anxiety and distress." To underline this warning, they showed her a darkened room resembling an isolation chamber, filled with complex electronic equipment. The man, unaware of his partner's experience, was then brought into the waiting room and the couple's ensuing interaction was covertly videotaped for 5 minutes.

People with different attachment styles showed distinct variations in their patterns of seeking and giving support, and the strongest differences were found between the securely attached and avoidant categories. Among securely attached women, those who were extremely upset sought more support from their partners than did those who were less frightened. In contrast, among avoidant women, extremely upset participants actually sought *less* support than did their less frightened counterparts. Almost one fifth of the women, mostly those classified as avoidant, did not even mention the stressful event to their partners! The men's attachment styles also played a role in the amount of support they offered. Securely attached men tended to offer more support to a partner who displayed more fear than to a partner who was less frightened. But among avoidant men, a different pat-

TABLE 11.1. An Example of Statements Measuring Attachment Styles in Adult Close Relationships.

Self-description	Attachment style	Basic beliefs about self, others, and love
I find it relatively easy to get close to others and am comfortable depending on them and having them depend on me. I don't often worry about being abandoned or about someone getting too close to me.	Secure	I am likable. Other people are generally good-hearted. Romantic love can last.
I am somewhat uncomfortable being close to others; I find it difficult to trust them completely, difficult to allow myself to depend on them. I am nervous when anyone gets too close, and often, love partners want me to be more intimate than I feel comfortable being.	Avoidant	I am not particularly easy to get to know. It's rare to find somebody you can really fall in love with. Romantic love rarely lasts.
I find that others are reluctant to get as close as I would like. I often worry that my partner doesn't really love me or won't want to stay with me. I want to merge completely with another person, and this desire sometimes scares people away.	Anxious	I have many self-doubts. I am not particularly easy to get to know. Few people are as willing as I am to commit themselves to a relationship. It's easy to fall in love.

Source: "Love as attachment: The integration of three behavioral systems" by P. Shaver, C. Hazan, & D. Bradshaw, in R. Sternberg & M. Barnes (Eds.), *The psychology of love* (pp. 80–82), 1988, New Haven, CT: Yale University Press. Reprinted with permission.

tern emerged: The more fear a woman displayed, the less support she was offered.

Regardless of their attachment styles, *all* the women in this upsetting situation were calmed if their partners made supportive comments. The most interesting result of this study is that the avoidant women tended not to ask for, and the avoidant men tended not to offer, this potentially effective interaction.

This study and other research (Reis & Patrick, 1996; Young & Acitelli, 1998) suggest that basic beliefs about self and others, as reflected in attachment styles, influence both people's trust in their partners' support and responsiveness and their own willingness to offer support. Securely attached partners, who turn toward one another for comfort, derive increased satisfaction from their relationship in the long term, compared to avoidant or anxious individuals. As a result of these processes, attachment styles pervasively influence the ways people attain intimacy and experience love. In general, securely attached people are highest in self-esteem and in happiness with their love relationships, and anxious people are lowest in both (Collins & Read, 1990; Simpson, 1990).

The effects of attachment style are so pervasive that they influence people's everyday social interactions, not just their closeness with romantic partners. In one study in which people filled out brief questionnaires following every social interaction for a week (Pietromonaco & Feldman Barrett, 1997), anxious individuals perceived their everyday interactions as involving greater intimacy and they self-disclosed more than others. Secure individuals, in contrast, felt higher self-esteem after routine social interactions. Unexpectedly, in interactions that involved conflict, anxious individuals reported more positive and less negative emotion than the other groups. The researchers explained this finding as resulting from the deep desire for intimacy and personal disclosure that is characteristic of people with an anxious attachment style. In a conflict or argument, the other party typically does respond to you and reveals his or her feelings—even if those feelings are negative! Thus conflict situations in some way suit the interpersonal goals of anxious individuals.

GENDER DIFFERENCES IN RELATIONSHIPS. It may come as no surprise that men and women often approach close relationships differently. Women's close relationships, particularly with same-sex friends, tend to be more intimate than men's (Reis, Senchak, & Solomon, 1985). This is because research shows that women are better at the skills of understanding, empathy, and emotional responsiveness that play such a key role in the self-disclosure process that builds intimacy (Reis & Patrick, 1996). This difference in intimacy is just one aspect of a more general principle: Men and women place different emphases on the various rewards that relationships offer (Tannen, 1990; P. H. Wright, 1982). Men prefer participating in enjoyable activities with their partners, and women generally prefer intimacy and sharing feelings.

In one study demonstrating the impact of these differences on heterosexual relationships, Catherine Surra and Molly Longstreth (1990) questioned dating couples about their activity preferences and conflicts in their relationships. They found that the sources of satisfaction with the relationship differed for men and women. The men's satisfaction depended mainly on the way the couple spent their time: The more time the men spent participating with their partners in activities they enjoyed, the happier they were. In contrast, women were satisfied when the couple successfully avoided arguments and conflict. In general, men care more about the rewards they can obtain from interacting with the partner. Women care more about the relationship itself; they are happiest when the relationship is going well (H. H. Kelley, 1979; P. H. Wright, 1982).

RELATIONSHIPS IN CULTURAL PERSPECTIVE. Existing research on relationships has a particular focus, which becomes clear if we consider relationships from a cross-cultural perspective. Most research, even studies of processes common to all types of close relationships, such as how people handle conflicts, has taken place in North America and has focused on heterosexual romantic relationships. This focus reflects an easily available pool of research participants: dating college students and married couples. However, the emphasis on relationships that are voluntary and often temporary fits well with the general characteristics of Western, independent cultures (Moghaddam and others, 1993). Researchers have largely neglected relationships that are permanent and unchosen, such as ties to kin and other social groups, which in interdependent cultures are even more important than dyadic (two-person) romantic connections (Moghaddam and others, 1993). Perhaps the focus on voluntary relationships is responsible for the strong theoretical focus on exchanges of rewards—on what each partner gets from the relationship—found in interdependence theory (Rusbult & van Lange, 1996).

When researchers cast their net beyond North America, many differences between cultures are found (Markus, Kitayama, & Heiman, 1996). For example, the nature of the early bond between mother and infant, which is central to conceptions of adult attachment, differs considerably in other industrialized nations from its patterns in the United States (LeVine and others, 1994). Our understanding of the full range of human relationships will be further enriched by more cross-cultural research and by theories that are sensitive to cultural assumptions and blind spots (Fiske, 1992).

Effects of Relationships

Relationships affect virtually all aspects of our lives, including physical health and mental well-being. Intimacy accounts for most of these benefits.

In chapter 4 we described research showing that the way we think about ourselves influences our feelings, our behaviors, and even our physical health. Relationships also affect these aspects of our lives, because a partner in a close relationship becomes part of ourself.

☐ **INTIMACY, SOCIAL SUPPORT, AND HEALTH.** The medical community was initially puzzled by research showing that **social support**—coping resources provided by significant others—can influence physical health as well as psychological well-being. The findings are now beyond dispute (Salovey and others, 1998; Uchino, Cacioppo, & Kiecolt-424, 1996). For example, people with cancer and other diseases who participate in support groups of fellow sufferers can obviously expect to receive comfort, reassurance, information, and advice. But it may surprise you to learn that they also have more effective immune-system responses and live longer than patients without such support (Goleman, 1990). One British study demonstrating this point focused on women with advanced breast cancer. Women who received the best available medical care and also attended support groups lived twice as long—an average of 37 months—as women who received the same excellent medical treatment but had no group support. The results of another study of more than 6,000 California residents, shown in Figure 11.6, suggest that social support has a marked impact on people's overall death rate (Berkman & Syme, 1979). A meta-analysis of over 50 such studies demonstrates that the effects of social support on physical health are pervasive, but they are stronger for support given to women rather than men, and stronger when the support is provided by family and friends rather than by strangers (Schwarzer & Leppin, 1989).

How does social support produce these striking benefits? Other people can provide practical help, from offering advice about problems to running errands for the patient. However, these concrete forms of assistance do not by themselves translate into the benefits of social support. Instead, social

Social support. Emotional and physical coping resources provided by other people.

FIGURE 11.6   Social support and physical health

■ Researchers questioned over 6,000 California residents about their social support. Nine years later, they calculated the death rate from all causes for individuals who initially had been categorized as having various levels of social support. This graph shows the rates for people aged 30 to 49, though findings were similar for other age groups. As you can see, both men and women who initially had higher levels of social support had lower death rates. (Data from Berkman & Syme, 1979.)

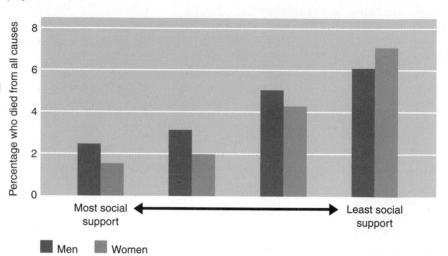

support offers opportunities for self-disclosure, companionship, and enjoyable interactions, and these seem to account for most of its benefits (Rook, 1987; Sarason, Shearin, Pierce, & Sarason, 1987; Wills, 1991). Relationships that are best for social support are those that involve high levels of intimacy and affection (Burleson, 1994; Reis & Franks, 1994). Thus, the same factors that provide the deepest satisfaction in our relationships in good times are also those that help most in bad times.

In general, married people are more likely to have a psychologically intimate relationship than unmarried people, although, as we will see, there are some exceptions to this generalization. The benefits of psychological intimacy mean, therefore, that marriage usually improves people's well-being, particularly men's, making them happier and more satisfied with their lives than unmarried people are (Veroff, Douvan, & Kukla, 1981). Again, happiness translates into health. In one study, married men aged 45 to 64 had just one half the death rate of unmarried men, even after other influences on health like income, smoking, drinking, and obesity were taken into account (Angier, 1990b). Remember, though, that it is psychological intimacy, not marriage itself, that produces these benefits. Many people, particularly women, find social support and intimacy in close friendships or nonmarital romantic relationships. And troubled marriages may bring not support but distress, which recent evidence suggests may translate directly into immune system malfunction (Kiecolt-424, Malarkey, Cacioppo, & 424, 1994; Rook & Pietromonaco, 1987).

GENDER AND SOCIAL SUPPORT. Deborah Tannen (1990, p. 49) described a woman who was upset about a scar left visible on her body by an operation. Here are the responses she obtained from two different people:

> *A:* "I know. It's like your body has been violated."
>
> *B:* "You can have plastic surgery to cover up the scar."

Did you guess that response *A* came from a woman and *B* from a man? Women are more likely than men to respond to someone's negative feelings with understanding and acceptance—to reassure the speaker that it's all right to feel bad, perhaps by sharing an account of a time when they had similar feelings. Men are more likely than women to take the initial disclosure as a complaint about a problem and to offer helpful advice on solving it. Tannen points out that women and men often misunderstand each other's approaches. A woman may feel that a problem-solving response belittles her feelings by failing to deal with them directly. In this particular episode, the woman was upset because she felt that B (her husband) *wanted* her to have plastic surgery, and that suggesting a solution meant that he was unconcerned about her current emotional state.

But men may be equally troubled by a woman's typical responses. When a woman responds to a man's concerns by saying "I know, sometimes I feel the same way," the man may feel that she is denying the uniqueness of his feelings and failing to contribute to a solution. Miscommunication might be less likely if each gender recognized the other's needs.

Emotional support is more helpful than problem solving to people who are ill or under stress (Rook, 1987; Wills, 1991). Since women are more likely to offer emotional support, it follows that people should feel healthier and happier after interacting with women than they do after interacting with men. And this is true. For both male and female college students, everyday

■ **Social support and health.** Researchers now know that supportive relationships can be just as important to good physical health as medical treatment and healthy living. Many of today's assisted living communities today employ aides whose primary responsibilities are to provide comfort and companionship to residents.

interaction with women is a more effective safeguard against loneliness than is interaction with men (Reis, 1986). Similarly, men seem to benefit more from marriage than women do, and, when a spouse dies, men are at greater risk for depression and physical illness than women are (Bernard, 1973; Reis, 1986).

Of course, this gender difference in psychological intimacy is largely a matter of preference rather than ability (Reis and others, 1985). Both men and women are able to engage in intimate, meaningful interaction and to provide emotional support. All people, regardless of gender, fare better psychologically and physically when they interact with close others in a psychologically and emotionally intimate way.

☐ **LOVE AND WORK.** Relationship troubles can interfere with a person's ability to concentrate on work, and the other side of this coin is that strong relationships can be a real benefit in the workplace. When Cindy Hazan and Philip Shaver (1990) investigated the impact of attachment styles on people's orientations toward work, they found that securely attached people value both love and work and are generally satisfied with their work and their co-workers. In contrast, avoidant individuals may immerse themselves in work to avoid dealing with other people—they may work late, for example, rather than confronting relationship problems. But although they may spend more hours in the workplace, avoidant individuals tend to be less satisfied with their work. Anxiously attached people also operate at a disadvantage. They fear rejection for low performance, enjoy their work less than others do, and may have difficulties concentrating on work unless they see it as an opportunity to gain love and respect from others. Thus, not only are close relationships central to our lives, but they also exert a powerful influence over specific aspects of our lives, such as our physical health and careers.

Romantic Love and Sexuality

Romeo and Juliet, Rhett Butler and Scarlett O'Hara, Madonna and Dennis Rodman—famous lovers of legend and lore feed our ideas about romance. Though high divorce rates suggest that many people fail to find the romance they seek, the ideal itself still influences how we act in relationships and how we feel about them. What is the mysterious force we call *romantic love* or *passion?* And how is it tied up with our ideas about sexuality and marriage?

Passionate Feelings

> Some relationships involve passionate feelings and emotions. Passionate emotions can arise quickly and are closely linked to sexual desires and behavior.

"I want my partner, physically, emotionally, mentally." "Sometimes I feel I can't control my thoughts; they are obsessively on my partner." "I eagerly look for signs indicating my partner's desire for me." These are items from the Passionate Love Scale, developed by Elaine Hatfield (1988). They suggest that *passionate love* involves, in addition to sexual feelings, a sense of intense longing for the partner, euphoric feelings of fulfillment and ecstasy when the relationship goes well, and anxiety and despair when it does not (Hatfield, 1988; Hatfield & Rapson, 1993). Other components of love, such as commitment, trust, intimacy, and attachment, are relatively quiet. When people talk about passionate or romantic feelings, they use words like *stormy, roller coaster, head-over-heels,* and *obsession.* They also add one crucial preposition to the word *love:* being *in* love means feeling not only warmth and affection for the partner, but also sexual attraction (Meyers & Berscheid, 1997).

Romantic love is quite different from liking (Z. Rubin, 1970). Sometimes we realize that the object of our hopeless adoration is someone totally unsuitable, a person we don't know very well or even like very much. As Ellen Berscheid (1988) has noted, the intransigent independence of passionate feelings from the other components of love

> *"can be testified to by anyone who has earnestly desired to be in love with another, often because the other* is *so likable, or because they* do *have all those qualities one desires (or ought to desire) in a mate, or because it would please one's parents, friends, or the other person; one can like the other so hard one's nose bleeds, but that—still—does not, and seemingly cannot, cause the liking state to be transcended and romantic love to appear." (p. 369)*

The vast majority of research on romantic relationships has examined heterosexual couples, though available evidence suggests that homosexual and heterosexual romantic relationships are much more alike than different (Kurdek, 1991; Leigh, 1989). In heterosexual relationships, men generally seem to be more romantic than women (K. L. Dion & Dion, 1988). For example, a study of college-student dating couples found that men tended to fall in love more quickly than women, while women fell *out* of love more readily (C. T. Hill and others, 1976).

Besides these gender differences, views on the mysterious and powerful force of passion differ from culture to culture. Most North Americans believe that romantic love is natural, desirable, and necessary for marriage (Simpson, Campbell, & Berscheid, 1986). However, most Chinese words for love have negative connotations, like *infatuation, unrequited love, sorrow* (Hatfield & Rapson, 1993). In China, more pragmatic attributes (like a high income) are viewed as desirable characteristics in a marriage partner; romantic love is viewed with some suspicion, as illicit and socially disruptive (Dion & Dion, 1988). Consistent with these cultural ideas, cross-national research finds that Americans are more likely than Russians or Japanese people to report experiencing romantic passion (Sprecher and others, 1994).

Passion *is* disruptive, as are other strong emotions. And, like all emotions, passion is linked to a set of beliefs about the beloved and motivations for specific types of action. The beliefs often idealize the partner: "For me, my partner is the perfect romantic partner" is another item from the Passionate Love Scale (Hatfield, 1988). The desired actions include sexual union and other types of closeness and contact with the beloved, such as touching or sustained eye contact. The high emotional value that lovers place on close contact may stem from the same innate attachment system

Calvin and Hobbes by Bill Watterson

Calvin and Hobbes © 1986 Watterson. Distributed by Universal Press Syndicate. Reprinted with permission.

that also serves to keep helpless infants in close proximity to their mothers (Bowlby, 1969; Hazan & Shaver, 1987).

Like all emotions, and like a roller coaster, passion has its peaks and valleys. When couples proclaim that they fell in love "at first sight," you can be sure that passion rather than commitment or intimacy is what they are describing. In fact, people often view passion as something that happens *to* them, as though they were struck by Cupid's arrow. Perhaps this helps explain why individuals who believe that external forces drive their lives are more likely to experience passionate love than are people who think they control their own fate (K. L. Dion & Dion, 1988).

The intense and sudden onset of passion at the beginning of a relationship is not surprising when you consider how important physical attractiveness is to initial attraction (R. J. Sternberg, 1986). However, after drawing people together, passion tends to fade as the relationship matures (R. J. Sternberg, 1988). Intimacy and commitment develop more slowly but become more important over time, giving a long-term close partnership quite a different character from the turbulent and frenzied feelings of its beginning.

As with many emotions, excited feelings that arise from other causes may intensify the experience of passion. As we saw in chapter 4, people cannot always accurately identify the causes of their emotional arousal. For this reason, anything that causes arousal can influence passionate feelings. A few minutes of exercise or a hilarious Steve Martin comedy routine, for instance, can intensify passionate feelings toward attractive others (G. L. White, Fishbein, & Rutstein, 1981; Zuckerman, 1979). The fact that arousal from external sources can intensify passionate feelings may explain the fact that, as we mentioned earlier, individuals with an anxious attachment style are more likely than others to fall head-over-heels in love, to experience obsessive preoccupation with the beloved, and to feel the emotional highs and lows that are characteristic of passion (Shaver and others, 1988). Similarly, adolescents who are highly anxious are particularly likely to experience passionate love (Hatfield, Sprecher, Pillemer, Greenberger, & Wexler, 1989).

In ordinary circumstances, where extraneous factors are not involved, what is the source of the arousal that underlies and strengthens passion? Ellen Berscheid (1988), who has been studying love for three decades, answered this question by saying: "If forced against a brick wall to face a firing squad who would shoot if not given the correct answer, I would whisper 'It's about 90 percent sexual desire as yet not sated' " (p. 373).

Sexual Attitudes and Behavior

People's attitudes about sex differ widely, depending in part on gender and personality differences. Some people see sex as an enjoyable activity even outside of a committed relationship; others see it as an expression of intimacy and commitment to the partner.

Do you think sexual activity is appropriate between people who like each other, even if they have not known each other very long? Between individuals who have a committed relationship but are not married? Between people of the same gender? Between a married person and someone other than his or her spouse? Does your opinion change depending on the kind of sexual activity—intercourse versus kissing and fondling, for example?

Researchers have asked such questions in surveys of the U.S. general public and of U.S. college students. As Table 11.2 shows, most people approve of sexual activity in a committed heterosexual relationship between

TABLE 11.2. Sexual Attitudes and Behaviors: Survey Results

Respondents	Statement	Percentage agreeing	
		Male	Female
	Premarital sex		
General public	A man and woman having sex relations before marriage is wrong only sometimes or not wrong at all.	69	58
College freshmen	A couple should live together for some time before deciding to get married.	58	47
College freshmen	If two people really like each other, it's all right for them to have sex even if they've known each other only a very short time.	66	39
	Extramarital sex		
General public	A married person having sexual relations with someone other than the married partner is wrong only sometimes or not wrong at all.	12	6
	Same-gender sex		
General public	Sexual relations between two adults of the same sex are wrong only sometimes or not wrong at all.	15	22
College freshmen	It is important to have laws prohibiting homosexual relations.	62	45
General public	Identifies self as homosexual or bisexual	2.8	1.4
General public (ages 18–44)	Reports that idea of sex with a same-sex partner would be "somewhat" or "very" appealing	6	6

Sources: Data from "Report: The sexual revolution?" by T. W. Smith, 1990, *Public Opinion Quarterly, 54,* 415–435; and *The American freshman: National norms for fall 1987* by A. W. Astin, K. C. Green, W. S. Korn, & M. Schalit, 1987, Los Angeles, CA: Higher Education Research Institute, University of California at Los Angeles. Reprinted with permission.

unmarried people. Indeed, premarital intercourse seems to be very common: One study of teenagers found that about 75% of men and 60% of women had engaged in sexual intercourse, before age 18 on the average (DeLamater & MacCorquodale, 1979). Attitudes toward other types of sex outside of marriage are more negative. A great majority of the public sees extramarital sex as wrong, though a recent survey estimated that 15% of married women and 25% of married men in the United States have had extramarital affairs (Laumann, Gagnon, Michael, & Michaels, 1994).

Gay and lesbian sexual activity is viewed almost as negatively. Contrary to the image of college students as sexually permissive, many students advocate laws against homosexual activities. In terms of actual behavior, while only about 3% of U.S. men identify themselves as gay or bisexual, about twice that percentage report having had at least one homosexual encounter since puberty (Laumann and others, 1994). The proportions for women are somewhat lower. None of these figures can be taken as valid for all time and all sorts of people, however. Patterns of sexual attitudes and behavior have been changing rapidly in recent decades, and the most recent available data suggest increased acceptance of homosexual activity among the general U.S. public. There has been a rise in the proportion saying it is wrong only sometimes or not at all, from 18% in 1990 to 32% in 1996 (Yang, 1997). Perhaps part of this shift is attributable to the greatly increased numbers of people who say that they have a friend or acquaintance who is gay or lesbian, which reached 56% of the adult population in 1996, more than double what it was a decade earlier (Yang, 1997).

Opinions are sharply divided on whether it's all right for unmarried people to engage in sex when they have known each other for a very short time. About two thirds of college men and one third of college women approve. Since the 1950s and 1960s, men's and women's attitudes toward sex have converged somewhat, but differences like this one still remain (Hendrick, Hendrick, Slapion-Foote, & Foote, 1985; Oliver & Hyde, 1993). Because of women's comparatively conservative stance, they tend to control the actual level of sexual intimacy in a relationship. That is, the traditional roles of males as initiators and females as gatekeepers apparently still hold (Surra & Longstreth, 1990).

PERSONALITY DIFFERENCES IN SEXUAL ATTITUDES. Although we have been discussing overall differences between men and women, the sexual attitudes and behaviors of individuals within each gender differ in systematic ways. Some people have what is termed a *restricted sociosexual orientation:* They seek closeness and commitment in a relationship before engaging in sex (Simpson & Gangestad, 1991). Individuals with an *unrestricted sociosexual orientation,* in contrast, have relatively permissive attitudes toward sex without commitment. When the two types are compared, unrestricted individuals report having had more "one-night stands" in the past, foresee having more sex partners in the future, and are more likely to maintain sexual relationships with more than one partner. Their relationships also involve less commitment, less love, and less psychological intimacy (Simpson & Gangestad, 1991). Perhaps as a result, unrestricted individuals' romantic relationships tend to break up relatively quickly (Simpson, 1987).

These findings suggest that people attach many different meanings to sexual activity. Some see it as an enjoyable activity even outside of a committed relationship. Others see it as an expression of intimacy and commitment

Chapter 5, pages 195 to 196, explained how a friendship across group lines can reduce people's prejudice not only against the friend's group, but against other out-groups as well.

to the partner. Because sexual activity has so many meanings, open communication about it is extremely important in a relationship. If one partner thinks sex is just good fun and the other assumes it means commitment, serious conflicts are bound to result. But what are the actual effects of sexual activity on a relationship? Does it, for example, strengthen a dating relationship, making it psychologically more intimate, or can it become a focus of conflict capable of driving the couple apart? Because sexual activity can be interpreted in so many different ways, its impact on relationship processes will also vary, depending on the individuals and their relationship.

Sex in the Context of a Relationship

Like other mutually enjoyable activities, sexual activity can strengthen a relationship. But it can also be a focus of conflict.

Some research shows that sexual intimacy is associated with increased satisfaction with the relationship. For instance, Jeffry Simpson (1987) studied the stability of relationships among dating couples who were not having sexual intercourse and among dating couples who were. He found that couples having intercourse were more likely to stay together over the course of 3 months.

However, over a longer time period, the picture is not so clear. Anne Peplau and her colleagues (Peplau, Rubin, & Hill, 1977) compared dating couples who had sexual intercourse within a month of their first date, those who had intercourse later (an average of 6 months after starting to date), and those who had not yet had intercourse at the time they were interviewed. The early-sex couples had more liberal sexual attitudes and engaged in sexual relations more often than the later-sex couples, and the women reported more sexual satisfaction. In contrast, the later-sex couples seemed to enjoy more emotional and psychological intimacy. They were more likely to say they were in love, they felt closer to their partners, and they were more likely to predict that they would marry the partner. Despite these differences, the two groups were equally satisfied with the relationships—and so were the couples in the study who had never had intercourse. Two years after the initial study, couples in all three groups reported similar outcomes: About 46% of the couples in all three groups had broken up, 34% were still dating, and 20% had married each other. Thus, neither the timing of sex nor the relative emphasis on psychological intimacy seemed to strongly affect the future of these dating relationships.

Satisfaction with sex is closely tied to relationship satisfaction among married couples (Reiss & Lee, 1988). One study, which compared happily married couples and troubled couples who had sought marital counseling, found that the happily married couples had sex more frequently (Birchler & Webb, 1977). This pattern was not unique to sexual activity, however: These couples did *many things* together more frequently, including participating in sports and social events. The more rewarding and mutually enjoyable the activities in a relationship, the warmer the partners' feelings are likely to be. Conversely, when a couple is dissatisfied with sex or other major components of the relationship, satisfaction with the relationship is also likely to decline.

The reasons for sexual dissatisfaction tend to differ for women and men. Women become dissatisfied if they see their sexual relationships as lacking warmth, love, and caring, whereas men who are dissatisfied want more frequent and varied sexual activity (Hatfield and others, 1989; Laumann and others, 1994). This gender difference, like other differences in sexual attitudes and behaviors, seems to diminish among older adults (Oliver & Hyde, 1993; Sprague & Quadagno, 1989). Sexual activity and satisfaction, however, can be maintained into old age. Although the frequency of sexual activity is lower among older adults than among younger adults, one study interviewed healthy adults ranging in age from 80 to over 100 and found that most were still sexually active (Bretschneider & McCoy, 1988).

People enjoy many types of activities with their partners. So why is sex such a unique and appropriate expression of love and intimacy in a close relationship? At least part of the answer is that sex uniquely combines the two fundamental processes that motivate people to form and maintain close relationships in the first place: mutual pleasure and enjoyment, and intimate self-disclosure (Reiss, 1986). These processes—giving and receiving pleasure, and knowing and being known—both flow from and reinforce the psychological link of partner to self, which is the underlying truth of an intimate relationship.

When Relationships Go Wrong

In the course of most relationships, periods of calm are interspersed with troubled times. When problems do develop, all the processes that helped the relationship bloom appear to go into reverse, speeding up the decline. Partners no longer seem to enjoy doing things together. Their attributions for each others' behaviors become more negative. Instead of intimate self-disclosures and support, they exchange angry words and bitter complaints, which lead to arguments and fights. Understanding the processes of relationship development and maintenance can also help us comprehend how relationships run aground at the very start or slowly deteriorate into conflict and breakup.

Interdependence and Conflict: Seeds of Trouble

Interdependence inevitably leads to disagreements and problems, but the impact of these problems on the relationship depends on how the couple handles them.

In fairy tales, the characters find true love and live happily ever after. Not so in real life, where interdependence inevitably breeds conflicts. The key issue is how couples handle them. How does trouble start, and what resources help people handle conflict constructively and avoid relationship meltdown?

Perhaps you recall a time in your own life when a partner changed—maybe the person lost interest in an activity you had previously enjoyed together or had a falling out with a mutual friend. Because of the interdependence in a close relationship, the change in your partner probably affected you as well. Personal change, illness, or disability can reduce one partner's willingness or ability to meet the other's needs. As one or both find that they derive fewer rewards from the relationship, their satisfaction and commitment eventually decline (Drigotas & Rusbult, 1992; Rusbult & van Lange, 1996).

External factors can also place stresses on relationships. If one person's job or family responsibilities increase, the resulting demands leave less time and energy for the partner. The birth of a couple's first child is a common

■ **Families aren't what they used to be.** In the 1950s, everyone knew, and many sympathized with, the Cleaver family from the hit TV show *Leave it to Beaver*. The family portrayed by this show, however, seems out of touch with the real pressures and stresses placed on today's families. How have social changes including changes in family size and composition and the prevalence of dual-career couples altered the sources of conflict in family relations?

source of stress for this reason: Children bring their parents love and joy, but they also force substantial changes in a couple's activities. One study found that after the baby's arrival, the husband had less time for independent activities, and the couple's joint activities came to more closely reflect the wife's preferences (Crawford & Huston, 1993).

Social norms can also create stress and conflict, by dictating that one partner should perform a particular task regardless of individual preferences or abilities. For example, women in heterosexual couples are generally expected to perform the bulk of the housekeeping chores, even if they also work at a paying job outside the home (Atkinson & Huston, 1984; Biernat & Wortman, 1991). This holds true whether the couple is unmarried or married (Denmark, Shaw, & Ciali, 1985). The imbalance in household responsibility is reinforced by economic factors. Women are paid on average only about two thirds as much as men for full-time, year-round work (Goldin, 1990), which tends to force men into the "breadwinner" role. Conflicts about who does what, such as how to share responsibility for housework, are among the most important causes of break-ups of both married and unmarried heterosexual relationships (Blumstein & Schwartz, 1983; Nettles & Loevinger, 1983).

A wide range of issues can spark relationship conflicts (Gottman, 1979). Leslie Baxter (1986), who asked people who had just ended dating relationships to write about the reasons for the break-ups, found several common themes.

- *Desire for autonomy,* or problems in dealing with interdependence, was cited by 27% of men and 44% of women.

- *Dissimilarity* was almost equally important for men (27%) and women (32%).

- *Lack of support,* or the feeling that the partner undermined rather than enhanced self-esteem, was less important for men (19%) than for women (33%).

- *Lack of openness and intimacy* was also a bigger problem for women (31%) than for men (8%).

- *Absence of romance or passion*—feeling that "the magic has gone"— was an issue for more men (19%) than women (3%).

Finally, an interesting study by Steven Beach and his colleagues (1998) found that envy arising from performance comparisons can spark bad feelings and relationship conflict. Have you and your partner ever worked for the same company, enrolled in the same course, or tried out for roles in the same play? If so, you know that you don't always feel great when your partner gets a glowing job evaluation, top grade, or starring role—if you didn't get as good an outcome yourself. At least with dating partners, areas that are high in self-relevance can become a kind of "romantic battleground" as each partner strives to establish and maintain a positive self-concept in the face of unfavorable comparisons with the partner (Beach and others, 1998). Married couples, in contrast, show concern for their partner's feelings as well as for the damage to their own egos when performance comparisons arise. Their commitment lets them handle the bad feelings that can be aroused by performance comparisons in ways that allow the relationship to survive.

Resources for Handling Conflict: Relationship Maintenance

Conflicts can be handled constructively when the partners hold strongly positive views of each other, when they are strongly committed to the relationship, and when they are securely attached.

Every relationship will eventually run into disagreements about activities, performance comparisons, or some of the other potholes just mentioned. Like an automobile, relationships then require maintenance to repair the damage and continue functioning. Several important resources allow couples to carry out this maintenance and handle conflicts constructively.

IDEALIZATION OF THE PARTNER. As we described earlier, romantic partners often idealize each other; that is, they hold images of the partner that are even more positive than the partner's self-image. You might think that idealization could set the relationship up for a fall when inevitable conflicts destroy the romantic illusions, but in fact idealization helps people deal with conflict. Sandra Murray and John Holmes (1997) found that among both dating and married couples, those with more positive illusions reported less overt conflict and fewer destructive ways of handling conflicts (such as avoidance or returning criticism for criticism). Even among couples with equivalent levels of overall satisfaction with their relationship, illusions had these positive effects. Favorable beliefs about the partner, then, even if they are so biased as to exceed reality, are one important resource that can help couples either avoid conflict or deal with it in useful and productive ways.

COMMITMENT. Commitment is the best predictor of a relationship's staying power over time (Bui and others, 1996; Rusbult, 1983). Strong feelings of commitment can motivate people to overlook their partners' flaws, to communicate about their needs, even to change their own behaviors in ways that help the relationship (Rusbult, Verette, Whitney, Slovik, & Lipkus, 1991). Commitment is also related to willingness to sacrifice for the partner, for example, giving up activities that your partner dislikes or moving to a boring town in the hinterlands because your partner gets a job there (van Lange and others, 1997). As you might imagine, dating couples who perform more of the sorts of constructive behaviors that are linked to commitment are more likely to stay together than couples who perform fewer of them (Berg & McQuinn, 1986).

ATTACHMENT STYLES. Handling conflicts is one of the many important aspects of relationships that is affected by people's attachment styles. Securely attached people generally have high levels of love, commitment, and satisfaction, which allow them to behave constructively when conflict arises (Kobak & Hazan, 1991; Simpson, 1990). They easily overlook a partner's faults or change their own behavior. In contrast, those with avoidant or anxious attachment styles tend to deal with conflict in less constructive ways—with outbursts of negative emotion, for example (Levy & Davis, 1988).

When Jeffry Simpson and his co-workers (Simpson, Rholes, & Phillips, 1996) brought dating couples into their laboratory to discuss a major problem in their relationship, they found that attachment styles influenced the actions and feelings resulting from the interaction. As Figure 11.7 shows, partners

FIGURE 11.7   Effects of attachment style when a couple discusses a major relationship problem

■ In a study by Jeffry Simpson and colleagues (1996), members of dating couples completed questionnaires identifying their attachment styles and then had a discussion of an issue that they identified as significant to their relationship. Discussion of an important relationship problem activates the underlying fears and concerns of anxiously attached individuals, resulting in strong negative feelings during the discussion. As a result, the discussion tends to damage the relationship, resulting in feelings of lessened love and commitment. Avoidant individuals do not experience the same strong negative feelings, but avoidant men tend to act cold and distant during the discussion.

who were anxious showed more stress and anxiety during the interaction, felt more anger toward their partners, and afterward saw their relationships as involving less love and commitment. In other words, discussing relationship problems is extremely difficult for anxious individuals because it activates their fears of abandonment and loss. Avoidant individuals, in contrast, did not display distress or anger during the interaction, nor did they rate their interactions as less close afterward. Avoidant men's behavior was distant and nonsupportive, though this was not true of avoidant women. Secure individuals actually viewed both their partner and their relationship more positively after discussing a major problem. Security of attachment is thus a resource that can allow a couple not only to defuse conflict and prevent it from harming the relationship, but even to turn it to advantage.

Conflict Processes

When one partner acts in ways that damage the relationship, the other partner may respond by trying to repair the damage and maintain the relationship. However, when such constructive responses are absent, a cycle of conflict may result.

The couple's resources, including positive beliefs about each other, commitment, and attachment styles, influence the ways they handle the inevitable bad times and problems.

RESPONDING TO NEGATIVE ACTS. Even in the happiest of relationships, one partner's actions will occasionally annoy or hurt the other. Rusbult and her colleagues (1991) investigated couples' patterns of *accommodation*, the processes of responding to a negative action by the partner. Constructive accommodations are actions that help maintain the relationship, including actively discussing problems, loyally waiting for the situation to improve, or forgiving the partner (McCullough, Worthington, & Rachal, 1997). In contrast, destructive responses, such as screaming at the partner or refusing to spend time together, actively endanger the relationship. A couple's patterns of accommodation, particularly the absence of negative responses rather than the presence of positive ones, influence relationship satisfaction. Constructive accommodation is more likely when people are committed to the relationship (Rusbult, Yovetich, & Verette, 1996). One point to ponder is that, although accommodation sounds like a thoroughly good thing (with its connotations of loyalty, forgiveness, and tolerance), it cannot be assumed to be appropriate in all situations. For women in a relationship with an abusive partner, for example, in many cases leaving the relationship rather than accepting the partner's destructive acts is the best course (Arriaga & Oskamp, in press).

Some evidence indicates that women accommodate more constructively than men do (Rusbult and others, 1991). This finding is consistent with women's general tendency to be comparatively open about their thoughts and concerns about relationships. Men are less likely to talk about how they feel and are more apt to express their unhappiness in nonverbal signs of coldness and distance (Levenson & Gottman, 1985; Tannen, 1990). Like other gender differences, these differing communication patterns can provide a rich soil for the seeds of misunderstanding. She may view his silence as rejection, a signal of declining intimacy and commitment. He may view her openness about her thoughts and feelings as threatening, without realizing that

■ **Breaking up partnerships, breaking up self.** Jealousy, declining intimacy, conflict: These processes come into play if the relationship goes sour. Because the partner becomes part of the self in close relationships, the losses suffered can have detrimental effects on the health and well-being of both partners.

she may verbalize fleeting negative thoughts without attaching great importance to them. If men and women realize that they view communication differently, they can make adjustments and lessen misunderstandings.

Unfortunately, misunderstandings and misinterpretations of a partner's goals and feelings are common when couples argue. And the more troubled the relationship, the more prone the partners are to misunderstand each other. The difficulty is specific to the problematic relationship, for the partners have no similar difficulty in interpreting the feelings and intentions of strangers (Noller & Ruzzene, 1991). When distressed couples misunderstand each other, negative biases in their interpretations may escalate conflict.

To demonstrate this process, one researcher asked one member of a couple to read descriptions of everyday situations, such as, "You and your husband are sitting alone on a winter evening. You feel cold" (Noller, 1980). The woman was asked to imagine that she wanted to know if her husband felt cold, too, and to say, "I'm cold, aren't you?" Based on her verbal and nonverbal messages, the husband then had to guess at the woman's intention, choosing among such alternatives as: "You wonder if only you are cold or if I am cold, too," or "You think I am being inconsiderate in not having turned up the heat by now, and you want me to turn it up right away." In distressed couples, husbands were more likely to pick negative alternatives, even when the intended message was neutral or positive.

ATTRIBUTION: YOU DID IT BECAUSE YOU DON'T LOVE ME. In happy relationships, minor annoyances do not have major consequences because attributions about the partner are positively biased (Fletcher & Fincham, 1991; Harvey & Omarzu, 1997). However, if this pattern is reversed—if the partners are unhappy and attributions are negatively biased—trouble lies ahead.

To investigate the role of attributions, researchers asked happy and unhappy married couples to read brief descriptions of positive or negative behaviors, imagine that their spouse had performed the behavior, and provide an explanation for it (Fincham & O'Leary, 1983). Happy partners offered benign attributions, viewing positive behaviors as reflecting the partner's likable dispositions and seeing negative behaviors as inadvertent minor mistakes. Unhappy partners showed the opposite bias, viewing the partner's actions with great suspicion. They attributed positive behaviors to aspects of the situation or other external forces, and they attributed negative acts to the partner's bad intentions or unlikable personality. They might think: "My partner is acting nice only because other people are around, not because she loves me," or "I don't care if he did have a bad day at work—this constant criticism is typical of someone as mean-spirited and selfish as he is." A shift toward negative attributions often precedes other indications of marital conflict, suggesting that attributions are a basic cause of relationship dissatisfaction (Bradbury & Fincham, 1990).

CYCLES OF CONFLICT. Negative attributions and unwillingness to accommodate constructively can release a vicious cycle of conflict, as each partner responds to the other's destructive behavior with an equally destructive reaction (Noller & Ruzzene, 1991). In a conversation, happy couples are likely to nod and smile at each other, to make eye contact, and to agree, whereas unhappy couples sneer, scowl, and shout, reciprocating each other's negative acts (Gottman and others, 1976). Ending such a cycle requires trust and the willingness to inhibit angry, hurtful impulses. Once a couple has raised their voices and exchanged insults, they find it very difficult to proceed immediately to a calm, logical approach to problem solving (D. R. Peterson, 1979). The first step must be *emotional* reconciliation, which usually has two aspects. They must put the problem in perspective ("It's not important enough to fight about"), and one partner must accept some blame for the conflict ("I guess I was wrong to do that, and I'll try to fix it"). In relatively mild conflicts, it is most often the man who tries to assuage negative feelings. However, when feelings run strongest, men seem less likely to do this, leaving responsibility for deescalation to women (Hatfield & Rapson, 1993). If the partner accepts a "peace offering" and makes a conciliatory move in return, anger can diminish and the parties can begin cooperating to solve the problem. Fortunately, constructive ways to handle conflict can be taught to couples, with a real impact on satisfaction and divorce rates. One study in Germany, for example, compared 55 couples who completed a 6-session program on effective communication and problem solving and 17 comparable couples who did not receive the training. Three years later, the trained couples not only reported more satisfaction and more positive communications in their relationship, but also had a lower rate of divorce (Hahlweg, Markman, Thurmaier, Engl, & Eckert, 1998).

HANDLING CONFLICTS IN EVERYDAY LIFE. Research on relationship conflicts suggests two constructive approaches to reducing your own conflicts.

- Try to avoid generalizing about the partner; instead, focus on discussing concrete actions. By doing so, you will help keep the problem in perspective and also avoid the tendency to become embroiled in arguments over negatively biased attributions. A conflict that has escalated from the behavioral level of "You did this" to the attributional level of "You always . . . ," "You never . . . ," or "You are such a . . ." becomes almost irresolvable (D. R. Peterson, 1983).
- Try to communicate about your feelings, perhaps with the words *I feel*. Contrast these statements: "You always leave the house so messy," versus "I feel upset when I see things left lying around the house." The first is accusatory and is likely to lead to pointless argument that avoids the real issue, such as: "I don't *always* . . . ," or "It

Similar processes are involved in the reduction of large-scale intergroup conflict, as we will see in chapter 13, pages 539 to 541.

You may recall that attributing problems to global and stable causes can also lead to trouble of another sort. It is a recipe for learned helplessness and depression, as we discussed in chapter 4, pages 139 to 140.

is not messy!" or "You sometimes leave messes, too." The "I feel" statement avoids these reactions because it is less likely to trigger defensiveness and it cannot really be contradicted—the partner is not likely to deny that the speaker feels upset. Most important, the statement focuses both partners' attention on the real problem, which is negative feelings. Because it correctly attributes the feelings to the person and not to the external situation, "I feel" invites appropriately focused problem solving (Gottman and others, 1976).

JEALOUSY. When real or imagined rivals appear on the scene, most people experience a twinge of jealousy. This familiar negative emotion may be especially strong if a person feels inadequate in the relationship or distrusts the partner's commitment (G. L. White, 1981). Any sign of the partner's interest in other people may seem to be a dress rehearsal for impending rejection and the end of the relationship.

Feelings of depression, anxiety, and anger may accompany jealousy. The depression and anxiety arise from the threatened loss of the valued relationship. Thus, they are similar to the feelings that would be aroused by other possible sources of loss, such as a serious illness. Anger, in contrast, is due to the loss of self-esteem from being rejected by the partner in favor of someone else (Mathes, Adams, & Davies, 1985). As you might expect, people whose attachment style is anxious experience jealous feelings more often, but their fear of losing the relationship makes them unlikely to express anger toward the partner. In contrast, securely attached people are less likely to experience jealousy. When they do, they are likely both to show their angry feelings toward the partner and to try to maintain the relationship (Collins & Read, 1990; Sharpsteen & Kirkpatrick, 1997). In fact, episodes of jealousy can end up strengthening a relationship, a surprising outcome reported by many couples (Fitness & Fletcher, 1993).

However, extreme jealousy can be profoundly destructive, particularly when an individual feels that his or her self-worth is completely dependent on the relationship. The rage and anger that can arise when a threat to the relationship is interpreted as a fundamental threat to self-esteem can lead even to suicide and murder. Jealousy is estimated to be a factor in as many as one quarter of all homicides (Salovey & Rodin, 1989).

DECLINING INTIMACY AND COMMITMENT. As conflicts escalate, the partners may spend less time together and become less open about their inner feelings. One important reason feelings are not shared is that many of them are likely to be negative. The growing distance diminishes the relationship's level of intimacy and, because intimacy is one of the most important rewards a relationship can offer, it speeds a downward spiral of dissatisfaction. Although the relationship may continue to satisfy needs for sociability or for sex, it no longer provides the feelings of self-validation and acceptance that spring from deeply intimate partnerships. In fact, low levels of intimacy, reflected in limited self-disclosure and low levels of attachment and love, characterize relationships that are destined for disintegration (Hendrick, Hendrick, & Adler, 1988; C. T. Hill and others, 1976).

Even strong commitment, the glue that holds relationships together, can break down under the stress of conflict and dissatisfaction. Because satisfaction with the relationship is one key ingredient in commitment, the partners may begin to perceive alternatives as more attractive when a relationship declines, and accumulated investments may no longer seem to be important barriers to leaving (Rusbult & van Lange, 1996). Unfortunately, this process feeds on itself: As you begin to view others as potential partners, those others note your potential availability and may in turn begin to pay you more attention. The comparison level against which you assess the benefits of this relationship thus starts to change. In other words, you will have a growing sense that the grass might be greener on the other side of the relationship fence.

☐ **RELATIONSHIP CONFLICT AND SOCIAL PROBLEMS.** Several significant social problems have their ultimate roots in conflicts in intimate relationships. Severe violent assaults are estimated to occur in about one in ten American marriages (Dutton, 1996). One study found that 25% of all violent crimes against women are committed by family members or people they have dated, compared with just 4% of violent crimes against men (T. Lewin, 1991). Violence and spousal abuse are related to the same factors that lead to relationship conflict and break-up in general, underlining their origin in fundamental relationship processes (Berscheid & Reis, 1998).

Why do women sometimes remain in abusive relationships? Though the question is an obvious one to ask, we should resist any implication that women should be blamed for their own victimization. Like abuse itself, at least part of the answer to this question flows from processes that operate in all relationships. One study of women who fled to a battered women's shelter found that whether or not they returned to the relationship depended on the same factors that determine commitment to a relationship in general: the quality of their alternatives and their investments in the relationship (Rusbult & Martz, 1995). If a women sees few or no alternatives and has invested years of time, she may well stay even if the relationship yields more costs than rewards.

Severe conflict in families can lead not only to violence but also to psychological problems for children. Recent large-scale studies of children in the United States and Britain examined the negative effects that are typically found in children whose parents have divorced (Cherlin and others, 1991). Like other research, these studies found that such children displayed more behavior problems and had lower school achievement than children from intact families. However, these researchers found that the problems usually appeared *before the parents separated.* Thus, these problems are not due to the trauma of divorce itself, as many people assume, but to conditions within intact but troubled families. As these studies indicate, the immediate costs of ending a conflict-filled relationship are sometimes easier to bear than the longer term costs of perpetuating it.

Break-Up and Aftermath

If a relationship breaks up, each partner usually blames the other for its general decline. Individuals cope more effectively if they feel they controlled the final separation. After the end of a close relationship, loneliness and other negative feelings are common.

THE BREAK-UP: YOUR FAULT, MY DECISION. Sometimes a relationship may reach the breaking point. In dating couples as well as marriages, women terminate heterosexual relationships more often than men do (J. D. Gray & Silver, 1990;

C. T. Hill and others, 1976). As you may recall, women are more distressed than men by relationship conflict, and that fact may explain why they more often pull the plug (Surra & Longstreth, 1990). But no matter who delivers the final word, the end of a relationship is often a lengthy and complex process, with repeated episodes of conflict and reconciliation (Cate & Lloyd, 1988). Each partner may feel victimized by the other, and their perceptions of responsibility for the relationship's decline may differ markedly. One study of divorced couples showed, not surprisingly, that each spouse primarily blamed the other for the decline of the relationship (J. D. Gray & Silver, 1990). However, the partners who felt that they controlled the separation itself coped more effectively with it. In dealing with the death of a relationship, as in so many other stressful events, feelings of psychological control are a key resource.

Chapter 4, pages 145 to 147, described how perceived control helps people cope with stressful events.

AFTER THE BREAK-UP: GRIEF AND DISTRESS FOR TWO. Most of us have been observers or participants in the break-up of more than one relationship and have seen first-hand that the psychological consequences of breaking up can vary. One sample of student dating couples found that the more depressed, lonely, and unhappy one partner felt after the break-up, the less the other partner did (Hill and others, 1976). Evidently, being the "breaker-upper" feels different from being the "broken-up-with." But whatever your role, because close relationships are so psychologically important, the experience of ending a relationship is almost always more negative than positive. If the partners cared deeply and helped each other in many ways, grief and distress are bound to occur. Such feelings arise even if the relationship's rewards were taken for granted before the break-up or if the interactions in the relationship were mostly negative (Berscheid, 1988; Simpson, 1987). A longitudinal study by Susan Sprecher (1999) underlines the fact that breaking up is usually not an easy decision. This research found that in couples that would later break up, their self-reports of various aspects of their relationship, such as satisfaction and commitment, became less positive before the final break. Interestingly, while satisfaction tended to diminish most, reports of love diminished least. This pattern means that for many couples, break-ups occur not because the partners "fall out of love," but because rising dissatisfaction and frustration from the relationship eventually outweigh the positive and loving feelings that are still present.

The cognitive and emotional consequences of the end of a close relationship can be long-lasting. People may reflect often and intensively on why the relationship ended, as they do concerning other important negative events (Harvey, Wells, & Alvarez, 1978). Because failures of relationships often leave the partners baffled about what went wrong, the search for causes may become somewhat obsessive as the person repeatedly reviews past events. Feelings of control, for example, knowing that you decided to end the relationship, or believing that you understand what happened, may influence the course of this stage (L. F. Clark & Collins, 1993). And understanding the causes of a relationship's end is an important learning experience that is likely to increase the chances of success in future relationships.

TILL DEATH DO US PART. Some close relationships are ended by death rather than break-up. The death of a spouse is regarded as the most stressful major life event (McCrae & Costa, 1988). It is also a particularly common one: Almost half of the population will experience it. The first year or two following the death of a spouse are marked by serious threats to mental and physical health (Hansson, Stroebe, & Stroebe, 1988). Most people eventually make it through this period and recover their previous levels of well-being, but a minority fail to recover even after several years. The most serious problems are likely to befall those whose spouses died unexpectedly and who believe that they have little control over their future (Stroebe, Stroebe, & Domittner, 1988), a belief that may cripple their ability to cope effectively. Social support from friends, self-help groups, or professional counselors can help the bereaved cope. Social support offers some of the rewards, such as opportunities to express inner feelings and to receive understanding and acceptance, that were part of the vanished relationship (Vachon and others, 1982).

LONELINESS. No matter what terminates a close relationship—death, conflict, or simple geographical separation—the end usually brings loneliness. Lonely people feel distress, desperation, boredom, and depression. They may even view themselves as unattractive or unlovable (Rubenstein, Shaver, & Peplau, 1979). Feeling lonely is not the same as being alone: Sometimes you can feel loneliest in the middle of a crowd. Rather, *loneliness* is an emotion arising from unmet needs for affection and self-validation from a psychologically intimate relationship (Shaver & Hazan, 1985). Loneliness is more a matter of lacking quality interactions—intimate ones—than of lacking quantity (Kraus, Davis, Bazzini, Church, & Kirchman, 1993). Intense feelings of loneliness are common not only after the end of a relationship but also when people move to a new area and are separated from their existing close relationships.

The most effective responses to loneliness include trying to find new ways to meet people and making something valuable out of solitude: learning a new skill or hobby, studying or working, or listening to music (Rook & Peplau, 1982). More negative reactions include dwelling on your bad qualities, or even drinking and drug use. A study of college students by Carolyn Cutrona (1982) found that those who thought of loneliness as arising from transitory, potentially controllable causes most easily overcame it. Students who saw their loneliness as resulting from stable, negative personal qualities, such as unattractiveness or shyness, were more likely to remain lonely for long periods of time.

Cutrona also found that lonely people who downplayed the importance of friendship and thought that only a romantic relationship could help them had a more difficult time. Perhaps this is because friends are easier to find than "that perfect someone." After all, as we have seen in this chapter, a close friendship can meet our needs for self-validation and psychological intimacy (Rook & Peplau, 1982). These, rather than the sexual expression found in a romantic relationship, bring most of the benefits of relationships.

UNREQUITED LOVE. So far we have been focusing on relationships that are mutual, but some of the most difficult relationship problems arise when love is not reciprocated. Roy Baumeister and Sara Wotman (1992) have found that there is pain on both sides in such a relationship, as you may know from your own experience. Of course, the rejected lover suffers the pangs of heartbreak and lost self-esteem. However, because this person often blindly maintains loving and hopeful feelings, he or she ultimately may have some positive memories of the episode, along with the disappointment. For the rejector, the picture is more thoroughly negative. Although

As we saw in chapter 4, pages 138 to 140, stable internal explanations for negative events may even turn an episode of loneliness into severe depression.

self-esteem initially may be bolstered by the rejected lover's obvious adoration, any benefits to self-esteem are often quickly supplanted by feelings of guilt, irritation, and even rage. Trying to be polite to the suitor may only raise false hopes.

Research indicates that more than half of all college women may have experienced daily letters and late-night phone calls from rejected suitors (Jason, Reichler, Easton, Neal, & Wilson, 1984). For those who must deal with a would-be lover, Elaine Hatfield and Richard Rapson (1993) recommend using what they term the "zombie" approach. When interaction is unavoidable, be polite and brief. Display no emotion, negative or positive, that might reward the pursuer; remember, emotional self-expression is a type of intimacy.

CONCLUDING COMMENTS

In concluding the chapter, we turn from conflict, break-up, and loneliness to something more positive: relationships that survive the challenges of time. Two factors are common to strong relationships in which the partners maintain and increase their love.

1. *The relationship satisfies many of the partners' individual needs.* Other people benefit us in many ways: as companions for leisure activities, as sources of social comparisons that help us understand ourselves, and as sources of validation for our beliefs and opinions. Relationships are most likely to meet our mastery needs in these ways when the partners are similar in their needs and desires, and when they reward each other to show love and caring.

2. *The relationship provides the partners with a sense of relatedness and connectedness.* As we indicated in chapter 6, belonging to a group can give people the sense that they have a special place in the social world and that others value their thoughts, feelings, and behaviors—their very presence. As you have seen, intimacy and self-disclosure in a close relationship with another individual can also fulfill this need.

The dual motives of seeking individual satisfaction and interdependent relatedness run as two parallel threads throughout many of the topics we have discussed in this chapter.

- Relationship development proceeds through the exchange of rewards as the partners satisfy each others' needs, and through the exchange of self-disclosures as the partners build the intimate linkage of partner to self.

- Gifts given and favors performed in a relationship have a dual meaning. The concrete act may be pleasant and rewarding in itself. The underlying messages of love and relatedness that each partner sends the other by kind and thoughtful acts become equally crucial.

- Gender differences in relationships reflect the dual motives of individual satisfaction and interdependent relatedness. Men generally

CHAPTER 11 THEMES

- **Construction of Reality**
  We use biased attributions to construct an idealized impression of a relationship partner.

- **Pervasiveness of Social Influence**
  In a close relationship, the partner becomes part of the self, influencing all aspects of thoughts, feelings, and behavior.

- **Striving for Mastery**
  Relationships with others help us obtain rewards and individual satisfactions.

- **Seeking Connectedness**
  Relationships with others help give us feelings of connectedness and belonging.

- **Valuing Me and Mine**
  We are biased to view relationship partners favorably when they become part of the self.

emphasize rewards, such as participating in enjoyable activities with the partner, and women often care more about intimacy, the self-disclosure of feelings, and intimate talks.

- Sexual behavior is particularly appropriate as an expression of relationship closeness because it fits with both motives: It is enjoyable and intimately self-disclosing.

The combination of these two powerful motives—the fact that at their best, close relationships can both help us find ourselves as individuals and find connection to valued others—makes relationships the most important components of our lives. As Charles Darwin wrote long ago (cited in Gould, 1991, p. 401): "Talk of fame, honor, pleasure, wealth, all are dirt compared to affection."

S U M M A R Y

 Initial Attraction. The formation of a relationship is often spurred by feelings of attraction or liking for another person. Attraction to strangers is strongly influenced by perceptions of physical attractiveness. People are also attracted to those with whom they have positive interactions. Interaction helps people to master the world and to find connectedness with others. In addition, interaction leads to familiarity, which increases liking.

Similarity also increases attraction by making positive interaction more likely, by suggesting that the other person likes the individual in return, and by validating the individual's beliefs and attitudes.

Thus, similarity, liking, and interaction all tend to cause one another. As a result, relationships tend to deepen and intensify over time.

From Acquaintance to Friend: Relationship Development. As a relationship begins to develop, the partners treat it as an **exchange relationship,** in which they reward each other to obtain rewards in return. As a relationship deepens, it may shift to a **communal relationship,** in which the partners reward each other to show affection and because they want to make each other happy. Relationship development also includes exchanges of self-disclosures as the partners come to know each other better. Self-disclosures increase liking and offer opportunities for sympathetic, supportive responses.

As the partners interact frequently and exchange rewards and self-disclosures, simple attraction and individual factors such as physical attractiveness become less important. Instead, the nature of the interaction between the partners becomes crucial, and each partner's liking for the other tends to be reciprocated.

Close Relationships. A **close relationship** is one marked by strong and frequent **interdependence,** meaning that each partner's thoughts, emotions, and behaviors influence the other's. A desire for closeness with a particular person seems to correspond to what people generally mean by "love." By necessity, most research on close relationships uses nonexperimental designs that leave some ambiguity about causal relations among variables.

Many processes are common to all types of close relationships, not just romantic ones. In a close relationship, the partner is incorporated into the self, just as an important social group membership may become part of one's identity. Relationship closeness also alters the way partners exchange rewards. In a close relationship, partners reward each other to show affection and because they want to make the partner happy.

Ongoing processes of self-disclosure and sympathetic support lead to psychological **intimacy,** marked by feelings of trust, closeness, and acceptance. As closeness increases, the partners feel a growing sense of **commitment** to each other.

Attachment styles describe differences in the ways people approach close relationships. Securely attached individuals are comfortable relying on the partner for support and acceptance. Avoidant individuals fear reliance on others, and anxious individuals worry that the partner will not be available and responsive. Gender and culture also play a role. Most relationship research has been conducted in Western, independent cultures.

Relationships affect virtually all aspects of our lives. **Social support** from others can improve both physical and mental health and well-being, and the most crucial components of social support appear to be intimacy and acceptance.

Romantic Love and Sexuality. Some relationships involve passionate feelings and emotions. Passionate emotions can arise quickly and are closely linked to sexual desires and behavior. People's attitudes about sex differ widely and depend in part on gender and personality. Some people see sex as an enjoyable activity even outside of a committed relationship; others see it as an expression of intimacy and commitment to the partner. Like other mutually enjoyable activities, sexual activity can strengthen a relationship. But it can also be a focus of conflict.

When Relationships Go Wrong. In any relationship, interdependence inevitably leads to disagreements and problems, but their impact on the relationship depends on how the couple handles them. Conflicts can be handled constructively when the partners hold strongly positive views of each other, when they are strongly committed to the relationship, and when they are securely attached.

When one partner acts in ways that damage the relationship, the other partner may respond by trying to repair the damage and maintain the relationship. However, when such constructive responses are absent, a cycle of conflict may result.

If a relationship breaks up, each partner usually blames the other for the general decline. Individuals cope more effectively if they feel they controlled the final separation, however. After the end of a close relationship, loneliness and other negative feelings are common.

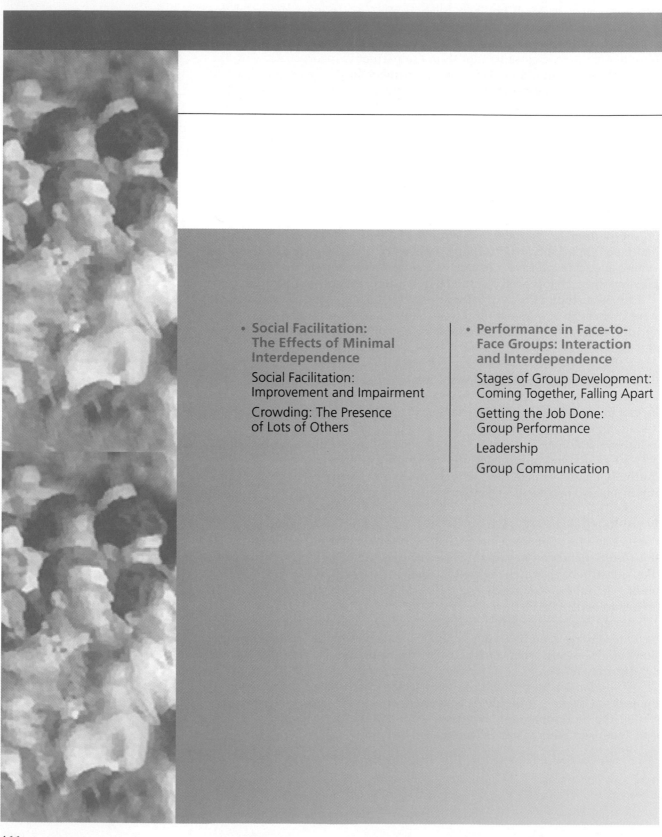

12

Interaction in Groups

The name *Harley-Davidson* was synonymous with *motorcycle* in the United States until high-quality, low-priced Japanese bikes suddenly flooded the market in the late 1970s, catching the U.S. company off guard. Harley-Davidson at that time was a poorly run organization. Its management and employees were often at odds, its product quality was low, and its workers were unmotivated. These problems were reflected in its sales, which soon dropped to only 4% of the U.S. market.

The challenges Harley-Davidson faced 2 decades ago are now widespread throughout the global airline, trucking, banking, automobile, electronics, and other manufacturing industries. As costs escalate and worldwide competition stiffens, industries must come to terms with the fact that the dual goals of high performance and a motivated and enthusiastic work force are more important than ever before.

These critical issues of efficiency and morale are not confined to the workplace, however. They characterize any group of people who interact for some shared purpose and rely on one another to accomplish common goals. Our aim in this chapter is to understand the consequences of group membership for *behavior*. To some extent, this topic has been woven throughout the earlier chapters. In chapter 9, for example, we looked at the ways juries and other groups make decisions. But decision making is often only a first step. Like the people at Harley-Davidson, most groups *act* on their decisions as they win or lose games, manufacture products, regulate work flow through an office, build roads, fight fires, undertake rescues, and treat patients. When people put their heads together—and their muscle and drive—their individual efforts are sometimes multiplied in astonishing ways, and the group can achieve goals far beyond the reach of any one member. The NASA group that put a man on the moon, the underdog French national soccer team that won the 1998 World Cup, and the legions of volunteers who staff the United Way are just a few examples of the remarkable achievements of group action. Of course, as Harley-Davidson's woes make clear, if a group is poorly organized or some of its members slack off, the efforts of hardworking members can be wasted.

Because the outcomes of group action are often strikingly different from the inputs of individual members—and sometimes very different from what is desired and intended—early theorists concluded that the behavior of a group has almost nothing to do with the individual characteristics of its members (Durkheim, 1898; LeBon, 1903). Rather, they argued, people lose their individuality in a group and, swept along by the crowd, no longer have a mind of their own. Although contemporary social scientists do not agree that individuals give up their autonomy to the group, they do recognize that being part of a group affects individual behavior in distinctive and sometimes dramatic ways. We saw in several earlier chapters that membership in groups defined by shared, socially significant features can influence people's thoughts, feelings, and behavior. The effects are even greater when people not only identify with a group but also interact with each other and are *interdependent:* relying on other members' actions as well as their own for mastery of material rewards and feelings of connectedness.

Groups differ in the degree of interaction and interdependence they share. At one extreme is a group of people who, like passengers on an airplane, are physically in the same place but who hardly interact and are only minimally interdependent. At the other end of the continuum are *face-to-face groups* like the decision-making groups we discussed in chapter 9 and those we focus on in most of this chapter. Members of face-to-face groups not only share socially relevant features but also interact and rely on each other to achieve specific goals. Like NASA and the French soccer team, they share values and coordinate their efforts to get things done. Their attempts to reach their goals are marked by intense communication and extensive interaction. The group's success often depends on just how well its leaders and members can manage the problems of interdependence. Indeed, the eventual rebuilding and success of Harley-Davidson was due in large part to its managers' ability to improve *both* production efficiency and worker satisfaction simultaneously (Willis, 1986).

Social Facilitation: Effects of Minimal Interdependence

Imagine that, as you jog along your usual route, you catch up with another jogger who runs alongside you for a couple of blocks. You greet each other with a friendly nod and perhaps check out each other's brand of running shoe, but otherwise you have no contact before you go your separate ways. A block later, you pass by a half-dozen people gathered on a front porch, and they look up and follow your progress down the street. Although your contact with your fellow jogger and with your temporary audience is minimal, their mere presence can influence your behavior in quite predictable ways.

Social Facilitation: Improvement and Impairment

Even when interdependence is minimal, the mere presence of others can produce arousal, either because the other people are highly evaluative or because they are distracting. Arousal improves performance of easy, well-learned behaviors, but can interfere with performance of novel or complex tasks.

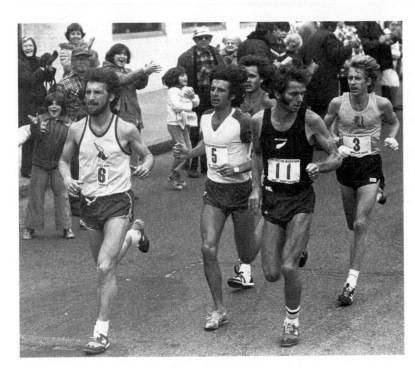

If you are like most people, you will run slightly faster in the presence of others than when you are alone (Worringham & Messick, 1983). This facilitating effect of other people on individual performance may seem familiar. In our discussion of the history of social psychology in chapter 1, we described Norman Triplett's (1898) observation that children winding line onto fishing reels worked more quickly when in the presence of others than when they were alone. Other research confirms the idea that the presence of others improves performance on a variety of simple tasks, from running to solving easy arithmetic problems (Guerin, 1986).

But is having others around always helpful? You may doubt this if you can remember standing in the glare of the footlights desperately trying to remember your lines or stumbling through a complex play on the basketball court before a crowd. And your answer would be correct, for research also shows that the presence of others can interfere with performance. On complicated and difficult tasks, from mazes to math problems to a newly learned tennis serve, our performance declines when others are present (C. F. Bond & Titus, 1983; Guerin, 1986). How can the presence of others both help and hurt performance?

EXPLAINING SOCIAL FACILITATION. In 1965, Robert Zajonc proposed an explanation of these apparently contradictory effects of the presence of others. According to Zajonc, the **social facilitation** effect occurs because the presence of others increases an individual's level of arousal, which in turn makes some behaviors easier and others more difficult. Arousal facilitates the performance of behaviors that are very accessible because they are simple, well learned, and highly practiced (often termed *dominant responses*) but it inhibits the performance of behaviors that are complex or new (*nondominant responses*). Accessibility should be a familiar concept by

> **Social facilitation.** The finding that in the presence of others highly accessible responses become more likely and less accessible responses become less likely.

now. You may recall that accessible thoughts and feelings are more likely to come to mind than are less accessible ones; similarly, accessible behaviors are more likely to be performed than are less accessible ones. Thus, the arousal caused by an audience may help a jogger to run faster, an entrant in a math contest to ace the easy problems, and a professional performer like Placido Domingo to shine in his well-learned concert routines. That same arousal may make it more difficult for a novice skier to complete a difficult course or for the math contestant to answer the tough final questions that will select the winner. When behaviors are complicated or not well learned, the arousal caused by the presence of others will detract from performance.

Because of the contradictory effects of arousal, the presence of an audience can even affect two people in quite opposite ways when they are performing the same task. For example, expert pool players, for whom good shots are highly accessible responses, performed better when an interested audience was close by than when they thought no one was watching. In contrast, poor players, for whom miscues were most accessible, succeeded on fewer shots when others watched (Michaels, Blommel, Brocato, Linkous, & Rowe, 1982). Zajonc's idea (1965) that other people cause arousal and that arousal improves performance of simple tasks but interferes with performance of difficult tasks, makes sense of these findings and has been confirmed by most subsequent research (C. F. Bond & Titus, 1983; Guerin, 1986).

Of course, these findings leave one question unanswered: Why does the presence of others lead to arousal? Zajonc (1965) believed that humans and other animals have an innate tendency to be aroused by other members of their species. But why is this so? Subsequent research points to two underlying causes: evaluation apprehension and distraction (Geen, 1991).

EVALUATION APPREHENSION. Most of the time, we want other people to value, include, and like us. In fact, our self-esteem is greatly affected by what others think of us. For these reasons, we may worry about whether onlookers are judging us in some way. As you jog past people, for example, you may suddenly be concerned about whether you look out of shape, and you may pull in your stomach and step up your pace. Research has confirmed that the presence of others who are in a position to judge us produces *evaluation apprehension* (M. J. Rosenberg, 1969) and that this apprehension changes our performance in the way predicted by social facilitation theory. One study, for example, demonstrated that apprehension can improve performance on simple aspects of a task and hinder it on complex aspects of the same task. Scott Bartis and his colleagues (Bartis, Szymanski, & Harkins, 1988) asked groups of participants to list various uses for a knife. Some participants were given the simple task of coming up with as many uses as possible. Others had the relatively challenging task of being as creative as possible. In each group, some participants believed the experimenter would evaluate their individual performance and others knew their responses would go into a common pool (where they could not be individually evaluated). As Figure 12.1 illustrates, the possibility of evaluation increased output on the simple task, and it decreased output on the intellectually more difficult task.

No wonder, then, that if you expect to succeed at a task (because it is easy, or it involves an accessible response, or you have succeeded at this task in the past), you will do better when you are observed, while the opposite is true if you expect to fail (Sanna & Shotland, 1990). Other researchers have provided evidence that evaluation, not mere presence, is the critical factor that affects

FIGURE 12.1   Effects of evaluation on simple and complex tasks

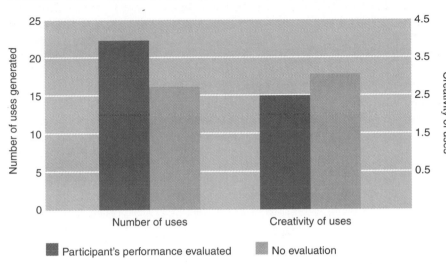

■ Some participants (*dark bars*) knew their individual task performance would be evaluated by the experimenter, while others (*light bars*) did not expect individual evaluations. When the task was fairly simple—generating as many suggestions as possible for ways to use a knife—evaluation improved performance, as shown by the bars on the left. However, when participants were given a much harder task—being as creative as possible in devising uses for the knife—evaluation had the opposite effect; it decreased their creativity (see scale on the right). (Data from Bartis and others, 1988.)

behavior. For example, the presence of actively supportive, nonevaluative observers—humans or even pets—neither provokes arousal nor interferes with performance (K. M. Allen, Blascovich, Tomaka, & Kelsey, 1991).

DISTRACTION. Other people can affect our performance not only by observing and evaluating us but also by creating *distraction.* Their mere presence causes us to think about them, to react to them, or to monitor what they are doing, and thereby deflects attention from the task at hand (Baron, 1986; Guerin, 1986). Researchers in one study, for example, had a person sit behind the participant in a location in which he or she could not possibly monitor the participant's performance. The presence of this person nevertheless improved the participant's performance on easy tasks and interfered with it on difficult ones (Schmitt, Gilovich, Goore, & Joseph, 1986). Such effects have also been found in nonhuman species. For example, centipedes run faster down a glass tube when other centipedes are placed in neighboring tubes than when the additional tubes are empty (Hosey, Wood, Thompson, & Druck, 1985). The centipedes presumably are not concerned about evaluation by the other centipedes. The effect seems to stem from distraction by the presence of others.

It is easy to understand why distraction could interfere with difficult tasks, but why would it improve performance on simple tasks? The answer seems to be that as our impulses to do two different things at once—concentrate on the task and react to others—start to conflict with each other, we become agitated and aroused (Geen, 1991). This arousal, like that caused by evaluation apprehension, can then improve performance on simple tasks and interfere with it on difficult ones. Figure 12.2 shows how the presence of others, even those with whom we do not interact, can make us worry about evaluation or can distract us.

Everyone has to perform in the presence of others from time to time, perhaps delivering an oral report in class or demonstrating a product to a new client. One way to avoid the disruptive effects of an audience is to make sure that your accessible responses—the ones most likely to be activated by arousal—are those that will help you to perform the task. You can make the

FIGURE 12.2 Multiple effects of the presence of others

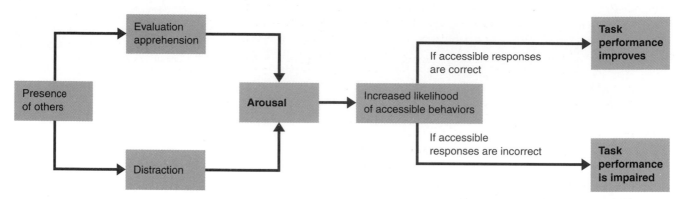

■ The presence of others can produce arousal, through either evaluation apprehension or simple distraction. Arousal increases the likelihood that people will perform the most accessible actions. With a simple or well-practiced task, highly accessible responses are likely to be correct and arousal improves performance. But if the task is complex or novel, accessible responses will not help much and arousal will impair task performance.

appropriate responses accessible by repeatedly practicing the task (Zajonc & Sales, 1966): Then arousal will work for you. Practice has the additional benefit of giving you self-confidence, so that you will not fear the audience's evaluation (Sanna & Shotland, 1990). It can also make your performance less vulnerable to distraction. Just as you can bike the familiar route from school to home without other thoughts getting in the way, practiced responses run from start to finish and resist interference.

☐ **SOCIAL FACILITATION IN THE WORKPLACE: MONITORING AND JOB PERFORMANCE.** In this technological age, observation and evaluation do not require the physical presence of an observer. Some employers monitor their employees' performances through electronic means, for example, by automatically recording the number of keystrokes clerical workers make per minute as they enter data into computers. Does this type of monitoring have the same social facilitation effects as the physical presence of observers? Yes. In an experiment by Jack Aiello and Kathryn Kolb (1995), highly skilled workers performed better when they knew they were being monitored than when they were unmonitored. On the other hand, monitoring decreased the performance of relatively unskilled workers. Monitoring also increased workers' feelings of stress. As this study shows, monitoring and evaluation may have similar effects whether the observers are actually present or are recording performance from afar. Like any form of social facilitation, monitoring sometimes decreases performance, which is the opposite of what employers who implement monitoring presumably expect.

Crowding: The Presence of Lots of Others

Crowding is another source of arousal that can improve performance on easy tasks and disrupt performance on difficult ones. However, the effects of crowding depend on people's interpretation of the situation and on their sense of control.

Being packed into a rush hour subway car or a standing-room-only auditorium is a forcible reminder of how strongly—and negatively—we can be affected by the presence of other people. Researchers studying the effects of crowding in college dormitories found that when three students are assigned to a room designed for two, both their contentment and their grades decline (Karlin, Rosen, & Epstein, 1979). Crowding can even be life threatening: Prisoners confined in crowded jail cells have higher death rates than those in more spacious facilities (McCain, Cox, & Paulus, 1980).

As you might have guessed, crowding has these negative effects because being crowded, like having an audience, is arousing. The arousal occurs for the same reasons: Crowds create many opportunities for evaluation and distraction. One study found, for example, that 10 strangers who were crammed into an 8-by-12-foot room had higher blood pressure and greater increases in other physiological indicators of arousal than did those occupying a larger room (Evans, 1979). Like the arousal produced by an audience, arousal induced by crowding can energize effort, thereby improving performance on simple tasks, such as cheering loudly at a football game, and impairing performance on complex tasks, such as making difficult judgments about the quarterback's passing skills (Hillery & Fugita, 1975; Paulus, Annis, Seta, Schkade, & Matthews, 1976).

☐ **CROWDING AND THE URBAN ENVIRONMENT.** Most social behavior, such as cooperating with others, helping those in need, and resolving conflicts, is complex. Since crowds can interfere with the performance of complex tasks, many people have suggested that living in a crowded city may disrupt social behavior. Crowding is indeed a popular scapegoat for society's ills. It has been blamed for the superficial and transitory relationships of modern life and for deviant behavior, mental illness, and poor physical health (Simmel, 1950). Although social life undoubtedly is affected by the size and density of community populations, the evidence that crowding causes widespread social problems is far from conclusive. Social beings are very adaptable. Cogni-

■ **Cultures define crowding.** Although research findings have long suggested that crowding triggers antisocial and unhealthful behavior, cross-cultural research indicates that responses to crowding depend on a culture's norms regarding appropriate behavior. Tokyo commuters routinely endure crowding as bad as what you see here and worse, yet they are generally far more orderly than commuters in other countries.

But one would here would increase arousal over a larger radius than he/she/it would in the US!

tive and social factors can help us buffer the arousal caused by crowding and thus limit its debilitating effects.

A sense of control seems to be a key factor in counteracting the negative effects of crowding. In one study of people working under crowded conditions, some participants were given an "escape button" to press if they needed to leave the situation (Sherrod, 1974). Although the participants never actually pressed the button, knowing they could control their situation helped these participants perform better than those who had no control. Another study packed people into an elevator to find out who would feel the least stress. Not surprisingly, that person was usually the individual standing by the control panel (J. Rodin, Solomon, & Metcalf, 1978). Similarly, a study in India found that residents in crowded housing who saw themselves as having control over their environment fared better than others (Ruback & Pandey, 1991). The presence of others, especially crowds of others, arouses us, but the effects on our behavior depend on how we interpret the situation, and particularly on the extent of our feelings of control.

These beneficial effects of perceived control should not surprise you, given our discussion in chapter 4, pages 149 to 151, of the many ways a sense of mastery or control acts as a buffer against stressful events.

Performance in Face-to-Face Groups: Interaction and Interdependence

If the minimal influence of other people who are present can influence our behavior, consider how much more potent is the effect of a face-to-face group. Members of such groups—families, flight crews, dance troupes, parent–teacher organizations, rock and roll bands, government commissions, and others—are highly interdependent. They are **socially interdependent** because they rely on one another for feelings of connectedness and positive emotional outcomes, such as respect, caring, and positive social identity. They are **task interdependent** because their mastery of material outcomes depends on working together to perform some collective task: a successful flight, the negotiation of teachers' contracts, or the design of a new health-care plan. Large or small, all face-to-face groups are characterized by some combination of social and task interdependence (J. M. Levine & Moreland, 1998).

Face-to-face groups have widely differing goals and purposes. For businesses, the group goal is profit; for university faculties, it is the production of new knowledge and well-rounded graduates; for boards of directors, it is a well-administered organization. Depending on their goals, groups demand different amounts of social or task interdependence. Social interdependence or connectedness is particularly important to *primary groups,* like families and close friends, which value their members just because they are members. Of course, these groups are also frequently task interdependent, as when they care for the yard, balance the budget, or organize vacations. *Secondary groups,* such as those found in most work settings, often exist for a specific purpose involving the mastery of rewards, so task interdependence is their defining feature. But as we all know, roles, status hierarchies, and friendships are inevitable in work settings, which means that work groups are also to some extent socially interdependent.

Indeed, every group faces the challenge of successfully managing both forms of interdependence to achieve high levels of productivity (in other words, mastery goals) and positive relationships among group members (connectedness goals). Managing these two forms of interdependence is a

Social interdependence. Reliance on other members of the group for feelings of connectedness, social and emotional rewards, and a positive social identity.

Task interdependence. Reliance on other members of a group for mastery of material outcomes that arise from the group's task.

challenge because they sometimes conflict. Fostering task interdependence, for example, can interfere with feeling good about being in the group, as when parents prohibit horseplay in an effort to keep children focused on their share of Saturday house cleaning. Social interdependence can similarly detract from task performance if office workers socialize so much that work falls behind schedule. To understand how such problems arise and how they can be solved, we need to look at what happens as groups come together and work toward their goals. Although most of our examples will involve work groups, the same processes operate in all groups working together to produce something.

Stages of Group Development: Coming Together, Falling Apart

Face-to-face groups usually go through different stages of formation, conflict, development, performance, and dissolution as they try to develop an identity and reach their goals. The passage of time can also have other direct effects on group process and performance.

In 1981, the Ashland Corporation, a manufacturer of air conditioners, convened a special task group. The team, composed of a team leader, "team advisers," and several production-line employees, was asked to turn a huge, empty factory building into a functioning production line for a newly designed series of compressors. The team had to select, order, and arrange for the installation of production machinery. It also was responsible for organizing and training the production-line workers in a way that maximized their efficiency and maintained extremely high quality standards. As the group began to work toward its goals over a period of months, it confronted a series of problems and challenges, which in turn influenced the group's structure and operation. These changes were not unique to the Ashland team. All groups, whether short-term, ad-hoc groups created to solve isolated problems or long-term groups that might take years to reach their goals, go through different stages of development (Eisenstat, 1990; Moreland & Levine, 1988; Tuckman, 1965; Wheelan, 1994). Although some groups go through all five of the stages described here, many others skip some steps, repeat earlier steps, or dissolve before they ever reach the later stages (Gersick, 1990).

1. *Forming.* In the initial stage of group development, members try to get to know each other, to find out what makes other members tick, and to see if they will fit in. Because members do not know each other well at this early stage, there is usually an intense focus on the group's leader (Wheelan, 1994). Ideally, this period of orientation enables each individual to understand the group's goals as well as its status relationships: who is central to the group and its task, who is less important. The Ashland team had several strengths at this stage: frequent interaction, both social and task interdependence, the members' developing feeling of attraction to the group and to the other members, and a belief in the group's uniqueness (Moreland, 1987). Managers facilitated the group's progress through this stage by giving group members time to get acquainted and by stressing the special nature of their task—a task that could not be completed without everyone's full cooperation.

2. *Storming.* Conflict is often evident in the second stage, and disagreements can be intense and emotional (Bales, Cohen, & Williamson, 1979; Tuckman, 1965). At this point, members already know each other, but they must resolve genuine disagreements about task and social interdependence. For the Ashland team, one conflict centered around a new leader's peering-over-the-shoulder style of management, which team members interpreted as a lack of confidence in their skills. Group members also clashed over priorities as production workers demanded training while trainers were absorbed in other matters. This particular conflict left the trainers feeling swamped and the workers feeling neglected (Eisenstat, 1990).

Deciding on group goals and the best ways to meet them is a common source of conflict at this stage, as members with different views jockey for position and coalitions and subgroups form among people with similar interests or agendas. But conflict may involve interpersonal as well as task issues. For example, one group member may feel betrayed by another's shift of position on an issue, or two members or subgroups may compete for the leader's attention and favor.

Conflict may die down when a majority forms and persuades the group to adopt its views. Sometimes, however, a minority dissenting opinion prevails. One person may have radical ideas that the majority initially resists but eventually adopts. In fact, many companies deliberately build in protection for "screwball" ideas, so that "storming" works to keep them on the cutting edge. In a classic case of persistent and effective dissent, a market researcher at Compaq Computer Corporation persuaded management to disregard surveys that predicted a limited market for a briefcase-size laptop computer. Many companies would not have been swayed by the dissent of a single person, but Compaq reaped big benefits because it did not simply try to suppress conflict, but allowed minority influence to prevail (Kotkin, 1986).

3. *Norming.* If the group survives the storming stage, harmony and unity usually emerge as consensus, cohesion, and a positive group identity develop. A sense of security and trust emerges when conflict declines as members' disagreements are resolved into a unified purpose (Wheelan, 1994). Members have internalized the group norms by this stage, so overt social influence, with its high potential for conflict, becomes less necessary. In this stage most members tend to be highly satisfied with the group and to agree about the group's purpose and the power and responsibilities of individual members. The Ashland team reached this stage as the deadline for shipping the first compressors drew near and team members realized that the plant's reputation rode on meeting the deadline with high-quality products. The group's purpose was finally clear, and everyone accepted the goal. As one worker put it, "Then everyone jelled together. . . . Nobody said no, everybody said yes. . . . It was smooth, and people [were] in a good mood" (Eisenstat, 1990).

4. *Performing.* With norms established, the group moves into the performance stage. In groups in which storming produces high-quality ideas and norming results in high productivity standards (Mayo, 1933), the performance stage is characterized by smooth management and high efficiency. Members cooperate to solve problems, make decisions, and generate output. They exchange information freely, handle disagreements productively, and exert social influence to achieve group goals. At this stage of the Ashland group's devel-

Recall from chapter 9, pages 363 to 369, that the best group decisions are made when a group considers as many dissenting and different perspectives as possible before reaching a consensus.

opment, employees who had completed their regular tasks helped their less experienced co-workers rather than taking it easy. People worked long hours and operated as a team. As one worker commented, "I surprise myself. . . . We work as one, not as separate individuals." As the initial shipments of the new compressors received extremely high ratings on quality tests, the new Ashland plant was declared a success. News that the factory could proceed to full production reinforced the team members' feeling that they had done a terrific job (Eisenstat, 1990).

5. *Adjourning.* Most groups, especially ad hoc groups put together for a specific purpose, eventually reach the end of their life span, the adjourning stage. Some, like the new factory team at Ashland, know from the outset that their lifetime is limited. Others dissolve because they have accomplished their goals. Still others fall apart when members lose interest, move away, or flee conflict (Rusbult, 1983; Thibaut & Kelley, 1959a). At a group's endpoint, members often gather to evaluate their work, give feedback to each other, and express their feelings about the group (Lundgren & Knight, 1978). The dissolution of a cohesive group can be stressful for members if group identification has taken place, because loss of the group entails a change in social identity. Members lose the benefits of others' skills and contributions and the security of others' support and companionship. When cohesion and interaction are particularly intense, the psychological impact of the adjourning of a group can be similar to that of a break-up of a close relationship, leaving the same feelings of grief and loneliness. Group members can prevent some of this stress if they prepare themselves for the adjournment by reducing group cohesion, stressing individual independence, and searching for new groups to join (Mayadas & Glasser, 1985).

Table 12.1 summarizes these five typical stages of group development, along with the task and social processes that characterize each stage.

TABLE 12.1 Stages of Group Development

Stage	Task Processes	Social Processes
Forming	Exchange of information, task exploration	Getting to know each other, self-disclosure, dependence on leader
Storming	Disagreement over goals and procedures	Disagreement over status, criticism of ideas, hostility, coalition formation
Norming	Formation of consensus and norms	Growth of cohesion and unity, positive group identity and connectedness
Performing	Goal-focused efforts, orientation toward mastery and task performance	Social influence, cooperation
Adjourning	Completion of tasks, dissolution of roles	Withdrawal, emotional expressions, reminiscence

Source: D. R. Forsyth, *Group dynamics,* 3rd ed., 1999, Pacific Grove, CA: Brooks/Cole; S. A. Wheelan, *Group processes: A developmental perspective,* 1994, Boston, MA: Allyn & Bacon.

OTHER EFFECTS OF TIME ON GROUP PROCESSES. Besides the typical progression through these developmental stages, time has other effects on the ways groups interact and deal with their tasks. Perhaps you have had the experience of working with a group on a long-term project for a class. If so, you may recall

■ **Task interdependence at work.** Most complex tasks require multiple forms of interdependence. These auto workers are celebrating producing their one millionth Jeep. The assembly of automobiles requires workers to complete specialized tasks in precise amounts of time. A worker that does not do so can halt the productivity of everyone on the assembly line.

that at a certain point, after getting to know each other in a relaxed way and developing and discarding various tentative plans, your group suddenly realized that time was passing and little concrete progress had been made. Connie Gersick (1989) proposed that many groups go through this process, which she termed the "mid-life crisis" because she found that it often occurred when about half of the group's total time remained. The reorientation spurred by the realization that time is growing short may trigger a radically different approach to the group's task, shifts in strategies, and a greater emphasis on productive work.

Janice Kelly and her colleagues (J. R. Kelly, Jackson, & Hutson-Comeaux, 1997; J. R. Kelly & Karau, in press) also found that time pressure alters the way groups approach their tasks. Groups under time pressure devote more of their interaction to clearly task-focused matters and differ from less pressured groups in the ways they share information and seek to influence each other. In some ways they perform better than groups with more time available. For example, because of their increased task focus, groups that have to write a proposal for a new program write more words per minute when they are under a tight deadline. Still, time pressure has its costs. Proposals that are written in a rush tend to be less creative and original than those written with more adequate time (Karau & Kelly, 1992).

Getting the Job Done: Group Performance

To achieve their performance goals, groups must maintain their motivation and avoid problems of coordination. Developing a common social identity helps to avoid such problems by encouraging cooperation for group goals, promoting social influence, and attracting and keeping valuable group members.

For most groups, performing is the crucial stage because the work of the group must be accomplished during this period. Whether the group carries through with a flawless performance or collapses into disarray will depend on the kinds of tasks it faces, the quality of the group effort, and the resources available for reaching goals and repairing damage to the group.

FORMS OF TASK INTERDEPENDENCE. According to Ivan Steiner (1972), group tasks differ in terms of the type of interdependence they require. With *additive tasks*, the potential performance of the group is approximately equal to the sum of the performances of the individual members and is generally better than any one member's performance. A tug-of-war is an additive task, as is typing in an office pool or joining others to push a stalled car out of an intersection. In additive tasks, individual effort is the key because the final outcome is roughly proportional to the number of individuals contributing and how much they give (Littlepage, 1991). But coordination is also important: One person tugging on the rope when all the others are resting will not ensure tug-of-war victory.

In *disjunctive tasks*, a group's performance is expected to be as good as the performance of its best individual member (Laughlin, VanderStoep, & Hollingshead, 1991). When one of a group of "idea people" comes up with a terrific concept for a new ad campaign and everyone else recognizes its merit, the task is disjunctive. In this case, interdependence means that the outcome will be a function of the individual skills and talents of the group members. Thus, education or training of individual members can improve group performance, as can the selection of members with the right mix of skills (Hackman, 1987). Coordination is important, too, because other members have to be careful not to get in the way of any individual member who can complete the task (Diehl & Stroebe, 1991; Littlepage, 1991).

Conjunctive tasks depend on every member playing his or her part. In this case, the group's performance is only as good as the performance of its worst member. Groups of mountain climbers, relay racers, or assembly-line teams are engaged in conjunctive tasks: Their slowest or weakest member determines whether and how quickly they achieve their goal. If three students agree that one will do the research for a report, a second will write it, and the third will deliver it in class, their grade will depend on how well each of them performs his or her part of the task. Coordination is very important in conjunctive tasks, so the group has to organize its members' activities. If coordination fails, so that two people do the research but nobody writes the presentation, the total task will remain undone.

Most tasks are *complex tasks*, which consist of subtasks that involve all forms of interdependence. In playing football, for example, some tasks are disjunctive (any of several players can block the opposing defensive end), whereas others are conjunctive (the quarterback must throw the pass and the receiver must catch it). Of course, the more complicated the task, the greater the need for planning and coordination to ensure that members' skills and efforts are appropriately allocated. And the more complicated the task, the greater the opportunity will be for the group's performance to multiply and surpass any possible effort by a single individual. At the same time, unfortunately, putting individuals' efforts together in complicated group tasks also provides many opportunities for things to go wrong.

GAINS AND LOSSES IN GROUP PERFORMANCE. "Two heads are better than one," and that certainly is one reason so much work is performed by groups. Groups do perform many tasks better than an individual could. Groups can multiply individual effort, provide a variety of skills that no one person possesses, and work together to complete tasks in parallel, rather than serial, fashion. Perhaps each Amish farmer has all the skills necessary to build a barn alone, but when all the members of his community pool their skills, labor, and enthusiasm, a barn can be raised in a day or two. The advantages of group effort are also evident on many cognitive tasks. For example, groups solve puzzles more quickly than individuals do (Laughlin, 1980). Members of the surgical team in an operating room can correct an error by one group member quickly, before its consequences become severe (Azar, 1994). And collective memory is also better: After watching a videotape portraying a police interrogation, groups of participants offered more accurate and detailed accounts of the event than those of individuals who worked alone (N. K. Clark, Stephenson, & Kniveton, 1990; Wegner, 1987).

Two heads may be better than one, but are they twice as good? That is, do groups perform as well as the same number of individuals working alone? Frequently the answer is no. Some research has evaluated the popular technique known as *brainstorming,* in which a group of people tries to generate a large number of ideas without criticizing or evaluating them, at least initially. The premise is that one person's idea, even if wild and unworkable, may be built on and improved by other group members (Osborn, 1953). The evidence indicates that while brainstorming groups do better than a single person, they usually come up with fewer ideas and ideas of poorer quality than those produced by the same number of individuals working separately (Diehl & Stroebe, 1991). The same is true for memory tasks: Although a group can remember more than a single individual, group performance is inferior to the combined information that can be recalled by an equal number of individuals working on their own (Wegner, 1987). Finally, groups sometimes display greater biases in judgment or decision-making tasks than do individuals provided with the same information (N. L. Kerr and others, 1996).

In cases like these, when groups do not amplify but actually diminish the sum of individual efforts, the cause is often a loss of either motivation or coordination among group members (J. M. Levine & Moreland, 1998).

LOSSES FROM DECREASED MOTIVATION: SOCIAL LOAFING. Sometimes working in a group leads people to slack off—to put less effort into the task than they would if working alone. As we noted in chapter 1, this loss of motivation, termed **social loafing,** was first studied in the 1880s by Max Ringelmann, a French agricultural engineer who was interested in group performance on very simple additive tasks (Kravitz & Martin, 1986). Over a century later, Ringelmann's early insights have been confirmed by laboratory experiments. In the study of social loafing illustrated in Figure 12.3, for example, college students were told to clap and cheer as loudly as they could. The amount of sound generated by each student's efforts decreased as the size of the group increased. Individual efforts seem quite literally to get lost in the crowd, and the degree of loss is substantial. In this study, an individual in a group of six made less than half the noise he or she made when clapping alone.

Social loafing is not restricted to simple motor tasks. When performance on cognitive tasks was measured, individuals in three-person brainstorming groups generated only 75% as many uses for a common object as they did when working alone. And working in groups, they made more than twice as many errors on a "vigilance" task of detecting brief flashes on

Social loafing. The tendency to exert less effort on a task when an individual's efforts are an unidentifiable part of a group than when the same task is performed alone.

FIGURE 12.3   Effects of social loafing

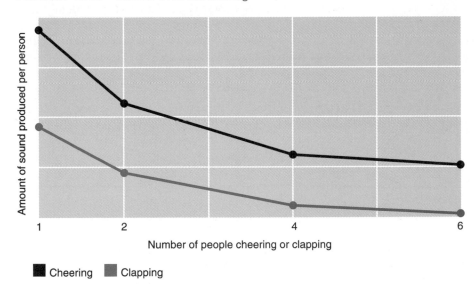

■ In this experiment, college students were told to clap or cheer as loudly as they could. Note that the noise produced by each person decreased as the number of people clapping or cheering together increased. Social loafing is most likely to occur if the task is unchallenging, if individual performances cannot be monitored, or if the individual's contribution to the group is dispensable. (Data from Latané, Williams, & Harkins, 1979.)

■ Cheering   ■ Clapping

a computer screen than they did when working alone (Harkins & Szymanski, 1989). Sharing responsibility can reduce effort no matter what the task is (Karau & Williams, 1993).

Why do people loaf on group tasks? To some extent, the nature of the task itself is a factor. Research indicates that social loafing occurs less often when tasks are interesting and involving (Brickner, Harkins, & Ostrom, 1986). But interdependence also plays a role. For example, when interdependence is minimal and individual roles are unimportant, as when the crowd sings the national anthem before a ball game begins, it is easy to let others pick up the slack (Karau & Williams, 1993; N. L. Kerr & Bruun, 1983). In contrast, social loafing is reduced when individual contributions are essential for success (Weldon & Mustari, 1988) or group members know that their individual contributions can be monitored (K. D. Williams, Harkins, & Latané, 1981; Zaccaro, 1984). Not surprisingly, people are also less likely to slack off when there is a clear standard against which the group's performance can be measured (Harkins & Szymanski, 1989) and when they can be sure that others are not taking it easy (N. L. Kerr & Bruun, 1983).

People's orientation toward the group also influences the tendency to loaf. Strong identification with the group decreases social loafing (Karau & Williams, 1997). For the same reason, women and members of interdependent cultures, who tend to be more group oriented than men and people from individualistic cultures, are less likely to engage in social loafing (Karau & Williams, 1993).

Finally, social loafing may be partly caused by an "illusion of group productivity" (Paulus, Dzindolet, Poletes, & Camacho, 1993): people's tendency to believe that their groups are even more productive than they really are. If you think your group is performing at an extremely high level, you may conclude that you do not have to push yourself hard to make contributions, so social loafing may result.

Beetle Bailey

As these findings indicate, to loaf or not to loaf seems to depend on both task and social interdependence. When individual performance is important for task mastery, social loafing declines. And when an individual's performance has implications for connectedness to the group, for example, when others can praise or condemn individual efforts, social loafing declines. In fact, when task and social interdependence are high, *social compensation* is sometimes observed, as one group member works extra hard to compensate for the weakness or lack of ability of another member (Karau & Williams, 1997).

LOSSES FROM POOR COORDINATION. Even when group members are trying hard, the group needs to be organized if it is to do the best possible work. As John Ruskin (1907/1963) observed, "Failure is less frequently attributable to either insufficiency of means or impatience of labor than to a confused understanding of the thing to be done" (p. 1). Members need assigned roles and a clear sense of their resources. They also need to be aware of one another's strengths and weaknesses, of how their actions contribute to group goals, and of who has a right to command and who has a duty to obey. Group performance suffers when group members leave crucial tasks undone, duplicate others' efforts, compete for personal resources and status, or get in each others' way—literally or figuratively. Interference caused by other group members' efforts appears to be a major reason for the inferior performance of groups on brainstorming tasks. Listening to others talk may distract group members from thinking up superior ideas or may even cause them to forget some ideas before they can be verbalized (Diehl & Stroebe, 1991; Stroebe & Diehl, 1991). Perhaps group brainstorming and memory tasks would be more successful if the group observed a moment of silence every few minutes to permit members to think without distraction.

☐ **POOR COORDINATION IN THE WORKPLACE.** Poor coordination on group tasks can be disastrous under some circumstances. Consider, for example, the life-and-death responsibilities of cockpit crews on commercial airliners. If these small groups fail to work well together in an emergency, the results can be tragic. An investigation of one crash found that the pilot failed to pay attention to the copilot's repeated but timid comments that the takeoff was not proceeding normally. In another incident, a flight engineer manually silenced a noisy alarm, leaving the pilot with the impression that it was a false warning (Foushee, 1984).

Airlines typically select pilots and copilots almost exclusively for their outstanding individual skills and knowledge, paying less attention to their interpersonal or communication skills. Unfortunately, research evidence indicates that successful performance of the flight crew may depend more on their coordination than on the skill of the individual group members (Foushee & Manos, 1981; Lanzetta & Roby, 1960). One study of a major airline's flight crews, using a realistic flight simulator, demonstrated this point (Harper, Kidera, & Cullen, 1971). The researchers found that about 25% of the simulated flights crashed because the copilot failed to take control of the aircraft when the captain faked a collapse during a final landing approach. As is the case with flight crews, errors made by teams of surgeons, anesthesiologists, and nurses in hospital operating rooms often reflect social and interpersonal failures rather than technical problems (Azar, 1994).

CURES FOR GROUP PERFORMANCE LOSSES. Loss of motivation and failures of coordination can undermine a group's ability to achieve its goals and can frustrate individual members as well. Nipping such problems in the bud seems a wise step for any organization, and available research evidence indicates that one particularly successful strategy is making group membership a positive part of members' social identity.

Organizations often try to achieve this goal by selling the "corporate culture," the set of values, beliefs, understandings, and norms shared by members of the organization (J. M. Levine & Moreland, 1991). To build a sense of group identity and cohesion, organizations create slogans and symbols, develop and distribute literature describing the principles that embody the company's ideals and goals, and introduce rituals, ceremonies, and awards. For example, the J.C. Penney department stores sell their employees on "The Penney Idea," a list of guiding principles that summarize the company's values and what it means to be a group member. In sports, teams have uniforms, mascots, and "Most Valuable Player" awards to promote players' cohesiveness and dedication to their teammates (Hogg & Abrams, 1988). All of these tactics are designed to give group members a strong sense of shared social identity. Former U.S. Secretary of Labor Robert Reich described a simple test he used when he visited organizations: He asked front-line workers to talk about their companies. "If the answers I get back describe the company in terms of 'they' or 'them,' I know it's one kind of company. If the answers include words such as 'we' or 'us,' I know it's another kind" ("Pronoun Test," 1993).

But even if corporate culture makes people feel good, can it help reach the organization's goals? The answer is yes. Building positive social interdependence often helps solve some of the problems of task interdependence (Mackie & Goethals, 1987). Organizations sell the corporate culture because it encourages group cohesion, and group cohesion increases group performance, as Brian Mullen and Carolyn Copper (1994) found in their meta-analysis of 49 studies of laboratory and nonlaboratory groups. The reason is that cohesion can be a strong remedy for many of the motivational and coordination losses that can render groups ineffective.

1. *Cohesive groups encourage cooperation.* Cohesive groups foster cooperation in the service of group goals, rather than competition for individual ones (Turner, 1987). Cooperation leads to positive feelings among group members and helps them work together to achieve group goals (Deutsch, 1949; Gaertner, Mann, Dovidio, Murrell, & Pomare, 1990; Sherif, 1966). For example, those who identify with a cohesive group are more likely to participate in and contribute to group activities than are members of noncohesive groups (Brawley, Carron, & Widmeyer, 1988). In sports like volleyball and baseball, cohesive teams are usually winning teams (Bird, 1977). However, this finding no doubt reflects the fact that success leads to cohesion, as well as the positive effect of cohesion on performance (Mullen & Copper, 1994).

One practical way to promote group goals is to make personal rewards clearly contingent on group outcomes. For example, students in "cooperative classrooms" work together to help each other learn and are graded on the basis of the entire group's performance, whereas students' grades in "competitive classrooms" are based on comparisons between group members. In the classroom as in the laboratory, mutual cooperation leads to positive feelings: Compared with members of competitive groups, cooperative group members generally like each other better. They also learn more. A meta-analysis of over 100 studies concluded that cooperative learning results in better classroom performance than is found in either competitive or individualistic situations (D. W. Johnson, Maruyama, Johnson, Nelson, & Skon, 1981).

Employers sometimes adopt a similar cooperative reward arrangement: a contingent pay system in which employees receive bonuses only when certain group goals (such as production levels) are met. One study of 66 large U.S. firms compared compensation packages among low-performing and high-performing companies. The study found that the companies with high performance records more often had packages that emphasized teamwork rather than individual competition (Schuster, 1985). These employers endorse the claim of W. Edwards Deming, the guru of managing for quality, that rewarding individual performance "annihilates long-term planning, builds fear, demolishes teamwork, and nourishes rivalry and politics" (Gabor, 1992). Indeed, General Motors Corporation's Cadillac Division, which adopted team-based rewards in 1989, credits them for the major turnaround that propelled Cadillac to a top-ranking place in customer satisfaction among American car-makers by 1991.

2. *Cohesive groups exercise social influence.* A sense of group belonging usually helps members form norms about the group's goals and its strategies for accomplishing those goals. Once consensus has been reached, those who identify with the group are likely to adhere to its norms (McGrath, 1984), and new members quickly absorb the group's "way of doing things" (Forsyth, 1999; J. R. Levine & Moreland, 1991). If a group is cohesive and has a high-performance norm, its members will be highly productive (Keller, 1986). Of course, if group norms block performance, productivity will be low (Roethlisberger & Dickson, 1939). In a demonstration of this point, researchers surveying more than 200 work groups found that job performance was related to group norms, which in turn were related to the labor–management climate (Seashore, 1954). Hostile management styles were associated with low-performance norms, and in these conditions, cohesive groups were less productive than noncohesive groups. Norms of high productivity

The ways in which groups form a consensus were described more thoroughly in chapter 9, pages 345 to 353. The ways in which these group norms influence group members' actions was the topic of chapter 10, especially pages 377 to 384.

tended to be found when management was supportive, and in these cases cohesive groups were the best performers. Experimental results confirm these findings (Schachter, Ellertson, McBride, & Gregory, 1951). What a cohesive group decides, group members usually do.

Reaching consensus also means the group no longer needs to spend time repeatedly renegotiating the issues. Members know what the group is set up to do and they know how to do it. These norms help both to eradicate motivation loss and to aid group coordination (Hackman, 1987). Consider, for example, the effect of norms on the goal of preparing a community meal. If the group has not reached a consensus, members may feel they have a right to work on the task they enjoy most; no one will do the dirty work, and there will be no dinner. Group norms, however, can specify that all the jobs must be done, that certain members have the right or obligation to do specific tasks, and that the tasks should be performed at certain times and in specific ways. Given these conditions, the community meal should proceed on schedule: When group norms match task demands, groups operate more smoothly.

3. *Cohesive groups attract and keep valued members.* When tasks are difficult, rewards are few, and conflict is frequent, potentially productive group members may slack off or drop out altogether. Member turnover can lessen a group's chances of achieving its goals, and it often represents the loss of a huge investment in training and skill development. Shared social identity acts as a counterforce by boosting people's liking for the group, their satisfaction with belonging, and their morale (Hackman, 1992; O'Reilly & Caldwell, 1985). Belonging to a cohesive group even helps people cope with stress, perhaps by offering them effective social support (Bowers, Weaver, & Morgan, 1996). You may recall that members of groups—even groups formed on the basis of arbitrary categorizations—tend to hold in-group members in higher esteem than out-group members (Hogg, 1987). This tendency is even stronger in cohesive face-to-face groups. Many Japanese businesses see group cohesion as a way to keep their workers productive and happy. They are famous for their efforts to ensure that employee morale is high and that performance is rewarded. Companies foster friendships between members; sponsor picnics, parties, and sports teams; and promise long-term employment. Company-sponsored computer dating services even encourage employees to marry within the company. Their efforts no doubt contribute to the fact that Japanese workers seldom change companies.

To review the many ways in which membership in a social group increases preference for in-group over out-group members, see chapter 6, pages 214 to 217.

Social identity can be such a powerful tool that it sometimes holds groups together when no material benefits are forthcoming. For example, groups with strong social identity often preserve (or even strengthen) their cohesion even when they lose or fail at important tasks (Brawley, Carron, & Widmeyer, 1987; D. M. Taylor, Doria, & Tyler, 1983). This occurred during the closing stages of the Second World War, when units of the German army, outnumbered, undersupplied, and with no chance of victory, continued to fight against all odds. They did so not because they believed deeply in Nazi ideology but because they were motivated by group loyalty forged by shared identity (Shils & Janowitz, 1948). Studies of U.S. soldiers in Europe and Vietnam tell a similar story of social interdependence motivating performance (Moskos, 1969; Stouffer and others, 1949).

FIGURE 12.4   Causes and cures of group productivity loss.

Source of productivity loss in groups	Motivation loss *Individuals diminish personal efforts, engage in social loafing.*	Coordination loss *Individuals interfere with each others' actions. Individuals fail to communicate effectively about group tasks.*
Remedy for productivity loss in groups	Cooperation: Individuals work toward group goals *Individuals maintain efforts even when contributions are not identifiable.*	Consensus: Individuals agree on goals and strategies *Individuals follow group norms. If norms are appropriate, high productivity results.*
Contribution of group cohesion to remedy	Individuals adopt group goals as their own.	Group exercises social influence over individuals.

■ Group productivity declines when individual members do not try hard to accomplish group goals—for example, when they engage in social loafing—or when the members' efforts are poorly coordinated. Group cohesion can help remedy both of these problems by encouraging individuals to cooperate for group goals and to follow the group consensus on goals and ways of achieving those goals.

We have seen that group performance can suffer from two basic types of problems. The first occurs when members stop trying or drop out because they do not care about group goals or are unwilling to waste their efforts while others slack off. These motivational losses are often remedied when people cooperate and identify with group goals, as shown in Figure 12.4. The second problem arises when members try hard but cannot coordinate their efforts effectively because members do not share common goals or interfere with each other. These coordination losses may be remedied when people identify with the group and follow its norms, at least when those norms favor high productivity. In this way, cohesion offers remedies for *both* motivational and coordination losses in groups. When group membership gives people a positive social identity, they are likely to take the group's goals as their own and to follow its norms in their behavior.

Leadership

Effective leaders enhance task performance and maintain social interdependence. The ways they do this must differ from situation to situation and from time to time. Sometimes, however, stereotypical thinking prevents the most effective leaders from emerging in groups. Some types of leadership may be associated with particularly strong impacts on group members.

Leadership. A process in which one or more group members are permitted to influence and motivate others to help attain group goals.

Whose job is it to make sure that groups fulfill their mastery and connectedness goals? As former U.S. president Dwight D. Eisenhower once wrote, "Leadership is the ability to decide what is to be done, and then to get others to want to do it." Leaders are crucial to the attainment of group goals. In fact, **leadership** can be defined formally as a process in which one or more group members are permitted to influence and motivate others to help attain group goals (Forsyth, 1999). Notice that in this definition the group grants the leader his or her power; as we noted in chapter 10, legitimate authority works only if the group accepts and agrees with it. The definition does not specify the route to power: Leaders may be appointed by an outside authority, elected by group members themselves, or simply emerge as a group interacts. Leaders may or may not be effective, but before we explore that issue, let's examine what leaders do.

WHAT DO LEADERS DO? The exercise of leadership generally involves two distinct types of behavior, those focused on decision making and task performance and those aimed at enhancing cohesion and liking among group members (Misumi, 1995; Stogdill, 1963). This pattern is understandable. Because people draw on groups both for mastery and concrete rewards stemming from task performance and for feelings of connectedness and belonging, groups require both task and social leadership. Task-related leader behaviors include telling group members what to do, criticizing poor performance, and coordinating others' activity. In contrast, relationship-oriented leadership involves being open, friendly, and approachable, treating group members as equals, and listening to group members' opinions. Both of these functions are vital to effective groups, and together they account for most of what leaders do (Mintzberg, 1980).

Early studies of interaction in small groups concluded that two different leaders often emerged, a task leader and a socioemotional leader, each specializing in one of these two types of behavior. These researchers argued that the task leader makes the decisions that translate into actual group performance. This individual typically makes task-focused comments, talks more than other members, and often addresses comments to the group as a whole rather than to individual members (Bales, 1953). According to early research, a second individual—typically the person who talks more than anyone else except the task leader—becomes the group's socioemotional leader. Most of this person's contributions are aimed at soothing feelings, maintaining harmony, and encouraging participation.

This presumed division of roles reflected the culture of the period in which this research was done. Researchers saw it as a "natural" and nearly universal pattern (Bales & Slater, 1955). After all, weren't families composed of husbands who exercised task leadership and wives who provided socioemotional support? More recently, reevaluation of these findings suggests that the pattern of separate task and socioemotional leaders is not truly universal (Burke, 1967). Leader behavior does tend to fall into two general categories, having to do with task performance versus relationship maintenance (Misumi, 1995; Stogdill, 1963). But a group does not require two separate leaders, for one person may be quite capable of leading the group to task completion and simultaneously taking care of the group's psychological well-being.

LEADERSHIP EFFECTIVENESS: PERSON OR SITUATION? Effective leaders can make or break countries, businesses, organizations, religions, clubs, sports teams, and even families. It is not surprising, then, that literally thousands of studies have tried to understand why some leaders have the capacity to inspire followers and others do not. When one considers the lives of Mohandas Gandhi or Martin Luther King, Jr., there is a strong temptation to attribute their in-

FIGURE 12.5   Contigency model of leadership

Degree of situational control	Characteristics of group and task	Most effective leadership style
High	Group members like and support leader. Goals are clear, task is straightforward. Leader has power over group members.	Task-oriented, directive leadership
Moderate	Group members like leader. Task is less clearly structured. Leader has little power over members. Group members dislike, distrust leader. Task is clearly structured. Leader has power over members.	Relationship-oriented leadership
Low	Group members dislike, distrust leader. Task is vague and unclear. Leader has little power over members.	Task-oriented, directive leadership

■ According to the contingency model of leadership, the most effective leadership style depends on the leader's and group's situation. When the situation allows high control, a directive and task-oriented leader can be most effective. The same leadership style also works well when conflict and ambiguity are extremely high, producing low control. In contrast, when either an unclear task or uncooperative group members produce moderate situational control, leaders are most effective when they adopt a relationship-oriented style to motivate group members toward task goals.

fluence to their unique personal attributes. This tendency may be one more example of the correspondence bias at work, leading us to attribute behavior to individual traits rather than to situational demands.

Despite the appeal of the idea that effective leadership depends on characteristics of the leader, researchers have had little success in identifying personality traits that universally characterize effective leaders. Indeed, these studies revealed that the same person could be an effective leader in one context (for example, in a cockpit crew) but ineffective in another (such as a community service organization). When researchers examined the relationship of leader behaviors to group outcomes, they found that giving socioemotional support consistently helped improve group morale. However, task-focused leader behaviors did *not* consistently improve group task performance; the effect varied for different types of groups and situations (Vroom, 1976). This suggests that while the types of behaviors a leader performs may depend on the leader's personality, whether or not those behaviors are effective in maximizing group performance depends less on who the leader is than on the characteristics of the situation in which leadership is needed.

This insight about the importance of the situation was developed by Fred Fiedler (1964) in his *contingency model of leadership,* which is based on two assumptions. First, leaders differ, especially in their personal characteristics: Some are task oriented and others care more about relationships. Second, leadership situations also differ, especially in the amount of control leaders have over group outcomes. The key aspect of contingency theory is its "matching" proposition: To maximize leadership effectiveness, the leader's style should match the type of leadership demanded by the situation, as Figure 12.5 shows.

When the group task requires lots of interpersonal interaction and cooperation, a socioemotionally oriented leader may be most effective. When the group takes on a difficult and complex task, group performance may be maximized by a task-oriented leader. Overall, Fiedler's model predicts that in situations in which leaders have either very high or very low levels of control, task-oriented leaders produce better performance. In contrast, relationship-oriented leaders are most effective where the leader has moderate control. The effectiveness of matching leader to task has been supported by a number of studies that have looked at such diverse groups as military units and basketball teams (Strube & Garcia, 1981).

Although some specific tasks may be best matched by a task-focused or relationship-oriented leader, most complex tasks require both leadership styles. In terms of group success, the leader's skill at handling one particular type of task may be less important than his or her ability to balance the two crucial elements of leadership as tasks and situations change (Hersey & Blanchard, 1982; Zaccaro, Foti, & Kenny, 1991). In fact, the essence of good leadership may be the flexibility to adjust the mix of social and task motivation that a group needs in a particular situation. A group that first fails to understand instructions but then becomes overconfident may need their leader to give task-oriented advice initially but need more socioemotional leadership in the later stage.

If groups always need to have the problems of mastery and connectedness solved, wouldn't a person who is high in both relationship and task concerns be the best leader for every situation (Blake & Mouton, 1980)? Most of the time, this is true. The most effective supervisors in settings as diverse as banks, factories, coal mines, and government offices are in fact those who score well in both task and social leadership (Bass, 1985; P. B. Smith & Tayeb, 1989). But for some particular groups and tasks, certain kinds of leadership behaviors may be unnecessary (S. Kerr & Jermier, 1978). For example, a skilled and experienced group working on a straightforward problem has little need for instructions on how to perform the task. An effective leader for this group will work to maintain positive feelings, group cohesion, and, therefore, motivation. In contrast, the leader of a cohesive unit may not need to worry about the interpersonal climate; in this situation, group effectiveness can be increased primarily by pushing task performance. In short, leadership is about the flexible exercise of social influence: Given a particular group performing a particular task, a good leader simultaneously maximizes both successful task performance and positive social identity.

☐ **COACHING LEADERSHIP IN YOUTH SPORTS.** Swimming teams, Little League baseball, youth soccer . . . if you have the impression that today's youngsters are heavily involved in sports activities you would be right! Estimates are that over 25 million children and 3 million adult supervisors and coaches are involved in the United States alone. Proponents of youth sports argue that they teach the benefits of cooperation and teamwork, self-control and discipline, and important lessons about dealing with success and failure, not to mention promoting physical fitness and other positive health habits. But the leadership of coaches is crucial if these worthy goals are to be attained. Ronald Smith and Frank Smoll (1996) studied coaches' behaviors and their effects on young athletes. They found that the children enjoyed their athletic experiences and teammates most and had the highest self-esteem when coaches gave positive feedback for good efforts as well as

■ **Coaches as leaders.** Studies have found that the adults who coach youth sports can have a profound impact on self-esteem, whether it is to empower or to erode it in the kids they must teach and motivate.

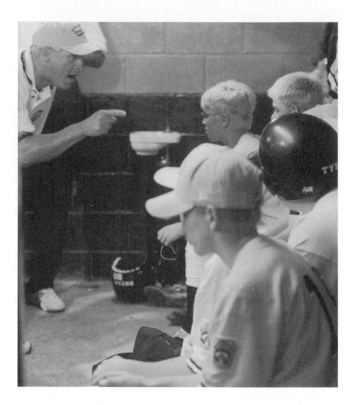

good performances, responded to mistakes with instruction about proper technique, and emphasized fun and personal improvement more than winning matches. In other words, a good mix of relationship-oriented leadership (encouragement) and task-oriented leadership (instruction, especially after a poor performance) carries the day. Unfortunately, along with these types of positive behaviors, coaches sometimes engaged in more negative acts, being punitive and critical toward the children. Though these behaviors occurred only rarely, when they did they had a dramatic negative impact on the children's attitudes and enjoyment.

R. E. Smith and Smoll (1997) also demonstrated that the behaviors that produce positive effects on young team members can be taught to coaches in brief workshops. When coaches who participated in these workshops were compared to those who attended an otherwise comparable coaching clinic focused on technical aspects of sport, their young athletes enjoyed sport participation more, increased in self-esteem, and decreased in performance anxiety. Perhaps the most important indicator of the effectiveness of the workshop is that only 5% of the athletes who played for the workshop-trained coaches failed to return for the sports program the next season, compared to about 26% for the other coaches.

Even though everyone presumably agrees that the chief goal of youth sports programs should be enjoyment, learning, and building positive attitudes rather than winning, you may still have one question about these results: Do the workshop-trained coaches, like other proverbial "nice guys," end up finishing last? No. They did not differ from the other coaches in their overall win/loss percentages in any of Smith and Smoll's studies (1997). So coaches do not have to choose between one leadership style that increases athletes' enjoyment and another style that wins matches. Instead, a single approach can attain the first (and more important) of these goals without sacrificing the second.

STEREOTYPES AND LEADERSHIP. Contingency theories make it clear that groups should choose leaders whose styles match the demands of the situation. Like so many other social decision makers, however, groups do not always base their judgments on all the available information, and superficial thinking sometimes seems to rule the day. For example, laboratory studies show that group members who talk a lot tend to be viewed as leaders (Littlepage, Schmidt, Whisler, & Frost, 1995; Sorrentino & Field, 1986). Groups do need guidance, so choosing a talker is not necessarily a bad idea. Unfortunately, the amount a group member talks seems to reflect mostly general personality traits like dominance, rather than the member's actual expertise on the group's task. But other members assume that those who talk are experts, so those who talk most have the most influence (Littlepage and others, 1995). When groups base their decision more on *how much* is said than on the *quality* of what is said, they may not select the best potential leaders (Hollander, 1985). Other irrelevant characteristics influence groups' choices of leaders as well: People who are taller or older than other group members, or who sit at the head of the table, tend to be treated as leaders and to exercise more influence than other members (Nemeth & Wachtler, 1974; Stogdill, 1974).

Stereotypic thinking may help explain the preponderance of males in leadership positions in business, government, religious, and military institutions. If people believe that competence and assertiveness are associated with leadership and that males are competent and assertive, they may turn to males for leadership (Lord, De Vader, & Alliger, 1986; Wagner & Berger, 1997). Thus, the expectation that males make good leaders creates a self-fulfilling prophecy in which males assume most leadership roles. A wealth of research data support this point. For example, a meta-analysis summarized 75 laboratory studies of mixed-sex informal groups that were allowed to interact without an appointed leader. When the group members later identified who had emerged as leaders, men were perceived as playing leadership roles more often than women were (Eagly & Karau, 1991). Groups turn to women only when their tasks require extensive social interaction, for example, in consensus-seeking tasks or negotiations (W. Wood, 1987).

Stereotypes also limit ethnic minorities' chances of rising to leadership positions. When a Los Angeles Dodgers executive commented in 1987 that African Americans "may not have some of the necessities" to be head coaches or executives, his remarks brought swift condemnation and vows of renewed

Sylvia

© 1982 By Nicole Hollander.

efforts to recruit African-American coaches and executives. Nevertheless, the upper management levels of most professional sports in the United States are still relatively unintegrated. Football is one of the worst offenders: As of 1992, African Americans made up 60% of the players but only 7% of the head coaches. Even team owners admit that lingering stereotypes bear some of the blame for this situation (Hammer, 1992). Of course, underrepresentation of minority group members in leadership positions is common throughout many types of business and government organizations, not only in sports.

Are groups hurting themselves by using such stereotypes to choose their leaders? Little research has examined ethnic differences, but meta-analyses of research on gender differences in leader effectiveness permit a partial answer to this question. The meta-analyses have looked at three related questions.

- *Who holds the group together?* In creating connectedness and cohesion, women leaders beat men hands down (Eagly, Makhijani, & Klonsky, 1992). Both groups and individual group members are happier when their boss is a woman. One reason may be that, at least in the laboratory, women leaders show more concern with morale and encourage more participation in decision making than men do (Eagly & Johnson, 1990).

- *Who gets the job done?* When it comes to mastery and task performance, studies of leaders in organizations show that, in general, women perform just as well as men on objective measures. However, the type of organization makes a substantial difference. In business, educational, and government organizations, women leaders slightly outperform men on the average. In contrast, in the military, men have been found to be much more effective leaders than women (Eagly and others, 1995).

- *Who do people believe make good leaders?* If we turn from objective measures of group performance to group members' *perceptions* of leader effectiveness, however, the story is different. In a number of studies in which a fixed set of leader behaviors are acted out by trained confederates or described in writing, research participants tend to rate female leaders as less effective than male leaders who perform exactly the same behaviors (Eagly and others, 1992). These judgments suggest that many people still doubt women's ability to lead, perhaps because women do not fit their stereotype of a leader (Hollander, 1985).

When research findings like those just discussed reveal the reality beyond the stereotypes, the power of stereotypic thinking to obstruct the selection of the best leader for the job becomes clear. Perhaps this is why so many of us have worked for an incompetent boss, an unlikable coach, or a disorganized chairperson at some point in our lives. One study shows that at least 60% of workers say that dealing with their supervisor is the most stressful aspect of their job (Freiberg, 1991b). Given the central role leaders play in coordinating both task and social interdependence in groups, perhaps it is time that stereotypical thinking about leadership went the way of the dinosaur.

GROUP NORMS AND LEADERSHIP. Some stereotypes of leaders may be held quite generally, such as those linking leadership to talking, sitting at the head of the table, or being male. But wouldn't you expect different types of groups to have distinctive stereotypes of leaders? For example, a quiet, book-loving English literature major might be considered an appropriate leader for a literary discussion group, while a loud, tough, physically strong individual might be expected to captain a Rugby football team. Thus, groups may pick leaders who in some way embody the group's stereotype, norms, or central defining attributes (Foti, Fraser, & Lord, 1982; Hogg, 1996). By the same token, a leader who matches the group's norms should be seen as particularly effective by group members. One study of college students meeting in groups to discuss a social issue illustrated this point. Designated group leaders who were close to the group's typical position on the issue were rated as more effective leaders (Hains, Hogg, & Duck, 1997). This effect was especially strong for members who identified with the group. Thus, when members identify with a group, making it a potential basis for their self-definition, leaders who most strongly embody the group's norms will be the most acceptable to group members, and especially effective as leaders. The study also showed an effect of general leader stereotypes: Leaders who were described as performing stereotypical leader behaviors, such as emphasizing group goals and letting other members know what was expected of them, were rated as more effective.

As you may recall from chapter 6, page 215, when people identify with a group, they especially like the other group members who most strongly personify group norms.

BEYOND THE ROUTINE: CHARISMATIC AND TRANSFORMATIONAL LEADERSHIP.
Jesus of Nazareth, Mohammad, and Gautama Buddha founded religious movements that have changed the lives of literally billions of followers over many centuries and that remain among the most powerful forces shaping our world today. Can research on leadership take us beyond the everyday world of business managers and sports coaches to shed light on the way such individuals can transform other people? The sociologist Max Weber (1921/1946), writing in the early part of this century, considered this question. He defined *charismatic leaders* as those who inspire extreme devotion and emotional identification on the part of their followers. This devotion allows these leaders to have profound effects on their followers. While most leaders help followers reach their existing goals, charismatic leaders may actually change their followers' goals, for example, turning them from seekers of worldly success into religious devotees practicing self-denial (House, Woycke, & Fodor, 1988).

Some theorists believe that aspects of charismatic leadership can be found in today's organizations, not just among the great leaders of history (Bass, 1990, 1997; House & Shamir, 1993). To have these profound effects, leaders must be self-confident and determined, as well as skilled and enthusiastic communicators. They take clear and strong stands and emphasize commitment to goals, optimistically express an attractive vision of the future, question old assumptions and traditions, and treat group members as individuals (Bass, 1997). Bass (1985) developed a questionnaire to identify leaders with these attributes, whom he termed *transformational leaders*. One study using this questionnaire examined 40 male and female Air Force officers, each leading a squadron of approximately 120 cadets (S. M. Ross & Offermann, 1997). The officers who scored high on the transformational leadership measure tended to be highly self-confident, pragmatic, and nurturant in their approach to their followers. (Given the military context of this study, it is interesting and perhaps unexpected that the high-scoring leaders tended to be high on nurturance and low on aggression and criticalness.) Replicating several other studies, these leaders had followers who were highly satisfied, demonstrating that transformational leadership can inspire followers to liking, respect, and admiration, if not life-changing devotion. However, the cadets serving under transformational leaders did not score any higher than others on objective measures of academic, athletic, or military performance.

Despite the mixed results in this and other studies, many organizations remain extremely interested in the concept of charismatic or transformational leadership and in the possibility of using aspects of this leadership style to increase their organization's effectiveness. Still, we should recognize that the life-changing potential of charismatic leadership can have a dark side. In 1978, over 900 members of the People's Temple group committed mass suicide at the urging of their leader, the Rev. Jim Jones. In a scenario eerily reminiscent of that earlier tragedy, Marshall Applewhite and nearly 40 other members of his Heaven's Gate group committed mass suicide in March 1997. They were following Applewhite's teaching that they had reached a new evolutionary stage in which their earthly "vehicles" or bodies would no longer be required, and that after shedding their bodies they would be picked up by a spaceship traveling with the Hale-Bopp comet. Tragedies like these remind us that charismatic leaders may use their extraordinary influence over their followers in destructive as well as positive ways.

Group Communication

High productivity and high morale can be achieved only through communication. Groups use both formal and informal channels to make sure communication is effective. Technology including video and electronic mail is now altering communication patterns and therefore many aspects of group performance.

Regardless of who leads and what the group's task is, leaders and groups have one primary weapon in the struggle to achieve high task efficiency while maintaining cohesion: communication. No wonder, then, that as group members share and exchange information, most of the talk is about getting the job done and feeling good while doing it (Bales, 1953).

MASTERY- AND CONNECTEDNESS-FOCUSED COMMUNICATION. The balance between task-focused and socioemotional communications is crucial if a group is to be effective (McGrath, 1984). If a group's performance suffers because of ineffective strategies or inadequate skills, the group must seek task-focused remedies, such as repeated instructions, new directions, or reminders of goals (Schachter, 1951). But when low cohesion is to blame for poor performance, remedies must have a socioemotional focus aimed at increasing positive interpersonal relationships and group identification. Over time, groups learn to alternate between a cluster of instrumental communications ("No, you do it *this* way") and a cluster of socioemotional ones ("Yes, you're doing a great job"), nurturing both task and social interdependence (Bales, 1953).

PATTERNS OF COMMUNICATION. How well messages like these are disseminated through an organization depends on *communication networks:* the typ-

FIGURE 12.6   Patterns of communication in groups

ical patterns in which messages are transmitted in that organization. In a centralized network, one person is the focus of all problem solving and decision making. The wheel and Y patterns shown in Figure 12.6 are typical centralized networks. A university in which department heads take their cases for new teaching facilities to a dean, who decides priorities and allocates resources, has a centralized communication network that fits the wheel pattern. In a decentralized network, in contrast, individuals can communicate freely with one another. For example, a university in which department heads meet together to discuss their needs and vote on the allocation of resources has an all-connect decentralized network, as shown in Figure 12.6.

Laboratory experiments have demonstrated that groups with centralized structures usually solve simple problems faster than groups using other structures. As members gather information, the central person is well situated to quickly coordinate it and make a correct decision. But when problems are complicated, a central individual may find the information and responsibilities overwhelming. In these situations, decentralized networks, in which communication can flow more freely, are more likely to produce accurate decisions. Business groups solving research and development problems and planning sales strategies thrive with decentralized networks (Shaw, 1954; Tushman, 1978).

A person's status within an organizational structure often determines the type of information that he or she communicates or receives. For example, instructions and evaluations may be transmitted more often by supervisors to subordinates, while requests and factual information are more likely to be transmitted upwards (Sias & Jablin, 1995). One disturbing finding is that, although good news about increased sales, research successes, and the

■ A group's success in accomplishing its tasks and the good feeling that its members have in working together depend on the group's ability to transmit task-focused and socioemotional messages. In centralized networks, most communication must pass through a single individual. In decentralized networks, individuals can communicate more freely with one another. Performance on simple tasks is faster and more accurate when networks are centralized, but performance on complex tasks benefits from decentralized communication. (Adapted from Shaw, 1954 and K. Davis & Newstrom, 1985.)

like travels upward quickly, bad news is much slower to arrive at the top (L. D. Browning, 1978; Jablin, 1982). This asymmetry is only natural: Wouldn't you rather tell your boss that his or her pet project is going well than that it is failing? Yet, as we saw in our discussion of groupthink in chapter 9, if bad news like the engineers' concerns about the reliability of the space shuttle Challenger's O-rings never reaches the ears of the top-level decision makers, tragically flawed decisions may result.

When formal routes of communication do not serve the group's needs, group members may rely on the "grapevine." The grapevine is an informal person-to-person network linking members in all directions. Group members use the grapevine to fill in gaps in information and to deal with uncertainty. Although not officially sanctioned by organizations, the grapevine can be surprisingly accurate and useful. One study showed that about 80% of grapevine items were work related rather than personal, and that from 70% to 90% of the details passed through the grapevine were accurate (K. Davis & Newstrom, 1985; Simmonds, 1985)!

TECHNOLOGY AND COMMUNICATION. You may have noticed that much of the research on communication in work groups was carried out before computers and video revolutionized communication. In many modern organizations, the telephone, fax, e-mail, and video conferences are displacing face-to-face interaction for brainstorming and resolving conflicts. Not surprisingly, the new technologies influence both how tasks are completed and how group members feel as they complete them.

Technology-mediated communication, that is, information sharing that occurs via video or e-mail, can be remarkably efficient at getting the job done. If you are sending a memo or leaving a message, you probably will get right to the point. Thus, because they emphasize the task-relevant features of the interaction, telephone calls and e-mail tend to lead to good performance on simple tasks.

There is also evidence that computer-mediated group decision making may be less vulnerable to problems like the premature consensus of groupthink and biases that polarize majority views. In one comparison of three-member groups of university administrators reaching decisions, group polarization was less likely after computer-mediated discussion than when the groups met face-to-face (T. W. McGuire, Kiesler, & Siegel, 1987). In another study, the electronically linked groups took longer to reach consensus and made more unconventional decisions (S. Kiesler & Sproull, 1992).

One reason technologically mediated communication allows groups to avoid some decision-making pitfalls is that it seems to promote more equal participation among members. When groups meet face to face, high-status members typically dominate the discussion (Rutter & Robinson, 1981; E. Williams, 1977). This was certainly the case when researchers arranged for university students of different levels to make decisions together: High-status group members like graduate students took up much more "air time" than lower-status first-year undergraduates. When the same groups made comparable decisions using e-mail, however, status inequalities in participation were reduced (Dubrovsky, Kiesler, & Sethna, 1991). Remember that if everyone participates, the group has a better chance of maximizing the potential of all its members to get the job done right. But lessened effects of status are not inevitable when electronic com-

You may remember from chapter 9, pages 345 to 352, that majority views typically dominate group discussion and determine group decisions.

munication is used. If the computer software prominently displays status cues (such as organizational titles) in e-mail messages, status effects may be as large or even larger than those found with traditional forms of communication (Weisband, Schneider, & Connolly, 1995).

Of course, groups do not focus solely on getting their job done. Like traditional channels of communication, electronic communication is used as much for enhancing connectedness as for attaining mastery through task performance. And because more people tend to participate in group-related activities through the electronic networks, group members are likely to feel better about the group and their place in it. The use of new communication technologies can thus make a difference to group cohesiveness and commitment. One survey of city government employees found that the level of commitment to the organization was higher among employees who used e-mail and electronic bulletin boards than among those who used more traditional and status-dominated forms of communication (Huff, Sproull, & Kiesler, 1989). These findings are nonexperimental, but they nevertheless suggest that the opportunity to participate actively in group communication increases group commitment.

Despite the advantages of high-tech communication channels, some aspects of communication are still achieved most effectively in face-to-face interaction. Thus, face-to-face gatherings like scientific conventions continue to thrive despite scientists' ready access to e-mail and other forms of electronic communication. Why? For one thing, people who work in groups are happier and more satisfied with their work than are those working alone.

■ **The new face of work . . . not face-to-face.** Today, many employees keep in touch with colleagues and with clients using computers, telephones, fax machines, and electronic mail. Research shows that such forms of communication often aid the performance of simple tasks by smoothing task interdependence and coordination. But today's trend toward working at home has another side, as the benefits of social interdependence—such as higher morale and better solutions to complex problems—can be lost.

Also important is the informal exchange of information, summed up by the maxim that conference attendees generally learn more in the cocktail parties and hallways than in the formal sessions. Perhaps most important, the emotional ties that develop from actual interaction seem essential for the growth of interpersonal trust and commitment, as well as group solidarity. Some purely electronic collaborations may fail because their members cannot develop the same level of trust as when they exchange jokes and gossip over lunch or trade idle chit-chat (Goldberg, 1997). Physical proximity seems to be essential for this type of frequent, informal interaction.

Electronic communication is also better for some types of tasks than for others. As we have said, for simple tasks like generating ideas or collecting information to make decisions, electronic communication works well, often as well or better than face-to-face interactions. But what about more complex tasks that involve negotiation or resolution of conflicts? The opportunity to read nonverbal cues like approval and disapproval or tension and relief gives face-to-face interaction an advantage in solving such complex interpersonal problems (Hollingshead, McGrath, & O'Connor, 1993; McGrath & Hollingshead, 1993; Rutter & Robinson, 1981).

Another problem with electronic communication is evident in a study of students who worked cooperatively on large-scale projects, either in face-to-face groups or by interactive videoconferencing (Storck & Sproull, 1995). After considerable collaborative work, each student rated how much he or she would like to work together in the future with other members of his or her group. The ratings in the face-to-face condition reflected mainly the other student's actual competence and task performance. Evidently it is easy to gain a solid impression of another's skills when interacting in person. In contrast, the ratings made by students in the videoconference condition were less influenced by the other individual's task skills and more by task-irrelevant characteristics, such as physical appearance and how effectively the person used the video medium. The effectiveness of real-world organizations may suffer if people are selected for collaborations based on such irrelevant factors rather than their task-related skills.

THE COMPUTER AS A GROUP MEMBER. A new possibility is coming into existence, based on today's powerful, networked computers. Instead of acting as a simple communications device (like a telephone) that allows us to interact with partners and teammates in other locations, the computer itself can become a partner or collaborator: researching, sorting, evaluating, or displaying information, and even recommending conclusions. Byron Reeves and Clifford Nass (1996) found that in many ways, people tend to treat interactive computers like fellow humans. For example, when people interact with a computer that provides information and makes suggestions in a decision-making task, whether or not the computer is identified as a "teammate" strongly affects reactions to it. In one condition of this study, the person and computer were both labeled as members of the "Blue Team" and instructions stated that their task performance would be evaluated jointly. In another condition, the computer was not labeled as a team member and people were told that they would be evaluated solely on their own work (with the computer there just to help). Although the computer's actual contributions were the same in all conditions, people liked the computer better and saw its contributions as more relevant and helpful when it was identified as a teammate. Perhaps most important, people actually changed their own decisions more to comply with the computer's suggestions when the computer was presented as a teammate than when it was there just to help! Of course, these effects parallel those we discussed in chapters 6 and 9: People like other people better, rate them more positively, and accept more social influence from them, when they share group membership.

Groups incorporate technological changes into their communication patterns. Nevertheless, although the means of communicating are new, the end remains the same: effective task performance and the maintenance of group morale. From the family to the board of directors, from the hobbyist club to the office staff, we spend much of our lives in groups, trying to get things done. Coordinating actions and feelings is not easy, and groups are sometimes derailed by loafing members, lack of direction, or infighting. But when responsive leadership and appropriate communication help keep everyone and everything on track, groups succeed where no single individual could.

CONCLUDING COMMENTS

 Social life centers on groups, so by understanding how they work we can better understand ourselves as social beings. Interdependence, the sharing of common experiences and of a common fate, is the key to all group processes. Most common-sense ideas about group interaction focus on task interdependence: on the need to coordinate individual skills, roles, and efforts so that the group contributes to mastery goals and obtains concrete rewards for members. This is certainly the focus that drives human-engineering approaches to personnel management, organizational behavior, and management science. Our message in this chapter is slightly different. Task interdependence is important, of course, but social interdependence may be even more important. Our need for a shared understanding of the social world and of our place in it and our concern for being positively connected to others manifest themselves in almost every aspect of our social behavior, and particularly our behavior in face-to-face groups.

The impact of social interdependence and the desire for group membership has been evident since the earliest research on group interaction and leadership. During much of that research, however, investigations viewed these social influences mainly as an impediment to the successful and efficient completion of group tasks. Thus, the social rewards of group membership and the development of group norms were seen as elements that interfered with the goals of production. Today's social psychology offers a different point of view. Far from working against effective task interdependence, social interdependence can exert a positive influence on group behavior. Social, not technological, solutions may be our best bet for eliminating many apparently task-related problems, such as failures of coordination, social loafing, and low productivity. A positive social identity can provide the consensus, cohesion, and cooperation needed to get the job done.

CHAPTER 12 THEMES

- **Construction of Reality**
  Groups define for their members what their tasks are and how to perform them.

- **Pervasiveness of Social Influence**
  Interaction and interdependence in face-to-face groups affects performance on many tasks.

- **Striving for Mastery**
  Face-to-face groups bring their members rewards of many kinds.

- **Seeking Connectedness**
  Face-to-face groups provide their members strong feelings of belonging and identity.

- **Valuing Me and Mine**
  When we value group membership, we frequently seek to act in the group's interest.

However, we must add a word of caution here. As chapter 6 made clear, cohesion and cooperation within the in-group often come at the cost of antagonism and hostility toward out-groups. And, as chapter 9 pointed out, a group can be so intent on feeling good about itself that its decisions and actions are vulnerable to groupthink. Thus, as we have argued before, the optimal solution is always one of balance. The sales group needs enough cohesion to keep morale high and attention focused on their sales goals, but not so much that they are in constant conflict with the production team. The local school board needs enough group identity to maintain its members' enthusiasm about solving the district's problems, but not so much that they suppress doubts and support one another in unrealistic and ill-advised decisions. In situations like these we all need to learn how to use a shared group identity to promote both positive feelings *and* effective group performance. Under ideal conditions, working together in groups can help us to see what we have in common and to cooperate to solve the problems that threaten us all.

SUMMARY

 Social Facilitation: The Effects of Minimal Interdependence. Even when interdependence is minimal, the mere presence of others can produce arousal, either because those others are highly evaluative or because they are distracting. Arousal improves the performance of easy, well-learned behaviors, but can interfere with performance of novel or complex tasks. This pattern is termed **social facilitation.**

Crowding is another source of arousal that can improve performance on easy tasks and disrupt performance on difficult ones. However, the effects of crowding depend on people's interpretation of the situation and on their sense of control.

Performance in Face-to-Face Groups: Interaction and Interdependence. The members of face-to-face groups interact with one another and also share both **task interdependence** and **social interdependence.** Face-to-face groups usually go through the different stages of formation, conflict, development, performance, and dissolution as they try to develop a shared identity and reach their goals. The passage of time can also have other direct effects on group process and performance.

To achieve their performance goals, groups must maintain their motivation and avoid problems of coordination. For example, groups must ensure that their members work hard and avoid **social loafing.** Developing a common social identity helps to avoid such problems by encouraging cooperation for group goals, promoting social influence, and attracting and keeping valuable group members.

Effective **leadership** enhances task performance and maintains social interdependence. The ways leaders do this must differ from situation to situation and from time to time. Sometimes, however, stereotypical thinking prevents the most effective leaders from emerging in groups. Some types of leadership may be associated with particularly strong impacts on group members.

High productivity and high morale can be achieved only through communication. Groups use both formal and informal channels to make sure communication is effective. Technology, including video and e-mail, is now altering communication patterns and therefore many aspects of group performance.

13

Aggression and Conflict

On June 19, 1954, two groups of 11-year-old boys tumbled out of buses to start summer camp in the Sans Bois mountains near Oklahoma City, Oklahoma. Robbers Cave State Park, named for the hideout of the notorious outlaw Jesse James, offered a 200-acre site with fishing, swimming, canoeing, hiking, and the usual camp games and sports. The new arrivals were ordinary White, middle-class boys with no record of school, psychological, or behavioral problems. They had nothing on their minds except high hopes for a fun-filled 3-week vacation.

The camp was more than it seemed, however. Unknown to the boys, their parents had agreed to let them participate in a field study of intergroup conflict set up by Muzafer Sherif and his colleagues—a study that came to be known as the Robbers Cave experiment (Sherif, Harvey, White, Hood, & Sherif, 1961). The boys did not know that the camp counselors and directors were social psychologists and research assistants. Nor, at first, did members of each group know that another group was sharing the campsite.

During the first week, as they took part in separate activities designed to promote group cohesion, each group developed norms and leaders. They gave themselves names, the Eagles and the Rattlers, and each group designed a flag. Toward the end of the week, the groups discovered each other. Seeing "those guys" using "our ball field" and "our hiking trails" sparked demands for a competition. The staff was only too pleased to arrange a 4-day tournament including baseball, tug-of-war, a treasure hunt, and other events. The experimenters even promised the winners a fancy trophy, shiny badges, and four-bladed pocketknives. Both groups practiced hard, cheered their teammates, and roundly booed and insulted the competition. Hostilities escalated as the tournament progressed, culminating in a flag burning when the Eagles lost the tug-of-war.

The Eagles ultimately won the tournament, collecting the trophy and the coveted pocketknives. But while they were taking a celebratory swim, the Rattlers raided their cabins and stole the prizes. The rivalry had turned into full-blown war, and the staff was kept busy silencing name calling, breaking up fist fights, and cleaning up after cabin raids and food fights. The experiment had transformed 22 perfectly normal boys into two gangs of brawling troublemakers, full of hostility and intent on exacting revenge for every real or imagined slight.

As you may have guessed, Sherif and his colleagues set up this situation to understand how intergroup hostilities develop and how they can be resolved. This is not a trivial issue: In the half-century since the end of the Second World War, more than 100 wars have raged. Unrest and hostility mar not only international relations but also interactions between ethnic, political, and religious groups. And conflict and violence occur among individuals as well as groups. Newspaper headlines scream of drive-by shootings, street crimes, spouse and child abuse, barroom fights, even, tragically, shootings in schools by young students themselves.

This chapter will examine the social and cognitive processes that underlie aggression and conflict at both the individual and intergroup levels. First, we will discuss whether the seeming pervasiveness of conflict and aggression means that these behaviors are fundamentally part of human nature, built in by evolution and therefore unalterable. Then we will describe the reasons that individuals act aggressively as well as the factors that can turn groups into rivals or deadly enemies. Finally, we will consider what social psychology tells us about ways to reduce conflict and violence, based on our understanding of the dynamics behind these processes. As we will see, the goal of reducing conflict will draw on virtually everything we know about how people perceive and interact with each other, and requires not only stopping open hostilities but moving beyond that to resolve differences in ways that benefit all parties.

Aggression, Conflict, and Human Nature

Defining Conflict and Aggression

When people have incompatible goals, they may attempt to harm each other. This intention is what defines behavior as aggressive.

Conflict is a perceived incompatibility of goals: What one party wants, the other party sees as harmful to its interests. Conflict between individuals and groups does not always lead to violence, of course, but is acted out in many forums: complaints between neighbors about loud parties, protracted litigation in courtrooms, bloody battles in war zones. Whether the conflict is between Coke and Pepsi, labor and management, or candidates competing for a desirable promotion on the job, individuals and groups in conflict try to belittle, outdo, or frustrate the opponent and to extend and protect their own interests. The conflict at the heart of these disputes frequently focuses on mastery of material resources and social rewards.

Aggression is an all-too-typical part of people's response to conflict. The term *aggression* is used in a variety of imprecise ways in everyday language: You might call a fast-talking salesperson or a defensive tackle aggressive. For social psychologists, the term is defined by the actor's motive: **Aggression** is behavior intended to hurt someone. Accidentally injuring someone in a football game is not aggression, but cursing out the referee is.

Conflict. A perceived incompatibility of goals between two or more parties.

Aggression. Behavior intended to harm someone else.

Even doing nothing at all, such as intentionally failing to warn a rival of impending danger, could be aggressive.

Origins of Conflict and Aggression

Humans have evolved to compete effectively for food and mates. Although the capacity to act aggressively may have helped, aggression has no special place in "human nature." Aggression is just one strategy among many others that humans use to attain rewards and respect in accordance with individual perceptions and social norms.

You may be wondering if social psychology, with its emphasis on beliefs, emotions, interpretations, and norms, can really explain conflict and aggression. Hasn't evolution built aggression into our very genetic make-up? And if it is part of our biological inheritance, doesn't that make it both inevitable and uncontrollable? The popular view of evolution's role in human aggression certainly sees evolution as shaping humans to be fundamentally and unalterably selfish. According to this "beast within" view (Klama, 1988), "survival of the fittest" has bred aggressive impulses into human brain and bone (Lorenz, 1966). From this perspective, it is "human nature" to be aggressive.

Modern evolutionary psychology offers a considerably more sophisticated view (D. M. Buss & Kendrick, 1998). According to this more recent perspective, "human nature" includes a wide variety of psychological mechanisms and motives that have contributed to survival and reproduction over the millennia. Competition for food and mates, especially among males, really means competition for status and resources. In most animal species as well as most human groups, those males with the highest status and the most resources father more offspring than do less fortunate males (D. M. Buss & Kendrick, 1998). But in human groups, at least, this does not mean that only the "caveman with the biggest club" has had the evolutionary advantage. In human societies, competition, like all other human behaviors, has taken on many forms. Any behavior that promoted and maintained status and resources, including the ability to form alliances with others, to learn from others instead of through experience, and to cooperate to overcome hardships, is likely to have become part of our genetic inheritance (D. M. Buss & Kenrick, 1998; Caporael, 1997; H. A. Simon, 1990). Far from concluding that aggression is the defining aspect of human nature, evolutionary psychology actually tells us that aggression is one technique *among many others* that humans use as they strive for mastery of material resources as well as respect and connectedness to others.

You will recognize these as the fundamental motives that we have discussed throughout this text. The specific techniques that people will use in the service of those motives in any particular situation depend, of course, on the relevant norms as well as the individual's assessment of a technique's likely success and effectiveness. In other words, both individual thought processes and social influence affect the experience and the expression of aggression, just as they do other biologically based motives. Think about hunger, for example. Experiencing hunger does not inevitably lead to eating. Unsocialized infants may get away with stuffing into their mouths any food (or nonfood) within reach, but adults in most societies satisfy their hunger in less direct ways. The ways we experience hunger, the items we define as food, and the ways we act when hungry are all strongly influenced by what and how we think, as well as the norms of the groups we live in. The triggering of aggressive impulses, and our decisions about whether to act on those impulses, are influenced by the same cognitive processes and the same social forces that have played such a big role in every other form of social behavior discussed in this text.

Interpersonal Aggression

As 19-year-old Herman Everett and two friends walked down a New York City street, a stranger approached and demanded Everett's stylish jacket. The three friends ignored the mugger: With three against one, they thought, what could he do? What he did was pull out a gun and fire, missing Everett but killing 20-year-old Bernard Richardson and wounding their other companion. Everett later reflected, "I think the reason he shot was he felt we disrespected him. Initially, I don't think he wanted to kill us. He just wanted to prove something to us" (Terry, 1991).

The young mugger who committed murder while trying to steal a jacket acted aggressively in two different ways. Threatening harm and demanding the jacket were instances of *instrumental aggression,* aggression used as a means to an end. The shooting of two people in an outburst of rage was *emotional aggression,* aggression as an end in itself. Aggression always involves the intention to harm someone. The road from intention to action is a long one, however, and it is posted with cognitive and social signs that can either check our aggressive impulses or hurry us along the path. What factors motivate one person to hurt another? How do norms regulate aggression? Social psychologists have tried to answer these and other questions in their research on aggression.

Studying Aggression

Aggression can be difficult to study experimentally because people are often unwilling to act aggressively when they are being observed. Researchers have used a variety of techniques to get around these problems.

Aggression in everyday life is, unfortunately, easy to observe. Researchers have watched as schoolchildren pushed, shoved, and punched each other on the playground, as professional sports teams crossed the boundary from rough play to violence, and as urban street gangs fought over territory and bragging rights. Some researchers have even used official records of violent crimes to test hypotheses about aggression.

Studying aggression in the laboratory is much more difficult than observing it elsewhere. For ethical reasons, researchers cannot set up situations in which people actually harm one another. In addition, adults are reluctant to act aggressively in a research setting where they know they are being observed. As a result, most laboratory researchers have relied on a few somewhat cumbersome techniques. In the most frequently used procedure, developed by Arnold Buss (1961), participants are told that they and another participant are in a study of the effects of punishment on learning. A rigged drawing assigns the participant to the "teacher" role, and the other participant, actually a confederate, is given the role of "learner." The teacher is instructed to deliver electric shocks to punish the learner for wrong answers. The intensity and duration of the shocks selected by the teacher on the "aggression machine" serve as measures of aggression. The learner, of course, never actually receives any shocks.

You might worry that measures like these lack construct validity. Do they really measure aggression as the researchers intend? What if participants deliver the shocks not with the intent to harm—the definition of aggression—but because they believe the shocks will facilitate learning? In response to such questions, researchers have demonstrated that people who are highly aggressive outside the laboratory also give the most shocks with the shock machine, indicating that the laboratory measure possesses some construct validity (Berkowitz & Donnerstein, 1982; Carlson, Marcus-Newhall, & Miller, 1989). The heavy reliance on a limited range of laboratory measures weakens the generalizability of the findings, however, and it is interesting to note the almost complete absence of research on one common, everyday form of aggression: verbal assaults such as insults, curses, or ethnic slurs. These, too, are delivered with the intent to harm. As we all realized as children, sticks and stones may break our bones, but names can also hurt us.

Despite the difficulties researchers face in investigating aggression, a number of clear patterns emerge from their studies. As you will see, many of these patterns appear consistently across different types of research, both in the lab and in the field. They show that aggression is usually triggered by perceptions and interpretations of some event or situation.

You may recall from chapter 10, pages 395 to 396, that Stanley Milgram adapted this method for his famous study of obedience to authority.

What Triggers Aggression?

Some aggression is triggered by potential rewards and is suppressed by perceived costs or risks. Sometimes, however, perceived provocation produces anger, which can set off aggression regardless of the consequences. Any negative emotion, in fact, can make aggression more likely.

A situation that appears to offer opportunities for gain makes instrumental aggression look tempting. Likewise, perceived provocation often sets off emotional aggression. Of course, what looks like an opportunity for gain to one person may not even be noticed by another. And behavior that is a red flag to one person may not bother someone else. Thus aggression, like so many other behaviors, depends on the individual's perceptions and interpretations of other people, their behavior, and the situations in which behavior occurs.

INSTRUMENTAL AGGRESSION: COUNTING MATERIAL COSTS AND REWARDS. Instrumental aggression occurs when people see an opportunity for gain: an unarmed young man wearing a trendy jacket, a lone woman withdrawing money from a cash machine, or an opponent blocking the goal as the referee looks the other way. Those adept at instrumental aggression become particularly good at sensing appropriate opportunities: The experienced purse

■ **An opportunity for aggression?**   Designers of ATM machines probably did not imagine them as a possible site for aggression, but users of the machines often sense the potential for danger in such situations. The combination of people with their backs turned and easy access to cash can offer an opportunity for gain that might make instrumental aggression more likely.

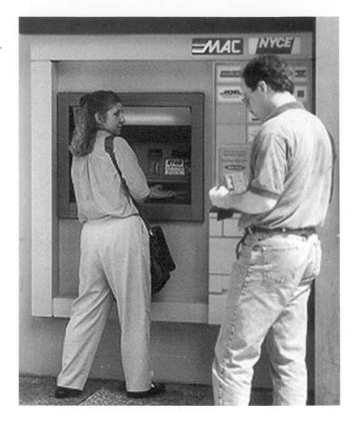

snatcher can spot the victims who are least able to resist effectively, and the schoolyard bully seems to zero in on smaller, weaker children. Cues that signal opportunities for gain are like billboards proclaiming, "Aggression pays."

When aggression pays, it becomes more likely (Bandura, 1973; G. R. Patterson, Littman, & Bricker, 1967). Perhaps it's no surprise, then, that children who believe aggression will lead to rewards or will prevent other kids from hurting them are the most aggressive in school (Perry, Perry, & Rasmussen, 1986). Nor is it surprising that teenage hockey players whose fathers applaud rough play are the most physically aggressive on the team (Ennis & Zanna, 1991). Conversely, when rewards are withdrawn, instrumental aggression usually subsides. Getting tough on terrorists—refusing to bargain with hijackers, hostage takers, and kidnappers—requires a heart of stone, but it eliminates the instrumental value of their tactics (B. Rubin, 1987). Even the threat of punishment can deter instrumental aggression, if the threat is believed (R. A. Baron, 1983a; Zillmann, 1979).

If instrumental aggression depends on mastery motivation, that is, on people's perceptions of potential rewards and costs, what factors influence those perceptions?

1. *Personal abilities.* For someone who is large and muscular or knows how to fight or to wield a knife or gun, aggression becomes easier— and a low perceived cost increases aggression. Children who think aggression is easy, or who have used it successfully to gain rewards in the past, are more likely to use it again (G. R. Patterson and others, 1967; Perry and others, 1986).

2. *Gender differences.* Aggression is usually easier and less risky for men than for women, so men find it more rewarding and less costly. In a meta-analysis of the research literature, Alice Eagly (1987) found that men are generally more likely to act aggressively than women, and this finding applies to both physical and verbal aggression. Eagly suggests that one reason for these differences is that men see aggression as less dangerous than women do.

3. *What do I have to lose?* Potential costs of aggression include retaliation from the intended victim, as well as the risk of being arrested, tried, and incarcerated. It may seem hard to understand why anyone would risk these severe consequences for gains that are often trivial—the average take in robberies and burglaries is only around $80 (Baumeister, 1997). To explain this phenomenon we must consider the perspective from which criminals, who come mostly from the poorest strata of society, assess their alternatives. First, for someone lacking education or living in an area without employment opportunities, aggression and crime may appear to be the only available means to resources and respect, even if they are accurately viewed as not very promising means (Gottfredson & Hirschi, 1990). Second, the risks of a criminal record or even a jail sentence might not loom as large for someone who, because of poverty, drug addiction, or lack of skills, has little hope of a secure and satisfying future in any case. Someone who has nothing has nothing to lose. For these reasons, poverty is the single most important factor in violence, including murder (H. Hill, Soriano, Chen, & LaFromboise, 1994).

EMOTIONAL AGGRESSION: PROTECTING SELF-ESTEEM AND STATUS. Unlike instrumental aggression, emotional aggression is not motivated by the calculus of material gain and loss. Propelled by "blind" fury, people sometimes act aggressively without regard even to the likelihood of immediate punishment (R. A. Baron, 1983a). The shooting of Bernard Richardson, one tragic example of emotional aggression, was prompted by the gunman's anger over perceived disrespect. This example reflects an important general truth: Angry feelings and impulses toward emotional aggression are usually provoked by a threat to self-esteem and status, for example, by being insulted, derogated, or disrespected (Baumeister, 1997). That is, needs to gain and maintain connectedness and respect motivate emotional aggression, just as desires for mastery of material rewards motivate instrumental aggression.

For this reason, threats to a positive self-image—being disrespected, ridiculed, or put down—are potent provocations that can lead to aggression. For example, in several recent cases where young schoolchildren committed shootings at school, news reports mentioned that these children had previously been socially rejected. Being coldly turned down when you ask someone for a date, being told by an angry co-worker that you have messed up an important job: Messages like these are likely to trigger thoughts that the evaluator is biased and unfair, and can lead to anger and aggressive action. Any blow to self-esteem is worse if it is public, because it is harder to just let an insult go by if others have witnessed the event. Thus, paradoxically, the presence of an audience may make violent responses to self-esteem threats more likely. One study found that more than half of murders were committed in front of an audience (Luckinbill, 1977).

People differ greatly in the ways they react to self-esteem threats. You may have heard that people who act aggressively typically have low self-esteem, but this is not the case. Aggression is more often committed by people with high self-esteem (Baumeister, 1997; Kernis, Grannemann, & Barclay, 1989). And not just anyone with high self-esteem, but those whose self-regard is fragile or insecure. Someone with stable and secure high self-esteem may brush off an insult or negative evaluation, knowing that it is off target. But someone whose high self-esteem is unstable, fluctuating with each new episode of social praise or rejection, is the person who reacts most strongly with anger and, sometimes, aggression.

Even among children, some are especially likely to interpret ambiguous acts as intentional disrespect and thus as threats to self-esteem. These youngsters tend to become chronically aggressive (Crick & Dodge, 1994). They may interpret unintentional collisions on the playground as deliberate and may then retaliate, possibly starting a cycle of violence. Although this perceptual bias has a strong role in emotional aggression, it has no impact on acts of instrumental aggression, such as bullying a younger child out of his lunch money (Dodge & Coie, 1987). Findings such as this support the belief that emotional aggression and instrumental aggression involve quite distinct psychological processes.

BEYOND PROVOCATION: NEGATIVE EMOTION AND AGGRESSION. Agitated by a loss, soccer fans riot, using stadium seat covers and planks from police barricades to assault the opposing fans. Frustrated by failure, a schoolboy continually bullies smaller children, even though it leads to rejection by his peers (J. M. Price & Dodge, 1989). As events like these demonstrate, emotional aggression is not limited to striking back at a provoker. In fact, one of the most influential early theories of aggression, *frustration-aggression theory*, held that any frustration—defined as the blocking of an important goal—inevitably triggers aggression (Dollard, Doob, Miller, Mowrer, & Sears, 1939). Early research evidence supported frustration-aggression theory, but critiques and conflicting data soon started to accumulate (N. E. Miller, 1941). More recently, Leonard Berkowitz (1989) outlined a broader model that also accounts for the original evidence linking frustration and aggression. According to Berkowitz, *any* negative feelings can set off aggression. Such feelings include not only frustration and anger but also pain, fear, and irritation. As Berkowitz (1993) put it, "We're nasty when we feel bad."

Berkowitz seems to be right. We now know that a variety of conditions that create negative feelings—unpleasant heat or painful cold, stressful noises, crowding, even noxious odors and air pollution—can trigger aggression (Berkowitz, 1989; Geen, 1998). The relationship between heat and aggression, for example, has been established in both field and laboratory studies (R. A. Baron, 1972; Rule, Taylor, & Dobbs, 1987). Examination of weather and crime records reveals that when the outdoor temperature is high, there is an increase in the incidence of violent crimes, including murder and rape (C. A. Anderson, 1987). But even negative feelings or frustration do not always lead to aggression, for norms strongly shape and control its expression.

Norms Promoting and Restraining Aggression

Social norms can either promote or restrain aggression. They can be activated by the behavior of models witnessed in person or in the media. Norms that limit aggression apply especially strongly to aggression against similar others or in-group members.

Because aggression is a potentially destructive force, virtually all societies and groups have norms that regulate it. This does not mean that all norms operate to squelch aggression. As you will see, group norms often promote aggressive behavior rather than restrain it.

NORMS PROMOTING AGGRESSION. According to one Chicago teenager, the code of the streets includes: "Never, ever, disrespect anybody." The reason? Norms in the teenager's neighborhood dictate violent responses to disrespect. "People won't fistfight. . . . They'd shoot me, step over my dead body and go about their business" (Terry, 1993). Urban gangs are not the only groups whose norms support aggression (M. W. Klein, 1969; Reicher, 1987). When aggressive school-age boys are more popular than less aggressive boys, schoolboy norms are promoting aggression (Price & Dodge, 1989). In some cultures, "crimes of passion" such as killing a romantic rival are judged leniently by public opinion and may even draw light sentences from the courts. When corporate managers fix prices and violate patent and copyright laws, their actions reflect a business norm that condones any action in the pursuit of profit. These business strategies, together with fraud and tax evasion, have caused more economic loss than theft and vandalism (President's Commission on Law Enforcement, 1967). When it comes to aggression, you cannot judge a book by its cover: Aggression seems to wear a suit as easily as it does expensive sneakers and gang colors.

Of course, norms that promote aggression differ from one society to another. International comparisons consistently show that the United States has one of the highest homicide rates in the world for young men between the ages of 15 and 24—22 per 100,000 (L. Howard, 1990). Among 21 industrial nations, no other country's rate was even one fourth as high as that. Israel's rate was 3.7, despite ongoing armed conflict in that country, and Japan and the major nations of Western Europe have rates below 1.5 per 100,000 young men. Sadly, several prevalent norms in mainstream U.S. culture promote aggression.

1. *The right to bear firearms and to use them.* In the United States, this right is viewed not only as a way to resist tyrannical government, as foreseen in the U.S. Constitution, but as a response to perceived threats to home or hearth. Many people in the United States believe it is appropriate for a householder to shoot an intruder in his or her home, and some states have passed laws explicitly providing immunity from prosecution in such situations. American public opinion even favors a tough line with petty criminals: In one case, a judge in Marion, Indiana, congratulated a defendant who shot and crippled a purse snatcher, saying, "My thanks, sir, for having tried to do something to help the problems in this country" (*Newsweek*, 1990a).

2. *The norm of family privacy.* The old saying that a man's home is his castle represents the idea that private homes are havens, safe from public intrusion. The norm of family privacy may exempt family life from public standards of behavior. In doing so, this norm often increases violence within the home (Berk & Newton, 1985; L. W. Sherman & Berk, 1984). Family members have several features that make them tragically frequent targets of aggression. Perhaps the most obvious is simply that they are there: They are easily accessible. Differences in size and power also make weaker family members less able

to retaliate. Finally, social norms condone aggression between parents and children that would not be tolerated between strangers. Imagine the quick action that would be taken if a restaurant owner slapped a customer's child for not eating his or her vegetables! Norms supporting traditional family power structures, though they are gradually changing, may also encourage violence against women and children (Straus, Gelles, & Steinmetz, 1980).

3. *The "culture of honor."* Though you might imagine that the highest homicide rates in the United States are found in densely populated urban areas, this is not the case. In 1996, for example, the murder rate in South Carolina (a mostly rural state) was over three times higher than that of densely populated Massachusetts. In fact, homicide rates tend to be highest in the generally rural and agricultural Southern states. What factor could explain this regional pattern, even outweighing the crowding and poverty so prevalent in the large cities of the North and East? One answer is provided by Richard Nisbett and Dov Cohen (1996): the persistence of what they term a "culture of honor" which involves a special readiness to respond with violence to perceived insults or threats of material loss. When the South was first settled, sheep and cattle herding were predominant occupations, and (with law enforcement essentially nonexistent) a herder had to be ready to use violence to defend himself against thieves and rustlers. Nisbett and Cohen argue that this cultural tendency has persisted to the present day. They cite survey data that show Southern White males, compared to those from other regions, are more likely to endorse aggression in defense of property or in retaliation for insults (D. Cohen & Nisbett, 1997). D. Cohen and others (D. Cohen, Nisbett, Bowdle, & Schwartz, 1996) even found that among students attending the University of Michigan, those from the South were more likely than students from Northern states to respond with anger to a staged insult in a laboratory study. The "culture of honor" thesis illustrates one way in which cultural differences in norms can influence when and whether people turn to aggression (Butterfield, 1998).

CULTURAL CUES TO VIOLENCE. In such a social context, it is no wonder that weapons, and especially guns, are strongly associated with the idea of aggression (Huesmann & Eron, 1984). If seeing a weapon cues thoughts of aggression, this in turn should make aggressive behavior more likely—and so it does, in an outcome termed the *weapons effect* (C. A. Anderson, Anderson, & Deuser, 1996; Berkowitz & LePage, 1967). In one nonlaboratory study of this effect, Charles Turner and his associates set up a booth at a campus carnival and invited students to throw sponges at a target person. Passersby threw more sponges when they could see a rifle that had been placed nearby than when no rifle was present (C. W. Turner, Simons, Berkowitz, & Frodi, 1977). Another study showed that motorists stopped by police officers acted more aggressively when the officers carried a holstered pistol than when they did not (Boyanowsky & Griffiths, 1982). The mugger who shot Bernard Richardson carried a gun. That gun not only made the mugger's aggression more deadly, it may also have made it more likely in the first place. The National Rifle Association, an organization that has long opposed any form of gun control, argues that guns don't kill, people do. But the evidence suggests otherwise. As Leonard Berkowitz (1965) put it, "The finger pulls the trigger, but the trigger may also be pulling the finger."

☐ **AGGRESSIVE CUES IN THE SPORTS ARENA.** Can learned cues increase athletes' aggression toward one another? Mark Frank and Thomas Gilovich (1988) think so. They hypothesized that in many Western countries, cultural associations may cause black uniforms to act as cues to thoughts of aggression and death, thereby encouraging aggressive behavior. To test this hypothesis, they looked at the relationship between uniform color and penalties incurred by professional hockey and football players. Sure enough, from the Pittsburgh Steelers to the Philadelphia Flyers, teams wearing black uniforms were penalized more often over 17 playing seasons than were teams wearing other colors. In fact, when a team changed to black uniforms during the course of its season, as the Pittsburgh Penguins did, their penalties increased. The uniform cue seems to influence both those wearing the uniforms (the teams become more aggressive) and those watching them (referees call more penalties against them). To replicate these effects in the laboratory, Frank and Gilovich formed college men into groups of three and told them that they could choose the game they wanted to play against another group of students. Each group was given either black or white "uniform" tops to wear over their regular clothing. Teams decked out in black were more likely than teams in white to choose "dart gun duel" or "chicken fights" over the less aggressive "block stacking" or "golf putting contest" games.

MODELS OF AGGRESSION. Not only culturally defined cues but also other people's actions offer clues to the norms appropriate in a situation. Models who demonstrate the appropriateness of nonviolent solutions to conflict can reduce aggression. Unfortunately, aggressive models not only show people ways to act aggressively but also send the message that an aggressive response is right, correct, and acceptable, and others soon imitate them (Bandura, Ross, & Ross, 1961, 1963). For example, at many sporting events, violence among fans is often preceded by aggressive play on the field (J. H. Goldstein, 1982).

Laboratory studies confirm the powerful impact that models have on aggressive behavior. Compared with those who had watched an innocuous film, people who had watched a film of a highly aggressive boxing match gave other participants stronger shocks on Buss's "aggression machine" (Bushman & Geen, 1990). Exposure to aggressive models makes violent behavior seem more appropriate because it stimulates aggressive thoughts and feelings (Bargh & Gollwitzer, 1993). It also makes people interpret ambiguous behaviors as more hostile, making retaliation to perceived provocations more likely (Carver, Ganellen, Froming, & Chambers, 1983).

Tragically, people often encounter aggressive models in their own homes. Children of abusive parents learn at an early age that aggression is both appropriate and acceptable. Indeed, until recently, surveys in the United States indicated that public opinion supported the physical punishment of children as legitimate and necessary (Gelles, 1972). Yet in the home, as elsewhere, violent acts teach violent norms. People who abuse their children or spouses tend to have been on the receiving end of child abuse themselves (Sugarman & Hotaling, 1989; Widom, 1989).

☐ **AGGRESSIVE MODELS IN THE MEDIA.** Even children from peaceful homes are exposed to an enormous amount of violence because of the amount of time they spend watching television. On average, children in the United

States watch 3.5 hours of TV each day, and during that time they see an average of 33 acts of violence (Heymann, 1989). Prime-time TV averages 5 violent acts per hour, whereas Saturday morning cartoons average 20 (Gerbner, Gross, Morgan, & Signorielli, 1986). Does aggressive media content stimulate viewers' aggression? Many studies have tried to answer this question.

In one study, researchers asked 141 parents how much television their kindergarten-age children watched, then visited the classrooms to observe the children's aggressive behavior at play (Singer & Singer, 1981). The children who viewed the most TV violence also behaved the most aggressively. However, this nonexperimental design is weak on internal validity and cannot show that TV viewing *causes* aggression. Other causal relationships could lead to the same pattern of results. For example, parental neglect could both make children aggressive and cause them to spend a lot of time watching TV. In another classic study, incarcerated delinquent boys were randomly assigned to view aggressive films or nonaggressive films every evening for a week (Parke, Berkowitz, Leyens, West, & Sebastian, 1977). The young men's aggressive behavior was observed both before and after the "film week," and boys who saw aggressive films committed more physical attacks than those who viewed neutral films. We can conclude that film viewing *caused* aggression because of the high internal validity of the experimental design, and this conclusion is supported by a meta-analysis of 28 different field experiments (W. Wood, Wong, & Chachere, 1991). However, most of these studies were relatively short term, examining the effects of only days or weeks of viewing.

Perhaps the most powerful findings on the issue come from longitudinal studies, which assess television viewing and aggressiveness over a long period of time to attempt to determine which variable causes the other. One ambitious study, which followed a group of participants for 22 years, found that those who watched more TV violence at age 8 were more likely to have been convicted for violent crimes by age 30 (Huesmann, 1986). These findings were confirmed in a 3-year multination study in the United States, Finland, Israel, and Poland (Huesmann & Eron, 1986). Though time consuming and costly to carry out, longitudinal research has important strengths: The variables can be measured in natural settings and strong causal conclusions can be drawn.

A simple conclusion can be drawn from all these different studies: aggressive media content can increase viewers' aggressive behavior (Hearold, 1986; Liebert & Sprafkin, 1988). Perhaps even more ominously, the effect seems to have a long life. Studies indicate that, over the long term, witnessing violence dulls our perceptions and numbs our reactions, eventually leading to indifference and acceptance. For example, boys who watch a great deal of violence on television are not aroused by viewing a brutal boxing match (Cline, Croft, & Courrier, 1973). Frequent viewers of "slasher" movies are relatively unconcerned about violence toward women (Donnerstein, Linz, & Penrod, 1987). Perhaps most unsettling, a recent study in the United States found that nearly 75% of violent scenes on TV, including cartoon shows viewed by very young children, involved no remorse, criticism, or penalty for the perpetrator (Wilson and others, 1998). What norms are these shows reinforcing? One of the authors of the study, Barbara Wilson, put the issue into context: "Even one televised depiction that encourages a child to drink poison or play with fire would surely come under great public attack. Here we have the average preschooler who's watching cartoons seeing over 500 high-risk portrayals that encourage aggression in a typical year" (National Public Radio, 1998).

NORMS RESTRAINING AGGRESSION. Of course, not all models and norms foster aggression. Most societies maintain and teach some norms that limit and inhibit violence. "Pick on someone your own size," like many other norms, forbids aggression against the weak and helpless. And although "an eye for an eye, a tooth for a tooth" seems to be a formula for revenge, its original purpose was to prevent retaliation from spiraling out of control.

Some groups have developed norms that effectively counteract violence. Anthropological reports indicate that among the Inuit of the Arctic, the Pygmies of Africa, and the Zuni and Blackfoot peoples of North America, controversy and conflict are avoided, physical violence is rare, and war is nonexistent (Gorer, 1968). Japanese social norms also dictate that it is often better to yield than fight, as reflected in the expression *Makeru ga kachi* "to lose is to win" (Alcock, Carment, & Sadava, 1988; Triandis, Bontempo, Villareal, Asai, & Lucca, 1988).

Norms are usually most effective in limiting aggression against other in-group members. Thus, similarity reduces aggression, and it does so for two reasons. First, as we have seen in chapter 6, shared group membership breeds liking, and fellow feeling is incompatible with aggression (P. A. Miller & Eisenberg, 1988). Second, the norms of most groups proscribe or strictly control aggression within the group so that cohesion can be maintained and group goals achieved. In-group members are protected by a norm that appears to warn, "Don't hurt me. I'm one of *us*." Unfortunately, as we will see, these norms are less likely to protect outsiders.

To Hurt or Not to Hurt:
Superficial and Systematic Thinking About Aggression

Situations that favor superficial thinking often favor aggression. Thinking carefully can reduce aggression, but many factors interfere with people's motivation and ability to process information carefully and evenhandedly, increasing the likelihood of aggression.

What if you really want to smack someone, but know it would be wrong? What happens when the messages we get from environmental cues, feelings, the anticipation of reward and punishments, and social norms conflict? Whether and how we turn to violence in such circumstances depends on how we deal with the relevant information.

When people are processing superficially, the most salient aspect of the environment or the most accessible attitude or norm "wins": Whatever grabs our attention most easily has the greatest impact on our behavior. The salience of costs or rewards, the behavior of models, and situational cues can all trigger aggressive behavior if the aggressor is processing superficially. In anger-inducing situations, the event that produced the anger is usually foremost in our attention. Thus conditions that favor superficial thinking are likely to favor aggression.

Unfortunately, a variety of factors can limit people's motivation and ability to engage in complex thinking (Zillmann, 1982).

1. *Individual differences in social reasoning ability.* Across situations and over time, some people are consistently more aggressive than others (Krebs & Miller, 1985; Olweus, 1979). One of the main reasons for this consistency is that some people are better able than others to think through a provoking situation and to come up with peaceful alternatives. Children with less ability to think of nonaggressive responses in social situations are more aggressive than children who can suggest more alternatives (Dodge & Crick, 1990; Huesmann, Eron, & Yarmel, 1987). This difference becomes even more pronounced as life grows more complicated. As tasks become more challenging or as interaction becomes more structured, social and cognitive skills are strained to their limits. Aggressive children are then even more likely to turn to violence (Dodge, Pettit, McClaskey, & Brown, 1986; J. C. Wright & Mischel, 1987).

   Sadly, there is evidence that the physical and emotional trauma of child abuse may diminish a child's ability to interpret social cues correctly and to generate imaginative responses to conflict situations (Dodge, Bates, & Pettit, 1990). These deficits in turn increase the child's own tendency to turn to aggression, which may be one important reason why abused children sometimes grow up to perpetuate abuse against their own spouses or children (Geen, 1998; Sugarman & Hotaling, 1989).

2. *Threat and emotional arousal.* Strong threat and intense emotions can reduce people's capacity to process information carefully, as we have seen many times throughout this text. Because strong emotions often accompany conflict, they temporarily interfere with careful processing just when it is most needed. The presence of weapons increases aggression even more strongly when people who are already

Situational cues can have similar effects on us in other contexts when we do not process thoroughly. The impact of heuristic cues on persuasion during superficial processing was discussed in chapter 7, pages 256 to 264, and the effect of physical and behavioral cues on the spontaneous formation of first impressions was discussed in chapter 3, pages 61 to 67.

aroused and angered (Berkowitz, 1993). In the same way, aggressive boys' tendency to see any bump or jostle as an act of aggression is magnified when they are very anxious (Dodge & Somberg, 1987). One study (J. R. Gray, 1999) found that when people were emotionally aroused by threat, they shifted to short-term thinking. In a conflict, this might lead them to seek the immediate rewards of aggressive action while ignoring or discounting its long-term costs.

3. *Alcohol use.* You may not be surprised to learn that drinking and violence often coincide (Bushman & Cooper, 1990; Ito, Miller, & Pollock, 1996). Alcohol is a factor in almost two thirds of homicides and in one third of rapes, burglaries, and assaults (Desmond, 1987; Wolfgang & Strohm, 1956). The statistics are less surprising, though no less shocking, when you realize that alcohol reduces people's capacity to process a wide range of information. Perceiving a restricted range of cues, a person under the influence of alcohol is likely to base his or her actions on whatever is most immediately obvious (Steele & Josephs, 1990). So alcohol by itself does not invariably lead to violence: People sometimes become jolly or weepy when they drink if they happen to focus on cues that push them in those directions. However, alcohol plus anger or threat is a surefire recipe for aggression (S. P. Taylor, Gammon, & Capasso, 1976). In addition to reducing our capacity to process a wide range of cues, alcohol exerts a second and equally dangerous influence. It lessens people's concern for factors that ordinarily restrain aggression: the potential costs and dangers of aggressive acts, the social norms that constrain aggression, and the cues that ordinarily inhibit aggression, such as expressions of pain from the victim (Baumeister, 1997; Schmutte & Taylor, 1980).

When factors like these are absent so that people have the time and capacity to consider deeply, they can intentionally try to activate the most appropriate, rather than the most accessible, cognitive structures (Yovetich & Rusbult, 1994). Given the opportunity, they can come up with alternatives to violence: talking over a conflict, weighing the costs and benefits of retaliation, compromising on a solution, realizing that an apparent provocation may have been accidental.

However, thinking extensively does not always guarantee a nonaggressive outcome. Sometimes people can direct their thinking towards rationalizing or justifying their aggressive impulses, even if norms against such behavior are present. To demonstrate this point, in one study the researcher arranged for students to be "accidentally" overpaid by a couple of dollars for their experimental participation (Bersoff, 1999). If the students thought the payment came out of the pocket of the graduate student who was in charge of the research, 50% pointed out the error. But if they thought the funds were provided by a big corporation, only 20% did so. Evidently motivated by even a small potential gain, the students redefined the applicable norm from "stealing is wrong" to "it is OK to take something that is not yours if nobody is really harmed" (Bersoff, 1999, p. 37). Other norms or attitudes that restrain aggression may be redefined or reinterpreted when a strong desire to act aggressively directs our thinking.

What explains interpersonal aggression? At this point you may be thinking that just about *anything* can cause aggression: feeling too hot or cold, drinking a beer, watching a violent movie, or even wearing black clothing. It is true that many different factors can push us in the direction of aggression, but all their effects can be understood in terms of the underlying processes shown in Figure 13.1. The process begins with perceptions of the person, the situation, and any provocation. The *desire* to hurt increases when potential rewards outweigh potential costs or when anger and other negative emotions are present. The desire to act aggressively does not always dictate action, however, because social norms and the actions of others also play a major role in initiating or restraining aggression. Violent models can show that violence is rewarded, offer evidence that aggression is normatively acceptable, and serve as a cue that makes aggressive thoughts and feelings more accessible. No wonder aggressive models are so potent in producing further aggression and that those aiming at reducing aggression in society have criticized the media for presenting so many aggressive models for public consumption.

But norms and models can also have a pacifying effect—if they are nonviolent and if they are brought to mind. This is one reason that it is so important to go beyond the immediate situation, and to think carefully about other cues, attitudes, and norms that oppose aggression. Unfortunately, this careful thought requires time, effort, and ability, resources that might not be available when people are pressed to make instant decisions or are stressed by anger or other strong negative emotions.

Thus interpersonal aggression is guided by fundamental cognitive and social processes. It is motivated by desires for mastery, connectedness, and esteem. It can be directed by firmly established or situationally accessible attitudes and norms, depending on whether or not we have the ability and motivation to think things through thoroughly. Not surprisingly, exactly these same processes apply also to aggression and conflict that pit group against group.

FIGURE 13.1 Multiple factors influence aggression

■ A perceived provocation in a particular situation may spur desires to aggress or may activate norms that either favor or restrain aggression. The way the person resolves potentially conflicting desires and norms will determine whether aggression occurs.

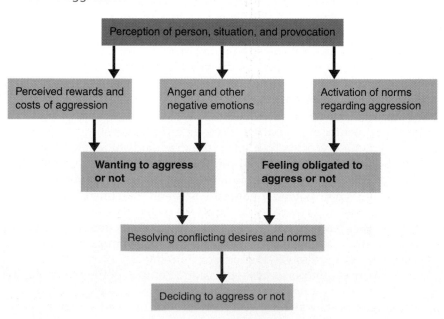

Intergroup Conflict

As we have seen, individuals all too frequently act to harm others. Unfortunately, groups aggress even more than individuals do! Nabith Berri, chief of one militia group in conflict-torn Lebanon, once stated, "When we deal with each other individually, we can be civilized . . . but when we deal with each other as groups, we are like savage tribes in the Middle Ages" (*Indianapolis Star*, 1989).

The greater aggressiveness of groups can be observed in the laboratory as well as in violent conflicts around the world (Insko & Schopler, 1998). For example, in a recent study the researchers had either two individuals or two 3-member groups participate in a construction activity (Mikolic, Parker, & Pruitt, 1997). To complete the activity successfully, the participants had to share the use of various materials such as paper, glue, and scissors, which were in short supply. One individual (or one group), a confederate of the experimenter, persistently withheld crucial materials, so that the researchers could examine the actual participants' responses to this frustration. Verbal responses on an intercom were coded into several categories, which could be placed in a clear order of severity. Participants always started with mild requests for cooperation. But when these requests had no effect, most of them escalated their responses in order of severity. For example, almost nobody made angry statements before trying requests, demands, and complaints, in that order.

Table 13.1 shows the responses from 41 individuals and 31 groups in this situation. Note that the groups systematically engaged in stronger responses than the individuals. In fact, though only one individual of the 41 went above the level of angry statements, more than half of the groups escalated beyond that level! Other studies similarly show that groups are more competitive than individuals. For example, participants given the task of allocating valu-

TABLE 13.1 Greater Competitiveness of Groups

Category	Example	Percent of individuals who went no higher than this category	Percent of groups who went no higher than this category
Requests	May I use the glue?	17	0
Demands	Give me the glue now!	20	0
Complaints	What's wrong with you? Why don't you share?	51	16
Angry statements	I'm mad now.	10	26
Threats	Give me the glue or else!	0	13
Harassment	I'm not giving you any more ribbon until you return the glue.	2	23
Abuse	You are a selfish swine.	0	23

Source: D. G. Pruitt, Social conflict, in D. T. Gilbert, S. T. Fiske, & G. Lindzey (Eds.), *Handbook of social psychology* 3rd ed., 1998, Vol. 2, pp. 470–503, Boston: McGraw-Hill.

able points to themselves and to others like their opponents less and make more competitive choices when playing in teams of two or three than they do when playing alone (Insko, Pinkley, Hoyle, & Dalton, 1987, Insko and others, 1988; McCallum and others, 1985). In fact, anything that increases a group's feeling of identity can boost its competitiveness (L. Gaertner & Schopler, 1998). To demonstrate this point, one group of researchers gave young members of informal handball teams bright orange jerseys to wear—emphasizing their identity as a group. This symbol of group solidarity was enough to increase their aggressiveness relative to their opponents who wore their usual street clothes (Rehm, Steinleitner, & Lilli, 1987).

Why are groups generally more aggressive than individuals? Like a jigsaw puzzle, the answer to this question has several pieces. We will discuss the reasons for the special competitiveness of groups as we describe the reasons and processes that underlie intergroup conflict.

Sources of Intergroup Conflict: The Battle for Riches and Respect

Most group conflict stems from competition for valued material resources or for social rewards like respect and esteem. Groups in conflict are often more attuned to social rewards than to material ones. People use social comparisons to determine acceptable levels of resources.

■ **The human price of war.** Victories and defeats are often measured in terms of material resources gained and lost. But the human cost of war goes far beyond such measures, as can be seen in the faces of these young Israeli soldiers weeping at the funeral of one of their comrades killed in Southern Lebanon. Similar experiences, of course, occur on both sides of the battlelines.

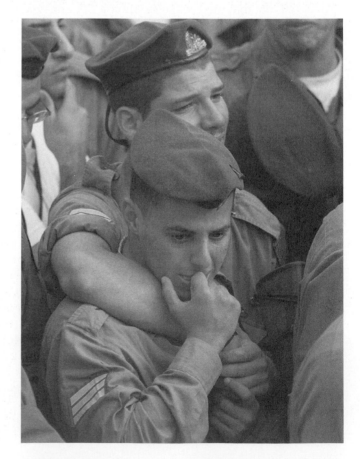

FIGURE 13.2 Competition increases solidarity and intergroup hostility

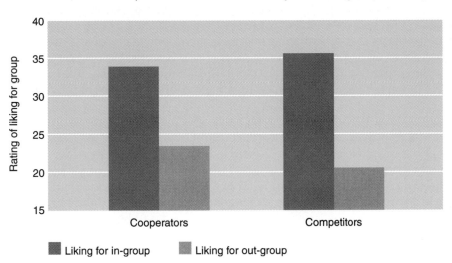

■ Two groups of participants either competed against one another or cooperated for rewards. Compared with the cooperators, those who competed liked their fellow in-group members better and disliked out-group members more. (Data from D. A. Taylor and Moriarty, 1987.)

Although groups are often more competitive and aggressive than individuals, groups and individuals generally enter into conflict for the same basic reasons: valued material resources or respect and esteem.

REALISTIC CONFLICT THEORY: GETTING THE GOODS. In the conflict between the Eagles and the Rattlers at Robber's Cave State Park, each group defended its swimming and playing territory, stole the other's prized possessions, and engaged in athletic competition spiced by the knowledge that only the winners would receive new pocketknives. The resulting dramatic escalation of hostilities provided good evidence for **realistic conflict theory.** This theory argues that intergroup hostility, conflict, and aggression arise from competition among groups for scarce but valued material resources (D. T. Campbell, 1965; LeVine & Campbell, 1972; M. Sherif, 1966). Just as the calculation of material costs and rewards motivates instrumental aggression by individuals, the potential gain or loss of material resources motivates intergroup aggression.

Laboratory research has confirmed that competition for scarce resources sours intergroup relations. Consider the way in which the potential for one group to win a reward can change intergroup interactions, for example. In this study two groups of students worked on tasks such as recommending a therapy program for a troubled adolescent or creating an advertising slogan for a new brand of toothpaste (D. A. Taylor & Moriarty, 1987). To set up a cooperative or competitive environment, researchers gave different instructions to the participants in the two groups. To create a cooperative environment, researchers told participants that proposals from the two groups would be combined to produce the best solution, and that both groups would be rewarded. In the competitive condition, participants heard that only the one group that came up with the best idea would receive the reward. The findings were consistent with predictions from realistic conflict theory. Compared with the cooperative groups, the groups in competition for the scarce and valued resource liked in-group members better and disliked out-group members more (see Figure 13.2).

Realistic conflict theory. The theory that intergroup hostility arises from competition among groups for scarce but valued material resources.

As the Rattlers and Eagles demonstrated, group competition can quickly escalate from dislike into hostility and aggression (Horwitz & Rabbie, 1982; Rapoport & Bornstein, 1987). Indeed, competition for real resources, such as land, jobs, and natural resources, has been implicated as one cause of the many conflicts that pit nation against nation and ethnic group against ethnic group (Brewer & Campbell, 1976; Gurr, 1970; Streufert & Streufert, 1986). When countries battle over the right to control strategic waterways or land rich in oil and minerals, realistic competition is probably at the root of the conflict.

SOCIAL COMPETITION: GETTING A LITTLE RESPECT. If groups fought only over material resources, intergroup conflict might be more easily resolved. After all, groups could learn to make do with a little less, resources could be more equally distributed, and more goods could be produced, all of which might help groups live side by side in relative satisfaction. Unfortunately, groups, like individuals, also fight over social goods: respect, esteem, and "bragging rights." And this is as true for adults as it is for small boys (D. Katz, 1965; Tajfel & Turner, 1979).

Consider a series of studies in which two groups of corporate executives attending a training program were assigned problem-solving tasks (Blake & Mouton, 1979, 1984). Researchers told the executives that experts would evaluate each team's performance, but they never mentioned competition, nor did they promise concrete rewards for performance. Nevertheless, the experience of being divided into groups and anticipating evaluation was apparently enough to produce conflict. In a virtual replay of the Eagles–Rattlers scenario, team spirit soared and intergroup antagonism emerged as group members huddled together during breaks and meals to plan strategies, analyze successful performances, and even hold pep rallies. In one version of the experiment, researchers asked representatives from each group to meet to evaluate the groups' products. These meetings almost always resulted in a deadlock, with each representative insisting his or her own group's work was best. When a neutral judge broke the deadlock, the losing team accused him of bias and incompetence. At one point the researchers had to break off the experiment to calm tempers and restore order.

What drives competition when no material resources whatever are at stake? If you think the answer has something to do with social identity, you're right. You may recall that people's desire to see their own groups as better than other groups can lead to intergroup prejudice. The same process can also contribute to outright conflict. People can even identify with groups formed on the basis of an arbitrary toss of a coin: They don't need to interact with other group members or even to know them, and they don't need to feel that their access to material resources is at risk. Research indicates that members of such "minimal groups" nevertheless act as if they were at odds with other groups, treating them in ways that fuel conflict. They downgrade the out-group's products, dislike out-group members as individuals, and discriminate against the out-group in allocating rewards (Brewer, 1979; J. C. Turner, 1980). Thus, people's strivings for positive social identity may plant the seeds of intergroup conflict.

THE SPECIAL COMPETITIVENESS OF GROUPS: GROUPS OFTEN VALUE RESPECT OVER RICHES. The first reason for the greater competitiveness of groups than individuals is this: When groups vie to be "Number One," social competition and the effort to outdo one's opponent frequently overshadow competition

Social identity theory and studies that demonstrate people's readiness to identify even with arbitrary, transient groups were discussed in chapter 6, especially pages 220 to 223.

for material resources (L. Gaertner & Schopler, 1998; C. A. Insko & Schopler, 1987). If the boys at summer camp had cared only about the badges and pocketknives, the researchers could have given those prizes to everyone. But do you think that would have satisfied the boys or reduced their desire to outdo the other group? Chester Insko and John Schopler (1998) have documented the way groups seek respect over riches in their studies of resource-allocation choices. In their studies, participants choose among several alternative ways to distribute points worth a small amount of money to their own group and to another group. Usually groups start by choosing alternatives that maximize the in-group's profit, paying little attention to the out-group's situation. As the play continues, however, the players' choices become more competitive—maximizing the advantage of the in-group over the out-group. In a display of supercompetitiveness, groups sometimes give up absolute gain in order to dominate their rivals (Brewer, 1979). And, of course, as soon as one side makes a competitive choice, the other retaliates.

Similar shifts occur in organizational and international conflicts. For example, nations begin wars knowing that either victory or defeat will exact an enormous cost in physical pain, economic ruin, and ecological devastation. Yet they sound the war drums anyway, accepting material costs in exchange for the chance of victory over their opponent. When competition for riches turns into competition for respect, winning becomes everything.

RELATIVE DEPRIVATION: WHEN IS ENOUGH ENOUGH? Perhaps conflict is understandable when material resources and respect are scarce. But even when this is not the case—when people seem to have adequate resources—they often continue to compete. Apparently, once people have the basic necessities of life, it becomes difficult to determine objectively how they are faring, and so they turn to comparisons with others to help them decide. This idea is central to **relative deprivation theory,** which suggests that social comparison, not objective reality, determines how satisfied or dissatisfied people are with what they have (Bernstein & Crosby, 1980; Crosby, 1976; Stouffer and others, 1949). It's not hard to see how this idea might apply in real life. If you had just bought a shiny new Chevrolet, you probably would feel pretty good about it—until your next-door neighbor proudly rolled *his* shiny new BMW into his driveway. Your Chevy is still exactly the same car, but suddenly you may not feel quite so proud of it. In fact, you may experience *egoistic relative deprivation*, a sense that you are doing less well than other individuals (Runciman, 1966).

Under many circumstances, however, the crucial comparison people make is not between themselves and other individuals, but between their group and other groups. *Fraternalistic relative deprivation* is the sense that one's group is not doing as well as other groups (Runciman, 1966). Like egoistic deprivation, fraternalistic deprivation has little to do with objective levels of adequacy or success. A group with little may be content if those around them also have little. Conversely, a group whose situation is improving may feel discontent if other groups seem to be improving at a faster rate. During the economic boom of the 1960s, for example, most people in the United States achieved substantial economic gains. Yet the 1960s were also a period of some of the worst racial violence in U.S. history, in part because African Americans saw their economic situation lagging behind that of Whites (Sears & McConahay, 1973). Fraternalistic deprivation is much more likely to cause intergroup conflict than is egoistic deprivation. Feelings of fraternalistic deprivation have been found to be directly related to

Relative deprivation theory. The theory that feelings of discontent arise from the belief that other individuals or other groups are better off.

conflicts between unemployed youths and the authorities in Australia (Walker & Mann, 1987), gay and lesbian groups and straight groups in Toronto (Birt & Dion, 1987), French and English speakers in Canada (Guimond & Dube-Simard, 1983), and Muslims and Hindus in India (Tripathi & Srivasta, 1981).

Escalating Conflict: Communication and Interaction That Make Things Worse

> Once conflict starts, poor communication can make it worse. In-group interaction hardens in-group opinion, threats are directed at the out-group, each group retaliate more and more harshly, and other parties choose sides. All of these processes tend to escalate the conflict.

Once conflict catches fire, the flames spread quickly. Persuasion, promises, and verbal sparring are replaced by attempted coercion, threats, and physical assault. And as new issues and disagreements come to light and inhibitions about breaking the peace dissolve, the arena of conflict broadens. Social competition may displace material competition as conflict escalates. The Rattlers and the Eagles certainly followed this pattern. Name calling soon moved on to flag burning and brawling, accompanied by food fights and midnight cabin raids.

What causes this pattern of escalating conflict? By now our answer should be familiar: The same social and cognitive processes responsible for other forms of social behavior play a role in conflict situations, too. Those processes, which can affect even the most well-intentioned individuals and groups, intensify conflict and cause opinions to harden.

We discussed why group polarization occurs and the many ways in which group discussion can make the majority opinion more extreme in chapter 9, pages 345 to 352.

TALKING TO THE IN-GROUP: POLARIZATION AND COMMITMENT. Discussion won't help if the only people you talk to are those who take your side. Talking things over with like-minded others pushes group members toward extreme views, a process called *group polarization*. As a result of group discussion, then, people may see their group's position as even more valid and valuable, and they may become even more firmly attached to it.

During discussion, we also become more committed to our views. As we explain and defend them, we marshal the best evidence, cite the strongest precedents, and organize every shred of support we can muster. We may pound the table for emphasis as we pick holes in the opposition's reasoning, seize on their slightest hesitations, and counter their every argument. These actions are unlikely to convince the opponents, but they can strengthen our own confidence and commitment (Brauer, Judd, & Gliner, 1995; Hovland and others, 1953). As group members see themselves getting worked up, they conclude that they must care a lot about the issues. At the same time, dissonance reduction processes ensure that their private attitudes line up with public positions, even if at first those public positions were just argued for effect without being fully believed. The very public nature of advocacy constitutes a commitment, which makes it even more difficult for group members to back down or change their minds.

To remind yourselves of the ways that self-perception processes and dissonance reduction can bring attitudes into lockstep with actions, review chapter 8, pages 292 to 312.

Of course, the same processes are also at work in the other group, so positions harden into extreme opposition. As in-group views are confirmed and out group arguments demolished, each group's position becomes entrenched at the extreme and each group's commitment intensifies (Staw & Ross, 1987). Now the battle lines between groups are drawn even more clearly.

THE SPECIAL COMPETITIVENESS OF GROUPS: WHEN CONFLICT ARISES, GROUPS CLOSE RANKS. Processes of commitment and polarization represent the second reason for the special competitiveness of groups. In situations of conflict, groups demand loyalty, solidarity, and strict adherence to group norms. The Eagles and Rattlers did this, forbidding any friendly contact or fraternization with the "enemy." This tight discipline permits no interaction or empathy with the out-group, widening the gap between the groups and making further conflict almost inevitable.

Leaders sometimes take advantage of the unifying effect of conflict to strengthen their hold on power. In a demonstration of this process, Jacob Rabbie and Frits Bekkers (1978) simulated a labor–management conflict in their laboratory at the University of Utrecht in the Netherlands. Some participants took the role of a union leader who could be removed from power by an election at any stage during the negotiations. Some students were in an unstable leadership position; just two negative votes could have removed them from office. Others held more stable positions; only a unanimous negative vote could have deposed them. Leaders whose jobs were shaky behaved more competitively in their negotiations with management, apparently to rally the rank and file around them. These laboratory findings remind us of a grim roster of real-world leaders who have taken their nations into wars and other misadventures to shore up power that was threatened by political rivals, economic troubles, or declining prestige.

TALKING TO THE OUT-GROUP: BACK OFF, OR ELSE! As positions harden, groups find it increasingly difficult to communicate productively. At this point persuasion and discussion often give way to threats and attempted coercion. Most people believe that threats—describing punishments that will follow unwanted behavior—increase their bargaining power and their chances of getting their way (Falbo & Peplau, 1980; Rothbart & Hallmark, 1988). Of course, since most people believe this, both groups tend to use threats, leaving neither group with an advantage. Each is thinking exactly the same thing, cursing the other's unwillingness to listen to reason, deciding that the language of force is the only language the opponent can understand. The reality, unfortunately, is that threats provoke counterthreats, diminish people's willingness to compromise, and, in the end, generate hostility.

To see how counterproductive threats can be, consider the findings from a study by Morton Deutsch and Robert Krauss (1960). They asked pairs of female participants to imagine themselves as owners of two rival trucking companies, named Acme and Bolt, whose profits were based on the speed with which they carried merchandise over roads to specific destinations. The most profit could be attained by taking the short central road rather than the long and winding bypass (see Figure 13.3). As the map shows, a potential source of conflict is built into the road layout: One section of the central road is only one lane wide. If both players reach this section at the same time, one must back up and let the other proceed. This problem was not insurmountable, however. Participants soon worked out a cooperative solution: They

FIGURE 13.3   Routes to conflict

■ In this study, each participant had to move her company's trucks from a starting point to a destination. Participants could save time and earn more money by going over the central road, but conflict arose because only one truck could pass through the one-lane section at a time. When one or both parties controlled gates on the central road and threatened to close them, the trucks had to take a long alternate route, losing money. (Adapted from Deutsch & Krauss, 1960.)

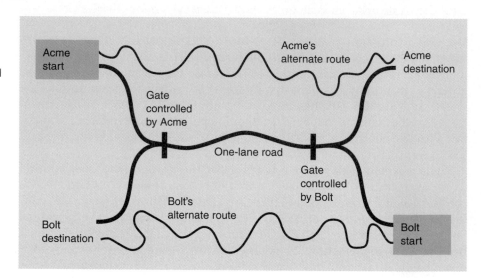

took turns making deliveries along the central road, each earning close to the maximum profit from the experimenter.

So far, so good. But then researchers introduced conditions that allowed the players to control something that could be used to threaten their opponent: a gate on the central road. By closing the gate, a player could force the opponent's truck to back up and take the bypass, costing extra time and lowering profits. In the *unilateral threat* condition, Acme controlled the only gate at one end of the one-lane stretch of road. In the *bilateral threat* condition, each company controlled a gate. As before, the companies were free to communicate to try to solve their differences.

How did the would-be trucking company operators react? When Acme could threaten Bolt with a gate closing, Bolt suffered quite a large loss, but Acme lost money, too, as her trucks sat idle on the road during confrontations. When both players could use the threat, matters were even worse: Both consistently lost money. And whether the threat was unilateral or bilateral, players' communications focused on the use and consequences of the threat rather than on ways of cooperating to resolve the conflict.

It may have occurred to you that nothing in the rules of the trucking game *forced* the players to threaten one another. They could have worked together, taking turns and happily raking in the money just like the players in the condition without any gates. But these findings indicate that the mere availability of a potential threat appears to be enough to bring about its use. Once people have coercive means at their disposal, they shift from reward-seeking to socially competitive behavior.

The irony is that, as we said earlier, threats usually are counterproductive. The threatened group may assume that aggression is inevitable no matter how it responds. And if it responds with a counterthreat, the first group's belief in the opponent's hostility and unwillingness to compromise will be confirmed (North, Brody, & Holsti, 1964). Threats and counterthreats almost invariably escalate in intensity rather than staying at the same level

(Tedeschi, Gaes, & Rivera, 1997). In laboratory simulations of international conflict, for example, other groups follow suit when one group stockpiles arms, and an arms race usually results (Kramer, 1989). Further, concerns over prestige and fears of losing face may make groups cling to their views more firmly, resolutely refusing to give in even when the potential costs are very high (Kaplowitz, 1990). Finally, when threats dominate communication, as they did when players controlled gates in the trucking game, they crowd out messages about cooperative solutions (Knudson, Sommers, & Golding, 1980). Communication can effectively deter and resolve conflict only when threats are not permitted or when opponents learn to avoid making threats that spark retaliation (Lawler, Ford, & Bleger, 1988; W. P. Smith & Anderson, 1975).

☐ **THREAT AND DETERRENCE IN INTERNATIONAL AFFAIRS.** What can laboratory research tell us about policies of deterrence between nations? A policy of deterrence is a political strategy in which one side threatens to use force in the hope of preventing an adversary's use of force (P. M. Morgan, 1983). Its central principle is that dangers arise when a potential aggressor believes its opponents are weak or vulnerable (Jervis, 1976). Proponents of these policies follow the maxim that "if you want peace, prepare for war." The lesson of history, however, suggests that if you prepare for war, you get war (Lebow & Stein, 1987). An analysis of two thousand years of international relations suggests that attempting to deter war by threats usually makes war more, not less, likely (Naroll, Bullough, & Naroll, 1974). Groups that stockpile resources in an effort at deterrence are often perceived as attempting to acquire an offensive edge in preparation for aggression. As a result, they often face escalating conflict from others who fear them (Hornstein, 1975). Speeches proclaiming defensive intentions are unlikely to persuade adversaries who feel threatened by an arms build-up.

Thus, deterrence, like other uses of threats, can backfire, eliciting counterthreats and escalation. This does not mean that it is wise for groups to neglect their defenses. As we have seen, intergroup conflict can stem from greed, and a group without power may appear as easy prey for strong aggressors who have little fear of retaliation. Such large differences in power leave the door open for those who would impose deadly "final solutions" to group conflict. Research indicates that groups roughly equal in power and ability use threats and coercion less often and achieve agreements more often than do parties with unequal power (Hornstein, 1975; Lawler and others, 1988). But even equality in power and command of threats cannot guarantee an absence of conflict: Recall that in the Acme–Bolt trucking game, the parties fared worst when they both controlled gates they could use as threats.

COALITION FORMATION: ESCALATION AS OTHERS CHOOSE SIDES. Conflicts often begin as one-on-one confrontations, but as positions harden, the participants—particularly the weaker side—may call on outside parties for help. *Coalition formation* occurs when two or more parties pool their resources to obtain a mutual goal they probably could not achieve alone (Koromita & Meek, 1978). Coalition formation tends to polarize multiple parties into two opposing sides (Mack & Snyder, 1957). When groups are in conflict, coalition formation is usually seen as a threatening action that, like most threats, only intensifies competition. Those excluded from the coalition may react with fear and anger, and they often form their own coalitions. As unaffiliated groups ally with one side or the other, differences become polarized and the dangerous allure of consensus convinces each side that it is right.

For all these reasons, the formation of coalitions and alliances between nations usually increases the possibility of armed hostility (Q. Wright, 1965). This point, as well as the failure of threats and deterrence, is illustrated by the beginning of the First World War. The scene was set when Austrian Archduke Francis Ferdinand was assassinated by a Serbian nationalist; leaders of the Austro-Hungarian empire retaliated by attacking Serbia. Even then, the conflict might have remained relatively localized, but the two parties' powerful allies stepped in. Serbia's ally Russia, viewing the Austrian attack as a pretext for a German-Austrian conquest of Europe, responded with military mobilization. Germany, feeling endangered, threatened war if Russia did not halt its mobilization. Russia's rejection of this demand led Germany to declare war, first on Russia and then on Russia's ally, France. The escalating hostilities finally drew another ally, Great Britain, into the war (Holsti & North, 1965; North and others, 1964). Not only did the build-up of allied associations make the conflict more rather than less likely, but it resulted in the deaths of more than 8 million soldiers from more than 19 countries.

Perceptions in Conflict: What Else Could You Expect From Them?

> As escalation continues, the in-group sees the out-group as totally evil and sees itself in unrealistically positive terms. Because the same biases characterize each group, each group's images of itself and its opponent tend to be similar. Emotion and arousal make these biases even worse.

As conflict escalates, groups' views of themselves and of their opponents change. These conflict-driven perceptions may have little basis in reality, but they affect the group's understanding of what is happening and why. This skewed understanding in turn becomes a guide for group behavior (R. K. White, 1965, 1977, 1984). When perceptions are negative, distrust and suspicion cast every action in the worst possible light. And self-fulfilling prophecies exert their own pressure: If one side expects the other to be hostile and devious, a vicious cycle can begin in which the other is *made* to be more hostile and devious.

POLARIZED PERCEPTIONS OF IN-GROUP AND OUT-GROUP. If mere categorization—with no hint of conflict or competition—can make people evaluate their own group more positively than the out-group, imagine how much stronger perceptual biases become in the midst of bloody conflict. In fact, groups enmeshed in conflict tend to develop three blind spots in their thinking.

1. *The in-group can do no wrong.* Biased perceptions cause members of the in-group to see their group as righteous and morally superior. Its every intention seems pure hearted, its every action justifiable.

Not surprisingly, groups in conflict almost always invoke religion to support their view. Leaders of warring parties in the Middle East have characterized their struggles as holy wars, and both the Germans and the Allies in the two World Wars were each confident that God was on *their* side. Abraham Lincoln spoke to this issue in his Second Inaugural Address, delivered at the height of the Civil War. Since the North was fighting slavery, wasn't God on its side? "Lincoln's conclusion was that God might not be on either side: 'The Almighty has his own purposes.' He later wrote to a political ally about that speech: '. . . I believe it is not immediately popular. Men are not flattered by being shown that there has been a difference of purpose between the Almighty and them' " (Safire, 1992).

2. *The out-group can do no right.* In contrast, the out-group is now seen as evil, even diabolical. In the recent war in the former Yugoslavia, Bosnian Muslim refugees spoke bitterly of Serbian former neighbors and friends who had turned informers or even taken up arms in the drive for "ethnic cleansing." The Serbians saw their opponents as equally despicable, insisting that their invasion of Bosnia was justified because of reports that Serbian babies were being fed to the lions in the Sarajevo zoo (Lane, Stanger, & Post, 1993). Perceptions like these dehumanize the enemy, supporting the idea that they are capable of doing anything to win, and therefore justifying any action taken against them.

3. *The in-group is all-powerful.* The in-group soon sees itself as having might as well as right on its side, leading to a preoccupation with appearing powerful, prestigious, tough, and courageous. This aggressive posturing, or what journalist Ross Barnet (1971) termed the "hairy chest syndrome," has dangerous side effects. The focus on winning may crowd out consideration of the merits or morals of in-group actions. The boasts of power may be seen as threats that deserve a response in kind (Lebow & Stein, 1987). Finally, the overconfident in-group may fall for its own rhetoric, just as it hopes the enemy will. United States policy in Vietnam offered many examples of overconfidence, as military and political leaders repeatedly promised that the next minor escalation, the next 25,000 troops, would be enough to do the job.

BIASED ATTRIBUTIONS FOR BEHAVIOR. Groups in conflict frequently attribute identical behaviors by the in-group and the out-group to diametrically opposed causes. One study carried out during the Cold War contrasted American college students' responses to similar military actions supposedly carried out by the United States or the Soviets (Oskamp & Hartry, 1968). Students considered, for example, sending aircraft carriers to patrol international waters off the coast of the other country. Participants who thought the United States had taken the actions against the Soviet Union saw them as more positive and more justifiable than did those who thought the Soviets had acted against the United States. In the context of conflict, attributions for in-group and out-group actions are biased in two different ways.

1. *In-group motives are positive; out-group motives are negative.* An in-group action is correct and justified: a protection of our rights, a measured defense against their hostile intentions. When the out-group carries out exactly the same action, it is seen as provocative:

If this pattern of attributions for behavior seems familiar, you're right. They are group-serving attributions, which were discussed in chapter 6, pages 215 to 216.

a revelation of aggression. We offer concessions, but they attempt to lure us with ploys. We are steadfast and courageous, but they are unyielding, irrational, stubborn, and blinded by ideology.

2. *Situations dictate in-group actions; character flaws prompt out-group actions.* People see their own group's actions as reasonable responses to difficult situations like the need to defend oneself from attack, to restrain internal unrest, to stand up for principle against compromise and corruption. Out-group actions, however, seem to be evidence of their flawed characters: Their military moves reflect aggressiveness; their harassment of dissidents reflects inhumanity, intolerance, and insecurity; their rejection of compromise reflects stubbornness and irrationality.

> This pattern of attributions is a group-level version of the actor–observer difference, in which we attribute our own behaviors to situations but other people's actions to their personalities. See chapter 4, pages 109 to 110.

In particular, we often fail to recognize how often fear motivates out-group actions (White, 1987). During the Cold War, fear of powerful Soviet forces largely motivated the U.S. arms build-up. Failing to understand this motivation, however, the Soviets took the build-up as threatening, and they responded with increased military production of their own. The U.S. side similarly reacted to their increase but not to the underlying Soviet fear. And so the cycle continued.

THE IMPACT OF EMOTION AND AROUSAL: MORE HEAT, LESS LIGHT. As conflict rises, people experience tension, anxiety, anger, frustration, and fear. Even participants in competitive games in the laboratory show obvious signs of stress: nervous laughter, increased sweating, and accelerated heart rate (Blascovich, Nash, & Ginsburg, 1978; Van Egeren, 1979). Not surprisingly, this emotional arousal affects processes of perception and communication and produces simplistic thinking. As complex thinking shuts down, decisions are based on simple stereotypes, snap judgments, and automatic reactions. If laboratory studies can generate such stress, imagine the pressure decision makers in real intergroup conflicts must experience (Milburn, 1977).

> Recall from chapter 5, pages 184 to 186, that these were just the circumstances that cause people to rely more on stereotypic views of others.

Philip Tetlock and his colleagues found evidence of a simplistic pattern of thinking when they analyzed former U.S. and Soviet leaders' portrayals of each other in several decades of public speeches (Suedfeld & Tetlock, 1977; P. E. Tetlock, 1988). During times of East–West crisis—the Berlin blockade, the Korean War, the Soviet invasion of Afghanistan—both sides' political statements reflected simplistic and stereotypic thinking about the out-group. The United States was seen as an imperialist aggressor and the Soviet Union as an "evil empire." When tensions relaxed, each side's statements about the other became more complex, acknowledging areas of agreement and common interests as well as continuing disputes. Editorials appearing in major newspapers in the United States, Canada, and the Soviet Union reflected these oversimplifications (Suedfeld, 1992). A study of United Nations speeches, shown in Figure 13.4, showed a similar pattern of simplification in the images used in Arab–Israeli exchanges during years in which war occurred.

There is an important lesson in all of this. People tend to perceive members of out-groups negatively, and anxiety, emotion, and tension strengthen this tendency. In stressful conflict situations, we may leap to the erroneous conclusion that our opponents are ignorant, are willfully misinterpreting evidence, and are fools whose self-interest or pernicious ideology blinds them to the truth. Of course, our opponents are viewing us in the same way.

FIGURE 13.4 Simplistic thinking appears when conflict escalates

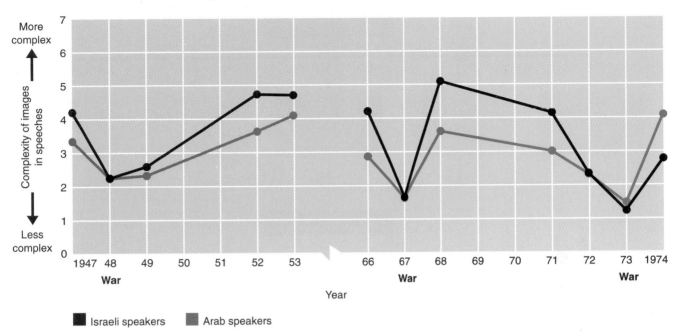

■ This study tracked the degree of complex thinking in verbal images of the opponent used in speeches by Arab and Israeli leaders in the United Nations. Note that the scores hit their lowest points in the years Arab–Israeli wars occurred. (Data from Suedfeld and Tetlock, 1977.)

As a result, neither side understands the other's perceptions or intentions, and, as Figure 13.5 illustrates, conflict may continue to escalate.

THE SPECIAL COMPETITIVENESS OF GROUPS: PEOPLE EXPECT GROUPS TO BE SUPERCOMPETITIVE, SO THEY REACT IN KIND. Biased and extreme perceptions of out-groups are a third reason that groups act more competitively than individuals. People *expect* groups to be highly competitive and hostile (Hoyle, Pinkley, & Insko, 1989). To demonstrate this, Nilanjana Dasgupta and her colleagues (Dasgupta, Banaji, & Abelson, 1997) showed students drawings of novel humanoid creatures called "Gs" and asked the students to judge how likely the Gs were to behave in various ways toward other creatures, "Hs," who were not shown in the pictures. Two aspects of the pictures were varied. If the Gs were all the same color (compared to different colors) or if they were standing close together (rather than scattered apart), the participants thought that they would be more likely to perform negative actions such as threatening the Hs. In other words, the more these cues of similarity and proximity suggested that the Gs were a *group* rather than separate individuals, the more negative were the observers' expectations for their actions (Abelson, Dasgupta, Park, & Banaji, 1998). And in the real world, of course, this expectation has a self-fulfilling quality (Hoyle and others, 1989). If you think your opponents will act competitively, you will probably try to beat them to it, either to deter them or at least to defend yourself (Insko, Schopler, Hoyle, Dardis, & Graetz, 1990).

Why does an expectation often elicit behavior that confirms it? To review the ways self-fulfilling prophecies produce behavior that corresponds with our expectations, see chapter 3, pages 93 to 95, and chapter 5, pages 188 to 190.

FIGURE 13.5 Social and cognitive processes in conflict escalation

■ Conflict between groups sets in motion a series of social and cognitive processes. Unfortunately, these processes usually harden each side's position and reinforce mutual negative views.

"Final Solutions": Eliminating the Out-Group

Ultimately, conflict may escalate into an attempt at total domination or destruction of the out-group. When power differences exist between the groups and the out-group is morally excluded, one group may try to eliminate the other.

As conflicts escalate, intergroup attitudes may harden, and mutual misperceptions can become oversimplified and overwhelmingly negative. An initially realistic conflict over valuable resources can then become a battle for social supremacy in which the primary concern is defeating the opponent, not controlling the resource. And in extreme cases, the goal can become total domination, exploitation, enslavement, or even extermination of the out-group (Allport, 1954b; Kaplowitz, 1990). Three factors seem particularly important in pushing a group to seek a "final solution" to intergroup differences once the groundwork of intergroup hostility and conflict has been laid.

1. *A difference in power between the groups translates desire into action.* Without power, no group can turn prejudice into discrimination, or discrimination into domination. But power gives a group the ability to attain its goals without fear of interference or retaliation, thereby increasing its ability and motivation to discriminate, dominate, and, possibly, eradicate a weaker opponent (Sachdev & Bourhis, 1985, 1991). As history shows, political repression, religious inquisitions, slavery, and genocide often follow (Opotow, 1990).

2. *Moral exclusion blocks moral outrage.* When we discussed moral exclusion in chapters 6 and 10, we noted that perceptions of out-group differences and inferiority can make one group indifferent to the plight of out-group members. If we place out-group members outside the boundaries of moral principles, regarding them as less than human, they can be treated in whatever way the in-group finds convenient or

■ **Excluding the out-group.** Power differences and indifference to others' plight can allow a stronger group to discriminate against, dominate, and possibly try to eradicate a weaker group. This ethnic Albanian mother and son were separated from her husband and his father and forced from their home into a tent city in Macedonia during ethnic conflict in neighboring Kosovo. Their lives are unlikely to ever be the same again.

profitable. Research suggests that moral exclusion is particularly likely when people harm others under orders from their in-group authorities (Bandura and others, 1996).

3. *Routinization produces desensitization.* As we saw in chapter 10, many who carry out crimes of politically and socially sanctioned evil begin with small, morally questionable deeds that gradually escalate into unthinkable acts (Kelman & Hamilton, 1989; Staub, 1989). Repetition of individual actions becomes routine, until at the extreme, even heinous acts like torture and murder become mundane. Such desensitization numbs the horror that naturally inhibits such brutality, allowing social atrocities to continue.

THE SPECIAL COMPETITIVENESS OF GROUPS: GROUPS OFFER SOCIAL SUPPORT FOR COMPETITIVENESS. This point constitutes yet another reason for the greater competitiveness of groups than individuals. Groups offer a rich soil for rationalizing behavior motivated by greed or by dislike for others. Taking advantage of others, putting our own self-interest above others' good, discriminating against or even massacring those whom we hate—these and similar actions rank high on the "don't do" list that parents, teachers, or religious figures teach to most of us. But in a group, competing with or even exploiting out-groups can be rationalized as a form of group loyalty—a motive that fits well with people's general tendency to look out for "me and mine." Those who harm or exploit members of the out-group may even view themselves as performing noble acts of altruism and self-sacrifice: After all, they are putting their own lives on the line for the sake of their valued in-group (Schopler and others, 1993).

As Roy Baumeister (1997) commented in his book on the nature of evil, "When someone kills for the sake of promoting a higher good, he may find support and encouragement if he is acting as part of a group of people who share that belief. If he acts as a lone individual, the same act is likely to brand him as a dangerous nut" (p. 190). So through history, nations as well as religious and political movements have acted in the name of the most exalted and worthy goals. Invasion of a less powerful neighbor nation is cloaked as self-defense, and murder of those who follow a different creed is obedience to God's revealed will. Individuals who participate in such acts of aggression have no need to formulate their own rationalizations for their evil acts, for their identification with the group does it for them. The power of groups to define norms for their members—to establish as unquestionably right what the group declares to be right—is the most fundamental reason that groups are so often more aggressive than individuals.

FINAL SOLUTIONS IN HISTORY. The effects of these forces can be seen in the events culminating in the Holocaust in Nazi Germany. Many of the conditions that set the stage for a "final solution" were already in place. Germany had been defeated in the First World War and had suffered economic hardships in the 1930s. The situation was ripe for a *scapegoat:* an enemy who, by bearing the blame for Germany's defeat and material ills, could enhance in-group cohesion and solidify leaders' power. Nazi ideologists drew on centuries of European anti-Semitism to emphasize supposed distinctions between in-group Aryans (supposedly racially pure Germanic folk) and out-group Jews. Negative perceptions and attitudes toward Jews flourished, and German Jews were blamed for the nation's problems.

The three forces that make "final solutions" possible were also operating. First, Nazis held all the high cards, particularly after Hitler's election as chancellor. Their control over the media, government, and military enabled them to enforce rules about every aspect of their victims' social, political, religious, and economic life. Jews as a group held little political power within Germany, and their appeals to other nations for rescue went largely unanswered. Second, the Nazis dehumanized the Jews, labeling them "worms" and "vermin," thereby excluding them from the sphere in which fair, just, or human treatment could be expected or demanded. Third, killers became desensitized to their acts through routine and repetition. For example, the special police squads who traveled through occupied Poland to round up and kill Jews reacted with shock and horror to their first participation in a massacre (C. R. Browning, 1992). They experienced strong emotions, drank heavily afterwards, and suffered from nightmares. But eventually killing people became no more than an unpleasant duty, and at the end of the day the men could sit around, laughing and joking over games of cards.

The Nazi Holocaust was unique in many respects, but the social-psychological processes that allowed it to happen are not. They can be found whenever one powerful group oppresses a weaker opponent. They were at work when Serbian gunmen herded 57 Muslim residents of the village of Koritnik into a cellar and tossed in grenades, joking that the victims' screams "sounded just like a mosque" (McAllister, 1992). The same processes played a part in the mutual massacres of Muslims and Hindus in India in 1948, the massacres of Tutsi and dissident Hutus by the Hutu-dominated government of Rwanda in 1994, massacres of Armenians by the Ottoman Turks early in this century, and White Americans' and Europeans' capture of Africans for sale into slavery. When one group holds power over another and begins to dominate or exploit them, negative stereotypes shade into dehumanization, and moral exclusion of the out-group is not far behind. Ultimately, as the processes shown in Figure 13.6

FIGURE 13.6 Two shifts in conflict

Source of conflict	Competition for material resources	→	Seeking benefits for in-group without much regard for what out-group receives
After escalation	Competition for social esteem	→	Seeking to outdo out-group, even if this would be costly for in-group
If out-group is also morally excluded and lacks power	Desire to completely dominate, exploit, or destroy out-group	→	Seeking "final solutions" that dehumanize the out-group

■ Conflicts often begin with realistic competition over material resources. If escalation occurs, groups may turn from seeking to do well for themselves to seeking to outdo their opponents. Winning, not prospering, then becomes the goal. In a context where the out-group is morally excluded and the groups have differential power, further escalation may result in a final shift in which the goal changes from outdoing the out-group to completely dominating or eliminating it.

operate, enslavement and genocide become acceptable actions justified by the superiority of the dominant group.

The social-psychological study of intergroup conflict yields many significant lessons, but perhaps the most important is that each of us is psychologically capable of hatred, dehumanization, and violence toward out-group members. Many of the New England ship captains who transported Africans to slavery in the Americas were regular churchgoers, fine family men, and respected leaders within their own communities (Deutsch, 1990). And as we noted in chapter 10, Nazi leaders viewed themselves as no more than ordinary citizens who cared about their families and did their job to protect them. Yet when groups are in conflict, social and cognitive processes—the same processes that sometimes produce empathy, bravery, altruism, and self-sacrifice—can conspire to produce extraordinary evil.

Resolving Conflict and Reducing Aggression

When we left the Rattlers and the Eagles at Robbers Cave State Park, they were thoroughly at odds with each other. Of course, their war did not spiral out of control like many international conflicts, but as childhood conflicts go, the hostility was pretty bad. Moreover, they displayed many of the earmarks of conflict discussed in the previous sections. The groups' negative feelings about each other escalated: "Those guys" became, in the slang of the day, "bums," "bad guys," "those damn campers," and "stinkers." The groups felt powerful: As the athletic tournament began, each team was supremely confident of winning. Group norms were strictly enforced. Anyone wanting to be friends or even seen speaking with a member of the other team was branded a traitor and ruthlessly brought into line with threats of bodily harm or ostracism.

Having aided and abetted the production of this intergroup hostility, the researchers at Robbers Cave now set about trying to resolve it. How could they do this? Reducing individual aggression or intergroup conflict may be possible if we draw on what we know about their causes. You will

It's interesting that task and social interdependence, the main issues that must be solved to reduce intergroup conflict, are the same issues that must be handled for a single group to perform effectively (chapter 12, pages 478 to 486).

see that many of the processes that increase aggression and conflict can be turned around to help reduce it (Deutsch, 1973; Pruitt, 1998). Efforts at reducing violence often involve altering people's immediate perceptions of others or the situational cues that may increase aggression. Some conflict-resolution strategies focus on reconciling the parties' concrete goals and aspirations, for example, by finding material outcomes that satisfy both individuals or groups. Other strategies encourage cooperation, to make former adversaries part of a new and more inclusive in-group. Our very ability to make this list offers some hope: Knowledge about the causes of aggression can now be recruited into the struggle against violence.

Altering Perceptions and Reactions

One approach to reducing aggression and conflict is to minimize or remove the cues that often cause individuals to commit aggressive acts and to encourage careful interpretation and identification with others.

Whether conflicts are between individuals or groups, an irrevocable line is crossed when one person first throws a punch or draws a gun. Acts that precipitate aggression can be discouraged by controlling situational cues and by encouraging people to reinterpret the situation and empathize with others.

MINIMIZE CUES FOR AGGRESSION. Some cues activate aggressive thoughts and feelings, making overt acts of aggression more likely. Many in the United States believe that the ready availability of weapons deters violence, but the evidence suggests just the opposite. When firearms are unavailable, violence not only is less deadly but also less likely. When Jamaica implemented strict gun control and censored gun scenes from television and movies beginning in 1974, robbery and shooting rates dropped dramatically (Diener & Crandall, 1979). When Washington, DC, passed a handgun-control law, the numbers of homicides and suicides involving guns decreased substantially. Importantly, the nation's capital experienced no offsetting increase in other methods of murder or suicide (Loftin, McDowall, Wiersema, & Cottey, 1991). Even if those inclined to murder simply pick up a knife or a lead pipe if no gun is handy, the outcome is not as deadly.

Fortunately, other cues can decrease aggression. A kind and gentle response, the presence of an infant, and even laughter in a tense situation can cue thoughts and feelings that are incompatible with aggression (P. A. Bell & Baron, 1990; Berkowitz, 1984). Even cues that normally produce aggression, such as guns, can decrease aggression if they provoke fear, anxiety, or disgust, as they do for many people (R. A. Baron, 1983b).

INTERPRET, AND INTERPRET AGAIN. Factors that make it difficult for people to think carefully, such as alcohol use, high emotion, or limited time to think, generally increase aggressive behavior. Thus, the old advice to "count to 10" before taking any action when you are angry is very sound. When you feel provoked, think hard about the other person's intentions: Perhaps he or she did not mean the action the way you took it. Kenneth Dodge's research shows that children who have problems processing social cues tend to display a bias in their reactions to ambiguous harmful actions. They tend to automatically react to them as intentionally hostile and, as a result, they act more aggressively in retaliation. But while their immediate reactions display this bias, their more considered reactions do not (Dodge & Newman, 1981). We can all learn from this finding. When a situation looks like a cause for angry retaliation or an opportunity for advantage through violence, we should try to see it in a different light before we respond.

PROMOTE EMPATHY WITH OTHERS. Aggression is easiest when victims are distanced and dehumanized. It is tempting to place one's enemies outside the realm of human sympathy, eliminating normative and moral restraints against violence. To avoid this temptation we need to intentionally reflect on their humanity and thus on the things they share with us. Similarity is a barrier to violence. This may seem to be a lofty ideal, but research suggests that it really is possible. Norma Feshbach and Seymour Feshbach (1982) trained elementary-school children to put themselves in other children's shoes, to recognize others' feelings, and to try to share their emotions. Compared with children in control groups, the children who engaged in this empathy training were much less aggressive in everyday playground activities. Empathy is fellow feeling, and fellow feeling is incompatible with aggression (P. A. Miller & Eisenberg, 1988).

Resolving Conflict Through Negotiation

Conflict resolution also involves the parties in trying to find mutually acceptable solutions, which requires understanding and trust. When direct discussion is unproductive, for example, because of cultural differences, third parties can intervene to help the parties settle their conflict.

TYPES OF SOLUTIONS. In addition to the factors just discussed that can discourage an immediate resort to violence in a conflict situation, there is also a longer range approach to conflict resolution that seeks solutions for the concrete disagreements that separate two individuals or groups. Sometimes solutions are dictated by one party, as when one nation overwhelms another by force or one person prevails in a lawsuit over another. In such cases, the

■ **Communicating to resolve conflict.** Unless parties in conflict communicate, the common interests that may provide a basis for integrative solutions may never be realized. After his election as Israeli Prime Minister in 1999, one of Ehud Barak's first acts was to reopen peace talks with Palestinian leader Yasser Arafat. Although many differences between the two sides remain, there is hope for peace in a region that has endured more than 50 years of ethnic and religious conflict.

conflict is resolved by an *imposed solution.* Not surprisingly, those who lose are usually dissatisfied with the outcome, and such solutions are rarely successful in ending conflict (Burke, 1970). Historians often point to the harsh terms of defeat imposed on Germany after the First World War as one of the factors that contributed to the rise of the Nazis and Germany's later aggression. Other conflicts are settled by *distributive solutions,* which involve mutual compromise or concessions that carve up a fixed-size pie. Examples of such solutions include international treaties that divide territory under dispute or union–management contracts that set workers' raises somewhere between the union's demands and management's proposals (R. Fisher & Ury, 1981). Compromise and concession mean that all parties must give up something they wanted, but the loss may be tolerable, particularly when compared to the cost of continued conflict.

Calvin and Hobbes by Bill Watterson

Integrative solutions are the best solutions because one side's gain is not necessarily the other's loss. These solutions are often termed *win–win solutions* because both sides can benefit simultaneously (Pruitt & Rubin, 1986). Imagine, for example, a resolution in which labor and management agree to split the increased profits from a new way of organizing production so that both sides come out ahead (Kimmel, Pruitt, Maganu, Konar-Goldband, & Carnevale, 1980; Pruitt & Lewis, 1977). One strategy that can lead to integrative solutions is log-rolling, in which each party gives up on issues that it considers less important but that the other group views as crucial (Pruitt, 1986). Although each party gets only some of its demands, it wins on the issues it considers most important. In an industry where employment is dropping as a result of foreign competition, for example, the union may accept limited pay raises to get guarantees of job security. Management's concessions on job security enable it to maintain wage scales that allow competitive pricing.

Finding an integrative solution generally requires creative thinking and an understanding of each party's interests, values, goals, and costs. Identifying an integrative solution is more difficult than locating some halfway point between the parties' demands. Integrative solutions attempt to satisfy the parties' underlying motives, rather than their explicit demands (R. Fisher & Ury, 1981), and they may offer the only way out of some difficult international conflicts. For example, Israel captured the Golan Heights region from Syria in 1967. Syria demands the return of this land and Israel refuses; neither party will accept a division of the territory between them. Some diplomats have suggested that an integrative solution might be possible, based on an analysis of the two parties' underlying needs rather than their contradictory claims to the same piece of landscape. Syria's main interest appears to be its national honor: International recognition of its sovereignty over the Golan Heights might satisfy it. Israel's overriding concern is military security: An ironclad guarantee that Syria could never mass troops and guns on the Golan might suffice. Both parties' most basic needs might be satisfied by a solution that restored the Golan Heights to Syria but guaranteed international monitoring to ensure that arms would never be placed there. Compared with solutions based on compromise, integrative solutions result in better outcomes for both parties, are more enduring, and produce better interparty relationships (Pruitt, 1986; L. Thompson, 1993).

ACHIEVING SOLUTIONS: THE NEGOTIATION PROCESS. Finding a solution to a conflict, particularly an integrative solution, requires the parties to communicate. **Negotiation** is reciprocal communication designed to reach agreement in situations in which some interests are shared and some are in opposition (R. Fisher & Ury, 1981; J. Z. Rubin & Brown, 1975). Diplomatic negotiations have successfully resolved international disputes over arms control, territory, and trade. Of course, not all negotiation is large scale and formal. We all negotiate with others virtually every day: when we discuss what movie to see with our friends, split up the work with our co-workers, or debate bedtime with our children.

The fundamental goal of negotiation is to help each party understand how the other interprets and evaluates the issues. Unfortunately, parties in conflicts often misperceive each other's position and goals, usually exaggerating their disagreement (L. Thompson & Hastie, 1990b). In one study demonstrating this point, 85% of the participants failed to realize, even after a period of negotiations, that they and their opponents agreed perfectly on one issue in contention (L. Thompson & Hastie, 1990a). These biased perceptions of adversaries lower the chances of an integrative solution. When one side proposes a solution, the other side automatically views it less favorably, reasoning that "if it's good for them it must be bad for us." This obstacle to integrative solutions is termed *reactive devaluation* (L. Ross & Nisbett, 1990).

One study demonstrated reactive devaluation in a conflict between Stanford University administrators and student groups demanding the university's divestment of stock holdings linked to the apartheid regime of South Africa (Stillinger, Epelbaum, Keltner, & Ross, 1989). Two possible compromises were proposed: one for divestiture only of those stocks specifically linked to the South African military or police; the other for setting a deadline for total divestiture 2 years in the future. Some students were told, truthfully, that the university was considering both proposals, and they rated them as nearly equally desirable. But other students, told that the university was about to enact one of the two proposals, rated it less satisfactory than the unchosen alternative. Apparently, when one party in a conflict takes a position, it triggers a search for hidden motives and a devaluation of that position by the other party.

> **Negotiation.** The process by which parties in conflict communicate and influence each other to reach agreement.

BUILDING TRUST. One of the priorities in negotiation is to build trust, so that parties will abandon their search for negative motives within each other's proposals. This is not easily accomplished because a history of bitter conflict is a poor foundation for trust. Even a sincere offer may be seen as a trick, a subterfuge designed to lull the opponent into a false sense of security. In such situations, trust must be built up by repeated displays of consistency between words and behavior (Lindskold, 1978).

Negotiators usually try to break conflicts into sets of small, manageable issues. By focusing on specific issues rather than just repeatedly stating their overall conflicting goals, negotiation can reverse the decline of trust that occurred during the commitment and escalation phases of the conflict. This reversal occurs in two ways. First, when one party successfully negotiates an issue with the opponent, liking and trust for the other party increase, perhaps making other issues easier to settle (L. Thompson, 1993). Second, when issues are narrow and specific, the parties in conflict have a better chance of accurately perceiving each other's positions rather than assuming the worst about them. Accurate perceptions of the other side's views and interests are the best hope for success in negotiation (L. Thompson & Hastie, 1990a, 1990b).

TRUST AND THE NORM OF RECIPROCITY. During the height of the Cold War, Charles Osgood (1962) and Amitai Etzioni (1962) independently suggested that reciprocal concessions could both build trust and reduce intergroup tensions. Osgood advised world governments to use *graduated and reciprocated initiatives in tension reduction (GRIT)* to deescalate conflicts.

The GRIT process begins when one side states its intention to reduce the conflict and makes a small concession to its opponent. The norm of reciprocity pushes the opposing group to make a small concession of its own or risk public condemnation. Of course, the party offering the first concession must walk a fine line between strength and weakness because total cooperation is often interpreted as an opportunity for exploitation (Reychler, 1979). If the opponent reciprocates with a concession, the first group follows with a slightly more significant concession. Again the opponent reciprocates with a greater concession, and a feeling of trust gradually builds as tensions wind down. Simulations of international negotiations in the laboratory have confirmed that reciprocal concessions may be effective in reducing international tensions (Lindskold, 1986).

☐ **GRIT AND INTERNATIONAL CONFLICTS.** The tactics recommended in the GRIT strategy have been used successfully in international relations. In June 1963, President John F. Kennedy, calling attention to the dangers of nuclear war, announced a unilateral halt to American atmospheric tests of nuclear weapons and promised not to resume testing unless another country did so first. Within 2 months, Soviet Premier Nikita Khrushchev ended the production of Soviet strategic bombers, agreed to the emergency communication hot line between Moscow and Washington, and signed a treaty limiting nuclear testing. Similarly, in 1977, Egyptian President Anwar Sadat's dramatic initiative of traveling to Jerusalem led to the Camp David peace talks and a treaty normalizing relations between Israel and Egypt. Cases like these suggest that GRIT shows promise in reducing international tensions (Druckman, 1990; Etzioni, 1967).

Remember from chapter 10, pages 387 to 390, that just as we feel obligated to return a favor for a favor, we feel obligated to follow a concession with a concession.

NEGOTIATING ACROSS CULTURAL LINES. Pervasive differences among cultures influence the way people negotiate just as they influence other types of social interaction (Adler, 1991; Casse, 1982). Negotiators from the United States prefer making small gains on the way to larger agreements and mixing competition and cooperation in the form of mutual concessions. In contrast, Russian negotiators generally start with extreme positions, make few concessions, and view their opponents' concessions as signs of weakness that should be exploited rather than reciprocated (Adler, 1991). Training in cultural styles and expectations for negotiation could be a valuable preparation for those who bargain with members of other cultures.

Another factor that comes into play when parties to a negotiation come from different groups is a greater emphasis on outcomes rather than perceptions of fairness (Tyler and others, 1998). When members of a common ingroup negotiate, they are concerned not only about how they stand in the final outcome, but also about being treated fairly and respectfully (Tyler & Lind, 1992). Thus, when conflict takes place within a group, fair treatment, politeness, and respect for all may win assent for an agreement, even if all cannot get what they want in terms of the concrete resources at stake. However, when negotiations cross group lines, concerns about fairness and respect recede, leaving the parties more interested in simply what they can get—potentially complicating the resolution of their dispute.

MEDIATION AND ARBITRATION: BRINGING IN THIRD PARTIES. Even if people share the same culture, direct communication is not always the best way to resolve conflicts. When opponents are too angry to discuss issues rationally or negotiators run out of ideas for resolving an impasse, third-party intervention may offer the best hope for a solution. The United Nations Security Council, baseball labor arbitrators, divorce mediators, moderators at a debate, and parents intervening in their children's squabbles are all third parties attempting to inhibit, regulate, or help resolve conflicts. Some negotiations involve *mediators* who help the opponents focus their discussion on the issues and reach a voluntary agreement. In *arbitration*, the third party has the power to hand down a decision after hearing the disputants present their arguments and information.

Third-party intervention has several advantages. First, mediators or arbitrators can arrange meeting agendas, times, and places so that these details don't themselves become sources of conflict (Raven & Rubin, 1976). Second, skillful intervention—mediation, in particular—can improve intergroup relationships. In one case, third parties were called in to mediate a dispute between public housing tenants and private homeowners in a small Canadian community. As a result of their work, intergroup attitudes improved, as did understanding of the complexity of each side's position (R. Fisher & White, 1976). The third advantage of third-party intervention is that, because outsiders bring fresh ideas, they may be able to offer more creative integrative solutions than those proposed by people deeply enmeshed in the conflict (R. Fisher & Ury, 1981). Finally, a skilled third party can leave room for graceful retreat and face saving when disputants lock themselves into positions they themselves realize are untenable (Pruitt, 1981). Thirdparty intervention may allow both sides to accept concessions without embarrassment. By doing so, it is more likely to lead to a mutually acceptable outcome than is unaided negotiations (J. Z. Rubin, 1980).

Intergroup Cooperation: Changing Social Identity

Conflict resolution can also be facilitated by having groups cooperate toward shared goals that can be attained only if both groups work together. Under the proper conditions, cooperative intergroup interaction reduces conflict.

After an athletic contest that marked the height of the Robbers Cave conflict, the researchers decided to see whether joint participation in some pleasant activity could reduce hostilities. They arranged for the boys to have meals at the same time and to watch a movie together. If you recall our discussion in chapter 5 of the conditions under which contact improves intergroup attitudes, you will not be surprised that the group contact did not help. Rather than providing the opportunity for consistently friendly interaction that disconfirmed stereotypes—the key to changing negative group perceptions—this kind of contact increased hostilities. The boys found that the shared meals provided perfect opportunities for food fights.

SUPERORDINATE GOALS. When simple contact failed, the researchers tried a different strategy. They engaged the groups in the pursuit of **superordinate goals,** which are goals that can be attained only if groups work cooperatively as a team. Examples of superordinate goals in political life are cooperation between agricultural and urban interests to increase the water supply for all, and cooperation between nations to eliminate greenhouse gases from the atmosphere to stop global warming. At Robbers Cave the superordinate goals were a series of "problems" that could be solved only if the teams worked together. For example, the staff staged a breakdown of the water supply, and the boys worked together to trace the water pipeline back into the hills. A movie was too expensive for either group alone to rent, so all the boys pooled their funds to pay the rental fee. Finally, after finding that the camp truck had broken down, they figured out how to restart the truck by pulling on a rope attached to its bumper. In contrast to the earlier competitive tug-of-war contests, the boys literally had to pull together, and, thanks to the driver's carefully calibrated foot pressure on the brake, it took the efforts of all the boys from both groups to get the truck moving.

Superordinate goals improved intergroup relationships, but not overnight. After repairing the water supply, the two groups mingled good-naturedly, but they capped the day off with a food fight. They rented the movie with pooled resources, but the two groups sat on opposite sides of the dining hall to watch it. After 6 days of cooperation, however, their previous hostilities were greatly decreased, as can be seen in Figure 13.7. In fact, when it was time to leave, they asked if they could travel home together on one bus. As the boys took their seats on the bus, the camp staff noticed that a Rattler was just as likely to sit next to an Eagle as to another Rattler (M. Sherif & Sherif, 1953). Superordinate goals have had similar success in eliminating other forms of experimentally induced conflict (Diab, 1970).

WHY DOES INTERGROUP COOPERATION WORK? Intergroup cooperation is not a foolproof cure for conflict. But when the right conditions exist, intergroup cooperation undermines many processes that contribute to conflict and it encourages positive interactions that can ultimately reduce prejudice (Allport, 1954b; Pettigrew, 1997, 1998). What are those conditions?

Superordinate goals. Shared goals that can be attained only if groups work together.

- *Cooperation should be for a valued common goal, which eliminates competition for material and social resources.* Rather than battling for pocketknives or bragging rights, the campers at Robbers Cave pooled their talents and resources to reach mutually desired goals.

- *Cooperation should provide repeated opportunities to disconfirm out-group stereotypes.* Remember that intergroup conflict arises from group differences as well as from competition over resources. As we saw at Robbers Cave, it took several bouts of cooperation to bring the Rattlers and Eagles together. Similar results are found in laboratory studies: A single cooperative episode often has quite limited effects (Lockhart & Elliot, 1981; Wilder & Thompson, 1980).

- *Cooperation should produce successful results.* If groups fail while working together, each is likely to blame the other, and hostility may even increase (Worchel, 1979; Worchel & Norvell, 1980). In contrast, success helps the intergroup climate, in part by allowing friendships to grow up across group lines (Pettigrew, 1997).

- *Cooperation should take place between equals, at least for the task at hand.* The Rattlers and the Eagles were all equally capable of pulling the bus and donating to the film fund.

- *Cooperation should be supported and promoted by social norms.* The goal of peaceable and respectful coexistence needs official institutional endorsement (Allport, 1954b; Amir, 1969). A few instances of cooperation cannot overwhelm intergroup hostility that is culturally ingrained and institutionally supported. Thus, for example, brief programs that bring together Israeli Jews and Arabs in Israel will not change intergroup perceptions if segregated communities continue to isolate one group from the other.

Intergroup cooperation resolves conflicts over concrete resources because it makes the out-group a source of rewards rather than punishments. Cooperation also resolves problems of esteem and status by creating friendships across

FIGURE 13.7   Cooperation cures conflict

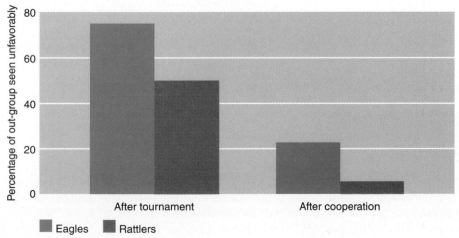

■ In the Robbers Cave experiment, hostility between Eagles and Rattlers reached a peak right after an athletic tournament. Researchers then arranged for the two groups to work together to achieve a series of superordinate goals that neither could attain alone. As the boys cooperated, intergroup hostility greatly declined. (Data from M. Sherif & Sherif, 1953.)

group lines and eventually fusing the warring parties into one new and improved in-group (Gaertner and others, 1989; Gaertner and others, 1990; Pettigrew, 1997). Figure 13.8 portrays this idea. As "we" and "they" become just "we," the new, larger group membership can be a source of self-esteem and a positive social identity (S. Feshbach & Singer, 1957; J. C. Turner, 1981). Even more importantly, "we" feelings decrease competition. In an experimental demonstration of this point, Roderick Kramer (1989) had small groups of participants play a game simulating an arms race. To create in-group feelings, some participants were reminded that all the groups had some features in common. Compared with participants not receiving the reminder, those with "we" feelings were much less likely to stockpile weapons. Similarly, in a study in which two groups of participants drew from a common resource pool, each took large amounts and quickly depleted the resource (Kramer & Brewer, 1984). However, when participants were reminded of their joint membership in a larger shared group, both groups cooperated more and used less of the resource.

Forming a new and more inclusive in-group works best in solving intergroup conflict if the original groups are permitted to retain some measure of distinctiveness rather than merging completely (Condor & Brown, 1988). For example, each group might perform distinct roles and tasks that contribute to the overall good (Brown, Condor, Matthews, Wade, & Williams, 1986; Brown & Wade, 1987; Deschamps & Brown, 1983). In this way, each group maintains its own cultural distinctiveness and its positive identity, but cooperating toward a greater goal improves its view of other groups (D. M. Taylor & Simard, 1979). The real ideal of a multicultural society is a tossed salad, not a melting pot. Every group's contribution is valued and respected for itself rather than as an indistinguishable part of a uniform whole. Cultural

FIGURE 13.8 Processes in conflict resolution

■ Just as social and cognitive processes can help escalate conflict, the processes involved in conflict resolution can build on themselves. Interventions that either help the groups settle the concrete issues in dispute or improve their feelings about each other can set the tone for further reductions in conflict.

differences then become opportunities for learning and mutual enrichment rather than bases for conflict (Deutsch, 1993).

Intergroup cooperation for superordinate goals holds the promise of true conflict resolution, rather than conflict management (S. P. Cohen & Arnone, 1988). Conflict resolution turns groups' basic strivings for mastery and connectedness toward positive ends. Previously hostile groups find ways to enhance their identities by cooperating, for example, in creating a truly multicultural society, rather than by outdoing one another. New symbols are created that reflect pride and respect for both sides, and the groups' old symbols of intransigence and hatred are allowed to slip into history. Just as conflict can build on itself and escalate, each step toward conflict resolution—whether aimed at task or social interdependence—can help to further reduce conflict, as Figure 13.8 shows. Peaceful relations will ultimately be possible when the world community finds ways to accommodate the needs of groups and nations not only for physical security and material resources, but also for positive and distinctive identities.

CONCLUDING COMMENTS

Whenever someone commits aggression, it is a safe bet that the person sees it as reasonable, well justified, even necessary. A man who kills in a barroom brawl sees himself as retaliating against the previous punch thrown by his victim or as defending his honor against an intolerable insult or slur. Muggers and robbers see themselves as taking what they need from those who have too much and whose losses will be covered by insurance in any case. It is worth repeating the eloquent statement by Martin Luther King, Jr. (1967), which we already quoted in chapter 6: "It seems to be a fact of life that human beings cannot continue to do wrong without eventually reaching out for some rationalization to clothe their acts in the garments of righteousness" (p. 72). The clothing is often so complete that people do not even feel guilty about their acts that harm others.

When individuals make their own interpretations of reality, they are deeply vulnerable to rationalizing their self-interest in these ways. As chapter 9 discussed, seeking consensus from others often helps us see situations clearly. For those who fail to rely on others' perceptions to check their own possibly skewed opinions, the result in all too many cases is the aggressive behavior of the outlaw: the petty bully, mugger, or murderer.

When groups commit aggression, they, too, rationalize their acts with high-sounding words and ideas. Exploiting, repressing, even massacring other groups are considered necessary to fulfill the glorious in-group's historical destiny or to redress past wrongs. Those outsiders are in any case less than fully human, so they do not deserve moral consideration.

When groups interpret reality for their members, they, too, are vulnerable to rationalizing their own self-interested desires for mastery of resources or for respect and esteem. The processes of conformity and groupthink can mean that no group members dare to speak out, even if they are capable of seeing things differently. The result in all too many cases is the aggressive behavior of groups of true believers: fanatical Nazis, Serbs bent on "ethnic cleansing," or Rwandan Hutus whipped by self-serving political leaders into a murderous frenzy against Tutsis.

Outlaws or true believers? Is that our choice for the world today? If it is, we would reluctantly point out that true believers are probably more dangerous. The civilized world thought it had put genocide behind it with the defeat of Nazi Germany and the Nuremberg war crimes trials, only to see intergroup conflict and massacre reemerge within a few years in India and Pakistan, Africa, even central Europe. Our opinion that true believers are probably a greater threat than outlaws is supported by the research reviewed in this chapter showing that groups are more aggressive than individuals.

But perhaps we need not choose between these two depressing alternatives. There is no single easy answer that works for every time and situation. Individuals cannot stand independent and reject group consensus without becoming easy prey for rationalized self-interest: That way lies the outlaw. Neither can individuals unthinkingly accede to the siren song of group consensus, which may rationalize and glorify group interests while dehumanizing opponents: That produces true believers. But each of us can try to balance our own individual perceptions and group consensus, applying plenty of thought—unclouded by strong emotion or immediate responses to threat. We must beware particularly of group-induced and group-sanctioned actions that victimize out-groups. History shows that group consensus that calls for aggressive action against outsiders, even when portrayed as necessary self-defense or a well-justified remedy for past injustices, requires the most searching moral scrutiny.

SUMMARY

 Aggression, Conflict, and Human Nature. When people are in **conflict,** or see their goals as incompatible, they may attempt to harm each other. This intention is what defines behavior as **aggression.**

Humans have evolved to compete effectively for food and mates. Although the capacity to act aggressively may have helped, aggression has no special place in "human nature." Aggression is just one strategy among many others that humans use to attain rewards and respect in accordance with individual perceptions and social norms.

Interpersonal Aggression. Aggression can be difficult to study experimentally, because people are often unwilling to act aggressively when they are being observed. Researchers have used a variety of techniques to get around these problems.

Some aggression is triggered by potential rewards and is suppressed by perceived costs or risks. Sometimes, however, perceived provocation produces anger, which can set off aggression regardless of the consequences. Any negative emotion, in fact, can make aggression more likely.

Social norms can either promote or restrain aggression. They can be activated by the behavior of models witnessed in person or in the media.

Norms that limit aggression apply with special force to aggression against similar others or in-group members.

Situations that favor superficial thinking often favor aggression. Thinking carefully can reduce aggression, but many factors interfere with people's motivation and ability to process information carefully and evenhandedly, increasing the likelihood of aggression.

Intergroup Conflict. Groups are generally even more competitive and aggressive than individuals.

Group conflict often stems from competition for valued material resources, according to **realistic conflict theory,** or for social rewards like respect and esteem. Groups in conflict are often more attuned to social rewards than to material ones. People use social comparisons to determine acceptable levels of resources, as described by **relative deprivation theory.**

Once conflict starts, poor communication can make it worse. In-group interaction hardens in-group opinion, threats are directed at the out-group, each group retaliates more and more harshly, and other parties choose sides. All of these processes tend to escalate the conflict.

As escalation continues, the in-group sees the out-group as totally evil and sees itself in unrealistically positive terms. Because the same biases characterize each group, each group's image of itself and that of its opponent tend to be similar. Emotion and arousal make these biases even worse.

Ultimately, conflict may escalate into an attempt at total domination or destruction of the out-group. When power differences exist between the groups and the out-group is morally excluded, one group may try to eliminate the other.

Resolving Conflict and Reducing Aggression. One approach to reducing aggression and conflict is to minimize or remove the cues that often cause individuals to commit aggressive acts, and to encourage careful interpretation and identification with others.

Conflict resolution also involves the parties in trying to find mutually acceptable solutions through **negotiation,** which requires understanding and trust. When direct discussion is unproductive, for example, because of cultural differences, third parties can intervene to help the parties settle their conflict.

Conflict resolution can also be facilitated by having groups cooperate toward **superordinate goals,** shared goals that can be attained only if both groups work together. Under the proper conditions, cooperative intergroup interaction reduces conflict.

14

Helping and Cooperation

As social beings, we often act, alone or in groups, to benefit other people. Some of these kindnesses are quite ordinary—we help an elderly neighbor do her shopping, drop some spare change into the collection box for an especially needy charity, or pool our resources and skills for a morning to build a playground in a rundown neighborhood. At other times we give generously of our effort and energy, volunteering to help battered women or victims of AIDS, spending hours to help a stranded motorist restart his car, or organizing the collection and shipping of medical supplies to the victims of hurricanes, earthquakes, and tidal waves. And sometimes, people even risk their own health and safety for others. Mother Teresa, who died in 1998, had risked disease and danger to live a life of dedication to the poorest and most needy in the slums of Calcutta, India. While rescuers airlifted those injured when a jet crashed in 1982 into an ice-covered river in Washington, DC, one survivor eventually lost his life after repeatedly giving up his place on a helicopter to others more seriously injured. And despite constant intimidation, arrests, and executions at the hands of their own Vichy government, the people of the French village of Le Chambon-sur-Lignon worked tirelessly together between 1937 and 1943 to hide and protect no fewer than 5,000 refugees, among them 3,500 Jews, from the systematic persecutions of the Third Reich.

Social psychologists call these everyday kindnesses as well as inspiring acts of heroism **prosocial behavior:** behavior that is intended to help or benefit others. As was the case with aggressive behavior, it is the intention with which action is carried out, rather than its consequences, that defines behavior as prosocial. In studying helping, social psychologists have looked at many kinds of behavior: giving aid in everyday situations, dramatic responses to emergencies, and long-term commitments of time, effort, and even personal risk. In laboratory studies, for instance, they have asked participants to aid others who are working on boring and repetitive tasks (Berkowitz & Daniels, 1963) or to volunteer to take the place of someone scheduled to receive painful electric shocks (Batson, Duncan, Ackerman, Buckley, & Birch, 1981). Outside the

Prosocial behavior. Behavior intended to help someone else.

laboratory, researchers have investigated why people donate blood and organs (Piliavin, Callero, & Evans, 1982), whether passengers in an elevator will help someone pick up handfuls of spilled pencils (Latané & Dabbs, 1975), and what circumstances affect responses to staged emergencies (Cramer, McMaster, & Bartell, 1988). This variety of research approaches means that researchers' conclusions about prosocial behavior often have high construct validity and good generalizability. What are their conclusions about what makes people help?

As you will see, helping and cooperation depend on how people interpret social situations and the social influences acting on them. We begin this chapter by exploring when people help. Indeed, it seems that for every example of heartwarming generosity, there are also examples of people turning away, failing to render much-needed aid, or ignoring and deflecting pleas for assistance. Understanding the individual and social forces that lead people to help also uncovers the circumstances under which people don't help, even when others seem to be in need.

We then turn to the tricky question of what motivates helping. We often label behaviors such as sending money to support starving children, biking to work to help improve the community's air quality, or delivering care parcels to the needy as altruism. But this term has a much more specific meaning, referring to one possible motive for helping: **Altruism** refers to the desire to benefit others for their own sake, without seeking personal rewards (Batson, 1991, 1998). Consider the following example. You donate $10 to someone collecting money for a homeless shelter. You intended to help the homeless, but also wanted to impress your companion with your generosity. Because this behavior involves an intention to help, it is an example of prosocial behavior. Is it also altruism? No, because altruism involves no intentional personal gain or reward, and that wasn't the case in this example. Some people argue that pure altruism doesn't exist—that helping is always in one way or another driven by **egoism,** the desire to obtain rewards for oneself. Can people never think, feel, or act for the greater good of others without being driven by self-interest? To answer this question, we need to go beyond the issue of when people help, and probe why. Is the tendency to help part of our genetic make-up? What motivates people to help others in distress or need? After we discuss this intriguing issue later in the chapter, we will consider how people actually make decisions about helping, whether under the time pressure and stress of a sudden emergency or with leisure to reflect and consider long-term helping commitments.

Understanding something about prosocial behavior provides a foundation for considering a very practical question: How can we promote more caring, helpful, and cooperative communities? In the last part of the chapter, we will see what suggestions for increasing the level of prosocial behavior in society emerge from social-psychological research.

When Do People Help?

Imagine walking back home from a trip to the neighborhood store one evening, carrying a half-gallon of milk. You notice a car stopped at the curb. You can hear fruitless attempts to start the motor. Although you glance repeatedly at the car, the elderly driver does not wave or gesture for help.

Altruism. Behavior intended to help someone else without any prospect of personal rewards for the helper.

Egoism. Behavior motivated by the desire to obtain personal rewards.

After a pause, the attempts to start the engine begin again and then cease. You see another pedestrian further down the street. After a casual glance over his shoulder at the sound of the sputtering engine, he walks on.

Would you help in such a situation? What questions might run through your mind before you decide whether or not to help? If you are like most people, the first and most crucial issue is whether help is actually needed. Like most social situations, those in which helping might be necessary are often ambiguous: Does the driver need help or not? But other questions soon follow: What should be done? And should you be the one to do it? Whether people are responding to an emergency, giving casual aid, or making a long-term commitment as a caregiver, helping behavior is affected by the same social and cognitive factors that influence all social behavior. Helping is crucially dependent on people's interpretation of a situation, but such perceptions don't take place in a social vacuum. As we saw in chapters 9 and 10, the actions of others are often crucially important to whether we act or not.

Is Help Needed And Deserved?

Helping is crucially dependent on people's perception of someone as both needing and deserving help. The ability and motivation to pay attention to others' needs influence whether people think help is needed, as does the behavior of other people in the situation. People are more likely to help those not held responsible for their own need.

NOTICING NEED. Imagine walking through your quiet neighborhood in the evening and hearing the motorist's repeated attempts to start the stranded car. Now imagine jostling your way down a busy city street, trying to tune out the roar of traffic and the honking of taxicabs. The driver of a car stopped by the sidewalk is trying in vain to start the motor. Although the first person's need is easy to notice, the second's may not be. Becoming aware of a need is usually the first step in the helping chain of events (Darley & Latané, 1968), and busy or noisy surroundings reduce the likelihood of people noticing that someone needs help (Korte, Ypma, & Toppen, 1975). No doubt this is one reason that people are more likely to help others in quiet, rural areas than in crowded cities (Eisenberg, 1991; R. V. Levine, Martinez, Brase, & Sorenson, 1994).

Some people are better able to see a need for help than others are. People who feel happy seem to pay more attention to others around them and are more likely to notice others' needs than sad people (Schaller & Cialdini, 1990). No wonder, then, that positive thinking often translates into positive actions. In a study demonstrating this point, researchers put one group of students in a good mood by telling them they had succeeded on a task, whereas another group were put in a bad mood by learning they had failed the task (Isen & Levin, 1972). When a confederate dropped a stack of books nearby, the happy students were more likely to help than the unhappy ones. Happy participants also remembered much more about the confederate and her actions. Because happy people's attention is turned outward, they are more attuned to others' needs for help.

Other people's reactions can also dictate whether or not we perceive a need. No one wants to foolishly rush in to help in a case that may not be an

You may recognize this as a state of pluralistic ignorance, discussed in detail in chapter 9, pages 357 to 358.

emergency after all. In fact, people sometimes fail to act because of *audience inhibition:* the fear of appearing foolish in front of others (Latané, Nida, & Wilson, 1981). So we usually keep calm and check to see what others present are doing. Perhaps in the example of the stalled car, the fact that the other passerby did not seem concerned would have made you less likely to help. Of course, if everyone else is also keeping calm while they check the reactions of others, everyone will conclude that no one else is upset and thus that help is not needed.

In one series of studies, experimenters arranged for smoke to pour into a laboratory room in which students were sitting completing questionnaires (Latané & Darley, 1968). When the students were alone, their concern at the unusual situation soon led them to seek help. But when two confederates in the room failed to react to the smoke, participants also did nothing. It is not the mere presence of others that facilitates or inhibits action, but what the actions of others tell us about the situation. For example, if an apparently blind confederate failed to react to the smoke, participants ignored the lack of response and went for help. But if the blind confederate failed to react to screams and cries of pain from a woman in an adjoining room, participants did nothing (A. S. Ross & Braband, 1973). When people notice that bystanders and passersby are unresponsive, that observation reduces the likelihood that they will help (R. E. Smith, Vanderbilt, & Callen, 1973).

JUDGING DESERVINGNESS. Even if you noticed a stranded motorist, a panhandler asking for change on a street-corner, or a person slumped in a doorway, would you offer help? Helping depends on whether we think help is deserved, and groups typically develop norms that dictate who does and does not deserve help (Caporael & Brewer, 1991). The norm of social responsibility, for example, suggests that those able to take care of themselves have a duty and obligation to assist those who cannot: the old, young, sick, helpless, or dependent (Berkowitz, 1972; Berkowitz & Daniels, 1963). Sometimes people are judged as deserving help simply because they have less than us: People who believe that they have more than their fair share often give valued resources to others or take less than they could (Mikula, 1980). In close relationships, norms dictate communal sharing of resources with others based on their need (M. S. Clark & Mills, 1979; Fiske, 1991). This norm is also prevalent in cohesive groups. Among the Moose people of West Africa, for example, even the most valuable resources, such as land and water in time of drought, are shared freely with anyone who asks for them (A. P. Fiske, 1991).

In many cultures, particularly in the individualistic cultures of the West, deservingness also depends on the attributions we make about controllability. If we think people are in need "through no fault of their own" (that is, due to an uncontrollable cause), we are more motivated to help. If, on the other hand, we perceive people as having "brought it on themselves" (a controllable cause), we think they don't deserve help and we are less likely to offer it (Reisenzein, 1986; G. Schmidt & Weiner, 1988). Thus, helping a person unconscious on the sidewalk seems more appropriate when the victim is ill than when he or she is drunk.

The importance of norms about controllability and deservingness helps explain why people who believe that opportunity for economic advancement is open to all, and who thus see poverty as the result of a lack of effort by the poor, are likely to oppose governmental programs to help those in need (Kluegel & Smith, 1986). Similarly, in another study, Canadian religious fundamentalists who perceived homosexuals and single mothers as responsible for their own group's unemployment problems were less likely to offer the group help (L. M. Jackson & Esses, 1997).

Is Helping Up to Me?

People sometimes help because social norms, their own standards, or the behavior of others show them that it is appropriate to do so. Not all norms promote helping, however, and sometimes the presence of other potential helpers can diminish the normative pressures to help.

Even when people recognize a need for help, recognition doesn't always translate into action. An event that took place on the streets of Queens, New York early one March morning in 1964 made this fact tragically clear (Latané & Darley, 1970).

The facts of the case are straightforward and brutal. Kitty Genovese was attacked by Winston Moseley, a 29-year-old machine operator, as she returned to her apartment from her night job. Bleeding from multiple stab wounds, Genovese staggered to a street corner, where she called for help. As lights in the surrounding apartments went on, her assailant returned and stabbed her again. Over half an hour after the attack began, Kitty Genovese finally died. Investigations showed that at least 38 people heard her cries for help or saw part of the attack, but none of them helped, not even by calling the police. Why didn't anybody help? What might have made them act differently?

WHEN HELPING SEEMS UNNECESSARY: DIFFUSION OF RESPONSIBILITY. To those who pondered this question, it was clear that the onlookers noticed that something was happening and realized that the situation was an emergency. Hearing the screams, nearby residents switched on their lights, and some looked out their windows. And although at first onlookers may have wondered if the dispute was between a husband and wife, Kitty Genovese herself made clear the seriousness of the situation with her screams: "My God, he stabbed me. Please help me, please help, I'm dying, I'm dying."

■ **Lending a helping hand.** Would you help this stranded motorist? If not, is it because you think he can handle the problem himself, or that he should have taken better care of his car? Decisions to help are often based on perceptions of whether the person in trouble needs and deserves help.

THE FAR SIDE   By GARY LARSON

Crossing the village, Mowaka is overpowered by army ants. (Later, bystanders were all quoted as saying they were horrified, but "didn't want to get involved.")

© 1992 FarWorks Inc. Reprinted with permission.

Although the press castigated the indifference of Genovese's neighbors, two social psychologists, John Darley and Bibb Latané (1968) were not so sure. The source of the bystanders' passivity, the researchers believed, lay in the presence of other onlookers, which influenced their decisions about whether helping was their responsibility or not. They decided to study this aspect of the helping situation in the laboratory.

Participants in Darley and Latané's study thought they had signed up for a group discussion about problems of college life. Supposedly to minimize embarrassment and to guarantee anonymity, each participant was seated alone in an intercom-equipped cubicle. Each person was told that his or her microphone would be activated for 2 minutes at a time, giving each person in turn a chance to talk while the other group members—but not the experimenter—listened. In reality, all of this was stage management. Only one person participated at a time, believing that one, two, or five other group members, represented by tape recordings, were also present.

Then came the emergency. The participant heard one of the other "group members," who had previously mentioned a susceptibility to epilepsy, suddenly begin to have a seizure. Speaking with increasing difficulty, he asked for help and then lapsed into silence. How did people react? As Figure 14.1 shows, the more other people the participants believed to be present, the less likely they were to help and the longer they delayed before seeking aid. Of those who thought that four others were present, only 62% ever came to the victim's aid. Don't assume the passive majority didn't care, however. Most were in the grip of anxiety and indecision, caught between behaving inappropriately by helping and behaving inappropriately by not helping.

Darley and Latané concluded that the number of participants in the group made a difference because when other people are present, responsibility is divided and each person feels less responsible for helping than when alone. This *diffusion of responsibility* explanation has been supported by additional studies showing that people who are alone when they notice an emergency feel that it is their personal responsibility to get involved, while far fewer do so when many other people are present and apparently able to help (Bickman, 1971; Schwartz & Gottlieb, 1980). In addition, a massive study conducted in 36 cities across the United States tested six different types of helping (including offering to help a blind person with a white cane cross a street, telling someone that he had "accidentally" dropped a pen from his pocket, and donating to the United Way). Helping was systematically lower in cities with higher population densities, suggesting that diffusion of responsibility also affects helping at the level of communities (R. V. Levine and others, 1994).

WHEN NORMS MAKE HELPING THE APPROPRIATE RESPONSE. The presence of others does not always inhibit helping, however. Individuals who hold leadership responsibility or people who have been specially designated as the person who should help do come through in emergency situations (Baumeister, Chesner, Senders, & Tice, 1988). And if one person rushes to offer help, many more may also do so: The first person serves as a model or example, implicitly defining helping as an appropriate response (Bandura, 1977b; Staub, 1978). Because we rely on others for information that helps us understand what is happening and gives us clues about what we should do, such models encourage others to do likewise. In one field study of the effect

FIGURE 14.1 Diffusion of responsibility: Lost in the crowd

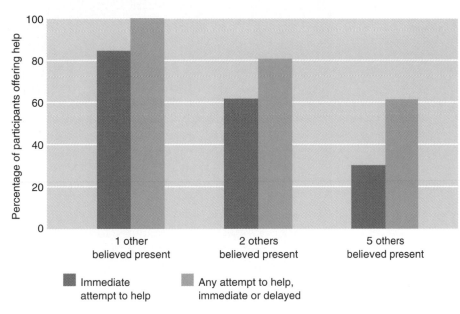

■ In this experiment, participants heard another participant having a "seizure" in what they believed was a group of two, three, or six people. (They actually heard recordings of other voices.) The more people participants believed to be present, the less likely the real participants were to help. (Data from Darley & Latané, 1968.)

of this social learning on helping, researchers stationed a motorist with an apparently disabled car at the side of the road. If drivers had recently seen another motorist helping out with a disabled car, they were more likely to offer aid than drivers who had not had the opportunity to see an altruistic model (Bryan & Test, 1967). And prosocial models can always be provided to help a good cause. When one group of researchers sought ways to increase the money contributed to worthy causes, they discovered that indicating that others had found giving to be an appropriate response—"We've already received contributions ranging from a penny up"—doubled the frequency of giving compared to a control condition (Cialdini & Schroeder, 1976). These findings provide further evidence of the power of social norms: In ambiguous situations, the way that other people (models) act has a big impact on our own behavior.

The importance of models became even clearer when social psychologists asked why some individuals have strong personal feelings of obligation that lead them to help others in unusual, costly, or dangerous ways (Schwartz, 1977). Why do such people help in situations in which others turn away? They often have been deeply influenced by personal examples, particularly their parents. Studies of heroic helpers, such as committed civil-rights workers in the segregated Southern United States in the 1960s and Gentiles who sheltered Jews from the Nazis during the Third Reich, have found that they often identify strongly with a parent who exemplified norms of concern for others (Oliner & Oliner, 1988; Rosenhan, 1970). Religious teachings can also make a difference: Among both college students and the general public, religiously committed individuals are more likely than the less committed to give time and money to help those they perceive as needy (Benson and others, 1980; Colasanto, 1989).

■ **The norms of helping.** Norms such as social responsibility, reciprocity, and social commitment often play a role in motivating helping behavior. When thousands of people—old and young, healthy and sick—turn out for walkathons to help raise money for charitable causes, the decision to participate is influenced by social norms as well as personal desires.

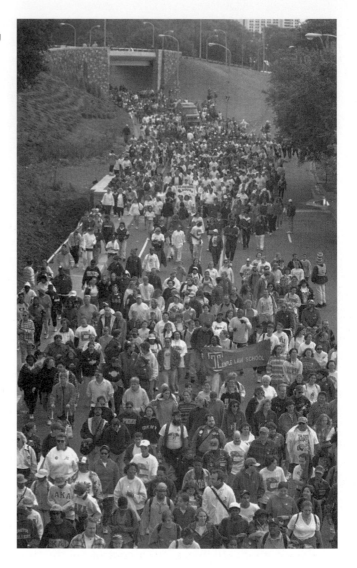

WHEN NORMS MAKE HELPING INAPPROPRIATE. Group norms dictate not only who gets help, but also who does not. Conservative estimates suggest that in the United States alone, at least 2 million young children, half of all adolescents, and as many as 2.5 million elderly people are the targets of physical violence from family members (Gelles & Cornell, 1985; Straus & Gelles, 1986). One factor contributing to their victimization is that some norms specify that intervening to help is socially inappropriate in some situations. The norm of family privacy, for example, makes people reluctant to intervene when they observe family violence, whether that violence involves a mother angrily slapping her child in a supermarket aisle, a man verbally abusing his wife on the street, or a grown child impatiently shaking an aging or forgetful parent. To demonstrate this point, Lance Shotland and Margaret Straw (1976) staged an attack by a man on a woman in front of male and female bystanders. Half the bystanders heard the victim say, "I don't know you!" while half heard her say, "I don't know why I ever married you!" Fully 65% of the bystanders tried to prevent the stranger's assault, compared to only 19% who intervened in the marital dispute. Why were people so reluctant to intervene in a family affair? People think wives would be embarrassed and upset by such intervention, and that husbands would likely turn on the would-be helper! Perhaps an increased awareness of and sensitivity to spousal abuse and date rape will gradually change norms that currently inhibit intervention in violence among intimates.

Norms restraining intervention in family violence can make bystanders reluctant to help even when a stranger assaults a woman. Over two thirds of participants shown a silent film of a man attacking a woman assumed that the attacker and the victim were dates, lovers, or spouses, although nothing in the film supported that conclusion (Shotland & Straw, 1976). The mental transformation of "dispute" into "domestic dispute" means that the most salient norms when a woman is being attacked may be not social responsibility or chivalry but: "that's family business" so "mind your own business."

Does the situation in which you passed the stranded motorist in the dark look a little more complicated now? The fact that the driver did not ask for help, and the unconcerned response of the only other passerby, may have suggested that help was not appropriate. Yet, with the departure of the other pedestrian, the entire responsibility for providing help fell to you. The elderly driver may not have been able to make even minor repairs himself, and might have been afraid to venture out of the car to phone for assistance. Would you help or not? As in every social situation, many pieces of information may need to be woven together before an appropriate response can be made.

Why Do People Help?
Helping for Mastery and Connectedness

Decades of research has provided some answers about when and how people will or will not help. But it is the bigger question that really intrigues social psychologists: Even if victims needed help, even if they were deserving, even if all the norms dictated that help should be given, people still would not help unless they were somehow motivated to do so. Ability and opportunity will not translate into behavior unless there is also desire. What are the fundamental motives behind helping? Why do we spend time, effort, and money, and sometimes even risk our lives, to benefit others?

Biologically Driven Helping: Is Helping in Our Genes?

Evolutionary principles suggest that some forms of helping, such as reciprocal helping or helping kin, have been naturally selected because they increase survival. In humans, however, cognitive and social processes mediate such biologically driven helping.

One possible answer is that human helping, or the lack thereof, is merely a product of natural selection: Our genes make us do it. At first glance it would seem that any kind of helping would violate the principles of natural selection. Surely, behaviors that reduce the likelihood that an organism will reproduce, such as giving some of its food to another, or diving off a bridge to rescue a drowning child, should be selected against, and soon die out in the population. In fact, some evolutionary scientists have argued that evolution has shaped humans, like other animals, to be fundamentally and unalterably selfish (Lorenz, 1966). But this does not mean that helping cannot occur. As modern evolutionary theorists point out, survival occurs at the level of the gene, and not the bearer of the gene (W. D. Hamilton, 1964). Thus some types of helping behaviors might enhance the likelihood that genes (though not necessarily the individual carrying them) will survive. There are two ways in which seemingly self-sacrificial helping could ensure survival of genes.

First, apparent helping sometimes involves a payoff for the helper as well as the helpee. "Cleaner fish" such as wrasse swim into the mouths of large fish such as grouper to eat ectoparasites. This provides food for the smaller fish and a cleaning for the big fish, which forgo snacking on the smaller fish. At the individual level, those who help are often repaid in kind. This type of reciprocal helping can evolve in species where individuals have the ability to remember other individuals who helped them in the past—or failed to do so (Trivers, 1971). Reciprocal helping occurs in humans as well as other species: As we noted in chapter 10, we often feel compelled to repay favors to those who have helped us. When helping engenders payback helping, those who help have a better chance of survival.

Second, helping kin may be like helping oneself. When individuals help relatives who share their genes, the genes have a better chance of survival, even if each individual carrier of them does not (W. D. Hamilton, 1964). For example, female ground squirrels often cry out in alarm when they notice a predator, and this behavior is especially likely if they are living with close kin rather than unrelated animals (P. W. Sherman, 1977). Making noise is riskier than quietly hiding, but if the alarm saves the lives of offspring, brothers, sisters, nieces, and nephews, then the squirrel's genes will survive to the next generation. Like ground squirrels, humans tend to help kin more than non-kin. For example, cross-cultural studies show that grandmothers, aunts, and other relatives are the most likely to adopt a child whose mother dies or is incapable of child rearing (Kurland, 1979).

The evolutionary explanation of helping has demonstrated that helping another person need not contradict the theory of natural selection and has suggested some possible behaviors that might promote genetically based forms of helping. The symbiotic relationships between grouper and wrasse and the self-sacrificial behavior of ground squirrels is probably genetically hardwired. But can such gene-driven forces explain the helping that goes on in the human race? In humans, behavior is much less the result of direct genetic impulse and much more the result of inherited but flexible processes that guide our behavior in diverse and changing environments (Batson, 1998). Helping in humans is much more likely to be the result of a naturally selected predisposition, or motivation, that can be activated and influenced by social or cognitive processes (M. L. Hoffman, 1981). Thus, even as the naturally selected nature of human helping must at some level be assumed, this line of thinking returns us to the real question of interest: What *motivates* people to help? As we will see, the answer involves the same two motives as all other forms of social behavior: our desires for mastery and concrete rewards, and for connectedness with others.

The norm of reciprocity and its powerful effect on behaviors was reviewed in chapter 10, pages 384 to 390.

You may recall that we discussed similar issues regarding the evolutionary basis of aggression in chapter 13, pages 505 to 506. Both helping and aggression are motivated by mastery and connectedness needs, and influenced by individual processing and social norms.

Helping for Mastery:
The Personal Rewards and Costs of Helping

Help may be motivated by perceived rewards or deterred by perceived costs or risks. These rewards and risks can be emotional: People sometimes help to alleviate their own distress at the victim's suffering.

REWARDS AND COSTS OF HELPING. The desire to help often depends on perceptions of the consequences of helping—on its potential rewards and costs. The upside of helping is its many rewards. One recent reviewer listed 11 material, social, or personal rewards that could be gained from helping and 9 material, social, or personal punishments that could be avoided if help was given (Batson, 1998). These benefits are often quite concrete: the gratitude of the victim, help in return via the norm of reciprocity, the cheers of a crowd of onlookers, or the thrill of making the evening news. Helping others pays—sometimes quite literally! A young boy recently made news by returning a wallet containing a large sum of money. When the owner failed to offer the youngster a reward, townspeople chipped in and gave the boy over $10,000! And just as the evolutionary theorists noted, helping often occurs for reciprocity credit. When we help someone, we expect to receive help in return at some future date. We may even help someone with that end in mind!

It is also the potential consequences of helping that can sometimes stop acts of generosity in their tracks. Consider this example. As several men in business suits stood watching, a 24-year-old woman dove into the Chicago River to rescue someone who had fallen in. Later, she reported, "One guy said, 'I have an appointment. I can't get my suit wet' " (*Newsweek*, 1990b). The cost of a ruined suit or a missed appointment seems trivial next to the possibility of saving a life, but it may deter helping. For example, participants in one study who thought they were a little late for their appointment with the experimenter were less likely to stop and assist an apparently ill confederate than those who thought they had plenty of time. This was true even though the participants were students studying to become ministers, and their appointment was to deliver a practice sermon on the Biblical parable of the Good Samaritan (Darley & Batson, 1973). The costs of helping can be many and varied: lost time, effort, embarrassment, money, social disapproval, or physical danger. Even when the need is clear and the victim seems deserving, people may not help if the costs appear too high.

The cost of helping is affected by a potential helper's abilities. Jumping into a river to rescue someone if you are not a strong swimmer could lead to two drownings instead of one. Remember that the first rule of lifesaving is: Don't become a victim yourself. But the more helping skills a person has, the lower the costs of helping. People with relevant abilities or training, for example, those with water-rescue or first aid skills, are more likely to offer direct help (Cramer and others, 1988). Perhaps someone with mechanical skills, confident of his or her ability to start a balky engine, would have been more likely to offer help to the stranded motorist we described earlier. Of course, training makes help not only more likely to be offered but also more likely to be effective. One study staged a bleeding emergency and found that people with Red Cross training were most likely to help the victim directly by applying pressure to the wound (Shotland & Heinold, 1985). Untrained individuals were equally likely to try to help in this obvious emergency—they phoned for an ambulance—but in the situation staged by the researchers, this indirect help probably would not have saved the victim.

The importance of perceived ability to help may explain Alice Eagly and Maureen Crowley's (1986) finding that men are more likely to help than women are. This conclusion is based on a meta-analysis of the research literature, which is heavily weighted toward studies of bystander intervention in emergencies. Indeed, Eagly and Crowley found that men perceive themselves as better able to help in most of the situations examined in research, such as assisting a motorist with a disabled car or carrying someone to safety—tasks requiring technical skills or physical strength. Thus, gender differences in helping probably reflect the types of helping that researchers have chosen to study. Other research shows that anyone (male or female) who sees himself or herself as independent, forceful, and dominant can have the confidence to help in emergency situations (Senneker & Hendrick, 1983).

EMOTIONAL REWARDS OF HELPING. Although helping sometimes pays quite literally, more often helping is its own reward: We feel good about ourselves because we helped others. Such internal rewards can be an even more powerful motivator of helping than external ones.

Because helping makes us feel good, people sometimes help to keep their spirits high (Isen, 1970). In one study, for example, participants who had been made to feel happy when they "happened" to find some money were asked to help the experimenter by reading a series of positive, upbeat or negative, depressing statements (Isen & Simmonds, 1978). Compared to people in a neutral mood, happy participants were more willing to read the positive sentences—and stay in a good mood—but were less willing to read the negative sentences that might make them feel blue. Thus, people who want to stay in a good mood may be particularly prone to good works, but only the kinds of good works that keep them feeling good.

People can help not only to stay in a good mood but also to escape from a bad mood. Thus, guilty people are often helpful people. The most successful donation collector for the entire international network of Save the Children agencies works the pavement Saturdays outside the local supermarket of one of your authors. As every passerby tries to maneuver into the market, he waves the pictures of needy recipients and reminds us, quite correctly, that we don't know how lucky we are. The ploy works. In experimental studies of the effects of guilt on helping, researchers have induced participants to break little rules or to tell little lies and then given them the opportunity to make up for their sins by helping. For example, some students in one study were induced to lie about having received advance information about a test. After taking the test, all participants were offered the chance to help the experimenter out on another project. Those who hadn't lied donated just 2 minutes of their time, whereas the guilt-laden fibbers spent an average of 63 minutes making up for their hidden transgression (McMillen & Austin, 1971). A clever field study of guilt makes the same point: Roman Catholics were solicited for donations to a worthy cause either on their way into confession or on their way out (H. B. Harris, Benson, & Hall, 1975). It's not hard to guess that those going in gave more than those coming out.

■ **Guilt and giving.** Seeing other people suffer can be unpleasant and doing something to remove that unpleasantness—handing money to someone less fortunate than ourselves, for example—can be as rewarding for the giver as for the recipient.

Other negative emotions can also increase our tendency to act charitably. If you just received a bad grade, had a falling out with a friend, or lost your address book, would you be more or less likely to help a stranger requesting aid? Most research indicates you would help more (Cialdini, Darby, & Vincent, 1973; Cialdini & Kenrick, 1976). The reason is that helping might distract you or reduce feelings like guilt, sadness, or disappointment. People know that helping makes them feel better, so those who want to feel better often offer their help.

People's tendency to help in order to make themselves feel better was clearly demonstrated in a study by Robert Cialdini and his colleagues (Cialdini and others, 1973). The researchers made one group of participants feel guilty about upsetting a stack of computer cards, while another group was not made to feel bad. Next, the researchers gave some of the guilty participants a compliment and others an unexpected payment for being in the experiment, ploys designed to put these participants back in a good mood. When all participants were then asked to do a favor, guilty ones were more likely to help than nonguilty ones—unless they had received a compliment or cash. Thus, doing a favor seemed to have the same effect as an external reward, getting people feeling better.

You may recall from chapter 13, page 510, that feeling bad can also make people commit aggressive acts. Can you think of other cases we have described in which the same inner state can have diverse effects on a person's behavior, depending on the way the person interprets the situation?

Understanding the reasons why people who are feeling bad are likely to help throws light on an apparent exception to that rule. Doing good to feel better depends on noticing opportunities to help. Unfortunately, deep depression and profound grief disengage their sufferers from the social world and replace social concern with self-absorption (Carlson & Miller, 1987). Thus, the self-focused attention characteristic of these states may blind people to opportunities to lift their spirits by helping. To demonstrate this negative effect, researchers asked participants to imagine in vivid detail that their best friend of the opposite sex was dying of cancer (W. C. Thompson, Cowan, & Rosenhan, 1980). The researchers' instructions focused some participants' attention on their own worry and grief, their own loss, their own sadness. Others were told to focus on their friend: his or her fear, uncertainty, and pain. Did sad thoughts increase helping? Even though everyone felt equally sad, the answer depended on the focus of attention. When the researcher asked for help with unrelated research, only 25% of the self-focused students volunteered. In contrast, 83% of those who were other-focused did so. If grief makes us think only of ourselves, it may keep us from using the warm glow of helping to cheer ourselves up.

Thus emotional costs and rewards can influence helping in several different ways. The ways in which emotions can produce both positive outcomes (increasing helping) and negative outcomes (decreasing helping) are summarized in Figure 14.2.

IS HELPING PURE EGOISM? As you may have realized, findings like this raise an intriguing question. If people help simply to maintain their own positive feelings or to relieve their own negative feelings, doesn't that mean that most helping is self-interested rather than truly altruistic? The *negative-state relief model* of helping answers this question with a solid "Yes" (Schaller & Cialdini, 1988). This theory begins with the assumption

FIGURE 14.2   Multiple effects of mood on helping

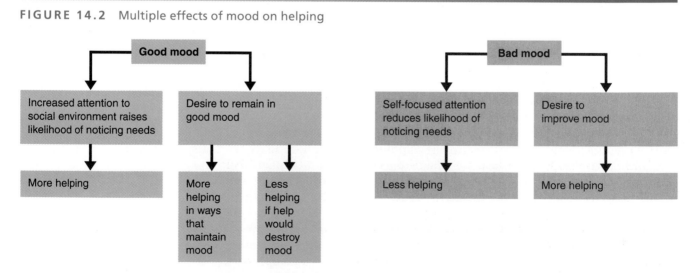

■ The effects of a positive or a negative mood on helping vary because they occur through several different processes. Both positive and negative moods have the ability to increase or decrease helping, depending on the circumstances.

that most people hate to watch others suffer. So their help is designed not to aid the victim for his or her sake, but to reduce the helper's own distress. Certainly the evidence we described above, showing that people feeling guilty or sad may help in an effort to feel better, is consistent with the negative-state relief model. The model also explains why people sometimes choose to walk away rather than help. Putting the victim "out of sight, out of mind" may be the easiest way to reduce distress. In fact, knowing that they are soon going to have a distracting experience—say, watch a comedy film—has been found to reduce people's helpfulness (Schaller & Cialdini, 1988). Distressed by the sight of starving refugees on a TV news program, will we write a check to a relief agency—or turn quickly to a variety show on another channel?

Thus proponents of the negative-state relief model believe that helping is based on egoism: Helping another is a means to self-benefit. The whole idea that helping only occurs when the cost–benefit trade-off is in the helper's favor suggests that it is the motive for mastery, and thus for positive consequences for the self, that dictates helping.

Helping for Connectedness: Empathy and Altruism

People are often motivated by a feeling of empathy to relieve another's suffering, regardless of personal rewards and costs.

Is egoism the only motive for benefiting another? Do people help only to gain rewards for themselves, or is true altruism—helping others as an end in itself—possible? And if so, how can we tell what a person's true motives are? Daniel Batson and his co-workers have conducted a number of clever studies that attempt to demonstrate the existence of true altruism (Batson, 1991, 1998). Imagine that you are a participant who has just arrived in their research laboratory. You learn that a second participant, Elaine, will be receiving mild electric shocks as she performs a task in another room. Your job will be to observe her performance through a window. As you watch, Elaine (who is, of course, actually a confederate) is hooked up to some equipment and the shocks apparently begin. Obviously upset after two shocks, she asks for a glass of water and tells the experimenter that she's been frightened of electricity ever since a childhood accident when a horse threw her into an electric fence. The experimenter hesitates. Perhaps Elaine shouldn't continue. The experiment could be canceled . . . or perhaps you (the real participant) would be willing to trade places with Elaine and take the remaining shocks for her? Would you suffer for someone else?

Batson and his colleagues (1981), who designed this scenario, expected participants' responses to depend on how they reacted emotionally to the victim's plight and on how easy it was to escape from the situation. Their *empathy-altruism model* suggests that people can experience two types of emotion when they see someone in trouble: personal distress, including alarm, anxiety, and fear, or empathic concern, including sympathy, compassion and tenderness. Personal distress motivates either egoistic helping—aimed at reducing the observer's own negative feelings—or escape, just as the negative-state relief model predicts. In contrast, feelings of empathic concern lead to altruistic behavior: helping designed to relieve the victim's suffering. People who are motivated in this way will help even if they could easily escape from the situation.

To test these ideas, the researchers manipulated participants' emotional responses to the situation and their ease of escape. To vary empathetic concerns, they told half of the participants that Elaine's personal values and interests were very similar to their own. Because similarity usually increases empathy, this information was designed to lead these participants to empathize with Elaine. The other half of the participants were told that she was quite different from them. To vary ease of escape, half of the participants (in the easy escape condition) were told they had to observe only 2 shocks, so when the experimenter asked them about changing places, the participants knew they could simply leave. The other half of the participants (in the difficult escape condition) were told they had to watch Elaine go through a series of 10 shocks.

The results of the experiment, as Figure 14.3 shows, were consistent with the empathy-altruism model. Participants who were not led to feel empathy acted differently depending on the ease of escape. A high percentage of those who could not escape—who knew they had to watch all 10 shocks—volunteered to take Elaine's place, presumably to avoid the distress of watching her suffer. However, the pattern was reversed for their low-empathy peers who could walk out the door. Most took advantage of the escape hatch, leaving Elaine to suffer out of their view. In contrast, participants who empathized with Elaine helped altruistically: Even when escape was easy, most offered to stay and take the shocks for her.

There is now a good deal of evidence supporting the idea that helping can be motivated by a true concern for and identification with the victim (Batson and others, 1991; Batson, Dyck, Brandt, & Batson, 1988; Dovidio, Allen, & Schroeder, 1990; A. P. Fiske, 1991; Toi & Batson, 1982). Studies show that, compared to those low in empathy, participants induced to feel empathy with a victim continue to feel bad if their attempts to help are unsuccess-

FIGURE 14.3   Does altruism exist?

■ For participants who did not empathize with Elaine, helping was a matter of avoiding personal distress. When escape was difficult—when participants could not simply leave the experiment—most volunteered to receive shocks in Elaine's place. But when an easy escape was available, most of the low-empathy participants left Elaine to suffer alone. In contrast, almost all those who empathized with Elaine volunteered to help her, regardless of the ease of escape. Their help must have been motivated by a focus on Elaine's feelings rather than by a desire to reduce their own distress. (Data from Batson and others, 1981.)

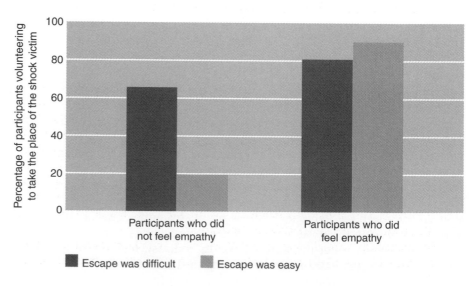

ful, even if the lack of success is fully justified (Batson & Weeks, 1996). Individuals who are particularly likely to think about the welfare and rights of other people, to feel concern and empathy for them, and to act on their behalf are more likely to feel distress in the presence of someone needing help (Penner, Fritzsche, Craiger, & Freifeld, 1995). Even in very young children, empathy for others' suffering can promote helping (Eisenberg & Fabes, 1991; Hoffman, 1981).

These findings should not surprise us, however. We already know that when people identify with another individual and feel connected to them, they pay as much attention to those others' outcomes as to their own. Even a minimal social connection between two individuals can turn a bystander into a likely helper. One study found that people who had given their name to a researcher, made eye contact with her, or joined her in a trivial conversation, were more likely than utter strangers to help her at a later time (Solomon and others, 1981). As the connections grow stronger, people are more likely to feel empathy for the other and more likely to help. No wonder, then, that people are more likely to help members of the same group, friends, and family than strangers (Schoenrade, Batson, & Brandt, 1986).

These results thus contradict the notion that most helpful actions are motivated simply by mastery motives: the prospect of maximizing personal rewards and minimizing personal costs. Instead, it appears that true altruism—acting with the goal of benefiting another—is alive and well in the repertoire of human behavior. Such actions depend on, and are often triggered by, a cognitive and emotional connection with another person. Among the many consequences of such connections is the motivation to increase another person's happiness and welfare regardless of the costs or benefits of such actions for the self.

Helping for Connectedness: Social Identification and Cooperation

In a social dilemma, rewards for each individual are in direct conflict with what is best for the group. However, people can be motivated by feelings of group connectedness to act for the good of the group, regardless of personal costs or benefits. When group identification increases commitment to shared goals and norms, social dilemmas can be successfully resolved.

Research on altruism indicates that the formation of a cognitive and emotional bond with another person, and the resulting feelings of empathy, can promote selfless helping of that other person. Such findings suggest that other types of connectedness might also promote helping that goes beyond pure egoism. Just as people identify with another individual, they can identify with and be closely bound to groups to which they belong. This suggests that group feeling might also act to increase helping where the goal is to benefit or promote the good of the group rather than the individual. Could such a feeling explain instances of heroism like a soldier throwing himself on a live grenade to save his buddies?

Some research already suggests that in-group members (even those who are not kin) are more likely to be the target of help than others. Similar others, and those perceived as sharing our values, usually end up receiving the most help (Dovidio, Piliavin, Gaertner, Schroeder, & Clark, 1991). During an election campaign, for example, passersby are more likely to give help (by picking up a stack of dropped leaflets) to those working for their own candidate than for the opposing candidate (Karabenick, Lerner, & Beecher, 1973). The tendency to help in-group members is even stronger in interdependent countries, where the in-group is even more important, than in individualistic Western cultures. For example, Chinese and Japanese participants are more likely to offer help to in-group members but less likely to help out-group members than are North Americans (M. H. Bond, 1988).

But the strongest test of the idea that helping and cooperation could occur to benefit a group regardless of costs and rewards for the individual would involve a situation in which the good of the individual was directly opposed to the good of the group. In such a situation, self-sacrificial behavior could only be interpreted as behavior designed to benefit the group, even at a personal cost. What social situations might reflect such a conflict of benefits?

SOCIAL DILEMMAS: SELF-INTEREST VERSUS GROUP INTEREST. In fact, we are all involved in just such situations. Consider the growing problem of air pollution, for example. Individuals use heat and air-conditioning, drive sporty automobiles with powerful engines, and buy convenience products manufactured from petroleum. From an individual's point of view, such behavior might make sense. As a society, however, our appetite for fossil-fuel energy—in industry, transportation, and housing—is pumping millions of tons of carbon dioxide into the atmosphere each year. This process produces global warming through the so-called "greenhouse effect" and may result in worldwide damage to agricultural productivity, changes in global weather patterns, and large increases in the levels of oceans and inland seas (Stern, 1992).

Can you see now why the study of such situations offers fascinating insights into the nature of human helping and cooperation? In these situations, if people do what makes sense from their individual points of view, the result is disaster for everyone. Thus pure self-interest is directly opposed to the best interests of the group, and vice versa. Such situations are **social dilemmas:** situations in which individual group members acting to benefit themselves bring harm to the group as a whole. If every fisherman catches as many fish as possible there are soon no fish for anyone; if everyone watches viewer-sponsored public television without contributing to its support, public television stations soon go off the air. Although social life is always characterized by tensions between individual and group goals, social dilemmas directly pit the individual against the group.

Because of this, social psychologists have set up laboratory situations that maintain the central feature of real-world social dilemmas: They pit individual goals against group interests. Although these studies never mimic all the complexities of actual large-scale dilemmas, they can offer insight into the social-psychological processes that come into play during two important types of social dilemma.

One response to social dilemmas, social loafing, was discussed in chapter 12, pages 480 to 482, because of its effects on group productivity.

Social dilemma. A form of interdependence in which the most rewarding action for each individual will, if chosen by all individuals, produce a negative outcome for the entire group.

1. *Replenishable resource dilemmas.* Replenishable resource dilemmas involve conflicts about the consumption of renewable resources, such as the world's rain forests or the populations of ocean fish. Individuals benefit personally by harvesting some of the resource. If enough

of the resource is left untouched, it can reproduce and replenish itself, so that harvesting can continue indefinitely. If too much of the resource is taken, however, reproduction cannot replenish the stock, and the resource disappears.

To study this type of situation in the laboratory, individuals take many turns "harvesting" a group resource for individual profit. For example, participants are told that a certain number of fish remain in a shared fishing spot. Each one then decides how many fish to take from the common resource pool. After everyone has made a decision, the total harvest is subtracted from the pool. The pool is then allowed to replenish itself by a set amount; for example, reproduction may increase the number of fish by 10% before the next trial. The same process continues for many trials (Messick and others, 1983).

Consider the rewards and costs faced by each participant in such a situation (see Table 14.1). For each individual, every fish caught means profit, and the more fish, the more profit. This is true regardless of whether other people use the resource or not. If the individual decides to take fewer fish, others might continue to overfish, so a cautious fisher could end up with reduced profit and still lose the resource. Regardless of what others do, that is, no matter whether you look at the first or the second row of the table, the individual is better off using than not using the resource. For the individual, the logic of the situation dictates taking more fish.

TABLE 14.1. Possible Outcomes in a Replenishable-Resource Dilemma

Individual's action	Use resource *Catch as many fish as possible.*	Do not use resource *Take the season off.*
Result if others use the resource	Short-term profit; resource is soon depleted.	No profit; resource is depleted anyway.
Result if others refrain from using the resource	Short-term profit; resource is not depleted.	No profit; resource is not depleted.

2. *Public goods dilemmas.* Another type of social dilemma arises over how public goods should be acquired or supported. A public good is one that has to be provided for everybody or nobody; it cannot be given to some and withheld from others. Unpolluted air, a strong national defense, and viewer-supported public broadcasting stations are all public goods. Because a public good is available to all, "free riders" are tempted to use it without paying for it.

To illustrate the underlying dilemma, consider Table 14.2, showing the situation faced by participants in an experiment by Linda Caporael and her colleagues (Caporael, Dawes, Orbell, & Van de Kragt, 1989). The researchers gave $5 to each of a group of seven participants. The participants were told that they would each receive a $10 reward—the public good—if at least four of them anonymously donated their $5 to the experimenter. If fewer than four people donated, however, no reward would be provided, and the donations would not be returned. Clearly, if every person donates, everyone ends up with $10. But is this really in the individual's best interest? How would you reason if presented with the dilemma? After all, if you donate but nobody else does, you lose your $5 and no public good is provided. By holding on to your $5 and collecting the bonus, you

TABLE 14.2. Possible Outcomes in an Experimental Social Dilemma

Individual action	Keep $5	Donate $5
Result if most others keep their $5	End up with $5	End up with nothing
Result if most others donate their $5	End up with $15	End up with $10

could even walk away with $15. Once again, your best bet as an individual seems to be free-riding, while hoping everyone else is a better citizen! The kicker is, of course, that if all individuals follow this entirely sensible course of action, no one will contribute and no one will have the benefit of the public good—in fact, all will be worse off than they might have been.

BEHAVIOR IN SOCIAL DILEMMAS. Faced with dilemmas like these, what do people do? Often they quite reasonably, but disastrously, follow their individual interests. Left to their own devices, almost every individual faced with a resource dilemma makes the same decision: to harvest as much as possible, even though the resource is rapidly depleted (Messick and others, 1983). This is especially true if people can't accurately estimate the size of the resource pool or if the pool is difficult to divide: Under these conditions people overestimate the size of their fair share, take more for themselves than will conserve the resource, and believe that others will do the same (Budescu, Rapoport, & Suleiman, 1990; Herlocker, Allison, Foubert, & Beggan, 1997). Of course, thinking that others will follow their own self-interest or actually seeing them do so provides selfish models, which makes people even more likely to harvest selfishly even when they realize the resource is being depleted (Messick and others, 1983; Schroeder, Jensen, Reed, Sullivan, and Schwab, 1983). After all, continuing to sacrifice when others are taking a free ride might make you feel like a sucker (Kerr & Bruun, 1983). In real life as in the laboratory, New England and North Sea fishermen have found that their operations have so depleted the once abundant offshore schools that their total catch is in steep decline. Even though their livelihoods are now endangered, taking action to solve the dilemma seems particularly difficult to do ("Plenty of fish in sea?", 1992).

Self-interest usually wins the day in public-goods dilemmas too. For example, only about 50% of participants in Caporael's study (Caporael and others, 1989) made $5 donations, and so only a few experimental groups collected the bonus. In an attempt to find out why, researchers looked at two possible motivations: the fear of wasting their donations and the greedy desire for profit (Rapoport & Eshed-Levy, 1989). To eliminate the influence of fear for some experimental groups, researchers offered to return the money if fewer than four participants made donations. To neutralize greed, they warned that if the $10 bonus was earned, nondonators as well as donators would go home with just $10. Only eliminating greed increased the number of donations (Caporael and others, 1989). Thus, greed seems to be the most important reason that most people fail to contribute.

STRUCTURAL SOLUTIONS IN SOCIAL DILEMMAS. In fact, selfish behavior is so prevalent in social dilemmas that often structural solutions, like the ones tested in this study, have to be imposed (N. L. Kerr, 1992, Messick & Brewer, 1983; Platt, 1973). By making laws or regulations, individual payoffs are changed and the dilemma is eliminated. A standard solution to a public-goods dilemma, for instance, is to levy taxes to pay for provision of the good: If everyone benefits, everyone should pay. In a resource-depletion dilemma, solutions usually involve setting quotas so that users can't deplete the resource. For example, international fishery commissions restrict the number of fish of different species that can be caught every year.

Unfortunately, structural solutions can generate about as many problems as they try to solve. First, structural solutions require an authority to impose them. Experimenters can easily set sanctions in laboratory game playing, and groups sometimes elect leaders to decide each member's share (Samuelson, Messick, Rutte, & Wilke, 1984). But who has the accepted authority to regulate use and misuse of the world's atmosphere or the proliferation of biological weapons? Only when a valuable resource is threatened to the point of extinction do people sometimes ask for some kind of authority to regulate their behavior (Sato, 1987). Second, structural solutions are often met with resistance. Even though New England fishermen are finding there aren't plenty more fish in the sea, they have resisted new regulations that would limit their catch and allow the fish stocks to be rebuilt ("Plenty of fish in sea?", 1992). Third, resistance necessitates a bureaucracy for monitoring compliance with no guarantee of successful enforcement (Yamagishi, 1986). Despite the existence of stiff penalties and routine inspection, the Chevron Oil Company was found to have illegally dumped oil products from off-shore rigs for years. Unless people willingly accept restraints on their behavior, structural solutions do not seem to be the answer for many of our most intractable global dilemmas.

Don't these findings support the idea that people are fundamentally selfish and that helping and cooperation never occur unless there is some personal gain? Perhaps. But before accepting this conclusion completely, consider some other findings from social dilemma research.

First, there are cultural and gender differences in people's responses to social dilemmas. We might expect to find more cooperation from women and in interdependent, group-oriented cultures. A meta-analysis of research on social loafing dilemmas found both of these predictions to be generally accurate (Karau & Williams, 1993). In studies of other types of dilemmas, some research found that Chinese students and manager trainees were more cooperative than their individualistic U.S. counterparts (Earley, 1989; Gabrenya, Wang, & Latané, 1985).

Second, some individuals behave in unselfish ways in resource dilemmas. In particular, individuals who generally prefer to cooperate make resource pools go further than people who like to compete (Liebrand & van Run, 1985; McClintock & Liebrand, 1988). Findings like this give social psychologists something to think about: If some of the people are helpful and cooperative some of the time, are there circumstances that would lead more people to act for the greater good more of the time? That is, are there conditions under which individuals tend to act for the good of the group rather than for their own selfish ends, and thus solve social dilemmas?

SOLVING SOCIAL DILEMMAS: SOCIAL IDENTIFICATION AND COOPERATION. In fact, under the right conditions, participants in social dilemmas show considerable helping and cooperation: agreeing to cut resource consumption and chipping in to pay for resources others can use. What makes people forego their own individual interests for the interests of the group? The factor that makes the difference is identification with the group as an important aspect of the individual's social identity. When group belonging becomes uppermost in peoples' minds, helping can be motivated by social identification, promoting the desire to benefit the group as a whole regardless of outcomes for the self. That is, individuals become concerned for "not me or thee but we" (Dawes, Van de Kragt, & Orbell, 1988).

When individuals identify with groups, three changes usually take place. First, the greater good of the group becomes the top priority (Caporael and others, 1989). Behaviors like contributing to a common good, which might appear foolish or naive from an individual point of view, seem loyal, trustworthy, and generous from the perspective of the group (P. E. Tetlock, 1989). For example, one study found that people who themselves identified and cooperated with a group rated others who also cooperated as more intelligent than noncooperators (Van Lange & Liebrand, 1991). Similarly, actions like free-riding, which may seem clever and sensible to the individual, may be viewed as despicable and treacherous by the group (Kuhlman, Brown, & Teta, 1992).

Second, when the group thinks and works together as one, people are more likely to assume that other group members will also be helping, rather than hurting, the group effort. There is no longer any need to worry that others will free-ride while you exercise self-control, nor will you take the opportunity to free-ride while others act responsibly (Caporael and others, 1989). In fact, when Caporael and her colleagues questioned people who contributed in their experimental groups, these participants said that they thought most others would contribute as well. Acting as you expect others to act—or, what is the same thing, trusting others to act the same way as you do—lets the entire group share the fruits of cooperation.

Third, internalized norms about cooperation become salient and group norms become good guides for individual action. Individuals in Caporael's study who thought that most others would contribute must have realized that they could keep their own $5—and still collect the bonus earned by others' contributions! Still, these individuals preferred to follow what they saw as a group norm of contributing rather than to maximize their individual earnings. The norm of commitment can have such a powerful effect that individuals who vow to cooperate during group discussion actually do so, even if they know their behavior is unlikely to solve the dilemma effectively (N. L. Kerr & Kaufman-Gilliland, 1993). People who identify strongly with their group are also more willing to accept imposed norms and solutions from authorities, because their strong bonds to their communities produce respect for those authorities (Tyler & Degoey, 1995).

Does shared group identity produce cooperative behavior in social dilemmas? Yes. Marilynn Brewer and Roderick Kramer (1986) created a laboratory situation in which individuals were faced with a resource dilemma. Students sat in individual cubicles with computer displays, but were led to believe that they were part of either a small 8-member group or a large 32-member group. In addition, some people in each condition were encouraged to develop group identification and some were not. The manipulation was subtle: Participants in the group identification condition were simply told that their payment for experimental participation would be decided for the group as a whole, rather than separately for each individual. Sharing a common fate in this way was enough to change their behavior, significantly

You might recognize the role of group identification in solving social dilemmas as similar to its role in solving other problems that groups face, as discussed in chapter 12, pages 483 to 486.

lowering the amount of resources participants drew from the common pool when given the opportunity.

How can the powerful effects of connectedness with a group be encouraged to increase such concern for the greater rather than the individual good? Several factors are important:

- *Communication among group members.* Laboratory studies have repeatedly demonstrated that when members of a group are allowed to discuss a dilemma before making their decisions, cooperation is enhanced (Orbell, Van de Kragt, & Dawes, 1988). For example, only 47% of participants in one study donated to a public good when no discussion was permitted, but discussion raised the figure to 84% (Caporael and others, 1989). And what did group members talk about? Mostly they worked on forming consensus around a norm for appropriate behavior, defining the meaning of deviance from the norm, and making promises to stick to the norm. Group discussion made them feel more connected, but it also committed them to promises of cooperation and sharing (Bouas & Komorita, 1996; Kerr & Kaufman-Gilliland, 1993). The difficulty of communication might be one reason that big groups often have a tougher time solving social dilemmas than smaller groups (Brewer & Kramer, 1986). When it comes to solving social dilemmas, small is beautiful (Edney, 1980).

- *Equality of opportunities and outcomes among group members.* If all group members use the same amount of a resource, that level of consumption becomes a norm for group members (Messick and others, 1983). Inequality of resource use reduces people's certainty about others' behaviors, weakens conformity pressures, diminishes personal efficacy, and makes people wonder if they are being exploited. It's not surprising that people feeling this way start to be concerned with their immediate self-interest rather than cooperation with the group. Inequality is a major roadblock to solving current problems of global pollution and resource depletion (Simons, 1992). The poorer nations wonder why environmental considerations should require them to use fewer resources than the already developed nations do. Why should they give up the promise of prosperity when the developed nations literally took the quick and dirty route to wealth?

- *Accessibility of group norms.* Keeping the value of acting in the group's best interest uppermost in everyone's mind gives it the best chance of guiding behavior. To demonstrate this point, some participants in one experiment listened to others talk about the value of group cooperation: "Maybe I could have gotten more if I was greedy, but I just couldn't do it. If I'm in a group, I'm going to try to do what helps the group, not just myself" (Sattler & Kerr, 1991, p. 760). When later faced with a social dilemma problem, these participants took less for themselves than did participants who had not heard the message. Compliance with such norms is more likely if the norm was developed fairly (Tyler & Smith, 1998), provides fair outcomes (Pruitt & Kimmel, 1977), and is endorsed by others (Orbell and others, 1988).

- *Linking individual efforts to the group good.* If people are given feedback that shows that their actions are effective, even on a small scale, they conserve more. Apparently, being able to see the effects of seemingly trivial actions like turning off unneeded lights or emptying the dishwater on flowerbeds creates a sense that personal actions do matter (C. L. Seligman, Becker, & Darley, 1981). Believing that their efforts make a difference makes people feel good, gives them a sense of psychological control, and increases the likelihood that they will act on their attitudes and norms, whether it means installing flow-restricted showerheads, subscribing to public television, or gathering signatures on petitions to stop nuclear weapons testing. When individuals are told: "Because you donated your share, the company was able to raise over $5000," they learn how their individual actions are magnified by the size of the group. The more members feel responsible for group success, the more likely they are to solve social dilemmas (Kerr, 1992).

Thus behavior that benefits others can sometimes be motivated because people come to care about the welfare of the group as a whole. Again, this conclusion should not surprise you given the many important changes, described in chapter 6, that can occur when people identify strongly with a group. Whereas altruism operates to benefit a single other individual, group identification can dictate helping to any member of any size group. In fact, feeling empathy for a single other member of a group experiencing a social dilemma may result in more resources being allocated to the favored other and fewer being allocated to the group as a whole (Batson and others, 1995, 1999). Thus altruism seems quite distinct from group identification, which seems necessary to solve social dilemmas. From work and sports teams, communities, and villages, to political parties, ethnic groups, and nations, group identification can be a powerful motivator of helping and cooperation. Group identification can also make our universal humanity salient, which might explain helping others who share nothing but this common bond. In this way, it can motivate helping for abstract groups like the poor, the starving, or, as when we consider global pollution, citizens of the earth. In hiding Jewish families from Nazi Germany, the villagers of Le Chambon may have been concerned not with themselves, not with their village, not even with Jews in particular, but with benefiting humanity. Such motivation is recognized by a special medal presented to those identified as having taken great risks to rescue others. The motto reads: "Whosoever saves one life, he has saved all of humanity" (cited in Batson, 1998).

Of course, using identification with a group to motivate helping and cooperation is not a perfect solution, nor is it always feasible. As we saw in chapter 6, cognitive and emotional identification with one group can often go hand in hand with rejection of other groups.

On the one hand, we may treat other members of our in-groups as we would ourselves like to be treated, producing high levels of self-sacrificial caring within the group. Even here, the more closely identified we are with a group, the more likely we are to help. On the other hand, when we fail to empathize with those whom we see as dissimilar from ourselves, we may morally exclude them, placing them outside the scope of norms and moral standards that might encourage helping. And despite the promise of group identification

FIGURE 14.4   Social dilemmas: Problems and remedies

Problems in solving social dilemmas	Motivation problems *Individuals seek personal rewards, undermining group benefits.*	Coordination problems *Individuals are unaware of others' choices.* *Individuals cannot trust others to cooperate.*
Remedies for social dilemmas	Task interdependence solutions: Change incentives for individuals. *Individuals seeking personal rewards now benefit group.* Social interdependence solutions: Individuals identify with group norms. *Individuals seek to act in ways that benefit the group.*	Task interdependence solutions: Individuals agree on appropriate actions. *Individuals assume others will cooperate.* Social interdependence solutions: Individuals follow group norms. *Norm of commitment keeps individuals cooperating.*
Contribution of group cohesion to remedy	Individuals adopt group goals as their own.	Group exercises social influence over individuals.

for solving global resource dilemmas, the groups involved are often enormous in size, have little in common, do not communicate, and are notably unequal in resource usage. These factors mean that it is difficult to create the sense of common group membership that may be the best hope of solving such dilemmas.

Nevertheless, as Figure 14.4 shows, feeling themselves to be part of a community can make people act more cooperatively, value group outcomes above individual ones, and forego self-interest in helping others for the benefit of the group as a whole. The future of our human group may depend on creating and maintaining that shared feeling of belonging.

■ Social dilemmas worsen when individuals seek to serve their own interests in opposition to group interests, and when individuals are unable to coordinate their actions to solve general problems.

Role of Superficial or Systematic Processing in Helping and Cooperation

The Impact of Processing

When desires and norms conflict, various factors may be considered superficially or thought through extensively before a decision about helping is made. Emotions can play a role in this process, for strong emotion disrupts extensive processing. When helping is a considered decision, though, it can result in a long-term commitment.

Sometimes it's relatively easy to decide whether or not to help, but more often we experience conflict over what to do. We may desperately want to come to the aid of a mugging victim but fear the risks and costs to ourselves. We may feel empathy for the toddler being spanked in the supermarket but feel that our intrusion into a "family affair" would be inappropriate. We may want to conserve water by taking shorter showers, but fear being made a sucker by those who will free-ride on our contributions. Many thoughts and emotions, attitudes, and norms can be activated in people's minds as they size up the victim, the need, and the situation in which help is needed.

The final decision to act or to turn away is also influenced by how these various facilitators or inhibitors of helping are processed. Sometimes the decision about whether to help or cooperate has to be made quickly and impulsively. At other times it is the product of extensive processing.

SPONTANEOUS HELPING, SUPERFICIAL PROCESSING. Emergencies are heart-stopping, adrenaline-pumping, sweaty-palm situations. The suffering of others causes anguish, distress, empathy, sadness, and guilt, and these strong emotions can motivate us to action, including helpful action (Dovidio and others, 1991). However, strong emotions also limit our ability to think things through carefully. In addition, emergencies usually don't allow much time for thought. The combination of arousal, emotions, and split-second timing usually leads people to respond to emergencies quickly and impulsively. That was certainly the case when local residents immediately went to the aid of the victims of an Air Borneo plane crash in Indonesia. When emergency personnel arrived on the scene, they credited many of the lives saved to the courageous actions of those who rushed to pull survivors from the wreckage before it sank or burned. When arousal is high and time for reflection is limited, people act on the basis of the most accessible motives or norms. In this case, the onlookers' empathy for the victims or their feelings of social responsibility must have outweighed thoughts of discomfort and danger.

PLANNED HELPING, SYSTEMATIC PROCESSING. Of course, instant help isn't always needed. Under such circumstances a would-be rescuer may give careful—even agonized—consideration to the available information. Someone may reflect on the victim's need, then on the possible cost and danger, then on feelings of personal responsibility and ability to help. Extensive thought can even reverse a first, quick reaction. When a Dutch couple with four children were asked to shelter a Jewish infant from the Nazis, they immediately reacted negatively. "This is going too far," they said. "We have given money to support and hide Jews—but we don't need a Jewish kid in the house!" (Oliner & Oliner, 1988, p. 69). Reflection, however, produced a change of heart. By the next morning they had made plans to save the infant: For example, the wife would pretend to be pregnant for a time to allay neighbors' suspicions about the sudden appearance of a new child.

One of the most typical forms of planned helping is volunteering, where people provide voluntary, sustained, and ongoing benefits to others, often for long periods of time. This kind of helping reflects the fact that both the initial decision to help and the decision to continue volunteering may result from considerable thought. As we have pointed out many times, decisions based on extensive thought produce long-lasting commitments that are not easily changed. When people repeatedly help others, they come to see themselves as helpful and altruistic, and these self-perceptions reinforce further helping (Deaux & Stark, 1996). This process explains why people who give blood a few times tend to become regular blood donors, for example (Piliavin and others, 1982). Repeated helping also builds perceptions of self-efficacy, the sense that one's actions are effective and meaningful. Self-efficacy also increases the likelihood that helpful attitudes and norms will be translated into helpful actions (Ajzen & Madden, 1986; Bandura, 1982). Such self-perceptions may be quite specific, as one aspect of the extensive thought given to volunteering is matching one's interests and talents with particular types of needs or ways to help (Benson and others, 1980; Clary and others, 1998).

Like helping in general, volunteering can be motivated by a number of different goals (Clary and others, 1998; Trudeau & Devlin, 1996). Recent work has identified six distinct motives: expressing personal values related to humanitarian concern for others; gaining understanding, new knowledge, and skills; socializing with friends and earning their approval; obtaining career benefits; helping solve personal problems; and enhancing self-esteem and personal growth (Clary and others, 1998). Note that these motives include egoistic concerns, for volunteering provides many material, social, and emotional benefits. But altruism also plays an important role in volunteer activity, with many volunteers motivated by humanitarian concerns for others and the opportunity to do something worthwhile for them. Group identification also motivates helping when volunteers help out of a sense of social obligation, or in order to create a better society or compensate for injustices to their group.

☐ **HELPING IN THE AIDS EPIDEMIC.** Over the past decade the AIDS epidemic has triggered a wave of volunteers who provide emotional support to and do household chores for people with AIDS, who staff counseling centers and hotlines, who care for infants born with AIDS, and who lobby the government on AIDS-related issues.

Like most volunteer work, these forms of helping usually involve considerable time, trouble, and financial cost to the helper. Helping people with AIDS also involves the special emotional costs of confronting personal tragedy, illness, and death. Why do people get involved in such activities? According to Mark Snyder and Allen Omoto (1992) and Louis Penner and Marcia Finkelstein (1998), who have conducted large surveys of active AIDS volunteers, the reasons vary from individual to individual. Some are motivated by personal feelings of obligation to help other people, others seek personal growth in skills and understanding, still others have connectedness concerns such as feelings of obligation to the gay community, and some simply want to feel better about themselves. Some motives may play more of a role when people initially decide to lend a hand, whereas others

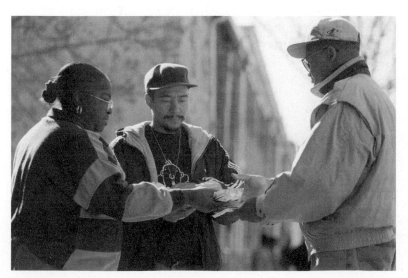

■ **The AIDS epidemic—a powerful motivator.** These members of the outreach program AIDS Delaware are distributing condoms and information in Wilmington, Delaware. The AIDS epidemic has brought out large numbers of volunteers, whose motives range from the personal growth and benefits that helping can bring to intense conviction that there is an obligation to selflessly help others who are suffering. The decision to give such time and effort to a cause is usually the result of considerable thought.

become important in the decision to stay involved. Regardless of the reasons people decide to become and remain involved, however, their decisions are the result of lengthy consideration.

AIDS volunteers thus illustrate that, as we have noted throughout this chapter, many different motives and norms can spur helping. Interestingly, M. Snyder and Omoto (1992) found that volunteers who expressed the seemingly more "selfish" desires for self-esteem and personal growth were more likely to stick with their service over the course of a year than were those driven by the more "humanitarian"-seeming motives. The researchers note that:

> Good, and perhaps romanticized, intentions related to humanitarian concern simply may not be strong enough to sustain volunteers faced with . . . tough realities and personal costs . . . Therefore, volunteer organizations . . . may want to remind volunteers of the personal rewards of their work rather than underscoring how volunteer efforts benefit clients and society. (p. 115)

On the other hand, Penner and Finkelstein found that altruistic motives were the best determinant of length of service (as did Clary & Orenstein, 1991, in a survey of volunteer crisis counselors), although this was more true of the male than of the female participants in their study. Since more than 90% of the males in the study were themselves homosexual, this may have made it easier for some of them to identify and empathize with the primary beneficiaries of their care, and in turn may have made altruistic concerns more salient (Batson, 1991; Penner & Finkelstein, 1998). The bottom line is that people help for many reasons and to fulfill many needs. Volunteers who perform actions that match their individual motivations derive more satisfaction and more enjoyment from their service and are likely to continue helping over the long haul (Clary and others, 1998; M. Snyder & Omoto, 1992).

By now you can see how many factors play a role in determining whether helping occurs or not. The process begins when the individual notices that help is needed. This perception may trigger thoughts about the costs and rewards of helping, feelings of empathy with the victim's suffering, group identification with the victim, or recognition of relevant norms. Although these kinds of information often work together to suggest that action should be taken to benefit another, sometimes competing thoughts, desires, feelings, and obligations have to be reconciled. This process may involve extensive thought or, when cognitive capacity is low, time is short, or emotional arousal is high, a quick snap judgment. The impact of these processes is illustrated in Figure 14.5. As this figure shows, individual processes and social forces work together to make helping and cooperation more or less likely.

Personality Differences in Helping

Personality factors related to helping and cooperation include differences in empathy and concern for others' welfare, as well as in self-efficacy or the confidence that one's actions will be effective.

Are some people just generally more helpful than others across a variety of different situations and types of help, such as rushing to assist in an emergency and volunteering regularly for charitable organizations? Despite the intuitive appeal of this idea, early research found little evidence of consistent personal-

FIGURE 14.5   Multiple factors influence helping

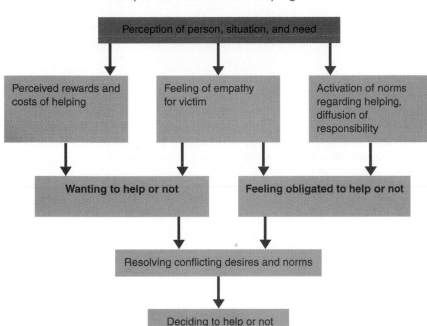

■ Perceptions of the person in need and of the helping situation influence people's desire to help or to refrain from helping. The desire to help (or not) will depend in part on an assessment of the rewards and costs involved in helping and on feelings of empathy with the victim. Perceptions of the person and situation also activate norms and influence feelings of obligation to help. Depending on how potential conflicts are resolved, the decision may be to offer help or to withhold it.

ity differences in helping (Piliavin, Dovidio, Gaertner, & Clark, 1981) and instead stressed the importance of situational factors such as the victim's perceived deservingness or diffusion of responsibility. More recently, however, consistent patterns have been identified in the types of people who are the most likely to help (Graziano & Eisenberg, 1997). These patterns underline the importance of the kinds of motives and processing patterns that we have already discussed. One personality variable that consistently increases helping is the tendency to empathize with others and to be concerned for others' welfare (M. H. Davis, 1983; Penner and others, 1995). People who are more empathetic naturally tend to be more emotionally moved by others' suffering, and therefore more motivated to help in large as well as small ways. Indeed, Oliner and Oliner (1988) found that heroic rescuers of Jews in the Third Reich tended to be more empathetic than others. The second personality variable associated with helping is self-efficacy, the confidence that one's actions are likely to be successful (Graziano & Eisenberg, 1997). Once empathetic concern is aroused, the belief that one *can* effectively help is crucial in setting helping behavior in motion. Like empathy, self-efficacy is related to small and short-term forms of help as well as to long-term patterns of volunteering, as Colby and Damon (1992) found in a study of 22 life-long altruists. The importance of these individual differences in empathy and self-efficacy underlines the way helping depends on both seeing others' need and seeing oneself as able to help.

Cooperating in social dilemmas is also related to general personality orientations. Some people generally prefer to cooperate in such situations, while others approach dilemmas from an individualist perspective, seeking to maximize their own rewards without regard for others' outcomes, and still others adopt a competitive perspective, evidently seeing dilemmas as opportunities to "win" more than the other players do (McClintock & Liebrand, 1988). Interestingly, people who generally cooperate in dilemmas also tend to help more in other ways, for example, by volunteering more hours of their time for a worthy cause (McClintock & Allison, 1989). This finding suggests that cooperatively seeking the group's good in a social dilemma and interpersonal forms of helping such as volunteering have common motivational roots.

Prosocial Behavior in Society

Help That Helps; Help That Hurts

Receiving help can have negative as well as positive consequences, especially if recipients cannot reciprocate because of an unequal power relationship between helper and helped or because receiving help makes them look and feel less competent.

Helpers usually feel good about themselves (Millar, Millar, & Tesser, 1988). But how does it feel to receive help? It depends on the recipient's need and on how being helped affects their self-esteem. Help that relieves physical suffering or mental anguish—a hot meal on an empty stomach, a safe escort across a busy street, or rescue from a house fire—is always welcome. Help that creates a positive relationship between helper and helped is welcome too. Cooperation builds trust and respect and helpers feel protective and proud of the person they benefited. Those on the receiving end of help and cooperation typically feel gratitude. The popular U.S. television show *Unsolved Mysteries* has a special segment on people searching for someone who helped them long ago—gave them a helping hand when they were down, nursed them through a long illness, showed faith in them as they started a difficult phase in life. Generally, the beneficiaries just want to say thank you.

However, receiving help is not always positive. First, help can make people feel that they owe a favor, and that can be a problem for those who are unable to reciprocate (Gross & Latané, 1974). People who cannot return a favor may resent the help and derogate their helper (J. D. Fisher, Nadler, & Whitcher-Alagner, 1982). Second, receiving help can make someone look and feel less capable or competent, robbing them of the pride and satisfaction that typically comes with success (D. T. Gilbert & Silvera, 1996).

The problem is that helping sends a mixed message. While help can convey a positive message of caring, it also has negative implications: "I am more powerful, more able, more in control than you—you need my help!" The beneficiary is left to wonder, "Do they think I'm worthy of help and encouragement? Or do they think I couldn't make it without special treatment?" This point has implications for the controversial topic of affirmative action. For example, governments, schools, and employers may implement programs to offer special help to members of groups that have traditionally suffered discrimination and exclusion. But the very existence of such programs, unless they are designed with extreme sensitivity, may imply that members of those groups somehow lack the ability to make it on their own.

Jeffrey Fisher and Arie Nadler (J. D. Fisher and others, 1982; Nadler & Fisher, 1986) call these opposing messages the self-supportive and the self-threatening aspects of receiving help. If recipients of help feel supported, they respond with gratitude. If the help seems threatening to their self-esteem, they dislike the helper and they may refuse future help. Perhaps this mixed message explains a familiar stereotype about gender differences in help-seeking: Men would rather get lost than ask for directions, whereas women don't mind asking a bit! Deborah Tannen (1990) argues that men are generally more sensitive to the status implications of requesting and receiving help, while women are more attuned to the positive relationships help can create.

Increasing Prosocial Behavior in Society

Helping in society can be increased by making needs clear, teaching and activating helping norms, fostering helpful self-concepts, focusing rather than diffusing responsibility, and promoting connectedness to engender empathy, altruism, and group identification.

For social psychologists, understanding helping and cooperation is more than just a theoretical concern. Helping is essential to group life and social functioning, and insights from research can show us how to increase both the giving of help and our chances of receiving it when we are in need.

1. *Reduce ambiguity:* Make the need for help and cooperation clear. If you are injured in a fall, don't rely on the fact that passersby can see that you are bleeding. Make your need obvious—by shouting "Help me," for example—to increase your chances of receiving aid (R. D. Clark & Word, 1972). The benefits of making the need for help clear have been demonstrated in studies of why people report crimes (Bickman, 1979; Bickman & Rosenbaum, 1977). Participants in these studies witnessed a staged shoplifting, which an experimental confederate interpreted for one group of participants ("Say, look at her. She's shoplifting. She put that in her purse") while remaining silent with the other group. Participants who had the event interpreted for them were more likely to report the crime than those who did not. Similarly, many people do not understand the nature of a social dilemma and how interdependent their own and the group's outcomes are.

2. *Increase internal attributions for helping and cooperation.* If you need your friends to donate blood for a family member who is seriously ill, one way to encourage their generosity is to foster a helpful self-concept, so motivation is internal rather than external. Daniel Batson and his colleagues have shown that people doing good deeds for their own sake rather than for external rewards are likely to see themselves as genuinely altruistic people and to get hooked on helping (Batson, Coke, Jasnoski, & Hanson, 1978; Batson, Fultz, Schoenrade, & Paduano, 1987). In their experiment, the researchers led people to attribute a helpful act either to external factors ("I guess we have no choice") or to their own compassion ("the guy really needed help"). When later asked to help on an unrelated task, more than twice as many "compassionate" participants volunteered. Similarly, people often give blood originally because of inducements and incentives, but after multiple donations they come to view themselves as giving and generous people. People who think of themselves as helpful are likely to help again (Piliavin and others, 1982). Similarly, linking individual efforts to the outcome of the group allows people a sense of self-efficacy, making it more likely that they will act on the group's behalf again.

3. *Teach norms that support helping and cooperation.* Families and schools can reinforce norms supporting social responsibility and prosocial behavior both by explicit teaching and by personal examples or models (Rushton, 1975). Research on the impact of the media on behavior confirms that seeing promotes doing (Johnston & Ettema, 1986). In one study, preschoolers who watched episodes of the U.S. television program *Mr. Rogers' Neighborhood*, which promotes compassion and cooperative social values, were more helpful than children who saw neutral or aggressive programs (A. K. Stein & Friedrich, 1972). Models like the heroic rescuers helping in the emergency situations portrayed on shows like *Rescue 911* can increase the accessibility of norms supporting helping, demonstrate possible ways to help, and make clear the positive consequences of helping (Krebs, 1970).

4. *Activate prosocial norms.* Social norms that support helping have to be brought to mind before they can guide behavior. In an emergency situation, directions like, "That small child needs help" or "That elderly man needs a coat over him" can activate norms of social responsibility to the old, young, and weak. In one condition of Bickman's crime-reporting study, the observer commented: "We saw the shoplifting. We should report it. It's our responsibility." Activating the norm boosted reporting of the incident to store management (Bickman, 1979; Bickman & Rosenbaum, 1977). Similarly, activating norms like, "Everyone should do their share" or "Every individual makes a difference" can increase cooperation for the collective rather than individual good. Making people self-aware often brings these group or personal standards to mind. Women who had just seen their own image on a television monitor were more likely than others to volunteer their time and money to a needy cause (Duval, Duval, & Neely, 1979). Similarly, passersby who had just had their picture taken were more likely than ordinary passersby to help when an experimenter staged a small accident nearby (Hoover, Wood, & Knowles, 1983).

5. *Infuse, don't diffuse responsibility.* Directions that activate norms are not particularly useful if they are broadcast to the world at large. Focusing responsibility on specific people makes normative pressures to help more insistent, just as diffusing responsibility among many people lessens each one's feelings of obligation to help. To get help, therefore, make it clear whom you want help from (Moriarty, 1975). If you are lying bleeding in the street, don't just shout, "Help me!", which might lead most people to convince themselves that someone else will do so. Focus on a particular individual and specifically ask that person to help: "You there in the red jacket! Help me now!"

6. *Promote identification with those who need help and cooperation.* No matter what the need—emergency or long term—a feeling of connectedness with the person in need breeds empathy and increases willingness to help. This principle—that we help others to whom we are connected as if we were helping ourselves—works with kin, friends, and in-groups. Connectedness is what motivates helping as an end in and of itself, and thus can sustain helping even if no personal rewards are involved. Perhaps this is why religious faith can be a powerful motivator for giving (Colasanto, 1989). The language of the scriptures—"love your neighbor," "children of Allah," and the "human family"—remind us of our connectedness with all humankind, increasing action that benefits others.

The diversity of these recommendations reflects the large number of fac
tors that can influence prosocial behavior, but the diversity should come as no
real surprise. Helping is a microcosm of human behavior: a series of judgments
influenced by what we see and who we are, by our groups and our norms, by
what we think and how we feel, until judgment culminates in action.

CONCLUDING COMMENTS

 When people provide help and benefits to other people, their activities inevitably reflect the same social and cognitive processes
that you have seen exemplified in every other chapter of this
book. Whether we deliver aid in an emergency situation or remain on the sidelines, whether we make charitable and philanthropic activities part of our lives or go about our own daily business depends vitally on a
true construction of reality. How we interpret cues and signs that help is
needed, and how others around us interpret those signals, work together to
determine whether helping seems appropriate and achievable. Going out of
our way to benefit others fulfils our fundamental need to be connected to
others, but because it can bring a variety of rewards in return, it also makes
us feel more competence and mastery of our environment. Research has often focused on the kinds of helping decisions that need to be made on the basis of rapid and superficial processing. Perhaps, though, the kinds of helping
that make an enduring difference to communities are more likely to result
from long-term, extensive weighing of the pros and cons of getting involved.

Because helping and cooperation reflect the same principles as all
other types of social behavior, we must interpret with caution statements
that self-sacrifice is the essence of what is means to be a social being. In
fact, we hope that as you've read this chapter the many parallels between
our propensity to help and our propensity to hurt, discussed in the previous chapter, have struck you. Examine Table 14.3 to see many of these parallels for yourself.

Seeing the connections between helping and cooperation and other
forms of social behavior also makes it clear that these aspects of social life
are not alone in having moral implications. Almost all aspects of social
behavior involve issues of right and wrong, including how people handle
conflicts in close relationships (chapter 11), whether they obey or disobey
destructive authorities (chapter 10), whether they stand up for their own
views or go along with the majority in the case of groupthink (chapter 9),
and whether they let their own group's self-interest dictate unjust treatment
of others (chapter 6), to mention just some examples. At the heart of all these
different behaviors lie the issues of responsibility and choice.

We are also used to thinking about helping and cooperating as occurring among those who meet face-to-face or interact on the street, in factories, in families, or in communities. We ordinarily don't reflect on the
fact that almost every aspect of our lives, even our long-term survival,
also depends on actions that involve others we never see. The rapid destruction of the global environment is less a failure of technology than a
failure to solve large-scale social dilemmas. This is true whether individual nations exploit renewable natural resources, such as fish populations

CHAPTER 14 THEMES

- **Construction of Reality**
  Interpretations of others'
  situations, not their actual
  needs, influence helping and
  cooperation.

- **Pervasiveness of Social
  Influence**
  Helping and cooperation are
  fundamentally shaped by social norms.

- **Striving for Mastery**
  Helping and cooperation
  are often motivated by the
  prospect of concrete rewards
  for the helper.

- **Seeking Connectedness**
  Helping and cooperation often
  flow from feelings of identification and connectedness with
  others.

- **Valuing Me and Mine**
  We are likely to treat fellow in-
  group members with cooperation and altruism.

- **Accessibility**
  The accessibility of norms
  can increase their impact on
  helping.

- **Superficiality Verus Depth**
  In-depth processing can promote long-term, committed
  helping.

TABLE 14.3. Parallels Between Prosocial and Aggressive Behavior

Parallel in:	Prosocial Behavior	Aggressive Behavior
Construction of reality	Many (sometimes conflicting) pieces of information (cues, attitudes, norms) influence whether helping occurs.	Many (sometimes conflicting) pieces of information (cues, attitudes, norms) influence whether aggression occurs.
Pervasive social influence	When situations are ambiguous, people sometimes look to others to see if helping is appropriate.	When situations are ambiguous, people sometimes look to others to see if aggression is appropriate.
	Norms—like the norm of reciprocity or the norm of "minding your own business"—can encourage or discourage helping.	Norms—like the norm of reciprocity or the norm "pick on someone your own size"—can encourage or discourage aggression.
Motivational principles	People sometimes help others purely for mastery of rewards it brings them.	Instrumental aggression and realistic conflict often occur as people strive for mastery of rewards.
	Because of connectedness needs, people often help others with whom they empathize or identify without regard to the costs involved.	When connectedness or respect is threatened, emotional aggression and intergroup conflict occur without regard to the costs involved.
	Empathy and identification are more likely when the victim is an in-group rather than an out-group member.	Aggression and competition over positive identity are more likely when the provokers are out-group rather than in-group members.
Processing principles	Information relevant to helping can be dealt with superficially or in great depth.	Information relevant to aggression and conflict can be dealt with superficially or considered in great depth.
	Factors that limit systematic processing—emotion or time constraints—make only the most salient cues likely to be used.	Factors that limit systematic thinking—emotion, alcohol, distracting stressors—increase the influence of salient cues.
	Systematic processing often increases prosocial behavior by increasing the impact of multiple pieces of information like accurate interpretation of need, empathy, and prosocial norms.	Systematic thinking often decreases aggression by increasing the impact of multiple pieces of information like accurate interpretation of provocation, nonaggressive norms, or alternative solutions, and by decreasing anger.

and energy sources, or such abstract "resources" as the earth's ability to eliminate pollution and recycle wastes. For example, biological and physical processes can absorb only limited amounts of emitted carbon dioxide and other "greenhouse gases." Because humans are producing so much more than that amount, the composition of the atmosphere is changing, leading many geoscientists to predict massive global climate changes. In the very near future, however, we will all have to learn to identify with larger groups so that our motives and abilities to benefit others extend beyond the usual sphere. Our current state of global interdependence is historically recent, and our sense of common purpose has not yet caught up to this situation. We have yet to learn that our choices to help and cooperate—as individuals and as nations—have implications beyond our private well-being and our national interest.

S U M M A R Y

 When Do People Help? Prosocial behavior, or behavior intended to help another person or group, is crucially dependent on people's perception of someone as both needing and deserving help. The ability and motivation to pay attention to others' needs influence whether people think help is needed, as does the behavior of other people in the situation. People are more likely to help those they see as deserving because they are not responsible for their own need.

People sometimes help because social norms, their own standards, or the behavior of others show them that it is appropriate to do so. Not all norms promote helping, however, and sometimes the presence of other potential helpers can diffuse responsibility, diminishing the normative pressures to help.

Why Do People Help? Helping for Mastery and Connectedness. Evolutionary principles suggest that some forms of helping, such as reciprocal helping or helping kin, have been naturally selected because they increase survival. In humans, however, cognitive and social processes mediate such biologically driven helping.

Help may be motivated by perceived rewards for the helper or deterred by perceived costs or risks. These rewards and risks can be emotional: People sometimes help to alleviate their own distress at the victim's suffering. In these cases helping is motivated by **egoism.**

People are often motivated by a feeling of empathy to relieve another's suffering, regardless of personal rewards and costs. This helping reflects **altruism,** because it is not motivated by even indirect or emotional rewards for the helper.

In a **social dilemma,** rewards for each individual are in direct conflict with what is best for the group. However, people can be motivated by feelings of group connectedness to act for the good of the group, regardless of personal costs or benefits. When group identification increases commitment to shared goals and norms, social dilemmas can be successfully resolved.

Role of Superficial or Systematic Processing in Helping and Cooperation. When desires and norms conflict, various factors may be considered superficially or thought through extensively before a decision about helping is made. Emotions can play a role in this process, for strong emotion disrupts extensive processing. When helping is a considered decision, though, it can result in a long-term commitment.

Personality factors related to helping and cooperation include differences in empathy and concern for others' welfare, as well as in self-efficacy or the confidence that one's actions will be effective.

Prosocial Behavior in Society. Receiving help can have negative as well as positive consequences, especially if recipients cannot reciprocate because of an unequal power relationship between helper and helped or because receiving help makes them look and feel less competent.

Helping in society can be increased by making needs clear, teaching and activating helping norms, fostering helpful self-concepts, focusing rather than diffusing responsibility, and promoting connectedness to engender empathy, altruism, and group identification.

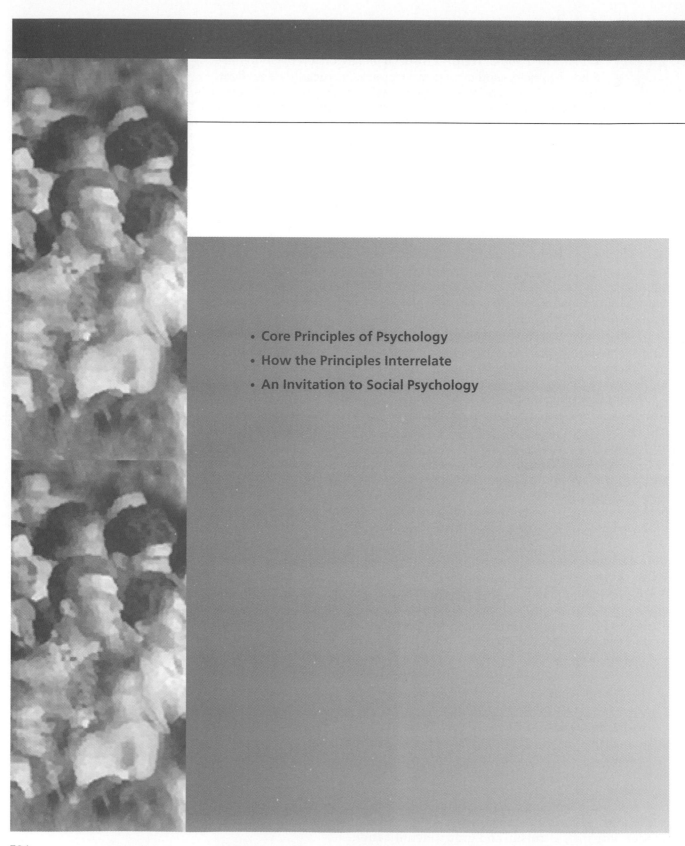

- Core Principles of Psychology
- How the Principles Interrelate
- An Invitation to Social Psychology

Epilogue

ow that we are at the end of our journey, we hope you have come
to appreciate the incredible diversity of behavior that social psychologists study. We also hope you noticed a few key ideas coming up
again and again as we described such diverse topics as impression formation, intergroup conflict, close relationships, and attitude change. In fact,
just as a limited number of chemical elements can be combined to form millions of different substances, so a set of basic principles can be seen to underlie all social behavior. It is this orderliness underlying diversity that makes
social psychology a unified field instead of a random collection of interesting
topics.

Core Principles of Social Psychology

The principles we highlighted throughout this text are those we see as most
important for understanding the findings and theories of social psychology.
Let's take a final look at how we can use these eight principles to help understand the wide range of social behavior we encounter in everyday life.

- Whether we are alone or with others, we construct social reality as
  we form impressions of other people and groups (chapters 3 and 5)
  and as we act in ways that reflect our own attitudes and group
  norms (chapters 8 and 10). This is why we so often react to unexpected, unusual, or ambiguous events by immediately turning to
  others and asking, "Do you smell gas?" or "Was that an earthquake?" or "So what have *you* heard about Bill?"

- The pervasive effects of social influence are evident when we conform to the opinions of important groups (chapter 9) and cooperate
  or compete with others (chapters 13 and 14). Next time you find
  yourself caught up in the latest clothing fad, realize that you just
  said something your dad always used to say, or feel uncomfortable

about expressing your political views, remind yourself of the power and pervasiveness of social influence.

- Our strivings for mastery explain why we want to form accurate opinions and attitudes about ourselves and others (chapters 4 and 7) and why we are capable of helping or harming others in order to gain rewards (chapters 13 and 14). This principle offers insights into why we work so hard to find out what instructors want in test answers, why group efforts can be so much more successful than any one person's efforts (chapter 12), and why we spend so much time trying to learn who we really are.

- We seek connectedness with others when we conform to group norms (chapters 9 and 12) and when we form close relationships with others (chapter 11). This principle explains why many people feel empty and incomplete when they lack intimate relationships, why the support of a good friend seems to make daily hassles as well as big crises easier to cope with, and why our memberships in groups and our relationships with others are some of the most important aspects of human life.

- Our desire to value me and mine is evident in our efforts to feel good about ourselves as individuals and as members of groups (chapters 4 and 6). It also helps explain why we act against out-group members while often behaving with kindness and altruism toward members of the in-group (chapters 13 and 14). Perhaps understanding the me-and-mine principle will alert you to the moments when your group puts others down just to make yourselves feel better. It may also help explain why news of an earthquake in a nearby state elicits more donations than news of a similar tragedy in some distant place.

- The processing principle of accessibility is responsible for our using easily grasped information to form our impressions of other people and our attitudes (chapters 3 and 7) and for the times we find ourselves conforming to accessible norms (chapters 6 and 10). After staring blankly at the rows of breakfast cereal in the supermarket, have you ever just grabbed the first one you could remember hearing about? Have you ever realized that you'd felt compelled to exchange gifts with someone you don't really like? Accessibility may have been at work.

- The principle of conservatism accounts for the persistence of first impressions and stereotypes (chapters 3 and 5) and also for the difficulties minorities experience in swaying a majority's opinion (chapter 9). If conservatism were not such a powerful influence on our thinking, advertisers wouldn't have to spend so much money trying to persuade us, and friends wouldn't have to work so hard to change our mistaken snap judgments.

- Finally, the principle of superficial versus extensive processing operates when we decide how much thought to devote to understanding a member of a stereotyped group (chapter 5) or to acting in accordance with our attitudes (chapter 8). This principle helps explain why we often make snap judgments when the stakes are low but give considerable thought to matters of importance.

Of course, these are just a few examples of the principles at work. We hope that as you review or reread the chapters, you will think of others. We also hope these principles will help you take a fresh look at events in your own lives. Perhaps you now see why making a good first impression at a job interview is important (conservatism), why you feel so good when your favorite team wins (me and mine), or why the whole world looks bleak when you're feeling low (accessibility). You may be better able to understand why people care so much about the majority point of view (connectedness) but also how the majority's opinion can sometimes be changed by minority dissent (systematic processing). If these ideas help you make sense of the world in which you live, our goals for this book have been achieved.

How the Principles Interrelate

Although we have described the eight principles separately so that you can see how they operate, we do not mean to suggest that they are unrelated to each other. They operate together, usually in a harmonious fashion.

Part of the reason we construct reality, for example, is because we want to master the environment, and part of the reason we influence others and accept social influence is because we seek connectedness. Social influence is important because we want to construct an appropriate and correct reality, and we need other people to do so. Accessibility helps us make judgments quickly and efficiently, which in turn helps us to master the environment we construct. It also means that we pay most attention to those closest to us, which helps us achieve connectedness and makes possible the give and take of social influence. The principle of conservatism, on the other hand, helps us maintain a stable view of the world—how would we be able to master the environment or form relationships with others if our views of them changed from minute to minute? Superficial versus systematic processing is the moderating principle, the fulcrum that keeps us balanced between the stability of conservatism and the flux of accessibility. For example, receiving unexpected or inconsistent information from those connected to us makes us think hard, opening the way for change.

Although the principles usually operate together to produce positive outcomes, they sometimes can result in conflicts and paradoxes. For example, the shortcuts we use to make inferences are often efficient routes to the right answer, but they sometimes lead us astray (chapter 3). Relying on social consensus often helps people master the environment and achieve connectedness, but it also can lead to mindless acceptance of a dangerous status quo (chapter 9). Thus, depending on the circumstances, the same motives and processes produce useful and valuable outcomes or misleading and destructive ones. In fact, almost every aspect of social behavior has an up side and a down side, whether that behavior is adherence to norms like obedience and reciprocity (chapter 10) or the biased thinking we use to elevate our self-esteem, sometimes by disparaging other people and groups (chapters 4 and 6).

These examples of ways in which the principles work with and against one another are not a complete list. We hope you have found other meaningful interrelationships that link different types and forms of social behavior.

An Invitation to Social Psychology

When you first picked up this textbook, you probably expected it to tell you how much social psychologists know. Were you surprised to discover how many things we *don't* know? Our understanding of social behavior still has many gaping holes and many unresolved issues because research in social psychology, like research in all fields of human knowledge, has been shaped by its historical development and social context. In the late 1800s, when researchers were just beginning to ask social-psychological questions, nobody could have written down the list of principles we just presented and used them to guide research. (Correspondingly, 20 years from now, the set of principles that social psychologists think are most important may have changed again.) Instead, as we have said, specific events have inspired and guided researchers' questions. The most important events for North American social psychology were the Nazi domination of Europe and the Second World War, which gave rise to research areas involving persuasion, prejudice, obedience to authority, and conformity.

As research traditions grew up around socially significant and culturally relevant issues, other areas were relatively neglected. For instance, the social effects of drug abuse, heterogeneity in the work force, and variations in family composition were not widespread enough to gain scientists' attention 50 years ago, but they certainly are today. Many important issues involving group identification, kin and friend relationships, and social stability and change have been neglected, perhaps because so much social-psychological research to date has been done in the individually oriented United States. As social psychology becomes a global enterprise, questions of more concern to non-Western societies may come to the fore. For example, the effects of social change are of particular importance to social psychologists in developing countries, who underscore that social psychology should be even more active as a positive force in bringing about and guiding such change. And though much is known about how people form and change attitudes on the basis of information, much less is known about the impact of values, ethics, and religious convictions on people's social behavior. These are just a few of the many areas in which social psychology needs to grow and develop.

We mention these gaps in knowledge and opportunities for development because we want you to understand that social psychology is a young science. One unfortunate characteristic that is almost inherent in the nature of textbooks is that they convey the impression that everything worth learning has already been learned: that all the *i*'s have been dotted, all the *t*'s have been crossed, and everyone agrees about everything. How boring social psychology would be if this were true. But it is not true; social psychologists are well aware of how much we still need to know about human social behavior. We guarantee that as you read these words, whatever the day or time, social psychologists somewhere—in their offices, laboratories, schools, businesses, hospitals, or out on the streets—are planning or carrying out research or reporting new findings. If that idea appeals to you and if you find yourself interested in the topics and issues social psychologists study, we invite you to consider becoming a social psychologist. You could help to shape the future of our science and contribute to what we know about the endlessly fascinating forms of human social behavior.

Photography Credits

Glossary

A

accessibility The processing principle that the information that is most readily available generally has the most impact on thoughts, feelings, and behavior.

actor-observer differences in attribution The tendency to attribute our own behaviors to situational causes while seeing others' acts as due to their inner characteristics.

aggression Behavior intended to harm someone else.

altruism Behavior intended to help someone else without any prospect of personal rewards for the helper.

association A link between two or more cognitive representations.

attachment styles People's basic securely attached, avoidant, or anxious orientation toward others in close relationships.

attitude A cognitive representation that summarizes an individual's evaluation of a particular person, group, thing, action, or idea.

B

BIRG (bask in reflected glory) A way of boosting self-esteem by identifying oneself with the accomplishments or good qualities of fellow in-group members.

C

causal attribution A judgment about the cause of a behavior or other event.

close relationship A relationship involving strong and frequent interdependence in many domains of life.

cognitive appraisal An individual's interpretation of a self-relevant event or situation that directs emotional responses and behavior.

cognitive dissonance An unpleasant state caused by people's awareness of inconsistency among various beliefs, attitudes, or actions.

cognitive processes The ways in which our memories, perceptions, thoughts, emotions, and motives influence our understanding of the world and guide our actions.

cognitive representation A body of knowledge that an individual has stored in memory.

commitment The combined forces that hold the partners together in an enduring relationship.

communal relationship A relationship in which people reward their partner out of direct concern and to show caring.

conflict A perceived incompatibility of goals between two or more parties.

conformity The convergence of individuals' thoughts, feelings, or behavior toward a social norm.

conservatism The processing principle that individuals' and groups' views of the world are slow to change and prone to perpetuate themselves.

construct validity The extent to which the independent and dependent variables used in research correspond to the theoretical constructs under investigation.

construction of reality The axiom that each person's view of reality is a construction, shaped both by cognitive processes (the ways our minds work) and by social processes (input from others either actually present or imagined).

constructs Abstract and general concepts that are used in theories and that are not directly observable.

contact hypothesis The theory that certain types of direct contact between members of hostile groups will reduce stereotyping and prejudice.

coping strategies   Efforts undertaken to reduce negative consequences of self-threatening events.

CORF (cut off reflected failure)   The act of criticizing or distancing oneself from an in-group or a group member who is viewed negatively.

correspondence bias   The tendency to infer an actor's personal characteristics from observed behaviors, even when the inference is unjustified because other possible causes of the behavior exist.

correspondent inference   The process of characterizing someone as having a personality trait that corresponds to his or her observed behavior.

D

debriefing   Informing research participants—as soon as possible after the completion of their participation in research—about the purposes, procedures, and scientific value of the study, and discussing any questions participants may have.

demand characteristics   Cues in a research setting that lead participants to make inferences about what researchers expect or desire and that therefore bias how the participants act.

dependent variable   A concrete measurement of a construct that is thought to be influenced by other constructs.

discrimination   Any positive or negative behavior that is directed toward a social group and its members.

door-in-the-face technique   A technique in which the influencer makes an initial request so large that it will be rejected, and follows it with a smaller request that looks like a concession, making it more likely that the other person will concede in turn.

E

egoism   Behavior motivated by the desire to obtain personal rewards.

elaboration   The generation of favorable or unfavorable reactions to the content of a message.

exchange relationship   A relationship in which people exchange rewards in order to receive benefits in return.

experimental research   A research design in which researchers randomly assign participants to different groups and manipulate one or more independent variables.

external validity   The extent to which research results can be generalized to other appropriate people, times, and settings.

F

face-to-face group   Two or more individuals who interact and influence each other.

false consensus effect   The tendency to overestimate others' agreement with one's own opinions, characteristics, and behaviors.

foot-in-the-door technique   A technique for increasing compliance with a large request by first asking people to go along with a smaller request.

G

group polarization   The process by which a group's initial average position becomes more extreme following group interaction.

groupthink   Group decision making that is impaired by the drive to reach consensus regardless of how the consensus is formed.

I

independent variable   A concrete manipulation or measurement of a construct that is thought to influence other constructs.

informed consent   Consent voluntarily given by an individual who decides to participate in a study after being told what will be involved in participation.

interdependence   A situation in which each person's thoughts, emotions, and behaviors influence those of other people.

internal validity   The extent to which it can be concluded that changes in the independent variable actually caused changes in the dependent variable in a research study.

intimacy   A positive emotional bond that includes understanding and support.

L

leadership   A process in which one or more group members are permitted to influence and motivate others to help attain group goals.

low-ball technique   A technique in which the influencer secures agreement with a request but then increases the cost of honoring the commitment.

M

mere exposure effect   People's tendency to prefer objects to which they have been more frequently exposed.

minimal intergroup situation   A research situation in which people are categorized, on an arbitrary or trivial basis, into groups that have no history, no conflicts of interest, and no stereotypes.

N

negotiation   The process by which parties in conflict communicate and influence each other to reach agreement.

nonexperimental research   A research design in which both the independent and dependent variables are measured.

norm of obedience to authority   The shared view that people should obey those with legitimate authority.

norm of social commitment   The shared view that people are required to honor their agreements and obligations.

norm of social reciprocity   The shared view that we are obligated to return to others the goods, services, and concessions they offer to us.

O

out-group homogeneity effect   The tendency to see the out-group as relatively more homogeneous and less diverse than the in-group.

P

persuasion   The process of forming, reinforcing, or changing attitudes by communication.

persuasion heuristic   An association of superficial cues with positive or negative evaluations, which allows people to evaluate an object quickly and without much thought.

pervasiveness of social influence   The axiom that other people influence virtually all of our thoughts, feelings, and behavior, whether those others are physically present or not.

prejudice   A positive or negative evaluation of a social group and its members.

priming   The activation of a cognitive representation to increase its accessibility and thus the likelihood that it will be used.

private conformity   Private acceptance of social norms.

prosocial behavior   Behavior intended to help someone else.

public conformity   Overt behavior consistent with social norms that are not privately accepted.

R

random assignment   The procedure of assigning participants to different experimental groups so that every participant has exactly the same chance as every other participant of being in any given group.

reactance   The motive to protect or restore a threatened sense of behavioral freedom.

realistic conflict theory   The theory that intergroup hostility arises from competition among groups for scarce but valued material resources.

reference group   Those people accepted as an appropriate source of information for a judgment because they share the attributes relevant for making that judgment.

relative deprivation theory   The theory that feelings of discontent arise from the belief that other individuals or other groups are better off.

replication   Conducting new studies in an effort to provide evidence for the same theoretically predicted relations found in prior research.

S

salience   The ability of a cue to attract attention in its context.

scientific theory   A statement that satisfies three requirements: It is about constructs; it describes causal relations; and it is general in scope, although the range of generality differs for different theories.

seeking connectedness   The motivational principle that people seek support, liking, and acceptance from the people and groups they care about and value.

self-awareness   A state of heightened awareness of the self, including our internal standards and whether we measure up to them.

self-categorization   The process of seeing oneself as a member of a social group.

self-complexity   The number and diversity of the self-aspects that people develop for different roles, activities and relationships.

self-concept   All of an individual's knowledge about his or her personal qualities.

self-discrepancy theory   The theory that people evaluate themselves against internal "ideal" and "ought" standards, producing specific emotional consequences.

self-enhancing bias   Any tendency to gather or interpret information concerning the self in a way that leads to overly positive evaluations.

self-esteem   An individual's positive or negative evaluation of himself or herself.

self-expression   A motive for choosing behaviors that are intended to reflect and express the self-concept.

self-fulfilling prophecy   The process by which one person's expectations about another become reality by eliciting behaviors that confirm the expectations.

self-monitoring   A personality characteristic defined as the degree to which people are sensitive to the demands of social situations and shape their behaviors accordingly.

self-perception theory   The theory that we make inferences about our personal characteristics on the basis of our overt behaviors when internal cues are weak or ambiguous.

self-presentation   A motive for choosing behaviors intended to create in observers a desired impression of the self.

social categorization   The process of identifying individual people as members of a social group because they share certain features that are typical of the group.

social change   The strategy of improving the overall societal situation of a stigmatized group.

social comparison theory   The theory that people learn about and evaluate their personal qualities by comparing themselves to others.

social desirability response bias   People's tendency to act in ways that they believe others find acceptable and approve of.

social dilemma   A form of interdependence in which the most rewarding action for each individual will, if chosen by all individuals, produce a negative outcome for the entire group.

social facilitation   The finding that in the presence of others highly accessible responses become more likely and less accessible responses become less likely.

social group   Two or more people who share some common characteristic that is socially meaningful for themselves or for others.

social identity theory   The theory that people's motivation to derive positive self-esteem from their group memberships is one driving force behind in-group bias.

social identity   Those aspects of the self-concept that derive from an individual's knowledge and feelings about the group memberships he or she shares with others.

social interdependence   Reliance on other members of the group for feelings of connectedness, social and emotional rewards, and a positive social identity.

social loafing   The tendency to exert less effort on a task when an individual's efforts are an unidentifiable part of a group than when the same task is performed alone.

social mobility   The strategy of individual escape, either physical or psychological, from a stigmatized group.

social norms   Generally accepted ways of thinking, feeling, or behaving that people in a group agree on and endorse as right and proper.

social processes   The ways in which input from the people and groups around us affect our thoughts, feelings, and actions.

social psychology   The scientific study of the effects of social and cognitive processes on the way individuals perceive, influence, and relate to others.

social support   Emotional and physical coping resources provided by other people.

stereotype   A cognitive representation or impression of a social group that people form by associating particular characteristics and emotions with the group.

stereotype threat   The fear of confirming others' negative stereotype of your group.

striving for mastery   The motivational principle that people seek to understand and predict events in the social world in order to obtain rewards.

subtype   A narrower and more specific social group, such as housewife or feminist, that is included within a broad social group, like women.

superficial processing   Relying on accessible information to make inferences or judgments, while expending little effort in processing.

superficiality versus depth   The processing principle that people ordinarily put little effort into dealing with information, but at times are motivated to consider information in more depth.

superordinate goals   Shared goals that can be attained only if groups work together.

symbolic prejudice   Hatred for out-groups that arises, together with the exaltation of in-group symbols, in response to perceived threat.

systematic processing   Giving thorough, effortful consideration to a wide range of information relevant to a judgment.

T

task interdependence   Reliance on other members of a group for mastery of material outcomes that arise from the group's task.

theory of planned behavior   The theory that attitudes, social norms, and perceived control combine to influence behavior.

V

valuing "me and mine"   The motivational principle that people desire to see themselves, and other people and groups connected to themselves, in a positive light.

References

1-day nerd surprised by some reactions. (1992, March 12). *Santa Barbara News Press.* p. A5.

Aaker, D. A., & Myers, J. G. (1987). *Advertising management.* Englewood Cliffs, NJ: Prentice-Hall.

Abelson, R. P., Dasgupta, N., Park, J., & Banaji, M. R. (1998). Perceptions of the collective other. *Personality and Social Psychology Review, 2,* 243–250.

Abelson, R. P., Kinder, D. R., Peters, M. D., & Fiske, S. T. (1982). Affective and semantic components in political person perception. *Journal of Personality and Social Psychology, 42,* 619–630.

Aboud, F. E. (1976). Self-evaluation: Information seeking strategies for interethnic social comparisons. *Journal of Cross Cultural Psychology, 7,* 289–300.

Aboud, F. E., & Taylor, D. M. (1971). Ethnic and role stereotypes: Their relative importance in person perception. *Journal of Social Psychology, 85,* 17–27

Abramovitch, I. (1997, August 12). Rap or rock? For dorm mates that may not be an easy negotiation. *The New York Times,* p. B3.

Abrams, J. (1991, August 31). Survey cites racism in housing. *Santa Barbara News Press,* p. A5.

Abramson, L. Y., Seligman, M. E. P., & Teasdale, J. (1978). Learned helplessness in humans: Critique and reformulation. *Journal of Abnormal Psychology, 87,* 49–74.

Adams, G. R., & Shea, J. A. (1981). Talking and loving: A cross-lagged panel investigation. *Basic and Applied Social Psychology, 2,* 81–88.

Adelmann, P. K., & Zajonc, R. B. (1989). Facial efference and the experience of emotion. *Annual Review of Psychology, 40,* 249–280.

Adler, N. J. (1991). *International dimensions of organizational behavior* (2nd ed.). Boston: PWS-Kent.

Adorno, T. W., Frenkel-Brunswik, E., Levinson, D. J., & Sanford, R. N. (1950). *The authoritarian personality.* New York: Harper.

Agnew, C. R., van Lange, P. A. M., Rusbult, C. E., & Langston, C. A. (1998). Cognitive interdependence: Commitment and the mental representation of close relationships. *Journal of Personality and Social Psychology, 74,* 939–954.

Aiello, J. R., & Kolb, K. J. (1995). Electronic performance monitoring and social context: Impact on productivity and stress. *Journal of Applied Psychology, 80,* 339–353.

Ailes, R. (1988). *You are the message.* New York: Doubleday.

Ainsworth, M., Blehar, M., Waters, E., & Wall, S. (1978). *Patterns of attachment.* Hillsdale, NJ: Erlbaum.

Ajzen, I. (1991). The theory of planned behavior. *Organizational Behavior and Human Decision Processes, 50,* 179–211.

Ajzen, I. (1996). The directive influence of attitudes on behavior. In P. M. Gollwitzer & J. A. Bargh (Eds.), *The psychology of action: Linking cognition and motivation to behavior* (pp. 385–403). New York: Guilford.

Ajzen, I., & Fishbein, M. (1977). Attitude-behavior relations: A theoretical analysis and review of empirical research. *Psychological Bulletin, 84,* 888–918.

Ajzen, I., & Fishbein, M. (1980). *Understanding attitudes and predicting social behavior.* Englewood Cliffs, NJ: Prentice-Hall.

Ajzen, I., & Madden, T. J. (1986). Prediction of goal-directed behavior: Attitudes, intentions, and perceived behavioral control. *Journal of Experimental Social Psychology, 22,* 453–74.

Alagna, S. W., & Reddy, D. M. (1984). Predictors of proficient technique and successful lesion detection in breast self-examination. *Health Psychology, 3,* 113–27.

Alcock, J. E., Carment, D. W., & Sadava, S. W. (1988). *A textbook of social psychology.* Scarborough, ON, Canada: Prentice-Hall.

Allen, B. P. (1988). Dramaturgical quality. *Journal of Social Psychology, 128,* 181–190.

Allen, K. M., Blascovich, J., Tomaka, J., & Kelsey, R. M. (1991). Presence of human friends and pet dogs as moderators of autonomic responses to stress in women. *Journal of Personality and Social Psychology, 61,* 582–589.

Allen, V. L. (1965). Situational factors in conformity. In L. Berkowitz (Ed.), *Advances in experimental social psychology* (Vol. 8, pp. 133–175). New York: Academic Press.

Allen, V. L. (1975). Social support for non-conformity. In L. Berkowitz (Ed.), *Advances in experimental social psychology* (Vol. 18, pp. 2–43). New York: Academic Press.

Allen, V. L., & Wilder, D. A. (1979). Group categorization and belief similarity. *Small Group Behavior, 10,* 73–80.

Allison, S. T., Mackie, D. M., Muller, M. M., & Worth, L. T. (1993). Sequential correspondence biases and perceptions of change: The Castro studies revisited. *Personality and Social Psychology Bulletin, 19,* 151–157.

Allison, S. T., Messick, D. M., & Goethals, G. R. (1989). On being better but not smarter than others: The Muhammad Ali effect. *Social Cognition, 7,* 275–295.

Allison, S. T., & Messick, D. M. (1985). The group attribution error. *Journal of Experimental Social Psychology, 21,* 563–579.

Allison, S. T., & Messick, D. M. (1990). Social decision heuristics in the use of shared resources. *Journal of Behavioral Decision Making, 3,* 195–204.

Alloy, L. B., & Abramson, L. Y. (1979). Judgment of contingency in depressed and nondepressed students: Sadder but wiser? *Journal of Experimental Psychology: General, 108,* 441–485.

Allport, F. H. (1924). *Social psychology.* Boston: Houghton Mifflin.

Allport, G. W. (1935). Attitudes. In G. Murchison (Ed.), *Handbook of social psychology,* Worchester, MA: Clark University Press.

Allport, G. W. (1954). The historical background of modern social psychology. In G. Lindzey (Ed.), *The handbook of social psychology* (Vol. 1, pp. 3–56). Cambridge, MA: Addison-Wesley.

Allport, G. W. (1954). *The nature of prejudice.* New York: Addison-Wesley.

Allport, G. W. (1958). *The nature of prejudice.* Garden City, NY: Doubleday Anchor.

Altman, I., & Taylor, D. A. (1973). *Social penetration.* New York: Holt, Rinehart, Winston

Alvaro, E. M., & Crano, W. D. (1996). Cognitive responses to minority- or majority-based communications: Factors that underlie minority influence. *British Journal of Social Psychology, 35,* 105–121.

Alvaro, E. M., & Crano, W. D. (1997). Indirect minority influence: Evidence for leniency in source evaluation and counterargumentation. *Journal of Personality and Social Psychology, 72,* 949–964.

Amir, Y. (1969). Contact hypothesis in ethnic relations. *Psychological Bulletin, 71,* 319–342.

Andersen, S. M. (1984). Self-knowledge and social inference: II. The diagnosticity of cognitive/affective and behavioral data. *Journal of Personality and Social Psychology, 46,* 294–307.

Andersen, S. M., & Baum, A. (1994). Transference in interpersonal relations: Inferences and affect based on significant-other representations. *Journal of Personality, 62,* 459–497.

Andersen, S. M., & Cole, S. W. (1990). "Do I know you?" The role of significant others in general social perception. *Journal of Personality and Social Psychology, 59,* 384–399.

Andersen, S. M., & Klatsky, R. L. (1987). Traits and social stereotypes: Levels of categorization in person perception. *Journal of Personality and Social Psychology, 53,* 235–246.

Andersen, S. M., & Ross, L. (1984). Self-knowledge and social inference: I. The impact of cognitive/affective and behavioral data. *Journal of Personality and Social Psychology, 46,* 280–293.

Anderson, C. A. (1987). Temperature and aggression: Effects on quarterly, yearly, and city rates of violent and nonviolent crime. *Journal of Personality and Social Psychology, 52,* 1161–1173.

Anderson, C. A., Anderson, K. B., & Deuser, W. E. (1996). Examining an affective aggression framework: Weapon and temperature effects on aggressive thoughts, affect, and attitudes. *Personality and Social Psychology Bulletin, 22,* 366–376.

Anderson, C. A., & Godfrey, S. S. (1987). Thoughts about actions: The effects of specificity and availability of imagined behavioral scripts on expectations about oneself and others. *Social Cognition, 5,* 238–258.

Anderson, C. A., Jennings, D. L., & Arnoult, L. H. (1988). Validity and utility of the attributional style construct at a moderate level of specificity. *Journal of Personality and Social Psychology, 55,* 979–990.

Anderson, N. H. (1981). *Foundations of information integration theory.* New York: Academic Press.

Andreoli, V., & Worchel, S. (1978). Effects of media, communicator, and message position on attitude change. *Public Opinion Quarterly, 42,* 59–70.

Angier, N. (1990, December 13). Anger can ruin more than your day. *New York Times.*

Angier, N. (1990, October 16). Marriage is lifesaver for men after 45. *The New York Times.*

Anthony, T., Copper, C., & Mullen, B. (1992). Cross-racial facial identification: A social cognitive integration. *Personality and Social Psychology Bulletin, 18,* 296–301.

Archer, D., Iratani, B., Kimes, D. B., & Barrios, M. (1983). Face-ism: Five studies of sex differences in facial prominence. *Journal of Personality and Social Psychology, 45,* 725–735.

Archer, R. L. (1980). Self-disclosure. In D. M. Wegner & R. R. Vallacher (Eds.), *The self in social psychology* (pp. 183–207). New York: Oxford University Press.

Arendt, H. (1965). *Eichmann in Jerusalem: A report on the banality of evil.* New York: Viking.

Arkes, H. R., Hackett, C., & Boehm, L. (1989). The generality of the relation between familiarity and judged validity. *Journal of Behavioral Decision Making, 2,* 81–94.

Arkin, R. M. (1981). Self-presentation styles. In J. T. Tedeschi (Ed.), *Impression management theory and social psychological research* (pp. 311–333). New York: Academic Press.

Arnold, M. B. (1960). *Emotion and personality.* New York: Columbia University Press.

Aron, A., & Aron, E. N. (1991). Love and sexuality. In K. McKinney & S. Sprecher (Eds.), *Sexuality in close relationships* (pp. 25–48). Hillsdale, NJ: Erlbaum.

Aron, A., Aron, E. N., & Smollan, D. (1992). Inclusion of Other in the Self scale and the structure of interpersonal closeness. *Journal of Personality and Social Psychology, 63,* 596–612.

Aron, A., Aron, E. N., Tudor, M., & Nelson, G. (1991). Close relationships as including other in the self. *Journal of Personality and Social Psychology, 60,* 241–253.

Aron, A., Paris, M., & Aron, E. N. (1995). Falling in love: Prospective studies of self-concept change. *Journal of Personality and Social Psychology, 69,* 1102–1112.

Aronson, E. (1969). The theory of cognitive dissonance: A current perspective. In L. Berkowitz (Ed.), *Advances in experimental social psychology* (Vol. 4, pp. 1–34). New York: Academic Press.

Aronson, E., & Carlsmith, J. M. (1963). Effect of severity of threat on the devaluation of forbidden behavior. *Journal of Abnormal and Social Psychology, 66,* 584–588.

Aronson, E., Fried, C., & Stone, J. (1991). Overcoming denial and increasing the intention to use condoms through the induction of hypocrisy. *American Journal of Public Health, 81,* 1636–1638.

Aronson, E., & Mills, J. (1959). The effect of severity of initiation on liking for a group. *Journal of Abnormal and Social Psychology, 59*, 177–181.

Aronson, E., & Worchel, S. (1966). Similarity versus liking as determinants of interpersonal attractiveness. *Psychonomic Science, 5*, 157–158.

Aronson, J., Blanton, H., & Cooper, J. (1995). From dissonance to disidentification: Selectivity in the self-affirmation process. *Journal of Personality and Social Psychology, 58*, 1062–1072.

Arriaga, X. B., & Oskamp, S. (Eds.). (in press). *Violence in intimate relationships.* Thousand Oaks, CA: Sage.

Asch, S. E. (1946). Forming impressions of personality. *Journal of Abnormal and Social Psychology, 41*, 258–290.

Asch, S. E. (1951). Effects of group pressure upon the modification and distortion of judgment. In H. Guetzkow (Ed.), *Groups, leadership, and men* (pp. 177–190). Pittsburgh, PA: Carnegie University Press.

Asch, S. E. (1955). Studies of independence and conformity: A minority of one against a unanimous majority. *Psychology Monographs, 70*, 1–70.

Asch, S. E. (1956). Opinions and social pressure. *Scientific American, 193*(5) 31–35.

Asch, S. E., & Zukier, H. (1984). Thinking about persons. *Journal of Personality and Social Psychology, 46*, 1230–1240.

Ashley, J. H. (1976). *Hospitals, paternalism, and the role of the nurse.* New York: Teachers College Press.

Ashmore, R. D. (1981). Sex stereotypes and implicit personality theory. In D. L. Hamilton (Ed.), *Cognitive processes in stereotyping and intergroup behavior* (pp. 37–81). Hillsdale, NJ: Erlbaum.

Ashmore, R. D., & Del Boca, F. K. (1981). Conceptual approaches to stereotypes and stereotyping. In D. L. Hamilton (Ed.), *Cognitive processes in stereotyping and intergroup behavior* (pp. 1–36). Hillsdale, NJ: Erlbaum.

Askenasy, H. (1978). *Are we all Nazis?* Secaucus, NJ: Lyle Stuart.

Astin, A. W., Green, K. C., Korn, W. S., & Schalit, M. (1987). *The American freshman: National norms for Fall 1987.* Los Angeles, CA: Higher Education Research Institute, University of California at Los Angeles.

Atkinson, J., & Huston, T. L. (1984). Sex role orientation and division of labor early in marriage. *Journal of Personality and Social Psychology, 46*, 330–345.

Axsom, D., & Cooper, J. (1985). Cognitive dissonance and psychotherapy: The role of effort justification in inducing weight loss. *Journal of Experimental Psychology, 21*, 149–160.

Axsom, D., Yates, S., & Chaiken, S. (1987). Audience response as a heuristic cue in persuasion. *Journal of Personality and Social Psychology, 53*, 30–40.

Azar, B. (1994, September). Teams that wear blinders are often the cause of tragic errors. *APA Monitor*, p. 23.

Babey, S. H., Queller, S., & Klein, S. B. (1998). The role of expectancy violating behaviors in the representation of trait knowledge: A summary-plus-exception model of social memory. *Social Cognition, 16*, 287–339.

Bagozzi, R. P., Baumgartner, H., & Pieters, R. (1998). Goal-directed emotions. *Cognition and Emotion, 12*, 1–26.

Bakan, D. (1966). *The duality of human existence.* Boston: Beacon Press.

Baker, S. M., & Petty, R. E. (1994). Majority and minority influence: Source position imbalance as a determinant of message scrutiny. *Journal of Personality and Social Psychology, 67*, 5–19.

Baldwin, M. W. (1992). Relational schemas and the processing of social information. *Psychological Bulletin, 112*, 461–484.

Baldwin, M. W., Carrell, S. E., & Lopez, D. F. (1990). Priming relationship schemas: My advisor and the Pope are watching me from the back of my mind. *Journal of Experimental Social Psychology, 26*, 435–454.

Baldwin, M. W., & Sinclair, L. (1996). Self-esteem and "if . . . then" contingencies of interpersonal acceptance. *Journal of Personality and Social Psychology, 71*, 1130–1141.

Bales, R. F. (1953). The equilibrium problem in small groups. In T. Parsons, R. F. Bales, & E. A. Shils (Eds.), *Working papers in the theory of action* (pp. 111–162). Glencoe, IL: Free Press.

Bales, R. F., Cohen, S. P., & Williamson, S. A. (1979). *SYMLOG: A system for the multiple level observation of groups.* New York: Free Press.

Bales, R. F., & Slater, P. E. (1955). Role differentiation. In T. Parsons & R. F. Bales (Eds.), *The family, socialization, and interaction process* (pp. 259–306). Glencoe, IL: Free Press.

Bandura, A. (1973). *Aggression: A social learning analysis.* Englewood Cliffs, NJ: Prentice-Hall.

Bandura, A. (1977a). Self-efficacy: Toward a unifying theory of behavioral change. *Psychological Review, 84*, 191–215.

Bandura, A. (1977b). *Social learning theory.* Englewood Cliffs, NJ: Prentice-Hall.

Bandura, A. (1982). Self-efficacy: Mechanism in human agency. *American Psychologist, 37*, 122–147.

Bandura, A. (1986). The explanatory and predictive scope of self-efficacy theory. Special Issue: Self-efficacy theory in contemporary psychology. *Journal of Social and Clinical Psychology, 4*, 359–373.

Bandura, A., Barbaranelli, C., Caprara, G. V., & Pastorelli, C. (1996). Mechanisms of moral disengagement in the exercise of moral agency. *Journal of Personality and Social Psychology, 71*, 364–374.

Bandura, A., Ross, D., & Ross, S. A. (1961). Transmission of aggression through imitation of aggressive models. *Journal of Abnormal and Social Psychology, 63*, 575–582.

Bandura, A., Ross, D., & Ross, S. A. (1963). Imitation of film-mediated aggressive models. *Journal of Abnormal and Social Psychology, 66*, 3–11.

Banner, L. W. (1983). *American beauty.* Chicago: University of Chicago Press.

Bargh, J. A. (1989). Conditional automaticity: Varieties of automatic influence in social perception and cognition. In J. S. Uleman & J. A. Bargh (Eds.), *Unintended thought* (pp. 3–51). New York: Guilford.

Bargh, J. A., Bond, R. N., Lombardi, W. J., & Tota, M. E. (1986). The additive nature of chronic and temporary sources of construct accessibility. *Journal of Personality and Social Psychology, 50*, 869–878.

Bargh, J. A., Chaiken, S., Raymond, P., & Hymes, C. (1996). The automatic evaluation effect: Unconditional automatic attitude activation with a pronunciation task. *Journal of Experimental Social Psychology, 32*, 104–128.

Bargh, J. A., & Gollwitzer, P. M. (1994). Environmental control of goal-directed action: Automatic and strategic contingencies between situations and behavior. In *Nebraska Symposium on Motivation* (vol. 41, p. 71–124). Lincoln: University of Nebraska Press.

Bargh, J. A., & Pietromonaco, P. (1982). Automatic information processing and social perception: The influence of trait information presented outside of conscious awareness on impression formation. *Journal of Personality and Social Psychology, 43*, 437–449.

Bargh, J. A., & Thein, R. D. (1985). Individual construct accessibility, person memory, and the recall-judgment link: The case of information overload. *Journal of Personality and Social Psychology, 49*, 1129–1146.

Barnet, R. (1971, November). The game of nations. *Harper's, 243*, 53–59.

Baron, R. A. (1972). Aggression as a function of ambient temperature and prior anger arousal. *Journal of Personality and Social Psychology, 21*, 183–189.

Baron, R. A. (1983a). The control of human aggression: An optimistic perspective. *Journal of Social and Clinical Psychology, 1*, 97–119.

Baron, R. A. (1983b). The control of human aggression: A strategy based on incompatible responses. In R. G. Geen & E. Donnerstein (Eds.), *Aggression: Theoretical and empirical reviews* (Vol. 2, pp. 173–190). New York: Academic Press.

Baron, R. A., Baron, P., & Miller, N. (1973). The relation between distraction and persuasion. *Psychological Bulletin, 80*, 310–323.

Baron, R. S. (1986). Distraction-conflict theory: Progress and problems. In L. Berkowitz (Ed.), *Advances in experimental social psychology* (Vol. 19, pp. 1–40). New York: Academic Press.

Baron R. S., & Roper, G. (1976). Reaffirmation of social comparison views of choice shift: Averaging and extremitization in an auto-kinetic situation. *Journal of Personality and Social Psychology, 35*, 521–530.

Baron, R. S., Vandello, J. A., & Brunsman, B. (1996). The forgotten variable in conformity research: Impact of task importance on social influence. *Journal of Personality & Social Psychology, 71*, 915–927.

Bar-Tal, D., & Bar-Tal, Y. (1988). A new perspective for social psychology. In D. Bar-Tal & A. W. Kruglanski (Eds.), *The social psychology of knowledge* (pp. 83–108). Cambridge, England: Cambridge University Press.

Bartis, S., Szymanski, K., & Harkins, S. G. (1988). Evaluation and performance: A two-edged knife. *Personality and Social Psychology Bulletin, 14*, 242–251.

Bass, B. M. (1985). *Leadership and performance beyond expectations.* New York: Free Press.

Bass, B. M. (1990). *Bass and Stogdill's handbook of leadership: Theory, research, and managerial applications* (3rd ed.). New York: Free Press.

Bass, B. M. (1997). Does the transactional-transformational leadership paradigm transcend organizational and national boundaries? *American Psychologist, 52*, 130–139.

Batson, C. D. (1975). Rational processing or rationalization?: The effect of disconfirming information on a stated religious belief. *Journal of Personality and Social Psychology, 32*, 176–184.

Batson, C. D. (1998). Altruism and prosocial behavior. In D. T. Gilbert, S. T. Fiske, & G. Lindzey (Eds.), *Handbook of social psychology* (4th ed., Vol. 2, pp. 282–315). New York: McGraw-Hill.

Batson, C. D. (1991). *The altruism question: Toward a social-psychological answer.* Hillsdale, NJ: Erlbaum.

Batson, C. D., Ahmad, N., Yin, J., Bedell, S. J., Johnson, J. W., Templin, C. M., & Whiteside, A. (1999). Two threats to the common good: Self-interested egoism and empathy-induced altruism. *Personality and Social Psychology Bulletin, 25*, 3–16.

Batson, C. D., Batson, J. G., Slingsby, J. K., Harrell, K. L., Peekna, H. M., & Todd, R. M. (1991). Empathic joy and the empathy-altruism hypothesis. *Journal of Personality and Social Psychology, 61*, 413–426.

Batson, C. D., Batson, J. G., Todd, M., Brummett, B. H., Shaw, L. L., & Aldeguer, C. M. R. (1995). Empathy and the collective good: Caring for one of the others in a social dilemma. *Journal of Personality and Social Psychology, 68*, 619–631.

Batson, C. D., Coke, J. S., Jasnoski, M. L., & Hanson, M. (1978). Buying kindness: effect of an extrinsic incentive for helping on perceived altruism. *Personality and Social Psychology Bulletin, 4*, 86–91.

Batson, C. D., Duncan, B. D., Ackerman, P., Buckley, T., & Birch, K. (1981). Is empathic emotion a source of altruistic motivation? *Journal of Personality and Social Psychology, 40*, 290–302.

Batson, C. D., Dyck, J. L., Brandt, J. R., & Batson, J. G. (1988). Five studies testing two new egoistic alternatives to the empathy-altruism hypothesis. *Journal of Personality and Social Psychology, 55*, 52–77.

Batson, C. D., Fultz, J., Schoenrade, P. A., & Paduano, A. (1987). Critical self-reflection and self-perceived altruism: When self-reward fails. *Journal of Personality and Social Psychology, 53*, 594–602.

Batson, C. D., & Weeks, J. L. (1996). Mood effects of unsuccessful helping: Another test of the empathy-altruism hypothesis. *Personality and Social Psychology Bulletin, 22*, 148–157.

Baumeister, R. F. (1982). A self-presentational view of social phenomena. *Psychological Bulletin, 91*, 3–26.

Baumeister, R. F. (1991). *Escaping the self: Alcoholism, spirituality, masochism, and other flights from the burden of selfhood.* New York: Basic Books.

Baumeister, R. F. (1997). *Evil: Inside human cruelty and violence.* New York: W. H. Freeman.

Baumeister, R. F. (1998). The self. In D. T. Gilbert, S. T. Fiske, & G. Lindzey (Eds.), *Handbook of social psychology* (4th ed., Vol. 1, pp. 680–740). Boston: McGraw-Hill.

Baumeister, R. F., Chesner, S. P., Senders, P. S., & Tice, D. M. (1988). Who's in charge here? Group leaders do lend help in emergencies. *Personality and Social Psychology Bulletin, 14*, 17–22.

Baumeister, R. F., & Leary, M. R. (1995). The need to belong: Desire for interpersonal attachments as a fundamental human motivation. *Psychological Bulletin, 117*, 497–529.

Baumeister, R. F., & Newman, L. S. (1994). How stories make sense of personal experiences: Motives that shape autobiographical narratives. *Personality and Social Psychology Bulletin, 20*, 676–690.

Baumeister, R. F., Smart, L., & Boden, J. M. (1996). Relation of threatened egotism to violence and aggression: The dark side of high self-esteem. *Psychological Review, 103*, 5–33.

Baumeister, R. F., & Wotman, S. R. (1992). *Breaking hearts: The two sides of unrequited love.* New York: Guilford.

Baumgardner, A. H., & Brownlee, E. A. (1987). Strategic failure in social interaction: Evidence for expectancy disconfirmation process. *Journal of Personality and Social Psychology, 52,* 525–535.

Baumrind, D. (1964). Some thoughts on ethics of research: After reading Milgram's "Behavioral Study of Obedience." *American Psychologist, 19,* 421–423.

Baxter, L. A. (1986). Gender differences in the heterosexual relationship rules embedded in break-up accounts. *Journal of Social and Personal Relationships, 1,* 29–48.

Baxter, T. L., & Goldberg, L. R. (1987). Perceived behavioral consistency underlying trait attributions to oneself and another: An extension of the actor-observer effect. *Personality and Social Psychology Bulletin, 13,* 437–447.

Beach, S. R. H., Tesser, A., Fincham, F. D., Jones, D. J., Johnson, D., & Whitaker, D. J. (1998). Pleasure and pain in doing well, together: An investigation of performance-related affect in close relationships. *Journal of Personality and Social Psychology, 74,* 923–938.

Bechtold, A., Naccarato, M. E., & Zanna, M. P. (1986). *Need for structure and the prejudice-discrimination link.* Paper presented at the annual meeting of the Canadian Psychological Association, Toronto.

Becker, B. J. (1986). Influence again: Another look at studies of gender differences in social influence. In J. S. Hyde & M. Linn (Eds.), *The psychology of gender: Advances through meta-analysis* (pp. 178–209). Baltimore: Johns Hopkins University Press.

Beggan, J. K. (1992). On the social nature of nonsocial perception: The mere ownership effect. *Journal of Personality and Social Psychology, 62,* 229–237.

Belch, G. E. (1981). An examination of comparative and noncomparative television commercials: The effects of claim variation and repetition on cognitive response and message acceptance. *Journal of Marketing Research, 18,* 333–349.

Bell, D. A. (1973). Racism in American courts: Cause for Black disruption or despair? *California Law Review, 761,* 165–203.

Bell, P. A., & Baron, R. A. (1990). Affect and aggression. In B. S. Moore & A. M. Isen (Eds.), *Affect and social behavior: Studies in emotion and social interaction* (pp. 64–88). New York: Cambridge University Press.

Bellah, R. N. and others. (1985). *Habits of the heart: Individualism and commitment in American life.* Berkeley, CA: University of California Press.

Belmore, S. M., & Hubbard, M. L. (1987). The role of advance expectancies in person memory. *Journal of Personality and Social Psychology, 53,* 61–70.

Bem, D. J. (1963). An experimental analysis of self-persuasion. *Journal of Experimental Social Psychology, 1,* 199–218.

Bem, D. J. (1967). Self-perception: An alternative interpretation of cognitive dissonance phenomena. *Psychological Review, 74,* 183–200.

Bem, D. J. (1972). Self-perception theory. In L. Berkowitz (Ed.), *Advances in experimental social psychology* (Vol. 6). New York: Academic Press.

Bem, S. (1981). Gender schema theory: A cognitive account of sex typing. *Psychological Review, 88,* 354–364.

Benson, P. L., Dehority, J., Garman, L., Hanson, E., Hochschwender, M., Lebod, C., Rohr, R., & Sullivan, J. (1980). Intrapersonal correlates of nonspontaneous helping behavior. *Journal of Social Psychology, 110,* 87–95.

Benson, P. L., Karabenick, S. A., & Lerner, R. M. (1976). Pretty please: The effects of physical attractiveness, race, and sex on receiving help. *Journal of Experimental Social Psychology, 12,* 409–415.

Bentler, P. M., & Speckart, G. (1979). Models of attitude-behavior relations. *Psychological Review, 86,* 452–464.

Berg, J. H. (1984). The development of friendship between roommates. *Journal of Personality and Social Psychology, 46,* 346–356.

Berg, J. H., & Archer, R. L. (1980). Disclosure or concern: A second look at liking for the norm-breaker. *Journal of Personality, 48,* 245–257.

Berg, J. H., & McQuinn, R. D. (1986). Attraction and exchange in continuing and noncontinuing dating relationships. *Journal of Personality and Social Psychology, 50,* 942–952.

Berglas, S., & Jones, E. E. (1978). Drug choice as a self-handicapping strategy in response to noncontingent success. *Journal of Personality and Social Psychology, 36,* 405–417.

Berk, R. A., & Newton, P. J. (1985). Does arrest really deter wife battery? *American Sociological Review, 50,* 253–262.

Berkman, L. F., Leo-Summers, & C., Horwitz, R. I. (1992). Emotional support and survival after myocardial infarction: A prospective population-based study of the elderly. *Annals of Internal Medicine, 117,* 1003–1009.

Berkman, L. F., & Syme, S. L. (1979). Social networks, host resistance, and mortality: A nine year follow-up of Alameda county residents. *American Journal of Epidemiology, 109,* 186–204.

Berkowitz, L. (1965). The concept of aggressive drive: Some additional considerations. In L. Berkowitz (Ed.), *Advances in experimental social psychology* (Vol. 2, pp. 301–329). New York: Academic Press.

Berkowitz, L. (1972). Social norms, feelings, and other factors affecting helping behavior and altruism. In L. Berkowitz (Ed.), *Advances in experimental social psychology* (Vol. 6). New York: Academic Press.

Berkowitz, L. (1984). Some effects of thoughts on anti- and prosocial influences of media events: A cognitive-neoassociationist analysis. *Psychological Bulletin, 95,* 410–427.

Berkowitz, L. (1989). The frustration-aggression hypothesis: An examination and reformulation. *Psychological Bulletin, 106,* 59–73.

Berkowitz, L. (1993). *Aggression: Its causes, consequences, and control.* New York: McGraw-Hill.

Berkowitz, L., & Daniels, L. R. (1963). Responsibility and dependency. *Journal of Abnormal and Social Psychology, 66,* 429–436.

Berkowitz, L., & Donnerstein, E. (1982). External validity is more than skin deep: Some answers to the criticisms of laboratory experiments. *American Psychologist, 37,* 245–257.

Berkowitz, L., & LePage, A. (1967). Weapons as aggression-eliciting stimuli. *Journal of Personality and Social Psychology, 7,* 202–207.

Bernard, J. (1973). *The future of marriage.* New York: Bantam.

Bernstein, M., & Crosby, F. (1980). An experimental examination of relative deprivation theory. *Journal of Experimental Social Psychology, 16,* 442–456.

Berry, D. S., & Brownlow, S. (1989). Were the physiognomists right? Personality correlates of facial babyishness. *Personality and Social Psychology Bulletin, 15,* 266–279.

Berry, D. S., & McArthur, L. Z. (1985). Some components and consequences of a babyface. *Journal of Personality and Social Psychology, 48,* 312–323.

Berscheid, E. (1988). Some comments on love's anatomy: Or, whatever happened to old-fashioned lust? In R. Sternberg & M. Barnes (Eds.), *The psychology of love* (pp. 359–374). New Haven, CT: Yale University Press.

Berscheid, E., & Reis, H. T. (1998). Attraction and close relationships. In D. T. Gilbert, S. T. Fiske, & G. Lindzey (Eds.), *Handbook of social psychology* (4th ed., Vol. 2, pp. 193–281). Boston: McGraw-Hill.

Berscheid, E., Snyder, M., & Omoto, A. M. (1989). The Relationship Closeness Inventory: Assessing the closeness of interpersonal relationships. *Journal of Personality and Social Psychology, 57,* 792–807.

Bersoff, D. M. (1999). Why good people sometimes do bad things: Motivated reasoning and unethical behavior. *Personality and Social Psychology Bulletin, 25,* 28–39.

Bickman, L. (1971). The effect of another bystander's ability to help on bystander intervention in an emergency. *Journal of Experimental Social Psychology, 7,* 367–379.

Bickman, L. (1974). The social power of a uniform. *Journal of Applied Social Psychology, 4,* 47–61.

Bickman, L. (1979). Interpersonal influence and the reporting of a crime. *Personality and Social Psychology Bulletin, 5,* 32–35.

Bickman, L., & Rosenbaum, D. P. (1977). Crime reporting as a function of bystander encouragement, surveillance, and credibility. *Journal of Personality and Social Psychology, 35,* 577–586.

Biernat, M., & Manis, M. (1994). Shifting standards and stereotype-based judgments. *Journal of Personality and Social Psychology, 66,* 5–20.

Biernat, M., & Wortman, C. (1991). Sharing of home responsibilities between professionally employed women and their husbands. *Journal of Personality and Social Psychology, 60,* 844–860.

Billig, M. (1976). *Social psychology and intergroup relations.* New York: Academic Press.

Billig, M., & Tajfel, H. (1973). Social categorization and similarity in intergroup behavior. *European Journal of Social Psychology, 3,* 27–52.

Binning, J. F., Goldstein, M. A., Garcia, M. F., & Scatteregia, J. H. (1988). Effects of preinterview impressions on questioning strategies in same- and opposite-sex employment interviews. *Journal of Applied Psychology, 73,* 30–37.

Birchler, G. R., & Webb, L. J. (1977). Discriminating interaction behavior in happy and unhappy marriages. *Journal of Consulting and Clinical Psychology, 45,* 494–495.

Bird, A. (1977). Team structure and success as related to cohesiveness and leadership. *Journal of Social Psychology, 103,* 217–223.

Birt, C. M., & Dion, K. L. (1987). Relative deprivation theory and responses to deprivation in a gay male and lesbian sample. *British Journal of Social Psychology, 26,* 139–145.

Blake, R. R., & Mouton, J. S. (1979). Intergroup problem solving in organizations: From theory to practice. In W. G. Austin and S. Worchel (Eds.), *The social psychology of intergroup relations* (pp. 19–32). Monterey, CA: Brooks/Cole.

Blake, R. R., & Mouton, J. S. (1980). *The versatile manager: A Grid profile.* Homewood, IL: Dow Jones-Irwin.

Blake, R. R., & Mouton, J. S. (1984). *Solving costly organizational conflicts.* San Francisco, CA: Jossey Bass.

Blanchard, F. A., & Cook, S. W. (1976). Effects of helping a less competent member of a cooperating interracial group on the development of interpersonal attraction. *Journal of Personality and Social Psychology, 34,* 1245–1255.

Blanton, H., Cooper, J., Skurnik, I., & Aronson, J. (1997). When bad things happen to good feedback: Exacerbating the need for self-justification with self-affirmations. *Personality and Social Psychology Bulletin, 23,* 684–692.

Blascovich, J., Nash, R. F., & Ginsburg, G. P. (1978). Heartrate and competitive decision making. *Personality and Social Psychology Bulletin, 4,* 115–118.

Blascovich, J., & Tomaka, J. (1996). The biopsychosocial model of arousal regulation. In M. P. Zanna (Ed.), *Advances in experimental social psychology* (Vol. 28, pp. 1–51). New York: Academic Press.

Blascovich, J., Wyer, N. A., Swart, L. A., & Kibler, J. L. (1997). Racism and racial categorization. *Journal of Personality and Social Psychology, 72,* 1364–1372.

Bless, H., Bohner, G., Schwarz, N., & Strack, F. (1990). Mood and persuasion: A cognitive responses analysis. *Personality and Social Psychology Bulletin, 16,* 331–345.

Bless, H., Clore, G. L., Schwarz, N., Golisano, V., Rabe, C., & Wolk, M. (1996). Mood and the use of scripts: Does a happy mood really lead to mindlessness? *Journal of Personality and Social Psychology, 71,* 665–679.

Blumstein, P., & Schwartz, P. (1983). *American couples: Money, work, sex.* New York: William Morrow.

Bodenhausen, G. V. (1990). Stereotypes as judgmental heuristics: Evidence of circadian variations in discrimination. *Psychological Science, 1,* 319–322.

Bodenhausen, G. V. (1993). Emotions, arousal and stereotyping judgments: A heuristic model of affect and stereotyping. In D. M. Mackie & D. L. Hamilton (Eds.), *Affect, cognition, and stereotyping: Interactive processes in group perception* (pp. 13–37). San Diego: Academic Press.

Bodenhausen, G. V., & Lichtenstein, M. (1987). Social stereotypes and information-processing strategies: The impact of task complexity. *Journal of Personality and Social Psychology, 52,* 871–880.

Bodenhausen, G. V., Schwarz, N., Bless, H., & Waenke, M. (1995). Effects of atypical exemplars on racial beliefs: Enlightened racism or generalized appraisals? *Journal of Experimental Social Psychology, 31,* 48–63.

Bodenhausen, G. V., Sheppard, L. A., & Kramer, G. P. (1994). Negative affect and social judgement: The differential impact of anger and sadness. *Special Issue: Affect on social judgements and cognition. European Journal of Social Psychology, 24,* 45–62.

Bohlen, C. (1992, October 20). Irate Russians demonize traders from Caucasus. *The New York Times,* p. A3.

Bolby, A., & Damon, W. (1992). *Some do care.* New York: Free Press.

Bond, C. F., Jr., & Brockett, D. R. (1987). A social context-persona lity index theory of memory for acquaintances. *Journal of Personality and Social Psychology, 52,* 1110–1121.

Bond, C. F., & Titus, L. J. (1983). Social facilitation: A meta-analysis of 241 studies. *Psychological Bulletin, 94,* 265–292.

Bond, M. H. (1988). *The cross-cultural challenge to social psychology.* Newbury Park, CA: Sage.

Bond, R., & Smith, P. B. (1996). Culture and conformity: A meta-analysis of studies using Asch's (1952b, 1956) line judgement task. *Psychological Bulletin, 119,* 111–137.

Boninger, D. S., Brock, T. C., Cook, T. D., Gruder, C. L., & Romer, D. (1990). Discovery of reliable attitude change persistence resulting from a transmitter tuning set. *Psychological Science, 1,* 268–271.

Boninger, D. S., Krosnick, J. A., & Berent, M. K. (1995). Origins of attitude importance: Self-interest, social identification, and value reference. *Journal of Personality & Social Psychology, 68,* 61–80.

Booth-Kewley, S., & Friedman, H. S. (1987). Psychological predictors of heart disease: A quantitative review. *Psychological Bulletin, 101,* 343–362.

Borgida, E., & Campbell, B. (1982). Belief relevance and attitude-behavior consistency: The moderating role of personal experience. *Journal of Personality and Social Psychology, 42,* 239–247.

Borgida, E., & Howard-Pitney, B. (1983). Involvement and the robustness of perceptual salience effects. *Journal of Personality and Social Psychology, 45,* 560–570.

Burnstein, R. F., Kale, A. R., & Cornell, K. R. (1990). Boredom as a limiting condition on the mere exposure effect. *Journal of Personality and Social Psychology, 58,* 791–800.

Bornstein, R. F., Leone, D. R., & Galley, D. J. (1987). The generalizability of subliminal mere exposure effects: Influence of stimuli perceived without awareness on social behavior. *Journal of Personality and Social Psychology, 53,* 1070–1079.

Bothwell, R. K., Brigham, J. C., & Malpass, R. S. (1989). Cross-racial identification. *Personality and Social Psychology Bulletin, 15,* 19–25.

Bouas, K. S., & Komorita, S. S. (1996). Group discussion and cooperation in social dilemmas. *Personality and Social Psychology Bulletin, 22,* 1144–1150.

Bourhis, R. Y., Giles, H., Leyens, J. P., & Tajfel, H. (1978). Psychological distinctiveness: Language divergence in Belgium. In H. Giles & R. St. Clair (Eds.), *Language and social psychology* (pp. 158–185). Oxford, England: Blackwell.

Boush, D. M., Friestad, M., & Rose, G. M. (1994). Adolescent skepticism toward TV advertising and knowledge of advertiser tactics. *Journal of Consumer Research, 21,* 165–175.

Bowers, C. A., Weaver, J. L., & Morgan, B. B., Jr. (1996). Moderating the performance effects of stressors. In J. E. Driskell & E. Salas (Eds.), *Stress and human performance* (pp. 163–192). Mahwah, NJ: Erlbaum.

Bowlby, J. (1969). *Attachment and loss: Vol. 1. Attachment.* New York: Basic Books.

Boyanowsky, E. O., & Griffiths, C. T. (1982). Weapons and eye contact as instigators or inhibitors of aggressive arousal in police-citizen interaction. *Journal of Applied Social Psychology, 12,* 398–407.

Bradbury, T. N., & Fincham, F. D. (1990). Attributions in marriage: Review and critique. *Psychological Bulletin, 107,* 3–33.

Branscombe, N. R. (1998). Thinking about one's gender group's privileges or disadvantages: Consequences for well-being in women and men. *British Journal of Social Psychology, 37,* 167–184.

Branscombe, N. R., & Wann, D. L. (1994). Collective self-esteem consequences of outgroup derogation when a valued social identity is on trial. *European Journal of Social Psychology, 24,* 641–657.

Branscombe, N. R., Wann, D. L., Noel, J. G., & Coleman, J. (1993). In-group or out-group extremity: Importance of the threatened social identity. *Personality and Social Psychology Bulletin, 19,* 381–388.

Brauer, M., Judd, C. M., & Gliner, M. D. (1995). The effects of repeated expressions on attitude polarization during group discussions. *Journal of Personality and Social Psychology, 68,* 1014–1029.

Brawley, L. R., Carron, A. V., & Widmeyer, W. N. (1987). Assessing the cohesion of teams: Validity of the Group Environment Questionnaire. *Journal of Sport Psychology, 9,* 275–294.

Brawley, L. R., Carron, A. V., & Widmeyer, W. N. (1988). Exploring the relationship between cohesion and group resistance to disruption. *Journal of Sport and Exercise Psychology, 10,* 199–213.

Bray, R. M., Johnson, D., & Chilstrom, J. T., Jr. (1982). Social influence by group members with minority opinions: A comparison of Hollander and Moscovici. *Journal of Personality and Social Psychology, 43,* 78–88.

Brean, H. (1958, March 31). What hidden sell is all about. *Life,* 104–114.

Breckler, S. J., & Wiggins E. C. (1989). Affect versus evaluation in the structure of attitudes. *Journal of Experimental Social Psychology, 25,* 253–271.

Brehm, J. W. (1956). Post-decision changes in desirability of alternatives. *Journal of Abnormal and Social Psychology, 52,* 384–389.

Brehm, J. W. (1966). *A theory of psychological reactance.* New York: Academic Press.

Bretschneider, J. G., & McCoy, N. L. (1988). Sexual interest and behavior in healthy 80- to 102-year-olds. *Archives of Sexual Behavior, 17,* 188–195.

Brewer, M. B. (1979). In-group bias in the minimal intergroup situation: A cognitive-motivational analysis. *Psychological Bulletin, 86,* 307–323.

Brewer, M. B. (1988). A dual process model of impression formation. In T. Srull & R. Wyer (Eds.), *Advances in social cognition* (Vol. 1, pp. 177–183). Hillsdale, NJ: Erlbaum.

Brewer, M. B. (1991). The social self: On being the same and different at the same time. *Personality and Social Psychology Bulletin, 17,* 475–482.

Brewer, M. B., & Campbell, D. T. (1976). *Ethnocentrism and intergroup attitudes: East African evidence.* New York: Halstead Press.

Brewer, M. B., Dull, V., & Lui, L. (1981). Perceptions of the elderly: Stereotypes as prototypes. *Journal of Personality and Social Psychology, 41,* 656–670.

Brewer, M. B., & Kramer, R. M. (1986). Choice behavior in social dilemmas: Effects of social identity, group size, and decision framing. *Journal of Personality and Social Psychology, 50,* 543–549.

Brewer, M. B., & Silver, M. (1978). Ingroup bias as a function of task characteristics. *European Journal of Social Psychology, 8,* 393–400.

Brewer, M. B., & Weber, J. G. (1994). Self-evaluation effects of interpersonal versus intergroup social comparison. *Journal of Personality and Social Psychology, 66,* 268–275.

Brickman, P., Coates, D., & Janoff-Bulman, R. (1978). Lottery winners and accident victims: Is happiness relative? *Journal of Personality and Social Psychology, 36,* 917–927.

Brickner, M. A., Harkins, S. G., & Ostrom, T. M. (1986). Effects of personal involvement: Thought-provoking implications for social loafing. *Journal of Personality and Social Psychology, 51*, 763–770.

Brief, A. P., Buttram, R. T., Elliott, J. D., Reizenstein, R. M., & McCline, R. L. (1995). Releasing the beast: A study of compliance with orders to use race as a selection criterion. *Journal of Social Issues, 51*, 177–194.

Brief, A. P., Dukerich, J. M., & Doran, L. I. (1991). Resolving ethical dilemmas in management: Experimental investigation of values, accountability, and choice. *Journal of Applied Social Psychology, 21*, 380–396.

Brigham, J. C. (1971). Ethnic stereotypes. *Psychological Bulletin, 76*, 15–33.

Brown, J. D. (1986). Evaluations of self and others: Self-enhancing biases in social judgment. *Social Cognition, 4*, 353–376.

Brown, J. D., & Smart, S. A. (1991). The self and social conduct: Linking self-representations to prosocial behavior. *Journal of Personality and Social Psychology, 60*, 368–375.

Brown, R., Condor, S., Matthews, A., Wade, G., & Williams, J. A. (1986). Explaining intergroup differentiation in an industrial organization. *Journal of Occupational Psychology, 59*, 273–286.

Brown, R., & Fish, D. (1983). The psychological causality implicit in language. *Cognition, 14*, 237–273.

Brown, R., & Smith, A. (1989). Perceptions of and by minority groups: The case of women in academia. *European Journal of Social Psychology, 19*, 61–75.

Brown, R., & Wade, G. (1987). Superordinate goals and intergroup behavior: The effects of role ambiguity and status on intergroup attitudes and task performance. *European Journal of Social Psychology, 17*, 131–142.

Brown, R. P., & Josephs, R. A. (1999). A burden of proof: Stereotype relevance and gender differences in math performance. *Journal of Personality and Social Psychology, 76*, 246–257.

Browning, C. R. (1992). *Ordinary men*. New York: Harper-Collins.

Browning, L. D. (1978). A grounded organizational communication theory derived from qualitative data. *Communication Monographs, 45*, 93–109.

Bruner, J. (1957). On perceptual readiness. *Psychological Review, 64*, 123–152.

Bruner, J. (1986). *Actual minds, possible worlds*. New York: Plenum.

Bryan, J. H., & Test, M. A. (1967). Models and helping: Naturalistic studies in aiding behavior. *Journal of Personality and Social Psychology, 10*, 222–226.

Budescu, D. V., Rapoport, A., & Suleiman, R. (1990). Resource dilemmas with environmental uncertainty and asymmetric players. *European Journal of Social Psychology, 20*, 475–487.

Budesheim, T. L., Houston, D. A., & DePaola, S. J. (1996). Persuasiveness of in-group and out-group political messages: The case of negative political campaigning. *Journal of Personality and Social Psychology, 70*, 523–534.

Bui, K.-V. T., Peplau, L. A., & Hill, C. T. (1996). Testing the Rusbult model of relationship commitment and stability in a 15-year study of heterosexual couples. *Personality and Social Psychology Bulletin, 22*, 1244–1257.

Bulman, R., & Wortman, C. (1977). Attributions of blame and coping in the "real world": Severe accident victims respond to their lot. *Journal of Personality and Social Psychology, 35*, 351–363.

Burger, J. M. (1986). Increasing compliance by improving the deal: The that's-not-all technique. *Journal of Personality and Social Psychology, 51*, 277–283.

Burger, J. M., Horita, M., Kinoshita, L., Roberts, K., & Vera, C. (1997). Effects of time on the norm of reciprocity. *Basic and Applied Social Psychology, 19*, 91–100.

Burgoon, M., Pfau, M., & Birk, T. S. (1995). An inoculation theory explanation for the effects of corporate issue/advocacy advertising campaigns. *Special issue: Communication and social influence. Communication Research, 22*, 485–505.

Burke, P. J. (1967). The development of task and social-emotional role differentiation. *Sociometry, 30*, 379–392.

Burke, R. J. (1970). Methods of resolving superior-subordinate conflict: The constructive use of subordinate differences and disagreements. *Organizational Behavior and Human Performance, 5*, 393–411.

Burleson, B. R. (1994). Comforting messages: Significance, approaches, and effects. In B. R. Burleson, T. L. Albrecht, & I. G. Sarason (Eds.), *Communication of social support: Messages, interactions, relationships, and community* (pp. 3–28). Thousand Oaks, CA: Sage.

Burnstein, E., & Vinokur, A. (1977). Persuasive argumentation and social comparison as determinants of attitude polarization. *Journal of Experimental Social Psychology, 13*, 315–332.

Bushman, B. J. (1998). Effects of warning and information labels on consumption of full-fat, reduced-fat, and no-fat products. *Journal of Applied Psychology, 83*, 97–101.

Bushman, B. J., & Baumeister, R. F. (1998). Threatened egotism, narcissism, self-esteem, and direct and displaced aggression: Does self-love or self-hate lead to violence? *Journal of Personality and Social Psychology, 75*, 219–229.

Bushman, B. J., & Cooper, H. M. (1990). Effects of alcohol on human aggression: An integrative research review. *Psychological Bulletin, 107*, 341–354.

Bushman, B. J., & Geen, R. G. (1990). Role of cognitive-emotional mediators and individual differences in the effects of media violence on aggression. *Journal of Personality and Social Psychology, 58*, 156–163.

Buss, A. (1961). *The psychology of aggression*. New York: Wiley.

Buss, D. M. (1994). The strategies of human mating. *American Scientist, 82*, 238–249.

Buss, D. M., & Kenrick, D. T. (1998). Evolutionary social psychology. In D. T. Gilbert, S. T. Fiske, & G. Lindzey (Eds.), *Handbook of social psychology* (3rd ed., Vol. 2, pp. 982–1026). Boston: McGraw-Hill.

Butler, L. D., Koopman, C., & Zimbardo, P. G. (1995). The psychological impact of viewing the film *JFK*: Emotions, beliefs, and political behavioral intentions. *Political Psychology, 16*, 237–257.

Butterfield, F. (1998, July 26). Southern curse: Why America's murder rate is so high. *The New York Times*, Week in Review section.

Byrne, D. (1971). *The attraction paradigm*. New York: Academic Press.

Cacioppo, J. T., & Petty, R. E. (1979). Attitudes and cognitive responses: An electro-physiological approach. *Journal of Personality and Social Psychology, 37,* 2181–2199.

Cacioppo, J. T., & Petty, R. E. (1982). The need for cognition. *Journal of Personality and Social Psychology, 42,* 116–131.

Cacioppo, J. T., & Petty, R. E. (1984). The need for cognition: Relationship to attitudinal processes. In R. McGlynn, J. Maddux, C. Stoltenberg, & J. Harvey (Eds.), *Social perception in clinical and counseling psychology.* Lubbock, TX: Texas Tech Press.

Cacioppo, J. T., & Petty, R. E. (1989). Effects of message repetition on argument processing, recall, and persuasion. *Basic and Applied Social Psychology, 10,* 3–12.

Cacioppo, J. T., Petty, R. E., Losch, M. E., & Kim, H. S. (1986). Electromyographic activity over facial muscle regions can differentiate the valence and intensity of affective reactions. *Journal of Personality and Social Psychology, 50,* 260–268.

Cacioppo, J. T., Petty, R. E., & Morris, K. J. (1983). Effects of need for cognition on message evaluation, recall, and persuasion. *Journal of Personality and Social Psychology, 45,* 805–818.

Cacioppo, J. T., Petty, R. E., & Sidera, J. (1982). The effects of a salient self-schema on the evaluation of proattitudinal editorials: Top-down versus bottom-up message processing. *Journal of Experimental Social Psychology, 18,* 324–338.

California case puts spotlight on jury coercion and peer pressure. (1992, July 17). *New York Times,* p. A23.

Campbell, A., Converse, P. E., & Rodgers, W. L. (1976). *The quality of American life.* New York: Russell Sage Foundation.

Campbell, D. T. (1963). Social attitudes and other aquired behavioral dispositions. In S. Koch (Ed.) *Psychology: A study of a science* (Vol. 6, pp. 94–172). New York: McGraw-Hill.

Campbell, D. T. (1965). Ethnocentric and other altruistic motives. In D. Levine (Ed.), *Nebraska Symposium on Motivation* (Vol. 13, pp. 283–311). Lincoln: University of Nebraska Press.

Campbell, D. T. (1967). Stereotypes and the perception of group differences. *American Psychologist, 22,* 817–829.

Campbell, J. D. (1990). Self-esteem and clarity of the self-concept. *Journal of Personality and Social Psychology, 59,* 538–549.

Campbell, J. D., Chew, B., & Scratchley, L. S. (1991). Cognitive and emotional reactions to daily events: The effects of self-esteem and self-complexity. *Journal of Personality, 59,* 473–505.

Campbell, J. D., & Fairey, P. (1985). Effects of self-esteem, hypothetical explanations, and verbalization of expectancies on future performance. *Journal of Personality and Social Psychology, 48,* 1097–1111.

Campbell, J. D., & Lavallee, L. F. (1993). Who am I? The role of self-concept confusion in understanding the behavior of people with low self-esteem. In R. F. Baumeister (Ed.), *Self-esteem: The puzzle of low self-esteem* (pp. 3–20). New York: Plenum.

Cantor, N., & Kihlstrom, J. F. (1987). *Personality and social intelligence.* Englewood Cliffs, NJ: Prentice-Hall.

Cantor, N., & Malley, J. (1991). Life tasks, personal needs, and close relationships. In G. Fletcher & F. Fincham (Eds.), *Cognition in close relationships* (pp. 101–126). Hillsdale, NJ: Erlbaum.

Caporael, L. (1997). The evolution of truly social cognition: The core configurations model. *Personality and Social Psychology Review, 1,* 276–298.

Caporael, L. R., & Brewer, M. B. (1991). Reviving evolutionary psychology: Biology meets society. *Journal of Social Issues, 47*(3), 187–195.

Caporael, L. R., Dawes, R. M., Orbell, J. M., & Van de Kragt, A. J. C. (1989). Selfishness examined: Cooperation in the absence of egoistic incentives. *Behavioral and Brain Sciences, 12,* 683–699.

Carli, L. (1990). Gender, language, and influence. *Journal of Personality and Social Psychology, 59,* 941–951.

Carli, L. L., & Leonard, J. B. (1989). The effect of hindsight on victim derogation. *Journal of Social and Clinical Psychology, 8,* 331–343.

Carlson, M., Marcus-Newhall, A., & Miller, N. (1989). Evidence for a general construct of aggression. *Personality and Social Psychology Bulletin, 15,* 377–389.

Carlson, M., & Miller, N. (1987). Explanation of the relation between negative mood and helping. *Psychological Bulletin, 102,* 91–108.

Carlston, D. E. (1994). Associated systems theory: A systematic approach to cognitive representations of persons. In T. K. Srull & R. S. Wyer (Eds.), *Advances in social cognition* (Vol. 7, pp. 1–78). Hillsdale, NJ: Erlbaum.

Carlston, D. E., & Skowronski, J. J. (1986). Trait memory and behavior memory: The effects of alternative pathways on impression judgment response times. *Journal of Personality and Social Psychology, 50,* 5–13.

Carlston, D. E., & Skowronski, J. J. (1994). Savings in the relearning of trait information as evidence for spontaneous inference generation. *Journal of Personality and Social Psychology, 66,* 840–856.

Carroll, J. M., & Russell, J. A. (1996). Do facial expressions signal specific emotions? Judging emotion from the face in context. *Journal of Personality and Social Psychology, 70,* 205–218.

Carter, S. (1991). *Reflections of an affirmative action baby.* New York: Basic Books.

Cartwright, D. (1979). Contemporary social psychology in historical perspective. *Social Psychology Quarterly, 42,* 82–93.

Cartwright, D., & Zander, A. (1960). Group cohesiveness: Introduction. In D. Cartwright & A. Zander (Eds.), *Group dynamics: Research and theory* (2nd ed., pp. 69–94). Evanston, IL: Row, Peterson.

Carver, C. S., Ganellen, R. J., Froming, W. J., & Chambers, W. (1983). Modeling: An analysis in terms of category accessibility. *Journal of Experimental Social Psychology, 19,* 403–421.

Carver, C. S., & Scheier, M. F. (1981). *Attention and self-regulation: A control theory approach to human behavior.* New York: Springer-Verlag.

Carver, C. S., & Scheier, M. F. (1990). Origins and functions of positive and negative affect: A control-process view. *Psychological Review, 97,* 19–35.

Cary, L. (1992, June 29). As plain as black and white. *Newsweek,* p. 53.

Cash, T. F., & Kilcullen, R. N. (1979). The eye of the beholder: Susceptibility to sexism and beautyism in the evaluation of managerial applicants. *Journal of Applied Social Psychology, 15,* 591–605.

Casse, P. (1982). *Training for the multicultural manager: A proactical and cross-cultural approach to the management of people.* Washington, DC: Society for Intercultural Education, Training, and Research.

Cate, R. M., & Lloyd, S. A. (1988). Courtship. In S. Duck (Ed.), *Handbook of personal relationships: Theory, relationships, and interventions*. Chichester, England: Wiley.

Chacko, T. I. (1982). Women and equal employment opportunity: Some unintended effects. *Journal of Applied Psychology, 67,* 119–123.

Chaiken, S. (1979). Communicator physical attractiveness and persuasion. *Journal of Personality and Social Psychology, 37,* 1387–1397.

Chaiken, S. (1980). Heuristic versus systematic information processing and the use of source versus message cues in persuasion. *Journal of Personality and Social Psychology, 39,* 752–756.

Chaiken, S. (1987). The heuristic model of persuasion. In M. P. Zanna, J. M. Olson, & C. P. Herman (Eds.), *Social influence: The Ontario Symposium* (Vol. 5, pp. 3–40). Hillsdale, NJ: Erlbaum.

Chaiken, S., & Baldwin, M. W. (1981). Affective-cognitive consistency and the effect of salient behavioral information on the self perception of attitudes. *Journal of Personality and Social Psychology, 41,* 1–12.

Chaiken S., & Eagly, A. H. (1976). Communication modality as a determinant of message persuasiveness and message comprehensibility. *Journal of Personality and Social Psychology, 34,* 605–614.

Chaiken, S., Liberman, A., & Eagly, A. H. (1989). Heuristic and systematic information processing: Within and beyond the persuasion context. In J. S. Uleman & J. A. Bargh (Eds.), *Unintended thought: Limits of Awareness, Intention, and Control* (pp. 212–252). New York: Guilford.

Chaiken, S., & Maheswaran, D. (1994). Heuristic processing can bias systematic processing: Effects of source credibility, argument ambiguity, and task importance on attitude judgement. *Journal of Personality and Social Psychology, 66,* 460–473.

Chaiken, S., Pomerantz, E. M., & Giner-Sorolla, R. (1995). Structural consistency and attitude strength. In R. E. Petty and J. A. Krosnick (Eds.), *Attitude strength: Antecedents and consequences* (pp. 387–412). Hillsdale, NJ: Erlbaum.

Charters, W. W., & Newcomb, T. M. (1958). Some attitudinal effects of experimentally increased salience of a membership group. In E. E. Maccoby, T. M. Newcomb, & E. L. Hartley (Eds.), *Readings in social psychology* (pp. 276–281). New York: Holt.

Chen, S., Shechter, D., & Chaiken, S. (1996). Getting at the truth or getting along: Accuracy- versus impression-motivated heuristic and systematic processing. *Journal of Personality and Social Psychology, 71,* 262–275.

Cherlin, A. J., Furstenberg, F. F., Jr., Chase-Lansdale, L., Kiernan, K. E., Robins, P. K., Morrison, D. R., & Teitler, J. O. (1991). Longitudinal studies of effects of divorce on children in Great Britain and the United States. *Science, 252,* 1386–1389.

Chu, D., & McIntyre, B. T. (1995). Sex role stereotypes on children's TV in Asia: A content analysis of gender role portrayals in children's cartoons in Hong Kong. *Communication Research Reports, 12,* 206–219.

Cialdini, R. B. (1984). Principles of automatic influence. In J. Jacoby & G. S. Craig (Eds.), *Personal selling* (pp. 1–27). Lexington, MA: Lexington Books.

Cialdini, R. B. (1993). *Influence: Science and practice* (3rd ed.). New York: HarperCollins.

Cialdini, R. B., & Ascani, K. (1976). Test of a concession procedure for inducing verbal, behavioral, and further compliance with a request to donate blood. *Journal of Applied Psychology, 61,* 295–300.

Cialdini, R. B., Borden, R. J., Thorne, A., Walker, M. R., Freeman, S., & Sloan, L. R. (1976). Basking in reflected glory: Three (football) field studies. *Journal of Personality and Social Psychology, 34,* 366–375.

Cialdini, R. B., Cacioppo, J. T., Bassett, R., & Miller, J. A., (1978). Lowball procedure for producing compliance: Commitment then cost. *Journal of Personality and Social Psychology, 36,* 463–476.

Cialdini, R. B., Darby, B. L., & Vincent, J. E. (1973). Transgression and altruism: A case for hedonism. *Journal of Experimental Social Psychology, 9,* 502–516.

Cialdini, R. B., & Kenrick, D. T. (1976). Altruism as hedonism: A social development perspective on the relationship of negative mood state and helping. *Journal of Personality and Social Psychology, 34,* 907–914.

Cialdini, R. B., Reno, R. R., & Kallgren, C. A. (1990). A focus theory of normative conduct: Recycling the concept of norms to reduce littering in public places. *Journal of Personality and Social Psychology, 58,* 1015–1026.

Cialdini, R. B., & Schroeder, D. A. (1976). Increasing compliance by legitimizing paltry contributions: When even a penny helps. *Journal of Personality and Social Psychology, 34,* 599–604.

Cialdini, R. B., Vincent, J. E., Lewis, S. K., Catalan, J., Wheeler, D., & Darby, B. L. (1975). Reciprocal concessions procedure for inducing compliance: The door in the face technique. *Journal of Personality and Social Psychology, 31,* 206–215.

Clark, K. B. (1965). *Dark ghetto: Dilemmas of social power.* New York: Harper & Row.

Clark, L. F., & Collins, J. E. (1993). Remembering old flames: How the past affects assessments of the present. *Personality and Social Psychology Bulletin, 19,* 399–408.

Clark, M. S., & Mills, J. (1979). Interpersonal attraction in exchange and communal relationships. *Journal of Personality and Social Psychology, 37,* 12–24.

Clark, M. S., & Taraban, C. (1991). Reactions to and willingness to express emotion in communal and exchange relationships. *Journal of Experimental Social Psychology, 27,* 324–336.

Clark, N. K., Stephenson, G. M., & Kniveton, B. H. (1990). Social remembering: Quantitative aspects of individual and collaborative remembering by police officers and students. *British Journal of Psychology, 81,* 73–94.

Clark, R. D., & Word, L. E. (1972). Why don't bystanders help? Because of ambiguity. *Journal of Personality and Social Psychology, 24,* 392–400.

Clary, E. G., & Orenstein, L. (1991). The amount and effectiveness of help: The relationship of motives and abilities to helping behavior. *Personality and Social Psychology Bulletin, 17,* 58–64.

Clary, E. G., Snyder, M., Ridge, R. D., Copeland, J., Stukas, A. A., Haugen, J., & Miene, P. (1998). Understanding and assessing the motivations of volunteers: A functional approach. *Journal of Personality and Social Psychology, 74,* 1516–1530.

Clement, R. W., & Krueger, J. (1998). Liking persons versus liking groups: A dual-process hypothesis. *European Journal of Social Psychology, 28,* 457–470.

Clifford, M. M. (1975). Physical attractiveness and academic performance. *Child Study Journal, 5,* 201–209.

Cline, V. B., Croft, R. G., & Courrier, S. (1973). Desensitization of children to television violence. *Journal of Personality and Social Psychology, 27,* 360–365.

Coch, L., & French, J. R. P., Jr. (1948). Overcoming resistance to change. *Human Relations, 1,* 512–532.

Codol, J. P. (1975). On the so-called "superior conformity of the self" behavior: Twenty experimental investigations. *European Journal of Social Psychology, 5,* 457–501.

Cohen, A. (1957). Need for cognition and order of communication as determinants of opinion change. In C. Hovland (Ed.), *The order of presentation in persuasion.* New Haven, CT: Yale University Press.

Cohen, D., & Nisbett, R. E. (1994). Self-protection and the culture of honor: Explaining southern violence. *Personality and Social Psychology Bulletin, 20,* 551–567.

Cohen, D., & Nisbett, R. E. (1997). Field experiments examining the culture of honor: The role of institutions in perpetuating norms about violence. *Personality and Social Psychology Bulletin, 23,* 1188–1199.

Cohen, D., Nisbett, R. E., Bowdle, B. F., & Schwarz, N. (1996). Insult, aggression, and the southern culture of honor: An "experimental ethnography. " *Journal of Personality and Social Psychology, 70,* 945–960.

Cohen, F. (1984). Coping. In J. D. Matarazzo et al. (Eds.), *Behavioral health* (pp. 261–274). New York: Wiley.

Cohen, M., & Davis, N. (1981). *Medication errors: Causes and prevention.* Philadelphia: G.F. Strickey Co.

Cohen, S., Doyle, W. J., Skoner, D. P., & Fireman, P. (1995). State and trait negative affect as predictors of objective and subjective symptoms of respiratory viral infections. *Journal of Personality and Social Psychology, 68,* 159–169.

Cohen, S. P., & Arnone, H. C. (1988). Conflict resolution as the alternative to terrorism. *Journal of Social Issues, 44*(2), 175–190.

Colasanto, D. (1989, November). Americans show commitment to helping those in need. *Gallup Report,* No. 290, 17–24.

Collins, N. L., & Miller, L. C. (1994). Self-disclosure and liking: A meta-analytic review. *Psychological Bulletin, 116,* 457–475.

Collins, N. L., & Read, S. J. (1990). Adult attachment, working models, and relationship quality in dating couples. *Journal of Personality and Social Psychology, 58,* 644–663.

Colvin, C. R., Block, J., & Funder, D. C. (1995). Overly positive self-evaluations and personality: Negative implications for mental health. *Journal of Personality and Social Psychology, 68,* 1152–1162.

Condon, J. W., & Crano, W. D. (1988). Inferred evaluation and the relation between attitude similarity and interpersonal attraction. *Journal of Personality and Social Psychology, 54,* 789–797.

Condor, S., & Brown, R. (1988). Psychological processes in intergroup conflict. In W. Stroebe, A. W. Kruglanski, D. Bar-Tal, & M. Hewstone (Eds.), *The social psychology of intergroup conflict* (pp. 3–26). New York: Springer-Verlag.

Cook, S. W. (1985). Experimenting on social issues: The case of school desegregation. *American Psychologist, 40,* 452–460.

Cook, T. D., & Campbell, D. T. (1979). *Quasi-experimentation.* Chicago: Rand McNally.

Cooley, D. H. (1902). *Human nature and the social order.* New York: Scribners.

Cooper, H. (1990). Meta-analysis and the integrative research review. In C. Hendrick & M. S. Clark (Eds.), *Review of personality and social psychology* (Vol. 11, pp. 142–163). Newbury Park, CA: Sage.

Cooper, H., & Good, T. (1983). *Pygmalion grows up: Studies in the expectation communication process.* New York: Longman.

Cooper, J., & Brehm, J. W. (1971). Prechoice awareness of relative deprivation as a determinant of cognitive dissonance. *Journal of Experimental Social Psychology, 7,* 571–581.

Cooper, J., & Fazio, R. H. (1984). A new look at dissonance theory. In L. Berkowitz (Ed.), *Advances in experimental social psychology* (Vol. 17, pp. 229–266). New York: Academic Press.

Cooper, J., Zanna, M. P., & Taves, P. A. (1978). Arousal as a necessary condition for attitude change following induced compliance. *Journal of Personality and Social Psychology, 36,* 1101–1106.

Copper, C., Mullen, B., Adrales, K., Asuncion, A., Gibbons, P., Goethals, G. R., Riordan, C., Schroeder, D., Sibicky, M., Tice, D., Worth, L., & Lipsitt, N., (1993). Bias in the media: The subtle effects of a newscaster's smile. In G. Comstock and F. Fischoff (Eds.) *Media Behavior,* Newbury Park, CA: Sage.

Corey, S. M. (1937). Professed attitudes and actual behavior. *Journal of Educational Psychology, 28,* 271–280.

Cosmides, L. (1989). The logic of social exchange: Has natural selection shaped how humans reason? Studies with the Wason selection task. *Cognition, 31,* 187–276.

Coulter, R. H., & Pinto, M. B. (1995). Guilt appeals in advertising: What are their effects? *Journal of Applied Psychology, 80,* 697–705.

Cousins, S. (1989). Culture and selfhood in Japan and the U.S. *Journal of Personality and Social Psychology, 56,* 124–131.

Cramer, R. E., McMaster, M. R., & Bartell, P. A. (1988). Subject competence and minimization of the bystander effect. *Journal of Applied Social Psychology, 18,* 1133–1148.

Crandall, C. S., & Cohen, C. R. (1994). The personality of the stigmatizer: Cultural world view, conventionalism, and self-esteem. *Journal of Research in Personality, 28,* 461–480.

Crano, W. D., & Alvaro, E. M. (1998). The context/comparison model of social influence: Mechanisms, structure, and linkages that underlie indirect attitude change. In W. Stroebe & M. Hewstone (Eds.), *European Review of Social Psychology* (Vol. 8, pp. 175–202). Chichester, England: Wiley.

Crano, W. D., & Chen, X. (1998). The leniency contract and persistence of majority and minority influence. *Journal of Personality and Social Psychology, 74,* 1437–1450.

Crano, W. D., Gorenflo, D. W., & Shackelford, S. L. (1988). Overjustification, assumed consensus, and attitude change: Further investigation of the incentive-aroused ambivalence hypothesis. *Journal of Personality and Social Psychology, 55,* 12–22.

Crawford, D. W., & Huston, T. L. (1993). The impact of the transition to parenthood on marital leisure. *Personality and Social Psychology Bulletin, 19,* 39–46.

Crick, N. R., & Dodge, K. A. (1994). A review and reformulation of social information-processing mechanisms in children's social adjustment. *Psychological Bulletin, 115,* 74–101.

Crocker, J., Hannah, D. B., & Weber, R. (1983). Person memory and causal attributions. *Journal of Personality and Social Psychology, 44,* 55–66.

Crocker, J., & Major, B. (1989). Social stigma and self-esteem: The self-protective properties of stigma. *Psychological Review, 96,* 608–630.

Crocker, J., Major, B., & Steele, C. M. (1998). Social stigma. In D. T. Gilbert, S. T. Fiske, & G. Lindzey (Eds.), *Handbook of social psychology* (4th ed., Vol. 2, pp. 504–553). Boston: McGraw-Hill.

Crocker, J., Voelkl, K., Testa, M., & Major, B. (1991). Social stigma: The affective consequences of attributional ambiguity. *Journal of Personality and Social Psychology, 60,* 218–228.

Crosby, F. (1976). A model of egoistic relative deprivation. *Psychological Review, 83,* 85–113.

Crosby, F. J., Pufall, A., Snyder, R. C., O'Connell, M., & Whalen, P. (1989). The denial of personal disadvantage among you, me, and all the other ostriches. In M. Crawford & M. Gentry (Eds.), *Gender and thought: Psychological perspectives* (pp. 79–99). New York: Springer-Verlag.

Cross, S. E., Kanagawa, C., Markus, H. R., & Kitayama, S. (1995). *Cultural variation in self-concept.* Unpublished manuscript, Iowa State University, Ames.

Croyle, R., & Cooper, J. (1983). Dissonance arousal: Physiological evidence. *Journal of Personality and Social Psychology, 45,* 782–791.

Crutchfield, (1955). Conformity and character. *American Psychologist, 10,* 191–198.

Csikszentmihalyi, M., & Figurski, T. J. (1982). Self-awareness and aversive experience in everyday life. *Journal of Personality, 50,* 15–28.

Cutrona, C. E. (1982). Transition to college: Loneliness and the process of social adjustment. In L. A. Peplau & D. Perlman (Eds.), *Loneliness* (pp. 291–309). New York: Wiley Interscience.

Dalcourt, P. (1996). Les stéréotypes sexuels dans la publicité québecoise télévisée: Le maintien d'une tradition. *Revue Québecoise de Psychologie, 17,* 29–42.

Darke, S. (1988). Effects of anxiety on inferential reasoning task performance. *Journal of Personality and Social Psychology, 55,* 499–505.

Darley, J. M., & Batson, C. D. (1973). From Jerusalem to Jericho: A study of situational and dispositional variables in helping behavior. *Journal of Personality and Social Psychology, 27,* 100–108.

Darley, J. M., & Fazio, R. H. (1980). Expectancy confirmation processes arising in the social interaction sequence. *American Psychologist, 35,* 867–881.

Darley, J. M., & Gross, P. H. (1983). A hypothesis-confirming bias in labelling effects. *Journal of Personality and Social Psychology, 44,* 20–33.

Darley, J. M., & Latané, B. (1968). Bystander intervention in emergencies: Diffusion of responsibility. *Journal of Personality and Social Psychology, 8,* 377–383.

Darwin, C. (1871/1909). *The descent of man.* New York: Appleton.

Dasgupta, N., Banaji, M. B., & Abelson, R. P. (1997, March). *Beliefs and attitudes toward cohesive groups.* Paper presented at Midwestern Psychological Association, Chicago.

David, B., & Turner, J. C. (1996). Studies in self-categorization and minority conversion: Is being a member of the out-group an advantage? *British Journal of Social Psychology, 35,* 179–199.

Davidson, A. R., & Jaccard, J. J. (1979). Variables that moderate the attitude-behavior relation: Results of a longitudinal survey. *Journal of Personality and Social Psychology, 37,* 1364–76.

Davidson, A. R., Yantis, S., Norwood, M., & Monano, D. E. (1985). Amount of information about the attitude object and attitude-behavior consistency. *Journal of Personality and Social Psychology, 49,* 1184–1198.

Davis, K., & Newstrom, J. W. (1985). *Human behavior at work: Organizational behavior* (7th ed.). New York: McGraw-Hill.

Davis, K. E., & Jones, E. E. (1960). Changes in interpersonal perception as a means of reducing cognitive dissonance. *Journal of Abnormal and Social Psychology, 61,* 402–410.

Davis, M. H. (1983). Empathic concern and muscular dystrophy telethon: Empathy as a multidimensional construct. *Personality and Social Psychology Bulletin, 9,* 223–229.

Dawes, R. M., & Smith, T. L. (1985). Attitude and opinion measurement. In G. Lindzey & E. Aronson (Eds.), *The Handbook of Social Psychology* (3rd Ed., Vol. 1, pp. 509–566). New York: Random House.

Dawes, R. M., Van de Kragt, A. J., & Orbell, J. M. (1988). Not me or thee but we: The importance of group identity in eliciting cooperation in dilemma situations: Experimental manipulations. *Acta Psychologica, 68,* 83–97.

Deaux, K. K., & Emswiller, T. (1974). Explanations of successful performance on sex-linked tasks: What is skill for the male is luck for the female. *Journal of Personality and Social Psychology, 29,* 80–85.

Deaux, K. K., & Hanna, R. (1984). Courtship in the personals column: The influence of gender and sexual orientation. *Sex Roles, 11,* 363–375.

Deaux, K. K., & Lewis, L. L. (1983). Components of gender stereotypes. *Psychological Documents, 13,* 25–34.

Deaux, K. K., & Lewis, L. L. (1984). Structure of gender stereotypes: Interrelationships among components and gender label. *Journal of Personality and Social Psychology, 46,* 991–1004.

Deaux, K. K., & Stark, D. E. (1996, May). *Identity and motive: An integrated theory of volunteerism.* Presented at the convention of the Society for the Psychological Study of Social Issues, Ann Arbor, MI.

DeBono, K. G. (1987). Investigating the social adjustive and value expressive functions of attitudes: Implications for persuasion processes. *Journal of Personality and Social Psychology, 52,* 279–287.

DeBono, K. G., & Harnish, R. (1988). Source expertise, source attractiveness, and processing of persuasive information: A functional approach. *Journal of Personality and Social Psychology, 55,* 541–546.

DeBono, K. G., & Snyder, M. (1995). Acting on one's attitudes: The role of a history of choosing situations. *Personality and Social Psychology Bulletin, 21,* 629–636.

Deci, E. L. (1971). Effects of externally mediated rewards on intrinsic motivation. *Journal of Personality and Social Psychology, 18,* 105–115.

Deci, E. L. (1975). *Intrinsic motivation.* New York: Plenum.

DeJong, W. (1979). An examination of self-perception mediation on the foot-in-the-door effect. *Journal of Personality and Social Psychology, 37,* 2221–2239.

DeJong, W. (1987). A short-term evaluation of project DARE (Drug Abuse Resistance Education): Preliminary indications of effectiveness. *Journal of Drug Education, 17,* 279–294.

DeLamater, J., & MacCorquodale, P. (1979). *Premarital sexuality: Attitudes, relationships, behavior*. Madison, WI: University of Wisconsin Press.

Denmark, F., Russo, N. F., Frieze, I. H., & Sechzer, J. A. (1988). Guidelines for avoiding sexism in psychological research. *American Psychologist, 43*, 582–585.

Denmark, F. L., Shaw, J. S., & Ciali, S. O. (1985). The relationship among sex roles, living arrangements, and the division of household responsibilities. *Sex Roles, 12*, 617–625.

Department of the Army. (1956). *The law of land warfare* (Field Manual No. 27–10). Washington, DC: U.S. Government Printing Office.

DePaulo, B. M., Lassiter, G. D., & Stone, J. I. (1982). Attentional determinants of success at detecting deception and truth. *Personality and Social Psychology Bulletin, 8*, 273–279.

Derlega, V. J., Wilson, M., & Chaikin, A. L. (1976). Friendship and disclosure reciprocity. *Journal of Personality and Social Psychology, 34*, 578–587.

Derlega, V. J., Winstead, B. A., Wong, P. T. P., & Hunter, S. (1985). Gender effects in an initial encounter: A case where men exceed women in disclosure. *Journal of Social and Personal Relationships, 2*, 25–44.

De Rivera, J. (1977). *A structural theory of the emotions*. New York: International Universities Press.

Deschamps, J. C., & Brown, R. (1983). Superordinate goals and intergroup conflict. *British Journal of Social Psychology, 22*, 189–195.

Desforges, D. M., Lord, C. G., Ramsey, S. L., Mason, J. A., Van Leeuwen, M. D., West, S. C., & Lepper, M. R. (1991). Effects of structured cooperative contact on changing negative attitudes toward stigmatized social groups. *Journal of Personality and Social Psychology, 60*, 531–544.

Desmond, E. W. (1987, November 30). Out in the open. *Time*, 80–90.

Deutsch, M. (1949). An experimental study of the effects of cooperation and competition upon group process. *Human Relations, 2*, 199–231.

Deutsch, M. (1973). *The resolution of conflict*. New Haven, CT: Yale University Press.

Deutsch, M. (1990). Psychological roots of moral exclusion. *Journal of Social Issues, 46*(1), 21–25.

Deutsch, M. (1993). Educating for a peaceful world. *American Psychologist, 48*, 510–517.

Deutsch, M., & Collins, M. E. (1951). *Interracial housing: A psychological evaluation of a social experiment*. Minneapolis, MN: University of Minnesota Press.

Deutsch, M., & Gerard, H. B. (1955). A study of normative and informational social influence upon individual judgment. *Journal of Abnormal and Social Psychology, 51*, 629–636.

Deutsch, M. & Krauss, R. M. (1960). The effect of threat upon interpersonal bargaining. *Journal of Abnormal and Social Psychology, 61*, 181–189.

Devine, P. G. (1989). Stereotypes and prejudice: Their automatic and controlled components. *Journal of Personality and Social Psychology, 56*, 5–18.

Devine, P. G., & Monteith, M. J. (1993). The role of discrepancy-associated affect in prejudice reduction. In D. M. Mackie & D. L. Hamilton (Eds.), *Affect, cognition, and stereotyping* (pp. 317–344). San Diego: Academic Press.

Dlab, L. N. (1970). A study of intragroup and intergroup relations among experimentally produced small groups. *Genetic Psychology Monographs, 82*, 49–82.

Diehl, M., & Stroebe, W. (1991). Productivity loss in idea-generating groups: Tracking down the blocking effect. *Journal of Personality and Social Psychology, 61*, 392–403.

Diener, E. (1980). Deindividuation: The absence of self-awareness and self-regulation in group members. In P. Paulus (Ed.), *The psychology of group influence*. Hillsdale, NJ: Erlbaum.

Diener, E., & Crandall, R. (1979). An evaluation of the Jamaican anticrime program. *Journal of Applied Social Psychology, 9*, 135–146.

Diener, E., & Wallbom, M. (1976). Effects of self-awareness on antinormative behavior. *Journal of Research in Personality, 10*, 107–111.

Dietrich, D. M., & Berkowitz, L. (1997). Alleviation of dissonance by engaging in prosocial behavior or receiving ego-enhancing feedback. *Journal of Social Behavior and Personality, 12*, 557–566.

Dijker, A. J. M. (1987). Emotional reactions to ethnic minorities. *European Journal of Social Psychology, 47*, 1105–1117.

Dindia, K., & Allen, M. (1992). Sex differences in self-disclosure: A meta-analysis. *Psychological Bulletin, 112*, 106–122.

Dion, K. K., & Berscheid, E. (1974). Physical attractiveness and peer perception among children. *Sociometry, 37*, 1–12.

Dion, K. K., Berscheid, E., & Walster, E. (1972). What is beautiful is good. *Journal of Personality and Social Psychology, 24*, 285–290.

Dion, K. L., & Dion, K. K. (1988). Romantic love: Individual and cultural perspectives. In R. Sternberg & M. Barnes (Eds.), *The psychology of love* (pp. 264–289). New Haven, CT: Yale University Press.

Dobzhansky, T. (1973). *Genetic diversity and human equality*. New York: Basic Books.

Dodge, K. A., Bates, J. E., & Pettit, G. S. (1990). Mechanisms of the cycle of violence. *Science, 250*, 1678–1683.

Dodge, K. A., & Coie, J. D. (1987). Social-information-processing factors in reactive and proactive aggression in children's peer groups. *Journal of Personality and Social Psychology, 53*, 1146–1158.

Dodge, K. A., & Crick, N. R. (1990). Social information-processing bases of aggressive behavior in children. Special Issue: Illustrating the value of basic research. *Personality and Social Psychology Bulletin, 16*, 8–22.

Dodge, K. A., & Newman, J. P. (1981). Biased decision-making processes in aggressive boys. *Journal of Abnormal Psychology, 90*, 375–379.

Dodge, K. A., Pettit, G. S., McClaskey, C. L., & Brown, M. (1986). Social competence in children. *Monographs of the Society for Research in Child Development, 51* (2, Serial No. 213).

Dodge, K. A., & Somberg, D. R. (1987). Hostile attributional biases among aggressive boys are exacerbated under conditions of threat to the self. *Child Development, 58*, 213–224.

Doise, W. (1978). *Groups and individuals: Explanations in social psychology*. Cambridge, England: Cambridge University Press.

Doise, W., & Sinclair, A. (1973). The categorization process in intergroup relations. *European Journal of Social Psychology, 3*, 145–157.

Doise, W., & Weinberger, M. (1973). Représentations musculines dans differentes situations de rencontre mixtes. *Bulletin de Psychologie, 26*, 649–657.

Dollard, J., Doob, L. W., Miller, M. E., Mowrer, O. H., & Sears, R. R. (1939). *Frustration and aggression*. New Haven: Yale University Press.

Donnerstein, E. I., & Linz, D. G. (1986). The question of pornography. *Psychology Today, 20*(12), 56–59.

Donnerstein, E., Linz, D., & Penrod, S. (1987). *The question of pornography: Research findings and policy implications*. New York: Free Press.

Doosje, B., Branscombe, N. R., Spears, R., & Manstead, A. S. R. (1998). Guilty by association: When one's group has a negative history. *Journal of Personality and Social Psychology, 75*, 872–886.

Dovidio, J. F., Allen, J. L., & Schroeder, D. A. (1990). Specificity of empathy-induced helping: Evidence for altruistic motivation. *Journal of Personality and Social Psychology, 59*, 249–260.

Dovidio, J. F., & Fazio, R. H. (1992). New technologies for the direct and indirect assessment of attitudes. In J. M. Tanur (Ed.), *Questions about questions: Inquiries into the cognitive bases of surveys* (pp. 204–237). New York: Russell Sage Foundation.

Dovidio, J. F., & Gaertner, S. L. (1993). Stereotypes and evaluative intergroup bias. In D. M. Mackie & D. L. Hamilton (Eds.), *Affect, cognition, and stereotyping: Interactive processes in group perception* (pp. 167–193). San Diego, CA: Academic Press.

Dovidio, J. F., Piliavin, J. A., Gaertner, S. L., Schroeder, D. A., & Clark, R. D. (1991). The arousal: cost-reward model and the process of intervention: A review of the evidence. In M. S. Clark (Ed.), *Prosocial behavior* (pp. 86–118). Newbury Park, CA: Sage.

Dowd, E. T., Hughes, S. L., Brockbank, L., Halpain, D., Siebel, C., & Siebel, P. (1988). Compliance-based and defiance-based intervention strategies and psychological reactance in the treatment of free and unfree behavior. *Journal of Counseling Psychology, 35*, 370–376.

Downs, A. C., & Lyons, P. M. (1991). Natural observations of the links between attractiveness and initial legal judgments. *Personality and Social Psychology Bulletin, 17*, 541–547.

Drigotas, S. M., & Rusbult, C. E. (1992). Should I stay or should I go? A dependence model of breakups. *Journal of Personality and Social Psychology, 62*, 62–87.

Druckman, D. (1990). The social psychology of arms control and reciprocation. *Political Psychology, 11*, 553–581.

Dubrovsky, V. J., Kiesler, S., & Sethna, B. N. (1991). The equalization phenomenon: Status effects in computer-mediated and face-to-face decision-making groups. *Human Computer Interaction, 6*, 119–146.

Duckitt, J., & Mphuthing, T. (1998). Group identification and intergroup attitudes: A longitudinal analysis in South Africa. *Journal of Personality and Social Psychology, 74*, 80–85.

Duke, L., & Morin, R. (1992, March 8). Focusing on race: Candid dialogue, elusive answers. *The Washington Post*, p. A35.

Dunning, D., Meyerowitz, J. A., & Holzberg, A. D. (1989). Ambiguity and self-evaluation: The role of idiosyncratic trait definitions in self-serving assessments of ability. *Journal of Personality and Social Psychology, 57*, 1082–1090.

Dunton, B. C., & Fazio, R. H. (1997). An individual difference measure of motivation to control prejudiced reactions. *Personality and Social Psychology Bulletin, 23*, 316–326.

Durkheim, E. (1898). *The rules of sociological method*. New York: Free Press.

Dutton, D. G. (1996). *The domestic assault of women*. Vancouver, Canada: University of British Columbia Press.

Duval, S., Duval, V. H., & Neely, R. (1979). Self-focus, felt responsibility, and helping behavior. *Journal of Personality and Social Psychology, 37*, 1769–1778.

Duval, S., & Wicklund, R. A. (1972). *A theory of objective self-awareness*. New York: Academic Press.

Dweck, C. S. (1986). Motivational processes affecting learning. *American Psychologist, 41*, 1040–1048.

Eagly, A. H. (1987). *Sex differences in social behavior: A social-role interpretation*. Hillsdale, NJ: Erlbaum.

Eagly, A. H. (1995). The science and politics of comparing women and men. *American Psychologist, 50*, 145–158.

Eagly, A. H., Ashmore, R. D., Makhijani, M. G., & Longo, L. C. (1991). What is beautiful is good, but . . .: A meta-analytic review of research on the physical attractiveness stereotype. *Psychological Bulletin, 110*, 109–128.

Eagly, A. H., & Carli, L. L. (1981). Sex of researchers and sex-typed communications as determinants of sex differences in influence-ability: A meta-analysis of social influence studies. *Psychological Bulletin, 90*, 1–20.

Eagly, A. H., & Chaiken, S. (1993). *The psychology of attitudes*. San Diego: Harcourt, Brace, Jovanovich.

Eagly, A. H., Chaiken, S., & Wood, W. (1981). An attributional analysis of persuasion. In J. H. Harvey, W. J. Ickes, & R. F. Kidd (Eds.), *New directions in attribution research* (Vol. 3, pp. 37–62). Hillsdale, NJ: Erlbaum.

Eagly, A. H., & Crowley, M. (1986). Gender and helping behavior: A meta-analytic review of the social psychological literature. *Psychological Bulletin, 100*, 283–308.

Eagly, A. H., & Johnson, B. T. (1990). Gender and leadership style: A meta-analysis. *Psychological Bulletin, 108*, 233–256.

Eagly, A. H., & Karau, S. J. (1991). Gender and the emergence of leaders: A meta-analysis. *Journal of Personality and Social Psychology, 60*, 685–710.

Eagly, A. H., Karau, S. J., & Makhijani, M. G. (1995). Gender and the effectiveness of leaders: A meta-analysis. *Psychological Bulletin, 117*, 125–145.

Eagly, A. H., Makhijani, M. G., & Klonsky, B. G. (1992). Gender and the evaluation of leaders: A meta-analysis. *Psychological Bulletin, 111*, 3–22.

Eagly, A. H., & Mladinic, A. (1989). Gender stereotypes and attitudes toward women and men. *Personality and Social Psychology Bulletin, 15*, 543–558.

Eagly, A. H., & Steffen, V. J. (1984). Gender stereotypes stem from the distribution of women and men into social roles. *Journal of Personality and Social Psychology, 46*, 735–754.

Eagly, A. H., Wood, W., & Chaiken, S. (1978). Causal inferences about communicators and their effect on opinion change. *Journal of Personality and Social Psychology, 36*, 424–435.

Earley, P. C. (1989). Social loafing and collectivism: A comparison of the United States and the People's Republic of China. *Administrative Science Quarterly, 34*, 565–581.

Easterbrook, J. A. (1959). The effect of emotion on cue utilization and the organization of behavior. *Psychological Review, 66*, 183–201.

Ebbesen, E. B., Kjos, G. L., & Konecni, V. J. (1976). Spatial ecology: Its effects on the choice of friends and enemies. *Journal of Experimental Social Psychology, 12*, 505–518.

Eberhard, J. L., & Fiske, S. T. (1996). Motivating individuals to change: What is a target to do? In C. N. Macrae, C. Stangor, & M. Hewstone (Eds.), *Stereotypes and stereotyping* (pp. 369–418). New York: Guilford.

Eckes, T. (1994). Explorations in gender cognition: Content and structure of female and male subtypes. *Social Cognition, 12*, 37–60.

Eckes, T., & Six, B. (1994). Fact and fiction in research on the relationship between attitude and behavior: A meta-analysis. *Journal of Social Psychology, 25*, 253–271. .

Edney, J. J. (1980). The commons problem: Alternative perspectives. *American Psychologist, 35*, 131–150.

Edwards, K., & von Hippel, W. (1995). Hearts and minds. The priority of affective versus cognitive actors in person perception. *Personality and Social Psychology Bulletin, 21*, 996–1011.

Eibl-Eibesfeldt, I. (1972). Similarities and differences between cultures in expressive movement. In R. A. Hinde (Ed.), *Nonverbal communication*. Cambridge, England: Cambridge University Press.

Eisenberg, N. (1991). Meta-analytic contributions to the literature on prosocial behavior. *Personality and Social Psychology Bulletin, 17*, 273–282.

Eisenberg, N., & Fabes, R. A. (1991). Prosocial behavior and empathy: A multimethod developmental perspective. In M. S. Clark (Ed.), *Prosocial behavior* (pp. 34–61). Newbury Park, CA: Sage.

Eisenberger, R., Cotterell, N., & Marvel, J. (1987). Reciprocation ideology. *Journal of Personality and Social Psychology, 53*, 743–750.

Eisenger, R., & Mills, J. (1968). Perception of the sincerity and competence of a communicator as a function of the extremity of his position. *Journal of Experimental Social Psychology, 4*, 224–232.

Eisenstat, R. A. (1990). Compressor team start-up. In J. R. Hackman (Ed.), *Groups that work (and those that don't)* (pp. 411–426). San Francisco: Jossey-Bass.

Eiser, J. R., & Sutton, S. R. (1977). Smoking as a subjectively rational choice. *Addictive Behaviors, 2*, 129–34.

Eiser, J. R., & van der Pligt, J. (1986). Smoking cessation and smokers' perceptions of their addiction. *Journal of Social and Clinical Psychology, 4*, 60–70.

Eiser, J. R., van der Pligt, J., Raw, M., & Sutton, S. R. (1985). Trying to stop smoking: Effects of perceived addiction, attributions for failure and expectancy of success. *Journal of Behavioral Medicine, 8*, 321–41.

Ekman, P. (1971). Universals and cultural differences in facial expression of emotion. In J. L. Cole (Ed.), *Nebraska symposium on motivation* (Vol. 19, pp. 207–283). Lincoln: University of Nebraska Press.

Ekman, P. (1992). Facial expressions of emotion: New findings, new questions. *Psychological Science, 3*, 34–38.

Ekman, P., Friesen, W. V., O'Sullivan, M., Chan, A., Diacoyanni-Tarlatzis, I., Heider, K., Krause, R., LeCompte, W. A., Pitcarin, T., Ricci-Bitti, P. E., Scherer, K., Tomita, M., & Tzauaras, A. (1987). Universals and cultural differences in the judgments of facial expressions of emotion. *Journal of Personality and Social Psychology, 53*, 712–717.

Ekman, P., & Friesen, W. V. (1974). Detecting deception from the body or face. *Journal of Personality and Social Psychology, 29*, 288–298.

Ekman, P., Friesen, W. V., & Ellsworth, P. (1972). *Emotion in the human face*. Elmsford, NY: Pergamon.

Ekman, P., & O'Sullivan, M. (1991). Who can catch a liar? *American Psychologist, 46*, 913–920.

Elkin, R. A., & Leippe, M. R. (1986). Physiological arousal, dissonance, and attitude change: Evidence for a dissonance arousal link and a "don't remind me" effect. *Journal of Personality and Social Psychology, 51*, 55–56.

Ellemers, N., Spears, R., & Doosje, B. (1997). Sticking together or falling apart: In-group identification as a psychological determinant of group commitment versus individual mobility. *Journal of Personality and Social Psychology, 72*, 617–626.

Ellemers, N., & van Knippenberg, A. (1997). Stereotyping in social context. In R. Spears

Ellsworth, P., & Carlsmith, J. M. (1973). Eye contact and gaze aversion in an aggressive encounter. *Journal of Personality and Social Psychology, 28*, 280–292.

Ennis, R., & Zanna, M. P. (1991). *Hockey assault: Constitutive versus normative violations.* Paper presented at Canadian Psychological Association convention.

Epstein, R., & Komorita S. S. (1966). Childhood prejudice as a function of parental ethnocentrism, punitiveness, and outgroup characteristics. *Journal of Personality and Social Psychology, 3*, 259–264.

Epstein, S. (1992). Coping ability, negative self-evaluation, and overgeneralization: Experiment and theory. *Journal of Personality and Social Psychology, 62*, 826–836.

Epstein, Y. M., Suedfeld, P., & Silverstein, S. J. (1973). The experimental contract: Subjects' expectations of and reactions to some behaviors of experimenters. *American Psychologist, 28*, 212–221.

Erb, H. P., Bohner, G., Schmalzle, K., & Rank, S. (1998). Beyond conflict and discrepancy: Cognitive bias in minority and majority influence. *Personality and Social Psychology Bulletin, 24*, 395–409.

Esser, J. K. (1998). Alive and well after 25 years: A review of groupthink research. *Organizational Behavior and Human Decision Processes, 73*, 116–141.

Esser, J. K., & Lindoerfer, J. S. (1989). Groupthink and the space shuttle Challenger accident: Toward a quantitative case analysis. *Journal of Behavioral Decision Making, 2*, 167–177.

Esses, V. M, Haddock, G., & Zanna, M. P. (1993). Values, stereotypes, and emotions as determinants of intergroup attitudes. In D. M. Mackie & D. L. Hamilton (Eds.), *Affect, cognition, and stereotyping: Interactive processes in group perception* (pp. 137–166). San Diego, CA: Academic Press.

Ethical Principles of Psychologists and Code of Conduct. (1992). Washington, DC: American Psychological Association.

Etzioni, A. (1962). *The hard way to peace*. New York: Collier.

Etzioni, A. (1967). The Kennedy experiment. *The Western Political Quarterly, 20,* 361–380.

Evans, G. W. (1979). Behavioral and physiological consequences of crowding in humans. *Journal of Applied Social Psychology, 9,* 27–46.

Falbo, T., & Peplau, L. A. (1980). Power strategies in intimate relationships. *Journal of Personality and Social Psychology 38,* 618–628.

Fazio, R. H. (1986). How do attitudes guide behavior? In R. M. Sorrentino & E. T. Higgins (Eds.), *The handbook of motivation and cognition: Foundations of social behavior* (pp. 204–243). New York: Guilford.

Fazio, R. H. (1989). On the power and functionality of attitudes: The role of attitude accessibility. In A. R. Pratkanis, S. J. Breckler, & A. G. Greenwald (Eds.), *Attitude structure and function* (pp. 153–179). Hillsdale, NJ: Erlbaum.

Fazio, R. H. (1990). Multiple processes by which attitudes guide behavior: The MODE model as an integrative framework. In M. P. Zanna (Ed.) *Advances in experimental social psychology* (Vol. 23, pp. 75–109). New York: Academic Press.

Fazio, R. H., Blascovich, J., & Driscoll, D. M. (1992). On the functional value of attitudes: The influence of accessible attitudes upon the ease and quality of decision-making. *Personality and Social Psychology Bulletin, 18,* 388–401.

Fazio, R. H., Chen, J., McDonel, E., & Sherman, S. J. (1982). Attitude accessibility, attitude-behavior consistency, and the strength of the object-evaluation association. *Journal of Experimental Social Psychology, 18,* 339–357.

Fazio, R. H., Effrein, E. A., & Falender, V. J. (1981). Self-perceptions following social interactions. *Journal of Personality and Social Psychology, 41,* 232–242.

Fazio, R. H., Jackson, J. R., Dunton, B. C., & Williams, C. J. (1995). Variability in automatic activation as an unobstrusive measure of racial attitudes: A bona fide pipeline? *Journal of Personality and Social Psychology, 69,* 1013–1027.

Fazio, R. H., & Zanna, M. P. (1981). Direct experience and attitude-behavior consistency. In L. Berkowitz (Ed.), *Advances in experimental social psychology* (Vol. 14, pp. 161–202). San Diego: Academic Press.

Fazio, R. H., Zanna, M. P., & Cooper, J. (1977). Dissonance and self-perception: An integrative view of each theory's proper domain of application. *Journal of Experimental Social Psychology, 13,* 464–479.

Feather, N. T. (1969). Attitude and selective recall. *Journal of Personality and Social Psychology, 12,* 310–319.

Fein, S. (1996). Effects of suspicion on attributional thinking and the correspondence bias. *Journal of Personality and Social Psychology, 70,* 1164–1184.

Fein, S., & Hilton, J. L. (1992). Attitudes toward groups and behavioral intentions toward individual group members: The impact of nondiagnostic information. *Journal of Experimental Social Psychology, 28,* 101–124.

Fein, S., & Spencer, S. J. (1997). Prejudice as self-image maintenance: Affirming the self through derogating others. *Journal of Personality and Social Psychology, 73,* 31–44.

Feingold, A. (1990). Gender differences in effects of physical attractiveness on romantic attraction: A comparison across five research paradigms. *Journal of Personality and Social Psychology, 59,* 981–993.

Feingold, A. (1992). Gender differences in mate selection preferences: A test of the parental investment model. *Psychological Bulletin, 112,* 125–139.

Feingold, A. (1992). Good-looking people are not what we think. *Psychological Bulletin, 111,* 304–341.

Felson, R. B. (1989). Parents and the reflected appraisal process: A longitudinal analysis. *Journal of Personality and Social Psychology, 56,* 965–971.

Fenigstein, A., Scheier, M. F., & Buss, A. H. (1975). Public and private self-consciousness: Assessment and theory. *Journal of Consulting and Clinical Psychology, 43,* 522–527.

Ferdman, B. M. (1989). Affirmative action and the challenge of the color-blind perspective. In F. A. Blanchard & F. J. Crosby (Eds.), *Affirmative action in perspective* (pp. 169–176). New York: Springer-Verlag.

Feshbach, N. (1980). *The child as "psychologist" and "economist": Two curricula.* Paper presented at the American Psychological Association convention.

Feshbach, N., & Feshbach, S. (1982). Empathy training and the regulation of aggression: Potentialities and limitations. *Academic Psychology Bulletin, 4,* 399–413.

Feshbach, S., & Singer, R. (1957). The effects of personality and shared threats upon social prejudice. *Journal of Abnormal and Social Psychology, 54,* 411–16.

Festinger, L. (1950). Informal social communication. *Psychological Review, 57,* 271–282.

Festinger, L. (1954). A theory of social comparison processes. *Human Relations, 7,* 117–140.

Festinger, L. (1957). *A theory of cognitive dissonance.* Stanford, CA: Stanford University Press.

Festinger, L., & Carlsmith, J. M. (1959). Cognitive consequences of forced compliance. *Journal of Abnormal and Social Psychology, 58,* 203–210.

Festinger, L., Pepitone, A., & Newcomb, T. (1952). Some consequences of de-individuation in a group. *Journal of Abnormal and Social Psychology, 58,* 203–210.

Festinger, L., Schachter, S., & Back, K. (1950). *Social pressures in informal groups: A study of human factors in housing.* Stanford, CA: Stanford University Press.

Fiedler, F. (1964). A contingency model of leadership effectiveness. In L. Berkowitz (Ed.), *Advances in experimental social psychology* (Vol. 1, pp. 149–190). New York: Academic Press.

Fincham, F., & O'Leary, K. D. (1983). Causal inferences for spouse behavior in maritally distressed and nondistressed couples. *Journal of Clinical and Social Psychology, 1,* 42–57.

Finlay, K. A., Trafimow, D., & Jones, D. (1997). Predicting health behaviors from attitudes and subjective norms: Between-subjects and within-subjects analyses. *Journal of Applied Social Psychology, 27,* 2015–2031.

Fishbein, M., & Ajzen, I. (1975). *Belief, attitude, intention, and behavior: An introduction to theory and research.* Reading, MA: Addison-Wesley.

Fisher, J. D., & Fisher, W. A. (1992). Changing AIDS-risk behavior. *Psychological Bulletin, 111,* 455–474.

Fisher, J. D., Nadler, A., & Whitcher-Alagner, S. (1982). Recipient reactions to aid. *Psychological Bulletin, 91,* 27–54.

Fisher, R., & Ury, W. (1981). *Getting to Yes: Negotiating agreement without giving in*. New York: Houghton Mifflin.

Fisher, R., & White, J. H. (1976). Intergroup conflicts resolved by outside consultants. *Journal of Community Development, 7*, 88–98.

Fiske, A. P. (1991). The cultural relativity of selfish individualism. In M. S. Clark (Ed.), *Prosocial behavior* (pp. 176–214). Newbury Park, CA: Sage.

Fiske, A. P. (1992). The four elementary forms of sociality: Framework for a unified theory of social relations. *Psychological Review, 99*, 689–724.

Fiske, A. P., Kitayama, S., Markus, H. R., & Nisbett, R. E. (1998). The cultural matrix of social psychology. In D. T. Gilbert, S. T. Fiske, & G. Lindzey (Eds.), *Handbook of social psychology* (4th ed., Vol. 2, pp. 915–981). Boston: McGraw-Hill.

Fiske, S. T. (1980). Attention and weight in person perception: The impact of negative and extreme behavior. *Journal of Personality and Social Psychology, 38*, 889–906.

Fiske, S. T. (1993). Controlling other people: The impact of power on stereotyping. *American Psychologist, 48,* 621–628.

Fiske, S. T. (1993). Social cognition and social perception. *Annual Review of Psychology, 44*, 155–194.

Fiske, S. T., & Neuberg, S. L. (1990). A continuum of impression formation, from category-based to individuating processes: Influences of information and motivation on attention and interpretation. In M. P. Zanna (Ed.), *Advances in experimental social psychology* (Vol. 23, pp. 1–74). New York: Academic Press.

Fiske, S. T., & Stevens, L. E. (1993). What's so special about sex? Gender stereotyping and discrimination. In S. Oskamp & M. Costanzo (Eds.), *Gender issues in contemporary society* (pp. 173–196). Newbury Park, CA: Sage.

Fiske, S. T., Bersoff, D. N., Borgida, E., Deaux, K., & Heilman, M. E. (1991). Social science research on trial: Use of sex stereotyping research in Price Waterhouse v. Hopkins. *American Psychologist, 46*, 1049–1060.

Fitness, J., & Fletcher, G. J. O. (1993). Love, hate, anger, and jealousy in close relationships. *Journal of Personality and Social Psychology, 65*, 942–958.

Flay, B. R., Ryan, K. B., Best, J. A., Brown, K. S., Kersell, M. W., d'Avernas, J. R., & Zanna, M. P. (1985). Are social-psychological smoking prevention programs effective? The Waterlook study. *Journal of Behavioral Medicine, 8*, 37–59.

Fleming, I., Baum, A., & Weiss, L. (1987). Social density and perceived control as mediators of crowding stress in high-density residential neighborhoods. *Journal of Personality and Social Psychology, 52*, 899–906.

Fletcher, G. J. O., & Fincham, F. D. (1991). Attribution processes in close relationships. In G. Fletcher & F. Fincham (Eds.), *Cognition in close relationships* (pp. 7–36). Hillsdale, NJ:Z Erlbaum.

Fletcher, G. J. O., & Haig, B. (1990). The layperson as "naive scientist": An appropriate model for personality and social psychology? Unpublished manuscript, University of Canterbury, Christchurch, New Zealand.

Flink, C., & Park, B. (1991). Increasing consensus in trait judgments through outcome dependency. *Journal of Experimental Social Psychology, 27*, 453–467.

Foerster, J., & Strack, F. (1996). Influence of overt head movements on memory for valenced words: A case of conceptual-motor compatibility. *Journal of Personality and Social Psychology, 71*, 421–430.

Folkman, S. (1984). Personal control and stress and coping processes: A theoretical analysis. *Journal of Personality and Social Psychology, 46*, 839–852.

Ford, C. S., & Beach, F. A. (1951). *Patterns of sexual behavior*. New York: Harper & Row.

Forgas, J. P. (1998). Asking nicely? The effects of mood on responding to more or less polite requests. *Personality & Social Psychology Bulletin, 24*, 173–185.

Forsyth, D. R. (1990). *Group dynamics*. Pacific Grove, CA: Brooks/Cole.

Forsyth, D. R. (1999). *Group dynamics* (3rd ed.). Pacific Grove, CA: Brooks/Cole.

Forsyth, D. R., Schlenker, B. R., Leary, M. R., & McCown, N. E. (1985). Self-presentational determinants of sex differences in leadership behavior. *Small Group Behavior, 16*, 197–210.

Foti, R. J., Fraser, S. L., & Lord, R. G. (1982). Effects of leadership labels and prototypes on perceptions of political leaders. *Journal of Applied Psychology, 67*, 326–333.

Foushee, H. C. (1984). Dyads and triads at 35,000 feet: Factors affecting group process and aircrew performance. *American Psychologist, 39*, 885–893.

Foushee, H. C., & Manos, K. L. (1981). Information transfer within the cockpit: Problems in intracockpit communications. In C. E. Billings & E. S. Cheaney (Eds.), *Information transfer problems in the aviation system*. NASA Report No. TP-1875. Moffett Field, CA: NASA-Ames Research Center.

Frable, D. E. S. (1989). Sex typing and gender ideology: Two facets of the individual's gender psychology that go together. *Journal of Personality and Social Psychology, 56*, 95–108.

Frable, D. E. S. (1997). Gender, racial, ethnic, sexual, and class identities. *Annual Review of Psychology, 48*, 139–162.

Fraley, R. C., & Waller, N. G. (1998). Adult attachment patterns: A test of the typological model. In J. A. Simpson & W. F. Rholes (Eds.), *Attachment theory and close relationships* (pp. 78–114). New York: Guilford.

Frank, M. G., & Gilovich, T. (1988). The dark side of self- and social perception: Black uniforms and aggression in professional sports. *Journal of Personality and Social Psychology, 54*, 74–85.

Freedman, J. L. (1965). Long-term behavioral effects of cognitive dissonance. *Journal of Experimental Social Psychology, 1*,145–155.

Freedman, J. L., & Fraser, S. C. (1966). Compliance without pressure: The foot-in-the-door technique. *Journal of Personality and Social Psychology, 4*, 195–202.

Freedman, J. L., & Sears, D. O. (1965). Warning, distraction and resistance to influence. *Journal of Personality and Social Psychology, 1*, 262–266.

Freiberg, P. (1991a, April). Self-esteem gender gap widens in adolescence. *APA Monitor*, p. 29.

Freiberg, P. (1991b, January). Surprise—most bosses are incompetent. *APA Monitor* p. 23.

Frenkel, O. J., & Doob, A. N. (1976). Post-decision dissonance at the polling booth. *Canadian Journal of Behavior Behavioral Science, 8*, 347–350.

Freund, T., Kruglanski, A. W., & Shpitzajsen, A. (1985). The freezing and unfreezing of impression primacy: Effects of need for structure and the fear of invalidity. *Personality and Social Psychology Bulletin, 11*, 479–487.

Frey, D. (1986). Recent research on selective exposure to information. In L. Berkowitz (Ed.), *Advances in experimental social psychology* (Vol. 19, pp. 41–80). New York: Academic Press.

Friedman, H. S., Riggio, R. E., & Casella, D. F. (1988). Nonverbal skill, personal charisma, and initial attraction. *Personality and Social Psychology Bulletin, 14*, 203–211.

Frijda, N. H. (1986). *The emotions.* Cambridge, England: Cambridge University Press.

Frijda, N. H., Kuipers, P., & ter Schure, E. (1989). Relations among emotion, appraisal, and emotional action readiness. *Journal of Personality and Social Psychology, 57*, 212–228.

Froming, W. J., Walker, G. R., & Lopyan, K. J. (1982). Public and private self awareness: When personal attitudes clash with societal expectations. *Journal of Experimental Social Psychology, 18*, 476–487.

Fukada, H. (1986). Psychological processes mediating the persuasion inhibiting effect of forewarning in fear arousing communication. *Psychological Reports, 58*, 87–90.

Fuller, R. G., & Sheehy-Skeffington, A. (1974). Effects of group laughter on responses to humorous materials: A replication and extension. *Psychological Reports, 35*, 531–534.

Funder, D. C., & Colvin, C. R. (1988). Friends and strangers: Acquaintanceship, agreement, and the accuracy of personality judgments. *Journal of Personality and Social Psychology, 55*, 149–158.

Furnham, A., & Gunter, B. (1984). Just world beliefs and attitudes towards the poor. *British Journal of Social Psychology, 23*, 265–269.

Gabor, A. (1992, January 26). Take this job and love it. *The New York Times*, 1F.

Gabrenya, W. K., Wang, Y., & Latané, B. (1985). Social loafing on an optimizing task: Cross-cultural differences among Chinese and Americans. *Journal of Cross Cultural Psychology, 16*, 223–242.

Gaertner, S. L., Dovidio, J. F., Anastasio, P. A., Bachman, B. A., & Rust, M. C. (1993). The common ingroup identity model: Recategorization and the reduction of intergroup bias. In W. Stroebe & M. Hewstone (Eds.), *European review of social psychology* (Vol. 4, pp. 1–26). Chichester, England: Wiley.

Gaertner, S. L., Mann, J. A., Murrell, A. J., & Dovidio, J. F. (1989). Reducing intergroup bias: The benefits of recategorization. *Journal of Personality and Social Psychology, 57*, 239–249.

Gaertner, S. L., Mann, J. A., Dovidio, J. F., Murrell, A. J., & Pomare, M. (1990). How does cooperation reduce intergroup bias? *Journal of Personality and Social Psychology, 59*, 692–704.

Gaertner, S. L., Mann, J. A., Dovidio, J. F., Murrell, A. J., & Pomare, M. (1990). How does cooperation reduce intergroup bias? *Journal of Personality and Social Psychology, 59*, 692–704.

Gaertner, S. L., & Schopler, J. (1998). Perceived ingroup entitativity and intergroup bias: An interconnection of self and others. *European Journal of Social Psychology, 28*, 963–980.

Gagnon, A., & Bourhis, R. Y. (1996). Discrimination in the minimal group paradigm: Social identity or self-interest? *Personality and Social Psychology Bulletin, 22*, 1289–1301.

Galizio, M., & Hendrick, C. (1972). Effect of music accompaniment on attitudes. *Journal of Applied Social Psychology, 2*, 350–359.

Gamson, W. A. (1992). The social psychology of collective action. In A. D. Morris & C. M. Mueller (Eds.), *Frontiers in social movement theory* (pp. 53–76). New Haven, CT: Yale University Press.

Gamson, W. A., Fireman, B., & Rytina, S. (1982). *Encounters with unjust authority.* Homewood, IL: Dorsey Press.

Gangestad, S. W. (1993). Sexual selection and physical attractiveness: Implications for mating dynamics. *Human Nature, 4*, 205–235.

Garcia-Marques, T. M. (1999). *The mind needs the heart: The mood-as-regulation-mechanism hypothesis.* Unpublished doctoral dissertation, University of Lisbon, Portugal.

Gardner, R. C., Lalone, R. N., Nero, A. M., & Young M. Y. (1988). Ethnic stereotypes: Implications of measurement strategy. *Social Cognition, 6*, 40–60.

Garofalo, J. (1997). Hate crime victimization in the United States. In R. C. Davis, A. J. Lurigio, and W. G. Skojan (Eds.), *Victims of crime* (2nd ed., pp. 134–145). Thousand Oaks, CA: Sage.

Geen, R. G. (1991). Social motivation. *Annual Review of Psychology, 42*, 377–391.

Geen, R. G. (1998). Aggression and antisocial behavior. In D. T. Gilbert, S. T. Fiske, & G. Lindzey (Eds.), *Handbook of social psychology* (3rd ed., Vol. 2, pp. 317–356). Boston: McGraw-Hill.

Geis, F. L., Brown, V., Jennings, J., & Porter, N. (1984). TV commercials as achievement scripts for women. *Sex Roles, 10*, 513–525.

Gelles, R. J. (1972). *The violent home: A study of physical aggression between husband and wife.* Beverly Hills, CA: Sage.

Gelles, R. J., & Cornell, L. P. (1985). *Intimate violence in families.* Beverly Hills, CA: Sage.

Gerard, H. B., & Rabbie, J. M. (1961). Fear and social comparison. *Journal of Abnormal and Social Psychology, 62*, 586–592.

Gerbner, G., Gross, L., Morgan, M., & Signorielli, N. (1986). Living with television: The dynamics of the cultivation process. In J. Bryant & D. Zillman (Eds.), *Perspectives on media effects* (pp. 17–40). Hillsdale, NJ: Erlbaum.

Gergen, K. J. (1965). Interaction goals and personalistic feedback as factors affecting the presentation of self. *Journal of Personality and Social Psychology, 1*, 413–424.

Gergen, K. J., & Gergen, M. M. (1988). Narrative and the self as relationship. In L. Berkowitz (Ed.), *Advances in experimental social psychology* (Vol. 21, pp. 17–56). San Diego, CA: Academic Press.

Gersick, C. J. (1989). Marking time: Predictable transitions in task groups. *Academy of Management Journal, 32*, 274–309.

Gersick, C. J. G. (1990). The students. In J. R. Hackman (Ed.), *Groups that work (and those that don't)* (pp. 89–111). San Francisco: Jossey-Bass.

Gibbons, F. X. (1978). Sexual standards and reactions to pornography: Enhancing behavioral consistency through self-focused attention. *Journal of Personality and Social Psychology, 36*, 976–987.

Gibbons, F. X., Eggleston, T. J., & Benthin, A. C. (1997). Cognitive reactions to smoking relapse: The reciprocal relation between dissonance and self-esteem. *Journal of Personality and Social Psychology, 72*, 184–195.

Gibbons, F. X., & Wicklund, R. A. (1982). Self-focused attention and helping behavior. *Journal of Personality and Social Psychology, 43*, 462–474.

Gilbert, D. T. (1991). How mental systems believe. *American Psychologist, 46,* 107–119.

Gilbert, D. T. (1998). Ordinary personology. In D. T. Gilbert, S. T. Fiske, & G. Lindzey (Eds.), *Handbook of social psychology* (4th ed., Vol. 2, pp. 89–150). Boston: McGraw-Hill.

Gilbert, D. T., & Jones, E. E. (1986). Perceiver-induced constraint: Interpretations of self-generated reality. *Journal of Personality and Social Psychology, 50,* 269–280.

Gilbert, D. T., & Krull, D. S. (1988). Seeing less and knowing more: The benefits of perceptual ignorance. *Journal of Personality and Social Psychology, 54,* 193–202.

Gilbert, D. T., Krull, D. S., & Malone, P. S. (1990). Unbelieving the unbelievable: Some problems in the rejection of false information. *Journal of Personality and Social Psychology, 59,* 601–613.

Gilbert, D. T., & Osborne, R. E. (1989). Thinking backward: Some curable and incurable consequences of cognitive busyness. *Journal of Personality and Social Psychology, 57,* 940–949.

Gilbert, D. T., Pelham, B. W., & Krull, D. S. (1988). On cognitive busyness: When person perceivers meet persons perceived. *Journal of Personality and Social Psychology, 54,* 733–740.

Gilbert, D. T., & Silvera, D. H. (1996). Overhelping. *Journal of Personality and Social Psychology, 70,* 678–690.

Gilbert, S. J. (1981). Another look at the Milgram obedience studies: The role of the gradated series of shocks. *Personality and Social Psychology Bulletin, 7,* 690–695.

Gilens, M. (1996). Race and poverty in America: Public misperceptions and the American news media. *Public Opinion Quarterly, 60,* 515–541.

Gilovich, T. (1990). Differential construal and the false consensus effect. *Journal of Personality and Social Psychology, 59,* 623–634.

Gioia, D. A., & Sims, H. P. (1985). Self-serving bias and actor-observer differences in organizations: An empirical analysis. *Journal of Applied Social Psychology, 15,* 547–563.

Glass, D. C. (1964). Changes in liking as a means of reducing cognitive discrepancies between self-esteem and aggression. *Journal of Personality, 32,* 491–549.

Glynn, C. J., Hayes, A. F., & Shanahan, J. (1997). Perceived support for one's opinion and willingness to speak out. *Public Opinion Quarterly, 61,* 452–463.

Goethals, G. R., Cooper, J., & Nacify, A. (1979). Role of foreseen, foreseeable, and unforeseeable behavioral consequences in the arousal of cognitive dissonance. *Journal of Personality and Social Psychology, 37,* 1179–1185.

Goethals, G. R., Messick, D. M., & Allison, S. T. (1991). The uniqueness bias: Studies of constructive social comparison. In J. Suls & T. A. Wills (Eds.), *Social comparison: Contemporary theory and research* (pp. 149–176). Hillsdale, NJ: Erlbaum.

Goethals, G. R., & Nelson, R. E. (1973). Similarity in the influence process: The belief-value distinction. *Journal of Personality and Social Psychology, 25,* 117–122.

Goffman, E. (1959). *The presentation of self in everyday life.* Garden City, NY: Doubleday.

Goldberg, C. (1997, February 25). Real-space meetings fill in the cyberspace gaps. *The New York Times,* p. A8.

Goldin, C. (1990). *Understanding the gender gap.* New York: Oxford University Press.

Goldstein, A. G., & Chance, J. E. (1985). Effects of training on Japanese face recognition: Reduction of the other-race effect. *Bulletin of the Psychonomic Society, 23,* 211–214.

Goldstein, J. H. (1982). Sports violence. *National Forum, 62*(1), 9–11.

Goleman, D. (1990, October 18). Support groups may do more in cancer than relieve the mind. *The New York Times.*

Goleman, D. (1992, December 15). New light on how stress erodes health. *The New York Times,* pp. B5, B9.

Gollwitzer, P. M. (1996). The volitional benefits of planning. In P. M. Gollwitzer & J. A. Bargh (Eds.), *The psychology of action: Linking cognition and motivation to behavior* (pp. 287–312). New York: Guilford.

Gollwitzer, P. M., & Moskowitz, G. B. (1996). Goal effects on action and congnition. In E. T. Higgins & A. W. Kruglanski (Eds.), *Social psychology: Handbook of basic principles* (pp. 361–399). New York: Guilford.

Gollwitzer, P. M., & Schaal, B. (1998). Metacognition in action: The importance of implementation intentions. *Personality and Social Psychology Review, 2,* 124–136.

Goodman, M. (1952). *Race awareness in young children.* Cambridge, MA: Addison-Wesley.

Goranson, R. E., & Berkowitz, L. (1966). Reciprocity and responsibility reactions to prior help. *Journal of Personality and Social Psychology, 3,* 227–232.

Gordon, R. A. (1996). Impact of ingratiation on judgments and evaluations: A meta-analytic investigation. *Journal of Personality and Social Psychology, 71,* 54–70.

Gordon, R. A., & Anderson, K. S. (1995). Perceptions of race-stereotypic and race-nonstereotypic crimes: The impact of response-time instructions on attributions and judgments. *Basic and Applied Social Psychology, 16,* 455–470.

Gorenflo, D. W., & Crano, W. D. (1989). Judgmental subjectivity/objectivity and locus of choice in social comparison. *Journal of Personality and Social Psychology, 57,* 605–614.

Gorer, G. (1968). Man has no "killer" instinct. In M. F. A. Montagu (Ed.), *Man and aggression* (pp. 27–36). New York: Oxford University Press.

Gorn, G. (1982). The effects of music in advertising on choice behavior: A classical conditioning approach. *Journal of Marketing Research, 46,* 94–101.

Gottfredson, M. R., & Hirschi, T. (1990). *A general theory of crime.* Stanford, CA: Stanford University Press.

Gottman, J., Notarius, C., Markman, H., Bank, S., Yoppi, S., & Rubin, M. (1976). Behavior exchange theory and marital decision making. *Journal of Personality and Social Psychology, 34,* 14–23.

Gottman, J. M. (1979). *Marital interaction: Experimental investigations.* New York: Academic Press.

Gould, S. J. (1978). Morton's ranking of races by cranial capacity. *Science, 200,* 503–509.

Gould, S. J. (1981). *The mismeasure of man.* New York: Norton.

Gould, S. J. (1991). *Bully for brontosaurus.* New York: W. W. Norton & Co.

Gouldner, A. W. (1960). The norm of reciprocity: A preliminary statement. *American Sociological Review, 25,* 161–178.

Gray, J. D., & Silver, R. C. (1990). Opposite sides of the same coin: Former spouses' divergent perspectives in coping with their divorce. *Journal of Personality and Social Psychology, 59,* 1180–1191.

Gray, J. R. (1999). A bias toward short-term thinking in threat-related negative emotional states. *Personality and Social Psychology Bulletin, 25,* 65–75.

Graziano, W., & Eisenberg, N. (1997). Agreeableness: Dimension of personality. In R. Hogan, J. Johnson, & S. Briggs (Eds.), *Handbook of personality* (pp. 795–825). San Diego, CA: Academic Press.

Green, D. P., Glaser, J., & Rich, A. (1998). From lynching to gay bashing: The elusive connection between economic conditions and hate crime. *Journal of Personality and Social Psychology, 75,* 82–92.

Greenberg, J., & Pyszczynski, T. (1985). The effect of an overheard ethnic slur on evaluations of the target: How to spread a social disease. *Journal of Experimental Social Psychology, 21,* 61–72.

Greenberg, M. S., & Westcott, D. R. (1983). Indebtedness as a mediator of reactions to aid. In J. D. Fisher, A. Nadler, & B. M. DePaulo (Eds.), *New directions in helping. Volume 1: Recipient reactions to aid* (pp. 85–112). New York: Academic Press.

Greene, G. (1980). *Ways of escape.* New York: Simon & Schuster.

Greenwald, A. G. (1968). Cognitive learning, cognitive response to persuasion, and attitude change. In A. Greenwald, T. Brock, & T. Ostrom (Eds.), *Psychological foundations of attitudes* (pp. 148–170). New York: Academic Press.

Greenwald, A. G. (1980). The totalitarian ego: Fabrication and revision of personal history. *American Psychologist, 35,* 603–618.

Greenwald, A. G., McGhee, D. E., & Schwartz, J. L. K. (1998). Measuring individual differences in implicit cognition: The implicit association test. *Journal of Personality and Social Psychology, 74,* 1464–1480.

Greenwald, A. G., Spangenberg, E. R., Pratkanis, A. R., & Eskenazi, J. (1991). Double-blind tests of subliminal self-help audiotapes. *Psychological Science, 2,* 119–122.

Greenwald, A. G., & Ronis, D. L. (1978). Twenty years of cognitive dissonance: Case study of the evolution of a theory. *Psychological Review, 85,* 53–57.

Gross, A. E., & Latané, J. G. (1974). Receiving help, reciprocation, and interpersonal attraction. *Journal of Applied Social Psychology, 4,* 210–223.

Gruenfeld, D. H. (1995). Status, ideology, and integrative complexity on the U. S. Supreme Court: Rethinking the politics of political decision making. *Journal of Personality & Social Psychology, 68,* 5–20.

Gruenfeld, D. H., Thomas-Hunt, M. C., & Kim, P. H. (1998). Cognitive flexibility communication strategy, and integrative complexity in groups: Public versus private reactions to majority and minority status. *Journal of Experimental Social Psychology, 34,* 202–226.

Guerin, B. (1986). The effects of mere presence on a motor task. *Journal of Social Psychology, 126,* 399–401.

Guimond, S., & Dube-Simard, L. (1983). Relative deprivation theory and Quebec Nationalist Movement: the cognitive-emotion distinction and the personal-group deprivation issue. *Journal of Personality and Social Psychology, 44,* 526–35.

Gurr, T. (1970). *Why men rebel.* Princeton, NJ: Princeton University Press.

Hacker, H. M. (1951). Women as a minority group. *Social Forces, 30,* 60–69.

Hackman, J. R. (1987). The design of work teams. In J. Lorsch (Ed.), *Handbook of organizational behavior* (pp. 315–342). Englewood Cliffs, NJ: Prentice-Hall.

Hackman, J. R. (1992). Group influences on individuals in organizations. In M. D. Dunnette & L. M. Hough (Eds.), *Handbook of industrial and organizational psychology* (2nd ed., Vol. 3., pp. 199–267). Palo Alto, CA: Consulting Psychologists Press.

Hadden, S. B., & Brownlow, S. (1991, March). *The impact of facial structure and assertiveness on dating choice.* Paper presented at the annual meeting of the Southeastern Psychological Association, New Orleans.

Hafer, C. L., Reynolds, K. L., & Obertynski, M. A. (1996). Message comprehensibility and persuasion: Effects of complex language in counterattitudinal appeals to laypeople. *Social Cognition, 14,* 317–337.

Hahlweg, K., Markman, H. J., Thurmaier, F., Engl, J., & Eckert, V. (1998). Prevention of marital distress: Results of a German prospective longitudinal study. *Journal of Family Psychology, 12,* 543–556.

Haines, H., & Vaughan, G. M. (1979). Was 1898 a "great date" in the history of experimental social psychology? *Journal of the History of Behavioral Sciences, 15,* 323–332.

Hains, S. C., Hogg, M. A., & Duck, J. M. (1997). Self-categorization and leadership: Effects of group prototypicality and leader stereotypicality. *Personality and Social Psychology Bulletin, 23,* 1087–1099.

Hamilton, D. L. (1981). Stereotyping and intergroup behavior: Some thoughts on the cognitive approach. In D. L. Hamilton (Ed.), *Cognitive processes in stereotyping and intergroup behavior* (pp. 333–354). Hillsdale, NJ: Erlbaum.

Hamilton, D. L., Driscoll, D., & Worth, L. T. (1989). *Journal of Personality and Social Psychology, 57,* 925–939.

Hamilton, D. L., & Gifford, R. K. (1976). Illusory correlation in interpersonal perception: A cognitive basis for stereotypic judgments. *Journal of Experimental Social Psychology, 12,* 392–407.

Hamilton, D. L., Katz, L. B., & Leirer, V. (1980). Organizational processes in impression formation. In R. Hastie, T. M. Ostrom, E. B. Ebbesen, R. S. Wyer, D. L. Hamilton, & D. E. Carlston (Eds.), *Person memory* (pp. 121–153). Hillsdale, NJ: Erlbaum.

Hamilton, D. L., & Mackie, D. M. (1990). Specificity and generality in the nature and use of stereotypes. In T. Srull & R. S. Wyer, Jr., (Eds.), *Advances in social cognition: Content and process specificity in the effects of prior experiences* (Vol. 3, pp. 99–110). Hillsdale, NJ: Erlbaum.

Hamilton, D. L., & Rose. T. L., (1980). Illusory correlation and the maintenance of stereotypic beliefs. *Journal of Personality and Social Psychology, 39,* 832–845.

Hamilton, D. L., & Sherman, S. J. (1989). Illusory correlations: Implications for stereotype theory and research. In D. Bar-Tal, C. F. Graumann, A. W. Kruglanski, & W. Stroebe (Eds.), *Stereotypes and prejudice: Changing conceptions* (pp. 59–82). New York: Springer-Verlag .

Hamilton, D. L., & Sherman, S. J. (1996). Perceiving persons and groups. *Psychological Review, 103,* 336–355.

Hamilton, D. L., Stroessner, S. J., & Mackie, D. M. (1993). The influence of affect on stereotyping: The case of illusory correlations. In D. M. Mackie and D. L. Hamilton (Eds.), *Affect, Cognition, and Stereotyping: Interactive processes in group perception* (pp. 39–61). San Diego, CA: Academic Press.

Hamilton, D. L., & Zanna, M. P. (1974). Context effects in impression formation: Changes in connotative meaning. *Journal of Personality and Social Psychology, 29,* 649–654.

Hamilton, V. L., & Sanders, J. (1992). *Everyday justice: Responsibility and the individual in Japan and the United States.* New Haven, CT: Yale University Press.

Hamilton, V. L., & Sanders, J. (1995). Crimes of obedience and conformity in the workplace: Surveys of Americans, Russians, and Japanese. *Journal of Social Issues, 51,* 67–88.

Hamilton, W. D. (1964). The genetical evolution of social behavior, I & II. *Journal of Theoretical Biology, 7,* 1–52.

Hammer, J. (1992, January 27). Business as usual. *Newsweek,* pp. 38–40.

Hammond, K. R. (1948). Measuring attitudes by error-choice: An indirect method. *Journal of Abnormal and Social Psychology, 43,* 38–48.

Han, S. & Shavitt, S. (1993). *Persuasion and culture: Advertising appeals in individualistic and collectivistic societies.* Unpublished manuscript, University of Illinois at Urbana, Champagne, IL.

Haney, C., Banks, C., & Zimbardo, P. (1973). Interpersonal dynamics in a simulated prison. *International Journal of Criminology and Penology, 1,* 69–97.

Hansson, R. O., Strobe, M. S., & Stroebe, W. (1988). In conclusion: Current themes in bereavement and widowhood research. *Journal of Social Issues, 44*(3), 207–216.

Harackiewicz, J. M. (1979). The effects of reward contingency and performance feedback on intrinsic motivation. *Journal of Personality and Social Psychology, 37,* 1352–1363.

Harber, K. D. (1998). Feedback to minorities: Evidence of a positive bias. *Journal of Personality and Social Psychology, 74,* 622–628.

Hardy, C., & Latané, B. (1986). Social loafing on a cheering task. *Social Science, 71,* 165–172.

Hare-Mustin, R. T., & Marecek, J. (1988). The meaning of difference: Gender theory, postmodernism, and psychology. *American Psychologist, 43,* 455–464.

Harkins, S. G., & Petty, R. E. (1983). Social context effects in persuasion: The effects of multiple sources and multiple targets. In P. Paulus (Ed.), *Basic group processes.* New York: Springer-Verlag.

Harkins, S. G., & Petty, R. E. (1987). Information utility and the multiple source effect. *Journal of Personality and Social Psychology, 52,* 260–268.

Harkins, S. G., & Szymanski, K. (1989). Social loafing and group evaluation. *Journal of Personality and Social Psychology, 56,* 934–941.

Harmon-Jones, E., Brehm, J. W., Greenberg, J., Simon, L., & Nelson, D. E. (1996). Evidence that the production of aversive consequences is not necessary to create cognitive dissonance. *Journal of Personality and Social Psychology, 70,* 5–16.

Harper, C. R., Kidera, G. J., & Cullen, J. F. (1971). Study of simulated airline pilot incapacitation: Phase II, subtle or partial loss of function. *Aerospace Medicine, 42,* 946–948.

Harris, M. B., Benson, S. M., & Hall, C. L. (1975). The effects of confession on altruism. *Journal of Social Psychology, 96,* 187–192.

Harris, M. J. (1991). Controversy and culmination: Meta-analysis and research on interpersonal expectancy effects. *Personality and Social Psychology Bulletin, 17,* 316–322.

Harris, M. J., & Rosenthal, R. (1985). Mediation of interpersonal expectancy effects: 31 meta-analyses. *Psychological Bulletin, 97,* 363–386.

Harvey, J. H., & Omarzu, J. (1997). Minding the close relationship. *Personality and Social Psychology Review, 1,* 224–240.

Harvey, J. H., Wells, G. L., & Alvarez, M. D. (1978). Attribution in the context of conflict and separation in close relationships. In J. H. Harvey, W. Ickes, & R. F. Kidd (Eds.), *New directions in attribution research* (Vol. 2, pp. 235–260). Hillsdale, NJ: Erlbaum.

Hasher, L., Goldstein, D., & Toppino, T. (1977). Frequency and the conference of referential validity. *Journal of Verbal Learning & Verbal Behavior,16,* 107–112.

Haslam, S. A., Oakes, P. J., Turner, J. C., & McGarty, C. (1995). Social categorization and group homogeneity: Changes in the perceived applicability of stereotype content as a function of comparative context and trait favourableness. *British Journal of Social Psychology, 34,* 139–160.

Hastie, R. (1984). Causes and effects of causal attribution. *Journal of Personality and Social Psychology, 46,* 44–56.

Hastie, R., & Kumar, P. A. (1979). Person memory: Personality traits as organizing principles in memory for behaviors. *Journal of Personality and Social Psychology, 37,* 25–38.

Hastie, R., & Park, B. (1986). The relationship between memory and judgment depends on whether the judgment task is memory-based or on-line. *Psychological Review, 93,* 258–268.

Hastie, R., Penrod, S. D., & Pennington, N. (1983). *Inside the jury.* Cambridge, MA: Harvard University Press.

Hastorf, A., & Cantril, H. (1954). They saw a game: A case study. *Journal of Abnormal and Social Psychology, 49,* 129–134.

Hatfield, E. (1988). Passionate and companionate love. In R. Sternberg & M. Barnes (Eds.), *The psychology of love* (pp. 191–217). New Haven, CT: Yale University Press.

Hatfield, E., & Rapson, R. L. (1993). *Love, sex, and intimacy.* New York: HarperCollins.

Hatfield, E., Sprecher, S., Pillemer, J. T., Greenberger, D., & Wexler, P. (1989). Gender differences in what is desired in the sexual relationship. *Journal of Psychology and Human Sexuality, 1,* 39–52.

Haugtvedt, C. P., & Petty, R. E. (1992). Personality and persuasion: Need for cognition moderates the persistence and resistance of attitude changes. *Journal of Personality and Social Psychology, 63,* 308–319.

Haugtvedt, C. P., & Wegener, D. T. (1994). Message order effects in persuasion: An attitude strength perspective. *Journal of Consumer Research, 21,* 205–218.

Hays, R. B. (1984). The development and maintenance of friendship. *Journal of Social and Personal Relationships, 1,* 75–98.

Hazan, C., & Shaver, P. (1987). Romantic love conceptualized as an attachment process. *Journal of Personality and Social Psychology, 52,* 511–524.

Hazan, C., & Shaver, P. (1990). Love and work: An attachment-theoretical perspective. *Journal of Personality and Social Psychology, 59,* 270–280.

Hearold, S. (1986). A synthesis of 1043 effects of television on social behavior. In G. Comstock (Ed.), *Public communications and behavior* (Vol. 1, pp. 65–133). New York: Academic Press.

Heatherton, T. F., & Nichols, P. A. (1994). Personal accounts of successful versus failed attempts at life change. *Personality and Social Psychology Bulletin, 20,* 664–675.

Heider, F. (1944). Social percpetion and phenomenal causality. *Psychological Review, 51,* 358–374.

Heider, F. (1958). *The psychology of interpersonal relations.* New York: Wiley.

Heilman, M. E., Simon, M. C., & Repper, D. P. (1987). Intentionally favored, unintentionally harmed? Impact of sex-based preferential selection on self-perceptions and self-evaluations. *Journal of Applied Psychology, 72,* 62–68.

Heilman, M. E., & Stopeck, M. H. (1985). Attractiveness and corporate success: Different causal attributions for males and females. *Journal of Applied Psychology, 70,* 379–388.

Heine, S. J., & Lehman, D. R. (1997). Culture, dissonance, and self-affirmation. *Personality and Social Psychology Bulletin, 23,* 389–400.

Helgeson, V. S., & Mickelson, K. D. (1995). Motives for social comparison. *Personality and Social Psychology Bulletin, 21,* 1200–1209.

Hemstrom, O. (1996). Is marriage dissolution linked to differences in mortality risks for men and women? *Journal of Marriage and the Family, 58,* 366–378.

Henderson-King, E. I., & Nisbett, R. E. (1996). Anti-black prejudice as a function of exposure to the negative behavior of a single black person. *Journal of Personality and Social Psychology, 71,* 654–664.

Hendrick, S., Hendrick, C., & Adler, N. L. (1988). Romantic relationships: Love, satisfaction, and staying together. *Journal of Personality and Social Psychology, 54,* 980–988.

Hendrick, S., Hendrick, C., Slapion-Foote, M. J., & Foote, F. H. (1985). Gender differences in sexual attitudes. *Journal of Personality and Social Psychology, 48,* 1630–1642.

Hensley, T. R., & Griffith, G. W. (1986). Victims of groupthink: The Kent State University Board of Trustees and the 1977 gymnasium controversy. *Journal of Conflict Resolution, 30,* 497–531.

Herlocker, C. E., Allison, S. T., Foubert, J. D., & Beggan, J. K. (1997). Intended and unintended overconsupmtion of physical, spatial, and temporal responses. *Journal of Personality and Social Psychology, 73,* 992–1004.

Herrett-Skjellum, J., & Allen, M. (1996). Television programming and sex stereotyping: A meta-analysis. In B. R. Burleson (Ed.), *Communication yearbook 19* (pp. 157–185). Thousand Oaks, CA: Sage.

Hersey, P., & Blanchard, K. H. (1982). *Management of organizational behavior* (4th ed.). Englewood Cliffs, NJ: Prentice-Hall.

Hewstone, M., Jaspars, J., & Lalljee, M. (1982). Social representations, social attribution and social identity: The intergroup images of "public" and "comprehensive" schoolboys. *European Journal of Social Psychology, 12,* 241–269.

Heymann, T. (1989). *On an average day.* New York: Fawcett Columbine.

Higgins, E. T. (1987). Self-discrepancy: A theory relating self and affect. *Psychological Review, 94,* 319–340.

Higgins, E. T. (1996a). Knowledge activation: Accessibility, applicability, and salience. In E. T. Higgins & A. W. Kruglanski (Eds.), *Social psychology: Handbook of basic principles* (pp. 133–168). New York: Guilford.

Higgins, E. T. (1996b). The "self digest": Self-knowledge serving self-regulatory functions. *Journal of Personality and Social Psychology, 71,* 1062–1083.

Higgins, E. T. (1998). Promotion and prevention: Regulatory focus as a motivational principle. In M. P. Zanna (Ed.), *Advances in experimental social psychology* (Vol. 30, pp. 1–46). New York.: Academic Press.

Higgins, E. T., & Bargh, J. A. (1987). Social cognition and social perception. *Annual Review of Psychology, 38,* 369–425.

Higgins, E. T., King, G. A., & Mavin, G. H. (1982). Individual construct accessibility and subjective impressions and recall. *Journal of Personality and Social Psychology, 43,* 35–47.

Higgins, E. T., & McCann, C. D. (1984). Social encoding and subsequent attitudes, impressions, and memory: "Context-driven" and motivational aspects of processing. *Journal of Personality and Social Psychology, 47,* 26–39.

Higgins, E. T., & Rholes, W. S. (1978). Saying is believing: Effects of message modification on memory and liking for the person described. *Journal of Experimental Social Psychology, 14,* 363–378.

Higgins, E. T., Rholes, W. S., & Jones, C. R. (1977). Category accessibility and impression formation. *Journal of Experimental Social Psychology, 13,* 141–154.

Higgins, E. T., Roney, C. J. R., Crowe, E., & Hymes, C. (1994). Ideal versus ought predilections for approach and avoidance distinct self-regulatory systems. *Journal of Personality and Social Psychology, 66,* 276–286.

Higgins, E. T., Shah, J., & Friedman, R. (1997). Emotional responses to goal attainment: Strength of regulatory focus as moderator. *Journal of Personality and Social Psychology, 72,* 515–525.

Hill, C. T., Rubin, Z., & Peplau, L. A. (1976). Breakups before marriage: The end of 103 affairs. *Journal of Social Issues, 32*(1), 147–168.

Hill, H., Soriano, F. I., Chen, A., & LaFromboise, T. D. (1994). Sociocultural factors in the etiology and prevention of violence among ethnic minority youth. In L. D. Eron, J. H. Gentry, & P. Schlegel (Eds.), *Reason to hope: A psychosocial perspective on violence and youth* (pp. 59–97). Washington, DC: American Psychological Association.

Hillery, J. M., & Fugita, S. S. (1975). Group size effects in employment testing. *Educational and Psychological Measurement, 35,* 745–750.

Hilton, J. L., & Darley, J. M. (1985). Constructing other persons: A limit on the effect. *Journal of Experimental Social Psychology, 21,* 1–18.

Hinsz, V. B., & Davis, J. H. (1984). Persuasive arguments theory, group polarization, and choice shifts. *Personality and Social Psychology Bulletin, 10,* 260–268.

Hiroto, D. S. (1974). Locus of control and learned helplessness. *Journal of Experimental Psychology, 102,* 187–193.

Hirschman, R. S., & Leventhal, H. (1989). Preventing smoking behavior in school children: An initial test of a cognitive-development program. *Journal of Applied Social Psychology, 19,* 559–583.

Hodgins, H. S., & Zuckerman, M. (1993). Beyond selecting information: Biases in spontaneous questions and resultant conclusions. *Journal of Experimental Social Psychology, 29*, 387–407.

Hoelter, J. W. (1985). The structure of self-conception: Conceptualization and measurement. *Journal of Personality and Social Psychology, 49*, 1392–1407.

Hoffman, C., & Hurst, N. (1990). Gender stereotypes: Perception or rationalization? *Journal of Personality and Social Psychology, 58*, 197–208

Hoffman, J. (1998, March 30). Police refine methods so potent, even the innocent have confessed. *The New York Times*, pp. A1, A17.

Hoffman, M. L. (1981). Is altruism part of human nature? *Journal of Personality and Social Psychology, 40*, 121–137.

Hoffman, M. L. (1986). Affect, cognition, motivation. In R. M. Sorrentino & E. T. Higgins (Eds.), *Handbook of motivation and cognition: Foundations of social behavior* (Vol. 1, pp. 244–280). New York: Guilford.

Hofling, C. K., Brotzman, E., Dalrymple, S., Graves, N., & Pierce, C. M. (1966). An experimental study in nurse-physician relationships. *Journal of Nervous and Mental Disease, 143*, 171–180.

Hogarth, R. M., & Einhorn, H. J. (1992). Order effects in belief updating: The belief-adjustment model. *Cognitive Psychology, 24*, 1–55.

Hogg, M. A. (1987). Social identity and group cohesiveness. In J. C. Turner (Ed.), *Rediscovering the social group: A self-categorization theory* (pp. 89–116). Oxford, England: Basil Blackwell.

Hogg, M. A. (1996). Social identity, self-categorization, and the small group. In E. H. Witte & J. A. Davis (Eds.), *Understanding group behavior, Vol. 2: Small group processes and interpersonal relations* (pp. 227–253). Mahwah, NJ: Erlbaum.

Hogg, M. A., & Abrams, D. (1988). *Social identifications*. London: Routledge.

Hogg, M. A., & Abrams, D. (1993). Toward a single-process uncertainty-reduction model of social motivation in groups. In M. A. Hogg & D. Abrams (Eds.), *Group motivation: Social psychological perspectives* (pp. 173–190). London: Harvester Wheatsheaf.

Hogg, M. A., Cooper-Shaw, L., & Holzworth, D. W. (1993). Group prototypicality and depersonalized attraction in small interactive groups. *Personality and Social Psychology Bulletin, 19*, 452–465.

Hogg, M. A., & Hains, S. C. (1998). Friendship and group identification: A new look at the role of cohesiveness in groupthink. *European Journal of Social Psychology, 28*, 323–341.

Hogg, M. A., & Hardie, E. A. (1991). Social attraction, personal attraction, and self-categorization: A field study. *Personality and Social Psychology Bulletin, 17*, 175–180.

Hogg, M. A., & Turner, J. C. (1987). Intergroup behavior, self-stereotyping and the salience of social categories. *British Journal of Social Psychology, 26*, 325–340.

Hollander, E. P. (1958). Conformity, status, and idiosyncrasy credit. *Psychological Review, 65*, 117–127.

Hollander, E. P. (1985). Leadership and power. In G. Lindsey & E. Aronson (Eds.), *The Handbook of Social Psychology* (3rd ed.), vol. 2, pp. 485–538. New York: Random House.

Hollingshead, A. B., McGrath, J. E., & O'Connor, K. M. (1993). Group task performance and communication technology: A longitudinal study of computer-mediated versus face-to-face work groups. *Small Group Research, 24*, 307–333.

Holsti, O. R., & North, R. (1965). The history of human conflict. In E. B. McNeil (Ed.), *The nature of human conflict* (pp. 155–171). Englewood Cliffs, NJ: Prentice-Hall.

Hoover, C. W., Wood, E. E., & Knowles, E. S. (1983). Forms of social awareness and helping. *Journal of Experimental Social Psychology, 19*, 577–590.

Hornstein, H. A. (1975). Social psychology as social intervention. In M. Deutch & H. A. Hornstein (Eds.), *Applying social psychology: Implications for research, practice, and training* (pp. 211–234). Hillsdale, NJ: Erlbaum.

Horowitz, M. J. (1987). *States of mind*. New York: Plenum.

Horwitz, M., & Rabbie, J. M. (1982). Individuality and membership in the intergroup system. In H. Tajfel (Ed.), *Social identity and intergroup relations* (pp. 241–274). New York: Cambridge University Press.

Hosey, G. R., Wood, M., Thompson, R. J., & Druck, P. L. (1985). Social facilitation in a "non-social" animal, the centipede Lithobius forficatus. *Behavioural Processes, 10*, 1–2.

House, R. J., & Shamir, B. (1993). Toward the integration of transformational, charismatic, and visionary theories. In M. M. Chemers & R. Ayman (Eds.), *Leadership theory and research: Perspectives and directions* (pp. 81–107). San Diego: Academic Press.

House, R. J., Woycke, J., & Fodor, E. M. (1988). Charismatic and noncharismatic leaders: Differences in behavior and effectiveness. In J. A. Conger and R. N. Kanungo (Eds.), *Charismatic leadership: The elusive factor in organizational effectiveness* (pp. 98–121). San Francisco: Jossey-Bass.

Hovland, C. I., Janis, I. L., & Kelley, H. H. (1953). *Communication and persuasion*. New Haven: Yale University Press.

Hovland, C. I., Lumsdaine, A., & Sheffield, F. (1949). *Experiments on mass communication*. Princeton, NJ: Princeton University Press.

Hovland, C. I., & Weiss, W. (1951). The influence of source credibility on communication effectiveness. *Public Opinion Quarterly, 15*, 635–650.

Howard, D. J. (1997). Familiar phrases as peripheral persuasion cue. *Journal of Experimental Social Psychology, 33*, 231–243.

Howard, J. A., Blumstein, P., & Schwartz, P. (1987). Social or evolutionary theories? Some observations on preferences in human mate selection. *Journal of Personality and Social Psychology, 53*, 194–200.

Howard, L. (1990, July 9). Periscope. *Newsweek*, 7.

Hoyle, R. H., Pinkley, R. L., & Insko, C. A. (1989). Perceptions of social behavior: Evidence of differing expectations for interpersonal and intergroup interaction. *Personality and Social Psychology Bulletin, 15*, 365–376.

Hsu, F. L. K. (1983). *Rugged individualism reconsidered*. Knoxville, TN: University of Tennesee Press.

Huesmann, L. R. (1986). Psychological processes promoting the relation between exposure to media violence and aggressive behavior by the viewer. *Journal of Social Issues, 42(3)*, 125–139.

Huesmann, L. R., & Eron, L. D. (1984). Cognitive processes and the persistence of aggressive behavior. *Aggressive Behavior, 10*, 243–251.

Huesmann, L. R., & Eron, L. D. (1986). *Television and aggressive child: A cross-national comparison*. Hillsdale, NJ: Erlbaum.

Huesmann, L. R., Eron, L. D., Klein, R., Brice, P., & Fischer, P. (1983). Mitigating the imitation of aggressive behaviors by changing childrens' attitudes about media violence. *Journal of Personality and Social Psychology, 44,* 899–910.

Huesmann, L. R., Eron, L. D., & Yarmel, P. W. (1987). Intellectual functioning and aggression. *Journal of Personality and Social Psychology, 52,* 232–240.

Huff, C., Sproull, L., & Kiesler, S. (1989). Computer communication and organizational commitment: Tracing the relationship in a city government. *Journal of Applied Social Psychology, 19,* 1371–1391.

Hull, J. G. (1981). A self-awareness model of the causes and effects of alcohol consumption. *Journal of Abnormal Psychology, 90,* 586–600.

Hull, J. G., & Young, R. D. (1983). Self-consciousness, self-esteem, and success-failure as determinants of alcohol consumption in male social drinkers. *Journal of Personality and Social Psychology, 44,* 1097–1109.

Hull, J. G., Young, R. D., & Jouriles, E. (1986). Applications of the self-awareness model of alcohol consumption: Predicting patterns of use and abuse. *Journal of Personality and Social Psychology, 51,* 790–796.

Humphrey, R. (1985). How work roles influence perception: Structural-cognitive processes and organizational behavior. *American Sociological Review, 50,* 242–252.

Hunt, W. A., Matarazzo, J. D., Weiss, S. M., & Gentry, W. D. (1979). Associative learning, habit and health behavior. *Journal of Behavioral Medicine, 2,* 111–124.

Hunter, C. E., & Ross, M. W. (1991). Determinants of health-care workers' attitudes toward people with AIDS. *Journal of Applied Social Psychology, 21,* 947–956.

Hurtz, W., & Durkin, K. (1997). Gender role stereotyping in Australian radio commercials. *Sex Roles, 36,* 103–114.

Hyde, J. S. (1979). *Understanding human sexuality.* New York: McGraw-Hill.

Ickes, W., & Simpson, J. A. (1997). Managing empathic accuracy in close relationships. In W. J. Ickes (Ed) *Empathic accuracy* (pp. 218–250). New York: Guilford.

Ikard, F. F., Green, D. E., & Horn, D. (1969). A scale to differentiate between types of smoking as related to the management of affect. *The International Journal of the Addictions, 4,* 649–659.

Indianapolis Star. (1989, September 12).

Insko, C. A. (1981). Balance theory and phenomenology. In R. Petty, T. Ostrom, & T. Brock (Eds.), *Cognitive responses and persuasion* (pp. 309–338). Hillsdale, NJ: Erlbaum.

Insko, C. A., Dreenan, S., Soloman, M. R., Smith, R., & Wade, T. J. (1983). Conformity as a function of the consistency of positive self-evaluation with being liked and being right. *Journal of Experimental Social Psychology, 19,* 341–358.

Insko, C. A., Hoyle, R. H., Pinkley, R. L., Hong, G.-Y., Slim, R. M., Dalton, B., Lin, Y.-H. W., Ruffin, P. P., Dardis, G. J., Bernthal, P. R., & Schopler, J. (1988). Individual-group discontinuity: The role of a consensus rule. *Journal of Experimental Social Psychology, 24,* 505–519.

Insko, C. A., Pinkley, R. L., Hoyle, R. H., & Dalton, B. (1987). Individual versus group discontinuity: The role of intergroup contact. *Journal of Experimental Social Psychology, 23,* 250–267.

Insko, C. A., & Schopler, J. (1987). Categorization, competition, and collectivity. In C. Hendrick (Ed.), *Group processes* (Vol. 8, pp. 213–251). New York: Sage.

Insko, C. A., & Schopler, J. (1998). Differential distrust of groups and individuals. In C. Sedikides, J. Schopler, & C. Insko (Eds.), *Intergroup cognition and intergroup behavior* (pp. 75–108). Mahwah, NJ: Erlbaum.

Insko, C. A., Schopler, J., Hoyle, R. H., Dardis, G. J., & Graetz, K. A. (1990). Individual-group discontinuity as a function of fear and greed. *Journal of Personality and Social Psychology, 58,* 68–79.

Insko, C. A., Thompson, V. D., Stroebe, W., Shaud, K. F., Pinner, B. E., & Layton, B. D. (1973). Implied evaluation and the similarity-attraction effect. *Journal of Personality and Social Psychology, 25,* 297–308.

Insko, C. A., & Wilson, M. (1977). Interpersonal attraction as a function of social interaction. *Journal of Personality and Social Psychology, 35,* 903–911.

Isen, A. M. (1970). Success, failure, attention, and reaction to others: The warm glow of success. *Journal of Personality and Social Psychology, 15,* 294–301.

Isen, A. M. (1987). Positive affect, cognitive processes, and social behavior. In L. Berkowitz (Ed.), *Advances in experimental social psychology* (Vol. 20, pp. 203–253). New York: Academic Press.

Isen, A. M., & Levin, P. F. (1972). The effect of feeling good on helping: Cookies and kindness. *Journal of Personality and Social Psychology, 21,* 384–388.

Isen, A. M., & Simmonds, S. F. (1978). The effect of feeling good on a helping task that is incompatible with good mood. *Social Psychology, 41,* 345–349.

Islam, M. R., & Hewstone, M. (1993). Intergroup attributions and affective consequences in majority and minority groups. *Journal of Personality and Social Psychology, 64,* 936–950.

Isozaki, M. (1984). The effects of discussion on polarization of judgment. *Japanese Psychological Research, 26,* 187–198.

Ito, T. A., Miller, N., & Pollock, V. E. (1996). Alcohol and aggression: A meta-analysis on the moderating effects of inhibitory cues, triggering events, and self-focused attention. *Psychological Bulletin, 120,* 60–82.

Jablin, F. M. (1982). Formal structural characteristics of organizations and superior–subordinate communication. *Human Communication Research, 8,* 338–347.

Jackman, M. R., & Senter, M. S. (1981). Beliefs about race, gender, and social class: different therefore unequal. In D. J. Treiman & R. V. Robinson (Eds.), *Research in stratification and mobility* (Vol. 2, pp. 309–335). Greenwich, CT: JAI Press.

Jackson, L. A., & Sullivan, L. A. (1989). Cognition and affect in evaluations of stereotyped group members. *Journal of Social Psychology, 129,* 659–672.

Jackson, L. A., Sullivan, L. A., Harnish, R., & Hodge, C. N. (1996). Achieving positive social identity: Social mobility, social creativity, and permeability of group boundaries. *Journal of Personality and Social Psychology, 70,* 241–254.

Jackson, L. M., & Esses, V. M. (1997). Of scripture and ascription: The relation between religious fundamentalism and intergroup helping. *Personality and Social Psychology Bulletin, 23,* 893–906.

Jacoby, J. (1984). Some social psychological perspectives on closing. In J. Jacoby & C. S. Criag (Eds.), *Personal selling* (pp. 73–92). Lexington, MA: Lexington Books.

Jacoby, J., & Hoyer, W. D. (1989). The comprehension/miscomprehension of print communication: Selected findings. *Journal of Consumer Research, 15,* 434–443.

Jacoby, J., Hoyer, W. D., & Sheluga, D. A. (1980). *Miscomprehension of televised communications.* New York: American Association of Advertising Agencies.

James, W. (1884). What is an emotion? *Mind, 9,* 188–205.

James, W. (1890). *Psychology.* New York: Holt.

Jamieson, D. W., & Zanna, M. P. (1983). *The lie detector expectation procedure: Ensuring veracious self-reports of attitude.* Paper presented to the Canadian Psychological Association, Winnipeg.

Janis, I. (1972). *Victims of groupthink.* Boston: Houghton Mifflin.

Janis, I. (1982). *Groupthink* (2nd ed.). Boston: Houghton Mifflin.

Janis, I. L., & Feshbach, S. (1953). Effects of fear-arousing communication. *Journal of Abnormal Social Psychology, 48,* 78–92.

Janis, I. L., Kaye, D., & Kirschner, P. (1965). Facilitating effects of "eating while reading" on responsiveness to persuasive communications. *Journal of Personality and Social Psychology, 1,* 181–186.

Janis, I. L., & Mann, L. (1965). Effectiveness of emotional role-playing in modifying smoking habits and attitudes. *Journal of Experimental Research in Personality, 1,* 84–90.

Janis, I. L., & Rife, D. (1959). Persuasibility and emotional disorder. In C. Hovland & I. Janis (Eds.), *Personality and Persuasibility.* New Haven, CT: Yale University Press.

Janis, I. L., & Terwilliger, R. (1962). An experimental study of psychological resistances to fear-arousing communication. *Journal of Abnormal and Social Psychology, 65,* 403–410.

Jason, L. A., Greiner, B. J., Naylor, K., Johnson, S. P., & Van Egenen, L. (1991). A large-scale, short-term, media-based weight loss program. *American Journal of Health Promotion, 5,* 432–437.

Jason, L. A., Reichler, A., Easton, J., Neal, A., & Wilson, M. (1984). Female harassment after ending a relationship: A preliminary study. *Alternative Lifestyles, 6,* 259–269.

Jennings, J., Geis, F. L., & Brown, V. (1980). Influence of television commercials on women's self-confidence and independent judgment. *Journal of Personality and Social Psychology, 38,* 203–210.

Jensen-Campbell, L. A., Graziano, W. G., & West, S. G. (1995). Dominance, prosocial orientation, and female preferences: Do nice guys really finish last? *Journal of Personality and Social Psychology, 68,* 427–440.

Jepson, C., & Chaiken S. (1990). Chronic issue-specific fear inhibits systematic processing of persuasive communications. *Journal of Social Behavior and Personality, 2,* 61–84.

Jervis, R. (1976). *Perception and misperception in international politics.* Princeton, NJ: Princeton University Press.

Johnson, D. W., Maruyama, G., Johnson, R. T., Nelson, D., & Skon, L. (1981). The effects of cooperative, competitive, and individualistic goal structures on achievement: A meta-analysis. *Psychological Bulletin, 89,* 47–62.

Johnson, E. J., & Tversky, A. (1983). Affect, generalization, and the perception of risk. *Journal of Personality and Social Psychology 45,* 20–31.

Johnson, M. P., & Ewens, W. (1971). Power relations and affective style as determinants of confidence in impression formation in a game situation. *Journal of Personality and Social Psychology, 37,* 1532–1538.

Johnson, R. D., & Downing, L. L. (1979). Deindividuation and valence of cues: Effects on prosocial and antisocial behavior. *Journal of Personality and Social Psychology, 37,* 1532–1538.

Johnson, R. W., Kelly, R. J., & LeBlanc, B. A. (1995). Motivational basis of dissonance: Aversive consequences or inconsistency. *Personality and Social Psychology Bulletin, 21,* 850–855.

Johnston, J., & Ettema, J. (1986). Using television to best advantage: Research for prosocial television. In J. Bryant & D. Zillman (Eds.), *Perspectives on media effects* (pp. 143–164). Hillsdale, NJ: Erlbaum.

Johnston, L., & Hewstone, M. (1992). Cognitive models of stereotype change. 3. Subtyping and the perceived typicality of disconfirming group members. *Journal of Experimental Social Psychology, 28,* 360–386.

Johnston, L., & Macrae, C. N. (1994). Changing social stereotypes: The case of the information seeker. *European Journal of Social Psychology, 24,* 581–592.

Jones, E. E. (1985). Major developments in social psychology during the last five decades. In G. Lindzey & E. Aronson (Eds.), *Handbook of social psychology* (Vol. I, pp. 47–107). New York: Random House.

Jones, E. E. (1990a). Constrained behavior and self-concept change. In J. M. Olson & M. P. Zanna (Eds.), *Self-inference processes: The Ontario Symposium* (Vol. 6, pp. 69–86). Hillsdale, NJ: Erlbaum.

Jones, E. E. (1990b). *Interpersonal perception.* New York: Freeman.

Jones, E. E., Brenner, K., & Knight, J. G. (1990). When failure elevates self-esteem. *Personality and Social Psychology Bulletin, 16,* 200–209.

Jones, E. E., & Davis, K. E. (1965). A theory of correspondent inferences: From acts to dispositions. In L. Berkowitz (Ed.), *Advances in experimental social psychology* (Vol. 2, pp. 219–266). New York: Academic Press.

Jones, E. E., & Gerard, H. B. (1967). *Foundations of social psychology.* New York: Wiley.

Jones, E. E., & Harris, V. A. (1967). The attribution of attitudes. *Journal of Experimental Social Psychology, 3,* 1–24.

Jones, E. E., & Nisbett, R. E. (1972). The actor and the observer: Divergent perceptions of the causes of behavior. In E. E. Jones, D. E. Kanouse, H. H. Kelley, R. E. Nisbett, S. Valins, & B. Weiner (Eds.), *Attribution: Perceiving the causes of behavior* (pp. 79–94). Morristown, NJ: General Learning Press.

Jones, E. E., & Pittman, T. S. (1982). Toward a general theory of strategic self-presentation. In J. Suls (Ed.), *Psychological perspectives on the self* (Vol. 1, pp. 231–262). Hillsdale, NJ: Erlbaum.

Jones, E. E., Rhodewalt, F., Berglas, S., & Skelton, J. A. (1981). Effects of strategic self-presentation on subsequent self-esteem. *Journal of Personality and Social Psychology, 41,* 407–421.

Jones, E. E., Rock, L., Shaver, K. G., Goethals, G. R., & Ward, L. M. (1968). Pattern of performance and ability attribution: An unexpected primacy effect. *Journal of Personality and Social Psychology, 10,* 317–340.

Jones, J. M. (1992). Understanding the mental health consequences of race: Contributions of basic social psychological processes. In D. N. Ruble, P. R. Costanzo, & M. E. Oliveri (Eds.), *The social psychology of mental health* (pp. 199–240). New York: Guilford.

Jones, R. A., & Brehm, J. W. (1970). Persuasiveness of one-sided and two-sided communications as a function of the awareness that there are two sides. *Journal of Experimental Social Psychology, 6,* 47–56.

Josephs, R. A., Larrick, R. P., Steele, C. M., & Nisbett, R. E. (1992). Protecting the self from the negative consequences of risky decisions. *Journal of Personality and Social Psychology, 62,* 26–37.

Josephs, R. A., Markus, H. R., & Tafarodi, R. W. (1992). Gender and self-esteem. *Journal of Personality and Social Psychology, 63,* 391–402.

Jost, J. T., & Banaji, M. R. (1994). The role of stereotyping in system-justification and the production of false consciousness. *British Journal of Social Psychology, 33,* 1–27.

Judd, C. M., & Kulik, J. A. (1980). Schematic effects of social attitudes on information processing and recall. *Journal of Personality and Social Psychology, 38,* 569–578.

Judd, C. M., & Park, B. (1988). Out-group homogeneity: Judgments of variability at the individual and group levels. *Journal of Personality and Social Psychology, 54,* 778–788.

Judd, C. M., Park, B., Ryan, C. S., Brauer, M., & Kraus, S. (1995). Stereotypes and ethnocentrism: Diverging interethnic perceptions of African American and White American youth. *Journal of Personality and Social Psychology, 69,* 460–481.

Judd, C. M., Smith, E. R., & Kidder, L. H. (1991). *Research methods in social relations* (6th ed.). Fort Worth, TX: Holt, Rinehart, & Winston.

A juror describes the ordeal of deliberations. (1992, May 6). *New York Times,* p. A13.

Kahle, L. R., & Berman, J. (1979). Attitudes cause behaviors: A cross-lagged panel analysis. *Journal of Personality and Social Psychology, 37,* 315–321.

Kahneman, D., & Miller, D. T. (1986). Norm theory: Comparing reality to its alternatives. *Psychological Review, 93,* 136–153.

Kalin, R., & Berry, J. W. (1982). The social ecology of ethnic attitudes in Canada. *Canadian Journal of Behavioral Science, 14,* 97–109.

Kallgren, C. A., & Wood, W. (1986). Access to attitude-relevant information in memory as a determinant of attitude-behavior consistency. *Journal of Experimental Social Psychology, 22,* 328–338.

Kalven, H. Jr., & Zeisel, H. (1966). *The American jury.* London: University of Chicago Press.

Kameda, T., Ohtsubo, Y., & Takezawa, M. (1997). Centrality in sociocognitive networks and social influence: An illustration in a group decision-making context. *Journal of Personality and Social Psychology, 73,* 296–309.

Kameda, T., & Sugimori, S. (1993). Psychological entrapment in group decision making: An assigned decision rule and a groupthink phenomenon. *Journal of Personality and Social Psychology, 65,* 282–292.

Kandel, D. B. (1978). Similarity in real-life adolescent friendship pairs. *Journal of Personality and Social Psychology, 36,* 306–312.

Kanter, R. (1977). *Men and women of the corporation.* New York: Basic Books.

Kaplan, M. F., & Miller, C. E. (1987). Group decision making and normative versus informational influence: Effects of type of issue and assigned decision rule. *Journal of Personality and Social Psychology, 53,* 306–313.

Kaplan, M. F., & Miller, C. E. (in press). Effects of differential status of group members on process and outcome of deliberation. *Group Processes and Interpersonal Relations.*

Kaplan, M. F., & Wilke, H. (in press). Cognitive and social motivation in group decision making. In J. P. Forgas, K. D. Williams, & L. Wheeler (Eds.), *The social mind: Cognitive and motivational aspects of interpersonal behavior.*

Kaplowitz, N. (1990). National self-images, perception of enemies, and conflict strategies: Psychopolitical dimensions of international relations. *Political Psychology, 11,* 39–82.

Karabenick, S. A., Lerner, R. M., & Beecher, M. D. (1973). Relation of political affiliation to helping behavior on election day, November 7, 1972. *Journal of Social Psychology, 91,* 223–227.

Karau, S. J., & Kelly, J. R. (1992). The effects of time scarcity and time abundance on group performance quality and interaction process. *Journal of Experimental Social Psychology, 28,* 542–571.

Karau, S. J., & Williams, K. D. (1993). Social loafing: A meta-analytic review and theoretical integration. *Journal of Personality and Social Psychology, 65,* 681–706.

Karau, S. J., & Williams, K. D. (1997). The effects of group cohesiveness on social loafing and social compensation. *Group Dynamics, 1,* 156–168.

Kardes, F. R., Sanbonmatsu, D. M., Voss, R. T., & Fazio, R. H. (1986). Self-monitoring and attitude accessibility. *Personality and Social Psychology Bulletin, 12,* 468–474.

Karlin, R. A., Rosen, L., & Epstein, Y. (1979). Three into two doesn't go: A follow-up of the effects of overcrowded dormitory rooms. *Personality and Social Psychology Bulletin, 5,* 391–395.

Kasser, T., & Ryan, R. M. (1996). Further examining the American dream: Differential correlates of intrinsic and extrinsic goals. *Personality and Social Psychology Bulletin, 22,* 280–287.

Kassin, S. M., & Kiechel, K. L. (1996). The social psychology of false confessions: Compliance, internalization, and confabulation. *Psychological Science, 7,* 125–128.

Kassin, S. M., & Wrightsman, L. S. (1985). *The psychology of evidence and trial procedure.* Beverly Hills, CA: Sage.

Katz, D. (1960). The functional approach to the study of attitudes. *Public Opinion Quarterly, 24,* 163–204.

Katz, D. (1965). Nationalism and strategies of international conflict resolution. In H. C. Kelman (Ed.), *International behavior: A social psychological analysis* (pp. 354–390). New York: Holt, Rinehart & Winston.

Katz, D., & Braly, K. W. (1933). Racial stereotypes of 100 college students. *Journal of Abnormal and Social Psychology, 28,* 280–290.

Katz, I. (1981). *Stigma: A social psychological analysis.* Hillsdale, NJ: Earlbaum.

Katz, I., & Hass, R. G. (1988). Racial ambivalence and American value conflict: Correlational and priming studies of dual cognitive structures. *Journal of Personality and Social Psychology, 55,* 893–905.

Keller, R. T. (1986). Predictors of the performance of project groups in R & D organizations. *Academy of Management Journal, 29,* 715–726.

Kelley, A. E., & Nauta, M. M. (1997). Reactance and thought suppression. *Personality and Social Psychology Bulletin, 23,* 1123–1132.

Kelley, H. H. (1950). The warm-cold variable in first impressions of persons. *Journal of Personality, 18,* 431–439.

Kelley, H. H. (1952). Two functions of reference groups. In G. E. Swanson, T. M. Newcomb, & E. L. Hartley (Eds.), *Readings in social psychology.* New York: Henry Holt.

Kelley, H. H. (1967). Attribution theory in social psychology. In D. Levine (Ed.), *Nebraska symposium on motivation* (Vol. 15, pp. 192–241). Lincoln, NE: University of Nebraska Press.

Kelley, H. H. (1972). Attribution in social interaction. In E. E. Jones and others (Eds.), *Attribution: Perceiving the causes of behavior* (pp. 1–26). Morristown, NJ: General Learning Press.

Kelley, H. H. (1979). *Personal relationships: Their structures and processes.* Hillsdale, NJ: Erlbaum.

Kelley, H. H., Berscheid, E., Christensen, A., Harvey, J. H., Huston, T. L., Levinger, G., McClintock, E., Peplau, L. A., & Peterson, D. L. (Eds.). (1983). *Close relationships.* San Francisco, CA: Freeman.

Kelly, J. R., Jackson, J. W., & Hutson-Comeaux, S. L. (1997). The effects of time pressure and task differences on influence modes and accuracy in decision-making groups. *Personality and Social Psychology Bulletin, 23,* 10–22.

Kelly, J. R., & Karau, S. J. (in press). Group decision making: The effects of initial preferences and time pressure. *Personality and Social Psychology Bulletin.*

Kelman, H. C. (1961). Processes of opinion change. *Public Opinion Quarterly, 25,* 57–78.

Kelman, H. C. (1973). Violence without moral restraint: Reflections on the dehumanization of victims and victimizers. *Journal of Social Issues, 29,* 25–61.

Kelman, H. C., & Hamilton, V. L. (1989). *Crimes of obedience: Toward a social psychology of authority and responsibility.* New Haven, CT: Yale University Press.

Kelman, H. C., & Hovland, C. I. (1953). "Reinstatement" of the communicator in delayed measurement of opinion change. *Journal of Abnormal and Social Psychology, 48,* 327–335.

Kelman, H. C., & Lawrence, L. (1972). Assignment of responsibility in the case of Lt. Calley: Preliminary report on a national survey. *Journal of Social Issues, 28*(19), 177–212

Keltner, D., Ellsworth, P. C., & Edwards, K. (1993). Beyond simple pessimism: Effects of sadness and anger on social perception. *Journal of Personality and Social Psychology, 64,* 740–752.

Kenny, D. A. (1991). A general model of consensus and accuracy in interpersonal perception. *Psychological Review, 98,* 155–163.

Kenny, D. A. (1994). Using the social relations model to understand relationships. In R. Erber & R. Gilmour (Eds.), *Theories for the study of relationships* (pp. 111–127). Hillsdale, NJ: Erlbaum.

Kenny, D. A., & DePaulo, B. M. (1993). Do people know how others view them? An empirical and theoretical account. *Psychological Bulletin, 114,* 145–161.

Kenrick, D. T., Sadalla, E. K., Groth, G., & Trost, M. R. (1990). Evolution, traits, and the stages of human courtship: Qualifying the parental investment model. *Journal of Personality and Social Psychology, 58,* 97–116.

Kernis, M. H., Grannemann, B. D., & Barclay, L. C. (1989). Stability and level of self-esteem as predictors of anger arousal and hostility. *Journal of Personality and Social Psychology, 56,* 1013–1022.

Kerr, N. L. (1992). Efficacy as a causal and moderating variable in social dilemmas. In W. Liebrand, D. Messick, & H. Wilke (Eds.), *A social psychological approach to social dilemmas* (pp. 59–88). New York: Pergamon Press.

Kerr, N. L., & Bruun, S. (1983). The dispensability of member effort and group motivation losses: Free rider effects. *Journal of Personality and Social Psychology, 44,* 78–94.

Kerr, N. L., & Kaufman-Gilliland, C. M. (1993). *Communication, commitment, and cooperation in social dilemmas.* Unpublished paper, Michigan State University, East Lansing, MI.

Kerr, N. L., MacCoun, R. J., Hansen, C. H., & Hymes, J. A. (1987). Gaining and losing social support: Momentum in decision making groups. *Journal of Experimental Social Psychology, 23,* 119–145

Kerr, N. L., MacCoun, R. J., & Kramer, G. P. (1996). Bias in judgment: Comparing individuals and groups. *Psychological Review, 103,* 687–719.

Kerr, S., & Jermier, J. M. (1978). Substitutes for leadership: Their meaning and measurement. *Organizational Behavior and Human Performance, 22,* 375–403.

Kiecolt-Glaser, J. K., Fisher, L. D., & Ogrocki, P. (1987). Marital quality, marital disruption, and immune function. *Psychosomatic Medicine, 49,* 13–34.

Kiecolt-Glaser, J. K., & Glaser, R. (1988). Psychological influences on immunity: Implications for AIDS. Special Issue: Psychology and AIDS. *American Psychologist, 43,* 892–898.

Kiecolt-Glaser, J. K., Malarkey, W. B., Cacioppo, J. T., & Glaser, R. (1994). Stressful personal relationships: Immune and endocrine function. In R. Glaser & J. K. Kiecolt-Glaser (Eds.), *Handbook of human stress and immunity* (pp. 321–339). San Diego: Academic Press.

Kiesler, C. A. (1971). *The psychology of commitment.* New York: Academic Press.

Kiesler, C. A., & Kiesler, S. B. (1964). Role of forewarning in persuasive communications. *Journal of Abnormal and Social Psychology, 68,* 547–549.

Kiesler, C. A., & Kiesler, S. B. (1969). *Conformity.* Reading, MA: Addison-Wesley.

Kiesler, S. B., & Mathog, R. (1968). The distraction hypothesis in attitude change. *Psychological Reports, 23,* 1123–1133.

Kiesler, S. B., & Sproull, L. (1992). Group decision making and communication technology. *Organizational Behavior and Human Decision Processes, 52,* 96–123.

Kim, H.-S., & Baron, R. S. (1988). Exercise and the illusory correlation: Does arousal heighten stereotypic processing? *Journal of Experimental Social Psychology, 24,* 366–380.

Kim, M., & Hunter, J. E. (1993). Attitude behavior relations: A meta-analysis of attitudinal relevance and topic. *Journal of Communication, 43,* 101–142.

Kimmel, M. J., Pruitt, P. G., Maganau, J. M., Konar-Goldband, E., & Carnevale, P. J. D. (1980). Effects of trust, aspiration, and gender on negotiation tactics. *Journal of Personality and Social Psychology, 38,* 9–22.

Kinder, D. R. (1986). The continuing American dilemma: White resistance to racial change 40 years after Myrdal. *Journal of Social Issues, 42*(2), 151–171.

Kinder, D. R., & Sears, D. O. (1985). Public opinion and political action. In G. Lindzey & E. Aronson (Eds.), *Handbook of social psychology* (Vol. II, pp. 659–742). New York: Random House.

King, M. L. (1967). *Where do we go from here? Chaos or community.* New York: Harper & Row.

Kinket, B., & Verkuyten, M. (1999). Intergroup evaluations and social context: A multilevel approach. *European Journal of Social Psychology, 29*, 219–238.

Kitayama, S., & Karasawa, M. (1997). Implicit self-esteem in Japan: Name letters and birthday numbers. *Personality and Social Psychology Bulletin, 23*, 736–742.

Kitayama, S., Markus, H. R., & Matsumoto, H. (1995). Culture, self, and emotion: A cultural perspective on "self conscious" emotions. In J. P. Tangney & K. W. Fischer (Eds.), *Self-conscious emotions: The psychology of shame, guilt, embarrassment, and pride* (pp. 366–383). New York: Guilford.

Kitayama, S., Markus, H. R., Matsumoto, H., & Norasak-kunkit, V. (1997). Individual and collective processes in the construction of the self: Self-enhancement in the United States and self-criticism in Japan. *Journal of Personality and Social Psychology, 72*, 1245–1267.

Kitayama, S., Takagi, H., & Matsumoto, H. (1995). Cultural psychology of Japanese self: I. Causal attribution of success and failure. *Japanese Psychological Research, 38*, 247–280.

Klama, J. [pseudonym for John Durant, Peter Klopfer, and Susan Oyama] (1988). *Aggression: The myth of the beast within.* New York: Wiley.

Kleck, R. E., & Strenta, A. (1980). Perceptions of the impact of negatively valued physical characteristics on social interaction. *Journal of Personality and Social Psychology, 39*, 861–873.

Klein, M. W. (1969). Violence in American juvenile gangs. In D. Mulvihill & M. Tumin, *Crimes violence: A staff report submitted to the National Commission on the Causes and Prevention of Violence* (Vol. 13, pp. 1427–1460). Washington, DC: U.S. Government Printing Office.

Klein, S. B., & Loftus, J. (1993). Behavioral experience and trait judgments about the self. *Personality and Social Psychology Bulletin, 19*, 740–745.

Klein, W. M., & Kunda, Z. (1992). Motivated person perception: Constructing justifications for desired beliefs. *Journal of Experimental Social Psychology, 28*, 145–168.

Kleinke, C. L., Meeker, F. B., & LaFong, C. (1974). Effects of gaze, touch, and use of name on evaluation of engaged couples. *Journal of Research in Personality, 7*, 368–373.

Klineberg, O. (1986). SPSSI and race relations in the 1950's and after. *Journal of Social Issues, 42*(4), 53–60.

Kluegel, J. R., & Smith, E. R. (1986). *Beliefs about inequality: Americans' views of what is and what ought to be.* Hawthorn, NY: Aldine de Gruyter.

Knapp, M. L. (1978). *Nonverbal communication in human interaction.* New York: Holt, Rinehart, Winston.

Knight, P. A., & Weiss, H. M. (1980). *Benefits of suffering: Communicator suffering, benefiting, and influence.* Paper presented at the American Psychological Association convention.

Knox, R. E., & Inkster, J. A. (1968). Postdecision dissonance at post time. *Journal of Personality and Social Psychology, 8*, 319–323.

Knudson, R. M., Sommers, A. A., & Golding, S. L. (1980). Interpersonal perception and mode of resolution in marital conflict. *Journal of Personality and Social Psychology, 38*, 751–763.

Kobak, R. R., & Hazan, C. (1991). Attachment in marriage: Effects of security and accuracy of working models. *Journal of Personality and Social Psychology, 60*, 861–869.

Kobrynowicz, D., & Biernat, M. (1997). Decoding subjective evaluations: How stereotypes provide shifting standards. *Journal of Experimental Social Psychology, 33*, 579–601.

Komorita, S. S., & Meek, D. D. (1978). Generality and validity of some theories of coalition formation. *Journal of Personality and Social Psychology, 36*, 392–404.

Korte, C., Ypma, I., & Toppen, A. (1975). Helpfulness in Dutch society as a function of urbanization and environmental input level. *Journal of Personality and Social Psychology, 32*, 996–1003.

Kotkin, J. (1986, February). The "SMART-TEAM" at Compaq Computer. *Inc.*, 48–56.

Kramer, R. M. (1989). Windows of vulnerability or cognitive illusions? Cognitive processes and the nuclear arms race. *Journal of Experimental Social Psychology, 25*, 79–84.

Kramer, R. M., & Brewer, M. B. (1984). Effects of group identity on resource use in a simulated commons dilemma. *Journal of Personality and Social Psychology, 46*, 1044–1057.

Kraus, L. A., Davis, M. H., Bazzini, D., Church, M. B., & Kirchman, C. M. (1993). Personal and social influences on loneliness: The mediating effect of social provisions. *Social Psychology Quarterly, 56*, 37–53.

Kraus, S. J. (1995). Attitudes and the prediction of behavior: A meta-analysis of the empirical literature. *Personality and Social Psychology Bulletin, 21*, 58–75.

Krauss, R. M., Freedman, J. L., & Whitcup, M. (1978). Field and laboratory studies of littering. *Journal of Experimental Social Psychology, 14*, 109–122.

Kraut, R. E. (1973). Effects of social labeling on giving to charity. *Journal of Experimental Social Psychology, 9*, 551–562.

Kravitz, D. A., & Martin, B. (1986). Ringelmann rediscovered: The original article. *Journal of Personality and Social Psychology, 50*, 936–941.

Krebs, D. L. (1970). Altruism—an examination of the concept and review of the literature. *Psychological Bulletin, 73*, 258–303.

Krebs, D., & Miller, D. (1985). Altruism and aggression. In G. Lindzey & E. Aronson (Eds.), *Handbook of social psychology* (3rd ed., Vol. 2, pp. 1–72). New York: Random House.

Krosnick, J. A. (1988a). Attitude importance and attitude change. *Journal of Experimental Social Psychology, 24*, 240–255.

Krosnick, J. A. (1988b). The role of attitude importance in social evaluation: A study of political preferences, presidential candidates evaluations, and voting behavior. *Journal of Personality and Social Psychology, 55*, 196–210.

Krueger, J., Ham, J. J., & Linford, K. M. (1996). Perceptions of behavioral consistency: Are people aware of the actor-observer effect? *Psychological Science, 7*, 259–264.

Krueger, J., & Rothbart, M. (1990). Contrast and accentuation effects in category learning. *Journal of Personality and Social Psychology, 59*, 651–663.

Kruglanski, A. W. (1975). The human subject in the psychology experiment: Fact and artifact. In L. Berkowitz (Ed.), *Advances in experimental social psychology* (Vol. 8, pp. 101–147). New York: Academic Press.

Kruglanski, A. W. (1988). *Lay epistemics and human knowledge: Cognitive and motivational biases.* New York: Plenum Press.

Kruglanski, A. W., & Freund, T. (1983). The freezing and unfreezing of lay-inferences: Effects on impressional primacy, ethnic stereotyping, and numerical anchoring. *Journal of Experimental Social Psychology, 19,* 448–468.

Kruglanski, A. W., & Mackie, D. M. (1990). Majority and minority influence: A judgmental process integration. In W. Stroebe & M. Hewstone (Eds.), *Advances in European social psychology* (Vol. 1, pp. 229–262). Chichester, England: Wiley.

Krull, D. S. (1993). Does the grist change the mill? The effect of the perceiver's inferential goal on the process of social inference. *Personality and Social Psychology Bulletin, 19,* 340–348.

Kuhlman, D. M., Brown, D., & Teta, P. (1992). Judgments of cooperation and defection in social dilemmas: The moderating role of judge's social orientation. In W. B. G. Liebrand & D. M. Messick (Eds.), *Social dilemmas: Theoretical issues and research findings* (pp. 111–132). Oxford, England: Pergamon Press.

Kuhn, D., & Lao, J. (1996). Effects of evidence on attitudes: Is polarization the norm? *Psychological Science, 7,* 115–121.

Kuhn, M. H., & McPartland, T. (1954). An empirical investigation of self attitudes. *American Sociological Review, 19,* 68–76.

Kunda, Z. (1990). The case for motivated reasoning. *Psychological Bulletin, 108,* 480–498.

Kunst-Wilson, W. R., & Zajonc, R. B. (1980). Affective discrimination of stimuli that cannot be recognized. *Science, 207,* 557–558.

Kurdek, L. A. (1991). Sexuality in homosexual and heterosexual couples. In K. McKinney & S. Sprecher (Eds.), *Sexuality in close relationships* (pp. 177–192). Hillsdale, NJ: Erlbaum.

Kurland, J. A. (1979). Paternity, mother's brother, and human sociality. In N. A. Chagnon & W. Irons (Eds.), *Evolutionary biology and human social behavior: An anthropological perspective* (pp. 145–180). North Scituate, MA: Duxbury Press.

Lagerquist, R. (1992, August 15). Band's not pretty, but the money's lovely. *Santa Barbara News Press,* p. B3.

Lalonde, R. N. (1992). The dynamics of group differentiation in the face of defeat. *Personality and Social Psychology Bulletin, 18,* 336–342.

Lane, C., Stanger, T., & Post, T. (1993, April 19). The ghosts of Serbia. *Newsweek,* 30–31.

Langer, E. J. (1975). The illusion of control. *Journal of Personality and Social Psychology, 32,* 311–328.

Langer, E. J., Blank, A., & Chanowitz, B. (1978). The mindlessness of ostensibly thoughtful action. *Journal of Personality and Social Psychology, 36,* 635–642.

Langer, E. J., & Rodin, J. (1976). The effects of choice and enhanced personal responsibility for the aged: A field experiment in an institutional setting. *Journal of Personality and Social Psychology, 34,* 191–198.

Lanzetta, J. T., & Roby, T. B. (1960). The relationship between certain group process variables and group problem-solving efficiency. *Journal of Social Psychology, 52,* 135–148.

LaPiere, R. T. (1936). Type-rationalizations of group antipathy. *Social Forces, 15,* 232–237.

LaPrelle, J., Hoyle, R. H., Insko, C. A., & Bernthal, P. (1990). Interpersonal attraction and descriptions of the traits of others: Ideal similarity, self similarity, and liking. *Journal of Research in Personality, 24,* 216–240.

Larson, J. R. Jr., Christensen, C., Abbott, A. S., & Franz, T. M. (1996). Diagnosing groups: Charting the flow of information in medical decision-making teams. *Journal of Personality and Social Psychology, 71,* 315–330.

Larwood, L., & Whittaker, W. (1977). Managerial myopia: Self-serving biases in organizational planning. *Journal of Applied Psychology, 62,* 194–198.

Lassiter, G. D., & Irvine, A. A. (1986). Videotaped confessions: The impact of camera point of view on judgments of coercion. *Journal of Applied Social Psychology, 16,* 268–276.

Latané, B., & Dabbs, J. M. (1975). Sex, group size, and helping in three cities. *Sociometry, 38,* 180–194.

Latané, B., & Darley, J. M. (1968). Group inhibition of bystander intervention in emergencies. *Journal of Personality and Social Psychology, 10,* 215–221.

Latané, B., & Darley, J. M. (1970). *The unresponsive bystander: Why doesn't he help?* New York: Appleton-Crofts.

Latané, B., Nida, S. A., & Wilson, D. W. (1981). The effects of group size on helping behavior. In J. P. Rushton & R. M. Sorrentino (Eds.), *Altruism and helping behavior* (pp. 287–313). Hillsdale, NJ: Lawrence Erlbaum Associates.

Latané, B., Williams, K., & Harkins, S. (1979). Many hands make light the work: The causes and consequences of social loafing. *Journal of Personality and Social Psychology, 37,* 822–832.

Latané, B., & Wolf, S. (1981). The social impact of majorities and minorities. *Psychological Review, 88,* 438–453.

Laughlin, P. R. (1980). Social combination processes of cooperative problem solving groups on verbal intellective tasks. In M. Fishbein (Ed.), *Progress in social psychology* (pp. 127–155). Hillsdale, NJ: Erlbaum.

Laughlin, P. R., VanderStoep, S. W., & Hollingshead, A. B. (1991). Collective versus individual induction: Recognition of truth, rejection of error, and collective information processing. *Journal of Personality and Social Psychology, 61,* 50–67.

Laumann, E. O., Gagnon, J. H., Michael, R. T., & Michaels, S. (1994). *The social organization of sexuality.* Chicago: University of Chicago Press.

Lavine, H., & Snyder, M. (1996). Cognitive processing and the functional matching effect in persuasion: The mediating role of subjective perceptions of message quality. *Journal of Experimental Social Psychology, 32,* 580–604.

Lawler, E. J., Ford, R. S., & Bleger, M. A. (1988). Coercive capability in conflict: A test of bilateral deterrence versus conflict spiral theory. *Social Psychology Quarterly, 51,* 93–107.

Leary, M. R. (1995). *Self-presentation: Impression management and interpersonal behavior.* Madison, WI: Brown & Benchmark.

Leary, M. R., Barners, B. D., & Griebel, C. (1986). Cognitive, affective, and attributional effects of potential threats to self-esteem. *Journal of Social and Clinical Psychology, 4,* 461–474.

Leary, M. R., Tambor, E. S., Terdal, S. K., & Downs, D. L. (1995). Self-esteem as an interpersonal monitor: The sociometer hypothesis. *Journal of Personality and Social Psychology, 68,* 518–530.

LeBon, G. (1903). *The crowd.* London: Unwin.

Lebow, R. N., & Stein, J. G. (1987). Beyond deterrence. *Journal of Social Issues, 43*(4), 5–71.

Leigh, B. C. (1989). Reasons for having and avoiding sex: Gender, sexual orientation, and relationship to sexual behavior. *Journal of Sex Research, 26,* 199–209.

Leippe, M. R., & Elkin, R. A. (1987). When motives clash: Issue involvement and response involvement as determinants of persuasion. *Journal of Personality and Social Psychology, 52,* 269–278.

Lemaine, G. (1974). Social differentiation and social originality. *European Journal of Social Psychology, 4,* 17–52.

Lemyre, L., & Smith, P. M. (1985). Intergroup discrimination and self-esteem in the minimal group paradigm. *Journal of Personality and Social Psychology, 49,* 660–670.

Lepore, L., & Brown, R. (1997). Category and stereotype activation: Is prejudice inevitable? *Journal of Personality and Social Psychology, 72,* 275–287.

Lepper, M. R., Greene, D., & Nisbett, R. E. (1973). Undermining children's intrinsic interest with extrinsic reward: A test of the "overjustification" hypothesis. *Journal of Personality and Social Psychology, 28,* 129–137.

Lerner, M. J. (1980). *The belief in a just world: A fundamental delusion.* New York: Plenum.

Lerner, M. J., & Miller, D. T. (1978). Just world research and the attribution process: Looking back and ahead. *Psychological Bulletin, 85,* 1030–1051.

Lerner, M. J., & Simmons, C. H. (1966). Observers' reaction to the "innocent victim:" Compassion or rejection? *Journal of Personality and Social Psychology, 4,* 203–210.

Lesar, T. S., Briceland, L., & Stein, D. S. (1997). Factors related to errors in medication prescribing. *Journal of the American Medical Association, 277,* 312–317.

Levenson, R. W., & Gottman, J. M. (1985). Six physiological and affective predictors of change in relationship satisfaction. *Journal of Personality and Social Psychology, 49,* 85–94.

Leventhal, H. (1970). Findings and theory in the study of fear communications. In L. Berkowitz (Ed.), *Advances in experimental social psychology* (pp. 119–186), (Vol. 5). New York: Academic Press.

Leventhal, H., Singer, R. P., & Jones, F. (1965). Effects of fear and specificity of recommendations upon attitudes and behavior. *Journal of Personality and Social Psychology, 2,* 20–29.

Levine, J. M. (1980). Reaction to opinion deviance in small groups. In P. B. Paulus (Ed.), *Psychology of group influence* (pp. 375–429). Hillsdale: NJ. Erlbaum.

Levine, J. M., & Moreland, R. L. (1991). Culture and socialzation in work groups. In L. B. Resnick, J. M. Levine, & S. D. Teasley (Eds.), *Perspectives on socially shared cognition* (pp. 257–279). Washington, DC: American Psychological Association.

Levine, J. M., & Moreland, R. L. (1998). Small groups. In D. L. Gilbert, S. T. Fiske, & G. Lindzey (Eds.), *Handbook of social psychology* (4th ed., Vol. 2, pp. 415–469). Boston: McGraw-Hill.

LeVine, R. A., & Campbell, D. T. (1972). *Ethnocentrism: Theories of conflict, ethnic attitudes and group behavior.* New York: Wiley.

LeVine, R. A., LeVine, S., Leiderman, P. H., Brazelton, T. B., Dixon, S., Richman, A., & Keefer, C. H. (1994). *Child care and culture: Lessons from Africa.* New York: Cambridge University Press.

Levine, R. V., Martinez, T. S., Brase, G., & Sorenson, K. (1994). Helping in 36 U. S. cities. *Journal of Personality and Social Psychology, 67,* 69–82.

Levinger, G. (1991). Commitment vs. cohesiveness: Two complementary perspectives. In W. H. Jones & D. Perlman (Eds.), *Advances in personal relationships* (Vol. 3, pp. 145–150). London: Jessica Kingsley.

Levinger, G., & Schneider, D. (1969). Test of the "risk is a value" hypothesis. *Journal of Personality and Social Psychology, 11,*165–169.

Levy, M. B., & Davis, K. E. (1988). Lovestyles and attachment styles compared: Their relations to each other and to various relationship characteristics. *Journal of Social and Personal Relationships, 5,* 439–471.

Lewicki, P. (1984). Self-schema and social information processing. *Journal of Personality and Social Psychology, 47,* 1177–1190.

Lewicki, P. (1985). Nonconscious biasing effects of single instances on subsequent judgments. *Journal of Personality and Social Psychology, 48,* 563–574.

Lewin, K. (1936). *Principles of topological psychology.* New York: McGraw-Hill.

Lewin, K. (1943). Forces behind food habits and methods of change. *Bulletin of the National Research Council, 108,* 35–65.

Lewin, K. (1947). Group decision and social change. In T. M. Newcomb & E. L. Hartley (Eds.), *Readings in social psychology* (pp. 330–344). New York: Henry Holt.

Lewin, K. (1948). *Solving social conflicts.* New York: Harper & Brothers.

Lewin, K. (1951). Problems of research in social psychology. In D. Cartwright (Ed.), *Field theory in social science* (pp. 155–169). New York: Harper & Row.

Lewin, T. (1991, January 17). Women found to be frequent victims of assaults by intimates. *The New York Times,* p. A12.

Lewin, T. (1992, January 8). Study points to increase in tolerance of ethnicity. *The New York Times,* p. A10.

Lewis, C. C. (1995). *Educating hearts and minds.* New York: Cambridge University Press.

Liberman, A., & Chaiken, S. (1996). The direct effect of personal relevance on attitudes. *Personality and Social Psychology Bulletin, 22,* 269–279.

Liberman, A., de La Hoz, V., & Chaiken, S. (1988). *Prior attitudes as heuristic information.* Paper presented at Western Psychological Association, Burlingame, CA.

Liberman, N., & Trope, Y. (1998). The role of feasibility and desirability considerations in near and distant future decisions: A test of temporal construal theory. *Journal of Personality and Social Psychology, 75,* 5–18.

Lieberman, S. (1956). The effects of changes in roles on the attitudes of role occupants. *Human Relations, 9,* 385–402.

Liebert, R. M., & Spratkin, J. (1988). *The early window: Effects of television on children and youth* (3rd ed.). New York: Pergamon Press.

Liebrand, W. B., & Van Run, G. J. (1985). The effects of social motives on behavior in social dilemmas in two cultures. *Journal of Experimental Social Psychology, 21,* 86–102.

Linder, D. E., Cooper, J., & Jones, E. E. (1967). Decision freedom as a determinant of the role of incentive magnitude in attitude change. *Journal of Personality and Social Psychology, 6,* 245–254.

Lindskold, S. (1978). Trust development, the GRIT proposal and the effects of conciliatory acts on conflict and cooperation. *Psychological Bulletin, 85,* 772–793.

Lindskold, S., (1986). GRIT: Reducing distrust through carefully introduced conciliation. In S. Worchel & W. G. Austin (Eds.), *Psychology of intergroup relations* (2nd ed., pp. 137–154). Chicago: Nelson Hall.

Lingle, J. H., & Ostrom, T. M. (1979). Retrieval selectivity in memory-based impression judgments. *Journal of Personality and Social Psychology, 37,* 180–194.

Linville, P. W. (1985). Self-complexity and affective extremity: Don't put all of your eggs in one cognitive basket. Special Issue: Depression. *Social Cognition, 3,* 94–120.

Linville, P. N. (1987). Self-complexity as a cognitive buffer against stress-related illness and depression. *Journal of Personality and Social Psychology, 52,* 663–676.

Linville, P. W., Fisher, G. W., & Salovey, P. (1989). Perceived distributions of the characteristics of ingroup and outgroup members. *Journal of Personality and Social Psychology, 57,* 165–188.

Lippmann, W. (1922). *Public opinion.* New York: Harcourt, Brace.

Lipsitz, A., Kallmeyer, K., Ferguson, M., & Abas, A. (1989). Counting on blood donors: Increasing the impact of reminder calls. *Journal of Applied Social Psychology, 19,* 1057–1067.

Liska, A. E. (1984). A critical examination of the causal structure of the Fishbein/Ajzen attitude-behavior model. *Social Psychology Quarterly, 47,* 61–74.

Littlepage, G. E. (1991). Effects of group size and task characteristics on group performance: A test of Steiner's model. *Personality and Social Psychology Bulletin, 17,* 449–456.

Littlepage, G. E., Schmidt, G. W., Whisler, E. W., & Frost, A. G. (1995). An input-process-output analysis of influence and performance in problem-solving groups. *Journal of Personality and Social Psychology, 69,* 877–889.

Lloyd, S., Cate, R., & Henton, J. (1982). Equity and rewards as predictors of satisfaction in casual and intimate relationships. *Journal of Psychology, 110,* 43–48.

Lockhart, W. H., & Elliot, R. (1981). Changes in the attitudes of young offenders in an integrated assessment centre. In J. Harbison & J. Harbison (Eds.), *A society under stress.* Somerset: Open Books.

Lockwood, P., & Kunda, Z. (1997). Superstars and me: Predicting the impact of role models on the self. *Journal of Personality and Social Psychology, 73,* 91–103.

Loewenstein, G. F., Thompson, L., & Bazerman, M. H. (1989). Social utility and decision making in interpersonal contexts. *Journal of Personality and Social Psychology, 57,* 426–441.

Loftin, C., McDowall, D., Wiersema, B., & Cottey, T. J. (1991). Effects of restrictive licensing of handguns on homicide and suicide in the District of Columbia. *New England Journal of Medicine, 325,* 1615–1620.

Loftus, E. F. (1974). The incredible eyewitness. *Psychology Today, 8*(7), 116–119.

Lombardi, W. J., Higgins, E. T., & Bargh, J. A. (1987). The role of consciousness in priming effects on categorization: Assimilation versus contrast as a function of awareness of the priming task. *Personality and Social Psychology Bulletin, 13,* 411–429.

Lord, C., & Lepper, M. R. (in press). Attitude representation theory. In M. P. Zanna (Ed.), *Advances in experimental social psychology* (Vol. 31). San Diego: Academic Press.

Lord, C. G., Lepper, M. R., & Mackie, D. (1984). Attitude prototypes as determinants of attitude-behavior consistency. *Journal of Personality and Social Psychology, 46,* 1254–1266.

Lord, C. G., Lepper, M. R., & Preston, E. (1984). Considering the opposite: A corrective strategy for social judgment. *Journal of Personality and Social Psychology, 47,* 1231–1243.

Lord, C. G., Ross, L., & Lepper, M. (1979). Biased assimilation and attitude polarization: The effects of prior theories on subsequently considered evidence. *Journal of Personality and Social Psychology, 37,* 2098–2109.

Lord, C. G., & Saenz, D. S. (1985). Memory deficits and memory surfeits: Differential cognitive consequences of tokenism for tokens and observers. *Journal of Personality and Social Psychology, 49,* 918–926.

Lord, R. G., De Vader, C. L., & Alliger, G. M. (1986). A meta-analysis of the relation between personality traits and leadership perceptions: An application of validity generalization procedures. *Journal of Applied Psychology, 71,* 402–410.

Lorenz, K. (1966). *On aggression.* New York: Harcourt Brace Jovanovich.

Lortie-Lusier, M. (1987). Minority influence and idiosyncrasy credit: A new comparison of the Moscovici and Hollander theories of innovation. *European Journal of Social Psychology, 17,* 431–446.

Losch, M. E., & Cacioppo, J. T. (1990). Cognitive dissonance may enhance sympathetic tonus, but attitudes are changed to reduce negative affect rather than arousal. *Journal of Experimental Social Psychology, 26,* 289–304.

Luckinbill, D. (1977). Criminal homicide as a situated transaction. *Social Problems, 25,* 176–186.

Luhtanen, R., Blaine, B., & Crocker, J. (1991, April). *Personal and collective self-esteem and depression in African-American and White students.* Paper presented at Eastern Psychological Association, New York.

Luhtanen, R., & Crocker, J. (1992). A collective self-esteem scale: Self-evaluation of one's social identity. *Personality and Social Psychology Bulletin, 18,* 302–318.

Lundgren, D. C., & Knight, D. J. (1978). Sequential stages of development in sensitivity training groups. *Journal of Applied Behavioral Science, 14,* 204–222.

Lydon, J. E., Jamieson, D. W., & Holmes, J. G. (1997). The meaning of social interactions in the transition from acquaintanceship to friendship. *Journal of Personality and Social Psychology, 73,* 536–548.

Lykken, D. T. (1985). The probity of the polygraph. In S. Kassin & L. Wrightsman (Eds.), *The psychology of evidence and trial procedure* (pp. 95–123). Beverly Hills, CA: Sage.

Maass, A., & Clark, R. D., III. (1983). Internalization versus compliance: Differential processes underlying minority influence and conformity. *European Journal of Social Psychology, 13,* 197–215.

Maass, A., Clark, R. D., III, & Haberkorn, G. (1982). The effects of differential ascribed category membership and norms on minority influence. *European Journal of Social Psychology, 12,* 89–104.

Maass, A., Salvi, D., Arcuri, L., & Semin, G. (1989). Language use in intergroup contexts: The linguistic intergroup bias. *Journal of Personality and Social Psychology, 57*, 981–993.

Maccoby, E. E. (1980). *Social development: Psychological growth and the parent-child relationship.* New York: Harcourt Brace Jovanovich.

MacCoun, R. J., & Kerr, N. L. (1988). Asymmetric influence in mock jury deliberations: Jurors' bias for leniency. *Journal of Personality and Social Psychology, 54*, 21–33.

Mack, R. W., & Snyder, R. C. (1957). The analysis of social conflict—Toward an overview and synthesis. *Journal of Conflict Resolution, 1*, 212–248.

Mackie, D. M. (1984). Social comparison in high- and low-status groups. *Journal of Cross-Cultural Psychology, 15*, 379–398.

Mackie, D. M. (1986). Social identification effects in group polarization. *Journal of Personality and Social Psychology, 50*, 720–728.

Mackie, D. M. (1987). Systematic and nonsystematic processing of majority and minority persuasive communications. *Journal of Personality and Social Psychology, 53*, 41–52.

Mackie, D. M., Asuncion, A. G., & Rosselli, F. (1992). The impact of positive affect on persuasion processes. In M. S. Clark (Ed.), *Emotion and social behavior. Review of personality and social psychology* (pp. 247–270). Newbury Park, CA: Sage.

Mackie, D. M., Gastardo-Conaco, C. M., & Skelly, J. J. (1992). Knowledge of the advocated position and the processing of in-group and out-group persuasive messages. *Personality and Social Psychology Bulletin, 18*, 145–151.

Mackie, D. M., & Goethals, G. R. (1987). Individual and group goals. In C. Hendrick (Ed.), *Group processes* (pp. 144–166). Beverly Hills, CA: Sage.

Mackie, D. M., & Hamilton, D. L. (Eds.). (1993). *Affect, cognition, and stereotyping: Interactive processes in group perception.* San Diego: Academic Press.

Mackie, D. M., Sherman, J. W., & Worth, L. T. (1993). On-line and memory based processes in group variability judgments. *Social Cognition, 11*, 44–69.

Mackie, D. M., & Worth, L. T. (1989). Cognitive deficits and the mediation of positive affect in persuasion. *Journal of Personality and Social Psychology, 57*, 27–40.

Mackie, D. M., Worth, L. T., & Asuncion, A. G. (1990). The processing of persuasive ingroup messages. *Journal of Personality and Social Psychology, 58*, 812–822.

MacLachlan, J., & Siegel, M. H. (1980). Reducing the costs of TV commercials by use of time compressions. *Journal of Marketing Research, 17*, 52–57.

Macrae, C. N., Bodenhausen, G. V., & Milne, A. B. (1998). Saying no to unwanted thoughts: Self-focus and the regulation of mental life. *Journal of Personality and Social Psychology, 74*, 578–589.

Macrae, C. N., Bodenhausen, G. V., Milne, A. B., & Jetten, J. (1994). Out of mind but back in sight: Stereotypes on the rebound. *Journal of Personality and Social Psychology, 67*, 808–817.

Macrae, C. N., Bodenhausen, G. V., Milne, A. B., Thorn, T. M., & Castelli, L. (1997). On the activation of social stereotypes: Moderating role of processing objectives. *Journal of Experimental Social Psychology, 33*, 471–489.

Maddux, J. E., & Rogers, R. W. (1980). Effects of source expertness, physical attractiveness, and supporting arguments on persuasion: A case of brains over beauty. *Journal of Personality and Social Psychology, 38*, 235–244.

Magnusson, S. (1981). *The flying Scotsman.* London: Quartet Books.

Magura, S., Saddiqi, Q., Shapiro, J., Grossman, J. I., Lipton, D. S., Marion, J. J., Weisenfeld, L., Amann, K. R., & Koger, J. (1991). Outcomes of an AIDS prevention program for methadone patients. *International Journal of the Addictions, 26*, 629–655.

Maheswaran, D., & Chaiken, S. (1991). Promoting systematic processing in low-motivation settings: Effect of incongruent information on processing and judgement. *Journal of Personality and Social Psychology, 61*, 13–33.

Major, B. (1994). From social inequality to personal entitlement: The role of social comaprisons, legitimacy appraisals, and group membership. In M. P. Zanna (Ed.), *Advances in experimental social psychology* (Vol. 26, pp. 293–348). San Diego, CA: Academic Press.

Malloy, T. E., & Albright, L. (1990). Interpersonal perception in a social context. *Journal of Personality and Social Psychology, 58*, 419–428.

Manis, M., Nelson, T. E., & Shedler, J. (1988). Stereotypes and social judgment: Extremity, assimilation and contrast. *Journal of Personality and Social Psychology, 55*, 28–36.

Mann, L., & Janis, I. L. (1968). A follow-up study on the long-term effects of emotional role playing. *Journal of Personality and Social Psychology, 44*, 657–671.

Manstead, A. S. R., Plevin, C. E., & Smart, J. L. (1984). Predicting mothers' choice of infant feeding method. *British Journal of Social Psychology, 23*, 223–231.

Manstead, A. S. R., Proffitt, C., & Smart, J. L. (1983). Predicting and understanding mothers' infant-feeding intentions and behavior: Testing the theory of reasoned action. *Journal of Personality and Social Psychology, 44*, 657–671.

Manstead, A. S. R., & van Eekelen, S. A. M. (1998). Distinguishing between perceived behavioral control and self-efficacy in the domain of academic achievement intentions and behaviors. *Journal of Applied Social Psychology, 28*, 1375–1392.

Marks, M. L. (1986, March 20). The question of quality circles. *Psychology Today*, 36–46.

Marks, M. L., Mirvis, P. H., Hackett, E. J., & Grady, J. F., Jr. (1986). Employee participation in a quality control circle program: Impact on quality of work life, productivity, and absenteeism. *Journal of Applied Psychology, 71*, 61–69.

Markus, H. (1977). Self-schemata and processing information about the self. *Journal of Personality and Social Psychology, 35*, 63–78.

Markus, H., & Kitayama, S. (1991). Culture and the self: Implications for cognition, emotion, and motivation. *Psychological Review, 98*, 224–253.

Markus, H., Kitayama, S., & Heiman, R. J. (1996). Culture and basic psychological principles. In E. T. Higgins & A. W. Kruglanski (Eds.), *Social pychology: Handbook of basic principles* (pp. 857–914). New York: Guilford.

Markus, H., Kitayama, S., & VandenBos, G. R. (1996). The mutual interactions of culture and emotion. *Psychiatric Services, 47*, 225–226.

Markus, H., & Nurius, P. (1986). Possible selves. *American Psychologist, 41*, 954–969.

Markus, H., Smith, J., & Moreland, R. L. (1985). Role of the self-concept in the perception of others. *Journal of Personality and Social Psychology, 49*, 1494–1512.

Markus, H., & Wurf, E. (1987). The dynamic self-concept: A social psychological perspective. *Annual Review of Psychology, 38*, 299–337.

Marques, J. M., & Yzerbyt, V. Y. (1988). The black sheep effect: Judgmental extremity towards ingroup members in inter- and intra-group situations. *European Journal of Social Psychology, 18*, 287–292.

Marques, J. M., Yzerbyt, V. Y., & Rijsman, J. B. (1988). Context effects on intergroup discrimination: In-group bias as a function of experimenter's provenance. *British Journal of Social Psychology, 27*, 301–318.

Marsh, R. L., Hicks, J. L., & Bink, M. L. (1998). Activation of completed, uncompleted, and partially completed intentions. *Journal of Experimental Psychology: Learning, Memory, and Cognition, 24*, 350–361.

Martin, C. L. (1987). A ratio measure of sex stereotyping. *Journal of Personality and Social Psychology, 52*, 489–499.

Martin, L. L., Seta, J. J., & Crelia, R. (1990). Assimilation and contrast as a function of people's willingness and ability to expend effort in forming an impression. *Journal of Personality and Social Psychology, 59*, 27–37.

Martin, L. L., Ward, D. W., Achee, J. W., & Wyer, R. S. (1993). Mood as input: People have to interpret the motivational implications of their moods. *Journal of Personality and Social Psychology, 64*, 317–326.

Martineau, P. (1957). *Motivation in advertising.* New York: McGraw-Hill.

Mathes, E. W., Adams, H. E., & Davies, R. M. (1985). Jealousy: Loss of relationship rewards, loss of self-esteem, depression, anxiety, and anger. *Journal of Personality and Social Psychology, 48*, 1552–1561.

May, R. B. (1976, December 30). Business Bulletin. *Wall Street Journal*, p. 1.

Mayadas, N., & Glasser, P. (1985). Termination: A neglected aspect of social group work. In M. Sundel, P. Glasser, R. Sarri, & R. Vinter (Eds.), *Individual change through small groups* (2nd ed., pp. 251–261). New York: Free Press.

Mayo, E. (1933). *The human problems of an industrial civilization.* New York: Macmillan.

McAdams, D. P. (1985). *Power, intimacy, and the life story: Personological inquiries into identity.* Homewood, IL: Dorsey.

McAdams, D. P., & Bryant, F. B. (1987). Intimacy motivation and subjective mental health in a nationwide sample. *Journal of Personality, 55*, 395–414.

McAlister, A., Perry, C., Killen, J., Slinkard, L. A., & Maccoby, N. (1980). Pilot study of smoking, alcohol and drug abuse prevention. *American Journal of Public Health, 70*, 719–721.

McAllister, J. F. O. (1992, August 17). Atrocity and outrage. *Time*, 21–24.

McArthur, L. A. (1972). The how and what of why: Some determinants and consequences of causal attribution. *Journal of Personality and Social Psychology, 22*, 171–193.

McArthur, L. Z. (1981). What grabs you? The role of attention in impression formation and causal attribution. In E. T. Higgins, C. P. Herman, & M. P. Zanna (Eds.), *Social cognition: The Ontario Symposium* (Vol. 1, pp. 201–246). Hillsdale, NJ: Erlbaum.

McArthur, L. Z., & Berry, D. S. (1987). Cross-cultural agreement in perceptions of babyfaced adults. *Journal of Cross Cultural Psychology, 18*, 165–192.

McArthur, L. Z., & Post, D. L. (1977). Figural emphasis and person perception. *Journal of Experimental Social Psychology, 13*, 520–535.

McCain, G., Cox, V. C., & Paulus, P. B. (1980). The effect of prison crowding on inmate behavior. Washington, DC: National Institute of Justice.

McCallum, D. M., Harring, K., Gilmore, R., Drenan S., Chase, J. P., Insko, C. A., & Thibaut, J. (1985). Competition and cooperation between groups and between individuals. *Journal of Experimental Social Psychology, 21*, 301–320.

McCauley, C. (1989). The nature of social influence in groupthink: Compliance and internalization. *Journal of Personality and Social Psychology, 57*, 250–260.

McCauley, C. (1998). Group dynamics in Janis's theory of groupthink: Backward and forward. *Organizational Behavior and Human Decision Processes,73*, 142–162.

McClintock, C. G., & Allison, S. T. (1989). Social value orientation and helping behavior. *Journal of Applied Social Psychology, 19*, 353–362.

McClintock, C. G., & Liebrand, W. B. (1988). Role of interdependence structure, individual value orientation, and another's strategy in social decision making: A transformational analysis. *Journal of Personality and Social Psychology, 55*, 396–409.

McConnaughey, J. (1998, March 28). Life could be a DUD if your initials are ILL conceived. *Lafayette Journal and Courier*, p. 1.

McConnell, J. D. (1968). Effect of pricing on perception of product quality. *Journal of Applied Psychology, 52*, 331–334.

McCrae, R. R., & Costa, P. T. (1988). Psychological resilience among widowed men and women: A 10-year follow-up of a national sample. *Journal of Social Issues, 44*(3), 129–142.

McCullough, M. E., Worthington, E. L., & Rachal, K. C. (1997). Interpersonal forgiving in close relationships. *Journal of Personality and Social Psychology, 73*, 321–336.

McFall, R. M. (1977). Parameters of self-monitoring. In R. B. Stuart (Ed.), *Behavioral self-management: Strategies, techniques, and outcomes.* New York: Brunner/Mazel.

McGarty, C., & Penny, R. E. (1988). Categorization, accentuation and social judgement. *British Journal of Social Psychology, 27*, 147–157.

McGill, A. L. (1989). Context effects in judgments of causation. *Journal of Personality and Social Psychology, 57*, 189–200.

McGrath, J. E. (1984). *Groups: Interaction and performance.* Englewood Cliffs, NJ: Prentice-Hall.

McGrath, J. E., & Hollingshead, A. B. (1993). Putting the "group" back in group support systems: Some theoretical issues about dynamic processes in groups with technological enhancements. In L. M. Jessup & J. S. Valacich (Eds.), *Group support systems: New perspectives* (pp. 78–96). New York: Macmillan.

McGrath, J. E., Kelly, J. R., & Rhodes, J. E. (1993). A feminist perspective on research methodology: Some metatheoretical issues, contrasts, and choices. In S. Oskamp & M. Costanzo (Eds.), *Gender issues in contemporary society* (pp. 19–37). Newbury Park, CA: Sage.

McGuire, T. W., Kiesler, S., & Siegel, J. (1987). Group and computer-mediated discussion effects in risk decision making. *Journal of Personality and Social Psychology, 52*, 917–930.

McGuire, W. J. (1964). Inducing resistance to persuasion: Some contemporary approaches. In L. Berkowitz (Ed.), *Advances in experimental social psychology* (Vol. 1, pp. 192–229). New York: Academic Press.

McGuire, W. J. (1969). The nature of attitudes and attitude change. In G. Lindzey & E. Aronson (Eds.), *Handbook of social psychology* (2nd ed., Vol. 3, pp. 136–314). Reading, MA: Addison-Wesley.

McGuire, W. J. (1985). Attitudes and attitude change. In G. Lindzey & E. Aronson (Eds.), *Handbook of social psychology* (3rd ed., Vol. 2, pp. 233–346). New York: Random House.

McGuire, W. J., & McGuire, C. V. (1981). The spontaneous self-concept as affected by personal distinctiveness. In M. D. Lynch, A. A. Norem-Hebeisen, & K. J. Gergen (Eds.), *Self-concept: Advances in theory and research* (pp. 147–171). Cambridge, MA: Ballinger.

McGuire, W. J., McGuire, C. V., Child, P., & Fujioka, T. (1978). Salience of ethnicity in the spontaneous self-concept as a function on one's ethnic distinctiveness in the social environment. *Journal of Personality and Social Psychology, 36,* 511–520.

McGuire, W. J., McGuire, C. V., & Winton, W. (1979). Effects of household sex composition on the salience of one's gender in the spontaneous self-concept. *Journal of Experimental Social Psychology, 15,* 77–90.

McGuire, W. J., & Padawer-Singer, A. (1978). Trait salience in the spontaneous self-concept. *Journal of Personality and Social Psychology, 33,* 743–754.

McKenna, K. Y. A., & Bargh, J. A. (1998). Coming out in the age of the Internet: Identity "demarginalization" through virtual group participation. *Journal of Personality and Social Psychology, 75,* 681–694.

McLachlan, A. (1986). The effects of two forms of decision reappraisal on the perception of pertinent arguments. *British Journal of Social Psychology, 25,* 129–138.

McMillen, D. L., & Austin, J. B. (1971). Effect of positive feedback on compliance following transgression. *Psychonomic Science, 24,* 59–61.

Medvec, V. H., Madey, S. F., & Gilovich, T. (1995). When less is more: Counterfactual thinking and satisfaction among Olympic medalists. *Journal of Personality and Social Psychology, 69,* 603–610.

Meeus, W. H. J., & Raaijmakers, Q. A. W. (1986). Administrative obedience: Carrying out orders to use psychological-administrative violence. *European Journal of Social Psychology, 16,* 311–324.

Meeus, W. H. J., & Raaijmakers, Q. A. W. (1987). Administrative obedience as a social phenomenon. In W. Doise & S. Moscovici (Eds.), *Current issues in European social psychology* (pp. 183–230). Cambridge: Cambridge University Press.

Meeus, W. H. J., & Raaijmakers, Q. A. W. (1995). Obedience in modern society: The Utrecht studies. *Journal of Social Issues, 51,* 155–176.

Mehrabian, A. (1972). *Nonverbal communication.* Chicago: Aldine.

Merikle, P. M. (1988). Subliminal auditory messages: An evaluation. *Psychology and Marketing, 5,* 355–372.

Merton, R. (1948). The self-fulfilling prophecy. *Antioch Review, 8,* 193–210.

Messick, D. M., & Brewer, M. B. (1983). Solving social dilemmas: A review. In L. Wheeler & P. Shaver (Eds.), *Review of personality and social psychology* (Vol. 4, pp. 11–44). Beverly Hills, CA: Sage.

Messick, D. M., Wilke, H., Brewer, M. B., Kramer, R. M., Zembe, P. E., & Lui, L. (1983). Individual adaptations and structural change as solutions to social dilemmas. *Journal of Personality and Social Psychology, 44,* 294–309.

Meyers, S. A., & Berscheid, E. (1997). The language of love: The difference a preposition makes. *Personality and Social Psychology Bulletin, 23,* 347–362.

Michaels, J. W., Blommel, J. M., Brocato, R. M., Linkous, R. A., & Rowe, J. S. (1982). Social facilitation and inhibition in a natural setting. *Replications in Social Psychology, 2,* 21–24.

Mickelson, K. D., Kessler, R. C., & Shaver, P. R. (1997). Adult attachment in a nationally representative sample. *Journal of Personality and Social Psychology, 73,* 1092–1106.

Mifflin, L. (1998, April 17). Increase seen in number of violent TV programs. *The New York Times,* p. A14.

Mikolic, J. M., Parker, J. C., & Pruitt, D. G. (1997). Escalation in response to persistent annoyance: Groups versus individuals and gender effects. *Journal of Personality and Social Psychology, 72,* 151–163.

Mikula, G. (1980). *Justice and social interaction.* New York: Springer-Verlag.

Milburn, T. W. (1977). The nature of threat. *Journal of Social Issues, 33* (1), 126–139.

Milgram, S. (1963). The behavioral study of obedience. *Journal of Abnormal and Social Psychology, 67,* 467–472.

Milgram, S. (1964). Issues in the study of obedience: A reply to Baumrind. *American Psychologist, 19,* 848–852.

Milgram, S. (1974). *Obedience to authority.* New York: Harper & Row.

Milgram, S. (1977, October). Subjects' reactions: The neglected factor in the ethics of experimentation. *Hastings Center Report,* pp. 19–23.

Millar, M. G., & Millar, K. U. (1996). The effects of direct and indirect experience on affective and cognitive responses and the attitude-behavior relation. *Journal of Experimental Social Psychology, 32,* 561–579.

Millar, M. G., Millar, K. U., & Tesser, A. (1988). The effects of helping and focus of attention on mood states. *Personality and Social Psychology Bulletin, 14,* 536–543.

Millar, M. G., & Tesser, A. (1986). Thought-induced attitude change: The effects of schema structure and commitment. *Journal of Personality and Social Psychology, 51,* 259–269.

Miller, D. T., & McFarland, C. (1987). Pluralistic ignorance: When similarity is interpreted as dissimilarity. *Journal of Personality and Social Psychology, 53,* 298–305.

Miller, D. T., & Ross, M. (1975). Self-serving biases in the attribution of causality: Fact or fiction? *Psychological Bulletin, 82,* 213–225.

Miller, D. T., & Turnbull, W. (1986). Expectancies and interpersonal processes. *Annual Review of Psychology, 37,* 233–256.

Miller, J. G. (1984). Culture and the development of everyday social explanation. *Journal of Personality and Social Psychology, 46,* 961–978.

Miller, J. G., Bersoff, D. M., & Harwood, P. L. (1997). Perceptions of social responsibilities in India and the United States: Moral imperatives or personal decisions. In L. A. Peplau & S. E. Taylor (Eds.), *Socioculutral perspectives in social psychology* (pp. 113–144). Upper Saddle River, NJ: Prentice-Hall.

Miller, L. E., & Grush, J. E. (1986). Individual differences in attitudinal versus normative determination of behavior. *Journal of Experimental Social Psychology, 22,* 190–202.

Miller, N., & Brewer, M. B. (1986). Categorization effects on ingroup and outgroup perception. In J. F. Dovidio & S. L. Gaertner (Eds.), *Prejudice, discrimination, and racism* (pp. 209–230). Orlando, FL: Academic Press.

Miller, N., Maruyama, G., Beaber, R. J., & Valone, K. (1976). Speed of speech and persuasion. *Journal of Personality and Social Psychology, 34*, 615–624.

Miller, N. E. (1941). The frustration-aggression hypothesis. *Psychological Review, 48*, 337–342.

Miller, P. A., & Eisenberg, N. (1988). The relation of empathy to aggressive and externalizing/antisocial behavior. *Psychological Bulletin, 103*, 324–344.

Miller, R. L., Brickman, P., & Bolen, D. (1975). Attribution versus persuasion as a means for modifying behavior. *Journal of Personality and Social Psychology, 31*, 430–441.

Miller, R. L., Seligman, C., Clark, N. T., & Bush, M. (1976). Perceptual contrast versus reciprocal concessions as mediators of induced compliance. *Canadian Journal of Behavioral Science, 8*, 401–409.

Miller, R. S. (1997). Inattentive and contented: Relationship commitment and attention to alternatives. *Journal of Personality and Social Psychology, 73*, 758–766.

Miller, S. M., & Mangan, C. E. (1983). Interacting effects of information and coping style in adapting to gynecologic stress: Should the doctor tell all? *Journal of Personality and Social Psychology, 45*, 223–236.

Millett, K. (1970). *Sexual politics.* Garden City, NY: Doubleday.

Mintzberg, H. (1980). *The nature of managerial work* (2nd ed.). Englewood Cliffs, NJ: Prentice-Hall.

Mischel, W., Ebbessen, E. B., & Zeiss, A. M. (1973). Selective attention to the self: Situational and dispositional determinants. *Journal of Personality and Social Psychology, 27*, 129–142.

Misumi, J. (1995). The development in Japan of the Performance-Maintenance (PM) Theory of Leadership. *Journal of Social Issues, 51*, 213–228.

Modigliani, A., & Rochat, F. (1995). The role of interaction sequences and the timing of resistance in shaping obedience and defiance to authority. *Journal of Social Issues, 51*, 107–124.

Moghaddam, F. M., Taylor, D. M., & Wright, S. C. (1993). *Social psychology in cross-cultural perspective.* New York: Freeman.

Monteith, M. J., Sherman, J. W., & Devine, P. G. (1998). Suppression as a stereotype control strategy. *Personality and Social Psychology Review, 2*, 63–82.

Mook, D. G. (1980). In defense of external invalidity. *American Psychologist, 38*, 379–388.

Moore, D. L., Hausknecht, D., & Thamodaran, K. (1986). Time compression, response opportunity, and persuasion. *Journal of Consumer Research, 13*, 85–99.

Moore, T. E. (1982). Subliminal advertising: What you see is what you get. *Journal of Marketing, 46*, 38–47.

Moorhead, G., Ference, R., & Neck, C. P. (1991). Group decision fiascoes continue: Space shuttle Challenger and a revised groupthink framework. *Human Relations, 44*, 533–550.

Moorhead, G., & Montanari, J. R. (1986). An empirical investigation of the groupthink phenomenon. *Human Relations, 39*, 399–410.

Moreland, R. L. (1987). The formation of small groups. In C. Hendrick (Ed.), *Group processes* (pp. 80–110). Beverly Hills, CA: Sage.

Moreland, R. L., & Beach, S. R. (1992). Exposure effects in the classroom: The development of affinity among students. *Journal of Experimental Social Psychology, 28*, 255–276.

Moreland, R. L., & Levine, J. M. (1988). Group dynamics over time: Development and socialization in small groups. In J. E. McGrath (Ed.), *The social psychology of time: New perspectives* (pp. 151–181). Newbury Park, CA: Sage.

Morgan, H. J., & Janoff-Bulman, R. (1994). Positive and negative self-complexity: Patterns of adjustment following traumatic versus non-traumatic life experiences. *Journal of Social and Clinical Psychology, 13*, 63–85.

Morgan, P. M. (1983). *Deterrence: A conceptual analysis.* Beverly Hills, CA: Sage.

Moriarty, T. (1975). Crime, commitment, and the responsive bystander: Two field experiments. *Journal of Personality and Social Psychology, 31*, 370–376.

Morris, M. W., & Peng, K. (1994). Culture and cause: American and Chinese attributions for social and physical events. *Journal of Personality and Social Psychology, 67*, 949–971.

Morton, T. L. (1978). Intimacy and reciprocity of exchange: A comparison of spouses and strangers. *Journal of Personality and Social Psychology, 36*, 72–81.

Moscovici, S. (1976). *Social influence and social change.* London: Academic Press.

Moscovici, S. (1980). Toward a theory of conversion behavior. In L. Berkowitz (Ed.), *Advances in experimental social psychology* (Vol. 13, pp. 209–239). New York: Academic Press.

Moscovici, S., & Lage, E. (1976). Studies in social influence. III: Majority versus minority influence in a group. *European Journal of Social Psychology, 6*, 149–74.

Moscovici, S., Lage, S., & Naffrechoux, M. (1969). Influence of a consistent minority on the responses of a majority in a color perception task. *Sociometry, 32*, 365–380.

Moscovici, S., & Personnaz, B. (1980). Studies in social influence. V: Minority influence and conversion behavior in a perceptual task. *Journal of Experimental Social Psychology, 16*, 270–282.

Moscovici, S., & Zavalloni, M. (1969). The group as a polarizer of attitudes. *Journal of Personality and Social Psychology, 12*, 125–135.

Moseley, R. (1998, April 5). Anti-foreigner bias sparks violent attacks. *Santa Barbara News Press,* p. A15.

Moskos, C. C., Jr. (1969). Why men fight: American combat soldiers in Vietnam. *Transaction, 7*(1), 13–23.

Mowen, J. C., & Cialdini, R. B. (1980). On implementing the door-in-the-face compliance technique in a business context. *Journal of Marketing Research, 17*, 253–258.

Mugny, G. (1975). Negotiations, image of the other, and the process of minority influence. *European Journal of Social Psychology, 5*, 209–228.

Mugny, G. (1982). *The power of minorities.* London: Academic Press.

Mugny, G., & Papastamous, S. (1980). When rigidity does not fail: Individualization and psychologization as resistances to the diffusion of minority innovations. *European Journal of Social Psychology, 10*, 43–62.

Mullen, B. (1987). Self-attention theory: The effects of group composition on the individual. In B. Mullen & G. R. Goethals (Eds.), *Theories of group behavior* (pp. 125–146). New York: Springer-Verlag .

Mullen, B. (1991). Group composition, salience, and cognitive representations: The phenomenology of being in a group. *Journal of Experimental Social Psychology, 27,* 297–323.

Mullen, B., Anthony, T., Salas, E., & Driskell, J. E. (1994). Group cohesiveness and quality of decision making: An integration of tests of the groupthink hypothesis. *Small Group Research, 25,* 189–204.

Mullen, B., Brown, R., & Smith, C. (1992). Ingroup bias as a function of salience, relevance, and status: An integration. *European Journal of Social Psychology, 22,* 103–122.

Mullen, B., & Copper, C. (1994). The relation between group cohesiveness and performance: An integration. *Psychological Bulletin, 115,* 210–227.

Mullen, B., Futrell, D., Stairs, D., Tice, D., Baumeister, R., Dawson, K., Riordan, C., Radloff, C., Goethals, G., Kennedy, J., & Rosenfeld, P. (1986). Newscasters' facial expressions and voting behavior of viewers: Can a smile elect a president? *Journal of Personality and Social Psychology, 51,* 291–295.

Mullen, B., & Hu, L. (1989). Perceptions of ingroup and outgroup variability: A meta-analytic integration. *Basic and Applied Social Psychology, 10,* 233–252.

Mullen, B., & Riordan, C. A. (1988). Self-serving attributions for performance in naturalistic settings: A meta-analytic review. *Journal of Applied Social Psychology, 18,* 3–22.

Mullen, B., Atkins, J. L., Champion, D. S., Edwards, C., Hardy, D., Story, J. E., & Vanderklok, M. (1985). The false consensus effect: A meta-analysis of 115 hypothesis tests. *Journal of Experimental Social Psychology, 21,* 262–283.

Muller, J. (1991, July 9). Subliminal ads debunked. *Santa Barbara News Press,* p. B6.

Mummendey, A., Simon, B., Dietze, C., Grunert, M., Haeger, G., Kessler, S., Lettgen, S., & Schaferhoff, S. (1992). Categorization is not enough: Intergroup discrimination in negative outcome allocations. *Journal of Experimental Social Psychology, 28,* 125–144.

Munro, G. D., & Ditto, P. H. (1997). Biased assimilation, attitude polarization, and affect in reactions to stereotype-relevant scientific information. *Personality and Social Psychology Bulletin, 23,* 656–653.

Murphy, P. L., & Miller, C. T. (1997). Postdecisional dissonance and the commodified self-concept: A cross-cultural examination. *Personality and Social Psychology Bulletin, 23,* 50–62.

Murphy, S., & Zajonc, R. (1993). Affect, cognition, and awareness: Affective priming with optimal and suboptimal stimulus exposures. *Journal of Personality and Social Psychology, 64,* 723–740.

Murray, S. L., & Holmes, J. G. (1997). A leap of faith? Positive illusions in romantic relationships. *Personality and Social Psychology Bulletin, 23,* 586–604.

Murray, S. L., Holmes, J. G., & Griffin, D. W. (1996). The self-fulfilling nature of positive illusions in romantic relationships: Love is not blind, but prescient. *Journal of Personality and Social Psychology, 71,* 1155–1180.

Myers, D. G., & Bishop, G. D. (1971). The enhancement of dominant attitudes in group discussion. *Journal of Personality and Social Psychology, 20,* 386–391.

Myers, D. G., & Kaplan, M. F. (1976). Group-induced polarization in simulated juries. *Personality and Social Psychology Bulletin, 2,* 63–66.

Myers, D. G., & Lamm, H. (1976). The group polarization phenomenon. *Psychological Bulletin, 83,* 602–627.

Nadler, A., & Fisher, J. D. (1986). The role of threat to self-esteem and perceived control in recipient reactions to help: Theory development and empirical validation. In L. Berkowitz (Ed.), *Advances in experimental social psychology* (Vol. 19, pp. 81–122). New York: Academic Press.

Naroll, R., Bullough, V. L., & Naroll, F. (1974). *Military deterrence in history: A pilot cross-historical survey.* Albany: State University of New York Press.

Natale, J. A. (1988). Are you open to suggestion? *Psychology Today, 22*(9), 28–30.

National Public Radio News. (1998, April 16). Barbara Wilson, quoted on *All Things Considered* broadcast.

Neisser, U. (1967). *Cognitive psychology.* New York: Appleton-Century-Crofts.

Nelson, L. J., & Miller, D. T. (1995). The distinctiveness effect in social categorization: You are what makes you unusual. *Psychological Science, 6,* 246–249.

Nelson, L. J., Moore, D. L., Olivetti, J., & Scott, T. (1997). General and personal mortality salience and nationalistic bias. *Personality and Social Psychology Bulletin, 23,* 884–892.

Nemeth, C. (1977). Interactions between jurors as a function of majority vs. unanimity decision rules. *Journal of Applied Social Psychology, 7,* 38–56.

Nemeth, C. (1986). Differential contributions of majority and minority influence. *Psychological Review, 93,* 1–10.

Nemeth, C. (1995). Dissent as driving cognition, attitudes, and judgements. *Social Cognition, 13,* 273–291.

Nemeth, C., & Chiles, C. (1988). Modelling courage: The role of dissent in fostering independence. *European Journal of Social Psychology, 18,* 275–280.

Nemeth, C., & Kwan, J. L. (1987). Minority influence, divergent thinking and detection of correct solutions. *Journal of Applied Social Psychology, 17,* 788–799.

Nemeth, C., Mayseless, O., Sherman, J. W., & Brown, Y. (1990). Exposure to dissent and recall of information. *Journal of Personality and Social Psychology, 58,* 429–437.

Nemeth, C., & Wachtler, J. (1974). Creating the perceptions of consistency and confidence: A necessary condition for minority influence. *Sociometry, 37,* 529–540.

Nemeth, C., & Wachtler, J. (1983). Consistency and the modification of judgments. *Journal of Experimental Social Psychology, 9,* 65–79.

Nemeth, C., Wachtler, J., & Endicott, J. (1977). Increasing the size of the minority: Some gains and losses. *European Journal of Social Psychology, 7,* 15–27.

Nettles, E. J., & Loevinger, J. (1983). Sex role expectations and ego level in relation to problem marriages. *Journal of Personality and Social Psychology, 45,* 676–687.

Neuberg, S. L. (1989a). Behavioral implications of information presented outside of conscious awareness: The effects of subliminal presentation of trait information on behavior in the prisoner's dilemma game. *Social Cognition, 6,* 53–64.

Neuberg, S. L. (1989b). The goal of forming accurate impressions during social interactions: Attenuating the impact of negative expectancies. *Journal of Personality and Social Psychology, 56,* 374–386.

Neuberg, S. L., & Fiske, S. T. (1987). Motivational influences on impression formation: Outcome dependency, accuracy-driven attention, and individuating processes. *Journal of Personality and Social Psychology, 53,* 431–444.

Newcomb, T. M. (1961). *The acquaintance process.* New York: Holt, Rinehart, & Winston.

Newsweek. (1990a, June 25). Perspectives, 15.

Newsweek. (1990b, May 21). Perspectives, p. 17.

Niedenthal, P. M. (1990). Implicit perception of affective information. *Journal of Experimental Social Psychology, 26,* 505–527.

Niedenthal, P. M., & Cantor, N. (1986). Affective responses as guides to category-based inferences. *Motivation and Emotion, 10,* 217–232.

Nields, D. (1991, May 27). The dirt on Shakespeare. *Newsweek,* p. 8.

Nigra, G. N., Hill, D. E., Gelbein, M. E., & Clark, C. L. (1988). Changes in the facial prominence of women and men over the last decade. *Psychology of Women Quarterly, 12,* 225–235.

Nisbett, R. E. (1987). Lay personality theory: Its nature, origin, and utility. In N. E. Grunberg, R. E. Nisbett, J. Rodin, & J. E. Singer (Eds.), *A distinctive approach to psychological research: The influence of Stanley Schachter* (pp. 87–117). Hillsdale, NJ: Erlbaum.

Nisbett, R. E., & Cohen, D. (1996). *Culture of honor: The psychology of violence in the South.* Boulder, CO: Westview Press.

Nisbett, R. E., & Wilson, T. D. (1977). Telling more than we can know. Verbal reports on mental processes. *Psychological Review, 84,* 231–259.

Noller, P. (1980). Musunderstandings in marital communication: A study of couples' nonverbal communication. *Journal of Personality and Social Psychology, 39,* 1135–1148.

Noller, P., & Ruzzene, M. (1991). Communication in marriage: The influence of affect and cognition. In G. Fletcher & F. Fincham (Eds.), *Cognition in close relationships* (pp. 203–234). Hillsdale, NJ: Erlbaum.

North, R. C., Brody, R. A., & Holsti, O. R. (1964). Some empirical data on the conflict spiral. *Peace Research Society International Papers, 1,* 1–14.

Nosanchuk, T. A., & Lightstone, J. (1974). Canned laughter and public and private conformity. *Journal of Personality and Social Psychology, 29,* 153–156.

Nuttin, J. M. (1987). Affective consequences of mere ownership: The name letter effect in twelve European languages. *European Journal of Social Psychology, 17,* 381–402.

Oakes, P. J., Haslam, S. A., Morrison, B., & Grace, D. (1995). Becoming an in-group: Reexamining the impact of familiarity on perceptions of group homogeneity. *Social Psychology Quarterly, 58,* 52–60.

Oakes, P. J., & Turner, J. C. (1980). Social categorization and intergroup behaviour: Does minimal intergroup discrimination make social identity more positive? *European Journal*

Oatley, K., & Johnson-Laird, P. N. (1987). Towards a cognitive theory of emotions. *Cognition and Emotion, 1,* 29–50.

Ogilvy, D. (1983). *Ogilvy on advertising.* New York: Vintage Books.

O'Keefe, D. J., & Figge, M. (1997). A guilt-based explanation of the door-in-the-face influence strategy. *Human Communication Research, 24,* 64–81.

O'Leary, A. (1990). Stress, emotion, and human immune function. *Psychological Bulletin, 108,* 363–382.

Oliner, S. P., & Oliner, P. M. (1988). *The altruistic personality.* New York: Free Press.

Oliver, M. B., & Hyde, J. S. (1993). Gender differences in sexuality: A meta-analysis. *Psychological Bulletin, 114,* 29–51.

Olson, J. M. (1990). Self-inference processes in emotion. In J. M. Olson & M. P. Zanna (Eds.), *Self-inference processes: The Ontario Symposium* (Vol. 6, pp. 17–42). Hillsdale, NJ: Erlbaum.

Olson, J. M., Roese, N. J., & Zanna, M. P. (1996). Expectancies. In E. T. Higgins & A. W. Kruglanski (Eds.), *Social psychology: Handbook of basic principles* (pp. 211–238). New York: Guilford.

Olweus, D. (1979). Stability of aggressive reaction patterns in males: A review. *Psychological Bulletin, 86,* 852–875.

Opinion Watch: On the front lines? (1991, August 5). *Newsweek,* pp. 23, 27.

Opotow, S. (1990). Moral exclusion and injustice: An introduction. *Journal of Social Issues, 46*(1), 1–20.

Orbell, J. M., Van de Kragt, A. J. C., & Dawes, R. M. (1988). Explaining discussion-induced cooperation. *Journal of Personality and Social Psychology, 54,* 811–819.

O'Reilly, C. A., & Caldwell, D. F. (1985). The impact of normative social influence and cohesiveness on task perceptions and attitudes: A social-information processing approach. *Journal of Occupational Psychology, 59,* 193–206.

Orne, M. T. (1962). On the social psychology of the psychological experiment: With particular reference to demand characteristics and their implications. *American Psychologist, 17,* 776–783.

Osborn, A. F. (1953). *Applied imagination.* New York: Scribner.

Osgood, C. E. (1962). *An alternative to war or surrender.* Urbana, IL: University of Illinois Press.

Oskamp, S., & Hartry, A. (1968). A factor-analytic study of the double standard in attitudes toward U. S. and Russian actions. *Behavioral Science, 13,* 178–188.

Ostrom, T. M. (1969). The relationship between the affective, behavioral, and cognitive components of attitude. *Journal of Experimental Social Psychology, 5,* 12–30.

Otten, S., Mummendey, A., & Blanz, M. (1996). Intergroup discrimination in positive and negative outcome allocations: Impact of stimulus valence, relative group status, and relative group size. *Personality and Social Psychology Bulletin, 22,* 568–581.

Ouellette, J. A., & Wood, W. (1998). Habit and intention in everyday life: The multiple processes by which past behavior predicts future behavior. *Psychological Bulletin, 124,* 54–74.

Owens, G., & Ford, J. G. (1978). Further consideration of the "What is good is beautiful" finding. *Social Psychology, 41,* 73–75.

Packard, V. (1971). *The hidden persuaders.* New York: D. McKay.

Paichelier, G. (1976). Norms and attitude change I: Polarization and styles of behavior. *European Journal of Social Psychology, 6,* 405–27.

Pallak, M. S., Cook. D. A., & Sullivan, J. J. (1980). Commitment and energy conservation. In L. Bickman (Ed.), *Applied social psychology annual* (Vol. 1, pp. 235–253). Beverly Hills, CA: Sage.

Pallak, S. R. (1983). Salience of a communicator's physical attractiveness and persuasion: A heuristic versus systematic processing interpretation. *Social Cognition, 2,* 156–168.

Palmer, E. L., & Dorr, A. (1980). *Children and the faces of television: Teaching, violence, selling.* New York: Academic Press.

Pandey, J., & Singh, A. K. (1986). Attribution and evaluation of manipulative social behavior. *Journal of Social Psychology, 126,* 735–744.

Park, B. (1986). A method for studying the development of impressions of real people. *Journal of Personality and Social Psychology, 51,* 907–917.

Park, B., & Judd, C. M. (1990). Measures and models of perceived group variability. *Journal of Personality and Social Psychology, 59,* 173–191.

Park, B., & Rothbart, M. (1982). Perception of out-group homogeneity and levels of social categorization: Memory for the subordinate attributes of in-group and out-group members. *Journal of Personality and Social Psychology, 42,* 1051–1068.

Parke, R. D., Berkowitz, L., Leyens, J. -P., West, S. G., & Sebastian, R. J. (1977). Some effects of violent and nonviolent movies on the behavior of juvenile delinquents. In L. Berkowitz (Ed.), *Advances in experimental social psychology* (Vol. 10, pp. 135–172). New York: Academic Press.

Patchen, M., Davidson, J. D., Hofmann, G., & Brown, W. R. (1977). Determinants of students' interracial behavior and opinion change. *Sociology of Education, 50,* 55–75.

Patterson, G. R., Littman, R. A., & Bricker, W. (1967). Assertive behavior in children: A step toward a theory of aggression. *Monographs of the Society for Research in Child Development 32* (5, Serial No. 113).

Patterson, M. L., Churchill, M. E., Burger, G. K., & Powell, J. L. (1992). Verbal and nonverbal modality effects on impressions of political candidates: Analysis from the 1984 presidential debates. *Communication Monographs, 59,* 231–242.

Paulus, P. B. (1988). *Prison crowding: A psychological perspective.* New York: Springer-Verlag.

Paulus, P. B., Annis, A. B., Seta, J. J., Schkade, J. K., & Matthews, R. W. (1976). Density does affect task performance. *Journal of Personality and Social Psychology, 34,* 248–253.

Paulus, P. B, Dzindolet, M. T, Poletes, G., & Camacho, L. M. (1993). Perception of performance in group brainstorming: The illusion of group productivity. *Personality and Social Psychology Bulletin, 19,* 78–89.

Pelham, B. (1991). On confidence and consequence: The certainty and importance of self-knowledge. *Journal of Personality and Social Psychology, 60,* 518–530.

Pendleton, M. G., & Bateson, C. D. (1979). Self-presentation and the door-in-the-face technique for inducing compliance. *Personality and Social Psychology Bulletin, 5,* 77–81.

Pennebaker, J. W. (1997). Writing about emotional experiences as a therapeutic process. *Psychological Science, 8,* 162–166.

Pennebaker, J. W., Kiecolt-Glaser, J. K., & Glaser, R. (1988). Disclosure of traumas and immune function: Health implications for psychotherapy. *Journal of Consulting and Clinical Psychology, 56,* 239–245.

Penner, L. A., & Finkelstein, M. A. (1998). Dispositional and structural determinants of volunteerism. *Journal of Personality and Social Psychology, 74,* 525–537.

Penner, L A., Fritzsche, B. A. Craiger, J. P., & Freifeld, T. R. (1995). Measuring the prosocial personality. In J. Butcher & C. D.

Spielberger (Eds.), *Advances in personality assessment* (Vol. 10, pp. 147–163). Hillsdale, NJ: Erlbaum.

Peplau, L. A., & Conrad, E. (1989). Beyond nonsexist research: The perils of feminist methods in psychology. *Psychology of Women Quarterly, 13,* 379–400.

Peplau, L. A., Rubin, Z., & Hill, C. T. (1977). Sexual intimacy in dating relationships. *Journal of Social Issues, 33,* 86–109.

Perdue, C. W., Dovidio, J. F., Gurtman, M. B., & Tyler, R. B. (1990). Us and them: Social categorization and the process of intergroup bias. *Journal of Personality and Social Psychology, 59,* 475–486.

Perez, J. A., & Mugny, G. (1990). Minority influence: Manifest discrimination and latent influences. In D. Abrams & M. Hogg (Eds.), *Social identity theory: Constructive and critical advances.* London, England: Harvester Wheatsheaf.

Perry, D. G., Perry, L. C., & Rasmussen, P. (1986). Cognitive social learning mediators of aggression. *Child Development, 57,* 700–711.

Perry, D. G., Williard, J. C., & Perry, L. C. (1990). Peers' perceptions of the consequences that victimized children provide aggressors. *Child Development, 61,* 1310–1325.

Peterson, C., Seligman, M. E., & Vaillant, G. E. (1988). Pessimistic explanatory style is a risk factor for physical illness: A thirty-five-year longitudinal study. *Journal of Personality and Social Psychology, 55,* 23–27.

Peterson, D. R. (1979). Assessing interpersonal relationships by means of interaction records. *Behavioral Assessment, 1,* 221–236.

Peterson, D. R. (1983). Conflict. In H. H. Kelley, E. Berscheid, A. Christensen, J. H. Harvey, T. L. Huston, G. Levinger, E. McClintock, L. A. Peplau, & D. L. Peterson (Eds.), *Close relationships* (pp. 360–396). San Francisco: Freeman.

Peterson, R. A. (1977). Consumer perceptions as a function of product, color, price, and nutritional labeling. In W. D. Perrault (Ed.), *Advances in consumer research* (pp. 61–62). Atlanta, GA: Association for Consumer Research.

Peterson, R. S., Owens, P. D., Tetlock, P. E., Fan, E. T., & Martorana, P. (1998). Group dynamics in top management teams: Groupthink, vigilance, and alternative models of organizational failure and success. *Organizational Behavior and Human Decision Processes, 73,* 272–305.

Pettigrew, T. F. (1958). Personality and sociocultural factors in intergroup attitudes: A cross-national comparison. *Journal of Conflict Resolution, 2,* 29–42.

Pettigrew, T. F. (1968). Race relations: Social and psychological aspects. In D. L. Sills (Ed.), *The international encyclopedia of the social sciences* (Vol. 13, pp. 277–282). New York: Macmillan.

Pettigrew, T. F. (1979). The ultimate attribution error: Extending Allport's cognitive analysis of prejudice. *Personality and Social Psychology Bulletin, 5,* 461–476.

Pettigrew, T. F. (1980). Prejudice. In S. Thernstrom (Ed.), *Harvard encyclopedia of American ethnic groups.* Cambridge, MA: Harvard University Press.

Pettigrew, T. F. (1997). Generalized intergroup contact effects on prejudice. *Personality and Social Psychology Bulletin, 23,* 173–185.

Pettigrew, T. F. (1998). Intergroup contact theory. *Annual Review of Psychology, 49,* 65–85.

Pettigrew, T. F., & Martin, J. (1987). Shaping the organizational context for black American inclusion. *Journal of Social Issues, 43,* 41–78.

Petty, R. E., & Cacioppo, J. T. (1977). Forewarning, cognitive responding, and resistance to persuasion. *Journal of Personality and Social Psychology, 35,* 645–655.

Petty, R. E., & Cacioppo, J. T. (1979). Effects of forewarning of persuasive intent and involvement on cognitive responses and persuasion. *Personality and Social Psychology Bulletin, 5,* 173–176.

Petty, R. E., & Cacioppo, J. T. (1981). *Attitudes and persuasion: Classic and contemporary approaches.* Dubuque, IA: Brown.

Petty, R. E., & Cacioppo, J. T. (1984). The effects of involvement on responses to argument quantity and quality: Central and peripheral routes to persuasion. *Journal of Personality and Social Psychology, 46,* 69–81.

Petty, R. E., & Cacioppo, J. T. (1986). *Communication and persuasion: Central and peripheral routes to attitude change.* New York: Springer-Verlag.

Petty, R. E., Cacioppo, J. T., & Goldman, R. (1981). Personal involvement as a determinant of argument-based persuasion. *Journal of Personality and Social Psychology 41,* 847–855.

Petty, R. E., Cacioppo, J. T., Haugtvedt, C., & Heesacker, M. (1986). *Consequences of the route to persuasion: Persistence and resistance of attitude changes.* Unpublished manuscript, University of Missouri, Columbia.

Petty, R. E., Haugtvedt, C. P., & Smith, S. M. (1995). Elaboration as a determinant of attitude strength: Creating attitudes that are persistent, resistant, and predictive of behavior. In R. E. Petty & J. A. Krosnick (Eds.), *Attitude strength: Antecedents and consequences* (pp. 93–130). Hillsdale, NJ: Erlbaum.

Petty, R. E., Priester, J. R., & Wegner, D. T. (1994). Cognitive processes in attitude change. In R. S. Wyer & T. S. Srull (Eds.), *Handbook of Social Cognition* (2nd ed., Vol. 2, pp. 69–142). Hillsdale, NJ: Erlbaum.

Petty, R. E., Schumann, D. W., Richman, S. A., & Strathman, A. J. (1993). Positive mood and persuasion: Different roles for affect under high- and low-elaboration conditions. *Journal of Personality and Social Psychology, 64,* 5–20.

Petty, R. E., & Wegener, D. T. (1998). Attitude change: Multiple roles for persuasion variables. In D. T. Gilbert, S. T. Fiske, & G. Lindzey (Eds.), *The handbook of social psychology 4th edition* (pp. 323–390). Boston: McGraw Hill.

Petty, R. E., Wells, G. L., & Brock, T. C. (1976). Distraction can enhance or reduce yielding to propaganda: Thought disruption versus effort justification. *Journal of Personality and Social Psychology, 34,* 874–884.

Pfau, M. (1995). Designing messages for behavioral inoculation. In E. Maibach & R. L. Parrott (Eds.), *Designing health messages: Approaches from communication theory and public health practice* (pp. 99–113). Thousand Oaks, CA: Sage.

Pfau, M., & Burgoon, M. (1988). Inoculation in political campaign communication. *Human Communication Research, 15,* 91–111.

Pfau, M., Kenski, H. C., Nitz, M., & Sorensen, J. (1990). Efficacy of inoculation strategies in promoting resistance to political attack messages: Application to direct mail. *Communication Monographs, 57,* 25–43.

Pfau, M., Tusing, K. J., Koerner, A. F., Lee W., Godbold, L. C., Penaloza, L. J., Yang, V. S., & Hong, Y. (1997). Enriching the inoculation construct: The role of critical components in the process of resistance. *Human Communication Research, 24,* 187–215.

Phillips, A. P., & Dipboye, R. L. (1989). Correlational tests of predictions from a process model of the interview. *Journal of Applied Psychology, 74,* 41–52.

Pietromonaco, P. R., & Feldman Barrett, L. (1997). Working models of attachment and daily social interactions. *Journal of Personality and Social Psychology, 73,* 1409–1423.

Piliavin, J. A., Callero, P. L., & Evans, D. E. (1982). Addiction to altruism? Opponent-process theory and habitual blood donation. *Journal of Personality and Social Psychology, 43,* 1200–1213.

Piliavin, J. A., Dovidio, J. F., Gaertner, S. L., & Clark, R. D. III (1981). *Emergency intervention.* New York: Academic Press.

Pines, A. M., Aronson, E., & Kafry, D. (1981). *Burnout: From tedium to personal growth.* New York: Freeman.

Pinto, M. B., & Priest, S. (1991). Guilt appeals in advertising: An exploratory study. *Psychological Reports, 69,* 375–385.

Pittman, T. S. (1975). Attribution of arousal as a mediator of dissonance reduction. *Journal of Experimental Social Psychology, 11,* 53–63.

Platt, J. (1973). Social traps. *American Psychologist, 28,* 641–651.

Platz, S. J., & Hosch, H. M. (1988). Cross-racial/ethnic eyewitness identification: A field study. *Journal of Applied Social Psychology, 18,* 972–984.

Plenty of fish in sea? Not anymore. (1992, March 25). *The New York Times,* p. A8.

Poll finds Whites use stereotypes. (1991, January 10). *The New York Times,* p. B10.

Pomerantz, E. M., Chaiken, S., & Tordesillas, R. S. (1995). Attitude strength and resistance processes. *Journal of Personality and Social Psychology, 69,* 408–419.

Postmes, T., & Spears, R. (1998). Deindividuation and antinormative behavior: A meta-analysis. *Psychological Bulletin, 123,* 1–22.

Pranulis, M., Dabbs, J., & Johnson, J. (1975). General anesthesia and the patient's attempts at control. *Social Behavior and Personality, 3,* 49–54.

Pratkanis, A. R. (1984). *Attitudes and memory: The heuristic and schematic functions of attitudes.* Unpublished doctoral dissertation, Ohio State University, Columbus, OH.

Pratkanis, A. R. (1989). The attitude heuristic and selective fact identification. *British Journal of Social Psychology, 28,* 257–263.

Pratkanis, A. R., Greenwald, A. G., Leippe, M. R., & Baumgardner, M. H. (1988). In search of reliable persuasion effects: III. The sleeper effect is dead. Long live the sleeper effect. *Journal of Personality and Social Psychology, 54,* 203–218.

Prentice, D. A. (1990). Familiarity and differences in self- and other-representations. *Journal of Personality and Social Psychology, 59,* 369–383.

Prentice, D. A., & Miller, D. T. (1993). Pluralistic ignorance and alcohol use on campus: Some consequences of misperceiving the social norm. *Journal of Personality and Social Psychology, 64,* 243–256.

Presidential Commission on the Space Shuttle Challenger Accident. (1986, June 6). (W. Rodgers, Chair.) Washington, DC: U.S. Government Printing Office.

President's Commission on Law Enforcement and Administration of Justice (1967). *The challenge of crime in a free society.* Washington, DC: U. S. Government Printing Office.

Price, J. M., & Dodge, K. A. (1989). Reactive and proactive aggression in childhood: Relations to peer status and social context dimensions. *Journal of Abnormal Child Psychology, 17,* 455–471.

Price, V. (1989). Social identification and public opinion: Effects of communicating group conflict. *Public Opinion Quarterly, 53,* 197–224.

Priester, J. R., Cacioppo, J. T., & Petty, R. E. (1996). The influence of motor processes on attitudes toward novel versus familiar semantic stimuli. *Personality and Social Psychology Bulletin, 22,* 442–447.

Priester, J. P., & Petty, R. E. (1996). The gradual threshold model of ambivalence: Relating the positive and negative bases of attitudes to subjective ambivalence. *Journal of Personality and Social Psychology, 71,* 431–449.

Pronoun test. (1993, August 4). *Globe and Mail* (Toronto), p. A18.

Pruitt, D. G. (1981). *Negotiation behavior.* New York: Academic Press.

Pruitt, D. G. (1986). Acheiving integrative agreements in negotiation. In R. K. White (Ed.), *Psychology and the prevention of nuclear war* (pp. 463–478). New York: New York University Press.

Pruitt, D. G. (1998). Social conflict. In D. T. Gilbert, S. T. Fiske, & G. Lindzey (Eds.), *Handbook of social psychology* (3rd ed., Vol. 2, pp. 470–503). Boston: McGraw-Hill.

Pruitt, D. G., & Kimmel, M. J. (1977). Twenty years of experimental gaming: Critique, synthesis, and suggestions for the future. *Annual Review of Psychology, 28,* 3–392.

Pruitt, D. G., & Lewis, S. A. (1977). The psychology of integrative bargaining. In D. Druckman (Ed.), *Negotiations: A social-psychological analysis* (pp. 161–192). New York: Halstead.

Pruitt, D. G., & Rubin, J. Z. (1986). *Social conflict: Escalation, stalemate, and settlement.* New York: Random House.

Pryor, J. B., & Merluzzi, T. V. (1985). The role of expertise in processing social interaction scripts. *Journal of Experimental Social Psychology, 21,* 362–379.

Psychological Bulletin, 121, 371–394.

Pyszczynski, T., & Greenberg, J. (1987). Self-regulatory perseveration and the depressive self-focusing style: A self-awareness theory of reactive depression. *Psychological Bulletin, 102,* 122–138.

Pyszczynski, T., Greenberg, J., & Holt, K. (1985). Maintaining consistency between self-serving beliefs and available data: A bias in information evaluation. *Personality and Social Psychology Bulletin, 11,* 179–190.

Quigley-Fernandez, B., & Tedeschi, J. T. (1978). The bogus pipeline as lie detector: Two validity studies. *Journal of Personality and Social Psychology, 36,* 247–256.

Rabbie, J. M., & Bekkers, F. (1978). Threatened leadership and intergroup competition. *European Journal of Social Psychology, 8,* 9–20.

Radin, C. (1992, September 9). Colleges compete for high-achieving black students. *Boston Globe,* pp. 1, 19.

Rank, S. J., & Jacobsen, C. K. (1977). Hospital nurses' compliance with medication overdose orders: A failure to replicate. *Journal of Health and Social Behavior, 18,* 188–193.

Rapoport, A., & Bornstein, G. (1987). Intergroup competition for the provision of binary public goods. *Psychological Review, 94,* 291–299.

Rapoport, A., & Eshed-Levy, D. (1989). Provision of step-level public goods: Effects of greed and fear of being gypped. *Organizational Behavior and Human Decision Processes, 44.*

Rasinski, K. A., Crocker, J., & Hastie, R. (1985). Another look at sex stereotypes and social judgments: An analysis of the social perceiver's use of subjective probabilities. *Journal of Personality and Social Psychology, 49,* 317–326.

Raven, B. H. (1998). Groupthink, Bay of Pigs, and Watergate reconsidered. *Organizational Behavior and Human Decision Processes, 73,* 352–361.

Raven, B. H., & Rubin, J. Z. (1976). *Social psychology: People in groups.* New York: Wiley.

Redfern, D. (1979). *Individual level and group level determinants of nurses' compliance with physicians' inappropriate medical orders.* Paper presented at the annual meeting of the American Psychological Association, New York.

Reeves, B., & Nass, C. (1995). *The media equation.* New York: Cambridge University Press.

Reeves, B., & Nass, C. (1996). *The media equation.* Cambridge, England: Cambridge University Press.

Regan, D. T. (1971). Effects of a favor and liking on compliance. *Journal of Experimental Social Psychology, 7,* 627–639.

Regan, D. T., & Kilduff, M. (1988). Optimism about elections: Dissonance reduction at the ballot box. *Political Psychology, 9,* 101–107.

Regan, P. C. (1998). What if you can't get what you want? Willingness to compromise ideal mate selection standards as a function of sex, mate value, and relationship context. *Personality and Social Psychology Bulletin, 24,* 1294–1303.

Rehm, J., Steinleitner, J., & Lilli, W. (1987). Wearing uniforms and aggression: A field experiment. *European Journal of Social Psychology, 17,* 357–60.

Reibstein, L. (January 26, 1998). Arguing at a fever pitch. *Newsweek,* pp. 66–69.

Reibstein, L., & Gideonse, T. (1997, October 20). Don't mess with Deepak: Chopra the peripatetic healer is also quite a fighter. *Newsweek,* 56–58.

Reicher, S. D. (1987). Crowd behavior as social action. In J. C. Turner (Ed.), *Rediscovering the social group: a self-categorization theory.* Oxford, England: Blackwell.

Reid, F. J. M. (1983). Polarizing effects of intergroup comparison. *European Journal of Social Psychology, 13,* 103–106.

Reingen, P. H. (1982). Test of a list procedure for inducing compliance with a request to donate money. *Journal of Applied Psychology, 67,* 110–118.

Reis, H. T. (1986). Gender effects in social participation: Intimacy, loneliness, and the conduct of social interaction. In R. Gilmour & S. Duck (Eds.), *The emerging field of personal relationships* (pp. 91–108). Hillsdale, NJ: Erlbaum.

Reis, H. T., & Franks, P. (1994). The role of intimacy and social support in health outcomes: Two processes or one? *Personal Relationships, 1,* 185–197.

Reio, H. T., & Patrick, B. C. (1996). Attachment and intimacy. Component processes. In E. T. Higgins & A. W. Kruglanski (Eds.), *Social psychology: Handbook of basic principles* (pp. 523–563). New York: Guilford.

Reis, H. T., Senchak, M., & Solomon, B. (1985). Sex differences in the intimacy of social interaction. *Journal of Personality and Social Psychology, 48,* 1204–1217.

Reis, H. T., Wheeler, L., Spiegel, N., Kernis, M., Nezlek, J., & Perri, M. (1982). Physical attractiveness in social interaction: II. Why does appearance affect social experience? *Journal of Personality and Social Psychology, 43,* 979–996.

Reisenzein, R. (1983). The Schacter theory of emotion: Two decades later. *Psychological Bulletin, 94,* 239–264.

Reisenzein, R. (1986). A structural equation analysis of Weiner's attribution-affect model of helping behavior. *Journal of Personality and Social Psychology, 50,* 1123–1133.

Reiss, I. L. (1986). A sociological journey into sexuality. *Journal of Marriage and the Family, 48,* 233–242.

Reiss, I. L., & Lee, G. R. (1988). *Family systems in America* (4th ed.). New York: Holt, Rinehart, & Winston.

Reychler, L. (1979). The effectiveness of a pacifist strategy in conflict resolution: An experimental study. *Journal of Conflict Resolution, 23,* 288–260.

Rhodewalt, F., & Agustsdottir, S. (1986). Effects of self-presentation on the phenomenal self. *Journal of Personality and Social Psychology, 50,* 47–55.

Rholes, W. S., & Pryor, J. B. (1982). Cognitive accessibility and causal attributions. *Personality and Social Psychology Bulletin, 8,* 719–727.

Ridgeway, J. (1991, April 28). A meeting with haters. *Parade,* p. 5.

Ringelmann, M. (1913). Recherches sur les moteurs animés: Travail de l'homme. *Annales de l'Institute National Agronomique, 2e série, tom Xii,* 1–40.

Robberson, M. R., & Rogers, R. W. (1988). Beyond fear appeals: Negative and positive persuasive appeals to health and self esteem. *Journal of Applied Social Psychology, 18,* 277–287.

Robinson, J., & McArthur, L. Z. (1982). Impact of salient vocal qualities on causal attribution for a speaker's behavior. *Journal of Personality and Social Psychology, 43,* 236–247.

Robinson, R., & Bell, W. (1978). Equality, success, and social justice in England and the United States. *American Sociological Review, 43,* 125–143.

Rodin, J. (1985). The application of social psychology. In G. Lindzey & E. Aronson (Eds.), *Handbook of social psychology* (Vol. II, pp. 805–882). New York: Random House.

Rodin, J., & Langer, E. J. (1977). Long-term effects of a control-relevant intervention with the institutionalized aged. *Journal of Personality and Social Psychology, 35,* 897–902.

Rodin, J., & Salovey, P. (1989). Health psychology. *Annual Review of Psychology, 40,* 533–579.

Rodin, J., Solomon, S., & Metcalf, J. (1978). Role of control in mediating perceptions of density. *Journal of Personality and Social Psychology, 36,* 988–999.

Rodin, M. J. (1987). Who is memorable to whom: A study of cognitive disregard. *Social Cognition, 5,* 144–165.

Roethlisberger, F. J., & Dickson, W. J. (1939). *Management and the worker.* Cambridge, MA: Harvard University Press.

Rofé, Y. (1984). Stress and affiliation: Activity theory. *Psychological Review, 91,* 235–250.

Rogers, R. W. (1983). Cognitive and physiological processes in fear appeals and attitude change: A revised theory of protection motivation. In J. T. Cacioppo & R. E. Petty (Eds.), *Social psychophysiology: A sourcebook.* New York: Guilford.

Rogers, R. W., Deckner, C. W., & Mewborn, C. R. (1978). An expectancy-value theory approach to the long-term modification of smoking behavior. *Journal of Clinical Psychology, 34,* 562–566.

Rogers, R. W., & Mewborn, R. (1976). Fear appeals and attitude change: Effects of a threat's noxiousness, probability of occurrence, and the efficacy of coping responses. *Journal of Personality and Social Psychology, 34,* 54–61.

Rogers, T. B. (1981). A model of the self as an aspect of the human information processing system. In N. Cantor & J. F. Kihlstrom (Eds.), *Personality, cognition, and social interaction* (pp. 193–214). Hillsdale, NJ: Lawrence Erlbaum Associates.

Rohrer, J. H., Baron, S. H., Hoffman, E. L., & Schwander, D. V. (1954). The stability of autokinetic judgments. *Journal of Abnormal and Social Psychology, 49,* 595–597.

The romance of science. (1995, August 13). *The New York Times Magazine,* p. 16.

Romer, D., Jamieson, K. H., & de Coteau, N. J. (1998). The treatment of persons of color in local television news: Ethnic blame discourse or realistic group conflict? *Communication Research, 25,* 286–305.

Ronis, D. L., & Kaiser, M. K. (1989). Correlates of breast self-examination in a sample of college women: Analyses of linear structural relations. *Journal of Applied Social Psychology, 19,* 1068–1084.

Rook, K. S. (1987). Social support versus companionship: Effects on life stress, loneliness, and evaluations by others. *Journal of Personality and Social Psychology, 52,* 1132–1147.

Rook, K. S., & Peplau, L. A. (1982). Perspectives on helping the lonely. In L. A. Peplau & D. Perlman (Eds.), *Loneliness.* New York: Wiley Interscience.

Rook, K. S., & Pietromonaco, P. (1987). Close relationship: Ties that heal or ties that bind? In W. H. Jones & D. Perlman (Eds.), *Advances in personal relationships* (Vol. 1, pp. 1–35). Greenwich, CT: JAI Press.

Roseman, I. J., Spindel, M. S., & Jose, P. E. (1990). Appraisals of emotion-eliciting events: Testing a theory of discrete emotions. *Journal of Personality and Social Psychology, 59,* 899–915.

Rosenbaum, M. E. (1986). The repulsion hypothesis: On the nondevelopment of relationships. *Journal of Personality and Social Psychology, 51,* 1156–1166.

Rosenberg, M. (1956). Cognitive structure and attitudinal affect. *Journal of Abnormal and Social Psychology, 53,* 367–372.

Rosenberg, M. (1965). *Society and the adolescent self-image.* Princeton, NJ: Princeton University Press.

Rosenberg, M. (1969). The conditions and consequences of evaluation apprehension. In R. Rosenthal & R. L. Rosnow (Eds.), *Artifact in behavioral research* (pp. 279–349). New York: Academic Press.

Rosenberg, M. (1979). *Conceiving the self.* New York: Basic Books.

Rosenberg, M., & Simmons, R. B. (1971). *Black & white self-esteem: The urban school child*. Washington, DC: The American Sociological Association.

Rosenberg, S., Nelson, C., & Vivekananthan, P. S. (1968). A multidimensional approach to the structure of personality impressions. *Journal of Personality and Social Psychology, 9*, 283–294.

Rosenberg, S. W., Kahn, S., & Tran, T. (1991). Creating a political image: Shaping appearance and manipulating the vote. *Political Behavior, 13*, 345–367.

Rosenfeld, P., Giacalone, R., & Tedeschi, J. T. (1984). Cognitive dissonances and impression management explanations for effort justification. *Personality and Social Psychology Bulletin, 10*, 394–401.

Rosenfield, D., & Stephan, W. G. (1981). Intergroup relations among children. In S. Brehm, S. Kassin, & F. Gibbons (Eds.), *Developmental social psychology* (pp. 271–297). New York: Oxford University Press.

Rosenhan, D. (1970). The natural socialization of altruistic autonomy. In J. Macaulay & L. Berkowitz (Eds.), *Altruism and helping behavior* (pp. 251–268). New York: Academic Press.

Rosenhan, D. L. (1973). On being sane in insane places. *Science, 179*, 250–258.

Rosenthal, R. (1969). Interpersonal expectations: Effects of the experimenter's hypothesis. In R. Rosenthal & R. L. Rosnow (Eds.), *Artifact in behavioral research* (pp. 181–277). New York: Academic Press.

Rosenthal, R. (1985). From unconscious experimenter bias to teacher expectancy effects. In J. B. Dusek, V. C. Hall, & W. J. Meyer (Eds.), *Teacher expectancies* (pp. 37–66). Hillsdale, NJ: Erlbaum.

Rosenthal, R. (1991). Meta-analysis: A review. *Psychosomatic Medicine, 53*, 247–271.

Rosenthal, R., & Fode, K. L. (1963). Three experiments in experimenter bias. *Psychological Reports, 12*, 491–511.

Rosenthal, R., & Jacobson, L. (1968). *Pygmalion in the classroom*. New York: Holt, Rinehart, & Winston.

Rosnow, R. L., & Fine, G. A. (1976). *Rumor and gossip: The social psychology of hearsay*. New York: Elsevier.

Ross, A. S., & Braband, J. (1973). Effect of increased responsibility on bystander intervention: II. The cue value of a blind person. *Journal of Personality and Social Psychology, 25*, 254–258.

Ross, L. (1977). The intuitive psychologist and his shortcomings: Distortions in the attribution process. In L. Berkowitz (Ed.), *Advances in experimental social psychology* (Vol. 10, pp. 174–221). New York: Academic Press.

Ross, L. D., Amabile, T. M., & Steinmetz, J. L. (1977). Social roles, social control, and biases in social-perception processes. *Journal of Personality and Social Psychology, 35*, 485–494.

Ross, L., Lepper, M. R., & Hubbard, M. (1975). Perseverance in self-perception and social perception: Biased attribution processes in the debriefing paradigm. *Journal of Personality and Social Psychology, 32*, 880–892.

Ross, L., & Nisbett, R. E. (1990). *The person and the situation: Perspectives of social psychology*. New York: McGraw-Hill.

Ross, M. (1989). The relation of implicit theories to the construction of personal histories. *Psychological Review, 96*, 341–357.

Ross, M., & Conway, M. (1986). Remembering one's own past: The construction of personal histories. In R. Sorrentino & E. T. Higgins (Eds.), *Handbook of motivation and cognition* (pp. 122–144). New York: Guilford.

Ross, M., McFarland, C., Conway, M., & Zanna, M. P. (1983). Reciprocal relation between attitudes and behavior recall: Committing people to newly formed attitudes. *Journal of Personality and Social Psychology, 45*, 257–267.

Ross, M., McFarland, C., & Fletcher, G. J. O. (1981). The effect of attitude on recall of past histories. *Journal of Personality and Social Psychology, 40*, 627–634.

Ross, M., & Sicoly, F. (1979). Egocentric biases in availability and attribution. *Journal of Personality and Social Psychology, 37*, 322–336.

Ross, S. I., & Jackson, J. M. (1991). Teacher's expectations for black males' and black females' academic achievement. *Personality and Social Psychology Bulletin, 17*, 78–82.

Ross, S. M., & Offermann, L. R. (1997). Transformational leaders: Measurement of personality attributes and work group performance. *Personality and Social Psychology Bulletin, 23*, 1078–1086.

Rosselli, F., Skelly, J. J., & Mackie, D. M. (1995). Processing rational and emotional messages: The cognitive and affective mediation of persuasion. *Journal of Experimental Social Psychology, 31*, 163–190.

Rothbart, M. (1981). Memory processes and social beliefs. In D. L. Hamilton (Ed.), *Cognitive processes in stereotyping and intergroup behavior* (pp. 145–182). Hillsdale, NJ: Erlbaum.

Rothbart, M., Dawes, R., & Park. B. (1984). Stereotyping and sampling biases in intergroup perception. In J. R. Eiser (Ed.), *Attitudinal judgment* (pp. 109–134). New York: Springer-Verlag .

Rothbart, M., Evans, M., & Fulero, S. (1979). Recall for confirming events: Memory processes and the maintenance of social stereotyping. *Journal of Experimental Social Psychology, 15*, 343–355.

Rothbart, M., Fulero, S., Jensen, C., Howard, J., & Birrel, P. (1978). From individual to group impressions: Availability heuristics in stereotype formation. *Journal of Experimental Social Psychology, 14*, 237–255.

Rothbart, M., & Hallmark, W. (1988). In-group-out-group differences in the perceived efficacy of coercion and conciliation in resolving social conflict. *Journal of Personality and Social Psychology, 55*, 248–257.

Rothbart, M., & John, O. P. (1985). Social categorization and behavioral episodes: A cognitive analysis of the effects of intergroup contact. *Journal of Social Issues, 41*, 81–104.

Rothenberg, R. (1991, July 23). Blacks are found to be still scarce in advertisements in major magazines. *The New York Times*, p. A7.

Ruback, R. B., & Pandey, J. (1991). Crowding, perceived control, and relative power: An analysis of households in India. *Journal of Applied Social Psychology. 21*, 315–344.

Rubenstein, C. M., Shaver, P., & Peplau, L. A. (1979). Loneliness. *Human Nature, 2*, 58–65.

Rubin, B. (1987). *Third world coup makers, strongmen, and populist tyrants*. New York: McGraw-Hill

Rubin, J. Z. (1980). Experimental research on third party intervention in conflict: Toward some generalizations. *Psychological Bulletin, 87*, 379–391.

Rubin, J. Z., & Brown, B. R. (1975). *The social psychology of bargaining and negotiation*. New York: Academic Press.

Rubin, M., & Hewstone, M. (1998). Social identity theory's self-esteem hypothesis: A review and some suggestions for clarification. *Personality and Social Psychology Review, 2*, 40–62.

Rubin, Z. (1970). Measurement of romantic love. *Journal of Personality and Social Psychology, 16*, 265–273.

Rubin, Z., Hill, C. T., Peplau, L. A., & Dunkel-Schetter, C. (1980). Self-disclosure in dating couples: Sex roles and the ethic of openness. *Journal of Marriage and the Family, 42*, 305–317.

Rudman, L. J., & Borgida, E. (1995). The afterglow of construct accessibility: The behavioral consequences of priming men to view women as sexual objects. *Journal of Experimental Social Psychology, 31*, 493–517.

Ruggiero, K. M., & Taylor, D. M. (1995). Coping with discrimination: How disadvantaged group members perceive the discrimination that confronts them. *Journal of Personality and Social Psychology, 68*, 826–838.

Ruggiero, K. M., & Taylor, D. M. (1997). Why minority group members perceive or do not perceive the discrimination that confronts them: The role of self-esteem and perceived control. *Journal of Personality and Social Psychology, 72*, 373–389.

Rule, B. G., Taylor, B. R., & Dobbs, A. R. (1987). Priming effects of heat on aggressive thoughts. *Social Cognition, 5*, 131–143.

Runciman, W. G. (1966). *Relative deprivation and social justice*. Berkeley, CA: University of California Press.

Rusbult, C. E. (1983). A longitudinal test of the investment model: The development (and deterioration) of satisfaction and commitment in heterosexual involvements. *Journal of Personality and Social Psychology, 45*, 101–117.

Rusbult, C. E., & Martz, J. M. (1995). Remaining in an abusive relationship: An investment model analysis of nonvoluntary commitment. *Personality and Social Psychology Bulletin, 21*, 558–571.

Rusbult, C. E., Martz, J. M., & Agnew, C. R. (1998). The Investment Model Scale: Measuring commitment level, satisfaction level, quality of alternatives, and investment size. *Personal Relationships, 5*, 357–391.

Rusbult, C. E., & van Lange, P. A. M. (1996). Interdependence processes. In E. T. Higgins & A. Kruglanski (Eds.), *Social psychology: Handbook of basic principles* (pp. 564–596). New York: Guilford.

Rusbult, C. E., Verette, J., Whitney, G. A., Slovik, L. F., & Lipkus, I. (1991). Accommodation processes in close relationships: Theory and preliminary empirical evidence. *Journal of Personality and Social Psychology, 60*, 53–78.

Rusbult, C. E., Yovetich, N. A., & Verette, J. (1996). An interdependence analysis of accommodation processes. In G. J. O. Fletcher & J. Fitness (Eds.), *Knowledge structures in close relationships: A social psychological approach* (pp. 63–90). Mahwah, NJ: Erlbaum.

Rushton, J. P. (1975). Generosity in children: Immediate and long-term effects of modeling, preaching, and moral judgment. *Journal of Personality and Social Psychology, 31*, 459–466.

Ruskin, J. (1907/1963). *The seven lamps of architecture*. London: Everyman's Library.

Russell, J. J. (1994). Is there universal recognition of emotion from facial expressions? A review of the cross-cultural studies. *Psychological Bulletin, 115*, 102–141.

Rutter, D. R., & Robinson, B. (1981). An experimental analysis of teaching by telephone. In G. M. Stephenson & J. H. Davis (Eds.), *Progress in applied social psychology* (Vol. 1, pp. 345–374). New York: Wiley.

Ryan, C. S. (1996). Accuracy of black and white college students' in-group and out-group stereotypes. *Personality and Social Psychology Bulletin, 22*, 1114–1127.

Ryan, C. S., & Bogart, L. M. (1997). Development of new group members' in-group and out-group stereotypes: Changes in perceived group variability and ethnocentrism. *Journal of Personality and Social Psychology, 73*, 719–732.

Ryan, R. M., & Grolnick, W. S. (1986). Origins and pawns in the classroom: Self-report and projective assessments of individual differences in children's perceptions. *Journal of Personality and Social Psychology, 50*, 550–558.

Ryen, A. H., & Kahn, A. (1975). The effects of intergroup orientation on group attitudes and proxemic behavior. *Journal of Personality and Social Psychology, 31*, 302–310.

Sachdev, I., & Bourhis, R. Y. (1985). Social categorization and power differentials in group relations. *European Journal of Social Psychology, 15*, 415–434.

Sachdev, I., & Bourhis, R. Y. (1991). Power and status differentials in minority and majority group relations. *European Journal of Social Psychology, 21*, 1–24.

Safire, W. (1992, August 27). God bless us. *The New York Times*, p. A15.

Sagar, H. A., & Schofield, J. W. (1980). Racial and behavioral cues in black and white children's perceptions of ambiguously aggressive acts. *Journal of Personality and Social Psychology, 39*, 590–598.

Sakai, H., & Andow, K. (1980). Attribution of personal responsibility and dissonance reduction. *Japanese Psychological Research, 22*, 32–41.

Salancik, G. R., & Conway, M. (1975). Attitude inference from salient and relevant cognitive content about behavior. *Journal of Personality and Social Psychology, 32*, 829–840.

Salovey, P., & Rodin, J. (1984). Some antecedents and consequences of social-comparison jealousy. *Journal of Personality and Social Psychology, 47*, 780–792.

Salovey, P., & Rodin, J. (1989). Envy and jealousy in close relationships. In C. Hendrick (Ed.), *Close relationships* (pp. 221–246). Beverly Hills, CA: Sage.

Salovey, P., Rothman, A. J., & Rodin, J. (1998). Health behavior. In D. T. Gilbert, S. T. Fiske, & G. Lindzey (Eds.), *Handbook of social psychology* (4th ed., Vol. 2, pp. 633–683). Boston: McGraw-Hill.

Samuelson, C. D., Messick, D. M., Rutte, C. G., & Wilke, H. (1984). Individual and structural solutions to resource dilemmas in two cultures. *Journal of Personality and Social Psychology, 47*, 94–104.

Sande, G. N., Goethals, G. R., & Radloff, C. E. (1988). Perceiving one's own traits and others': The multifaceted self. *Journal of Personality and Social Psychology, 54*, 13–20.

Sanitioso, R., Kunda, Z., & Fong, G. T. (1990). Motivated recruitment of autobiographical memory. *Journal of Personality and Social Psychology, 59*, 229–241.

Sanna, L. J., & Shotland, R. L. (1990). Valence of anticipated evaluation and social facilitation. *Journal of Experimental Social Psychology, 26*, 82–92.

Sarason, B. R., Shearin, E. N., Pierce, G. R., & Sarason, I. G. (1987). Interrelations of social support measures: Theoretical and practical implications. *Journal of Personality and Social Psychology, 52*, 813–832.

Sato, K. (1987). Distribution of the cost of maintaining common resources. *Journal of Experimental Social Psychology, 23*, 19–31.

Sattler, D. N., & Kerr, N. L. (1991). Might versus morality explored: Motivational and cognitive bases for social motives. *Journal of Personality and Social Psychology, 60*, 756–765.

Saxe, L., Dougherty, D., & Cross, T. (1985). The validity of polygraph testing: Scientific analysis and public controversy. *American Psychologist, 40*, 355–366.

Schachter, S. (1951). Deviation, rejection and communication. *Journal of Abnormal and Social Psychology, 46*, 190–207.

Schachter, S. (1959). *The psychology of affiliation.* Stanford, CA: Stanford University Press.

Schachter, S., Ellertson, N., McBride, D., & Gregory, D. (1951). An experimental study of cohesiveness and productivity. *Human Relations, 4*, 229–238.

Schachter, S., & Singer, J. (1962). Cognitive, social, and physiological determinants of the emotional state. *Psychological Review, 69*, 379–399.

Schafer, M., & Crichlow, S. (1996). Antecedents of groupthink. *Journal of Conflict Resolution, 40*, 415–435.

Schaller, M., Asp, C. H., Rosell, M. C., & Heim, S. J. (1996). Training in statistical reasoning inhibits the formation of erroneous group stereotypes. *Personality and Social Psychology Bulletin, 22*, 829–844.

Schaller, M., & Cialdini, R. B. (1988). The economics of empathic helping: Support for a mood management motive. *Journal of Experimental Social Psychology, 24*, 163–181.

Schaller, M., & Cialdini, R. B. (1990). Happiness, sadness, and helping: A motivational integration. In E. T. Higgins & R. M. Sorrentino (Eds.), *Handbook of motivation and cognition* (Vol. 2, pp. 265–296). New York: Guilford.

Scheier, M. F., & Carver, C. S. (1977). Self-focused attention and the experience of emotion: Attraction, repulsion, elation, and depression. *Journal of Personality and Social Psychology, 35*, 625–636.

Schein, E. H. (1956). The Chinese indoctrination program for prisoners of war: A study of attempted brainwashing. *Psychiatry, 19*, 149–172.

Schell, T. L., Klein, S. B., & Babey, S. H. (1996). Testing a hierarchical model of self-knowledge. *Psychological Science, 7*, 170–173.

Scher, S., & Cooper, J. (1989). Motivational basis of dissonance: The singular role of behavioral consequences. *Journal of Personality and Social Psychology, 56*, 899–906.

Schiller, J. C. F. (1882). *Essays, esthetical and philosophical, including the dissertation on the "Connexions between the animal and the spiritual in man."* London: Bell.

Schittekatte, M. (1996). Facilitating information exchange in small decision-making groups. *European Journal of Social Psychology, 26*, 537–556.

Schlenker, B. R. (1982). Translating actions into attitudes: An identity-analytic approach to the explanation of social conduct.

In L. Berkowitz (Ed.), *Advances in experimental social psychology* (Vol. 15). New York: Academic Press. pp. 193–247.

Schlenker, B. R. (1985). Identity and self-identification. In B. R. Schlenker (Ed.), *The self and social life* (pp. 65–100). New York: McGraw-Hill.

Schlenker, B. R., Dlugolecki, D. W., & Doherty, K. (1994). The impact of self-presentations on self-appraisals and behavior: The power of public commitment. *Personality and Social Psychology Bulletin, 20*, 20–33.

Schlenker, B. R., & Forsyth, D. R. (1977). On the ethics of psychological research. *Journal of Experimental Social Psychology, 13*, 369–396.

Schmalz, J. (1992, October 11). Gay politics goes mainstream. *The New York Times Magazine*, pp. 18–21, 29, 41.

Schmidt, G., & Weiner, B. (1988). An attribution-affect-action theory of behavior: Replications of judgments of help-giving. *Personality and Social Psychology Bulletin, 14*, 610–621.

Schmidt, W. E. (1990, December 13). White men get better deals on cars, study finds. *The New York Times.*

Schmitt, B. H., Gilovich, T., Goore, N., & Joseph, L. (1986). Mere presence and social facilitation: One more time. *Journal of Experimental Social Psychology, 22*, 242–248.

Schmutte, G. T., & Taylor, S. P. (1980). Physical aggression as a function of alcohol and pain feedback. *Journal of Social Psychology, 110*, 235–244.

Schneider, D. J. (1973). Implicit personality theory: A review. *Psychological Bulletin, 79*, 294–309.

Schoeneman, T. J., & Rubanowitz, D. E. (1985). Attributions in the advice columns: Actors and observers, causes and reasons. *Personality and Social Psychology Bulletin, 11*, 315–325.

Schoenrade, P. A., Batson, C. D., & Brandt, J. R. (1986). Attachment, accountability, and motivation to benefit another not in distress. *Journal of Personality and Social Psychology, 51*, 557–563.

Schofield, J. (1978). School desegregation and intergroup relations. In D. Bar-Tal & L. Saxe (Eds.), *Social psychology of education: Theory and research* (pp. 329–364). New York: Wiley.

Schofield, J. W. (1986). Causes and consequences of the color-blind perspective. In J. F. Dovidio & S. L. Gaertner (Eds.), *Prejudice, discrimination, and racism* (pp. 231–254). Orlando, FL: Academic Press.

Schopler, J., Insko, C. A., Graetz, K. A., Drigotas, S., Smith, V. A., & Dahl, K. (1993). Individual-group discontinuity: Further evidence for mediation by fear and greed. *Personality and Social Psychology Bulletin, 19*, 419–431.

Schroeder, D. A., Jensen, T. D., Reed, A. J., Sullivan, D. K., & Schwab, M. (1983). The actions of others as determinants of behavior in social trap situations. *Journal of Experimental Social Psychology, 19*, 522–539.

Schuman, H., & Johnson, M. P. (1976). Attitudes and behavior. *Annual Review of Sociology, 2*, 161–207.

Schuster, J. R. (1985, May). Compensation plan design. *Management Review*, 21–25

Schwartz, S. H. (1977). Normative influences on altruism. In L. Berkowitz (Ed.), *Advances in experimental social psychology* (Vol. 10, pp. 221–279). New York: Academic Press.

Schwartz, S. H., & Gottlieb, A. (1980). Bystander anonymity and reaction to emergencies. *Journal of Personality and Social Psychology, 39,* 418–430.

Schwarz, N. (1999). Self-reports: How the questions shape the answers. *American Psychologist, 54,* 93–105.

Schwarz, N., Bless, H., & Bohner, G. (1991). Mood and persuasion: Affective states influence processing of persuasive communications. In M. P. Zanna (Ed.), *Advances in experimental social psychology* (Vol. 24, pp. 161–199). San Diego: Academic Press.

Schwarz, N., & Clore, G. L. (1983). Mood, misattribution, and judgments of well-being: Informative and directive functions of affective states. *Journal of Personality and Social Psychology, 45,* 513–523.

Schwarz, N., & Clore, G. L. (1988). How do I feel about it? Informative functions of affective states. In K. Fiedler & J. Forgas (Eds.), *Affect, Cognition, and Social Behavior* (pp. 44–62). Toronto: Hogrefe.

Schwarzer, R., & Leppin, A. (1989). Social support and health: A meta-analysis. *Psychology and Health, 3,* 1–15.

Schwarzwald, J., Bizman, A., & Raz, M. (1983). The foot-in-the-door paradigm: Effects of second request size on donation probability and donor generosity. *Personality and Social Psychology Bulletin, 9,* 69–79.

Schwarzwald, J., Raz, M., & Zvibel, M. (1979). The efficacy of the door-in-the-face technique when established behavioral customs exist. *Journal of Applied Social Psychology, 9,* 576–586.

Sears, D. O., (1988). Symbolic racism. In P. Katz & D. Taylor (Eds.), *Eliminating racism: Profiles in controversy* (pp. 53–84). New York: Plenum.

Sears, D. O., & Allen, H. M., Jr. (1984). The trajectory of local desegregation controversies and whites' opposition to busing. In N. Miller & M. Brewer (Eds.), *Groups in contact: The psychology of desegregation* (pp. 123–151). New York: Academic Press.

Sears, D. O., & McConahay, J. B. (1973). *The politics of violence: The new urban blacks and the Watts riot.* Boston: Houghton Mifflin.

Seashore, S. E. (1954). *Group cohesiveness in the industrial work group.* Ann Arbor, MI: Institute for Social Research.

Sedek, G., & Kofta, M. (1990). When cognitive exertion does not yield cognitive gain: Toward an informational explanation of learned helplessness. *Journal of Personality and Social Psychology, 58,* 729–743.

Sedikides, C. (1990). Effects of fortuitously activated constructs versus activated communication goals on person impressions. *Journal of Personality and Social Psychology, 58,* 397–408.

Sedikides, C., & Skowronski, J. J. (1993). The self in impression formation: Trait centrality and social perception. *Journal of Experimental Social Psychology, 29,* 347–357.

Segal, H. A. (1954). Initial psychiatric findings of recently repatriated prisoners of war. *American Journal of Psychiatry, 61,* 358–363.

Segal, M. W. (1974). Alphabet and attraction: An unobtrusive measure of the effect of propinquity in a field setting. *Journal of Personality and Social Psychology, 30,* 654–657.

Seligman, C. L., Becker, J., & Darley, J. M. (1981). Encouraging residential energy conservation through feedback. In A. Baum & J. Singer (Eds.), *Advances in environmental psychology* (Vol. 3, pp. 53–91). Hillsdale, NJ: Erlbaum.

Seligman, M. E. P. (1975). *On depression, development, and death.* San Francisco: Freeman.

Seligman, M. E. P., & Maier, S. F. (1967). Failure to escape traumatic shock. *Journal of Experimental Psychology, 74,* 1–9.

Senneker, P., & Hendrick, C. (1983). Androgyny and helping behavior. *Journal of Personality and Social Psychology, 45,* 916–925.

Shanab, M. E., & Yahra, K. A. (1977). A behavioral study of obedience in children. *Journal of Personality and Social Psychology, 35,* 530–536.

Sharpsteen, D. J., & Kirkpatrick, L. A. (1997). Romantic jealousy and adult romantic attachment. *Journal of Personality and Social Psychology, 72,* 627–640.

Shaver, P., & Hazan, C. (1985). Incompatibility, loneliness, and "limerence. " In W. Ickes (Ed.), *Compatible and incompatible relationships* (pp. 163–186). New York: Springer-Verlag.

Shaver, P., & Hazan, C. (1988). A biased overview of the study of love. *Journal of Social and Personal Relationships, 5,* 473–501.

Shaver, P., Hazan, C., & Bradshaw, D. (1988). Love as attachment: The integration of three behavioral systems. In R. Sternberg & M. Barnes (Eds.), *The psychology of love* (pp. 68–99). New Haven, CT: Yale University Press.

Shaver, P., Schwartz, J., Kirson, D., & O'Connor, C. (1987). Emotion knowledge: Further exploration of a prototype approach. *Journal of Personality and Social Psychology, 52,* 1061–1086.

Shavitt, S. (1990). The role of attitude objects in attitude functions. *Journal of Experimental Social Psychology, 26,* 124–148.

Shaw, M. E. (1954). Some effects of unequal distribution of information upon group performance in various communication nets. *Journal of Abnormal and Social Psychology, 49,* 547–553.

Shaw, M. E. (1976). *Group dynamics: The psychology of small group behavior* (2nd ed.). New York: McGraw-Hill

Sheppard, B. H., Hartwick, J., & Warshaw, P. R. (1988). The theory of reasoned action: A meta-analysis of past research with recommendations for modifications and future research. *Journal of Consumer Research, 15,* 325–343.

Sherif, C. W. (1979). Bias in psychology. In J. A. Sherman & E. T. Beck (Eds.), *The prism of sex: Essays in the sociology of knowledge* (pp. 93–133). Madison, WI: University of Wisconsin Press.

Sherif, M. (1936). *The psychology of social norms.* New York: Harper.

Sherif, M. (1966). *In common predicament: Social psychology of intergroup conflict and cooperation.* Boston: Houghton Mifflin.

Sherif, M., Harvey, O. J., White, B. J., Hood, W. E., & Sherif, C. W. (1961). *Intergroup conflict and cooperation: The robbers cave experiment.* Normon, OK: University of Oklahoma Press/Book Exchange.

Sherif, M., & Sherif, C. W. (1953). *Groups in harmony and tension.* New York: Harper.

Sherman, J. W., & Klein, S. B. (1994). Development and representation of personality impressions. *Journal of Personality and Social Psychology, 67,* 972–983.

Sherman, J. W., Klein, S. B., Laskey, A., & Wyer, N. A. (1998). Intergroup bias in group judgment processes: The role of behavioral memories. *Journal of Experimental Social Psychology, 34,* 51–65.

Sherman, L. W., & Berk, R. A. (1984). The specific deterrent effects of arrest for domestic assault. *American Sociological Review, 49,* 261–272.

Sherman, P. W. (1977). Nepotism and the evolution of alarm calls. *Science, 197,* 1246–1253.

Sherman, S. J. (1980). On the self-erasing nature of errors of prediction. *Journal of Personality and Social Psychology, 39,* 211–221.

Sherman, S. J., Chassin, L., Presson, C. C., & Agostinelli, G. (1984). The role of the evaluation and similarity principles in the false consensus effect. *Journal of Personality and Social Psychology, 47,* 1244–1262.

Sherrod, D. (1974). Crowding, perceived control, and behavioral aftereffects. *Journal of Applied Social Psychology, 4,* 171–186.

Shih, M., Pittinsky, T. L., & Ambady, N. (1999). Stereotype susceptibility: Identity salience and shifts in quantitative performance. *Psychological Science, 10,* 80–83.

Shils, E. A., & Janowitz, M. (1948). Cohesion and disintegration in the Wehrmacht in World War II. *Public Opinion Quarterly, 12,* 280–315.

Shotland, R. L., & Heinold, W. D. (1985). Bystander response to arterial bleeding: Helping skills, the decision-making process, and differentiating the helping response. *Journal of Personality and Social Psychology, 49,* 347–356.

Shotland, R. L., & Straw, M. K. (1976). Bystander response to an assault: When a man attacks a woman. *Journal of Personality and Social Psychology, 34,* 990–999.

Showers, C. (1992). Compartmentalization of positive and negative self-knowledge: Keeping bad apples out of the bunch. *Journal of Personality and Social Psychology, 62,* 1036–1049.

Shrauger, J. S., & Schoeneman, T. J. (1979). Symbolic interactionist view of self-concept: Through the looking glass darkly. *Psychological Bulletin, 86,* 549–573.

Sia, T. L., Lord, C. G., Blessum, K. A., Ratcliff, C. D., & Lepper, M. R. (1997). Is a rose always a rose? The role of social category exemplar change in attitude stability and attitude-behavior consistency. *Journal of Personality and Social Psychology, 72,* 501–514.

Sias, P. M., & Jablin, F. M. (1995). Differential superior-subordinate relations, perceptions of fairness, and coworker communication. *Human Communication Research, 22,* 5–38.

Silka, L. (1989). *Intuitive judgments of change.* New York: Springer-Verlag.

Silver, M., & Geller, D. (1978). On the irrelevance of evil: The organization and individual action. *Journal of Social Issues, 34,* 125–136.

Silverstein, L. (1965). *Defense of the poor in criminal cases in American state courts.* Chicago: American Bar Foundation.

Simmel, G. (1950). *The sociology of Georg Simmel.* New York: Free Press.

Simmonds, D. B. (1985). The nature of the organizational grapevine. *Supervisory Management,* 39–42.

Simon, B. (1992). The perception of ingroup and outgroup homogeneity: Reintroducing the intergroup context. In W. Stroebe & M. Hewstone (Eds.), *European review of social psychology* (Vol. 3, pp. 1–30). Chichester, England: Wiley.

Simon, B. (1998). Individuals, groups, and social change: On the relationship between individual and collective self-interpretations and collective action. In C. Sedikides & J. Schopler (Eds.), *Intergroup cognition and intergroup behavior* (pp. 257–282). Mahwah, NJ: Erlbaum.

Simon, B., & Brown, R. (1987). Perceived homogeneity in minority-majority contexts. *Journal of Personality and Social Psychology, 53,* 703–711.

Simon, B., & Hamilton, D. L. (1994). Self-stereotyping and social context: The effects of relative in-group size and in-group status. *Journal of Personality and Social Psychology, 66,* 699–711.

Simon, B., Loewy, M., Sturmer, S., Weber, U., Freytag, P., Habig, C., Kampmeier, C., & Spahlinger, P. (1998). Collective identification and social movement participation. *Journal of Personality and Social Psychology, 74,* 646–658.

Simon, H. A. (1990). A mechanism for social selection and successful altruism. *Science, 250,* 1665–1668.

Simon, L., Greenberg, J., & Brehm, J. (1995). Trivialization: The forgotten mode of dissonance reduction. *Journal of Personality and Social Psychology, 68,* 247–260.

Simons, M. (1992, March 17). North-South chasm is threatening search for environmental solutions. *The New York Times,* p. A5.

Simpson, J. A. (1987). The dissolution of romantic relationships: Factors involved in relationship stability and emotional distress. *Journal of Personality and Social Psychology, 53,* 683–692.

Simpson, J. A. (1990). Influence of attachment styles on romantic relationships. *Journal of Personality and Social Psychology, 59,* 971–980.

Simpson, J. A., Campbell, B., & Berscheid, E. (1986). The association between romantic love and marriage: Kephart (1967) twice revisited. *Personality and Social Psychology Bulletin, 12,* 363–372.

Simpson, J. A., & Gangestad, S. W. (1991). Personality and sexuality: Empirical relations and an integrative theoretical model. In K. McKinney & S. Sprecher (Eds.), *Sexuality in close relationships* (pp. 71–92). Hillsdale, NJ: Erlbaum.

Simpson, J. A., Gangestad, S. W., & Lerma, M. (1990). Perception of physical attractiveness: Mechanisms involved in the maintenance of romantic relationships. *Journal of Personality and Social Psychology, 59,* 1192–1201.

Simpson, J. A., Ickes, W., & Blackstone, T. (1995). When the head protects the heart: Empathic accuracy in dating relationships. *Journal of Personality and Social Psychology, 69,* 629–641.

Simpson, J. A., Rholes, W. S., & Nelligan, J. S. (1992). Support seeking and support giving within couples in an anxiety-provoking situation: The role of attachment styles. *Journal of Personality and Social Psychology, 62,* 434–446.

Simpson, J. A., Rholes, W. S., & Phillips, D. (1996). Conflict in close relationships: An attachment perspective. *Journal of Personality and Social Psychology, 71,* 899–914.

Sinclair, R. C., Mark, M. M., & Clore, G. L. (1991). *Mood, misattribution, and persuasion: The informational impact of mood on processing strategy.* Unpublished manuscript, University of Alberta, Canada.

Singer, J. L., & Singer, D. G. (1981). *Television, imagination, and aggression: A study of preschoolers.* Hillsdale, NJ: Erlbaum.

Singleton, R., Jr. (1979). Another look at the conformity explanation of group-induced shifts in choice. *Human Relations, 32,* 37–56.

Skaalvik, E. M. (1986). Sex differences in global self-esteem. *Scandinavian Journal of Educational Research, 30,* 167–179.

Skinner, M., & Stephenson, G. M. (1987). The effects of intergroup comparison on the polarization of opinions. *Current Psychological Research, 1*, 49–61.

Skowronski, J. J., & Carlston, D. E. (1989). Negativity and extremity biases in impression formation: A review of explanations. *Psychological Bulletin, 105*, 131–142.

Smith, E. R. (1977). Single-sex colleges and sex-typing. *Journal of Social Issues, 33*, 197–199.

Smith, E. R. (1991). Illusory correlation in a simulated exemplar-based memory. *Journal of Experimental Social Psychology, 27*, 107–123.

Smith, E. R. (1993). Social identity and social emotions: Toward new conceptualizations of prejudice. In D. M. Mackie & D. L. Hamilton (Eds.), *Affect, cognition, and stereotyping: Interactive processes in group perception* (pp. 297–315). San Diego: Academic Press.

Smith, E. R. (1998). Mental representation and memory. In D. Gilbert, S. T., Fiske, G. Lindzey, *Handbook of social psychology* (4th ed. Vol. 1, pp. 391–445). Boston: McGraw-Hill.

Smith, E. R., Coats, S., & Walling, D. (1999). Overlapping mental representations of self, in-group, and partner: Further response time evidence and a connectionist model. *Personality and Social Psychology Bulletin, 25*, 873–882.

Smith, E. R., & Ho, C. (1999). Prejudice as intergroup emotion: Integrating relative deprivation and social comparison explanations of prejudice. In I. Walker & H. Smith (Eds.), *Relative deprivation: Specification, development, and integration*. Boulder, CO: Westview Press.

Smith, E. R., & Kluegel, J. R. (1982). Cognitive and social bases of emotional experience: Outcome, attribution, and affect. *Journal of Personality and Social Psychology, 43*, 1129–1141.

Smith, E. R., & Miller, F. D. (1979). Salience and the cognitive mediation of attribution. *Journal of Personality and Social Psychology, 37*, 2240–2252.

Smith, E. R., & Zárate, M. A. (1992). Exemplar-based model of social judgment. *Psychological Review, 99*, 3–21.

Smith, H. J., & Spears, R. (1996). Ability and outcome evaluations as a function of personal and collective (dis)advantage: A group escape from individual bias. *Personality and Social Psychology Bulletin, 22*, 690–704.

Smith, H. J., & Tyler, T. R. (1997). Choosing the right pond: The impact of group membership on self-esteem and group-oriented behavior. *Journal of Experimental Social Psychology, 33*, 146–170.

Smith, M. B., Bruner, J. S., & White, R. W. (1956). *Opinions and personality*. New York: Wiley.

Smith, P. B., & Bond, M. H. (1993a). *Across cultures*. Boston: Allyn & Bacon.

Smith, P. B., & Bond, M. H. (1993b). *Social psychology across cultures: Analysis and perspectives*. New York: Harvester Wheatsheaf.

Smith, P. B., & Tayeb, M. (1989). Organizational structure and processes. In M. Bond (Ed.), *The cross-cultural challenge to social psychology*. Newbury Park, CA: Sage.

Smith, R. E., & Smoll, F. L. (1996). *Way to go, Coach! A scientifically validated approach to coaching effectiveness*. Portola Valley, CA: Warde Publishers.

Smith, R. E., & Smoll, F. L. (1997). Coaching the coaches: Youth sports as a scientific and applied behavioral setting. *Current Directions in Psychological Science, 6*, 16–21.

Smith, R. E., Vanderbilt, K., & Callen, M. B. (1973). Social comparison and bystander intervention in emergencies. *Journal of Applied Social Psychology, 3*, 186–196.

Smith, S. M., & Shaffer, D. R. (1995). Speed of speech and persuasion: Evidence for multiple effects. *Personality and Social Psychology Bulletin, 21*, 1051–1060.

Smith, S. S., & Richardson, D. (1983). Amelioration of deception and harm in psychological research: The important role of debriefing. *Journal of Personality and Social Psychology, 44*, 1075–1082.

Smith, T. W. (1990). Report: The sexual revolution? *Public Opinion Quarterly, 54*, 415–435.

Smith, W. P., & Anderson, A. J. (1975). Threats, communication and bargaining. *Journal of Personality and Social Psychology, 32*, 76–82.

Smyth, M. M., & Fuller, R. G. C. (1972). Effects of group laughter on responses to humorous materials. *Psychological Reports, 30*, 132–134.

Snyder, C. R., & Higgins, R. L. (1988). Excuses: Their effective role in the negotiation of reality. *Psychological Bulletin, 104*, 23–35.

Snyder, C. R., Lassegard, M. A., & Ford, C. E. (1986). Distancing after group success and failure: Basking in reflected glory and cutting off reflected failure. *Journal of Personality and Social Psychology, 51*, 382–388.

Snyder, C. R., Smith, T. W., Augelli, R. W., & Ingram, R. E. (1985). On the self-serving function of social anxiety: Shyness as a self-handicapping strategy. *Journal of Personality and Social Psychology, 48*, 970–980.

Snyder, M. (1974). The self-monitoring of expressive behavior. *Journal of Personality and Social Psychology, 30*, 526–537.

Snyder, M. (1982). When believing means doing: Creating links between attitudes and behavior. In M. Zanna, E. T. Higgins, & C. P. Herman (Eds.), *Consistency in social behavior: The Ontario symposium* (Vol. 2, pp. 105–130). Hillsdale, NJ: Erlbaum.

Snyder, M., Berscheid, E., & Glick, P. (1985). Focusing on the exterior and the interior: Two investigations of the initiation of personal relationships. *Journal of Personality and Social Psychology, 48*, 1427–1439.

Snyder, M., Berscheid, E., & Matwuchuk, A. (1988). Orientations toward personnel selection: Differential reliance on appearance and personality. *Journal of Personality and Social Psychology, 54*, 972–979.

Snyder, M., & DeBond, K. G. (1985). Appeals to image and claims about quality: Understanding the psychology of advertising. *Journal of Personality and Social Psychology, 49*, 586–597.

Snyder, M., & Gangestad, S. (1982). Choosing social situations: Two investigations of self-monitoring processes. *Journal of Personality and Social Psychology, 43*, 123–135.

Snyder, M., & Haugen, J. A. (1995). Why does behavioral confirmation occur? A functional perspective on the role of the target. *Personality and Social Psychology Bulletin, 21*, 963–974.

Snyder, M., & Kendzierski, D. (1982). Acting on one's attitudes: Procedures for linking attitude and behavior. *Journal of Experimental Social Psychology, 18*, 165–183.

Snyder, M., & Omoto, A. M. (1992). Volunteerism and society's response to the HIV epidemic. *Current Directions in Psychological Science, 1*, 113–116.

Snyder, M., & Swann, W. B., Jr. (1976). When actions reflect attitudes: The politics of impression management. *Journal of Personality and Social Psychology, 34,* 1034–1042.

Snyder, M., & Swann, W. B. (1978). Behavioral confirmation in social interaction: From social perception to social reality. *Journal of Personality and Social Psychology, 36,* 1202–1212.

Snyder, M., Tanke, E. D., & Berscheid, E. (1977). Social perception and interpersonal behavior: On the self-fulfilling nature of social stereotypes. *Journal of Personality and Social Psychology, 35,* 656–666.

Solarz, A. (1960). Latency of instrumental responses as a function of compatibility with the meaning of eliciting verbal signals. *Journal of Experimental Psychology, 59,* 239–245.

Solomon, H., Solomon, L. Z., Arnone, M. M., Maur, B. J., Reda, R. M., & Rother, E. O. (1981). Anonymity and helping. *Journal of Social Psychology, 113,* 37–43.

Sorrentino, R. M., & Field, N. (1986). Emergent leadership over time: The functional value of positive motivation. *Journal of Personality and Social Psychology, 50,* 1091–1099.

Spears, R., Doosje, B., & Ellemers, N. (1997). Self-stereotyping in the face of threats to group status and distinctiveness: The role of group identification. *Personality and Social Psychology Bulletin, 23,* 538–553.

Spears, R., & Oakes, P. J. (Eds.). *The social psychology of stereotyping and group life* (pp. 208–235). Oxford, England: Blackwell Publishers.

Spence, J. T., Deaux, K., & Helmreich, R. L. (1985). Sex roles in contemporary American society. In G. Lindzey & E. Aronson (Eds.), *Handbook of social psychology* (3rd ed., Vol. 2, pp. 149–178). New York: Random House.

Spencer, S. J. (1994). The effect of stereotype vulnerability on women's math performance (Doctoral dissertation, Department of Psychology, University of Michigan, 1994). *Dissertation Abstracts International: Section B: the Sciences & Engineering, 54(7-B),* 3903.

Sprague, J., & Quadagno, D. (1989). Gender and sexual motivation: An exploration of two assumptions. *Journal of Psychology and Human Sexuality, 2,* 57–76.

Sprecher, S. (1989). The importance to males and females of physical attractiveness, earning potential and expressiveness in initial attraction. *Sex Roles, 21, 591–607.*

Sprecher, S. (1999). "I love you more today than yesterday": Romantic partners' perceptions of changes in love and related affect over time. *Journal of Personality and Social Psychology, 76,* 46–53.

Sprecher, S., Aron, A., Hatfield, E., Cortest, A., Potapova, E., & Levitskaya, A. (1994). Love: American style, Russian style, and Japanese style. *Personal Relationships, 1,* 349–369.

Srull, T. K. (1981). Person memory: Some tests of associative storage and retrieval models. *Journal of Experimental Psychology: Human Learning and Memory, 7,* 440–463.

Srull, T. K., & Brand, J. F. (1983). Memory for information about persons: The effect of encoding operations upon subsequent retrieval. *Journal of Verbal Learning and Verbal Behavior, 22,* 219–230.

Srull, T. K., Lichtenstein, M., & Rothbart, M. (1985). Associative storage and retrieval processes in person memory. *Journal of Experimental Psychology: Learning, Memory, and Cognition, 11,* 316–345.

Srull, T. K., & Wyer, R. S. (1980). Category accessibility and social perception: Some implications for the study of person memory and interpersonal judgment. *Journal of Personality and Social Psychology, 38,* 841–856.

Stalder, D. R., & Baron, R. S. (1998). Attributional complexity as a moderator of dissonance-produced attitude change. *Journal of Personality and Social Psychology, 75,* 449–455.

Stangor, C., Lynch, L., Duan, C., & Glass, B. (1992). Categorization of individuals on the basis of multiple social features. *Journal of Personality and Social Psychology, 62,* 207–218.

Stangor, C., & Schaller, M. (1996). Stereotypes as individual and collective representations. In C. N. Macrae, C. Stangor, & M. Hewstone (Eds.), *Stereotypes and stereotyping* (pp. 3–40). New York: Guilford.

Stasser, G., & Stewart, D. (1992). Discovery of hidden profiles by decision-making groups: Solving a problem versus making a judgment. *Journal of Personality and Social Psychology, 63,* 426–434.

Stasser, G., Taylor, L. A., & Hanna, C. (1989). Information sampling in structured and unstructured discussions of three- and six-person groups. *Journal of Personality and Social Psychology, 57,* 67–78.

Stasson, M. F., & Hawkes, W. G. (1995). Effect of group performance on subsequent individual performance: Does influence generalize beyond the issues discussed by the group? *Psychological Science, 6,* 305–307.

Staub, E. (1978). *Positive social behavior and morality.* New York: Academic Press.

Staub, E. (1989). *The roots of evil: The origins of genocide and other group violence.* Cambridge, UK: Cambridge University Press.

Staw, B. M. (1974). Attitudinal and behavioral consequences of changing a major organizational reward: A natural field experiment. *Journal of Personality and Social Psychology, 29,* 742–751.

Staw, B. M., & Ross, J. (1987). Behavior in escalation situations: Antecedents, prototypes, and solutions. *Research in Organizational Behavior, 9,* 39–78.

Steele, C. M. (1975). Name calling and compliance. *Journal of Personality and Social Psychology, 31,* 361–369.

Steele, C. M. (1988). The psychology of self-affirmation: Sustaining the integrity of the self. In L. Berkowitz (Ed.), *Advances in experimental social psychology* (Vol. 21, pp. 261–302). San Diego, CA: Academic Press.

Steele, C. M. (1992, April). Race and the schooling of black Americans. *Atlantic Monthly,* pp. 68–78.

Steele, C. M. (1997). A threat in the air: How stereotypes shape intellectual identity and performance. *American Psychologist, 52,* 613–629.

Steele, C. M., & Aronson, J. (1995). Stereotype threat and the intellectual test performance of African Americans. *Journal of Personality and Social Psychology, 69,* 797–811.

Steele, C. M., & Josephs, R. A. (1990). Alcohol myopia: Its prized and dangerous effects. *American Psychologist, 45,* 921–933.

Steele, C. M., & Lui, T. J. (1983). Dissonance processes as self-affirmation. *Journal of Personality and Social Psychology, 45,* 5–19.

Steele, C. M., & Southwick, L. (1985). Alcohol and social behavior I: The psychology of drunken excess. *Journal of Personality and Social Psychology, 48*, 18–34.

Steele, C. M., Southwick, L. L., & Critchlow, B. (1981). Dissonance and alcohol: Drinking your troubles away. *Journal of Personality and Social Psychology, 41*, 831–846.

Steele, C. M., Spencer, S. J., & Lynch, M. (1993). Self-image resilience and dissonance: The role of affirmational resources. *Journal of Personality and Social Psychology, 64*, 885–896.

Stein, A. K., & Friedrich, L. K. (1972). Television content and young children's behavior. In J. Murray, E. Rubenstein, & C. Comstock (Eds.), *Television and social learning*. Washington, DC: U. S. Government Printing Office.

Stein, L. (1967). The doctor-nurse game. *Archives of General Psychiatry, 16*, 699–703.

Stein, N. L., Liwag, M. D., & Wade, E. (1996). A goal-based approach to memory for emotional events: Implications for theories of understanding socialization. In R. D. Kavanaugh, B. Zimmerberg, & S. Fein (Eds.), *Emotion: Interdisciplinary perspectives* (pp. 91–118). Mahwah, NJ: Erlbaum.

Steiner, I. (1972). *Group process and productivity*. New York: Academic Press.

Stephan, C. W., & Stephan, W. G. (1984). The role of ignorance in intergroup relations. In N. Miller & M. Brewer (Eds.), *Groups in contact: The psychology of desegregation* (pp. 229–255). New York: Academic Press.

Stephan, W. G. (1987). The contact hypothesis in intergroup relations. In C. Hendrick (Ed.), *Review of Personality and Social Psychology* (Vol. 9, pp. 13–40), Newbury Park: Sage.

Stephan, W. G., & Rosenfield, D. (1978). Effects of desegregation on racial attitudes. *Journal of Personality and Social Psychology, 36*, 795–804.

Stephan, W. G., & Stephan, C. W. (1985). Intergroup anxiety. *Journal of Social Issues, 41*, 157–175.

Stern, P. C. (1992). Psychological dimensions of global environmental change. *Annual Review of Psychology, 43*, 269–302.

Sternberg, L. (1990). *From velleity to specific plans: How planning affects attitude, intention, behavior relations*. Unpublished doctoral dissertation, Purdue University, West Lafayette, IN.

Sternberg, R. J. (1986). A triangular theory of love. *Psychological Review, 93*, 119–135.

Sternberg, R. J. (1988). Triangulating love. In R. J. Sternberg & M. L. Barnes (Eds.), *The psychology of love* (pp. 119–138). New Haven, CT: Yale University Press.

Sternberg, R. J., & Grajek, S. (1984). The nature of love. *Journal of Personality and Social Psychology, 47*, 312–329.

Sterngold, J. (1992, May 21). Japan cuts back on fingerprinting. *The New York Times*, p. A4.

Sternthal, B., Dholakia, R., & Leavitt, C. (1978). The persuasive effect of source credibility: A test of cognitive response analysis. *Journal of Consumer Research, 4*, 252–260.

Stewart, D. D., & Stasser, G. (1995). Expert role assignment and information sampling during collective recall and decision making. *Journal of Personality and Social Psychology, 69*, 619–628.

Stewart, J. E. (1985). Appearance and punishment: The attraction-leniency effect in the courtroom. *Journal of Social Psychology, 125*, 373–378.

Stillinger, C., Epelbaum, M., Keltner, D., & Ross, L. (1989). *The reactive devaluation barrier to conflict resolution*. Unpublished manuscript, Stanford University, Stanford, CA.

Stock, R. W. (1995, October 19). Wearing the gray badge of courage. *The New York Times*, p. B5.

Stogdill, R. M. (1963). *Handbook for the leader behavior description questionnaire—Form XII*. Columbus, OH: Ohio State University.

Stogdill, R. M. (1974). *Handbook of leadership: A survey of theory and research*. New York: Free Press.

Stolzfus, N. (1992, September). Dissent in Nazi Germany. *Atlantic Monthly*, pp. 87–94.

Stone, J., Wiegand, A. W., Cooper, J., & Aronson, E. (1997). When exemplification fails: Hypocrisy and the motive for self-integrity. *Journal of Personality and Social Psychology, 72*, 54–65.

Stoner, J. A. (1961). *A comparison of individual and group decisions involving risk*. Unpublished master's thesis, MIT, Cambridge, MA.

Storck, J., & Sproull, L. (1995). Through a glass darkly: What do people learn in videoconferences? *Human Communication Research, 22*, 197–219.

Storms, M. D. (1973). Videotape and the attribution process: Reversing actors' and observers' points of view. *Journal of Personality and Social Psychology, 27*, 165–175.

Stouffer, S. A. (1949). *The American soldier*. Princeton, NJ: Princeton University Press.

Stouffer, S. A., Suchman, E. A., DeVinney, L. C., Star, S. A., & Williams, R. M., Jr. (1949). *The American soldier: Adjustment during army life* (Vol. 1). Princeton, NJ: Princeton University Press.

Strack, F., Martin, L. L., & Stepper, S. (1988). Inhibiting and facilitating conditions of the human smile: A nonobtrusive test of the facial feedback hypothesis. *Journal of Personality and Social Psychology, 54*, 768–777.

Strack, F., Schwarz, N., Bless, H., Kubler, A., & Wanke, M. (1989). Awareness of the influence as a determinant of assimilation versus contrast. *European Journal of Social Psychology, 23*, 53–62.

Strauman, T. J., & Higgins, E. T. (1988). Self-discrepancies as predictors of vulnerability to distinct syndromes of chronic emotional distress. *Journal of Personality, 56*, 685–707.

Strauman, T. J., Lemieux, A. M., & Coe, C. L. (1993). Self-discrepancy and natural killer cell activity: Immunological consequences of negative self-evaluation. *Journal of Personality and Social Psychology, 64*, 1042–1052.

Straus, M. A., & Gelles, R. J. (1986). Societal change and change in family violence from 1975 to 1985 as revealed by two national surveys. *Journal of Marriage and the Family, 48*, 465–479.

Straus, M. A., Gelles, R. J., & Steinmetz, S. K. (1980). *Behind closed doors: Violence in the American family*. New York: Anchor Press.

Streufert, S., & Streufert, S. C. (1986). The development of internation conflict. In S. Worchel & W. G. Austin (Eds.), *Psychology of intergroup relations* (2nd ed., pp. 134–152). Chicago: Nelson-Hall.

Stroebe, W., & Diehl, M. (1991). You can't beat good experiments with correlational evidence: Mullen, Johnson, and Sala's meta-analytic misinterpretations. *Journal of Basic and Applied Social Psychology, 12,* 25–32.

Stroebe, W., & Stroebe, M. S. (1986). Beyond marriage: The impact of partner loss on health. In R. Gilmour & S. Duck (Eds.), *The emerging field of personal relationships* (pp. 203–224). Hillsdale, NJ: Erlbaum.

Stroebe, W., Stroebe, M. S., & Domittner, G. (1988). Individual and situational differences in recovery from bereavement: A risk group identified. *Journal of Social Issues, 44*(3), 143–158.

Stroessner, S. J., & Mackie, D. M. (1992). The impact of induced affect on the perception of variability in social groups. *Personality and Social Psychology Bulletin, 18,* 546–554.

Strube, M. J., & Garcia, J. E. (1981). A meta-analytic investigation of Fiedler's contingency model of leadership effectiveness. *Psychological Bulletin, 90,* 307–321.

Struch, N., & Schwartz, S. H. (1989). Intergroup aggression: Its predictors and distinctness from in-group bias. *Journal of Personality and Social Psychology, 56,* 364–373.

Stryker, S. (1980). *Symbolic interactionism.* Menlo Park, CA: Benjamin/Cummings.

Study shows TV depiction of Lations to be negative. (1994, September 7). *Purdue Exponent,* p. 5.

Suedfeld, P. (1992). Bilateral relations between countries and the complexity of newspaper editorials. *Political Psychology, 13,* 601–632.

Suedfeld, P., & Tetlock, P. E. (1977). Integrative complexity of communications in international crises. *Journal of Conflict Resolution, 21,* 169–184.

Sugarman, D. B., & Hotaling, G. T. (1989). Violent men in intimate relationships: An analysis of risk markers. *Journal of Applied Social Psychology, 19,* 1034–1048.

Sumner, W. G. (1906). *Folkways.* New York: Ginn.

Surra, C. A., & Bohman, T. (1991). The development of close relationships: A cognitive perspective. In G. Fletcher & F. Fincham (Eds.), *Cognition in close relationships* (pp. 281–306.). Hillsdale, NJ: Erlbaum.

Surra, C. A., & Longstreth, M. (1990). Similarity of outcomes, interdependence, and conflict in dating relationships. *Journal of Personality and Social Psychology, 59,* 501–516.

Svenson, O. (1981). Are we all less risky and more skillful than our fellow drivers? *Acta Psychologica, 47,* 143–148.

Swann, W. B., & Ely, R. J. (1984). A battle of wills: Self-verification versus behavioral confirmation. *Journal of Personality and Social Psychology, 46,* 1287–1302.

Swann, W. B., & Hill, C. A. (1982). When our identities are mistaken: Reaffirming self-conceptions through social interaction. *Journal of Personality and Social Psychology, 43,* 59–66.

Swann, W. B., Hixon, J. G., & de la Ronde, C. (1992). Embracing the bitter "truth": Negative self-concepts and marital commitment. *Psychological Science, 3,* 118–121.

Swann, W. B., & Read, S. J. (1981). Acquiring self-knowledge: The search for feedback that fits. *Journal of Personality and Social Psychology, 41,* 1119–1128.

Swartley, W. M. (1983). *Slavery, Sabbath, war, and women.* Scottsdale, PA: Herald Press.

Sweeney, P. D., & Gruber, K. L. (1984). Selective exposure: Voter information preferences and the Watergate affair. *Journal of Personality and Social Psychology, 46,* 1208–1221.

Symons, C. S., & Johnson, B. T. (1997). The self-reference effect in memory: A meta-analysis.

Szybillo, G. J., & Heslin, R. (1973). Resistance to persuasion: Inoculation theory in a marketing context. *Journal of Marketing Research, 10,* 396–403.

Tait, R., & Silver, R. C. (1989). Coming to terms with major negative life events. In J. S. Uleman & J. A. Bargh (Eds.), *Unintended thought* (pp. 351–382). New York: Guilford.

Tajfel, H. (1972). La catégorization sociale. In S. Moscovici (Ed.), *Introduction à la psychologie sociale* (Vol. 1, pp. 272–302). Paris: Larousse.

Tajfel, H. (1978). *Differentiation between social groups: Studies in the social psychology of intergroup relations.* London: Academic Press.

Tajfel, H., Billig, M. G., Bundy, R. P., & Flament, C. (1971). Social categorization and intergroup behavior. *European Journal of Social Psychology, 1,* 149–178.

Tajfel, H., & Turner, J. C. (1979). An integrative theory of intergroup conflict. In W. G. Austin & S. Worchel (Eds.), *The social psychology of intergroup relations* (pp. 7–24). Monterey, CA: Brooks/Cole.

Tajfel, H., & Wilkes, A. L. (1963). Classification and quantitative judgment. *British Journal of Psychology, 54,* 101–114.

Tak, J., Kaid, L. L., & Lee, S. (1997). A cross-cultural study of political advertising in the United States and Korea. *Communication Research, 24,* 413–430.

Tannen, D. (1990). *You just don't understand.* New York: Ballantine Books.

Taylor, C. R., & Stern, B. B. (1997). Asian-Americans: Television advertising and the "model minority" stereotype. *Journal of Advertising, 26,* 47–61.

Taylor, D. A., & Moriarty, B. F. (1987) Ingroup bias as a function of competition and race. *Journal of Conflict Resolution, 31,* 192–199.

Taylor, D. M., Doria, J., & Tyler, J. K. (1983). Group performance and cohesiveness: An attribution analysis. *Journal of Social Psychology, 119,* 187–198.

Taylor, D. M., & Jaggi, V. (1974). Ethnocentrism and causal attribution in a south Indian context. *Journal of Cross Cultural Psychology, 5,* 162–171.

Taylor, D. M., & Simard, L. M. (1979). Ethnic identity and intergroup relations. In D. J. Lee (Ed.), *Emerging ethnic boundaries* (pp. 155–174). Ottawa, Canada: University of Ottawa Press.

Taylor, D. M., Wright, S. C., Moghaddam, F. M., & Lalonde, R. N. (1990). The personal/group discrimination discrepancy: Perceiving my group, but not myself, to be a target for discrimination. *Personality and Social Psychology Bulletin, 16,* 254–262.

Taylor, S. E. (1975). On inferring one's attitude from one's behavior: Some delimiting conditions. *Journal of Personality and Social Psychology, 31,* 126–131.

Taylor, S. E. (1981). A categorization approach to stereotyping. In D. L. Hamilton (Ed.), *Cognitive processes in stereotyping and intergroup behavior* (pp. 83–114). Hillsdale, NJ: Erlbaum.

Taylor, S. E. (1983). Adjustment to threatening events: A theory of cognitive adaptation. *American Psychologist, 38,* 1161–1173.

Taylor, S. E., & Brown, J. D. (1988). Illusion and well-being: A social psychological perspective on mental health. *Psychological Bulletin, 103*, 193–210.

Taylor, S. E., Falke, R. L., Shoptaw, S. J., & Lichtman, R. R. (1986). Social support, support groups, and the cancer patient. *Journal of Consulting and Clinical Psychology, 54*, 608–615.

Taylor, S. E., & Fiske, S. T. (1975). Point of view and perceptions of causality. *Journal of Personality and Social Psychology, 32*, 439–445.

Taylor, S. E., Fiske, S. T., Etcoff, N. L., & Ruderman, A. J. (1978). Categorical and contextual bases of person memory and stereotyping. *Journal of Personality and Social Psychology, 36*, 778–793.

Taylor, S. E., & Lobel, M. (1989). Social comparison activity under threat: Downward evaluation and upward contacts. *Psychological Review, 96*, 569–575.

Taylor, S. P., Gammon, C. B., & Capasso, D. R. (1976). Aggression as a function of alcohol and threat. *Journal of Personality and Social Psychology, 34*, 938–941.

Tedeschi, J. T. (Ed.). (1981). *Impression management theory and social psychological research*. New York: Academic Press.

Tedeschi, J. T., Gaes, G. G., & Rivera, A. N. (1977). Aggression and the use of coercive power. *Journal of Social Issues, 33*(1), 101–125.

Telch, M. J. et. al. (1982). Long-term follow-up of a pilot project on smoking prevention in adolescents. *Journal of Behavioral Medicine, 5*, 1–8.

Tempest, R. (1990, June 27). French official loses job after rent-a-crowd caper. *Los Angeles Times*, pp. A1, A16.

Tennen, H., & Affleck, G. (1993). The puzzles of self-esteem: A clinical perspective. In R. F. Baumeister (Ed.), *Self-esteem: The puzzle of low self-esteem* (pp. 241–262). New York: Plenum.

Terkel, S. (1992). *Race*. New York: The New Press.

Terry, D. (1991, February 4). Project tenants see island of safety washing away. *The New York Times*, pp. A1, B4.

Terry, D. (1993, April 11). Fear and ghosts: The world of Marcus, 19. *The New York Times*, pp. A1, A11.

Terry, D. J., & Hogg, M. A. (1996). Group norms and the attitude-behavior relationship: A role for group identification. *Personality and Social Psychology Bulletin, 22*, 776–793.

Tesser, A. (1978). Self-generated attitude change. In L. Berkowitz (Ed.), *Advances in experimental social psychology* (Vol. 11, pp. 288–338). New York: Academic Press.

Tesser, A. (1988). Toward a self-evaluation maintenance model of social behavior. In L. Berkowitz (Ed.), *Advances in experimental social psychology* (Vol. 21, pp. 181–227). San Diego, CA: Academic Press.

Tesser, A. (1993). The importance of heritability in psychological research: The case of attitudes. *Psychological Review, 100*, 129–142.

Tesser, A., & Collins, J. E. (1988). Emotion in social reflection and comparison situations: Intuitive, systematic, and exploratory approaches. *Journal of Personality and Social Psychology, 55*, 695–709.

Tesser, A., & Cornell, D. P. (1991). On the confluence of self processes. *Journal of Experimental Social Psychology, 27*, 501–526.

Tetlock, P. E. (1983). Accountability and complexity of thought. *Journal of Personality and Social Psychology, 45*, 74–83.

Tetlock, P. E. (1985). Accountability: The neglected social context of judgement and choice. *Research in Organizational Behavior, 7*, 297–332.

Tetlock, P. E. (1988). Monitoring the integrative complexity of American and Soviet policy rhetoric: What can be learned? *Journal of Social Issues, 44* (2), 101–131.

Tetlock, P. E. (1989). The selfishness-altruism debate: In defense of agnosticism. *Behavioral and Brain Sciences, 12*, 723–724.

Tetlock, P. E., Peterson, R. S., McGuire, C., Chang, S., & Feld, P. (1992). Assessing political group dynamics: A test of the groupthink model. *Journal of Personality and Social Psychology, 63*, 403–425.

Tetlock, R. E. (1985). Integrative complexity of American and Soviet foreign policy rhetoric: A time-series analysis. *Journal of Personality and Social Psychology, 49*, 1565–1585.

The New York Times. (1992, June 28). Turning the tables: A reverse questionnaire. P. F23.

Thibaut, J. J., & Kelley, H. H. (1959). *The psychology of groups*. New York: Wiley.

Thompson, L. (1993). The impact of negotiation on intergroup relations. *Journal of Experimental Social Psychology, 29*, 304–325.

Thompson, L., & Hastie, R. (1990a). Judgment tasks and biases in negotiation. In B. H. Sheppard, M. H. Bazerman, & R. J. Lewicki (Eds.), *Research in negotiation in organizations* (Vol. 2, pp. 31–54). Greenwich, CT: JAI Press.

Thompson, L., & Hastie, R. (1990b). Social perception in negotiation. *Organization Behavior and Human Decision Processes, 47*, 98–123.

Thompson, M. M., & Zanna, M. P. (1995). The conflict individual: Personality-based and domain-specific antecedents of ambivalent social attitudes. *Journal of Personality, 63*, 259–288.

Thompson, T. L., & Zerbinos, E. (1995). Gender roles in animated cartoons: Has the picture changed in 20 years? *Sex Roles, 32*, 651–673.

Thompson, W. C., Cowan, C. L., & Rosenhan, D. L. (1980). Focus of attention mediates the impact of negative affect on altruism. *Journal of Personality and Social Psychology, 38*, 291–300.

Thompson, W. C., Fong, G. T., & Rosenhan, D. L. (1981). Inadmissible evidence and juror verdicts. *Journal of Personality and Social Psychology, 40*, 453–463.

Thoresen, C. E., & Low, K. G. (1990). Women and the Type A behavior pattern: Review and commentary. *Journal of Social Behavior and Personality, 5*, 117–133.

Tilker, H. A. (1970). Socially responsible behavior as a function of observer responsibility and victim feedback. *Journal of Personality and Social Psychology, 49*, 420–428.

Tindale, R. S., & Davis, J. H. (1983). Group decision making and jury verdicts. In H. H. Blumberg, A. P. Hare, V. Kent, & M. F. Davies (Eds.), *Small groups and social interaction* (Vol. 2, pp. 9–38). New York: Wiley.

Tindale, R. S., Davis, J. H., Vollrath, D. A., Nagao, D. H., & Hinsz, V. B. (1990). Asymmetrical social influence in freely interacting groups: A test of three models. *Journal of Personality and Social Psychology, 58*, 438–449.

Toi, M., & Batson, C. D. (1982). More evidence that empathy is a source of altruistic motivation. *Journal of Personality and Social Psychology, 43*, 281–292.

Tomaka, J., Blascovich, J., Kibler, J., & Ernst, J. M. (1997). Cognitive and physiological antecedents of threat and challenge appraisal. *Journal of Personality and Social Psychology, 73*, 63–72.

Tommasini, A. (1996, April 9). Music history: One woman wielding a baton. *The New York Times*, p. B1.

Tourangeau, R., & Rasinski, K. A. (1988). Cognitive processes underlying context effects in attitude measurement. *Psychological Bulletin, 103*, 299–314.

Tourangeau, R., Rasinski, K. A. Bradburn, N., & D'Andrade, R. (1989). Belief accessibility and context effects in attitude measurement. *Journal of Experimental Social Psychology, 25*, 401–421.

Trafimow, D., & Finlay, K. A. (1996). The importance of subjective norms for a minority of people: Between-subjects and within-subjects analyses. *Personality and Social Psychology Bulletin, 22*, 820–828.

Trafimow, D., & Fishbein, M. (1994a). The importance of risk in determining the extent to which attitudes affect intentions to wear seat belts. *Journal of Applied Social Psychology, 24*, 1–11.

Trafimow, D., & Fishbein, M. (1994b). The moderating effect of behavior type on the subjective norm-behavior relationship. *Journal of Social Psychology, 134*, 755–763.

Trafimow, D., & Sheeran, P. (1998). Some tests of the distinction between cognitive and affective beliefs. *Journal of Experimental and Social Psychology, 34*, 378–397.

Trafimow, D., Triandis, H. C., & Goto, S. G. (1991). Some tests of the distinction between the private self and the collective self. *Journal of Personality and Social Psychology, 60*, 649–655.

Triandis, H. C. (1977). *Interpersonal behavior*. Monterey, CA: Brooks/Cole.

Triandis, H. C. (1980). Values, attitudes, and interpersonal behavior. In H. Howe & M. Page (Eds.), *Nebraska Symposium on Motivation* (Vol. 27, pp. 195–260). Lincoln: University of Nebraska Press.

Triandis, H. C. (1994). Major cultural syndromes and emotion. In S. Kityama, & H. R. Markus (Eds.), *Handbook of industrial and organizational psychology* (2nd ed., Vol. 4, pp. 285–308). Palo Alto, CA: Consulting Psychologists Press.

Triandis, H. C., Bontempo, R., Villareal, M. J., Asai, M., & Lucca, N. (1988). Individualism and collectivism: Cross-cultural perspectives on self-ingroup relaitonships. *Journal of Personality and Social Psychology, 54*, 323–338.

Tripathi, R. C., & Srivasta, R. (1981). Relative deprivation and intergroup attitudes. *European Journal of Social Psychology, 11*, 313–318.

Triplett, N. (1898). The dynamogenic factors in pacemaking and competition. *American Journal of Psychology, 9*, 507–533.

Trivers, R. L. (1971). The evolution of reciprocal altruism. *Quarterly Review of Biology, 46*, 35–57.

Trivers, R. L. (1972). Parental investment and sexual selection. In B. Campbell (Ed.), *Sexual selection and the descent of man 1871–1971* (pp. 136–172). Chicago: Aldine.

Trope, T., & Mackie, D. M. (1987). Sensitivity to alternatives in social hypothesis-testing. *Journal of Experimental Social Psychology, 23*, 445–459.

Trope, Y. (1986). Identification and inferential processes in dispositional attribution. *Psychological Review, 93*, 239–257.

Trope, Y., Bassok, M., & Alon, E. (1984). The questions lay interviewers ask. *Journal of Personality, 52*, 90–106.

Trope, Y., & Thompson, E. P. (1997). Looking for truth in all the wrong places? Asymmetric search of individuating information about stereotyped group members. *Journal of Personality and Social Psychology, 73*, 229–241.

Trost, M. R., Cialdini, R. B., & Maas, A. (1989). Effects of an international conflict simulation of perceptions of the Soviet Union: A FIREBREAKS backfire. *Journal of Social Issues, 45*, 139–158.

Trudeau, K. J., & Devlin, A. S. (1996). College students and community service: Who, with whom, and why? *Journal of Applied Social Psychology, 26*, 1867–1888.

Tuckman, B. W. (1965). Developmental sequences in small groups. *Psychological Bulletin, 63*, 384–399.

Turnbull, W., Miller, D. T., & McFarland, C. (1990). Population-distinctiveness, identity, and bonding. In J. M. Olson & M. P. Zanna, (Eds.), *Self-inference processes: The Ontario Symposium* (Vol. 6, pp. 115–133). Hillsdale, NJ: Erlbaum.

Turner, C. W., Simons, L. S., Berkowitz, L., & Frodi, A. (1977). The stimulating and inhibiting effects of weapons on aggressive behavior. *Aggressive Behavior, 3*, 355–378.

Turner, J. C. (1980). Fairness or discrimination in intergroup behavior? A reply to Braithwaite, Doyle, and Lightbrown. *European Journal of Social Psychology, 10*, 131–47.

Turner, J. C. (1981). The experimental social psychology of intergroup behavior. In J. C. Turner & H. Giles (Eds.), *Intergroup behavior* (pp. 66–101). Chicago, IL: University of Chicago Press.

Turner, J. C. (1982). Towards a cognitive redefinition of the social group. In H. Tajfel (Ed.), *Social identity and intergroup relations*. Cambridge, England: Cambridge University Press.

Turner, J. C. (1991). *Social influence*. Pacific Grove, CA: Brooks/Cole.

Turner, J. C., Hogg, M. A., Oakes, P. J., Reicher, S. D., & Wetherell, M. S. (1987). *Rediscovering the social group: a self-categorization theory*. Oxford, England: Blackwell.

Turner, J. C., Sachdev, I., & Hogg, M. A. (1983). Social categorization, interpersonal attraction and group formation. *British Journal of Social Psychology, 22*, 227–239.

Turner, M. E., Pratkanis, A. R., Probasco, P., & Leve, C. (1992). Threat, cohesion, and group effectiveness: Testing a social identity maintenance perspective on groupthink. *Journal of Personality and Social Psychology, 63*, 781–796.

Tushman, M. L. (1978). Technical communication in research and development laboratories: The impact of project work characteristics. *Academy of Management Journal, 21*, 624–645.

Tyler, T. R., & Degoey, P. (1995). Collective restraint in social dilemmas: Procedural justice and social identification effects on support for authorities. *Journal of Personality and Social Psychology, 69*, 482–497.

Tyler, T. R., & Lind, E. A. (1990). Intrinsic versus community-based justice models: When does group membership matter? *Journal of Social Issues, 46*(1), 83–94.

Tyler, T. R., & Lind, E. A. (1992). A relational model of authority in groups. In M. P. Zanna (Ed.), *Advances in experimental social psychology* (Vol. 25, pp. 115–191). New York: Academic Press.

Tyler, T. R., Lind, E. A., Ohbuchi, K. -I., Sugawara, I., & Huo, Y. J. (1998). Conflict with outsiders: Disputing within and across cultural boundaries. *Personality and Social Psychology Bulletin, 24,* 137–146.

Tyler, T. R., & Smith, H. J. (1998). Social justice and social movements. In D. T. Gilbert, S. T. Fiske, & G. Lindzey (Eds.), *Handbook of social psychology* (4th ed., Vol. 2, pp. 554–594). Boston: McGraw-Hill.

Uchino, B. N., Cacioppo, J. T., & Kiecolt-Glaser, J. K. (1996). The relationship between social support and physiological processes: A review with emphasis on underlying mechanisms and implications for health. *Psychological Bulletin, 119,* 488–531.

Uleman, J. S., Hon, A., Roman, R. J., & Moskowitz, G. B. (1996). On-line evidence for spontaneous trait inferences at encoding. *Personality and Social Psychology Bulletin, 22,* 377–394.

Unnikrishnan, N., & Bajpai, S. (1996). *The impact of television advertising on children.* New Dehli, India: Sage.

Vachon, M. L., Roger, J., Lyall, W. A., Lancee, W. J., Sheldon, A. R., & Freeman, S. J. J. (1982). Predictors and correlates of adaptation to conjugal bereavement. *American Journal of Psychiatry, 139,* 998–1002.

Vallacher, R., & Wegner, D. M. (1987). What do people think they're doing? Action identification and human behavior. *Psychological Review, 94,* 3–15.

Vanbeselaere, N. (1991). The different effects of simple and crossed categorization: A result of the category differentiation process or of differential category salience? In W. Stroebe & M. Hewstone (Eds.), *European Review of Social Psychology* (Vol. 2, pp. 247–278). Chichester, England: Wiley.

van den Putte, B., Hoogstraten, J., & Meertens, R. (1996). A comparison of behavioural alternative models in the context of the theory of reasoned action. *British Journal of Social Psychology, 35,* 257–266.

Van Egeren, L. F. (1979). Cardiovascular changes during social competition in a mixed-motive game. *Journal of Personality and Social Psychology, 37,* 858–864.

Van Gyn, G. H., Wenger, H. A., & Gaul, C. A. (1990). Imagery as a method of enhancing transfer from training to performance. *Journal of Sport and Exercise Psychology, 12,* 366–375.

van Knippenberg, D., & Wilke, H. (1991). Social categorization and attitude change. *European Journal of Social Psychology, 18,* 395–406.

van Knippenberg, D., & Wilke, H. (1992). Prototypicality of arguments and conformity to ingroup norms. *European Journal of Social Psychology, 22,* 141–155.

van Lange, P. A., & Liebrand, W. B. (1991). Social value orientation and intelligence: A test of the Goal Prescribes Rationality Principle. *European Journal of Social Psychology, 21,* 273–292.

van Lange, P. A. M., Rusbult, C. E., Drigotas, S. M., Arriaga, X. B., Witcher, B. S., & Cox, C. L. (1997). Willingness to sacrifice in close relationships. *Journal of Personality and Social Psychology, 72,* 1373–1395.

Vanman, E. J., & Miller, N. (1993). Applications of emotion theory and research to stereotyping and intergroup relations. In D. M. Mackie & D. L. Hamilton (Eds.), *Affect, cognition, and stereotyping: Interactive processes in group perception* (pp. 213–238). New York: Academic Press.

Vanman, E. J., Paul, B. Y., Ito, T. A., & Miller, N. (1997). The modern face of prejudice and structural features that moderate the effect of cooperation on affect. *Journal of Personality and Social Psychology, 73,* 941–959.

Veroff, J., Douvan, E., & Kukla, R. A. (1981). *The inner American: A self-portrait from 1957 to 1976.* New York: Basic Books.

Vonk, R. (1995). Effects of inconsistent behaviors on person impressions: A multidimensional study. *Personality and Social Psychology Bulletin, 21,* 674–685.

Vroom, V. H. (1976). Leadership. In M. D. Dunnette (Ed.), *Handbook of industrial and organizational psychology* (pp. 1527–1552). Chicago: Rand McNally.

Wagner, D. G., & Berger, J. (1997). Gender and interpersonal task behaviors: Status expectation accounts. *Sociological Perspectives, 40,* 1–32.

Wahl, M. (1989). EyePOPing persuasion. *Marketing Insights, 22,* p. 130.

Waldman, S. (1991, May 6). Watering the grass roots: How to buy a "spontaneous" popular uprising. *Newsweek,* p. 35.

Walker, I., & Mann, L. (1987). Unemployment, relative deprivation, and social protest. *Personality and Social Psychology Bulletin, 13,* 275–283.

Walster, E., Aronson, V., Abrahams, D., & Rottman, L. (1966). The importance of physical attractiveness in dating behavior. *Journal of Personality and Social Psychology, 4,* 508–516.

Walster, E., & Festinger, L. (1962). The effectiveness of "overheard" persuasive communications. *Journal of Abnormal and Social Psychology, 65,* 395–402.

Walzer, M. (1970). *Obligations.* Cambridge, MA: Harvard University Press.

Watson, D., & Pennebaker, J. W. (1989). Health complaints, stress, and distress: Exploring the central role of negative affectivity. *Psychological Review, 96,* 234–254.

Weber, M. (1921/1946). The sociology of charismatic authority. In H. H. Gertz & C. W. Mills (Trans. & Eds.), *From Max Weber: Essays in sociology* (pp. 245–252). New York: Oxford University Press.

Weber, R., & Crocker, J. (1983). Cognitive processes in the revision of stereotypic beliefs. *Journal of Personality and Social Psychology, 45,* 961–977.

Wech, C E., Lundstrum, R. H., & Moore, A. (1989). Bogus-pipeline effects on self-reported college student drug use, problems, and attitudes. *The International Journal of the Addictions, 24,* 1003–1010.

Wegener, D. T., & Petty, R. E. (1995). Flexible correction processes in social judgment: The role of naive theories in corrections for perceived bias. *Journal of Personality and Social Psychology, 68,* 36–51.

Wegener, D. T., & Petty, R. E. (1997). The flexible correction model: The role of naive theories of bias in bias correction. In M. P. Zanna (Ed.), *Advances in experimental social psychology* (Vol. 29, pp. 141–208). Mahwah, NJ: Erlbaum.

Wegener, D. T., Petty, R., & Smith, S. M. (1995). Positive mood can increase or decrease message scrutiny: The hedonic contingency view of mood and message processing. *Journal of Personality and Social Psychology, 69,* 5–15.

Wegner, D. M. (1987). Transactive memory: A contemporary analysis of the group mind. In B. Mullen & G. R. Goethals (Eds)., *Theories of group behavior* (pp. 185–208). New York: Springer-Verlag.

Wegner, D. M. (1994). Ironic processes of mental control. *Psychological Review, 101,* 34–52.

Wegner, D. M., & Vallacher, R. R. (1986). Action identification. In R. M. Sorrentino & E. T. Higgins (Eds.), *Handbook of motivation and cognition: Foundations of social behavior* (pp. 550–582). New York: Guilford.

Weiner, B. (1985). An attributional theory of achievement motivation and emotion. *Psychological Review, 92*, 548–573.

Weinstein, N. D. (1987). Unrealistic optimism about susceptibility to health problems: Conclusions from a community-wide sample. *Journal of Behavioral Medicine, 10*, 481–500.

Weir, W. (1984). Another look at subliminal "facts. " *Advertising Age*, 46.

Weisband, S. P., Schneider, S. K., & Connolly, T. (1995). Computer-mediated communication and social information: Status salience and status differences. *Academy of Management Journal, 38*, 1124–1151.

Weldon, E., & Mustari, E. L. (1988). Felt dispensability in groups of coactors: The effects of shared responsibility and explicit anonymity on cognitive effort. *Organizational Behavior and Human Decision Processes, 41*, 330–351.

Wellesley College Center for Research on Women. (1992). *How schools shortchange girls: The AAUW Report*. Washington, DC: American Association of University Women Educational Foundation.

Wells, G. L., & Gavanski, I. (1989). Mental simulation of causality. *Journal of Personality and Social Psychology, 56*, 161–169.

Wells, G. L., & Petty, R. E. (1980). The effects of overt head-movements on persuasion: Compatibility and incompatibility of responses. *Basic and Applied Social Psychology, 1*, 219–230.

Wetherell, M. S. (1987). Social identity and group polarization. In J. C. Turner (Ed.), *Rediscovering the social group: A self-categorization theory*. London: Blackwell.

Wheelan, S. A. (1994). *Group processes: A developmental perspective*. Boston, MA: Allyn & Bacon.

Wheeler, L. (1974). Social comparison and selective affiliation. In T. Huston (Ed.), *Foundations of interpersonal attraction* (pp. 309–330). New York: Academic Press.

White, G. L. (1981). A model of romantic jealousy. *Motivation and emotion, 5*, 295–310.

White, G. L., Fishbein, S., & Rutstein, J. (1981). Passionate love: The misattribution of arousal. *Journal of Personality and Social Psychology, 41*, 56–62.

White, R. K. (1965). Images in the context of international conflict: Soviet perceptions of the U. S. and the U. S. S. R. In H. C. Kelman (Ed.), *International Behavior: A social-psychological analysis* (pp. 236–276). New York: Holt, Rinehart & Winston.

White, R. K. (1971). Selective inattention. *Psychology Today*, pp. 47–50, 78–84.

White, R. K. (1977). Misperception in the Arab-Israeli conflict. *Journal of Social Issues, 33*, 190–221.

White, R. K. (1984). *Fearful warriors: A psychological profile in U. S. -Soviet relations*. New York: Free Press.

White, R. K. (1987). Underestimating and overestimating others' fear. *Journal of Social Issues, 43*(4), 105–110.

White, R. W. (1959). Motivation reconsidered: The concept of competence. *Psychological Review, 66*, 297–333.

Whyte, G., Saks, A., & Hook, S. (1997). When success breeds failure: The role of self-efficacy in escalating commitment to a losing course of action. *Journal of Organizational Behavior, 18*, 415–432.

Wicker, A. W. (1969). Attitudes versus actions: The relationship of verbal and overt behavioral responses to attitude objects. *Journal of Social Issues, 25*, 41–78.

Wicklund, R. A., & Brehm, J. W. (1976). *Perspectives on cognitive dissonance*. Hillsdale, NJ: Erlbaum.

Widom, C. S. (1989). The cycle of violence. *Science, 244*, 160–166.

Wierzbicka, A. (1994). Emotion, language, and cultural scripts. In S. Kitayama & H. R. Markus (Eds.), *Emotion and culture: Empirical studies of mutual influence* (pp. 133–196). Washington, DC: American Psychological Association.

Wilder, D. A. (1977). Perception of groups, size of opposition, and social influence. *Journal of Experimental Social Psychology, 13*, 253–268.

Wilder, D. A. (1981). Perceiving persons as a group: Categorization and intergroup relations. In D. L. Hamilton (Ed.), *Cognitive processes in stereotyping and intergroup behavior* (pp. 213–258). Hillsdale, NJ: Erlbaum.

Wilder, D. A. (1984). Intergroup contact: The typical member and the exception to the rule. *Journal of Experimental Social Psychology, 20*, 177–94.

Wilder, D. A. (1986). Social categorization: Implications for creation and reduction of intergroup bias. In L. Berkowitz (Ed.), *Advances in experimental social psychology* (Vol. 19, pp. 291–355). New York: Academic Press.

Wilder, D. A. (1990). Some determinants of the persuasive power of in-groups and out-groups: Organization of information and attribution of independence. *Journal of Personality and Social Psychology, 59*, 1202–1213.

Wilder, D. A., & Shapiro, P. (1991). Facilitation of outgroup stereotypes by enhanced ingroup identity. *Journal of Experimental Social Psychology, 27*, 431–452.

Wilder, D. A., & Shapiro, P. N. (1984). Role of out-group cues in determining social identity. *Journal of Personality and Social Psychology, 47*, 342–348.

Wilder, D. A., & Shapiro, P. N. (1988). Role of competition-ind uced anxiety in limiting the beneficial impact of positive behavior by out-group members. *Journal of Personality and Social Psychology, 56*, 60–69.

Wilder, D. A., & Thompson, J. E. (1980). Intergroup contact with independent manipulations of in-group and out-group interaction. *Journal of Personality and Social Psychology, 38*, 589–603.

Wilke, H., & Lanzetta, J. T. (1970). The obligation to help: The effects of amount of prior help on subsequent helping behavior. *Journal of Experimental Social Psychology, 6*, 488–493.

Wilke, H., & Lanzetta, J. T. (1982). The obligation to help: Factor affecting response to help received. *European Journal of Social Psychology, 12*, 315–319.

Wilke, W. L., & Farris, P. W. (1975). *Consumer information processing: perspective and implications for advertising*. Cambridge, MA: Marketing Science Institute.

Williams, A., & Giles, H. (1998). Communication of ageism. In M. C. Hecht (Ed.), *Communicating prejudice* (pp. 136–160). Thousand Oaks, CA: Sage.

Williams, E. (1977). Experimental comparisons of face-to-face and mediated communication: A review. *Psychological Bulletin, 84*, 963–976.

Williams, J. E., & Best, D. L. (1982). *Measuring sex stereotypes: A thirty-nation study*. Beverly Hills, CA: Sage.

Williams, K. D., Harkins, S., & Latané, B. (1981). Identifiability as a deterrent to social loafing: Two cheering experiments. *Journal of Personality and Social Psychology*, 40, 303–311.

Williams, L. (1991a, April 30). When blacks shop, bias often accompanies sale. *The New York Times*, pp. A1, A9.

Williams, L. (1991b, November 30). In a 90's quest for black identity, intense doubts and disagreement. *The New York Times*, pp. A1, A7.

Williamson, G. M., & Clark, M. S. (1989). Providing help and desired relationship type as determinants of changes in moods and self-evaluations. *Journal of Personality and Social Psychology*, 56, 722–734.

Willis, R. (1986). Harley Davidson comes roaring back. *Management Review*, March, 20–27.

Wills, T. A. (1991). Social support and interpersonal relations. In M. S. Clark (Ed.), *Prosocial behavior* (pp. 265–289). Beverly Hills, CA: Sage.

Wilson, T. D., & Dunn, D. S. (1986). Effects of introspection on attitude-behavior consistency. Analyzing reasons versus focusing on feelings. *Journal of Experimental Social Psychology*, 22, 249–263.

Wilson, T. D., Gilbert, D. T., & Wheatley, T. P. (1998). Protecting our minds: The role of lay beliefs. In V. Yzerbyt, G. Lories, & B. Dardenne (Eds.), *Metacognition: Cognitive and social dimensions* (pp. 171–201). New York: Sage.

Wilson, T. D., Houston, C. E., & Meyers, J. M. (1998). Choose your poison: Effects of lay beliefs about mental processes on attitude change. *Social Cognition*, 16, 114–132.

Wilson, T. D., Laser, P. S., & Stone, J. I. (1982). Judging the predictors of one's own mood: Accuracy and the use of shared theories. *Journal of Experimental Social Psychology*, 18, 537–549.

Wilson, T. D., Lisle, D. J., Schooler, J. W., Hodges, S. D., Klaaren, K. J., & LaFleur, S. J. (1993). Introspecting about reasons can reduce post-choice satisfaction. *Personality and Social Psychology Bulletin*, 19, 331–339.

Wittenbrink, B., Judd, C. M., & Park, B. (1997). Evidence for racial prejudice at the implicit level and its relationship with questionnaire measures. *Journal of Personality and Social Psychology*, 72, 262–274.

Wolfgang, M., & Strohm, R. B. (1956). The relationship between alcohol and criminal homicide. *Quarterly Journal of Studies on Alcohol*, 17, 411–425.

Wood, J. V. (1989). Theory and research concerning social comparisons of personal attributes. *Psychological Bulletin*, 106, 231–248.

Wood, J. V., Taylor, S. E., & Lichtman, R. R. (1985). Social comparison in adjustment to breast cancer. *Journal of Personality and Social Psychology*, 49, 1169–1183.

Wood, W. (1982). Retrieval of attitude relevant information from memory: Effects on susceptibility to persuasion and on intrinsice motivation. *Journal of Personality and Social Psychology*, 42, 798–810.

Wood, W. (1987). Meta-analytic review of sex differences in group performance. *Psychological Bulletin*, 102, 53–71.

Wood, W., Christensen, P. N., Hebl, M. R., & Rothgerber, H. (1997). Conformity to sex-typed norms, affect, and the self-concept. *Journal of Personality and Social Psychology*, 73, 523–535.

Wood, W., Kallgren, C., & Preisler, R. (1985). Access to relevant information in memory as a determinant of persuasion. *Journal of Experimental Social Psychology*, 21, 73–85.

Wood, W. Lundgren, S., Ouellette, J. A., Busceme, S., & Blackstone, T. (1994). Minority influence: A meta-analytic review of social influence processes. *Psychological Bulletin*, 115, 323–345.

Wood, W., Pool, G. J., Leck, K., & Purivs, D. (1996). Self-definition, defensive processing, and influence: The normative impact of majority and minority groups. *Journal of Personality and Social Psychology*, 71, 1181–1193.

Wood, W., Rhodes, N., & Beik, M. (1995). Working knowledge and attitude strength: An information processing analysis. In R. E. Petty & J. A. Krosnick (Eds.), *Attitude strength: Antecedents and consequences*, (pp. 283–313). Hillsdale, NJ: Erlbaum.

Wood, W., Wong, F., & Chachere, J. (1991). Effects of media violence on viewers' aggression in unconstrained social interaction. *Psychological Bulletin*, 109, 371–383.

Woodside, A. G., & Davenport, J. W. (1974). Effects of salesman similarity and expertise on consumer purchasing behavior. *Journal of Marketing Research*, 11, 198–202.

Woolfolk, R. L., Novalany, J., Gara, M. A., Allen, L. A., & Polino, M. (1995). Self-complexity, self-evaluation, and depression: An examination of form and content within the self-schema. *Journal of Personality and Social Psychology*, 68, 1108–1120.

Wootton, B. H. (1997, April). Gender differences in occupational employment. *Monthly Labor Review*, 15–24.

Worchel, S. (1979). Cooperation and the reduction of intergroup conflict: Some determining factors. In W. G. Austin & S. Worchel (Eds.), *The social psycholgy of intergorup conflict* (pp. 262–273). Monterey, CA: Brooks/Cole.

Worchel, S., Lee, J., & Adewole, A. (1975). Effects of supply and demand on ratings of object value. *Journal of Personality and Social Psychology*, 32, 906–914.

Worchel, S., & Norvell, N. (1980). Effect of perceived environmental conditions during cooperation on intergroup attraction. *Journal of Personality and Social Psychology*, 38, 264–772.

Word, C. O., Zanna, M. P., & Cooper, J. (1974). The nonverbal mediation of self-fulfilling prophecies in interracial interaction. *Journal of Experimental Social Psychology*, 10, 109–120.

Worringham, C. J., & Messick, D. M. (1983). Social facilitation of running: An unobtrusive study. *Journal of Social Psychology*, 121, 23–29.

Worth, L. T., & Mackie, D. M. (1987). Cognitive mediation of positive affect in persuasion. *Social Cognition*, 5, 76–94.

Wortman, C., Adesman, P., Herman, E., & Greenberg, R. (1976). Self-disclosure: An attributional perspective. *Journal of Personality and Social Psychology*, 33, 184–191.

Wright, J. C., & Mischel, W. (1987). A conditional approach to dispositional constructs: The local predictability of social behavior. *Journal of Personality and Social Psychology*, 53, 1159–1177.

Wright, P. H. (1982). Men's friendships, women's friendships and the alleged inferiority of the latter. *Sex Roles*, 8, 1–20.

Wright, Q. (1965). Escalation of international conflicts. *Journal of Conflict Resolution*, 9, 434–449.

Wright, S. C., Aron, A., McLaughlin-Volpe, T., & Ropp, S. A. (1997). The extended contact effect: Knowledge of cross-group friendships and prejudice. *Journal of Personality and Social Psychology, 73,* 73–90.

Wu, C., & Shaffer, D. R. (1987). Susceptibility to persuasive appeals as a function of source credibility and prior experience with the attitude object. *Journal of Personality and Social Psychology, 52,* 677–688.

Wyer, R. S., & Srull, T. K. (1989). *Memory and cognition in its social context.* Hillsdale, NJ: Erlbaum.

X, M. (1966). *The autobiography of Malcolm X.* New York: Grove Press.

Yalom, I. D. (1985). *The theory and practice of group psychotherapy.* New York: Basic Books.

Yamagishi, T. (1986). The provision of a sanctioning system as a public good. *Journal of Personality and Social Psychology, 51,* 110–116.

Yang, A. S. (1997). Trends: Attitudes toward homosexuality. *Public Opinion Quarterly, 61,* 477–507.

Young, A. M., & Acitelli, L. K. (1998). The role of attachment style and relationship status of the perceiver in the perceptions of romantic partner. *Journal of Social and Personal Relationships, 15,* 161–173.

Younger, J. C., Walker, L., & Arrowood, A. J. (1977). Post-decision dissonance at the fair. *Personality and Social Psychology Bulletin, 3,* 247–287.

Yovetich, N. A., & Rusbult, C. E. (1994). Accommodative behavior in close relationships: Exploring transformation of motivation. *Journal of Experimental Social Psychology, 30,* 138–164.

Yzerbyt, V., Rocher, S., & Schadron, G. (1997). Stereotypes as explanations: A subjective essentialistic view of group perception. In R. Spears, P. J. Oakes, N. Ellemers, & S. A. Haslam (Eds.), *The social psychology of stereotyping and group life* (pp. 20–50). Cambridge, England: Blackwell.

Zaccaro, S. J. (1984). Social loafing: The role of task attractiveness. *Personality and Social Psychology Bulletin, 10,* 99–106.

Zaccaro, S. J., Foti, R. J., & Kenny, D. A. (1991). Self-monitoring and trait-based variance in leadership: An investigation of leader flexibility across multiple group situations. *Journal of Applied Psychology, 76,* 308–315.

Zajonc, R. B. (1965). Social facilitation. *Science, 149,* 269–274.

Zajonc, R. B. (1968). Attitudinal effects of mere exposure. *Journal of Personality and Social Psychology, 9* (Monograph Suppl. No. 2, part 2).

Zajonc, R. B. (1980). Feeling and thinking: Preferences need no inferences. *American Psychologist, 35,* 151–175.

Zajonc, R. B. (1998). Emotions. In D. T. Gilbert, S. T. Fiske, & G. Lindzey (Eds.), *Handbook of social psychology* (4th ed., Vol. 1, pp. 591–634). Boston: McGraw-Hill.

Zajonc, R. B., & Sales, S. M. (1966). Social facilitation of dominant and subordinate responses. *Journal of Experimental Social Psychology, 2,* 160–168.

Zanna, M. P., Kiesler, C. A., & Pilkonis, P. A. (1970). Positive and negative attitudinal affect established by classical conditioning. *Journal of Personality and Social Psychology, 14,* 321–328.

Zanna, M. P., & Rempel, J. K. (1988). Attitudes: A new look at an old concept. In D. Bar-Tal & A. Kruglanski (Eds.), *The social psychology of knowledge* (pp. 315–334). New York: Cambridge University Press.

Zárate, M. A., & Smith, E. R. (1990). Person categorization and stereotyping. *Social Cognition, 8,* 161–185.

Zebrowitz, L. A., & Collins, M. A. (1997). Accurate social perception at zero acquaintance: The affordances of a Gibsonian approach. *Personality and Social Psychology Review, 1,* 204–223.

Zebrowitz, L. A., Tenenbaum, D. R., & Goldstein, L. H. (1991). The impact of job applicants' facial maturity, sex, and academic achievement on hiring recommendations. *Journal of Applied Social Psychology, 21,* 525–548.

Zillman, D. (1979). *Hostility and aggression.* Hillsdale, NJ: Erlbaum.

Zillman, D. (1982). Transfer of excitation in emotional behavior. In J. T. Cacioppo & R. E. Petty (Eds.), *Social psychophysiology* (pp. 215–240). New York: Guilford.

Zimbardo, P. G. (1970). The human choice: Individuation, reason, and order versus deindividuation, impulse, and chaos. In W. J. Arnold & D. Levine (Eds.), *Nebraska Symposium on Motivation 1969* (Vol. 17, pp. 237–307). Lincoln: University of Nebraska Press.

Zimbardo, P. G. (1977). *Shyness.* New York: Jove.

Zimbardo, P. G., Banks, W. C., Haney, C., & Jaffe, D. (1973, April 8). The mind is a formidable jailer: A Pirandellian prison. *The New York Times Magazine,* 38–60.

Zuckerman, M. (1979). *Sensation seeking: Beyond the optimal level of arousal.* Hillsdale, NJ: Erlbaum.

Zuckerman, M., DePaulo, B. M., & Rosenthal, R. (1981). Verbal and nonverbal communication of deception. In L. Berkowitz (Ed.), *Advances in experimental social psychology* (Vol. 14, pp. 1–59). New York: Academic Press.

Author Index

Subject Index